FRUSTRATION
AND
FORCE MAJEURE
SECOND EDITION

AUSTRALIA
Law Book Co.
Sydney

CANADA and USA
Carswell
Toronto

HONG KONG
Sweet & Maxwell Asia

NEW ZEALAND
Brookers
Wellington

SINGAPORE and MALAYSIA
Sweet & Maxwell Asia
Singapore and Kuala Lumpur

CCNT. T

Commemorative Medals of the Coronation of King Edward VII
(above) by F. Bowsher showing the originally planned,
and (below) unsigned showing the actual date of the coronation.

Photographs reproduced by kind permission of the Ashmolean Museum, Oxford

FRUSTRATION
AND
FORCE MAJEURE

SECOND EDITION

by

Sir Guenter TREITEL, Q.C., D.C.L., F.B.A.
Honorary Bencher of Gray's Inn;
Formerly Vinerian Professor of English Law

THOMSON
™
SWEET & MAXWELL

Published in 2004 by
Sweet & Maxwell Limited of
100 Avenue Road London NW3 3PF
http://www/sweetandmaxwell.co.uk
Typeset by MFK Mendip
Printed in England by MPG Books Ltd, Bodmin, Cornwall

A CIP catalogue record for this
book is available from the British Library

 ISBN 0 421 77820 2

ISBN 0-421-77820-2

9 780421 778207

PREFACE

This edition takes account of more than 40 cases decided, and of much new legislation passed, in the ten years since the publication of its predecessor. Some of these developments relate directly to the subject-matter of the book; that is, to the legal effects of supervening events on contracts. Others relate to changes in, so to speak, contiguous areas: contract law is well know for the interlocking character of its parts, so that changes in any one of them is necessarily reflected in many of the others.

The first group of changes includes, for example, the *Gamerco* case (1995), one of the few judicial discussions of the effect of the Law Reform (Frustrated Contracts) Act, 1943; *The Kriti Rex* (1996) and *The Marine Star (No2)* (1996), and many other cases, on the construction of *force majeure* clauses; the *Harbinger* case (2000) on the question just what contracting parties might mean by the phrase "in perpetuity"; and *Johnson & Co (Barbados) v NSR* (1997) on the effect of compulsory acquisition on contracts for the sale of land.

An example of the second kind of change is provided by amendments to the Sale of Goods Act 1979 made in 1995 (by the Sale of Goods (Amendment) Act) and in 2002 (by the Sale and Supply of Goods to Consumers Regulations). The discussion of the relationship between frustration and the passing of risk is substantially revised in the light of this legislation. Another example of this type of change is provided by *The Great Peace* (2002) which has prompted further reflection on the relationship between frustration and mistake. There are also many significant changes in the discussion of the legal consequences of frustration. In particular, an extended treatment of the effects of insurance on the powers of adjustment exercisable under the 1943 Act replaces the briefer discussion of this topic in the previous edition.

While the book deals mainly with English law, it to some extent adopts a comparative approach. Without attempting to give a comprehensive account of the law on the topic of foreign systems, it does look to some such systems for rules, concepts and examples which help with an understanding and evaluation of the English rules. The text takes account of changes and proposed changes (not yet in their final form) to the American Uniform Commercial Code and of changes to the German Civil Code which took effect in January 2002.

The book originated in seminars taught (more than once) at the Law School of Southern Methodist University where part of the work on this edition was done in 2003. I am grateful for the help that I was given there, especially by the staff of the Underwood Law Library. The help that I have had from the staff of the Codrington Library of All Souls College, even after my retirement, has also been invaluable. I am grateful, too, to Birke Häcker for providing the text of the new German legislative provisions and for discussions of their effects; to Professor Jonathan Rose for supplying me with the material relating to the proposed changes to the Uniform Commercial Code; and to Professor Colin Tapper for continuing to help by retrieving electronic information. It is a pleasure also to acknowledge the help of Dr Henry Kim of the Ashmolean Museum for help with the frontispiece. My thanks go, finally, to the publishers for their help and forbearance in countless ways.

Work on this edition was finished on March 1, 2004

A conversation with an academic visitor to Oxford from another discipline and another continent is worth recording. With reference, no doubt, to my great age, he asked whether I was still working. Well, yes, I was just then dealing with the proofs of a book. What was its title? *Frustration and Force Majeure*. Was that my autobiography?

GHT
Oxford
July 10, 2004

CONTENTS

CONTENTS

CHAPTER 3

IMPOSSIBILITY IN GENERAL: DESTRUCTION OF SUBJECT-MATTER

CHAPTER 4

OTHER TYPES OF IMPOSSIBILITY

CHAPTER 5
PARTIAL AND TEMPORARY IMPOSSIBILITY

CHAPTER 6
IMPRACTICABILITY

CHAPTER 7
FRUSTRATION OF PURPOSE

CHAPTER 8
ILLEGALITY

CHAPTER 12
CONTRACTUAL PROVISIONS FOR SUPERVENING EVENTS

CHAPTER 13
FORESEEN AND FORESEEABLE EVENTS

CHAPTER 14
SELF-INDUCED FRUSTRATION

CONTENTS

CHAPTER 15
EFFECTS OF FRUSTRATION

CHAPTER 16
NATURE OF THE DOCTRINE

TABLE OF UK CASES

TABLE OF CASES FROM OTHER JURISDICTIONS

Table of Cases from Other Jurisdictions

TABLE OF UK LEGISLATION

TABLE OF OTHER LEGISLATION

TABLE OF EC LEGISLATION

TABLE OF VIENNA CONVENTION REFERENCES

TABLE OF RESTATEMENT REFERENCES

CHAPTER 1

INTRODUCTION

I. TWO CONFLICTING PRINCIPLES

This book is about a conflict between two principles. The first is the **1–001** principle of sanctity of contract, sometimes expressed in the Latin maxim *pacta sunt servanda*. This principle insists on the literal performance of contracts in spite of the fact that events occurring after the contract was made have interfered with the performance of one party, or reduced its value to the other; it is based on the view that one of the main purposes of contract as a legal and commercial institution is precisely to allocate the risks of such events. It takes the position that, once those risks have been so allocated by the parties, they should, as a general rule, not be re-allocated in a different manner by the courts. On the other hand, the principle of sanctity of contract, like many legal principles, is not considered to express an absolute value. It is qualified by a counter-principle that parties who enter into contracts often do so on the basis of certain shared, but unexpressed assumptions. This counter-principle is also sometimes expressed in a Latin phrase, *rebus sic stantibus*. Its effect is that contractual obligations may be discharged by supervening events where these have brought about a change of circumstances so significant as to destroy a basic assumption which the parties had made when they entered into the contract.

II. NO THEORY OF IMPOSSIBILITY

In discussing the conflict between sanctity of contract and discharge by **1–002** supervening events, two further principles of the common law of contract must be kept in mind. The first is that most[1] common law systems have not followed the original civil law principle that there can be no contract

---

[1] For a different statutory approach, see Indian Contract Act 1872, s.56 ("An agreement to do an act impossible in itself is void"); criticised by Pollock, *Principles of Contract* (13th ed.), p.229.

to do what is impossible[2] (*impossibilium nulla obligatio*[3]). This position has been repeatedly rejected in English law. As long ago as 1706 Holt C. J. said that: "when a man will for a valuable consideration undertake to do an impossible thing, though it cannot be performed, yet he shall answer in damages."[4] In modern cases, statements are similarly to be found to the effect that English law has no difficulty in recognising that parties can effectively enter into a contract "requiring one of them to do the impossible".[5] The statements which assert the nullity in civil law systems of obligations to do the impossible, and those asserting the (possible) validity of such obligations in common law systems, refer for the most part to cases of antecedent impossibility. They are, therefore, not our prime concern in this book, which deals with cases of supervening impossibility. There are indeed many cases in which such (supervening) impossibility is regarded by the common law as a ground of discharge.[6] But it is by no means invariably so regarded: the common law sees no greater difficulty in holding a party liable where his performance has become impossible, than in holding him liable where the impossibility existed *ab initio*. The explanation for this difference between civil and common law lies in the original approach of the two groups of systems to remedies. According to this approach, enforced performance was assumed in civil law systems to be the primary remedy,[7] and was obviously inappropriate when the performance in question was, or had become, impossible. This might be so even when the impossibility results from what to a common lawyer would appear to be a plain breach[8]: in such cases civil law often reached the same result as the common law, making the party who is responsible for the impossibility liable for compensation; but it felt a conceptual difficulty about the actual enforceability of the impossible obligation. In the common law, where the primary remedy for breach of contract is by means of a money judgment, no similar difficulties are felt. Performance

---

[2] *e.g.* Swiss Code of Obligations, Art.20I; Zweigert and Kötz, (trs. Weir), *Introduction to Comparative Law* (2nd ed.), p.525. For recent changes in German law on this topic, see below after n.13.

[3] Dig. 50.17.185.

[4] *Thornborow v Whitacre* (1706) 2 Ld. Raym. 1164, 1165; *cf.* below, para.2–009 at n.63.

[5] *Eurico SpA v Phillip Brokers (The Epaphus)* [1987] 2 Lloyd's Rep. 215 at 218; *cf. Baily v De Crespigny* (1869) L.R. 4 Q.B. 180 at 185; *Joseph Constantine SS Line v Imperial Smelting Corp Ltd* [1942] A.C. 154 at 163; *Jones v St John's College* (1870) L.R. 6 Q.B. 115 at 127; *Richco International Ltd v Bunge & Co Ltd (The New Prosper)* [1991] 2 Lloyd's Rep. 93 at 99.

[6] See Ch.3, below.

[7] See Treitel, *Remedies for Breach of Contract: a Comparative Account*, esp. pp.51, 56.

[8] *e.g.* disposal of the subject-matter of the contract (amounting to what an English lawyer would regard as a breach) is regarded as a case of impossibility for the purposes of BGB § 275; the same assumptions underlie, *e.g.* BGB §§ 323, 325 and 326. In English law, "impossibility" is sometimes used in this sense in discussions of anticipatory breach: *e.g.* in *Heyman v Darwins* [1942] A.C. 356, 397 ("impossibility created by his own act"). Plainly, such impossibility is not a ground of discharge: *cf.* below, para.14–009.

of an obligation to pay money is never considered to be impossible, so that an action for an agreed sum (which is conceptually a kind of specific enforcement) cannot be resisted on this ground. And impossibility in performing an obligation of some other content (whether to transfer a thing, or to render a service) is no conclusive objection to an award of damages for failing to render the performance in question. The closest English law analogy to the civil law principle that impossibility led to nullity of an obligation is to be found in the rule of equity that "the court does not compel a person to do what is impossible"[9]: *i.e.* that it will refuse in such a case to order specific performance.[10] Such refusal does not, of course, preclude an award of damages. Looked at in this way, the divergence between civil and common law in cases of impossibility was less striking than may at first sight appear; for in some cases in which an obligation was regarded by civil lawyers as void for impossibility, the party who had promised to do the impossible thing might be liable in damages, *e.g.* because he was at fault in concluding the contract when he knew, or should have known, of the impossibility, (though sometimes such liability was restricted to one to compensate the other party for his reliance loss)[11]; or because the terms of the contract are considered to include a guarantee that performance was (or would be) possible[12]; or because one party was responsible for the impossibility.[13] Recent developments in German law show a considerable convergence between civil and common law approaches to this topic. Before the coming into force in 2002 of amendments to the Civil Code (BGB), that Code provided that a contract for an impossible performance was null (*nichtig*).[14] This provision has been repealed so that antecedent impossibility is no longer a ground of invalidity.[15] Instead, impossibility is a bar to a claim for (specific) performance[16] but not to one for damages: the creditor of the impossible

---

[9] *Forrer v Nash* (1865) 35 Beav. 167, 171.

[10] Treitel, *The Law of Contract* (11th ed.), p.1029; Both common law and civil law principles are reflected in the amendments to the Sale of Goods Act 1979 made by the Sale and Supply of Goods to Consumers Regulations 2002, SI 2002/3045, reg.5. S.48A 2(a) provides that where non-conforming goods are delivered to a buyer, then the buyer has the right "to require the seller" to "repair or replace" the goods and by s.48E(2) the court may enforce the seller's obligation to repair or to replace by ordering specific performance. But it cannot do so where repair or replacement is "impossible" since in such a case "the buyer must not require" the seller to do either of these things: s.48B(3)(a).

[11] See Treitel, *Remedies for Breach of Contract: a Comparative Account*, pp.88–89.

[12] *e.g.* Seuff. A. 65 Nr 160 (1910) (seller of 1,000 boxes of potatoes on a named steamer held to have guaranteed the presence of that quantity when in fact only 106 were on board).

[13] Above, n.8.

[14] Former BGB § 306.

[15] BGB § 311a(1).

[16] BGB § 275(1); see also § 257(2) and (3) for obstacles not amounting to impossibility.

performance is entitled at his option to damages (for loss of his bargain) or to reliance loss[17] except where the debtor at the time of contracting was neither aware of the obstacle to performance nor responsible for failing to be aware of it.[18] These two bases of liability can scarcely apply to cases of supervening impossibility (which are our concern); but the further concepts of the debtor's being liable because he was responsible[19] for the impossibility by reason of being at fault[20] or of having guaranteed that performance was possible[21] may well apply to such cases.

III. STRICT CONTRACTUAL LIABILITY

1–003 The second point relates to the standard of liability; and here it is important to emphasise that, at common law, liability for breach of contract is often strict: that is, a party may be in breach even though his failure or inability to perform is not due to any want of care or diligence on his part.[22] The mere fact that supervening events occurring without his fault have interfered with or even prevented performance is therefore not sufficient to bring the doctrine of discharge into operation. This point is most readily illustrated by the case of a seller of unascertained generic goods who is cut off by supervening events from the only source of supply to which he could reasonably have been expected to resort,[23] or who cannot ship the goods from the contractually designated country of origin because it turns out that no shipping space is available there during the time specified in the contract for shipment.[24] In such cases, the contract is not discharged: lack of fault is not a sufficient (though it may be a necessary[25]) condition for the operation of the doctrine of discharge. It does not follow that such contracts can never be discharged by supervening events. Thus the case in which goods cannot be shipped because shipping space is unavailable may be contrasted with one in which the port of shipment designated in the contract is destroyed by an earthquake: there can be little doubt that in the latter case the contract would be discharged. The distinction between the two situations can be explained by saying that the seller undertakes to obtain shipping space, but that neither party undertakes that the port will continue to exist.

---

[17] BGB §§ 275(4), 311a(2), 283, 284.

[18] BGB § 311a(2), sentence 2.

[19] BGB § 280(1).

[20] BGB § 276(1).

[21] *ibid; cf.* above, n.12.

[22] *Raineri v Miles* [1981] 1 A.C. 1050 at 1086; see generally Treitel in Bos and Brownlie (eds.), *Liber Amicorum for Lord Wilberforce*, p.185.

[23] See, *e.g. Barnett v Javeri & Co* [1916] 2 K.B. 390; *P J Van der Zijden Wildhandel v Tucker & Cross* [1975] 2 Lloyd's Rep. 240; *Intertradex SA v Lesieur Torteaux SARL* [1978] 2 Lloyd's Rep. 509; and those of the soyabean cases (discussed in Ch.13, below) in which the sellers were held liable.

[24] *Lewis Emanuel & Son Ltd v Sammut* [1952] 2 Lloyd's Rep. 629.

[25] Below, Ch.14.

The latter point is simply an assumption, made by both parties, on which performance of the contract depends. Even the undertaking to obtain shipping space, does not extend to all imaginable situations: it has, for example, been held that the doctrine of discharge could apply where most of the shipping space which was expected to be available for transporting the goods from the country of origin to that of the contractual destination had been requisitioned during the First World War, thus wholly disrupting the seaborne trade between those countries for a period of some years.[26] The crucial factor here was that of delay: the contract expressly provided for suspension where performance was "hindered," and it was held that performance need not be resumed when some years later shipping conditions returned to normal. A similar point can be made in relation to the failure of a charterer to provide a cargo. His liability for such failure is strict[27]; but if he provides the cargo the contract may be discharged as a result of delays in loading caused by events beyond his control, such as strikes at the port of loading.[28] Again it can be said that the charterer undertakes that there will be a cargo, but not that manpower will be available to load it. Another way of stating the distinction is to say that a contracting party takes the risk of some events of the kind here considered (the availability of the goods, or of shipping space) but not of others (prolonged disruption of communications due to war, delays caused by strikes): thus it has been said that the outcome depends on whether the party claiming to be discharged has (or has not) taken "the risk of the contingency's occurrence".[29] But this type of statement is, with respect, unhelpful. It can refer either to risk allocation by the agreement, or to risk allocation by law. On the former view, it adds nothing to the formulation put forward above, under which the result depends on the undertakings of the parties with respect to the event. On the latter view, it simply restates the problem of drawing the borderline between strict liability and discharge, without carrying any further the process of determining where and how that line should be drawn.

---

[26] *Acetylene Co of G.B. v Canada Carbide Co* (1922) 8 Lloyd's Rep. 456; and see below, para.5–042.

[27] *Sociedad Financiera etc. v Agrimpex etc. (The Aello)* [1961] A.C. 135 (overruled on another point in *E L Oldendorff & Co GmbH v Tradax Export SA (The Johanna Oldendorff)* [1974] A.C. 479); *Kawasaki Steel Corp v Sardoil SpA (The Zuhio Maru)* [1977] 2 Lloyd's Rep. 552; *cf. Hills v Sughrue* (1846) 15 M. & W. 252 (where the shipowner undertook to supply the cargo and this undertaking was described at 261 as "absolute"); *Kurt A Becher GmbH v Roplak Enterprises SA (The World Navigator)* [1991] 2 Lloyd's Rep. 23 (time of loading); *The Athanasia Cominos* [1990] 1 Lloyd's Rep. 277 at 282; and *Effort Shipping Co Ltd v Linden Management SA (The Giannis NK)* [1998] A.C. 605 at 619, 624 (shipper's "warranty" that cargo is not dangerous).

[28] *Pioneer Shipping v BTP Tioxide (The Nema)* [1982] A.C. 724.

[29] e.g. *Transatlantic Financing Corp v US*, 363 F. 2d 312, 316 (1966); and see below, para.3–008, at n.41.

IV. CONTRACTUAL LIABILITY BASED ON FAULT

1–004   The preceding discussion concerns the borderline between strict liability and discharge; but it is also necessary to refer to the relationship between the doctrine of discharge and cases in which contractual liability is based on fault. These are cases in which a party who has undertaken to perform a service or to achieve some result is not liable if he has exercised reasonable care in rendering the service, or if he has used due diligence to bring about the result. If that party complies with that standard, but the result specified or expected by the other party is not achieved, then the former party is not in breach. This is often the position where professional services are rendered, for example, by a surgeon who conducts an operation or by a lawyer who represents his client in litigation.[30] Similar reasoning may apply where the achievement of the result is prevented by some supervening event. For example, a contract may require a party to use due diligence to obtain the consent of a third party, necessary to its performance or to the use intended to be made by the other party of its subject-matter. This would be the position where the contract required a party to obtain an export or import licence,[31] or to obtain planning permission or some other form of official consent. Refusal of such consent may be, or result from, a supervening event, such as a change in the policy of the planning or licensing authority.[32] If the party who was required by the contract to make the reasonable efforts does make them and nevertheless fails to obtain the requisite consent, he is under no liability. But the reason for this is not that the supervening event has discharged him from his duty of diligence: it is rather that he has performed that duty.[33] The point is of practical significance since the legal consequences of discharge by supervening events for which a party is not responsible, and of discharge by performance, differ significantly: in particular, the legislation which specifies the effects of discharge by impossibility and frustration[34] does not apply to discharge by performance. Again the possibility exists that in cases of the kind just described the contract may be discharged by supervening events. This is true, not only in the obvious

---

[30] *e.g. Clark v Kirby-Smith* [1964] Ch. 506; *Eyre v Measday* [1986] 1 All E.R. 488; *Thake v Maurice* [1986] Q.B. 644.

[31] See below, para.8–014.

[32] *e.g. Maritime National Fish Ltd v Ocean Trawlers Ltd* [1935] A.C. 524.

[33] See the discussion of *A V Pound & Co Ltd v M W Hardy Inc* [1956] A.C. 588 in *Benjamin's Sale of Goods* (6th ed.), paras 18–294 to 18–296, and below, para.8–020. An alternative ground on which the party in question may escape liability is that the condition of obtaining the consent is on its true construction not promissory but contingent, so that that party has not made any promise even to make reasonable efforts to bring it about: see *Total Gas Marketing Board Ltd v Arco British Ltd* [1998] 2 Lloyd's Rep. 209; for the distinction between contingent and promissory conditions, see Treitel, *The Law of Contract* (11th ed.) p.62.

[34] The Law Reform (Frustrated Contracts) Act 1943 applies "where a contract . . . has become impossible of performance or been otherwise frustrated" and so would not cover the situation discussed in the text at n.33, above.

case where the effect of such an event is to prevent the party who is under an obligation of diligence from pursuing the course of conduct which he has undertaken to perform: *e.g.* where a party who had undertaken to render professional services dies. It is equally true where, though that course of conduct is not prevented, the event makes it impossible to achieve the object to be attained: *e.g.* where a contract obliged a seller to make reasonable efforts to obtain an export licence, and the export of such goods of the contract description was then absolutely prohibited. In such a case the seller would not be bound even to make reasonable efforts, for it is settled that he is under no liability if he can show that the licence would certainly have been refused, even if he had made such efforts.[35]

V. SUPERVENING AND ANTECEDENT EVENTS: FRUSTRATION AND MISTAKE

Our concern in this book is with the effect on contracts of supervening events, *i.e.* with events which occur after the conclusion of the contract. The effect of antecedent events, *i.e.* those which had already taken place at the time of contracting, is governed by principles which may in some respects be related to those which apply to supervening events,[36] but it is submitted that the two sets of principles are nevertheless distinct. The distinction, in English terminology, can be summed up by saying that antecedent events may make the contract void for mistake, while supervening events may discharge it by frustration. For example, in a number of the coronation cases, to be discussed in Ch.7, contracts were discharged when, after they had been made, the processions were

1–005

---

[35] See *Re Anglo-Russian Merchant Traders and John Batt & Co (London) Ltd* [1917] 2 K.B. 679; *Benjamin's Sale of Goods* (6th ed.), para.18–285.

[36] *cf.* Pollock, *Principles of Contract* (13th ed.), p.246; Anson, *Principles of the Law of Contract* (19th ed.), p.350; this view is no longer found in more recent editions of Anson: see now 28th ed., p.530, restricting the operation of the doctrine of discharge to "supervening" events. *cf.* also Lord Haldane (dissenting) in *Bank Line Ltd v Arthur Capel & Co.* [1919] A.C. 435, at 445; *Associated Japanese Bank (International) Ltd v Crédit du Nord SA* [1989] 1 W.L.R. 255 at 264 ("related areas"); *William Sindall plc v Cambridgeshire CC* [1994] 1 W.L.R. 1016 at 1039; *Grains Fourrage SA v Huyton* [1997] 1 Lloyd's Rep. 628 at 630 ("analogous concepts"). See also the reference to the frustration case of *Krell v Henry* [1903] 2 K.B. 740 in the mistake case of *Bell v Lever Bros Ltd* [1932] A.C. 161 at 226 and the words "whether as to existing or future facts" *ibid.* at 226–227; the reliance on frustration cases in the mistake case of *Great Peace Shipping Ltd v Tsavliris Salvage (International) Ltd (The Great Peace)* [2002] EWCA Civ 1407; [2003] Q.B. 697 at [61]–[76] (as to which see below, para.1–007, at nn.67–68 and contrast below, para.1–008, at n.74. For the citation in the United States of decisions on supervening events in cases actually concerned with antecedent obstacles to performance, see, for example, *Stees v Leonnard*, 20 Minn. 448 (1874), below, paras 3–056 to 3–057, and *Kinzer Construction Co v State*, 125 N.Y.S. 46 (1910). For the position taken by the American Law Institute's Restatement of the Law, 2d, Contracts (hereinafter Restatement 2d) on cases of antecedent impracticability or frustration, see below, para.1–010.

cancelled.[37] In one of these cases, however, the processions had (unknown to the parties) already been cancelled before the contract was made, and the contract was held to be void for mistake[38]: this shows that mistake can make a contract void even though it consists of a belief as to the future, so long as the belief is already false at the time of contracting. One can, in relation to these cases, also make the point that the line between antecedent and supervening events is not always easy to draw. It is, for example, not wholly clear on which side of the line a case would have fallen if the contract had been made after the King had fallen ill, but before his illness had been diagnosed or found to be sufficiently serious to warrant the postponement of the coronation. A somewhat similar point arose in *Amalgamated Investment & Property Co Ltd v John Walker & Sons Ltd*,[39] where a contract was made for the sale of a London warehouse which the purchaser (as the vendor knew) intended to redevelop. Before the contract was made, a government official had decided that the warehouse ought to be listed as a building of special architectural or historic interest. But the actual listing only took place after the conclusion of the contract: its effect was to make it very much harder to obtain permission to redevelop, and (according to the purchaser's evidence) to reduce the value of the property by some £1,500,000 below the contract price of £1,710,000. The Court of Appeal held that the purchaser was not entitled to relief on the ground either of mistake or of frustration. The point here to be emphasised is that these two doctrines were considered as *separate* grounds for relief, and that it is implicit in this approach that one of them could have prevailed in spite of the rejection of the other. Yet the distinction between their respective factual bases would have been a fine one, and to make legal consequences depend on such fine factual distinctions might be thought undesirable.

Nevertheless, the analogy between initial invalidity on the ground of mistake and discharge under the doctrine of frustration is imperfect for a number of reasons. There are, in particular, three distinctions between the two doctrines, and one can also make a point about their historical development.

The first distinction relates to the state of mind of the parties. The type of mistake with which frustration is said to be analogous is mistake which nullifies consent[40] (also described as "common" mistake), *i.e.* a fundamental mistake of both parties as to the subject-matter of the contract. Inherent in the notion of "mistake" is the idea that the parties entertain an affirmative belief in the existence of a state of affairs when in fact that state of affairs does not exist, *e.g.* in the existence of the subject-matter, when in fact it has been destroyed. If the parties entertain no such belief, their state of mind cannot be described as mistake; the law relating to the effect of mistake on contracts distinguishes between indifference

---

[37] See below, paras 7–006 to 7–014.

[38] *Griffith v Brymer* (1903) 19 T.L.R. 434.

[39] [1977] 1 W.L.R. 164; *cf.* also *Smith Coney & Barret v Becker Gray & Co* [1916] 2 Ch. 87, where both frustration and mistake were considered.

[40] See n.42, below; Treitel, *The Law of Contract* (11th ed.), p.286.

and mistake.[41] In cases of mistake, it is also a requirement for relief that the mistake must induce the contract.[42] The position is different in cases of actual or alleged discharge by frustration, where the parties often have no affirmative belief as to the event, which may have taken them wholly by surprise. They need not *believe* that the event *will not* occur. It does not, indeed, logically follow from this distinction that parties should be denied relief in respect of antecedent obstacles to performance merely because they did not affirmatively believe that such obstacles did not exist.[43] But, whatever the ground of such relief may be, it cannot be mistake,[44] and English law recognises no other ground for relief in such cases.[45] Nor, for reasons to be discussed below, should it do so.

The second distinction relates to the legal effects of the two doctrines. Mistake makes a contract void[46] *ab initio*, while frustration only discharges it with effect from the occurence of the frustrating event.[47] It follows that no action can be brought to enforce any obligation alleged to have been imposed by a contract which is void for mistake, while such actions can be brought in respect of obligations which have arisen under a frustrated contract before the time of discharge.[48] The latter proposition has been modified by statute in respect of money payable before discharge,[49] but this modification is subject to significant exceptions[50] and in any event does not extend to a number of other applications of the principle that obligations accrued before discharge remain enforceable.[51] Moreover, in

---

[41] *cf. Gillman v Gillman* (1946) 174 L.T. 272 (where the court was concerned with the type of mistake required to substantiate the defence of *non est factum*).

[42] This is inherent in the notion that the mistake "nullifies ... consent" (*Bell v Lever Bros Ltd* [1932] A.C. 161 at 217) and also in the definition of the requirement that the mistake must be "fundamental." In relation to a mistake as to quality this, it is submitted, means that the mistake must relate to a quality by reference to which the parties have identified the subject-matter: Treitel, *The Law of Contract* (11th ed.), p.292. The requirement of inducement appears more explicitly in relation to mistake which negatives consent (or "mutual" mistake): see, *e.g. Mackie v European Assurance Soc* (1869) 21 L.T. 102; *Fellowes v Gwydyr* (1829) 1 Russ. & My. 83.

[43] See, *e.g. Kinzer Construction Co v State*, 125 N.Y.S. 46 (1910), discussed below, para.3–058.

[44] In the United States Restatement 2d, Ch.11, § 266 provides for relief in such cases of antecedent "impracticability and frustration;" and such relief is evidently regarded as distinct from the relief for mistake provided for in Ch.6 of the Restatement 2d: see below, para.§ 1–010.

[45] Contrast the *Kinzer* case, n.43, above with *M'Donald v Corporation of Worthington* (1892) 9 T.L.R. 21 at 239.

[46] *Associated Japanese Bank (International) Ltd v Crédit du Nord SA* [1989] 1 W.L.R. 255 at 268; *cf. Great Peace Shipping Ltd v Tsavliris Salvage (International) Ltd (The Great Peace)* [2002] EWCA Civ 1407; [2003] Q.B. 697 at [82], [85].

[47] Below, para.15–011. For cases in which the effect of the event is not clear as soon as it occurs, see below, Ch.9.

[48] See the example given below, para.15–011.

[49] Law Reform (Frustrated Contracts) Act 1943, s.1(2); below, para.15–050.

[50] *ibid.* s.2(5), below, paras 15–089 *et seq.*

[51] See below, para.15–066.

so far as the effects of discharge are now regulated by the provisions of the Law Reform (Frustrated Contracts) Act 1943, those provisions clearly apply only to supervening events: in the words of s.1(1) they apply, "where a contract ... *has become* impossible of performance or been otherwise frustrated and the parties thereto have for that reason been discharged from *further* performance of the contract. ..." These words clearly contemplate discharge by supervening events, and the whole structure of the Act is based on the assumption that discharge occurs by reason of a change of circumstances occurring after the conclusion of an effective contract.[52] Indeed, the point is so clear that no attempt has ever been made to apply the Act to cases of mistake as to circumstances in existence at the time of contracting.[53]

1–007   The third point is of a more practical nature. It is said to be a requirement of invalidity on the ground of mistake that the mistake must be "fundamental",[54] and the same expression is used to make the point that it is only a "fundamental" change of circumstances which brings the doctrine of discharge into play.[55] But the word "fundamental" is used in the law of contract with many shades of meaning; and the use of this single word to refer to tests of mistake and frustration should not obscure the fact that the standards of "fundamentality" required for their operation are distinct. One may concede that if the degree of difference between facts as they are and as they are supposed to be is sufficiently serious to amount to a fundamental mistake, then the same degree of difference between facts as they are at the time of contracting and as they later turn out to be (by reason of a supervening event) will also be sufficiently serious to discharge the contract under the doctrine of frustration. But the converse is by no means necessarily true: events which frustrate a contract would not necessarily make it void for mistake if, unknown to the parties they had already happened when the contract was made. Two illustrations may be given in support of this suggestion. First, we have already noted that in *Griffith v Brymer*,[56] one of the coronation cases, a contract was held void for mistake on the ground that the Coronation had already been postponed when the parties, without being aware of this fact, entered into the contract. Since that decision, however, the scope of the doctrine of mistake as to the subject-matter has been restrictively interpreted in *Bell v*

---

[52] See the frequent use in the Act of the phrase "before the time of discharge": this clearly contemplates events occurring after the conclusion of an effective contract.

[53] The assumption that the 1943 Act does not apply to cases of antecedent impossibility giving rise to an operative mistake is supported by *Great Peace Shipping Ltd v Tsavliris Salvage (International) Ltd (The Great Peace)* [2002] EWCA Civ 1407; [2003] Q.B. 679 at [161].

[54] See Treitel, *The Law of Contract* (11th ed.), pp.286 *et seq.*

[55] e.g. *British Movietonenews Ltd v London and District Cinemas* [1952] A.C. 166 at 185, *Sir Lindsay Parkinson Ltd v Commissioners of Works* [1949] 2 K.B. 632 at 667, both approved in *Davis Contractors Ltd v Fareham UDC* [1956] A.C. 696 at 722, and see *ibid.* at 723.

[56] (1903) 19 T.L.R. 434, above, para.1–005.

Lever Bros Ltd,[57] and it is an open question whether *Griffith v Brymer* has survived that decision of the House of Lords.[58] Doubts were indeed at one time also expressed about *Krell v Henry*,[59] where a contract which had been made before the Coronation was postponed was held to have been frustrated by the postponement, but these doubts have not prevailed.[60] Secondly, we shall see that in the Suez cases (to be discussed in Ch.4) it was held that contracts of sale and contracts of carriage were not frustrated by the closure of the canal, since the difference between carrying the goods via Suez and via the Cape was not sufficiently "fundamental". Such cases do not rule out the possibility that a contract of carriage might be frustrated by the blocking of a contemplated route where use of the only route remaining open *would* require the carrier to render a performance "fundamentally" different from that which he would have rendered, had he been able to use the contemplated route. Yet it is unlikely that the contract would be held void for mistake if the contemplated route had (without the knowledge of the parties) been already blocked when the contract was made. Again, we have seen that a party can be liable for failing to perform an undertaking to do the impossible: *e.g.* to deliver goods from a specified ship at a specified port which (unknown to the parties) the ship was incapable of entering[61]; but the party who had given that undertaking could be discharged if, after the contract had been made, an event happened which made it impossible to get into the port: *e.g.* "if a sudden storm had silted up the harbour".[62] Such contrasting examples form the basis for the submission that a stricter standard of what is "fundamental" is applied at common law in cases of alleged mistake than in cases of alleged frustration.[63] It is submitted that this distinction can be justified on the practical ground that it is easier to discover present facts than to foresee the future, and correspondingly easier to discover existing obstacles to performance than to foresee or guard against obstacles which may arise in the future, or because a contracting party is more likely, on the true construction of the contract, to have undertaken responsibility for an unknown existing, than for an unexpected future, state of affairs.[64] The view that the test for a mistake which makes a contract void under the rules laid down in *Bell v Lever Bros Ltd* is stricter

---

[57] [1932] A.C. 161.

[58] *Griffith v Brymer* is cited with apparent approval in the frustration case of *Fibrosa Spolka Akcyjna v Fairbairn Lawson Combe Barbour Ltd* [1943] A.C. 32 at 82 and in the mistake case of *The Great Peace*, above, n.53 at [67].

[59] [1903] 2 K.B. 740.

[60] See below, paras 7–011 to 7–014; *The Great Peace*, above, n.53, at [66].

[61] *Eurico SpA v Phillip Brothers (The Epaphus)* [1987] 2 Lloyd's Rep. 215 at 218; *Richco International Ltd v Bunge & Co. Ltd (The New Prosper)* [1991] 2 Lloyd's Rep. 93 at 99; above, para.1–002.

[62] *The Epaphus*, above, n.61, at 220; *cf. Bell v Lever Bros Ltd* [1932] A.C. 161 at 218, *per* Lord Atkin, approving the formulation of counsel (Sir John Simon KC).

[63] *cf. Jan Albert (HK) Ltd v Shu Kong Garment Factories Ltd* [1990] H.K.L.R. 317.

[64] *Great Peace Shipping Ltd v Tsavliris Salvage (International) Ltd (The Great Peace)* [2002] EWCA Civ 1407; [2003] Q.B. 697 at [85].

than that for frustration appears to be reflected in a recent mistake case[65] in which the Court of Appeal relied to a considerable extent on the analogy of frustration cases[66] but nevertheless added that the test of frustration might "not be adequate in the context of mistake"[67] and that "circumstances where a contract is void as a result of common mistake are likely to be less common than instances of frustration".[68] Such statements show that the analogy between invalidity on the ground of mistake and discharge by frustration is, at best, imperfect. It should therefore occasion no surprise that references to the doctrine of "absolute contracts"[69] and to *Paradine v Jane*[70] (to be discussed in Ch.2) continued to be made in cases of antecedent impossibility,[71] even after the basis of the modern doctrine of discharge by supervening impossibility was laid in *Taylor v Caldwell.*[72] It follows *a fortiori* that factors which were not only in existence but also known to the parties at the time of contracting cannot be relied on as grounds of frustration.[73]

1–008   The differences so far listed appear to support the judicially expressed view that mistake is "a different juristic concept"[74] from frustration, in that the two are brought into operation by circumstances which differ significantly from each other (and differ not only in respect of the time at which the obstacle to performance arises), and in that they give rise to different legal effects. The same view is also supported by a curious aspect of the history of the matter. The origin of the doctrine of discharge by supervening events is generally traced back to the judgment of Blackburn J. in *Taylor v Caldwell*[75] in 1863. Only four years later, Blackburn J. delivered the judgment of the court in the leading mistake case of *Kennedy v Panama Royal Mail Co.*,[76] but that judgment contains no reference to *Taylor v Caldwell*, even though that case was cited by counsel in the *Kennedy* case.[77] Nor is there any reference to *Taylor v Caldwell* in *Clifford v Watts*,[78] a case which was also concerned with antecedent impossibility, even though in that case the result resembled *Taylor v Caldwell* in that the impossibility did, on the true construction of the contract, provide the defendant with an excuse. Conversely, *Taylor v Caldwell* does not refer to cases of

---

[65] *The Great Peace*, above.
[66] *ibid.* at [61]–[76].
[67] *ibid.* at [83].
[68] *ibid.* at [85].
[69] Below, paras 2–001 *et seq.*
[70] (1647) Aleyn 26, below, para.2–002.
[71] *e.g.* in *Clifford v Watts* (1870) L.R. 5 C.P. 577, at 586, and see below, para.2–033.
[72] (1863) 3 B. & S. 826, below, para.2–024.
[73] *McAlpine Humberoak Ltd v McDermott International Inc* (1992) 58 B.L.R. 1.
[74] *Joseph Constantine SS Line v Imperial Smelting Corp Ltd* [1942] A.C. 154 at 186; *cf. Bell v Lever Bros Ltd* [1932] A.C. 161 at 237; *Fibrosa Spolka Akcyjna v Fairbairn Lawson Combe Barbour Ltd* [1943] A.C. 32 at 80.
[75] Above, n.72.
[76] (1867) L.R. 2 Q.B. 580, where the mistake was not "fundamental" and so did not make the contract void.
[77] *ibid.* at 581.
[78] (1870) L.R. 5 C.P. 577.

antecedent impossibility such as *Couturier v Hastie*,[79] which had been decided only seven years earlier. It is not necessary here to enter into the debate whether *Couturier v Hastie* was indeed a case of mistake[80] or one which turned on the construction of the contract.[81] The point here is simply that it was concerned with an antecedent obstacle to performance, and that it was not regarded in *Taylor v Caldwell* as relevant to the development of the emerging doctrine of discharge by supervening events.

The preceding discussion is concerned with the different effects of antecedent and supervening obstacles to performance under the common law doctrines of mistake and frustration. It remains to consider the effect, in the present context, of the equitable rules relating to mistake, and in particular the relation between discharge of contract under the doctrine of frustration and the jurisdiction which was formerly thought to exist in equity to set a contract aside where both parties had entered into it under a mistake,[82] even though that mistake was not so serious as to amount to a "fundamental" one in the narrow common law sense established in *Bell v Lever Bros Ltd*.[83] It was certainly arguable that the types of mistake for which equity gave relief by way of rescission were so broadly defined as to include all events which, if they had occurred after the contract, would have frustrated it. Indeed the definition of mistake for this purpose may actually have been wider than that of a change of circumstances which is sufficiently serious or "fundamental" to bring the doctrine of frustration into play. It can also be said that the equitable jurisdiction resembled frustration in that it did not declare the contract void, but only voidable. But if there was an analogy between the type of mistake for which rescission was available only in equity and the type of supervening event which discharges a contract under the doctrine of frustration, then that analogy is, at least for the time being, deprived of its legal significance by *The Great Peace*,[84] where the Court of Appeal held that there was no longer any equitable power to rescind contracts for mistakes which were not "fundamental" in the narrow common law sense. This decision was based primarily on the ground that the former equitable power to rescind could not be reconciled with the strict common law requirement of a "fundamental" mistake as defined in *Bell v Lever Bros Ltd*.[85] However the Court of Appeal in *The Great Peace* seems also to have taken the view that the requirement, stated in some of the frustration

---

[79] (1856) 5 H.L.C. 673.
[80] *Barrow, Lane & Ballard Ltd v Phillips & Co Ltd* [1929] 1 K.B. 574 at 582 ("failure of consideration and mistake").
[81] Atiyah, 73 L.Q.R. 487.
[82] See the cases stretching from *Solle v Butcher* [1950] 1 K.B. 671 to *West Sussex Properties Ltd v Chichester DC*, June 28, 2000, CA, and Treitel, *The Law of Contract* (11th ed.), pp.318–319, where further references to the cases and other literature are given.
[83] [1932] A.C. 161; Treitel, *op. cit.*, pp.286–294.
[84] *Great Peace Shipping Ltd v Tsavliris Salvage (International) Ltd (The Great Peace)* [2002] EWCA Civ 1407; [2003] Q.B. 697.
[85] [1932] A.C. 161.

cases, of a supervening event making performance "something *radically* different from that which the parties contemplated when [the contract] was concluded"[86] imposed a stricter standard than that which had been applied in the cases which had allowed rescission for mistake in equity; and that those cases were open to objection precisely because, in at least some of them, there was no such *radical* difference between the facts (in existence at the time of contracting) as they were and as they were believed to be. Moreover, even if the House of Lords were in some future case to reject the part of the reasoning of *The Great Peace* which denies the existence of an equitable power to rescind contracts for mistakes which are not "fundamental" in the common law sense,[87] there would still be many other differences (than the one just noted[88]) between, on the one hand, any such hypothetically revived equitable jurisdiction to rescind for mistake and, on the other, discharge by frustration. In the first place, the equitable jurisdiction to rescind for mistake was discretionary,[89] while once a frustrating event is found to have occurred the contract is automatically brought to an end,[90] without any scope for judicial discretion. Secondly, the equitable jurisdiction was one to set the contract aside *on terms*,[91] while frustration leads to total discharge.[92] It is true that, under the Law Reform (Frustrated Contracts) Act 1943, the court has certain discretionary powers to make adjustments in respect of expenses incurred[93] and valuable benefits conferred[94] under frustrated contracts. But these powers have only a limited scope, and in cases to which they do not extend English courts have no analogous common law power to make adjustments. The powers conferred by the Act, moreover, apply only to discharge by supervening (and not to invalidity on the ground of antecedent) events, so that they do not extend to the types of cases in which rescission for mistake was available in equity.[95] Under the former equitable jurisdiction in cases of mistake, the court could even give a party the option of upholding the contract on terms which removed or at least reduced the prejudice suffered by the other party as a result of the mistake.[96] There is no similar power, even under the 1943 Act, to make

---

[86] *The Great Peace*, above, n.84, at [63], italics supplied.

[87] It would be open to the House of Lords to take this step without disapproving of the actual decision in *The Great Peace* which can be justified on the grounds that (1) equity should not intervene in a charterparty case since in such cases certainty was of paramount importance (see the judgment of Toulson J., November 9, 2001 at [126]) and (2) there was "no injustice in the result": [2002] EWCA Civ 1407 at [166].

[88] Above, n.86.

[89] *Mills v Fox* (1887) 37 Ch.D. 153.

[90] Below, para.15–002.

[91] *Solle v Butcher* [1950] 1 K.B. 671; *Grist v Bailey* [1967] Ch. 532, esp. at 543.

[92] Below, para.15–010.

[93] s.1(2) proviso, below, para.15–071.

[94] s.1(3), below, para.15–060

[95] *Great Peace Shipping Ltd v Tsavliris Salvage International Ltd (The Great Peace)* [2002] EWCA Civ 1407; [2003] Q.B. 697 at [161]; above, para.1–006.

[96] See the authorities cited in n.91, above.

such an order in cases of frustration. Finally, the exercise of the equitable jurisdiction in cases of mistake may have been restricted to cases in which the party claiming relief was not at fault,[97] and in which it was "unconscientious" for the other party to insist on his rights under the contract after becoming aware of the mistake.[98] The former restriction may be compared with the rule that a party cannot rely on "self-induced" frustration[99]; but the conscience of the party resisting discharge is never regarded as an issue in cases in frustration. The equitable principles governing rescission for mistake were, therefore, no less than those of common law are, (though for different reasons) radically different from the concept of discharge by supervening events under the doctrine of frustration.

The position described in paras 1–005 to 1–009 above may be summarised by saying that English law distinguishes in many significant ways between relief for mistake in cases of antecedent, and relief for frustration in cases of supervening, impossibility or certain other obstacles to performance. In the United States, the Restatement 2d takes what may be called an intermediate position. While §§ 261 and 265 provide for relief in cases of supervening impracticability[1] and frustration, relief for "existing impracticability or frustration" is dealt with in § 266[2] and this differs not only from relief for supervening impracticability or frustration, but also from relief for mistake.   **1–010**

Two distinctions are drawn[3] between cases of antecedent and cases of supervening events. First, relief in respect of antecedent impracticability or frustration is available only to a party who at the time of contracting had no reason to know of the facts on which the claim for relief was based; and this requirement must be contrasted with the view that, in the case of a claim for relief in respect of supervening events, the fact that such events were foreseeable does not "necessarily" preclude discharge.[4] Secondly, the effect of antecedent impracticability or frustration is "to prevent a

---

[97] *Solle v Butcher* [1950] 1 K.B. 671 at 693; *Harrison & Jones Ltd v Bunten & Lancaster Ltd* [1953] 1 Q.B. 646 at 654; *Laurence v Lexcourt Holdings Ltd* [1978] 1 W.L.R. 1128; *The Lloydiana* [1983] 2 Lloyd's Rep. 313 at 318; *Associated Japanese Bank International Ltd v Crédit du Nord SA* [1989] 1 W.L.R. 255 at 270.

[98] *e.g. Hitchcock v Giddings* (1817) 4 Price 135; *Bettyes v Maynard* (1882) 46 L.T. 766; but see *Riverlate Properties Ltd v Paul* [1975] Ch. 133 at 140–141.

[99] Below, para.14–002.

[1] For the concept of "impracticability," see below, Ch.6.

[2] In the Uniform Commercial Code (UCC), s.2–615 (which provides for "Excuse by Failure of Presupposed Conditions") is stated to apply only in cases of "unforeseen *supervening* circumstances" (Comment 1). By contrast, s.2–613 (which deals with the effect of "Casualty to Identified Goods") "applies whether the goods were already destroyed at the time of contracting without the knowledge of the parties or whether they were destroyed subsequently" (Comment 2). S.2–613 runs together (with considerable modifications) the rules stated in Sale of Goods Act 1979, ss.6 and 7.

[3] See § 266, Comment a.

[4] Restatement 2d, § 261, Comments b and c, § 265, Comment a; and see below, Ch.13.

duty from arising",[5] while the effect of supervening circumstances of this kind is "to discharge a duty that has already arisen".[6]

With regard to the relationship between relief for antecedent impracticability or frustration and relief for mistake as to a basic assumption, the scheme of the Restatement 2d envisages that often the same circumstances will justify relief on either ground; and where this is the position, "the party entitled to relief may ... choose the ground on which he will rely".[7] However there are also significant differences between the two grounds for relief. The first is that, in American law, the effect of a mistake of both parties as to a basic assumption is to make the contract, not void (as in English law),[8] but "voidable by the adversely affected party".[9] The effect of antecedent impracticability or frustration, by contrast, is that no duty to render the performance in question arises,[10] so that the party adversely affected by the antecedent circumstances need not take any steps to avoid the contract. It follows that he is not affected by the rules which limit the power of avoidance for mistake, *e.g.* by the rule that the power to avoid for mistake may be lost by lapse of time.[11] The second difference relates to the grounds for relief. Relief for mistake is not available to a party who "bears the risk of mistake"[12] and this phrase is thought to cover a wider range of cases that the phrase "unless the language or circumstances indicate the contrary",[13] which excludes relief for antecedent impracticability or frustration.

Thus the Restatement 2d draws a tripartite distinction between cases of (1) mistake, which makes a contract voidable; (2) antecedent impossibility or frustration, which prevents a contractual duty from arising; and (3) supervening impracticability or frustration which discharges a contractual duty after it has arisen. It recognises considerable overlap between the first two of these categories but does not regard them as precisely co-extensive, apparently showing a greater readiness to grant relief in favour of a party who can establish antecedent impracticability or frustration than in favour of one who can establish only mistake. This distinction appears to be based on the view that impracticability or frustration can give rise to "extreme hardship"[14] while mistake results only in a "material imbalance"[15] between the two performances, and that such a consequence is regarded

---

[5] Restatement 2d, § 266, Comment a; § 266(1) and (2) ("no duty ... arises").

[6] Restatement 2d, § 266, Comment a; § 261 ("duty ... is discharged").

[7] *ibid*, § 266, Comment a.

[8] *i.e.* because consent is nullified under the principles stated in *Bell v Lever Bros Ltd* [1932] A.C. 161 (where the mistake was not sufficiently fundamental to make the contract void).

[9] Restatement 2d, § 152(1).

[10] Above, n.5.

[11] Restatement 2d, § 381(2).

[12] *ibid.*, § 152(1).

[13] *ibid.*, § 266(1) and (2).

[14] *ibid.*, Introductory Note to Ch.6, at p.380.

[15] *ibid.*

as "much less extreme"[16] than the hardship resulting from impracticability or frustration. The method used for giving effect to the distinction is to provide that relief for mistake is not available where a party "bears the risk of the mistake"[17] and this exception to such relief is said to be "much broader"[18] than the exception to relief for impracticability or frustration in the "relatively narrow"[19] case where "the language or the circumstance indicate the contrary."[20] It is submitted that very little, if any, of this reasoning applies in English law. In the first place, it is to a considerable extent based on the American concept of a mistake as to a basic assumption which makes a contract voidable and which covers a range of cases wider than that of a fundamental mistake which makes a contract void at common law.[21] The American concept is, it seems, closer to the former rule of English Law by which a contract could be set aside in equity for a mistake that did not make it void at law[22]; but the most recent decision of the Court of Appeal has denied that English law recognises any power to rescind a contract on this ground.[23] Secondly, there is no trace in English law of the distinction between the first two of the categories described above. Antecedent impossibility is not *per se* a ground for relief,[24] though relief in respect of it may, as already noted, be granted either on the ground of mistake or so as to give effect to the true construction of the contract.[25] Thirdly, in so far as the distinction between categories (1) and (2) is based on the ground that the hardship resulting from mistake is "much less extreme[26] than that resulting from impracticability or frustration, it is submitted that the reasoning of the Restatement 2d is at variance with the approach of English law. The reasoning, it is true, is used by the Restatement 2d in the context of *antecedent* impracticability or frustration; but if this can result in "extreme hardship",[27] then the same must be true of *supervening* impracticability or frustration, and there is no support in English law for the view that *greater* hardship is required to discharge a contract on the ground of frustration

---

[16] *ibid.*

[17] Restatement 2d, §§ 152, 154.

[18] *ibid.*, Introductory Note to Ch.6, p.380.

[19] *ibid.*, § 261.

[20] *ibid.*, § 152(1).

[21] See the criticism of *Bell v Lever Bros Ltd* [1932] A.C. 161 in *Williston on Contracts*, (rev. ed.), para.1570, n.3 and *ibid.*, para.1544; a considerable number of the illustrations of contracts voidable for mistake given in Restatement 2d, §§ 152 and 153 would not, it is submitted, satisfy the English requirement of a "fundamental" mistake.

[22] *i.e.* the rule based on the line of cases running from *Solle v Butcher* [1950] 1 K.B. 671 to *West Sussex Properties Ltd v Chichester DC*, June 28, 2000, cited in *Great Peace Shipping Ltd v Tsavliris (International) Ltd (The Great Peace)* [2002] EWCA Civ 1407; [2003] Q.B. 697 at [150].

[23] *The Great Peace*, above, n.22.

[24] Above, para.1–002.

[25] Above, para.1–008, at nn.80 and 81.

[26] See above, at n.16.

[27] See above, at n.14.

than to make it void at common law[28] for mistake. If anything, the contrary is the case: that is, for the reasons given in para.1–007 above, English law applies a *more* exacting standard of what is "fundamental" for the purpose of making a contract void for a mistake as to existing facts than it does for the purpose of discharging a contract by supervening events under the doctrine of frustration.

---

[28] There may formerly have been such a distinction between discharge by frustration and rescission for mistake in equity: see *The Great Peace*, above, n.22, at [63]; para.1–009 at nn.86, 88.

CHAPTER 2

DEVELOPMENT

I. THE DOCTRINE OF *PARADINE V JANE*

(1) Introduction

Paradine v Jane[1] is generally regarded as the authority for what has become   2–001
known as the doctrine of absolute contracts. The case was frequently cited
in later decisions in which the court held that supervening events had
not discharged a party from the contractual obligation in suit; and it
continued so to be cited even after *Taylor v Caldwell*,[2] which is now
generally considered to have established the doctrine of discharge by
supervening events, a doctrine which has come in English law to be known
as the doctrine of frustration.[3] Account must also be taken of the fact that
many of the actual decisions in which *Paradine v Jane* was applied are still
regarded as good law.[4] In discussing that case, a number of questions
therefore present themselves: what actually was decided? what subsequent
applications were made of the decision? and how much of what was
decided (in the case itself and in later applications of it) still survives? The
ensuing discussion is confined to the first two of these questions; the third
will be considered after we have discussed the impact of *Taylor v Caldwell*.

(2) The decision itself

The facts in *Paradine v Jane* were that the tenant of a farm was sued for rent   2–002
and pleaded that for part of the period to which the claim related he had
been dispossessed by "Prince Rupert, an alien born, enemy to the King[5]

---

[1] (1647) Aleyn 26; Kiralfy, *A Source Book of English Law*, p.22; Ibbetson, "Absolute
   Liability in Contract", in (ed. Rose), *Consensus ad Idem, Essays in the Law of
   Contract in Honour of Guenter Treitel*, 1.
[2] (1863) 3 B. & S. 826.
[3] For the various meanings of "frustration," see below, paras 2–044 to 2–050.
[4] See below, paras 2–033 to 2–034, 11–003, 11–017 to 11–022.
[5] Ibbetson, *op. cit.*, p.31 criticises this description of Prince Rupert on the ground
   that he was "the King's nephew and effective commander of his army". The first
   of these points is hardly compelling (King George V and Kaiser Wilhelm II were

and kingdom ... with an hostile army of men," so that the defendant was prevented from taking the profits of the land. The lessor demurred to this plea, so that the facts alleged in it must be assumed to have been true; and it was held that the tenant was nevertheless liable in debt for rent under the lease in respect of the period during which he was so dispossessed. One narrow ground for the decision was that the tenant had not pleaded that the entire force which had dispossessed him were alien enemies, the point being that, to the extent that this was not the case, the tenant would have had a remedy over against the wrongful dispossessors. But the court went on to give a wider ground, under which the tenant was liable "though the whole army had been alien enemies".[6] In reaching this result, the court drew a distinction between two situations and laid down two propositions. It will be convenient in the ensuing discussion to refer to these as the first and second propositions in *Paradine v Jane* and to note at this point that it is the second proposition which has been the more influential, so much so that the first is commonly overlooked or disregarded and that references to the doctrine of *Paradine v Jane*, or to the doctrine of absolute contracts, are to the second proposition only. The two situations between which the judgment distinguishes, and the propositions of law applicable to them, are as follows: (1) "Where the law creates a duty or charge and the party is disabled to perform it without any default in him, and hath no remedy over, there the law will excuse him. As in the case of waste, if a house be destroyed by tempest or by enemies, the lessee is excused ..." (2) "But when the party by his own contract creates a duty or charge upon himself, he is bound to make it good, if he may, notwithstanding any accident by inevitable necessity, because he might have provided against it by his contract. And therefore if a lessee covenant to repair a house, though it be burnt by lightning or thrown down by enemies, yet he ought to repair it".[7] This distinction calls for a number of comments.

(3) Distinction between the two propositions

2–003 First, the distinction between cases "where the party by his own contract creates a duty" and those "where the law creates a duty" is not the same as the modern distinction between contractual and non-contractual duties: no doubt the latter phrase applies where the duty is now regarded as arising in tort,[8] but it is not restricted to such cases. Thus a tenant's duty

---

cousins) and the force of the second may well have been diminished by events in the Civil War, such as the fact that Prince Rupert was dismissed from his command in 1645 after the surrender of Bristol and that at the time of the decision of *Paradine v Jane* the King was, in effect, prisoner of the Parliamentarians: see 17 D.N.B. 410, *et seq.*; C V Wedgwood, *The King's War*, 461 at 571 and *passim*.

[6] (1647) Aleyn 26 at 27.

[7] *ibid.*

[8] *e.g. Carstairs v Taylor* (1871) L.R. 6 Ex. 217 at 223, applying the first proposition in *Paradine v Jane* to a tort case.

not to commit waste is given in *Paradine v Jane* as an example of a duty created by law, even though it arises out of contract just as much as his duty to pay rent or his duty to perform an express covenant to repair. Some of the duties arising out of the relationship of bailor and bailee are likewise regarded for the present purpose as having been created by law, even where the relationship is contractual,[9] and we shall see that the performance of such duties may be excused by supervening events.[10] The distinction drawn in *Paradine v Jane* more closely resembles the modern distinction between *express* terms and certain *implied* terms. The implied terms in question are those which the law implies or imposes (in the absence of contrary agreement) to give expression to a number of duties which *prima facie* arise out of certain types of contracts, or (in other words) to terms which form "legal incidents of those ... kinds of contractual relationship."[11] In modern terminology, such terms have come to be known as "terms implied in law".[12] A tenant's obligation not to commit waste can be said to fall into this category.[13] The point of the distinction between the two situations described in *Paradine v Jane* is that "accident by inevitable necessity" is no defence to an action on an express contractual promise; but the judgement seems to recognise that such circumstances can be a defence to an action for breach of an implied promise or of a "legal incident" of a contract. This is made plain by the contrast between the two examples given: a tenant is not liable for waste "if a house be destroyed by tempest" but is liable for breach of an express covenant to repair a house "though it be burnt by lightning".

(4) Events affecting the counter-performance for the performance in suit

The second point arises out of the citation in subsequent cases of the   2–004
dictum from *Paradine v Jane* (quoted above) as to the tenant's liability on his express covenant to repair. Such citations were so frequent as apparently to give rise to the impression that *Paradine v Jane* was an action against the tenant for breach of a covenant to repair,[14] when actually it was an action for rent. It was, in other words, a case in which the supervening event affected, not the performance which was being sued for, but the counterperformance for that performance: that is, the enjoyment by the tenant of the subject-matter of the lease. In a later case it was indeed suggested that *Paradine v Jane* was a case where "The Court ...

---

[9] *cf. Sandeman Coprimar SA v Transitos y Transportes Integrales SL* [2003] EWCA Civ 113; [2003] Q.B. 1270 at [63] ("bailment and contract often go hand in hand").

[10] Below, para.2–012.

[11] *Mears v Safecar Securities Ltd.* [1983] Q.B. 54 at 78.

[12] See Treitel, *The Law of Contract* (11th ed.), pp.206–211.

[13] *ibid.*, p.11.

[14] *Paradine v Jane* is, for example, cited as an authority covering this situation in *Chitty on Contracts* (2nd ed., 1834), p.569 and in *Hall v Wright* (1859) E.B. & E. 765 at 775.

saw a cross remedy for the tenant ...".[15] This might suggest that the court regarded the lessor as being liable for his inability to render a performance made impossible by the supervening event. But the only actual reference in *Paradine v Jane* to a "remedy over" is in the cases "where the law creates a duty", *e.g.* in cases of waste: the point appears to be that, if the tenant has a remedy against a third party who is responsible for the damage then the tenant is responsible to the landlord even though the damage occurred "without any default in him" (*i.e.* the tenant). There is no suggestion that, on the assumed facts of the case, the tenant had any "cross remedy" against the landlord.[16] A conceivable ground for such a remedy might have been on the landlord's covenant for quiet possession; but such a remedy is most unlikely to have been available. There is no record of any such express covenant, and a claim on an implied covenant, even if then available,[17] would have fallen into the first of the two groups of cases distinguished in *Paradine v Jane: i.e.* within the group "where the law creates a duty" so that the landlord would have been excused by supervening disability occurring "without any default in him". Another way of reaching the same conclusion would be to say that the implied covenant amounts only to an undertaking that the tenant's possession will not be interrupted by the landlord or by the lawful acts of those claiming through him[18]: this is certainly the modern view, under which, on facts resembling *Paradine v Jane*, the landlord would not be in breach.[19] This would also normally be true even if there were an express covenant, which *prima facie* extends to interruptions of the kind just described and also to those arising from claims by title paramount.[20] In the modern law, this "means an eviction due to the fact that the lessor had no title to grant the term"[21]; but in *Paradine v Jane* the tenant's eviction was not due to any defect in the landlord's title: it was the result of an act of naked force on the part of a stranger. An express covenant might, no doubt, have been drafted so as to make the landlord liable even for a dispossession of this kind, but there is no hint that the lease contained any such unusual

---

[15] *Brown v Quilter* (1764) Amb. 619 at 621; as to this case, see further para.2–007, below.

[16] The judgment at most envisages a remedy against a third party: *e.g.* against dispossessors if they were not alien enemies: see above before n.6; *cf. Monk v Cooper* (1727) 2 Str. 763, discussing the possibility of a tenant's remedy against a third party who might have been responsible for destruction of the house by fire. There is no reference to this point in the report of *Monk v Cooper* in 2 Ld. Raym. 1477.

[17] See Megarry and Wade, *Law of Real Property* (6th ed.), para.14–196; Hill and Redman, *Law of Landlord and Tenant*, para.936.

[18] Hill and Redman, above, paras 935, 936.

[19] Some of the older authorities may have gone further in, *e.g.* giving a remedy to the tenant in respect of distress by a superior landlord: see Hill and Redman, above, para.936, n.3; but not in respect of tortious interference by a third party since the tenant then had his remedy against the wrongdoer: *Hayes v Bickerstaff* (1675) Vaugh. 118.

[20] Hill and Redman, above, paras 935, 936.

[21] *Matthey v Curling* [1922] A.C. 180 at 227.

covenant. It is most unlikely, therefore, that any "cross remedy" against the landlord would have been available to the tenant. The probable reason for this conclusion is not that the landlord was "excused" by reason of the supervening events; it is rather that his contractual responsibility did not, in the first place, extend to the state of affairs which those events brought about. In any case, nothing was decided in *Paradine v Jane* (even by inference) as to the liability of the landlord. The only point actually decided was that the tenant remained liable for rent even on the assumption that he was deprived of possession of the premises by an event for which neither party was responsible. On this point, the decision was followed in many later cases in which it was similarly held that liability for rent was not discharged by the supervening destruction of the premises by fire, flood[22] or enemy action.[23]

(5) Events affecting the performance in suit

A third point relates to the scope of the doctrine of *Paradine v Jane*. The language of the second proposition in that case is certainly wide enough to extend to the case where performance of the defendant's own promise (and not merely that of the counter-promise for it) is prevented as a result of some "accident by inevitable necessity". This view is at first sight supported by the dictum in *Paradine v Jane*, making the tenant of a house liable on his express covenant to repair it, "though it be burnt by lightning or thrown down by enemies"[24]; and by many subsequent cases in which that dictum was applied so as to hold the tenant liable on his repairing covenant in such circumstances.[25] No doubt a landlord would be similarly liable for breach of his express covenant to repair. Here, however, one must beware of an ambiguity in the word "repair". No doubt if the owner of a car (or indeed of a house) employed a contractor to "repair" it, in the sense of putting right some defect in it, the destruction of the car (or house) would in the modern law *prima facie* discharge the contract; for its subject-matter or a thing essential for its performance would have disappeared.[26] But in the law of landlord and tenant, a tenant's covenant to "repair" the premises, or to repair and keep them in repair, or to deliver them up at the end of the tenancy in good and tenantable repair, may, on its true construction, require the tenant to reinstate the building[27] even if it or part of it has been destroyed as a result of a supervening calamity such as fire or flood,[28] or as a result of the order of a

---

[22] For such cases, see below, para.2–007.

[23] *London and Northern Estates Ltd v Schlesinger* [1916] 1 K.B. 20; below, para.11–021.

[24] (1647) Aleyn 26 at 27.

[25] Below, para.2–007.

[26] cf. *Appleby v Myers* (1867) L.R. 2 C.P. 651, below, para.4–015.

[27] It will not necessarily have this effect: see *Lurcott v Whakely & Wheeler* [1911] 1 K.B. 905 at 919.

[28] *e.g. Bullock v Dommitt* (1796) 6 T.R. 650; *Redmond v Dainton* [1920] 2 K.B. 256.

public authority.[29] If so, the covenant simply *means* that the tenant must, in the event of the destruction of the building, restore it to its former state. Thus a covenant by a tenant to "repair" the house which is the subject-matter of the tenancy, and a contract by a builder to make specified "repairs" to the same house, may impose obligations of very different content: destruction of the house may make it impossible to perform the latter, but not the former, obligation. The cases holding a tenant liable on a covenant to repair after destruction of the premises[30] do not make him liable for failing to do what is impossible. In *Paradine v Jane* performance of the covenant to repair might, indeed, have been impossible during the period of the tenant's dispossession, so that he would have had an excuse for *delay* in executing the repairs; but the question of the tenant's liability for such delay was not in issue, nor even discussed in the dictum relating to repairs.

2–006   Similar problems can arise in the law of insurance. In *Brown v Royal Insurance Co*[31] buildings were insured against fire risks for £1,500 under a policy giving the insurers the right to reinstate them instead of paying claims. The buildings having been destroyed by fire, the insurers elected to reinstate, and after they had begun to do so a public authority, acting under statutory powers, caused the building to be taken down as a dangerous structure. This was held to be no defence to a claim by the insured for damages. One view of the case was that "the fact that performance has become impossible is no excuse for their [the insurers'] not performing it (*i.e.,* the contract)"[32]: this is reminiscent of the second proposition in *Paradine v Jane.* Another view is that performance had *not* become impossible but only "more expensive ..., but that is no answer"[33]: this view is in turn comparable with the repairing covenant dictum in *Paradine v Jane*: if such a covenant, on its true construction, imposes an obligation to reinstate, it may involve the covenantor in unexpected expense, but there is no impossibility of performance.

(6) Applications of the doctrine in later cases between landlord and tenant

2–007   The doctrine of *Paradine v Jane,* or the reasoning of the case so far as it relates to express covenants, was followed in many subsequent cases between landlord and tenant. These cases fall into two overlapping groups.

In the first group, it was held that a tenant remained liable for rent in spite of the destruction by fire or flood or tempest of buildings on the land.[34] At common law, this was so even though the landlord had insured

---

[29] *e.g. Lurcott v Wakely & Wheeler* [1911] 1 K.B. 905.
[30] Below, nn.36–44.
[31] (1859) 1 E. & E. 853; and see below, para.2–031.
[32] (1859) 1 E. & E. 853 at 859.
[33] *ibid.* at 860.
[34] *Carter v Cumming* (1666) 1 Cas. in Ch. 84; *Walton v Waterhouse* (1673) 2 Wms. Saund. 422 n.2; *Monk v Cooper* (1727) 2 Ld. Raym. 1477; 2 Str. 763; *Bullock v*

the premises and had been paid the sum insured in consequence of the destruction of the premises.[35] In the second group of cases, it was held that the tenant could be liable on his covenant to repair in case of destruction of the premises by some such calamity[36]; where the tenant covenanted to insure and repair, his liability to repair was held not to be limited by the amount of the insurance.[37] The tenant's liability on his covenant to repair was based simply on the construction of that covenant, which in the cases in question was regarded as imposing a duty on the tenant to keep the premises in repair irrespective of the cause of their disrepair. Indeed, such a construction was not confined to covenants in leases: in one case[38] it was applied to a contract to build a bridge and to keep it in repair for seven years, so that the contractor was liable when during those seven years the bridge was washed away "by a great unusual and extraordinary flood".[39] In a passage remiscent of *Paradine v Jane*, Lord Kenyon C.J. said that "if the defendants had chosen to except any loss of this kind, it should have been introduced into this contract by way of exception".[40] In the reported cases concerning leases, such exceptions were by no means uncommon: thus in a number of these cases the tenant's covenant to repair is qualified in that loss or damage by fire is expressly excepted. It is at this point that the two lines of cases overlap, for although in such cases a tenant was not liable on the repairing covenant in the event of destruction of the premises by fire, he nevertheless remained liable for rent[41]; while the mere fact that fire was excepted from the tenant's covenant to repair was held not to impose any duty to repair on the landlord.[42] Even where each party covenanted to repair (*e.g.* where the landlord and the tenant covenanted respectively to keep the exterior and interior in repair) accidental destruction of the premises did not liberate the tenant from his liability for rent,[43] his covenant to pay rent and the landlord's covenant to repair being evidently regarded as "independent,"[44] so that the tenant's remedy would be a cross-claim for damages.

The common law position as stated above was at one time doubted in equity. It was said that, where the tenant's covenant excepted liability for

---

Dommitt (1796) 6 T.R. 650; *River Wear Commissioners v Adamson* (1877) 2 App. Cas. 743 at 748.

[35] *Belfour v Weston* (1786) 1 T.R. 310 at 312; *Lofft v Dennis* (1859) 1 E. & E. 474.

[36] *Bullock v Dommitt*, n.34, above; *Walton v Waterhouse*, n.34, above; *cf. Chesterfield v Bolton* (1739) 2 Com. 627.

[37] *Digby v Anderson* (1815) 4 Campb. 275.

[38] *Company of Proprietors of the Brecknock & Abergavenny Canal Navigation v Pritchard* (1796) 6 T.R. 750.

[39] *ibid.* at 750.

[40] *ibid.* at 752.

[41] *Monk v Cooper* (1727) 2 Ld. Raym. 1477; 2 Str. 763; *Belfour v Weston* (1786) 1 T.R. 310.

[42] *Holtzapffel v Baker* (1811) 18 Ves. Jr. 115; the same assumption seems to have been made in *Waters v Weigall* (1794) 2 Anst. 575.

[43] *Leeds v Cheetham* (1827) 1 Sim. 146.

[44] *Marshall v Schofield* (1882) 52 L.J.Q.B. 58 at 60. For the concept of "independent" promises, see Treitel, *The Law of Contract* (11th ed.), p.763.

fire and the landlord had received the proceeds of his insurance against fire, he could be restrained from suing for rent until he had reinstated the premises.[45] Lord Nottingham evidently regarded the landlord's failure to reinstate as akin to eviction[46] and so providing the tenant with a remedy under the landlord's express covenant for quiet enjoyment. But this analogy was later criticised on the ground that such a remedy was available only in respect of defects of title and the view that the tenant could rely on equity to escape from the rule in *Paradine v Jane* did not prevail.[47]

(7) Performance of promise in suit becoming impossible

2-008   The foregoing discussion shows that neither the decision in *Paradine v Jane* itself,[48] nor the later cases between landlord and tenant in which the reasoning of that decision was applied, actually support the proposition that a party is liable in spite of the fact that his *own* performance has become impossible. Further situations can, indeed, be imagined in which performance of the obligations in suit might be affected by impossibility. This would, for example, have been the case if in *Paradine v Jane* the tenant had promised to pay a "rent" consisting of a specified quantity out of crops to be grown by him on the demised land, or of a specified proportion of such crops: performance of the tenant's promise would have been literally impossible during the period of his dispossession. Similarly, a natural catastrophe might not only have destroyed buildings on the land but have made their re-erection impossible, at least in the then existing state of technology: for example, if the land had been seriously and permanently flooded to such an extent that it could not be drained. If taken literally, the second of the two propositions in *Paradine v Jane* (quoted above)[49] would extend to such situations; but no actual decision goes to the length of holding a tenant liable on such facts.

To find cases in which a party was held liable, under the doctrine of *Paradine v Jane*, for failing to render a performance which became impossible one has to turn to cases involving the carriage of goods by sea. A sketchily reported case decided before *Paradine v Jane* is *Tompson v Miles*,[50] where the defendant contracted to deliver goods in London (evidently under a contract of carriage[51]). The goods were later put on a boat which was overturned "by the violence of wind and water" and this

---

[45] *Brown v Quilter* (1764) Amb. 619 at 621; *cf. Steele v Apsley* (1773) cited in *Doe v Sandham* (1787) 1 T.R. 705 at 708.

[46] *Brown v Quilter*, above, at 621.

[47] *Hare v Groves* (1763) 3 Anst. 687; *cf. Waters v Weigall* (1794) 2 Anst. 575; but Lord "Northington's" (Nottingham's?) view in *Brown v Quilter*, n.45, above, is cited with apparent approval by Lord Kenyon C.J. in *Cutter v Powell* (1795) 6 T.R. 320 at 323.

[48] (1647) Aleyn 26.

[49] Above, para.2–002.

[50] (1591) I Rolle's Abridgement Conditions G. 9.

[51] This is clear from the report in Camb. U.C. MS Ee 6.12 f.91; I am grateful to Professor D.J. Ibbetson for supplying me with this text.

fact was said not to provide any excuse for the defendant.[52] Other obstacles to the performance of charterparties were likewise held to have no effect on the contract in a number of cases decided between *Paradine v Jane* and the development of the modern doctrine of discharge. One such case was *Shubrick v Salmond*[53] which arose out of a voyage charter to carry rice from Winyaw (in South Carolina). The charterparty contained an express covenant on the part of the shipowner "to go thither", but the ship was prevented by bad weather from leaving Madeira and so failed to reach Winyaw within the period specified. The shipowner was held liable, Lord Mansfield saying that, "The words are positive and express that he should go thither".[54] This language, as well as Lord Mansfield's reference to cases in which tenants were held liable for rent although the premises had been destroyed by fire, seem to indicate that he had *Paradine v Jane* in mind, a view evidently taken by the reporter.[55] It is reinforced by Wilmot J.'s observation that if the shipowner "had not expressly covenanted to go to this port; and had been unavoidably prevented, without any default in himself; it might have been a different case."[56]

In a later case[57] it was held that a shipowner was not excused where an **2–009** "embargo" (*i.e.* detention of the ship) prevented him for two years from carrying the goods to the agreed destination; and Lawrence J. expressly relied on *Paradine v Jane* in support of this conclusion. The fact that the defendant's arguments in these cases differed from that of the defendant in *Paradine v Jane*, in that the supervening event affected the shipowners' *own* performance, while in *Paradine v Jane* it affected the counter-performance expected by the tenant, is not mentioned by the court. Nor is it mentioned in other charterparty cases in which it was held that a defendant was not absolved where supervening events prevented him from performing his express undertaking. Thus it was held in *Barker v Hodgson*[58] that a shipper was liable for failing to load a cargo even though the failure was due to a pestilence making the performance of his undertaking to load "impracticable"[59]; it is interesting to note that this case was cited with approval by Blackburn J.[60] five years *after* his famous judgment in *Taylor v*

---

[52] The action was against the carrier for damages. In *Chitty on Contracts* (2nd ed., 1834), the case is cited with a wrong reference to 7 T.R. 384. This refers to a passage in *Cook v Jennings* (1797) 7 T.R. 381 which is not concerned with the carrier's *liability*. It decides the different point that a carrier whose ship is wrecked "by violence of wind and waves" is not *entitled* to freight. The reason for this is that he has not performed a condition precedent to the cargo-owner's liability to pay—not that the contract is discharged.

[53] (1765) 3 Burr. 1637.

[54] *ibid.* at 1640.

[55] Who cites *Paradine v Jane* in his footnote to the report.

[56] (1765) 3 Burr. 1637 at 1640.

[57] *Hadley v Clark* (1799) 8 T.R. 259.

[58] (1814) 3 M. & S. 267.

[59] *ibid.* at 269.

[60] In *Ford v Cotesworth* (1869) L.R. 4 Q.B. 127. See further below, para.2–025, at n.92 and para.2–032, at nn.41 to 43.

Caldwell.[61] The word "impracticable" might suggest that there was no actual impossibility,[62] but other charterparty cases do apply the same principle where there was such impossibility. For example, where shipment was prevented by an embargo at the foreign port of shipment, it was said that "If a man undertakes what he cannot perform, he shall answer for it ..."[63] *A fortiori*, it was held in *Hills v Sughrue*[64] that a charterer was not excused from performance of his undertaking to provide "a full cargo of guano" merely by reason of the fact that, on the ship's arrival at the port of loading, there was no guano there. The undertaking to provide the cargo was described as "absolute" or "positive".[65] The court also seems to have attached some importance to the high freight rate, saying that "it looks very much like a contract for supplying goods at that price"[66]: *i.e.*, the charterer's strict liability[67] for supplying a cargo was likened to the strict liability of a seller who has undertaken to deliver unascertained generic goods. Conversely, shipowners were held liable where loading was prevented by an embargo placed (or likely to be placed) on their vessels[68]: in one such case,[69] *Paradine v Jane* was cited in the judgments to support this conclusion. Again, a shipowner was held liable for refusing to set sail for a port which was under blockade,[70] but the reasoning seems to be that the blockade might have been lifted by the time of the ship's arrival there and that the contract might have amounted to a speculation on the length of the blockade. In his direction to the jury, Tindal C.J. said that, if the blockade had still continued when the ship arrived at the named port, the charterer would have been entitled to no more than nominal damages: this seems to indicate that failure to enter the blockaded port would have been a breach, but one that would have caused no loss. But the view that failure to proceed to a blockaded port would amount to a breach was qualified in *Pole v Cetcovich*[71] where the owner of an Austrian ship was held not liable for failing to proceed to Copenhagen which was being blockaded by French warships in the course of a war between Austria and France. One factor influencing the decision appears to have been that the captain was not bound to expose his ship to danger: thus the court asked rhetorically whether, if a violent storm had arisen, the captain would not have been "justified in delaying his

---

[61] (1863) 3 B. & S. 826.

[62] *cf.* below Ch.6.

[63] *Bligh v Page* (1801) 3 B. & P. 295n., followed in *Sjoerds v Luscombe* (1812) 16 East 201; *cf. Spence v Chodwick* (1847) 10 Q.B. 517.

[64] (1846) 15 M. & W. 253, probably a case of antecedent impossibility: see below, para.2–032, at n.46.

[65] (1846) 15 M. & W. 253 at 261.

[66] *ibid.*

[67] *cf.* above, para.1–003.

[68] *Hadley v Clark* (1799) 8 T.R. 259; *Atkinson v Ritchie* (1809) 10 East 530.

[69] *Atkinson v Ritchie*, above, at 533.

[70] *De Medeiros v Hill* (1831) 5 C. & P. 182.

[71] (1860) 9 C.B.N.S. 430.

departure till the storm abated?"[72] But the actual decision was based on the ground that the contract did not specify any particular time for proceeding to Copenhagen, so that the shipowner's contractual duty was merely to go there without unreasonable delay, and (in view of the blockade) his delay had not been unreasonable. Accordingly, the decision was said not to "qualify the rule that a party contracting to do a thing must do it at all events or pay the penalty of his inability to perform the contract which he has entered into".[73] *Pole v Cetcovich* is concerned with the definition of the shipowner's obligation, particularly with regard to the time of performance, rather than with the question whether that obligation was discharged by supervening events.

II. EARLY QUALIFICATIONS OF THE DOCTRINE OF ABSOLUTE CONTRACTS

The doctrine of absolute contracts, as stated in *Paradine v Jane*, was never   2–010
of universal application, but was subject to a number of significant qualifications. Some of these can be regarded as applicable to cases outside the scope of the doctrine; others as exceptions to it. So far as the scope of the doctrine is concerned, it is important to recall[74] that *Paradine v Jane* states *two* propositions, the first of which applies "where the law creates a duty" and the second "when the party by his own contract creates a duty or charge upon himself"; and that the second proposition (which states the doctrine of absolute contracts) is that the party in question "is bound to make it good, if he may, not withstanding any accident by inevitable necessity."

(1) "If he may": supervening illegality

In determining the scope of the doctrine, the first question is: what, in the   2–011
above statement is meant by the words "if he may?" Do they mean "if he can" (in the sense of being *able* to do something), or "if he is allowed" (in the sense of being legally permitted to do something)? From the context, it seems that they cannot have the former meaning, for to give them this meaning would make the statement largely self-contradictory.[75] One of the points that the statement seems to be making is precisely that a party may be liable in spite of the fact that what he promised has become impossible. That is certainly the view taken in some of the later cases (such as the charterparty cases discussed above[76]) even though it was not decided in *Paradine v Jane* itself.[77] On the other hand, to interpret the

---

[72] *ibid.* at 437. For a modern statement of the same principle, see *Kuwait Petroleum Corp v I & D Oil Carriers Ltd (The Houda)* [1994] 2 Lloyd's Rep. 541 at 547–549.
[73] (1860) 9 C.B.N.S. at 439; *cf. The Houda*, above, at 555.
[74] Above, para.2–002.
[75] *Joseph Constantine S.S. Line v Imperial Smelting Co Ltd* [1942] A.C. 158 at 184.
[76] Above, para.2–009.
[77] Above, para.2–004.

words in the latter sense merely imposes a limited restriction on the scope of the doctrine of absolute contracts, namely that a party may be discharged even from his duty to perform an express contractual promise by a supervening legal prohibition or legal compulsion. The point was put (perhaps rather quaintly) in another seventeenth century case: if an Act of Parliament compels a person to do what he has covenanted not to do, "the statute repeals the covenant".[78] While this statement deals with legal compulsion, the same restriction on the scope of the doctrine of absolute contracts is more commonly illustrated by legal prohibition. The point is made in some of the charterparty cases already discussed,[79] in which supervening *impossibility* was held not to be a ground of excuse; but in a number of these cases the courts emphasise that performance had not become unlawful, thus indicating that such supervening *illegality* would have led to a different result.[80] In accordance with these dicta, it was held that a charterparty was dissolved when, following the outbreak of the Crimean War, the port of destination became an enemy port[81]; and the view that such supervening illegality (even by foreign law[82]) had this effect was reaffirmed (after *Taylor v Caldwell*[83]) in a judgment expressly based on the assumption that *Paradine v Jane* was "at present" still good law.[84] This restriction on the scope of the doctrine of absolute contracts appears to be based on the principle of public policy that parties must not be given inducements to violate the law.[85] In *Atkinson v Ritchie* this principle is given an even wider scope: it is said to apply where performance, though not illegal, would be contrary to public policy. The actual decision was that the owner of a chartered ship was not justified in sailing her away from St Petersburg by rumours of an impending Russian "embargo" (not actually imposed till six weeks later) on British vessels. But Lord Ellenborough C.J. said that the contract would have been discharged, not only if it had "become illegal", but also if "by reason of a change in the political relations and circumstances of this country" the contract had "become incapable of being any longer carried into effect without derogating from the clear public duty which a British subject owes to his Sovereign and the State of which he is a member".[86] He added that "this new public duty" could arise only if the change of circumstances had actually taken place, and if "the danger ... to the public interest [was]

---

[78] *Brewster v Kitchell* (1679) 1 Salk. 198.

[79] Above, para.2–009.

[80] *Atkinson v Ritchie* (1809) 10 East 530 at 534; *Barber v Hodgson* (1814) 3 M. & S. 267 at 270; *Spence v Chodwick* (1847) 10 Q.B. 517 at 529; *cf. Cunningham v Dunn* (1878) 3 C.P.D. 441 at 449; and see *Jacobs v Crédit Lyonnais* (1884) 12 Q.B.D. 598, as explained in *Ralli Bros. v Compania Naviera Sota y Aznar* [1920] 2 K.B. 287 at 292 on the ground that there was *no* illegality by foreign law.

[81] *Esposito v Bowden* (1857) 7 E. & B. 763.

[82] Below, para.8–054.

[83] (1863) 3 B. & S. 826.

[84] *The Teutonia* (1871) L.R. 3 A. & E. 395 at 411.

[85] *cf.* below, Ch.8.

[86] (1809) 10 East 530 at 534–535; *cf.* also *Touteng v Hubbard* (1802) 3 B. & P. 291, discussed below at para.5–037.

clear immediate and certain"[87]; and neither of these requirements had been satisfied when the ship had sailed away. Later cases, while upholding the principle of discharge by illegality,[88] have not followed up the suggestion of discharge by supervening events which made performance contrary to public policy but fall short of making it illegal.

(2) **Bailment: duty of bailee**

The second qualification of the doctrine of absolute contracts concerns 2–012 cases of bailment. In *Taylor v Caldwell*, Blackburn J., after referring to "the great case of *Coggs v Bernard*"[89] stated this qualification as follows: "if the performance of the promise of the ... bailee to return the things lent or bailed becomes impossible because it has perished, this impossibility (if not arising from the fault of the ... bailee from some risk which he has taken upon himself[90]) excuses the ... bailee from the performance of his promise to redeliver the chattel."[91] So, for example, the bailee of a horse was held not to be liable for failure to return it when the horse had died without any default on the bailee's part before the bailor had requested its return.[92] Such cases again seem to fall outside the scope of the doctrine of absolute contracts rather than to constitute to an exception to it. *Coggs v Bernard* specifies in detail the standard of duty owed by various types of bailee: this may, for example, depend on whether the bailee is a gratuitous bailee or a bailee for reward. Two points are relevant in the present context in relation to these rules. First, such cases of bailment can, in terms of the judgment in *Paradine v Jane*, be described as cases in which "the law creates a duty" which can arise even in the absence of any contractual relationship between the bailor and the bailee or sub-bailee who relies on the supervening event as a ground of discharge.[93] They therefore come within the first of the two propositions stated in that case, rather than within the second proposition, which is the one which enshrines the doctrine of absolute contracts.[94] Secondly, even that doctrine does not prevent contracting parties from expressly or impliedly stipulating that a contracting party undertakes no more than to exercise reasonable care, or some lower standard (such as the same degree or care which he exercises in his own affairs). If, in spite of observing the promised degree of care, that party fails to achieve the objective

---

[87] (1809) 10 East. 530 at 535.

[88] Below, Ch.8.

[89] (1703) 2 Ld. Raym. 909.

[90] This reference to risks taken by the bailee may be to the common carrier's liability at common law for loss of or damage to the goods unless caused by act of God or of the Queen's enemies or inherent vice.

[91] (1863) 3 B. & S. 826 at 838–839. (In the report, the verb does not agree with its subject).

[92] *Williams v Lloyd* (1628) W. Jones 179: it will be seen that the exception was established before *Paradine v Jane.*

[93] See *K H Enterprise v Pioneer Container* [1994] 2 A.C. 324 at 336, citing *Gilchrist Watt and Sanderson Pty Ltd v York Products Pty Ltd* [1970] 1 W.L.R. 1262.

[94] See above, para.2–002.

contemplated by the contract, he is not in breach: the reason for this is not, strictly speaking, that he is excused but that he has performed all that he undertook to do. That, perhaps, is why the bailment cases to which Blackburn J. refers are no longer referred to in modern discussions of frustration.[95] There is also, in these cases, no question of any protection of the *bailor* by reason of the supervening event: it seems to be assumed that there is no outstanding obligation on his part. If there were (*e.g.* because he had promised to pay a periodic charge for the safe custody of the thing) the effect of the perishing of the thing would presumably be to bring that obligation to an end since the most obvious meaning of the undertaking to pay would be that payment should continue only for so long as the service for which it was to be made continued to be rendered. The bailor would be entitled to rely on the general principle that, under a contract for services, the rendering of those services is (unless otherwise agreed) a condition precedent to the entitlement of the party who is to render them to the agreed remuneration.[96] References to an "excuse" from a contractual obligation can have many meanings; it should not be assumed that they necessarily denote discharge under what has become known as the doctrine of frustration.

(3) **Personal service: effects of death or unavailability**

2-013   The third qualification of the doctrine of absolute contracts concerns contracts the performance of which required the continued availability of a particular person.[97] In one case, for example, a surety who had promised to pay the creditor £70 unless the debtor either paid the creditor or surrendered his body to prison was held to be discharged by the death of the debtor before proceedings to secure his arrest had begun.[98] The same principle applied to contracts of apprenticeship or of service: these were dissolved by the death of either party.[99] There is some support for two extensions of this principle. First, the contract might be dissolved by disability giving rise to a permanent incapacity to perform personal services. This appears from the guarded judicial statement that "where a contract depends upon personal skill and the act of God renders it impossible, as for instance in the case of a painter employed to paint a picture who is struck blind, it may be that performance might be

---

[95] Though there is a brief reference to the passage from *Taylor v Caldwell* here under discussion in Palmer, *Bailment* (2nd ed.), pp.1267–1268.

[96] Treitel, *The Law of Contract* (11th ed.), p.762.

[97] *Hyde v Dean & Canons of Windsor* (1596) Cro. Eliz. 552; *Marshall v Broadhurst* (1831) 1 C. & J. 403 at 406; *Wentworth v Cock* (1839) 10 Ad. & E. 42 at 45–46.

[98] *Sparrow v Southgate* (1622) W. Jones 29.

[99] *Taylor v Caldwell* (1863) 3 B. & S. 826 at 836 (death of apprentice); *Whincup v Hughes* (1871) L.R. 6 C.P. 78 (death of a master: no case of this kind is cited or otherwise referred to in *Taylor v Caldwell*); *cf. Farrow v Wilson* (1869) L.R. 5 C.P. 744 (death of employer).

excused."[1] This statement was made five years before *Taylor v Caldwell*, where Blackburn J., with equal caution, says that in such circumstances performance might "perhaps"[2] be excused. It is clear from the context that the performance which, in these examples of personal incapacity, is said to be "excused" is that of the party suffering from the incapacity. The converse problem can also arise of the effect of one party's incapacity on the other party's duty to render the counter-performance promised by the latter. This problem can be illustrated by contrasting two cases concerning claims by mariners for their wages.

The first case is *Beale v Thompson*,[3] where a seaman had signed on for a voyage from Hull to St Petersburg and thence to London. A diplomatic dispute having arisen between Great Britain and Russia, the ship was detained at St Petersburg, and in November 1800 the crew were taken off by the Russian authorities and "marched into the interior".[4] They were allowed back on board in May 1801 (the diplomatic dispute having in the meantime been settled) and the ship afterwards completed her voyage, earning freight. The shipowners, moreover, received compensation for the detention from the Russian government. In these circumstances, it is scarcely surprising that the crew's claim for wages at the contractual rate of £5 10s. per month was upheld, even though it included payment for the period during which the crew were temporarily prevented, by reason of their internment, from rendering any services. The result was not unjust as the owners had been compensated from another source. The case was later explained on the ground that, whatever effect the original internment of the crew may have had on the contracts with them, they were later taken back and completed the voyage.[5] This point is reflected in Lord Ellenborough's statement in *Beale v Thompson* that even if (contrary to his view) there was any breach by the crew, this had been waived[6] when they were taken back by the owners.

Such emphasis on the completion of the voyage serves also to **2–014** distinguish *Beale v Thompson* from the contrasting case of *Melville v De Wolf*,[7] where the claimant was a mariner who had signed on for a voyage from England to the Pacific and back. When the ship reached Montevideo, it appeared that the captain had shot another member of the crew; and a tribunal set up at Montevideo under the Merchant Marine Act 1850 ordered the claimant to be taken off the ship and sent to England to give evidence at the captain's trial for murder. The trial ended in an acquittal, and it was not practicable after its conclusion for the claimant to rejoin the ship. Wages were paid to the claimant up to the time

---

[1] *Hall v Wright* (1858) E.B. & E. 746 at 749, *per* Crompton J. in the Ct of Exch; Crompton J.'s view that the defendant was liable, on the facts of *Hall v Wright*, was the one which prevailed: see the discussion of the case at n.17, below.

[2] (1863) 3 B. & S. 826 at 836.

[3] (1804) 4 East 546.

[4] *ibid.* at 548.

[5] *Horlock v Beal* [1916] 1 A.C. 486 at 494, 500, 511.

[6] (1804) 4 East 546 at 564.

[7] (1855) 4 E. & B. 844.

of his having been taken off the ship, and the action was brought for wages after that time. It is not without interest to record that Blackburn appeared as counsel for the claimant and argued that the defendant was liable for the wages in suit because "the case resembles that of use and occupation for premises which have been burnt down"[8]—an obvious reference to the cases following *Paradine v Jane*.[9] In rejecting the claim, Lord Campbell C.J. said that no blame could be attached to the claimant, so that there had been "no forfeiture of wages" (*i.e.* of those which had become due before he was taken off the ship); "but [the claimant] cannot be considered as having earned the wages in dispute".[10] This merely amounts to saying that the claimant had failed to perform a condition precedent to his entitlement to those wages[11]; but the judgment goes beyond this narrow proposition when it adds that, since "the relation of employer and employee could not be renewed within the scope of the original hiring ... the contract must be considered as having been dissolved by the supreme authority of the state, which is binding on both parties".[12] This seems to be the language of the modern doctrine of discharge, under which the employer would be no more entitled to call for resumption of services under the contract, than he was liable to pay for them once they ceased to be rendered. So far as the latter point was concerned, *Beale v Thompson* was distinguished on the ground that there the voyage was completed by the crew. One can also make the point that the interruption in *Beale v Thompson* was only temporary, while in *Melville v De Wolf* there was a finding that it was not practicable for the claimant to rejoin the ship.

2–015   A further, and controversial, group of cases consists of those in which supervening events do not bring about any actual inability to perform a "personal" contract, but merely make such performance dangerous to the life or health of a party. *Lawrence v Twentiman*[13] appears to have decided that, "If a man covenant to build a house before such a day, and then the plague is there before the day and continues there till after the day, this excuses him from the breach of the covenant for not doing it before the day; for the law does not wish to compel him to venture his life for this, but he must do it afterwards". In other words, the contract is not discharged, but suspended. Suspension would probably not be available in the modern law,[14] but discharge by danger to a person's health is now accepted as a possibility.[15] An American case decided before *Taylor v Caldwell* supports this view: a person who had been employed to work at a sawmill was held to be justified in leaving before the end of the period of employment as he reasonably feared that he would fall victim to a cholera epidemic which

---

[8] *ibid.* at 848.
[9] See above, para.2–007.
[10] (1855) 4 E. & B. 844 at 849.
[11] *cf.* above, para.2–012 at n.96.
[12] (1855) 4 E. & B. 844 at 849.
[13] 1 Rolle's Abridgement Condition G. pl. 10 (p.450), cited in *Hall v Wright* (1858) E. B. & E. 746 at 758 and doubted *ibid.* at 790.
[14] See below, para.15–034.
[15] See below, para.4–021.

had broken out in the vicinity of the mill.[16] In England the scope of this exception to the doctrine of absolute contracts was, however, restricted by the controversial case of *Hall v Wright*.[17] In an action for breach of promise of marriage, the defendant pleaded that he was "afflicted by a dangerous bodily disease which occasioned frequent and severe bleeding from his lungs and by reason of which the defendant was and still is incapable of marriage without great danger to his life and therefore unfit for the married state: where of the plaintiff had notice before the commencement of the action". The jury found that the facts pleaded by the defendant were true except with regard to the allegation of the plaintiff's having notice "which they negatived". On these findings, the four judges of the Court of Exchequer were evenly divided, and the Exchequer Chamber held the defendant liable by a majority of four to three. Two members of the majority relied on *Paradine v Jane*, and one of these (Martin B.) said that "to admit exceptions of this kind utterly destroys the certainty of the law".[18] A factor that weighed with the majority was that the defendant's illness had not made performance by him impossible (as in the example of the painter who was struck blind) but merely dangerous. But in earlier decisions danger to health or life had been regarded as providing an excuse for non-performance of "personal" contracts[19]; and a number of narrower grounds for the decision can be extracted from the majority judgments: for instance, that the defendant's incapacity might have been caused by his voluntary conduct[20]; that the illness merely gave each party a right to rescind but that they had decided in spite of the illness to go ahead with the marriage and that the defendant had *then* deserted the plaintiff[21]; and that the plaintiff might have relied on the defendant's incapacity but that he could not rely on his own.[22] Later courts have regarded the decision as giving rise to considerable difficulty,[23] and perhaps the best explanation for it lies in the special characteristics of the former action[24] for breach of promise of marriage. Although technically this was a contractual action, it had many of the characteristics of an action in tort: *e.g.* it gave rise to a claim for punitive damages[25] and the death of either party was a bar to the action.[26] In the present context, the point to be emphasised is that the purpose of the action was generally to recover damages for a past injury; and this would scarcely be assuaged by the supervening incapacity of the promisor. The point is reflected in statements to the effect that, even if the defendant's promise could not

---

[16] *Lakeman v Pollard*, 43 Me. 463 (1857); below, para.4–022.

[17] (1858) E. B. & E. 746.

[18] *ibid.* at 789. The other judge to rely on *Paradine v Jane* was Williams J. at 791.

[19] See at nn.13, 16 above; *cf. Pole v Cetcovitch* (1860) 9 C.B.N.S. 430 at 437 (above, para.2–009, at n.72).

[20] Martin B. at 789–790.

[21] Crompton J. at 750.

[22] Williams J. at 792.

[23] See *Jefferson v Paskell* [1916] 1 K.B. 57 at 70.

[24] It was abolished by Law Reform (Miscellaneous Provisions) Act 1970, s.1.

[25] *Quirk v Thomas* [1916] 1 K.B. 516 at 527, 531, 538.

[26] *Finlay v Chirney* (1887) 20 Q.B.D. 494 at 497–498.

be specifically enforced, and even if it was not in the circumstances reasonable for him to marry the plaintiff, that was no reason why he should not pay her damages.[27] *Hall v Wright* is best regarded as a special exception, of limited scope, to the general principle that supervening physical incapacity might discharge contracts of a "personal" nature. The case does not seem to have intended to question that principle; certainly it is not treated as having had any such effect in *Taylor v Caldwell*, where Blackburn J. refers to the case, quoting from it the example of the painter who is struck blind[28]: this example is taken from one of the judgments[29] which holds the defendant liable on the facts of *Hall v Wright*.

(4) Sale of goods: destruction of "specific" goods

2–016   A fourth qualification of the doctrine of absolute contracts was said by Blackburn J. in *Taylor v Caldwell* to arise in certain cases involving the sale of goods. The example that he gives is that of a sale of "specific chattels" to be delivered on a future day, which perish without the fault of the seller after the property in them has passed to the buyer but before the day fixed for delivery. The significance of the passing of property was that risk generally passed with property, a rule stated in the first edition of *Blackburn on Sale*.[30] It followed that: "the purchaser must pay the price and the vendor is excused from performing his contract to deliver, which has thus become impossible."[31] A number of points arise from this alleged qualification of the doctrine of absolute contracts.

First, in one obvious respect the result resembles that in *Paradine v Jane*[32]: the buyer must pay the price (just as the tenant in *Paradine v Jane* had to pay the rent) even though he does not obtain the counter-performance, *i.e.* delivery of the goods. The only respect in which the example may differ from *Paradine v Jane* is that in Blackburn J.'s example the seller is said to be excused. The corresponding question in *Paradine v Jane* would have been whether the landlord was excused, but that question was simply not in issue, there being no allegation of any breach of covenant on his part.[33] If Blackburn J.'s object was to find an example of a case in which *both* parties were discharged,[34] he would have done better to discuss the case of an agreement to sell specific goods which perish before (not after) the risk has passed to the buyer: in such a case the seller is discharged from his obligation to deliver *and* the buyer from his obligation

---

[27] (1858) E.B. & E. 746 at 790–791, *per* Martin B. and Williams J.

[28] See para.2–013 at nn.1 and 2, above.

[29] See para.2–013 at n.1, above.

[30] At 152. See now Sale of Goods Act 1979, s.20(1); the various exceptions to this general rule, discussed in paras 3–010 *et seq.*, below do not affect the present discussion.

[31] (1863) 3 B. & S. 826 at 837. For the relationship between risk and the modern doctrine of frustration, see below, paras 3–007 *et seq.*

[32] (1647) Aleyn 26, above, para.2–002.

[33] See above, para.2–004.

[34] See below, paras 2–039 to 2–048.

to pay the price.[35] But perhaps when *Taylor v Caldwell* was decided that development still lay in the future. It is usually associated with the case of *Howell v Coupland*[36] where a seller of potatoes to be grown on specified land was held not liable when the crop failed as a result of potato blight, without any default of the seller. In the Court of Queen's Bench, Blackburn J. based this result on *Taylor v Caldwell*,[37] from which it may be deduced that he regarded the buyer, no less than the seller, as having been excused.[38] Actually the buyer's liability was not in issue, and the Court of Appeal seemed to be content to make the point that *the seller* had not entered into an "absolute contract".[39]

Secondly, the authority on which Blackburn J. in *Taylor v Caldwell* relies for his sale of goods qualification to the doctrine of absolute contracts is *Rugg v Minett*[40] which, in modern terminology, was scarcely a contract for the sale of "specific"[41] goods, but rather one of goods to be taken from an identified source. The sale was of turpentine in casks to be filled by the seller from the cargo of a named ship.[42] Evidently, the turpentine was in two large casks from which 25 smaller casks were to be filled, each with a specified amount; and what was then left in the two original casks was to be sold as an unspecified amount. The claimant bought 24 of the resulting 27 lots; and after some of the smaller casks had later been filled, the whole of the turpentine was destroyed by an accidental fire. A claim by the buyer for repayment of a deposit which he had paid failed in respect of the casks which had been filled, but succeeded in respect of those which had not yet been filled. It must have been assumed that the buyer could have been sued for the price of the casks which had been filled, but that he was not liable for the price of those which had not been filled. According to Lord Ellenborough C.J., these consequences followed from the passing of property,[43] and hence of risk, in the casks which had been filled—not

2–017

---

[35] See now Sale of Goods Act 1979, s.7; below, para.3–004.

[36] (1874) L.R. 9 Q.B. 462; affirmed (1876) 1 Q.B.D. 258.

[37] L.R. 9 Q.B. 462 at 465.

[38] See below, para.2–039.

[39] (1876) 1 Q.B.D. 258 at 261, 263 (basing the result on the construction of the contract); see below, paras 4–049 to 4–051.

[40] (1809) 11 East 210.

[41] See the definition of "specific goods" in Sale of Goods Act 1979, s.61(1): "goods identified and agreed on when a contract of sale is made"; below, para.3–013. The point is not affected by the amendment to this definition made by Sale of Goods (Amendment) Act 1995, s.2(d), which extends the meaning of "specific goods" so as to include "an undivided share specified as a fraction or percentage of goods identified and agreed on as aforesaid". See further n.42, below.

[42] *i.e.* the sale was of an undifferentiated part not specified as a fraction or percentage of an identified bulk. Such a sale is not one of "specific goods" within the definition quoted in the previous note: see *Re Wait* [1927] 1 Ch. 606; Sale of Goods Act 1979, s.20A(1) ("specified quantity of *unascertained* good").

[43] Property presumably passed in the contents of each of the smaller casks as these were filled, the goods becoming ascertained at this stage. Under s.20A of the Sale of Goods Act 1979 (as inserted by s.1 of the Sale of Goods (Amendment) Act 1995) property could now pass even while the goods were still unascertained

from any doctrine of discharge. The distinction between these two sets of rules will be further discussed in Ch.3. Here it is only necessary to make the point that the linkage between property and risk was established well before *Taylor v Caldwell*: it is (as already noted) stated in the first edition of *Blackburn on Sale* which had been published in 1845. In *Taylor v Caldwell*, Blackburn J. says that in *Rugg v Minett* "it seems ... rather to have been taken for granted than decided that the destruction of the thing sold excused the vendor from fulfilling his contract to deliver on payment".[44] The point was not "decided" since no claim for damages was made by the buyer, who sued only for the return of his deposit. In such an action, the buyer's duty to pay may have been indirectly in issue, but the same can hardly be said with regard to the seller's duty to deliver. Thus it is not easy to see how any point about the seller's liability was even "taken for granted". It may be possible to infer from the passing of risk that the seller was no longer liable: this depends on exactly what is meant by the passing of risk, a point to be further discussed in Ch.3. On this reasoning, the seller would only have been "excused" with regard to the casks that were filled. His excuse with regard to those which were not filled was not established until *Howell v Coupland*. We have seen[45] that, in the Court of Queen's Bench in that case, Blackburn J. regarded the seller's excuse as being based on *Taylor v Caldwell*, and if the rule excusing the seller is derived from *Taylor v Caldwell* it can scarcely form one of the bases of that decision in cases of the kind illustrated by *Rugg v Minett*, *i.e.* those in which the sale was not one of "specific chattels" in the common law sense[46] and would not now be one of "specific goods" as defined by the Sale of Goods Act 1979 because at the time of the contract the goods were neither "identified and agreed on"[47] nor an undivided share "specified as a fraction or percentage"[48] of such goods.

2-018   A case which does appear to concern the destruction of *specific* goods is *Hinde v Whitehouse*[49] where the sale was of *numbered* lots of sugar in a bonded warehouse, on the terms that the goods were to be at the purchaser's risk from the "time of sale". After the time of contracting, but before that of delivery and payment, the sugar was destroyed by fire. The sugar was held to have been at the risk of the buyer when it was destroyed, as the property in it had passed to the buyer before that time. The actual outcome of the case was that the seller recovered damages of £110; and the report does not indicate how this sum was assessed or why the seller did not claim the price of £1,265 11s.3d. But the significant point for the present purpose is the importance attached to the passing of property, and hence of risk. One can infer from this that the buyer would have been

---

but only to the extent to which the buyer has paid "the price"; and it is an open question whether the payment of a deposit would satisfy this requirement.

[44] (1863) 3 B. & S. 826 at 837.
[45] Above, para.2–016 n.37.
[46] *Taylor v Caldwell* (1863) 3 B. & S. 826 at 837.
[47] Sale of Goods Act 1979, s.61(2), definition of "specific goods".
[48] *ibid.*, as amended by Sale of Goods (Amendment) Act 1995, s.2(d).
[49] (1807) 7 East 558.

under *no* liability if the goods had been destroyed *before* the passing of property and risk. The case would then have been one in which a buyer would have been entitled to rely on the destruction of specific goods by way of defence to a claim for refusal to accept and pay for the goods. Such reasoning would have come closer than *Rugg v Minett* to establishing the proposition advanced by Blackburn J. in *Taylor v Caldwell* and quoted above; but again it would have been based on the passing of risk and it would have told us nothing directly about any possible liability of the seller. It is, indeed, a puzzling feature of the development of this branch of the law that in his formulation of the sale of goods rule in *Taylor v Caldwell* Blackburn J. refers only to the transfer of property and not to the transfer of risk, although even before that case he clearly regarded the linkage between the two concepts as well established.[50] So far as the release of the seller by destruction of the goods is concerned, it is also interesting to note how the topic is dealt with in the second edition of *Blackburn on Sale* (1885). There we find the proposition that, "If the goods perish without any fault on the part of the vendor, he is relieved from his obligation to deliver ..."[51]; but, significantly, it is not supported by any pre-1863 decisions in which the contract concerned sale of goods.

(5) **Admiralty: effects on contracts of shipwreck or capture**

A fifth possible qualification of the doctrine of absolute contracts appears to have existed in Admiralty and to have been recognised to some extent by the common law courts. In discussing contracts involving personal service, we have already considered cases in which mariners were, without any breach on their part, taken off their ships and so prevented from performing the agreed work. There is also the converse possibility that such prevention may result from the supervening unavailability, not of the crew, but of the ship. This possibility is illustrated by *The Elizabeth*,[52] which concerned a seaman's claim for wages. The claimant had signed on for a voyage from Portsmouth to St Petersburg and back to Portsmouth. After the ship had taken on a cargo, she "without the default of any person" went aground in the Baltic on September 26, 1818. In consequence she was so seriously damaged that she was unable to complete her voyage during that year's Baltic season; and when this became clear the captain, on October 21, discharged the crew who (apparently with some assistance from the captain) returned to England, reaching London in the following January. The ship was repaired in Sweden and was brought back to England by a Swedish crew in April 1819. The owners admitted liability for wages up to the time of the crew's discharge, while the crew claimed wages up to the time of the return of the ship. Sir William Scott steered a middle course between these positions. He evidently did not regard the discharge of the crew as wrongful and held that they were entitled to their wages till they reached England, plus the cost of their journey home: this, he said,

2–019

---

[50] Above, para.2-016 n.30.
[51] At 230.
[52] (1819) 2 Dods. 403.

was "all that they could have had under their . . . contract".[53] In fact, some minor variation of the contract was involved since the contract voyage was to Portsmouth, while the wages awarded were until the return of the crew to London. Even setting this point aside, the contract was clearly not "discharged" in October (when it became clear that the ship would not be able to complete her intended voyage during the 1818 season), for the wages continued to be payable until the following January. Nevertheless, some of the remarks made by Sir William Scott are of interest when compared with the doctrine of absolute contracts.

2–020   First, it is obviously with some indignation that he rejects the argument that the crew were entitled to their wages until April. If such a right existed, the master would be "bound to keep his crew in an unemployed state, living on shore, keeping holiday all winter, at the expense of his owners, who were to continue all that time to pay, *pro opere et labore*, by virtue of the contract, though no work or labour can be performed; and thus the price of industry was to be regularly paid to unoccupied idleness!"[54] Where a misfortune had "arisen from *vis major*, the act of God which neither party had in contemplation at the time of the contract, it seems hardly just that the whole inconvenience should fall upon one party, while a new and unexpected benefit is to arise from this common calamity—the benefit of living in ease and safety on shore at the expense of the other".[55] Put in another way, the owners' grievance would have been that they would have had to pay without getting the counter-performance for which they had bargained. That was of course, exactly the grievance of the tenant in *Paradine v Jane*, but there it did not engage the sympathy of the court. What landlords were expected to provide in return for the rent was (to say the least) more narrowly interpreted that what seamen were expected to provide for their wages; in this respect the common law may well have reflected prevailing social attitudes. Lord Nottingham, indeed, had taken the position that, "A man should not pay rent for what he cannot enjoy, and that occasioned by an accident which he did not undertake to stand to . . .".[56] In the law of the landlord and tenant, that argument did not prevail, even in equity,[57] but the point made by Lord Nottingham is similar to that made by Sir William Scott in his reference to a "holiday all winter at the expense of the owners".

Secondly, Sir William Scott refers, in another dictum, to an apparently then well-recognised principle of maritime law: "A total loss by wreck happens. This operates as a total loss of wages".[58] A somewhat similar point had been made by Lord Ellenborough C.J. in the earlier and contrasting case of *Beale v Thompson*,[59] another case concerning seamen's wages. One aspect of that case has already been discussed, namely the

---

[53] *ibid.* at 410.
[54] *ibid.* at 411.
[55] *ibid.* at 408–409.
[56] *Brown v Quilter* (1764) Amb 619 at 621.
[57] See above, para.2–007.
[58] (1819) 2 Dods. 403 at 408.
[59] (1804) 4 East 546.

effect of the fact that the crew were forcibly taken off the ship by the Russian authorities; it will be recalled that the crew were nevertheless entitled to their wages.[60] So far as this aspect of the case is concerned, internment in Russia could scarcely be regarded in the same light as the "holiday" in Sweden (even if only a winter one) allegedly claimed by the crew in *The Elizabeth*.[61] Another crucial distinction between the two cases was that in *Beale v Thompson* the crew had eventually worked the ship home, while in *The Elizabeth* they had not. But in the present context the principal point of interest in *Beale v Thompson* was that the Russian authorities had seized the ship as well as the crew; and even if the crew had been left on board the ship could not have left St Petersburg. So far as this aspect of the case was concerned, it is interesting to note the assumption made "on all sides" and apparently viewed with approval by Lord Ellenborough C.J. that "the effect of capture is to dissolve the contract, both for freight and wages, between the respective parties thereto".[62] It is not difficult to see that claims for wages and freight would be defeated by the fact that the capture would prevent the occurrence of the conditions precedent on which these payments would have been due: wages would be due only when freight was paid on the completion of the voyage (freight being then "the mother of wages"[63]), and freight would become due only on delivery of the cargo at the contractual destination (it being clearly assumed that there was no stipulation for advance freight). But it would not follow that the contracts would be dissolved: in *Atkinson v Ritchie*[64] Lord Ellenborough himself was to hold (only five years later) that a threatened detention of (or "embargo" on) British ships at St Petersburg did not relieve the shipowner from liability in damages for sailing away. His reliance there on *Paradine v Jane* at least casts some doubt on the assumption made in *Beale v Thompson*[65] if the phrase "to dissolve the contract for both" is to be taken literally; though a distinction can be drawn between the actual "capture" envisaged in that dictum and the prospective "embargo" (in fact imposed six weeks later) in *Atkinson v Ritchie*.[66]

A final possibility is to argue that the qualification to the doctrine of **2–021** absolute contracts recognised in the dicta in *Beale v Thompson*[67] and in *The Elizabeth*[68] is based on the principle (already discussed) which applies to cases of supervening physical incapacity in contracts of personal services. That principle clearly applies where the personal incapacity is that of the employer: *e.g.* on his death. It can be argued that loss or capture of the

---

[60] See above, para.2–013.

[61] Above, at n.54.

[62] (1804) 4 East 546 at 559.

[63] For use of this well-worn phrase, see *e.g. Cutter v Powell* (1795) 6 T.R. 320 at 321.

[64] (1809) 10 East 530.

[65] Above, n.62.

[66] See, however, *Pole v Cetcovitch* (1860) 9 C.B.N.S. 430 (where prospective capture was held to excuse a shipowner's delay in performing a charterparty).

[67] Above, n.62.

[68] Above, n.52.

ship likewise creates an "incapacity" on the part of the shipowner to receive the contractual services; and that incapacity of either party discharges both. But in cases of the present kind, the "incapacity" (if it can be so described) did not affect the *person* of the employer; and, where the incapacity affected merely the workplace, it is very doubtful whether any principle of discharge was recognised outside the area of maritime law. One wonders what the effect of the supervening events in *Paradine v Jane*[69] might have been on contracts of employment between the defendant and his farm labourers. When yearly hirings were common, this could have been a significant question[70] and similar problems could have arisen where commercial or industrial premises were destroyed during the currency of long-term contracts of employment. The trend towards short-term contracts would have reduced the significance of such problems and may account for the scarcity of modern authority on the point. Such authority as there is seems to indicate that the employer would be discharged *only* where it appeared from the term of the contract that the services were to be performed only at the workplace which, by reason of the supervening events, has become unavailable.[71]

III. *TAYLOR V CALDWELL* AND LOSS ALLOCATION

(1) The bases of the doctrine of discharge

2–022   *Taylor v Caldwell*[72] is generally regarded as a turning point in this branch of the law, as the case in which the law moved away from the doctrine of absolute contracts to the modern doctrine of discharge by supervening events. The change was brought about by the familiar judicial technique[73] of deducing a general principle from a series of particular examples. In *Taylor v Caldwell*, Blackburn J. relies on three of the mitigations of the doctrine of absolute contracts which have been discussed above: cases in which death or permanent physical incapacity prevent performance of a contract for personal services, cases in which specific goods are sold and

---

[69] (1647) Aleyn 26, above, para.2–002.

[70] According to a dictum in *Cutter v Powell* (1795) 6 T.R. 320 at 326 in cases of a yearly hiring the general rule was that the servant was to get his wages "for the time he serves, though he does not continue in service for the whole year"—but this seems to refer to the case where the servant leaves or is disabled, rather than to the case where his workplace become unavailable.

[71] *e.g. Turner v Goldsmith* [1891] 1 O.B. 544; *cf.* also *Minnevitch v Café de Paris (Londres) Ltd.* [1936] 1 All E.R. 884, below, para.5–058 (where the contract was not discharged).

[72] (1863) 3 B. & S. 826.

[73] Also used by Blackburn J. in another famous judgment, that in *Rylands v Fletcher* (1866) L.R. 1 Ex. 265, affirmed (1868) L.R. 3 H.L. 330. It is interesting to note that, while in *Rylands v Fletcher*, Blackburn J. used this technique to *create* a principle of strict liability in tort, in *Taylor v Caldwell* he used it to the opposite effect: *i.e.* to *qualify* a principle of strict liability in contract. Perhaps he saw a greater need to protect proprietary than contractual rights.

perish after the property in them has passed to the buyer, and cases in which the subject-matter of a bailment was destroyed without any default on the part of the bailee. From these examples, he deduces the general principle which applies where "from the nature of the contract, it appears that the parties must ... have known that it could not be fulfilled unless ... some particular specified thing continued to exist".[74] He states the effect of the principle to be that "the parties shall be excused in case, before breach, performance becomes impossible from the perishing of the thing without default of the contractor".[75] It is a significant feature of this formulation that "the parties" are excused, or, as the judgment later puts it, "*both* parties are excused".[76] That is actually a surprising conclusion, which is not directly supported by the three examples from which the general principle purports to be derived.

In the personal service cases, the only point made by Blackburn J. is that the person who is to render the services (or, in the case of apprentice, the father who also covenants that they are to be rendered) is excused by the death or incapacity of that person[77]: the liability of the *other* party is not under discussion. No doubt that liability will often simply not arise since generally the promise of the other party will be one to pay money, and performance of the services will be a condition precedent to the accrual of that party's liability to make the payment.[78] Blackburn J.'s proposition would have been more completely supported by authority to the effect that the other party was excused from some other promise: *e.g.* by discussion of the question whether the incapacity of an apprentice could discharge the master from his obligation to teach; but the judgment contains no reference to this possibility.

Similarly, in the bailment cases the only point made by Blackburn J. is that the perishing of the subject-matter "excuses the ... bailee from his promise to redeliver the chattel" so long as it does not arise "from the fault of the ... bailee from some risk which he has taken upon himself".[79] As already noted, there is, in this example, no question of any excuse protecting the *bailor*, for it is assumed that there is no outstanding obligation on his part; but such a question would arise if there were some such obligation: *e.g.* where the bailor had promised to pay a periodic charge for the safe-custody of the thing. Under Blackburn J.'s general principle, that obligation would presumably be discharged[80]; and in this respect the general principle would go beyond the examples from which it is derived.

---

[74] (1863) 3 B. & S. 826 at 833.

[75] *ibid.* at 834.

[76] *ibid.* at 840 (italics supplied).

[77] *ibid.* at 836.

[78] *e.g. Cutter v Powell* (1795) 6 T.R. 320 (where there is accordingly—and appropriately—no reference to the doctrine of absolute contracts as stated in *Paradine v Jane* (1647) Aleyn 26, above, para.2–002).

[79] (1863) 3 B. & S. 826 at 839.

[80] *ibid.* at 840 ("both parties are excused").

Even more remarkable is the use made of the example of the sale of specific goods which perish after the property (and hence the risk) in them has passed to the buyer. As already noted, in this situation Blackburn J. makes it clear that the seller is excused but the buyer is not[81]; and so the case is not one in which "both parties are excused".[82] Indeed the buyer's position resembles that of the tenant in *Paradine v Jane*[83] in that he must pay without getting the benefit for which he had bargained. Blackburn J.'s sale of goods example differs in nature from *Paradine v Jane* only in explicitly stating that the party whose performance has become impossible (*i.e.* the seller) is excused. In *Paradine v Jane* this point was not in issue since no claim was made against the landlord.[84]

(2) The decision in *Taylor v Caldwell*

2–024   *Taylor v Caldwell*[85] does not itself very closely resemble any of the three groups of cases on which it purports to be based; the significance of the case lies in the general principle which Blackburn J. (rightly or wrongly) derived from some of the early mitigations of the doctrine of *Paradine v Jane*. The facts of *Taylor v Caldwell* are worth stating in some detail, so as to bring out a number of unusual features of the case. The contract, made on May 27, 1861, provided that the defendants were to let the plaintiffs have the use of the Surrey Gardens and Music Hall (it is interesting to note the order) "for the purpose of giving a series of four grand concerts" on June 17, July 15, August 5 and August 19, 1861. The plaintiffs were to pay £100 in respect of each concert "in the evening of the said respective days"; they also agreed to provide the artistes (one of whom, a Mr Sims Reeves,[86] was named in the contract) who were to perform at the concerts. The contract went on to give the plaintiffs the right to certain box-office receipts, and it gave them the right to advertise the concerts at the entrance to the Gardens one week before each of the specified days. The defendants, for their part, undertook not only to make the premises available, but also to maintain specified side-shows in the Gardens. On June 11, the Music Hall was destroyed by fire, and "the destruction ... was so complete that ... the concerts could not be given as intended"[87]; the cause of the fire appears to have been the carelessness of a plumber in leaving an unattended flame in the roof of the Hall.[88] The plaintiffs

---

[81] *ibid.* at 837; above, para.2–016.

[82] (1863) 3 B. & S. 826 at 840.

[83] (1647) Aleyn 26.

[84] See above, para.2–004.

[85] (1863) 3 B. & S. 826.

[86] Evidently a well-known tenor who wrote a number of books, including *The Life of Sims Reeves by Himself* (1888); this disappointingly contains no reference to the destruction of the Surrey Music Hall in 1861.

[87] (1863) 3 B. & S. 826 at 832–833.

[88] See the report of the trial in *The Times*, December 19, 1861 (where the statement that the payments of £100 were to be made by the defendants to the plaintiffs has evidently transposed the parties).

claimed damages in respect of the expenses[89] which they had incurred in advertising and preparing for the concerts. Their claim was dismissed on the ground that "in contracts in which the performance depends on the continued existence of a given person or thing, a condition is implied that the impossibility of performance arising from the perishing of the person or thing shall excuse the performance".[90] A number of points arising from this formulation call for comment.

First, it is significantly narrower than that found earlier in the judgment,[91] the "performance" which is excused being only that which has become impossible. This was the only point which actually arose for decision in *Taylor v Caldwell*, where no attempt was made to enforce any of the plaintiffs' undertakings. It is nevertheless clear that Blackburn J. regards the destruction of the Hall as excusing the plaintiffs no less than the defendants: according to the concluding paragraph of the judgment, "both parties are excused, the plaintiffs from taking the gardens and paying the money, the defendants from performing their promise to give the use of the Hall and Gardens and other things".[92] The significance of the discharge of both parties will be more fully discussed below.[93]

The second point is that, by restricting his formulation to "the impossibility of performance arising from the perishing of the person or thing"[94] Blackburn J. skilfully avoids any direct conflict with *Paradine v Jane*[95] since there the subject-matter had not perished. The treatment of that case in *Taylor v Caldwell* merits some further comment. The case is cited by counsel for the plaintiffs,[96] but there is no direct reference to it in the judgment, which does, however, refer to a note in *Williams' Saunders*[97] where in turn *Paradine v Jane* is cited. The doctrine of *Paradine v Jane* is, moreover, restated in *Taylor v Caldwell*: "There seems to be no doubt that where there is a positive contract to do a thing not in itself unlawful, the contractor must perform it or pay damages for not doing it, although in consequence of unforeseen accidents, the performance of his contract has become unexpectedly burdensome or even impossible."[98] Blackburn J. (sitting in the Court of Queen's Bench) was in no position to deny the validity of this rule, which has been "recognised as the general rule by all the Judges in the much discussed case[99] of *Hall v Wright*"[1]: that was a

---

[89] According to the report in *The Times*, above, the amount claimed was £58.

[90] (1863) 3 B. & S. 826 at 839.

[91] *ibid.* at 834, quoted above, at n.75.

[92] (1863) 3 B. & S. 826 at 840.

[93] See below, paras 2–039 *et seq.*

[94] Above, at n.90.

[95] (1647) Aleyn 26.

[96] (1863) 3 B. & S. 826 at 831.

[97] *Walton v Waterhouse*, 2 Wms. Saund (6th ed.), p.421, n.2 cited in *Taylor v Caldwell* (1863) 3 B. & S. 826 at 833.

[98] *ibid.*

[99] An expression echoed in *Jefferson v Paskell* [1916] 1 K.B. 57 at 70, where *Hall v Wright* (1858) E.B. & E. is said to have been "much observed upon". For a discussion of *Hall v Wright*, see above, para.2–015.

[1] (1863) 3 B. & S. 826 at 833.

decision of the Exchequer Chamber and so binding on the Queen's Bench. Indeed, five years after *Taylor v Caldwell* Blackburn J. himself restated what is clearly recognisable as the doctrine of *Paradine v Jane*: "where a party has either expressly or impliedly undertaken without any qualification to do anything, and does not do it, he must make compensation in damages, though the performance was rendered impracticable by some cause over which he had no control."[2] This may be an attenuated version of *Paradine v Jane*, in that what is "impracticable" is not the same as what is "impossible"—but the citation in the same judgment of an earlier decision[3] applying the doctrine of *Paradine v Jane* makes it doubtful whether Blackburn J. here intended to attach any importance to the distinction (to be more fully discussed in Ch.6) between impossibility and impracticability. Nor does it seem that in *Taylor v Caldwell* he intended to make an abrupt departure from the principle of *Paradine v Jane*—a principle which had been repeatedly applied in the two centuries preceding *Taylor v Caldwell*. The significance of *Taylor v Caldwell* lies rather in its formulation of an exception to the doctrine of *Paradine v Jane*. The development was no doubt facilitated by the fact that in *Taylor v Caldwell* the action was brought against the party whose performance had become impossible, while in *Paradine v Jane* it was only the counter-performance for the promise in suit which was affected by the supervening event. It is also significant that the formulation of the exception took a form which made it possible for later judges to extend the scope of the exception, so that in course of time what was the exception has become the general rule, and conversely. An important reason why the exception was capable of being thus extended beyond its original scope (applicable only to the perishing of a particular person or thing) lay in its rationale, which restricted the old general rule to cases where the contract was "positive and absolute, and not subject to any condition express or implied".[4] The reference, in particular, to implied conditions allowed for flexibility, being capable of application where supervening events *other than* the "perishing" of a person or thing interfered with performance. Accordingly, *Taylor v Caldwell* forms the starting point for the development of the modern doctrine of discharge, even though it did not at once create that doctrine.

---

[2] *Ford v Cotesworth* (1868) L.R. 4, Q.B. 127 at 138. It will be recalled, too, that in *Melville v De Wolf* (1855) 4 E. & B. 844 at 848 Blackburn had, as counsel, relied on what was evidently the doctrine of *Paradine v Jane*: see above, para.2–014, at n.8. *cf.* his approval during the argument in *Geipel v Smith* (1872) L.R. 7 Q.B. 404 at 407 of counsel's proposition closely resembling the then traditional formulation of the doctrine of absolute contracts. For other statements of the doctrine after *Taylor v Caldwell*, see *Nickolls v Marsland* (1876) 2 Ex.D. 1 at 4 and below, para.2–033, at nn.53–38.
[3] *Barker v Hodgson* (1814) 3 M. & S. 267, cited in *Ford v Cotesworth*, above, at 138.
[4] *Taylor v Caldwell* (1863) 3 B. & S. 826 at 833.

(3) **Advantages of the doctrine of discharge**

The modern doctrine of discharge, which has its roots in *Taylor v Caldwell*,   2–026
is generally thought to provide a better solution, than that provided by the
doctrine of absolute contracts, to the problems of loss allocation which
arise where performance is prevented by supervening events for which
neither party to the contract is responsible. In explaining this view, it will
be convenient to make use of a set of terminological distinctions which are
familiar to civil lawyers though they have not in the past been commonly
found in English (or other common law) discussions of the topic. We shall
refer to the person who has undertaken the performance which has
become impossible as the debtor of that performance and the other party
as the creditor of that performance (their roles as debtor and creditor are,
or course, reversed in relation to the counter-performance for the now
impossible performance). The effect of the doctrine of discharge is that
the debtor of the now impossible performance is excused from his duty to
render it, while the creditor of that performance is excused from
rendering the counter-performance, *i.e.* (usually) from having to pay a
sum of money for the performance which had been promised by the
debtor. In the most common contractual situation, in which some
performance other than a payment of money is to be exchanged for such a
payment, the effect of the doctrine of *Taylor v Caldwell* is that the
"performance risk" of the now impossible performance is on the creditor
of that performance (*i.e.* he will neither receive the performance nor be
entitled to damages for non-performance) while the "price risk", or
"counter-performance risk"[5] is on the debtor of the now impossible
performance (*i.e.* he will not be entitled to the promised counter-
performance, which is usually the money promised by the creditor to the
debtor in exchange for the performance which has become impossible).
The statement in *Taylor v Caldwell* that "both parties are excused"[6] has the
effect that each party bears one of these two risks. The plaintiffs in that
case were the creditors of the impossible performance and were not
entitled to damages for the defendants' failure to render it, while the
defendants, who were the debtors of the impossible performance, were (it
was assumed, though not actually decided) not entitled to the agreed
price. This division of the two risks operates as a kind of loss-splitting.
There would be no such loss-splitting if both the performance risk and the
payment risk had come to rest on the same party, *i.e.* if the plaintiffs in
Taylor v Caldwell had been entitled to damages and had not been liable for
the price, or if the defendants had not been liable in damages but had
been entitled to the price. We shall see that in some of the coronation
cases to be discussed in Chs 7 and 15 the latter result was in fact reached.[7]

---

[5] The terms "performance risk" and "payment (or counter-performance) risk"
are borrowed from German law, which distinguishes, *e.g.* between "*Leistungsge-
fahr*" and "*Preisgefahr*": see Larenz, *Schuldrecht* (14th ed.), Vol.I, pp.308–310;
Esser & Schmidt, *Schuldrecht* (6th ed.), Vol.I, pp.314, 317.

[6] (1863) 3 B. & S. 826 at 840.

[7] *e.g. Chandler v Webster* [1904] 1 K.B. 493, below, para.15–047.

Criticism of these cases, and their eventual reversal,[8] can be explained by saying that cases in which the hirer was liable to pay in spite of having no claim against the other party were open to objection precisely because they united the performance risk and the payment risk in the same party (*i.e.* in the hirer). *Paradine v Jane*[9] is similarly thought to have united these, two risks in the tenant, and this is why *Taylor v Caldwell*[10] (which divides the two risks) is regarded as providing, in general, the preferable result. Strictly speaking, in making this comparison, reference should be made to the doctrines generally derived from the two cases, rather than to the decisions themselves. *Paradine v Jane* is actually concerned only with the payment risk and holds this risk to be on the creditor of the performance which had been interfered with (it would be question-begging to say that it had become impossible), *i.e.* the tenant was liable for rent in spite of having been, without the landlord's default, deprived of possession. The performance risk (*i.e.* the question whether the landlord was liable in respect of the tenant's loss of possession) was not in issue; and if it had received a negative answer, the probable reason for this was that the landlord had made no relevant promise[11]—not that he was excused from performing any obligation which he had undertaken. A different performance risk is dealt with in the much cited and frequently applied dictum in *Paradine v Jane* to the effect that the tenant of a house is liable on his express covenant to repair although the house is "burnt by lightning or thrown down by enemies."[12] Here the debtor of the performance which is affected by the supervening event is the tenant, and the performance risk is on him. At first sight, this may appear to be contrary to the modern rule which generally places the performance risk on the creditor. But, as has been suggested above,[13] the dictum on tenants' covenants to repair is not concerned with impossibility at all: it is concerned with the cause of the disrepair, rather than with the possibility of remedying it. There is nothing impossible about *executing* the repairs: the question is simply whether, on the true construction of the covenant, the tenant's promise extends (as it has commonly been held to do) to damage or destruction of the kind which has occurred.

2-027   The crucial difference between the two leading cases is in their underlying assumptions. These are that in *Paradine v Jane* the performance risk and the payment risk are united in one party (both being borne by the tenant) while in *Taylor v Caldwell* they are divided, thus splitting the loss. It may be noted that, so long as the two risks are divided, loss-splitting occurs, no matter how the division is made. Thus in a case like *Taylor v Caldwell* loss-splitting would have occurred not merely by holding that the defendants were neither liable in damage nor entitled to the price, but also by holding that they were so liable, provided that they were also so

---

[8] See below, paras 15–048, 15–050.

[9] (1647) Aleyn 26, above, para.2–002.

[10] (1863) 3. B. & S. 826, above, para.2–024.

[11] See above, para.2–004.

[12] (1647) Aleyn 26 at 27, above, para.2–002.

[13] See above, para.2–005.

entitled. The latter position was, in substance, that taken by those who sought to justify *Paradine v Jane* by arguing that the tenant there had (or should have had) a cross-claim against the landlord[14]; but if such a claim had been made it would probably have failed for the reason already given,[15] *i.e.* because the landlord had not made any promise extending to the type of "eviction" which occurred. The modern view is that loss-splitting is more satisfactorily achieved by placing the performance risk on the creditor of the impossible performance and the price risk on the debtor, rather than by adopting the converse solution of putting the performance risk on the debtor and the price risk on the creditor. One reason for this choice between these two solutions may rest on intuition or common sense: where performance has become impossible without a party's default, it is a natural reaction to say that he should not be liable for failing to render it, and that the other party should not have to pay for a performance which he does not receive. Another reason for preferring this approach is that it discourages the multiplicity of claims which would be the consequence of its converse: if, in *Taylor v Caldwell*, the plaintiffs had been entitled to damages but liable for the price, each party would have needed to sue the other. From this point of view a solution by which neither party can sue the other is more elegant and more economical than one under which each can sue the other; and both solutions equally provide a form of loss-splitting.

Even in the modern law, the concentration of the performance and price risks in one party survives in cases in which the "risk of loss" is said to have passed at a certain stage in the performance of the contract. If, for example, the risk of loss has passed to a buyer of goods, and the goods are then destroyed before delivery, the buyer (the creditor of the impossible performance) bears both the performance risk (he cannot claim damages) and the price risk (he must pay). This is because where goods are destroyed after the risk of loss has passed the doctrine of discharge (under which the price risk would be on the seller) is excluded.[16] The buyer's position is then similar to that of the tenant in *Paradine v Jane*, and indeed one modern view of that case is that the result there is to be explained on the ground that the risk of loss had passed to the tenant on execution of the lease.[17]

The discussion of loss allocation under the modern doctrine of discharge has so far been based on the simple assumption that the contract belongs to the normal type of bilateral contract under which a thing or a service is supplied in exchange for a sum of money. It follows from the doctrine of discharge that the person to whom the thing or service was to be supplied cannot recover damages in respect of the benefit that he expected to derive from it, while the prospective supplier cannot recover the agreed remuneration or price. Thus in *Taylor v Caldwell*

2–028

---

[14] See *Brown v Quilter* (1764) Amb. 619, above, para.2–007.
[15] See above, para.2–004.
[16] Below, para.3–007.
[17] Megarry and Wade, *The Law of Real Property* (6th ed.), para.14–189; but see below, paras 11–004 to 11–005.

the defendants could not have claimed the promised payments of £100 per night; nor could the plaintiffs have claimed damages for loss of their expected profits. In fact no such claims were made: the only claim was one by the plaintiffs for their wasted expenditure. The result of the decision was that the *whole* of this loss had to be borne by the plaintiffs; and it is questionable whether this was an altogether satisfactory solution. One possible argument is that the outcome was just since the defendants had also incurred expenses on the side-shows. But there are no grounds for supposing that there was equality in the two sets of expenses; and in any event it appears that the Gardens remained open, and that charges were made for admission,[18] so that the defendants' expenses were not wholly wasted. It also appears that the defendants received some compensation for their loss through insurance of the Hall[19]; and the cost to them of the insurance was presumably reflected in the payments of £100 per night which were to be made by the plaintiffs. It further seems reasonable to suppose that the defendants could have recovered damages for negligence or breach of contract from the plumber whose carelessness led to the fire[20]; and that in such an action damages could have been recovered for loss of profits suffered as a result of the destruction of so obviously a profit-earning thing as the Music Hall. The effect which should be given to these various factors is by no means easy to determine; but it is clear that *Taylor v Caldwell*, while representing an advance on the doctrine of absolute contracts, does not by any means provide the ideal solution of the problem of allocating the loss which results from wasted expenses. We shall return to these questions when discussing the effects of discharge.[21]

(4) Survivals of the doctrine of absolute contracts

2–029   Although the doctrine of discharge has now in general displaced the doctrine of *Paradine v Jane*, the latter doctrine does still survive to some extent. The cases in which it survives can be divided broadly into two groups. The first can be said to consist of historical survivals: that is, of cases in which the doctrine still applies to certain types of contracts merely because it had been applied to such contracts before *Taylor v Caldwell* was

---

[18] According to *The Times*, June 12, 1861: "By 5 o'clock the flames were entirely subdued and most of the engines had left, but they were scarcely out of sight when the band of the Gardens commenced playing and an announcement was posted informing the public that the price of admission was one shilling."

[19] From *The Times*, June 13, 1861, it appears that the defendants were themselves lessees of the Hall, and that, "The building is insured, and, it is believed, to the full amount". It is not clear whether the insurance was in the names of the defendants or of their lessors; in the latter event the defendants would have had rights in respect of the application of the insurance moneys under Fires Prevention (Metropolis) Act 1774, s.83. *Quaere* whether moneys payable to the defendants' lessor but applied for the benefit of the defendants by virtue of the 1777 Act would now fall within Law Reform (Frustrated Contracts) Act 1943, s.1(5), discussed below, paras 15–079 *et seq.*

[20] See above, para.2–024, at n.88.

[21] See below, paras 15–019, 15–078.

decided. The second consists of cases in which the doctrine continues to apply because the reasoning on which it was based still retains its force in relation to them.

(a) *Historical survivals*

In discussing the doctrine of absolute contracts, we saw that its most frequent application was to leases, in which its effect was that the destruction of buildings on the demised premises did not discharge the tenant's covenant to pay rent or his covenant to repair.[22] These rules have proved to be extraordinarily tenacious. They continued to be applied in cases decided after *Taylor v Caldwell*: in such cases it was (for example) held that the tenant of a house at common law[23] remained liable for rent after the house had been destroyed by enemy action,[24] and that such destruction did not relieve him from liability under his covenant to repair[25]; nor presumably would it relieve a landlord from any covenant which he may have made to repair. The pre-*Taylor v Caldwell* cases which follow *Paradine v Jane* continue, moreover, to be regarded as authoritative in modern works on real property and landlord and tenant.[26] The reason why the doctrine of absolute contracts has proved to be so tenacious in this branch of the law is that before the *National Carriers* case[27] in 1981 it was doubtful whether leases of land could ever be frustrated, and that, even in that case, the House of Lords emphasised that the frustration of such a lease would be a very rare event. The exact effects of the *National Carriers* case on the old landlord and tenant cases which applied *Paradine v Jane* remain to be worked out; but for the moment the general assumption appears to be that they are still good law. This assumption is interestingly reflected in the Landlord and Tenant Act 1985 which provides that the statutorily implied landlord's repairing covenant "shall not be construed as requiring the lessor ... to rebuild or reinstate the premises in the case of destruction or damage by fire, or by tempest, flood or other inevitable accident ...".[28] This statutory language seems to be a distant echo of *Paradine v Jane*, the draftsman evidently thought that the landlord needed the express statutory exemption. Whether this is a correct interpretation of the authorities is another matter: it is at least arguable that an *implied* covenant to repair does not fall within the doctrine of absolute contracts but rather within the first of the two propositions in *Paradine v Jane*, *i.e.* within that which applies "where the law creates a duty": here destruction "by tempest"[29] is said to operate as

2–030

---

[22] See above, para.2–007.

[23] For special statutory provisions, see Landlord and Tenant (War Damage) Act 1939, s.1.

[24] *Whitehall Court Ltd v Ettlinger* [1920] 1 K.B. 680.

[25] *Redmond v Dainton* [1920] 2 K.B. 256.

[26] *e.g.* Megarry and Wade, *The Law of Real Property* (6th ed.), para.14–189; Hill and Redman, *Law of Landlord and Tenant*, para.1128.

[27] *National Carriers Ltd v Panalpina (Northern) Ltd* [1981] A.C. 625; below, Ch.11.

[28] s.11(2)(b).

[29] (1647) Aleyn 26 at 27; above, para.2–002.

an excuse for the tenant (in cases of waste), and there seems to be no reason why it should not correspondingly excuse the landlord from liability under a covenant implied in law.

2–031   A second situation (which somewhat resembles that of the repairing covenant cases) arose out of fire insurance policies giving the insurer the option of either paying the sum insured or reinstating the premises. We have seen that in *Brown v Royal Insurance Co*[30] the insurer, having elected to reinstate, was not excused by a subsequent order of the local authority for the demolition of the premises, two judges taking the view that performance had not become impossible (but only more expensive) and a third that, even though performance had become impossible, that was no excuse. *Brown's* case seems to have survived *Taylor v Caldwell*, having been cited with approval in the House of Lords in 1922,[31] though it may be significant that the approval occurred in a case in which a plea of frustration was rejected because the subject-matter was a lease of land and it was then thought that the doctrine of frustration did not apply to such leases. The view has been expressed that, if the problem of *Brown's* case arose today, the court would have to consider whether the contract was frustrated.[32] It seems, however, highly unlikely that frustration would occur, since in the case put there is no impossibility of doing the very thing promised. The further question arises whether the contract would be frustrated if, after reinstatement had begun, the buildings suffered further damage or destruction by some supervening event (other than one of the perils insured against) for which neither party was responsible. The answer to this question would depend on the rules relating to the passing of risk in building contracts (to be discussed in Ch.3)[33] since the effect of the insurer's election to reinstate is to turn the insurer's promise into a contract of this kind.[34]

2–032   The third group of cases, to which the doctrine of absolute contracts was applied before *Taylor v Caldwell*, arose out of contracts for the carriage of goods by sea. In such cases it was, for example, held that a shipper was not discharged by prohibition or by pestilence making it dangerous for him to load a cargo,[35] or by a foreign embargo,[36] or by inability to procure a cargo[37]; and that an embargo or certain other supervening events preventing the prosecution of the voyage did not excuse the shipowner.[38] The fate of some of these cases has been significantly different from that of the landlord and tenant cases; and the reason for the difference is that

---

[30] (1859) 1 E. & E.; above, para.2–006 and see below, para.3–056.

[31] In *Matthey v Curling* [1922] 2 A.C. 180 at 229.

[32] *MacGillivray and Parkington on Insurance Law* (10th ed.), para.21–09.

[33] See below, paras 3–051 *et seq.*

[34] *MacGillivray and Parkington on Insurance Law* (10th ed.), para.21–06.

[35] *Bligh v Page* (1801) 3 B. & P. 295n; *Barker v Hodgson* (1814) 3 M. & S. 267.

[36] *Hadley v Clarke* (1789) 8 T.R. 259; *Sjoerds v Luscombe* (1812) 16 East 201.

[37] *Hills v Sughrue* (1846) 15 M. & W. 253 (as to which see below, n.46).

[38] *Shubbrick v Salmond* (1765) 3 Burr. 1637; *Hadley v Clark* (1799) 8 T.R. 259; *Atkinson v Ritchie* (1809) 10 East 530.

it was recognised soon after *Taylor v Caldwell* that the new doctrine of discharge did apply to charterparties.[39] Indeed, it was in charterparty cases that important developments of the doctrine of discharge took place in the early part of the twentieth century.[40] One of the older cases referred to above was, indeed, cited with approval by Blackburn J. five years after *Taylor v Caldwell*,[41] but the case has been judicially doubted[42] and is now generally doubted by textwriters,[43] even though it has not been specifically overruled. The same is true of a number of other charterparty cases which, before *Taylor v Caldwell*, had applied the doctrine of absolute contracts.[44] The one rule from the old charterparty cases which clearly has survived is that a party who undertakes to provide a cargo is strictly liable for failure to do so.[45] This rule appears to have originated in cases of *antecedent* impossibility,[46] where strict liability is arguably more appropriate[47] than it would be in cases of supervening impossibility. The possibility that the obligation to provide a cargo (though it has been described as "absolute"[48]) may be excused by *supervening* events is therefore not wholly to be ruled out.

(b) *Survivals based on the reasoning of* Paradine v Jane

More significant than possible historical survivals of the doctrine of absolute contracts are those cases in which the reasoning of *Paradine v Jane* can still appropriately be applied today, even though they may arise from situations to which that reasoning had not been applied before *Taylor v Caldwell*. The reasoning, it will be recalled, was that, "notwithstanding any accident by inevitable necessity", a party was bound by a duty created by

2–033

---

[39] *e.g.* in *Jackson v Union Marine Insurance Co Ltd* (1874) L.R. 10 C.P. 125.

[40] *e.g.* in *Tamplin SS Co Ltd v Anglo-Mexican Petroleum Co Ltd* [1916] 2 A.C. 379; *Scottish Navigation Co Ltd v Souter* [1917] 1 K.B. 222; *Bank Line Ltd v Arthur Capel & Co* [1919] A.C. 435; *Hirji Mulji v Cheong Yue SS Co Ltd* [1926] A.C. 497.

[41] *Barker v Hodgson*, above, n.35 cited in *Ford v Cotesworth* (1868) L.R. 4 Q.B. 127 at 134.

[42] *Ralli Bros v Compañia Naviera Sota y Asznar* [1920] 2 K.B. 287 at 291, 296, 297 and 300.

[43] *Barker v Hodgson*, above, is disapproved in *Scrutton on Charterparties* (20th ed.), p.312, n.17; Carver, *Carriage by Sea* (13th ed.), paras 986–988, 1034 (but see *ibid.* paras 796 and 1822, n.47); *Dicey and Morris on the Conflict of Laws* (11th ed.), p.1225, n.86 (the case is no longer cited in later editions of this work).

[44] *Bligh v Page*, above, n.35 and *Sjoerds v Luscombe*, above, n.36, doubted in *Scrutton, op. cit.* at 312, n.17 and in the *Ralli Bros* case, at 291–292, 301–302; *Hadley v Clarke* (1799) 8 T.R. 259 (doubted in *Metropolitan Water Board v Dick, Kerr & Co* [1918] A.C. 119 at 127).

[45] *Hills v Sughrue*, above, n.37; *Soc Financiera, etc. v Agrimpex, etc. (The Aello)* [1961] A.C. 135 (overruled, but on another point, in *E L Oldendorff & Co GmbH v Tradax Export SA (The Johanna Oldendorff)* [1974] A.C. 479).

[46] *Hills v Sughrue*, above, n.45, appears to have been such a case and follows *Bute v Thompson* (1844) 13 M. & W. 487 where antecedent impossibility was held not be a defence to an action for minimum rent under a mining lease.

[47] See above, para.1–007.

[48] *Hills v Sughrue* (1846) 15 M. & W. 253 at 261.

his own contract "*because he might have provided against it by his contract*".[49] Subject to one significant emendation (to be noted below) there are situations in which this reasoning still retains its force today. The point has been well put in an American case by Learned Hand J.: "No doubt we have gone a long way since *Paradine v Jane* ... but a promise still involves risks that the promisor may find it burdensome or even impossible to meet ... Its very purpose is to give assurance to the promisee against hazards of the future."[50]

One group of cases concerns antecedent impossibility. In one English case[51] of this kind, the reasoning of *Paradine v Jane* was approved after *Taylor v Caldwell*, though on the facts that reasoning did not apply as, on the true construction of the contract, no undertaking to do what turned out to be impossible (namely to extract from land, which was the subject of a mining lease, more clay than the land contained) had been given. More directly in point are American cases concerning building contracts. These will be more fully considered in Ch.3.[52] Here it is necessary only to say that they were cases in which contractors claimed to be discharged from their obligations to erect buildings on specified sites when the buildings collapsed (sometimes repeatedly[53]) because the sites were incapable of sustaining their weight. In rejecting such claims, the courts relied[54] on the reasoning of *Paradine v Jane*; and this reasoning continues to have greater force in such cases of antecedent impossibility than it normally does in cases of supervening impossibility. The reason for this distinction has already been given: it is, in general, easier to discover present facts than to foresee the future.[55] The contractor in these cases could (and arguably should) have investigated the site before entering into the contract: in this sense, it can be said that he had the opportunity of providing by his contract against the difficulty which he encountered. If he fails to make any such provision, the contract is more likely (than in cases of unexpected supervening obstacles to performance) to be construed as one by which he undertook responsibility for the difficulties which have arisen from the antecedent state of the site. For this reason, too, the contractor is unlikely to be able to claim relief on the ground of mistake.[56]

2–034   A second group of cases concerns the liability of sellers who are prevented by the occurrence of a supervening event (or by the non-

---

[49] (1674) Aleyn 26 at 27.

[50] *Companhia de Navegaceo Lloyd Brasileiro v CC Blake*, 34 F. 2d 616 at 619 (1929).

[51] *Clifford v Watts* (1870) L.R. 5 C.P. 577 at 586.

[52] See below, paras 3–056 to 3–058.

[53] See *Stees v Leonnard*, 20 Minn. 455 (1874), below, para.3–056.

[54] See the citation in *Stees v Leonnard*, above, of *School District v Bennet* 3 Dutcher 513, 518 (1859).

[55] See above, para.1–007.

[56] *Watkins v Carrig*, 21 A. 591 (1941), so far as it concerns the validity of the *original* contract; contrast *Kinzer Construction Co v Stat*, 125 N.Y.S. 46 (1910) where the contractor recovered on a *quantum meruit* basis in respect of work done under a contract the full performance of which was "impossible" by reason of antecedent obstacles; see further below, para.3–058.

occurrence of such an event where it was expected to occur) from performing their obligation to ship goods as required by the contract. One such case is *Ashmore & Son Ltd v CS Cox & Co*,[57] where Manila hemp had been sold on the terms that shipment was to be made "from a port or ports in the Philippine Islands between May 1 and July 31, 1898 ...". The sellers were unable to make such a shipment on account of the Spanish–American war and were held to be in breach on the ground that their undertaking to ship was an "absolute" one.[58] An alternative explanation of the case is that there was evidence of the availability of a shipment of the contract description, which the sellers could have acquired afloat.[59] But it is interesting to note that counsel for the buyer relied on *Paradine v Jane* while counsel for the seller relied on *Taylor v Caldwell*; and that it was nevertheless the buyer who prevailed. Another such case is *Lewis Emanuel & Son Ltd v Sammut*[60] where a contract was made for the sale of potatoes to be shipped from Malta between April 14 and 24. During that period, no ship capable of taking the potatoes on board left Malta, so that it was impossible for the seller to ship them during the contractual shipment period. He was nevertheless held liable in damages, on the ground that: "The seller, being on an island, must make sure that shipping space is available before he commits himself to an absolute contract."[61] That is language reminiscent of *Paradine v Jane*, and one can explain it on the ground that, in such export contracts, it is common for the seller to safeguard himself by means of a clause which qualifies his obligation, *e.g.* by making it "subject to shipment". In other words, the reasoning of *Paradine v Jane* still has force where the position is not merely that the party *might* have provided against the event by his contract, but where it is *reasonable* to expect him to do so. The trouble with the doctrine of absolute contracts was that it applied to *both* these situations; and, where it was *not* reasonable to expect a party to provide for the event, the doctrine came to be regarded as an unsatisfactory way of allocating the loss resulting from the event, and therefore to be superseded by the doctrine of discharge.

IV. Trends Affecting the Development of the Doctrine

In discussing the judgment in *Taylor v Caldwell*,[62] we saw that Blackburn J. **2–035** there formulated the doctrine of discharge in a way which facilitated its development and expansion[63]; and in the years following that case the

---

[57] [1899] 1 Q.B. 436; *cf.* also the discussion of *Jacobs v Crédit Lyonnais* (1884) 12 Q.B.D. 589 below, para.12–021.

[58] [1899] 1 Q.B. at 442.

[59] *ibid.* at 440; *Benjamin's Sale of Goods* (6th ed.), para.19–126; and see below, para.4–044.

[60] [1959] 2 Lloyd's Rep. 629.

[61] *ibid.* at 642.

[62] (1863) 3 B. & S. 826.

[63] See above, para.2–025.

doctrine entered into an initial period of growth. It was extended in the first place to various groups of cases in which performance had indeed become impossible, but had done so otherwise than by reason of the perishing of a "given person or thing"[64]: *e.g.* to cases where a thing necessary for the performance of the contract was permanently or temporarily requisitioned,[65] or in some other way became temporarily unavailable for the purpose of performance,[66] or where the impossibility affected only the method of performance,[67] or where the subject-matter was not a specific thing, but was one to be taken from an identified source which failed.[68] An even more striking extension of the doctrine was made in cases in which the supervening event had not made performance by either party impossible at all but can be said to have frustrated the purpose of the contract. This was the position in the coronation cases to be discussed in Ch.7 below.[69] In a number of these cases, contracts had been made for the hire of rooms or seats overlooking the routes of the processions planned for the coronation of King Edward VII; and such contracts were held to have been discharged when the coronation was postponed on account of the illness of the King. In the leading case of *Krell v Henry*[70] this was held to be the position even though the contract contained no express reference to the coronation.[71] Performance was not physically or literally impossible: the rooms were available for use by the hirer on the days in question, and of course it was not impossible for him to pay the agreed fee. But it was held that the doctrine of discharge was not restricted to cases where the supervening event made performance physically impossible: it also applied "to cases where the event which renders the contract incapable of performance is the cessation or non-existence of an express condition or state of things going to the root of the contract and essential to its performance".[72]

2–036   This extension of the doctrine of discharge did not escape criticism since it could, if misapplied, lead to the situation in which a party would be entitled to relief merely because a supervening change of circumstances had turned the contract, for that party, into a very bad bargain.[73] But these criticisms have not prevailed and the doctrine of discharge is now generally thought to have been correctly applied to coronation cases such as *Krell v Henry*;[74] for it can fairly be said that the hirer in that case would have suffered unacceptable hardship if he had been held to his contract in

---

[64] (1863) 3 B. & S. 826 at 839.

[65] *e.g. Re Shipton, Anderson & Co* [1915] 3 K.B. 676; *Bank Line Ltd v Arthur Capel* [1919] A.C. 435.

[66] *e.g. Jackson v Union Marine Insurance Co Ltd* (1874) L.R. 10 C.P. 125.

[67] *e.g. Nickoll & Knight v Ashton Edridge & Co* [1901] 2 K.B. 126.

[68] *e.g. Howell v Coupland* (1876) 1 Q.B.D. 258.

[69] See below, paras 7–006 to 7–014.

[70] [1903] 2 K.B. 740; see further para.7–010, below.

[71] In this respect, *Krell v Henry* is unique among the coronation seat cases: see below, para.7–010.

[72] [1903] 2 K.B. 740 at 748.

[73] See below, para.7–011.

[74] See below, para.7–011 at n.76.

the altered circumstances. But English cases provide few other illustrations of discharge on the ground of frustration of purpose,[75] and they seem not to have adopted the converse notion of discharge on the ground of "impracticability",[76] *i.e.* on the ground that supervening events have made performance more expensive or otherwise more onerous for the party claiming discharge. Thus in the *British Movietonenews* and *Davis Contractors* cases[77] (to be further discussed in Ch.6) pleas of discharge on such grounds were rejected; and a number of dicta in the House of Lords similarly adopt a restricted approach to the doctrine. In this vein it has, for example, been said that "an increase of expense is not a ground of frustration",[78] that the doctrine of frustration was only to be applied "within very narrow limits",[79] that "it by no means follows that disappointed expectations lead to frustrated contracts",[80] and that the doctrine was "not lightly to be invoked to relieve contracting parties of the normal consequences of imprudent commercial bargains".[81]

At first sight, a less strict approach to the doctrine may seem to have been taken by Lord Hailsham L.C. in the *National Carriers* case, where he described as "untenable" the "proposition that the doctrine was not to be extended".[82] But the purpose of this observation was to make the point that the doctrine could apply to contracts generally: thus suggestions that it did not apply to particular types of contracts, such as time charters or demise charters, or leases of land, have from time to time been rejected by the courts.[83] The actual decision in the *National Carriers* case was that events which temporarily prevented a tenant of a warehouse from putting it to its intended use were not sufficiently serious to discharge the contract. In this respect the case, so far from departing from, actually illustrates, the view that the doctrine of discharge is "not lightly to be invoked".

This approach to the doctrine of discharge reflects the importance which the English courts have come, in the interests of commercial certainty, to attach to the principle of sanctity of contract. It can fairly be described as a trend to restrict the operation of the doctrine after its initial period of growth; and in the English cases the trend is illustrated by an increasing amount of negative evidence. The First World War did indeed

2–037

---

[75] See below, para.7–035.

[76] See below, para.6–021.

[77] [1952] A.C. 166; [1956] A.C. 696.

[78] *Tsakiroglou & Co Ltd v Noblee Thorl GmbH* [1962] A.C. 93 at 115.

[79] *ibid.*

[80] *Davis Contractors Ltd v Fareham UDC* [1956] A.C. 696 at 715.

[81] *Pioneer Shipping v BTP Tioxide (The Nema)* [1982] A.C. 724 at 752; *cf. Atisa SA v Aztec AG* [1983] 1 Lloyd's Rep. 579 at 584; *J Lauritzen A/S v Wijsmuller BV (The Super Servant Two)* [1990] 1 Lloyd's Rep. 1 at 8.

[82] *National Carriers Ltd v Panalpina (Northern) Ltd* [1981] A.C. 675 at 689; *cf. ibid.* at 694, 712.

[83] *Bank Line Ltd v Arthur Capel & Co* [1919] A.C. 435 (time charters); *Blane Steamships Ltd v Minister of Transport* [1951] 2 K.B. 965 (demise charters); *National Carriers Ltd v Panalpina (Northern) Ltd* [1981] A.C. 675 (leases of land).

give rise to a significant number of cases[84] in which contracts were held to have been discharged by supervening impossibility. By contrast, there were hardly any reported[85] Second World War cases in which contracts were held to have been discharged by supervening impossibility, as opposed to supervening illegality.[86] The Suez crisis of 1956 led to severe commercial disruption, but it produced only two reported cases in which frustration was successfully pleaded. Both these cases were later overruled.[87] When the Suez Canal was again closed in 1967, pleas of frustration met with no more success[88]; and the "energy crisis" resulting from further hostilities in the Middle East in 1973 did not lead to any reported cases in England in which frustration was even raised as a defence.[89] All this is not to say that the doctrine of discharge may not be applied where performance is actually prevented; it was, for example, applied in a number of cases in which shipowners were prevented from rendering the agreed services under time charters because their ships were trapped in port for long periods after the outbreak of hostilities in 1980 between Iran and Iraq.[90]

---

[84] Especially charterparty cases such as *Scottish Navigation Co Ltd v WA Souter & Co* [1917] 1 K.B. 222 and *Bank Line Ltd v Arthur Capel & Co* [1919] A.C. 435, discussing earlier authorities; *cf.* also sale of goods cases such as *Acetylene Co of GB v Canada Carbide Co* (1922) 8 Ll.L. Rep. 456. See also Report of the Committee appointed by the Board of Trade to consider the position of British Manufacturers and Merchants in respect of Pre-War Contracts, Cd. 8975 (1918).

[85] There were some: *e.g. Morgan v Manser* [1948] 1 K.B. 184.

[86] In three leading Second World War cases, the alleged ground of frustration was supervening illegality: they were the *Fibrosa* case (*Fibrosa Spolka Akcyjna v Fairbairn Lawson Combe Barbour Limited*) [1943] A.C. 32 and the *Denny Mott* case (*Denny, Mott & Dickson Limited v James B Fraser & Company Limited*) [1944] A.C. 265 (below, paras 8–005, 7–021) in which the contracts were held to be frustrated, and the *Cricklewood* case (*Cricklewood Property and Investment Trust v Leighton's Investment Trust Limited*) [1945] A.C. 221 (below, para.11–015) in which the plea of frustration failed.

[87] *Carapanayoti & Co Ltd v ET Green Ltd* [1959] 1 Q.B. 131; overruled in the *Tsakiroglou* case [1962] A.C. 93; and *Soc Tunisiene d'Armement v Sidermar SpA (The Massalia)* [1961] 2 Q.B. 278; overruled in *Ocean Tramp Tankers Corp v V/O Sovfracht (The Eugenia)* [1964] 2 Q.B. 226.

[88] For the Suez cases, see further, paras 4–071 to 4–083, below.

[89] See below, para.6–024. In a number of American cases, it was argued (generally without success) that the contracts were discharged by these events on the ground of "impracticability": below, paras 6–009 to 6–016 for an exceptional case giving relief on this ground, see *Aluminum Corp of America v Essex Group Inc*, 499 F. Supp. 53 (1980), below, para.6–018. In *Florida Power & Light Company v Westinghouse Electric Corporation*, 826 F. 2d. 239 (1987) relief was granted on account of a combination of impossibility in the contemplated method of performance and "impracticability": see below, paras 4–061 and 6–034.

[90] *Kodros Shipping Corp v Empresa Cubana de Fletes (The Evia) (No2)* [1983] 1 A.C. 736; *Kissavos Shipping Co v Empresa Cubana de Fletes (The Agathon)* [1982] 2 Lloyd's Rep. 211; *International Sea Tankers Inc v Hemisphere Shipping Co Ltd (The Wenjiang) (No 2)* [1983] 1 Lloyd's Rep. 400; *Vinava Shipping Co Ltd v Finelvet AG (The Chrysalis)* [1983] 1 Lloyd's Rep. 503.

In the Suez cases there was (with one exception[91]) no such prevention: performance had merely become more onerous for the party alleging frustration. There is now a marked judicial reluctance to apply the doctrine in such circumstances.

It has been suggested above that this reluctance is primarily based on the importance now attached to the principle of sanctity of contract. At a more practical level, it is further supported by two related points. The first is the tendency of contracting parties to "draft out" possible causes of frustration by making express provisions either for specific obstacles to performance, or for such obstacles in general: *e.g.* in "Suez clauses"[92] which began to make their appearance after the first Suez crisis, and in the *force majeure* and similar clauses to be discussed in Ch.12. The second is the point, already noted in connection with *Taylor v Caldwell,* that total discharge of the contract may not be a satisfactory way of allocating the loss which results from the supervening event.[93] Often it may be more reasonable to adopt some compromise solution: for example, in some of the coronation seat cases the contracts provided that, if the procession were cancelled, the ticket-holder should be entitled to use the ticket on the day when the procession eventually did take place[94]; the Suez clauses mentioned above specified (sometimes in considerable detail) which party was to bear any extra expense which might be incurred, should the Canal again be closed[95]; and *"force majeure"* clauses may provide that, in cases of temporary impossibility, performance is to be *postponed,* at least for a limited time, at the end of which discharge may follow if the impossibility persists.[96] A contract could also by express provisions vary the normal *consequences* of discharge: this possibility is illustrated by another of the coronation cases in which the contract provided that, if the procession were cancelled, the ticket-holder should get his money back, less a percentage to cover the other party's expenses.[97] In the absence of such express provisions, the English courts had no power to *modify* the contract; nor was there in English law any half-way house between holding that the contract was totally and automatically discharged (if the supervening event was sufficiently drastic for this purpose) and that it remained in full force (if the event was not of this character).[98] Certain powers to make

---

[91] *i.e. The Eugenia* [1964] 2 Q.B. 226 (above n.87); but there the fact that the ship was trapped in the Canal did not lead to frustration as it was due to the charterer's prior breach of the contract: see below para.14–022.

[92] Below, n.95.

[93] See above, para.2–028.

[94] For contracts containing such provisions, see *Clark v Lindsay* (1903) 19 T.L.R. 202 and *Victoria Seats Agency v Paget* (1902) 19 T.L.R. 16 (first contract).

[95] *Achille Laura v Total Societa Italiana per Azioni* [1969] 2 Lloyd's Rep. 65; *DJ Henry Ltd v Wilhelm V Clasen* [1973] 1 Lloyd's Rep. 159.

[96] *e.g.* GAFTA Form 100 cl.22, discussed in *Bremer Handelsgesellschaft mbH v Vanden Avenne-Izegem PVBA* [1978] 2 Lloyd's Rep. 109, below, para.12–029.

[97] *Victoria Seats Agency v Paget* (1902) 19 T.L.R. 16 (second contract); *cf. Elliott v Crutchley* [1903] 2 K.B. 476, [1904] 1 K.B. 565, [1906] A.C. 7 (below, para.15–069).

[98] See below, para.15–040.

adjustments in respect of expenses incurred for the purpose of performance and in respect of benefits conferred by part performance before discharge do now exist by statute,[99] but these powers have a limited scope. The desire of contracting parties to provide for compromise solutions where supervening events disrupt performance has thus given a further impetus to the process of making express contractual provisions for such events, and this process has tended further to narrow the scope of the doctrine of frustration since that doctrine is excluded where the parties have expressly provided for the effects on their contract of the event which has interfered with its performance.[1]

V. DISCHARGE OF BOTH PARTIES

2–039   In discussing *Taylor v Caldwell* we saw that Blackburn J. concluded that "both parties are excused"[2]; that this statement was not directly supported by the particular examples from which Blackburn J. derived his general principle[3]; and that the statement was not strictly necessary for the actual decision of the case, in which the court was concerned only with the liability of the defendants: their obligation to supply the Music Hall could not be performed because of the fire, but that event clearly did not make it impossible for the plaintiffs to perform their principal obligation to make the agreed payments. It is more doubtful whether it prevented the plaintiffs from performing their other obligation, namely to engage the artistes for the concerts, and whether indeed the plaintiffs were under any obligation to hold the concerts at all. On a literal reading of the contract, they had a right, but not a duty, to give the concerts; though it is arguable that an obligation to give them might have been implied if the defendants had a financial interest in the giving of the concerts (it is not entirely clear whether the plaintiffs' rights to box-office receipts extended to all, or only to some, such receipts). The contract in *Taylor v Caldwell* was, in any event, a somewhat unusual one: it was a kind of joint enterprise in which each party undertook to render a performance other than the payment of money. The more usual bilateral contract consists of an exchange of promises whereby one party (A) promises to provide a thing or a service and the other (B) to pay for it in money. Where the contract is of this kind, supervening events may make it impossible for A to perform his promise, but performance of B's promise, being simply one to pay money, cannot in law become impossible (though it may become illegal[4]). Blackburn J. does not explain why an event which makes it impossible for

---

[99] Law Reform (Frustrated Contracts) Act 1943, s.1(2) proviso and s.1(3); below, paras 15–071, 15–073.

[1] See below, para.12–001.

[2] (1863) 3 B. & S. 823 at 840, above, para.2–022; *cf. Horlock v Beal* [1916] 1 A.C. 486 at 525.

[3] See above, para.2–022.

[4] See *Libyan Arab Foreign Bank v Bankers Trust Co* [1989] Q.B. 728 at 749, recognising that "an obligation to pay money can be frustrated" by illegality.

only one party to perform his promise nevertheless discharges both parties.

In England, this conclusion was, indeed, not immediately accepted, even after *Taylor v Caldwell*. One type of case in which it was doubted concerned time charters. Under such a contract, the shipowner undertakes to render services for a specified or ascertainable time by making his ship available to the charterer who in return undertakes to make periodic payments of hire. There was at one time some support for the view that the detention or requisition of the ship did not discharge the charterer: he could still pay the agreed hire, and what use he made of the ship was of no concern to the shipowner.[5] But in two early twentieth-century cases[6] Lord Sumner rejected this argument and held that the detention or requisition of the ship could discharge both parties to a time charter. His explanation for this result was that: "It is [the parties'] common object which is frustrated, not merely the individual advantage which one party or the other might have gained from the contract. If so, what the law provides must be a common relief from this common disappointment and an immediate termination of the obligation as regards future performance."[7]

This reasoning has been criticised in other common law jurisdictions. Thus in Australia Latham C.J. has said[8]: "There is some difficulty in specifying the 'common object' of the parties to a contract ... contracting parties are not partners. They are engaged in a common venture only in a popular sense." In a contract for the sale of goods, "the acquisition of the goods is no more and no less a common object than the receipt of the price". The idea of a "common object" comes from the "peculiar

2–040

---

[5] *Scottish Navigation Co Ltd v Souter* [1916] 1 K.B. 675 at 681; *cf. Admiral Shipping Co Ltd v Weidner Hopkins & Co* [1916] 1 K.B. 429 at 437; this statement may be explicable on the narrower ground that in *this* charter there was in fact "no object in common contemplation". Both decisions were reversed on appeal, sub nom. *Scottish Navigation Co Ltd v Souter* [1917] 1 K.B. 222, where it was stressed that the contracts were not ordinary time charters but charters for "one Baltic round" (which could not be accomplished on account of the outbreak of the First World War). The argument that "the adventure on the part of the owners of the ship was that she should earn freight" had earlier been used even in a voyage charter case: see *Hudson v Hill* (1874) 43 L.J.C.P. 273 at 279, though it had been clear ever since *Jackson v Union Marine Insurance Co Ltd* (1874) L.R. 10 C.P. 125 (below, para.5–039) that such a charter could be frustrated. In *Tamplin SS Co v Anglo-Mexican Petroleum Co Ltd* [1916] 2 A.C. 397 at 424–425 Lord Parker also seems to take the view that time charters cannot be frustrated by requisition of the ship. For similar views expressed in the Court of Appeal in that case, see [1916] 1 K.B. 485 at 494.

[6] *Bank Line Ltd v Arthur Capel & Co* [1919] A.C. 435; *Hirji Mulji v Cheong Yue SS Co* [1926] A.C. 497. The same view had been taken by the Court of Appeal in *Countess of Warwick SS Co v Le Nickel SA* [1918] 1 K.B. 372; *cf.* also *Scottish Navigation Co Ltd v Souter* [1917] 1 K.B. 222 at 237.

[7] *Hirji Mulji* case, above, n.6, at 507. Contrast *Brown v Turner Brightman & Co* [1912] A.C. 12 (performance of time charter not "prevented" or "hindered" within a "strikes" clause by charterer's inability, as a result of a strike, to secure a cargo).

[8] *Scanlan's New Neon Ltd v Tooheys Ltd* (1943) 67 C.L.R. 169 at 197.

characteristics" of charterparty cases. Presumably, one such characteristic is that each party has to do some act other than to pay cash. Such "peculiar characteristics" are by no means confined to charterparties: another illustration of them is (as already noted) provided by *Taylor v Caldwell* itself, where the plaintiffs undertook to "find and provide, at their own sole cost, all the necessary artistes for the ... concerts"[9] as well as to pay the hire.

In the United States, a point similar to Latham C.J.'s has been made by Corbin: "each of the two parties to a contract has an object or purpose for which he joins the transaction. These purposes are not identical ... There is no 'purpose of the contract'; instead there are the purposes of the parties to the contract."[10] Thus in a case like *Taylor v Caldwell*, the plaintiffs' purpose was to get the use of the Music Hall (leaving the side shows out of account); while the purpose of the defendants was to get the £100 per night (again leaving out of account the possible benefit to them of the increased number of visitors which the grand concerts might attract to the Gardens). Critics of the "common object" theory do not, however, deny that both parties are discharged and two explanations for this conclusion have been put forward in the United States.

2–041   One, given by Corbin,[11] is that in a case such as *Taylor v Caldwell* the defendants are discharged by impossibility, while the plaintiffs are discharged because their purpose in entering into the contract (*i.e.* to secure the use of the Hall) is frustrated. This is an unusual use of the notion of "frustration of purpose", which normally refers to cases in which there is no impossibility on either side[12] (as in the coronation cases, to be discussed in Ch.7). Corbin recognises this when he describes those cases as ones in which it is the "further and ultimate purpose" of the parties which is frustrated. In view of the multiplicity of senses in which the expression "frustration" is already used,[13] Corbin's use of the phrase "frustration of purpose" in the two senses just described (*i.e.* relating to an *immediate* and to an *ultimate* purpose) scarcely promotes clarity, and no further use of the sense which he gave it in explaining *Taylor v Caldwell* will be made in this book. This sense also seems to be an unnecessary one, for it does not seem to add anything of substance to the second explanation for the discharge of both parties (to be discussed below) which has been given in the United States.

This second explanation is that, in a case like *Taylor v Caldwell*, the defendants were discharged by supervening impossibility, while the plaintiffs were discharged by what used to be (and sometimes still is) called "failure of consideration", a misleading expression for which the

---

[9] (1863) 3 B. & S. 826 at 830.

[10] *Contracts*, para.1322. For similar reasoning in an English charterparty case (in which the actual decision turned on the direction to the jury on another point) see *Hudson v Hill* (1874) 43 L.J.C.P. 273 at 279, quoted in n.95, above.

[11] *Corbin, Contracts*, para.1332.

[12] See below, paras 7–001, 7–011.

[13] See below, paras 2–044 to 2–050.

Restatement 2d[14] substitutes the more informative phrase "failure in performance". This view has considerable support in the United States[15] and is adopted by § 261 of the Restatement 2d which provides that "where, after a contract is made, a party's performance is made impracticable without his fault by the occurrence of an event, the non-occurrence of which was a basic assumption on which the contract was made, *his* duty to render that performance is discharged" (emphasis added). To find out how the *other* party's duty is affected, we have to look at other provisions of the Restatement 2d. The starting point is the Introductory Note to Ch.11[16]; "The obligor [*i.e.* the plaintiff in *Taylor v Caldwell*] may claim that he will not receive the agreed exchange [*i.e.* the use of the Music Hall] for his own performance [*i.e.* the payments of £100 per night] because some circumstance [*i.e.* the destruction of the Music Hall] has discharged the obligee's [*i.e.* the defendant's] duty to render the agreed exchange on the ground of impracticability. ...." The principle which discharged the plaintiffs in *Taylor v Caldwell,* is then stated in § 237 (to which we are referred in Ch.11 by § 267): "... it is a condition of each party's remaining duty to render performances under an exchange of promises that there be no uncured material failure by the other party to render any such performance at an earlier time" (and where the performances were to be exchanged simultaneously, § 238 requires each party either to render or to show that he is able to render performance as part of the simultaneous exchange). The important point is that § 237 refers to *failure* in performance: not to *breach*. It therefore excuses the plaintiffs in *Taylor v Caldwell,* even though the defendants are discharged by the destruction of the Music Hall and so are not in breach. Again both parties are discharged, but the Restatement's explanation for this result differs from that given in England.

The Uniform Commercial Code manages to sit on both sides of this conceptual fence.[17] Section 2–615(a) follows what may be called the American conceptual structure, which has just been outlined. It merely provides that "Delay in delivery or non-delivery ... by a seller ... is not a breach of *his* duty under a contract of sale if performance as agreed has been made impracticable by the occurrence of a contingency the non-occurrence of which was a basic assumption on which the contract was

---

[14] § 237.

[15] See Corbin, paras 1320, 1322; Corbin (1947) 29(3) Jl of Comp. Int. Law 7; *Earn Line SS Co v Sutherland SS Co Ltd,* 254 F. 126 at 131 (1918); *Kowal v Sportswear by Revere Inc,* 22 N.E. 2d 778 at 781 (1967) and see the citations from Restatement 2d in the text below. Other American decisions however seem to adopt the English approach stated at n.97, above, *e.g. The Isle of Mull,* 278 F. 131 (1921).

[16] Restatement 2d, Vol.II, p.310.

[17] Draft proposed amendments to the sections of the UCC discussed in this paragraph do not affect the substance of the reasoning contained in it. Further discussion here of the proposed amendments to Arts 2, 2A and 7 of the Code would be premature as it is uncertain whether the proposals are in their final form, or to what extent they will gain acceptance by the relevant legislatures. The draft here referred to is that issued by the American Law Institute dated April 18, 2003.

made" (emphasis added). In cases of non-delivery, the buyer is excused simply because the goods have not been delivered (s.2–507(1)): not because of the impracticability which prevents the seller from delivering; and in cases of delay in delivery a similar result follows from the buyer's right to reject under the "perfect tender" rule of s.2–601(a), which (as a general rule) entitles him to reject "if the goods or the tender of delivery fail in any respect to conform to the contract". These last two provisions excuse the buyer where the supervening events make it impracticable for the seller to perform his duty to deliver. Section 2–615 gives rise also to an entirely separate problem where those events make it impracticable for the *buyer* to perform his duty to take delivery. Here Comment 9 to s.2–615 suggests that the buyer may be able to rely on "the reason of" the section, *i.e.* on discharge by impracticability of his performance.[18] The present point is that the buyer may be discharged, (even though performance of his own duty to pay is not impracticable at all) where the seller's duty to deliver is discharged by impracticability.

By contrast to s.2–615(a), s.2–613(a) seems to adopt the English conceptual structure. It provides that, if goods identified when the contract is made are totally destroyed before the risk of loss passes to the buyer, "the contract is avoided".[19] This closely resembles the corresponding phrase in s.7 of the Sale of Goods Act 1979 ("the agreement is avoided"). If s.2–613(a) had followed the conceptual structure of s.2–615(a), one would have expected s.2–613(a) to say that failure by the seller to deliver was not a breach of his duty under the contract. One could then conclude that failure by the buyer to pay was not a breach of his duty either, precisely because the loss had occurred before the risk had passed him.

2–043   Under the second of the two American views discussed above, the defence of the party whose performance has not become impossible "is often described as failure of consideration".[20] It is probable that this very terminology accounts for the fact that this explanation of that party's discharge is not now commonly[21] found in England; indeed in *National*

---

[18] See below, para.4–059.

[19] This phrase was also found in the American Uniform Sales Act, s.8; this Act is now superseded by UCC, Art.2. The draft amendments to the UCC referred to in n.17, above substitutes, for the phrase quoted in the text above, the phrase "the contract is terminated". The point of the change is said to be that it "clarifies that pre-termination breaches are preserved". In English law, the same consequence follows from the principles stated in para.15–010, below.

[20] *e.g.* Corbin, *Contracts*, para.1320.

[21] It is occasionally found in English cases: *e.g.* in *Herne Bay Steamboat Co v Hutton* [1903] 2 K.B. 683 at 691; *Grimsdick v Sweetman* [1909] 2 K.B. 740 at 744; it may (for the reason given at paras 7–014, 7–024, below) be significant that the alleged ground of discharge in these cases was not impossibility but frustration of purpose, and that the plea of discharge failed in both cases. A somewhat similar argument for the discharge of both parties is used in *Scottish Navigation Co Ltd v Souter & Co* [1917] 1 K.B. 222 at 237. For an English work which uses "failure of consideration" reasoning in this context, see McElroy and Williams,

Carriers Ltd v Panalpina (Northern) Ltd,[22] the argument that such discharge was based on failure of consideration was specifically rejected in the House of Lords. The reason for this rejection seems to lie in an old terminological habit. The phrase "failure of consideration" is most commonly found in English law in the context of a restitutionary claim, *i.e.* one by a party, who had paid money for an agreed counter-performance, to recover back the money on the ground that he has not received that counter-performance.[23] In English law the general rule, now much qualified,[24] is that such a claim will only succeed if the payor has not received *any part* of the agreed performance; or, as it is traditionally put, he must show that there has been a "total failure of consideration". The word "total" is thus almost instinctively prefaced by English lawyers to the phrase "failure of consideration". Yet it is equally clear that a contract may be discharged by supervening events in spite of the fact that they do not *totally* prevent performance.[25] This was the position in *Taylor v Caldwell*[26] itself, where the Music Hall was destroyed but the Gardens (which formed part of the subject-matter of the contract) remained available; and the contract was discharged because its *main* purpose (the giving of the four grand concerts) could no longer be carried out. Thus one reason why the "failure of consideration" explanation has not found favour in the English courts is that, if the phrase were linked (as it usually has been) with the word "total", the explanation would unduly narrow the scope of the doctrine of discharge. The rejection of the explanation is thus based in part on terminological, rather than on logical grounds. But another, somewhat more satisfactory, reason why there is so little support for the explanation in the English cases is that English lawyers are reasonably well satisfied with Lord Sumner's explanation, quoted above,[27] in which he refers to the "common object" of the parties. It may be conceded that, in a contract for the sale of goods the buyer's object is to get the goods while the seller's is to get the price. But it makes perfectly good sense, in the case of most contracts, to say that the parties have a common object; and this is well understood by both of them. Suppose that a person who has contracted to sell his car for £5,000 were asked to say what he had contracted about. He would surely reply, "I have sold my car"—not, "I have contracted to receive £5,000". Similarly, in the case of a time charter, Lord Sumner has said that the owner's object was "not only to get hire [*i.e.*

Impossibility of Performance, Part 2; *cf.* Williams, *The Law Reform (Frustrated Contracts) Act 1943,* p.22.

[22] [1981] A.C. 625 at 687, 702.

[23] See *Fibrosa Spolka Akcyjna v Fairbairn, Lawson Combe, Barbour Ltd* [1943] A.C. 32.

[24] See Goff and Jones, *The Law of Restitution* (6th ed.), paras 19–007 to 19–009; Treitel, *The Law of Contract* (11th ed.), pp.1050–1052.

[25] See below, para.5–002 (partial impossibility). A dictum in *Modern Transport Co Ltd v Duneric SS Co* [1917] 1 K.B. 370 at 377 requiring "entire failure of consideration" in cases of temporary impossibility is out of line with other cases on this topic discussed below, para.5–054.

[26] (1863) 3 B. & S. 823.

[27] See above, para.2–039, at n.7.

the payment] but to afford services".[28] The "common object" of the parties in such cases can be described as the *exchange* of the car for the price, or of the services for the hire. Such a common object may be defeated by supervening impossibility resulting from such events as the destruction of the car[29] or the requisition of the ship or her prolonged detention[30] without the fault of either party. Contracting parties quite commonly have the same object in view, even though they expect to benefit from it in different ways. This reasoning applies not only in cases of supervening impossibility, but also in cases in which the contract is discharged by frustration of purpose even though there was no impossibility. In *Krell v Henry*,[31] for example, the "common object" of the parties was the provision of facilities for watching the coronation processions[32]: this was what one party had to sell and the other wanted to buy. That common object was defeated even though one party expected to benefit from it by receiving a sum of money and the other by seeing the processions. Whenever such common objects are defeated, it makes practical sense to say that performance of the contract has been frustrated. It follows that both parties will be discharged even though it affects only the performance to be rendered by one of them.

VI. "FRUSTRATION": A NOTE ON TERMINOLOGY

2–044   The expression "frustration" is used in a variety of senses; as Lord Devlin has said, "We are very slovenly about the way in which we use expressions like 'frustration'".[33] At least four usages are established: they refer respectively to frustration of contract, frustration of the adventure, frustration of purpose and frustrating breach.

(1) Frustration of contract

2–045   The expression "frustration of contract" refers to the whole doctrine of discharge by supervening events, irrespective of the type of event which brings about discharge. In this sense, a contract is said to be "frustrated" whether discharge occurs by supervening destruction of the subject-matter, or by its temporary unavailability, or by frustration of purpose (in the sense to be discussed below)[34] or by supervening illegality. This usage has, indeed, been criticised: for example, by Lord Wright when he

---

[28] *Bank Line Ltd v Arthur Capel & Co* [1919] A.C. 435 at 453.
[29] *e.g.* under Sale of Goods Act 1979, s.7; it is assumed that the risk has not yet passed to the buyer (below, para.3–012).
[30] As in the *Bank Line* case, above, n.28, and above, para.2–037, n.90.
[31] [1903] 2 K.B. 740; above, para.2–035, below, para.7–010.
[32] *cf.* the description of the subject-matter in such cases as "a room with a view" in *Great Peace Shipping Ltd v Tsavliris Salvage (International) Ltd (The Great Peace)* [2002] EWCA Civ 1407; [2003] Q.B. 679 at [66].
[33] [1966] C.L.J. 192 at 206.
[34] Below, para.2–047, and Ch.7.

described "frustration of contract" as "an elliptical expression", adding that "the fuller and more accurate phrase is 'frustration of the adventure or of the commercial or practical purpose of the contract' "[35]; and by Mustill L.J. when he said "Strictly ... it is the adventure which is frustrated, not the contract".[36] But (as the word "strictly" in the phrase just quoted seems to concede), these are criticisms of a terminology which is generally accepted; indeed, Lord Wright, in the speech to which reference has just been made, accepts that: "the phrase ... commonly used is 'frustration of contract'[37] or more shortly 'frustration' "—though he adds that "the fuller and more accurate phrase is 'frustration of the adventure or of the contract.' "[38] The common usage of "frustration" to refer to the entire doctrine of discharge also finds legislative recognition in the opening words of Law Reform (Frustrated Contracts) Act 1943: "Where a contract ... has become impossible of performance or been otherwise frustrated."[39] Clearly the draftsman regarded supervening impossibility as a type of frustration. Commonwealth legislatures have used the expression "Frustrated Contracts Act"[40] in the same sense.

(2) **Frustration of the adventure**

This phrase might, from the dicta of Lord Wright and Mustill L.J. which have been quoted above, appear to be merely a more accurate way of describing "frustration of contract". It is, however, submitted that the expression "frustration of the adventure" refers to a particular type of event which may discharge a contract. In this sense, it is both narrower than "frustration of contract" which refers generally to discharge by supervening events, irrespective of their nature; and it is also different in kind: "frustration of contract" refers to the *legal effect* of the supervening events (*i.e.* to the discharge of the contract) while "frustration of the adventure" refers to one particular kind of *cause* of discharge. Thus we can, for example, say that a contract can be discharged (or frustrated) by events such as either destruction of the subject-matter or frustration of the adventure. It makes sense to say that a contract may be frustrated by frustration of the adventure; but to say that a contract is frustrated by frustration of contract makes no sense, or is mere repetition. Most commonly, "frustration of the adventure" refers to cases in which performance has not become permanently impossible, but has been

2–046

---

[35] *Joseph Constantine SS Line v Imperial Smelting Corp* [1942] A.C. 154 at 182; *cf.* *Heyman v Darwins Ltd* [1942] A.C. 356 at 400–401, *per* Lord Porter ("The contract is not frustrated. Its future performance, or the adventure, is frustrated").

[36] *FC Shepherd & Co Ltd v Jerrom* [1987] Q.B. 301 at 323.

[37] *e.g. Re Thornett & Fehr and Yuills* [1921] 1 K.B. 219 at 227 ("no frustration ... of the contract").

[38] *Joseph Constantine* case, above, p.182.

[39] s.1(1).

[40] *e.g.* Victoria: Frustrated Contracts Act 1959; British Columbia: Frustrated Contracts Act 1974; New South Wales: Frustrated Contracts Act 1978; South Australia: Frustrated Contracts Act 1988.

merely affected by temporary obstacles which are later removed: for example, by temporary requisition or temporary delay to the arrival of a ship.[41] The point is well put in a definition of "frustration of the adventure" by Bailhache J. as "the happening of some unforeseen delay ... of such a character as that by it the fulfilment of the contract in the only ways in which fulfilment is contemplated and practicable is so inordinately postponed that its fulfilment when the delay is over will not accomplish the only object or objects that both parties to the contract had in view when the contract was made ...,"[42]; this definition was later approved in the Court of Appeal[43] though the actual decision in which it was given was reversed. Delay may not be the only illustration of "frustration of the adventure", but the phrase is generally used to refer to cases of discharge where the impossibility which supervenes is either not total or not permanent.[44]

(3) Frustration of purpose

2–047　This expression is here used to refer to cases in which there is *no* "impossibility", even of a temporary nature, in rendering the performance promised by each party, for example, to cases such as the coronation cases (to be discussed in Ch.7[45]). In those cases, it was perfectly possible for one party to supply the premises or facilities which he had undertaken to supply, and there was no impossibility affecting the other party's counter-performance (usually, a payment of money); but the purpose for which the contracts had been made could no longer be achieved because of the postponement of the coronation. In one sense, such cases could be described as cases of "frustration of the adventure"; but they go beyond the cases described in the preceding paragraph. In those cases, performance on one side is actually prevented, if only for a limited time, and discharge can result from the length of time over which the prevention or impossibility extended. In cases of frustration of purpose, there is no such prevention at all, but discharge may nevertheless occur because the literal performance of one party's duty has become useless to the other. The fact that the coronation was merely postponed,

---

[41] *e.g. Hudson v Hill* (1874) 43 L.J.C.P. 273 at 278 ("delay ... so long as to frustrate the mercantile adventure ..."); *Lloyd Royal Belge SA v Stathatos* (1917) 34 T.L.R. 70 at 72 ("such interruption ... as to amount to a frustration of the commercial adventure"); *Heilgers & Co v Cambrian SN Co Ltd* (1917) 34 T.L.R. 72 ("frustration of the adventure"); *cf. Geipel v Smith* (1872) L.R. 7 Q.B. 404 ("frustration of the very object").

[42] *Admiral Shipping Co Ltd v Weidner, Hopkins & Co* [1916] 1 K.B. 429 at 436–437.

[43] *Scottish Navigation Co Ltd v Souter & Co* [1917] 1 K.B. 222 at 242, 250; *cf. Bank Line Ltd v Arthur Capel & Co* [1919] A.C. 435 at 442; *cf. ibid.* at 445 ("frustration of ... commercial object"); *Jackson v Union Marine Insurance Co* (1874) L.R. 10 C.P. 125 at 148 ("the voyage ... is frustrated"); *Horlock v Beal* [1916] 1 A.C. 486 at 513 ("frustration of the voyage").

[44] See the discussion of partial and temporary impossibility in Ch.5, and also the discussion of impossibility in the method of performance in Ch.4.

[45] See below, paras 7–006 to 7–014.

not permanently cancelled, does not affect this point. In the "frustration of the adventure" cases a short delay (say of one week) might not have discharged the contract,[46] because the contracts in those cases were not contracts to be performed on a fixed day or days. In at least most of the coronation cases the facilities for viewing were to be provided on a specified day or on two specified days. The crucial fact in these cases was not the length of the delay before the processions eventually took place (of about six weeks in relation to one of the processions and of about four months in relation to the other[47]), but the fact that the processions did not take place on the *only* day or days on which the facilities were, under the relevant contracts, to be made available. The length of the delay could be relevant only where the contract expressly provided for flexibility in this respect[48]; but where this was the position the express provisions in question were held to have excluded the doctrine of discharge, so that there was no scope for the application of the notion of "frustration of the adventure" by long delay.

In the United States, the distinction between discharge by impossibility (or impracticability[49]) was at one time so sharply drawn that, in the original version of the Restatement, the two concepts were discussed at widely separate points.[50] The reason for this arrangement may have been that discharge by mere frustration of purpose was formerly viewed in the United States with some hostility.[51] When this hostility subsided, the arrangement of the Restatement was in turn criticised[52] as it tended to overemphasise the differences between the two grounds of discharge, and to attach insufficient significance to the features which they had in common. The Restatement 2d accordingly treats them in the same chapter,[53] while devoting separate sections to discharge by supervening "Impracticability"[54] and by "Frustration".[55] English law, too, regards them as illustrations of a single principle of discharge by supervening events; but the distinction between them is nevertheless significant not only from an analytical, but also from a practical, point of view, for the rules which govern discharge are in some respects stricter in cases of supervening frustration of purpose than they are in cases of supervening impossibility.[56]

2–048

---

[46] *e.g.* such a short delay would not have discharged the charterparty in *Bank Line Ltd v Arthur Capel & Co* [1919] A.C. 435 or that in *Jackson v Union Marine Insurance Co* (1874) L.R. 10 C.P. 125.

[47] See below, para.7–006.

[48] See provisions of the kind discussed above, para.2–038, at n.94.

[49] For "impracticability," see below, Ch.6.

[50] Frustration of purpose in § 288; impossibility in §§ 454–459, with no more than a cross-reference to frustration of purpose in § 454, Comment *b.*

[51] See below, para.7–033.

[52] Corbin, *Contracts*, para.1322.

[53] Ch. 11.

[54] § 261.

[55] § 265.

[56] See below, paras 7–014, 7–017, 7–024.

(4) **Frustrating breach**

2–049   This expression refers to the type of breach which is sufficiently serious to justify the victim's rescission of the contract, in the sense that it gives the victim the option of refusing, on account of the breach, to perform his own part of the contract, and to accept further performance from the party in breach.[57] As Devlin J. has pointed out,[58] this use of the expression "frustration" antedates its use in the context of the doctrine of discharge by supervening events, and indeed the establishment of that doctrine as a general principle of English law. Obviously cases of "frustrating breach" are distinct from the doctrine of discharge by supervening events (the "doctrine of frustration") since that doctrine cannot be invoked by a party whose "default" brings about, or amounts to, the supervening event which interferes with performance; and for this purpose a "frustrating breach" clearly amounts to default.[59]

2–050   The position is, however, complicated by the fact that failure in performance does not necessarily amount to a breach, for a party who fails to perform may be entitled to rely on an excuse for non-performance. Such an excuse may be provided either by the general law or by an express provision of the contract.[60] Where such an excuse applies, the party failing to perform is not in breach, so that there can be no question of a "frustrating breach". But there is room for an analogous concept of "frustrating failure": that is, of an excused failure in one party's performance which gives the other party an option to rescind,[61] without automatically discharging the contract under the "doctrine of frustration".[62] An excused failure to perform may, moreover, produce yet a third consequence: that of operating only as a temporary or partial excuse for the party whose performance is prevented,[63] and of sometimes making a corresponding temporary or partial excuse available to the other party.[64] Which of these three legal consequences flows from an excused failure in performance depends on the degree of its seriousness. The highest degree of seriousness is required to bring about automatic discharge under the "doctrine of frustration"; a lower degree of seriousness, equivalent to that required in cases of "frustrating breach", is required to give rise to an option to rescind; while no requirement of seriousness need be satisfied where a party simply relies on the event as an excuse for partial or temporary non-performance (as, *e.g.* where a short temporary illness operates as a temporary excuse for non-performance by an employee of his obligation to work).

---

[57] *e.g. Tarrabochia v Hickie* (1856) 1 H. & n.183 at 185: *McAndrew v Chapple* (1866) L.R. 1 C.P. 643 at 649 ("frustrates the intention of the parties").

[58] *Universal Cargo Carriers Corp v Citati* [1957] 2 K.B. 401 at 430–431.

[59] See below, para.14–010.

[60] See Treitel, *The Law of Contract* (11th ed.), pp.835–838.

[61] *ibid.*, p.659.

[62] This was, for example, the position in *Poussard v Spiers & Pond* (1876) 1 Q.B.D. 410; see below, para.5–060, for further discussion of the distinction drawn in the text above.

[63] *e.g. H R & S Sainsbury Ltd v Street* [1972] 1 W.L.R. 834.

[64] *e.g. Minnevitch v Café de Paris (Londres) Ltd* [1936] 1 All E.R. 884.

CHAPTER 3

IMPOSSIBILITY IN GENERAL: DESTRUCTION OF SUBJECT-MATTER

I. INTRODUCTION

Supervening impossibility of performance may bring about the discharge of a contract but will by no means always have this effect; conversely a contract may be discharged by a supervening event which does not make its performance impossible at all but only frustrates its purpose. The position was well summed up by Lord Simon in the *Joseph Constantine* case[1]: "Discharge by supervening impossibility is not a common law rule of general application like discharge by supervening illegality; whether the contract is terminated or not depends on its terms and the surrounding circumstances in each case ... Some kinds of impossibility may in some circumstances not discharge the contract at all. On the other hand, impossibility is too stiff a test in other cases".[2] Our concern in this chapter is to identify various kinds of supervening impossibility and to consider when they are capable of discharging the contract. We have already noted that a party may be liable, even though supervening events have made his performance impossible, where his duty to perform the obligation is a strict one,[3] or where it is still appropriate to apply the doctrine of absolute contracts to the particular circumstances giving rise to the impossibility.[4] A further situation in which impossibility is not a ground of discharge is illustrated by cases, to be discussed later in this chapter, in which the effects of impossibility are governed by the rules as to the passing of risk.[5] There is also the point that impossibility which is only partial or temporary, or which affects only the method of performance, will not of

3–001

---

[1] *Joseph Constantine SS Line Ltd v Imperial Smelting Corp Ltd* [1942] A.C. 154 at 163–164.

[2] The reference here is to coronation cases such as *Krell v Henry* [1903] 2 K.B. 740, below, para.7–010 where the contract was discharged by frustration of purpose even though there was no impossibility of performance.

[3] See above, paras 1–002, 1–003.

[4] See above, para.2–033.

[5] See below, paras 3–007 *et seq.*

itself discharge the contract: it will do so only if it is of the degree of seriousness which will be described in the discussion (in later chapters) of these types of impossibility.[6]

II. OBJECTIVE AND SUBJECTIVE IMPOSSIBILITY

3–002   The distinction between "objective" and "subjective" impossibility appears to be derived from civil law systems[7] in which the former was more readily than the latter regarded as a ground of discharge. For this purpose, impossibility was regarded as objective when performance could not be rendered by anyone and as subjective when it could not be rendered by the promisor because of some disability personal to himself, but could be rendered by others. It must be emphasised that it does not follow from the distinction that subjective impossibility can never provide the debtor with a defence: this point is reflected in the new § 275(1)[8] of the German Civil Code by which a claim for (specific) performance is excluded if performance is impossible "for the debtor or for anyone"; and such impossibility may further be a ground of excuse where the debtor is not considered to be responsible for the circumstances giving rise to it. A similar principle of excuse based on "subjective" impossibility was applied in a Swiss case[9] in which a tenant of premises let for use as a dentist's practice was prevented from carrying on the practice by legislation requiring practitioners to hold a diploma which she did not hold and which she could not, in view of her somewhat advanced age, reasonably have been expected to obtain. It was held that she was discharged from her obligations under the lease, the court saying that "relative" (as opposed to "absolute") impossibility was a sufficient ground of discharge.

On the other hand, subjective impossibility is not necessarily a defence to a claim for damages. In particular, a debtor who has undertaken to deliver generic goods[10] or to pay money cannot escape such liability merely because the source from which he expected to obtain the goods or the money has failed without fault on his part. In such cases, liability is strict,[11] the debtor being regarded as having taken the risk[12] of being able to procure the goods or the money. An alternative explanation for this rule is that there is, in such cases, *no* impossibility, subjective or objective,

---

[6] See below, paras 4–060 to 4–083 and Ch.5.

[7] See in Switzerland, Von Tuhr/Peter, *Allgemeiner Teil des Schweizerischen Obligationenrechts* (3rd ed.), p.263; *cf.* in France, Mazeaud & Chabas, *Leçons de Droit Civil* (9th ed.), Vol.II, p.576 (requiring "absolute" impossibility).

[8] Which came into force on January 1, 2002. The distinction between "Unmöglichkeit" (impossibility in its "objective" sense) and "Unvermögen" ("subjective" impossibility) formerly contained in the now repealed §§ 275 and 279 has been abandoned.

[9] BGE 57 III 532, November 10, 1931; *cf.* Bucher, *Schweizerisches Obligationenrecht*, p.176.

[10] See below, para.3–018, for the meaning of this expression.

[11] See above, para.1–003.

[12] See (new) BGB § 276(2), referring to "*Beschaffungsrisiko*" (procurement risk).

generic goods or money being in contemplation of law always available from some source.

In the context of supervening impossibility the distinction between objective and subjective impossibility formerly had some vogue in the United States. It was drawn by the first Restatement[13] in the terms stated in para.3–002, above; its legal consequence was that objective impossibility could, but subjective impossibility of itself could not, be a ground of discharge.[14] The treatises of Williston[15] and Corbin[16] draw the distinction in similar terms and give it substantially the same effect. It followed that in cases of (e.g.) temporary or partial impossibility *two* questions (at least) could arise: (1) was the impossibility objective or subjective? and (2) was it sufficiently serious to form a ground of discharge? But such reasoning was also criticised on the ground that the distinction between objective and subjective impossibility was often hard to draw and in any event an unnecessary one.[17] It was, for example, hard to say whether a serious illness which prevented a promisor from performing services of a personal nature constituted objective or subjective impossibility. According to the first Restatement, the impossibility in such a case "is objective as well as subjective."[18] But this analysis does not seem to be based on the nature of the impossibility: it merely states the legal conclusion that the impossibility in the case put (however it may be classified) can operate as a ground of discharge. In response to such criticism the importance of the distinction in the United States has declined: the Restatement 2d recognises its existence[19] but makes no use of it. Nor is the distinction used in modern English cases on the topic. These would accept the view that performance of an obligation to deliver generic goods, or one to pay money, is not discharged merely because the promisor's intended source of goods of the contract description, or of money, has failed. English cases do not make it clear whether the reason for this result is that there is in such cases thought to be *no* impossibility (in the sense that the promisor could have made use of another source),[20] or simply that liability is regarded as strict.[21] They certainly do not explain the result by saying that the impossibility is only "subjective" and that "subjective impossibility" is not a ground of discharge. In this respect, therefore, they support the view that the distinction between the two types of impossibility is an unnecessary and an unhelpful one. This is also true of the case (put above) in which serious illness interferes with the performance of a contract to render personal services. In such a case, it seems better to go straight to the question

---

[13] § 455.
[14] *ibid.*
[15] *Williston on Contracts* (3rd ed.), para.1932.
[16] Corbin, *Contracts*, para.1322.
[17] Patterson, 24 Col. L.R. 355 (1924).
[18] § 455, Illustration d.
[19] § 261, Comment e, the substance of which is repeated in *Farnsworth on Contracts* (2d ed.) Vol.II, pp.557–558.
[20] *cf.* below, paras 4–053, 4–059.
[21] *cf.* above, para.1–003.

whether the illness is sufficiently serious to discharge the contract, than to discuss the intermediate question whether the impossibility is subjective or objective. The answer to the latter question has, in itself, no practical significance: it is only a step (and an unnecessary one) towards the solution of the problem of discharge. We shall therefore follow the current practice of the English courts in disregarding the distinction between "objective" and "subjective" impossibility.

III. DESTRUCTION OF THE SUBJECT-MATTER

3–004   The most obvious situation in which performance becomes impossible is that in which the subject-matter of a contract is destroyed between the time when the contract was made and the time when it should have been performed. Such destruction of the subject-matter is commonly[22] a ground of discharge. Thus in *Taylor v Caldwell*[23] the destruction of the Music Hall discharged the contract under which the Hall was to be made available for the purpose of giving the four concerts on the specified days. A statutory illustration of discharge on the same ground is provided by s.7 of the Sale of Goods Act 1979, under which an agreement for the sale of specific goods is avoided if the goods perish without the fault of either party before the risk of loss has passed to the buyer.[24] Section 2–613(a) of the Uniform Commercial Code similarly provides that a contract for the sale of goods "identified when the contract is made" is avoided[25] if the goods suffer casualty without fault of either party and "if the loss is total". A similar principle would apply where services were to be rendered in relation to, or by use of, a specific thing, and that thing was then destroyed before the services had been rendered or fully rendered. For example, a contract to carry goods in a particular ship, or one to repair that ship, could be discharged by the destruction of the ship. Similarly, a contract to re-roof a house could be discharged by destruction of the house before completion of the work[26]; and a contract to service a car could be discharged if before the work was done the car was destroyed in a road accident. In cases of this kind, the subject-matter of the contract could be said to be either the thing in question (the ship, the house or the car) or the services to be rendered. On the latter view, such cases would fall into the category of contracts discharged by the destruction of a thing essential for their performance: this group of cases will be further discussed in Ch.4.

---

[22] But not always: see the discussion of "passing of risk" at paras 3–007 *et seq.*, below.

[23] (1863) 3 B. & S. 826, above, para.2–024.

[24] See further paras 3–013, 3–020, below.

[25] For the proposed amendment of the section by the substitution of "terminated" for "avoided", see above, para.2–042, n.17: for further discussion of the UCC, s.2–613, see below, para.3–015. *cf.* (in cases of chattel leases) UCC, s.2A–221(a).

[26] *cf. Appleby v Myers* (1867) L.R. 2 C.P. 651; *Anglo-Egyptian Navigation Co v Rennie* (1875) L.R. 10 C.P. 271.

IV. Total Destruction, Partial Destruction

The ensuing discussion is concerned with destruction of the entire 3–005
subject-matter of the contract. Cases of partial destruction are further
considered in Ch.5. "Partial destruction" there refers to the destruction
of some severable part of the subject-matter of the contract, resulting from
an event which does not affect the physical integrity of the rest of that
subject-matter, *e.g.* destruction by fire of half the cargo of a ship, leaving
the other half undamaged. Such cases are to be distinguished from those
in which the supervening event causes damage to the entire subject-matter
of the contract without wholly destroying any part of it, *e.g.* where the
entire cargo of a ship is contaminated, so that no part of it escapes
unharmed, but it is not totally destroyed. Damage or deterioration of this
kind can vary almost infinitely in its degree of seriousness, but for the
purpose of the present discussion only two situations need to be
contrasted.

In the first, the subject-matter is so seriously damaged that it is regarded
as having been destroyed even though it has not been physically
annihilated or literally ceased to exist: even in *Taylor v Caldwell* itself it
seems that the four walls of the Music Hall remained standing.[27] The same
point is further illustrated by *Asfar & Co v Blundell*[28] where a ship carrying
a quantity of dates sank, and the cargo was so contaminated by sewage as
to become "for business purposes something else"[29] (though the ship was
later raised and the dates were sold for £2,400 "for the purpose of
distillation into spirit".[30]) An action was brought by the carriers (who were
charterers of the ship) against the insurers of the freight; and the insurers
were held liable on the ground that there had been a total loss of the
freight on the dates. It is essential to this reasoning that the carriers could
not have sued for the freight, *i.e.* that the contract of carriage was
discharged because "the dates had been so deteriorated that they had
become something which was not merchantable as dates".[31] Similarly, in
Duthie v Hilton[32] it was held that freight could not be recovered on a cargo
of cement which had solidified, before freight had become due, as a result
of an accidental fire, leading to the scuttling of the ship. It was said that
"the goods ... were destroyed ... and ceased to exist as cement".[33]

---

[27] *The Times,* June 12, 1861; *cf.* as to the meaning of "destroyed" in the case of a
building, *Heart of America Lumber Co v Welbelove,* 28 F. Supp. 619 (1939), where,
however, the assertion that the Parthenon had been "destroyed by the
explosion which shattered it in 1687" is open to some doubt.

[28] [1896] 1 Q.B. 123.

[29] *ibid.* at 128 (and see below, para.3–016); *cf. Terkol Rederiene v Petroleo Brasileiro
(The Badagry)* [1985] 1 Lloyd's Rep. 395 at 399; and (in the context of breach)
Dakin v Oxley (1864) 15 C.B.N.S. 646 at 667; *Montedison SpA v Croma SpA (The
Caspian Sea)* [1980] 1 W.L.R. 48.

[30] [1896] 1 Q.B. 123 at 128.

[31] *ibid.*

[32] (1870) L.R. 4 C.P. 138.

[33] *ibid.* at 143.

3–006   The second situation is that in which the deterioration is merely such that the subject-matter is no longer in conformity with the contract, though it can still be dealt with (no doubt for a lower price) as an article belonging to the same general commercial category. Such deterioration would not be regarded as the equivalent of destruction so as to bring about the automatic discharge of the contract, though it might well give the party prejudiced by the non-conformity a right to rescind the contract on account of the non-conformity.[34]

3–006   The various distinctions drawn above can be illustrated by reference to the leading case of *Taylor v Caldwell* itself. The case was actually one of only partial destruction: the contract referred to "the Surrey Gardens and Music Hall" and only the Hall was affected by the fire.[35] Even parts of the Hall survived the fire,[36] but it was reasonable to regard the destruction of the Hall as total for the purpose of the doctrine of discharge. If the fire had caused less serious damage (*e.g.* damage reducing the seating capacity of the Hall by one quarter) it seems unlikely that the contract would have been discharged. The case would then have raised the issues whether the defendant's duty in respect of the condition of the Hall was a strict one or one of care only; and whether the plaintiffs would have been entitled to rescind the contract on account of the damage which had occurred.[37]

V. Discharge and Rules Governing Risk[38]

3–007   At first sight, it might seem obvious that destruction of the subject-matter by a supervening event outside the control of the parties should discharge the contract. In discussing *Taylor v Caldwell*, we saw that the effect of discharge in such cases had the effect of splitting the loss caused by the supervening event[39]; and that this loss-splitting effect could be explained by saying that discharge divided two risks which we described as the performance risk and the payment risk. The former was on the party *to* whom, and the latter on the party *by* whom, the now impossible performance was (or would, but for the supervening event have been) owed: hence in *Taylor v Caldwell* the effect of the destruction of the Hall was that on the one hand the defendants were not liable in damages,

---

[34] It would have this effect if the non-conformity were sufficiently serious to justify rescission, or if it fell within an exception to the requirement of serious failure in performance (*e.g.* if it amounted to a breach of condition). A defect can be sufficiently serious for this purpose while falling short of the higher degree of seriousness required to bring the doctrine of discharge into play: *cf.* the discussion of *Poussard v Spiers and Pond* (1876) 1 Q.B.D. 410 in para.5–060, below.

[35] See below, para.5–003 for a discussion of this aspect of the case.

[36] Above, n.27.

[37] For an American solution (probably not available in England) see the discussion of the UCC, s.2–613(b), below, para.3–016.

[38] Sealey [1972B] C.L.J. 225.

[39] See above, para.2–026.

while, on the other, the plaintiffs were not liable for the agreed price.[40]

The risk-distribution just described is, however, by no means of universal application. Under special rules applicable to certain specific types of contracts, it is varied by rules of law which specify a point at which (before performance has been completed) "risk of loss" passes from one party to the other. Before that time, both the performance and payment risks are borne by the party who was to render the now impossible performance; after it, they are borne by the other party. While the doctrine of discharge *divides* the two risks between the parties, the special rules as to the "passing of risk" *unite* them in one party. To this extent, therefore, the special rules as to risk in specific types of contract displace the doctrine of discharge. This does not mean that the doctrine of discharge cannot be brought into operation by other events affecting the performance of such contracts, such as impossibility in the method of performance, delay or illegality. The special rules as to risk deal only with supervening events which affect the physical integrity of the subject-matter. In such cases, their effects are radically different from those of the doctrine of discharge. That difference can be summed up by saying that under the doctrine of discharge *both* parties are discharged from *all* their obligations under the contract while, under the special rules as to the passing of risk of loss, *one* party may be discharged from *some* of his obligations.

Our concern at this stage is with special rules as to passing of risk in specific types of contracts which operate so as to *displace* the doctrine of discharge. In English law, the expression "risk" is most commonly used in connection with such rules. In the United States however, that expression is used both in this sense and also in a different sense, namely to determine the scope of the doctrine of discharge by asking which party has, under the express or implied terms of the contract, undertaken "the risk of a contingency's occurrence".[41] The reference here is to the allocation of "risks" (of whatever nature) by the terms of the contract and is of general application; it reflects the nature of contract as a mechanism for the allocation of certain commercial or financial risks (such as those of price or currency fluctuations or those of insolvency). However, merely because a contract for the sale of goods to be delivered on credit at a future date may allocate such "risks", it does not follow that it also, by its terms or nature, allocates the risk of the destruction of the goods before the performance by the parties of their duties to deliver and pay for them. The ensuing discussion of the "passing of risk" is concerned with risks of

3–008

---

[40] (1863) 3 B. & S. 826 at 840.

[41] *e.g. Transatlantic Financing Corp v US*, 363 F. 2d 312 at 316; *cf. Farnsworth on Contracts* (2nd ed.) Vol.II, p.543; Restatement 2d, Ch.11, Introductory Note, pp.310–311; for criticism of this terminology, see above, para.1–003; for its occasional use in England, see *National Carriers Ltd v Panalpina (Northern) Ltd* [1981] A.C. 675 at 712; *Amalgamated Investment & Property Co Ltd v John Walker & Sons Ltd* [1977] 1 W.L.R. 164 at 173 ("risk of listing": this is a purely financial, and not a physical, risk); *cf.* the view of the Privy Council in *E Johnson & Co (Barbados) Ltd v NSR Ltd* [1997] A.C. 400 at 406 ("risk of interference with land-owning rights by the Crown").

the latter kind and with their allocation, not by the terms of the contract or by its nature (as described above), but by rules of law (though these can be excluded by contrary agreement). These rules, are, moreover, not of general application: they apply only to the specific types of contracts to be discussed below. The operation of such rules, and their relationship with the doctrine of discharge, will be illustrated by reference to contracts for the sale of goods, contracts for the sale of land, and building contracts.

The special rules as to the "passing of risk" to be discussed below most obviously govern the effects of destruction of the subject-matter between the conclusion of the contract and its performance. Destruction which has already taken place when the contract is made raises (in English law[42]) issues of mistake,[43] or of the express or implied undertakings as to the existence of the subject-matter given by the party whose performance is affected by the destruction.[44] Conversely, destruction which occurs after the performance affected by it has been rendered in full cannot discharge the contract: the party who has rendered the performance will have been discharged *by performance* and the other party cannot rely on the destruction as a ground for relieving him from his duty to render the agreed counter-performance (*i.e.* usually, to pay the agreed price). If, for example, conforming goods are duly delivered under a contract of sale, and property in them has passed to the buyer, then the subsequent destruction of those goods obviously cannot discharge the buyer from his duty to pay the price. This is so even if the destruction occurred on the day after such performance by the seller, but the sale was on credit terms, so that the price was not payable until six months later. The point may seem to be an obvious one, but it does need to be made because, in relation to some of the types of contracts to be discussed below, it is sometimes said that risk passes,[45] or that it should pass,[46] on completion of performance. Such statements really mean that risk does not, or should not, *pass* at all, but that it *remains* on the party whose performance is affected by the destruction, though he will of course be discharged once that performance has been rendered in full. That, as we shall see, is the *prima facie* rule in building contracts.[47] By contrast, where goods are sold to a buyer who does not deal as consumer,[48] the risk can truly be said to *pass*,[49] in

---

[42] The point is reflected by the fact that the Sale of Goods Act 1979 devotes *separate* sections to the destruction of specific goods *before* and *after* the contract was made (ss.6 and 7). In the United States, these two situations are dealt with in the *same* section (UCC, s.2–613) and this fact is one of the bases of the concept of "existing impracticability or frustration", discussed in Restatement 2d, § 266: see Reporter's Note to Comment a above, para.1–010.

[43] See above, para.1–005.

[44] *e.g. Couturier v Hastie* (1856) 5 H.L.C. 673.

[45] *e.g.* below, para.3–054.

[46] *e.g.* below, para.3–047.

[47] See below, para.3–056.

[48] For the position where the buyer does deal as consumer, see below, para.3–009, n.70.

[49] *cf.* Sale of Goods Act 1979, s.20, marginal note, as substituted by the Regulations cited in 3–009, n.70, above ("passing of risk").

that a point may come after the contract was made and before the seller has performed his duty to deliver the goods,[50] at which the risk of the destruction of the goods is no longer on the seller but must be borne by the buyer.[51] There is finally the possibility that risk may pass as soon as the contract is made. That is the general English common law rule in contracts for the sale of land[52] and may also sometimes be the English position in contracts for the sale of goods.[53]

(1) **Sale of goods**

Where goods are sold to a buyer who does not deal as consumer,[54] the general rule of English law is that risk passes (unless otherwise agreed) with property.[55] For the detailed rules as to the passing of risk and property, reference should be made to works on the sale of goods[56]; but a number of points of general interest must be made here since they affect the scope of the doctrine of discharge by supervening impossibility.   **3–009**

First, the rule which links risk with property is in practice commonly displaced, so that risk passes before property. For example, the general rule is that property cannot pass until the goods are ascertained[57]; and since goods which form an undifferentiated part of a larger bulk are unascertained, it formerly followed that property in such goods could not pass until the goods became ascertained,[58] normally by being separated from the bulk.[59] Where the sale is of a specified quantity of unascertained goods which form part of a bulk which is identified either in the contract or by subsequent agreement between the parties, property in an undivided share in the bulk can now, by virtue of amendments to the Sale of Goods Act 1979 made in 1995 ("the 1995 Reforms") pass to the extent to which the buyer has paid for the goods.[60] Property passes in such cases, not

---

[50] Even delivery is not necessarily *full* performance of the seller's obligations under the contract, *e.g.* where the sale is on credit, performance of the seller's duty to transfer the property (s.2(1)) is likely to remain unperformed at the point of delivery.

[51] See below, para.3–009. The German BGB neatly expresses the distinction in the text by providing that risk under a contract of sale "passes" on delivery (§ 446); while risk under a contract for the execution of works the risk is "borne" by the contractor till "acceptance" of the works (§ 644) unless the other party is in default (in which case the risk does "pass" to that party).

[52] See below, para.3–027.

[53] *e.g.* by virtue of the joint operation of Sale of Goods Act 1979, s.18, r.1 and s.20(1) (but as to the former, see below, para.3–010, n.76).

[54] See n.48, above, and n.70, below, for the position where the buyer does deal as consumer.

[55] Sale of Goods Act 1979, s.20(1).

[56] *e.g. Benjamin's Sale of Goods* (6th ed.), Chs 5 and 6.

[57] Sale of Goods Act 1979, s.16.

[58] *Re Wait* [1927] 1 Ch. 606.

[59] For other methods of ascertainment, see below, para.3–012, n.13.

[60] Sale of Goods Act 1979, s.20A, as inserted by Sale of Goods (Amendments) Act 1995, s.1(3).

because the goods are regarded as having become ascertained, but in spite of the fact that they remain unascertained[61]; and where the requirements of the 1995 Reforms are not met (*e.g.* because the buyer has not paid the price),[62] the former general rule[63] (preventing the passing of property in goods which are unascertained) continues to apply to sales of goods which form an undifferentiated part of an identified bulk. However, even where no property passes under such a contract, it is nevertheless possible for the risk to pass, *e.g.* under a contract for the sale of 200 out of the 1,000 tons shipped in bulk on a named ship,[64] or of a specified quantity of oil out of a larger quantity lying in designated storage tanks.[65] Even where goods are ascertained, risk may pass before property: this possibility is illustrated by sales on c.i.f. or f.o.b. terms, where it is common for risk to pass on shipment,[66] and where in the case of goods sold in transit it may even pass retrospectively as from shipment[67]; but where it is equally common for property to pass only at the later stage when shipping documents are taken up and payment is made.[68] It is, conversely, possible for property to pass before risk. This would, for example, be the position where payment precedes delivery but the parties agree that the goods are to remain at the seller's risk until delivery.[69] Where goods are sold to a buyer who deals as consumer, the goods similarly remain at the seller's risk until they are delivered to the consumer[70]; and this rule applies even though property may have passed to the buyer and he has paid for the goods before

---

[61] See the reference to "unascertained goods" in Sale of Goods Act 1979, s.20A(1).

[62] See *ibid.*, s.20A(3). The requirements of s.20A would also not be met if identification of the bulk occurred otherwise than "in the contract or by subsequent agreement between the parties": see *Benjamin's Sale of Goods* (6th ed.) para.18–261. The passing of property may also be prevented or delayed by contrary agreement: see s.20A(2).

[63] Above, n.57.

[64] See *Inglis v Stock* (1884) 12 Q.B.D. 564 at 573, 577, affirmed (1885) 10 App. Cas. 263, where Lord Blackburn at 273 similarly said that the seller was entitled to the price in spite of the fact that the goods had perished; *Margarine Union GmbH v Cambay Prince SS Co Ltd (The Wear Breeze)* [1969] 1 Q.B. 219 at 253–254. If the quantity were expressed not as a "specified quantity" but as a fraction or percentage (*e.g.* half the cargo of a named ship) the goods would be specific by virtue of the amendment to the definition of "specific goods" in Sale of Goods Act 1979, s.61(1), made by Sale of Goods (Amendment) Act 1995, s.2(d). The passing of property would therefore be governed by s.18, r.1 of the 1979 Act: as to this, see below, para.3–010.

[65] *Sterns Ltd v Vickers Ltd* [1923] 1 K.B. 78.

[66] *Benjamin's Sale of Goods* (6th ed.), paras 19–106, 20–086. The possibility of the buyer dealing as consumer in such contracts is so remote that the special rule as to the passing of risk which applies where the buyer deals as consumer (below, at n.70) does not call for consideration in relation to them.

[67] *Benjamin's Sale of Goods* (6th ed.), para.19–106.

[68] *ibid.* paras 19–099, 20–082.

[69] *ibid.* para.6–603.

[70] Sale of Goods Act 1979, s.20(4) as inserted by Sale and Supply of Goods to Consumers Regulations 2002, SI 2002/3045, reg.4.

delivery. Similarly, where the goods are unascertained because they consist of a specified quantity out of an identified bulk, the buyer may acquire property as an undivided share in them by virtue of the rules stated above,[71] but if he dealt as consumer the goods would remain at the seller's risk until the quantity bought had been delivered to him.[72] Risk may also remain on the seller wholly or in part under other rules of law, *e.g.* where goods which have been sold to a buyer who does not deal as consumer are to be carried by sea under circumstances in which it is usual to insure and the seller fails to give the buyer notice enabling him to insure.[73] This rule was never likely to apply where the buyer dealt as consumer, and the Sale of Goods Act 1979 now in terms provides that it no longer applies to cases of this kind.[74]

The second point is that in contracts for the sale of goods the doctrine of discharge is more likely to be displaced by the operation of the rules as to risk if under those rules the risk can pass at an early, rather than at a late stage of the performance of the contract. In this context, it is important to state again that s.20(1) of the Sale of Goods Act 1979 provides that, unless otherwise agreed, risk passes to the buyer with property, though this rule no longer applies where the buyer deals as consumer[75]; and to note that s.18, r.1 of the Sale of Goods Act 1979 provides that, in the case of an unconditional contract for the sale of specific goods in a deliverable state, property passes when the contract is made, unless a different intention appears. Section 18, r.1 is now commonly displaced because (in the words of Diplock L.J.) "In modern times very little is needed to give rise to the inference that property in specific goods is to pass only on delivery or payment".[76] But where s.18, r.1 and the general rule in s.20(1) do apply there is no scope at all for discharge by destruction of the goods after the conclusion of the contract. From this point of view, the general rule of English law stands in sharp contrast with systems under which the passing of risk is not linked with the passing of property and occurs, generally speaking, at a later stage in the performance of the contract than it does under the rules laid down by s.20(1) of the Sale of Goods Act 1979 with regard to the passing of risk and as to passing of property laid down in s.18 of the Act.[77] Indeed, this is now the position in English law where, the buyer deals as consumer[78]: the goods remain at the seller's risk until they are delivered to the consumer. There is likewise more scope (than under s.20(1)) for the operation of the doctrine of discharge under the American Uniform Commercial Code, which provides that, as a general

3–010

---

[71] Above, n.60.

[72] Above, n.70.

[73] Sale of Goods Act 1979, s.32(3).

[74] Sale of Goods Act 1979 s.32(4), as inserted by Sale and Supply of Goods to Consumers Regulations 2002, SI 2002/3045, reg.4.

[75] See above, para.3–009, n.70.

[76] *R V Ward Ltd v Bignall* [1967] 1 Q.B. 534 at 545. Contrast *Shogun Finance Ltd v Hudson* [2003] UKHL 62; [2004] 1 All E.R. 215, at [47], where, however, no reference is made to Diplock L.J's dictum quoted in the text above.

[77] Especially s.18, r.1.

[78] See above, para.3–009, n.70.

rule, risk passes (unless otherwise agreed) on receipt of the goods if the seller is a merchant and on tender of delivery if he is not.[79] To the extent that these events are likely to occur later than the passing of property in English law, there is more scope for the operation of the doctrine of discharge by destruction of the goods under the Uniform Commercial Code than there is under s.20(1) of the Sale of Goods Act 1979. There is similarly more scope (than under s.20(1)) for the doctrine of discharge under the Vienna Convention on Contracts for the International Sale of Goods,[80] under which the general rule is that risk passes when the buyer "takes over" the goods.[81] Paradoxically, however, under these systems risk may actually pass earlier than under s.20(1) of the Sale of Goods Act 1979 where (in the words of the Uniform Commercial Code) "the contract requires or authorises the seller to ship the goods by carrier"[82] but "does not require him to deliver at a particular destination" or where (in the words of the Vienna Convention) "the contract of sale involves carriage of the goods and the seller is not bound to hand them over at a particular place".[83] In such cases risk passes (under the Uniform Commercial Code) "when the goods are duly delivered to the carrier"[84] or (under the Vienna Convention) when they are "handed over to the first carrier for transmission to the buyer in accordance with the contract of sale".[85] In English law, by contrast, in such cases risk normally passes (unless the buyer deals as consumer[86]) on shipment,[87] that is, when the goods are

---

[79] UCC, s.2–509(3). This subs. concentrates on the role in which the *seller* deals and may from this point of view be contrasted with the Sale of Goods Act 1979, s.20(4) (above, para.3–009, n.70), under which the crucial question is whether the *buyer* deals as consumer. However, by virtue of the definition of dealing as consumer in Sale of Goods Act 1979, s.61(5A) (cross-referring to Unfair Contract Terms Act 1977, s.12, as now amended by Sale and Supply of Goods to Consumers Regulations 2002, SI 2002/3045, reg.14) the buyer can so deal only if the seller acts in the course of a business. Under the proposed amendments to the UCC (above, para.2–042, n.17,) risk under s.2–509(3) is to pass on receipt of the goods by the buyer irrespective of whether the seller is a merchant.

[80] The Convention has at the time of writing not been ratified by the UK.

[81] Vienna Convention, Art.69(1); and see paras 6–048, 15–043, below.

[82] UCC, s.2–509(1).

[83] Vienna Convention, Art.67(1).

[84] UCC, s.2–509(1)(a).

[85] Vienna Convention, Art.67(1).

[86] Sale of Goods Act 1979, s.20(4), as inserted by Sale and Supply of Goods to Consumers Regulations 2002, SI 2002/3045, reg.4. S.20(4) provides that the risk remains with the seller until the goods "are delivered *to the consumer*" and by virtue of s.32(4) of the Act (as inserted by reg.4) delivery of the goods to the carrier is no longer *prima facie* deemed to be a delivery to the buyer (*i.e.* the consumer) even where by virtue of s.32(1) it would be so deemed where the buyer had *not* dealt as consumer.

[87] See above, para.3–009, at n.66. Under Sale of Goods Act 1979, s.32(1), delivery of goods to a carrier may be deemed to be a delivery to the buyer, but subs.(1) says nothing about risk, the passing of which does not depend on delivery where the buyer does not deal as consumer; and where he does so deal (so that risk remains with the seller until delivery by virtue of s.20(4)), s.32(1) does not

actually placed on board the ship.[88] Since destruction or serious deterioration of goods cannot discharge a contract of sale after the risk has passed, but may in some of the situations to be discussed below have this effect where it takes place before the passing of risk,[89] the possibility of discharge in the present type of case is somewhat greater in English law than in the other systems described: in English law (but not in the other systems) discharge can occur if the goods are destroyed between their receipt by the carrier and their being put on board ship.

A contract of sale may expressly provide that risk is to pass at some time other than that specified in the various legislative provisions referred to above; and, to the extent that such contract terms are valid, they will affect the doctrine of discharge. There is no doubt as to the validity of a contract term displacing the rules as to risk laid down in s.20(1) of the Sale of Goods Act 1979,[90] in the Uniform Commercial Code[91] and in the Vienna Convention[92]; but it is less clear whether such a term can effectively exclude the English rule that, where the buyer deals as consumer, the goods remain at the risk of the seller until they are delivered to the consumer. Section 20(4) of the Sale of Goods Act (which lays down this rule) differs from s.20(1) in not containing the words "unless otherwise agreed" or words to the same effect. The mere omission of these words does not, however, conclude the question whether s.20(4) can be excluded or varied by contrary agreement providing for risk to pass to the consumer before delivery to him.[93] Such a term would, however, sometimes deprive the buyer of rights conferred on him by Pt 5A of the 1979 Act,[94] *e.g.* if the goods were damaged after the contract so as no longer to conform to the contract "at the time of delivery".[95] Thus the term would be an exemption clause within the Unfair Contract Terms Act 1977,[96] and if the non-conformity amounted to breach of an implied term under ss.13 to 15 of the 1979 Act, then the term would be void by virtue of the 1977 Act.[97] But this reasoning would not apply where the non-

---

apply: see s.32(4), as inserted by Sale and Supply of Goods to Consumers Regulations 2002, SI 2000/3045, reg.4.

[88] See, *e.g. Pyrene Co Ltd v Scindia Navigation Co Ltd* [1954] 2 Q.B. 402, where risk was assumed not to have passed under an f.o.b. contract precisely because the goods had not yet crossed the ship's rail when they were damaged. For a similar meaning of "shipment" in another context, see *Mowbray Robinson & Co v Rosser* (1922) 91 L.J.K.B. 524; for a slightly wider meaning see *Customs & Excise Commissioners v APS Samex* [1983] 1 All E.R. 1043 at 1051.

[89] *e.g.* where the goods are specific: Sale of Goods Act 1979, s.7, below, para.3–013.

[90] s.20(1) begins with the words "unless otherwise agreed".

[91] s.2–509(4).

[92] Art.6.

[93] See Sale of Goods Act 1979, s.55(1).

[94] As inserted by Sale and Supply of Goods to Consumer Regulations 2002, SI 2002/3045, reg.5.

[95] Sale of Goods Act 1979, s.48A(1)(b).

[96] s.13(1)(a).

[97] s.6(2)(a).

conformity amounted only to breach of an express term[98]; nor would it apply where the goods had been totally destroyed, so that the seller's breach would be by way of non-delivery (and not by way of delivery of non-conforming goods). In such cases, the term would, under the Unfair Contract Terms Act 1977, be ineffective except in so far as it satisfied the requirement of reasonableness[99]; and where the term had not been individually negotiated it would by virtue of the Unfair Terms in Consumer Contracts Regulations 1999 not be binding on the consumer if it were "unfair" within the meaning of those Regulations.[1] Neither the requirement of reasonableness under the 1977 Act nor that of fairness under the 1999 Regulations *necessarily* lead to the invalidity of a term purporting to exclude the rule laid down in s.20(4) of the 1979 Act that the goods remain at the seller's risk until they are delivered to the consumer. A further argument in favour of such invalidity can be based on the ultimate source of s.20(4) of the 1979 Act. Section 20(4) and Pt 5A of the 1979 Act were introduced into the 1979 Act by Regulations[2] made in 2002 to give effect in the United Kingdom to an EC Directive,[3] Art.7.1 of which provides that "contractual terms ... which ... waive or restrict the rights resulting from this Directive shall, as provided by national law, not be binding on the consumer". Since the Directive must be taken into account in interpreting the Regulations,[4] (and hence the provisions which they add to the 1979 Act,) Art.7.1 supports the view that a term purporting to exclude or vary these provisions (including s.20(4)) would not bind the consumer, though it could bind the seller, *e.g.* if in the case of a credit sale it provided that risk was not to pass, even after delivery, before payment in full.

(a) *Destruction of goods after passing of risk*

3–011 Where goods are destroyed after the risk has passed to the buyer, the contract is not discharged by the destruction of the goods: the statement that risk has passed *means* that the buyer must pay the price[5] even though the goods have been destroyed, and that the seller is under no further liability in respect of his inability (in consequence of the destruction) to deliver them. The latter point is obviously one of greater practical

---

[98] Breach of such a term can constitute non-conformity for the purpose of Pt 5A of the 1979 Act: see s.48F.

[99] s.3(1) ("where one of them deals as consumer"); s.3(2)(a).

[1] SI 1999/2083, regs 5(1) and 8.

[2] *i.e.* those cited in n.94, above.

[3] 1999/44.

[4] See *Chitty on Contracts* (29th ed.), para.15–008.

[5] This statement refers to his *duty* to pay the price. Whether the *action* for the price is available depends on other factors specified in Sale of Goods Act 1979, s.49, which makes the action available (1) where the property has passed or (2) where the price is payable "on a day certain irrespective of delivery". Contrast UCC, s.2–709(1)(a), making the action for the price available (*inter alia*) where conforming goods are "lost or damaged within a commercially reasonable time after the risk of their loss has passed to the buyer". The purpose of the "reasonable time" requirement is obscure.

importance in systems of law (such as English law) in which the passing of risk is not (unless the buyer deals as consumer[6]) connected with delivery, than in systems (such as the Uniform Commercial Code or the Vienna Convention) in which there is, as a general rule, such a connection. But although the destruction of the goods after passing of risk will discharge the seller's duty *to deliver* them, it will not totally discharge him from all his outstanding obligations. The contract may, for example, oblige him to transfer shipping documents (such as carriage and insurance documents) to the buyer, so as to enable the buyer to obtain the benefits of the contracts contained in, or evidenced by, those documents; and such obligations will survive the destruction of the goods after the risk has passed.[7] The legal consequence of the destruction of the goods after the passing of risk thus provides a good illustration of the proposition formulated above: its effect is to discharge some of the obligations of one of the parties (*i.e.* of the seller), while leaving those of the buyer in force. If, by contrast, performance of the contract became illegal by virtue of a supervening prohibition, it would be totally discharged, *i.e.* both parties would be discharged from all their obligations under it.

A buyer may be under a duty not only to pay for the goods but also to "accept"[8] them and to take delivery[9] of them. The duty to accept normally means no more than a duty not wrongfully to reject the goods, but the duty to take delivery may require a positive act, such as providing boxes, or a ship into which the goods can be loaded, or removing the goods from the seller's premises. There would normally be no point in calling on the buyer to perform such acts after the goods had been destroyed; but it should be recalled that goods may be regarded as having (for present purposes) been "destroyed" even though they are not wholly annihilated but are so seriously damaged as to have become "for business purposes something else".[10] If this happens after the passing of risk, the buyer may nevertheless still be obliged to remove the seriously deteriorated goods, and so to clear the seller's storage space.

(b) *Destruction of goods before passing of risk*

One might expect the statement that risk has *not* passed to mean the exact   **3–012**
converse of the statement that risk has passed, *i.e.* that the seller's duty to deliver the goods is not discharged, and that the buyer is under no liability to pay for them. It would follow that the contract could not be discharged by destruction of the goods before (any more than it could be discharged by their destruction after) the passing of risk. But the law does not present such a neat symmetrical appearance. The main reasons for this lack of symmetry are the special treatment of the destruction of *specific* goods

---

[6] Sale of Goods Act 1979, s.20(4), above, para.3–009, at n.70.
[7] *e.g. Manbré Saccharine Co Ltd v Corn Products Co Ltd* [1919] 1 K.B. 198 (c.i.f. contract).
[8] Sale of Goods Act 1979, s.27.
[9] Sale of Goods Act 1979, s.37.
[10] See above, para.3–005, n.29.

before the risk has passed, and the difficulty in identifying "the goods" in many cases of destruction before the passing of risk.

Risk cannot normally[11] pass until after the goods to which the contract relates have become ascertained, *i.e.* identified in accordance with the contract,[12] or perhaps in some other way,[13] or until after the bulk of which they form a part (even though an undifferentiated part) has similarly been identified. Where the goods are destroyed *after* the passing of risk, it is therefore normally possible to say with some degree of assurance that the goods which have been destroyed were indeed "the goods" which were the subject-matter of the contract (though even this could be difficult in a case of part-destruction of the identified bulk of which the goods formed an undifferentiated part).[14] But where the destruction is alleged to have taken place *before* the passing of risk, it will often be much less clear that what was destroyed was indeed the subject-matter of the contract. Risk may not have passed precisely because the goods were unascertained, and where they were unascertained because they were purely generic (and not an undifferentiated part of an identified bulk) it will not be possible to say that what was destroyed was indeed the subject-matter of the contract. But it is also possible for the risk not to have passed for some other reason than that described above, *e.g.* because, even though the goods were identified as the subject-matter of the contract at the time of destruction, the property in them has not passed and there is no evidence of contrary agreement excluding the general rule that risk passes with property[15]; or because the buyer has dealt as consumer[16]; or because the sale is on c.i.f. or f.o.b. terms and the goods have not been shipped.[17] Hence, while destruction of the goods after the passing of risk can never be a ground of discharge, it is possible for the doctrine of discharge to apply in cases of

---

[11] It is arguable that there is an exception to the normal rule where goods are sold in transit on c.i.f. terms so that risk passes "as from" shipment (at n.55, above). But even in this situation the better view is that a seller cannot "appropriate" to the contract goods already lost at the time of appropriation: see below, para.3–021, at nn.9–10; on this view, risk does not pass unless at the time of loss the goods are ascertained, or at least form part of an identified bulk.

[12] *Re Wait* [1927] 1 Ch. 606 at 630.

[13] *Thames Sack & Bag Co Ltd v Knowles* (1918) 88 L.J. K.B. 585 at 588, *e.g.* perhaps, by "exhaustion" as described in *Karlshamns Oljefabriker v Eastport Navigation Co (The Elafi)* [1981] 2 Lloyd's Rep. 679 at 684 and Sale of Goods Act 1979, s.18, r.5(3), as inserted by Sale of Goods (Amendment) Act 1995, s.1(2); or by "consolidation" as described in *Benjamin's Sale of Goods* (6th ed.), para.18–254. These two processes relate to the "ascertainment" of goods forming an undifferentiated part of a bulk, a situation in which risk can pass even without "ascertainment:" above, para.3–008.

[14] The difficulty may be solved by contractual provisions for *pro rata* distribution, as in *The Arpad* (1935) 51 Ll.L. Rep. 115 (a case which was several times litigated). For the possibility of *pro rata* division in the absence of such express provisions, see below, paras 5–023 *et seq. cf. Benjamin's Sale of Goods* (6th ed.), paras 18–272, 18–317.

[15] Sale of Goods Act 1979, s.20(1).

[16] *ibid.*, s.20(4).

[17] *Benjamin's Sale of Goods* (6th ed.), paras 19–106, 19–110, 20–086.

destruction of goods before the passing of risk. For the purpose of determining whether it does apply, it is necessary to distinguish between four types of case.

(i) Specific goods

Section 7 of the Sale of Goods Act 1979 provides that an agreement for the sale of "specific" goods[18] is avoided if the goods "perish" without any fault on the part of either party after the making of the agreement and before the risk has passed to the buyer. This section amounts to a statutory application of the doctrine of discharge. In the normal case of such "perishing", performance of the seller's duty to deliver the goods[19] and to transfer the property in them[20] will become impossible to perform; and this will also be true of the buyer's duty to accept the goods.[21] Impossibility will not indeed affect the buyer's duty to pay, but this will be discharged on the ground (already explained[22]) of impossibility affecting the agreed exchange of the goods for the price. Section 7 may, it seems, apply even though some of the duties described above have been performed. This would be the position where the goods had been delivered and accepted, but the property in them (and hence the risk[23]) had been retained by the seller on the ground that the goods had not been paid for.[24] In such a case, the seller would be discharged from his duty to transfer property and the buyer from his duty to pay the price.

(a) Fractions and percentages. The 1979 Act defines "specific goods" to mean "goods identified and agreed on when the contract is made," and includes in the definition "an undivided share, specified as a fraction or percentage"[25] of goods so identified and agreed on. A contract for sale of "half the cargo of cotton shipped on the *Peerless*" may therefore fall within s.7. Whether it does fall within the section depends on whether property has passed to the buyer, who may acquire property in an undivided share in the bulk in accordance with the intention of the parties relating to the passing of property in specific goods.[26] If he has acquired such property, the contract at this stage becomes (in a terminology of the Act) a "sale" as opposed to an "agreement to sell"[27] and s.7 ceases to apply to it.[28] If, however, property has not passed (*e.g.* because it was intended to pass only on payment and payment has not been made), then s.7 does apply to the contract, and the contract will be avoided under that section if the whole

3–013

3–014

---

[18] Defined in s.61(2): see above, para.2–016, below para.3–014.

[19] Sale of Goods Act 1979, s.27.

[20] *ibid.* s.2.

[21] *ibid.* s.27.

[22] See above, para.2–043.

[23] Sale of Goods Act 1979, s.20(1).

[24] See *R V Ward Ltd v Bignall* [1967] 1 Q.B. 537 at 545.

[25] Sale of Goods Act 1979, s.61(1), definition of "specific goods".

[26] *Benjamin's Sale of Goods* (6th ed.), para.5–129; Law Commissions' Paper on *Sale of Goods Forming Part of a Bulk* (Law Com. No.215, Scot. Law Com. No.145, 1993), paras 5.5, 5.6.

[27] See s.2(6).

[28] *Benjamin's Sale of Goods* (6th ed.), para.6–030.

of the cargo is destroyed before risk has passed to the buyer. If only part of the cargo is destroyed, then it is submitted that the result will depend on the rules to be discussed in Ch.5, relating to partial failure of a source of supply.[29]

3–015   *(b) "Without . . . fault".*   Section 7 does not apply if the destruction of the goods is due to the "fault"[30] of either party, *e.g.* the agreement would not be avoided if the goods had disintegrated because of a defect in them amounting to a breach of the seller's express or implied undertakings as to description or quality.[31] It seems that, to exclude s.7 in this way, the "fault" must be a cause of the perishing of the goods. Thus if the goods suffered from a defect amounting to a breach of contract but were destroyed by some other cause (*e.g.* by an accidental fire) the contract could be avoided under s.7. Such avoidance would, however, not prejudice any claim for damages in respect of loss which the buyer might have suffered in consequence of the defect *before* the goods were destroyed.[32]

Buyer or seller might also be at "fault" in respect of delay in making, or taking, delivery. Such fault will prevent the passing of risk "as regards any loss which might not have occurred but for such fault".[33] Where delivery is delayed as a result of the "fault" of the seller, and the passage of risk is thus deferred, this rule may at first sight appear to extend the scope of s.7. But if the destruction of the goods is caused by the delay, then the goods will not have perished "without fault on the part of the seller", so that the agreement will not be avoided under s.7. There may however be avoidance under the section where the delay might have caused the loss, but it was actually attributable to some other cause which would have operated even if there had been no delay.[34] The rules relating to the effect on risk of delay in making or taking delivery do not apply where the buyer deals as consumer.[35] In such cases, the goods remain at the seller's risk until they are delivered to the buyer even though delivery is delayed through the fault of the buyer[36]; and where the delay results from the fault of the seller the *whole* risk remains with him, and not only the risk of loss "which might not have occurred without such fault".[37]

---

[29] See below, paras 5–010 *et seq.*

[30] Defined in Sale of Goods Act 1979, s.61(1) to mean "wrongful act or default", a phrase which clearly includes breach of contract, even where liability for such breach is strict. And see below, para.14–007.

[31] In particular, because of breach of the terms implied by Sale of Goods Act 1979, ss.13–15.

[32] See below, para.15–011.

[33] Sale of Goods Act 1979, s.20(2).

[34] *cf.* the reasoning of *Demby Hamilton & Co v Barden* [1949] 1 All E.R. 435 at 437 (dealing with the converse case of delay resulting from the "fault" of the buyer).

[35] Sale of Goods Act 1979, s.20(4), as inserted by Sale and Supply of Goods to Consumers Regulations 2002, SI 2002/3045, reg.4.

[36] *ibid.*

[37] See above, at n.33.

(c) "Perish". Section 7 refers only to the case in which the goods "perish"; but the principle that destruction of the subject-matter need not involve its total physical annihilation[38] applies for the purpose of determining whether damage to goods is so serious that they can be said to have "perished". The test, here as elsewhere, is whether the goods have "become for business purposes something else",[39] and if the goods in the cases of *Asfar & Co v Blundell*[40] and *Duthie v Hilton*[41] (discussed above) had been specific and the subject-matter of a sale, they would, it is submitted, have been regarded as having "perished" for the purpose of s.7. Whether damage or deterioration is of this nature can obviously raise difficult questions of construction and of degree: exactly what is the description of the goods and how serious is the deterioration? Two cases may be contrasted. In *Horn v Ministry of Food*[42] a contract was made for the sale of potatoes which became rotten "with the result that they could not be used" but it was "not found that the use of the word 'potatoes' was inapposite with reference to them".[43] One ground for holding that the contract was not avoided under s.7 was that the deterioration occurred *after* the risk had passed to the seller; but it was also held that the potatoes had not "perished". On the other hand, in the New Zealand case of *Rendel v Turnbull & Co*[44] a contract was made for the sale of "table potatoes" and it was held that the goods had "perished"[45] when they became unfit for human consumption. The different ways in which the parties described the subject-matter may serve to distinguish the two decisions.

In its requirement that goods must "perish", s.7 may be contrasted with s.2–613 of the Uniform Commercial Code, which distinguishes between cases in which "the loss is total"[46] and those in which "the loss is partial or the goods have so deteriorated as no longer to conform to the contract".[47] Automatic avoidance[48] results only in cases of total loss.[49] Where the loss is partial, or the goods deteriorate, s.2–613(b) gives the buyer a choice: he can either treat the contract as avoided or accept the goods with an allowance in respect of the partial loss or deterioration (but without any

---

[38] See above, para.3–005.

[39] *Asfar & Co v Blundell* [1896] 1 Q.B. 126 at 128.

[40] See above, para.3–005.

[41] (1870) L.R. 4 C.P. 138, above, para.3–005.

[42] [1948] 2 All E.R. 1036.

[43] *ibid.* at 1039.

[44] (1908) 27 N.Z.L.R. 1067.

[45] Within the New Zealand equivalent of Sale of Goods Act 1979, s.6 (which deals with the effect of the perishing of the goods *before* the time of contracting).

[46] s.2–613(a).

[47] s.2–613(b). The distinction drawn in the text above is also used in relation to chattel leases by UCC, s.2A–221.

[48] For a proposed terminological change, see above, para.3–004, n.17.

[49] Contrast Indian Contract Act 1930, s.8, applying the rule of *automatic* avoidance not only where the goods have "perished" but also where they have become "so damaged as no longer to answer to their contractual description".

right to damages).[50] Section 7 of the Sale of Goods Act 1979 gives the buyer no such choice. Goods may indeed "perish" for the purpose of the section, even though they have not totally ceased to exist, if they have been so seriously damaged as to have become "for business purposes something else" (as in the examples already given). But where this is the case the contract is "avoided" by operation of law, not by choice of the buyer; nor can the buyer insist on delivery at a reduced price. We shall see, however, that in cases of partial destruction of goods to be taken from an identified source, English law does reach a result resembling that envisaged in s.2–613(b) of the Uniform Commercial Code.[51] The fact that that provision does distinguish between "total" loss on the one hand, and partial loss and deterioration on the other, makes it probable that the concept of "total" loss under the Code will be interpreted somewhat more narrowly than that of "perishing" in s.7 of the Sale of Goods Act; and that in this respect the scope of the principle of automatic discharge will be correspondingly narrower under the Code than it is under the Act.

3–017   (d) *"Specific" or "identified" goods*. The scope of that principle will, on the other hand, be wider under the Code than under the Act in that s.7 applies only where the goods are "specific" while s.2–613 makes the somewhat different concept of "identified" goods. Goods are "specific" for the purpose of s.7 if they are "identified and agreed on at the time a contract of sale is made" or if they consist of "an undivided share specified as a fraction or percentage" of goods so identified and agreed on.[52] It has been held in England that where the sale is of a specified quantity of goods which form an undifferentiated part of an identified bulk (*e.g.* 200 tons out of the cargo of the *Peerless*, consisting of 1,000 tons[53]), then the goods are neither ascertained nor specific for the purpose of other provisions of the Act,[54] though property can now, under certain conditions, pass to the buyer in such goods.[55] However there is no reason to suppose that they would be "specific" for the purpose of s.7[56]: they would be so regarded only if the sale were of the whole cargo of an identified ship or of a fraction or percentage of such a cargo. By contrast, the Uniform Commercial Code more broadly provides that an "undivided

---

[50] The "casualty" is required in s.2–613 to have occurred "without fault of either party" and "fault" is defined in s.1–201(16) to mean "wrongful act omission or breach." Hence "without fault" means (*inter alia*) that the seller was not in breach in respect of the partial loss or damage.

[51] See below, para.5–013.

[52] Sale of Goods Act 1979, s.61(1), as amended by Sale of Goods (Amendment) Act 1995, s.2(d), above, para.3–014.

[53] *cf. Re Wait* [1927] 1 Ch. 606; *Re Goldcorp Exchange* [1995] 1 A.C. 74, where the contract was not regarded as one "for a sale ex bulk" (at 89–90).

[54] *i.e.* ss.16, 52.

[55] By virtue of s.20A of the 1979 Act, as inserted by s.1(3) of the 1995 Act: see above, para.3–009.

[56] s.20A(1) refers to them as "unascertained".

share in an identified bulk of fungible[57] goods" can be "identified"[58]; and these words cover an undivided share whether it is expressed as a specified quantity or as a fraction or percentage. In this respect, the American concept of "identified" goods is wider than the English concept of "specific" goods; but in being applicable only to goods which are "fungible", the American concept is narrower than its English counterpart. The concept of "fungible" goods is by no means free from difficulty since, in legal systems which make use of it, there are two quite different definitions of "fungible" goods, and these in turn must be distinguished from the concept of "generic" goods,[59] though the two ideas are sometimes confused.[60]

Under one definition, "fungible" goods are those which in the ordinary course of business are dealt with by weight, number or measure[61]; this concept (though not the term "fungible"[62]) goes back to Roman law,[63] where it was used to describe those things which could be the subject-matter of a loan for use (*mutuum*). This was a contract which required the borrower to return, not the very thing lent to him, but an equivalent quantity. The subject-matter of such a contract could be fungible goods as well as money.[64] Under another definition, "fungible" goods are those "of which each particle is identical with every other particle",[65] or (somewhat more broadly) those "of which any unit is, by nature or usage of trade, the equivalent of any other like unit."[66] Goods such as vegetable crops may be treated as "equivalent" by usage of trade, even though each particle is not "identical" with every other particle: indeed, if taken literally, this requirement of "identicalness" could scarcely ever be satisfied except perhaps in the case of bulk liquids. Under the definitions so far given, the test of fungibility is objective,[67] but the Uniform Commercial Code introduces the notion of fungibility by agreement,

---

[57] The UCC's definition of "fungible" goods was contained in s.1–201(17); in the 2002 edition it is replaced, without change of substance, by s.1–201(18), but this version seems at the time of writing not to have been widely adopted by State legislatures.

[58] UCC s.2–105(4) (to become s.2–105(3) under the proposed amendments to Art.2 referred to in para.2–042, n.17, above).

[59] See Esser & Schmidt, *Schuldrecht Allgemeiner Teil* (6th ed.), Vol.1, p.191; Guhl, *Das Schweizerische Obligationenrecht* (7th ed.), p.46.

[60] Especially in French law: see Mazeaud, Mazeaud & Chabas, *Leçons de Droit Civil* (9th ed.), Vol.II(1), Nos 1082, 1119–1120.

[61] German Civil Code (BGB), § 91.

[62] See Buckland, *A Textbook of Roman Law* (2nd ed.), p.463.

[63] Dig. 12. 1. 2. 1.

[64] Buckland, n.62, above, at p.463.

[65] *Williston on Sales* (rev ed.), para.159.

[66] UCC s.1–201 (17); s.1–201(18) in the 2002 edition (above, para.3–017, n.57).

[67] Esser & Schmidt, n.59 above, at p.191; in French law a subjective test is sometimes stated, *e.g.* Mazeaud & Mazeaud; *Leçons de Droit Civil* (5th ed.), Vol.III(2), No. 1356, but these authors give to "fungible" the same meaning as "generic" and the test for the latter category is generally regarded as subjective: see below, at n.76.

under which the test of fungibility depends, at least in part, on the intention of the parties: it provides that "goods which are not fungible shall be deemed fungible ... to the extent that under a particular agreement ... unlike units are treated as equivalent".[68] Thus stacks of hay, bales of cotton, or animals forming part of a herd or flock can be fungible by agreement.[69] If, however, it is a term of a contract that particular units of goods which are either objectively or subjectively the "equivalent" of others are to be delivered, then those units are not fungible, since "among fungibles there are no right and wrong units".[70] In the absence of extended fungibility by agreement, typical illustrations of fungible goods include "grain in an elevator or oil in a storage tank"[71]; rather less obviously, mass produced goods are also fungible if any one item so produced is, as a matter of business, regarded as the equivalent of another.[72]

Although the Uniform Commercial Code uses the "equivalence" test (in the modified form described above) in order to determine fungibility, it also refers in this context to the "weight, number or measure" test. In dealing with the sale of an "undivided share in a bulk of fungible goods," it provides that any quantity of such a bulk "agreed upon by number, weight or other measure may ... be sold".[73] These words do not, however, here define the concept of fungibility: they merely refer to one possible method of ascertaining the quantity of goods so sold. Such ascertainment may also be made in other ways, *e.g.* by selling "any agreed proportion of such a bulk".[74]

3–018   Generic goods (in legal systems which make use of this concept) are goods which belong to a class which is defined by reference to common characteristics possessed by all goods of that class, but which are not otherwise identified[75]; they are identified by reference to general rather than to particular distinguishing factors. The extent of the class is said to depend on the intention of the parties,[76] who may define the class broadly or narrowly, *e.g.* as wheat, or as American wheat, or as American winter wheat,[77] or even (it seems) as branded goods even though these are produced only by a single factory.[78] It follows that the extent of the class

---

[68] UCC, s.1–201(17); above, n.66.

[69] *Casinelli v Humphrey Supply Co*, 183 P 523, at 525 (1919); *Williston on Sales* (rev. ed.), para.159.

[70] *Stamford Extract Mfg Co v Oakes Mfg Co*, 9 F. 2d 301 at 302 (1925).

[71] UCC, s.2–501, Comment 5.

[72] Palandt, *Bürgerliches Gesetzbuch* (57th ed.), § 91, Comment 2.

[73] UCC, s.2–105(4). In the proposed amendments to the UCC (above, para.2–042, n.17) the definition is contained, with modifications, in the proposed s.2–105(3).

[74] *ibid.*

[75] Guhl, above, n.59, p.46.

[76] Esser & Schmidt, n.59, above, p.191; Palandt, above n.72, § 91, Comment; § 243, Comment 1(b).

[77] Von Tuhr/Peter, *Allgemeiner Teil des Schweizerischen Obligationenrechts* (3rd ed.), p.54.

[78] RGZ 57, 116, RG February 27, 1904.

depends on subjective criteria (as opposed to the, in general, objective criteria which determine whether goods are fungible). Goods may be generic without being fungible, *e.g.* "a Turner drawing".[79] More commonly, generic goods are also fungible: the typical commodity sale of a quantity of unascertained oil or grain would fall into both categories; this would also be true of the sale of a new mass-produced car of a specified manufacture and model[80] (though a contract for the sale of a second-hand car would not fall into either category.[81])

English law does not make use of the concepts of fungible or generic goods in the sense that there are no special rules which govern dealings in such goods. The nearest English law comes to adopting the concept of fungible goods is in the definition of "bulk" inserted into the Sale of Goods Act 1979 in 1995.[82] It is part of this definition that any goods forming part of the bulk "are interchangeable with any other goods therein of the same number or quantity". This part of the definition of bulk to some extent draws on the definition of "fungible" goods given above.[83] With regard to generic goods, the nearest English equivalent to the concept of the genus which is subjectively determined is that of unascertained goods sold by description.[84] In English discussions of the effect on a contract of the perishing of goods, reference is sometimes made to the somewhat misleading maxim *genus numquam perit*.[85] This might suggest the existence in English law of a category of generic goods, but the reference is simply to unascertained goods of the contract description. The maxim is misleading in the sense that if the genus is sufficiently restricted by the intention of the parties, then it clearly *can* perish, as in the case of a genus consisting of goods which are made only in a particular factory[86] to which the contract does not refer and which is destroyed with all its stock. The maxim may in such cases express a legal conclusion (*i.e.* that the perishing of the genus has no effect on the obligation of one, or conceivably of both, parties) even if it can be shown to be untrue in a factual sense. Whether this is indeed the position is further discussed in paras 4–053 to 4–056, below.

A contract for the sale of goods not yet in existence and forming part of   **3–019**
a bulk to be taken from an identified source would not be one for the sale of "specific goods" within s.7. Thus the section would not apply where part of a growing crop, or of a crop to be grown on identified land was

---

[79] *Münchener Kommentar zum Bürgerlichen Gesetzbuch*, (4th ed.), § 243, Comment II.1.

[80] Above, n.72.

[81] Palandt, above, n.72, § 91, Comment 3.

[82] Sale of Goods Act 1979, s.61(1), definition of "bulk", inserted by Sale of Goods (Amendment) Act 1995, s.2(a).

[83] See above, para.3–017, nn.65, 66.

[84] By contrast to the example given at n.79 above, the sale of a specific picture attributed to a named artist has been held not to be a sale "by description". *Harlingdon & Leinster Enterprises Ltd v Christopher Hull Fine Art Ltd* [1991] 1 Q.B. 564.

[85] *e.g. Benjamin's Sale of Goods* (6th ed.), para.6–035.

[86] Above, at n.78.

sold[87]; though we shall see that the failure of the crop may discharge the contract at common law.[88] Under the Uniform Commercial Code, "identification" in such cases occurs "when the crops are planted or otherwise become growing crops" if they are to be harvested "within twelve months or the next normal harvest season after contracting whichever is longer".[89] It is, however, far from clear whether the failure of such a crop would lead to avoidance under s.2–613 or be a ground of excuse under the doctrine embodied in s.2–615.[90] The point is an important one because the effects of the two sections differ in a number of significant respects.[91]

It is an open question whether an agreement for the sale of the *whole* of an identified growing crop, or of a crop to be grown on identified land, could be an agreement for the sale of "specific" goods within s.7. In *Kursell v Timber Operators & Contractors Ltd*[92] a contract for the sale of "all the merchantable timber" growing in a named forest in Latvia on a specified date was held to have been frustrated when a prohibition imposed by the Latvian Government made it impossible for the purchaser to cut the timber and remove it, in accordance with the terms of the contract. It was said[93] that property had not passed to the buyer, but this conclusion was not expressly based on the view that the goods were not specific, and other reasons for it can be suggested, *e.g.* that the timber was not in a deliverable state, or that it had not yet been paid for. It remains, therefore, arguable that, where the agreement covers *all* the goods to be produced and taken from an identified source, it is one for the sale of specific goods, so that the destruction of those goods, after they have come into existence but before the risk in them has passed to the buyer, can avoid the agreement under s.7.[93a] The goods in such a case can be regarded as "identified and agreed upon when the contract is made", in the sense that there is no doubt that the contract must relate to all goods brought into existence from the identified source: the only doubt is as to

---

[87] *Howell v Coupland* (1876) 1 Q.B.D. 258, as explained in *HR & S Sainsbury Ltd v Street* [1972] 1 W.L.R. 834.

[88] See below, para.4–049.

[89] UCC, s.2–501(1)(c).

[90] s.2–615, Comment 5 indicates that a case of the kind described in the text above would be dealt with under s.2–615 rather than under s.2–613. Comment 9 to s.2–615, on the other hand, refers specifically to sale of "crops to be grown on designated land"; it says that such a case could fall within either section, but it fails to specify which party can choose between the two provisions.

[91] *e.g.* the principle of pro rata division is available under s.2–615(b) (below, para.5–023) but not under s.2–613, while the principle of price reduction is available under s.2–613(b) but not under the enacting words of s.2–615 (though it might conceivably be available under Comment 6). Comment 5 (above, n.90) could be read to refer to the case where the source is not "identified" within s.2–501(1)(c), *e.g.* because the sale is of part of a crop which is not yet planted.

[92] [1927] 1 K.B. 298.

[93] At 312, 314.

[93a] See the discussion of *Kursell's* case [1927] 1 K.B. 298, above, at n.92.

the quantity to which the contract will attach. If, moreover, a contract for the sale of the whole of a crop to be grown on identified land can be one for the sale of specific goods, then it seems to follow from the statutory definition of such goods,[94] that the same can also be true of a contract for the sale of a fraction or percentage of such a crop. However, where the contract was one for the sale of a specified quantity of goods forming part of an identified bulk (a concept that seems to include a crop growing on identified land), then the contract would be one for the sale of unascertained goods[95] since it would not at the time of contracting be certain to which goods the contract related; nor would the goods in such a case be "specific" within the statutory definition.[96] This is true whether the bulk is already in existence when the agreement is made, or whether (as in the growing crop cases) it is only to come into existence at a later date.

In English law, the significance of the question discussed above is, for practical purposes, relatively small where the *whole* of the bulk or source is destroyed; for in such a case the contract will be discharged at common law, even though the goods are *not* "specific".[97] The only practical consequence of the distinction arises when the exact legal *effects* of discharge are considered, since cases of frustration by destruction of "specific" goods are excepted from the provisions of the Law Reform (Frustrated Contracts) Act 1943.[98] The distinction is of greater importance in cases of *partial* destruction, especially in legal systems which lay down different rules for such cases according to whether the goods are or are not what an English lawyer would call specific goods. This, on one view, is the position under the American Uniform Commercial Code[99]; such cases of partial destruction will be further discussed in Ch.5.] 3–020

(ii) Unascertained goods sold simply by description

At the opposite extreme to a contract for the sale of specific goods is an agreement for the sale of unascertained goods simply by description (or a contract for the sale of "generic" goods), *e.g.* of 5,000 tons of wheat of a specified grade, origin or type. The seller may intend to appropriate a particular lot of such wheat to the contract, *e.g.* the 5,000 tons stored in a particular elevator or on board a particular ship. If that lot is destroyed before the risk has passed, the contract is clearly not discharged, so that the seller is bound to procure another 5,000 tons of such wheat and to deliver it under the contract[1-2] while the buyer is bound to accept and pay 3–021

---

[94] Sale of Goods Act 1979, s.61(1), definition of "specific goods"; see above, para.3–016, at n.52.

[95] Sale of Goods Act 1979, s.20A(1) ("unascertained goods").

[96] Above, at n.94.

[97] *Howell v Coupland* (1876) 1 Q.B.D. 258; below, para.4–049.

[98] Law Reform (Frustrated Contracts) Act, s.2(5)(c); below, para.15–095.

[99] Above, at nn.90, 91.

[1-2] *cf.* the assumption made in the many "soyabean" cases (below, paras 12–036 *et seq.*) in which sellers were held not to be protected by the "prohibition" and "*force majeure*" clauses in the contract. These were cases, not of destruction of the subject-matter, but of unavailability of a particular source.

for it. Of course, if the seller fails to tender such delivery, the buyer is not bound to pay, but this follows from the rule that delivery and payment are concurrent conditions.[3] There is no doubt that the seller's failure to tender will make him liable in damages.[4] This may be so even though in fact the seller is unable to obtain an alternative supply of goods of the contract description, so that it becomes "impossible for [him] to fulfil his bargain".[5] All this is not to say that a contract for the sale of unascertained goods can never be frustrated[6]: the present point is simply that it will not be frustrated by the destruction of the goods which the seller intended to appropriate to the contract; for before the goods are actually appropriated there can (at least in general) be no question that the goods are still at his risk. There may, indeed, be an exception[7] to this last statement in the case of c.i.f. contracts, in which risk may pass with retrospective effect by virtue of the rule that risk can pass "as from shipment".[8] Hence one view is that unascertained goods sold by description under such a contract may be at the buyer's risk before they are appropriated to the contract, so that the seller can appropriate to the contract goods of that description lost between the time of the contract and the time of appropriation, and that the buyer would be bound to pay the price.[9] But the better view is that a c.i.f. seller is not entitled to make an appropriation of goods already lost.[10] Even if he were so entitled, the situation would be one in which the destruction of the goods had taken place *after* the passing of risk, while our present concern is with the situation in which the goods are destroyed *before* risk has passed. And frustration by destruction of the goods would be

---

[3] Sale of Goods Act 1979, s.28; *cf.* UCC, s.2–507(1).

[4] This follows *a fortiori* from cases such as *Ashmore & Son v C S Cox & Co* [1899] 1 Q.B. 436 (above, para.2–034) and *Blackburn Bobbin Co Ltd v T W Allen & Sons* [1918] 2 K.B. 467 (below, para.4–054), where there was no destruction of goods but the seller was cut off by war-time conditions from his intended source.

[5] *per* McCardie J. in the *Blackburn Bobbin* case (above) at first instance [1918] 1 K.B. 540 at 550.

[6] See the discussion of *Acetylene Co of G B v Canada Carbide Co* (1922) 8. Ll.L. Rep. 456 at para.5–043, below.

[7] For another exception where the goods are to be, and are, manufactured by the seller and deteriorate on account of the buyer's delay in taking delivery, see *Demby Hamilton & Co Ltd v Barden* [1949] 1 All E.R. 435, where such goods were held to be "the goods" within what is now Sale of Goods Act 1979, s.20(2) in spite (it seems) of the fact that the seller was not legally bound under the contract to deliver those goods, though it would have been hard for him to find a substitute.

[8] *The Julia* [1949] A.C. 293 at 309; for further references see *Benjamin's Sale of Goods* (6th ed.), para.19–106.

[9] This view is said to be supported by dicta in *C Groom Ltd v Barber* [1915] 1 K.B. 316 at 324 and in *Manbré Saccharine Corp v Crown Products Ltd* [1919] 1 K.B. 198 at 203: see Feltham [1975] J.B.L. 273; for a different interpretation see *Benjamin's Sale of Goods* (6th ed.), para.19–079.

[10] *Re Olympia Oil and Cake Co and Produce Brokers Co* [1915] 1 K.B. 233 at 237 (actual decision reversed on proof of custom [1916] 1 A.C. 314 and doubted in *Produce Brokers Co Ltd v Olympia Oil Co Ltd* [1917] 1 K.B. 320 at 329–330); *Benjamin's Sale of Goods* (6th ed.), paras 19–080, 19–109.

excluded in both situations, the effect of the destruction of the goods in each of them being governed by the rules relating to risk.

(iii) Unascertained goods becoming ascertained

The situation discussed in para.3–021 above may be varied by supposing that the contract is one for the sale of unascertained goods and that the seller has, after the conclusion of the contract, notified the buyer that he intends to perform by delivering a particular lot, thus appropriating[11] it to the contract and becoming bound to deliver those particular goods under the contract. If those goods are then destroyed before the risk in them has passed to the buyer, the contract is certainly not avoided under s.7 of the Sale of Goods Act 1979, since that section only applies to "specific goods", *i.e.* (in the present context) to "goods identified and agreed upon when the contract was made"[12]; and in the case put the goods were only identified after the contract was made. But the destruction of goods may frustrate a contract for the sale of goods in cases falling outside s.7[13]; and the question, in the case put, is whether the contract is frustrated under the general principles of common law which apply to a contract for the sale of goods, except in so far as they are inconsistent with the provisions of the Sale of Goods Act 1979.[14]

The question put above most obviously concerns the liability of the seller: if the goods which he has appropriated are destroyed before the risk has passed and before payment has become due, there can be no question of the buyer's being bound to pay for those goods. One reason for this is that the statement that the goods are at the seller's risk *means* that the buyer is not so liable.[15] A second reason is that delivery and payment are, unless otherwise agreed, concurrent conditions[16]; and in the case put there can, *ex hypothesi*, be no delivery of the destroyed goods. But the first of these two reasons may apply even where the second does not, *i.e.* where the contract provides for payment before delivery. In relation to such a payment, the statement that risk has not passed to the buyer appears to mean that the buyer is entitled to the return of his payment if it has been made.[17] It should follow that he is relieved from his liability to make the

---

[11] In the "contractual" (as opposed to the "proprietary") sense of indicating which particular goods are to be delivered. For the distinction between these two senses of "appropriation," see *Benjamin's Sale of Goods* (6th ed.), para.18–181.

[12] Sale of Goods Act 1979, s.61(1). The inclusion in this definition of fractions and percentages of goods so identified (above, para.3–014) does not affect the point here under discussion.

[13] See the discussion of *Howell v Coupland* (1876) 1 Q.B.D. 258, below, para.4–049.

[14] Sale of Goods Act 1979, s.62(2).

[15] *cf.* (for the converse situation) above, para.3–011.

[16] Sale of Goods Act 1979, s.28; *cf.* UCC, s.2–507(1).

[17] *cf. Fibrosa Spolka Akcyjna v Fairbairn, Lawson Combe, Barbour Ltd* [1943] A.C. 32; *The Julia* [1949] A.C. 293 where risk had not passed (see *Benjamin's Sale of Goods* (6th ed.), para.18–270). Neither of these cases is directly relevant to the question whether destruction of the goods would have frustrated the contract, the cause of frustration having been supervening illegality in the first, and impossibility (due to war) in reaching the contractual destination in the second.

payment if it has not been made, for it would be absurd to hold the buyer liable to make a payment which the seller was then obliged to return to him as soon as it was made.[18] The position would of course be different where goods were ascertained and then destroyed *after* risk had passed to the buyer: in such a case he would be liable for the price if not paid and not entitled to its return if it had already been paid.[19]

Although it is clear that destruction of goods which were unascertained when sold but became ascertained before the passing of risk discharges the buyer from his duty to pay *for those goods*, the answer to two further questions is much less clear.

3–023   The first question is whether the seller is *entitled* to substitute a second appropriation for that relating to the goods which have been destroyed; and if the seller takes this course the question will arise whether the buyer is merely liberated by the destruction of the first lot from his duty to accept and pay for *those* goods, or whether he is freed from liability to accept and pay for *any* goods which may subsequently be tendered under the contract. This will depend in the first place on the construction of the contract. If the contract provides for the appropriation to be made by means of a notice of appropriation, it may be an express[20] or an implied[21] term of the contract that, once such a notice has been given, it is not to be withdrawn. If that is the true meaning of the contract, then the seller clearly cannot effectively make a substitute appropriation and require payment for it in the event of the destruction of the originally appropriated goods. If, on the other hand, the contract is merely one for the sale of unascertained goods and contains no provision as to how an appropriation is to be made, or as to the effects of a notice of appropriation, then, the position may well be different. Here the courts might by analogy invoke the principle which applies where a seller tenders goods which do not conform with the contract. If the buyer rejects those goods and the seller within the time allowed by the contract makes a fresh tender which is in conformity with the contract, then the buyer is obliged to accept the goods so tendered and to pay for them.[22] In the situation with which we are concerned (*i.e.* where the goods which were originally

---

[18] See *French Marine v Compagnie Napolitaine, etc* [1921] 2 A.C. 494 at 511, cited with approval in the *Fibrosa* case [1943] A.C. 32 at 53–54. For analogous reasoning in cases of breach, see *McDonald v Denys Lascelles Ltd* (1933) 48 C.L.R. 457, cited with approval in *Johnson v Agnew* [1980] A.C. 367 at 396 and in *Hyundai Heavy Industries Ltd v Papadopoulos* [1980] 1 W.L.R. 1129 at 1141.

[19] *e.g.* where goods had been appropriated to a c.i.f. contract and were then destroyed before tender of documents: *Benjamin's Sale of Goods* (6th ed.), para.19–077.

[20] See, *e.g. Ross T Smyth & Co Ltd v T D Bailey, Son & Co* [1940] 3 All E.R. 60; *Getreide Import Gesellschaft mbH v Itoh & Co (America) Ltd* [1979] 1 Lloyd's Rep. 592.

[21] See *Borrowman Phillips & Co v Free & Hollis* (1878) 4 Q.B.D. 500 at 504; *Benjamin's Sale of Goods* (6th ed.), para.19–021.

[22] *Tetley v Shand* (1871) 25 L.T. 658; *cf. Borrowman, Phillips & Co v Free & Hollis* (1878) 4 Q.B.D. 500; and see Treitel, *The Law of Contract* (11th ed.), p.754.

appropriated are then destroyed) the buyer may not have rejected, or indeed have been entitled to reject, the original appropriation (which is assumed to be in accordance with the contract). But where the goods appropriated to the contract are destroyed after appropriation and before the risk in them has passed, the buyer is released from his duty to accept and pay for them just as much as if he had rejected them. Nor will he usually be prejudiced by having to accept and pay for a second lot of goods appropriated to the contract after destruction of the first lot: being a buyer of unascertained goods by description he has, at least initially, no greater interest in delivery of one lot of goods of that description rather than in delivery of another. He might acquire such an interest by reselling the goods by reference to the first appropriation, but the destruction of the goods would release him from that contract, either under s.7, if goods to be acquired by him can be "specific", or, if this possibility is rejected, at common law.[23] The only hardship to the buyer might then be that he could not pass on the substitute goods to his sub-buyer and so be left holding those goods on a market which may have fallen. It is however, possible to make allowance for this possibility by holding that the buyer must accept and pay for the second appropriation unless he can establish that he would thereby suffer some prejudice which he would not have suffered, if the goods first appropriated had not been destroyed. It is submitted that the buyer's duty to accept a second tender would be qualified in this way where the original appropriation was rejected on account of the seller's breach[24]; and there seems to be no reason why a similar rule should not apply where an appropriation becomes ineffective by reason of the accidental destruction of the originally appropriated goods before the passing of risk.

The second question is whether, after destruction of the originally   3–024
appropriated goods, the seller is *bound* to procure other goods and to appropriate them to the contract. This question is closely related to the question whether the buyer is bound to accept a substitute appropriation; for at first sight it would seem that a court would not impose an obligation on a seller to make a tender which the buyer was free to reject. There seems, remarkably, to be no direct authority on this question. It has been held that, where a seller of unascertained goods on c.i.f. terms purports by notice to appropriate goods which never existed at all, the buyer can accept that notice; and if he does accept it the seller will be liable for his inability to deliver in accordance with the appropriation.[25] The seller will also be bound by the appropriation, in the sense that he will not, on discovering that the appropriation related to non-existent goods, normally

---

[23] On the ground that the goods were to be taken from an identified source which had failed; below, para.4–049.

[24] *cf. Benjamin's Sale of Goods* (6th ed.), para.20–052.

[25] *Waren Import Gesellschaft Krohn & Co v Alfred C Toepfer (The Vladimir Ilich)* [1975] 1 Lloyd's Rep. 322 (where the buyer lost his rights by *rejecting* the appropriation of non-existent goods, so enabling the seller to make a fresh, and effective, appropriation).

be entitled to substitute an appropriation of other goods which are in existence: he will be so entitled only if the buyer rejects the appropriation and if the seller is then able to substitute one relating to existing goods within the time allowed by the contract.[26] The position as stated above may to some extent depend on the special rule that in a c.i.f. contract the validity of a notice of appropriation "depends upon form and timing and not upon factual accuracy".[27] But in the situation with which we are concerned it is not necessary to invoke this special rule since the appropriation, when made, *was* factually accurate: the goods did exist at the time of appropriation and were destroyed later. Hence the original appropriation is valid quite apart from any special provisions in the contract as to notice of appropriation, or special rules relating to c.i.f. contracts; and this validity is not affected by the subsequent destruction of the goods.

For the purpose of determining whether the seller is under any obligation to make a fresh appropriation it is again necessary to distinguish (in accordance with the preceding discussion) between cases in which the buyer is not, and those in which he is, bound to accept a fresh appropriation. If the contract on its true construction meant that, once an original appropriation had been made, the buyer's duty to accept and pay existed *only* in relation to the goods so appropriated, then it would normally be pointless to require the seller to make a further tender which the buyer was free to reject. It would follow that the contract would be discharged even though the case fell outside s.7 of the Sale of Goods Act 1979; but such a conclusion would not be unduly surprising since that section does not exhaustively specify the circumstances in which the destruction of goods sold leads to the discharge of the contract of sale, as opposed to being governed by the rules as to risk. This appears from the cases to be discussed below,[28] of the sale of goods to be taken from a specified bulk or source, and of the sale of alternatives.[29] But the question whether the seller is liable for failing to make a fresh appropriation will arise only if the buyer has asked for such an appropriation; and a buyer who had behaved in this way would, it is submitted, be taken to have waived any right, which he might otherwise have had, to reject the second appropriation. In these circumstances there would be no absurdity or hardship to the seller in requiring him to make the second appropriation and so to give effect to the normal meaning of the statement that risk remains with the seller, *i.e.* that he is not discharged from his obligations. The contract being originally one for the sale of unascertained goods, its performance has not in any literal sense become impossible. One could argue that such impossibility had arisen because the first appropriation had turned the contract into one to deliver *exclusively* the goods to which

---

[26] As in *The Vladimir Ilich*; see previous note.
[27] *The Vladimir Ilich*, above, n.25, at 329; *PT Putrabi Adyamulia v Société des Epices (The Intan 6 V 360A SN)* [2003] 2 Lloyd's Rep. 700 at [9].
[28] See below, paras 4–048 to 4–056.
[29] See below, para.3–026.

that appropriation referred[30]; but in the case put the buyer would be precluded from relying on that interpretation of the contract.

If, on the other hand, the contract did not (as a matter of construction) mean that the buyer's obligation to accept and pay was to arise *only* in respect of the goods originally appropriated, then there would be no injustice or absurdity in requiring the seller to make a fresh appropriation in the event of the destruction of the goods originally appropriated before the risk had passed to the buyer; and it is submitted that he should be required to make such an appropriation. Such a conclusion would merely give effect to the normal meaning of the statement that the risk was still on the seller.

(iv) Goods forming an undifferentiated part of a larger bulk

A contract for the sale of a specified quantity of goods forming an   **3–025**
undifferentiated part of an identified bulk (*e.g.* of "200 out of the 1,000 tons of hay in my barn") is not one for the sale of "specific" goods.[31] The destruction even of the whole of the bulk cannot therefore avoid the contract under s.7 of the Sale of Goods Act 1979, nor does any other rule laid down in the Act apply to such a case. But there seems to be no doubt that the contract would be discharged by the destruction of the whole bulk, and the best view is that this result follows from the doctrine of discharge, which is one of the rules of common law stated to apply to contracts for the sale of goods unless inconsistent with the 1979 Act.[32] This view is supported by the cases (to be more fully discussed in Ch.4[33]) in which the contract is for the sale of goods which are not yet in existence, or which are to be acquired by the seller, and in which the contract provides that they are to be taken from a specified source which later fails, *e.g.* where the contract is for the sale of part of a crop to be grown on designated land. If the crop wholly fails without any default on the part of the seller, the contract will be discharged[34] even though the goods are clearly not specific, so that s.7 cannot apply[35]; and one explanation for this result is that discharge takes place under the general common law doctrine. That doctrine should, *a fortiori*, apply where the contract is for the sale of a specified quantity forming part of an identified bulk already in existence and owned by the seller at the time of contracting; and it is this situation with which we are here concerned.[36]

---

[30] The notice of appropriation in *The Vladimir Ilich*, above, n.25, seems to have been treated as having this effect.

[31] *cf. Re Wait* [1927] 1 Ch. 606. Sale of Goods Act 1979, s.20A(1) regards the goods sold as "unascertained" in such a case.

[32] Sale of Goods Act 1979, s.62(2).

[33] See below, paras 4–048 to 4–052.

[34] *cf. Howell v Coupland* (1876) 1 Q.B.D. 258 (where the sale was of *part* of an expected crop).

[35] Contrast *Kursell v Timber Operators & Contractors Ltd* [1927] 1 K.B. 298 (discussed above, para.3–019) where the *whole* of a growing crop was sold.

[36] Hence the situation could not fall under Sale of Goods Act 1979, s.5(2), which deals with "future goods" and has been regarded as an alternative basis for

A contract for the sale of goods forming an undifferentiated part of an identified bulk can be a contract for the sale of specific goods if the part sold is expressed as a fraction or percentage of the whole[37] (*e.g.* "half the hay in my barn"). Section 7 could apply to such a case so that the destruction of the whole bulk could avoid the contract under that section. The exact effect of partial destruction of the bulk on such a contract awaits judicial determination. It would seem that if one-half or less than one-half of the bulk was destroyed, the contract would be enforceable by either party; if more than one-half were destroyed, the outcome would depend on the rules relating to partial failure of a source of supply, discussed in Ch.5.[38]

(v) Alternatives

3–026   The question of the impact of the doctrine of frustration on alternative obligations depends on a number of distinctions to be more fully discussed in Ch.10. At this stage it is necessary only to make the point that there are circumstances in which a contract which originally imposed such an obligation may, at a later stage, by reason of one party's election communicated to the other, become one to perform one of those alternatives, but not the other. For example, a contract may be made for the sale of "my Rolls or my Bentley" on the terms that the seller is to have the right to choose which car is to be delivered. If the seller communicates his intention to deliver the Rolls, and that car is subsequently destroyed before the risk has passed to the buyer, then it seems that the contract is discharged even though the Bentley is still available.[39] Yet the contract is not one for the sale of "specific goods"[40]: certainly it could not be said that it was so for the purpose of the rule by which property in specific goods can pass as soon as the contract is made.[41] The position appears to be the same for the purpose of s.7: at the time of the contract, neither car can be identified as the eventual subject-matter of the contract. Here again frustration takes place under the general common law doctrine which applies to contracts for the sale of goods unless inconsistent with the 1979 Act.[42] It should be added that if, in the case put, the Rolls had been destroyed *before* the seller had made his election, he would have had to deliver the Bentley. But if the contract had provided for delivery of the Rolls, with an option given to the seller to substitute the Bentley, then destruction of the Rolls before the seller had exercised the option (and before risk had passed) would discharge the contract: such a contract

---

cases such as *Howell v Coupland*, above, n.34; see *Re Wait* [1927] 1 Ch. 606 at 631; *HR & S Sainsbury Ltd v Street* [1927] 1 W.L.R. 834 at 837.

[37] Sale of Goods Acts 1979, s.61(1), definition of "specific goods", above, para.3–017.

[38] See below, paras 5–010 *et seq.*

[39] *Atlantic Lines & Navigation Co Inc v Didymi Corp & Leon Corp (The Didymi and the Leon)* [1984] 1 Lloyd's Rep. 583 at 585.

[40] See above, para.3–017, at n.52.

[41] Sale of Goods Act 1979, s.18, r.1.

[42] *ibid.* s.62(2).

would impose an obligation to deliver the Rolls unless the seller exercised the option granted to him.[43] The contract would appear to be one for the sale of specific goods so that discharge would occur under s.7.

(2) Sale of land

Land is commonly bought for the sake of the structures on it and questions as to the passing of risk can arise when those structures are damaged or destroyed between the making of the contract and the time fixed for its completion. In theory, such questions can also arise where the land itself is "destroyed", *e.g.* by being washed away by a river,[44] or as a result of an earthquake or some similar natural catastrophe; but (no doubt because of the relatively stable geological conditions which normally prevail in England) the English decisions provide no actual example of a contract affected by such natural disasters, though the possibility is occasionally mentioned in dicta.[45]

3–027

The present English rule is that risk passes to a buyer of land on the conclusion of the contract. After tracing the development of this rule, we shall attempt to evaluate it and to consider various judicial and legislative departures from it, as well as further mitigations of it by insurance and by express contractual provisions.

(a) *Development of the rule that risk passes on contract*

The early authorities provide no clear answer to the question when risk passes under a contract for the sale of land. According to the report in Vernon of *Cass v Rudele*[46] specific performance was in that case ordered of a contract for the sale of four houses in Jamaica, in spite of the destruction of the houses before completion. But later dicta cast doubt on the accuracy of the report and indicate that the destruction did not take place until after the vendor had made "a title ... by conveyance executed".[47] Moreover, in 1724 Sir Joseph Jekyll M.R. had taken a different view from that supported by Vernon's report of *Cass v Rudele*. In *Stent v Bailis* he had said that: "If I should buy a house, and before such time as by the articles I am to pay for the same, the house be burnt down by casualty of fire, I shall not in equity be bound to pay for the house."[48] This conclusion was based on the principle that it was "against natural justice that anyone should pay

3–028

---

[43] *cf. Reardon Smith Lines Ltd v Ministry of Agriculture, Fisheries and Food* [1963] A.C. 691, discussed below, para.10–006.

[44] See *Amundson v Severson*, 170 N.W. 633 (1919) (where a large part of the land had been "washed away and eroded by the Missouri River", but the vendor's claim failed as he had been unable to show good title).

[45] *e.g. Cricklewood Property and Investment Trust Ltd v Leighton's Investment Trust Ltd* [1945] A.C. 221 at 229 ("if ... some vast convulsion of nature swallowed up the property altogether, or buried it in the depths of the sea"); *cf. National Carriers Ltd v Panalpina (Northern) Ltd* [1981] A.C. 675 at 700.

[46] (1692) 2 Vern. 280.

[47] See *Mortimer v Capper* (1782) 1 Bro. C.C. 156 at 158 citing *Poye v Roots* (unreported); *White v Nutt* (1702) 1 P. Wms. 62, n.2.

[48] (1724) 2 P. Wms. 217 at 219.

for a bargain which he cannot have".[49] Similar reasoning is found in those later eighteenth-century equity cases (discussed in Ch.2) which had cast some doubt on the scope of the doctrine of absolute contracts, as stated in *Paradine v Jane*.[50] It was, for example, suggested that, in certain circumstances, a tenant might in equity be able to rely on the destruction of the premises by fire as a defence to a claim for rent; and the reason for this suggestion was that "a man should not pay rent for what he cannot enjoy".[51] But this view was rejected in later equity cases,[52] and it may be that it was these later cases which Lord Eldon had in mind when in *Paine v Meller*[53] he described Sir Joseph Jekyll's dictum (quoted above) as unsupported by authority and as having been "overruled by subsequent cases".[54]

Further dicta of Lord Eldon's in *Paine v Meller*[55] appear to be the basis of the generally accepted[56] modern view that the risk of loss passes to the purchaser of land at the time of the conclusion of the contract. Lord Eldon there rejected the purchaser's argument that he was excused on account either of the destruction by fire of the houses which were the subject-matter of the sale, or of the fact that the vendor had allowed his insurance on them to lapse. He added that destruction of the houses might actually make the property *more* desirable for the purchaser on the ground that it would facilitate what would now be called redevelopment "and it would be impossible to say to the purchaser, willing to take the land without the house, because much more valuable on account of this project, that he shall not have it".[57]

3–029   To a modern reader, this last remark would appear to indicate that Lord Eldon was thinking of what would now be called the doctrine of frustration, rather than of the rules as to risk. The doctrine of frustration would, indeed, lead to the automatic discharge of both parties,[58] but no such consequence would follow from the rules as to risk.[59] If, for example, a valuable antique vase were sold and then (without fault of either party) smashed into several hundred fragments after the risk had passed to the buyer, it might well be that the buyer would wish to claim delivery with a

---

[49] *ibid.* The same argument is used in *Skelly Oil Co v Ashmore*, 365 S.W. 2d 582 (1963): "It is not equitable to make a vendee pay a vendor for something the vendor cannot give him."

[50] See above, para.2–007.

[51] *Brown v Quilter* (1764) Amb. 619 at 621.

[52] See above, para.2–007.

[53] (1801) 6 Ves. 349.

[54] *ibid.* at 352.

[55] Above, n.53.

[56] Some doubts on the point are referred to in the Law Commission's Working Paper No.109, Pt I, which nevertheless accepts "the prevailing rule" that risk passes to the purchaser on the conclusion of the contract: see para.1.1 and *cf.* para.1.41. That view is also accepted by the Law Commission's subsequent Report: Law Com. No. 191, para.2.2.

[57] (1801) 6 Ves. 349 at 352.

[58] See below, para.15–002.

[59] See above, para.3–007.

view to restoring the vase,[60] and there seems to be no reason why his claim should not be upheld. Of course if the buyer did not want the fragments and was merely seeking to avoid liability for the price, he might argue either that the risk had not passed or that the contract had been frustrated: either argument would, if accepted, lead to his being held not liable. It is when the buyer seeks to enforce the contract (as in Lord Eldon's last-quoted example) that the distinction between them is significant.

Although Lord Eldon's example seems to be cast in terms of what a modern reader would regard as the doctrine of frustration, the actual judgment in *Paine v Meller* is nevertheless generally regarded as the origin of the English rule that risk under a contract for the sale of an interest in land passes on contract. The judgment does not, indeed, use the word "risk", but it does rely on an argument frequently found in connection with risk. Lord Eldon justifies his view that the purchaser is not excused by saying: "As to the effect of the accident itself, no solid objection can be founded on that simply; for if the party by the contract has become in equity owner of the premises they are his to all intents and purposes."[61] Implicit in this reasoning is the link (already discussed in relation to sale of goods[62]) between risk and property: the purchaser bears the risk from the conclusion of the contract, because the contract makes him owner from that time. An explicit reference to risk (though in Latin) is made 14 years later in *Harford v Purrier*,[63] where land deteriorated in consequence of being left untenanted between contract and completion, and this was held to be no ground for refusing specific performance to the vendor. Sir Thomas Plumer V.C. refers to *Paine v Meller* in support of the proposition that gains and losses "fall upon the person to whom the Court holds the Estate to belong",[64] having previously stated that the estate was considered to be the purchaser's "from the time of the contract".[65] He adds that the rule is the same in the civil law, citing Justinian's *Institutes*[66] for the proposition that "*periculum rei statim ad emptorem pertinet*". Actually the rationale of this civil law rule cannot be the same as that stated in *Paine v Meller* since in Roman law property did not pass on contract[67]; but the two sets of rules are analogous in that under both, risk could be transferred when the contract was made, or at least, in Roman law, when the contract became "*perfecta*".[68]

---

[60] Example based on Williams, *The Breaking and Remaking of the Portland Vase* (B.M.P., 1989).

[61] (1801) 6 Ves. Jun. 349 at 352. The legislative abolition (in Barbados) of the doctrine of equitable conversion for purposes of devolution only has been held not to affect the present point: see *E Johnson & Co (Barbados) Ltd v NSR Ltd* [1997] A.C. 400 at 407.

[62] Sale of Goods Act 1979, s.20(1); above, para.3–009.

[63] (1815) 1 Madd. 532.

[64] *ibid.* at 539.

[65] *ibid.*

[66] III. 24.3.

[67] C. 2, 3, 20.

[68] Zulueta, *The Roman Law of Sale*, p.31.

3–030   The rule that risk in a contract for the sale of land passes on contract is recognised in other nineteenth-century cases,[69] in one of which the rule is finally expressed in terms of "risk" by Sir George Jessell M.R.: "If anything happens to the estate between the time of sale and the time of completion of the purchase, it is at the risk of the purchaser."[70] Judicial references to "risk" in the present context are also common in the United States,[71] where there are many different solutions to the problem of risk in contracts for the sale of land.[72]

3–031   In England what may be called the rule in *Paine v Meller* (*i.e.* that risk passes on contract) has come to be generally, if in some quarters reluctantly,[73] regarded as settled law. The only at first sight discordant case is *Bacon v Simpson*[74] where the seller had contracted to transfer to the defendant a leasehold house together with certain articles of furniture; and the house and a "great part" of the furniture were destroyed before the time fixed for completion. The case differs from those discussed above in that the seller sued, not in equity for specific performance, but for damages at common law; and one plea was that the seller was not ready and willing to convey the furniture. In support of this plea, counsel for the defendant argued, *inter alia*, that the contract was "entire".[75] It seems to have been this argument (rather than the further argument that *the house*, as well as the furniture, remained the seller's property and at her risk) which was accepted by the court in rejecting the seller's claim. Thus Lord Abinger C.B. said that "*The goods* being in great measure destroyed by fire put it out of her [*i.e.* the seller's] power to [deliver them]".[76] The judgments of Parke and Alderson BB. are to the same effect; only Gurney B. seems to base his judgment in part on the destruction of the house. All the judgments seem to assume that the goods were still at the seller's risk when they were destroyed, an assumption which can perhaps be justified on the ground that property had not passed either because the goods were not in a deliverable state[77] or because the price was yet to be fixed. If this assumption is accepted, and if the contract was indeed "entire", the case can be read as not taking any position on the question which party bore the risk of the destruction of the house.[78] In modern conditions it is unlikely that a transaction under which the purchaser of a house agreed also to buy furniture in the house at a valuation would be regarded as

---

[69] *e.g. Robertson v Skelton* (1849) 12 Beav. 260; *Rayner v Preston* (1881) 18 Ch.D. 1 at 7.

[70] *Lysaght v Edwards* (1876) 2 Ch.D. 499 at 507.

[71] *e.g. Skelly Oil Co v Ashmore*, 365 S.W. 2d 582 (1963); Uniform Vendor and Purchaser Risk Act; Uniform Land Transactions Act, s.2–406 (not yet adopted); below, paras 3–043 *et seq.*

[72] See below, paras 3–039 to 3–043.

[73] See above, para.3–028, n.56.

[74] (1837) 3 M. & W. 78.

[75] *ibid.* at 83.

[76] *ibid.* at 86 (italics supplied).

[77] *ibid.* at 83.

[78] Counsel's reference to the already discredited dictum in *Stent v Bailis* (see above nn.48 and 54) drew no comment from the court.

giving rise to an "entire contract". More probably, such a transaction would, in accordance with the intention of the parties, be regarded as giving rise to two separate (though related) contracts, one for the sale of the house and the other for the sale of the furniture. The risk of destruction of the house would therefore pass in accordance with the rule in *Paine v Meller*, while the risk of destruction of the goods would pass in accordance with the rules discussed earlier in this chapter.

(b) *Evaluation of the rule*

Criticism of the rule[79] that risk passes to a purchaser of land on contract is   3–032
of two kinds. The first questions the legal assumptions on which the rule is based, *i.e.* that the contract is specifically enforceable notwithstanding the destruction of structures on the land, and that such destruction therefore cannot be a ground of frustration. The second is based on the practical consequences of the rule.

(i) Specific enforceability

Discussion of the development of the rule indicates that at least one basis   3–033
of it was that, by virtue of the contract, the purchaser had become in equity owner of the land. Hence the rule can be regarded as an application of the principle (which also generally applies in the case of sale of goods[80]) that the risk of loss should be borne by the owner. But it is said that the assumption on which this alleged justification of the rule is based is open to question. The reason why equitable ownership is normally transferred on contract is that a contract for the sale of land is specifically enforceable,[81] and that specific performance of such a contract is normally ordered as a matter of course.[82] Nevertheless specific performance remains a discretionary remedy. If, for some reason, specific performance is refused, then (it is said) the purchaser does not become equitable owner of the land; and if that is the position, then (so the argument continues) the purchaser should not bear the risk. Moreover, one reason why an order of specific performance may be refused is that the order would cause unacceptable hardship to the defendant[83]; and (it is said) the buyer would suffer such hardship in having to pay the full price after destruction of the buildings for the sake of which he had bought the land. In such a case, therefore, equitable ownership would not be transferred by the contract.[84]

This line of argument is, however, not wholly compelling. The linkage of risk with equitable ownership does indeed have support in the authorities considered earlier in this chapter as a basis of the rule that risk passes to the purchaser on contract. But, as the sale of goods cases

---

[79] See generally Stone, 13 Col.L.Rev. 369 (1913); Law Commission Working Paper No.109 (1988) and the consequent Report (Law Com.191, 1990).

[80] Sale of Goods Act 1979, s.20(1), above, para.3–009; and see n.89, below.

[81] *cf. Walsh v Lonsdale* (1882) 21 Ch.D. 9; *Jerome v Kelly* [2004] UKHL 25; [2004] 2 All E.R. 835, at [31], [32].

[82] See Fry, *Specific Performance* (6th ed.), para.62.

[83] *e.g. Patel v Ali* [1984] Ch. 283; Treitel, *The Law of Contract* (11th ed.), pp.1026–1027.

[84] Stone, 13 Col.L.Rev. 369, 386 (1913).

indicate, the linkage between risk and property is only a general principle. We saw in discussing those cases that risk and property are not uncommonly separated[85] and there seems to be no reason why such separation should not occur in contracts for the sale of land. To make the passing of risk in such cases *necessarily* dependent on the specific enforceability of the particular contract in each individual case would lead to an unacceptable degree of uncertainty, particularly in view of the discretionary nature of the remedy of specific performance. It would become impossible to tell which party bore the risk of accidental damage or destruction until it had been judicially determined whether any special factors were present to displace the normal rule that a contract for the sale of land was specifically enforceable. It is submitted that the possible exercise of the court's discretion to refuse specific performance should be disregarded in determining when the risk has passed. If risk is to be linked to specific enforceability, it is submitted that the test should be whether the court has jurisdiction to order specific performance, not whether in its discretion it decides to exercise that jurisdiction.[86] There is no doubt that, in the case of contracts for the sale of land, the court does have such jurisdiction.

(ii) Frustration

3–034   A second criticism of the rule that risk passes on contract is that a contract for the sale of land can be frustrated, and that the destruction of buildings on the land should be a ground of frustration, at least if it occurs when neither equitable nor legal ownership has passed to the buyer. Again it is submitted that this criticism is less than compelling. Although it seems to be accepted that the doctrine of frustration can apply to contracts for the sale of land,[87] it does not follow that the destruction of buildings on the land between contract and completion can be a ground of frustration. The whole point of the relationship between risk and frustration is that, if the risk has passed, destruction of the subject-matter can no longer be a ground of frustration.[88] To revert again to a sale of goods analogy, if specific goods were destroyed *after* the risk in them had passed to the buyer, the contract would neither be avoided under Sale of Goods Act 1979 nor discharged under the common law doctrine of frustration: the buyer would have to pay the price even though the goods were destroyed before delivery.[89] Indeed, this is the very point made by Blackburn J. in the

---

[85] See above, paras 3–009, 3–010.

[86] *cf.* the similar test adopted in *Wroth v Tyler* [1974] Ch. 30 for the purpose of determining whether the court has jurisdiction to award damages "in substitution for specific performance" under the power now conferred by Supreme Court Act 1981, s.50.

[87] *Amalgamated Investment and Property Co Ltd v John Walker & Co Ltd* [1977] 1 W.L.R. 164 (where the plea of frustration failed for the reason stated at below, para.7–030).

[88] See above, para.3–007.

[89] It is assumed in the above example that the buyer did not deal as consumer; if he did so deal, the goods would remain at the seller's risk until delivery to the consumer by virtue of Sale of Goods Act 1979, s.20(4), above, para.3–010.

sale of goods example which he gives in *Taylor v Caldwell*.[90] One cannot rely on the general frustratability of contracts for the sale of land as an argument against the passing of risk on contract since the whole point of saying that risk has passed is that the contract *cannot* subsequently be frustrated by one particular type of event, namely the destruction of the subject-matter or part of it. That is why the rule in *Paine v Meller* is stated sometimes in the form that risk passes to the purchaser on contract,[91] and sometimes in the form that a contract for the sale of land cannot be frustrated by destruction of the buildings on it.[92] So far as the purchaser's liability is concerned, the two statements mean the same thing. To say that the doctrine of frustration can apply to contracts for the sale of land does not (any more than the corresponding statement in relation to contracts for the sale of goods) tell us anything about *when* the risk of loss passes from seller to buyer.

(iii) Practical consequences

Criticism of the theoretical bases of the rule in *Paine v Meller*[93] does not necessarily lead to the conclusion that the rule should be rejected; nor can such criticism perform the constructive role of suggesting what might be put in place of the rule if it were to be rejected. In this connection, it is interesting to note that the theoretical basis of the general rule that under a contract for the sale of *goods* risk passes with property has given rise to little debate in England.[94] The merit (or lack of merit) of that rule is judged by practical considerations and it is no doubt such considerations which account for the recent change in the law by which the general rule no longer applies where the buyer of goods deals as consumer and by which the goods in such cases remain at the seller's risk until they are delivered to the consumer.[95] Such practical considerations should likewise be used to determine when it would be appropriate for risk to pass under contracts for the sale of land. **3–035**

At first sight, the English rules as to risk in sale of goods and sale of land seem closely to resemble each other. Under the general sale of goods rule, risk passes (unless otherwise agreed) with property[96]; and property in goods which are specific (as land which is the subject-matter of a sale always is) passes as soon as the contract is made, unless a different intention appears.[97] Hence risk under a contract for the sale of specific goods can pass (as it does under a contract for the sale of land) as soon as the contract is made. In fact, however, the apparent resemblance between

---

[90] (1863) 3 B. & S. 826 at 837; above, para.2–016.

[91] See above, para.3–030, at n.70.

[92] Treitel, *The Law of Contract* (11th ed.), p.895 (also referring to passing of risk).

[93] (1806) 6 Ves. 349, above, para.3–027.

[94] For criticism of the rule in the United States, on the practical ground that it gave rise to uncertainty, see White & Summers, *Uniform Commercial Code* (4th ed.), Vol.I, p.248; Llewellyn, 15 N.Y.U.L. Rev. 159 at 182–191.

[95] Sale of Goods Act 1979, s.20(4), as inserted by Sale of Goods to Consumers Regulations 2002, SI 2002/3045, reg.4, above, para.3–010.

[96] Sale of Goods Act 1979, s.20(1).

[97] *ibid*. s.18, r.1.

the two sets of rules is deceptive, mainly because the rule that property in specific goods passes as soon as the contract is made is quite commonly excluded by evidence of contrary intention.[98] Perhaps for this reason, the practical operation of the English sale of goods rule has not had to bear the same weight of criticism as that which has been directed at the sale of land rule; though the recent change in the sale of goods rule in cases of sales to consumers[99] no doubt reflects the view that hardship could be caused to consumers if risk passed to them before the goods were delivered to them and so before they could take steps to protect the goods or were likely to be covered by insurance in respect of them. Similar practical considerations may account for the fact that, in the United States and under the Vienna Convention on Contracts for the International Sale of Goods, the tendency is to link the passing of risk with the transfer of possession.[1]

There may also be another reason why the general English sale of goods rule as to risk has attracted less criticism than the sale of land rule. No doubt in both types of contract the rule as to risk can be excluded by inferences drawn from the circumstances and from the nature of the transaction. Thus in overseas sales of goods, risk and property commonly pass at different times. Normally this leads to the consequence that risk passes before property: thus it is common for risk to pass on or as from shipment[2] and property to pass only on payment against shipping documents.[3] But it is also possible for the converse situation to arise in such contracts, *i.e.* for property to pass before risk. This would, for example, be the position where goods had been shipped in pursuance of an f.o.b. contract, but the seller had not given the buyer a notice enabling the buyer to insure the goods during their sea transit.[4] If those goods were destroyed during that transit, it seems that the contract could be discharged under s.7 of the Sale of Goods Act 1979 notwithstanding the passing of property. From a commercial point of view, this seems to be a sensible result; and it can be argued that the transfer of proprietary interests in land should similarly not of itself draw with it consequences as to risk. The question of risk should depend on consideration of commercial convenience rather than on the legal theory that a contract for the sale of land operates to transfer equitable title.

3–036   From a practical point of view the rule that risk passes to the purchaser of land as soon as the contract is made is likely to be inconvenient for two related reasons. First, there is always an appreciable[5] (and sometimes a

---

[98] *RV Ward Ltd v Bignall* [1967] 1 Q.B. 534 at 545.

[99] Above, at n.95.

[1] UCC, s.2–509(3); Vienna Convention, Art.69(1); above, para.3–010.

[2] See above, para.3–009.

[3] *ibid.*

[4] Sale of Goods Act 1979, s.32(3); *Benjamin's Sale of Goods* (6th ed.), paras 18–217 to 18–220. S.32(3) does not apply where the buyer deals as consumer: see s.32(4), as inserted by Sale and Supply of Goods to Consumers Regulations 2002, SI 2002/3045, reg.4; but in the case of an f.o.b. contract the buyer is unlikely so to deal.

[5] *e.g.* of four weeks.

long[6]) interval between contract and completion. Secondly during that interval it is generally the vendor, not the purchaser, who remains in possession of the property, so that the purchaser is in fact unable to protect the property against loss or damage: this is the position in the normal case in which the purchase price is payable in full in exchange for possession, and the purchase-money is paid either out of the purchaser's own resources or with the aid of a mortgage provided by a building society or a bank. An alternative (if now rare) possibility is for finance in effect to be provided by the vendor under a contract allowing the purchase price to be paid in instalments, possession being given at once (or on payment of the first instalment) but title remaining in the vendor until all the instalments have been paid if full. In such cases the interval between contract and completion is likely to be a considerable one, but for most of that interval the purchaser will be in possession and so be the party best able to protect the property against loss or damage. Hence the present criticism of the rule in *Paine v Meller* would not be apposite to cases of this kind.

Criticism can also be levelled at the rule in *Paine v Meller* in so far as that rule is stated in the form that the destruction after contract of buildings on the land sold is not a ground of frustration. One possible justification of this position is that it exemplifies the underlying principle on which the doctrine of frustration is based: namely that a contract should be discharged only when supervening events make the performance which remains possible fundamentally different from that originally bargained for.[7] From this point of view, the argument is that the purchaser's principal object in entering into the contract is to acquire title to the land. This object is said not to be defeated by the destruction of the buildings on the land; indeed, in equity it is achieved as soon as the contract is made, and once the main object of a contract has been achieved that contract cannot be frustrated by subsequent events. In the case of the ordinary purchase of a dwelling house, this line of argument is open to the obvious objection that it takes a technical or artificial approach to the question: what was the purchaser's principal purpose in entering into the contract? That purpose is, in a practical sense, more plausibly described as the acquisition of a residence than as the acquisition of an equitable (or even of a legal) interest in the land[8]; and, as it can fairly be said to be a purpose contemplated by both parties, its failure would (if risk had not passed) *prima facie* frustrate the contract.

The merit of the rule in *Paine v Meller* is that it promotes certainty. At first sight, it might seem that certainty would equally be promoted if a rule   **3–037**

---

[6] In *Patel v Ali* [1984] Ch. 283, four years had passed between contract and the purchaser's claim for specific performance. No question of damage to the property arose, but the claim failed for reasons discussed below, para.6–042.

[7] See below, para.16–006.

[8] An argument similar to that stated in the text above has been accepted in the case of frustration of leases: see *National Carriers Ltd v Panalpina (Northern) Ltd* [1981] A.C. 675. For the present purpose leases are analogous to sales, though in other respects the analogy is imperfect: see below, para.3–049.

were adopted under which risk passed at some other fixed or readily ascertainable time, *e.g.* on completion or at the time fixed for completion or on transfer of possession. But if risk passed at some such time after the time of contracting, then between those two points the doctrine of frustration could apply, just as it can apply to contracts for the sale of goods where the goods are "specific" and "perish" before the risk has passed to the buyer.[9] Land which is the subject-matter of a contract for the sale of land is in practice always "specific", but it scarcely ever[10] literally "perishes". The application of the doctrine of frustration to such contracts would therefore depend on whether the damage (usually to structures on the land) was sufficiently serious to bring the doctrine of discharge into operation. This is, indeed, the position reached under many of the departures (in other jurisdictions[11]) from the rule in *Paine v Meller*. The uncertainty which results from such departures makes it hard to tell which party will have to bear the loss resulting from damage or destruction occurring after contract, and hence which party will have to insure against that loss. Such uncertainty may be mitigated by legislative or contractual provisions designed to exclude the doctrine of frustration in the event of damage to or destruction of buildings on the land. But the vague or open-textured nature of such provisions[12] leads to their falling far short of achieving a significant degree of certainty or predictability. They are also open to the objection that, while they may be more just (than the present English rule) to the purchaser, they are likely to cause hardship to the vendor. When a dwelling-house is sold, the vendor will commonly enter into a second contract to buy another dwelling, in the expectation of receiving the proceeds of the sale of the house sold under the original contract. His liability under that second contract is unlikely to be affected by discharge of the first (by reason of damage to the subject-matter of the first contract); and his liability to forfeiture of his deposit and in damages under the second contract will lead to losses which are unlikely to be covered by insurance.

(c) *Departures and mitigations*

3–038   Attempts to deal with the defects, or alleged defects, of the rule that risk in sale of land passes on contract have taken a variety of forms. In some jurisdictions, there have been common law departures from the rule; in others the rule has been modified by legislation or such modification has been proposed. Its effects have also been mitigated by insurance and by contractual provisions excluding or modifying the rule.

(i) Common law departures

3–039   In the United States, the cases support a variety of solutions. Some States follow the rule in *Paine v Meller*; others leave the risk with the seller till transfer of legal title; others provide for the passing of risk at the time

---

[9] Sale of Goods Act 1979, s.7, above, para.3–013.
[10] See above, para.3–027 at n.45.
[11] See below, paras 3–040, 3–043.
[12] See below, paras 3–043, 3–047.

agreed for the transfer of legal title; while yet others put the risk of loss on the party in possession when the loss occurs.[13] Of particular interest is the so-called "Massachusetts rule", which provides for an intermediate solution, distinguishing between two situations.

The first is that in which the value of the buildings "constitutes a large part of the total value of the estate, and the terms of the agreement show that they constituted an important part of the subject-matter of the contract".[14] In this type of case, "the contract is to be construed as subject to an implied condition that it shall no longer be binding if, before the time for the conveyance to be made, the buildings are destroyed by fire. . . . The contract is no longer binding upon either party"[15]; and the purchaser can recover back any payment which he has made. The solution, in cases of this kind, is (in English terms) that the contract is frustrated. As it is "no longer binding upon either party", what we have called the "price risk"[16] falls on the vendor and what we have called the "performance risk"[17] falls on the purchaser: that is, the vendor is not entitled to the price, while the purchaser is not entitled to damages. Under the rules as to passing of risk, both these risks would (as already noted) be united in one party. Under those rules, only one party would be discharged from some of his obligation; in the situation now under discussion, the "Massachusetts rule" wholly discharges both parties. It seems that risk can pass under the "Massachusetts rule" at the "time for the conveyance to be made", unless the delay in making conveyance is due to the vendor's default.

The second situation dealt with by the "Massachusetts rule" is that in which "the change in the value of the estate is not so great, or if it appears that the buildings did not constitute so material a part of the estate to be conveyed as to result in an annulling of the whole contract . . .".[18] It seems that this second situation requires further subdivision in that it covers (a) cases in which damage occurs to buildings which do constitute an "important part" of the subject-matter, but that damage is only slight; and (b) cases in which the buildings damaged or destroyed do not form an "important part" of the subject-matter at all (as might be the case where derelict buildings stood on land bought for the sake of minerals contained in it). In either of these cases, however, the result is the same: "specific performance may be decreed with compensation for any breach of the agreement, or relief may be given in damages."[19] The contract is not frustrated, since the difference between the performance promised by the vendor and that remaining possible is not sufficiently serious or fundamental. It is this test (which has nothing to do with the rules as to

3–040

---

[13] See 3 American Law of Property, para.11.30.

[14] *Hawkes v Kehoe*, 79 N.E. 766 at 767 (1907).

[15] *Hawkes v Kehoe*, n.14, above, cited with approval in *Libman v Levenson*, 128 N.E. 13 at 14 (1920), in turn cited with approval in *Skelly Oil Co v Ashmore*, 365 S.W. 2d. 582 at 589 (1963).

[16] See above, para.2–026.

[17] *ibid.*

[18] *Hawkes v Kehoe*, n.14, above.

[19] *ibid.*

passing of risk[20]) which distinguishes the cases within the second situation from those within the first. To put the point in another way, the "Massachusetts rule" approaches the problem *not* as one of risk but as one of frustration. In neither of the two cases falling within the second situation would it be correct to deduce, from the availability of specific performance to the vendor, that the risk has passed to the purchaser, for the solution envisages that the purchaser may have "compensation for any breach of the agreement or relief may be given in damages".[21] The exact circumstances in which such monetary adjustment is available are not entirely clear. In particular, it is not clear whether the vendor's liability in respect of damage or destruction is strict: in other words, whether it extends to cases in which the loss was the result of circumstances wholly beyond his control. The phrase "compensation for any breach of the agreement" may well be intended to exclude liability in cases of this kind.

(ii) Legislation

3–041 Legislative modification of the rule that risk passes to a purchaser of land on the conclusion of the contract is most widespread in the United States, where the Uniform Vendor and Purchaser Risk Act was originally approved by the Commissioners for Uniform State Laws in 1935 and has, at the time of writing, been adopted (sometimes with modifications[22]) in 13 of the States. Under the Act, the crucial stage for the purpose of passing risk is no longer the transfer of equitable title on contract. Instead the Act looks to the transfer of legal title or of possession; and for this purpose it makes use of what English lawyers would call the device of the implied term. It provides that a contract for the sale of realty, is, unless otherwise agreed, to be interpreted as giving rise to the following rights and duties.

First, the Act in s.1(a) deals with the situation in which destruction occurs "when neither the legal title nor the possession ... has been transferred". If at this stage "all or a material part" of the subject-matter is destroyed without the purchaser's fault, then: "the vendor cannot enforce the contract and the purchaser is entitled to recover any portion of the price that he has paid." Thus the risk is no longer on the purchaser from the time of contracting; but destruction of the subject-matter does not frustrate the contract (in the English sense): there is nothing in s.1(a) to prevent the purchaser from enforcing the contract, should he wish to do so, in spite of the destruction of a material part (*e.g.* where he has bought for redevelopment). Nor does s.1(a) take any position on the question of the liability of the vendor in respect of the destruction, where this is due to an event beyond his control. In New York, some light may be shed on this question by an addition to s.1(a): this provides that if "an immaterial part" of the subject-matter has been destroyed without fault of the purchaser the contract remains enforceable by both parties but there shall

---

[20] Risk seems to pass when "conveyance [is] to be made": see the passage quoted at n.15, above.

[21] *ibid.*

[22] As in New York: see below.

be an abatement of the purchase price "to the extent of the destruction". It seems that this abatement is available whether the claim to enforce the contract is made by the vendor or by the purchaser, and that there is nothing to prevent the purchaser from enforcing the contract even where the damage is serious. It seems that the purchaser's right to abatement should be available in the latter case since it is scarcely plausible that this right should be less extensive in cases of serious, than in cases of slight, damage. Under s.1(a), a purchaser cannot be compelled to perform in cases of serious damage, but if he wishes to do so because the damage has *increased* the value of the property (*e.g.* by facilitating redevelopment planned by the purchaser) there will be no room for an abatement of the price. There is the further possibility that serious damage may reduce the value of the property but still leave that value above the contract price, *e.g.* because the market had moved in the purchaser's favour. In such a case it is arguable that he should be able to enforce the contract subject to an abatement of the price in respect of the damage.

Secondly, the Act deals in s.1(b) with the situation in which destruction **3–042** occurs "when either the legal title or possession ... has been transferred". If after one of these events has occurred "all or any part" of the subject-matter is "destroyed without fault of the vendor", then "the purchaser is not relieved from his duty to pay the price nor is he entitled to recover any portion thereof that he has paid". Nothing is said in so many words about any possible liability of the vendor in respect of the destruction; but it seems that the words "without fault" are intended to exclude any such liability.

The Uniform Act differs from the "Massachusetts rule"[23] in two ways. First, it does not treat the problem of total destruction as one of frustration, but as one of risk. Secondly, it lays down a clear rule as to the time or times at which risk passes to the purchaser, *i.e.* on transfer of legal title or of possession. Before these events occur the risk of total destruction is on the vendor and the same is true of the risk of destruction "of a material part". There is some ambiguity in this phrase; for "material" in this context may mean either "significant" or "serious". It seems that the latter is the intended meaning (as in the Massachusetts rule): if so, the Act seems to divide the risk in the sense that the risk of serious damage is on the vendor while the risk of damage which is significant but not serious is not explicitly dealt with by the Act except under the New York amendment to s.1(a). There seems, however, to be nothing in the unamended text of s.1(a) to prevent courts in other States from allowing a monetary adjustment to a purchaser in respect of destruction of an "immaterial" part.

The position is somewhat clearer under the Uniform Land Transactions Act, which was approved by the Commissioners for Uniform State Laws in 1978 but has not at the time of writing been adopted in any State. Under that Act risk again passes on conveyance or transfer of possession (whichever occurs earlier).[24] If loss occurs before such passing of risk the

---

[23] See above, paras 3–039 and 3–040.
[24] s.2–406(c).

position depends on whether the loss does or does not amount to a "substantial failure of the real estate to conform to the contract".[25] If there is such a substantial failure, the purchaser can *either* cancel the contract and recover any part of the price which he has paid *or* enforce the contract with (at his choice) a reduction of the agreed price or with the benefit of the seller's insurance.[26] If there is no such substantial failure, the buyer must "accept the real estate, but is entitled (at his choice) to a reduction of the price or the benefit of the seller's insurance".[27] Any loss occurring after the passing of risk does not discharge the buyer from his obligations[28] (and presumably does not impose any obligations on the seller). The Act clearly treats risk and what English lawyers would call frustration as separate principles, for it devotes separate sections to the passing of risk of loss[29] and to excuse on the ground of delay or non-performance where "performance has been made impracticable by the occurrence of a contingency the risk of which the parties did not assume would be borne by the party whose performance has been made impracticable".[30] In this last sentence, "risk" does not seem to refer to "risk of loss" but is used in the more general sense in vogue in the United States as an explanation of the common law doctrine of discharge: reference to this usage has already been made.[31]

3-043   The above provisions of both Uniform Acts apply only to real property,[32] *i.e.* not to leaseholds; the 1978 Act expressly so provides. Both apply not only to physical loss or damage but also to "taking by eminent domain",[33] an expression roughly equivalent to the English "compulsory purchase". This topic is further discussed in Ch.4.[34]

Legislation in a number of other common law jurisdictions has also amended the rule that risk passes on contract. This is, for example, the effect of the Victorian Sale of Land (Amendment) Act 1982 which entitles the purchaser of a dwelling-house to rescind the contract if, before the purchaser becomes entitled to possession or to receipt of the rents and profits, the dwelling-house has been so destroyed or damaged so as to be unfit for occupation as such.[35] This rule cannot be excluded by the contract.[36] The New South Wales Conveyancing (Passing of Risk) Amendment Act 1986 provides that risk in respect of damage to land

---

[25] s.2–406(b)(1).

[26] *ibid.*

[27] s.2–406(b)(2).

[28] s.2–407(d).

[29] s.2–406.

[30] s.2–407, the section of the Act which corresponds to UCC, s.2–615, more fully discussed at paras 6–003 *et seq.*, below.

[31] See above, para.1–003.

[32] Uniform Vendor and Purchaser Risk Act, s.1 ("contract for the purchaser and sale of realty"); Uniform Land Transaction Act, s.2–406(a) ("This section does not apply to transfers of leaseholds").

[33] See ss.1 and 2–406(b) respectively.

[34] See below, paras 4–005 to 4–009.

[35] s.34(1).

[36] s.34(3).

shall not pass till either completion of the sale or the time stipulated by the contract (*i.e.* for the passing of risk), so long as this is after the time when the purchaser enters into, or is entitled to enter into "possession" (an expression defined to include occupation and receipt of income from the land).[37] The Act goes on to make elaborate provisions[38] giving the purchaser the right to rescind the contract where the property is "substantially damaged" and to price reduction in respect of damage, whether substantial or not[39]; and giving the court power to refuse specific performance against the vendor if the land has been substantially damaged and the court thinks that it would be unjust or inequitable to require him to complete the sale.[40] The parties can contract out of these provisions except where the subject-matter of the sale is a dwelling-house.[41] These Acts illustrate the desire of legislators to avoid hardship to purchasers, but seem to have little regard for the interests of vendors who, in reliance on the contract, have entered into a further contract to buy a new dwelling. They also give rise to uncertainty by virtue of the difficulty of applying such concepts of "unfitness" and "substantial" damage, and of the judicial discretions which the New South Wales Act confers.

(iii) Insurance

A further mitigation of the rules as to passing of risk under contracts for the sale of land appears to result from the practice of owners of buildings to insure them. In England the original common law position was, indeed, that this practice was of no avail to a purchaser to whom (in accordance with the general rule) the risk had passed on contract. In *Rayner v Preston*[42] a house was damaged by fire between contract and completion; and it was held that the vendor need not account to the purchaser for money which he had received in respect of the damage under his policy of insurance against damage caused by fire. The vendor was moreover later held liable[43] to repay to the insurers the money which he had received from them on the ground that the policy was a contract to indemnify him against loss and that he had suffered no loss[44] as he had received from the purchaser the full price for which he had agreed to sell the property before it was damaged.

American cases were divided on these points. Some States which followed the rule that risk passed on contract also followed the rule in

3–044

---

[37] Conveyancing Act 1919, s.66K (as inserted by the 1986 Act referred to in the text above).

[38] *ibid.* s.66L.

[39] *ibid.* s.66M.

[40] *ibid.* s.66N.

[41] *ibid.* s.66O.

[42] (1881) 18 Ch.D. 1.

[43] *Castellain v Preston* (1883) 11 Q.B.D. 380.

[44] Contrast *Lonsdale and Thompson Ltd v Black Arrow Group plc* [1993] Ch. 361, where the vendor had suffered loss as he had undertaken in a lease of the premises to insure them against fire and to lay out the insurance money in reinstating the premises.

Rayner v Preston,[45] but a majority of those States which followed the former rule rejected the latter, so that the vendor was held to be trustee of the insurance money for the purchaser.[46] Even in a State which rejected (or modified) the rule that risk passed on contract, it was nevertheless held that the purchaser was entitled to enforce the contract with an abatement of the purchase price equal to the amount of the insurance money received by the vendor. In *Skelly Oil Co v Ashmore*[47] this was held to be the case, even though the purchaser had bought the property for redevelopment, and intended to demolish the buildings which had been destroyed and in respect of which the insurance money had been paid. It cannot, however, be said that in the *Skelly Oil* case the destruction caused the purchaser no loss since the buildings were let to a tenant and the purchaser would (had the buildings not been destroyed) have been entitled to rent under the lease. At the very least, this benefit had to be balanced against the fact that the cost of redevelopment was reduced (and the process of development accelerated) by the fire which gave rise to the insurance claim.

3–045   In England s.47(1) of the Law of Property Act 1925 appears to have been intended to alter the common law position stated above. The subsection provides that "where after the date of any contract for sale or exchange of property[48] money becomes payable under any policy of insurance maintained by the vendor in respect of any damage to or destruction of property included in the contract, the money shall, on completion of the contract, be held or receivable by the vendor on behalf of the purchaser ...". The subsection can be excluded by contrary agreement.[49] The purchaser's rights under it are further subject to "the payment by the purchaser of the proportionate part of the premium from the date of the contract"[50]; and "to any requisite consent of the insurers".[51] The exact force of these last words is not entirely clear. They may refer to the general principle that a policy indemnifying the insured against loss is not assignable where it is a "personal" contract in which the insurer relies on the personal integrity or claims record of the insured.[52] The spirit of this rule could be violated if a purchaser of land were in possession between contract and completion, especially if the interval

---

[45] *Brownell v Board of Education of . . . Saratoga Springs,* 146 N.E. 630 (1925).

[46] *Brady v Welsh,* 204 N.W. 235 (1925), describing this as the majority view; *Dubin Paper Co v Insurance Co of North America,* 63 A. 2d 85 (1949).

[47] 365 S.W. 2d 582 (1963), where the court was divided by four to three on this issue.

[48] Defined by s.205(1)(xx) to include "any interest in ... personal property". Section 47(1) can accordingly apply to a contract for the sale of goods, though the phrase "on completion of the contract" is scarcely apposite in relation to such a contract. *cf.* below, para.15–025.

[49] s.47(2)(a).

[50] s.47(2)(c).

[51] s.47(2)(b).

[52] *e.g. Peters v GAFLAC* [1937] 4 All E.R. 628 (motor insurance); contrast *Siu Yin Kwan v Eastern Insurance Co Ltd* [1994] 2 A.C. 199 (employer's liability insurance).

between these two events were a considerable one,[53] and if loss or damage of a kind covered by the vendor's policy occurred while the purchaser was so in possession. But there would be no such violation of the spirit of the rule if (as is now more usual in the case of sales of residential property) it was the vendor who remained in possession during the interval between contract and completion. Perhaps it is for this reason that the subsection refers to "the *requisite* consent of the insurers": this wording seems to indicate that such consent is not invariably "*requisite*".

It is generally agreed that s.47(1) was intended to reverse the rule in *Rayner v Preston*[54] so as to allow the purchaser (who has to pay the price in spite of the destruction or damage) to obtain the benefit of the vendor's insurance; but it is disputed whether the subsection has succeeded in achieving that result.[55] One possible view is that the reasoning of *Rayner v Preston* continues to apply: since (so the argument runs) risk passes on contract, the vendor is entitled to be paid the price in spite of the destruction or damage; if he is so paid, he suffers no loss; and hence no money is "payable" to him under his policy of insurance.[56] But no English decision supports this view and it is submitted that s.47(1) should not be interpreted in a way which would wholly defeat its purpose, so long as there is an alternative interpretation which does not do violence to the words of the subsection. Such an alternative interpretation can be supported by arguing that the subsection clearly distinguishes between the two stages of contract and of completion, and refers to insurance money "payable" *between those two stages*. During the period between these two stages it is uncertain whether the vendor will suffer loss, since the contract may go off as a result of the default of either party, or it may be rescinded, *e.g.* for misrepresentation. Thus it is submitted that between contract and completion the money is "payable under a policy of insurance" and the former rules of common law[57] governing the destination of such money have been superseded by s.47(1). Those common law rules now apply only in cases which are excepted from s.47(1), *e.g.* in cases where the subsection is excluded by the terms of the contract of sale, or where the consent of the insurers is "requisite" but has not been obtained. It is now common to exclude s.47 by contract[58]; but

---

[53] As in the instalment sale cases described at above, para.3–036.

[54] See, *e.g.* Law Commission Working Paper No. 109, para.2.10. If the contract of sale contained a covenant by the vendor to insure, it has been said that the position would be the same "even apart from" s.47 of the Law of Property Act 1925: *Lonsdale & Thompson Ltd v Black Arrow Group plc* [1993] Ch. 361 at 370.

[55] For a legislative attempt to put the point beyond doubt, see Victorian Sale of Land Act 1962., s.35(2), as inserted by Sale of Land (Amendment) Act 1982.

[56] Law Commission Working Paper No.109, paras 2–16, 2–17; *cf.* Megarry and Wade, *The Law of Real Property* (6th ed.), para.12–057; Cheshire and Burn, *Modern Real Property* (16th ed.), p.132, n.14 likewise express reservations about the utility of s.47(1).

[57] At nn.42, 43, above.

[58] See below, para.3–047.

since the same common provision also leaves the risk with the vendor it has the effect of also excluding the rule in *Rayner v Preston*.[59]

3–046   Even if the purchaser is to some extent protected by the vendor's insurance against the passing of risk on contract, that protection may for various reasons be less than satisfactory. The vendor's insurance may be for less than the amount required to make good the loss or damage; the loss or damage caused by the particular event which has occurred may not be covered by the policy; and the insurer may be able to avoid liability under the policy on the ground of the vendor's misrepresentation or non-disclosure. For these reasons, purchasers are normally advised to take out their own insurance on exchange of contracts, and may indeed be required by their mortgagees to do so. On the other hand, vendors will normally wish to remain insured until completion, so as to cover the possibility that the contract may be rescinded by either party, thus in effect throwing the risk back on the vendor. It follows that during the period between contract and completion the premises are likely to be insured by both parties.[60] The cost of the transaction was thus increased to no good purpose and in a way that provided a windfall for insurers, who received two premiums while being liable once only for the amount for which the property was insured.

(iv) Contractual modification

3–047   The practical problems arising from the English common law rule that risk passes on contract are therefore not satisfactorily solved by the practice of vendors (or even of both parties) to insure and the Law Commission has proposed that the rule should be changed so that, unless otherwise agreed, the risk of physical damage to the property should pass to the purchaser "on completion of the contract rather than when the contract was made".[61] As already noted, this formulation is somewhat misleading since there can be no question of risk passing once the contract has been fully performed.[62] What is meant by the recommendation is that risk should not pass *before* completion[63]; and it follows that the effects of loss or destruction before that time would be governed by the law relating to the effects of failure to perform, which may (if the damage is sufficiently serious) lead to frustration. At the same time it was recognised that the result which would follow from the proposed legislative change of the common law rule as to passing of risk could also be achieved without legislation if it became common practice for parties by the express terms of their contract to exclude the common law rule that risk passes on contract. Such a practice appears to have arisen as a result of the now

---

[59] (1881) 18 Ch.D. 1: the rule is excluded because, risk being with the vendor, he will suffer loss if the buildings are destroyed between contract and completion.
[60] See Law Com. No.191, paras 2.17 to 2.19.
[61] *ibid.*, para.2.25.
[62] See above, para.3–008.
[63] *cf.* the formulation in the New South Wales legislation cited at n.37, above: "risk ... shall not pass ... until ... the completion of the sale".

common use of the Standard Conditions of Sale.[64] These expressly provide that "the seller retains the risk until completion".[65] They also specify certain legal consequences which follow if the physical state of the property makes it (before completion) unusable for its purpose: in such a case the buyer may rescind the contract,[66] and the seller may also rescind where the property has become unusable as a result of damage against which he could not reasonably have insured, or which he cannot legally make good (*e.g.* where the property has been destroyed and he cannot get planning permission to rebuild it).[67] These express provisions for the legal effect of the damage would also exclude the doctrine of frustration, which might (but for them) apply (on the analogy of Sale of Goods Act 1979, s.7) on the ground that specific property was "destroyed" without fault of either party before the risk had passed to the buyer. The Standard Conditions further provide that the vendor is to be under no obligation to the buyer to insure,[68] and that s.47 of the Law of Property Act 1925 is not to apply.[69] As these Standard Conditions are in common use and as they lead in substance to the change advocated by the Law Commission, no legislative change is for the present recommended, but the Commission has indicated that the position would require reconsideration if the practical operation of the Standard Conditions should fail to achieve its object of largely eliminating the objections raised by the Commission to the common law rule that risk passes on contract.[70]

(v) Sales of houses in course of construction

The preceding discussion is concerned with the effect of the destruction   3–048
of buildings on a contract for the sale of land with those buildings already on it at the time of contracting. They do not apply where a developer sells land with a house *to be built on it*. Such a contract contains two elements: a sale of the land and an undertaking to build the house on it. The latter element of the contract is governed, not by the rules as to risk which apply to contracts for the sale of land, but by the rules as to risk which govern building contracts.[71] It follows that destruction of the partly completed house will not frustrate the contract and that the builder must (unless the contract otherwise provides) do the work again at no extra charge. The practical result of this rule is exactly the opposite to that of the rule in *Paine v Meller*.[72] The point must again be made that the present rule, leaving the risk in cases of this kind with the developer, only means that the contract will not be frustrated *merely* by the destruction of the partly completed building. It does not exclude the possibility that the contract

---

[64] Law Com. No.191, para.3.2, reproducing Condition 5.1. The 2d edition (1992) of the Standard Conditions retains this provision: see [1992] New L.J. 1013.
[65] Condition 5.1.1.
[66] Condition 5.1.2(a).
[67] Condition 5.1.2.(b).
[68] Condition 5.1.3.
[69] Condition 5.1.4.
[70] Law Com. No.191, paras 3.11, 3.12.
[71] See below, paras 3–051 to 3–062.
[72] (1801) 6 Ves. 349.

may be frustrated on other grounds. Thus where a landslip not only destroyed a partly completed block of flats, but also delayed the construction of the block for two-and-a-half years, it was held that a contract for the sale of one of the flats had been frustrated *by the delay*; for in the interval market conditions had changed to such an extent as to make performance at the end of the delay radically different from that originally undertaken.[73]

(vi) Analogy of frustration of leases of land

3–049   In discussions of risk passing under a contract for the sale of land, reference is sometimes made to the question of frustration of leases[74]; but although the two questions are related there are also significant differences between them.[75]

One point of apparent similarity is the argument, which was formerly regarded as an obstacle to the frustration of leases, that the effect of a lease was to vest a legal estate in the tenant; and that, after this had happened, the contract could no longer be frustrated.[76] This conclusion was, moreover, sometimes explained on the ground that, on execution of the lease, the risk had passed to the tenant.[77] The argument resembles that of *Paine v Meller*,[78] and subsequent cases, which base the passing of risk on the transfer (by virtue of the contract) of equitable ownership to a purchaser.[79] Indeed, the argument is stronger in that the execution of the lease vests a legal, and not merely an equitable, title in the tenant. Yet the argument is no longer regarded as compelling: in the *National Carriers* case[80] the House of Lords took the view that a lease could, in spite of the tenant's acquisition of a legal title, be frustrated. However on the actual facts of that case no question of risk of destruction of, or damage to, the premises directly arose. The warehouse which was the subject-matter of the lease was not damaged or destroyed: the tenant's complaint was that he could not make the intended use of it because the local authority had temporarily blocked the only access road. His argument was that he was discharged by alleged frustration of purpose[81]: not by destruction of the subject-matter. The tenant's argument failed because the interference with his intended use was not sufficiently serious; but the House of Lords recognised that the doctrine of frustration could, in exceptional

---

[73] *Wong Lai Ying v Chinachem Investment Co* (1979) 13 Build.L.R. 81; *cf.* below, para.5–042.

[74] See Ch.11.

[75] *National Carriers Ltd v Panalpina (Northern) Ltd* [1981] A.C. 675 at 695 ("not parallel") and at 705 ("false analogy").

[76] See below, para.11–004.

[77] Megarry and Wade, *The Law of Real Property* (6th ed.), p.691; *National Carriers Ltd v Panalpina (Northern) Ltd* [1981] A.C. 675 at 695.

[78] (1801) 6 Ves. 349.

[79] See above, paras 3–027 to 3–031.

[80] *National Carriers Ltd v Panalpina (Northern) Ltd* [1981] A.C. 675.

[81] This was also the position in *Tay Salmon Fisheries Co v Speedie*, 1929 S.C. 593, and in the American cases concerning leases of "saloons" and other business premises, discussed at below, paras 7–020, 7–023 and 7–024.

circumstances, apply to a lease of land. It has also been recognised in principle that frustration of purpose may similarly discharge a contract for the sale of land,[82] though in the case in question the argument again failed, this time on the ground that the purpose (of redeveloping land) was not that of both parties but that of the purchaser only.[83] Our concern in this section is with risk of physical damage or destruction: the fact that this risk may pass to the purchaser on contract does not preclude discharge by other supervening events such as delay, illegality or frustration of purpose.

Although the *National Carriers* case was one of frustration of purpose, some of the illustrations of possible grounds of discharge given in that case do concern events which affect the physical integrity of the subject-matter of the lease, *e.g.* the destruction of an upper-storey flat or the innundation of the premises or their collapse into the sea.[84] These examples suggest that under a lease such risks do not necessarily pass to the tenant on execution of the lease. If this is the case even though the tenant has acquired a legal interest in the land, then it is arguable that the position should not be different where a purchaser had acquired only an equitable interest by virtue of the conclusion of a contract of sale. However it is submitted that there is a significant difference between the two types of transactions,[85] in that a lease gives rise to continuing reciprocal obligations while a contract of sale is performed and thus discharged by performance of a single act on each side (*i.e.* by payment and conveyance). Perhaps for this reason, it is less common[86] to find references to the passing of risk in discussions of the frustration of leases than in discussions of the frustration of contracts for the sale of land.

3–050

Even before the *National Carriers* case, there was authority for the view that an *agreement* for a lease (as opposed to an executed lease) could be frustrated.[87] This situation came close to the rule in *Paine v Meller* in that the person who had agreed to take the lease had, by virtue of the agreement, an equitable interest in the land.[88] Yet he could rely on subsequent events as a ground of discharge. Again, however, the point must be made that, in the leading case[89] which recognises this possibility, the ground of discharge was not the destruction of or damage to buildings

---

[82] See *Amalgamated Investment and Property Co Ltd v John Walker & Co Ltd* [1977] 1 W.L.R. 164.

[83] *cf.* below, para.7–030.

[84] *National Carriers Ltd v Panalpina (Northern) Ltd* [1981] A.C. 675 at 690, 691, 700; *cf.* the less extreme example given at 701 of a house becoming unfit for occupation by reason of a coastal erosion.

[85] *cf.* n.75, above and below, para.11–005.

[86] Though not unknown: see n.77, above, for references.

[87] *Denny Mott & Dickson v James B. Fraser & Co Ltd* [1944] A.C. 265 (a decision not confined to Scots law: see *National Carriers Ltd v Panalpina (Northern) Ltd* [1981] A.C. 675 at 704); *Rom Securities Ltd v Rogers (Holdings) Ltd* (1968) 205 E.G. 427 (failure to obtain planning permission); *cf. Property Discount Corp Ltd v Lyon Group Ltd* [1981] 1 W.L.R. 300 at 305; below, paras 11–013 to 11–024.

[88] *Walsh v Lonsdale* (1882) 21 Ch.D. 9.

[89] *i.e.* the *Denny Mott* case, n.87, above.

on the land: it was the supervening illegality of their use for the purpose specified in the contract. The argument that it is inappropriate to talk of the passing of risk in a relationship which involves continuing reciprocal obligations applies to an agreement for a lease no less than to an actual lease.

The foregoing discussion distinguishes the relationship of landlord and tenant from that of vendor and purchaser. Where the holder of a leasehold interest contracts to sell it, the relationship between him and his purchaser falls into the latter category and is governed by the rules as to risk discussed earlier in this section, *i.e.* by the rule in *Paine v Meller*[90] and its various qualifications, and not by the rules as to frustration of leases.[91]

(3) **Building contracts**

(a) *Introduction*

3–051   Discussions of the effect on building contracts of damage to or destruction of the works are not, in the English authorities or books, commonly cast expressly in terms of "risk".[92] This is perhaps because it is harder to think of the "passing" of risk in relation to acts to be performed by a party than in relation to things to be delivered by him.[93] Nevertheless, the problems which arise in relation to things which are destroyed can also arise in relation to acts to be done by a party by means of which he has contracted to bring about a specified result, as is typically the case under a building contract. If before that result is achieved, the product of the contractor's work is destroyed, two questions arise. The first is whether the contractor can recover the payment which he was to receive on completion of the work (or any part of that payment); the second is whether he is legally bound to repeat the work, at no extra charge. These two questions are analogous to those which arise where a seller of unascertained goods is prevented from delivering the goods which he had intended to deliver because those goods have been destroyed. In such a case, the answers to the questions whether the seller is entitled to the price and bound to appropriate other goods depend on whether the risk has passed from the seller to the buyer. In building contracts the two questions put above similarly depend on whether the risk is still on the contractor or can be said to have passed to the customer. Thus references to risk are found in discussions of the problem by civil lawyers,[94] who regard the first of the two questions put above as concerning the "price risk" and the second as

---

[90] (1801) 6 Ves. 349, above, para.3–029.

[91] See below, para.11–005.

[92] For a reference to risk, see *Hudson's Building and Engineering Contracts* (11th ed.), para.4–248; *cf. Appleby v Myers* (1867) L.R. 2 C.P. 651 at 659, where Blackburn J. refers to the passing of risk in the materials used by the builder.

[93] *cf.* above, para.3–050 at n.85.

[94] *e.g.* Esser and Weyers, *Schuldrecht* (6th ed.), Vol.II, Besonderer Teil, pp.257 *et seq.*; Koziol and Wesler, *Grundriss des Bürgerlichen Rechts* (7th ed.), p.354; *cf.* Guhl, *Das Schweizerische Obligationenrecht* (7th ed.), p.488; Mazeaud and Mazeaud, *Leçons de Droit Civil* (5th ed.), Vol.III (2), No.1365.3.

concerning the "performance risk".[95] A widely adopted principle in civil law systems is that "risk" of the work remains on the contractor until "acceptance" or "completion" or "transfer" of the work. References to "risk" are also commonly found in American authorities on the topic.[96]

(b) *Possible solutions*

Solutions to the problem of the passing of risk under building contracts can proceed along three lines. One possibility is to follow the starting, or general, principle governing sales (whether of goods or of land), *i.e.* to link the passing of risk with the passing of property.[97] Since the normal principle in the case of a building contract is that the property in materials passes to the building owner as soon as the materials are incorporated in the structure,[98] risk would, on this view, pass from time to time as such incorporation occurred in the course of the work. A second possibility is to link the passing of risk to the payment terms of the contract,[99] so that risk would pass on (and not before) completion of the stages of the work at which various instalments of the price became due; in the case of a contract requiring the builder to complete the entire work before becoming entitled to payment, risk would *prima facie* remain on him until completion. A third possibility is to say that the risk remains with the contractor until some single, and fairly easily definable, stage in the performance of the contract has been reached, such as completion of the work. This solution could be based on the analogy of those systems in which risk under a contract for the sale of goods passes on delivery[1]; or on that of the civil law rule, stated above, under which risk under a contract for the execution of works remains on the contractor until "acceptance" or "completion" or "transfer" of the work.[2] It should be added that, although the discussion that follows is mainly concerned with contracts to carry out building work on land, there is no reason of principle why

3–052

---

[95] For the distinction between these two risks, see above, para.2–026.

[96] *Hartford Fire Insurance Co v Riefolo Construction Co*, 410 A.2d 658 at 663 (1980), citing earlier authorities.

[97] This possibility seems to have attracted Blackburn J. in *Appleby v Myers* (1867) L.R. 2 C.P. 651 at 659; see also *ibid.* at 652–653 (in argument).

[98] *ibid.* at 659.

[99] Again this possibility derives some support from *Appleby v Myers*, where one reason why the builder's claim failed was that he had "contracted to do an entire work for a specific sum, and [could] recover nothing unless the work be done ..." (at 661). But this explanation does not answer the "performance risk" question, *i.e.* whether the builder is bound to do the work again.

[1] *e.g.* UCC, s.2–509(3); Vienna Convention on Contracts for the International Sale of Goods, Art.69(1). Sale of Goods Act 1979, s.20(4) (above, para.3–010) applies this principle where the buyer deals as consumer.

[2] *e.g.* German BGB § 644; Swiss CO, Art.376 (price risk); Art.376 II puts the risk of the material on the supplier; French CC, Art.1790 (price risk); Arts 1788, 1789 make the performance risk depend on whether the contractor supplies labour and material, or labour only.

contracts to build a chattel, or to do work on it, should not be governed by the same rules.[3]

3–053   Of the three possible solutions, it is submitted that the first two are open to practical objections which do not apply to the third, and that the third solution is therefore to be preferred. One such objection is that, if the passing of risk is linked to the passing of property, or to the payment of instalments, risk will pass from time to time over what may (in the case of a major construction project) be a very long period. It is true that risk may similarly not pass instantaneously under a contract for the sale of goods, *e.g.* where a contract for the sale of oil on c.i.f. or f.o.b. terms provides that property and risk is to pass at the permanent hose connection of the carrying vessel.[4] But the period during which risk passes in such a case is relatively short, while in the case of a building contract the period is likely to extend over months or even years. To split the risk between the parties over such a long period is likely to increase the difficulties and costs of insurance. This objection would also apply if risk were linked to the payment term. Of course a provision in the contract calling for payment by instalments would determine the price risk in the sense that the contractor would be entitled to the instalment once the specified stage had been reached, irrespective of the subsequent destruction of what had then been done. However it does not follow that such a provision would settle the performance risk, *i.e.* the question whether the contractor was bound to complete the specified work, an obligation which (if it existed) would necessarily require him to repeat the work for which he had already been paid and which had been rendered useless by the supervening event. Linking the passing of risk to the payment term also gives rise to the difficulty that that term is not always given literal effect. Under the so-called doctrine of substantial performance, payment is said sometimes to be due even before the point specified in the payment term (*i.e.* full and exact completion of performance) has been reached.[5] It would be difficult to determine whether risk should pass when payment is held to be due under this doctrine, or (on the other hand) whether risk should remain with the builder until performance strictly in accordance with the contract had been completed.[6] The first two possibilities are, finally, open to the objection that during the progress of the works the contractor is in practice likely to be in control of what is being done, and therefore to be in a better position than the owner to take precautions against loss or damage.

---

[3] *e.g. Menetone v Athawes* (1746) 3 Burr. 1592 (contract to repair ship); *Anglo-Egyptian Navigation Co v Rennie* (1875) L.R. 10 C.P. 271 at 571 (contract to install new machinery in a ship).

[4] See, *e.g.* the contract between Sonatrach and Vanol in *Enichem Anic SpA v Ampelos Shipping Co Ltd (The Delfini)* [1990] 1 Lloyd's Rep. 252.

[5] See Treitel, *The Law of Contract* (11th ed.), pp.787–788 (doubting the existence of the doctrine).

[6] See *Hartford Fire Insurance Co v Riefelo Construction Co*, 410 A. 2d 658 (1980), reflecting the view that risk had passed on "substantial completion".

The third possible solution, *i.e.* that which links risk to some *single* point in the performance of the contract, has the merit of being free from the practical objections which arise from solutions under which risk passes in stages during the performance of the contract. Whether it has the further merit of making the risk pass at an appropriate time obviously depends on the point selected by it for the passing of risk. There are three possibilities: that risk should pass on the conclusion of the contract (as in the English sale of land rule[7]); that it should pass at some point between the conclusion of the contract and completion of performance (as in the general English sale of goods rule under which risk passes with property, which in turn may well pass before delivery[8]); or that it should not "pass" during the performance of the contract at all, but remain with the contractor until completion of performance.[9] From a practical point of view, it is submitted that the third of the above possibilities is more appropriate than the other two for the reason already given, namely that until completion the contractor is in a better position than the owner to protect the works against loss or damage. This third solution is also the one which enjoys the greatest measure of support among the authorities which are discussed below. For the purpose of this solution, completion of performance would *prima facie* be taken to have occurred when the structure to be erected by the builder is ready for the purpose for which, in the contemplation of both parties, it was intended to be used.[10]

The view that risk under a building contract remains with the contractor until completion of the work is sometimes said to cause hardship to the contractor, but placing the risk on the owner would cause corresponding hardship to him. These points are further considered below,[11] but at this stage it is interesting to compare the criticism of the "builder's risk" rule with that of the "purchaser's risk" rule in contracts for the sale of land: the substance of the former criticism is that risk passes too late (or does not strictly "pass" at all), while that of the latter is that risk passes too early.[12] *Any* rule as to passing of risk is capable of causing hardship to the party at risk at the moment of the casualty. The law can do no more than to select a point for the passing of risk which will put the risk on the party best able to take precautions against loss in the majority of cases. The party *prima facie* at risk can, of course, generally[13] protect himself by express contractual provisions as to the passing of risk, or by insurance; and the price which he charges for his services are likely to be adjusted accordingly.

---

[7] See above, para.3–027.
[8] See above, paras 3–009, 3–010.
[9] See above, para.3–008.
[10] *Hartford Fire Insurance Co v Riefolo Construction Co*, 410 A. 2d 658 at 664 (1980).
[11] See below, para.3–060, at n.45.
[12] See above, para.3–036.
[13] Where a buyer of goods deals as consumer, the seller's power to exclude or vary the rule that the goods remain at his risk until they are delivered to the consumer (Sale of Goods Act 1979, s.20(4)) is certainly limited, and may be wholly excluded, by law: see above, para.3–010.

3–055   In discussing the question of risk under building contracts, a distinction
has to be drawn between two types of cases: those in which the contract is
to build an entire, new structure, and those in which the contract is one to
do work on an existing structure.[14] The distinction is more clearly drawn,
and more fully discussed, in American than in English authorities, but it is
recognised in England[15] no less than in the United States. After discussing
cases which fall clearly into one or the other category it will be necessary to
consider a group of intermediate or borderline cases.

(i) Contracts to build an entire structure

3–056   Here the rule is that (unless otherwise agreed) the structure is at the
builder's risk until completion. Hence if the structure is destroyed or
damaged before completion the builder will have to do the work again for
no extra charge, even though the destruction or damage is in no way due
to his "fault", *e.g.* if the partially completed structure is destroyed by an
accidental fire.[16] In the United States the rule is generally illustrated by
reference to the case of *Stees v Leonnard,*[17] where a builder contracted to
build a house on a site designated in the contract. The house collapsed
when partly complete; the builder began to rebuild, but again the house
collapsed, apparently because of the unsuitability of the site which was said
to be "loose, spongy and soft". The builder was held to be in breach.
Three points must in the present context be emphasised with regard to
this decision.

First, the reasoning of the case is based on an indirect quotation of the
doctrine of absolute contracts as stated in *Paradine v Jane.*[18] The
subsequent abandonment of that doctrine in cases following *Taylor v
Caldwell*[19] might therefore be thought to have undermined *Stees v
Leonnard.* But where destruction of the subject-matter is governed by the
rules as to risk the doctrine of discharge does *not* apply; and therefore it is
not inconsistent with the latter doctrine to say that the structure remains
at the builder's risk until completion. *Stees v Leonnard* is therefore

---

[14] Restatement 2d, Contracts, § 263, Illustrations 3 and 4; Williston on *Contracts*
(3rd ed.), paras 1964, 1965; Corbin, *Contracts*, para.1338; *Farnsworth on Contracts*
(2nd ed.), Vol.II, para.9.5.

[15] *Hudson's Building and Engineering Contracts* (11th ed.), para.4–248 ("destruction
... of the place where the work is to be done").

[16] English cases supporting this rule include *Company of the Proprietors of the
Brecknock and Abergavenny Canal Navigation v Pritchard* (1796) 6 T.R. 750, above,
para.2–007; *Brown v Royal Insurance Co* (1859) 1 E. 4 E. 853, above, para.2–006;
Jackson v Eastbourne Local Board (1885) *Hudson's Building Contracts* (8th ed.) 174,
H.L., where a contract for the erection of a sea wall expressly provided that the
contractor was to be "answerable for all accidents and damages from or by seas,
winds etc".

[17] 20 Minn. 448 (1874).

[18] (1647) Aleyn 26 at 27, above, para.2–002. The court in *Stees v Leonnard*, above,
cites *School Trustees of Trenton v Bennet*, 3 Dutcher 513 at 518 (1859), which in
turn cites *Paradine v Jane*, above.

[19] (1863) 3 B. & S. 826, above, para.2–024.

regarded as correctly decided by the Restatement 2d,[20] and the "builder's risk" rule continues to be stated in later American cases.[21]

The second point is that *Stees v Leonnard* was concerned with antecedent rather than with supervening obstacles to performance. But this distinction was evidently not regarded as significant by the court, which relied in its judgment on a number of earlier authorities two of which concerned supervening,[22] one antecedent,[23] and one both antecedent and supervening obstacles.[24] It is, indeed, arguable that failure to overcome antecedent obstacles (which the builder might have discovered) is a stronger ground for holding the builder liable than is failure to overcome supervening ones.[25] English and New Zealand authorities certainly support the view that a builder who fails to overcome antecedent obstacles is liable, precisely because he might have discovered such obstacles.[26] That reasoning does not apply to supervening obstacles beyond the control of the parties; but *Stees v Leonnard* is nevertheless considered in the United States to apply in cases of this kind.[27] From the judgment it seems clear that the result would have been the same if the partly completed building had been destroyed by a supervening event, such as an accidental fire.

The third point is that *Stees v Leonnard* was not a case in which the obstacle to performance gave rise to any impossibility at all. As the court pointed out, the builder could have performed if he had laid stronger foundations or if he had properly prepared the site by draining it,[28] and the cost of doing this would probably not have been so great (in proportion to the agreed price) as to attract the operation even of the American doctrine of "impracticality",[29] to be discussed in Ch.6. This would also have been true if the destruction of the house had been due to a wholly supervening event, such as an accidental fire. Such a case may seem to bear some superficial resemblance to *Taylor v Caldwell*,[30] but the case is more truly analogous to that of a seller of unascertained goods in

---

[20] Restatement 2d, Contracts, § 266, Illustration 8 and Comment b, where the decision is explained, not on the ground that the building was at the builder's risk, but on the ground that the doctrine of discharge was excluded by evidence of contrary intention; *cf.* above, para.2–033. The "builder's risk" rule is, however, recognised by Restatement 2d, Contracts, § 263, Illustration 3.

[21] *e.g. Rowe v Peabody*, 93 N.E. 604 (1911); *Keeling v Schastey & Vollmer*, 124 p.445 (1912); *Hartford Fire Insurance Co v Riefolo Construction Co*, 410 A. 2d 658 at 663 (1980).

[22] *Adams v Nichols*, 19 Pick. 275 (1837); *School District v Dauchy*, 25 Conn. 530 (1857).

[23] *Dermott v Jones*, 2 Wallace 1 (1864).

[24] *School Trustees of Trenton v Bennett*, 3 Dutcher 513 (1859).

[25] *cf.* above, para.1–007.

[26] *M'Donald v Corporation of Worthington* (1892) 9 T.L.R. 21 at 230; *Wilkin & Davies Construction Co Ltd v Geraldine Borough* [1958] N.Z.L.R. 985.

[27] See above, n.20.

[28] 20 Minn. 448 at 455.

[29] *cf.* below, para.6–017.

[30] (1863) 3 B. & S. 826, see above, para.2–024.

whose hands the particular goods which he intended to appropriate (or indeed those which he had appropriated, but in which the risk had not yet passed) are destroyed.[31] He can (and must) still perform, though at greater expense to himself than he had originally envisaged; and this is also true of the builder in our example of the destruction of the partly completed structure by a supervening event.

3-058   This line of argument does not, however, rule out the possibility of discharge where the supervening event not only destroys the partly completed building but also makes its re-erection in accordance with the contract impossible. The possibility of discharge in such circumstances is hinted at by a dictum in a later case, according to which there is no discharge unless performance is "prevented ... by the act of God",[32] though this is said not to include destruction of the building by fire. One type of case in which discharge could occur is that in which the site itself ceases to exist, or to be suitable for building purposes (e.g. in consequence of being contaminated by toxic waste). Another is that in which time was of the essence and in which the supervening event made it impossible to complete the work within the time specified in the contract, e.g. where a contract was made to complete a stand at a football ground in time for the beginning of the season, and the nearly completed stand was destroyed by fire the day before the season began. In such a case, the builder might be excused from liability for the delay,[33] even if not from his duty to rebuild the stand. Similar reasoning may apply where the obstacle to performance, though not making it impossible to erect the structure, does make it impossible to do so in accordance with the specifications of the contract. In an American case of this kind,[34] performance was said to be "impossible", and the contract to have been dissolved, even though the obstacle to performance was an antecedent one (namely the condition of the soil); it is interesting to note that the authorities on which the court relied were cases of supervening (not antecedent) obstacles to performance. English authority suggests that an antecedent obstacle would not be a ground on which the contractor could claim relief,[35] but does not exclude the possibility of such relief where supervening events make it impossible to complete the work in accordance with the contractual specifications.

(ii) Contract to work on an existing structure

3-059   The second type of case is that in which the builder is to do work on an existing structure belonging to the owner, e.g. by way of maintenance,

---

[31] See above, para.3–021.

[32] *Keeling v Schastey & Vollmer*, 124 p.445 at 446 (1912); cf. *Jackson v Eastbourne Local Board* (1885), *Hudson on Building Contracts* (4th ed.) 81 at 94, where Lord Watson reserved the question whether the contractor would be liable if he met "with serious impediments which necessarily alter the character of the work and are due to causes which were not and could not reasonably have been in contemplation of either party at the time of contracting".

[33] cf. below, para.5–034.

[34] *Kinzer Construction Co v State*, 125 N.Y.S. 46 (1910).

[35] Above, at n.26.

extension or repair. Here the destruction of the existing structure can frustrate the contract. For example, where a contract is made to re-roof a house, the contract is discharged if when the work is partly completed the house is destroyed by an accidental fire.[36] Plainly, *the house* in such a case is not at the builder's risk. In England, this position is supported by *Appleby v Myers*,[37] where a contract to install machinery in a factory was discharged when the factory was burnt down. A contract to install new machinery in a ship would likewise be discharged by the loss of the ship.[38] Where the builder is under this rule discharged from his obligation to complete the agreed work, the owner is likewise discharged from his obligation to pay the contract price[39]; but a remedy may be available to the builder under restitutionary or similar principles to be discussed in Ch.15. The chances of securing such relief appear to be greater in the United States than in England.[40]

Although, in cases of this kind, the structure on which the work is to be done is not at the builder's risk, he does bear the risk of his own work where it is only the product of that work which is destroyed. Thus the actual facts of *Appleby v Myers* were distinguished from an example given in the judgment: "Had the accidental fire left the defendant's premises untouched and only injured a part of the work which the plaintiffs had already done ... the plaintiffs under such a contract as this must have done that part over again, in order to fulfil their contract to complete the whole ...".[41] Here again, there is *prima facie* no impossibility affecting the builder's performance, since the builder can generally repeat the work, though in doing so he will incur unexpected expense; but it is possible to think of exceptional cases in which this reasoning would not apply. One such case would be that in which the contract required the builder to use some unique component, *e.g.* where he had contracted to install a particular antique mantelpiece in the owner's drawing room. In such a case, even if the contract were not one for the *sale* of the mantelpiece, the contract would be discharged on the analogy of s.7 of the Sale of Goods Act 1979[42] if when the loss of the mantelpiece occurred the risk had not

---

[36] Restatement 2d, Contracts, § 262, Illustration 3; *Keeling v Schastey & Vollmer*, 124 P. 445 (1912).

[37] (1867) L.R. 2 C.P. 651.

[38] *Anglo-Egyptian Navigation Co v Rennie* (1875) L.R. 10 C.P. 271; the Exchequer Chamber, *ibid.* at 571, would have decided the case on a different ground but suggested a submission to arbitration, a suggestion in which the parties evidently acquiesced.

[39] See above, paras 2–039 *et seq.*

[40] Below, para.15–058; see the discussion of cases resembling *Appleby v Myers* (above, n.37) in *B P Exploration (Libya) Ltd v Hunt* [1979] 1 W.L.R. 783–801; actual decision affirmed, subject to relatively minor variations, [1983] 2 A.C. 352.

[41] (1867) L.R. 2 C.P. 651 at 660; *cf.* the example given by Blackburn J. at 654 (during the argument): "Suppose a riotous mob entered the defendant's premises and broke the machinery before the work was complete....".

[42] See above, para.3–013.

yet passed from the builder to the owner. If the submissions made above are accepted, the builder would bear the risk until completion of the work.

The only question actually at issue in *Appleby v Myers* was whether the builder was entitled to be paid for, or in respect of, the partly completed work; and in this context it can be argued that the dictum quoted above simply amounts to an application of the English rule that a party who fails to complete performance of an entire obligation cannot recover the agreed remuneration, or any part of it, or even a reasonable sum.[43] But the dictum is wide enough to cover the builder's liability as well as his rights, *i.e.* it seems to mean not only that the builder is, in the case put, not entitled to be paid, but also that he is liable in damages if he fails or refuses to do "that part over again."[44]

(iii) Intermediate cases

3–060   In borderline cases, the distinction between contracts to build a new structure and contracts to work on an existing one can give rise to obvious factual difficulties. Where, for example, the contract is one to extend, or to add to, existing buildings, the distinction might depend on whether the new structures were attached to the original ones, or on what proportion the one bore to the other. The difficulty of drawing the line has enabled courts to extend the second group of cases so as to reduce the scope of the rule that the work is at the builder's risk until completion. In the United States, this process has been justified on the ground that the "builder's risk" rule can cause hardship to the builder and that its scope should therefore be narrowed.[45] The argument is not wholly convincing. Where damage to the structure results from antecedent obstacles (such as the condition of the soil) the builder is often more likely than the owner to have (or to have access to) the skills needed to discover the obstacles; and an English case of this kind explicitly makes the point that he should have done so "to see if he can do the work upon the terms mentioned in the specification".[46] Where the damage results from supervening events outside the control of both parties (such as accidental fire or storm) there is little to choose between the hardship which will be suffered by the builder in having to do the work twice and that which will be suffered by the owner in having to pay for it twice. Even if the hardship to the builder were thought to be the more severe, there is the further question from just which risk he ought to be relieved; from the performance risk (*i.e.* from his liability in damages if he fails to do the work again) or from the price

---

[43] This is indeed the reasoning of the concluding paragraph of Blackburn J.'s judgment in which, at 660–661, he applies the principle of (*inter alia*) *Cutter v Powell* (1795) 6 T.R. 320: see below, para.15–057.

[44] Above, at n.41.

[45] Gilmore, *The Death of Contract*, pp.77–79.

[46] *M'Donald v Corporation of Worthington* (1892) 9 T.L.R. 21 and 330. There seems to be more force in this practical consideration than in the view, taken in some civil law systems, that responsibility for defects in the site should be taken by the owner on the analogy of his responsibilities for defects in material supplied by him: see German BGB, § 645, Swiss CO, Arts.378 I; contrast French CC, Art.1792.

risk (*i.e.* from the need to do the work again in order to earn his pay)? In the United States, the two questions are linked, in that the common law recognises that a party who has partly performed a contract which is then discharged by supervening impossibility is entitled to a reasonable recompense.[47] In England, there was no such entitlement at common law,[48] and the question whether the court has a statutory discretion to make an award in respect of such partial performance remains on the authorities an open one.[49] Hence there has so far been less temptation in England to expand the second category at the expense of the first. A further reason for the absence of such a trend in England is that the problem is in practice likely to be solved by express contractual provisions as to responsibility for both antecedent and supervening obstacles, and as to insurance. These practices probably account for the lack of modern case law on the topic.

The leading American case which illustrates the borderline here under discussion is *Butterfield v Byron*,[50] where the contract was one for the construction of a new house, but was in the nature of a joint enterprise between landowner and builder. The contract provided that the house was to be erected on the plaintiff's land; that "the grading, excavating, stone-work, brick-work, painting and plumbing" were to be done by the plaintiff; and that the rest of the work was to be done by the defendant. The destruction of the partly completed house before the date fixed for performance was held to discharge the contract. The court took the view that: "it was like a contract to make repairs on the house of another. [The defendant's] undertaking and duty to go on and finish the work was upon an implied condition that the house, the product of their joint contributions, should remain in existence."[51] In other words, the court did not apply the "builder's risk" rule, but held that the contract was discharged by supervening impossibility. It is obvious that the defendant should not, in such a case, be required to rebuild the entire structure at his own expense, but it is less obvious that he should be discharged if the plaintiff were willing to repeat the part of the works which he had undertaken to do. This point did not arise since the plaintiff made no offer to repeat his part of the work, nor did the defendant require him to do so. The plaintiff in fact had no personal interest in the outcome of the action, which was brought on behalf of his insurers to recover (*inter alia*) instalments which had been paid to the defendant as the work had progressed. This claim succeeded on the grounds that the sum to be paid under the contract "was an entire sum for the performance of the contract, and that the payments made were merely advances on account of it, and that, on his failure to perform the contract, there was a failure of

3–061

---

[47] See *Butterfield v Byron*, 27 N.E. 667 (1891) and below, para.15–058.

[48] *Appleby v Myers* (1867) L.R. 2 C.P. 651; unless the obligation to do the work was not "entire": *Menetone v Athawes* (1764) 3 Burr. 1592 (cited in *Appleby v Myers* at 660); below, para.15–064.

[49] Above, n.40.

[50] 27 N.E. 667 (1891); see also *Keeling v Schastey & Vollmer*, 124 P. 445 (1912).

[51] 27 N.E. 667 at 668.

consideration which gave the plaintiff the right to sue for money had and received ...".[52] But success on the plaintiff's claim was counterbalanced by the defendant's right to recover a reasonable sum for the work which he had done. In England a somewhat similar result would now be reached under statute: the plaintiff could recover back his payments, less an allowance to the defendant in respect of the latter's expenses[53]; while the question whether the defendant could recover anything in respect of a "valuable benefit" obtained by the plaintiff before the contract was discharged remains an open one.[54]

3–062   In *Butterfield v Byron* a significant factor was that part of the work was to be done *by the owner* of the site, for whom the house was to be built. It has been suggested that the rule in that case equally applies where (as is now common) work on a building project is carried out by a number of sub-contractors and that such contractors are thus "protected" by the rule in *Butterfield v Byron* if the entire project is destroyed before completion.[55] This is no doubt true in the sense that no sub-contractor can be under a duty to rebuild the entire structure so that the specialist operation to be carried out by him (*e.g.* the electrical work or the plastering) can be accomplished. To this extent, the work done by each sub-contractor would not be at his risk, but it does not follow that he would not be bound to repeat the work if the general contractor rebuilt the structure to the point at which it was again fit to incorporate the work to be done by the sub-contractor. It is, moreover, possible for the owner to contract directly with the various contractors whose combined work is needed to complete the structure in question. In an American case apparently of this kind,[56] the court applied "the general rule that the risk of loss during construction rests with the builder", so that the contractors were bound to make good loss caused by fire when between 90 per cent and 95 per cent of the agreed work had been done. The case shows that it is something of an exaggeration to say that specialist sub-contractors were all "safely sheltered under"[57] the rule in *Butterfield v Byron*: that rule will not apply where the specialists are not truly sub-contractors but all enter into direct contracts with an owner who does not himself perform any part of the building work.

---

[52] *ibid.* at 669.
[53] Law Reform (Frustrated Contracts) Act 1943, s.1(2); below, paras 15–050, 15–071.
[54] See above para.3–059, n.40 and para.15–064, below, discussing the position under s.1(3) of the Law Reform (Frustrated Contracts) Act 1943.
[55] Gilmore, *The Death of Contract*, p.78.
[56] *Hartford Fire Insurance Co v Riefolo Construction Co*, 410 A. 2d 658 (1980).
[57] Gilmore, above, n.55; *cf.* Kessler and Gilmore, *Contracts: Cases and Materials* (2nd ed.), p.769.

Chapter 4

OTHER TYPES
OF IMPOSSIBILITY

I. Introduction

In this chapter we shall consider the effects on contracts of impossibility   **4–001**
other than that which arises from the destruction of the subject-matter.
The cases show that discharge may result where the subject-matter is not
destroyed but merely becomes unavailable; where something which is
essential for the purpose of performance (but which is not actually the
subject-matter of the contract) is destroyed or becomes unavailable; where
the contract cannot be performed because of the death or unavailability of
a particular person; where a particular source becomes unavailable, and
where the impossibility affects only the method of performance. Although
it is convenient to divide the cases into these categories, we shall see that
there is some overlap between them. They are, moreover, not exhaustive:
it is possible to imagine other types of impossibility, of which the cases
provide no illustrations, but which may nevertheless be a ground of
discharge.

II. Unavailability of The Subject-Matter

A contract may be discharged where the subject-matter of the contract,   **4–002**
though it is not destroyed, becomes unavailable for the purpose of
performance by reason of its ceasing to be at the disposal of the parties.
Such cases must be distinguished from those in which the subject-matter
continues to be at the disposal of the parties but can no longer be used for
the intended purpose. In cases of the latter kind, the ground of discharge
(if any) is frustration of purpose, arising from the fact that the parties can
no longer use the subject-matter for one particular purpose: this ground
of discharge will be discussed in Ch.7. In the cases to be discussed in the
present chapter, the ground of discharge is impossibility arising from
the fact that (at least for a limited time) the parties can no longer deal with
the subject-matter at all.

(1) Unavailability in general

4–003   One group of cases which illustrates discharge by supervening unavailability concerns requisition of the subject-matter, or its lawful seizure or compulsory acquisition by a public authority. For example, in *Re Shipton Anderson & Co*[1] a contract for the sale of a specific parcel of wheat was discharged when, before property in the goods had passed, the wheat was requisitioned; in *Dale SS Co Ltd v Northern SS Co Ltd*[2] a contract for the sale of a ship in the course of being built by a third party was discharged when the ship was requisitioned; in *Bank Line Ltd v Arthur Capel & Co*[3] a time charter was discharged when the ship named in it was requisitioned; and in *BP Exploration (Libya) Ltd v Hunt*[4] a contract to operate, and share in the profits of, an oilfield in Libya was discharged when the interests of both contracting parties in the oilfield were expropriated by the Libyan Government. Where (as in the *Bank Line* case) the requisition is only temporary, the question of discharge depends on a number of further factors to be discussed in Ch.5.[5] On a similar principle, a contract may be discharged if government regulations prevent one party from dealing with its subject-matter in accordance with the contract, *e.g.* where a seller of paper was ordered by a wartime proclamation to reduce supplies to his customers to a proportion of the amounts supplied to them before the outbreak of war.[6]

A charterparty may similarly be discharged where the ship is detained so as to become unavailable for the performance of the contract. This possibility is illustrated by a number of cases arising out of the Gulf War between Iran and Iraq: in these cases, the prolonged detention of ships which had been time-chartered had the effect of discharging the contracts.[7] Where a charterparty specifies a voyage, either because it is a voyage charter or because it is a so-called "time charter trip", the contract may similarly be discharged if, as a result of war, the ship is detained and therefore unable to accomplish the specified voyage. This was the position in *Scottish Navigation Co Ltd v Souter & Co*[8] where two charterparties were

---

[1] [1915] 3 K.B. 676. Counsel for the buyer argued that Sale of Goods Act 1979 (formerly 1893), s.7 excused the seller *only* where the goods "perished"; but the court rejected the buyer's claim for damages for non-delivery on common law principles, without reference to the section.

[2] (1918) 34 T.L.R. 271.

[3] [1919] A.C. 435; *cf. Texas Co v Hogarth Shipping Corp Ltd*, 256 U.S. 619 (1921).

[4] [1983] 2 A.C. 352; *cf. Kursell v Timber Operators and Contractors Ltd* [1927] 1 K.B. 298.

[5] See para.5–046, below.

[6] *E Hulton & Co Ltd v Chadwick & Taylor Ltd* (1918) 34 T.L.R. 230.

[7] *e.g. Kodros Shipping Corp of Monrovia v Empresa Cubana de Fletes of Havana (The Evia)* [1983] 1 A.C. 736; *Kissavos Shipping Co SA v Empresa Cubana de Fletes (The Agathon)* [1982] 2 Lloyd's Rep. 211; *International Sea Tankers Inc v Hemisphere Shipping Co Ltd (The Wenjiang) (No2)* [1983] 1 Lloyd's Rep. 400; *Vinava Shipping Co v Finlivet A C (The Chrysalis)* [1983] 1 Lloyd's Rep. 503; *cf. Adelfamar SA v Silos e Mangimi Martini (The Adelfa)* [1988] 2 Lloyd's Rep. 466, para.4–010, below.

[8] [1917] 1 K.B. 222; *cf. Lloyd Royal Belge SA v Stathatos* (1917) 34 T.L.R. 70.

concluded for respectively one and two "Baltic rounds", *i.e.* for trips from United Kingdom to Baltic ports and back, to be paid for by the time taken to accomplish those voyages. The contracts were held to have been frustrated when the ships were detained by the Russian authorities shortly after the outbreak of the First World War, it having previously become in fact impossible (even shortly before the war) for the ships to leave the Baltic. The possibility of discharge by such unavailability is distinct from the possibility of discharge by illegality resulting from the prohibition against trading with the enemy.[9] In *Scottish Navigation Co Ltd v Souter* the ship was detained in a port controlled by an allied power, and no question of trading with the enemy arose; and in the Gulf War cases no such question could arise because the war in question was not one in which the United Kingdom was a belligerent. Hostilities (whether amounting to a "war" or not) may also interfere with the performance of a charterparty by blocking the route of shipment. Here the argument that the contract is discharged is generally based on an alleged impossibility in the method of performance[10] and not on alleged unavailability of the ship. The latter argument could be available in cases of this kind where the blocking of the route also had the effect of trapping the ship.[11]

In the case of a voyage charter, the contract may be discharged, not only   **4–004** when it is the ship, but also when it is the cargo, which becomes unavailable for the purpose of performing the contract, *e.g.* when, because of a strike at the charterer's installations at the port of loading, it becomes impossible to load the cargo.[12] On the same principle it was held in an American case that a voyage charter for the carriage of copra was discharged when, during the Second World War, the United States Government ordered the ship to carry wool instead of copra.[13]

Cases of this kind raise the question just what can be said to constitute the "subject-matter" of a contract. Time and voyage charters are not contracts for the hire of the ship: they are contracts for services,[14] with the special characteristic that they can be performed only by use of the

---

[9] See below, para.8–004. For an example of discharge on the ground of illegality in such circumstances, see *Avery v Bowden* (1855) 5 E. & B. 714; (1856) 6 E & B. 953.

[10] *e.g.* in the Suez cases, discussed below, paras 4–071 to 4–083.

[11] *cf. Embiricos v Sydney Reid & Co* [1914] 3 K.B. 45 (below, para.9–002) and *Ocean Tramp Tankers Corp v V/O Sovfracht (The Eugenia)* [1964] 2 Q.B. 226, where the charterer could not rely on the detention as a ground of frustration as it was "self-induced": below, para.14–010.

[12] *e.g. Pioneer Shipping v BTP Tioxide (The Nema)* [1982] A.C. 724; *cf.* also the cases discussed in Ch.10, in some of which frustration resulting from the unavailability of one of a number of alternative cargoes is recognised as a possibility.

[13] *Jackson v Royal Norwegian Government*, 177 F. 2d 694 (1949). Learned Hand J. dissented on the ground that the shipowners had not done all that they could reasonably have been expected to do to get the order lifted.

[14] *Ellerman Lines v Lancaster Maritime Co (The Lancaster)* [1980] 2 Lloyd's Rep. 497 at 500; *Scandinavian Trading Co AB v Flota Petrolera Ecuatoriana (The Scaptrade)* [1983] 2 A.C. 694; *Hyundai Merchant Marine Co Ltd v Karander Maritime Inc (The*

specified ship. It is this feature which makes it plausible to regard the ship as the subject-matter of the contract, while in a contract for the services of a plumber the latter's tools would plainly not be so regarded. In the case of most contracts for services, the subject-matter of the contract could with equal plausibility be regarded either as the services themselves or as the thing in respect of which they were to be rendered, *e.g.* in the case of a contract to paint a house as (1) the house-painter's services or (2) the house itself. It follows that the contract could be discharged by (a) the conscription of the house-painter[15] or (b) the requisition of the house.[16] Similarly, the subject-matter of a voyage charter could be regarded as (i) the shipowner's services (to be rendered by means of the ship) or (ii) the cargo; and so such a contract could be discharged by the unavailability of (a) the ship or (b) the cargo. In practice the second possibility does not often arise since most cargoes are generic in nature so that the contractual cargo does not become unavailable merely because of the unavailability of the particular cargo which the shipper had intended to ship. But if the contract were one to carry a specific cargo (*e.g.* a specific piece of machinery) it could be frustrated by an event such as the requisition of that cargo. Similar arguments are unlikely to apply to time charters, since these do not impose any obligations on the charterer to supply a cargo: the subject-matter of such contracts is simply to provide services (for the time and within the geographical range, if any, specified in the contract) by use of the ship. And since a demise charter is a contract for the hire, not of services, but of the ship[17] it can scarcely be doubted that the subject-matter of the contract can only be the ship. Similarly, in the case of a simple sale, it is always the thing sold which is the subject-matter of the contract. It would make no sense to regard the price as the subject-matter since this can never be destroyed or (in contemplation of law) become unavailable, though payment of it may become illegal.

(2) Compulsory purchase and requisition of land

4–005   In the United States, certain legislative provision as to the passing of risk under a contract for the sale of realty are contained in the Uniform Vendor and Purchaser Risk Act and the Uniform Land Transactions Act. These provisions have been discussed in Ch.3[18]; the point to be made here is that they apply, not only where the subject-matter is "destroyed," but also where it is "taken by eminent domain" (and so becomes unavailable for the purpose of performing a contract). These Acts do not in terms provide for discharge of the contract even where the whole of the subject-

---

Niizura) [1996] 2 Lloyd's Rep. 66 at 72; *Homburg Houtimport BV v Agrosin Private Ltd (The Starsin)* [2003] UKHL 12; [2004] 1 A.C. 715 at [119].

[15] See below, para.4–024.

[16] See below, para.4–014.

[17] See *Baumwoll Manufacture v Furness* [1893] A.C. 8; *BP Exploration Operating Co Ltd v Chevron Transport Shipping Co Ltd* [2000] UKHL 50; [2003] 1 A.C. 97 at [78], [79].

[18] See above, para.3–049.

matter is so taken: they provide for a more complex set of legal consequences (than simple discharge of the contract) where the taking occurs while the subject-matter is still at the vendor's risk. In this respect they differ from both the English[19] and the American[20] legislative provisions for the avoidance of a contract for the sale of "specific" or "identified" goods by the total destruction of the goods. But this seems merely to reflect the American view (to be discussed in Ch.15[21]) that total automatic dissolution of the contract is not (as it is in the English common law[22]) the only possible legal effect of the common law doctrine of discharge, or of its statutory counterparts in the legislation affecting contracts for the sale of goods.

The same point can be made of the Pennsylvania case of *West v Peoples* **4–006** *First National Bank & Trust Co*,[23] where the parties had in March 1941 entered into a "joint venture" agreement for six years to develop a 142-acre site belonging to the defendant. The work in relation to the development was to be done by the plaintiff and the expense to be borne by him; in return he was to receive a half share in the profits of the venture. The work was delayed in consequence of restrictions imposed after "World War II began on December 7, 1941"[24] (the day of the Japanese attack on Pearl Harbour); and the parties agreed to extend the duration of the contract. During this extended period, in 1946 and 1947, parts of the land, amounting to 58 acres, were "condemned ... for the purpose of a limited access highway with elaborate traffic interchanges"[25] but the parties went on dealing with each other as if the agreement still subsisted; it was not until 1948 that the defendant first indicated that it regarded the agreement as no longer in force. The court held that the "condemnation" did not of itself terminate the contract: since "the extent of the devastating effect of the condemnation [was] not ... entirely clear, it was up to the parties themselves to decide, and to indicate to one another, whether they considered the agreement as terminated".[26] This reasoning might seem to support the conclusion that termination had to be effected by agreement of both parties. But that was evidently not the view of the court, which regarded the contract as having been eventually "terminated through no fault of [the plaintiff's] own",[27] apparently by the election of the defendant; and the ground on which that election was justified seems to have been "impossibility".[28] In England, frustration

---

[19] Sale of Goods Act 1979, s.7, above, para.3–013.

[20] UCC, s.2–613(a); above, para.3–016.

[21] See below, paras 15–005, 15–023, 15–034, 15–035, 15–037 to 15–039.

[22] See below, paras 15–002, 15–010.

[23] 106 A. 2d 427 (1954).

[24] *ibid.* at 430.

[25] *ibid.* at 430.

[26] *ibid.* at 432; the court presumably took this view because the unavailability was only partial: *cf.* below, para.5–002.

[27] 106 A. 2d 427 at 433 (1954).

[28] See the references *ibid.* to the discussion of "impossibility" as a ground of discharge in *Williston on Contracts*, para.1972.

would operate automatically or not at all,[29] and termination by election (or rescission) would be available only in cases of breach or excused non-performance,[30] but no such breach or non-performance by the plaintiff as could justify the defendant's termination of the contract was alleged. An English court could perhaps hold that the contract had been discharged by the "condemnation" but that the defendant was until 1948 estopped by convention from relying on such discharge.[31] It should be added that the contract was *not* one for the sale of land by the defendant to the plaintiff: the court held that no interest in the land ever passed under the contract to the plaintiff, so that he was not entitled to any share in the compensation payable in the "condemnation" proceedings.[32] But the case illustrates the possibility that a contract may be discharged in consequence of the compulsory taking of the subject-matter by a public authority acting under statutory powers. In this respect it more closely resembles *B P Exploration (Libya) Ltd v Hunt*[33] than the cases in which a contract is made for the sale of land which is then requisitioned before completion of the sale.

The English cases distinguish between the situation in which a compulsory purchase order is made in respect of the land which is the subject-matter of a contract of sale and those in which the land is actually requisitioned and possession is taken by the requisitioning authority.

4-007   The first of these situations is illustrated by *Hillingdon Estates Co v Stonesfield Estates Ltd*[34] where a contract had been made in 1938 for the sale of land for residential development. Part of the contract was completed in the same year, but the rest remained uncompleted, apparently without breach on either side, when war broke out in September 1939. Completion of this part had still not taken place in 1949 when a local authority, acting under statutory powers, made a compulsory purchase order in respect of the land in question and served a notice to treat.[35] Vaisey J. held that the contract was not frustrated and that the vendor was entitled to specific performance. One possible ground for the decision is that the doctrine of frustration "does not usually operate in the case of contracts for the sale of land"; but it is unlikely that this explanation would now be accepted.[36] A second possible ground for the decision lies in the excessive delay in completion: it was said that the purchaser's

---

[29] See below, para.15–002.

[30] See above, para.2–050; and the discussion of cases such as *Poussard v Spiers and Pond* (1876) 1 Q.B.D. 410 at below, para.5–063.

[31] *cf.* the reference to "estoppel" and "waiver" in the *West* case, 106 A. 2d 427 at 432 (1954). For estoppel by convention in the context of the English law of contract, see Treitel, *The Law of Contract* (11th ed.), pp.119–124. For estoppel or waiver and frustration, see below, para.15–004.

[32] 106 A. 2d 427 at 432. For the plaintiff's right to restitution in respect of services rendered by him under the agreement, see below, para.15–058.

[33] [1983] 2 A.C. 352; above, para.4–003, n.4.

[34] [1952] Ch. 627.

[35] *ibid.* at 631.

[36] The doctrine of frustration was assumed to apply to contracts for the sale of land in *Amalgamated Investment & Property Co v John Walker & Co Ltd* [1977] 1

position should not be better than it would have been if he had completed on time and not delayed in doing so for some 12 years.[37] This looks like a version of the principle that a party cannot rely on self-induced frustration,[38] and we shall see that this principle can apply even though the conduct of that party does not amount to an actual breach of the contract.[39] Here it seems that the delay was not of this character, for the judgment expressly disclaims the need to decide which (if either) of the two parties was in breach.[40] A third possible ground for the decision was that, "subject to the payment of the purchase-money" the purchasers were "to be regarded as owners of the land"[41]. This resembles the reasoning of *Paine v Meller*[42] and suggests that the risk of compulsory acquisition (like that of physical damage) passes on contract to the purchaser. This was the explanation of the *Hillingdon* case given by the Privy Council in *E Johnson & Co (Barbados) Ltd v NSR Ltd*,[43] where, after a contract for the sale of land had been made, and before the date fixed in the contract for completion, the Crown issued a notice of intended compulsory purchase of the land. This was held not to have frustrated the contract (so that the buyer's purported rescission of it was wrongful) because "on the conclusion of a contract for the sale of land the risk passes to the purchaser".[44] This reasoning involves some extension of the rule as to passing of risk derived from *Paine v Meller*,[45] for that rule refers (like those relating to the passing of risk in contracts for the sale of goods)[46] to the risk of physical damage and not to financial risks of the kind at issue in cases of the present kind. In the *Hillingdon* case, the view that frustration was excluded by the passing "risk" is also hard to reconcile with the emphasis placed in that case on the fact that "the date for completion is long past",[47] for this would be irrelevant if the risk of compulsory acquisition had passed on contract. The final reason for the decision in that case is that the requirements of the doctrine of frustration had not been satisfied, since, although the compulsory purchase order had "very much altered the situation", it had not "altered it in such a fundamental or catastrophic manner as to justify the court in holding that the whole contract had been frustrated".[48] The purchaser would of course get the compensation payable by the acquiring authority; and where there was a long interval between the contract and the compulsory purchase,

---

W.L.R. 164, where the plea of frustration failed for reasons to be stated at below, para.7–030.

[37] [1952] Ch. 627 at 635.
[38] See below, para.14–002.
[39] See below, paras 14–013, 14–014.
[40] [1952] Ch. 627 at 636.
[41] *ibid.* at 632.
[42] (1801) 6 Ves. 349; above, para.3–027,
[43] [1997] A.C. 400.
[44] *ibid.* at 406
[45] Above, n.42.
[46] *Benjamin's Sale of Goods* (6th ed.), para.6–001.
[47] [1952] Ch. 627 at 632.
[48] *ibid.* at 634.

this compensation might be more, or less, than the price payable under the contract. The compulsory purchase order could be regarded simply as an event which occurred after the contract and affected the value of its subject-matter; and after the contract the risk of any fall, no less than the chance of an increase, in value should be the purchaser's. The mere making of the order before the time fixed for completion therefore does not affect the binding force of the contract. If, however, the land is taken over by the acquiring authority in pursuance of the order *after* the time fixed in the contract for completion but *before* the hearing, then the court will not order *specific* performance since it can no longer order the vendor to convey.[49] However, as the contract is not frustrated, the purchaser's repudiation of it or his failure to perform it is a breach making him liable in damages and to the forfeiture of his deposit.[50]

4–008   In the *Hillingdon* case, the court was concerned simply with the effect of the *making* of the compulsory purchase order. At the time when the contract was to have been completed the vendor could have performed his part of the contract by transferring title and possession; and the mere making of the order, and the consequent service of a notice to treat did not prevent him from performing these obligations. From this point of view, the *Hillingdon* case is to be contrasted with a group of three cases in which land was sold on the terms that vacant possession should be given on completion, and the land was then requisitioned under the Defence (General) Regulations 1939 before completion was due to take place. One such case is *Cook v Taylor*,[51] where a notice requisitioning premises had been served six days before completion was due[52] and the keys of the property were handed over to the requisitioning authority; and Simonds J. held that the vendor was not entitled to specific performance.[53] A similar case is *James Macara Ltd v Barclay*[54] where again a notice of requisition had been served before the day fixed for completion. It was held by the Court of Appeal that "actual entry" was not necessary for the exercise of the power of requisition, and that such exercise had given the acquiring authority the immediate right to possession,[55] so that the vendor was unable to give vacant possession and the purchaser was entitled to the return of his deposit. The final case in this group is *Re Winslow Hall Estates*[56] where a notice of intention to requisition had been served on the vendor before the date fixed for completion and Bennett J. held (on a vendor and purchaser summons) that the purchaser was not entitled to rescind the contract. The case was distinguished in *Cook v Taylor* on

---

[49] *E Johnson & Co (Barbados) Ltd v NSR Ltd* [1997] A.C. 400.
[50] *ibid.*
[51] [1942] Ch. 349.
[52] *ibid.* at 353.
[53] The keys were received by the requisitioning authority "on the same day" (*i.e.* the day on which the notice was served): [1942] 2 All E.R. 85 at 86; this fact is not stated in the *Law Reports*.
[54] [1945] K.B. 148.
[55] *E Johnson & Co (Barbados) Ltd v NSR Ltd* [1997] A.C. 400 at 407.
[56] [1941] Ch. 503.

the ground that in *Cook v Taylor* possession had been taken by the requisitioning authority when, before the date fixed for completion, the keys of the property were handed to it,[57] while nothing of this kind had occurred in the *Winslow Hall* case. But in the *James Macara* case there was no equivalent act of taking actual or even symbolical possession. The mere giving of the notice of requisition was regarded as a taking of possession and so deprived the vendor of the power of giving vacant possession under the contract. The terms of that notice were, moreover, not significantly different from those of the notice in the *Winslow Hall* case. That case was cited by counsel in the *James Macara* case[58] but not there referred to in the judgment of the Court of Appeal. In view of the difficulty of reconciling these two cases, the *Winslow Hall* case must be regarded as a somewhat doubtful authority.[59]

None of the three cases discussed in para.4–008, above contains any reference to the doctrine of frustration and their relation to that doctrine is more than a little obscure. *Cook v Taylor* and the *James Macara* case seem to be based on the view that the vendor in those cases was in breach of his express promise to give vacant possession: "that was his bargain and he must fulfill it and cannot insist on the purchaser performing some bargain which he did not enter into."[60] The case of destruction of the premises by fire or flood (events which, it was accepted, would not preclude enforcement by the vendor) was distinguished on the ground that there was "no express bargain in relation to fire or flood".[61] This emphasis on the vendor's *express* promise is reminiscent of the reasoning of *Paradine v Jane*,[62] though none of the requisition cases goes so far as to hold the vendor liable in damages for his inability (in consequence of the requisition) to give vacant possession. His failure to do so seems merely to have justified the purchaser's rescission and consequent right to the return of his deposit. That right was held to arise at common law, independently of the court's discretion to order the return of a deposit under s.49(2)[63] of the Law of Property Act 1925. Nor does it seem that the power, conferred on the court by s.1(2) of the Law Reform (Frustrated Contracts) Act 1943,[64] to order the return of payments made under a

4–009

---

[57] See above, n.53.
[58] [1945] K.B. 148 at 151.
[59] All three of the cases cited at nn.51–56, above, are cited with apparent approval by the Privy Council in *E Johnson & Co (Barbados) Ltd v NSR Ltd* [1997] A.C. 400 at 408, but no attempt is made to resolve the apparent conflict between the *Winslow Hall* and *James Macara* cases.
[60] *Cook v Taylor* [1942] Ch. 349 at 353; *cf.* the reference to the vendor's breach in *James Macara Ltd v Barclay* [1945] K.B. 148 at 153.
[61] *Cook v Taylor* [1942] Ch. 349 at 354.
[62] (1627) Aleyn 26; above, para.2–002 In *Cook v Taylor*, above, at 352 it was assumed that an implied promise to give vacant possession would have sufficed in that case, and this reasoning seems to be at variance with the basis of the distinction between the two propositions in *Paradine v Jane*, as explained in para.2–002 above.
[63] *James Macara Ltd v Barclay* [1945] K.B. 148 at 156.
[64] See below, para.15–050.

frustrated contract would be relevant in cases of this kind. In the *James Macara* case one reason why this power could not be invoked was that the requisition occurred before the date specified in the 1943 Act[65]; but a now more significant reason why the Act could not apply was that the contract was not frustrated but terminated by the purchaser on account of the vendor's breach (or perhaps of his non-performance, whether amounting to a breach or not).[66] The point that termination was at the purchaser's election could also be significant for other purposes, *e.g.* if the financial terms on which the land was requisitioned were sufficiently attractive to the purchaser to make him wish to enforce the contract.[67]

(3) **Court order affecting the subject-matter**

4–010   The subject-matter of a contract may become unavailable for the purpose of the performance of the contract at as a result of a court order affecting it. A hypothetical example of this possibility is provided by Restatement 2d § 264, Illustration 4, according to which a seller of a specific piece of machinery is not liable if a third party, by falsely alleging ownership of the machine, obtains a court order enjoining the seller from dealing with the machine. But the scope of the doctrine of discharge in cases of this kind is likely to be a narrow one; for the Illustration goes on to make the point that the seller would not be discharged if he had failed to use due diligence to have the injunction lifted[68] or if it was due to his fault that the third party had grounds for obtaining the injunction.

In an English case,[69] a shipowner on whose ship goods had been shipped by a person who was not their owner, and who had not acted with the authority of the owner, was ordered by a New York court to deliver the goods up to their owner. This was held not to amount to a "restraint of princes" within the terms of the bill of lading,[70] but to give the shipowner a defence to a claim by the transferee of the bill of lading on the equitable ground that the claim amounted to a fraud on the owner of the goods. "Seizure under legal process" would now provide a carrier with a defence under a bill of lading governed by the Hague or Hague-Visby Rules[71]; but that excuse would arise, not under the general doctrine of discharge, but by virtue of the special provisions of the Rules.

The possibility of discharge as a result of a court order is recognised in the American case of *Peckham v Industrial Securities Co,*[72] where

---

[65] See s.2(1) of the 1943 Act.

[66] *cf.* above, para.4–006, at n.30.

[67] For undesirable effects of automatic termination of time charters where the compensation for requisition exceeds the hire payable under the contracts, see below, paras 15–007 to 15–009.

[68] *cf.* above, para.4–004, n.13.

[69] *Finlay v Liverpool & Great Western SS Co Ltd* (1870) 23 L.T. 251.

[70] *ibid.* at 254; the reasoning on this point is curiously reminiscent of *Paradine v Jane* (1647) Aleyn 26 at 27, above, para.2–002.

[71] Carriage of Goods by Sea Act 1971, Sch., art.IV(2)(g); US Carriage of Goods by Sea Act 1936, s.4(2)(g).

[72] 113 A. 799 (1929).

performance of a contract for the sale of shares was prevented when one of the shareholders obtained an injunction restraining the sale. But the actual outcome of the case was that the plea of discharge failed because the company was unable to show that it could not have obtained the lifting of the injunction. The plea of discharge will often fail in cases of this kind since the fact that the court order was made (or not lifted) will commonly be due to some degree of "fault" of the party claiming discharge, and accordingly it will attract the operation of the rule that a party cannot rely on "self-induced" frustration.[73] On this ground, a seller of goods was again held liable in another American case,[74] in which he was unable to deliver the goods because they had been taken in execution in legal proceedings against him. Such execution may occur, of course, even though the seller was not guilty of "fault" in the sense of want of care or diligence: the execution may result from breach of a contract with a third party when the duty broken under that contract was one giving rise to strict liability.[75] If this amounts to "fault" as against the other party to the contract from which the seller now claims (by virtue of the execution) to be discharged, the scope of the doctrine of discharge in cases of the present kind will be significantly reduced. But the doctrine can apply where the court order is obtained by a third party for whose conduct the party claiming to be discharged is not responsible, so long as the order is not the result of any breach of a contract between that party and the third party. This was the position in *The Adelfa*[76] where a voyage charterer successfully relied as a ground of frustration on the arrest of the ship in legal proceedings which had been taken at the port of discharge by the receivers of the cargo; those proceedings were regarded (in the present litigation) as unjustified and do not appear to have been based on any breach by the charterers of any contract between them and the receivers.

In the United States, the scope of the doctrine of discharge in cases of the present kind is further limited by the rule as to burden of proof on the issue of self-induced frustration. Under this American rule as to burden of proof, it will be up to the party claiming to be discharged to show that it was not his "fault" that the court order was made, or not lifted.[77] Under the English rule as to burden of proof,[78] the burden would be on the other party to the contract to show that the party claiming discharge was at fault in this respect. The further possibility that a court order may frustrate a contract by prohibiting an agreed or mutually contemplated method of performance is discussed later in this chapter.[79]

---

[73] See below, para.14–002.
[74] *Western Drug Supply Co v Board of Administrators of Kansas*, 187 P. 701 (1920); *cf. Klauber v San Diego Street Car Co*, 30 P. 555 (1892).
[75] *cf.* above, para.1–003.
[76] *Adelfamar SA v Silos e Mangimi Martini (The Adelfa)* [1988] 2 Lloyd's Rep. 466, below, para.14–004.
[77] See below, para.14–025.
[78] *ibid.*
[79] *Codelfa Construction Pty Ltd v State Rail Authority of New South Wales* (1982) 149 C.L.R. 337, below, para.4–060.

(4) **Theft of subject-matter**

4–011   The cases so far considered all concern the unavailability of the subject-matter as a result of an act or order affecting it carried out or made by some organ of the state. The subject-matter of a contract may also become unavailable (without being destroyed) by the act of a third party, in particular where the subject-matter is stolen. A case in which the theft had occurred *before* the time of contracting was *Barrow Lane & Ballard Ltd v Phillip Phillips & Co.*[80] It was there held that a contract for the sale of a specific "indivisible parcel"[81] of 700 bags of nuts, of which 109 bags had been "fraudulently abstracted or misdelivered"[82] before the contract was made, was void under s.6 of the Sale of Goods Act 1979, since *the parcel* of 700 bags no longer existed and had therefore "perished" without the knowledge of the seller when the contract was made. It seems reasonable to suppose that the parcel would similarly be regarded as having "perished" for the purpose of s.7 of the Act, and that the contract would therefore have been avoided, if the theft had occurred after the making of an agreement for the sale of the parcel and before the risk had passed[83] to the buyer. Such a decision could be based on the special circumstance that the parcel of 700 nuts no longer existed as such. It would not follow that, if a contract were made for the sale of, for example, a specific picture which was then stolen, the picture would be regarded as having "perished" for the purpose of s.7. But a contract may be discharged by events falling outside s.7, and in the case put there seems to be no reason why the general principle of discharge by unavailability of the subject-matter should not apply. Unavailability which is due to theft may, indeed be temporary (unless the thing stolen is consumable or has its identity altered by the thief, for instance, where objects made of precious metal are melted down). The statistically low chance of recovering stolen property would, however, make it likely in the majority of cases that theft of the subject-matter of the contract would discharge the contract on the ground of unavailability.

(5) **Negative contracts**

4–012   A somewhat similar principle to that of discharge by unavailability of the subject-matter can apply to negative contracts. For example, in *Baily v De Cespigny*[84] a lease of land contained a covenant that the lessor would not build on certain adjoining land. The covenant was held to have been discharged when the adjoining land was compulsorily acquired by a railway company which then erected a station and other buildings on that land.

---

[80] [1929] 1 K.B. 574.

[81] *ibid.* at 581.

[82] *ibid.* at 582.

[83] Contrast *Bevington v Dale* (1902) 7 Com. Cas. 112 (where goods were stolen after the risk had passed and it was held that the buyer remained liable for the price).

[84] (1869) L.R. 4 Q.B. 180; for criticism on the case on another point, see below, para.15–007.

(6) Miscellaneous cases

Impossibility may arise where the performance of a contract depends on   4–013
the continuation of a state of affairs which, after the making of the
contract, ceases to exist. On this ground, contracts under which two
students were employed as officers of a university students' union were
held to have been frustrated when the university, acting under statutory
powers, imposed a new constitution on the union, expelled the two
students, and banned them from the university campus.[85] On a similar
principle, the contract (if any) by which a person holds a public office can
be discharged if the office is abolished by statute.[86] A contract with a
public authority for the erection of public works could likewise be
discharged by legislation declaring such contracts to be void.[87]

III. DESTRUCTION OR UNAVAILABILITY OF A THING ESSENTIAL FOR PERFORMANCE

The principle of discharge may apply when a thing is destroyed which is   4–014
not the subject-matter of the contract but is one the continued existence
or availability of which is essential for the performance of the contract. As
the discussion in a previous section of this chapter shows, the question just
what constitutes the subject-matter of a contract is not always easy to
answer, or may be susceptible of more than a single answer.[88] Thus even if
one took the view that the subject-matter of a voyage charter under which
a specific cargo were to be carried was the ship (and the ship alone) the
contract could nevertheless be frustrated by unavailability of the specific
cargo on the ground that the availability of that cargo was essential for the
performance of the contract. Similarly, a contract to paint frescoes in a
church would no doubt be discharged by the destruction of the church,
even if the subject-matter of the contract were regarded as the work of the
artist, rather than the church itself.[89] The same point can be made in
relation to a situation discussed in Ch.2, where we saw that a seaman's
contract of service could be discharged by the loss or capture of the ship[90]:

---

[85] *Anyanwu v South Bank Student Union (No. 2), The Times*, December 5, 2003.

[86] *Reilly v R.* [1934] A.C. 176.

[87] See *Gulf Bank KSC v Mitsubishi Heavy Industries Ltd* [1994] 1 Lloyd's Rep. 323; the
actual decision was concerned, not with the principal contract, but with an
ancillary contract of "counter-indemnity" given by the contractor to its bank in
respect of payments which might be made by the bank under an "advance
payments guarantee" issued by the bank to the public authority at the
contractor's request. The counter-indemnity was (at least arguably) saved from
discharge by its express terms (*cf.* below, para.8–056) and was not within the
express provisions of the legislation which had discharged the construction
contract.

[88] See above, para.4–004.

[89] *cf.* Lord Bramwell's example in *Jackson v Eastbourne Local Board* (1885) 2 *Hudson
on Building Contracts* (4th ed.) 81 at 96 (contract to build a toll-house on a
bridge which is then washed away).

[90] See above, paras 2–019 to 2–021.

here again it seems that the subject-matter of the contract is the service to be rendered and the ship a thing essential for its performance. It is possible to imagine other cases in which a contract would be discharged by the destruction or unavailability of a thing even though that thing is clearly not the subject-matter of the contract. For example, in the case of a contract to ship goods from a particular port, it could not be said that the port was the subject-matter of the contract; but the contract would no doubt be discharged if the port were destroyed by an earthquake. Such a case could be explained on the ground that the port was a thing, the continued existence or availability of which was essential to the performance of the contract. An alternative possible view would be that in this example the unavailability affected the method of performance.[91] But this view is less plausible in relation to the further situations to be discussed in para.4–015. These situations support the view that there is an independent principle of discharge by destruction or unavailability of a thing essential for performance. That view is also supported by the analogous rule of discharge by the death, incapacity or unavailability of a person whose continued availability is essential for performance.[92]

4–015   Where the ground on which frustration is claimed is the destruction or unavailability of a thing which is not itself the subject-matter of the contract, the question arises whether that thing is indeed essential for performance. The point may be illustrated by reference to contracts for the sale of goods to be manufactured by the seller. If the contract provides that the goods are to be manufactured by the seller in his factory, then the factory is essential for performance and its destruction will discharge the contract.[93] On the other hand, in *Turner v Goldsmith*[94] a contract was made for the sale of goods to be "manufactured *or sold*" by the seller. It was held that the contract was not discharged by the destruction of the seller's factory, since he acted not only as a manufacturer but also as a dealer in goods of the kind in question. In an Indian case[95] a contract was made for the sale of cloth "from the Victoria Mills," a factory belonging to a third party. These words were said to be "purely descriptive" and, although the point did not arise for decision, it seems that the destruction of the factory would not have discharged the contract.

A similar distinction exists where a contract is made for the supply of goods which are to be installed in specified premises or to be used there. In *Appleby v Myers*[96] a contract to install machinery in a factory and to maintain the machinery for two years was held to be discharged when the

---

[91] *cf. Clarksville Lane Co v Harriman*, 44 A. 527 (1895), para.4–060, below (drying up of stream).

[92] See below, para.4–026.

[93] Restatement 2d, § 263, Illustration 2.

[94] [1891] 1 Q.B. 544.

[95] *Ganga Saran v Ram Charam Ram Gopal* [1952] S.C.R. 36, where the factory belonged to a third party who failed to make the agreed delivery. For the situation where the contract contains no reference to the factory, see below, paras 4–053 to 4–056.

[96] (1867) L.R. 2 C.P. 651.

factory was destroyed before the work of installing the machinery had been completed. On the other hand, in the American case of *Sechrest v Forest Furniture Co*[97] a contract was made for the manufacture and sale of plywood drawer bottoms which the buyer intended to use in his factory. It was held that the contract was not discharged when the factory was destroyed by fire, so that the buyer was liable for the price. The two cases may be distinguished on the ground that, in *Appleby v Myers* the services under the contract were to be rendered by the supplier in the factory which was destroyed while the supplier's performance in the *Sechrest* case could be and was completed even though the buyer's factory had ceased to exist. The buyer's only hope of claiming discharge would be under the doctrine of "frustration of purpose"; but this hope is (as we shall see[98]) a faint one.

IV. DEATH OR UNAVAILABILITY OF A PARTICULAR PERSON

(1) Effect of death on "personal" contracts

The death of a party may discharge a contract which is "personal" in the sense of requiring personal performance from one or both of the parties. For example, a contract of apprenticeship, employment or agency is terminated by the death of either party.[99] In contracts of apprenticeship, the rule that termination results from the death of the master, no less than from that of the apprentice, can be explained on the ground that each party is to render services to the other: the master is to teach, and the apprentice to work. Thus in *Whincup v Hughes*[1] it was the death of the master which discharged the contract, while the judgment of Blackburn J. in *Taylor v Caldwell*[2] is in part based on the then already established rule that such a contract was discharged by the death of the apprentice. The rule that a contract of employment or agency is discharged by the death of the employee or agent is similarly based on the fact that that party had undertaken to render services of a personal nature; while the rule that the contract is discharged by the death of the employer or principal appears to be based on the fact that the employment or agency relationship is one involving personal confidence and that it is an implied term of a contract of employment that the employer will not without reasonable cause so conduct himself as to destroy or seriously damage the relationship of trust

4–016

---

[97] 141 S.E. 2d 292 (1965).

[98] See below, paras 7–035, 7–036.

[99] *e.g. Whitehead v Lord* (1852) 7 Ex. 691 at 694 (solicitor's retainer terminated by death of client); *Campanari v Woodburn* (1854) 15 C.B.N.S. 400; *Taylor v Caldwell* (1863) 3 B. & S. 826 at 835; *Pool v Pool* (1889) 58 L.J.P. 67; *Farrow v Wilson* (1869) L.R. 4 C.P. 744; *Graves v Cohen* (1930) 46 T.L.R. 121 and see above, para.2–013; Restatement 2d, § 262, Illustration 8; *Kowal v Sportswear by Revere Inc*, 222 N.E. 2d 778 (1967). For special agency rules, see below, paras 4–028, 4–029.

[1] (1871) L.R. 5 C.P. 78.

[2] (1863) 3 B. & S. 826 at 836.

and confidence between the parties.[3] Such a contract therefore requires the continued existence of both parties.

Similar reasoning can apply also to contracts which are not contracts of employment or agency, but which are contracts to render services of a personal nature, *e.g.* a contract to write a book would be discharged by the death of the author.[4] The same rule can apply to contracts requiring the personal performance of services of a professional nature. For example, in *Stubbs v Holywell Railway Co* the death of a person who had been appointed as consulting engineer to supervise specified works was held to have "dissolved the contract".[5] Again, if A sold his business to B on the terms that A would for a specified period assist B in the operation of the business, A's death within that period could discharge the contract.[6] For the present purpose the question whether a contract was "personal" would seem to depend on the same factors as those which determine whether a contract is "personal" for the purpose of the rule that the benefit of a "personal" contract cannot be assigned,[7] and that such a contract cannot be vicariously performed.[8] In these contexts, the personality of a seller of goods can no doubt be important to the buyer (*e.g.* where the goods are to be manufactured by the seller or where the buyer on other grounds relies on the seller's reputation in respect of quality or other aspects of performance). It is also possible for the seller to rely on the personality of the buyer, *e.g.* where the sale is on credit and the seller relies on the buyer's skill as a retailer[9] (to realise the means of payment from his disposal of the goods). In the former case, the seller could not delegate performance to another manufacturer,[10] and in the latter, the buyer could not assign the benefit of the contract; and where this is the position it is submitted that the death of the party who could not delegate performance or assign the benefit of the contract would, on similar grounds, also discharge the contract.

4–017 If the contract is not of this "personal" nature, it is not discharged by the death of either party. For example, the death of a party engaged "to fill a tract of land"[11] would not discharge the contract. On the same principle, the death of either party would not discharge a contract for the sale of goods which did not contain any "personal" elements of the kind described in the preceding paragraph. Thus it has been said that a contract for the sale of a piano (not being one of the seller's own

---

[3] *Malik v BCCI* [1998] A.C. 20; for discussion of the question whether there is also such an implied term in contracts of agency, see *Bowstead and Reynolds on Agency* (17th ed.,), para.7–001.

[4] *Taylor v Caldwell*, above n.2, at 835.

[5] (1867) L.R. 2 Ex. 311 at 313.

[6] *Mullen v Wafer* 480 S.W. 2d 332 (1972).

[7] See Treitel, *The Law of Contract* (11th ed.), pp.693–695.

[8] *ibid.* pp.756–757.

[9] *Cooper v Micklefield Coal & Lime Co Ltd* (1912) 107 L.T. 457.

[10] *Johnson v Raylton Dixon & Co* (1881) 7 Q.B.D. 438; *cf. Peters, Flamman & Co v Kohstad Municipality*, 1919 A.D. 423.

[11] Restatement 2d, § 262, Illustration 9.

manufacture) would not be discharged by the death of the seller[12]; and in *Wentworth v Cock*[13] it was held that a contract to make monthly deliveries of slate for one year was not discharged by the death of the buyer during that year. The death of either party would similarly not discharge a contract to construct business premises; though the contract between an architect engaged in connection with such a venture and his client would be one for the "personal" services of the architect[14] and would therefore be discharged by the architect's death.

In some cases, greater difficulty can arise in drawing the line between "personal" and other contracts. In the Canadian case of *Re Witwicki*[15] a contract by which a son undertook to supply his parents with the necessities of life was held not to have been discharged by the son's death: his obligations under the contract were said to be purely financial, so that they could be performed by his estate. The case is perhaps a borderline one, since it could be argued that the contract was based on assumptions about the son's personal earning power. A contract of this kind may also be "personal" where the recipient of the allowance undertakes obligations under it. This was the position in *James v Morgan*[16] where the father of an illegitimate child promised the child's mother a weekly allowance until the child was 14 and the mother in return promised the father to maintain and bring up the child. On the mother's death it was held that the contract was discharged as it was "a personal contract which she alone could carry out. It was she alone who could give that special care that the father was anxious that the child should have".[17]

Another group of contracts in which it is not easy to draw the line between "personal" and other contracts are those for services in relation to the formation of a company or the underwriting of an issue of new shares. In *Re Worthington*[18] such a contract ("for procuring the subscription of the various shares") was held not to be one for "personal services," so that it was not terminated by the death of the person who had agreed to provide underwriting services, and his estate was held liable in damages. In the American case of *Kelley v Thompson Land Co*,[19] on the other hand, a contract to render similar services in the formation of a company was held to be discharged by the death of the person who was to render them, since the financial skills of that person were a crucial element in the contract. This view seems to be preferable to that taken in *Re Worthington*;[20] though "personal" considerations would no longer be

---

[12] *Siboni v Kirkman* (1836) 1 M. & W. 418 at 423.

[13] (1839) 10 A. & E. 42.

[14] *Stubbs v Holywell Railway Co*, above, n.5.

[15] (1979) 101 D.L.R. (3d) 430.

[16] [1909] 1 K.B. 564.

[17] *ibid.* at 566.

[18] [1914] 2 K.B. 299.

[19] 164 S.E. 667 (1932).

[20] *cf. Collins v Associated Greyhound Racecourses Ltd* [1930] Ch. 1 (underwriting contract held to be of a "personal" nature for the purpose of the rule that an undisclosed principal cannot enforce such a contract made by his agent as the third party had relied on the agent's reputation and integrity).

relevant where nothing more was to be done by the underwriter than to pay for the shares which he had agreed to take up: such a liability can be enforced against his executors.[21]

(2) Supervening incapacity

Where the contract is one which would be discharged by the death of a party, it may likewise be discharged by that party's supervening incapacity. For example, a contract to paint a picture would (it seems) be discharged if the painter were struck blind[22]; a contract to write a book would be

4–018 discharged by the supervening insanity of the author[23]; a contract to act in a play or to give a musical performance could be discharged by the actor's or performer's illness on the day or days fixed for the performance[24]; the relationship of principal and agent is terminated by the insanity of either party[25]; and in jurisdictions which regarded engagements to marry as having contractual force it seems that the supervening insanity of either party would discharge the contract.[26]

(a) *Physical and legal incapacity*

4–019 In the present context "incapacity" generally refers to physical inability to perform the contract, rather than to any supervening legal incapacity. The painter who is struck blind suffers from no legal incapacity, and the point of the example of the author who becomes insane appears to be, not that he may suffer from a legal disability, but that it is assumed (rightly or wrongly) that his disturbed state of mind will prevent him from writing his book. These examples show that supervening *legal* incapacity[27] is not necessary to bring about discharge; nor, it is submitted, would it be sufficient. This submission is based on the rules relating to the effect of mental illness which is already in existence at the time of contracting. Such illness is not of itself a ground of invalidity: it is merely a ground on which the party suffering from the illness can avoid the contract if the other party knew of his condition.[28] Since for this purpose such

---

[21] *Warner Engineering Co Ltd v Brennan* (1913) 30 T.L.R. 391.

[22] *Hall v Wright* (1858) E.B. & E. 746 at 749, cited with approval in *Taylor v Coldwell* (1863) 3 B. & S. 826 at 836. Dismissal of an employee on account of a supervening incapacity resulting from an injury at work which is *not* sufficiently serious to frustrate the contract may amount to a breach of duty under Disability Discrimination Act 1995, s.6: see *Collins v Royal National Theatre Trust* [2004] EWCA Civ 144, [2004] 2 All E.R. 851, where no attempt was made to argue that the incapacity was so serious as to frustrate the contract.

[23] *Jackson v Union Marine Insurance Co* (1874) L.R. 10 C.P. 125 at 145.

[24] *cf. Robinson v Davison* (1871) L.R. 6 Ex. 269, below, para.5–034; Indian Contract Act 1872, s.56, Illustration (e).

[25] *Drew v Nunn* (1879) 4 Q.B.D. 661; *Yonge v Toynbee* [1910] 1 K.B. 215; below, para.4–028.

[26] Indian Contract Act 1872, s.56, Illustration (b).

[27] *cf.* below, para.4–038, for certain cases of legal incapacity.

[28] *Moulton v Camroux* (1849) 4 Ex. 17; *Imperial Loan Co v Stone* [1892] 1 Q.B. 599; and see Treitel, *The Law of Contract* (11th ed.), p.557.

knowledge must exist at the time of contracting, mental illness occurring after that time cannot, of itself, be a ground of discharge. Even if the mental illness is so serious as to result in the patient's property being subject to the control of the court,[29] the contract is not (when the illness existed at the time of contracting) void. It merely does not bind the patient to the extent to which it attempts to dispose of such property, and it does bind the other party.[30] Again it follows that if such illness supervenes, the contract is not frustrated, though it can no longer be enforced to the extent to which it amounts to an attempt to dispose of the patient's property. The only one of the above examples to which this reasoning might not have applied was that of the breach of a promise of marriage (an example which is now obsolete in England[31]). Here it could have been argued that the contract to marry was discharged because the marriage itself would have been void at canon law on the ground of one party's lack of mental capacity to enter into it.[32]

(b) *Agency*

The application of the above principles at first sight gives rise to some conceptual difficulty in relation to the law of agency. Here it has been held that a power of attorney was "void" on the ground that it had been executed by a person of "unsound mind" who did not "know what he was doing"[33]; and it has been said to be a "general rule of law that a lunatic cannot appoint an agent".[34] A similar rule has been applied in cases of the supervening insanity of the principal. This has been held to terminate the actual (though not the apparent) authority of the agent, at least where the principal was "so far afflicted with insanity as to be disabled from acting for himself"[35] or where the principal had "become so far insane as to have no mind": in such a case "perhaps he ought to be deemed dead for the purpose of contracting".[36] In all these statements it is the fact of the principal's insanity (actual or supervening) which is regarded as decisive. They give rise to difficulty because they make no reference to the agent's knowledge of the insanity; and it is this factor of knowledge which is normally decisive in determining the validity of contracts with mental

4–020

---

[29] Under Pt VII of the Mental Health Act 1983. This Part of the 1983 Act will be repealed and replaced by other provisions for judicial administration of the property of persons of impaired mental capacity if the Mental Capacity Bill is passed in the form in which it was introduced in June 2004.

[30] *Re Walker* [1905] 1 Ch. 160; *Re Marshall* [1920] Ch. 284; *cf. Baldwyn v Smith* [1900] 1 Ch. 588.

[31] Law Reform (Miscellaneous Provisions) Act 1970, s.1.

[32] See Cretney Masson and Bailey-Harris, *Principles of Family Law* (7th ed), para.2–038; by statute, the marriage in such a case is now voidable: Matrimonial Causes Act 1973, s.12.

[33] *Daily Telegraph Newspaper Co v McLaughlin* [1904] A.C. 776 at 779; *Elliot v Ince* (1857) De G. M. & G. 475.

[34] *Gibbons v Wright* (1954) 91 C.L.R. 423 at 445.

[35] *Drew v Nunn* (1879) 4 Q.B.D. 661 at 666.

[36] *ibid.* at 669; *cf.* also *Yonge v Toynbee* [1910] 1 K.B. 215, below, paras 4–028, 4–029.

patients.[37] The statements are, however, all concerned with the agent's *authority* rather than with the *contract* of agency: indeed, in the leading case[38] on the effect of the principal's supervening insanity there was *no* contract at all between principal and agent (who were husband and wife). The statements also all appear to be concerned with forms of "insanity" so extreme as to give rise in fact to an incapacity to continue the relationship of principal and agent. Thus they can be explained on the ground that, in the present context, a factual (as opposed to a legal) incapacity suffices to bring a contract to an end. This reasoning can also be extended to the case of the supervening mental incapacity of the agent, to which the same legal rule is generally considered to apply[39] (although the authorities all deal with the incapacity of the principal). In other words, the mental illness of the agent should terminate the agency if it is so serious as to prevent the agent from carrying out his duties as such. By no means all forms of what is now recognised as mental illness would necessarily have this effect.

The preceding discussion is concerned with the effect of supervening mental illness on contracts made by individuals, this being the only type of supervening legal incapacity which can affect such persons.[40] Different considerations apply to the supervening legal incapacity of corporations: these are discussed below.[41]

(c) *Disability leading to risk of injury to health*

4–021 The principle of discharge by supervening incapacity has been extended to cases in which a party receives medical advice that his health would be injured by performance, or continued performance, of the contract. In *Condor v The Barron Knights*[42] the claimant (aged 16) was employed as a drummer in a band on the terms that he was to perform for seven nights a week. This level of activity led to his suffering a nervous breakdown and the contract was held to have been discharged on his receiving medical advice that he would suffer another, more serious, breakdown if he performed for more than three or four nights a week. The general principle of discharge by reason of the risk of injury to health resulting from the employee's incapacity or special susceptibility appears to be well established in spite of the difficulties of reconciling that principle with the decision in *Hall v Wright*.[43] It was there held that it was no defence to an action for breach of promise of marriage that performance of the promise had become dangerous (but not impossible) for the promisor. The case is

---

[37] Above, n.28.

[38] *Drew v Nunn*, above, n.35.

[39] *e.g. Bowstead and Reynolds on the Law of Agency* (17th ed.), Art.5.

[40] It is arguable that supervening legal incapacity may result from a contracting party's becoming an alien enemy. The ground of discharge in such a case is, however, supervening illegality (below, para.8–004); our present concern is with supervening impossibility.

[41] See below, para.4–033.

[42] [1966] 1 W.L.R. 87.

[43] (1858) E.B. & E. 746.

discussed in Ch.2,[44] where it is suggested that the result is explicable by reason of its special circumstances and of the special characteristics of the action for breach of promise of marriage.

The common law authorities discussed above envisage the possibility of discharge only where performance of the contract would endanger the health of the party claiming discharge. Danger to mental health is for this purpose clearly sufficient[45]; but the further question arises whether the contract would be discharged if its performance would cause severe distress to one of the parties. An example of this type of situation, discussed by some German writers, would be the case of a comedian who had suffered a bereavement shortly before the day of the performance for which he had been engaged, or whose child was on that day dangerously ill.[46] The effect of such events is, however, not to discharge both parties, but merely to provide the party suffering from the misfortune in question with an excuse for non-performance. In English law, it seems unlikely that such circumstances would have even this effect. In *Turner v Mason*[47] it was held that a domestic servant who absented herself, contrary to her employer's orders, so as to visit her mother who was ill and allegedly "in peril of death", had committed a breach which justified her summary dismissal. The case is now discredited insofar as it holds that any single act of disobedience of a lawful order of itself justifies summary dismissal,[48] but not on the point that the employee was in breach. Circumstances of this kind clearly do not frustrate the contract (it would be absurd to suggest that they entitled the *employer* to treat himself as discharged); and they do not provide even the employee with a legally recognised excuse for non-performance.

(3) Risk of illness or injury related to place of work

The cases discussed in para.4–021, above must be distinguished from another group in which the alleged obstacle to the performance of a contract of employment arises, not from the supervening personal disability or susceptibility of the employee, but from unexpected risks related to his place of work. One group of cases shows that the employee is justified in leaving, or in refusing to proceed to, the place in question, on the ground that his life or safety would be in immediate danger there. But in some of these cases the employees recovered damages,[49] on the ground that their refusal was justified and therefore not a ground on which the

4–022

---

[44] See above, para.2–015.

[45] As in *Condor v The Barron Knights*, above, n.42.

[46] See, *e.g.* Larenz, *Schuldrecht* (14th ed.), Vol.I, p.134.

[47] (1845) 14 M. & W. 112.

[48] See *Laws v London Chronicle (Indicator Newspapers) Ltd* [1959] 1 W.L.R. 698; *Gorse v Durham CC* [1971] 1 W.L.R. 775 at 781.

[49] *Ottoman Bank v Chakarian* [1930] A.C. 277 (treated as a case of employer's breach in *Johnstone v Bloomsbury Health Authority* [1992] Q.B. 333 at 349, 351); contrast *Bouzourou v Ottoman Bank* [1930] A.C. 271 (where the employee's refusal was not justified as there was *no* immediate danger to his life).

employer was entitled to dismiss them; and in others they recovered their wages,[50] on the ground that, though they had failed to perform their "entire" obligations to work before becoming entitled to be paid, this failure had been brought about by the wrongful act of the employer. In these cases, therefore, the employees were held entitled to *enforce* the contracts, which were clearly not frustrated. The danger which justified their refusal was accordingly not a ground of discharge, but rather an excuse for non-performance available at their option to the employees.[51] In a mid-nineteenth century American case[52] an employee was held to be justified in leaving his place of work because the outbreak of a cholera epidemic exposed him to a high risk of infection there. There was no question of any breach by the employer, and the employee recovered no more than a reasonable sum for his work. This result is consistent with the theory of discharge, which in the United States (though not in England) can occur at the option of one party and can give rise to a common law claim for a reasonable sum for work done before discharge.[53] But in England
it is at least equally plausible to say that the case was one of excuse for non-performance rather than one of frustration, for in English law frustration automatically discharges *both* parties[54]; and it would seem that the epidemic would not have justified the employer in discharging the employee if the latter had (like most of his fellow employees) chosen to remain at his place of work.

4–023   The case which comes closest to supporting the view that the contract was discharged by events of the kind described above is *Liston v SS Carpathian (Owners)*.[55] The claimants had signed on as seamen for a voyage from the United Kingdom to Port Arthur, Texas, and back. At Port Arthur, news of the outbreak of the First World War reached the men, together with information that there was a risk of capture by enemy warships. The men refused to go to sea unless they were promised extra pay; such a promise was made and the homeward voyage was safely accomplished. The action was for the recovery of the extra amount promised; and (at least as the law then stood[56]) this action could not succeed if, in working the ship home, the men did no more than to perform what they were bound under the original contract to do. Coleridge J. upheld the claim. He said that risk

---

[50] *O'Neill v Armstrong, Mitchell & Co* [1895] 2 Q.B. 418, where the reference at 422 to the "peace adventure" having been "frustrated" cannot (in spite of the citation of *Appleby v Myers* (1867) L.R. 2 C.P. 651) be a reference to frustration of the contract as the employee recovered wages due under it; *Palace Shipping Co v Caine* [1907] A.C. 386.

[51] A similar principle underlies the statutory right of an employee not to be subjected to any detriment on the ground of his refusal to expose himself to serious and imminent danger at work: see Employment Rights Act 1996, s.44(1)(d) and (e).

[52] *Lakeman v Pollard*, 43 Me. 463, 69 Am. Dec. 77 (1857); above, para.2–015.

[53] See below, paras 15–018, 15–058.

[54] See below, para.15–002.

[55] [1915] 2 K.B. 42.

[56] See now *Williams v Roffey Bros & Nicholls (Contractors) Ltd* [1991] 1 Q.B. 1.

of capture was not in the contemplation of the parties at the time of contracting; and, that risk having subsequently arisen, "the crew were justified in ... refusing to proceed on the voyage, and that being so they were discharged from their obligation to sail". He added that "A risk to life has in certain circumstances ... been held to be a ground for the discharge of the contract. But that is not the guiding point of my judgment in this case".[57] The first of these statements refers to the discharge only of the claimants ("they were discharged ...") and can be interpreted as meaning that the danger of capture provided them with an excuse for non-performance. It does not appear that *the contract* was regarded as having been frustrated: on the contrary, in its varied form it was enforced. Only the second statement refers to "the discharge *of the contract*," presumably with the result that, in the situation described in it, both parties would be discharged. On the actual facts, the shipowner could perhaps have claimed to be discharged on the ground that it was not reasonable to expect him to expose his ship to the risk of capture. Some of the early cases on the topic (discussed in Ch.2) proceed on this basis.[58] It is also arguable that an employer should not be obliged to expose his employees to risks in respect of which he could incur liability to them. But it seems that no such argument would have been available in the *Liston* case, where no criticism is directed at the employers' conduct in entering into the agreement by which the ship was worked home in spite of the supervening risk of capture.

(4) **Unavailability of party**

A contract which requires a party to render "personal" services may be discharged as a result of that party's unavailability for the purpose of performance (no less than by his death or incapacity). For example, such a contract may be discharged by that party's conscription or internment.[59] Unavailability resulting from the imprisonment of a party in consequence of his conviction on a criminal charge cannot generally be relied on by that party as a ground of discharge, since a party cannot rely on "self-induced" frustration[60]; but it seems that it could be so relied on by the other party.[61] Arrest of a party on a criminal charge of which that party is later acquitted is much less likely to provide even the other party with a ground of discharge. In *Mount v Oldham Corporation*[62] the headmaster and proprietor of a school for maladjusted children was arrested on a   **4–024**

---

[57] [1915] 2 K.B. 42 at 47.

[58] See above, para.2–032.

[59] *e.g. Morgan v Manser* [1948] 1 K.B. 184; *cf. Autry v Republic Productions*, 180 P. 2d 888 (1947); *Peters, Flamman & Co v Kohstad Municipality*, 1919 A.D. 423.

[60] See below, paras 14–020 to 14–021.

[61] *ibid.*

[62] [1973] Q.B. 309. *cf. Boyo v Lambeth LBC* [1994] I.C.R. 727, where employers ultimately abandoned the argument that a contract of employment had been frustrated by the arrest and release on bail of one of their employees on criminal charges which were later dismissed.

charge of indecency of which, some six months later, he was acquitted. In the interval between his arrest and his trial he was released on bail on the condition that he did not return to the school pending his trial; and the staff of the school continued to carry on its activities. It was held that a contract by which a local authority had agreed to send children to the school was not frustrated by these events. One reason for this conclusion was that "the position of the headmaster was not so very personal"[63]; another was that the absence was only temporary and not of such a length as to discharge the contract.

(5) **Inability to receive performance**

4–025   In the cases so far considered we have been concerned with the death, incapacity or unavailability of the person who is to *render* the personal performance, rather than with that of the person *to whom* it is to be rendered. There is an apparent exception in cases of discharge by the death of an employer, but the exception is more apparent than real. Although an employer is of course the recipient of the personal services of the employee, he also owes duties to the employee and it is the personal nature of those duties which accounts for the discharge of the contract by the death of the employer. But there is a further group of cases in which it is only the capacity of a party to *receive* performance which is affected by that party's death or incapacity. This was the position in an American case[64] in which it was held that a contract to give dancing lessons was discharged when the pupil was so seriously injured that he could no longer dance. The pupil himself did not owe any duties of a personal nature under the contract: his only duty was to pay the agreed fees. His continuing to be capable of dancing was a state of affairs essential to performance, which had become impossible in the same sense in which a contract to put a roof on a house would become impossible by the destruction of the house. A contract to render medical services would similarly be discharged by the death of the patient. Cases of this kind must be distinguished from those in which the supervening event merely frustrates one party's purpose in entering the contract. Thus it has been suggested in an Australian case that a contract to make a wedding dress would not be discharged "if the wedding goes off without 'default' on the part of the lady"[65] who had ordered the dress. A case somewhat nearer the line would be that in which a person who had booked holiday accommodation died or became too ill to travel before the appointed time. It seems that in principle the contract could be frustrated on such grounds, but in practice the doctrine of frustration is likely to be excluded in such cases by express provisions as to insurance against such events, and as to cancelling charges. In the case of "package" holidays the point is now dealt with by the Package Travel, Package Holidays and Package

---

[63] [1973] Q.B. 309 at 316.
[64] *Parker v Arthur Murray Inc*, 295 N.E. 2d 487 (1973).
[65] *Scanlan's New Neon Ltd v Tooheys Ltd* (1943) 67 C.I.R. 169 at 201.

Tours Regulations 1992.[66] In contracts governed by these Regulations[67] there is an implied term that "where the consumer is prevented from proceeding with the package the consumer may transfer his booking" to another suitably qualified person, so long as the consumer gives due notice to the other party to the contract.[68] The effect of this provision is that the contract is not frustrated, but that the consumer is given a right to vary it if circumstances such as illness prevent him from proceeding.

(6) **Death, incapacity or unavailability of third party**

A contract may be discharged by the death or incapacity of a third party: for example, a contract between A and B by which B undertook to paint a portrait of C would be discharged by the death of C (at least, if the contract was one to paint the portrait "from life," and not from a photograph). Similarly the death or incapacity of a child could discharge a contract between the child's parents and a school for the child's education,[69] though in practice the doctrine of frustration is likely to be excluded, at least in cases of incapacity, by the express provisions of the contract as to the payment of fees notwithstanding the illness of the pupil. In the foregoing examples, the contract did not require any performance from the third party. Where it does call for such performance, and that performance is of a personal nature, the third party's incapacity is, *a fortiori*, a ground of discharge. Thus in *Boast v Firth*[70] an action was brought on an apprenticeship deed against the father of the apprentice in respect of the apprentice's failure to render the agreed services. The father successfully relied on the "permanent illness" of the apprentice as a ground of discharge. In an American case[71] it was similarly held that a contract, by which A agreed with B to produce a play in B's theatre featuring a named actor C, was discharged by C's incapacity resulting from medical advice that his performing on the specified days would injure his health by aggravating a "throat condition" from which he was then suffering. A contract between A and B to give a concert featuring a named singer C would similarly be discharged if C were arrested, or refused entry to the country in which the concert was to be held, because he had been found to be illegally in possession of drugs. C himself might not be able to rely on such circumstances as a ground of discharge of his contract with A, because his incapacity would be due to his "fault"[72]; but this fault could not be imputed to A so as to deprive him of the defence of frustration against B. In all the above cases, the continued availability of the third party is essential to the performance of the contract, which accordingly

4–026

---

[66] SI 1992/3288, giving effect to Council Dir. 90/314.
[67] SI 1992/3288, reg.3(1) (packages sold or offered for sale in the UK; for definition of "offered" and "package" see *ibid.*, reg.2).
[68] *ibid.*, reg.10(1).
[69] *Simeon v Watson* (1877) 46 L.J.C.P. 679; *Holton v Cook*, 27 S.W. 2d 1017 (1930).
[70] (1868) L.R. 4 C.P. 1.
[71] *Wasserman Theatrical Enterprises v Harris*, 77 A. 2d 329 (1950).
[72] See para.14–020, below.

becomes impossible to perform when that availability ceases. They must be distinguished from cases where the death or incapacity merely frustrates the purpose of one of the parties in entering into the contract. The distinction may be illustrated by varying an example given in para.4–025 above[73]: a contract under which A agreed to make a wedding dress for B would not become impossible to perform as a result of the death of B's fiancé; nor is it likely that the frustration of B's purpose would in such a case be a ground of discharge since B's purpose of marrying the particular man who later died is unlikely to be a common purpose of A and B.[74]

(7) **Death, etc. after performance of "personal" obligations**

4–027   Even where a contract is "personal" in nature, it will be discharged only to the extent that, at the time of the death or incapacity, the performance of obligations of a personal nature remains outstanding. For example, the death of an agent engaged to sell his principal's products on commission discharges the obligation of the agent to endeavour to effect sales and also the principal's obligation to co-operate with the agent (*e.g.* by providing samples); but it has been held in the United States not to discharge any obligation which the contract may impose on the principal to pay commission on orders placed before, but executed after, the agent's death,[75] at least where such orders can be executed without any further activity on the part of the agent. The application of this rule in England at first sight gives rise to some difficulty in view of the generally strict insistence on the rule that frustration operates automatically on the occurrence of the frustrating event.[76] But it seems that the enforceability of the agent's right to commission in the case put could be explained on the ground that the commission was *earned* before, though it did not become *payable* until after, the death of the agent.[77] It seems that the same rule applies where an employee is incapacitated or dies after he has performed his duty to work, so that he or his estate can recover holiday pay which had become due at the date of discharge, even though it was not payable till after that date.[78]

(8) **Special agency rules**

4–028   The common law rule that the death or incapacity of a principal automatically terminated a contract of agency, and that it also terminated the agent's authority, could be a source of hardship both to the agent and to third parties.

---

[73] Above, at n.65.

[74] For the requirement of such a *common* purpose, see below, para.7–014.

[75] *Kowal v Sportswear by Revere Inc*, 222 N.E. 2d. 778 at 781 (1967).

[76] See below, para.15–002.

[77] *cf.* (in another context) *Colonial Bank v European Grain & Shipping Co (The Dominique)* [1989] A.C. 1056; *Bowstead and Reynolds on Agency* (17th ed.), para.7–041.

[78] *Re Wil-Low Cafeterias Inc*, 111 F. 2d 429 (1940), disapproving *Donlan v City of Boston*, 111 N. E. 718 (1916).

One source of hardship to the agent was that termination resulted even though the agent was unaware of the supervening event. Thus in *Yonge v Toynbee*[79] a solicitor was conducting litigation on behalf of a client who became insane. After this had happened, but before the solicitor had heard of it, he took further steps in the action. It was held that the other party to the litigation could recover damages from the solicitor for breach of implied warranty of authority in respect of the costs incurred by that party in the litigation after the solicitor's authority had come to an end by reason of the client's insanity. Such liability for breach of warranty is strict[80]: it made no difference that the solicitor had acted in good faith and with due diligence. Another source of hardship to the agent is that he might give credit to the principal, for example, by advancing money to him after the conclusion of the contract, in the expectation of recouping amounts so advanced out of the commission which he expected to earn. At common law, this did not make the agency irrevocable on the ground that it was "coupled with an interest"[81]; and a power of attorney was revoked by the principal's death even where it was so "coupled".[82]

A possible source of hardship to the third party was that he might be unable to enforce the contract against the principal. Thus in *Blades v Free*[83] a contract made through an agent could not be enforced by the third party against the estate of a principal who (unknown to either the third party or to the agent) had died before the contract was made. But this hardship was mitigated where the circumstances were such that the third party could rely, as against the principal, on the doctrine of apparent or ostensible authority.[84] Thus although the principal's insanity terminates the agent's actual authority even where the agent has no notice of it, such insanity will not terminate any apparent or ostensible authority which the agent may have; and in *Drew v Nunn*[85] it was therefore held that the third party could enforce a contract made by the agent on behalf of the principal, after the latter had become insane, on the ground that the agent's apparent or ostensible authority had not been terminated by a supervening incapacity of the principal, of which the third party was unaware. It is submitted that the agent's apparent authority can similarly survive the principal's death and that the third party's claim in a case like *Blades v Free*[86] would therefore now be upheld.

If the third party can rely against the principal on the doctrine of apparent authority, then the agent's liability for breach of implied warranty should be excluded, since that liability arises only where the third   **4–029**

---

[79] [1910] 2 K.B. 215.

[80] *Collen v Wright* (1857) 8 E. & B. 647; approved in *Starkey v Bank of England* [1903] A.C. 114.

[81] *Smart v Sandars* (1848) 5 C.B. 895; to make the power of attorney irrevocable on this ground, the "interest" had to exist independently of the agency.

[82] *Watson v King* (1815) 4 Camp. 272.

[83] (1829) 9 B. & C. 167.

[84] See *Bowstead and Reynolds on Agency* (17th ed.), Arts 22, 74–76; Treitel, *The Law of Contract* (11th ed.), pp.712–716.

[85] (1879) 4 Q.B.D. 661.

[86] Above, n.83.

party has *no* claim against the principal.[87] This possibility was not considered in *Yonge v Toynbee*,[88] where the court was concerned only with the termination of the agent's *actual* authority and did not consider the question of the possible liability of the principal on the basis of apparent or ostensible authority. The reason for this may be that the damages suffered by the third party did not result from his inability to enforce a contract or disposition of property against the principal, but rather from acts which the principal, by reason of insanity, no longer had any power to do at all. Where the third party's loss results from the fact that the agent's actual authority to bind the principal by a contract has come to an end, the third party's rights are more likely to be governed by *Drew v Nunn*, for even an insane person is by no means incapable of incurring liability on contracts, and for this purpose it should make no difference whether he enters into a contract personally or through an agent.

Two Acts of Parliament have mitigated the hardships which might result from the common law rule that a contract of agency, and the actual authority of an agent, were automatically terminated by the death or incapacity of the principal. They apply where the authority of the agent is conferred under a power of attorney, *i.e.* by a deed.[89]

The first of these Acts is the Powers of Attorney Act 1971: this provides that a power of attorney which is expressed to be irrevocable and is given to secure a proprietary interest of, or the performance of an obligation owed to, the donee shall not be revoked by the donor without the consent of the donee, or by the donor's death, incapacity or bankruptcy, so long as the interest or obligation secured by it remains in being.[90] The Act also protects third parties who deal in good faith with the donee of a power which is expressed to be irrevocable and to be given by way of security. Such persons are entitled to assume (unless they know the contrary) that the power cannot be revoked except by the donor acting with the consent of the donee, and that it has not been revoked in this way.[91]

The second Act is the Enduring Powers of Attorney Act 1985.[92] This makes provision for powers of attorney executed in a prescribed form and expressed to continue in spite of the donor's supervening mental

---

[87] See, *e.g. Rainbow v Howkins* [1904] 2 K.B. 322; criticised in *McManus v Fortescue* [1907] 2 K.B. 1 at 6 (but that case can be explained on the ground that the third party there knew of the agent's want of authority).

[88] [1910] 1 K.B. 215.

[89] Powers of Attorney Act 1971 s.1(1), as amended by Law of Property (Miscellaneous Provisions) Act 1989, s.1 and Sch.1, para.6(a); *Bowstead and Reynolds on Agency* (17th ed.,), para.3–011, cited in *Gregory v Turner* [2003] EWCA Civ 183; [2003] 1 W.L.R. 1149 at [66].

[90] s.4.

[91] s.5(3); special protection is provided for transferees under stock exchange transactions by s.6.

[92] Cretney and Lush, *Enduring Powers of Attorney* (4th ed.). The 1985 Act will be repealed and "enduring" powers of attorney be replaced by "lasting" ones (with savings for enduring powers already in existence) if the Mental Capacity Bill is passed in the form in which it was introduced in June 2004.

incapacity.[93] To create such an "enduring power" the donor need only have the capacity to understand the act of conferring authority on the donee: it is not necessary for the donor to have the mental capacity of managing his or her own affairs.[94] An enduring power is not revoked by the supervening incapacity of the donor,[95] but when such incapacity occurs the power is, in effect, suspended[96] until it is registered by the court.[97] Once an enduring power has been registered, it can no longer be revoked by the donor of the power; it can be revoked only with the consent of the court.[98] The Act further protects the donee of the power and third parties in a number of cases: if they act in good faith in ignorance of the donor's supervening mental incapacity[99]; if they act in good faith in pursuance of an instrument which is registered as an enduring power in spite of not being a valid power of attorney; if an enduring power is invalidly revoked (*i.e.* by the donor without the consent of the court); and if the instrument, though valid as a power of attorney, was not a valid *enduring* power though purporting to be one, and the power has been revoked by the donor's supervening mental incapacity.[1]

(9) Dissolution of corporations

According to the Restatement 2d, the rule by which the death of an individual can discharge a contract can apply by analogy to the dissolution of a corporation but will seldom apply to such cases since the dissolution will normally be due to the voluntary act or fault of the corporation.[2] Hence the doctrine of frustration will be excluded by the principle that a party cannot rely on self-induced frustration.[3] It is submitted, however, that the issues raised by the dissolution of a corporation in the present context are more complex than this analysis might suggest; for in this context (as of course in many others) the analogy between the death of an individual and the dissolution of a corporation is imperfect. On the death of a natural person, that person continues legally to be represented by his estate, so that contracts with that person can be enforced by or against the estate in actions brought by or against his executors or administrators. When, on the other hand, a corporation is dissolved it simply ceases to exist as a legal person and there is (as a general rule) no surviving legal entity by or against which any contract to which the corporation was a

4–030

---

[93] s.2.
[94] *Re K* [1988] Ch. 310. For the burden of proof on this issue, see *Re W (Enduring Power of Attorney)* [2001] Ch. 609.
[95] s.1(1)(a).
[96] s.1(1)(b).
[97] Under s.6. Execution of a second power of attorney in favour of different donees from those named in the first is no bar to registration of the first: *Re E (Enduring Power of Attorney)* [2001] Ch. 364.
[98] ss.7(1)(a), 8(3).
[99] s.1(1)(c).
[1] s.9.
[2] Restatement 2d, § 262, Comment a.
[3] See below, para.14–002.

party can be enforced. Such a contract must then come to an end because one party to it has ceased to exist,[4] and even if this is due to the "fault" of the former corporation, it has no legal successor which can be made liable in respect of that fault.

In the case of a company incorporated under the Companies Acts, dissolution of the company will be preceded by winding-up proceedings, which may be voluntary or by order of the court[5]; and it is at this stage that questions might seem to arise as to the applicability of the doctrine of frustration and in particular of the principle that a party cannot rely on self-induced frustration. Again, however, it is in practice unlikely that such questions will arise since the common law doctrine of frustration will in the majority of cases be displaced by legislative provisions which apply to the winding up of companies. One such provision is that which entitles the company's liquidator to disclaim "onerous property,"[6] an expression which includes "an unprofitable contract".[7] Such a disclaimer does not, however, frustrate the contract: "any person sustaining loss or damage in consequence of the disclaimer" is entitled to prove for that loss or damage in the winding up; and the disclaimer, while it determines the rights and liabilities of the company, does not (except so far as is necessary to secure the release of the company) affect the rights and liabilities of any other person.[8] Another such provision is that which gives the court power, on the application of a person who is entitled to the benefit or subject to the burden of a contract with the company, to rescind the contract.[9] Again it is clear that the contract is not frustrated: rescission is by order of the court and may be ordered subject to the payment of damages for non-performance of the contract. It should be emphasised again that these provisions apply during winding up, *i.e.* before the company is actually dissolved.

4–031   At common law, the position is similarly that a contract was not discharged merely because the company was in the process of being wound up. In *British Waggon Co v Lea & Co*[10] a company which had contracted to let out railway wagons and to keep them in repair for seven years passed a resolution for voluntary winding up; and the court rejected as "altogether untenable" the other contracting party's argument that the company had thereby incapacitated itself from performing the contract. The court emphasised that "personal performance" by the company was not of the essence of the contract, which could be satisfactorily performed by a second company to which the company, which had originally entered into the contract, had assigned the benefit of it. This may suggest that the result would have been different if the contract *had* contained a "personal" element. This might well be the case now that persons who

---

[4] *e.g. Salton v New Beeston Cycle Co* [1990] 1 Ch. 43.
[5] Insolvency Act 1986, s.73(1).
[6] *ibid.*, s.178(2).
[7] *ibid.*, s.178(3).
[8] *ibid.*, s.178(4).
[9] *ibid.*, s.186.
[10] (1880) 5 Q.B.D. 149.

supply professional or similar services may for commercial or fiscal reasons contract to do so through a company. Even in such cases, however, it is submitted that the contract would not be dissolved merely because the company was being wound up, though discharge might follow if the person who was to render the services died, or was incapacitated or became unavailable for the purpose of performance. If the contract was discharged on this ground, damages would not be available to the other party, as they are under the statutory provisions stated above. Those provisions only assume that discharge does not result merely from the commencement of the winding up process: it does not follow that frustration may not follow on other grounds.

In *Measures Bros Ltd v Measures*[11] it was held that, after the appointment of a director had been terminated by a winding-up order, the company could no longer enforce against the director a covenant in restraint of trade contained in the terms of his appointment. The reason for this was not, however, that the contract was frustrated, but that the company could not enforce the director's part of it after it had incapacitated itself from performing its own part.

So far we have considered the effect of dissolution (or proceedings leading to dissolution) only as between the company and the party who had contracted with it. Dissolution of the company can also affect third parties. For example, the dissolution of a company can terminate the authority of an agent, such as a solicitor appointed to act on its behalf in litigation[12]; and such termination may make the agent liable to third parties for breach of implied warranty of authority.[13] Conversely, a contract between A and B for the supply of goods to a corporation could be frustrated by the dissolution of that corporation.   **4–032**

The foregoing discussion does not in theory exclude the possibility that a contract may be discharged by the winding up of a company. This result could follow if after the conclusion of the contract legislation were passed ordering the corporation (or a class of corporations to which the corporation in question belonged) to be wound up, or dissolving the corporation.[14] In practice, however, such legislation is likely to make express provisions for any outstanding rights and liabilities (including those arising under contracts) in existence when the legislation comes into force. Examples of legislation of this kind (which relate more frequently to corporations created by special statute than to those incorporated under the Companies Acts) can be found in Acts of Parliament nationalising or privatising certain corporate enterprises,[15] or transferring public functions from one body corporate to another.

---

[11] [1900] 2 Ch. 248.

[12] *Salton v New Beeston Cycle Co* [1900] 1 Ch. 43.

[13] The contrary view was taken in *Salton's* case, above; but on this point the case was disapproved in *Yonge v Toynbee* [1910] 1 K.B. 215.

[14] Restatement 2d, § 262, Comment a.

[15] *e.g.* Telecommunications Act 1984, s.60(1); Electricity Act 1989, s.65(1). For judicial consideration of provisions of a similar nature, see *Re British Concrete Pipe Association* [1983] 1 All E.R. 203.

(10) **Supervening incapacity of corporation**

4–033   It is also necessary to consider the effect on a contract of the supervening incapacity of a corporation: this may arise from an alteration of the objects of the corporation, so that a contract which was within those objects when that contract was made ceases to be within those objects before the time when the contract is to be performed.

If the corporation is a company incorporated under the Companies Acts[16] and alters the objects clause of its Memorandum of Association after the contract in question was made, there are two reasons why the alteration will not discharge the contract. The first is that s.35(1) of the Companies Act 1985[17] provides that (as a general rule[18]) the validity of any act done by the company is not to be called into question on the ground of lack of the company's capacity by reason of anything in (or, presumably, not in) its Memorandum of Association. It follows that the contract cannot be challenged on the ground of supervening lack of capacity. Nor can members of the company restrain it from performing the contract since such proceedings do not lie in respect of a legal obligation arising from a previous act of the company.[19] The other party to the contract will therefore have the usual remedies for its breach. He will not need to rely on s.35A(1) of the 1985 Act, which provides that, in favour of a person dealing with the company in good faith, the power of the directors to bind the company shall be deemed to be free of any limitations under the company's constitution; for when the contract was made there were, in the type of case here under consideration, no such limitations. The second reason why the alteration will not discharge the contract is that the alteration results from the voluntary act of the company, so that once again the principle would apply, that a party cannot rely on "self-induced" frustration. This second reason can be of some practical importance in the present context in those exceptional cases in which the general rule of s.35(1) (stated above) does not apply.[20]

The provisions of the Companies Act 1985 described above do not apply to corporations created by special statute or to corporations created by Royal Charter whose capacity is nevertheless defined or limited by statute.[21] Such corporations remain subject to the *ultra vires* doctrine[22] under which a contract which was beyond the statutory powers of the corporation when it was made is void in law. It would seem in principle to be possible for a

---

[16] Companies Act 1985, s.735(1)(a), defining "company" for the purposes of the Act; by virtue of this definition, the discussion to n.20, below applies only to companies incorporated under the Acts.

[17] As substituted by Companies Act 1989, s.108(1).

[18] For exceptions, see Companies Act 1985, s.35(4), as substituted by Companies Act 1989, s.108(1); Charities Act 1993, s.65(1) (charitable companies and certain transactions with directors).

[19] Companies Act 1985, ss.35(2), 35A(4), as substituted by Companies Act 1989, s.108(1).

[20] See n.18, above.

[21] *e.g. Hazell v Hammersmith and Fulham Borough Council* [1992] 2 A.C. 1.

[22] *Ashbury Ry Carriage & Iron Co v Riche* (1875) L.R. 7 H.L. 653.

contract which was within those powers when it was made to be discharged by subsequent legislation depriving the company of the legal power to perform the contract in question. For example, an agreement to sell a specific object could be frustrated by legislation depriving the corporation of its power to alienate either that specific object or all objects of the class to which it belonged. In such a case it could certainly not be said that the corporation was seeking to rely on "self-induced" frustration. The question whether the contract was actually frustrated would depend on the construction of the supervening legislation: the issue would be whether the legislation was in such terms as to apply only to future transactions, or whether it had retrospective effect.

At common law, the *ultra vires* doctrine does not apply to corporations created by Royal Charter[23] and so the foregoing discussion does not apply to such corporations where their legal capacity is *not* defined or limited by statute. Nor does the doctrine apply to limited liability partnerships which, by virtue of being registered under the Limited Liability Partnerships Act 2000 have become bodies corporate[24]: this follows from s.1(3) of the Act, which provides that such a partnership "has unlimited capacity".

(11) Dissolution of partnerships

Where a contract is made with a partnership, the effect of the dissolution of the partnership on the contract depends on a number of distinctions. The first relates to the cause of the dissolution; the second turns on the construction of the contract.   4–034

(a) *Cause of the dissolution*

Dissolution may result either from the voluntary act of the partners or from some other event, such as the death of a partner.   4–035

(i) Voluntary dissolution

This kind of dissolution (*e.g.* by notice given by one partner to the others) cannot be relied on by the partners as a ground of frustration since a party cannot rely on self-induced frustration. If it has any effect on the contract, it is a wrongful repudiation which the other party can accept as a ground for bringing the contract to an end,[25] without prejudice to his right to damages (though these may be reduced on account of his failure to mitigate if it was reasonable to expect him to continue the contractual relationship with the remaining members of the firm after the retirement of one[26]). The position is the same where the partnership is for a fixed   4–036

---

[23] *Case of Sutton's Hospital* (1613) 10 Co. Rep. 1 at 306; *Wenlock v River Dee Co* (1885) 36 Ch. D. 374 at 385; *Jenkin v Pharmaceutical Society* [1921] 1 Ch. 392 at 398; *Institution of Mechanical Engineers v Cane* [1961] A.C. 696 at 724; *Hazell v Hammersmith & Fulham LBC* [1992] 2 A.C. 1 at 39; the point is left open in *Credit Suisse v Allerdale BC* [1997] Q.B. 306 at 336.

[24] See ss.1(2), 2 and 3 of the Act.

[25] *Brace v Calder* [1895] 2 Q.B. 253; *cf. Tunstall v Condon* [1980] I.C.R. 786.

[26] In *Brace v Calder*, above, the injured party was held to have failed to mitigate in this way when he refused an offer of re-employment from the newly constituted firm, and he recovered only nominal damages.

term and the partners enter into a contract with a third party for a period exceeding the length of that term. On the expiry of the term of the partnership, the partners will then be in breach of the contract with the third party, who will be entitled to rescind on account of that breach.[27]

(ii) Dissolution by death of a partner

4–037 A partnership is, unless the partnership articles otherwise provide, dissolved by the death of a partner.[28] The dissolution of the partnership on this ground would not appear to amount to a breach and could be a ground of frustration. This conclusion is less obvious in the case of a partnership than in the case of a corporation, since a partnership does not, as such, have legal personality: thus the contract is not, as a matter of legal theory, with the firm, but with the partners; and, as their liability is joint and several,[29] it can be argued that on the death of a partner the survivors and the executors of the deceased remain both liable and entitled under it. Where the contract is not of a "personal" nature, this conclusion has indeed been reached. In *Phillips v Alhambra Palace Co*[30] the claimants were a "troupe of music-hall performers" who had entered into a contract with "the Alhambra Palace Company" to give musical performances at the latter's premises. The company was actually a partnership, but neither this fact, nor the composition of the partnership was known to the claimants. After the death of one of the partners, the claimants recovered damages for breach of the contract from the two surviving partners and the executors of the one who had died. If, on the other hand, the contract is of a personal nature, the death of a partner can bring it to an end, *e.g.* if the contract is one of agency or employment.[31] Such a contract could, indeed, be frustrated even where the death of a partner did *not* bring the partnership to an end because (as is common in the case of large professional partnerships) the articles expressly provide that the death of a partner is not to have this effect.[32] If the relationship of an agent or employee was one of personal confidence with a particular partner, the contract might be frustrated on the ground that the relationship had come to an end (even if the partnership had not) on the death of that partner. On the other hand, the contract would not be dissolved by the death of a partner if the composition of the partnership was a matter of indifference to the other contracting party, so that the contract was not a "personal" contract in the sense in which that word is understood in this branch of the law.

---

[27] *Briggs v Oates* [1990] I.C.R. 473.

[28] Partnership Act 1890, s.33(1).

[29] *ibid.*, s.9.

[30] [1900] 1 Q.B. 69.

[31] See *Tasker v Shepherd* (1861) 5 H. & N. 575 (employment of agent by partnership terminated by death of one of the partners); *Friend v Young* [1897] 2 Ch. 421 (employment of partnership as agent terminated by death of one of the partners); *Bowstead and Reynolds on Agency* (17th ed.), p.565 (describing the contract as "frustrated.")

[32] Partnership Act 1890, s.33(1) recognises the validity of such provisions.

(iii) Dissolution by mental illness and other incapacity

If a partner becomes a mental patient whose property is subject to the   4–038
control of the court under the Mental Health Act 1983,[33] then the court is
empowered by that Act to make an order for the dissolution of a
partnership of which the patient is a member.[34] The effect of such an order
could be to frustrate a contract between the firm and a third party; it is
submitted that it would have this effect in the same circumstances as those
which would frustrate a contract where the partnership was dissolved by
death. Under s.36(b) of the Partnership Act 1890, the court may also, on an
application by a partner, decree the dissolution of a partnership "when a
partner, other than the partner suing, becomes in any other way [*i.e.* other
than through mental illness] permanently incapable of performing his part
of the partnership contract". This provision seems to refer to physical,
rather than to legal, incapacity,[35] and would seem to be broad enough to
cover both cases in which the "incapacity" was, and those in which it was
not, due to the voluntary act of the partner suffering from the incapacity. In
accordance with the principles already stated it would seem that a decree
dissolving the partnership under s.36(b) would be a ground of frustration
only where the "incapacity" was not due to the partner's voluntary conduct.

The foregoing discussion is concerned with the effect of a court order
dissolving the partnership on a contract between the firm and a third
party: it is not concerned with the effect of a partner's mental illness or
other incapacity on the contract of partnership itself. The fact that the
statutory provisions described above provide for dissolution by court order
seems to suggest that the contract of partnership is not discharged under
the common law doctrine of frustration; for such discharge would be
automatic, and so would not require the intervention of the court.

(b) *Construction of the contract*

The contract may be construed as being *either* a contract with the partners   4–039
constituting the firm when the contract was made *or* one with the partners
who may constitute the firm from time to time; no doubt the latter
construction is now the more likely to be adopted where the contract is
with a large firm of frequently fluctuating membership. If the contract is
of the first of these kinds, dissolution of the firm by the death of a partner
can be a ground of frustration[36] and clearly will be such a ground if the

---

[33] Mental Health Act 1983, Pt VII. For the proposed repeal and replacement of
Part VII of the 1983 Act, see above, para.4–019 n.29.

[34] *ibid.*, s.96(1)(g).

[35] See *Whitwell v Arthur* (1865) 35 Beav. 140, on which s.36(b) seems to be based. It
was there held that *temporary* paralysis of one member of a partnership of two
chemists was not a ground for ordering dissolution; but it seems that the
decision would have been different if the disability had been permanent.

[36] This possibility is recognised in *Briggs v Oates* [1990] I.C.R. 473 at 483, where the
effect on a contract of employment of the "death or bankruptcy or incapacity"
of a member of the employer firm is left open. Bankruptcy, though a ground for
dissolution of the partnership under Partnership Act 1890, s.33(1) would
probably not be a ground of frustration of a contract with a third party since it is
likely to be regarded as due to the fault of a member of the firm. Moreover

contract is of a "personal" nature. If the contract is of the second kind, it would seem to follow that the contract would not be frustrated by the death of a partner even if that death dissolved the partnership. Nor could it be argued that the contract was frustrated on the ground that the continued existence of any particular partner was vital to the continuation of the contractual relationship between the firm and the other contracting party: such an argument would be inconsistent with the assumed meaning of the contract as one with the members of the firm from time to time.

(c) *Limited liability partnerships*

4-040   The problems discussed in paras 4–034 to 4–039 with regard to the effects of the death or incapacity of a partner on the continued existence of the partnership, and hence on contracts between third parties and the firm, cannot arise (or at least arise in the same form) where the partnership is a limited liability partnership registered under the Limited Liability Partnership Act 2000. Such a partnership is a body corporate,[37] so that the death of a partner, though it no doubt results in that person's ceasing to be a member of the partnership,[38] has no effect on the continued existence on the body corporate. It follows that the death of a partner cannot normally have any of the effects (discussed in para.4–037, above) on contracts with third parties that result from the death of a member of an ordinary partnership. Even where the third party entered in the contract with the limited liability partnership in reliance on some personal skill or other characteristic of a particular member of the partnership, it seems unlikely that the contract would be frustrated by the death of that partner (any more than a contract with a company incorporated under the Companies Acts would be frustrated by the death of one of its directors whose personal qualities induced the third party to enter into that contract). The effect on contracts with third parties of the dissolution (in other ways[39]) of a limited liability partnership is more likely to be governed by the rules which determine the effect on such contracts with companies (discussed in paras 4–030 and 4–031, above) than on the rules discussed in para.4–039, above.

V. UNAVAILABILITY OF A PARTICULAR SOURCE

4-041   A contract may be frustrated if its subject-matter is to be taken from a particular source which fails, or otherwise becomes unavailable, after the

---

"incapacity" (if the reference is to mental incapacity) might not have any effect on a contract with a third party at all since it would not of itself dissolve the partnership. Section 33(1) of the Partnership Act 1890 contains no reference to such incapacity nor would dissolution of the partnership follow from the common law rules as to the contractual capacity of mental patients.

[37] Limited Liability Partnerships Act 2000, s.1(2); see also ss.2 and 3.

[38] See ss.4(3), 7(1)(a); for the cessation of membership by events such as the partner's bankruptcy, see s.7(1)(b)–(d).

[39] See s.14 (insolvency and winding up).

time of contracting. This could, for example, be the position where a contract was made for the sale of goods which were to be taken from a particular crop, and that crop later failed; or where the contract was one for the sale of goods to be exported from a particular country, and such export was later prevented by prohibition of export, or by some natural disaster (even though this did not destroy or damage the goods themselves). Our present concern is with cases in which the source fails completely; further problems which arise when the source fails in part only will be considered in Ch.5.[40] The question to be considered here is in what circumstances the total failure of a source of supply can be a ground of discharge.

(1) Has the source failed?

Before the question just put is reached, a preliminary issue may arise: namely, whether the source of supply has indeed failed; or, to put the point in another way, how the source is to be defined.   **4–042**

(a) *In general*

An issue of this kind arose in *Gelling v Crispin*[41] where a contract had been   **4–043** made for the sale of "New South Wales wheat". Later the government of that State compulsorily acquired all wheat in the State, except for wheat already in transit to other States. Two reasons were given for holding that the contract was not discharged: first, the government had not compulsorily acquired all wheat in the State (wheat in transit being excepted), and secondly the compulsory purchase related only to wheat in the State: it remained possible for the seller to acquire "New South Wales wheat" which had been exported before the compulsory acquisition, and to deliver wheat so acquired to the buyer in performance of his contract with the buyer, so that the source had not failed.

(b) *Application to c.i.f. contracts: the general rule*

The second of the two lines of reasoning just stated is often applied where   **4–044** goods are sold on c.i.f. terms which specify a place or country of shipment, or otherwise indicate a country of origin, and a subsequent event prevents shipment from that place or country. The effect of the argument is that the seller will not be discharged in such circumstances by the common law doctrine of frustration; for as a general rule a c.i.f. seller can perform either by shipping goods of the contract description or by acquiring such goods already afloat and appropriating them to the contract[42]; so that if one such method of performance becomes impossible, the other must be

---

[40] See below, paras 5–010 to 5–032.

[41] (1917) 23 C.L.R. 443.

[42] *J H Vantol Ltd v Fairclough, Dodd & Jones Ltd* [1955] 1 W.L.R. 642 at 646 (reversed *ibid.* at 1302, but restored [1957] 1 W.L.R. 136; the actual decision is discussed at below, para.12–028); *Benjamin's Sale of Goods* (6th ed.), para.19–011. UCC, s.2–320 does not expressly refer to the possibility of the seller's performing his duty by buying afloat; but Comment 8, para.2, assumes that he can perform in

adopted.[43] One case of this kind was *Ashmore & Son v CS Cox & Co*[44] where c.i.f.[45] sellers of Manila hemp to be shipped from the Philippine Islands had been prevented by war from shipping goods of the contract description but were nonetheless held to be in breach on the ground that their undertaking was an "absolute"[46] one. This aspect of the case has been discussed in Ch.2[47]; and the decline of the doctrine of absolute contracts as a general principle,[48] may account for later criticisms of the case in a number of decisions at first instance.[49] But one of these was later overruled by the House of Lords,[50] while *Ashmore & Son v CS Cox & Co* has been approved in the Court of Appeal.[51] A significant feature of the case is that, although the war had prevented the sellers from shipping hemp from the Philippines, there had within the contract period been a shipment "of hemp which, had it been a shipment of the [sellers] would have satisfied the [buyers]".[52] Hence the decision could now be explained on the ground that the source had not failed since there were goods available which the seller could, and should, have bought afloat so as to put himself into the position of being able to perform his contract.

The argument that a c.i.f. seller who is prevented from shipping must buy afloat can also prevent him from relying on express contractual provisions for supervening events, such as *force majeure* clauses.[53] Whether the seller can rely on the clause in such circumstances depends on its construction; authorities on this question will be discussed in Ch.12.[54]

(c) *C.i.f. contracts: the exception*

4–045   An exception to the general rule, that a c.i.f. seller who is prevented from shipping goods must buy afloat, was created in the cases which arose when the United States authorities in June 1973 imposed a ban on the export of soyabean meal from that country.[55] The cases were concerned with the

---

this way. Under the proposed amendments to the UCC (above, para.2–042, n.17), s.2–320 is to be deleted.

[43] See below, para.10–002.

[44] [1899] 1 Q.B. 436.

[45] See the reports in 68 L.J. Q.B. 75; 4 Com. Cas. 48.

[46] Subject to an exclusion clause which was held, on construction, not to apply.

[47] See above, para.2–034.

[48] See above, para.2–029, where we saw that in the present context the doctrine may survive.

[49] *Carapanayoti v ET Green Ltd* [1959] 1 Q.B. 131 at 137; *Albert D Gaon v Société Interprofessionalle des Oléagineux Fluides Alimentaires* [1959] 2 Lloyd's Rep. 30 at 42 (there is no reference to this point to the Law Reports: [1960] 2 Q.B. 318); *Lewis Emanuel & Son Ltd. v Sammut* [1959] 2 Lloyd's Rep. 629 at 640.

[50] *Carapanayoti v ET Green*, above, overruled in *Tsakiroglou v Noblee Thorl GmbH* [1962] A.C. 93.

[51] *Blackburn Bobbin Co Ltd v TW Aleen & Sons Ltd* [1918] 2 K.B. 467 at 470.

[52] [1899] 1 Q.B. 436 at 438.

[53] *e.g. PJ van der Zijden Wildhandel v Tucker & Cross Ltd* [1975] 2 Lloyd's Rep. 240.

[54] See below, paras 12–022 to 12–024.

[55] See generally Ch.12, below, and *Benjamin's Sale of Goods* (6th ed.), paras 18–312 to 18–322.

effect of this embargo on c.i.f. sales of United States soyabean meal to buyers many of whom then contracted to resell, so that "string" or "circle" contracts were formed under which each seller had "already made arrangements to ship the goods by himself or some shipper higher up in the string".[56] The resulting "chains" of buyers and sellers commonly had 20 to 30 (and sometimes as many as 100) "links".[57] All the contracts in question were made on the terms set out in Form 100 of the Grain and Feed Trade Association, and this form contained "prohibition" and "*force majeure*" clauses, excusing the sellers in specified events, provided that certain conditions (*e.g.* as to giving notice of an obstacle to performance) were complied with. The effect of the export embargo was to push prices up steeply,[58] so that buyers claimed damages from the sellers who were unable to deliver; while the sellers relied on the *force majeure* and prohibition clauses. For reasons to be considered in Ch.12[59] many such buyers' claims succeeded; but one argument was resolved in favour of the sellers. That argument was that the contracts were on c.i.f. terms; that, although the sellers could not ship United States soyabean meal because of the embargo, there was United States soyabean meal afloat which had been shipped before the embargo had come into force; and that the sellers should have bought such soyabean meal and appropriated it to their contracts with their buyers. That argument was rejected on the ground that, in the special circumstances of these cases, the application of the ordinary rule (that a c.i.f. seller who cannot ship must buy afloat) would drive prices to "unheard-of levels".[60] The special circumstances were that the goods were to come from a specified country; that, in the case of "string" contracts, it was impossible to tell *which* seller was required to buy afloat; and that, if every seller in each string tried to buy afloat, the result would be to create an extreme pressure on prices, since, in relation to the contractual commitments of the sellers, the amount of soyabean meal of the contract description available afloat when the embargo was imposed was severely limited. In such circumstances, the seller can rely on the clause because he cannot obtain goods of the contract description "by the exercise of any means reasonably open to him".[61]

Similar reasoning was applied when the embargo was lifted in   **4–046** September 1973 with regard to *future* contracts. It was held that sellers

---

[56] *Tradax Export SA v André & Cie* [1976] 1 Lloyd's Rep. 416 at 423.

[57] *Cook Industries Inc v Meunerie Liègeois SA* [1981] 1 Lloyd's Rep. 359 at 364.

[58] *Bremer Handelsgesellschaft mbH v Vanden Avenne-Izegem PVBA* [1978] 2 Lloyd's Rep. 109 at 122. The contract price on April 5, 1973, was $239.50 per ton; the embargo was imposed on June 27, 1973; on July 10, 1973 the market price had risen to $635 per ton; on September 10, 1973 it had fallen back to $215 per ton: see [1977] 1 Lloyd's Rep. 133 at 143.

[59] See below, paras 12–033 to 12–039.

[60] *Tradax Export SA v André & Cie* [1976] 1 Lloyd's Rep. 416 at 423; this part of the reasoning of the Court of Appeal was approved by the House of Lords in *Bremer Handelsgesellschaft mbH v Vanden Avenne-Izegem PVBA* [1978] 2 Lloyd's Rep. 109 at 115, 125.

[61] *André & Cie SA v Tradax Export SA* [1983] 1 Lloyd's Rep. 254 at 258; *Continental Grain Export Corp v STM Grain Ltd* [1979] 2 Lloyd's Rep. 460 at 473.

were not then bound to go into the market to procure the amounts that they had been unable to deliver under *existing* (pre-embargo) contracts which called for delivery in September; for to have required all sellers in a string of contracts to do this in the "limited market" for goods shipped in September would have driven prices up to "levels just as unheard of"[62] as those that would have been reached if such sellers had been obliged to buy afloat when the embargo was originally imposed.

(d) *Scope of the exception*

4–047   In discussing the scope of the exception to the normal rule, that a c.i.f. seller who is prevented from shipping must acquire goods afloat, the first point to note is that the cases which establish the exception were concerned, not with discharge under the common law doctrine of frustration, but with excuse of the seller under express contractual provisions. The significance of this point is further emphasised in Ch.6.[63]

Apart from this restriction, there is some doubt as to the scope of the exception in cases of the kind so far discussed. One view is that "if shipment is prevented by *force majeure* the shipper is under no obligation to buy afloat"[64]; but if this is to be taken literally it is, with respect, too wide, and inconsistent with cases which hold that a c.i.f. seller cannot (where buying afloat is possible) rely on a *force majeure* clause merely because shipment has been prevented.[65] A second view is that the exception is restricted to the particular facts (including the provisions of the contracts)[66] in the soyabean meal cases cited above, in one of which it was said that there was no duty to buy afloat "in circumstances such as the present"[67] and "in the context of this particular system of purchase and sale of goods".[68] This view is, in turn, probably too narrow. The justification for the exception suggests that the important factors for determining its scope are that the contract should specify the country of origin; that shipment from that country should be prevented (whether by prohibition of export or by *force majeure*); and that the contract should be one of a "string" or "circle" of contracts, leading back to a relevant shipper[69] who, at the time of the contract in question, had made, or undertaken to make, arrangements to ship goods intended for appropriation to that contract.[70] It is in this situation that attempted performance of

---

[62] *Cook Industries v Tradax Export SA* [1983] 1 Lloyd's Rep. 327 at 344, affirmed [1985] 2 Lloyd's Rep. 454.

[63] See below, para.6–038.

[64] *Bremer Handelsgesellschaft mbH v Vanden Avenne-Izegem PVBA*, above, n.60, at 121.

[65] e.g. *PJ van der Zijden Wildhandel NV v Tucker & Cross Ltd* [1975] 2 Lloyd's Rep. 240.

[66] See *Warinco AG v Fritz Mautner* [1978] 1 Lloyd's Rep. 151 at 154 (*per* Megaw L.J.).

[67] *Bremer Handelsgesellschaft mbH v Vanden Avenne-Izegem PVBA*, above, n.60, at 125.

[68] *ibid.* at 131.

[69] See below, para.12–037.

[70] *Warinco AG v Fritz Mautner* [1978] 1 Lloyd's Rep. 151 at 156 (*per* Bridge L.J.); *cf. ibid.* at 154 (*per* Megaw L.J.); *Bunge SA v Deutsche Conti-Handelsgesellschaft mbH* [1979] 2 Lloyd's Rep. 435 at 439; it is submitted that these views are to be preferred to the suggestion of Lord Denning M.R. in *Bremer Handelsgesellschaft*

a duty to buy afloat could lead to the extreme pressure on prices which is said to justify the exception.

The exception in one respect goes beyond the situations so far discussed. It can apply where a limited supply of goods is available for reasons other than that they had already been shipped at the time of the supervening event. This possibility arose in the soyabean cases because the embargo was subject to certain "loopholes": it did not apply to goods which, when it was imposed, were already being loaded or were on lighters destined for an exporting vessel.[71] If all sellers in string contracts tried to buy the limited quantity of available "loopholes" goods, prices would again be driven up to "unheard-of levels"[72]; and the exception was accordingly extended to this situation. The case[73] in which the extension was made further suggests that a seller could rely on the exception *without* having to show that he was a seller in a "string" of contracts or that he had (before the embargo was imposed) "made arrangements to ship the goods by himself or through some shipper higher in the string".[74] This suggestion gives rise to difficulties which will be further considered in Ch.12.[75]

(2) Effect of failure of the source

Where the source of supply has indeed failed, the question whether the contract is discharged depends on a distinction between three groups of cases.   4-048

(a) *Source expressly referred to in the contract*

The first group consists of cases in which the contract expressly refers to the source of supply. The typical situation is that which has arisen in the "growing crop" cases in which a farmer has agreed to sell a crop (or part of a crop) to be grown on land which is specifically referred to in the contract. The leading English case is *Howell v Coupland*[76] where the defendant, a farmer, contracted to sell to a potato merchant 200 tons of potatoes to be grown "on [the defendant's] land in Whaplode". The defendant duly planted that land with potatoes, and also planted potatoes on other land which he had at Holbeach; but the crops were attacked by disease, so that only 79.5 tons were produced. The defendant delivered the 79.5 tons (even though his contract did not oblige him to deliver the   4-049

---

mbH v Finagrain, etc., SA [1981] 2 Lloyd's Rep. 259 at 265, that *no* string need be established for the purpose of the exception.

[71] For further problems arising in relation to these "loopholes", see below, para.12–038.

[72] Above, n.60.

[73] *Bunge SA v Kruse* [1979] 1 Lloyd's Rep. 279, affirmed on other grounds [1980] 2 Lloyd's Rep. 142 and referred to with apparent approval on this point in *André & Cie v Tradax Export SA* [1983] 1 Lloyd's Rep. 254 at 267.

[74] Above, at n.56.

[75] See below, para.12–039.

[76] (1876) 1 Q.B.D. 258, affirming (1874) L.R. 9 Q.B. 462. For similar American cases, see *Ontario Deciduous Fruit Growers' Association v Cutting Fruit-Packing Co*, 66 P. 28 (1901); *Holly Hill Fruit Products Inc v Bob Staton Inc*, 275 So. 583 (1973).

potatoes from Holbeach); and it was held that he was not liable for his failure to deliver the remainder of the 200 tons which he had agreed to sell. In the Court of Queen's Bench,[77] Blackburn J. regarded the case as being governed by the principle stated in *Taylor v Caldwell, i.e.* that if parties contract on the basis of the continued existence of a "particular specified thing",[78] or of a "particular ... chattel",[79] then they are discharged by the "perishing of the thing".[80] In the Court of Appeal, Mellish L.J. likewise regarded the contract as "an agreement to sell what may be called specific things"[81] and said that therefore neither party was liable if performance became impossible. These expressions of opinion gave rise to the view that *Howell v Coupland* was the basis of s.7 of the Sale of Goods Act 1979,[82] under which an agreement for the sale of specific goods is avoided if the goods perish without fault of either party before the risk has passed to the buyer.[83] It is, however, clear that the potatoes in *Howell v Coupland* were not "specific goods" within the definition of that term in the Sale of Goods Act[84]: only 200 tons out of the expected crop were sold, and a contract for the sale of a specified quantity to be taken from an identified bulk was not then[85] and is not now one for the sale of "specific" goods.[86] It is also uncertain whether an agreement for the sale even of the *whole* of an identified growing crop, or of a crop to be grown on designated land, can be "specific goods" for the purpose of the Sale of Goods Act.[87] These difficulties may account for the fact that the other judgments in the Court of Appeal in *Howell v Coupland* are more equivocal than that of Mellish L.J. Thus Lord Coleridge C.J. (after referring to *Taylor v Caldwell*) says that the "true ground" of the decision in the court below was based on the "simple and obvious construction"[88] of the agreement; while Bagally L.J. and Cleasby B. do not refer either to *Taylor v Caldwell* or to "specific goods". These difficulties are reflected in subsequent judicial

---

[77] (1874) L.R. 9 Q.B. 462 at 465.

[78] (1863) 3 B. & S. 826 at 833.

[79] *ibid.* at 839.

[80] *ibid.* at 834.

[81] (1876) 1 Q.B.D. 258 at 262.

[82] See the comment to s.7 in Chalmers, *Sale of Goods Act 1893* (1st ed., 1894).

[83] See above, para.3–013.

[84] Sale of Goods Act 1979, s.61(1), definition of "specific goods", above, para.3–017.

[85] *Re Wait* [1927] 1 Ch. 606, discussing the meaning of "specific" in Sale of Goods Act 1979, s.52 before the amendments to that definition referred to in n.86, below.

[86] As a result of amendments to the Sale of Goods Act 1979, s.61 made by the Sale of Goods (Amendment) Act 1995, parts of an identified bulk expressed as *fractions* or *percentages* are now "specific goods" within the definition of that expression in s.61(1); but a contract for the sale of a specified quantity out of such a bulk remains one for the sale of unascertained goods: see s.20A(1).

[87] See *Kursell v Timber Operators and Contractors Ltd* [1927] 1 K.B. 298, discussed above, para.3–019.

[88] (1876) 1 Q.B.D. 258 at 261.

discussions of *Howell v Coupland.* According to these,[89] the case is now to be explained in one of two ways.

First, it can be regarded as an application of the rule, stated in s.5(2) of the Act, that there may be "a contract for the sale of goods the acquisition of which by the seller depends on a contingency which may or may not happen", *i.e.* the contract was conditional on the coming into existence of at least 200 tons from the crop at Whaplode. On this view, the failure of the specified source to produce the quantity of goods to which the contract referred did not *discharge* the contract, but amounted to a failure of a condition precedent, so that the seller's obligation *never accrued at all.* This analysis was, indeed commonly adopted in cases concerned with contracts under which goods were sold "to arrive" in, or "on arrival of" a named ship. Such contracts are no longer common, but they were extensively considered in the older authorities.[90] According to these, such a contract was normally construed as subject to a double condition precedent, *i.e.* at the arrival both of the ship and of the quantity of goods specified in the contract.[91] It followed that the seller was not liable if the ship or the goods did not arrive,[92] so long as the non-arrival was "due to accidental circumstances and not due to any fraud of the seller",[93] and so long as it was not due simply to his failure to ship[94]; if the non-arrival was due to such failure, the seller was liable (even in the absence of fraud) on the principle that a party is liable for wrongfully preventing the occurrence of a condition precedent.[95] The construction of such contracts as subject to a double condition precedent was not, however, invariably adopted. Sometimes is was held that the seller's obligation was conditional only on the arrival of the ship (even though she contained no goods of the contract description),[96] or that the seller had "warranted" that goods of the contract description had been shipped.[97] Such a "warranty" would not,

4-050

---

[89] *Re Wait* [1927] 1 Ch. 606, at 631; *HR & S Sainsbury Ltd v Street* [1972] 1 W.L.R. 834 at 837.

[90] See *Benjamin's Sale of Goods* (6th ed.), paras 21–022 to 21–028, on which the following summary is based. *cf.* UCC, s.2–613 so far as it applies to "no arrival, no sale" terms, below, para.15–017. Under the proposals for amending UCC, Art.2 (above, para.2–042, n.17), the reference to such contracts is to be deleted from s.2–613.

[91] *Johnson v Macdonald* (1842) 9 M. & W. 600 at 606. There is some support for the view that there was "no sale" until the condition occurred: *Hollis Bros & Co Ltd v White Sea Timber Trust Ltd* [1936] 3 All E.R. 895 at 900; but it is submitted that the preferable view is that stated in *Johnson v Macdonald,* above, at 605: "the language of the contract renders *the performance of it* conditional on a double event". *Lovatt v Hamilton* (1839) 5 M. & W. 639 at 644 states the condition to be "precedent" even though the contract there provided that it was to "*become* void" in the event of non-arrival.

[92] *Johnson v Macdonald,* above; *Boyd v Sifkin* (1809) 2 Camp. 326.

[93] *Hawes v Humble* (1809) 2 Camp. 327a.

[94] *Barnett v Javeri & Co* [1916] 2 K.B. 390.

[95] See *Mackay v Dick* (1881) 6 App. Cas. 251; *Thompson v ASDA-MFI Group plc* [1988] Ch. 241.

[96] *Hale v Rawson* (1858) 4 C.B.N.S. 85.

[97] *Gorrissen v Perrin* (1857) 2 C.B. 681.

however, exclude the possibility of frustration if the contract was for the sale of goods to arrive in a named ship and the failure of the goods to arrive was due to the loss of the ship, or to some other accident affecting the ship, or if delivery at the specified destination became illegal.[98] It was also possible for the arrival condition to be subsequent rather than precedent, *e.g.* where the contract provided that it was to be "void" if the ship should fail to arrive,[99] or if the ship or the goods should be lost,[1] or if the ship should arrive without goods of the contract description on board.[2] In such cases, the effect of the failure of the specified event to occur would no doubt resemble frustration in that it would operate as a ground of discharge, but it would so operate under an express contractual provision, rather than under the common law doctrine of frustration.[3] The same would be true if a contract for the sale of the whole, or part of, a growing crop provided that the contract was to become void if the crop failed.

4–051   The second of the judicial explanations[4] of *Howell v Coupland* is that the decision is preserved by what is now s.62(2)[5] of the Sale of Goods Act 1979, under which the "rules of the common law ... except in so far as they are inconsistent with the provisions of this Act ... apply to contracts for the sale of goods". *Howell v Coupland* can thus be regarded as authority for the common law rule that a contract for the sale of goods to be taken from a source to which express reference is made in the contract will be discharged at common law if the source fails without the fault of either party. There is no reason to suppose that this rule is to be restricted to the facts of *Howell v Coupland*, *i.e.* to the sale of only a specified quantity out of a growing crop. The case for discharge of the contract would certainly be no weaker, and could plausibly be regarded as stronger, if the contract had been for the sale of the whole crop to be grown on the seller's land at Whaplode, or of a fraction or percentage of that crop.[6]

For the purpose of the rule in *Howell v Coupland*, it is necessary to specify the source with some degree of particularity. The mere description of goods by a name having certain regional or geographical associations does not necessarily amount to a sufficient indication that the goods are to

---

[98] *Barnett v Javeri & Co* [1916] 2 K.B. 390 at 394; *Benjamin's Sale of Goods* (6th ed.), para.21–028; *cf. Nickoll & Knight v Ashton Edridge & Co* [1900] 2 K.B. 126, below, para.4–062.

[99] *Lovatt v Hamilton* (1839) 5 M. & W. 639, but see above, n.91.

[1] *Lovatt v Hamilton*, above. *Johnson v Macdonald* (1842) 9 M. & W. 600.

[2] *cf. Lovatt v Hamilton*, above.

[3] *cf.* below, para.12–019.

[4] See above, n.89.

[5] Formerly Sale of Goods Act 1893, s.61(2), which is the subsection referred to in the authorities cited in n.89, above.

[6] The question whether such goods could be "specific" within s.61(2) would depend on the unresolved point referred to in above, para.4–049, at n.87; the answer would now be the same whether the sale was of the whole crop or of a fraction or percentage of it: see the amendment to the definition of "specific goods" made by the Sale of Goods (Amendment) Act 1995. s.2(d).

come from a specified source. In a South African case[7] it was accordingly said that a seller of "white Kaffir corn" would not be discharged even if he could show a total failure of the South African corn crop. The sale was regarded simply as one of generic goods; and this will often be true where the name of some locality has come to be attached in the trade to some commodity (such as Pershore plums, Worcester apples or Cheddar cheese) regardless of the actual place of origin of the goods in question.

The rule in *Howell v Coupland* furthermore applies only where it is clear that the specified source is intended to be exclusive. Thus where a contract of agency referred to shirts to be "manufactured or sold" by the principal, it was held that the contract was not frustrated by the destruction of the principal's factory.[8] The position would be the same where a contract of sale referred to several sources and the one which the seller intended to use failed, while another or others remained available. Under the rules relating to alternatives,[9] the contract would, in general, not be discharged. Similarly, where a contract of carriage was to be performed by the use of one of two named ships, the contract would not be frustrated merely on account of the loss of one of those ships.[10] The rule that a c.i.f. contract is not frustrated if shipment is prevented, so long as it remains possible for the seller to buy afloat,[11] could be explained on the same ground. But the preferable view of such cases is that the source has not failed at all: *prima facie*, it is simply "goods which have been shipped" not "goods which have been shipped by the seller".

A party is excused by the failure of a designated source of supply only   4–052
where that failure is not due to his want of care or diligence. Where a farmer is excused in the growing crop cases, it is always assumed that he has duly planted and cultivated his crop. If this were not the case, he would be liable: as Blackburn J. said in *Taylor v Caldwell*, the impossibility must occur "without default of the contractor"[12]; and he repeated the point in the present context when, in *Howell v Coupland*, he said that the result in that case would have been different if the crop had failed through the "default" of the seller.[13] A seller would similarly be in default where his failure to deliver goods of the contract description was due to the fact that the packaging to be provided by him for the goods was defective, or not of the dimensions or capacity required by the contract.[14] Similar reasoning can apply where the contract is for the sale of goods to be produced by the seller's supplier at a plant named in the contract between buyer and seller. In such a case, destruction of that plant may frustrate the

---

[7] *Herschman v Shapiro & Co*, 1926 T.P.D. 367 (where the failure was not in fact total).

[8] *Turner v Goldsmith* [1891] 1 Q.B. 544.

[9] Below, Ch.10.

[10] *J. Lauritzen A/S v Wijsmuller B V (The Super Servant Two)* [1990] 1 Lloyd's Rep. 1.

[11] See above, para.4–044.

[12] (1863) 3 B. & S. 826 at 834.

[13] (1874) L.R. 9 Q.B. 462 at 465.

[14] *Lebeaupin v Crispin* [1920] 2 K.B. 714 at 718; *cf. Fyffes Group Ltd v Reefer Express Line Pty Ltd (The Kriti Rex)* [1996] 2 Lloyd's Rep. 171 at 196; and see below, para.15–028.

contract, but this result will not follow merely because the supplier, working below capacity, has failed to produce an amount sufficient to enable the seller to perform his contract with the buyer. In an American case of this kind, the seller was said to be at fault as he had failed to show that he could not "by a timely contract ... have assured himself of a sufficient supply for its needs"[15]: he had simply failed to make an adequate supply contract. Yet a further illustration of the same principle is provided by the American case of *El Rio Oils (Canada) Ltd v Pacific Coast Asphalt Co.*[16] The plaintiff and the defendant were associated companies; the plaintiff agreed to supply oil from certain wells on specified land to the defendant, who in turn agreed to sell all the asphalt produced from that oil to a third party (the intervenor). The plaintiff refused to supply the oil to the defendant who in turn failed to supply the asphalt to the intervenor. One of the issues was whether the defendant was liable to the intervenor for breach of its contract to supply the asphalt. In spite of the fact that the oil was to be obtained from a specified source, the court held the defendant liable to intervenor, relying on the distinction drawn by Restatement, § 455 between subjective and objective impossibility. Now that this distinction has gone out of fashion in the United States,[17] one can explain the case on the ground that the court, in another part of its judgment, ordered specific performance of the plaintiff's undertaking to supply the oil to the defendant. It would seem that, where such a remedy is available to the seller, he cannot rely on breach of the supply contract as discharging him from his own obligations to his buyer under the contract of sale. Such an order may, however, not be available, *e.g.* where the goods are of such a kind that the seller (who is the buyer under the supply contract) can readily obtain similar goods from another source.[18] But if those similar goods are not of the description contained in the sale contract, they cannot be delivered in performance of *that* contract; so that the seller may be discharged from his obligation under the sale contract if that contract is exclusively for the sale of goods obtained from the named supplier.[19]

(b) *Unspecified source intended by one party only*

4–053   The second group of cases consists of those in which the contract contains no express reference to any source of supply; the seller intends to use a particular source of supply, but the buyer does not know this. The contract in such a case is simply one for the sale of unascertained generic goods; and if the source intended by the seller fails he is not excused but must procure goods of the contract description from another source. This was

---

[15] *Canadian Industrial Alcohol Co v Dunbar Molasses Co,* 179 N.E. 383 at 384 (1932); *cf.* below, at n.24.

[16] 213 P. 2d (1949).

[17] See above, para.3–003.

[18] *Chitty on Contracts* (29th ed.), para.27–011.

[19] See above, para.4–049. For view that the seller must make over his rights against the supplier to his buyer as a condition of claiming excuse from liability to the buyer, see UCC s.2–615, Comment 5; below, para.15–023.

the position in *Blackburn Bobbin Co Ltd v TW Allen & Sons Ltd*[20] where a sale of "Finland Birch timber" provided that the goods were to be delivered at Hull between June and November 1914. The seller did not keep stocks of "Finland Birch timber" in England but usually got such timber by shipping it through the Baltic, and this became impossible[21] as a result of the outbreak of the First World War in August 1914. It was held that the contract was not discharged since the buyer did not know that the seller kept no such stocks in England or that "Finland Birch timber" was normally shipped through the Baltic. A *fortiori* a seller cannot rely, by way of excuse, on the fact that a change of government policy in the country from which he intended to export the goods had made it more expensive for him to do so, his intention not being known to (let alone shared by) the buyer.[22] Another common example of the operation of the same principle is that a seller of goods is not excused where he is let down by the supplier from whom he expected to get the goods and who is *not* named in the contract. This point is illustrated by the *Intertradex*[23] case which arose out of a sale of 800 tonnes of Mali groundnut expellers. The seller knew, but the buyer did not, that these were produced by only one supplier, and this source of supply failed because of a mechanical breakdown at that sole supplier's factory. It was held that seller was not discharged. Such a result seems to be eminently reasonable as the seller presumably had a remedy against the supplier; or, if he did not (because that supplier had excluded liability for delays due to mechanical breakdown), the seller should have correspondingly excluded liability to his buyer. If he fails to do so, he can also be said to be at "fault" in failing to make a proper supply contract (*i.e.* one which matches his obligations under the contract of sale), so that frustration would be excluded on that ground.[24] The seller can be liable even though the goods were described as being of a certain brand which is used exclusively by the supplier from whom the seller had intended to obtain the goods, but who had failed to supply them.[25]

(c) *Source not expressly specified but intended by both parties*

The third and most controversial situation is that in which the contract contains no express reference to a source of supply but *both* parties contemplate that the goods (or other subject-matter) will be taken from a particular source, and that source then fails. In the New Zealand case of

4–054

---

[20] [1918] 2 K.B. 467; *cf. Greenway Bros v Jones* (1915) 32 T.L.R. 184; *Exportelisa SA v Giuseppi & Figli Soc Coll* [1978] 1 Lloyd's Rep. 433; Restatement 2d, § 263, Illustration 1; *Bunge Corp v Miller*, 381 F. Supp. 176 (1974); *Colley v Bi State Inc*, 586 P. 2d 908 (1978).

[21] The case was one of impossibility, not of illegality, as no question arose of trading with the enemy.

[22] *Beves & Co Ltd v Farkas* [1953] 1 Lloyd's Rep. 103.

[23] *Intertradex SA v Lesieur Torteaux SARL* [1978] 2 Lloyd's Rep. 509, affirming [1977] 2 Lloyd's Rep. 146.

[24] *Atisa SA v Aztec AG* [1983] 2 Lloyd's Rep. 579 at 585; *Canadian Industrial Alcohol Co v Dunbar Molasses Co*, 179 N.E. 383 at 384 (1932).

[25] *Re Thornett & Fehr and Yuills* [1921] 1 K.B. 219.

Spence v Shiel[26] evidence to this effect was indeed rejected as inadmissible under the parol evidence rule. It followed that a contract for the sale of potatoes by a farmer was not discharged by the failure of the seller's crop, since there was nothing in the contract itself to indicate that the potatoes were to be taken from the seller's land. But it is probable that such evidence would now be admitted under one of the growing list of cases which constitute exceptions to the parol evidence rule, or which fall outside its scope: for example as evidence to identify the subject-matter of the contract,[27] or as an aid to construction.[28] Thus *Spence v Shiel* may be contrasted with the American case of *Squillante v California Lands Inc*[29] where a grower of grapes had agreed to sell 10 carloads of grapes, but because of heat damage was able to produce only five carloads. He delivered those five and was held not liable for the balance, the court relying on the fact that he was not a dealer but a grower, and (in the light of this fact) construing the contract as one for the sale of grapes to be grown on the seller's land. In Australia the same conclusion has been supported on the grounds that the buyer had inspected the crop and that delivery was to be made at the seller's premises.[30] Another possibility is that the court will rely on evidence of this kind to rectify (or, in American terminology, to reform) the document in which the contract is set out, so as to include a reference to the land on which the goods were to be produced.[31] For these purposes it is, necessary to show that both parties intended, not merely that the goods were to come from the mutually contemplated source, but that it was to be a *term of the contract* that the goods should come from that source. The construction and rectification techniques, in other words, incorporate a reference to the source into the contract and so bring the case into the first of our three groups.[32] They leave open the question whether, in the absence of even such a judicially incorporated reference, the contract may still be discharged because of the failure of a source contemplated by both parties.

4–055   In the United States, discussion of this point begins with the 1892 Minnesota case of *Anderson v May*.[33] A contract was made for the sale of 591 bushels of beans grown by the seller (a farmer); he alleged that the contract was for the sale of beans to be grown on his market gardening farm near Red Wing, but the contract contained no reference to any particular land. Only 152 bushels were delivered and to a claim for damages by the buyer, the seller pleaded that an unexpected early frost had so injured the crop that he could not deliver the entire quantity. It was held that this was no excuse. Just as the buyer would have been obliged to accept a crop grown

---

[26] (1910) 30 N.Z.L.R. 88.
[27] Treitel, *The Law of Contract* (11th ed.), p.199.
[28] *ibid.*, pp.197–198; *cf. Campbell v Hostetter Farms Inc*, 380 A 2d 463 (1977).
[29] 44 P. 2d 81 (1935).
[30] *Ockerby & Co Ltd v Murdock* (1916) 19 W.A.R. 1; affirmed (1916) 22 C.L.R. 420.
[31] As in *Snipes Mountain Co v Benz Bros & Co*, 298 P. 714 (1931).
[32] *i.e.* that discussed above, paras 4–049 to 4–052.
[33] 52 N.W. 530 (1892).

on other land ("though not ... previously cultivated by"[34] the seller), so the seller was not excused merely because the crop on particular land had failed. The court referred to *Howell v Coupland,*[35] but distinguished that case on the ground (apparently) that there the contract had expressly specified the land on which the crop was to be grown. Exactly what was decided in *Anderson v May* is obscure because of a number of special features of the case. The contract was not simply one for the sale of beans: it provided that the farmer should "*raise,* sell and deliver them". Moreover, the report does not make it clear whether only the seller contemplated that the beans were to be grown on his farm at Red Wing or whether both parties contemplated this. According to the Restatement (§ 460, Illustration 3) and the Restatement 2d (§ 263, Illustration 7) this is the crucial point: these Illustrations conclude that, where *both* parties contemplate that the crop will be grown on a particular piece of land, and the crop there fails, then the farmer is excused; but Restatement 2d, § 263, Illustration 8 holds the farmer liable if the parties have "no *common* understanding *where* [not 'by whom'] the beans will be grown".

The Uniform Commercial Code deals with the problem in three of the comments to s.2–615. Comment 9 says that the section applies (so that the seller may be discharged) "to the case of a farmer who has contracted to sell crops to be grown on *designated* land". But Comment 5 says that the section applies "where a particular source of supply is shown by the circumstances to have been *contemplated* or assumed by *the parties*"; and Comment 4 says that the section can apply in cases of "*local* crop failure." These Comments do not make it at all clear how *Anderson v May* would be decided under s.2–615. The case clearly does not fall within Comment 9; but it is less clear whether the source of supply was "contemplated" within Comment 5. We have seen that there was no finding that particular land was contemplated but that it was contemplated that the beans would be grown by the farmer. Does it follow from this that the source of supply was "contemplated ... by the parties" (*i.e.* both of them)? Or did it turn the crop failure into a "local" one within Comment 4? Is the reasoning of the court in *Anderson v May* perhaps a little unrealistic? If the beans were to be grown by the seller, is it not likely that the frost would have affected other land in the same vicinity? In 1892, the seller's farming operations are unlikely to have covered a wide geographical area, so it is probable that the same frost would have affected them all.

In England, there is little authority on the question whether the failure of a source of supply contemplated by both parties, but not referred to in the contract, is a ground of discharge.

Re Badische Co[36] is sometimes said to support the view that failure of a   **4–056** mutually contemplated (but not expressly specified) source of supply discharges the contract. In that case, a contract for the supply of chemicals was held to have been discharged by illegality, on the outbreak of the First World War, because both parties intended the goods to be obtained from

---

[34] *ibid.* at 530.
[35] (1876) 1 Q.B.D. 258; above, para.4–049.
[36] [1921] 2 Ch. 331.

Germany. However, it should be emphasised that the alleged ground of discharge was not supervening impossibility but supervening illegality. It would have been contrary to public policy to have allowed the contract to subsist after the outbreak of war, and this would have been so whether the enemy source was specified or merely contemplated. Where supervening illegality is alleged to be the ground of discharge, the court has to take considerations of public interest into account. In this respect, such cases differ from those concerned with supervening impossibility, in which the court is concerned only with loss-allocation between the parties.[37] *Re Badische Co* is therefore not an authority which yields a rule which can safely be applied in "growing crop" or other physical impossibility cases. Analogous reasoning applies to a later case in which a contract for the sale of Argentinian maize was said to be frustrated when the export of maize of the contract description from Argentina became illegal by the law of that country.[38]

Lipton Ltd v Ford,[39] is equally inconclusive for a different reason. The contract was for the sale "50 tons Scotch Raspberries (Blairgowrie)". Blairgowrie was a raspberry growing *district* in Scotland where the sellers' principals owned some (but not all) of the raspberry-growing land. They had sold 1,276 tons of the 1916 crops to various buyers but because of a drought only 913 tons were produced on their land. Of this amount 363 tons were requisitioned by the government; and the sellers were unable to obtain further supplies from other growers. The disputed question was whether the requisition was valid; and the buyers *conceded* that, if the requisition was valid, the growers were released to the extent of the requisition. It was on the basis of this concession that the partial failure of the contemplated (but not stipulated) source released the sellers in part.

These English cases do not firmly establish the American position (taken by the Restatement, the Restatement 2d and the Uniform Commercial Code) that failure of a mutually contemplated source can be a ground of discharge; so that it is uncertain how an English court would deal with the problem. In a "growing crop" case, it seems probable that the American view would be followed in England, *i.e.* that the seller would be discharged where *both* parties "contemplated" the source of supply. It is less clear whether the English Courts would take the same view in the cases where the seller was cut off from a foreign source by prohibition of export or import, or by impossibility resulting from war. It is true that in the *Blackburn Bobbin* case the Court of Appeal stressed that the buyer did not know of the seller's need to get in a supply from abroad[40]; and one might deduce from this that, if *both* parties had contemplated that need, then the seller would have been discharged. On the other hand, it

---

[37] *cf.* below, para.8–002.

[38] *Société Co-operative Suisse des Céréales v La Plata Cereal Co SA* (1947) 80 Ll.L. Rep. 530; illegality by foreign law gives rise to issues of public policy even though these are not identical to those which arise where the contract becomes illegal by English law: below, para.8–054.

[39] [1917] 2 K.B. 647.

[40] [1918] 2 K.B. 467 at 470, 471; above, para.4–053.

can be argued that it is now common for commodity dealers to protect themselves by clauses expressly providing for interference with performance by "prohibition of export" or "*force majeure*" clauses; and that a seller who did not protect himself by such a clause, or by specifying the source, would now be held liable, even though the source was contemplated by both parties.

(d) *Failure of source affecting buyer's capacity to perform*

The preceding discussion deals only with the possibility that failure of a particular source of *supply* may affect the capacity of a *seller* to perform. It is also possible for supervening events to have the converse effect of affecting the capacity of a *buyer* to perform. **4–057**

(i) Capacity to take delivery

The first possibility is that the buyer's capacity to take delivery may be impaired. In English law, this gives rise to no special difficulty since the doctrine of frustration is expressed in general terms, so as to apply equally to the obligations of both parties. But we have noted that in the United States, s.2–615 of the Uniform Commercial Code in terms operates only to excuse the seller[41]; it is only in Comment 9 to that section that the possibility is recognised that a similar excuse may operate in favour of the buyer. One illustration of this possibility is provided by *Akins v Riverbank Canning Co*[42] where a cannery had contracted to buy tomatoes on the terms that it was to provide the boxes into which the tomatoes were to be delivered. The contract provided that, in the case of "shortage of boxes" reduced quantities were to be taken. The actual decision was that the cannery was bound to allocate the available boxes among its various suppliers,[43] so that it was partially excused by an express contractual term. It seems that, in the absence of such an express term, there might now be an excuse provided by law under Comment 9. Another possibility is that the contract might provide for delivery to be taken at a named port or on a named ship, and the port or the ship might subsequently become unavailable.[44] Such cases are, however, concerned with impossibility in the method of performance[45]: they are not truly analogous to failure of a specified source. Comment 9 also gives the example of goods bought "for a particular construction venture" which is subsequently cancelled. Again this is not analogous to failure of a source: the case put is not one of impossibility but one of frustration of purpose; and in the example given it is very doubtful whether the contract would be discharged on this ground.[46] Similarly, decided cases suggest that, in the example given in Comment 9, the plea of frustration would fail. It has, for example, been held that a buyer of industrial equipment was not discharged merely **4–058**

---

[41] See above, para.2–042.
[42] 183 P. 2d 86 (1947).
[43] *cf.* below, para.5–031.
[44] *Benjamin's Sale of Goods* (6th ed.), paras 20–015, 20–095.
[45] See below, paras 4–062 to 4–068.
[46] See below, para.7–035.

because the factory in which he intended to install it was destroyed,[47] and that a buyer of goods is not normally discharged merely because his purpose of exporting them was frustrated.[48] The buyer is likely to be able to rely on such events as a ground of excuse only where it is an express or implied term of the contract that the goods which form the subject-matter of the contract were bought for the purpose which has become impossible to achieve.

(ii) Capacity to pay

4–059 The most obvious analogy to failure of the seller's source of supply is failure of the buyer's source of funds. Since the source of payment is generally a matter of indifference to the seller, that source will normally be within the contemplation of the buyer only and so its failure will not discharge the contract: the buyer must get other funds from elsewhere for, in contemplation of law, the payment of money is never impossible. The point is illustrated by *Universal Corp v Five Ways Properties Ltd*,[49] where a contract was made for the sale of a property known as Dorset House (in London) for £885,000. To make payments due under the contract, the purchasers intended to use money in their bank in Nigeria; but a change in exchange control regulations in that country delayed the transmission of the money so that it did not arrive till after the completion date. It was held that the purchasers' inability to get the money from Nigeria in time did not discharge them since the source of payment was contemplated by one party only. In the United States, it has similarly been held that a contract for the sale of land is not discharged by failure of the buyer's intended source of funds.[50] *A fortiori* a contract for the sale of goods is not frustrated merely because the buyer's supply of the currency in which payment was to be made has become exhausted and cannot be replenished by him.[51] Events affecting the buyer's ability to pay could, however, be a ground of discharge where the contract *specified* a source of payment and that source later failed.

VI. Method of Performance Impossible

(1) In general

4–060 A contract may be discharged if it provides for a method of performance which subsequently becomes impossible. A simple example is provided by the American case of *Clarksville Land Co v Harriman*,[52] where a contract was

---

[47] *Sechrest v Forest Furniture Co*, 141 S.E. 2d 202 (1965).

[48] *Congimex, etc. SARL v Tradax Export SA* [1983] 1 Lloyd's Rep. 250.

[49] [1979] 1 All E.R. 552; *cf. Francis v Cowcliffe* (1977) 33 P. & C.R. 368.

[50] *Christie v Pilkington*, 273 S.W. 2d 533 (1954).

[51] *Congimex SARL (Lisbon) v Continental Grain Export Corp (New York)* [1979] 2 Lloyd's Rep. 346 at 353; *cf. Janos Paczy v Haendler & Naterman GmbH* [1981] 1 Lloyd's Rep. 302.

[52] 44 A. 527 (1895); *cf. Hackfield v Castle* 198 P. 1041 (1921), below, para.4–075, at n.84.

made to float logs to a mill down a specified stream. The contract was discharged when the stream dried up.

(a) *Stipulated and contemplated methods*

In the *Clarksville* case, the contract expressly referred to the method of performance which became impossible. But the Australian *Codelfa*[53] case shows that a contract can be frustrated where the impossibility affects a method of performance which was not specified in the contract but was merely contemplated by the parties. A contract to build a suburban railway specified the time for completion (130 days) and this time was fixed on the assumption that the contractors would work "round the clock", three shifts a day, and with no restriction on Sunday working. The defendants (who had commissioned the work) represented to the contractors that no injunction could be issued against them in respect of noise and nuisance caused by the work. This advice was based on a misconstruction of the relevant legislation; and, after the contractors had started work, third parties did obtain injunctions against them, restraining them from working between 10pm and 6am. In settlement of the third parties' claim, the contractors also agreed not to work on Sundays. The result was that the contractors could neither work three shifts a day, nor complete within 130 days. The defendants granted the contractors extensions of time but eventually cancelled the contract. It was held by a majority of the High Court of Australia that the contract had been discharged (so that the contractors were entitled to a *quantum meruit* for work done after discharge). Although the contract did not specify three shift working, it had been made on the assumption that such working would be possible: "performance by means of a two shift operation, necessitated by the grant of the injunction, was fundamentally different from that contemplated by the contract".[54] The case is special in that it can be argued that discharge was in part the consequence of supervening illegality (which is not in all respects governed by the same rules as those which apply to supervening impossibility).[55] As Aikin J. said: "it became unlawful to perform the work in a manner which would have complied with the requirement of the contract."[56] Brennan J. dissented on the ground that the injunction was not a supervening event: even before the injunction was issued, it was illegal to do the work in the manner contemplated by the contract. As we shall see, it is not always easy to distinguish between antecedent and the supervening illegality.[57]

The view that a contract can be discharged by impossibility affecting a contemplated (as opposed to a stipulated) method of performance is also supported by the American case of *Florida Power & Light Company*

4–061

---

[53] *Codelfa Construction Pty Ltd v State Rail Authority of New South Wales* (1982) 149 C.L.R. 337.
[54] *ibid.* at 363.
[55] See below, para.8–002.
[56] *Codelfa* case, above, n.53, at 381.
[57] See below, paras 8–009, 8–020, 8–024.

v Westinghouse Electric Corporation.[58] In that case, a contract for the construction of a nuclear power plant obliged the contractor to "remove and dispose of" irradiated fuel as it saw fit for a period of 10 years. It was contemplated, at the time of contracting (but not expressly provided), that the contractor would perform this obligation by reprocessing the fuel. By reason of a change in government policy, reprocessing could not be carried out during the 10-year period specified for the performance of the obligation to "remove and dispose"; and this impossibility in the contemplated method of performance was held to have discharged the obligation.[59]

The Suez cases, to be discussed later in this chapter,[60] give some further support to the view that a contract may be discharged by supervening impossibility in a method of performance that is merely contemplated. In some of those cases, the contracts certainly contained no *express* stipulation as to the method of performance[61]; but it was not for this reason that it was held that the contracts were not discharged. This conclusion was based on the fact that the difference between the contemplated method of performance (which had become impossible) and another method (which remained open) was not sufficiently serious or "fundamental" to bring about discharge.[62] The cases do not rule out the possibility of discharge where the difference between the two methods *is* of this serious kind. The same view is also indirectly supported by the *Florida Power* case, where the court also rejected the further argument that the obligation to "remove and dispose" could have been performed by the alternative method of storing (as opposed to reprocessing) the irradiated fuel. The main ground for rejecting the argument was that suitable storage facilities does not exist at the relevant time[63]; but even the existence of such facilities at that time would not have precluded discharge since disposal *by storage* differed fundamentally from the contemplated method of disposal *by reprocessing,* in that the reprocessing would have yielded a profit to the contractor of some $18m while storage would have led to the contractor's suffering a loss of approximately $80m.[64]

---

[58] 826 F. 2d 239 (1987).

[59] *ibid.* at 265.

[60] Below, paras 4–071 *et seq.*

[61] There was no express reference to the Suez route in *Transatlantic Financing Corp v US,* 363 F. 2d 312 (1966), *Palmco Shipping Inc v Continental Ore Corp (The Captain George K)* [1970] 2 Lloyd's Rep. 21 or *American Trading and Production Corp v Shell International Marine,* 453 F. 2d 939 (1972), though in the last two cases a term providing for shipment via Suez was probably to be implied. In *Tsakiroglou & Co Ltd v Noblee Thorl GmbH* [1962] A.C. 93 there was neither an express nor an implied term for shipment via Suez.

[62] See below, paras 4–073, 4–078, 4–079.

[63] 826 F. 2d 239 at 277.

[64] *ibid.* The concept is analogous to that of the availability of a "commercially reasonable" substitute in UCC s.2–614(1), below, paras 4–064 to 4–068, not directly applicable in the *Florida Power* case where the contract was not one for the sale of goods.

Where the method which has become impossible is expressly specified in the contract, it may seem obvious that the impossibility should discharge the contract. But in some situations the application of the principle of discharge to cases of this kind can give rise to considerable difficulties.

(b) *Impossibility affecting method of delivery*

Suppose that a contract for the sale of goods contains stipulations as to the manner of making or taking delivery and that the specified method of performance becomes impossible. The goods may still be available and the question then arises whether delivery must be made and taken in some other way. Most of the cases concern the duty of the seller to make delivery, but problems of the same kind can arise with regard to the duty of the buyer to take delivery.

4–062

An apparently simple case is *Nickoll & Knight v Ashton Edridge & Co*[65] (the *Orlando* case) where a contract for the sale of cottonseed provided that the goods were "to be shipped per steamship *Orlando* from Alexandria during the month of January 1900". In December 1899, the *Orlando* went aground in the Baltic, so that she could not get to Alexandria in January 1900. The seller relied on this fact as a ground of discharge so as to justify his refusal to deliver cottonseed on some other vessel. The motive for the seller's refusal was presumably that the market price of cottonseed had risen. One can infer this from the fact that the buyer claimed damages based on the amount by which the market price exceeded the contract price. A majority of the Court of Appeal held that the contract was frustrated, so that the seller was not liable. In practical terms, the result amounted to a windfall for the seller, who was released from what had turned out, for him, to be an unfavourable bargain by reason of the increase in the market price of the cottonseed, and this increase was in no way attributable to the event which had frustrated the contract (*i.e.* to the stranding of the ship). The result in the *Orlando* case was scarcely the sort of satisfactory allocation (or division) of loss which the doctrine of discharge is meant to provide. The result would have been even less satisfactory if the seller had actually had the cottonseed in stock at Alexandria, for he would then have been able to make an actual profit out of frustration by selling the cottonseed to a third party at the higher market price which prevailed after the stranding of the *Orlando*.[66] But this appears not to have been the position. The seller had indeed contracted to buy the cargo from one Behrend (who seems to have been his undisclosed principal) but that contract was on the same terms, except as to commission, as the contract between seller and buyer.[67] It follows that the seller could no more enforce his contract against Behrend than the buyer could enforce his contract against the seller. Whether Behrend had the cottonseed in stock, or merely expected to acquire it when the *Orlando* arrived, does not appear from the reports of the case.

---

[65] [1901] 2 K.B. 126.

[66] *cf.* the discussion of *Tsakiroglou & Co Ltd v Noblee Thorl GmbH* [1962] A.C. 93, below, para.4–073.

[67] These facts appear from 69 L.J.Q.B. 640 and 82 L.T. 761.

4–063   Although the outcome in the *Orlando* case is thus open to criticism, there are certain special factors in the case which may account for the decision. The first is that the contract had been made on a printed form which provided for shipment "per ship or ships" and that the parties had deleted these words and substituted "per steamship *Orlando*". The majority of the court construed this stipulation as providing that the contract was to be performed *only* by shipment on the *Orlando*, while Vaughan Williams L.J. (who dissented) took the view that it was intended only for the benefit of the buyer (so that he would, for example, not have been bound to accept shipment on a sailing ship) and that he should be able to "waive" the stipulation and enforce the contract without it. The second is that the buyers could have bought another cargo when they had notice of the stranding and when the price had risen only a little, but that they had not done so. This factor should, however, affect, not the issue of liability, but that of damages, being relevant to the question whether the buyers should have taken reasonable steps to mitigate their loss. For this purpose the decisive time should, it is submitted, not be the time when the buyers knew of the stranding of the *Orlando*, but the time when it became clear to them that the sellers would not deliver on another ship.

The *Orlando* case was followed in the Australian case of *Cornish & Co v Kanematsu*[68] where a contract was made for the sale of Japanese onions c.i.f Sydney, "shipment per P&O steamer sailing from Japan about the 8th September". Because of a strike in London, the P&O steamer which was to have sailed from Japan at about that time did not do so. It was held that the seller was not liable in damages for failing to ship as agreed. Superficially, this looks very much like the *Orlando* case, but in commercial terms the issue was very different. There was no evidence of price fluctuations in *Cornish & Co v Kanematsu* and the seller was not trying to get out of the contract. On the contrary, he had offered to ship by other ships but the buyer had refused to agree to this variation of the contract as those ships did not go directly to Sydney. The proposed variation in the method of performance may well have been prejudicial to the buyer, so that his refusal to agree to it may have been more readily justifiable than the seller's refusal to agree to substitute shipping arrangements in the *Orlando* case.

4–064   Both the above cases may be contrasted with the American case of *Whitman v Anglum*.[69] A contract for the sale of 175 quarts of milk per day for one year (from April 1914 to April 1915) provided that the buyer was "to come and get the milk at No. 1 Wawarme Avenue ...", the premises at which the seller produced the milk. On November 23, 1914, the seller, his cattle and premises were quarantined during an outbreak of "hoof and mouth" disease; the seller was not allowed to leave the premises; his cows there were killed, and the removal from the premises of products which might carry infection was prohibited. Between November 22, 1914 and March 13, 1915, the seller delivered no milk, and it was held that the buyer was entitled to damages. The court's conclusion was based largely on the

---

[68] (1913) 3 S.R. (N.S.W.) 83.
[69] 103 A. 114 (1918).

view that the contract was "absolute and unconditional",[70] but it was also said that it did not follow, from the fact that the buyer could no longer "come and get" the milk from the premises specified in the contract, "that the contract could not be performed substantially, if not literally."[71] One can argue that the substance of the provision as to taking delivery was that the buyer should bear the cost of collection, not that the exact place from which the milk was to be collected was important to either party. It is also interesting to note that the contract expressly provided that the buyer should pay for his daily 175 quarts "just the same" even if he failed to take it; and that if the seller failed to supply it he was to pay to the buyer the difference between the contract price and the cost of "cover". The case provides an early illustration of what has become known in the oil business as a "take or pay" clause.[72]

In the United States, the *Orlando* case has been followed in a charterparty case[73]; but contracts for the sale of goods which raised problems of this kind would now fall within Uniform Commercial Code, s.2–614(1). This provides that: "where without fault of either party the agreed berthing, loading, or unloading facilities fail or an agreed type of carrier becomes unavailable or the agreed manner of delivery otherwise becomes commercially impracticable but a commercially reasonable substitute is available, such substitute performance must be tendered and accepted." In determining the effect of this provision, the crucial question is what amounts to a "commercially reasonable substitute".

One test for determining this question is to ask to what extent a party   **4–065** would be prejudiced by having to make, or to accept, such substitute performance. On this test, the decision in the *Orlando* case[74] would have gone the other way: that is, the buyer's claim would have succeeded, unless the seller could have shown that shipment on another ship would have been in some way less advantageous to him than shipment on the *Orlando*; and this may seem to be a better result than that actually reached in that case. In *Whitman v Anglum*,[75] the test would yield the same result as that reached by the court: that is, the buyer would still win, unless the seller could show that delivery at premises other than those described in the contract was more (or significantly more) burdensome to him than delivery strictly in accordance with the contract. It is not clear how s.2–614(1) would operate where the substitute performance was significantly more burdensome for one party but not for the other. This possibility is illustrated by *Cornish & Co v Kanematsu*,[76] where it might be "commercially" reasonable for the seller to put the goods on a steamer other than a P&O one, but not

---

[70] *ibid.* at 114.
[71] *ibid.* at 115.
[72] *cf.* below, para.6–015 but see *Petrogas Processing Ltd v Westcoast Transmission* [1988] 4 W.W.R. 699 (affirmed on other grounds [1989] 4 W.W.R. 272) for the application of the doctrine of discharge to a contract containing such a clause.
[73] *Texas Co v Hogarth Shipping Co Ltd*, 256 U.S. 619 (1921).
[74] Above, n.65.
[75] Above, n.69.
[76] Above, n.68.

be "commercially" reasonable to require the buyer to accept delivery on a vessel which was neither a P&O steamer nor went directly to Sydney. Presumably in such a case the seller is not bound to tender a substitute performance (even though to do so would not prejudice *him*) if the buyer is not bound to accept it, and indicates that he will refuse to do so.

4–066   A second possible test of what is a commercially reasonable substitute is based on the general principle that the provisions of the Code can be "varied by agreement".[77] Section 2–614(1) is, in other words, probably[78] not intended to deprive the parties of their freedom of contract, in the sense that if they make it clear that performance by the stipulated method was to be *exclusive,* and if that method "becomes unavailable or commercially impracticable", then there is no need either to tender or to accept a "commercially reasonable" substitute. If the purpose of the stipulation as to shipment in the *Orlando* case was to specify an exclusive method of performance, then that case would (on this test) go the same way (*i.e.* in favour of the seller) under s.2–614(1).

Subject to this last point, s.2–614(1) is capable of providing a better solution on facts such as those in the *Orlando* case than that reached by the majority of the Court of Appeal; but there is considerable doubt whether any principle resembling that of s.2–614(1) would be recognised in English law, in which there is no comparable legislative provision. The doubt arises because historically s.2–614(1) is in part based on the American case of *Meyer v Sullivan,*[79] where a contract for the sale of wheat provided for delivery "free on board Kosmos steamer at Seattle" in September 1914. Because of war-time conditions, no *Kosmos* steamer sailed from Seattle during September 1914 and, the price of the wheat having risen, the seller refused to deliver. He was held liable, partly because of proof of a West Coast custom that "f.o.b. clauses were used in connection with the price of the wheat and not the place of delivery",[80] and that delivery under contracts on f.o.b. terms was to be taken at the dock (rather than on board ship); and partly because any provision as to delivery on a steamer (as opposed to at the dock) was for the benefit of the buyer and could be waived by him. But such special factors would not be necessary for the purpose of s.2–614(1), which would require the seller to deliver at the dock, even in the absence of such a custom (unless, presumably, the seller could show that he would be seriously prejudiced by having to

---

[77] UCC, s.1–101(3) and (4); replaced in the 2002 version (above, para.3–017, n.57) by s.1–302.

[78] Under the provisions cited in the previous note "obligations of reasonableness" cannot be disclaimed but the parties "may by agreement determine the standards by which the performance of such standards are to be measured if such standards are not manifestly unreasonable". Specifying an exclusive method of performance would appear to fall within the words last quoted.

[79] 181 P. 847 (1919), cited in UCC, s.2–614, Comment 1.

[80] 181 P. 847 at 849 (1919). This reasoning is criticised as "uncommercial" in UCC s.2–319, Comment 1, though without reference to *Meyer v Sullivan* (above), but that case is cited with apparent approval in s.2–614, Comment 1. In the draft proposals for amendment of UCC, Art.2, (above, para.2–042 n.17) s.2–319 is to be deleted.

deliver in this way, or that the stipulated manner of delivery was intended to be exclusive). The result in *Meyer v Sullivan* is also approved by the Restatement 2d, Illustration 3 to § 270 being based on that case. But in England the opposite conclusion was reached in *Maine Spinning Co v Sutcliffe*[81] where a contract for the sale of wool was held on its true construction to provide for delivery "f.o.b. Liverpool". War-time regulations made it illegal for the seller to put the goods on board a ship; and it was held the seller was not bound to deliver simply at Liverpool. This may look like a strange decision because normally under an f.o.b. contract the seller is bound to pay the cost of getting the goods on board[82] and to require him to deliver simply at Liverpool would save him expense and so at first sight would not prejudice him. In the Australian case of *Cohen & Co v Ockerby & Co Ltd* it was therefore said that, where shipment had become impossible or illegal, an f.o.b. buyer did have the right to have the goods delivered short of the ship, *e.g.* at a wharf or at the seller's warehouse, "unless it can be shown that the seller thereby sustains some detriment."[83–84] Such a detriment might, *e.g.* be suffered by the seller if, in consequence of being required to deliver short of the ship, he lost some fiscal advantage available by law only to exporters[85]; or if he found that goods which he had sold cheaply for export were thrown back on the home market, where they might be sold in competition with him by his buyer.[86] It is also possible for any right which the buyer might (by virtue of the above suggestion) have to take delivery short of the ship to be excluded by an express term of the contract. The buyer would, *e.g.* have no such right where the contract provided that it was to be cancelled if shipment should be prevented by blockade or war[87] and such an event did indeed prevent shipment. The above statements in *Cohen & Co v Ockerby & Co* do not make it clear which party has the burden of proving that the seller would not be prejudiced by having to deliver short of the ship; but as this would be an essential part of the buyer's cause of action it is submitted that the burden of proof on this issue would normally be on him. Nor could an f.o.b. buyer normally claim delivery short of the ship by "waiving" the stipulation as to delivery on board, for normally a party can waive a stipulation only if it is wholly for his benefit; and the stipulation as to the place of delivery is one which, in the present situation, can clearly benefit either party. The only sense in which the buyer can be said to waive the stipulation is that, if he requests delivery at some point short of the

---

[81] (1918) 87 L.J.K.B. 382.

[82] *Benjamin's Sale of Goods* (6th ed.), para.20–018; *cf.*, in the United States, UCC, s.2–319(1)(c), to be deleted under the proposed reforms to Art.2 (above, para.2–042, n.3a).

[83–84] (1917) 24 C.L.R. 288 at 299; and see *Benjamin's Sale of Goods* (6th ed.), para.20–015.

[85] *cf. Wackerbath v Masson* (1812) 3 Camp. 270.

[86] For damages that might be recoverable *for misrepresentation* on the buyer's part in such a case, *cf. Clef Aquitaine SARL v Laporte Materials (Barrow) Ltd* [2001] Q.B. 488.

[87] As in *Cohen & Co v Ockerby & Co Ltd* : see (1917) 24 C.L.R. 288 at 300–301.

ship, then delivery at that point will amount to performance of the seller's duty to deliver the goods.[88]

4–067   Just as an f.o.b. seller is not bound to deliver at a place other than that specified in the contract as the place of shipment, so he is not entitled to do so. In *Petrotrade Inc v Stinnes Handel GmbH*,[89] a contract for the sale of gasoline called for delivery to be made f.o.b. Antwerp, and the seller, being unable to make delivery there within the contract period, offered instead to deliver the goods at Flushing, which was closer than Antwerp to the point at which the ship (to be provided by the buyer[90]) on which the goods were to be shipped was waiting. Delivery at Flushing would therefore presumably have saved the buyer some expense, but it was held that the buyer was nevertheless justified in rejecting the seller's offer as the stipulation as to the place of delivery was a condition (being part of the description of the goods[91]). The case was not one of impossibility, the seller having simply failed to make an adequate supply contract and so being in breach; but the reasoning suggests that, even if delivery at Antwerp had become impossible, the seller would not have been entitled to deliver, and that the buyers would not have been bound to accept delivery, at Flushing. The case should be contrasted with *Neill v Whitworth*[92] where cotton was sold "to arrive ... at Liverpool ... the said cotton to be taken from the quay". After the cotton had been discharged on the quay at Liverpool, the sellers, to avoid costs that would have been incurred by leaving it on the quay, moved it to a warehouse. *Prima facie*, this benefited the buyers by saving them the expense of moving the cotton from the quay; and it was held that their refusal to take it from the warehouse was not justified "providing that the warehouse does not impose on them *any* additional expense or undue delay".[93] No such prejudice having been suffered by the buyers,[94] their claim for damages for non-delivery was accordingly rejected. The case is again one in which there was no impossibility in the specified method of delivery; and it seems that, if there had been such impossibility (not brought about by a breach on the part of the sellers[95]), then the buyers would *a fortiori* not have been justified in refusing to accept delivery from the warehouse. To this extent, the rule there laid down resembles that contained in s.2-614(1) of the Uniform Commercial Code. *Neill v Whitworth* was, however concerned only with the buyers' duties and not with their rights: it leaves open the question whether the sellers would have been bound to deliver from the warehouse

---

[88] See *Henderson & Glass v Rushmore & Co* (1920) 10 Ll.L. Rep. 727, where on the facts no "waiver" was established.

[89] [1995] 1 Lloyd's Rep. 142.

[90] *Benjamin's Sale of Goods* (6th ed.), paras 20–001, 20–003, 20–042.

[91] On the analogy of the rule that stipulations as to the time of shipment form part of the description of the goods: *Bowes v Shand* (1877) 2 App. Cas. 455.

[92] (1866) L.R.1 C.P. 683; affirming 18 C.B. N.S. 435.

[93] *ibid.* at 442 (emphasis added).

[94] The sellers had offered to pay the expense of moving the goods, and even to return them to the quay.

[95] It seems that the seller's tender of delivery from the warehouse would seem to have been a breach, though not (as was held) a repudiatory one.

if delivery from the quay had become impossible or illegal. If one adapted the dictum just quoted[96] to this situation, the sellers would have been bound to make such delivery only if it did not impose on them "*any* additional expense"; and this condition would be hard to satisfy.

The foregoing account shows that there is some conflict between American statutory rules on this subject and the rules which are stated in the English and Australian cases; but it seems that the conflict may be less acute than at first sight appears. In deciding whether a substitute is "commercially reasonable" in the Uniform Commercial Code terminology, and whether (in the language of the English and Australian cases) it occasions a "detriment"[97] or "additional expense or undue delay"[98] to the party claiming excuse, the courts probably have regard, at least to some extent, to similar factors. American law is explicit in its recognition of the duty to make and take a performance which is a "commercially reasonable substitute". English law may recognise, and does not as a general principle[99] deny, a duty to make and to take, performance by a method which is *less* onerous than the stipulated method which has become impossible, so long as the change in the method does not cause any other prejudice to the party who is asked to make (or, as the case may be, to take) it. Moreover English law may recognise that impossibility in an agreed method of performance which is *not* intended to be exclusive does not discharge a contract if the agreed method relates to a matter which is not of fundamental importance: this appears from dicta in the Suez cases, to be discussed below.[1] Indeed, these dicta seem to go some way beyond Uniform Commercial Code, s.2–614(1) in suggesting that performance by a substitute method could be required even though it imposed considerable extra expense (than the agreed method which had become impossible) on the party required to render it; but the actual decisions are distinguishable from the situation here under discussion in that they do not (for the most part) deal with impossibility in performing in an *expressly stipulated* way, and certainly not with a method which is intended to be exclusive.

Perhaps the most plausible conclusion is that the difference between the English and American approaches is largely one of emphasis. English law has not in terms accepted the American view that there is a duty to make use of a "commercially reasonable" substitute method where the stipulated method becomes impossible. But if the stipulation is of major importance, a substitute will not be commercially reasonable, so that s.2–614(1) will not apply; while if the stipulation is of only minor importance, impossibility of performing in the stipulated manner may not discharge the contract even in English law and a substitute will be reasonable within s.2–614(1). The two approaches may occasionally produce different results, or different

4–068

---

[96] Above, at n.93.

[97] Above, at n.84.

[98] Above, at n.93.

[99] *i.e.* apart from the English cases relating to f.o.b. contracts discussed in above, paras 4–066, 4–067.

[1] See below, para.4–075.

prima facie assumptions (as in the f.o.b. cases discussed above)[2]; but more often they are likely to lead to the same practical results.

One point not dealt with by s.2–614(1) is who should bear the extra expense of tendering the "commercially reasonable substitute", or of accepting it, where such acceptance occasioned extra expense. Presumably the *whole* of this falls on the party required to perform (or to accept performance) in this way.

(c) *Impossibility affecting method of payment*

4–069   The foregoing discussion is concerned with cases in which supervening impossibility affects the method by which a supplier of goods or services was to perform his obligations under the contract. At first sight, the corresponding problem of the effect of supervening events on the obligation of the other contracting party to pay for those goods and services cannot arise, since the payment of money cannot in law become impossible. An obligation to pay money may indeed be discharged (wholly or in part) by supervening illegality by the law of the country where that obligation was to have been performed.[3] But if the contract does not in terms require any act to be done which is illegal by the law of that country, no such excuse will operate merely because one party intended to adopt a method of payment which would involve the doing of such an act. Thus in *Toprak Mahsulleri Ofisi v Finagrain Cie Commerciale*[4] a contract for the sale of wheat by American sellers to Turkish buyers c.i.f. Turkish ports provided for payment by irrevocable letter of credit to be "opened in Sellers' favour with and confirmed by a first class U.S. or West European Bank ...". It was held that the buyers were not excused by their failure to obtain Turkish exchange control permission since the sellers were "not in the least concerned as to the method by which the Turkish buyers [were] to provide that letter of credit".[5] At first instance it was said that it would have made no difference even if both parties had contemplated the method of performance which was subsequently prevented, so long as the contract did not actually require that method to be adopted.[6]

It seems that, where a contract did require a specified method of payment to be adopted, the contract could be discharged if that method subsequently became impossible. That might, for example, be the position if a contract of sale called for payment by a letter of credit to be opened with a named bank, and that bank went out of existence before the letter of credit was opened. Whether the contract was actually frustrated by such impossibility in the stipulated method of performance would, it is submitted, depend on whether the identity of the named bank was

---

[2] See above, paras 4–066, 4–067.

[3] *Libyan Arab Foreign Bank v Bankers Trust Co* [1989] Q.B. 728 at 749; *cf. Ralli Bros v Compania Naviera Sota y Aznar* [1920] 2 K.B. 287 (a case of partial excuse rather than one of frustration); and see below, para.8–030.

[4] [1979] 2 Lloyd's Rep. 98.

[5] *ibid.* at 114.

[6] *ibid.* at 107.

regarded by the parties as a matter of fundamental importance. *Prima facie* the stipulation would have this effect since it would have provided for an exclusive method of performance: certainly, if the named bank had continued to exist, the seller would be entitled to rescind the contract if the buyer tendered a letter of credit opened at another bank.[7] But two possible contrary arguments merit consideration. The first is that the letter of credit is only the primary source of payment and that, if this source fails, the seller is normally entitled to sue the buyer for the price.[8] But in spite of this rule there can be no doubt that the seller is entitled to the additional security of the specified bank's promise, even though in a particular case that security may fail. The second contrary argument is that the security of the letter of credit and the identity of the issuing bank may be a matter of importance only to the seller, and that it would be strange if in these circumstances the buyer could rely on the fact of the bank's having ceased to exist as a ground of discharge. But it is by no means inconceivable that the use of a different bank could (as well as subjecting the seller to additional risks) impose additional burdens on the buyer.[9] At least where this is the case, such an impossibility in the method of payment would, it is submitted, be a ground of frustration.

The cases so far discussed are concerned with events which affect the method of payment and which may discharge a contract because the originally specified method has become impossible or illegal. A contract may also be discharged for the quite different reason that, unless the stipulated method is varied, it will be impossible or illegal for the party *to whom* the payment was to be made to perform his obligations under the contract. This was the position in *Nile Co for the Export of Agricultural Crops v H & J M Bennett (Commodities) Ltd,*[10] where a contract had been made relating to the sale of potatoes to be exported to the United Kingdom from Egypt by an Egyptian Public Sector company. The potatoes were to be shipped f.o.b. Egyptian ports and payment was to be made *against documents*, which usually reached the buyer after the goods. The contract was held to have been frustrated when an Egyptian Ministerial Regulation required payment instead to be made *in advance by confirmed letter of credit*, since the difference between this method of payment and that specified in the contract was "fundamental".[11] Frustration of the contract is at one stage in the judgment explained in terms both of "supervening illegality" and "impossibility",[12] without at this stage making it clear on which of these alternative grounds the decision is based. The view that the decision is based on illegality by foreign law is perhaps supported by the fact that the

4–070

---

[7] *cf. Benjamin's Sale of Goods* (6th ed.), para.19–200.

[8] *W J Alan & Co v El Nasr Export & Import Co* [1972] 2 Q.B. 189 at 212; *E D & F Man v Nigerian Sweets and Confectionery Co* [1977] 2 Lloyd's Rep. 50; *Saffron v Société Minière Cafrika* (1958) 100 C.L.R. 231 at 243–244.

[9] *e.g.* because the buyer has a controlling interest in the named bank (as in the *E D & F Man* case, above).

[10] [1986] 1 Lloyd's Rep. 555.

[11] *ibid.* at 582.

[12] *ibid.* at 581 and *cf.* at 580.

authorities cited[13] are of this kind. On the other hand, it plainly had not become illegal for payment to be made against documents: the effect of the Egyptian regulations was not to prohibit payment[14] in accordance with the contract, but to prohibit the export of the potatoes unless a different method of payment were adopted. The impossibility, in other words, was one affecting the obligations of the seller, even though it resulted from a Regulation affecting the method of payment: the crucial factor was that the seller was unable (unless the altered method of payment were adopted) to perform his obligation to ship the goods in Egypt. As Evans J. said: "the agreement required the [sellers] to load the potatoes at Egyptian ports and to obtain the necessary documents from the authorities there. The supervening illegality, or impossibility of performing these acts in Egypt is sufficient to frustrate the contract even if it is governed by English law ...".[15] The "illegality" was one arising under foreign law; and according to one view discharge in such cases is based, not on the same ground of public policy as that which applies in cases of supervening illegality by English law, but on different policy considerations[16] or (as the dictum just quoted may suggest) on the ground that performance in the foreign country has become impossible by reason of the change in the law there.

(2) The Suez cases[17]

4–071   These cases arose when the Suez Canal was blocked as a result of hostilities in the Middle East in 1956 and again in 1967 (when it remained blocked until further hostilities there in 1973; these did not lead to any further Suez cases, but did lead to the "energy crisis" cases to be considered in our discussion of impracticability in Ch.6).[18] The Suez cases fall into two groups: those concerning contracts of sale and those concerning contracts of carriage. The sale cases were litigated only in England; the carriage cases both in England and in the United States.[19]

(a) *The sale cases*

4–072   These all concern contracts on c.i.f. terms. Under such contracts, the seller charges an inclusive price covering the cost of the goods, insurance and freight; he is bound to make (or procure) a contract for the carriage of goods to the c.i.f. destination; and that contract must be for the carriage of the goods by the route which is usual and customary at the time, not when the contract of sale was made, but when the contract of carriage was,

---

[13] At 581.

[14] As in the *Ralli Bros* case [1920] 2 K.B. 287, as to which see below, para.8–030.

[15] At 581. Actually the contract was held to be governed by Egyptian law.

[16] See below, para.8–054.

[17] Birmingham, 20 Hastings L.J. 1393 (1969).

[18] See below, paras 6–009 *et seq.*

[19] The author has not found any Suez case decided outside England or the United States, with the possible exception of the decision of the German Bundesgerichtshof in Vers R. 61, 821 (where, however, that court applied English law).

or ought to have been, made.[20] It is possible, but unusual, for the route to be specified in the contract; it was not so specified in any of the Suez sale cases. In these cases, the sellers argued that the closure of the canal discharged the contracts: their motive for advancing this argument was to avoid the extra expense of shipping the goods via the Cape of Good Hope. As the c.i.f. price included the freight element, this cost would (if the contract remained in force) fall entirely on the sellers, reduce their profit and possibly lead to a loss (in the sense that the cost of performance could exceed the contract price).

The seller's argument succeeded in the first of the reported Suez cases, **4–073** *Carapanayoti & Co Ltd v E T Green Ltd*,[21] where McNair J. regarded the availability of the Suez route as a fundamental assumption on the basis of which both parties contracted. But this view was rejected in two later cases: in the *Gaon*[22] case and in the *Tsakiroglou* case,[23] the latter being the only one of the Suez cases to reach the House of Lords. In that case, an agreement had been made on October 4, 1956 for the sale of 300 tons of Sudanese groundnuts c.i.f. Hamburg. The contract provided for shipment from Port Sudan during November/December 1956 (actually the parties had by mistake used a form which called for shipment from a *West* African port, but it was found that Port Sudan was the intended port of shipment). When the contract was made, both parties contemplated that shipment would be via the Suez Canal, but the Canal was blocked on November 2, 1956, and not reopened until well after the end of the contractual shipment period. It was held that the closure of the Canal did not discharge the contract. The case was not one in which a *stipulated* method of performance became impossible since the contract did not expressly provide for shipment via Suez; nor could any such stipulation be implied. The seller's duty was to ship via the route which was usual and customary when shipment should have been made[24]; that route was the route via the Cape of Good Hope; and it would be inconsistent with that duty to imply a term specifying the different Suez route. It is true that, at the time of contracting, the buyer, no less than the seller, contemplated that shipment would be via Suez, but it was a matter of indifference to the buyer whether the goods were shipped by the Suez route or by the Cape route. As the contract did not expressly or impliedly refer to the Suez route, it had not in any sense become impossible to perform: it remained possible for the seller to put the goods on a ship bound for Hamburg. This method of performance was different from that contemplated and certainly would have caused the seller considerable additional expense; the voyage via the

---

[20] *Benjamin's Sale of Goods* (6th ed.), paras 19–001, 19–025, 19–030 and 19–031; UCC, s.2–320(2)(a) (which makes no reference to the route of shipment). This section is to be deleted under the proposals for reform of Art.2 (above, para.2–042, n.17).

[21] [1959] 1 Q.B. 131.

[22] *Albert D. Gaon & Co v Soc Interprofessionelle des Oléagineux Fluides Alimentaires* [1960] 2 Q.B. 348.

[23] *Tsakiroglou & Co Ltd v Noblee Thorl GmbH* [1962] A.C. 93.

[24] Above, n.20.

Cape would have been two-and-a-half-times as long and twice as expensive as that via the Canal. Nevertheless it was held that the difference between the two methods of performance was not sufficiently "fundamental" to discharge the contract. Three factors help to account for this conclusion.

4–074   First, shipment via the Cape, while causing the seller additional expense, would not prejudice the *buyer* in any way: the goods were not of a kind which would deteriorate during the time taken by the longer voyage; nor did the buyer have any "seasonal" need for them which would be left unfulfilled by this delay.

Secondly, a c.i.f. contract can be said by its nature to allocate the risk of fluctuations in freight rates.[25] By charging an inclusive price including freight in a contract for goods to be shipped on a future date, the seller takes the risk of increases in freight rates, just as he takes the risk of increases in the price of goods. Conversely, the buyer takes the risk that freight rates might fall; and there is no case which even remotely suggests that a fall in freight rates would be a ground on which a buyer could claim to be discharged.

Thirdly, the decision may have been influenced by the way in which prices moved. The contractual shipment period ended in December 1956. By early January 1957, the price of groundnuts had risen to £68 15s. per ton, against the contract price of £50. It appears from the reports that 300 tons of groundnuts were held to the seller's order in a warehouse in Port Sudan on November 1, 1956[26]; and, if the contract had been discharged, the seller could have resold those goods to a third party (instead of appropriating them to his contract with the buyer). At the market price in early January, such a sale would have yielded £18 15s. per ton more than the price payable under the original contract, while the extra cost of shipping the goods via the Cape would have been no more than £7 10s. per ton, leaving the seller better off by £11 15s. per ton. On the contract quantity of 300 tons, this would have left him with a windfall profit of £3,375, and such a result would have been inconsistent with the purpose of the doctrine of discharge, which is intended to allocate losses, not to enable a party to take advantage of the supervening event so as to profit from it. In discussing the *Orlando* case,[27] we noted that the result there was open to the objection that it allowed the seller to escape from a bargain which (quite apart from the frustrating event) had turned out for him to be a bad one.[28] The objection to allowing a party to rely on the doctrine of frustration would be all the stronger where discharge would enable that party, not merely to avoid a

---

[25] *cf. Blyth & Co v Richards Turpin & Co* (1916) 85 L.J.K.B. 1425, where a c.i.f. seller remained liable in spite of the fact that freight rates had nearly trebled: he was not protected by an express provision for suspension, should shipment be prevented; and *Companhia de Navegaceo Lloyd Brasileiro v C G Blake Co*, 34 F. 2d 616 (1929), where a c.i.f. seller was not excused by an increase in the cost of procuring shipping space caused by (apparently) the knock-on effect in the United States of the 1926 General Strike in the United Kingdom.

[26] See [1960] 2 Q.B. 318 at 320, and *cf. ibid.* at 326.

[27] [1901] 2 K.B. 126; above, para.4–062.

[28] See above, para.4–052.

potential loss, but to make an actual profit. In discussing cases of temporary impossibility, we shall see that the courts do not favour the use of the doctrine of frustration where it leads to such a result[29]; and the decision in the *Tsakiroglou* case is consistent with this judicial policy.

In the *Tsakiroglou* case, the contract did not expressly specify the route of shipment; and in a c.i.f. contract a term which did specify the route would be an uncommon one, though stipulations for direct shipment (*i.e.* without calling at an intermediate port) are occasionally found.[30] The further question arises what the position would have been if the contract in the *Tsakiroglou* case had expressly provided for shipment via Suez, or if the House of Lords had accepted the argument that such a term must be implied.[31] Lord Simonds said that: "it does not automatically follow that, because one term of the contract, *e.g.* that goods shall be carried by a particular route, becomes impossible of performance, the whole contract is thereby abrogated."[32] The other members of the House of Lords expressed no opinion on the point; but presumably Lord Simonds' view is an illustration of the general principle that inability to perform a term of minor importance does not of itself discharge a contract, *e.g.* the contract in *Taylor v Caldwell*[33] would not have been discharged if only one of the side-shows had been destroyed (or made unavailable). On this principle, unavailability of even a contractually specified route would discharge a contract only if the route was of fundamental importance, as it might be if the buyer had resold the goods under a contract making the route part of the description of the goods, so that his sub-buyer could reject goods shipped by another route.[34] But in the Suez cases there was no evidence of such facts. In relation to c.i.f. contracts, Lord Simonds' dictum gives rise to some difficulty; for if the carriage documents do not comply with the contract of sale the buyer is entitled to reject them[35]; and it is hard to see why a seller should be bound to procure carriage documents which the buyer is entitled to reject. One possible answer to this objection is that the parties in Lord Simonds' example may not have intended the route to be exclusive; though this would be an unusual interpretation of such a provision. Of course, if (as in the *Tsakiroglou* case) it was the buyer who sought to enforce the contract, he could by taking this course of action, be

---

[29] See the discussion of *Tamplin SS Co v Anglo-Mexican Petroleum Co* [1916] A.C. 397 in *Metropolitan Water Board v Dick Kerr & Co* [1918] A.C. 119 at 129, below, para.5–053, but see *The Isle of Mull*, 278 F. 131 (1921), and generally below, paras 15–007 to 15–009.

[30] *e.g. Cornish & Co v Kanematsu* (1913) 13 S.R. (N.S.W.) 83; *Bergerco USA v Vegoil Ltd* [1984] Lloyd's Rep. 440.

[31] *cf. Re L Sutro & Co and Heilbut, Symons & Co* [1917] 2 K.B. 348, where the Court of Appeal was divided on the point of construction but not on the point of principle. The actual decision may require reconsideration: see *Tsakiroglou* case [1962] A.C. 93 at 113.

[32] [1962] A.C. 93 at 112.

[33] (1863) 3 B. & S. 826; above, para.2–024; *cf.* below, para.5–002 (partial impossibility).

[34] See *Hackfield & Co Ltd v Castle*, 198 P. 1041 (1921) (f.o.b. contract).

[35] See *Benjamin's Sale of Goods* (6th ed.), paras 19–031, 19–042.

taken to have waived his right to reject the carriage document on account of its non-conformity with the contract. The difficulty considered here is, in any event, one which arises because of the special nature of a c.i.f. contract, under which the shipping documents must be strictly in conformity with the contract.[36] At a more general level Lord Simonds' dictum shows that the crucial distinction is not between stipulated and contemplated methods of performance; impossibility affecting the former is not *per se* sufficient to discharge the contract, while impossibility affecting the latter *may* be a ground of discharge if it relates to a matter which is regarded by both parties as being one of fundamental importance.[37]

4–076   The result of cases such as the *Tsakiroglou* case may seem to be hard on the seller (at least in some cases); but one has to emphasise that in c.i.f. sales of commodities parties generally bargain on equal terms; that freedom of contract prevails; and that a seller, where his bargaining position permits it, can easily "contract out" of the result reached by the House of Lords in the leading case. There are two ways in which he can do this.

4–077   First, he can enter into a different type of contract: that is, in the *Tsakiroglou* case he could have sold f.o.b. Port Sudan instead of c.i.f. Hamburg. In that case the cost of carriage—and consequently any increase in freight rates—would have fallen on the buyer who certainly could not have successfully argued that the contract had been discharged by the closure of the Suez Canal. One reason for this would be that an f.o.b. contract, while naming, or requiring one of the parties[38] to name, the port of shipment,[39] does not usually[40] say anything about the destination, let alone the route. Another is that under such a contract the buyer takes the risk of increases in freight rates, just as the seller takes it when the sale is on c.i.f. terms. The very fact that there are two standard types of contract, of which one places this risk on the buyer and the other on the seller, is a ground for not reallocating that risk (once the parties have made their choice) by applying the doctrine of discharge.

A second, less radical possibility is simply to provide specifically for the event. This was in fact done, after the first Suez crisis, in *DI Henry Ltd v*

---

[36] *Cehave NV v Bremer Handelsgesellschaft mbH (The Hansa Nord)* [1976] Q.B. 44 at 70; *Benjamin's Sale of Goods*, (6th ed.), para.19–142.

[37] As in the "banana" example given in below, para.4–080; *cf.* (in another context), the *Codelfa* case (1982) 149 C.L.R. 337; above, para.4–061; and the *Florida Power* case, 826 F. 2d 239 (1987); above, para.4–061.

[38] *Prima facie*, that party is the buyer: see *David T Boyd & Co Ltd v Louis Louca* [1973] 1 Lloyd's Rep. 209; *Benjamin's Sale of Goods* (6th ed.), para.20–014.

[39] *cf.* UCC, s.2–319(c) ("f.o.b. port of shipment"); in English law and commercial practice, "f.o.b." (without more) refers to such a contract. Under the proposed amendments to UCC, Art.2 (above, para.2–042, n.17), s.2–319 is to be deleted.

[40] For exceptions, see above, n.34; *Bulk Oil (Zug) AG v Sun International Ltd* [1984] Lloyd's Rep. 531 ("Destination ... in line with exporting Government's policy"). Specification of the destination, not in the contract but in the buyer's shipping instructions, raises different issues: see *Benjamin's Sale of Goods* (6th ed.), para.20–098.

Clasen[41] where a c.i.f. contract contained a provision which read "Cape surcharge buyer's account". This did not alter the general character of the contract. It meant that, if freight rates rose because of the closure of the Suez Canal, the buyer would have to pay for *this* increase. But if they rose for some *other* reason, that (other) increase, would have to be absorbed by the seller: to this extent, the contract retained the characteristics of a normal c.i.f. sale.

(b) *The carriage cases*

Most of these cases concern voyage charters by which the carrier agrees to   4–078
carry the shipper's goods from one named port to another, for a fixed remuneration (the freight) which is commonly calculated on the amount of cargo carried. Prolongation of the voyage by reason of the closure of the Canal prejudiced the carrier in that he would get no more than the agreed freight for carrying the goods to the contractual destination, while the cost which he would incur in earning the freight would rise because of the extra length of the voyage. Accordingly, it would be the carrier who would argue that the contract was discharged.

Such an argument was upheld in the earliest of the reported English cases on this topic, *The Massalia*,[42] where a ship had been chartered for the carriage of iron ore from a port on the East coast of India to Genoa; the charterparty provided: "Captain to telegraph 'Martisider Genoa' on passing Suez Canal". The contract had been made on October 18, 1956; the Canal was blocked on November 2. The ship began loading *thereafter* and then sailed via the Cape of Good Hope; this voyage was twice as long as the voyage via the Suez would have been. After the ship had sailed, the carrier claimed that the contract had been discharged, and that he was entitled to a reasonable remuneration of 195s. per ton, as against the agreed freight of 134s. per ton. The claim was upheld because the contract imposed an obligation to go via Suez and the "highly circuitous"[43] route which the carrier had to take was, in the view of the judge (though not in that of the arbitrator), fundamentally different from that contracted for.

But *The Massalia* was overruled in *The Eugenia*[44]; and all the other voyage charterparty cases arising out of the Suez crises reject the carrier's plea of discharge. In the American case of *Glidden v Hellenic Lines Ltd*[45], the contract provided for the carriage of the goods from India to the United States "via Suez, Cape or Panama, at owner's [*i.e.* shipowner's] option" and was held not to have been discharged by the closure of the Suez Canal. This result could be explained on the ground that the contract provided for alternative methods of performance only one of which was affected by the closure of the Suez Canal.[46] But no such alternatives were expressly mentioned in another American case, *Transatlantic Financing Corp v US*[47] in

---

[41] [1973] 1 Lloyd's Rep. 159.
[42] *Soc Tunisienne d'Armement v Sidermar SpA (The Massalia)* [1961] 2 Q.B. 278.
[43] *ibid.* at 307.
[44] *Ocean Tramp Tankers Corp v V/O Sovfracht (The Eugenia)* [1964] 2 Q.B. 226.
[45] 275 F. 2d 253 (1960).
[46] See below, para.10–001.
[47] 363 F. 2d 312 (1966).

which the contract was to carry wheat from Galveston, Texas, to Bandar Shapur in Iran. When the contract was made (on October 2, 1956) the usual and customary route was via Suez but after the ship had sailed (on October 27), the Canal was blocked (on November 2). Accordingly, the ship proceeded via the Cape of Good Hope, adding 3,000 miles to what would have been a 10,000 mile voyage and about $44,000 to the shipowner's costs (which on a voyage via Suez would have been $306,000). These changes were held not to be sufficiently fundamental to discharge the contract.

4–079   In the *Transatlantic Financing* case, the contract made no express reference to Suez; but this was not the decisive factor. In other words, a voyage charter would not be discharged merely because the contract did refer to Suez. This is implicit in the overruling of *The Massalia* (where the contract contained such a reference) by *The Eugenia*; and the point is made explicit in two further voyage charterparty cases. The first is the English case of *The Captain George K.*[48] where the contract was to carry sulphur from a port on the East coast of Mexico to Kandla in India. The contract provided that the master should telegraph his estimated arrival date 96 hours before arriving off, and 72 hours after passing, Suez. The distance between the two ports via Suez was 9,700 miles; via the Cape of Good Hope it was 12,100 miles (or 1.25 times as long) but the ship had got as far as the Eastern Mediterranean (only three miles from the entrance to the Canal) when the Canal was closed, so that she had to retrace her course and to steam 18,400 miles (nearly twice the originally contemplated distance). The shipowners claimed that the original contract was discharged and that they were entitled to an additional payment of some $68,000 (the amount of the originally stipulated freight is not stated in the report) in respect of the extra length of the voyage. But Mocatta J. (who as counsel had argued successfully for discharge in *The Massalia*) held that there was not a sufficiently fundamental difference, between the voyage contemplated, and that accomplished, to discharge the contract. *American Trading and Production Corp v Shell International Marine*[49] was a very similar American case. The charterparty was for the carriage of oil from Beaumont/Smith's Bluff, Texas, to Bombay; part of the contractual freight was 85 cents per ton for the passage through the Suez Canal. The voyage via Suez would have taken 9,705 miles; the ship had got to within 84 miles of Port Said when the Canal was closed and then had to steam 18,055 miles to reach Bombay. A claim for an extra payment of $132,000 (as against the contractual freight of $417,000) was again rejected: there had been no discharge. There can be little doubt that, in these two cases it would have been a breach for the shipowners to have gone to India by a different route, if the Canal had not been closed; and that this breach would have given the charterers a right to damages (though probably not a right to rescind the contract).[50] But the mere fact that the contract in each

---

[48] *Palmco Shipping Inc v Continental Ore Corp (The Captain George K.)* [1970] 2 Lloyd's Rep. 21.
[49] 453 F. 2d 939 (1972).
[50] *ibid.* at 942; *cf. Glidden v Hellenic Lines Ltd*, 275 F. 2d 253 at 257 (1960).

of these two cases was (at least by implication) one to carry the goods via Suez was not decisive on the issue of discharge.

Indeed, an implication to use the Suez route could arise, even though   4–080 the contract contained no express reference to Suez, by virtue of the rule that the carrier must proceed by the route which is the usual one at the time of contracting.[51] For this reason, the contract in the *Transatlantic Financing*[52] case would by implication have been one to carry the goods via Suez, but it was nevertheless not discharged by the closure of the Canal. Thus even the failure of an expressly or impliedly *stipulated* method of performance will not discharge a contract if that method is not of fundamental importance, unless the parties have made it clear that they intend the stipulated method to be exclusive.

The voyage charter cases show that it is very difficult for the closure of a contemplated or even of a specified route to discharge a contract of carriage, so long as another practicable (though more expensive) route is available[53] (the North-West passage to Alaska would scarcely suffice). But it is not impossible to think of examples in which the contract would be discharged. A contract to carry bananas from Port Sudan to Port Said would be one such example – especially if the cargo would deteriorate on the longer voyage via the Cape. Another example is given by Restatement 2d, § 261, Illustration 10: if the ship had been actually trapped in the Canal and detained there, the carrier's duty to carry the goods would be discharged at least if (as the illustration seems to assume) the ship remains so trapped for a long period, and if the fact that the ship had been trapped was not due to the fault of the charterer.[54] Indeed, one could imagine in such a case that *the charterer* might claim discharge because of the resulting long delay in delivering of the goods. Between the 1967 and 1973 wars, some ships were trapped in the Suez Canal for six years; but contracts to carry goods in them do not appear to have been the subject of any litigation. Analogous cases arising out of the Gulf War between Iran and Iraq indicate that *time* charters relating to such ships would be discharged by their prolonged inability to render the agreed service[55]; but our present concern is with voyage charters.

Just as the sale cases may be thought to be hard on the seller, so the   4–081 present group of carriage cases can be said to be hard on the carrier, who has to accomplish a longer voyage—in some cases, nearly twice as long as that contemplated—for no extra reward. But the decisions in the carriage

---

[51] *Scrutton on Charterparties* (20th ed.), pp.256–257.

[52] Above, n.47.

[53] No such alternative was available in *Clarksville Land Co v Harriman*, 44 A. 527 (1895), above, para.4–060.

[54] As it was in *Ocean Tramp Tankers Corp v V/O Sovfracht (The Eugenia)* [1964] 2 Q.B. 226 (where the charterer had committed a breach of contract by ordering the ship into the Canal).

[55] *Kodros Shipping Corp of Monrovia v Empresa Cubana de Fletes (The Evia) (No 2)* [1983] A.C. 736; *Kissavos Shipping Co SA v Empresa Cubana de Fletes (The Agathon)* [1982] 2 Lloyd's Rep. 400; *International Sea Tankers Inc v Hemisphere Shipping Co Ltd (The Wenjiang) (No2)* [1983] 1 Lloyd's Rep. 400; *Vinava Shipping Co v Finelvet AC (The Chrysalis)* [1983] 1 Lloyd's Rep. 503.

cases seem to reflect a correct judicial appreciation of the commercial risks undertaken by the parties: a voyage charter *prima facie* puts the risk of increased carriage costs on the carrier. And, as in the sale cases, he can shift that burden (if his bargaining power permits) to the shipper; and the methods by which he can do this are in principle the same as those already considered in connection with the sale cases.

The first is to provide specifically for the event by a Suez Clause. This was done in the *Achille Laura* case,[56] where a voyage charter contained a complicated provision requiring the charterer to make extra payments in respect of the increased distance to be travelled in the event of a closure of the Suez Canal.

The second is to alter the nature of the transaction so as in effect to throw the risk of the closure of the Canal (and the consequent extra length of the voyage) on the charterer. This was done in *The Eugenia*,[57] where a Soviet trading corporation wanted to have a quantity of steel girders carried from the Black Sea to India. They entered into a contract with the owners of *The Eugenia*; the contract was negotiated in the summer of 1956 when both parties realised that the Suez Canal might be closed. The Soviet corporation agreed to enter into not a voyage charter, but what has become known as a "time charter trip". This provided that the ship, which was at Genoa when the contract was made, was to proceed from there "via the Black Sea and thence to India" (thus in effect specifying a *voyage*) but that payment was to be made by reference to the capacity of the ship and the *time* taken to accomplish the voyage ("45 shillings per ton on the steamer's dead weight capacity per calender month from the time of the vessel's delivery to her redelivery"). Obviously, this type of contract was intended to put the risk of a prolongation of the voyage (whether resulting from closure of the Canal or from some other cause), on the charterers: payment was to be made by reference to the time taken and not (as in a voyage charter) by reference to the quantity of cargo carried. Such charters have become common: they are a standard device for putting the risk of delays on charterers. *The Eugenia* differs from the voyage charter cases in that it was the charterers (not the shipowners) who claimed that the extra time which the voyage round the Cape would have taken (138 instead of 108 days) discharged the contract. The argument was rejected on exactly the same grounds as in the voyage charter cases: the difference between the two voyages was not sufficiently great to amount to a fundamental one; and the cargo was not of such a nature that it would have suffered from the extra length of the voyage.

4–082 In fact, there were further complications in *The Eugenia*. The charterers had sub-chartered the ship to another Soviet state trading corporation (at a profit of 5 per cent) which, in breach of the charter, ordered the ship into the Canal on October 31, after hostilities had begun; and she did not emerge until January 7, 1957, still from the North end of the Canal. But the charterers could not rely on *this* delay as a ground of discharge as it was

---

[56] *Achille Laura v Total SpA* [1969] 2 Lloyd's Rep. 65.
[57] *Ocean Tramp Tankers Corp v V/O Sovfracht (The Eugenia)* [1964] 2 Q.B. 226.

due to their "fault".[58] Therefore they had to argue that the contract would have been discharged even if they had *not* ordered the ship into the Canal: and it was this argument which was rejected by the court. The reasoning is the same as that of the voyage charter cases, but the practical result is the exact opposite: under a "time charter trip", it is the charterer who has to bear the extra cost of the longer voyage.

(c) *Conclusion*

In the Suez cases, all the English and American decisions (except for two early cases which were later overruled[59]) agree in the result. In none of them was the closure of the Canal, and the consequent imposition of unexpected costs on one of the parties, regarded as a ground of discharge.[60] This unanimity is relevant to the question (which will be discussed in Ch.6) to what extent "impracticability" is in either system a ground of discharge. Here it need only be noted that the Suez cases were not cases of "pure" impracticability, *i.e.* not cases where the *only* ground on which discharge was claimed was that supervening events had made performance considerably more onerous for the party claiming discharge. They were, instead, cases of actual impossibility affecting a contemplated, or in some instances an agreed, method of performance. Such impossibility was held not to be a ground of discharge, even though it resulted in the imposition of considerable additional burdens on one of the parties. This fact would seem to indicate that a similar result should be reached where corresponding burdens arise from "pure" impracticability, unaccompanied by impossibility of any kind, *e.g.* from a steep and unexpected increase of the charges payable for passage of the Canal.

4–083

(3) **Alternative methods**

The effect of supervening events on alternative obligations is discussed in Ch.10. We shall see that, as a general rule, supervening impossibility affecting one or more alternatives is not a ground of discharge so long as at least one alternative remains possible.[61] At this point we need only note some applications of this general rule to contracts which, expressly or by implication, provide for alternative methods of performance. One illustration of this situation is provided by the American case of *Board of Education v Townsend*,[62] where the defendant wished to acquire a plot of land belonging to the plaintiff for the purpose of building a railroad across that land. The parties accordingly agreed that the plaintiff's plot was to be exchanged for one belonging to the defendant, and that the defendant would "remove" a brick school building standing on the

4–084

---

[58] See below, para.14–010.

[59] *i.e.* the *Carapanayoti* case [1959] 1 Q.B. 131, overruled in the *Tsakiroglou* case [1962] A.C. 93 (above, para.4–073) and *The Massalia* [1961] 2 Q.B. 278, overruled in *The Eugenia* [1964] 2 Q.B. 278 (above, para.4–078).

[60] See below, paras 6–017, 6–019, for a discussion of the Suez cases in this context.

[61] See below, para.10–001.

[62] 59 N.E. 223 (1900).

plaintiff's land and "rebuild" it on the land which the defendant was giving in exchange. Before the defendant could perform this undertaking, the school house was blown down by a violent wind; and the defendant argued that his covenant had become impossible to perform. The court rejected the argument on the grounds that there were two ways of performing the covenant: (i) by moving the house as it stood, using jacks and rollers; and (ii) by tearing it down and using the materials for reconstructing it. "Though the former mode of performance became impossible, the latter was not".[63] The court was also influenced by the fact that the defendant had received the full consideration for its promise: the site of the school had been conveyed to the defendant and the railroad had been built over it.

4–085   English cases provide many other illustrations of the principle that a contract is not discharged merely because one of a number of methods of performance has become impossible. It has, for example, been held that a contract to ship goods to, or from, one of two or more ports is not frustrated merely because shipment to or from the particular port intended by the party who was entitled to make the choice subsequently became impossible or illegal, so long as shipment to or from at least one port in the contractual range remained possible and lawful.[64] The same general rule also applies where the obligation to perform in alternative ways is imposed, not by the terms of the contract, but by law. Thus the general rule (already considered)[65] that a c.i.f. seller is under a duty either to ship goods or to buy goods already afloat (and appropriate them to the contract) can be described as one requiring alternative methods of performance. We have seen that the seller is not discharged merely because shipment has become impossible or illegal, and that, in general, the seller must then perform by buying afloat,[66] though the soyabean cases have established an exception to this general rule.[67]

VII. RESULT ACHIEVED BY OTHER MEANS

4–086   We have seen that a contract can be frustrated by the destruction or unavailability of a thing essential for its performance: for example, a contract to install machinery in a factory can be frustrated by the destruction of the factory.[68] There is also a converse situation, commonly discussed under the heading of impossibility by German and Austrian writers, in which a contract is made for the purpose of achieving a particular result and that result is then achieved by other means.[69] Examples given of this type of situation include a contract to free a stranded

---

[63] *ibid.* at 225.

[64] *Seabridge Shipping Ltd v Antco Shipping Ltd (The Furness Bridge)* [1977] 2 Lloyd's Rep. 367; *Warinco AG v Fritz Mauthner* [1978] 1 Lloyd's Rep. 151. And see *Glidden v Hellenic Lines Ltd*, 275 F. 2d 253, above, para.4–078.

[65] See above, para.4–044.

[66] *ibid.*

[67] See above, para.4–045.

[68] *Appleby v Myers* (1867) L.R. 2 C.P. 651; above, para.4–015.

[69] See Esser & Schmidt, *Schuldrecht* (6th ed.), Vol.I, p.325, and nn.70–73, below.

ship which, before the contractor can reach her, is refloated by natural forces[70]; a contract by which an ambulance is summoned to take an accident victim to hospital who, before the ambulance arrives, is conveyed to the hospital by a passing doctor[71]; a contract to tow to a garage a broken-down car which is started up by a passer-by before the towing vehicle reaches it[72]; and a contract by which a plumber is summoned to unblock a pipe which, before the plumber arrives, unblocks itself.[73] In such cases, it is sometimes said that performance has become impossible[74] though another view is that these cases are more appropriately brought within the principle that relief may be given (in German law) where the commercial basis of the contract (*Geschäftsgrundlage*)[75] has disappeared. The latter view was some-times preferred on the ground that impossibility led, under provisions of the Civil Code which have now been repealed, to discharge of the obligation of both parties,[76] while more flexible remedies were (and continue to be) available under the doctrine of the disappearance of the basis of the contract.[77] This reasoning has less force now that impossibility, while a bar to claims for specific enforcement,[78] may leave open claims for damages[79]; though the content of those rights would differ from those available where the court awarded the more flexible remedy of an adaptation of the contract on the ground that its commercial basis had disappeared or been disrupted.[80]

The question how to classify or to deal with such cases seems not to have arisen in England. No doubt some of the situations discussed could be dealt with under the principle that a party cannot rely on self-induced frustration[81]: this could apply to the case of the broken-down car, where it could be argued that the owner, having summoned professional assistance, is responsible if he then voluntarily allows the work to be done by a passer-by.[82] But this analysis can scarcely be applied where the result

4–087

---

[70] Larenz, *Schuldrecht* (14th ed.), Vol.I, p.315; Larenz, *Geschäftsgrundlage and Vertragserfüllung*, p.100; Koziol & Wesler, *Grundriß des Bürgerlichen Rechts* (7th ed.), Vol.I, p.212.

[71] Larenz, *Schuldrecht* (Vol.I) above, (n.70), p.315.

[72] *ibid.* p.303.

[73] Koziol & Wesler, above, n.70, p.354.

[74] *e.g.* Koziol & Wesler, above, nn.70 and 73, and (*semble*) Esser & Schmidt, above, n.69.

[75] *e.g.* Larenz, nn.70 and 73, above.

[76] Former §§ 275, 323 of the BGB.

[77] See below, paras 6–011, 15–037.

[78] New §§ 275(1), 326(1) of the BGB, in force January 1, 2002.

[79] See new § 275(4) of the BGB (above).

[80] See new § 313 of the BGB (above).

[81] See below, para.14–002.

[82] There is perhaps a faint analogy between the situation described above and that which arose in *Great Peace Shipping Ltd v Tsavliris Salvage (International) Ltd (The Great Peace)* [2002] EWCA Civ 1407; [2003] Q.B. 697. In that case vessel A, which was under charter to the defendants, had got into distress at sea, and the defendants had chartered vessel B to render escort services to vessel A. The defendants then found that vessel C, which was also under charter to them, was

which the contractor was to achieve was instead brought about by forces of nature, as in the case of the stranded ship which is refloated by winds or tides. No doubt salvage agreements will commonly make express provision for such events and so exclude the doctrine of frustration. It is also arguable that, if the result is achieved by the normal operation of natural forces, the doctrine of frustration is excluded on the ground that the allegedly frustrating event was foreseeable.[83] But this argument would not be available where the event which achieved the result was of a wholly unexpected and unforeseeable kind, such as a tide which was entirely abnormal for the season in question. In such a case it is at least arguable that the contract had been discharged on the analogy of the principle of discharge by the unavailability of a thing essential for performance[84]: it could be said that a state of affairs, the continuation of which was necessary if the contract was to be performed, had ceased to exist without the fault of either party. Total discharge of the contract might, indeed, be an unsatisfactory solution in the cases put, in which the contractor should recover at least his out-of-pocket expenses. But that is part of the more general point that the English rule, by which frustration gives rise to automatic, total dissolution of the contract,[85] can (even after its statutory modification)[86] sometimes lead to unsatisfactory results.

---

closer than vessel B to vessel A and the services were rendered by vessel C. They sought to avoid liability on the charter of vessel B on the ground of a mistake as to the position of vessel B relative to that of A; and this defence failed as the mistake was not sufficiently fundamental: see Treitel, *The Law of Contract*, (11th ed.), pp.288, 319. No attempt was made to argue that the arrival on the scene of vessel C or the provision by her of the escort services had *frustrated* the charter party of vessel B; and it seems likely that any such attempt would have failed on the ground (among others) stated at n.81, above.

[83] See below, para.13–001.
[84] See above, para.4–014.
[85] See below, paras 15–002, 15–010, 15–069.
[86] By Law Reform (Frustrated Contracts) Act 1943, below paras 15–071, 15–073.

Chapter 5

PARTIAL AND TEMPORARY IMPOSSIBILITY

In this chapter, we shall consider the effects on a contract of (1) the partial destruction or unavailability of its subject-matter, or of a thing essential for its performance and (2) the temporary unavailability of the subject-matter or of one of the parties to the contract, or of a thing or person essential for the performance of the contract. These two topics are related in the sense that in many cases[1] the question whether the contract is discharged will turn on the extent to which the partial or temporary impossibility prejudices one or both parties, or on whether it "frustrates" their "adventure". Indeed, the phrase "frustration of the adventure" seems to have originated in cases of temporary impossibility,[2] though the word "frustration" is now more appropriately used to refer to cases in which the contract is discharged even though there is *no* impossibility in performing it at all.[3]

5–001

I. PARTIAL IMPOSSIBILITY IN GENERAL

(1) As a ground of discharge

The operation of the doctrine of discharge in cases of partial impossibility is illustrated by the leading case of *Taylor v Caldwell*[4] itself. The contract in that case related to "the Surrey Gardens and Music Hall" and was discharged by the destruction of the Hall even though the Gardens (with their many attractions) survived and remained in operation,[5] and even though reduced facilities for theatrical and musical performances in an

5–002

---

[1] This is not necessarily true of all cases of temporary impossibility: *e.g.* not of those in which performance is to be rendered *only* on a fixed day (below, para. 5–029).
[2] See above, para.2–046.
[3] Below, Ch.7.
[4] (1863) 3 B. & S. 926; for in full account of the facts, see above, para.2–024.
[5] See above para.2–028, n.18.

adjoining building remained available.[6] The contract was discharged because its *main purpose* (the giving of the four grand concerts) was defeated. Although the contrary is sometimes suggested,[7] it is not necessary to show that performance should have become *wholly* impossible: such a requirement would be inconsistent with the actual decision in *Taylor v Caldwell*. On the other hand, partial impossibility would not have discharged the contract if it had not defeated the main purpose of the contract,[8] *e.g.* if only the facilities for some (or even all) of the side-shows to be provided by the defendants had been destroyed.

(2) **Position where contract is not discharged**

5-003   Two further questions would have arisen in the case of such partial (but not frustrating) supervening impossibility of the kind just described. The first would have related to the claimants' liability to make the agreed payments of £100 per night, and the second to the defendants' liability in respect of their inability to perform in full.

(a) *Liability of recipient of the partial performance*

5-004   If, in the example given at the end of para.5–002, above, the claimants in *Taylor v Caldwell* had continued with their plans to give the four grand concerts, they would (it seems) have had to make the promised payments in full,[9] even though the absence of one or more of the side-shows had made the enterprise less profitable. Their liability would have been reduced to one to pay a proportionate amount only if the contract had been severable in respect of the facilities to be provided, and in *Taylor v Caldwell* this seems not to have been the case. The contract may, indeed, have been severable[10] in respect of time, so that total impossibility affecting only one of the four concerts could have discharged the contract in respect of that occasion alone.[11] But that is not the present hypothesis, under which partial impossibility affects all four occasions alike.

The preceding discussion has been based on the assumption that the claimants had given the concerts in spite of the partial impossibility affecting the side-shows; but a further possibility is that they might have wished to refuse to continue performance on the ground of such impossibility. They might be entitled to do so under the rules relating to recission for failure in performance, even though the partial impossibility

---

[6] *The Times*, June 13, 1861, reports that: "a smaller building, connected by a short passage, has entirely escaped, thus enabling the lessees [*i.e.* the defendants] to carry on their entertainment, thought not to the usual extent."

[7] See *Grimsdick v Sweetman* [1909] 2 K.B. 740 at 746; but this was a case not of impossibility, but of "frustration of purpose", and where such "frustration" is only partial the requirements for discharge are stricter than they are in cases of partial *impossibility* (see below, para.7–024).

[8] Restatement 2d, § 270(a).

[9] *cf.* Restatement 2d, § 270, Illustration 4.

[10] See below, para.15–031.

[11] *cf. Stubbs v Holywell Ry Co* (1867) L.R. 2 Ex. 311.

was not sufficiently serious to frustrate the contract.[12] The distinction is a matter of degree, and hence a difficult one to draw, but it is submitted that partial impossibility might not be sufficiently serious to defeat the main purpose of the contract but nevertheless be such as to cause the sort of serious prejudice to one party which will provide that party with a ground for rescinding the contract.[13] That might, for example, have been the case if a supervening event in *Taylor v Caldwell* had made it impossible to provide *any* of the side-shows in the Gardens. The main object of the contract—the giving of the four grand concerts in the Hall—could still have been achieved; but the profitability of the venture could have been so seriously affected as to have given the hirers the right to rescind the contract. For this purpose it would not have been necessary to show that the defendants were in breach[14]: it would have been enough to show that there had been a failure in performance of a sufficiently serious kind. There is an important practical difference between the effects of the two concepts in that frustration operates automatically,[15] while rescission depends on the election of the party prejudiced by the event.[16] Thus on destruction of the Hall the contract was discharged so that the hirers were no longer entitled to use the facilities in the Gardens, but on destruction of the facilities for the side-shows they might well have been entitled, but not bound, to continue to use the Hall.

The distinction between partial impossibility which frustrates a contract and partial impossibility which merely gives a party the option to rescind may be illustrated by the American case of *West v Peoples First National Bank and Trust Company*[17] which has been discussed in Ch.4. It will be recalled that in that case a contract for the redevelopment of a 142 acre site was held to have been "terminated"[18] in consequence of the compulsory acquisition of part of the site, and that it is far from clear whether this termination resulted from the doctrine of discharge, from the election of one party, or from the consent of both. In the United States, it may not be necessary to distinguish sharply between the first two modes of termination since discharge in consequence of impossibility is not necessarily automatic (as it is in England[19]), but sometimes depends on the election of the party prejudiced.[20] In England the result would be more appropriately explained on the ground that the partial impossibility,

5–005

---

[12] For a similar point in relation to temporary impossibility, see above, para.2–050; below, para.5–057.

[13] For a discussion of this degree of seriousness, see Treitel, *The Law of Contract* (11th ed.), pp.769–778. For the submission that a failure in performance may be sufficiently serious to justify rescission at the injured party's election, without being sufficiently serious to discharge the contract automatically under the doctrine of frustration, see below, para.5–060.

[14] Treitel, *op. cit.*, p.759.

[15] Below, para.15–002.

[16] Treitel, *op. cit.* (n.13), p.844.

[17] 106 A. 2d 427 (1954); above, para.4–006.

[18] 106 A. 2d 427, 433.

[19] Below, para.15–002.

[20] Below, paras 15–014 to 15–018.

though not sufficiently serious to frustrate the contract, nevertheless gave the party prejudiced by it a right to rescind the contract.

(b) *Liability of the party rendering the partial performance*

5–006   This problem can be illustrated by reverting to the example based on *Taylor v Caldwell, i.e.* to the situation in which only the facilities for providing one or more of the side-shows in the Gardens had been destroyed, so that the contract was not frustrated, and the hirers had not attempted to rescind it but had continued with their plans for giving the four grand concerts in the Hall. Their box-office receipts might have been diminished by reason of the reduction in the facilities in the Gardens (which the contract had obliged the defendants to provide); and the question would then have arisen whether in such a case of non-frustrating partial impossibility the defendants would have been liable for this reduction in the hirers' expected profits. This is a little developed area of English law, but it seems in principle possible for supervening partial impossibility which is not sufficiently serious to be a ground of frustration nevertheless to provide a party with an excuse for partial non-performance.[21] The cases to be considered later in this chapter recognise the existence of this possibility in cases of the partial failure of a source of supply[22] and in cases of temporary impossibility[23]; and there seems to be no reason why it should not also exist in cases of partial impossibility. It is clear that such an excuse will be recognised only where the partial impossibility occurs without the "fault" of the party seeking to rely on the excuse,[24] for if he were at fault there would be no good reason for relieving him from liability for loss flowing from such fault. What is less clear is whether absence of fault is *sufficient* to bring the excuse into operation. The answer to this question, it is submitted, depends on the standard of the defendant's liability under the contract.[25] If that liability were strict, mere absence of fault would not, in cases of partial impossibility, give rise to an excuse for non-performance; though total impossibility might nevertheless be a ground of frustration, since strict liability is not necessarily absolute liability.[26] If, on the other hand, the defendant were, under the contract, liable only for "fault",[27] partial impossibility occurring without fault would provide him with a partial excuse for non-performance and could, if sufficiently serious, also frustrate the contract.

---

[21] Treitel, *The Law of Contract* (11th ed.), p.835.

[22] See *HR & S Sainsbury Ltd v Street* [1972] 1 W.L.R. 834; below, para.5–013.

[23] See *Minnevitch v Café de Paris (Londres) Ltd* [1936] 1 All E.R. 884; below, para.5–058.

[24] *cf.* above, para.4–052; *HR & S Sainsbury Ltd v Street* [1972] 1 W.L.R. 834 at 835 ("through no fault of his").

[25] *cf.* above, para.1–003.

[26] *e.g.* the duty of a seller of goods by description to procure goods of the contract description is strict, but it does not follow that such a contract cannot be frustrated: *cf.* below, para.5–042.

[27] See above, para.1–004.

(3) **Partial frustration?**

In some civil law systems, partial destruction of the subject-matter can lead   5–007
to the same type of relief in respect of that part as would be available in
respect of the whole in cases of total destruction. In German law, for
example,[28] this result can follow from provisions of the Civil Code by
which in cases of impossibility the creditor's claim for (specific)
performance is excluded "insofar as" (*soweit*) performance is impossible,[29] and his claim for damages is excluded if the debtor is not
responsible for the failure in performance[30]; while the creditor's liability
to render the agreed counter-performance (*i.e.* usually to pay the agreed
price) is correspondingly reduced.[31] For the purpose of these rules a
distinction is, however, drawn between impossibility which renders the
part performed or remaining possible "of no interest"[32] to the creditor
and partial impossibility which does not have this effect. In the former
(but not in the latter) case, the creditor has the right to terminate the
contract[33] and if he exercises this right the special rules applicable to
partial impossibility cease to apply. The distinction between the two
situations may be illustrated by reference once again to *Taylor v Caldwell*.[34]
On the actual facts of the case, the hirers had (presumably) no "interest"
in the Gardens and the side-shows, so that as the contract was not
severable,[35] the defendants would (under the German rules) have been
under no liability; but if the facilities for one or more of the side-shows had
been accidentally destroyed the contract would have remained in being,
the defendants would have been under no liability in respect of their
inability to provide the side-shows, and the amount which the hirers had
promised to pay would have been reduced in respect of that inability on
the part of the defendants.

These rules have no direct counterpart in English law, under which, in   5–008
cases of partial impossibility, the contract is either frustrated or remains in
force. There is no such concept as partial or temporary frustration on
account of partial or temporary impossibility.[36] Under rules considered
elsewhere in this chapter, partial or temporary impossibility which occurs
without the fault of one party may, indeed, give the debtor an excuse for
non-performance and the creditor an option to rescind.[37] But where that

---

[28] For similar rules in Austrian and Swiss law, see Koziol & Wesler, *Grundriß des
Bürgerlichen Rechts*, p.216; for special application to leases, see Austrian Civil
Code § 1105; Von Tuhr/Escher, *Allgemeiner Teil des Schweizerischen Obligationen-
recht* (3rd ed.), Vol.II, p.133.

[29] BGB § 275(1).

[30] BGB §§ 275(4), 280(1), sentence 2, 283.

[31] BGB § 326(1), sentence 1.

[32] BGB § 323(5), sentence 1.

[33] *ibid.*

[34] (1863) 3 B. & S. 826.

[35] Above, para.5–004.

[36] For discussion of the contrary view, as applied to partial failure of a specified
source, see below, para.5–030.

[37] Above, para.5–003; below, para.5–060.

option is exercised the termination of the contract results from the election of one of the parties, whereas the civil law rules discussed above appear to bring about partial discharge by operation of law. The concept of partial discharge in English law is restricted to obligations which are "severable",[38] whether in point of time or otherwise.

In the United States, the Uniform Commercial Code, s.2–613(b)[39] expressly deals with the case where, without fault of either party, goods which were identified when the contract was made, are partially destroyed before the risk has passed to the buyer. In such a case, the buyer is given the option of either treating the contract as avoided[40] or accepting the goods "with due allowance from the contract price for the deficiency in quantity but without further right against the seller". As already noted,[41] this provision has no direct counterpart in the United Kingdom Sales of Goods Act 1979, though where the goods are such as are normally sold by weight, measure or number, similar results may in practice often be reached.[42] The further point to be noted here is that s.2–613(b) differs from the civil law provisions relating to partial impossibility in that its operation depends on the choice of that buyer, and that this choice is unfettered in the sense that, if he wishes to avoid the whole contract, he need not show that he has "no interest" in the performance of the part remaining possible. In extreme cases, the courts might perhaps hold that the general good faith requirement of the Uniform Commercial Code, s.1–203 (now renumbered s.1–304[43]) would preclude the buyer from avoiding the contract, *e.g.* where the part destroyed was relatively small; where the shortfall caused little or no prejudice to the buyer, and where his motive for treating the contract as avoided was that the market price of the goods had fallen below the contract price. In English law, the buyer's right to reject in such circumstances may be excluded by law (so long as the buyer does not deal as consumer) if the part destroyed was so small that it would be unreasonable for the buyer to reject the amount which the seller was able to deliver.[44]

(4) **Impossibility in method of performance**

5-009   The Restatement 2d in two of its Illustrations appears to classify impossibility in the method of performance as partial impossibility. Thus it so classifies impossibility in delivering goods at a specified place or on a

---

[38] *Stubbs v Holywell Ry Co* (1867) L.R. 2 Ex. 311; *cf.* Law Reform (Frustrated Contracts) Act 1943, s.2(4).

[39] *cf.* French Civil Code, art.1601(2) (partial destruction of goods which have been sold).

[40] Under the proposed amendments to Art.2 of the UCC (above, para.2–042, n.17) "terminated" is to be substituted for "avoided".

[41] Above, para.3–016.

[42] See the discussion of *HR & S Sainsbury Ltd v Street* [1972] 1 W.L.R. 834, and the effect on such a case of Sale of Goods Act 1979, s.30(1), below, paras 5–013, 5–014.

[43] See above, para.3–017, n.57.

[44] See Sale of Goods Act 1979, s.30(2A); below, paras 5–014; 15–066; 15–017, n.26.

specified ship.[45] In favour of this classification, it can be said that the same test which determines the issue of frustration in cases of partial impossibility is also often applied where the impossibility lies in the method of performance: in both types of contract, the question is whether, after the supervening event, performance of the contract would be fundamentally different from that originally undertaken.[46] Nevertheless it is submitted that there are both analytical and practical grounds for treating the two types of impossibility as distinct. From an analytical point of view, it seems that, where a specified method of performance becomes impossible, the *promised* performance in fact becomes *wholly* impossible. In the Suez charterparty cases,[47] *e.g.* it became wholly impossible to perform the (expressly or impliedly promised[48]) voyage via Suez, though it remained possible to carry the goods by an alternative route, such as that via the Cape. In cases such as *Taylor v Caldwell*,[49] by contrast, performance became only partly impossible, and this would have been true whether it had been the Hall or the facilities for the side-shows that had been destroyed. From a practical point of view, the distinction is important because the tests applied in some cases of impossibility in the method of performance are plainly inapplicable to cases of partial impossibility. Thus in the Suez charterparty cases frustration was excluded because the alternative Cape route was regarded as a commercially satisfactory substitute for the Suez route, so that there was no fundamental difference between the two routes. But in *Taylor v Caldwell* it would have been beside the point for the defendants to have shown that they had at their disposal another hall which was equally suitable for the giving of the four grand concerts. The distinction cannot be explained away on the ground that the contract in *Taylor v Caldwell* expressly referred to the particular Hall; for in some of the Suez charterparty cases the contracts likewise expressly referred to Suez,[50] and even where they did not it was an implied term of such contracts that this route (if customary at the time of contracting) would be taken.[51]

II. PARTIAL FAILURE IN A SOURCE OF SUPPLY

In the following discussion, it will be assumed that the source is specified in the contract, so that there would be no doubt that its *total* failure would discharge the contract.[52] We shall first discuss in general terms the questions

5–010

---

[45] § 270, Illustrations 2 and 3. These illustrations are based respectively on *Whitman v Anglum*, 103 A. 114 (1918) and *Meyer v Sullivan*, 181 P. 847 (1921), discussed at above, paras 4–064, 4–066.

[46] Above, paras 4–073, 5–002.

[47] Above, paras 4–078 to 4–082.

[48] See below, nn.50 and 51.

[49] (1863) 3 B & S. 826.

[50] Above, para.4–078.

[51] Above, para.4–079.

[52] Above, para.4–049.

which arise where the source fails only in part, and then consider certain special problems which can arise from the partial failure of a single source from which a supplier (usually of goods, but conceivably of services)[53] intends to perform contracts with more than one customer. Many of the older cases concern agricultural produce expected to be grown on specified land; but an increasing number of more recent cases have concerned contracts for the sale of goods to be derived from a particular foreign source which fails in full to yield the expected supply because of restrictions on the export of goods from the country in question.

(1) Effect of partial failure of source: in general

5–011 Where the circumstances are such that the total failure of a source would discharge a contract of sale,[54] the partial failure of that source normally has the following legal consequences.

(a) *Excuse to extent of deficiency*

5–012 First, the seller is excused to the extent of the deficiency. This was the position in *Howell v Coupland*[55] where the contract was for the sale of part of a crop of potatoes to be grown on specified land and that crop failed in large part. The seller delivered the quantity grown on the specified land (as well as a quantity of potatoes grown by him on other land), and the only point actually decided was that he was not liable in damages for failing to deliver the balance of the contract quantity. The grounds for the decision are more fully discussed in Ch.4.[56] Here it need only be noted that, in so far as he had delivered the potatoes grown on land other than that specified in the contract, the seller seems to have gone beyond what was legally required of him.

(b) *Duty generally to deliver what is produced*

5–013 The second legal consequence of the partial failure is that, normally, the seller must deliver the quantity which the source actually yields; this point is of obvious practical importance since the partial failure of the source is likely to lead to a shortage of supply and hence to an increase in the market price of the commodity in question. The rule is illustrated by *H R & S Sainsbury Ltd v Street*,[57] where a farmer had agreed to sell the whole of a crop of barley of "about 275 tons", to be grown on specified land, at a price of £20 per ton. For reasons largely outside the farmer's control, and not involving any breach of contract on his part, the crop yielded only 140 tons, which the farmer sold to a third party for £27.50 per ton. It was held that the farmer was liable in damages to his original buyer for failing to deliver to him the 140 tons. The contract was not discharged: the effect of

---

[53] *e.g. J Lauritzen A/S v Wijsmuller BV (The Super Servant Two)* [1990] 1 Lloyd's Rep. 1
[54] *i.e.* where the source is specified in the contract, and, sometimes, where it is contemplated by both parties: above, paras 4–049 to 4–052, 4–054 to 4–056.
[55] (1876) 1 Q.B.D. 258.
[56] Above, paras 4–049 to 4–052.
[57] [1972] 1 W.L.R. 834.

the partial crop failure was merely to provide the seller with an excuse for non-performance to the extent of the shortage.[58] In this respect, the rule can be compared with the similar rule which applies in certain cases of temporary impossibility, *e.g.* with that which governs one of the effects of temporary illness on contracts to render personal services.[59]

It is open to question whether the rule just stated should be applied if so large a part of the crop fails as to make it uneconomical to harvest the rest. This was the position in *International Paper Co v Rockefeller*,[60] where the contract was for the sale of timber growing on specified land, to be delivered over a period of five years at the rate of 6,000 cords per annum for a price of $5.30 a cord. After three years (when 12,000 cords remained to be delivered) there was a fire in which the timber, except for 500 cords standing on a hilltop, was destroyed; and these 500 cords could be harvested only at a cost of $20 per cord. It was held that seller was excused with regard to the part of the timber which had been destroyed, but not with regard to the 500 cords which had survived the fire. The case is cited with seeming approval by the Restatement 2d[61] and by Uniform Commercial Code, s.2–614, Comment 1. But it is submitted that a crop can be wholly "destroyed" as a matter of business even though the destruction is not literally total,[62] and that the better view is that this was what had happened in *International Paper Co v Rockefeller*.

(c) *Effect of partial failure on buyer's duties*

The third legal consequence (or group of legal consequences) of the   5–014
partial failure of a source of a seller's supply relates to the position of the buyer; and this is more favourable than that of the seller. If the seller tenders less than the quantity sold, the general rule[63] is that the buyer can reject the tender. In English law this rule is laid down by s.30(1) of the Sale of Goods Act 1979, which provides that "where the seller delivers a quantity of goods less than he contracted to sell, the buyer may reject them". In the United States, the Uniform Commercial Code contains no provision directly comparable to s.30(1), but the same result follows from the "perfect tender" rule of s.2–601(a), which provides that, in general,[64] "if the goods or the tender of delivery fail in any respect to conform to the contract the buyer may ... reject the whole". The buyer's rights of rejection can be excluded by contrary provision in the contract.[65] The buyer is also liable to pay for the part actually delivered if he elected to

---

[58] Above, para.5–006.

[59] Below, para.5–058.

[60] 146 N.Y.S. 371 (1914).

[61] § 272, Reporter's note to Comment c.

[62] Above, para.3–005.

[63] For an exception, see below, at nn.70–77.

[64] There are many exceptions to the "perfect tender" rule: these are stated in Treitel, *Remedies for Breach of Contract*, pp.364–365.

[65] As in *Goldsborough Mort & Co v Carter* (1914) 19 C.L.R. 419, below, at n.79. See Sale of Goods Act 1979, s.30(5): UCC, s.2–601 similarly contains the qualification "unless otherwise agreed." See also s.1–102(3), now replaced by s.1–302(a) in the new version of Art.1 (above, para.3–017, n.57).

accept tender of the quantity (falling short of that agreed) which the source had actually provided. In England, the concluding words of s.30(1) of the Sale of Goods Act 1979 expressly provide that, if the buyer accepts delivery of less than the agreed quantity of goods, "he must pay for [those accepted] at the contract rate". The position is the same under Uniform Commercial Code, s.2–601(b), which provides that the buyer may "accept the whole"; and, if he does so, s.2–607(1) requires him "to pay at the contract rate for any goods accepted". It is possible that Uniform Commercial Code, s.2–613(b) might also apply to cases of partial failure of a specified source and produce the result that the buyer can "accept the goods with due allowance from the contract price for the ... deficiency in quantity". This provision is discussed elsewhere in this book[66]; here the only point to be noted is that, if it does apply to cases of the present kind, it can lead to a result which may be different in financial terms from that which would be reached under ss.2–601(b) and 2–607(1), for "due allowance"[67] is not necessarily calculated "at the contract rate".[68] In comparing the English and American positions, it should finally be noted that Uniform Commercial Code, s.2–601(c) gives the buyer a third option in providing that he may "accept any commercial unit or units and reject the rest". In case of short delivery, this option seems not to be open to the buyer in English law.[69]

Section 30(1) of the Sale of Goods Act 1979 is subject to a statutory exception, introduced in 1994[70] and now contained in s.30(2A) of the Act. This subsection provides that, where the buyer does not deal as consumer and the quantity of goods delivered to him is less than the quantity contracted for,[71] then the buyer may not reject the goods if the shortfall is "so slight that it would be unreasonable for him to do so" (*i.e.* to reject). The purpose of s.30(2A) was to prevent what were thought to be abuses of the right to reject,[72] *e.g.* where a buyer rejected goods on a falling market

---

[66] Above, para.3–016; below, para.15–016.

[67] UCC, s.2–613(b).

[68] *ibid.* s.2–607(1).

[69] *Benjamin's Sale of Goods* (6th ed.), para.8–041. The "right of partial rejection" conferred on the buyer by Sale of Goods Act 1979, s.35A (inserted by Sale and Supply of Goods Act 1994, s.3) does not appear to alter the position in cases of the present kind, in which it is assumed that the goods are (except with regard to quantity) in conformity with the contract with regard to quality and description. To this extent, the goods delivered are conforming goods; and where the buyer accepts any *conforming* goods he must accept them all: *Benjamin, op. cit.*, para.12–061. *cf.* Law Commissions' Report on *Sale and Supply of Goods* (Law Com. No 160; Scot Law Com. No 104) Pt 6, dealing separately with "Partial Rejection" (paras 6.06–6.16) and "Remedies for Delivery of the Wrong Quantity" (paras 6.17–6.23).

[70] By Sale and Supply of Goods Act 1994, s.4(2) implementing a Report of the Law Commissions on *Sale and Supply of Goods*, above, para.6.20.

[71] See s.30(2A)(a); a corresponding provision for the case where the seller delivers *more* than he contracted to sell is made in s.30(2A)(b) but is not our concern here. Dealing as consumer is defined in s.61(5A).

[72] See Report (above, n.70), para.6.20 and *cf. ibid.*, para.4.18.

on account of a comparatively slight[73] discrepancy between the quantity specified in the contract and that delivered. On the other hand, the difficulty of predicting just when a discrepancy is "so slight that it would be unreasonable" is a regrettable source of uncertainty; and this defect in s.30(2A) is at least mitigated by the further provision that the subsection (among others) is "subject to any usage of trade, special agreement or course of dealing between the parties".[74] Section 30(2A) can thus be excluded by express agreement and it is submitted that it could be also excluded by a term (commonly found in commodity contracts) which provides for a margin (*e.g.* 2,000 tons 5 per cent more or less). It was settled before the introduction of s.30(2A) that such a margin must not be exceeded[75]; and it is submitted that this position is not effected by the subsection. It is submitted that such a stipulation would be regarded as a "special agreement" excluding s.30(2A)[76]; in support of this submission, it can be argued that a stipulation for a margin itself achieves the objective of preventing abuses of the right to reject, at least within the specified limits; and that these limits should be respected by the courts, particularly in the non-consumer cases to which the operation of s.30(2A) is restricted. Where the buyer deals as consumer, his right to reject delivery of the wrong quantity is not affected by the subsection.[77]

In cases of partial failure of a source of supply, the buyer's right to reject **5-015** short delivery is of little practical importance, for the failure will normally drive up prices, so that the buyer will not wish to reject the amount which the seller can deliver. An analogous question can, however, arise where a partial export embargo is imposed and later relaxed, so that the seller is then able to ship the balance due under the contract. The relaxation of the embargo is likely to cause prices to fall back and the buyer, having accepted the original part-shipment, may then be unwilling to accept the balance. Unless the terms on which the original part-shipment was accepted indicate that the buyer is to be under no further liability, the buyer is then bound to accept the balance of the quantity specified in the contract.[78]

---

[73] Even before the introduction of s.30(2A); a minimal discrepancy did not justify rejection: *Shipton, Anderson & Co v Weil Bros & Co* [1912] 1 K.B. 574 (excess of 55lbs over 4,950 tons; the same would apply to a minimal shortfall).

[74] s.30(5).

[75] *Tamvaco v Lucas (No1)* (1859) 1 E.& E. 581; unless the discrepancy is trivial: see n.73, above.

[76] For exclusion of s.30(2A) by "usage of trade" in cases of c.i.f. and f.o.b. sales, see *Benjamin's Sale of Goods* (6th ed.), paras 19–012, 20–038.

[77] This follows from the opening words of s.30(2A), implementing the policy stated in Report (above, n.70), para.6.20.

[78] *André & Cie v Cook Industries Inc* [1987] 2 Lloyd's Rep. 463 (one of the soyabean cases discussed in above, para.4–045; and below, paras 12–036 *et seq.*; the buyer's reluctance to accept the balance may have been influenced by the price movements described at para.4–045, n.58, above).

(d) *Express contractual provisions*

5–016   The rules which normally determine the effect of the partial failure of a specified source may be varied by express provisions of the contract. In an Australian case,[79] for instance, a contract for the sale of a specified number of sheep from a named sheep-station provided that if the number delivered turned out to be smaller or greater than that stated in the contract "the purchaser shall pay for the number … so delivered". Because of adverse weather conditions, many of the sheep died, and the actual decision was that the seller could in these circumstances rely on the principle of *Howell v Coupland*[80] as a defence to a claim for damages for short delivery. But there seems to be little doubt that the contractual provision quoted above would have precluded the buyer from exercising his normal right to reject the sheep delivered on the ground that the number delivered fell short of that which the seller had contracted to sell. Similarly, the normal rule that the seller must deliver the quantity actually produced can be excluded by an express contractual provision stating that the contract is to be of no effect if the source to which it refers yields less than the specified quantity. Clauses of this kind were sometimes found in contracts for the sale of goods "to arrive" on a named ship.[81] If the contract was not expressly conditional on arrival of the full contract quantity, it would be a question of construction whether, in the event of the arrival of less than that quantity, the seller was to be wholly free from liability or to be excused only to the extent of the deficiency, and whether the buyer was entitled to reject the quantity which arrived on the ground that it fell short of the quantity specified in the contract.[82] The view that the seller was liable for no more than the quantity which arrived, and that the buyer must accept and pay for that quantity, would clearly prevail where the contract provided that the missing quantity was to be written off the contract quantity, or that the contract was to be void to the extent of the deficiency. Such clauses are sometimes found in c.i.f. contracts.[83]

(2) **Effect of partial failure: more than one contract**

5–017   The problem here to be considered most commonly arises where a seller has entered into contracts with a number of buyers to supply each of them with a specified quantity of goods from the same designated source. That source then fails in part, with the result that, though the seller is not prevented from performing one (or some) of those contracts, he is prevented from performing them all. Many of the modern cases on this topic have arisen because the goods were to be taken from a foreign source which ceased to be freely available to the seller because of export

---

[79] *Goldsborough Mort & Co v Carter* (1914) 19 C.L.R. 419.
[80] (1876) 1 Q.B.D. 258, above, para.4–049.
[81] *e.g. Lovatt v Hamilton* (1839) 5 M. & W. 639. For other cases concerning sales of goods "to arrive" (see above, para.4–050).
[82] See, *Benjamin's Sale of Goods* (6th ed.), para.21–023.
[83] See *ibid.* para.19–006.

restrictions imposed by the authorities of the country of origin.[84] Some at least of these cases are cases of supervening illegality by foreign law, rather than cases of physical impossibility. It is nevertheless convenient, for two reasons, to discuss them here, rather than in Ch.8, which deals with supervening illegality. First, there is some dispute on the question whether, in cases of supervening illegality by foreign law, the basis of discharge is indeed impossibility or some principle of public policy.[85] Secondly, in resolving questions of the kind here under discussion, the courts have treated partial failure of the source in the same way whether it has resulted from physical impossibility or from foreign export restrictions; there has been no suggestion in the decided cases that the two types of cases should be governed by different principles.

(a) *Possible solutions*

In discussing possible solutions of the problem stated at the beginning of para.5–017, above, it will be convenient to take the simple example of a farmer who, reasonably expecting his land to yield a crop of 1,000 tons, agrees to sell 200 tons to be grown on that land to each of five buyers. If there is then a partial crop failure, so that the land yields no more than 600 tons, there are four possible solutions. After examining these possibilities, we shall consider the extent to which they (or some of them) are supported by the authorities. **5–018**

(i) All contracts discharged

The first possibility is to say that all the contracts are discharged because the seller cannot perform them all in full. This is an unattractive solution in the partial crop failure example given above because it would leave the seller free to go into the market and there to sell the whole 600 tons which had actually been produced at the higher prices which would probably prevail because of the shortage. In English law, this first possible solution would also give rise to a further difficulty, because under it *both* parties would be automatically discharged.[86] Yet if the seller delivered 200 tons to any one buyer, that buyer should have no cause for complaint. In American law, there would be no such difficulty: discharge is not necessarily automatic, the buyer's own performance would not be impossible and there would be no "failure of consideration" if the whole quantity bought by him were tendered.[87] **5–019**

(ii) No contract discharged

The second possibility is to say that none of the contracts is discharged. Discharge (so the argument runs) must be due to an event beyond the control of the party invoking the doctrine of discharge. If the seller chooses to deliver 200 tons to each of three of the five buyers, his inability to deliver anything to the other two is due to his own choice, and therefore his contracts with those two cannot be discharged. According to an **5–020**

---

[84] As in the soyabean cases, above, para.4–054; below, para.12–036.
[85] Below, para.8–054.
[86] Above, para.2–039; below, para.15–002.
[87] Above, para.2–041.

analogous case[88] concerning contracts of carriage, the doctrine of discharge would in our example be excluded on the ground that a party cannot rely as a ground of discharge on an inability to perform which is due to his own act or "election".[89] But the seller in the case has no really *free* choice: he cannot perform all the contracts in full. If he had sold the whole 1,000 tons to one buyer, he would have had an excuse with regard to the shortfall of 400 tons.[90] The fact that he sold equal parts of the expected crop to each of five buyers does not seem to be a sufficiently significant ground for depriving him of that excuse. The argument that discharge of two of the contracts would be due to the seller's "election" could also be met by imposing legal restrictions on his right to choose between the five buyers, as under the second alternative of the third possible solution, to be stated in para.5–021, below. We shall see that the authorities provide some support for the imposition of such restrictions.[91]

(iii) Some contracts discharged

5–021   The third possibility is to say that *some* of the contracts are discharged, so that, if the seller delivers to three of the buyers, his contracts with the other two are discharged. There are two versions of this possibility. One is that the seller has a free choice in deciding to which of the buyers he will deliver (in which case he is likely to choose those who have agreed to pay the highest price). The other is that he must deliver to such of the buyers as may be designated by law, for example, he may be required to deliver to those who had made the earliest contracts, or to act reasonably in making his choice.

(iv) Allocation of available supplies

5–022   The fourth possibility is to say that the seller must, and need only, allocate supplies between the various buyers, *e.g.* on a *pro rata* basis. On this basis he would, in our example have to deliver 120 tons to each buyer and he would be excused under each contract with regard to the balance of 80 tons.

For the reasons given above, it is submitted that neither of the first two solutions should be adopted, unless the contract on its true construction provided for one of them.[92] The effective choice should therefore be between the third and fourth solutions.

(b) *Principle of allocation in American law*

5–023   In the United States, there was support for the principle of *pro rata* division even before it was given legislative force by the provision of the Uniform Commercial Code to be discussed below. It obviously applies where the

---

[88] *J Lauritzen A/S v Wijsmuller BV (The Super Servant Two)* [1990] 1 Lloyd's Rep. 1, following *Maritime National Fish Ltd v Ocean Trawlers Ltd* [1935] A.C. 524; for a full discussion of these cases, see below, paras 14–023, 14–024.

[89] Below, para.14–015.

[90] *HR & S Sainsbury Ltd v Street* [1972] 1 W.L.R. 834, above, para.5–011.

[91] Below, paras 5–021, 5–027, 5–028.

[92] *cf. Tennants (Lancashire) Ltd v C S Wilson & Co Ltd* [1917] A.C. 495, where the contract in terms allowed the seller to suspend deliveries to *all* his buyers.

contract expressly provided for such division[93] but it is regarded as applicable even in the absence of such a provision in the treatises on contracts of Williston[94] and Corbin.[95] It is also supported by § 464 of the Restatement,[96] but in a restricted form: it does not apply where the buyer had at the time of contracting been given reason by the seller to believe that the seller (a) had not entered into contracts to supply other customers from the same source, and (b) would not enter into such contracts.[97] In such cases the seller is liable for failing to deliver the agreed quantity. It seems to be assumed that if the buyer *does* know that the seller had already entered into a contractual commitment towards another customer, then the buyer's claim is postponed to that of the earlier customer. A similar restriction is supported by an Australian case[98] in which the contract was expressly "subject to export quota" and this was held to mean that it was subject to the seller's getting a quota sufficient to satisfy the buyer after fulfilling previous contracts of which the buyer knew.

The restriction stated in the Restatement, § 464, is not in terms repeated in the Uniform Commercial Code, s.2–615(b),[99] which adopts the principle of allocation of available supplies (*prima facie* on a *pro rata* basis[1]) and extends it in two respects. It allows the seller, when making an allocation, to take into account not only other buyers to whom he had sold goods from the source which had partly failed, but also "regular customers not ... under contract" and even his "own requirements",[2] though only "for further manufacture". These last words would prevent him from making an allocation to himself for the purpose of resale, so as to take advantage of the rising market which is likely to have resulted from the partial failure of the source. The right of the seller to make an allocation to himself is illustrated by *Campbell v Hostetter Farms Inc*[3] where a farmer had agreed to deliver 20,000 bushels of corn to be grown by him. His crop having failed in part, he delivered only just over 10,000 bushels, keeping some 2,000 bushels to feed his own stock. This course of action was held to be justified under s.2–615(b), so that the farmer was held not

---

[93] *Ranney-Davies Mercantile Co v Shawano Canning Co*, 206 P. 337 (1922).

[94] para.1962.

[95] para.1342.

[96] "Ratable apportionment" (§ 464(1)).

[97] This is the effect of the Restatement, § 464(2).

[98] *Bowring & Walker Pty Ltd v Jackson's Corio Meat Packing (1965) Pty Ltd* [1972] 1 N.S.W.R. 277; see further below, para.5–027.

[99] *cf.* s.2A–405(b), applying the same rules to chattel leases.

[1] Comment 10 refers to "proration".

[2] A provision perhaps inspired by the German decision in RGZ 91, 312 (RG, December 7, 1917), where a farmer who had contracted to supply a specified quantity of milk was excused in part in consequence of shortages due to facts beyond his control. He was allowed to keep enough to continue to run his own farm because the contract was construed as one for the *surplus* product of the farm. The influence of German law on the Uniform Commercial Code is a topic which cannot be further pursued here. *cf.* Treitel, *Remedies for Breach of Contract*, p.141.

[3] 380 A. 2d 463 (1977).

to be in breach. The above two extensions of the principle of *pro rata* division which are made by the Uniform Commercial Code are only partly followed by the Restatement 2d, which in § 272, Illustration 5, allows the seller to take account of the needs of his regular customers, when making the allocation[4] but makes no reference to the seller's own needs. It is submitted that both of the extensions are of questionable merit; and that the better view is that priority should be given to customers who have entered into binding contracts with the seller. Such customers take the risk that there may be a glut and that prices may *fall.* If there is a shortage, they should correspondingly be treated more favourably than regular customers who have not made any contractual commitment; and, *a fortiori,* than the seller himself. Indeed, the Uniform Commercial Code seems to some extent to recognise the force of this argument. The overriding principle (stated in s.2–615(b)) is that the allocation is to be made "in any manner which is fair and reasonable"; and Comment 11 amplifies this not very helpful statement by saying that "in cases of doubt ... contract customers should be favoured and supplies pro-rated evenly among them regardless of price". There is no explicit suggestion here that the time sequence in which the contracts were made is of any significance but at least the courts are not precluded from taking this factor into account. Another factor that might be relevant is that the quantity produced was very small, *e.g.* if 1,000 tons were sold and only 100 tons were produced, it might not be reasonable to divide such a small amount between five buyers.

5–024   A buyer to whom an allocation is made under s.2–615(b)) is not bound to accept it. On receipt of notification of an allocation, he may either terminate the contract or modify it by agreeing to take the reduced quantity[5]; if he fails to modify the contract within a reasonable time, not exceeding 30 days, the contract lapses.[6] It is not clear what happens then to the "lapsed" share, *i.e.* whether the seller can keep it, or whether it must, in turn, be divided among the other buyers. These provisions as to notification of allocation and modification of the contract can obviously apply in terms only to buyers under contract and not to regular customers not under contract. But a seller who reduced a contract buyer's share on the basis that he also had a regular customer, who then did not take up his allocation, would not be acting in a "manner which [was] fair and reasonable"[7] if he did not in good faith offer to make a supply to that customer, who presumably ought to have a reasonable time in which to decide whether or not to accept the offer.

In Ch.3, we saw that the Uniform Commercial Code did not make it clear whether crop-failure cases were to be dealt with under s.2–615 or

---

[4] For a statement of the duty "to prorate", see § 272, Comment c.

[5] s.2–616(1). UCC, s.2A–406 applies the same rules to most chattel leases as s.2–616 applies to sales.

[6] s.2–616(2). The proposed amendments to UCC, Art.2 (above, para.3–042, n.17) substitute "is terminated" for "lapses".

[7] s.2–616(b).

under s.2–613.[8] The point is of crucial importance in the present context since s.2–613 simply entitles the buyer, in case of partial loss, to "accept the goods", without making any provision for *pro rata* division where each of several buyers buys a part of an identified bulk which is then partially destroyed. Under s.2–613 there could therefore be a scramble for priorities. It is to be hoped that the fairer provisions of s.2–615 would be applied where the subject-matter of the sale was physically divisible. That would leave scope for the application of s.2–613 where such division was not possible; this type of case is further discussed later in this chapter.[9]

(c) *Principle of allocation in English law*

In English law there is no legislative provision for allocation of supplies; but   5–025
it is significant that in the United States the principle of allocation was recognised as a matter of common law[10] well before its legislative recognition in Uniform Commercial Code, s.2–615(b). In discussing the English authorities, a distinction must be drawn between two types of cases: those in which the seller relies by way of excuse on express contractual provisions (such as *force majeure*, prohibition of export, or similar clauses) and those in which he relies on the common law doctrine of frustration.

(i) Where the seller relies on excuse under express contractual provisions

In this group of cases there is considerable support for some form of the   5–026
principle of *pro rata* division (though with significant differences from the American position described above). The first case of this kind is *Tennants (Lancashire) Ltd v CS Wilson & Co Ltd,*[11] where support for the principle is somewhat tentative. A contract for the sale of magnesium chlorate to be delivered in instalments over a period of one year provided that the seller should be entitled to suspend performance in the event of "short supply ... hindering ... delivery". War-time conditions prevented him from obtaining enough to supply *all* his buyers, though he could (at a higher price than that due under the contract) have got enough to supply one buyer such as the claimants. All the other buyers acquiesced in the situation and it was held that the words quoted above protected the seller from liability to the claimants. This conclusion on its face supports the first of the possible solutions outlined in paras 5–018 to 5–019, above, *i.e.* the view that *all* the contracts were suspended. But in the circumstances there was no force in the normal objection to this solution, that it enabled the seller to profit from the supervening event by reselling the available supply, since the seller was not a producer but a middleman who could himself procure goods of the contract description only at the higher prices brought about by the war-time conditions, and since in any event his duty to deliver was only suspended. The principle of *pro rata* division is

---

[8] See above, para.3–019; UCC, s.2–615, Comments 5 and 9; s.2–501(1)(c), making it clear that growing crops can be "identified", so that s.2–613 can apply to them.
[9] Below, para.5–029.
[10] Above, para.5–023.
[11] [1917] A.C. 495.

supported by dicta in the case, to the effect that, if the claimants were entitled to anything, their entitlement would be to *no more* than their *pro rata* share of the quantity which the sellers could have obtained.[12]

5–027   Further support for various forms of the principle of *pro rata* division is provided by the soyabean cases (already mentioned),[13] in which sellers relied on *force majeure* and prohibition of export clauses in the contracts. The point which is of interest in the present context is that the export embargo imposed by the United States authorities was not total, but was subject to "loopholes": it did not extend to goods which (when it took effect) were in the process of being loaded or which were already on lighters and destined for exporting vessels. Hence a seller who had a defence under the *force majeure* or prohibition clauses might nevertheless have had some goods of the contract description at his disposal. In one such case, it was said that where such limited quantities (insufficient for all the seller's contractual commitments) were available, no buyer was entitled to more than his *pro rata* share[14]: this purely negative proposition does not go to the extent of affirmatively stating that each buyer is entitled to such a share. The view that each buyer is so entitled is, however, supported by dicta in another of the soyabean cases[15]; while, a dictum in a case not connected with the soyabean embargo (in which the seller relied on a *force majeure* clause) states that a buyer cannot complain if (in cases of the present kind) the seller allocates the whole of his limited supply to an *earlier* buyer[16]: this statement tends to support the third, rather than the fourth, of the possible solutions outlined above.[17] The solution of settling the claims of competing buyers on a temporal, rather than on a *pro rata*, basis was also adopted in an Australian case[18] but there the court relied on the special circumstance that the buyer who made the claim was, when he entered into his contract with the seller, aware of the fact that the seller had entered into contracts with other buyers.[19] The cases so far considered thus do not provide a clear answer to the question whether

---

[12] *ibid.* pp.511–512.

[13] Above, para.4–045.

[14] *Bremer Handelsgesellschaft mbH v Vanden Avenne-Izegem PVBA* [1978] 2 Lloyd's Rep. 109 at 115, 128, 131 (where the exact method of allocation to be adopted is left open).

[15] *Bremer Handelsgesellschaft mbH v C Mackprang Jr* [1979] 1 Lloyd's Rep. 221 at 224; the question is left open in *Continental Grain Export Corp v STM Grain Ltd* [1979] 2 Lloyd's Rep. 460 at 473.

[16] *Intertradex SA v Lesieur Torteaux SARL* [1978] 2 Lloyd's Rep. 509 at 513; *cf. Continental Grain Export Corp v STM Grain Ltd* [1979] 2 Lloyd's Rep. 460 at 473. It is assumed that the clause gives some protection to the seller; if not (and if there is no frustration) he is liable to all the buyers, as in *Hong Guan & Co v R Jumabhoy* [1960] A.C. 684; *cf. Coastal (Bermuda) Petroleum Ltd v VTT Vulcan Petroleum SA (The Marine Star)* [1993] 1 Lloyd's Rep. 329 at 332–333.

[17] Above, para.5–021.

[18] *Bowring and Walker Pty Ltd v Jackson's Corio Meat Packing (1965) Pty Ltd* [1972] 1 N.S.W.R. 277.

[19] *cf.* above, para.5–023.

the claims of the competing buyers are to be settled on a *pro rata* or on a temporal basis.

Some further help in answering this question may be derived from dicta in English cases according to which a seller is required to do no more than to act reasonably in allocating the limited supplies which remain available after partial failure of the source.[20] In deciding the issue of reasonableness, the court could have regard to the order in which the seller's contracts with the various buyers had been made; but it could also have regard to other circumstances. For example, it could hold that the seller was not bound to allocate his limited supplies *pro rata* if the quantity remaining available after partial failure of the source was so small that its division among several buyers would make no commercial sense.[21] The requirement of reasonableness is also stated in Uniform Commercial Code, s.2–615(b), but there it determines, not the existence of the duty to allocate supplies, but the manner in which that duty is to be performed. The section begins by stating that the seller "*must* allocate production …" and then goes on to say that "he *may* so allocate … in any manner which is fair and reasonable". The English dicta supporting the test of reasonableness seem to apply that test to the existence of a duty to allocate, no less than to its performance. Since the test of reasonableness raises (at least in part) a question of law, it imposes a legal restriction on the seller's choice in that it requires him to deliver to those buyers (or to that buyer) who may be designated by law. Thus the present group of English cases is consistent both with the third and with the fourth of the possible solutions outlined in paras 5–018 to 5–022, above. There will often be no difference between them, since *pro rata* division will commonly be a reasonable solution.

So far as *pro rata* division is concerned, there is one point on which there is a clear difference between the English position and that taken by the Uniform Commercial Code. In English law, a seller is not (when allocating supplies) allowed to take into account the needs or expectations of regular customers not under contract. The point was decided in *Pancommerce SA v Veecheema BV*,[22] where the Uniform Commercial Code provision allowing the seller to allocate part of the available supply to such customers was considered and rejected. The Court of Appeal there held that if a seller had a *legal* obligation to deliver to his buyer and also a moral obligation to deliver to another person (to whom he had made a non-contractual promise of a "first refusal"), then the fact that he could not perform both the legal and the moral obligation was not a justification for reducing the amount to be delivered to the buyer. Much less would the seller's own

---

[20] *Continental Grain Export Corp v STM Grain Ltd* [1979] 2 Lloyd's Rep. 460 at 473; *Bremer Handelsgesellschaft mbH v Continental Grain Co* [1983] 1 Lloyd's Rep. 269 at 292, 293 (where the seller had no excuse as he had failed to identify the "relevant shipper"; below, para.12–037).

[21] *Bremer Handelsgesellschaft mbH v Continental Grain Co* [1983] 1 Lloyd's Rep. 269 at 293.

[22] [1983] 2 Lloyd's Rep. 304.

needs be a ground on which he could reduce the amount due to the buyer.[23] That is, a seller who, after a partial embargo or crop failure allocated to himself part of the quantity remaining available would be liable[24] to that extent if he failed to deliver the whole of that quantity to a buyer of at least that amount. For the reasons already stated,[25] it would be wrong to allow the seller to keep part of the quantity remaining available for his own purposes and so to benefit at the buyer's expense from the rising market prices likely to result from the embargo or crop failure.

5–029   *Pro rata* division assumes that the subject-matter can be physically divided without impairing or destroying its commercial nature. The point may be illustrated by supposing that a farmer, expecting five calves to be born to his herd, sells one calf to each of five buyers, and that (for reasons beyond his control) only three calves are born. Even in the United States, where the principle of *pro rata* division has a wider scope than in English law, and even if the contract contains a *force majeure* or similar clause, the principle of *pro rata* division cannot apply in such a case[26] and the third of the solutions outlined in para.5–021, above should be adopted. If, in the example just given, the seller delivers the calves that are born to three of the buyers, and if his choice of those three buyers is a reasonable one, it is submitted that his contracts with the other two buyers ought to be discharged.

(ii) Where the seller relies on the common law doctrine of frustration

5–030   The preceding discussion shows that there are English cases which give some support, at least in dicta, to the principle of allocation (whether *pro rata* or on some other basis) of supplies which remain available after partial failure of a source of supply. Those cases are, however, all concerned with the effect of such partial prevention of performance on the operation of express contractual provisions which excuse the seller in the events which have occurred. None of them directly raises the issue whether the principle of allocation can apply where the seller relies, not on such an express contractual provision, but on discharge under the common law doctrine of frustration. In cases of the latter kind, there may be two difficulties in applying the principle of allocation.[27] One is that frustration is said to lead to automatic total discharge,[28] while allocation of supplies would amount to modification of the contracts. It is, however, possible to point to various possible mitigations of the rule of automatic

---

[23] *cf. Maritime National Fish Ltd v Ocean Trawlers Ltd* [1935] A.C. 524, where a charterer's attempt to prefer his own needs for a licence to his duties to the shipowner similarly failed on similar grounds; see further below, para.14–023.

[24] On the principle of *HR & S Sainsbury Ltd v Street* [1972] 1 W.L.R. 834, above, para.5–013.

[25] Above, para.5–023.

[26] One could invoke the most famous of all judgments: I Kings 3, 25.

[27] *J Lauritzen A/S v Wijsmuller BV (The Super Servant Two)* [1989] 1 Lloyd's Rep. 148 at 158; [1990] 1 Lloyd's Rep. 1 at 8.

[28] Below, para.15–002.

total discharge[29] and the possibility that the courts might create a further such exception in the present context should not (it is submitted) be wholly ruled out. A second difficulty is that allocation may be regarded as an "election" by the seller, so as to bring into operation the rule that a party cannot rely on frustration which is "self-induced".[30] It is submitted that this objection, too, should not be regarded as conclusive. It could be met by arguing that the method of allocation (whether on a *pro rata* or temporal basis, or by reference to the standard of reasonableness) is laid down by law[31]: if so, the allocation is not determined by the election of the seller. A further possible approach is to say that the seller can rely on partial failure of a specified source, not as a ground of frustration, but as a partial excuse for non-performance. We have seen such an excuse is available where a partial crop failure, occurring without the fault of the seller, prevents him from fully performing a contract with a single buyer.[32] It is submitted that there is no compelling reason why this principle should not apply where a shortage of supply results from some other cause (*e.g.* from an export embargo) and where the seller has made contracts with more than one buyer.

(d) Scope of principle of allocation

In discussing the principle of allocation, we have so far considered only cases in which the partial failure of a source affects the capacity of a *seller* to perform contracts with more than one buyer. Similar problems can arise where events of this kind affect the *buyer's* capacity to perform the agreed method of taking delivery. This would be the position where a buyer had entered into contracts with several sellers and the contracts required him to provide the receptacles into which the goods were to be delivered. Reference has already been made to an American case of this kind,[33] in which the contract expressly provided for reduced quantities to be taken in the event of "shortage of boxes", and in which it was held that the buyer must allocate the available boxes, in accordance with the principle of the Restatement, § 464. It seems that, even in the absence of the contractual term excusing the buyer, he would now have a similar defence under the Uniform Commercial Code, s.2–615(b) if he reasonably allocated the available boxes among his sellers. The case would not, indeed, fall directly within that provision, since s.2–615 deals in terms only with events affecting the *seller's* performance. But the excuse provided by s.2–615 can apply also in favour of a buyer,[34] and there seems to be no reason why the principle of allocation of available means of taking delivery should not likewise apply so as to qualify the buyer's excuse. Events

---

[29] *e.g.* in cases of "divisible contracts"; see *Stubbs v Holywell R* (1867) L.R. 2 Ex. 331 (below, para.15–031); or of "self-induced" frustration: see *F C Shepherd & Co Ltd v Jerrom* [1987] Q.B. 301 (below, paras 14–020 to 14–021).

[30] *Bank Line Ltd v Arthur Capel Ltd* [1919] A.C. 434 at 452; below, para.14–022.

[31] Above, para.5–028.

[32] See *HR & S Sainsbury Ltd v Street* [1972] 1 W.L.R. 834; above, para.5–013.

[33] *Akins v Riverbank Canning Co*, 183 P. 86 (1947), above, para.4–058.

[34] UCC, s.2–615, Comment 9; above, para.4–058.

affecting the buyer's ability to pay would not normally be a ground of discharge; but they might exceptionally have this effect where the contract specified a particular source of payment which later failed.[35] If the source failed in part, and the buyer had entered into contracts with more than one seller specifying that source, it seems that the principle of *pro rata* division could apply, each seller's duty to deliver being correspondingly reduced.

5–032   The principle of allocation is most commonly considered in relation to contracts of sale. But its formulation in the Restatement and in the Restatement 2d is perfectly general, so that it could apply to contracts other than sales, *e.g.* where a person's capacity to render services is restricted, but not extinguished, by supervening events. In such a case that person may be *pro tanto* excused by the supervening event; and if he has contracted to render the services to more than one person the principle of allocation (whether *pro rata* or on some other basis) could in appropriate circumstances be applied. In the case of contracts to render personal services, the restriction of the party's capacity will usually involve temporary impossibility (to be discussed later in this chapter)[36]; but it is also possible to imagine a case in which the impossibility would be partial. A singer might, for example, contract to give 10 performances within a specified period and then, before the beginning of that period, suffer illness and receive medical advice to the effect that, if he gave more than six performances within that period, he would further endanger his health.[37] If the performances were to be given under contracts with more than one impresario, it might be reasonable for the singer to allocate amongst them the performances which remained possible.

Partial impossibility to render services can also result from circumstances which affect, not the person of the contracting party, but rather the designated means of rendering the services. This would, for example, be the position where a carrier by sea had contracted to render services by carrying goods in specified ships, and his capacity to render those services was then reduced by the loss (without his fault) of one or more of those ships.[38] If the contracts in question had been made with more than one prospective shipper, it is arguable that the principle of allocation should apply. Once again, however, the point must be made that the partial performance thus available to each shipper must make commercial sense.[39] If a carrier could no longer perform all his contracts with a number of shippers to carry goods from Piraeus to Hamburg, it would make no sense for him partly to perform each contract by carrying the agreed quantity for each shipper to Lisbon; but it might well make sense for him to carry a proportion of the agreed quantity for each shipper all the way to the agreed destination.

---

[35] Above, para.4–059.

[36] Below, para.5–065.

[37] For discharge on such a ground, see above, para.4–021.

[38] *cf. J Lauritzen A/S v Wijsmuller BV (The Super Servant Two)* [1990] 1 Lloyd's Rep. 1; below, para.14–024.

[39] *cf.* above, para.5–023.

III. TEMPORARY IMPOSSIBILITY IN GENERAL

Temporary impossibility arises where a thing or person essential for the performance of a contract becomes temporarily unavailable, or when a state of things essential for such performance ceases temporarily to exist[40]; it may arise *either* at the time when performance ought to have begun *or* at some later stage during the performance of the contract. Such temporary impossibility does not of itself discharge the contract. One group of cases which illustrates this position consists of those (to be further discussed in paras 5–056 to 5–060, below) which concern the effects of temporary illness on a long-term contract of employment, or on one which, though it is terminable by fairly short notice, is in fact intended, and likely, to continue for an indefinite time. We shall see that such an illness does not discharge the contract, though it has certain other legal effects. Similarly, where the headmaster of a school for maladjusted children was imprisoned for six months on a criminal charge of which he was later acquitted, his temporary unavailability did not frustrate a contract between him and a local authority to send children to his school.[41] It has likewise been held in the United States that a building contract was not discharged by temporary unavailability of building materials (though this fact gave the contractor an excuse for delay in completing the work)[42]; and that the temporary closure of a school during an influenza epidemic did not discharge a contract to provide a bus service to the school for a period of eight-and-a-half months.[43]

5–033

While, therefore, temporary impossibility is not of itself a ground of frustration, there are situations in which it can have the effect of discharging the contract. These can conveniently be divided into two groups. The first comprises cases in which the contract specifies a time for performance and this time is of the essence of the contract. The second (and much larger) group consists of those cases in which it is the length of the delay, or its effects, which are the grounds of discharge. After discussing these two groups of cases, we shall consider the legal effects of delays which are not such as to discharge the contract.

The cases here to be discussed must be distinguished from those in which the burdens of one party are increased simply because, as a result of a supervening event, performance simply takes longer than expected and therefore increases *either* the costs that will be incurred by one party *or* the charges payable by the other (where these are measured by the time taken for performance). This was the position in the Suez cases, discussed in Ch.4,[44] in which the closure of the Canal was held not to discharge the

---

[40] For an illustration of the latter possibility, see *Minnevitch v Café de Paris (Londres) Ltd* [1936] All E.R. 884 (below, para.5–058) where the contract was not frustrated.

[41] *Mount v Oldham Corp* [1973] Q.B. 309; above para.4–024.

[42] *Peerless Cas Co v Weymouth Gardens Inc*, 215 F. 2d 362 (1954).

[43] *Montgomery v Board of Education etc*, 131 N.E. 497 (1921).

[44] Above, paras 4–071 to 4–083.

contract. These are sometimes described as cases of "prolonged delay"[45] but they differ from the cases here to be discussed, which deal with delays that *postpone* or *interrupt* performance, as opposed to merely *prolonging* it.

IV. TIME OF THE ESSENCE

5–034 A contract will be discharged by temporary impossibility where it is one which can be performed *only* on the day or days over which the temporary impossibility extends. One illustration of this situation is provided by *Robinson v Davison*,[46] where a contract under which a pianist was to give a concert on a specified day was held to have been discharged, on the principle of *Taylor v Caldwell*,[47] by the illness of the pianist on that day. In such a case, the unavailability may be temporary, but the resulting impossibility can, in the contractual context, be said to be total, since time is of the essence of the contract. The same is true where a voyage charter provides that the ship is to load between specified dates and she is requisitioned, and remains under requisition, for the whole of the period so specified: in an American case of this kind,[48] the contract was said to have been dissolved, again on the principle of *Taylor v Caldwell*. It seems that, for the purpose of the present rule, the date (or other time or period) fixed for performance must be specified in the contract; and it must be clear from the terms of the contract or from the surrounding circumstances, that performance at that time is regarded as vital. If these conditions are satisfied the unavailability at the specified time of a thing or person essential for performance will discharge the contract.

5–035 Such a conclusion may appear to promote justice in the sense that in *Robinson v Davison*[49] it might be thought unjust to have made the defendant liable for loss of the profits which the claimant expected to make from the concert. On the other hand, the claimant suffered loss, not only of the profits which he expected to make, but also in respect of expenses resulting from the cancellation of the concert; and the case presents an unusual (if minor) feature which bears on this point. The principal claim for loss of profits was indeed rejected; but there was also a claim for a small additional sum of £2 13s. 9d. in respect of the extra expense to which the claimant had been put because he was notified of the pianist's illness by a letter reaching him only on the day of the proposed concert, instead of being so notified by a telegram which would have reached him on the previous day. This claim succeeded at the trial on the ground that the defendant was in breach of an implied term of the contract to take reasonable steps to notify the claimant of the pianist's

---

[45] *Eridania SpA v Rudolf A Oetker (The Fjord Wind)* [1999] 1 Lloyd's Rep. 307 at 329, affirmed without reference to this point [2000] 2 Lloyd's Rep. 191.
[46] (1871) L.R. 6 Ex. 269.
[47] (1863) 3 B. & S. 826, cited in *Robinson v Davison* (above, n.45) at 275.
[48] *Texas Co v Hogarth Shipping Corp Ltd*, 256 U.S. 619 (1921).
[49] (1871) L.R. 6 Ex. 269.

illness; and this result was upheld (with some apparent reservations)[50] in the Court of Exchequer. In this respect, the case is significant in showing an early awareness of the point that the doctrine of discharge does not always provide an entirely satisfactory allocation of loss.[51] But it does give rise (at least in English law) to a doctrinal difficulty: if the effect of frustration is to produce total automatic discharge of the contract,[52] how can an implied term of that contract survive discharge? Perhaps a modern court could resolve this difficulty by describing the obligation to give reasonable notice as arising out of a collateral contract which could survive the frustration of the main contract. The collateral contract could then itself be discharged by frustration, *e.g.* if the main (and hence the collateral) contract in *Robinson v Davison* had been between the plaintiff and the pianist herself (instead of with the latter's husband) and the pianist had been rendered unconscious at the relevant time, and so become unable to give the notice. A similar point could be made by arguing that the implied term gave rise to an ancillary obligation which survived discharge, on the analogy of the rule that such an obligation can survive rescission for breach.[53] There is, for example, judicial support for the view that arbitration clauses survive the frustration of the contract in which they are contained[54]; and the principle of such survival of ancillary obligations appears to be of general application.[55] It is again possible for the ancillary obligation itself to be frustrated by events making *its* performance impossible[56]; but supervening impossibility affecting only the principal obligation will not discharge the ancillary one.

For the present purpose, a time of performance may be specified by reference to an event, even though the contract does not specify a date: for example, "if A engages B to make a drawing ... of some present event, for an illustrated paper, and B is attacked with blindness which will disable him for six months"[57] (presumably extending over the time of the occurrence of the event in question). A modern variation of this example would be the engagement of a cameraman to cover such an event and his inability, through illness, to perform the service on the day of the event; such an illness could discharge the contract.

---

[50] *ibid.* at 275–276.

[51] *cf.* the discussion of *Taylor v Caldwell* (1863) 3 B. & S. 826 on this point above, para.2–029.

[52] Below, para.15–002.

[53] Treitel, *The Law of Contract* (11th ed.), p.851.

[54] See the reference to frustration in *Heyman v Darwins Ltd* [1942] A.C. 356 at 383, 400–401; *Kruse v Questier* [1953] 1 Q.B. 669; *Government of Gibraltar v Kenney* [1956] 2 Q.B. 410.

[55] *Yasuda Fire & Marine Insurance Co of Europe Ltd v Orion Marine Insurance Underwriting Agency Ltd* [1995] 1 Lloyd's Rep. 525 (inspection of documents clause).

[56] *e.g.* by destruction of the documents in the above *Yasuda* case.

[57] *Jackson v Union Marine Insurance Co Ltd* (1874) L.R. 10 C.P. 125 at 145.

V. Length and Effects of Delay

5–036   A contract which does not expressly specify a time for performance, or one in which the time for performance, though specified, is not of the essence, may nevertheless be discharged by reason of the length of the delay resulting from temporary impossibility. The cases in this group are divisible in to four sub-groups, in at least the first three of which the crucial factor is the effect of the delay.

(1) **Delay making performance useless to the party to whom it is to be rendered**

5–037   In the first group of cases, the effect of the delay which results from the temporary impossibility is such as to make the delayed performance useless for the contractually contemplated purpose to the party to whom that performance was to be rendered. An example of this situation was given in *Jackson v Union Marine Insurance Co Ltd*, where it was said that a charterparty, by which a ship was "to go from Newport to St. Michael's ... in time for the fruit season",[58] would be discharged if the ship were stranded and did not again become available for service until the fruit season was over. The example is based on the earlier case of *Touteng v Hubbard*,[59] where a Swedish ship was chartered to proceed to the island of St Michael's (in the West Indies) to load a cargo of fruit, but was prevented from reaching that island by war-time embargo "laid by the British Government on foreign ships in the nature of reprisals and partial hostility".[60] The decision that the British charterer was not liable for his refusal to continue to perform was based on the consideration of public policy that, if British subjects were so liable to foreign shipowners, the British Government might be inhibited from imposing such an embargo. Hence the contract was discharged, on grounds analogous to supervening illegality,[61] even while the doctrine of absolute contracts still prevailed.[62] The actual decision has been approved[63]; though dicta in it to the effect that if the ship had been a British ship the charterer would have had to supply a cargo even though the ship had been prevented by the embargo from reaching St Michael's till after the end of the fruit seasons have been rightly questioned.[64] No doubt a charterer is under a strict duty to provide a cargo, but this merely means that his inability to procure goods of the contract description does not of itself excuse his failure to load.[65] It does

---

[58] *ibid.* at 143.
[59] (1802) 3 B. & P. 291.
[60] *ibid.* at 298.
[61] See below, para.8–002.
[62] See above, para.2–011.
[63] *Geipel v Smith* (1872) L.R. 7 Q.B. 404 at 412.
[64] *Jackson v Union Marine Insurance Co Ltd* (1874) L.R. 10 C.P. 125 at 143, 146.
[65] *Hills v Sughrue* (1846) 15 M. & W. 253, apparently a case of antecedent, not supervening, impossibility; for the significance of this point, see above, paras 1–007, 2–032.

not follow that the contract cannot be discharged if his inability is due to the late arrival of the ship on account of temporary impossibility affecting the performance of the shipowner's obligation.

The "fruit season" example discussed above differs from the case in   **5–038** which time is of the essence since in the example no actual dates for performance are specified. It may, indeed, be possible for time to be of the essence where the contract requires performance within a specified *period* (rather than on a specified *date*), *e.g.* where a contract for the sale of goods requires them to be shipped within a specified month.[66] Even this suggestion gives rise to some difficulty since the buyer can reject an *early* (no less than a *late*) shipment[67]; but in any event it presupposes that the shipment period is either specified in the contract or precisely ascertainable by reference to the terms of the contract. Time may also be specified by reference to an event; but an expression such as "in time for the fruit season" is not, it is submitted, sufficiently precise to be capable of making time of the essence. There is also the point that the example assumes unavailability for the *whole* of the fruit season, totally preventing use of the ship for the purpose of loading fruit. The phrase "in time for the fruit season" might bear various meanings: by the beginning of the season, before the end of the season, or by some intermediate point between these two extremes. It seems unlikely that the contract would be frustrated if the fruit season lasted for two months and the supervening event delayed the ship so that she arrived only one week after the season had begun; nor, on the other hand, would the contract be likely to survive if the ship arrived so late in the season that the amount of fruit available on her arrival was such that only a small part of the anticipated cargo could be loaded. If the stipulation made time of the essence, it could be expected to provide clear-cut answers to such questions. In fact the test to be applied appears to be the vaguer one, whether *substantial* prevention of the contemplated purpose had resulted from the delay.[68] The answer to this question would depend on the length of the delay and not (as it would where time was of the essence) on the mere fact that delay had occurred, so that the contractual time limits could no longer be strictly[69] observed.

The distinguishing feature of the "fruit season" example is that the   **5–039** contract in it *expressly* refers to a seasonal element. But this does not seem to be necessary to bring about discharge on the ground that delay resulting from temporary impossibility has made performance useless to one party. Even in the absence of such an express reference, the contract may be construed as referring to, or as having been made for the purpose of accomplishing, a particular "adventure"; and the temporary impossibility may be so long as to make the prosecution of that adventure impossible. This seems to have been the position in *Jackson v Union Marine*

---

[66] See *Benjamin's Sale of Goods* (6th ed.), para.18–232.

[67] *Bowes v Shand* (1877) 2 App. Cas. 455.

[68] *cf.* the test applied in cases such as *Pioneer Shipping v BTP Tioxide (The Nema)* [1982] A.C. 724, above, para.5–052.

[69] For the strictness of the requirement where a stipulated time is expressed to be of the essence, see *Union Eagle Ltd v Golden Achievement Ltd* [1997] A.C. 514.

Insurance Co Ltd[70] itself. In that case, a ship had been chartered to carry rails from Newport to San Francisco; the charterparty was made in November 1871 and did not specify any date or period for performance, but it did provide that the ship was to proceed to Newport with all possible dispatch (dangers and accidents of navigation excepted). While the ship was on her way from Liverpool to Newport in January 1872, she ran aground (but without any breach of contract on the part of the carrier) and was not repaired until the following August. The shipowner claimed on a policy of insurance of freight, and the claim succeeded on the ground that the freight had been lost as the charterparty had been discharged. The contract was to be "read as a charter for a definite voyage or adventure", so that there was "necessarily an implied condition that the ship should arrive at Newport in time for it".[71] Again the vital factor appears to be the length of the delay: it seems unlikely that the contract would have been discharged if the delay resulting from the stranding of the ship had lasted, not for seven months, but for seven days. Such a short delay would not have turned the voyage remaining possible into one substantially or fundamentally different from that originally undertaken; and, where time is not of the essence, delay will not, of itself, result in such a substantial or fundamental difference. A delay in prosecuting a voyage may also, by reason of its length, expose the cargo to serious risks of damage or deterioration and could for this reason result in the frustration of a voyage charterparty.[72]

5–040   The length of the delay was, again, the ground of frustration in *Lloyd Royal Belge SA v Stathatos*,[73] where a time charter for "one round trip Gibraltar to the States" entitled the charterers to cancel if the ship was not delivered by December 10. The ship was detained by the Admiralty on December 2, and not released till the following February 10, when the ship sailed for New York, performing services for the charterers without prejudice to their rights. The charterparty was held to have been discharged as there had been "such interruption of the common object of the parties as to amount to frustration of the common adventure".[74] The reason why the charterers relied on frustration, rather than on the cancellation clause, seems to have been that they wished to recover back advance payments of hire; but this claim failed since under the law as it

---

[70] (1874) L.R. 10 C.P. 125.

[71] *ibid.* at 142. The suggestion in *Hudson v Hill* (1874) L.R. 43 L.J.C.P. 273 at 279, that the shipowner's only purpose in such cases is to earn freight, seems to be inconsistent with the reasoning of *Jackson's* case (above, n.70) as well as with that of later cases explaining why supervening impossibility affecting only one party's performance operates so as to discharge both parties: above, para.2–039.

[72] *Eridania SpA v Rudolf A Oetker (The Fjord Wind)* [1999] 1 Lloyd's Rep. 307 at 333 (affirmed without reference to this point [2000] 2 Lloyd's Rep. 191); on the facts, frustration was excluded as the delay was due to the carrier's breach in failing to exercise due diligence to make the ship seaworthy.

[73] (1917) 34 T.L.R. 70.

[74] *ibid.* at 72.

then stood a person who had paid money under a contract which was later frustrated had no right to the return of that payment.[75]

A case on the other side of the line is *Braemont SS Co Ltd v Andrew Weir &* **5–041** *Co*[76] where a ship had been time-chartered for a trip from a port in New South Wales to one in South America. The charterer intended her to carry a cargo of coal but was prevented by a strike from loading coal for three weeks after the ship had been placed at his disposal. Although a charterparty of this kind can be frustrated by the temporary unavailability of the cargo[77] (no less than by that of the ship) it was held that the delay was not such as to frustrate the "commercial adventure".[78]

It should be noted that (in the terminology explained in Ch.2)[79] the issue in the cases and examples which have been discussed above is distinct from that which arises in the cases of "frustration of purpose" to be discussed in Ch.7. In those cases, the contract may be discharged in spite of the fact that there is *no impossibility* affecting the performance of either party.[80] In the present group of cases, one party's performance does become temporarily impossible, and the question is whether the contract is discharged *by that impossibility*.

(2) Delay making performance more onerous to the party rendering it

In this group of cases, the effect of the delay which results from temporary **5–042** impossibility is to increase the burdens of the party by whom the performance which has been temporarily prevented would have to be rendered if the contract were not discharged by the delay.

The most obvious way in which performance can become more burdensome to the party who is to render it is by increasing the cost of performance to him. A simple illustration of this possibility is provided by the American case of *Village of Minneota v Fairbanks, Morse & Co*,[81] in which performance of a building contract was prevented by war-time conditions for five years; and the contract was discharged because, by the end of that period, the costs of labour and materials had increased to an extent which could not have been contemplated when the contract was made. The same principle was applied in the English case of *Acetylene Co of G B v Canada*

---

[75] *Chandler v Webster* [1904] K.B. 493, overruled in *Fibrosa Spolka Akcyjna v Fairbairn Lawson Combe Barbour Ltd* [1943] A.C. 32 so as to allow recovery where there has been a total failure of consideration. For the question whether the more extensive right of recovery conferred by s.1(2) of the Law Reform (Frustrated Contracts) Act 1943 would extend to charters such as that in *Lloyd Royal Belge SA v Stathatos*, see the discussion of s.2(5)(a) of the Act, below, para.15–091. For express provisions for the return of hire under frustrated time charters, see below, paras 15–048, 15–084.

[76] (1910) 15 Com.Cas. 101.

[77] *Pioneer Shipping v BTP Tioxide (The Nema)* [1982] A.C. 724 (consecutive voyage charter) above, para.4–004; below, para.5–052.

[78] (1910) 15 Com.Cas. 101 at 110.

[79] Above, paras 2–044 to 2–050.

[80] Below, para.7–001.

[81] 31 N.W. 2d 920 (1948); *cf.* Restatement, § 462; Restatement 2d, § 269.

Carbide Co[82] where a contract for the sale of carbide to be shipped from Canada to the United Kingdom provided that shipment was to begin in 1917. The war-time requisitioning of all available ships made shipment impossible at the agreed time, and it remained impossible until 1920. It was held that the seller was no longer bound to ship when performance again became possible, since by then market conditions had radically changed.

The principle of these cases was applied, and in some respects extended, in *Metropolitan Water Board v Dick, Kerr & Co*,[83] where contractors agreed in July 1914 to construct a reservoir within six years; in the event of delays "however occasioned", they were to be allowed an extension of time. In February 1916, the contractors were required by a war-time Government Order to stop the work and to sell their construction plant. It was held that the contract was frustrated; and the case in two respects goes beyond those considered in the preceding paragraph. First, the contract was frustrated in spite of the fact that it expressly provided for delays, this provision being narrowly construed so as not to cover the very serious delay resulting from the Government intervention. Secondly, frustration occurred in spite of the fact that the delay was to a considerable extent prospective: it had not yet run its course at the time of the proceedings, but it was probable (when discharge was claimed) that it *would* last for so long that conditions would have radically changed by the time that performance again became possible. These aspects of the case are considered later in this book.[84]

5-043 Delay can make a contract more burdensome for the party whose performance has become temporarily impossible, not only because of the fact that performance at the end of the delay is more expensive than it would have been, if no such delay had occurred, but also because of the costs which would be incurred by that party if he had to hold himself in readiness to perform until the temporary obstacle to performance had been removed. This possibility is illustrated by *Geipel v Smith*,[85] where the actual decision is based on an express term of the contract rather than on the common law doctrine of frustration,[86] but much of the court's reasoning is applicable to that doctrine. The case arose out of a charterparty under which a cargo of coal was to be carried to Hamburg, with an exception for "restraint of princes". This exception was held to protect the shipowner from liability for refusal to load when Hamburg was blockaded by the French fleet in the course of the Franco-Prussian War. The argument that the shipowner should have loaded the cargo so as to be

---

[82] (1922) 8 Ll.L. Rep. 456; for similar German cases see RGZ 90, 102; RGZ 94, 455 RGZ 94, 68.

[83] [1918] A.C. 119.

[84] Below, paras 9–009, 12–008.

[85] (1872) L.R. 7 Q.B. 404.

[86] Blackburn J. in *Geipel v Smith* makes no reference to *Taylor v Caldwell* (1863) 3 B. & S. 826, perhaps regarding that case as being applicable only to cases of *destruction* of the subject-matter; but the doctrine of discharge is now clearly of wider scope.

ready to set off for Hamburg as soon as the blockade was lifted was rejected, Blackburn J. saying that such a course of action would "frustrate the very object of the contract, namely the speedy transport of the shipper's goods, and the remunerative employment of the shipowner's vessel".[87] Cockburn C.J. likewise refers to the *possible* prejudice to both parties from the delay[88]; but the party who would have been *actually* prejudiced by the delay was no doubt the shipowner. In this respect, the case differs from *Jackson v Union Marine Insurance Co Ltd*,[89] where it was the charterer who was prejudiced by the ship's delay in reaching the port of loading.

In *Robert H Dahl v Nelson, Donkin*,[90] the issue again arose under an **5–044** express term of the contract rather than under the common law doctrine of frustration. The case concerned a charterparty under which the ship was to proceed "to London Surrey Commercial Docks or so near thereto as she may safely get". When the ship reached London, the dock authorities refused to admit her to the docks; this refusal was due, not to the fault of either party, but to congestion in the docks, which would have prevented the ship from entering the docks for five weeks. She therefore proceeded to Deptford Buoys, where the shipowner unloaded her after the charterers had refused to do so. It was held that the shipowner's action was justified (so that he was entitled to recover the cost of unloading, as well as demurrage) because it had become "impossible"[91] for the ship to complete the voyage by proceeding to the named docks. It should be emphasised that the effect of the impossibility was not to frustrate the contract but to justify the shipowner's act of delivering the cargo at the alternative destination mentioned in the contract, and to require the charterers to take delivery there. The reason for this conclusion is again that extra costs would have been incurred by the shipowner in having to keep his ship waiting outside the dock until the temporary obstacles to delivering the cargo there had ceased to exist. If the contract had not contained the words "or so near there to as she may safely get" it is highly unlikely that the contract would have been discharged by the temporary impossibility of reaching the Surrey Commercial Docks. For this purpose, a much longer delay would have been necessary. *Robert H Dahl v Nelson Donkin* should not, therefore, be regarded as an authority on temporary impossibility as a ground of frustration.

It should be emphasised that the mere fact that market conditions have **5–045** changed in the course of a delay in performance is not sufficient to bring about discharge. Many delays are not due to even temporary impossibility, but to factors such as shortages of labour and materials; and in principle such obstacles can be overcome by paying more for the services or goods which are in short supply. The consequence of so overcoming them may, indeed, be to make the contract unprofitable, and so it may raise the

---

[87] (1872) L.R. 7 Q.B. 404 at 412.
[88] *ibid.* at 410.
[89] (1874) L.R. 10 C.P. 125; above, para.5–039.
[90] (1881) 6 App. Cas. 38.
[91] *ibid.* at 57.

question (to be discussed in Ch.6) whether the contract should be discharged on the ground of "impracticability". The issue in such cases is whether the contract can be discharged (on the ground that performance has become severely more burdensome to one party) *without* being affected by impossibility. Our present concern is with cases in which there *is* impossibility of a temporary nature, and in which the extra burdens which delayed performance would impose on one party would not have arisen but for such impossibility.

(3) **Delay increasing value of performance of party rendering it**

5-046 In this group of cases, the party whose performance is temporarily impossible would be prejudiced by having to perform when the obstacle to performance is removed; but the prejudice would arise in a different way from that considered in paras 5-042 to 5-045, above. It would result, not from extra expense to that party, but from the fact that, by the time performance was once again possible, he would expect to be paid considerably more for it under a contract made at that time, than the amount payable under the contract which is alleged to have been frustrated. No doubt in many cases the main reason why he would expect to be paid more would be that the cost of performance to him would have risen; but this is not necessarily true. The point may be illustrated by reference to the American case of *Autry v Republic Productions*,[92] where a contract was made in 1938 between an actor and a film studio by which the actor was to act in a specified number of films at specified rates of pay; the contract gave the studio options to renew and a further such option was granted in 1942. The actor joined the army in that year and was released three years later. It was held (*inter alia*) that he was no longer bound by the contract to make the number of films comprised in the various options at the originally agreed rates of pay; for by the time of his release from the armed forces conditions in the film industry (including rates of pay) had radically changed since the conclusion of the contract.

It seems that the difficult case of *Bank Line Ltd v Arthur Capel & Co*[93] can be explained on similar grounds. The case arose out of a time charter for one year made on February 16, 1915; the year was to run from the time at which the ship was placed at the charterer's disposal; it was contemplated that this would happen in April 1915, so that the contract was said to be "in substance, though not in form, an April to April charter". The ship had not been delivered by the end of April; on May 11, 1915 she was requisitioned; and she was not released until September 1915. The House of Lords held that the contract had been frustrated by the requisition so that the charterers were not entitled to damages for non-delivery of the ship. Lord Sumner said that the September to September charter, the performance of which would have remained possible, was "as a matter of business quite a different thing[94] from the April to April charter originally

---

[92] 180 P. 2d 888 (1947).
[93] [1919] A.C. 435.
[94] *ibid.* at 460.

concluded. Exactly why he took this view is not altogether clear. The delay does not seem to have interfered with the use which the charterer intended to make of the services of the ship; indeed it was the charterer who sought to enforce the contract, while the shipowner relied on the requisition as a ground of discharge. It is at first sight hard to see what prejudice (let alone what serious prejudice) the shipowner would have suffered by being held to the contract for one year from September. Certainly it does not seem that the cost of performance to him was so much (if at all) increased by the delay as to constitute a ground of frustration. The shipowner's real motive for arguing that the contract was frustrated seems to have been that by September market conditions had changed, in the sense that freight rates had risen,[95] so that the amount which the shipowner could then have charged for the services of the ship would have exceeded the hire due under the charterparty; the amount of this excess over the period of the charterparty appears to have been £31,000.[96] At first sight, the result in the *Bank Line* case is open to the objection that, to this extent, the shipowner profited from frustration, and that this was an improper application of the doctrine of discharge, the object of which is to provide for a fair allocation of losses resulting from the supervening event.

There are however certain special factors in the *Bank Line* case which   **5–047** indicate that the shipowner would indeed have been prejudiced if the contract had remained in force. One such factor is that the length of the requisition, when it originally took effect, was uncertain, so that the contract, if it had remained in force, would *for an indefinite time* have restricted the shipowner's freedom to dispose of the ship or of her services. In this connection it must be stressed that, though the period of the charterparty was fixed, the time of its commencement was not: the 12 months were to run from the time at which the ship was placed at the disposal of the charterer, and at the time of the requisition she had not yet been placed at his disposal. The fact that the requisition actually lasted for less than half of the period of the charterparty, therefore, cannot be regarded as decisive: there was at least a probability that it might have lasted much longer.[97] The same reasoning would not necessarily have applied if the ship had *already* been placed at the charterer's disposal when she was requisitioned. In one such case,[98] in which a ship which had been chartered for 12 months was placed at the charterer's disposal in April 1915 and was *then* requisitioned for some five-and-a-half months, it was held that the contract remained in force. These facts in many ways resemble those of the *Bank Line* case but differ from it in the crucial

---

[95] See *Modern Transport Co Ltd v Duneric SS Co* [1917] 1 K.B. 370 at 376. For a discussion of this case (in which the relevant dates were in some respects similar to those in the *Bank Line* case) see below, para.5–054.

[96] This was the amount of the damages which would have been awarded by the majority of the Court of Appeal, who had taken the view that the contract had not been discharged: see [1919] A.C. 435 at 441.

[97] *cf.* below, paras 9–002, 9–003.

[98] *Modern Transport Co Ltd v Duneric SS Co* [1917] 1 K.B. 370; below, para.5–054.

respect that, when the requisition took effect, there was no doubt as to the time at which the period of 12 months specified in the charterparty would expire. Hence there was no such uncertainty as that which was likely to cause prejudice to the shipowner in the *Bank Line* case. Further prejudice to the shipowners in that case may have been caused by the fact that in June 1915 both parties apparently regarded the contract as at an end. The point is significant (even though the views of the parties are not decisive on the issue of frustration),[99] in that the shipowners seem to have acted in reliance on this shared view: they had obtained the release of the ship by supplying a substitute vessel to the Admiralty and had sold the ship to a third party. The final result in the *Bank Line* case can, it is submitted, be justified by reference to special factors discussed in this paragraph.

(4) **Proportion of delay to the performance bargained for**

5–048   In many of the cases of temporary impossibility so far discussed, the claim by the party seeking to enforce the contract was for performance *in full* after the temporary impossibility had come to an end. In some of those cases, the contract was held to have been discharged, so that no further performance at all had to be rendered; in others it was held to subsist, so that when performance again became possible, the contract had to be performed in full after the specified date or period. These are the only two available solutions where the contract calls for a single act to be done at or within a specified time (*e.g.* where it calls for 1,000 tons of soyabeans to be delivered in June) or for a single result to be achieved by the end of a specified time (*e.g.* where the contract is for the construction of a reservoir to be completed in 1920), and a supervening event makes adherence to that timetable impossible. The outcome then will be either (1) that no soyabeans need be delivered, or that no further work need be done on the reservoir; or (2) that the 1,000 ton must be delivered after June, or that the reservoir must be completed after 1920. But there is a further available solution where the contract not only specifies the period during which performance is to be rendered, but also measures the amount of that performance by the time taken to render it. This is commonly the position where the contract is one to render services for a specified period and within specified limits of time, *e.g.* where services are to be rendered under a contract of employment or under a time charterparty. In such cases, one possible consequence of holding that the contract is not discharged is that performance must be rendered for the *balance (if any) of the contract period* (after the temporary impossibility has come to an end) rather than for the *whole of the period but at a later time* (with the period of temporary impossibility being added on at the end of the specified time, rather like "injury time" in certain games). A claim of the latter kind was made in the *Bank Line* case where the contract specified a performance period without (as already noted)[1] fixing the date when it was to begin: the 12 month period was to run from the time when the ship was placed at the charterer's

---

[99] *Hirji Mulji v Cheong Yue SS Co Ltd* [1926] A.C. 497 at 507; below, para.15–003.
[1] Above, para.5–047.

disposal, and it was that event which was held up by the requisition. But where the contract specified both the period of performance and the dates over which it was to extend, claims for the balance remaining possible (as opposed to claims for performance over a later period equivalent to the whole contract period) have been made in a number of the cases to be discussed below.

(a) *No performance remaining possible*

Claims of the kind just described can succeed only where performance for some part of the contract period remains possible. If the temporary impossibility lasts, or is likely to last,[2] for so long that *no* part of the agreed performance can be rendered, the contract will be discharged. One illustration of this situation is provided by *Countess of Warwick SS Co v Le Nickel SA*,[3] where a ship had been delivered under a 12 month time charterparty in March 1915 and was then requisitioned in October 1915. At that time, the general expectation was that ships so requisitioned would not be released before the end of the war, and that this ship would not be released in time for her to perform further services under the charter. It followed that the charterparty was frustrated, so that the charterer was not liable for hire after the requisition. Similar results were reached in a group of more recent cases in which ships which had been time-chartered were detained for long periods in the course of the Gulf War between Iran and Iraq[4]: in these cases, the contracts were frustrated (so that the charterers ceased to be liable for hire) as soon as it became clear that the detention would extend beyond the period of the charterparties. Other illustrations of the same principle are provided by employment cases in which the contracts were frustrated because the employee suffered from so serious an illness as to make it unlikely that he would ever be able to resume the work for which he was engaged.[5] Similarly in *Horlock v Beal*[6] a contract to serve on a ship as second mate for a two-year voyage was frustrated when the ship's crew were interned by the German authorities shortly after the outbreak of the First World War and it became clear that the contractual voyage could no longer be accomplished.

(b) *Some performance remaining possible*

Where performance for some balance of the contract period remains (or is likely to remain) possible, and a claim is made in respect of that balance,

5–049

5–050

---

[2] Below, para.9–002.

[3] [1918] 1 K.B. 372; the somewhat sketchily reported case of *Heilgers & Co v Cambrian SN Co Ltd* (1917) 34 T.L.R. 72 seems to be another case of this kind.

[4] *Kodros Shipping Corp of Monrovia v Empresa Cubana de Fletes of Havana (The Evia)* [1983] 1 A.C. 736; *Kissavos Shipping Co SA v Empresa Cubana de Fletes (The Agathon)* [1982] 2 Lloyd's Rep. 211; *International Sea Tankers Inc v Hemisphere Shipping Co Ltd (The Wenjiang) (No2)* [1983] 1 Lloyd's Rep. 400; *Vinava Shipping Co v Finelvet AG (The Chrysalis)* [1983] 1 Lloyd's Rep. 503. *cf. Scottish Navigation Co Ltd v Souter* [1917] 1 K.B. 222; *Hirji Mulji v Cheong Yue SS Co Ltd* [1926] A.C. 497.

[5] See *Hart v AR Marshall & Sons (Bulwell) Ltd* [1977] 1 W.L.R. 1067; the actual decision appears to be based on the principle stated in below, para.5–056.

[6] [1916] 1 A.C. 486.

the tests which have so far been discussed in relation to temporary impossibility obviously cannot apply. The test of discharge cannot be whether performance after the delay has become useless to the party to whom it was to be rendered, for it is that very party who claims the balance remaining possible and it is implausible to suggest that he would do so if such performance were useless to him. Nor can the test be whether performance after the end of the temporary impossibility has (by reason of a change in commercial conditions) become more burdensome or less remunerative to the party who was to render it, since that party is not being asked to do anything after the time during which he originally undertook to perform. The test, in cases of the present kind appears to turn rather on the ratio which the part remaining possible bears, or is likely to bear, to the whole of the specified performance: the lower that ratio, the more likely it is that the contract will be discharged. It will be convenient to refer to this test as "the proportionality test".

5–051   The difference between this test and that applied in the situation considered in paras 5–037 to 5–047, above can be illustrated by contrasting *Autry v Republic Productions*[7] with the English case of *Morgan v Manser*.[8] The latter case arose out of a contract between an entertainer and his agent, made in February 1938 and expressed to last for 10 years. During the Second World War the entertainer was conscripted in 1940 and it then seemed likely that he would remain in the armed forces for a very long time; in fact he was not demobilised until February 1946. Thereafter, he was sued for breach of a term in the 1938 contract, by which he had undertaken not to use the services of any other agent or manager during the subsistence of that contract. It was held that the contract was discharged by the entertainer's conscription, and this conclusion seems to have been based on the likely length (in 1940) of the interruption of performance. The case differs from the *Autry* case in that it does not seem that the agent was trying to extend the contract by the number of "lost" years; he was merely trying to enforce the balance of the original 10-year contract. As the entertainer had agreed to be tied to the agent for that period, it is not at all obvious why he was released on being conscripted. One possible explanation is that conditions in the entertainment industry after the war were radically different from those which had prevailed before the war. But the ground of frustration was not the war but the entertainer's conscription. Had he been exempt from conscription (*e.g.* on grounds of age or health) there could have been no question of frustration. Another possible explanation for the result is the view, expressed in some cases, that wars, and their attendant disruptions, are "presumed to be likely to continue so long"[9] as to frustrate contracts made temporarily impossible by them. Put so broadly, this explanation

---

[7]   180 P. 2d 888 (1947); above, para.5–046.

[8]   [1948] 1 K.B. 184.

[9]   *Geipel v Smith* (1872) L.R. Q.B. 404 at 414; *cf. Unger v Preston Corp* [1942] 2 All E.R. 200 at 203; *Benjamin's Sale of Goods* (6th ed.), para.18–300; but the presumption is rebuttable: *Vinava Shipping Co Ltd v Finelvet AG (The Chrysalis)* [1983] 1 Lloyd's Rep. 503 at 511.

proves too much since there are cases in which temporary impossibility arising from war-time conditions was held not to be a ground of frustration.[10] One can perhaps account for the result in *Morgan v Manser* by saying that, on the facts, it was reasonable to assume in 1940 that the conscription would last for the whole, or substantially the whole, of the contract period.

The further cases in which claims have been made in respect of the balance of the performance remaining possible fall into two groups: the first concerns charterparties and the second contracts for personal service.

(i) The charterparty cases

The proportionality test[11] was applied in *The Nema*[12] where a "consecutive voyage" charterparty was made for six or seven voyages (at the charterer's option) beginning in April and ending in December 1979, to carry titanium slag from the charterer's loading installations at Sorel (a Canadian port) to Calais or Hartlepool. After one voyage had been accomplished, the charterer's loading installations at Sorel were strike-bound from June till October, so that no more than two or three further voyages could have been accomplished. In arbitration proceedings, the charterparty was held to have been frustrated, the arbitrator saying: "The result [of the strike] will be that *The Nema* will only perform three of the seven contractual voyages at most; this ... constitutes something radically different from that originally undertaken by the owners of the vessel". The House of Lords held that the arbitrator had not misdirected himself and so declined to interfere with his decision. The reason why the contract was discharged seems to have been that the part of it which could still have been performed amounted only to a small proportion of the whole obligation undertaken; and this prejudiced the shipowner in that his remuneration depended on the freight to be earned on each voyage.

A case which applies the same proportionality test but falls on the other side of the line is *Tamplin SS Co v Anglo-Mexican Petroleum Co*,[13] where a tanker was chartered for five years from December 1912 to December 1917; in February 1915, when the charterparty still had nearly three years to run, the ship was requisitioned during the First World War and converted into a troopship. This interference with performance caused no prejudice to the charterers, since the compensation paid by the Government for the requisition exceeded the agreed hire; but the ship's owners claimed that the contract was frustrated. The House of Lords rejected the claim, but only by a narrow majority, so that the case is evidently a borderline one. In the view of the majority, the proportion which the part which it might be possible still to perform bore to the

5–052

---

[10] *e.g. Tamplin SS Co v Anglo-Mexican Petroleum Co* [1916] 2 A.C. 397; *cf. Modern Transport Co Ltd v Duneric SS Co* [1917] 1 K.B. 370.

[11] Above, para.5–050.

[12] *Pioneer Shipping v BTP Tioxide (The Nema)* [1982] A.C. 724.

[13] [1916] 2 A.C. 397. For a similar application of the "proportionality" test in a case of frustration of purpose (below, para.7–034), see *National Carriers Ltd v Panalpina (Northern) Ltd* [1981] A.C. 675.

original contract was sufficiently large for the contract to remain in force: "There may be many months during which this ship will be available for commercial purposes before the five years have expired."[14] It should be noted that the effect of the requisition fell to be determined by reference to the state of probabilities at or near the time when the requisition occurred.[15] In practice, courts no doubt take account of later events, but the *Tamplin* case was decided before either the requisition or the chartered period had come to an end. Thus the House of Lords had to speculate as to the length of the requisition, and perhaps indirectly as to the length of the war. But even if the majority may in the light of later events be thought to have speculated wrongly on either or both of these matters, that is no criticism of the decision.

5–053   Another factor which may have weighed with the majority in the *Tamplin* case was that it was the *owners* who claimed that the contract was discharged; and if their claim had succeeded they would have gained a windfall profit from the requisition in the shape of the amount by which the compensation paid by the Government exceeded the hire payable under the charterparty. At any rate, this is the ground on which the case is explained in a later decision of the House of Lords.[16] It has, indeed, been suggested that, if the compensation paid by the Government had fallen short of the agreed hire, and if the shipowners had therefore tried to enforce the contract, they would not have been able to do so. The case (it is said) would then have "fallen within the lines of *Horlock v Beal*"[17]: *i.e.* the contract would have been frustrated. The difficulty with this view is that in *Horlock v Beal*[18] the temporary impossibility was such as to cover the *whole* contract period, while in the *Tamplin* case the majority of the House of Lords did not regard the temporary impossibility as likely to continue for the whole term of the charterparty, or even for so long as to make it unreasonable to require the parties to continue to perform their obligations when performance would (in reasonable probability) again become possible. There is also some difficulty in accepting the view that frustration could have been claimed by one party (the charterer) on account of an interference with performance which did not make the plea

---

[14] [1916] 2 A.C. 397 at 405; *cf. Port Line Ltd v Ben Line Steamers Ltd* [1958] 2 Q.B. 146 at 162; this seems also to be a basis of one of the judgments (that of Scrutton L.J.) in *Leiston Gas Co v Leiston-cum-Sizewell UDC* [1916] 2 K.B. 428 at 440 (a case of alleged frustration of purpose: below, para.7–017).

[15] Below, para.9–002.

[16] *Metropolitan Water Board v Dick, Kerr & Co* [1918] A.C. 119 at 129; but see *Heilgers & Co v Cambrian SN Co Ltd* (1917) 34 T.L.R. 72, where the shipowner was allowed to profit in this way from frustration. In *Modern Transport Co Ltd v Duneric SS Co* [1917] 1 K.B. 370 it was accepted that the charterer was entitled to the compensation for requisition, but only, apparently, on the assumption (which there prevailed) that the contract was *not* discharged). See also below, para.15–007. For this aspect of the *Bank Line* case [1919] A.C. 435, see above, para.5–046.

[17] *Metropolitan Water Board v Dick Kerr & Co* [1918] A.C. 119 at 129.

[18] [1916] 1 A.C. 486; above, para.5–049.

available to the other (the shipowner). This might be a desirable view, but we shall see that it does not represent English law.[19]

The view that a claim by the shipowners in the *Tamplin* case would have failed (if the compensation for requisition had fallen short of the contractual hire) is also, at least at first sight, inconsistent with *Modern Transport Co Ltd v Duneric SS Co*,[20] where the Court of Appeal relied on the *Tamplin* case to uphold just such a claim. The *Modern Transport* case concerned a time charter for 12 months from the time of the ship's being placed at the charterer's disposal, restraints of princes being excepted. The ship was delivered for service on April 15, 1915; in May she was requisitioned; she was placed at the disposal of the Admiralty on June 4; in November she was released; and on December 4 she was again available for service under the charterparty. The compensation for requisition was at the rate of only £1,220 15s per month, as against the monthly rate of hire of £2,350 due under the charterparty, and for so long as the ship was under requisition the charterers refused to pay hire. But when she was released market conditions had changed so that at this time the charterers tendered the hire due for the following month, while the owners sought to withdraw the ship. Neither party seems to have alleged frustration.[21] The charterers sought an injunction to restrain the shipowners from withdrawing the ship, while the shipowners claimed hire in respect of the period that the ship was under requisition; they agreed to reduce this claim by the amount received by them from the Government as compensation for the requisition. The Court of Appeal held that the shipowners were entitled to hire for the period during which the ship had been under requisition (less the amounts received by them from the Government); that they would have been entitled to withdraw the ship, but that they had waived their right to do so by submitting their claim for hire during the period of requisition to arbitration. So far as the claim for hire was concerned, Swinfen Eady L.J. said that the requisition was "for less than one half the period of the time charter"[22] and that the *Tamplin* case showed that this was not sufficient to bring the charterparty to an end. Bankes L.J. likewise said that this aspect of the case was governed by the *Tamplin* case. A passage in the judgment of Swinfen Eady L.J. in which he appears to base his conclusion also on the fact that there was "no entire failure of consideration"[23] gives rise, however, to more difficulty. One possible interpretation of this passage is that a contract cannot be frustrated by temporary impossibility so long as *any* part of the promised

---

[19] Below, para.15–002.

[20] [1917] 1 K.B. 370, affirming [1916] 1 K.B. 726. There are minor discrepancies between the statements of the facts in the two reports; the account in the text above follows that in [1917] 1 K.B. 370.

[21] Indeed, counsel for the charterers expressly disclaimed such an argument: see [1917] 1 K.B. 370 at 373, while counsel for the shipowners claimed that the *Tamplin* case [1916] 2 A.C. 397 (where the contract was held not to have been frustrated) was indistinguishable.

[22] [1917] 1 K.B. 370 at 377.

[23] *ibid.*

performance remains possible; but it is clearly inconsistent with cases such as *The Nema*[24] and some of the authorities relating to contracts for personal services, to be discussed in paras 5–055 and 5–056, below. An alternative (and from the context more plausible) interpretation of the passage is that there was no "failure of consideration" at all as the shipowner had undertaken to provide the use of the ship only subject to "restraints of princes" (and not absolutely); but while this exception no doubt protected him from liability it does not follow that it gave him any right to the charterer's counter-performance. "Failure of consideration" in this context refers to failure in performance, not to breach; and in *Jackson v Union Marine Insurance Co Ltd*[25] (where the charterparty contained an exception for perils of the sea) it was said that the words of the exception "excuse the shipowner but give him no right".[26] A third possible interpretation is that any failure of consideration which may have occurred was not total since, even if the charterers were deprived of the use of the ship, they were entitled[27] to the compensation for the requisition paid by the Government and so received some benefit under the contract. The difficulty with this view is that there is very little support in English law for the view that the charterers were indeed entitled, as a matter of common law, to the compensation paid to the shipowners by the Admiralty: this question is further discussed in Ch.15.[28] The discussion of these difficulties with the reasoning of the *Modern Transport* case is not intended as any criticism of the actual result there reached. This is, with respect, an excellent piece of loss-splitting, the charterer having to bear the loss incurred by reason of the low rate of Government compensation, but being entitled to the benefits resulting from the subsequent rise in market rates.

(ii) The personal services cases

5 055   Reference has already been made to *Morgan v Manser*[29] where a 10-year contract between an entertainer and his agent, made in 1938, was held to have been frustrated by the entertainer's conscription in 1940, even though he was released from the armed forces in 1946; and we have suggested that this result can be explained on the ground that in 1940 it was likely that no resumption of performance would be possible. Similar

---

[24] [1982] A.C. 724 above, para.5–052.

[25] (1874) L.R. 10 C.P. 125.

[26] *ibid.* at 144. See further below, para.12–012, and *cf. Blane Steamships Ltd v Minister of Transport* [1951] 2 K.B. 965, where the words of a charterparty excused *the charterer*, but gave him no rights.

[27] [1917] 1 K.B. 370 at 378, *per* Swinfen Eady L.J., who in the context of a shipbuilding contract again expressed a similar view in *Dale SS Co Ltd v Northern SS Co Ltd* (1918) 34 T.L.R. 271 at 272. The same view appears to be taken by Lord Loreburn in *Tamplin SS Co v Anglo-Mexican Petroleum Co* [1916] 2 A.C. 397 at 405.

[28] Below, paras 15–019 *et seq*. It is possible for such entitlement to be conferred by special war-time legislation, but no reference to any such legislation is made in the *Modern Transport* case.

[29] [1948] 1 K.B. 184; above, para.5–051.

reasoning may explain *Unger v Preston Corporation*[30] where a refugee from Germany was interned in 1940 as an enemy alien (although his sympathies lay on the allied side) and his contract to serve a local authority as a school medical officer was held to have been frustrated. The court regarded *Horlock v Beal*[31] as indistinguishable and the reference to that case suggests that the court in *Unger's* case considered that there was in 1940 no prospect of the resumption of performance of the contract. The fact that the contract was terminable on three months' notice should not be regarded as decisive; for the principles here under discussion can apply not only where a contract of employment is expressly for a fixed long term but also where the contract, though providing for relatively short periods of notice, is intended to give rise to an enduring relationship[32]

The above cases should be contrasted with *Nordman v Rayner & Sturgess*[33] where it was held that a commission agency which was to last for five years from July 1914 (subject to a power to terminate it at the end of the first year) was not frustrated by the internment of the agent as an enemy alien in September 1914, shortly after the beginning of the First World War. The agent, though of German nationality, was of French origin and anti-German sympathies, and he was released from internment after only one month. In these circumstances, the internment was "not ... sufficient to cause a substantial frustration of the business venture".[34]

That test has also been applied to determine whether a contract of employment is frustrated by a temporary illness. Frustration does not result merely from the fact that the employee suffers from an illness which prevents him from working for only a short time (relative to the length of the contract)[35]; but the contract will be discharged if the illness continues for so long as to put an end to the possibility of performance "in a business sense".[36] This would be the position where the illness had made resumption of work within a reasonable time a practical impossibility.[37] For this purpose it would be relevant that the employer needed, with some degree of urgency, to replace the employee who had fallen ill, *e.g.* because the employee was one of a team which could not continue to carry out its appointed task unless a substitute were appointed,[38] or because for some

5–056

---

[30] [1942] 2 All E.R. 200.

[31] [1916] 1 A.C. 486; above, para.5–049.

[32] *Notcutt v Universal Equipment Co (London) Ltd* [1986] 1 W.L.R. 641; Howarth [1987] C.L.J. 47.

[33] (1916) 33 T.L.R. 87.

[34] *ibid.* at 88.

[35] *Jackson v Union Marine Insurance Co Ltd* (1874) L.R. 10 C.P. 125 at 144 ("a short illness would not suffice"); *Storey v Fulham Steel Works Co* (1907) 24 T.L.R. 89; *Marshall v Harland & Wolff Ltd* [1972] 1 W.L.R. 899; *Williams v Watsons Luxury Coaches* [1990] I.C.R. 536.

[36] *Jackson v Union Marine Insurance Co Ltd* (1874) L.R. 10 C.P. 125 at 145.

[37] *e.g. Notcutt v Universal Equipment Co (London) Ltd* [1986] 1 W.L.R. 461; *cf. Watts v Monmouthshire CC* (1968) 66 L.G.R. 171, explained in *Vermeer v Derby CC* [2003] EWHC 2708 as a case of termination by resignation.

[38] *e.g. Hart v AR Marshall (Bulwell) Ltd* [1977] 1 W.L.R. 1067.

other reason the employer's operations could not be continued without someone who had the employee's skills or qualifications.

In assessing the effect of the interruption, it is also necessary to have regard to the nature of the contract. In *E C Shepherd & Co Ltd v Jerrom*[39] an apprentice was sentenced to Borstal training for a period which was likely to last for 39 weeks.[40] This was held to frustrate his four-year contract of apprenticeship which, when the sentence was imposed, still had two years to run, since in this type of contract continuity of training was considered to be of vital importance. Whether the court would have taken the same view of an interruption of the same length which was due to illness, is perhaps open to question.

Somewhat different considerations apply where performance of the contract becomes temporarily illegal as well as impossible. This was the position in *Marshall v Glanvill*[41] where, during the First World War, a commercial traveller volunteered for service in the armed forces four days before he would have been conscripted. His contract of employment was frustrated since under war-time legislation its performance became illegal as soon as he had joined the armed forces. It seems that this result is based on the consideration of public policy which can prevent the suspension of contracts after their performance has become illegal[42]; though in *Marshall v Glanvill* an additional ground for the decision was that the employee's service in the armed forces was likely to last for so long as to discharge the contract on the ground of temporary impossibility, quite apart from any question of illegality.

VI. OTHER LEGAL EFFECTS OF TEMPORARY IMPOSSIBILITY

5-057   Temporary impossibility which is not sufficiently serious to frustrate a contract may have a number of other legal effects; in this respect it resembles partial impossibility.[43]

(1) Excuse for non-performance

5-058   First, the party whose performance is temporarily impossible may have a temporary excuse for non-performance.[44] For example, even where the illness of an employee was not of such a duration as to frustrate his contract of employment, the employee would not be in breach of the contract through failing to work while he was ill.[45] The excuse can, it seems, extend

---

[39] [1987] Q.B. 301.

[40] See *ibid.* at 320. Contrast *Chakki v United Yeast Ltd* [1982] I.C.R. 140, where the employee was granted bail after sentence and later placed on probation.

[41] [1917] 2 K.B. 87.

[42] Below, para.8–055.

[43] *cf.* above, paras 5–013, 5–014; Stannard, 46 M.L.R. 738.

[44] For a similar effect of partial impossibility, see above, para.5–013.

[45] *Jackson v Union Marine Insurance Co Ltd* (1874) L.R. 10 C.P. 125 at 145 ("no action will lie against him"); *Poussard v Spiers & Pond* (1876) 1 Q.B.D. 410 at 414

to cases in which the employee is temporarily prevented from performing by other causes beyond his control: the example has been given of a teacher who is locked in a school lavatory "through no fault of his own".[46] The same principle can apply to temporary impossibility in other types of contracts. It has, for example, been held that a tenant was not in breach of his covenant to redevelop a site by a specified date where the redevelopment was prevented by an order listing a building on the site as one of special architectural interest.[47] In these cases, the excuse is provided by law. It is obvious that an excuse provided by an express term of the contract can apply to temporary impossibility which does not frustrate the contract, *e.g.* where delay in the performance of a charterparty, or of a building contract, results from circumstances for which the carrier or building contractor is, by the express terms of the contract, to be under no liability.

A supervening event may give a temporary excuse for non-performance, not only to the party by whom services are to be rendered under a contract, but also to the person to whom those services are to be rendered. For example, the temporary illness of a pupil may provide him or his parents with a temporary excuse for not making payments under a contract to provide education or other instruction to the pupil.[48] A similar point is illustrated by *Minnevitch v Café de Paris (Londres) Ltd,*[49] where a group of musicians known as the Harmonica Rascals contracted with the defendant to give variety performances at the Café from December 26, 1935 to January 25, 1936; the contract contained a "no play, no pay" clause. On January 20, 1936, King George V died, and all places of public entertainment remained closed on that day and on the following day. It was held that the defendant was not in breach in failing to give the Harmonica Rascals a chance to play on those two days; but that he was in breach in refusing to give them such a chance on the next four days (the remaining period of their engagement).

The possibility that a supervening event may give one party a temporary excuse for non-performance (without discharging the contract) is not restricted to contracts for the provision of services. It was, for example, applied in the American case of *Patch v Solar Corp*[50] where an agreement was made granting a licence to use a patent; the agreement was expressed to last for the duration of the patent, so long as the licensee paid $5,000 per annum. The patented article was incorporated in washing machines, the manufacture of which was prohibited during the Second World War. It was held that the contract was not discharged, but that the licensee was entitled to use the patent after the end of the war, without having to keep up the annual payments of $5,000 during the war.

5–059

("not any breach"); contrast *Bettini v Gye* (1876) 1 Q.B.D. 183 at 189 (employer "must ... seek redress by a cross-claim for damages").

[46] *Sim v Rotherham Metropolitan BC* [1987] Ch. 216 at 254.
[47] *John Lewis Properties v Viscount Chelsea* [1993] 2 E.G.L.R. 77.
[48] *Simeon v Watson* (1877) 46 L.J.Q.B. 679; *cf.* above, para.4–026.
[49] [1936] 1 All E.R. 884.
[50] 149 F. 2d 558 (1945), cert. denied 326 U.S. 741.

(2) **Option to rescind**

5–060   So far, we have considered two legal consequences of temporary impossibility: the first is wholly to discharge the contract by operation of law, while the second is merely to provide *one* party with an excuse for non-performance. Between these two extremes, there is an intermediate position, which is illustrated by *Poussard v Spiers and Pond.*[51] That case concerned a contract by which Mme Poussard was to sing the leading female part in a new opera to be produced by the defendants; the engagement was for three months, if the opera ran for so long. Some days before the opening night, she fell ill, and the defendants engaged a substitute to sing her part for one month. A week after the opening night, Mme Poussard recovered her health and voice and claimed her part, but the defendants refused to take her back. It was held that their refusal was justified because her failure to appear on the opening night (though not amounting to a breach as it was due to illness) was a sufficiently serious failure in performance to provide the defendants with a ground for rescinding the contract. At first sight, it may seem that the contract was discharged by impossibility, since, in consequence of the supervening event, failure to perform was not a breach by either party; and this view may appear to derive some support from the occasional citation of *Poussard v Spiers and Pond* in cases of discharge under the doctrine of frustration, apparently as an illustration of that doctrine. In the *Bank Line* case, *e.g.* Lord Sumner referred to *Poussard's* case as "transferring the rule in *Jackson's* case from a steamship to a prima donna"[52] – a remark perhaps inspired by the fact that Blackburn J. in *Poussard's* case places some reliance on *Jackson's* case.[53] Nevertheless it is submitted that *Poussard's* case was not one of discharge frustration. Such discharge operates automatically,[54] and the better view is that there was no such automatic discharge in *Poussard's* case. The singer's illness had two effects; first, it gave Mme Poussard a temporary excuse for non-performance; and secondly, it gave the defendants an option to dismiss her[55]; for this purpose, a serious failure in performance suffices, even though it does not amount to a breach.[56] If Mme Poussard had been a great operatic star and the defendants had wished (after she had recovered from her illness) to hold her to the remaining part of her engagement, they would have been

---

[51]   (1876) 1 Q.B.D. 410.

[52]   [1919] A.C. 435 at 457; *cf. ibid.* at 461. For other references to *Poussard's* case in the context of frustration see *Robert H Dahl v Nelson Donkin* (1881) 6 App. Cas. 38 at 52 ("entitled *either of them* ... to treat the contract as at an end"); *Tamplin SS Co Ltd v Anglo-Mexican Petroleum Co Ltd* [1916] 2 A.C. 397 at 421; *J. Lauritzen A/S v Wijsmuller BV (The Super Servant Two)* [1989] 1 Lloyd's Rep. 148, at 153, affirmed [1990] 1 Lloyd's Rep. 1. *cf.* also Restatement 2d, § 268, where Illustrations 1 and 2 are, according to the Reporter's Note "suggested by ... *Poussard v Spiers and Pond*".

[53]   See (1876) 1 Q.B.D. 410 at 414.

[54]   Below, para.15–002.

[55]   See Treitel, *The Law of Contract* (11th ed.), pp.844–846.

[56]   *ibid.*, p.759.

entitled to do so (though not to claim specific performance of her undertaking).[57] The illness had consequences which were sufficiently serious to justify rescission of the contract by the defendants. But, because of its comparatively short duration, the illness was not of the greater degree of seriousness which is required to discharge both parties automatically, by operation of law; it would not have made performance of the contract after Mme Poussard had recovered from her illness fundamentally different from that originally undertaken.

The distinction drawn above between the two degrees of seriousness in the failure of performance may (like all matters of degree) be hard to formulate precisely, but is, it is submitted, nevertheless real. A much quoted statement of the test which has to be satisfied to justify rescission by an injured party is that of Diplock L.J. in the *Hong Kong Fir* case: according to this test, the event relied on (*i.e.* the failure in performance) must be such as to deprive the injured party of "substantially the whole benefit which it was the intention of the parties that he should obtain . . .".[58] This test was, in terms, formulated for the purpose of determining only the question whether the failure was sufficiently serious to "discharge *one* of the parties from further performance of his undertakings".[59] It has, indeed, been said to be "applicable alike to both frustration and to fundamental breach",[60] but it is respectfully submitted that an event may have a sufficiently serious effect to satisfy Diplock L.J.'s test (quoted above) *without* frustrating the contract. To put the point in another way, there is a significant difference between saying that an event deprives a party of "substantially the whole benefit"[61] which he was intended to obtain and saying that an event turns (or would turn) performance after it into "quite a different thing"[62] from that bargained for. The point can be illustrated by the *Tamplin* case,[63], where the interference with performance was held *not* to have been sufficiently serious to frustrate the contract but where a similar interference with performance might (if due to the shipowner's breach or even excused non-performance) well have justified rescission by the charterer. Conversely, in *Poussard v Spiers and Pond*,[64] the interference

[57]   *cf. Lumley v Wagner* (1852) 1 D.M. & G. 604.

[58]   *Hong Kong Fir Shipping Co Ltd v Kawasaki Kisen Kaisha Ltd* [1962] 2 Q.B. 26 at 65.

[59]   *ibid.*

[60]   *Great Peace Shipping Ltd v Tsavliris Salvage (International) Ltd (The Great Peace)* [2002] EWCA Civ 1407; [2003] Q.B. 697 at [82]; there is some support for this view in the paragraph following that in the *Hong Kong Fir* case from which the quotation at n.58, above is taken.

[61]   Above, n.58.

[62]   *Bank Line Ltd v Arthur Capel & Co* [1919] A.C. 435 (above, para.5-046) at 460.

[63]   *Tamplin SS Co v Anglo-Mexican Petroleum Co* [1916] 2 A.C. 397.

[64]   Above, n.51. There is no reference in Blackburn J.'s judgment in *Poussard v Spiers and Pond* to his earlier judgment in *Taylor v Caldwell* (1863) 3 B. & S. 826 (above, para.2–024), though the former judgment does refer to *Jackson v Union Marine Insurance Co Ltd* (1874) L.R. 10 C.P. 125 which in turn refers at 148 to *Taylor v Caldwell*. Perhaps Blackburn J. still regarded the latter case as applicable only to impossibility arising from "the *perishing* of the person or thing" (at 840, italics supplied): *cf.* above, para.5–043, n.86.

with performance (due to excused non-performance) was held to justify rescission of the contract at the election of the defendants, but it by no means follows that the contract was frustrated. The distinction here drawn can, it is submitted, be accounted for by reference to the difference in legal effect between events which justify rescission by the injured party and those which lead to frustration. Rescission is a mechanism which discharges "one of the parties"[65] and does so only at that party's election, while frustration discharges both parties and does so automatically,[66] without any election. The legal consequences of frustrating events being thus more drastic than those of events which entitle a party to rescind,[67] it is reasonable that more stringent requirements should be imposed to lead to the former, than to the latter, result.

5–061 The distinction drawn above between cases in which temporary impossibility discharges a contract, and those in which it merely gives the party to whom the temporarily impossible performance was due an option to rescind is, however, often blurred. The reason for this is that, if the only interest of that party is to escape from liability under the contract, and if he has rescinded, then he will succeed on either basis, so that it will often be unnecessary to decide between them. In the cases here under discussion, it is also assumed that the other party has an excuse for non-performance, so that he will not be subject to the secondary liability in damages which is normally imposed on the defaulting party in consequence of rescission for breach.[68] There are, however, situations in which the distinction is of practical importance. One is where the party to whom the temporarily impossible performance was due has *not* rescinded. Here he can avoid liability only if the delay is sufficiently serious to frustrate the contract: if it merely gives him the option to rescind, and he has failed to exercise it, he remains liable.[69] A second is where that party has not rescinded and wishes to enforce the contract after the temporary impossibility has come to an end. He can clearly do so if the effect of the delay is merely to give him an option to rescind, but not if its effect is to frustrate the contract. A third situation in which the distinction between the two processes is of practical importance would arise if either party wished to invoke the provisions of the Law Reform (Frustrated Contracts) Act 1943.[70] This Act applies where a contract "has become impossible of performance ... and the parties thereto have *for that reason* been discharged from the further performance of the contract".[71] It follows that the Act would not apply where the impossibility would not of itself

---

[65] *Hong Kong Fir* case, above, n.58, at 65.

[66] Below, para.15–002; above, para.2–039.

[67] *cf.* above, para.2–050; for further discussion of the distinction between frustration and rescission for breach, see below, para.15–005.

[68] Treitel, *The Law of Contract* (11th ed.), p.851.

[69] *ibid.*, p.855; *cf. Loates v Maple* (1903) 88 L.T. 288, where the crucial point appears to be the statement at 291 that "the defendant does not say that he rescinded [the contract]".

[70] Below, paras 15–049, 15–061, 15–071, 15–073.

[71] s.1(1) (italics supplied).

discharge the contract, but would only give an option to rescind to the party who, in consequence of it, had failed temporarily to receive the agreed performance.

For these practical grounds, it is necessary to distinguish between the two types of situation; but where no such grounds exist it is not always clear, especially in the older authorities, whether the decisions, and the examples given in the judgments, are based on frustration or on rescission for failure in performance. Two cases, one on each side of the line, illustrate the difficulty of drawing the distinction.

5–062

The first is *Jackson v Union Marine Insurance Co Ltd*[72] the facts of which have already been stated.[73] For the present purpose, one significant point is that the issue there did not arise directly between the parties to the charter. The claim was by one of those parties (the shipowner) against his insurers on a policy against loss of freight, and it was upheld on the ground that the charterer had been discharged, by the length of the delay, from his liability under the contract. A further significant point is that the charterer had rescinded the charterparty[74] on account of the delay; and in the circumstances it therefore made no practical difference whether his discharge from liability resulted automatically, *i.e.* by operation of law under the doctrine of frustration, or (on the other hand) as a result of his exercise of his option to rescind. Some of the examples given in Bramwell B.'s judgment may seem to support the latter view in that they conclude that the party failing to receive performance at the agreed time may engage a substitute[75]: this conclusion tells us nothing about the liability of the party whose performance is delayed, should the other party wish to claim it after the temporary impossibility has come to an end. On the other hand, the judgment places no emphasis on the fact that the charterer rescinded the contract. And, in discussing the effect of the exception for perils of the sea, Bramwell B. says that it does not "take away the right the other party [*i.e.* the charterer] would have had, if the non-performance had been a breach of contract, to retire from the engagement: and if one party may, so may the other".[76] The concluding words indicate that both parties are discharged (in consequence of the delay caused by the excepted peril) by operation of law rather than by the election of one of them: in other words, that the case is one of discharge by frustration rather than one of discharge consequent on rescission. This view is further supported by the citation in *Jackson's* case of *Taylor v Caldwell*[77]; and by the fact that *Jackson's* case is regarded as an authority on frustration in many later decisions.[78]

---

[72] (1874) L.R. 10 C.P. 125.

[73] Above, para.5–039.

[74] See (1874) L.R. 10 C.P. 125 at 126, 127, *per* Cleasby B. (dissenting).

[75] *ibid.* at 145 ("may hire a fresh servant", "might procure someone else").

[76] *ibid.*; *cf.* at 144 ("when I think *he* (*i.e.* the charterer) is [discharged] I think *both* are").

[77] (1863) 3 B. & S. 826, cited in *Jackson's* case at 148.

[78] *e.g.* in *Tamplin SS Co v Anglo-Mexican Petroleum Co* [1916] 2 A.C. 397 at 404, 415–418, 424; *Metropolitan Water Board v Dick Kerr & Co* [1918] A.C. 119 at 135; *Bank*

5–063   The second case which illustrates the difficulty of distinguishing between automatic discharge by frustration and discharge consequent on one party's election to rescind is *Tully v Howling*,[79] where a charterer was held to be justified in refusing to accept the services of the ship under a 12-month consecutive voyage charterparty by reason of a two-month delay (due to unseaworthiness) in making the ship available. References in the judgments to the fact that the delay "frustrated the object of the adventure"[80] may at first sight seem to indicate that the contract was discharged under the doctrine of frustration. But the word "frustrated" (or one of its derivatives) is commonly used in relation to a breach (or justified non-performance) which justifies rescission[81]; and in *Tully v Howling* it seems to be used in this sense. This view is supported by the fact that Mellish L.J. relies[82] on the analogy of short delivery as a justification for rejection under a contract for the sale of goods, for it is clear that the shortage will provide such a justification even though it does not reach the degree of seriousness which would be required to frustrate the contract.[83] Nor is this degree of seriousness required by s.30(2A) of the Sale of Goods Act 1979, under which a buyer who does not deal as consumer cannot reject short delivery where the shortage is "so slight that it would be unreasonable" for him to reject. This subsection merely excludes the right to reject for shortages that are trivial; and a shortage is not a frustrating event merely because it is not trivial.

(3) Wages during sickness

5–064   Where temporary illness is not sufficiently serious to frustrate a contract of employment, the *prima facie* rule is that the employee is entitled to be paid wages during sickness.[84] The right to such wages will cease, as a matter of common law,[85] if the illness is sufficiently serious to entitle the employer to terminate the contract, and the employer exercises his option to do so.[86] The *prima facie* common law right to wages during sickness can also be displaced by an express contrary provision or by circumstances from which a contrary provision can be implied. To establish such an implied term, it is not necessary to show that the employee would, at the time of contracting, have agreed that he should not be paid during sickness.[87] The

---

Line Ltd v Arthur Capel & Co [1919] A.C. 435 at 461; *Joseph Constantine SS Line Ltd v Imperial Smelting Corp Ltd* [1942] A.C. 154 at 165.

[79] (1877) 2 Q.B.D. 182.

[80] *ibid.* at 189; *cf. ibid.* at 184.

[81] See above, paras 2–049, 2–050.

[82] (1877) 2 Q.B.D. 182 at 188.

[83] Sale of Goods Act 1979, s.30(1); above, paras 5–013, 5–014.

[84] *Marrison v Bell* [1939] 2 K.B. 187; *Mears v Safecar Securities Ltd* [1983] Q.B. 54 at 79. *cf.* Employment Rights Act 1996, s.64.

[85] No attempt is made in this book to deal with statutory sick pay.

[86] As in *Poussard v Spiers and Pond* (1876) 1 Q.B.D. 410, above, para.5–060.

[87] *Mears v Safecar Securities Ltd* [1983] Q.B. 54 at 74, disapproving *Orman v Saville Sportswear Ltd* [1960] 1 W.L.R. 1065, and following *O'Grady v Saper* [1940] 2 K.B. 469.

rule can be displaced by other circumstances indicating that a term excluding the right to sick pay ought to be implied, *e.g.* by the practice of the employers not to make such payments and the failure of the employee to claim that such payments were due.[88]

(4) **Allocation of available time**

In paras 5–015 to 5–025 above, we considered various solutions to the   **5–065** problems which could arise where a party had entered into more than one contract to supply goods to be taken from a particular source, and where the partial failure of that source then led to a situation in which he could perform some of those contracts but not all. One such solution was to require that party to allocate the available supply between his customers *pro rata*, or on some other basis.

Problems of this kind can arise also in cases of temporary impossibility. For example,[89] an actor, a musical performer or a carrier may contract to render services to a number of persons within a specified period, and the contract may leave the exact dates (within that period) on which the services are to be rendered for future determination by notice given, or demand made, by one of the contracting parties. Before the dates have been fixed in this way, performance may become temporarily impossible, and it may be that full performance of all the contracts cannot be rendered within that part of the contract period remaining available. The question would then arise whether the party who can no longer perform all his contracts in full should allocate the remaining time, or in other words his capacity to render services in the remaining part of the contract period, between the various parties with whom he has contracted. For example, it might be argued that if a singer who had contracted to give a total of nine concerts for three impresarios in a specified period of three weeks should be required to give one (and no more than one) concert for each of them if he were prevented by illness from performing during the first two of those weeks. There appears to be no authority which supports such a solution in cases of temporary impossibility; but if the principle of allocation can apply in cases of partial impossibility, there seems to be no good reason why it should not also apply where the impossibility is temporary.

---

[88] *Mears v Safecar Securities Ltd*, above, n.87.

[89] This example differs from the similar one given in above, para.5–032, in which the singer's capacity is reduced over the *whole* of the contract period.

CHAPTER 6

IMPRACTICABILITY

I. IMPRACTICABILITY DISTINGUISHED FROM IMPOSSIBILITY

In this chapter, we shall consider the question whether, and if so in what circumstances, a contract may be discharged on the ground that its performance, though it remains possible, has become impracticable. It will be convenient first to consider (in outline) the position in American law,[1] where a doctrine of discharge by impracticability is now generally regarded as established. The purpose of that discussion will be to gain some understanding of the nature and practical effects of the doctrine, and so to prepare the ground for a discussion of the question whether impracticability, of itself, can also be regarded as a ground of discharge in English law. It is clear that English law does recognise that a contract may be discharged, even though there is no impossibility, under the doctrine of frustration of purpose. That doctrine will be discussed in Ch.7, where the distinction between it and the doctrine of discharge by impracticability will be explained.[2]

6–001

As originally formulated in *Taylor v Caldwell*, the doctrine of discharge applied only where performance became "impossible".[3] That, in itself, is something of a relative term. It has been suggested[4] that even *Taylor v Caldwell* itself was not a case of literal impossibility, since "by the expenditure of huge sums of money" the music hall could probably have been rebuilt "in time for the scheduled concerts"; but it would have been wholly unreasonable to have required the defendants to take such steps. Whether something is "impossible" depends in part on the amount of trouble and expense which one is prepared to incur to achieve it and in part on the current state of technology. The point can be illustrated by an example given by Sir Frederick Pollock who, in 1876, suggested that "an agreement to make a practicable flying machine need not be regarded as

---

[1] The discussion will be restricted to a selection of typical cases; no attempt will be made to present a complete survey of the American authorities.
[2] Below, paras 7–001 to 7–004.
[3] (1863) 3 B. & S. 826 at 834.
[4] Fuller and Eisenberg, *Basic Contract Law* (3rd ed.), p.801.

absolutely impossible".[5] This may be contrasted with the example given as late as 1962 by Corbin of "absolute" impossibility: "no-one", he wrote, "can go to the moon".[6] One can alter the example by supposing that a contract had been made for the sale of some mineral of which supplies on Earth had later run out, but which remained plentifully available on the moon. Performance might not then be literally impossible; but no one would expect the seller to go to the moon to get the goods and he would not be liable for failing to do so. He might, indeed, be liable on the ground that he had made an absolute contract to procure and supply generic goods, but such liability can arise in spite even of "absolute" impossibility.[7]

II. IMPRACTICABILITY AS A GROUND OF DISCHARGE IN AMERICAN LAW

6–002   The examples given in para.6–001, above are extreme and even absurd; but in the United States the view is now commonly expressed that there is a range of more realistic situations in which contracts may be discharged, even though performance has not become "impossible", on the ground of "impracticability".

(1) General statements

6–003   General statements of the principle of discharge by impracticability are to be found in a number of rather confusing (if not self-contradictory) passages from the Restatement 2d and in the Comments to s.2–615 of the Uniform Commercial Code. The Restatement 2d, § 261, Comment d defines "impracticability" so as to include "extreme and unreasonable difficulty, expense, injury or loss to one of the parties". It goes on to give some examples of impracticability: "A severe shortage of raw materials or of supplies due to war, embargo, local crop failure, unforeseen shutdown of major sources of supply or the like, which ... causes a marked increase in cost may bring the case within the rule .. ". These examples are borrowed from Comment 4 to Uniform Commercial Code, s.2–615 which provides for "excuse by failure of presupposed conditions"[8] where the

---

[5] *Principles of Contract* (12th ed.), p.229, referring to the lst ed. (1876), p.365.

[6] *Contracts* (1962), para.1325; a view also expressed by Pollock, *Principles of Contract* (1st ed., 1876), p.325, but nearly 90 years earlier.

[7] The case would fall within the principle of "strict" contractual liability: above, para.1–005.

[8] s.2–615, section caption, which is part of the Act: UCC, s.1–109, now replaced by s.1–107 (see above, para.3–017, n.57). In the phrase quoted above, one can again detect signs of the influence of German law on the UCC (*cf.* above, para.5–023, n.2): "presupposed conditions" seems to be an attempt to translate the German "*Vorraussetzungen*" as used (at least formerly) in this context: for a brief account of the history of this concept, see Zweigert and Kötz, *Introduction to Comparative Law* (trs. Weir) (2nd ed.), p.556. The phrase "failure of presupposed

agreed performance has been "made impracticable[9] by the occurrence of a condition, the non-occurrence of which was a basic assumption on which the contract was made ...". But Comment 4 also explains or qualifies this principle by saying that: "increased cost alone does not excuse performance unless the rise in cost is due to some unforeseen contingency which alters the essential nature of the performance. Neither is a rise or a collapse in the market in itself a justification, for that is exactly the type of business risk which business contracts made at fixed prices are intended to cover." In a somewhat similar vein, the Restatement 2d, § 261, Comment d tells us that: "'Impracticability' means more than impracticality. A mere change in the degree of difficulty or expense due to such causes as increased wages, prices of raw materials or costs of construction, unless well beyond the normal range, does not amount to impracticability." In spite of the confusing nature of these statements, the general message which they seem to be intended to convey is that a contracting party may be discharged if, as a result of unexpected supervening events, performance of the contract, though remaining physically possible, has become severely more burdensome for that party. The principle has also been referred to as one of "commercial impracticability".[10] All such expressions seem to mean the same thing: their common feature is that the contract may be discharged even though no *physical* (or legal) obstacle has arisen which would prevent its performance or make such performance unlawful.

(2) Origins

In the United States, the case to which the doctrine of discharge by impracticability is usually traced back (and which is still a frequently cited authority on the subject) is *Mineral Park Land Co v Howard*,[11] where a contract had been made by which the defendants agreed to take all the gravel required for a particular construction project from the plaintiff's land for a payment of 5¢ per cubic yard. Only about half the agreed quantity was taken and the plaintiff claimed damages for failure to take the remainder. The claim was rejected on the grounds that all the gravel which the defendants had not taken was below the water level and could only have been extracted at the "prohibitive cost"[12] of 10 or 12 times the usual cost of such an operation; and that use of this gravel in the construction project would have caused delays because it would have been necessary to dry the gravel before such use. In a much quoted dictum, the court said that "a thing is impossible in legal contemplation when it is not

6–004

---

conditions" does not occur in the corresponding UCC, s.2A–405 (on chattel leases) or in Uniform Land Transactions Act, s.2–407, below, n.9.

[9] *cf.* "impracticability" in the corresponding s.2–407 of the Uniform Land Transactions Act (not yet in force).

[10] *e.g. Asphalt International Inc v Enterprise Shipping Corp SA*, 667 F. 2d 261 at 266 (1981).

[11] 156 P 458 (1916).

[12] *ibid.* at 459.

practicable"[13]; and it added that "the defendants were not binding themselves to take what is not there".[14] The case may be contrasted with *Watkins v Carrig*[15] where the plaintiff had contracted to excavate a cellar for the defendant at a stated price. Soon after the work was begun, solid rock was encountered and it was agreed that the plaintiff should remove this at a unit price which was about nine times greater than that specified in the contract. The issue was whether this subsequent promise by the defendant was supported by consideration, and the court held that it was so supported.[16] But it rejected the argument that the original contract was voidable for mistake, and so evidently took the view that, if no promise to pay extra had been made, the plaintiff would have been obliged to do the work at the originally agreed price.

Both the above are cases of antecedent (rather than supervening) impossibility. English law would probably classify them as raising issues of mistake rather than of frustration and would probably deny relief since it applies stricter standards in cases of mistake than in those of frustration. The reason for this (as suggested earlier in this book[17]) is that it is easier to find out existing facts than to foresee the future or that, on the true construction of the contract, a party is more likely to have undertaken responsibility for an unknown existing, than for an unexpected future, state of affairs. In English law, the buyer's best hope of escaping from liability on facts such as those of the *Mineral Park* case would be to rely on the construction of the contract, *e.g.* by arguing that the usual commercial sense of "gravel" in a contract of the kind in question was "gravel above the water line". One might in this respect compare the case with cases such as *Clifford v Watts*,[18] where a tenant who had promised to dig 1,000 tons of clay and to pay a royalty of 2s.6d. per ton was held not liable for failing to extract the full quantity when it turned out that there was not so much clay in the land: he had not warranted that the full contract quantity could be extracted. It is interesting to note that the court in the *Mineral Park* case based its conclusion in part on American decisions which resemble *Clifford v Watts*.[19] But the latter case was actually one of physical impossibility and so gives no support to the view that a defendant can rely on any increase in the cost of his own performance as a ground of discharge.[20]

6–005   The statement in the *Mineral Park* case that "a thing is impossible in legal contemplation when it is not practicable"[21] is there taken from *Beach on Contracts*,[22] where the only authority cited for it is a dictum in the English

---

[13] *ibid.*

[14] *ibid.*

[15] 21 A. 2d 591 (1941).

[16] For the present standing of the case in England on this point, see *Chitty on Contracts* (29th ed.), para.3–069.

[17] Above, para.1–007.

[18] (1876) L.R. 5 C.P. 577.

[19] Though *Clifford v Watts* itself is not cited.

[20] See below, para.6–027.

[21] 156 p.458 at 459.

[22] Vol.I, para.216.

case of *Moss v Smith*. Maule J. there expressed himself in somewhat different terms. He said: "In matters of business, a thing is said to be impossible when it is not practicable; and a thing is impracticable when it can only be done at an excessive or unreasonable cost."[23] Two points should be noted about this statement. First, Maule J. refers to things which are said to be impossible "in matters of business," and not (as Beach would have it) "in contemplation of law". Secondly, Maule J.'s statement was made in the context of the doctrine of "constructive total loss". This originated in the law of marine insurance, under which a ship was considered to be totally lost when the cost of repairing her exceeded her value when repaired.[24] The principle on which the doctrine is based appears from the next sentence of judgment in *Moss v Smith*: "A man may be said to have lost a shilling when he had dropped it in deep water, though it might be possible by some very expensive contrivance to recover it."[25]

It is in this context of constructive total loss that we find a modern application of "impracticability," (and reliance on Uniform Commercial Code, s.2–615 and on Restatement 2d, §261, though outside the field of marine insurance) in *Asphalt International v Enterprise Shipping Corp SA*.[26] The case concerned a time charter of the defendant's ship for three years. During this period the ship was, without the fault of anyone for whom the defendant was responsible, so severely damaged that the cost of repairing her was $1.5 million, but her market value before she was damaged was only half that amount. The defendant advised the charterer that he regarded the ship as a constructive total loss, sold her for scrap for $157,500 and collected insurance payments of $1,335,000 on his hull insurance. The court held that the ship had become a constructive total loss, so that the defendant was not liable for breach of the charterparty. It described the case as one of "commercial impracticability",[27] and said that to oblige the defendant to rebuild a "virtually demolished vessel" would "require a type of performance essentially different from that for which [the charterers] contracted".[28] The case raises yet again the question whether the application of the doctrine of discharge here resulted in a satisfactory splitting or allocation of loss.[29] At first sight, the result in the *Asphalt International*[30] case is open to the objection in that it left the defendant with a large windfall profit (of $961,000[31]) from its insurance. This aspect of the case will be further considered in our

---

[23] (1850) 9 C.B. 94 at 103.

[24] See Marine Insurance Act 1906, s.60; Arnould, *Marine Insurance* (16th ed.), Ch.29.

[25] (1859) 9 C.B. 94 at 103. *cf.* the example given in Germany by Larenz, *Schuldrecht* (14th ed.), Vol.I, p.99 (dropping of a ring on the ocean floor).

[26] 667 F. 2d 261 (1981). Contrast *Hanjin Shipping Co Ltd v Zenith Chartering Corp (The Mercedes Envoy)* [1995] 2 Lloyd's Rep. 559, below, para.6–022.

[27] 667 F. 2d 261 at 266.

[28] *ibid.*

[29] For a discussion of a similar point relating to *Taylor v Caldwell* (1863) 3 B. & S. 826, see above, para.2–028.

[30] 667 F. 2d 261 (1981).

[31] 667 F. 2d 261 at 266 (1981).

discussion in Ch.15 of the effects of discharge.[32] The point to be emphasised here is that "constructive total loss" is a well-established doctrine in maritime law, so that it was scarcely necessary in the *Asphalt International* case to invoke the general doctrine of "impracticability".

6–006 A similar point applies to the reasoning of *Northern Corporation v Chugach Electric Association*[33] where a contractor undertook to do work for a public utility on the construction of a dam in Alaska. The contract required the contractor to take the necessary building material from a specified quarry and to haul it from there across the ice to the building site. While the contractor was attempting to perform this operation, its vehicles on several occasions broke through the ice and two of the contractor's men were killed. The contract was held to be discharged; and the actual ground for the decision seems to have been that performance by the contemplated method was "impossible".[34] But the court added that, even if it were "technically possible"[35] to perform the contract (*e.g.* by using another method of transporting the material) the contract would nevertheless have been discharged by commercial impracticability because the cost of such a method of performance "would be so disproportionate to that reasonably contemplated by the parties as to make the contract totally impractical[36] in commercial sense".[37] The court relied on the *Mineral Park* case[38] and on an earlier Alaskan case[39] in which a contract contemplated the moving of equipment across a frozen river at point A; this proved to be impossible because the ice there was too thin, but it would have been possible at point B, 70 miles further north. It was held that on these facts no summary judgment could be given against the contractor and that there was a triable issue that the contract was discharged. It was not decided that the contract *was* discharged: this must be doubtful in view of the Suez cases.[40] That doubt appears to extend, also, to the *Chugach* case itself, where the Suez cases are not cited. No doubt the actual decision was influenced by what the court evidently regarded as the intransigent attitude of the public utility after the contractor's attempt to perform had led to loss of life. Like the *Mineral Park* case, the *Chugach* case does not seem to raise issues of *supervening* impossibility: there is, for example, no suggestion that the difficulties encountered by the contractor resulted from a spell of unexpectedly mild weather.

---

[32] Below, para.15–022.

[33] 518 P. 2d 76 (1974)

[34] *ibid.* at 80.

[35] *ibid.* at 81.

[36] The subtle distinction drawn in Restatement 2d, § 261, Comment d, between "impracticability" and "impracticality" seems to have escaped the court. It seems to have also escaped the drafters of the Uniform Land Transactions Act, s.2–407, which is headed "Impracticality" while "impracticability" is used in the body of the section.

[37] 518 P. 2d 76 at 81 (1974).

[38] 156 P. 458 (1916); above, para.6–004.

[39] *Merl F Thomas v State*, 396 P. 2d 76 (1964).

[40] Above, paras 4–071 to 4–083.

(3) **Impracticability due to market movements**

6–007
The American cases so far considered give some support (at least in dicta) to the view that literal impossibility is not always necessary to bring about discharge and that for this purpose it may suffice to establish "impracticability" arising from the additional cost of, or other unexpected obstacles to, performance. But these cases do not touch upon the question whether mere market movements, however violent, can be sufficient to bring about discharge. Most of the cases which raise this issue concern sellers who argue that they should be discharged because the costs of what they have agreed to supply (or their costs of production) have risen to wholly unexpected levels above the contract price; but a few also deal with the converse question, whether a steep fall in the value of what the buyer has agreed to buy, to levels well below the contract price, can discharge the buyer. These look like mirror-image questions; and indeed it is sometimes argued[41] that the seller ought not be "excused" (so as, in effect, to be able to charge more) when production costs or market prices rise because he would not admit a similar argument on the part of his customer, who (it is said) cannot claim a similar "excuse" (or a price reduction) where seller's production costs or the market prices which he has to pay for a supply of the goods have fallen. But the argument is only a superficially attractive one because the cases are not true mirror images. The seller's loss is theoretically infinite—prices of his raw materials or other costs can (in theory) continue to rise without limit. The buyer's loss (so far as it is due to falling values) can never exceed the contract price. Perhaps this is why Uniform Commercial Code, s.2–615 in terms excuses only sellers[42]: their claim to release is more plausible than that of the buyers.

6–008
The typical situation to be discussed here is that in which parties enter into a fixed term contract, sometimes extending over several years, and then some supervening event occurs which causes the supplier's costs to rise sharply. The contract either provides for fixed prices throughout its duration, or (more commonly nowadays) contains provisions for "flexible pricing" but the formula adopted by the parties is alleged by one of them to be inadequate to deal with the extent of the price fluctuation which has occurred. The question is whether that party can claim to be discharged on this ground.

In the United States the argument that such factors may discharge the contract certainly cannot be rejected out of hand. This appears from two of the cases arising from the "energy crisis" which occurred when, in consequence of hostilities in the Middle East in 1973, the supply of oil coming from OPEC countries was restricted and the price of crude oil

---

[41] *e.g.* in *Maple Farms Inc v City School District of the City of Elmira*, 352 N.Y.S. 2d 784 at 790 (1974).

[42] For the extension of the principle of s.2–615 to excuse buyers, see Comment 9 and above, para.4–058. UCC, s.2A–405 similarly in terms excuses only lessors and suppliers. Uniform Land Transactions Act, s.2–407, by contrast, excuses both parties.

quadrupled. In the first of these cases, *Gay v Seafarer Fiberglass Yachts*,[43] the defendant argued that he should be released from a contract to build and deliver a yacht for a fixed price of $25,946; he relied on the facts that the cost of polyester resin (a petro-chemical derivative which was to be used in building the hull) had risen "sharply" because of the energy crisis, and that other components had gone up in price for the same reason. It was held that the seller had at least an arguable case along these lines, so that the buyer was not entitled to summary judgment. Moreover, in the second case, *Mansfield Propane Gas Co v Folger Gas Co*[44] the defendant had agreed to sell to the plaintiff the latter's requirements of propane gas, up to a maximum of 10 million gallons. The defendant was held entitled to reduce the amount deliverable under the contract by virtue of the allocation provision of Uniform Commercial Code, s.2–615 (b).[45] Here the seller relied on the *shortage* resulting from the "energy crisis" rather than on the increase in cost. The buyer did not even try to argue that s.2–615 was not, in principle, applicable. His argument was simply that he ought to be preferred to other customers because he had (while they had not) a written contract, and one which specified the maximum quantity; and it was this argument which was rejected by the court. Such cases show that, in the United States, the judiciary and the profession regarded as plausible the argument, that cost increases or general shortages *may* operate as a ground of discharge; and this view is also supported by dicta in many of the cases (to be discussed below) in which, on the facts, the courts concluded that there was no discharge. The general trend of decisions is in this direction: most of the recent cases, even in the United States, have rejected the argument that steep rises in costs (or falls in value) are grounds of discharge. These cases can be divided into several groups.

(a) *Discharge claimed by sellers on account of rising prices or costs*

6–009   In the first, sellers of goods claim that sharp increases in the market prices of their raw materials or supplies are a ground of discharge under Uniform Commercial Code, s.2–615. In the following discussion, we shall consider a selection of typical cases of this kind. Most, but not all, of these cases are concerned with the "energy crisis" of 1973.

Eastern Airlines Inc v Gulf Oil Corp[46] forms a convenient starting point for this discussion since it makes use of a number of arguments which appear with some regularity in later cases. Gulf had agreed to supply Eastern with the latter's requirements of aviation fuel for a period of about four-and-a-half years from 1972. The contract contained a price-escalation clause, but the amounts by which this entitled Gulf to raise its prices under the

---

[43] 14 U.C.C. Rep. Serv. 1335 (1974).

[44] 204 S.E. 2d 625 (1974); *cf. Intermar Inc v Atlantic Richfield Co*, 364 F. Supp. 82 (1973).

[45] Above, para.5–023.

[46] 415 F. Supp. 429 (1975). For a similar result in a German "energy crisis" case, see J.Z. 1978, 235 (but contrast RGZ 100, 130 (1920), where a contrary conclusion was reached in an earlier case raising a somewhat similar problem).

contract fell far short of the "400 per cent"[47] increase in the market price consequent on the energy crisis. The argument that this increase released Gulf by "impracticability" was rejected on a number of grounds. First, the court relied on the English and American Suez cases,[48] and on other American cases[49] which "similarly strictly construe the doctrine of commercial impracticability".[50] With regard to the Suez cases, the court might (as has been suggested in para.4–083, above) have strengthened its reasoning by pointing out that they were not cases of "pure" impracticability but cases in which there was actual impossibility in the contemplated or stipulated method of performance. If such impossibility, when combined with increased cost, was not a ground of discharge, then *a fortiori* increased cost alone should not have this effect. Secondly, the court pointed out that "the events associated with the energy crisis were reasonably foreseeable at the time the contract was executed"[51] so that Gulf could have protected itself against the resulting price increases by express provisions in the contract. Thirdly, the parties had specified the extent to which prices might be raised in a "price escalation" clause in the contract: the court inferred from this that they intended to be bound by the standard[52] specified in that clause. Fourthly, Gulf had failed to prove how much it had cost them to produce each gallon of aviation fuel, or that they were losing or had lost money on the contract with Eastern. And fifthly, Gulf had actually increased its profits in 1974 (the year after the beginning of the energy crisis) by more than 25 per cent over its previous year's profits. The point is an important one: large-scale enterprises (such as major oil companies) are capable of turning steep price-rises to their *general* advantage; and accordingly the mere fact that they suffer losses on *individual* contracts should not be a ground for discharging those contracts.

In the *Publicker Industries*[53] case there was a similar long term contract **6–010** for three years to supply "Ethanol". The contract contained a price-escalation clause which was subject to a ceiling of 28.5¢ per gallon; as a result of the energy crisis a major component of Ethanol, ethylene, rose in price from 21.2¢ to 37.2¢ per gallon, so that the seller stood to lose 10¢ per gallon of Ethanol, or $5 to 8 million in all on the full contract quantity. The case for discharging the seller was stronger than the *Eastern Airlines* case in that the seller *had* proved its prospective loss; but even so its plea of discharge failed. The main reason for rejecting it was that, by making the price-escalation subject to a ceiling, the parties had shown that they

---

[47] 415 F. Supp. 429 at 434.

[48] Above, paras 4–071 to 4–083.

[49] *e.g.* the *Maple Farms* case, above, n.41 and *Neal-Cooper Grain Co v Texas Gulf Sulphur Co*, 508 F. 2d 283 (1974); for these cases, see below, para.6–012; and *cf.* the later case of *Nora Springs Co-operative Co v Brandau*, 247 N.W. 2d 744 (1976), below, n.78.

[50] 415 F. Supp. 429 at 438.

[51] *ibid.* at 441.

[52] "Posting" in Platts-Oilgram.

[53] *Publicker Industries Inc v Union Carbide Corp*, 17 U.C.C. Rep. Serv. 989 (1973).

"intended the risk of a substantial and unforeseen rise in [the] cost [of ethylene] to be borne by the seller".[54] The court also indicated that it was not aware of any case in which "something less than a 100% increase has been held to make a seller's performance 'impracticable'".[55]

It does not, of course, follow that a 100 per cent increase is sufficient to bring about discharge. Certainly, such an increase in the *market price* of the product sold was not regarded as sufficient in *Virginia Electric & Power Co v Westinghouse Electric Corp* (the *VEPCO* case) of which unfortunately no full report is available.[56] Westinghouse had contracted to sell uranium to VEPCO and other public utilities; the contracts specified quantities (about 40 million lbs.) and delivery periods and prices ranging from $8 to $12 per pound. When (as a result of the energy crisis)[57] the market price had risen by more than 100 per cent, Westinghouse claimed discharge under s.2–615 from part of its obligation (it was willing to deliver uranium at its disposal) and argued that it stood to lose some $2–5 billion if it were held to the contracts. Apparently, Westinghouse had not intended to *produce* all the uranium but to *buy* at least some of it in the market, and so it would indeed suffer heavy losses if it were held to the contracts. But the plea of discharge was rejected, rightly, it seems, for Westinghouse in selling uranium in these circumstances must—like anyone who sells short for future delivery—be taken to have accepted the risk of market fluctuations. The judge urged the parties to come to a settlement[58]; to encourage them to do so, he left open the exact amount of damages; and he imposed on the buyers the burden of showing that they had acted reasonably to mitigate their loss by making a substitute contract, thus departing from the normal rule which puts the burden of proof in respect of this issue on the party in breach.[59] He also left open a question (to be discussed later in this chapter)[60]: namely, whether a court can make equitable adjustments under s.2–615 where it does not find in favour of total discharge.

6–011   Such a course of action is, indeed, suggested by s.2–615, Comment 6, which says that where "neither sense nor justice is served by either answer when the issue is posed in flat terms of 'excuse' or 'no excuse'", then "adjustments" should be made under other provisions of Art.2[61] "especially the sections on good faith[62] on insecurity and assurance[63]

---

[54] *ibid.* at 992.

[55] *ibid.*

[56] For brief reports, see 887 ATTR No 887–A15 (1978); *Washington Post*, October 28, 1978, P.D8; *Wall Street Journal*, October 30, 1978, p.10. See also Duesenberg, (1977) 32 Buis. Lawyer 1089; Joskow (1977) Jl. of Legal Studies 119.

[57] Joskow, *op. cit.* argues that the increase was due at least partly to other factors.

[58] As apparently they did: see *Wall Street Journal*, August 5, 1980.

[59] See, in England, *Roper v Johnson* (1873) L.R. 8 C.P. 167; and, in the United States, *Apex Mining Co v Chicago Copper Chemicals Co*, 306 F. 2d 725 at 738 (1962).

[60] Below, paras 6–011, 6–018.

[61] Comment 6 refers to "this Article".

[62] The reference appears to be to UCC s.1–203, now superseded by s.1–304 (see above, para.3–017, n.57), though this is plainly not part of "*this* Article" (in the words of s.2–615, Comment 6).

[63] *i.e.* s.2–609.

and on the reading of all provisions [of the Code] in the light of their purposes".[64] It is perhaps not fanciful to detect in Comment 6 (as elsewhere in the Uniform Commercial Code)[65] traces of German influence, for the Comment envisages a course of action which is scarcely distinguishable from the practice of German courts to order the "adaptation" of a contract where changed circumstances have destroyed the commercial basis (*Geschäftsgrundlage*).[66] But in the American case of *Iowa Electric Power Co v Atlas Corp*[67] a seller's attempt to persuade the court to impose such a solution (by modifying the contract in the light of changed circumstances to be discussed below) met with no success. Rather curiously, the seller there relied, not on the three sections referred to in Comment 6, but on two other sections of the Code. The first was s.2–716(2), which lays down that a decree of specific performance "may include such terms . . . as to payment of the price . . . as the court may deem just". But it was held that this was not intended to give the court a power to adjust the price: it was intended rather to deal with such matters as the time, place and manner of payment. The second was s.2–209, which deals with the modification of contracts; but this also did not help the sellers as it contemplated a modification by agreement (after bargaining in good faith), and not one imposed by the court. The facts of the *Iowa Electric* case were that a contract had been made in 1973 for the sale of 700,000 lbs. of uranium yellowcake to be delivered in the years 1975–78; the contract contained a price escalation clause and was varied in 1976 when the buyer agreed to an increase in the price and was given an option to buy a further 250,000 lbs. Between 1972 and 1977 the market price rose from $5.95 to $43 per pound; and the seller's costs exceeded the contract price by 50–58 per cent. The seller's plea of discharge was rejected because at least some of the factors leading to the price increase were foreseeable; because the increase in the seller's costs was in part due to the seller's own corporate decisions; because the seller had made other highly profitable contracts covering the period in question and had so spread the risk of market fluctuations (an argument which had also been used in the *Eastern*

---

[64] *i.e.* s.1–102(1) and (2), now s.1–103(a) (and see n.62 above). Again these provisions are not part of "this Article", *i.e.* Art.2.

[65] *cf.* above, paras 5–023 n.2, 6–003 n.8.

[66] The doctrine of "*Wegfall der Geschäftsgrundlage*" (disappearance of the commercial basis of the contract) was developed by the German courts, relying on the general good faith provision of BGB § 242. It attracted some academic criticism on the grounds that the almost boundless forms of available relief (termination, partial termination, adaptation, modification) gave rise to uncertainty and constituted an interference with private autonomy of a kind that could be justified only in times of extraordinary crises: see, *e.g.* Esser & Schmidt *Schuldrecht* (6th ed), p.341; Larenz, *Geschäftsgrundlage and Vertragserfül-lung*, pp.116–124; Emmerich, *Das Recht der Leistungsstörungen*, pp.277, 281. But these criticisms do not deny the existence of the doctrine, and as a result of amendments to the BGB it is now codified in § 313 under the heading "*Störung der Geschäftsgrundlage*" (disturbance of the commercial basis of the contract).

[67] 467 F. Supp. 128 (1978).

Airlines[68] case); and because cost increases of only 50–58 per cent were not enough to bring about discharge: again the court refers to the (somewhat imperfect[69]) analogy of the Suez cases.[70]

6–012   The reluctance of the American courts to uphold a seller's plea of impracticability alleged to result from price or cost increases is by no means confined to the energy crisis cases and may be illustrated by reference to two further cases having no apparent connection with that crisis. In the *Maple Farms* case,[71] a contract had been made for the supply of milk to a school for the school year 1973–74. The court rejected the seller's claim that he was discharged on the ground of impracticability by a 23 per cent increase in the price of raw milk. Two reasons were given: first, that the increase was "not totally unexpected"[72]; and secondly that, even if it was unexpected, the contract had allocated the risk to the seller, the "very purpose of the contract" being "to guard against fluctuation in the price of milk as a basis for the school budget".[73] Yet the court added (perhaps somewhat inconsistently with its second reason) that a point "could conceivably be reached" at which the increase would be "so disproportionate to the risk assumed as to amount to impracticability".[74] In the *Neal-Cooper* case,[75] the seller relied partly on shortage of supply and partly on extra cost (due to Canadian government restrictions on mining) to excuse his failure to perform in full a contract for the sale of potash. The defence failed as the difficulties facing the seller had arisen because of the seller's own decision to shift his mining operations to Canada. He could have performed by continuing to use US sources; and the mere fact that the contract had become "economically burdensome and unattractive"[76] was not a ground of discharge.

(b) *Discharge claimed by buyers because of increased cost of taking delivery*

6–013   It will be recalled that the unexpectedly high cost of taking delivery was the ground on which the buyer's defence succeeded in the *Mineral Park* case[77] in which the American doctrine of impracticability can be said to have originated. But in the more recent *Nora Springs* case[78] it was held that a buyer of corn was not excused from taking delivery by a shortage of boxcars making it, apparently, more expensive for him to take delivery. The buyer's argument here is substantially the same as that of the sellers in the cases considered in paras 6–009 to 6–012, above, *i.e.* that the extra cost of his own performance should discharge him. It was rejected on the same

---

[68] 415 F. Supp. 429 (1975); above, para.6–009.

[69] Above, para.6–009.

[70] Above, paras 4–071 to 4–083.

[71] *Maple Farms Inc v City School District of Elmira*, 352 N.Y.S. 2d 4784 (1974).

[72] *ibid.* at 789.

[73] *ibid.* at 790.

[74] *ibid.*

[75] *Neal-Cooper Grain Co v Texas Sulphur Co*, 508 F. 2d 208 (1974).

[76] *ibid.* at 293; *cf. 407 East 61st St. Garage Inc v Fifth Avenue Corp*, 244 N.E. 2d 37 at 41 (1968); *Schmidt v CP Builders Inc*, 320 N.Y.S. 2d 460 (1971).

[77] 156 P. 458 (1916); above, para.6–004.

[78] *Nora Springs Co-operative Co v Brandau*, 247 N.W. 2d 744 (1976).

ground, and indeed in the same words, as those used, in the *Neal-Cooper* case[79]: to establish impracticability, it was not enough to show that the contract had become "economically burdensome and unattractive"[80] to the buyer. Again, the court does not absolutely rule out the possibility of discharge by "impracticability" in cases of this kind: it says that the buyer "did not show any increased cost would be so prohibitive as to change the nature of its corn contract with the seller".[81] In other words, the buyer *might* be excused but only in an extreme case.

(c) *Discharge claimed by buyers because of falling values*

In this group of cases the buyer's case is not that the cost of his own **6–014** performance has gone up, but that the value to him of the seller's performance has gone down. The simplest case is that in which the buyer's only ground for claiming discharge is that the market value of the goods has fallen. Such a claim was rightly rejected in the *Hancock Paper* case,[82] where a buyer of coated paper (used to make milk cartons) claimed to be discharged by reason of a decline in the market price of the goods. The court, relying on Comment 4 to Uniform Commercial Code, s.2–615,[83] said that the decline in the market price was "exactly the sort of risk which a fixed-price contract was intended to cover".[84] Once again, however, the court did not absolutely rule out the possibility that a decline in the market price might, in an extreme case, be a ground for excuse; for it added that the decline here did "not reach the level of severity required to excuse performance"[85] under either the Restatement or the Uniform Commercial Code formulations. As has been suggested in para.6–007 above, it would require most exceptional circumstances to excuse a *buyer* on such grounds since his risk (unlike the seller's) is limited: he cannot lose more than the contract price.

Two further cases[86] arose from what may be called the "reverse energy crisis", *i.e.* from the decline in fuel prices after the energy crisis of 1973. In these cases long-term contracts for the supply of fuel had been made with buyers who later claimed that the use to which they had intended to put the goods was no longer profitable but would, on the contrary, result in a loss to them. The cases were not (as will be suggested later)[87] cases of frustration of purpose (thought that ground of discharge was argued): the

---

[79] Above, n.75.

[80] 247 N.W. 744 at 748 (1976).

[81] *ibid.*

[82] *Hancock Paper Co v Champion International Corp*, 424 F. Supp. 285 (1975).

[83] Presumably, in particular, on the phrase "collapse in the market"; it is not obvious why this should (as the context in Comment 4 seems to suggest) excuse *the seller*. Perhaps the point is that the collapse may prevent the seller from making the requisite supply contracts.

[84] 424 F. Supp. 285 at 290.

[85] *ibid.*

[86] *Northern Illinois Gas Co v Energy Co-operative Inc*, 461 N.E. 2d 1049 (1984); *Northern Indiana Public Service Co v Carbon County Coal Co*, 799 F. 2d 265 (1986); to be discussed below, paras 6–015, 6–016.

[87] Below, para.6–015.

buyers could still use the goods for the intended purpose, but to do so was unprofitable. The ground of discharge therefore had to be impracticability; but in each case the argument that the contract had been discharged on this ground was rejected.

6–015   In the *Northern Illinois*[88] case a contract had been made in 1973 to supply naphtha to the plaintiffs for 10 years or until 56 million barrels had been supplied. Naphtha was used in the production of natural gas; by 1979–80, the demand for natural gas was falling while the contract price of the naphtha was increasing under a flexible pricing clause in the contract. The buyers, having unsuccessfully applied to the State authorities for permission to increase their rates to consumers, now argued that the contract of sale was discharged. The court was prepared to assume that Uniform Commercial Code, s.2–615 could (by virtue of Comment 9[89]) apply so as to discharge a buyer; but it held that this contract was not discharged either on the ground of frustration of purpose or on that of impracticability. The buyers' purpose was not frustrated; they were not prevented from using the naphtha for the purpose of producing gas; they were prevented only from increasing their rates. Moreover, each of the alleged grounds of discharge failed because the circumstances relied on by the buyers were foreseeable, both on the particular facts of the case and on general grounds. The buyers knew, even before the conclusion of the contract, that the demand for natural gas was falling, but nevertheless entered into the long-term contracts in question; and, as a general proposition, fluctuations in the market prices of oil and gas, which might adversely affect either party, must be regarded as foreseeable. The court also relied on two special terms of the contract. The first was a "take or pay"[90] clause, well known in the industry, by which the buyers bound themselves to pay for specified quantities, whether they took delivery or not: this was said to negative any assumption that the buyers should have any continuing need for the seller's product. The second was a flexible pricing clause: this was said to have been intended to insulate the seller from market risks and shift them to the buyers (though it seems that, if the market had moved the other way, the clause might have had the opposite effect). The court also stressed that the buyers had not shown that they could have operated *only* at a loss if they continued to be bound by the contracts, or that failure to discharge them would lead to grave injustice. It followed that the buyers were liable under naphtha contracts, though their liability was limited by a liquidated damages clause in those contracts.

6–016   A similar "reverse energy crisis" situation arose in the *Northern Indiana*[91] case where a 20-year contract for the supply of coal by a mining company to an electricity company was made in 1978; the contract specified a fixed

---

[88] Above, n.86.
[89] See above, para.4–058.
[90] For a discussion of such clauses, see *International Minerals & Chemical Corp v Llano Inc*, 770 F. 2d 879 (1985), where a price reduction was allowed under another term of the contract.
[91] Above, n.86.

minimum price and contained a "price escalation" clause which had by 1985 driven the price of the coal up from its original base of $24 per ton to $44 per ton. By this time, it was cheaper for the buyers to buy electricity from other producers than to produce it from the coal supplied by the sellers; and in 1983 the buyers had indeed been ordered by an "economy purchase order" issued by the Public Service Commission to take this course and not to increase their charges to customers to recover the higher cost of themselves generating electricity from the coal which was the subject-matter of the contract. The buyers claimed discharge, or at least suspension, of the contract on various grounds. Reliance on a *force majeure* clause failed since this applied only if the buyers were "prevented" from making use of the coal and there was no such prevention by the economy purchase order: again the point was made that this did not prevent the buyers from using the coal but only from passing on the cost of so doing by increasing their charges. The argument of discharge by impracticability was also rejected. The court left open the question whether Uniform Commercial Code, s.2–615 could apply in Indiana so as to discharge buyers (Indiana not having adopted Comment 9)[92] but it recognised the possibility that a buyer (no less than a seller) might be discharged by an analogous common law doctrine of impracticability. This doctrine, however, could not apply where the contract had explicitly allocated the risk of the change of circumstances alleged to constitute the ground of discharge; and the effect of the long-term contract, (specifying a minimum fixed price) which had been made in this case, was to allocate this risk to the buyers. In this context, an argument used in rebutting the defence based on the *force majeure* clause is significant: the contract fixed a minimum price and provided for increases in that price, but not for any reductions in it. A further argument against allowing the buyers to rely on the defence was based on the relative bargaining strength of buyer and seller. Where a "small" seller (*e.g.* a farmer) sells to a "large" buyer (*e.g.* a grain elevator company), the court should be more inclined to make the impracticability defence available to the seller than to make it available to the buyer, since the large buyer is more likely to be able to "buffer"[93] (or spread) the risk of price fluctuations. In the *Northern Indiana* case, the sale was indeed by a "small" seller to a "large" buyer, but the impracticability defence was being invoked by the party less likely to be able to rely on it, *i.e.* by the "large" buyer. In comparing English and American rules on this subject, it is interesting to note that the remedy against the buyers was limited to damages: specific performance was refused[94] since damages were an adequate remedy and specific performance would be economically wasteful (leading to the production of coal at a cost exceeding its market value). The court rejected the argument that specific performance should be ordered so as to promote the continued production of the coal

---

[92] See above, para.4–058.
[93] 799 F. 2d 265 at 278 (1986).
[94] *cf.* below, para.6–042 for refusal of specific performance on account of changes in circumstances which do *not* discharge the contract at law.

and so to preserve a mining community, saying that the miners were neither parties to the proceedings nor third-party beneficiaries of the contract.

(d) Contracts for the supply of services

6–017   This group of cases concerns contracts for services in which the party who is to supply them argues that he should be discharged because the cost to him of rendering them has been greatly increased by supervening events. In the American Suez cases (which all concerned voyage charters)[95] such extra cost was combined with the factor of impossibility in a contemplated or stipulated method of performance. In spite of this additional factor, the plea of discharge was uniformly rejected in these cases; but it should be stressed that in them the extra cost of the voyage via the Cape, though considerable, was not immense. In the *Transatlantic Financing* case[96] the extra cost was $44,000, as against the agreed freight of $306,000; in the *American Trading* case[97] the claim was for an extra payment of $132,000, as against $417,000 due under the contract. These are low percentages (14.4 and 31.6) when compared with those in the *Mineral Park* case[98] (about 1,000 per cent), and even when compared with the energy crisis cases, if one assumes a four-fold increase in the price of crude oil. The American Suez cases leave open the possibility that a contract may be discharged if the stipulated or contemplated method becomes impossible and either no other method is available or, though another method is available, it involves the contractor in an increase of expense "so excessive as to justify the application of the impossibility doctrine".[99] This was the position in the *Florida Power*[1] case where the contemplated method of performance would have yielded to the contractor a profit of $18–20 million and the alternative method, had it been possible, would have resulted in a loss of $80 million (a difference of 400 to 500 per cent). Such a difference can be said to give rise to a sufficiently serious or fundamental change to discharge the contract, even in English law.[2] In such a case, however, discharge would again result, not from "pure" impracticability,[3] but from impracticability combined with other factors, such as impossibility or illegality in the stipulated or contemplated method of performance.

Another situation in which discharge may be claimed of a contract containing a service element is that in which a manufacturer contracts to develop and deliver a new product and then finds that his development

---

[95]   Above, paras 4–078 to 4–080.
[96]   *Transatlantic Finance Corp v US*, 363 F. 2d 312 (1966).
[97]   *American Trading & Production Corp v Shell International Marine*, 453 F. 2d 939 (1972); [1972] 1 Lloyd's Rep. 463.
[98]   156 P. 458 (1916), above, para.6–004.
[99]   *Florida Power & Light Co v Westinghouse Electric Corp*, 826 F. 2d 239 at 277 (1987).
[1]   Above, n.99; above, para.4–056.
[2]   *cf.* the example given in above, para.4–080 of the effect of the closing of the Suez Canal on a contract to carry bananas from Port Sudan to Port Said.
[3]   *cf.* above, para.4–083 and below, paras 6–030 to 6–034.

expenditure turns out to be unexpectedly large, so that the contract will result in a loss to him. But there are at least two reasons why such a claim is likely to be rejected. The first is that the case is one of antecedent difficulty to which, as has already been suggested,[4] more stringent tests should be applied than those which are appropriate in cases of supervening impossibility. The second is that a manufacturer who makes a fixed-price contract for a new product, the cost of which is essentially speculative, would normally be considered to have taken the risk that development costs will turn out to be larger than expected.[5] Conversely, it seems that a claim for discharge would for similar reasons be rejected where the cost increase prejudiced the party to whom the services were to be rendered or to whom the new product was to be supplied, *e.g.* where a new product to be developed by the manufacturer was to be paid for on a cost-plus basis. The position was similar in one of the English Suez cases[6] concerning a "time charter trip", *i.e.* one under which the voyage was to be paid for by reference (*inter alia*) to the time taken to accomplish it. Here it was the charterer (not, as in the voyage charter cases, the shipowner) who raised the plea of discharge, but without success. Again it must be pointed out that the percentage by which the cost of a voyage via the Cape would have exceeded that of a voyage via Suez was relatively modest: the length of the voyage would have been increased from 108 to 138 days, *i.e.* by no more than 27.8 per cent.

The most controversial in the present group of cases involving contracts for services is *Aluminum Corp of America v Essex Group Inc*[7] (the *ALCOA* case). The contract in that case was made in 1967 and was to run for 16 (or at the option of Essex for 21) years. It provided that Essex was to deliver alumina to ALCOA which was to smelt them (*i.e.* turn them into aluminium) for a charge fixed initially at 15¢ per pound. The parties realised that in the course of such a long-term contract ALCOA's costs might vary from time to time; and the contract accordingly contained a flexible pricing formula, allowing ALCOA to increase its prices to take account of increases in respect of certain elements in its costs. Unfortunately for ALCOA, that formula did not make adequate allowance for the steep increase in the price of electricity resulting from the 1973 energy crisis; and electricity was major element in the cost of smelting. The result of that increase was that ALCOA (which had made a profit of $9 million from the contract before the increase in the cost of electricity) stood to lose some $60 million if the contract ran its full course: at least, that was the argument presented at the time of the trial, before the subsequent fall in oil prices. It was held that ALCOA was entitled to relief on the ground of (*inter alia*) impracticability; and this relief took the form of substituting a different flexible pricing formula for that agreed by the

6–018

---

[4] Above, para.1–007.
[5] See *US v Wegematic Corp*, 360 F. 2d 674 (1966).
[6] *Ocean Tramp Tankers v V/O Soufracht (The Eugenia)* [1964] 2 Q.B. 226; above, para.4–081.
[7] 499 F. Supp. 53 (1980).

parties. Under the formula imposed by the court, ALCOA still stood to make some losses under the contract, but the court's intervention was intended to reduce these losses to manageable proportions. Such a result appears to be very much open to question.[8] When parties enter into such long-term contracts and provide in them for flexible pricing within specified limits, they seem thereby to have allocated the risk of cost or price fluctuations which fall outside those limits. That seems to be the reasoning of the later *Northern Illinois*[9] and *Northern Indiana*[10] cases and (although the *ALCOA* case is not cited in either of these cases) their reasoning seems to be preferable to that of the *ALCOA* case. The result reached in that case is objectionable not only on the ground that it interferes with the parties own allocation of risks, but also on the ground that it leads to uncertainty.[11] It is, moreover, one-sided: there is no suggestion that Essex could have claimed relief, had the contract turned out to be highly profitable for ALCOA (though in this connection it is necessary to repeat the point that Essex's potential loss could not exceed the contract price, while ALCOA's was theoretically without limit). There is, finally, the point that the subsequent *fall* in energy prices seems to undermine ALCOA's case (*i.e.* the argument that ALCOA would necessarily have suffered a large loss if the contract had been allowed to run its full course). The pricing formula imposed by the court does, indeed, take this possibility into account; but it ignores the fundamental point that it is undesirable for a court to grant relief from long-term contracts on the basis of assumptions about future market movements, especially when these assumptions turn out to be wrong. The decision in the *ALCOA* case might derive some indirect support from Uniform Commercial Code, s.2–615, Comment 6,[12] though curiously the opinion does not refer to this Comment; but a similar argument failed in the *Iowa Electric* case[13]; and in any event the *ALCOA* case was not a case of sale of goods so that neither s.2–615, nor any of the Comments to that section, was directly applicable to the case.

---

[8] See, *e.g.* Dawson, 64 B.U. Law Rev. 1, 26 (1984); White & Summers, *Uniform Commercial Code* (4th ed.), Vol.I, pp.173–174; in support of the decision, on the other hand, see *e.g.* Speidel, 76 N.W.U.L.R. 396. For a German case in which similar relief was given (but in which the contract contained *no* flexible pricing clause) see RGZ 100, 130 (1920).

[9] Above para.6–015.

[10] Above, para.6–016. There is also no reference to the *ALCOA* case in the *Florida Power* case, above, n.1, even though in the latter case the court mentions the doctrine of discharge by impracticability with evident approval (*e.g.* at 254, 262). The *Florida Power* case was, as noted in para.6–017 above, not one of "pure" impracticability.

[11] *cf.* the criticism referred to in above, para.6–011, n.66, of the German remedy of modifying or adapting the contract to changed circumstances.

[12] Above, para.6–011.

[13] *Iowa Electric Light & Power Co v Atlas Corp*, 467 F. Supp. 128 (1978), above, para.6–011.

(e) *Conclusion*

In the foregoing discussion of the American cases on the effect of   6–019
impracticability due to market movements, it is possible to identify a
number of recurring themes:

(1)   The possibility that such circumstances may afford a ground of
      discharge is regarded as one which is in principle arguable, though
      the argument rarely[14] succeeds.

(2)   One reason why the argument often fails is that the extent of the
      market fluctuation in question is regarded as foreseeable.[15]

(3)   Another common reason for rejecting the argument of discharge
      is that the extent of the market fluctuation is often said to be
      insufficient to bring about a fundamental change of circumstances.

(4)   The party claiming discharge often fails to demonstrate the effect of
      the market fluctuation on the contract in question, *e.g.* he fails to
      show that an increase in the price of a particular raw material will be
      directly translated into a loss resulting from the performance of the
      contract.

(5)   The party claiming discharge may make a profit out of the market
      movement as a whole; if so, his claim to be discharged from the
      particular contract in question (even if it has become unprofitable)
      is considered to have little merit.

(6)   Where the contract contains a price-escalation clause, the court has
      been inclined to rely on it to exclude discharge. The argument is
      that such a clause is evidence of the parties' intentions to allocate
      risks, so that any fluctuations in costs or values which the clause does
      not take into account is at the risk of the party on whom it may fall.
      On the other hand, the courts have also relied on the *absence* of a
      flexible pricing clause as evidence of intention to allocate the risk of
      supervening events.

(7)   The essentially speculative nature of a long-term contract is regarded
      in the United States (as in England[16]) as an argument against
      discharge by reason of changing market conditions.

---

[14] It was influential in the *Florida Power* case, 826 F. 2d 239 (1987) above, paras
4–061, 6–017), but even there impracticability was combined with other factors
and so not the sole ground of decision.

[15] The statements to this effect in some of the "impracticability" cases discussed
are not inconsistent with the view, often expressed in the United States, that
foreseeability, or even foresight, is not decisive: see Restatement 2d, § 265,
Comment a; and see further below, paras 13–010 to 13–015. They can be
regarded as applications of the test, formulated in *Mishara Const Co v Transit-
Mixed Concrete Corp*, 310 N.E. 2d 363 at 367 (1974): was the contingency "one
which the parties could reasonably have foreseen *as a real possibility*" (emphasis
added).

[16] *Larrinaga v Société Franco-Américaine des Phosphates de Medulla* (1923) 92 L.J.K.B.
455, below, para.12–003.

(8)   In some of the American "impracticability" cases which have been considered in the foregoing discussion, reference is made to the Suez cases, and in some of those cases the question is indeed formulated in the terms whether closure of the Canal "rendered performance commercially impracticable".[17] As already suggested above,[18] however, the Suez cases are not cases of "pure" impracticability: they are cases in which increased cost is combined with impossibility in a contemplated (or sometimes in a stipulated) method of performance. They therefore present a stronger case for discharge than that presented by impracticability (in the sense of increased cost) alone. The fact that the contracts were, nevertheless, upheld without modification in all these cases is therefore a strong indication of the restrictive attitude of the American courts towards impracticability as a ground of discharge.

(9)   The case for giving relief to a seller of goods or services on the ground of increases in the market price or other costs is generally stronger than the case for giving relief to the buyer on the ground of a fall in the market price of what he has contracted to buy. The justification for this further restriction on the scope of the doctrine of impracticability is that increases in market prices or costs can expose a seller to a theoretically unlimited loss, while the loss which falls in market price may cause to the buyer cannot exceed the contract price. The only type of case in which the loss which the buyer may suffer is also theoretically without limit is that in which he has to bear the costs of taking delivery, and those costs rise. It is, perhaps, no coincidence that the *Mineral Park*[19] case (in which the American doctrine of impracticability can be said to have originated) was a case of this kind.

III. IMPRACTICABILITY IN ENGLISH LAW

(1) Introduction

6-020   The foregoing discussion shows that "impracticability" (as opposed to "impossibility") is recognised as a ground of discharge in the United States. At the same time, the American courts have become distinctly reluctant to regard increased cost or difficulty of performance as in themselves sufficient for this purpose. The question now to be considered is whether English law recognises the doctrine of discharge by impracticability even to this limited extent.

It is appropriate to begin this discussion with a curious point. In Comment 4 to s.2–615 of the Uniform Commercial Code, the principle of

---

[17]   *e.g. Transatlantic Finance Corp v US*, 363 F. 2d 312 at 315 (1963).
[18]   Above, paras 4–083, 6–009.
[19]   156 P. 458 (1918), above, para.6–004.

discharge by impracticability[20] is not supported (as one might expect) by the citation of any American authorities, such as the *Mineral Park* case.[21] Instead, the only authority cited in support of it is the English case of *Ford & Sons (Oldham) Ltd v Henry Leetham & Sons Ltd.*[22] This may give rise to the impression that the principle is derived from English law[23]; but that impression would be totally misleading since *Ford & Sons (Oldham) Ltd v Henry Leetham & Sons Ltd* was not an authority on the common law doctrine of discharge, whether by impossibility or impracticability, at all. The case arose out of a contract for the sale of wheat which contained an express provision excusing the seller if shipment of wheat to this country was prevented by prohibition of export imposed by the country of origin, or by hostilities or by certain other specified causes. It was held that the seller could rely on this clause when, in consequence of the outbreak of the First World War, the export of wheat was prohibited by some (but not by all) of the countries from which wheat had usually been exported to England, with a consequent "material"[24] increase in the price of wheat. In reaching this conclusion, the court was concerned, not with any question of discharge under the general law, but only with the construction of the express contractual provision on which the seller relied.[25]

Such express provisions for supervening events often excuse one or both parties in circumstances falling short of those which would bring the common law doctrine of discharge into operation: indeed this is one of their chief commercial purposes. If they did not have this effect, they would simply provide excuses where the common law already produced the same result (though they might provide for a more satisfactory regulation[26] of the exact legal consequences of the supervening event). It follows that "impracticability" which can bring such an express provision into effect[27] would not, merely for that reason, suffice to discharge a party

---

[20] The word "impracticable" does not actually occur in Comment 4, but it does occur in s.2–615(a) and in the statement of principle in Comment 1; and Comment 4 is clearly intended as an explanation of this principle.

[21] 156 P. 458 (1916); above, para.6–004. Perhaps the reason why this case is not cited in the Comments to s.2–615 is that the case concerned an excuse for the *buyer*, while s.2–615 is mainly concerned with circumstances excusing the *seller*. But according to Comment 9 a buyer can also rely on the principle of s.2–615.

[22] (1915) 21 Com.Cas. 55.

[23] *cf.* also the Canadian case of *Petrogas Processing Ltd v Westcoast Transmission Co Ltd* [1988] 4 W.W.R. 699, where one ground for the decision at first instance was discharge on grounds analogous to the American doctrine of impracticability but the court relied, not on any of the American impracticability cases, but on English authorities. On appeal the decision was affirmed on other grounds: [1989] 4 W.W.R. 272.

[24] (1915) 21 Com.Cas. 55 at 60.

[25] Below, para.12–023.

[26] See below, paras 15–007 to 15–008 for criticism of the English rule of total automatic discharge by frustration.

[27] See, *e.g.* the charterparty in *Ellis Shipping Corp v Voest Alpine Intertrading (The Lefthero)* [1992] 2 Lloyd's Rep. 109, entitling the shipowner to cancel if a rise in insurance rates made continued performance "economically unfeasible".

under the common law doctrine; and it will be argued in paras 6–022 to 6–028 below that it generally does not have this effect in English law.

(2) Impracticability not generally a ground of discharge

6–021   Statements to the effect that a contract may be discharged if its performance has become "impracticable" are occasionally found in English cases: for example, in *Horlock v Beal*, Lord Loreburn said "the performance of this contract became impossible, which means impracticable in a commercial sense".[28] To the same effect are statements concerning the scope of the dictum in *Moss v Smith*[29] (quoted in para. 6–005, above) on the subject of impracticability. It has been said that this dictum was "applicable generally to mercantile contracts"[30]; and one can infer from this that it is not considered to be restricted to cases of constructive total loss. The point is significant in view of the fact that the American *Mineral Park* case, and hence the American doctrine of discharge by impracticability, is indirectly based on the dictum in *Moss v Smith*.[31] One can also point to judicial statements which formulate excuses for non-performance in terms of "commercial impossibility"[32] or of what is "commercially impracticable"[33] or which tentatively leave open the possibility that "serious impediments"[34] may be a ground of discharge; though it must be emphasised that these statements are all concerned with the operation of express contractual provisions and not with the common law doctrine of discharge. It has also been said that, where a contract provides for alternative methods of performance, it may be discharged if one becomes impossible and the other will involve "prohibitive"[35] cost. Moreover, courts do not always distinguish sharply between impracticability and impossibility. Thus in one of the cases of discharge resulting from unavailability of a ship to perform services under a charterparty, the further performance of the contract was described in consecutive pages of

---

[28] [1916] 1 A.C. 486 at 492; *cf. Nile Co for the Export of Agricultural Crops v H & JM Bennett (Commodities) Ltd* [1986] 1 Lloyd's Rep. 555 at 581.

[29] (1859) 9 C.B. 94 at 103; above, para.6–005.

[30] *Horlock v Beal* [1916] 1 A.C. 486 at 499; *cf. Robert H. Dahl v Nelson Donkin* (1881) 6 App. Cas. 38 at 52.

[31] Above, paras 6–004 to 6–005.

[32] *e.g. Blane Steamships v Minister of Transport* [1951] 2 K.B. 9654 at 989; *Seabridge Shipping Ltd v Antco Shipping Ltd (The Furness Bridge)* [1977] 2 Lloyd's Rep. 367 at 377; *Terkol Rederierne v Petroleo Brasileiro SA (The Badagry)* [1985] 1 Lloyd's Rep. 395 at 399.

[33] *Naylor Benzon & Co Ltd v Hirsch* (1917) 33 T.L.R. 432 at 433, where the phrase was used in relation to the scope of an express provision in the contract for obstacles to performance: *cf.* below, paras 6–035 to 6–036; *Owners of Steamship Matheos v Louis Dreyfus & Co* [1925] A.C. 654 at 660; but see below, para.6–036 for the context in which this phrase was used (at n.20).

[34] *Jackson v Eastbourne Local Board* (1885) 2 *Hudson on Building Contracts* (4th ed.), 81 at 94, H.L.

[35] *Edward Grey & Co v Tolme & Runge* (1915) 31 T.L.R. 551 at 553.

the same judgment as "quite impracticable in a commercial sense"[36] and as "impossible".[37]

Some further support for the same view is provided by the Report, made in 1918, of a Committee appointed by the Board of Trade "to consider the position of British Manufacturers and Merchants in respect of Pre-War Contracts".[38] After stating the common law doctrine of discharge by supervening impossibility, the Report says that "Impossibility for this purpose means commercial impossibility".[39] But it proceeds to qualify this position in a way that seems to anticipate some of the American statements quoted in para.6–003, above: "Mere increase in cost of performance, unless to an enormous and extravagant extent, does not make it impossible. A man is not prevented from performing by economic unprofitableness, unless the pecuniary burden is so great as to amount to physical prevention."[40] It seems to have been the apparent harshness of this position which led to the appointment of the Committee, but the Report did not recommend any further legislation going beyond a number of war-time measures of restricted scope.

In England, support for the view that "impracticability" or "commercial impossibility" can, of themselves, be grounds of discharge is, however, confined to dicta and to extra-judicial statements.[41] The English cases do not provide a single clear illustration of discharge on such grounds alone[42]; and the possibility of such discharge appears to have been denied on a number of occasions in the House of Lords. Thus in *Tenants (Lancashire) Ltd v CS Wilson & Co Ltd*, Lord Loreburn seems to have had second thoughts,[43] for he said that "the argument that a man can be excused from performance of his contract when it becomes 'commercially' impossible ... seems to me a dangerous contention which ought not to be admitted unless the parties have plainly contracted to that effect",[44] *i.e.* by an express provision for excuse in that event. Similar hostility to "impracticability" or mere "commercial impossibility" as a ground of discharge is expressed in a number of other cases in which difficulties or extra expense resulting from the First World War were relied on as

6–022

---

[36] *Scottish Navigation Co Ltd v Souter & Co* [1917] 1 K.B. 222 at 236.

[37] *ibid.* at 237; *cf. Blane Steamships v Minister of Transport* [1951] 2 K.B. 965 at 989 ("commercially impossible") with *ibid.* at 996 ("impossible").

[38] Cd. 8975 (1918). Lord Buckmaster and Mr F.D. MacKinnon (later Mackinnon L.J.) were members of the Committee.

[39] para.10.

[40] *ibid.*; *cf.* above, para.6–003 for the similar American restrictions on the scope of discharge by impracticability.

[41] Above, n.39; Beatson in (ed. Rose), "Consensus ad Idem", essays in *Law of Contract in Honour of Guenter Treitel*, p.123.

[42] *i.e.* on grounds of "pure" impracticability: see above, para.4–083, below, paras 6–030 to 6–034.

[43] *cf.* above, n.28.

[44] [1917] A.C. 495 at 510; *cf. Shearson Lehman Hutton Inc v Maclaine Watson & Co Ltd* [1989] 2 Lloyd's Rep. 570 at 608 (holding that a commodity contract had not been frustrated by the closing of the relevant market).

grounds of discharge. Thus in *Blackburn Bobbin Co Ltd v TW Allen & Co*,[45] the contract was not discharged even though the circumstances described earlier in this book had made it "practically impossible for the vendor to deliver",[46] and McCardie J. expressed the view that it could not be "said that grave difficulty on the part of the vendor in procuring the contract articles will excuse him from the performance of his bargain".[47] Increases in the price of the goods to be supplied[48] or in the price of the seller's raw materials[49] or in other costs of the seller[50] have likewise been held not to be a ground of discharge. And in a case in which the increases in the costs of services to be supplied by one party were described as "devastating", no attempt was made even to argue that the contract had been discharged.[51] In another case a chartered ship had been so severely damaged that it was "not commercially viable"[52] to repair her; and again no attempt was made to rely on these circumstances as a ground of frustration.

6–023   Similar hostility to the principle of discharge by impracticability is expressed in the *British Movietonenews*[53] case, which arose out of a contract which had been made during the Second World War for the supply of newsreels to cinemas. After the end of the war, the cinema owners argued that the contract had been discharged by the fact that the war was over and by the following further changes in the surrounding circumstances: it was no longer necessary in the national interest to save film; there were no longer patriotic grounds for showing any particular newsreels; and newsreels were no longer uniform, as they had been during the war. In the Court of Appeal, it had been held that this "uncontemplated turn of events"[54] had discharged the contract; but this reasoning was disapproved, and the decision was reversed, by the House of Lords. Lord Simon said: "The parties to an executory contract are often faced, in the course of carrying it out, with a turn of events which they did not at all anticipate—a wholly abnormal rise or fall in prices, a sudden depreciation of currency, an unexpected obstacle to execution or the like. Yet this does not of itself affect the bargain they have made."[55] Almost certainly, the actual facts of the *British Movietonenews* case would not be held to fall within even the American doctrine of discharge discussed in Part II of this

---

[45] [1918] 1 K.B. 540; affirmed [1918] 2 K.B. 467.

[46] [1918] 1 K.B. 540 at 551; above, para.4–053.

[47] [1918] 1 K.B. at 545.

[48] *S Instone & Co Ltd v Speeding Marshall & Co Ltd* (1916) 33 T.L.R. 202 (88 per cent increase).

[49] *E Hutton & Co Ltd v Chadwick Taylor & Co Ltd* (1918) 34 T.L.R. 230.

[50] *Blythe & Co v Richards, Turpin & Co* (1916) 85 L.J.K.B. 1425 (increase in seller's freight charges making c.i.f. contract unprofitable for seller).

[51] *Finland Steamship Co Ltd v Felixstowe Dock & Ry Co* [1980] 2 Lloyd's Rep. 287; the parties there had agreed that extra payments were to be made, and the only issue before the court was as to the scope of that agreement.

[52] *Hanjin Shipping Co Ltd v Zenith Chartering Corp (The Mercedes Envoy)* [1995] 2 Lloyd's Rep. 559 at 563.

[53] *British Movietonenews Ltd v London District Cinemas* [1952] A.C. 166.

[54] [1951] 1 K.B. 190 at 201.

[55] [1952] A.C. 166 at 185.

chapter, but the passage quoted suggests a rejection of the very principle of "impracticability" as an independent ground of discharge. We have seen that Restatement 2d suggests that a price increase *"well beyond the normal range"*[56] may lead to discharge. Yet this is the very situation in which Lord Simon would deny that the contract would be discharged: "a *wholly abnormal* rise or fall in prices" would not "affect the bargain [the parties] have made." Statements in later cases to the same effect include one by Lord Radcliffe that "it is not hardship or inconvenience or material loss itself which calls the principle of frustration into play"[57]; and one by Lord Simonds which asserts, without qualification, that "an increase of expense is not a ground of frustration".[58] The widely held judicial view which such statements support is, no doubt, based on the desire to avoid the uncertainty to which a doctrine of discharge by mere impracticability can give rise, or (to put the same point in another way) to the tendency of such a doctrine to undermine the sanctity of contract. English law has tended to place greater emphasis than American law on the related requirements of certainty and of the sanctity of contract, even though the result of doing so might occasionally appear to be harsh to one of the parties. It seems that the mitigation of such hardship should, in the view of the English courts, be achieved, not by a broad doctrine of discharge, uncertain in its operation,[59] but by express contractual provisions, or, in times of general economic dislocation (*e.g.* by war) through special legislative intervention.[60]

The contrast between English and American law can further be   **6–024** illustrated by reference to the energy crisis cases. In the United States, it was clearly regarded as arguable that the crisis might discharge a party[61]; in one case it was assumed or conceded that it has this effect[62]; in another case relief (though not amounting to discharge) was granted to the party prejudiced by the increase in energy costs[63]; while dicta in cases arising out of other events recognise the possibility of discharge through sharp market

---

[56] § 261, Comment d; above, para.6–003.

[57] *Davis Contractors Ltd v Fareham UDC* [1956] A.C. 696 at 729; below, para.6–025.

[58] *Tsakiroglou & Co Ltd v Noblee Thorl* [1962] A.C. 93 at 115; above, paras 4–073 to 4–074.

[59] The German doctrines of commercial impossibility and disappearance of the commercial basis of the contract (*Wegfall der Geschäftsgrundlage*) have been criticised precisely on the ground of the uncertainty of their operation. But these criticisms have not prevailed, the latter doctrine having been given statutory force by one of the new provisions of the BGB (§ 313) which came into force in 2002: *cf.* above, para.6–011, n.66.

[60] *e.g.* Courts (Emergency Powers) Act 1917, s.1; Courts (Emergency Powers) Act 1943; Liabilities (War Time Adjustments) Acts 1941–1944.

[61] *Gay v Seafarer Fiberglass Yachts*, 14 U.C.C. Rep. Serv. 1335 (1974); above, para. 6–008.

[62] *Mansfield Propane Gas Co v Folger Gas Co*, 204 S.E. 2d 625 (1974); above, para. 6–008.

[63] *Aluminum Co of America v Essex Group Inc*, 499 F. Supp. 53 (1980); above, para. 6–018.

fluctuations, though denying it on the facts of the particular cases,[64] or granting it on, at least partly, other grounds.[65] In England, by contrast, there is only a single contract case arising out of the energy crisis which has found its way into the law reports. That case is *Sky Petroleum Ltd v VIP Petroleum Ltd,*[66] where an oil company cut off deliveries of petrol, which it had contracted to make to a filling station, on the ground, not of increased costs, but of alleged shortage of supply. The only question raised by the case was whether the filling station's remedy was in damages or by the way of specific relief; and because no substitute was readily available to the filling station, specific relief was ordered. In the present context, the interesting point is that counsel for the oil company did not even attempt to argue that the contract had been discharged by the energy crisis. By contrast in the American case of *Eastern Airlines Inc v Gulf Oil Corp*[67] such an argument was put forward by counsel, though it was rejected by the court. The two cases are distinguishable in that price does not seem to have been an issue in the *Sky Petroleum* case (presumably because the contract provided for flexible pricing in a way that adequately protected the seller); but it is noteworthy that not a single reported English decision raises the issue whether the increase in a supplier's costs which resulted from the energy crisis of itself provided a ground for discharge. One can think of various economic factors which may account for this state of affairs, *e.g.* that by 1973 England had had recent experience of more severe inflation than the United States; and that the coal, gas and electricity suppliers were public utilities owned by the state (though the oil industry for the most part was not); but, even so, the difference in approach between the two systems is a striking one. In the United States, the argument of discharge by "impracticability" may only rarely have succeeded in the energy crisis (and "reverse" energy crisis) cases, but it is one that cannot be dismissed out of hand. In England the total absence of authority on the point suggests that the argument has not been regarded even as a plausible one.[68]

6–025   While the energy crisis cases indicate a difference in the general approach to impracticability adopted by the two systems, the negative proposition that impracticability (in the American sense) is not a ground of discharge in English law, cannot strictly be proved; it can only be made more probable by reference to examples in which such a defence has been recognised in the United States but rejected in England. Examples of this kind turn out, however, to be somewhat elusive. A convenient starting

---

[64] See above, paras 6–012, 6–013, 6–014.

[65] *Florida Power & Light Corp v Westinghouse Electric Corp,* 826 F. 2d 239 (1987); above paras 4–061, 6–017, below, paras 6–033, 6–034.

[66] [1974] 1 W.L.R. 576; *Tower Hamlets LBC v British Gas, The Times,* March 23, 1982 (affirmed, without reference to the present point, *The Times,* December 14, 1983) may be an energy crisis case, but this is not clear from the sketchy report. For this case see below, para.6–038.

[67] 415 F. Supp. 429 (1975); above, para.6–009.

[68] *cf.* also above, at n.51 for a similar failure to rely on a "devastating" increase in cost as a ground of discharge.

point for this discussion is the decision of the House of Lords in *Davis Contractors Ltd v Fareham UDC*,[69] a case which can be regarded as an illustration of the English attitude towards impracticability. The contract in that case was one to build 78 houses for a price of £94,000. The houses were to be built in eight months, but because of labour shortages the work took 22 months, and the costs incurred by the builders in doing it rose to £115,000 (though the costs "unavoidably incurred" by reason of the delay were said to amount to no more than £17,651).[70] The builders' argument that these events had discharged the contract was rejected on the ground that the events which had caused the delay, and the increase in costs, were within the ordinary range of commercial probability. The case may be indicative of the English attitude towards "impracticability" but the outcome does not reveal any actual difference between the English and the American approaches; for in an almost contemporaneous similar American case[71] the court reached the same result and did so for similar reasons. Moreover, the percentage by which costs had increased in the *Davis Contractors* case was relatively low: it amounted to less than 23 per cent of the contract price and such an increase would not have come even close to bringing the American doctrine of discharge by impracticability into play. A similar point can be made about the Suez cases[72] which, as already noted,[73] were not cases of "pure" impracticability. In these cases, both English and American courts regarded the point that the closure of the Canal (and the consequent increase in cost to one party) had discharged the contract as an arguable one, but both consistently rejected it. Again it should be emphasised that in each of those cases the amount by which the costs of the party prejudiced by the closure of the Canal rose in consequence of that event (or the extra remuneration claimed by that party), was relatively low when expressed as a fraction of the contract price, hardly ever exceeding one-third of that price.[74]

It is less easy to answer the question how an English court would   6–026
approach a problem such as that which arose in the American *Mineral Park*

---

[69] [1956] A.C. 696; *cf. Chaucer Estates v Fairclough Homes* [1991] E.G.C.S. 65.

[70] [1956] A.C. 696 at 701.

[71] *Peerless Cas Co v Weymouth Gardens Inc*, 215 F. 2d 362 (1954).

[72] Above, paras 4–071 to 4–083.

[73] Above, paras 4–083, 6–009.

[74] For the percentage increases in some of the Suez cases, see above, para.6–017; in the *Tsakiroglou* case [1962] A.C. 93 the seller's costs increased by no more than 15 per cent of the contract price; in *The Captain George K* [1970] 2 Lloyd's Rep. 21 (above, para.4–079) the report does state the amount of additional freight claimed and the contractual rate of freight per ton, but not the amount of the cargo, so that it is impossible to tell what percentage increase was claimed; but the facts closely resemble the *American Trading* case 453 F. 2d 939 (1972) (above, para.4–079) where the increase amounted to 31.6 per cent. It is perhaps significant that the highest percentage increase revealed by the cases was that of 45 per cent in *The Massalia* [1961] 2 Q.B. 278 (above, para.4–078) and that the contract there was held to have been frustrated; but that case was overruled in *The Eugenia* [1964] 2 Q.B. 236.

case.[75] Probably the English approach would be to emphasise that the obstacle to performance existed at the time of contracting and that the party prejudiced by it was not excused by it as he could have discovered it before entering into the contract and accordingly have taken it into account in the terms of the contract.[76] That was certainly the view taken in *M'Donald v Corporation of Worthington*[77] where a building contractor claimed to be discharged from a contract to build a sewer for a local authority on the ground that performance was "impracticable (by reason of water in the soil)"[78] or that it was "impossible to carry out the work as mentioned in the specification" because of "moist ground".[79] The plea of discharge was rejected on the ground that the contractor should have investigated the site: "to see if he can do the work upon the terms mentioned in the specification. He takes the risk."[80] The same result was reached in the New Zealand case[81] where, again, groundwater presented an obstacle to the installation of a sewage plant. The case was discussed as one of alleged "frustration",[82] but the decision can be explained on the ground, not only that the obstacle was not sufficiently serious, but also that it was already in existence at the time of contracting. These cases can certainly be said to take an approach to antecedent impracticability different from that taken in the *Mineral Park* case. But we have seen that even in the United States *Watkins v Carrig*[83] takes a stricter view of such impracticability, so that once again the difference between the English and American positions is by no means clear-cut.

6–027   Nor do the cases considered in para.6–026, above touch on the question how an English court would deal with a problem similar to that which arose in the *Mineral Park* case if the obstacle to performance were indeed not an antecedent but a supervening one. Such a problem would, for example, arise if a contract were made to extract a specified quantity of coal from a mine, and if afterwards the mine were flooded, or an earthquake so altered the nature of the strata, that the coal could be extracted only at a prohibitive cost. It is unlikely that English law would regard the increase in cost as being, of itself, a ground of discharge; but might it take the view that the contract was discharged on the ground that the physical operations to be performed after the flood or earthquake were fundamentally different from those which were within the contemplation of the parties when the contract was made? Moreover might a similar argument be applied where events of this kind interfered with the performance of a building contract? No confident answers can be given to these questions. Certainly, they are not conclusively determined

---

[75] 156 P. 458 (1916); above, para.6–004.
[76] *cf.* above, paras 1–007, 6–004.
[77] (1892) 9 T.L.R. 21 and 230.
[78] *ibid.* at 21.
[79] *ibid.* at 230.
[80] *ibid.* at 230.
[81] *Wilkins & Davis Construction Co Ltd v Geraldine Borough* [1958] N.Z.L.R. 985.
[82] *ibid.* at 988 *et seq.*
[83] 21 A. 2d 591 (1941); above, para.6–004.

by the building contract cases considered in para.6–026, above. Those were cases of antecedent obstacles, which are governed by stricter standards than cases of supervening obstacles.[84] In particular the argument commonly used in them, that the contractor could have discovered the obstacle by investigating the site before entering into the contract, is plainly inapplicable where the obstacle arises only after the time of contracting. Our examples perhaps show that in cases of this kind the distinction between impossibility and impracticability becomes hard to draw. In one sense, performance is not impossible: the object to be achieved by the contract can still be achieved. But if it can be achieved only in a manner totally different from that contemplated, it would not be an abuse of language to say that the task contemplated under the original contract had become an impossible one to perform.

The preceding discussion shows that it is hard to formulate the exact difference between English and American law on discharge by "impracticability". But there are certainly differences of emphasis in the approaches adopted by the two systems. One cannot, for example, imagine an English court deciding a case in the way which the *ALCOA*[85] case was decided in the United States. Even there, that decision is regarded as controversial, but it is the product of a climate of opinion which has no counterpart in English law. The case may be contrasted with the (in some respects analogous) case of *Wates Ltd v GLC*[86] where a contract to build houses for a local authority provided that the amounts to be paid to the building contractor might be increased in accordance with an agreed formula. The contractor's costs then rose much faster than had been anticipated (though by no means to such an extent as in the *ALCOA* case); and the contractor's argument that the contract had been discharged was rejected, precisely because parties had expressly provided in their contract for events which had occurred. A contrast between two hypothetical examples points in the same direction as that between the *ALCOA* and *Wates* cases. The first is taken from the English case of *Brauer & Co (Great Britain) Ltd v James Clark (Brush Materials) Ltd.*[87] The actual decision (to be more fully discussed in para.6–035, below) was that a seller was not excused under an express *force majeure* clause in the contract merely because a change in the export regulations in the country of origin of the goods had required him to pay his supplier there an amount in excess of the price fixed in his contract with the buyer. But Denning L.J. said that the position might have been different if the seller's costs had increased a *hundredfold*.[88] Even this dictum does not necessarily mean that such an increase would discharge the seller under the common law doctrine of frustration; indeed, if it did mean this it would seem to be inconsistent with the judicial statements quoted in para.6–023, above. It may, in the context of the *Brauer* case, mean merely that the hundredfold

6–028

---

[84] Above, para.1–007.
[85] 499 F. Supp. 53 (1980); above, para.6–018.
[86] (1983) 25 Build L.R. 1.
[87] [1952] 2 All E.R. 497.
[88] [1952] 2 All E.R. 497 at 501.

increase would bring the *force majeure* clause into operation, or that it would excuse the seller on the ground that, in general, a seller who is under an obligation to obtain an export licence need do no more than take reasonable steps to that end.[89] Whatever its precise meaning or status may be, the dictum should be contrasted with a corresponding passage in the Restatement 2d which refers to an "abrupt *tenfold* increase in cost to the seller"[90] as a possible ground of discharge. The difference between this and Denning L.J.'s example of a *hundred fold* increase can be said to be that between fantastic and unlikely contingencies. Such a distinction obviously lacks precision, and this may be one reason why American courts have found it so hard to determine the extent of the doctrine of discharge by impracticability. Thus on the one hand it has been said that Uniform Commerical Code, s.2–615 "abandons the old rule of impossibility" and replaces it with "the less stringent test of impracticability".[91] But it is significant that this statement occurs in a case in which the contract was not discharged[92]; and it should be contrasted with the almost con-temporaneous statement that "recent American cases ... strictly construe the doctrine of commercial impracticability"[93]; and with repeated judicial statements to the effect that "the fact that performance has become economically more burdensome is not sufficient for performance to be excused".[94] The chance of obtaining relief on the sole ground that rising costs have made performance "impracticable" may not be good in the United States, especially after the criticisms which have been levelled at the *ALCOA* case[95]; but in England a case based on such impracticability alone is virtually hopeless and is indeed generally regarded as unarguable. The preponderance of English judicial opinion (cited in para.6–023, above) appears to be hostile to the existence of a doctrine of discharge by "impracticability" (in the American sense); and this view is supported by negative evidence of the energy crisis cases, *i.e.* by the lack of any English cases in which the point was even argued that rising costs occasioned by the crisis could be a ground of discharge. One can conclude that no English decision supports a general rule of discharge by impracticability

---

[89] See *Benjamin's Sale of Goods* (6th ed.), paras 18–285, 18–286.

[90] Introductory note to Ch.11 (Vol.2, p.311); *cf.* the German decision in RGZ 101, 79 (fifteenfold increase in the price of a car a ground of discharge).

[91] *Neal-Cooper Grain Co v Texas Gulf Sulphur Co*, 508 F. 2d 283 at 293 (1974).

[92] For a similar statement, see *Florida Power & Light Co v Westinghouse Electric Corp*, 826 F. 2d 239 at 254, contrasting "the traditional version of impossibility" with "the modern, more liberal, doctrine of commercial impracticability". The contract in that case *was* held to have been discharged, but not on grounds of "pure" impracticability: see above, paras 4–061, 4–083 and below, paras 6–030, 6–034.

[93] *Eastern Airlines Inc v Gulf Oil Corp*, 415 F. Supp. 429 at 438 (1975).

[94] *Neal-Cooper Grain Co v Texas Gulf Sulphur Co*, 508 F. 2d 283 at 293; *Companhia de Navegaceo Lloyd Brasileiro v CG Blake Co*, 34 F. 2d 616 at 619 (1929); *cf. 407 East 61st Garage v Fifth Avenue Corp*, 244 N.E. 2d 37 at 41 (1968); *Schmidt v CP Builders Inc*, 320 N.Y.S. 2nd 460 at 461 (1971); *Nora Springs Co-operative Co v Brandau*, 247 N.W. 2d 744 at 748 (1976).

[95] Above, para.6–018.

and that a number of dicta of high authority appear emphatically to reject such a rule.

(3) Exceptional or special cases

The general approach of English law, described above, is subject to a 6–029 number of possible exceptions or qualifications. None of these, however, goes so far as to support the view that the doctrine of discharge can apply in cases of "pure" impracticability, that is, in those in which nothing more appears than that one party will suffer even severe financial or commercial hardship resulting from increased cost or commercial difficulty of that party's performance. These exceptional or special cases are the subject-matter of the following discussions. In those discussed in paras 6–030 to 6–040, discharge is claimed on the ground of changes in economic conditions, while in those discussed in paras 6–041 and 6–042 such claims are motivated by other factors.

(a) *Impracticability combined with other factors*

A contract may be discharged, not by impracticability alone, but by this 6–030 factor combined with some additional factor such as temporary impossibility, impossibility in the method of performance or illegality. These possibilities are discussed in paras 6–031 to 6–034, below. Although discharge in some such cases is sometimes said to result from impracticability (*e.g.* in the form of additional expense to the party claiming to be discharged), they are not cases of "pure" impracticability and do not support the view that the increased expense alone, not accompanied by the additional factor in question, would of itself be a ground of discharge.

(i) Impracticability and temporary impossibility

In discussing the effect of temporary impossibility, we saw that contracts 6–031 were in some cases discharged because, when performance again became (or was expected to become) possible, circumstances had (or would be likely to have) so radically changed as to make performance at that later date fundamentally different from that originally undertaken. This was, for example, the ground on which delays resulting from government action in the First World War were held to have discharged the contract of sale in the *Acetylene*[96] case and the contract to build the reservoir in the *Metropolitan Water Board*[97] case. The delays were thought to produce fundamental changes in the performance required respectively of the seller and of the building contractor because they had led, or were likely to lead, to steep rises in the cost of performance of those parties. Such prejudice to one of the contracting parties could be described as "impracticability"; but cases of this kind are not cases of discharge by impracticability alone. In them, performance had for some considerable period, been actually impossible, and it was this factor, combined with the increased cost of performing at the end of the delay, which led to

---

[96] *Acetylene Co of GB v Canada Carbide Co* (1922) 8 Ll.L. Rep. 456; above, para.5–042.
[97] *Metropolitan Water Board v Dick Kerr & Co* [1918] A.C. 119; above, para.5–042.

discharge. One can test the point by contrasting such cases with those in which the contract is *ab initio* a very long-term one (extending over a period equal in length to that covered by the delay in the temporary impossibility cases). In such a case the fact that circumstances had changed by the end of the *originally agreed* period would not be a ground of discharge: on the contrary, such a contract is considered to allocate the risk of such changes,[98] whether their effect is to increase the cost of performance to one party, or to reduce its value to the other.

6–032   A similar point can be made about the converse situation which arose in the American *Autry* case,[99] where the actor would have been prejudiced, if he had been held to his contract to make the specified number of films, after his release from the armed forces, at the originally agreed rates of pay, since these were far lower than those which prevailed after the end of the temporary impossibility. The "impracticability" here takes the form, not of increased cost to the actor of his performance, but of a decline in the relative value of the counter-performance; and again it is combined with actual, though temporary, impossibility. But for this factor, the actor would simply have made a bargain which would have turned out badly, if he had committed himself to a long-term engagement at fixed rates of pay. The English case of *Morgan v Manser*[1] gives rise to difficulty precisely because no attempt was made there to enforce the contract beyond the originally agreed term; but since the ground of discharge does not appear to have been any increase in the cost of performance to the actor, or any fall in the value of the counter-performance due to him, it does not seem that the case raised any issue of impracticability.

(ii) Impracticability and impossibility in method of performance

6–033   Where a stipulated or contemplated method of performance becomes impossible, but another method remains available, the question whether the contract is frustrated depends on whether there is a radical or "fundamental" difference between the former and latter method. In the Suez cases[2] it was held that the extra costs, incurred by the party prejudiced by the closure of the Canal were not, in proportion to the costs that would have been incurred by that party but for that event, sufficiently great to give rise to such a "fundamental" difference. But it is inherent in the reasoning of those cases that if the increase had been sufficiently great to give rise to such a difference (or if, for some other reason, performance by the method remaining possible had been "fundamentally different" from performance by the stipulated or contemplated method[3]), then the contracts could have been discharged.[4] Again, however, such discharge would have followed, not from "pure" impracticability, but from

---

[98] *Larrinaga v Société Franco-Américaine des Phosphates de Medulla* (1923) 92 L.J.K.B. 455.

[99] *Autry v Republic Productions Inc*, 180 P. 2d 888 (1947); above, para.5–046.

[1] [1948] 1 K.B. 184; above, para.5–051.

[2] Above, paras 4–071 *et seq.*

[3] See the examples given in para.4–080, above, after n.53.

[4] *cf.* the American case of *Florida Power & Light Company v Westinghouse Electric Corp*, 826 F. 2d 239 (1987), above, para.4–061.

impracticability (usually in the form of greatly increased expense) coupled with a form of impossibility (*i.e.*, in the method of performance).[5] It again does not follow that increased cost alone, without any concomitant impossibility, would have been a ground of discharge.

(iii) Impracticability and illegality

The possibility of discharge by this combination of circumstance may be illustrated by the situation in which a contract is made for the provision of specified services and the law is then changed so as to make performance illegal unless the contractors who are to render the services take additional precautions, not required when the contract is made, in the interests of safety or public health. The extra expense which has to be incurred by the contractors may then be so large (in relation to the amount payable for the services) as to make it "commercially impossible"[6] for the contract to be performed and so frustrate it. Such circumstances can be said to amount to a kind of "impracticability", leading to discharge[7]; but this result will, more significantly, be based on the special consideration of public policy on which discharge is based in cases of supervening illegality.[8] It therefore does not follow that the contract would be discharged by impracticability alone if the same amount of extra expense had to be incurred simply by commercial factors such as increased costs of labour or fuel, without any additional element of supervening illegality.

6–034

(b) *Express provisions*

A contracting party may claim to be discharged (or at least temporarily excused), not under the general doctrine of discharge, but under an express provision of the contract, such as a *force majeure* or "prohibition of export" clause. Such a clause may on its true construction apply in circumstances amounting to impracticability. This was the position in *Ford & Sons (Oldham) Ltd v Henry Leetham Ltd*[9] which, as already noted, is the only case cited in the comments to Uniform Commercial Code, s.2–615 in

6–035

---

[5] It is, perhaps, significant that in the *Florida Power* case (above, n.4) the court refers at 265 and 277 to discharge under the doctrine of "impracticability/impossibility".

[6] *William Cory & Son Ltd v Corporation of London* [1951] 1 K.B. 8 at 13 and (on appeal) [1951] 2 K.B. 476 at 483.

[7] It seems to have been so regarded in the *William Cory* case, above, n.6, where the change in the law was made by the local authority to which the services were under the contract to be rendered. The actual decision was merely that the authority had not, by *making* the new byelaw's in 1948 committed a *breach* of the contract and it was "not disputed" that the contract was frustrated on the byelaw's coming into force in 1950: [1951] 1 K.B. 8 at 13; [1951] 2 K.B. 476 at 483.

[8] Below paras 8–001 to 8–003; in the present context, the public interest requires the service provider not to be given any incentive to perform the services without taking the precautions required by the change in the law. Public policy considerations (of a different kind) may also in part account for the American decision in *Florida Power & Light Co v Westinghouse Electric Corp*, 826 F. 2d 239 (1987), above, paras 4–061, 6–033.

[9] (1915) 21 Com.Cas. 55; above, para.6–020.

support of the American doctrine of impracticability. The fact that the seller there was cut off from some of his normal sources of supply would certainly not have discharged him under the common law doctrine, but was (on the true construction of the clause) held to excuse him in that case. There is, moreover, nothing to stop parties from expressly providing that the contract is to be discharged or suspended in the event of supervening impracticability, or if performance should become "economically unfeasible"[10] or if a change of circumstances should cause "hardship"[11] to one party. Such express provisions can have the effect of incorporating the concept of impracticability into the contract by express agreement, and even of extending its scope.

Force majeure and similar provisions for supervening events will not, however, necessarily be construed so as to protect a party merely because an event of the kind specified in the clause has occurred and has made performance more onerous or more expensive for that party. For example, in *Brauer & Co (Great Britain) Ltd v James Clark (Brush Materials) Ltd*[12] a contract for the sale of Brazilian piassava contained a provision by which the contract was to become void should shipment be prevented by prohibition of export, or by various other specified causes such as revolution or riot or *force majeure* or plague. The contract prices ranged from £118 to £163 per ton according to quality. Subsequently, the Brazilian authorities announced that they would grant export licences only if prices were paid to the sellers' Brazilian supplier which exceeded the contract price by between £20 and £40 per ton. It was held that the sellers were not protected by the *force majeure* clause. In a later case it was likewise held that a seller was in such circumstances not protected by a prohibition of export clause.[13] Similarly, in *B & S Contracts Ltd v Victor Green Publications Ltd*[14] it was held that a building contractor, who had agreed to erect exhibition stands, was not protected by a *force majeure* clause when his employees made demands for severance pay and threatened to strike if the demands were not met. It was said that the contractor could have "bought off" the strike by taking reasonable steps, *i.e.* by paying the men with money provided by way of an "advance" offered by the other contracting party: he was not entitled to insist that the "advance" should be paid as an extra, *i.e.* in addition to the contract price, and to refuse to perform unless it was so paid. This view of his obligations was further supported by the fact that the clause began with the words "Every effort will be made to carry out" the contract.

6–036   Clauses of the kind here under discussion are also subject to a further restriction: they do not normally protect a party where he can perform in alternative ways only one of which is affected by an event specified in the

---

[10] As in *Ellis Shipping Corp v Voest Alpine Inter-trading (The Lefthero)* [1992] 2 Lloyd's Rep. 109.

[11] See ICC Brochure No 421 (*Force Majeure* and Hardship).

[12] [1952] 2 All E.R. 497.

[13] *Exportelisa SA v Guiseppe & Figli Soc Coll* [1978] 1 Lloyd's Rep. 433; *cf.* also *Beves Ltd v Farkas* [1953] 1 Lloyd's Rep. 103.

[14] [1984] I.C.R. 419.

clause,[15] *e.g.* where a c.i.f. seller is prevented from shipping, but not from buying goods afloat. This general rule is however subject to an exception which was developed in the soyabean cases. The circumstances in which this exception applies have been discussed in Ch.4,[16] where we saw that the reason for the exception was that, if all the sellers in the frequently long chains of contracts were required to buy afloat, then prices would be driven up to "unheard-of levels".[17] This is the language of impracticability, and so it is not surprising to find Lord Wilberforce saying, when he approved the exception, that to require the sellers in these circumstances to buy afloat would be "impracticable and commercially unsuitable".[18] A similar point emerges from the earlier *Matheos* case,[19] in which a voyage charterparty for the carriage of wheat provided that delays caused by frost or ice were not to count as laydays. The ship was frozen in at the port of loading so that she could not be loaded either from the quay or by lighters, but it remained theoretically possible to load her manually, *i.e.* by carrying the wheat across the ice. This method of loading was described as "commercially impracticable"[20] so that the charterer was held to be protected by the "frost and ice" exception. But such statements and decisions merely mean that "impracticability" may bring an express provision into operation. Such a conclusion is scarcely surprising, since express provisions of this kind are often intended to provide a party with an excuse precisely where he would not be discharged under the general common law doctrine.[21] The fact that such a clause may, on its true construction cover "impracticability" therefore does not support the view that "impracticability" could discharge the contract if it contained no such clause, or if the events giving rise to the "impracticability" did not fall within the clause. Indeed, the view that in these circumstances "impracticability" would *not* be a ground of discharge receives some support from the many soyabean cases in which sellers could not bring themselves within the express "prohibition" and "*force majeure*" clauses (*e.g.* because they could not identify the person at the head of the string who was to ship the goods).[22] In all these cases the sellers were held liable: in none of them was the steep rise in prices (from \$239.50 to \$635 per ton)[23] following the imposition of the embargo regarded as a ground of discharge at common law. Such an argument might not have stood much chance of success even in the United States since the extent of the price rise would probably have been regarded as insufficient, and since the parties were usually dealers in commodities whose losses on some

---

[15] Above, para.4–044; below, paras 10–002, 12–023, 12–029.
[16] Above, paras 4–045 to 4–047.
[17] *Tradax Export SA v André et Cie* [1976] 1 Lloyd's Rep. 416 at 423.
[18] *Bremer Handelsgesellschaft mbH v Vanden Avenne-Izegem PVBA* [1978] 2 Lloyd's Rep. 108 at 115.
[19] *Owners of Steamship Matheos v Louis Dreyfus & Co* [1925] A.C. 654.
[20] *ibid.* at 660.
[21] Below, para.12–016.
[22] *i.e.* the "relevant shipper:" see below, paras 12–037, 12–040.
[23] See above, para.4–046, n.58.

contracts might well have been balanced by gains on others.[24] Nevertheless it seems to be significant that in only one[25] of the soyabean cases was any attempt made to invoke the common law doctrine of discharge, and that this attempt was not pressed. In all the others, counsel for the sellers relied only on the express *force majeure* and prohibition clauses. The "impracticability" which could be said to result from the risk of driving prices up to "unheard-of levels" was, in other words, regarded as relevant only for the purpose of deciding that those provisions could apply in spite of the fact that it was theoretically possible for the sellers to buy afloat and so to put themselves in the position of being able to perform.

(c) *Long-term contracts of indefinite duration*

6–037   This group of cases concerns long-term contracts for the supply of goods or services. The contracts in these cases in some respects resemble those in the American energy crisis cases but differ from them in the crucial respect that the contracts do not specify the time during which the supply is to be maintained. The flavour of such cases is perhaps best caught by the nineteenth-century French *Canal de Craponne* case,[26] where a contract for the supply of water had been made in 1567 and over 300 years later the court rejected the supplier's claim that he should be relieved on the ground that, by then, the cost of supplying the water had risen considerably above the price fixed by the contract for the supply. It is worth noting that the supplier claimed, not to be discharged from the contract, but to be entitled to a judicially imposed increase in his charges. Such a remedy is available in French administrative law, *e.g.* where the supply is to be made to a public authority[27]: in this context the need to ensure performance by the supplier and hence the maintenance of services to the public is thought to prevail over the principle of sanctity of contract, so that the remedy was available even in respect of a contract which specified the time for which the supply was to be made.[28] Relief from long-term supply contracts (whether of indefinite duration or for a fixed term) by reason of changes in circumstances is also available under other civil law systems; it may take the form either of discharge[29] or of a variation[30] of the contract or of a right to terminate the contract by notice

---

[24] *cf.* above, para.6–009.

[25] *i.e.* in *Bremer Handelsgesellschaft mbH v Vanden Avenne Izegem PVBA* at first instance [1977] 1 Lloyd's Rep. 133 at 163, below, para.12–019; the decision was eventually varied by the House of Lords [1978] 1 Lloyd's Rep. 109.

[26] Cass. Civ., 6 March 1876, D.P. 1876. 1. 197.

[27] CE, March 30, 1916, D. 1916. 3. 25.

[28] The contract in the case cited in the previous note specified a duration of 30 years.

[29] *e.g.* in the Swiss "Stauweiher" case, BG, September 10, 1919, BGE 45 II 386 (1919).

[30] *e.g.* in German cases such as RGZ 100, 130 (1920), where a lease was varied so as to allow a landlord to charge a higher rent when the cost of performing his obligation to provide steam had arisen to 10 times the agreed rent. Such "variation" or "adaptation" of contracts on the ground of *Wegfall der Geschäftsgrundlage* (disappearance of the commercial basis) has long been

"for an important reason" (*aus wichtigem Grund*).[31] In English law the courts certainly have no power at common law to vary the contract in the light of changing circumstances; nor do they distinguish for this purpose between contracts with public authorities[32] and contracts between private persons. The problem in English law is whether contracts within the present group may be discharged and, if so, on what ground.

The leading English case on this topic is *Staffordshire Area Health Authority v South Staffordshire Waterworks Co*,[33] where a hospital had, in 1919, agreed to give up its right to take water from a well to a waterworks company, and that company had in return promised that it would "at all times hereafter" supply water to the hospital, at prices fixed in the contract. By 1975, the cost to the company of supplying the water had risen to over 18 times the contract price and the company gave seven months' notice to the hospital to terminate the contract. The Court of Appeal held that the notice was effective, but its members differed in their reasons for this result. Lord Denning M.R. held that, although the contract on its literal construction meant that it was intended to continue "in perpetuity",[34] it had "cease(d) to bind" because "the situation has changed so radically since the contract was made".[35] This seems to mean that he regarded the contract as having been frustrated by the change of circumstances which had taken place between 1919 and 1975. But this view is, with respect, open to question as it is based on the very passages of Lord Denning's own judgment in the *British Movietonenews* case[36] which, in that case, had been disapproved by the House of Lords.[37] Goff and Cumming-Bruce L.JJ. based their decision in the *Staffordshire* case on the different ground that the words "at all times hereafter" were not to be taken literally; that they merely obliged the waterworks company to supply water at all times *during*

---

recognised as a remedy in German law: see above, paras § 6–011, n.66, 6–023, n.59 and below, para.15–037 at n.51; it is given legislative recognition in the new § 313 of the BGB: see next note.

[31] See the new BGB, § 314, introduced as one of the amendments of the BGB which came into force in 2002. The new § 314 appears to be a generalisation of the similar rule applicable by virtue of BGB § 626 (using almost identical language) to contracts of employment; the words *"bis zur vereinbarten Beendigung"* (until the end of the agreed term) indicate that it can apply to contracts of fixed no less than to those of indeterminate duration. It appears to be intended to cover cases such as *Poussard v Spiers and Pond* (1876) 1 Q.B.D. 410, above, para.5–060, where the reason for termination by one party is the failure of the other (whether amounting to a breach or not) to perform the latter's obligation. There is no reference in the new § 314 to any power to order adaptation (*Anpassung*) of a long-term contract in the light of changed circumstances; but in cases of the kind described in n.30, above, this form of relief continues to be available under the new BGB § 313, headed *Störung der Geschäftsgrundlage* (disturbance of the commercial basis).

[32] See, *e.g. Davis Contractors v Fareham UDC* [1956] A.C. 696.

[33] [1978] 1 W.L.R. 1387.

[34] *ibid.* at 1394.

[35] *ibid.* at 1398.

[36] [1951] 1 K.B. 190, esp. at 200.

[37] [1952] A.C. 166; above, para.6–023.

the existence of the agreement; that the agreement on its true construction was intended to be one of indefinite (rather than one of perpetual) duration and that the case fell within the general principle that in commercial agreements of indefinite duration a term is often implied entitling either party to terminate by reasonable notice.[38] This seems to be the preferable basis for the decision in the sense that it is consistent with other cases concerning agreements of indefinite duration; and in that it is not inconsistent with the views expressed by the House of Lords in the *British Movietonenews* case. The view that the contract was discharged by a radical change of circumstances also makes it hard to explain why the contract was (as Lord Denning said) terminated *by notice*[39]: it should (on his view) have been discharged automatically, by operation of law,[40] when the radical change occurred. The difficulty of fixing a point at which such discharge might have taken place is another ground for preferring the majority view to that of Lord Denning. The majority view was followed in the *Tower Hamlets*[41] case where a contract to supply gas to a local authority at a fixed price failed to specify its duration and was held, on its true construction, to be an agreement for six years certain and thereafter subject to termination by one year's notice. The contract was made in January 1971, and the notice of termination took effect in December 1978, so that the agreement actually ran for nearly eight years. The judge pointed out that, if Lord Denning were right in the *Staffordshire* case, then, in the *Tower Hamlets* case, the "enormous increase in the market price" of gas which occurred in the year ending March 1975, would have justified termination by notice *in that year.* This was a view which the trial judge in the latter case necessarily had to reject once he had held that the contract, on its true construction, was intended to last for a minimum of six years.

6–039 The *Staffordshire* case would go the same way in the United States quite irrespective of the Uniform Commercial Code, s.2–615 or of any doctrine of "impracticability". The governing provisions would be s.2–309(2) and (3) which provide for termination by reasonable notice[42] "where the

---

[38] *e.g. Martin-Baker Aircraft Co v Flight Refuelling Equipment Ltd* [1955] 2 Q.B. 556; *cf.* Commercial Agents (Council Directive) Regulations 1993, SI 1993/3053 (implementing Directive 86/653), reg.15(1); reg.15(2) specifies periods of notice; contrast *Watford DC v Watford RDC* (1988) 86 L.G.R. 524, below, para.6–040. On this ground, the court in the *Staffordshire* case would probably have approved of the result in the Swiss *Stauweiher* case, above, n.29 and have held that the contract in the French *Canal de Craponne* case, above n.26, could have been terminated on reasonable notice (though the remedy of *variation* there sought would not be available in English law).

[39] [1978] 1 W.L.R. 1387 at 1399.

[40] Below, para.15–002.

[41] *Tower Hamlets LCB v British Gas, The Times,* March 23, 1982 (affirmed without reference to this point, *The Times,* December 14, 1983); the majority view in the *Staffordshire* case was also approved in the *Watford* case, above, n.38.

[42] Under the proposed amendments to Art.2 of the Code (above, para.2–042, n.17) it will become possible for the parties to provide that no notice need be given, if such a term is not manifestly unreasonable: see the proposed last sentence of s.2–309(3) and the new Comment 11.

contract provides for successive performances but is indefinite in duration". These subsections do not apply to contracts for a fixed term; and it follows from the reasoning of the majority in the *Staffordshire* case that the decision there would have gone the other way, if the contract had been for a fixed term (as it was in the *ALCOA* case).[43] This view is supported by the later *Kirklees* case[44] where an agreement giving a transport company the sole right to operate transport services into certain local authority areas was made in 1930 and expressed to last for 99 years; it provided that the local authorities were to have a share of the profits. The responsibility of the authorities for operating transport services was vested in a new authority in 1972. It was held that no term could be implied into the 1930 agreement for terminating the agreement before the end of the 99 years, nor was the contract frustrated. Hence the transport company was not discharged from its obligation *to pay over the share of the profits.* There were no facts in this case suggesting impracticability and the transport company was not seeking to be discharged from its duty *to provide the services,* but the decision shows that the reasoning of the majority in the *Staffordshire* case does not apply to fixed term contracts. This restriction on the scope of that decision seems (with respect) to be correct in principle; for if parties enter into a fixed term fixed price contract they must *prima facie* be taken thereby to have allocated the risks of market fluctuations. If the parties are not prepared to accept these risks (or to accept them in full) they can adopt the practice of providing in the contract itself for flexible pricing. The very fact that this practice is now common in long-term contracts indicates that the parties' failure to adopt it amounts to a deliberate allocation of these risks.

Even an agreement of indefinite duration is not necessarily terminable on reasonable notice. Uniform Commercial Code, s.2–309(2) provides that such agreements may be so terminated "unless otherwise agreed" and in English law the usual implication of a right to determine such contracts on reasonable notice may likewise be negatived by the express terms of the contract. This possibility is illustrated by *Harbinger UK Ltd v GE Information Services Ltd*[45] where A undertook to supply software to B's customers and to license its use by B and those customers; the agreement also obliged A to provide support and maintenance services to the customers "in perpetuity". Although it was accepted that these words did not mean "for ever", they were nevertheless held to exclude A's right to terminate the obligation to supply the specified services by reasonable notice: that obligation remained in force (even after the termination of the principal supply obligation by due notice given under another clause of the agreement) for so long as the customers continued to ask, and were willing to pay, for the services in question. The distinction between the meaning of the words "in perpetuity" and the words "at all times hereafter" (which were held in the *Staffordshire* case[46] not to exclude the

6–040

---

[43] 499 F. Supp. 53 (1980); above, para.6–018.
[44] *Kirklees MBC v Yorks Woollen District Transport Co* (1978) 77 L.G.R. 448.
[45] [2000] 1 All E.R. (Comm) 166.
[46] [1978] 1 W.L.R. 1387; above, para.6–038.

right to terminate on reasonable notice) may not at first sight be obvious; but the interpretation of the former phrase in the *Harbinger* case can, with respect, be said to have given effect to the intention of the parties since it must have been clear to both of them that, without the support services, the utility of the software to the customers would be, to say the least, significantly reduced. There is also no suggestion that this interpretation of the relevant term in that case locked the suppliers into a fixed pricing structure for a protracted period; for the services were to be rendered in relation to a rapidly changing technology and would cease to be called for once that technology had been superseded.[47] There is, therefore, no more than a superficial resemblance between the practical issues raised by the *Staffordshire* and *Harbinger* cases.

The implication of a term allowing termination of a contract of indefinite duration by reasonable notice may also be displaced by circumstances other than the wording of the contract. This possibility is illustrated by *Watford Borough Council v Watford Rural District Council*[48] where an agreement was made in 1963 by which cemeteries, previously owned jointly by the claimants and the defendants, were henceforth to be run by the claimants, the defendants paying a contribution towards the running costs according to an agreed formula. In 1984, the defendant gave notice terminating the agreement because of an "unacceptable" increase in the cost of their contribution. The notice was held to be ineffective: the agreement was intended to provide for the discharge of a public duty under the Burial Acts, and the duty was "perpetual in nature".[49] Hence no term could be implied for termination on reasonable notice. There was no suggestion of any change in circumstances which could lead to discharge; but it is at least clear that *mere* increase in costs will not suffice.

(d) *Breakdown in diplomatic and commercial relations*

6–041   A contract may be discharged, not because performance becomes more expensive, or less profitable, but for wholly different, and not purely commercial, reasons. In *The Playa Larga*[50] sugar had been sold c.i.f. Chilean port by a Cuban state trading organisation to a body controlled by a Chilean state trading organisation. When the contract was made, Cuba and Chile were both ruled by Marxist governments; but before deliveries had been completed, the Marxist government in Chile was overthrown. As a result, diplomatic relations between the two countries were severed and there was a complete breakdown of commercial relations between them. It was held that the contract was discharged even though its performance was neither impossible nor (as yet) illegal (though it later became illegal by a Cuban law, providing an additional ground of discharge). The ground of discharge was not financial hardship to the seller: it was simply

---

[47] See [2000] 1 All E.R. (Comm) 166 at 170.
[48] (1988) 86 L.G.R. 524.
[49] *ibid.* at 536. *cf. Islwyn BC v Newport BC* [1994] 6 Admin. L.R. 386.
[50] *Empresa Exportadora de Azucar v Industria Azucarera Nacional SA (The Playa Larga)* [1983] 2 Lloyd's Rep. 171.

that, in the altered political conditions, there was no practical possibility of the implementation of the contract by either party.[51] In these circumstances the court took the view that the contract was no longer intended by either party to be binding, and this result could be said to turn on what might perhaps be called political impracticability. But the decision would not, it is submitted, support the view that a contract between two private parties would be discharged merely because its performance would involve trade between two countries which had ceased, before performance had been completed, to have diplomatic relations with each other. Nor would it support the view that a serious dispute between parties on a matter unrelated to their contract would normally discharge it merely by reason of making future co-operation between them unlikely. In a Swiss case of this kind[52] it was held that a contract by which the defendant had agreed to allow his wife's parents to live in his house would be discharged, when the defendant and his wife were divorced, if the divorce was not due to the defendant's fault; but in England the parties' inability to co-operate would not be a ground of discharge, though it would be a factor relevant to the issue whether specific relief should be ordered.[53] *The Playa Larga* was, it is submitted, a highly exceptional case in which the crucial facts were that the breakdown in diplomatic and commercial relations was between governments which controlled the entire trade between the two countries in question, and that the parties to the contracts of sale were state entities controlled by those governments.

(e) *Refusal of specific relief*

It has been suggested in para.6–016, above that supervening events which do not discharge the contract may nevertheless be grounds for refusing specific relief. The point extends even to cases in which the contract is of such a kind that specific performance of it would normally be ordered as a matter of course, *e.g.* where it is a contract for the sale of land. The possibility of such refusal is illustrated by *Patel v Ali*,[54] where the defendant had contracted to sell her house and there was then a long delay, for which neither she nor the purchaser was responsible, during which the contract remained unperformed. During this period (of some four years) the defendant was overtaken by a series of disastrous changes of circumstances. Her husband became bankrupt and was later sent to prison, she developed bone cancer, and she had to have a leg amputated, thus becoming immobile and greatly dependent on her neighbours (especially as she spoke little English). Shortly after the amputation, she gave birth to her second (and three years later to her third) child. It was held that the contract could not be *specifically* enforced against the vendor: "equitable relief may ... be refused because of an unforeseen change of

6–042

---

[51] *ibid.* at 188.

[52] BG, July 10, 1956, BGE 82 II 332.

[53] See *Warren v Mendy* [1989] 1 W.L.R. 853; similar reasoning has been used to explain the rule that an agreement to enter into a partnership will not be specifically enforced: *England v Curling* (1844) 8 Beav. 128 at 137.

[54] [1984] Ch. 281.

circumstances not amounting to legal frustration."[55] On the other hand, "mere pecuniary difficulties" would "afford no excuse".[56] Thus the purchaser of a house will not be denied specific performance merely because the vendor, on a rising market, finds it difficult to acquire comparable alternative accommodation with the proceeds of sale.[57] Moreover *Patel v Ali* decided only that specific performance was not an appropriate remedy. The defendant remained liable in damages, and she could presumably have paid these by raising a further loan on the security of the house, which would, in the state of the market at the time, be likely to have increased in value between the time of the contract and that of the hearing. This reasoning would not, indeed, apply if the house had fallen in value, but in that case the claim to enforce the contract (whether specifically or by way of damages) would in all probability have been made *by* the vendor, rather than *against* her. In neither type of claim would such a change in market value be a ground of discharge.

(4) Inflation

6–043   Earlier in this chapter, the question was considered whether a contract might be discharged on the ground that the cost of supplying some particular commodity or service had increased, so as to make the contract an unprofitable one for one of the parties. The same type of question may arise from the *general* process of inflation, as opposed to an increase in the cost of supplying *particular* goods or services. This general process of inflation can give rise to two distinct legal problems: that of revalorisation and that of discharge.

(a) *Revalorisation*

6–044   The first of these problems is whether, after a period of severe inflation, a debt contracted before (or near) the beginning of that period can be effectively paid in the contractually specified units of the now depreciated currency. This is not regarded by common lawyers as a problem of discharge by supervening events since the debtor is willing (and indeed generally anxious) to perform the contract literally. The question is whether his obligations should be varied in the light of the drastically changed value of the monetary units in which it was expressed, so as to impose on the debtor an obligation different from that originally undertaken by him. In systems of law in which such a remedy is available, a court could, for example, order a tenant to pay a rent higher than that reserved by his lease[58]; in a case like the *Staffordshire*[59] case, revalorisation

---

[55]   *ibid.* at 288. For refusal of specific relief even where the supervening change of circumstances did not discharge the contracts, see also the *Northern Illinois* case, 461 N.E. 2d 1049 (1984) and the *Northern Indiana* case, 799 F. 2d 265 (1986), above, paras 6–015, 6–016.

[56]   *Patel v Ali* [1984] Ch. 281 at 288.

[57]   *Mountford v Scott* [1975] Ch. 258; *cf. Easton v Brown* [1981] 3 All E.R. 278.

[58]   *e.g.* RGZ 100, 130 (1920), above, para.6–037 n.30; Larenz, *Schuldrecht* (14th ed.), Vol.I, pp.127, 137–138.

[59]   [1978] 1 W.L.R. 1387; above, para.6–038.

could (in such systems) lead to an order compelling the hospital to pay for the water supply at a rate higher than that fixed by the contract. In fact, no such issue was raised by that case: the question simply was whether the waterworks company had been discharged from its obligation to continue to supply water to the hospital. No doubt in cases of this kind a decision to the effect that the contract has been discharged, or that it has been duly terminated by notice, may lead to fresh negotiations between the parties, and these may in turn lead to an agreement to pay an increased amount; but this process is obviously quite different from that of imposing an obligation to make such a payment on an unwilling party by order of the court. There is also the possibility that, where services had been rendered under a contract before frustration, or in ignorance of it, the court may sometimes award to the party who has rendered them a reasonable remuneration[60] at rates of pay which differ from those fixed by the contract; but such a remedy is available only in respect of past acts and so would not "revalorise" the paying party's obligation for the future.

The principle of revalorisation of debts has not been recognised in England[61]; but some support for it may at first sight seem to be provided by American cases resulting from the collapse of the Confederate currency during the Civil War. One such case was *Effinger v Kenny*,[62] which concerned a promissory note made in 1863, payable in Confederate dollars in 1865. When the promissory note was made, the Confederate dollar was worth one-third, but when payment became due it was worth only one-twentieth, of a US dollar. The Supreme Court held that the amount to which the payee was entitled (in US dollars) was to be calculated by reference to the value of the Confederate in relation to the US dollar at the time when the note was made, and not by reference to the relationship between the two currencies when the note became due. This result could be regarded as a kind of revalorisation; but the reasoning of the case emphasises the special characteristics of the Confederate dollar as a means of payment which was (in the opinion of the US courts) illegal and void. The court recognised that, where no such factor was present, a contract calling for payment in a lawful currency would entitle the payee only to the contractually specified amount of that currency, however much the value of that currency might have declined. Thus *Effinger v Kenny* and similar cases are best explained as turning on the special characteristics of the Confederate currency, and are not to be regarded as providing support for a general common law principle of revalorisation.

(b) *Discharge*

Our principal concern in this book is not with revalorisation but with discharge: in other words, not with the question whether the obligations of the party who had agreed to pay money should be varied in the light of a drastic fall in the value of the currency in which the obligation was

6–045

---

[60] Below, paras 15–003, 15–041.

[61] See *Anderson v Equitable Life Insurance Society of the United States* (1926) 42 T.L.R. 302.

[62] 115 U.S. 566 (1885), discussing earlier authorities on the point.

expressed, but with the question whether such a fall can release the person *to whom* the payment was to be made from his obligation to perform his part of the contract. This question is one on which English cases provide little guidance; but such authority as there is seems to be opposed to the view that a party can rely on inflation as a ground of discharge merely because it has in real terms reduced the benefit that he expected to gain under the contract. In the passage already quoted from the *British Movietonenews* case "a sudden depreciation of currency" is listed, together with "a wholly abnormal rise or fall in prices", as one of the types of events which will "not in itself affect the bargain [the parties] have made"[63] —*i.e.* which will not lead to discharge. The passage from which this quotation is taken continues: "If, on the other hand, a consideration of the terms of the contract in the light of the circumstances when it was made, shows that [the parties] never agreed to be bound in the fundamentally different situation which has now emerged, the contract ceases to bind at that point …". This sentence could be interpreted to refer back to the types of events previously listed, including inflation,[64] so that these events could discharge a contract if they produced a "fundamentally different situation". More probably, however, the reference is to *other* events, *e.g.* to events such as temporary impossibility giving rise to such long delays as to make performance when it again becomes possible fundamentally different from that originally contemplated by the parties.[65] There is a similarly equivocal quality about a dictum of Lord Roskill in *National Carriers Ltd v Panalpina (Northern) Ltd* which refers to "inflation" as one of the "circumstances in which the doctrine [of frustration] has been invoked, sometimes with success, *sometimes without*".[66] It is not clear whether inflation falls within the former or within the latter group of circumstances. Another dictum which more strongly supports the view that inflation is not a ground of discharge occurs in *Wates Ltd v GLC*. "Things may have turned out differently from what the parties contemplated in that inflation increased, not at a trot or at a canter, but at a gallop. But that difference in degree or tempo was not so radical a difference from the inflation contemplated and provided for as to frustrate the contract."[67] Again, one can make the point that the inflation which occurred was of the order of 20–25 per cent; and that the dictum leaves open the possibility of discharge where inflation is of such a "degree or tempo" that it does amount to a "radical … difference" from anything that the parties could have contemplated.

6-046   In the United States, *Willard v Tayloe*[68] supports the view that depreciation of currency may affect the remedy available against a party prejudiced by the depreciation. The case arose out of a contract for the sale of land which provided for payment to made in "Dollars", an

---

[63] [1952] A.C. 166 at 185; above, para.6–023.
[64] *cf.* Mann, *The Legal Aspects of Money* (5th ed.), pp.117–118.
[65] Above, para.5–042.
[66] [1981] 1 A.C. 675 at 712.
[67] (1987) 25 Build. L.R. 1 at 35.
[68] 75 U.S. 577 (1869).

expression intended by the parties to refer to gold dollars. Subsequently paper dollars became legal tender but at the time of the proceedings these were worth only just over one-third of the gold dollars by reference to which the parties had contracted. It was held that the purchaser was not entitled to specific performance on tender in paper dollars of the amount specified in the contract. All that the case actually decided was that the remedy of specific performance was not available to the purchaser: it did not decide that the contract was discharged. The suggestion has been made that the difference in value between the gold and paper currencies could also have been taken into account in an action for damages.[69] Even if this suggestion were accepted, it would not follow that the contract would be discharged merely by depreciation of the paper currency; the difference might be relevant only to the *measure* of damages.

While English and American authorities do not support the possibility of discharge by depreciation of currency, they cannot be said wholly to rule it out. The inflation experienced in those countries in the 1970s and 1980s may have been severe, but it was not extreme; and Corbin[70] in the United States, as well as Mann[71] in England, have suggested that extreme depreciation of currency might be a ground of discharge. If these suggestions were accepted, it seems likely that inflation would have to be more extreme in England than in the United States to bring about discharge. Reference has been made in para.6–028, above to the corresponding difference between the effects on contracts of cost increases of particular items (as opposed to the general process of inflation). We have seen that such increases do not normally discharge contracts; but that the Restatement 2d suggests that a "disaster" giving rise to "an abrupt *tenfold* increase in cost to the seller" may be a ground of discharge[72]; while a corresponding English dictum refers to a *hundredfold* increase in cost as a possible excuse for the seller, and then only in the context of a contract containing an express *force majeure* clause and imposing on the seller a duty to take no more than reasonable steps to overcome the increase in cost.[73] It seems that nothing short of such an extreme depreciation of currency would be regarded as sufficient to discharge a contract in English law; a distinction might be drawn between severe inflation and the total collapse of the currency. These possibilities must be regarded as speculative; and for a number of reasons the question whether they represent the law is unlikely to be resolved by judicial decision. Where inflation is not of the extreme kind described above, it would be likely to be within the contemplation of the parties, or to be dealt with by the terms of the contract, *e.g.* by providing for payments under the contract to be "index-linked"[74]; and the common law doctrine

---

[69] Corbin, *Contracts*, para.1360.
[70] *ibid.*
[71] *The Legal Aspects of Money* (5th ed.), p.118.
[72] Above, para.6–028, n.90.
[73] Above, para.6–028, n.88.
[74] *Nationwide BS v Registrar of Friendly Societies* [1983] 1 W.L.R. 1226 (index-linked mortgage).

of discharge would probably be excluded on one of those grounds.[75] Where, on the other hand, the inflation was so extreme as to amount to a total collapse of the currency, it is likely that its effects on contracts would be dealt with by legislation, so that questions of the kind which have been raised here would not need to be resolved by common law principles.

(5) Currency fluctuations

6–047   A problem similar to that of the effects of inflation on contracts can arise where a debtor whose business dealings are carried on in one currency makes a long-term contract under which his obligations are expressed in, or defined by reference to, a different currency. In *Multiservice Bookbinding Ltd v Marden*[76] premises in England were mortgaged in 1966 for £36,000. The mortgage contained a "Swiss franc uplift clause" by which the amount repayable as capital was to depend on the value of the Swiss franc in relation to sterling. Ten years later, the mortgagor gave notice of his intention to redeem the mortgage; by this time the pound sterling was worth only 4 Swiss francs, as against 12 at the time of the mortgage transaction. As a result, the capital sum due to the mortgagees (taking into account earlier repayments) was £87,000. It was held that the mortgagor had no grounds for relief, either under the doctrine of frustration or on equitable principles. The decisions can scarcely be said to have inflicted hardship on the mortgagor since he had presumably benefited from the increase in the value of the property in the 10 years which had elapsed since the loan was made. Without the clause, the mortgagee would have been repaid in pounds sterling, the value of which would have been eroded by inflation, and it seems unlikely that the interest payments which he would have received (at the rates which then prevailed) would have provided him with adequate compensation for this capital loss.

IV. VIENNA CONVENTION

6–048   Article 79(1) of the Vienna Convention on Contracts for the International Sale of Goods provides that: "A party is not liable for a failure to perform any of his obligations if he proves that the failure was due to an impediment beyond his control and that he could not reasonably be expected to have taken the impediment into account at the time of the conclusion of the contract or to have avoided or overcome it or its consequences." This provision, however, exempts the impeded party only from liability in damages: it does not prevent the other party "from exercising any right other than to claim damages under this Convention".[77] The other party can, for example, exercise his right to declare the contract avoided if the failure is such as to satisfy the conditions (laid

---

[75] Below, Chs 12, 13.
[76] [1919] Ch. 84.
[77] Art.79(5).

down elsewhere in the Convention) in which this right arises.[78] The legal consequences of the "impediment" are quite different from those of frustration at common law.[79] The exemption provided by Art.79 may be partial or temporary,[80] and the contract is not discharged automatically but only (if at all) at the other party's election to declare it avoided. In all these respects, the effect of Art.79 is more closely analogous to the effect (in English law) of an excuse for non-performance in circumstances falling short of frustration, than to the total and automatic discharge which is the legal consequence of frustration.[81]

There is no clear answer to the question whether "impracticability" (as opposed to impossibility) can amount to an "impediment" within Art.79(1). It has been suggested that, in this respect, the Convention "stands somewhere between the most strict and the most liberal of the domestic systems"[82]; that "under very narrow conditions 'impediment' also includes 'unaffordability' "[83]; and that the words of Art.79 are "very elastic" and that they may well be "differently interpreted in different national courts".[84] The question is for the present unlikely to come before the English courts[85] since at the time of writing the United Kingdom has not ratified the Convention. But if the question were to arise in England, one argument that could be put forward would be that, just as the effects of the exemption provided by Art.79(1) are less drastic than those of frustration, so its requirements should be less exacting and should be satisfied by at least some kinds of impracticability which are not recognised as grounds of total discharge under English domestic law. Even if the Convention were ratified by the United Kingdom, questions as to the scope of Art.79(1) are unlikely to come frequently before the courts, since contracts for the international sale of goods now commonly contain express terms dealing with the effects of supervening events. Such terms will prevail over Art.79 since the Convention permits contracting parties "to derogate from or vary the effects of any of its provisions".[86]

---

[78] See Arts 49, 64, 72 and 73. For the other party's right to "require performance", see below, para.15–044.

[79] See further below, para.15–043.

[80] This follows from the words "any of his obligations" in Art.79(1) and from Art.79(3); see further below, para.15–043.

[81] See above, paras 5–058 to 5–063 and below, para.15–043.

[82] Honnold, *Uniform Law for International Sales* (2nd ed.), p.542.

[83] Schlechtriem, *Uniform Sales Law*, p.102.

[84] Nicholas, 105 L.Q.R. 201 at 235; *cf.* Tallon in (ed.) Bianca and Bonnel, *Commentary on the International Sales Law*, p.577.

[85] The possibility cannot be ruled out as the parties may by express reference incorporate the Convention into a contract that would not otherwise be subject to it.

[86] Art.6 (which is subject to an exception which is not relevant for the purpose of this discussion).

Chapter 7

FRUSTRATION OF PURPOSE

I. Introduction

Frustration of purpose is, in a sense, the mirror-image of impracticability. **7–001** The typical contract is an arrangement under which one party agrees to supply a thing or a service or some other facility to the other, and the latter agrees to pay a sum of money for it. In cases of impossibility, the contract is discharged because the supervening event has made it impossible for the former party to supply the thing, service or facility. In cases of alleged impracticability there is no such impossibility, but the normal position is that the *supplier* argues that the cost of providing the thing, service or facility has risen, or that other difficulties of so doing have increased, to such an extent that he should be discharged. In cases of alleged frustration of purpose it is normally the *recipient* of the thing, service or facility who argues that the contract should be discharged. His own obligation, being merely one to pay money, cannot have become impossible, nor has any impossibility affected the obligation of the supplier, which can still be performed. But the recipient's case is that the contract should be discharged because the supplier's performance is no longer of any use to the recipient for the purpose for which both parties had intended it to be used. This was the ground of discharge recognised in the "coronation cases" to be discussed in paras 7–006 to 7–014, below; and the other examples of alleged frustration of purpose, discussed later in this chapter,[1] are of a similar nature. Frustration of purpose thus resembles impracticability in that it can lead to discharge of contracts in cases falling short of impossibility; and for this reason the doctrines are sometimes regarded as equivalents,[2] or are confused with each other.[3] But they differ in that generally in cases of impracticability discharge is claimed by the supplier of the thing, service or facility which is to be supplied under the contract, while in cases of frustration of purpose it is the recipient who claims that the contract has been discharged.

---

[1] Below, paras 7–015 *et seq.*
[2] *e.g. Downing v Stiles*, 635 P. 2d 808 at 811 (1981).
[3] See below, para.7–002, and below, at n.8.

It must, however, be stressed that this distinction between the two doctrines is only generally, and not invariably, true. The point can be illustrated by referring back to the American *Mineral Park*[4] case, and by assuming that the case had been one of discharge by supervening (rather than by antecedent) impracticability. In that case, it was the buyer who relied on impracticability because the contract obliged him, not merely to pay for the gravel, but also to extract it; and it was the difficulty and cost of that operation which turned out to be far greater than the parties had supposed it to be. Similarly, in the American *Nora Springs*[5] case it was the buyer who sought to rely on "impracticability" arising from shortage of box-cars and from the alleged extra expense of obtaining "a substitute method of carrier".[6] The buyer's argument was rejected as the shortage of box-cars had not been clearly proved, nor had the buyer shown "any increased costs so prohibitive as to change the nature of its corn contracts"[7] with the seller. The court's reference to the Uniform Commercial Code, s.2–615 (and especially to Comment 9) indicates that the ground of decision was that the requirements of discharge by impracticability had not been satisfied. The court indeed somewhat confusingly adds: "Thus the Code expressly recognises the doctrine of 'commercial frustration'."[8] This remark, however, merely illustrates the point that, where discharge occurs, or is alleged to occur, in spite of the fact that performance has not become impossible, courts sometimes fail to distinguish clearly between impracticability and frustration of purpose. The buyer's argument was not that the corn had become useless to him, but that the cost of taking delivery had increased. That amounted to his relying on impracticability, not on frustration of purpose. A similar argument may be raised by a "buyer" of services where the method of calculating the payment to be made for them is such that the amount of that payment is sharply increased by supervening events. This was the position in *The Eugenia*,[9] where it was the charterers who argued that the contract had been frustrated by the closure of the Suez Canal since this would have increased the amount to be paid by them as that amount depended on the time taken to accomplish the voyage. This argument was rejected for reasons which have already been discussed.[10] But the present point relates to the structure of the argument, which would in the United States be classified under the heading of impracticability, thus showing that an argument of impracticability may be raised by a recipient, no less than by a supplier, of services. A similar point could arise where building work was to be done on a "cost-plus" basis and a supervening event led to a steep rise in the builder's costs, or where similar factors affected the

---

[4] *Mineral Park Land Co v Howard*, 156 P. 458 (1916); above, para.6–004.
[5] *Nora Springs Co-operative Co v Brandau*, 247 N.W. 2d 744 (1976); above, para.6–013.
[6] At 748.
[7] *ibid.*
[8] *ibid.*
[9] *Ocean Tramp Tankers Corp v V/O Sovfracht (The Eugenia)* [1964] 2 Q.B. 226.
[10] Above, para.4–081.

amount to be paid by the buyer under a contract to develop and supply an article for a price which depended on the seller's costs.[11]

Cases of the kind discussed above would have raised issues of frustration
of purpose if the thing or service to be supplied under the contract had, as a result of supervening events, ceased to be of use for the purpose contemplated by the parties at the time of contracting. Such an issue would, for example, have arisen in the *Mineral Park*[12] case if the bridge-building project for which the gravel was to have been used had been abandoned; or in *The Eugenia*[13] if the charterparty had been concluded to enable the charterers to perform in a particular contract of sale, and that contract had then been cancelled by the other party to it. That is not to suggest that in such cases an argument of frustration of purpose would have prevailed: the point relates only to the nature of the argument and not to its prospects of success.

In discussing the American doctrine of impracticability, we saw that buyers sometimes sought to invoke this doctrine on the ground that there had been a fall in the market price of what they had agreed to buy (as in the *Hancock Paper*[14] case); or on the ground that, though the buyers were still able to use the subject-matter for the purpose originally contemplated, they could only do so at a loss (as in the *Northern Illinois Gas*[15] and *Northern Indiana Public Service Co*[16] cases). In the latter case Posner J. said that the buyer's "defense is more properly frustration than impracticability".[17] This statement is based on Posner J.'s view of the relationship between the two doctrines, as expressed in the following passage from the same judgment: "To deal with the rare case where the buyer or (more broadly) the paying party might have a good excuse based on some unforeseen change in circumstances, a new rubric was thought necessary, different from 'impossibility' (the common law term) or 'impracticability' the [Uniform Commercial] Code term[18] picked up in the Restatement (Second) of Contracts, s.261 (1979), and it received the name 'frustration'. Rarely is it impossible for the payor to pay; but if something has happened to make the performance for which he would be paying worthless to him, an excuse for not paying, analogous to impracticability or impossibility, may be available to him."[19] It is however, with respect, open to doubt whether "frustration" (of purpose) is an accurate

---

[11] *cf. US Wegematic Corp*, 360 F. 2d 674 (1966), where the alleged "impracticability" was antecedent and the argument based on it failed: see above, para.6–017.

[12] Above, n.4.

[13] Above, n.9.

[14] *Hancock Paper Co v Champion International Corp*, 424 F. Supp. 285 (1975); above, para.6–014.

[15] *Northern Illinois Gas Co v Energy Co-operative Inc*, 461 N.E. 2d 1049 (1984); above, para.6–015.

[16] *Northern Indiana Public Service Co v Carbon County Coal Co*, 799 F. 2d 265 (1986); above, para.6–016.

[17] 799 F. 2d at 277.

[18] Actually this American usage antedates the UCC, being found (for example) in the original Restatement, § 454.

[19] 799 F. 2d 265 at 276.

description of the buyer's argument in the *Northern Indiana* case. That argument seems to have been, not that the coal was of no use to the buyer for the contractually contemplated purpose, but rather that it was too expensive. In this respect, the situation in the *Northern Indiana* case differed from that in the coronation cases[20] in which the "buyers" did not allege that the windows or seats from which they had hoped to watch the processions had become too expensive; their argument was that, after the cancellation of the processions, those facilities had become wholly useless to them for the contractually contemplated purpose. In the *Northern Indiana* case, the legal position was further complicated by the fact that the doctrine of discharge by frustration of purpose was not recognised in Indiana law.[21] Consequently, the buyer's argument had to be based on impracticability, and as we saw in para.6–016, above that argument failed. But it would be misleading to say that it failed merely because it was raised by the buyer, or that a claim that the contract has been discharged by supervening events (other than those making performance impossible) must be classified as one of frustration merely because it is raised by a buyer or by some other "paying party". Some of the cases discussed above[22] show that the defence of impracticability can be available to the "paying party", or (in our terminology) to the *recipient* of the performance which has been made more expensive or more onerous for that party by the supervening event. The statement that "impracticability" operates as a defence for the supplier while "frustration" operates as one for the recipient of that performance is no more than an approximation; it may be generally but it is not universally true.

7–003   Just as the defence of "impracticability" is sometimes raised by the recipient, so the defence of frustration of purpose may occasionally be raised by the supplier. Thus in *Re Comptoir Commercial Anversois and Power Sons & Co*[23] wheat was sold by a seller in New York to a buyer in Antwerp, the seller expecting to receive the price in New York by there selling drafts on the buyer. This expectation was defeated because war-time conditions made it impossible so to sell the drafts. The seller's claim that the contract had been frustrated was rejected on the ground that the way in which the seller dealt with the drafts was not a matter of concern to the buyers, so that no *common* purpose had been frustrated. The point which is of interest here is that, if there had been such a common purpose, the argument of frustration of purpose could have succeeded even though it was raised by the seller.

The view that "frustration" necessarily refers to a defence raised by the "paying party" is also inappropriate where the contract is not one for the simple exchange of goods, services or facilities to be provided by one party for money to be paid by the other. The point may be illustrated by the Australian *Brisbane* case,[24] where a company owned land which it wished to

---

[20] Below, paras 7–006 *et seq.*
[21] 799 F. 2d. 265 at 276.
[22] *i.e.* those discussed at nn.4–9, above.
[23] [1920] 1 K.B. 868.
[24] *Brisbane City Council v Group Projects Pty Ltd* (1979) 145 C.L.R. 143.

develop for residential purposes and promised the city council that, in return for the city's help in securing permission for the development from the appropriate government department, it (the company) would execute certain works, mainly on other land. That permission was later obtained, but before this happened the company's land had been compulsorily acquired by the Crown, so that the residential development could no longer take place. It was held that the company was discharged from its obligation to execute the promised works; and reference by Stephen J.[25] to the coronation cases indicates that his decision is based (rightly or wrongly[26]) on the doctrine of frustration of purpose: the services of the city, or their results, were no longer of any use to the company.[27] In such a case the company (which successfully relied on the doctrine of frustration of purpose) can scarcely be described as "*the* paying party". The case was one in which *each* party can be said to have "paid" by services for the services of the other; so that it cannot be said that only one was the supplier and only the other the recipient of the services. Yet the case is properly to be classified as one of frustration of purpose because the performance of one party had become *useless* to the other. Cases of impracticability, by contrast, are those in which a party claims discharge on the ground that his own performance has become *severely more onerous.*

Frustration of purpose and impracticability are, however, closely related **7–004** doctrines in that both envisage discharge in circumstances falling short of impossibility. Both are therefore open to the objection that they tend to subvert the sanctity of contract. The value of this concept is, indeed, treated with scepticism in the American *Opera Company of Boston* case,[28] but there the phrase "sanctity of contracts" appears to be used to refer to the former doctrine of absolute contracts,[29] which no longer prevails.[30] The phrase now more properly refers to the idea that "contract" should be regarded as a mechanism on which parties can place a reasonable degree of reliance when allocating risks between themselves. Discharge by supervening impossibility may qualify this function of contract and show that parties cannot place absolute reliance on their contracts for this purpose. But where discharge is claimed in circumstances falling short of impossibility the court must beware of granting relief merely because supervening events have turned the contract into a bad bargain for the party claiming relief. It is the exercise of judicial caution in such circumstances which gives effect to the requirement of sanctity of contract in its modern sense. It is interesting to note that such considerations

---

[25] *ibid.* at 161; Murphy J. (at 164) agreed with Stephen J.

[26] See below, para.7–032 at n.27.

[27] This conclusion caused no hardship to the city since its interest in the works was based on the assumption that residential development would take place; and once it became clear that this would not happen the city's "particular concern comes to an end": (1979) 145 C.L.R. 143 at 163.

[28] *Opera Company of Boston v Wolf Trap Foundation for the Performing Arts*, 817 F. 2d 1094 at 1097 (1986).

[29] See the reference *ibid.* to *Paradine v Jane* (1647) Aleyn 26, above, para.2–002.

[30] Above, para.2–025.

appear to have been influential in England in cases of impracticability, while in the United States their influence was formerly more marked in cases of frustration of purpose. To put the point in another way, discharge by impracticability is in origin an American doctrine,[31] which the English courts have been reluctant to accept[32]; while discharge by frustration of purpose originated, as a legal doctrine, in the English coronation cases[33] and was at one time viewed with considerable suspicion in the United States, where one writer as late as 1953 described it as "a rejected doctrine".[34] This view has not been without influence in the United States: as we saw in discussing the *Northern Indiana* case,[35] the doctrine of discharge by frustration of purpose has not been accepted in all States. Nevertheless it is clear that any initial hostility which may once have been felt in the United States towards the doctrine of frustration of purpose no longer represents the prevailing view. The following discussion will, indeed, show that illustrations of discharge by frustration of purpose are more commonly found in American than in English decisions, and that it is (to say the least) doubtful whether some of the American cases which apply the doctrine would be followed in England. The doctrine of discharge by frustration of purpose is, moreover, accepted in terms by the Restatement[36] and by the Restatement 2d,[37] which, with reference to that doctrine, states that "in recent years the courts have shown an increasing liberality in discharging obligors on the basis of such extraordinary circumstances".[38]

II. ILLUSTRATIONS OF THE DOCTRINE

7–005   In the rest of this chapter, we shall first trace the development of the doctrine by discussing a number of groups of cases in which it has been invoked, and then attempt to assess its status in the present law.

(1) The coronation cases[39]

7–006   These cases arose when the coronation of King Edward VII was postponed because of the illness of the King. Many contracts had been made in

---

[31] Above, paras 6–003 to 6–006.
[32] Above, paras 6–021 to 6–028.
[33] Below, paras 7–006 *et seq.*
[34] Anderson, 3 De Paul L. Rev. 1 (1953); Hay, 164 Ac P. 231–245–250 (1964). For the view that the scope of "frustration" is similarly narrower in India (since s.56 of the Contract Act 1872 refers only to cases where performance "becomes impossible"), see *Dalmia Dairy Industries Ltd v National Bank of Pakistan* [1978] 2 Lloyd's Rep. 223 at 251–253; but contrast Pollock, *Principles of Contract* (13th ed.), p.229, where s.56 of the 1872 Act is criticised and the author concludes that "It does not appear ... that there has in practice been any material divergence from English law" in the cases decided under s.56.
[35] 799 F. 2d. 265 (1986); above, para.7–002.
[36] § 288.
[37] § 265.
[38] Restatement 2d, Introductory Note to Ch.11 (Vol.II, p.310).
[39] McElroy and Williams, 4 M.L.R. 241; 5 M.L.R. 1.

anticipation of the coronation, *e.g.* for the hire of rooms, or of seats on stands, from which the hirers or ticket-holders expected to be able to watch the processions which had been planned. Performance of these contracts did not, by reason of the supervening events, become impossible or even impracticable. It remained possible for the owners to provide the rooms or seats, and for the hirers or ticket-holders to occupy them and to look out on an ordinary day's London traffic; but this would, for them, have been a pointless exercise. They therefore claimed that the contracts were discharged on the ground of frustration of purpose, *i.e.* because the facilities to be provided by the owners were no longer of any use for the contractually contemplated purpose. Two legal issues were raised by the coronation cases: first, whether the contracts were discharged by the cancellation of the originally planned festivities; and secondly, what were the exact legal effects of discharge, especially in relation to payments made or to be made under the contracts.[40] Before discussing these questions, something must be said of the factual background to this group of cases, as this to some extent affected the course of the litigation and as it is relevant to the evaluation of the results reached in some of the cases.

In December 1901, it was announced that the coronation of King Edward VII was to take place on June 26, 1902.[41] On that day, there was to be a procession from Buckingham Palace to Westminster Abbey and back; this was referred to as "the Coronation Procession". On the following day, there was to be a second procession called "the Royal Progress", the highlight of which was to be a visit to the City of London. Maps showing the routes of both processions were published in the press.[42] On the day after the Royal Progress there was to be a naval review at Spithead. The King fell ill on June 24, and at 10am on that day the decision was taken to operate on him for a form of appendicitis. After recovering from this operation, the King was crowned on August 9, and the procession on that day followed the same route as that which had originally been planned for June 26.[43] Evidently, however, the King had not regained sufficient strength to take part in a second procession on the day following his coronation (which in any event was a Sunday); and for some time the fate of the Royal Progress was in doubt. It was originally said to have been "abandoned", though the same announcement added that the King "hope[d] to be able to drive through some of the streets South of the Thames in the autumn".[44] The date for this event was not fixed until September 20, when it was announced that it would take place on October 25; this announcement added that "the precise route will be announced

---

[40] See further below, paras 15–047 to 15–052.
[41] *The Times*, December 10, 1901.
[42] *The Times*, June 9, 1902; for the route of the Royal Progress see also *The Times*, January 25, 1902.
[43] See the announcement in *The Times*, July 15, 1902.
[44] *ibid.* It is perhaps significant that all the litigated cases concerned seats or windows in streets north of the Thames.

later".[45] It was finally announced on October 7,[46] when it became clear that the route to be followed on October 25 would cover much, but not all, of the ground that would have been covered by the Royal Progress originally planned for June 27.[47] Of particular interest to readers of the coronation cases are the facts that both the original and the revised routes traversed Pall Mall,[48] but that, while the original route included St James's Street,[49] that street was omitted from the revised route. The revised procession duly took place on October 25, but it must have been a less colourful, and no doubt a less profitable, occasion than the originally planned Royal Progress would have been in June; for by October many of the foreign dignitaries who were to have participated in the event, as well as many of the foreign tourists who were expected to have paid to watch the Royal Progress, would have returned to their homes. The question was how the losses resulting from the postponement and curtailment of the planned celebrations were to be allocated.

7–007   For the most part, this question was no doubt resolved without litigation. Reports in *The Times*[50] indicate that some sellers of tickets for seats on stands were prepared to refund the money which had been paid for the seats, or to refund the money less an allowance (presumably to cover their additional expenses), or to allow ticket-holders to use their tickets on the days on which the processions eventually did take place. This last solution would have given rise to obvious difficulty for foreign visitors who had bought tickets for the Royal Progress and were no longer in London in October; and it would not work at all where the seat or window was on the originally planned route for that procession but not on the route eventually taken. Some of the contracts (or agreed variations of contracts) in the reported cases provide for similar solutions.[51] It also appears that owners of some of the stands had insured against the risk of cancellation or postponement[52]: in view of the age of the King, who was over 60 at the time, this was clearly a sensible precaution and one which would be likely to have been taken by those who, in selling tickets, had acted in the course of a business. But other contracts were made, not by persons so acting, but by private individuals who happened to be owners or tenants of rooms overlooking the routes of the processions, and in these contracts there were

---

[45] *The Times*, September 20, 1902.

[46] *The Times*, October 7, 1902.

[47] The differences between the two routes appear from a comparison of the map published in *The Times*, June 9, 1902 with the list of streets given in the announcement in *The Times*, October 7, 1902.

[48] Where subject-matter of the contract in *Krell v Henry* [1903] 2 K.B. 740 (below, para.7–010) was situated.

[49] Where the subject-matter of the contract in *Griffith v Brymer* (1903) 19 T.L.R. 434 (below, para.7–008) was situated.

[50] June 26, 1902.

[51] *e.g. Victoria Seats Agency v Paget* (1902) 19 T.L.R. 16; below, para.7–010; *Clark v Lindsay* (1902) 88 L.T. 198; below, para.7–009.

[52] *The Times*, June 26, 1902.

no provisions for the event, nor (so far as appears from the reports) was either party covered by insurance against cancellation or postponement.

The cases on this subject fall into two groups: those in which the originally planned processions or other celebrations had already been cancelled when the contracts were made, and those in which the cancellation came after the conclusion of the contracts. In the latter group of cases, no attempt was ever made to distinguish between cases in which at the time of contracting the King may already have been ill but his illness had not been diagnosed, and those in which he fell ill only after the contract was made. Speculation on the former point could have given rise to great uncertainty and it seems that lawyers took account only of the easily verifiable fact whether, when the contract was made, the cancellation or postponement had already been announced.

(a) *Post-cancellation contracts*

The first case in this group was *Griffith v Brymer*,[53] where the claimant had paid £100 for the hire of the defendant's rooms at 8 St James's Street for the purpose of viewing the coronation procession on June 26. The contract had been made at 11am on June 24, neither party knowing that the decision to operate on the King had been taken just an hour earlier. It was held that the contract was "void" on the ground of "missupposition of the state of facts"[54] (*i.e.* for mistake) and that the claimant was entitled to the return of the £100. Of all the coronation cases, this was the only one in which a claim for the return of money paid succeeded; and this result can be supported on the ground that it is unlikely that the defendant could have suffered any loss (beyond that which the cancellation had already caused him) by acting in reliance on the supposed contract between the time of the agreement and that of the discovery of the true state of affairs. He may, however, by entering into the agreement have incurred an agency fee,[55] and his refusal to return the £100 may also have been motivated by the fact that he was disappointed in his expectation of being able to let the rooms again on the day of the Royal Progress, for the revised route of this procession (as eventually held in October) did not pass his premises.[56] But this disappointment had nothing to do with the claimant, whose contract related only to the coronation procession. How such a case would be decided now must be regarded as an open question. On the issue of mistake, one possible view is that *Griffith v Brymer* cannot stand after a stricter test of what amounts to a fundamental mistake was adopted by the House of Lords in *Bell v Lever Brothers Ltd*.[57] If it could not,

7–008

---

[53] (1903) 19 T.L.R. 434.

[54] *ibid.*

[55] The report (above n.53) refers to "Messrs. Pope, Roach & Co., the defendant's agents", but it does not specify the circumstances in which their commission was to become due.

[56] Above, at n.49.

[57] [1932] A.C. 161. See above, para.1–007, at n.47. For the citation with approval of *Griffith v Brymer* in cases decided since *Bell v Lever Bros Ltd*, see *Fibrosa Spolka Akcyjna v Fairbairn Lawson Combe Barbour Ltd* [1943] A.C. 32 at 80, 82; *Great Peace*

the result would be reversed, so that the defendant would be able to keep the payment of £100, even though the agency fee had been only £10. If the contract were still regarded as void for mistake there would be no possibility of splitting this loss under the Law Reform (Frustrated Contracts) Act 1943[58] since the case would not be one of discharge by supervening events, but one of nullity by reason of antecedent events.[59] It was formerly arguable that somewhat similar loss-splitting adjustments could be made in cases of mistake by virtue of the equitable jurisdiction to rescind contracts on terms for mistakes which were not sufficiently fundamental to make the contract void at law.[60] But this way of dealing with the problem is no longer available (at least below the level of the House of Lords) now that the Court of Appeal has held that the equitable jurisdiction described above no longer exists in English law.[61] In the United States a similar possibility does, however, appear to exist since mistakes of the kind here under discussion make a contract voidable[62] (and not void) and the Restatement 2d envisages that "relief on such terms as justice requires"[63] may be given where a contract is voidable for mistake.

7–009   The only other case in this group is *Clark v Lindsay*[64] where a contract for the hire of rooms at 29 Ludgate Hill, to view the Royal Progress was made at 12 noon on June 24, neither party knowing that the processions had been cancelled two hours earlier. Almost immediately after the contract had been made the hirer learnt from a newspaper that the decision had been taken to operate on the King, and he at once claimed the return of the £50 which he had paid. After some discussion, the parties agreed on a compromise by which, if the procession were postponed, the hirer was to have the use of the room on the day when the procession eventually did take place. The hirer argued that the originally planned procession "with the foreign princes and so forth"[65] never took place at all, but the court held that the compromise had barred any right which the hirer might otherwise have had to reclaim the £50. In view of the circumstances in which that compromise was reached, it seems that the hirer had taken the risk of the change in the character of the procession.

Shipping Ltd v Tsavliris Salvage (International) Ltd (The Great Peace) [2002] EWCA Civ 1407; [2003] Q.B. 697 at [67].

[58] *i.e.* under the proviso to s.1(2), relating to expenses: below, para.15–071.

[59] s.1(1) of the 1943 Act makes is clear that the Act only applies in cases of discharge by *supervening* events; and the view that it does not apply where the contract is void for mistake (as to facts in existence when the alleged contract was made) is supported by *Great Peace Shipping Ltd v Tsavliris Salvage (International) Ltd (The Great Peace)* [2002] EWCA Civ 1407; [2003] Q.B. 697 at [161].

[60] See above, para.1–009, n.82.

[61] *Great Peace Shipping Ltd v Tsavliris Salvage (International) Ltd (The Great Peace)* [2002] EWCA Civ 1407; [2003] Q.B. 697, above, para.1–009.

[62] Restatement 2d, § 152(1).

[63] *ibid.*, § 158(2); *cf.* below, para.15–078.

[64] (1902) 88 L.T. 198.

[65] *ibid.* at 200.

(b) *Pre-cancellation contracts*

This (much larger) group of cases concerns contracts made before the cancellation or postponement of the planned festivities. Where the contract expressly provided for these possibilities, the doctrine of discharge was excluded. This was the position in *Victoria Seats Agency v Paget*[66] where two contracts for the hire of rooms to watch the Royal Progress were under consideration. One provided for the hire of the room on June 27 "or such other day as the said processions should pass the premises. Should the processions not pass the premises, I agree to refund the money". The second contract was in similar terms except that it provided that, if the procession were abandoned, the hirer should get back his money less 10 per cent. In both cases, claims for the return of the money failed, rightly since the contracts provided better and more flexible solutions. The position would on such facts be the same today since the express contractual provisions for the event would generally exclude the doctrine of discharge.[67]

Where the contract contained no such express provisions, the question whether it was discharged by frustration of purpose gave rise to more difficulty. *Krell v Henry*[68] is usually regarded as the leading case on this topic, though its facts present some highly unusual features. Mr Krell, who had rooms at 56A Pall Mall, overlooking the routes of both processions, had gone abroad in March 1902 and instructed his solicitor to let the rooms. In June, Mr Henry saw an announcement in the windows of the rooms, stating that they were to be let for viewing the coronation processions. By an exchange of letters between him and Mr Krell's solicitor on June 20, Mr Henry agreed to take the rooms for "the days but not the nights" of June 26 and 27, for a price of £75; of this sum, £25 was paid on June 20, and the balance was to be paid on June 24. These letters made no reference to the coronation, and in this respect *Krell v Henry* is unique among the coronation cases. It is also unique in its payment provisions in that part of the money promised to Mr Krell was paid before the processions were cancelled, while the balance did not become due until after that event: it was due "on" June 24, and this meant that Mr Henry was not bound to pay it till midnight,[69] while the cancellation occurred at 10am, on that day. It was held that the contract had been discharged by the cancellation of the processions, so that Mr Krell was not entitled to the £50 which was to have been paid on June 24. On the other hand, Mr Henry abandoned his counterclaim for repayment of the £25

---

[66] (1902) 19 T.L.R. 16.
[67] Below, para.12–002. It seems unlikely that the validity of the terms under consideration in the *Victoria Seats* case would be affected by the legislation, considered in para.12–018, below, which restricts the effectiveness of certain standard form contracts.
[68] [1903] 2 K.B. 740.
[69] See now *Tradax Export SA v Dorada Compania Naviera SA (The Lutetian)* [1982] 2 Lloyd's Rep. 140; *Afovos Shipping Co v Pagnan (The Afovos)* [1983] 1 W.L.R. 195.

already paid,[70] no doubt because the Court of Appeal had in the meantime decided that money paid before the processions had been cancelled could not be recovered back by the payor.[71] The end-result can therefore be described as a form of rough loss-splitting: Mr Henry did not have to pay the £50, while Mr Krell kept the £25 and this sum would cover any expenses which he might have incurred in connection with the transaction: for example, the fee that he presumably paid to his solicitor for negotiating the contract with Mr Henry. The loss-splitting was of course no more than rough, since there is no evidence of the relationship between the £25 which Mr Krell was allowed to keep and the expenses actually incurred by him. Legislation now provides that Mr Krell would have to pay back the £25 subject to the court's power to allow him to retain out of that sum the whole or any part of his actual expenses.[72] This is a more satisfactory solution than that reached in the actual case, at least where the amount paid before discharge exceeds the actual expenses. But *Krell v Henry* itself represents an advance on the "all or nothing" solutions which the common law had generally reached where a contract was held to have been discharged by supervening events.

7-011   The debate to which *Krell v Henry* gave rise is however concerned, not with such details of adjustment in consequence of discharge, but with the more fundamental question whether the doctrine of discharge should have been applied at all in the circumstances of the coronation cases. When those cases were decided, they stood for a new principle: namely that, even though performance had not become impossible (in the sense that the room or seat remained available and could be paid for), the contracts were discharged because their purpose, of enabling the hirers to watch the processions (or one of them) had been frustrated. On the one hand, there were obvious dangers in such a rule since it was, in theory, capable of extension to many cases in which a contract had simply, as a result of supervening events, become for one of the parties a bad bargain. The doctrine of discharge by frustration of purpose, and the decision in *Krell v Henry*, have therefore been criticised, both in England[73] and in Australia[74]; and we have noted that in the United States the doctrine has

---

[70] At first instance, this counterclaim had been upheld by Darling J.: (1902) 18 T.L.R. 823.

[71] *Blakeley v Muller* [1903] 2 K.B. 760n (cited under its alternative name of *Hobson v Pattenden* in *Great Peace Shipping Ltd v Tsavliris Salvage International Ltd (The Great Peace)* [2002] EWCA Civ 1407; [2003] Q.B. 679 at [65]). cf. *Lumsden v Barton* (1902) 19 T.L.R. 53; *Civil Service Co-operative Soc v General Steam Navigation Co* [1903] 2 K.B. 756. Such cases would now fall within Law Reform (Frustrated Contracts) Act 1943, s.1(2); below, paras 15–049 to 15–052.

[72] *ibid.* and below, para.15–071.

[73] *Blackburn Bobbin Co Ltd v TW Allen & Sons Ltd* [1918] 1 K.B. 540 at 551–552 (affirmed [1918] 2 K.B. 467); *Larrinaga v Société Franco-Américaine des Phosphates de Medulla* (1923) 92 L.J.K.B. 455 at 459; *Maritime National Fish Ltd v Ocean Trawlers Ltd* [1935] A.C. 524 at 529 ("not to be extended").

[74] *Scanlan's New Neon Ltd v Tooheys Ltd* (1943) 67 C.L.R. 169 at 191–194.

not been universally accepted.[75] On the other hand, the decision in *Krell v Henry* has been approved in many other English[76] and American[77] decisions, while in Australia earlier criticisms of the case have more recently been rejected.[78] The most elaborate judicial discussion is in the American *Northern Indiana* case,[79] where Posner J. advances two principal arguments in support of *Krell v Henry*. These may be labelled the insurance argument and the postponement argument.

The insurance argument is that the owner of the rooms was in a better position than the hirer to cover the risk by insurance and so should not be entitled to the promised payment. On the facts of *Krell v Henry*, this is however an argument of doubtful weight. In the case of such a "one-off" contract, neither party would be likely to consider the possibility of insuring. The owner of the premises might well be covered by some form of household insurance, but this would be unlikely to cover the risk in question. The insurance argument would have more substance in relation to tickets on stands which had been especially erected for the purpose of viewing the procession. We have noted that at least some of the stand holders had insured against cancellation or postponement,[80] and where they had done so this might be[81] regarded as an argument for supporting a conclusion similar to that reached in *Krell v Henry*, *i.e.* that the ticket-holder was not liable for the price of the ticket.[82] But this was not the issue raised in any of the cases concerning tickets on stands. In all those cases, the ticket-holders had already paid and were suing for the return of those

---

[75] *e.g.*, it has not been accepted in Indiana: above, para.7–002, at n.21; *cf.* para.7–004 at n.34.

[76] *e.g. Horlock v Beal* [1916] 1 A.C. 486 at 513; *Scottish Navigation Co Ltd v WA Souter & Co* [1917] 1 K.B. 222 at 228, 244. For the citation of *Krell v Henry* with apparent approval in mistake cases, see *Bell v Lever Bros Ltd* [1932] A.C. 161 at 226 and *Great Peace Shipping Ltd v Tsavliris Salvage (International) Ltd (The Great Peace)* [2002] EWCA Civ 1407; [2003] Q.B. 697 at [68].

[77] *e.g. Alfred Marks Realty Co v "Churchills"*, 153 N.Y.S. 264 (1915); *The Abbaye v U.S. Motor Cab Co*, 128 N.Y.S. 697 (1911); *Lloyd v Murphy* 153, P. 2d 47 at 49–50 (1944).

[78] *Codelfa Construction Pty Ltd v State Rail Authority of New South Wales* (1982) 149 C.L.R. 337 at 358.

[79] 799 F. 2d 265 at 277 (for discussion of this case on the issue of impracticability, see above, para.6–016).

[80] Above, para.7–007.

[81] For the view that the insurance should be disregarded in deciding whether "impracticability" should be a defence, see *Asphalt International Inc v Enterprise Shipping Corp SA*, 667 F. 2d 261 at 266, discussed above, para.6–005 and below, para.15–022.

[82] The present point is that the fact of the standholder's having insured may be relevant to the question *whether* a person who had agreed to pay for a ticket should be discharged. This is a different question from that of the relevance of sums payable under policies of insurance on the *effects* of discharge under the Law Reform (Frustrated Contracts) Act 1943: see s.1(5) of that Act, discussed below, paras 15–079 *et seq*. The assumption underlying that subsection is that the contract has been discharged: see s.1(1) of the Act.

payments[83]; and their claims were rejected at the time, though they would now be upheld.[84] Presumably, the standholders had included a proportion of their insurance costs (as part of their overheads) in the price of the tickets. So the decisions are open to the objection that the ticket-holders had paid indirectly for the insurance, but had got no benefit from it. The force of this argument must, indeed, depend on exactly what risk the stand-holders had covered by their insurance. It is not clear from contemporary accounts whether the insurance was against total loss of the opportunity of seeing the processions (and hence of the business expected to result from the sale of that opportunity) or against the extra cost of maintaining the stands from June 26 to August 9, or against the fall in the value of the opportunity of seeing the Royal Progress on account of its long postponement till October 25, when it must have been a very different kind of event from that originally planned. In German law, at least if the insurance was of the first of these kinds, the stand-holders would be required to make over the benefit of a proportionate part of the insurance[85]; if they failed to do so they would be in breach, and this might be regarded as a better solution than that reached in the English cases of the kind here under discussion.

7–012   The essence of Posner J.'s second, or "postponement," argument is that the owner of the rooms still had them at his disposal when the coronation eventually did take place; that he could make his anticipated profit by again letting the rooms then, and that it would therefore be unjust to allow him to recover, or to keep, money promised, or paid, to him in respect of the originally planned processions. This argument, too, is not wholly compelling; in particular, it overlooks a number of points in the factual background to the coronation cases.[86] In the "window" cases, the profits were considerably reduced by the change between the character of the originally planned Royal Progress and the procession which took its place in October; and in some of these cases the owner's profits were still further reduced by the fact that the route of the October procession differed from that of the Royal Progress which was to have taken place in June.[87] The "postponement" argument also ignores the wasted expenditure of the party seeking to uphold the contract. This was a factor even in some of the "window" cases[88]; and it must have been significant in all the "stand" cases: in these cases, the seats for the Coronation Procession could indeed have been relet, but only at the extra expense of maintaining the stands until August 9. In both types of cases the owner (or stand-holder) would also have to bear any expenses connected with reletting, such as agency or legal fees. Finally the "postponement" argument seems to involve a paradox in so far as it suggests that Mr Krell's claim for the balance of £50 would have been

---

[83] *e.g. Blakeley v Muller* [1903] 2 K.B. 760n; and see below, para.15–047.

[84] Law Reform (Frustrated Contracts) Act 1943, s.1(2); below, paras 15–049 *et seq.*

[85] BGB § 285; below, para.15–020.

[86] Above, para.7–006.

[87] See the discussion above, para.7–008 of *Griffith v Brymer* (1903) 19 T.L.R. 434.

[88] *e.g. Lumsden v Barton* (1902) 19 T.L.R. 53, (where lunch and wine seem to have been included in the price specified in the contract).

strengthened if (to imagine the unthinkable) the coronation had been wholly cancelled because a Republic had been declared. It seems, on the contrary, that such a drastic change of circumstances would have been more, rather than less, likely to discharge the contract.

Further difficulty arises in reconciling *Krell v Henry* with a number of other cases, both actual or hypothetical, in which it has been held or said that the contracts would not be discharged.

One such hypothetical case is the example given in *Krell v Henry* itself of   **7-013**
a contract to take a cab to Epsom on Derby Day "at a suitably enhanced price".[89] Such a contract, it is said, would not be discharged if the Derby were cancelled. Another such hypothetical case is put in the Australian case of *Scanlan's New Neon Ltd v Tooheys Ltd*: a bride orders a wedding dress, both the bride and her dressmaker knowing that the dress was "required for, and only for, the purposes of a wedding between the customer and a particular man. The wedding goes off without 'default' on the part of the lady. No-one would suggest that the lady is under no liability to pay for the dress, or even that she was entitled to cancel the order if the dress was partly made."[90] The solution is perhaps not as obvious as this dictum suggests, and it may also be significant that it appears to be restricted to the situation in which the dressmaker has wholly or partly performed, thus leaving open the possibility of discharge where the contract was wholly executory.

There are also many actual cases which have rejected the argument of discharge by frustration of purpose. Some of these will be discussed later in this chapter, *e.g.* those in which frustration of a buyer's export or import purpose[91] or of his purpose to redevelop land[92] was held not to be a ground of discharge. But in the present context the most interesting contrast with *Krell v Henry* is provided by another of the coronation cases. This was *Herne Bay Steamboat Co v Hutton*,[93] where a contract had been made for the hire of a pleasure boat at Spithead on June 28, 1902, "for the purpose of viewing the naval review[94] and for a day's cruise round the fleet; also on Sunday June 29th, for similar purposes". The hirer had apparently intended to sell seats on the boat to those who wished to see the naval review, and no doubt suffered loss in consequence of the cancellation of the review, even though the fleet remained at Spithead. The court regarded the contract as one for the hire of a boat for sight-seeing, and held that the fact that one of the anticipated attractions (the review) had failed to materialise was not a ground of discharge.

Even if it is accepted that there should be no discharge in any of the   **7-014**
hypothetical and actual examples considered above, *Krell v Henry* is properly regarded as falling on the other side of the line. The contract in

---

[89] [1903] 2 K.B. 740 at 750–751.
[90] (1943) 67 C.L.R. 169 at 201.
[91] Below, paras 7–026, 7–027.
[92] *Amalgamated Investment & Property Co Ltd v John Walker & Co Ltd* [1977] 1 W.L.R. 164; below, para.7–030.
[93] [1903] 2 K.B. 683.
[94] Which had formed part of the planned coronation celebrations.

that case was not simply one which granted a licence to use the rooms at an unusually high price. It was a contract to provide facilities for viewing the coronation processions, or, as Lord Phillips M.R. has said, one for "a room with a view".[95] There was not, indeed, any undertaking in it that the processions would take place, or that they could be viewed from the rooms. In this respect, the contract differed from the contract that is made by buying a theatre or concert ticket; performance of such a contract would become impossible if supervening events led to the cancellation of the play or concert. In *Krell v Henry* there was no such impossibility, or (as the Restatement 2d puts it) "no impediment to performance by either party".[96] But it was the common purpose of both parties that facilities for viewing the processions should be provided: in the words of Vaughan Williams L.J., the provision of such facilities was the crucial point "as much for the lessor as the hirer".[97] In the other examples, there was either no such common purpose (though the wedding-dress example is perhaps near the line), or the common purpose was not wholly defeated. The latter point reflects a recurrent feature of the cases on frustration of purpose, which shows that the approach of the law to partial frustration of purpose differs from that which it adopts to partial impossibility. In cases of partial impossibility, a contract can be discharged if its *main* purpose can no longer be achieved[98]; but in cases of frustration of purpose the courts have applied the more rigorous test of asking whether *any* part of the contractual purpose (other than a part which was wholly trivial) could still be achieved: if so, they have refused to apply the doctrine of discharge.[99] The *Herne Bay* case fell far short of satisfying this test. The naval review may have formed the hirer's principal inducement to enter into the contract, but the continued presence of the fleet at Spithead also provided a considerable and unusual attraction, and it was one of the purposes of the contract to give the hirer the opportunity of taking advantage of this attraction for commercial purposes. In *Krell v Henry*, by contrast, it was no part of the contractual purpose that Mr Henry should be able to look out of the window to watch the ordinary London traffic which continued to pass down Pall Mall on the two days in question. *Krell v Henry* seems, with respect, to have been correctly decided on the basis that it was the common purpose of both parties that facilities for watching the processions were to be provided under the contract, and the cancellation of the processions had prevented the achievement of that common purpose (though literal performance of the contract had not become impossible).[1] This emphasis on the requirement that the purpose of *both* parties must be frustrated is found also in other English and American

---

[95] *Great Peace Shipping Ltd v Tsavliris Salvage (International) Ltd (The Great Peace)* [2002] EWCA Civ 1407; [2003] Q.B. 697 at [66].
[96] § 265, Comment a.
[97] [1903] 2 K.B. 740 at 751.
[98] Above, para.5–002.
[99] *cf.* below, paras 7–017, 7–020, 7–024.
[1] *cf. Lloyd v Murphy,* 153 P. 2d 47 at 50 ("actual but not literal failure of consideration").

cases.[2] It means that the supervening event must prevent one party from supplying, and the other from obtaining, what the former had contracted to provide and the latter to acquire under the contract. In this sense, formulations of the doctrine in terms of the frustration of the purpose of *both* parties are preferable to those (occasionally found) which refer to the frustration of the purpose of *one* party only.[3] The point can be illustrated by supposing that, in *Krell v Henry*, the coronation had taken place as planned but Mr Henry had fallen ill and so been unable to watch the processions. In that case, his purpose might have been frustrated, but the same could not have been said of Mr Krell's purpose: that purpose, being the provision of viewing facilities, would have been accomplished. Accordingly it is submitted that on such facts, the contract should not have been discharged.

In the United States, there are of course no coronation cases. A somewhat similar situation did, indeed, arise in January 1985, when a spell of unusually cold weather led to the cancellation of the parade that was to have marked the inauguration of President Reagan for his second term of office. But no litigation resulted as money which had been paid by would-be spectators was repaid voluntarily.[4] It is not inconceivable that the drafting of the relevant contracts was affected by the English coronation cases, which are widely discussed in American legal literature.[5]

(2) **The black-out cases**

These are cases in which long-term contracts were made for the provision of illuminated advertising signs or of street-lighting systems. During the currency of the contracts, war-time black-out regulations were then imposed, so that the signs or street-lamps could no longer lawfully be lit; and the question arose whether the contracts were discharged (so that the agreed "rental" or service charge was no longer payable) on the ground that the purpose of the contract had been frustrated. It should be noted that, for two reasons, these cases were not cases of alleged discharge by supervening illegality. The first such reason was that the regulations prohibited only one possible use of the subject-matter, *e.g.* in the advertising sign cases it was not the erection and maintenance of the signs, but only their illumination, and then only by night, which was prohibited. The second reason was that the contracts merely required the facilities for illumination to be made available, while the prohibition

7–015

---

[2] *e.g. Congimex, etc., SARL v Tradax Export SA* [1983] 1 Lloyd's Rep. 250 at 253; *Brown v Oshiro*, 156 P. 2d 250 at 253 (1945); *cf.* above, para.2–039.

[3] *e.g.* Restatement 2d, § 265 ("a party's principal purpose") and Comment a ("*his* purpose").

[4] *New York Times*, January 25, 1985.

[5] *e.g.* Restatement 2d, § 265, Illustration 1 is said in the Reporter's note to be based on (*inter alia*) *Krell v Henry* [1903] 2 K.B. 740; this case is also fully discussed in *Williston on Contracts* (3rd ed.), para.1954, Corbin, *Contracts*, para.1355, and *Farnsworth on Contracts*, para.9.7.

related only to their use.[6] In discussing this group of cases, it will be convenient to begin by contrasting an American with an Australian case, in which different conclusions were reached on broadly similar facts; and then to consider which of these opposing views would be likely to be supported in England.

The American case is *20th Century Lites v Goodman*,[7] where a contract was made for the "lease" of an "electrical advertising display" in Los Angeles; the object of the display was to advertise the defendant's "drive-in" restaurant, which was in a side-street. The display was to be provided by the plaintiff for three years from September 3, 1941. On December 7, 1941 (the day of the Japanese attack on Pearl Harbor) war broke out between the United States and Japan; and black-out (or "dim-out") regulations were imposed on the west coast, though not until August 5, 1942, some two months after the Battle of Midway had made Japanese attacks on the continental United States highly unlikely; but this state of affairs did not receive official recognition until November 1, 1943, when an order was made "abolishing the dim-out requirements".[8] The plaintiff's claim for the monthly payments to be made under the agreement after August 1942 was dismissed on the ground of frustration of purpose; that this was the ground of decision is made clear by the court's reliance[9] on § 288 of the (First) Restatement, in which the principle of frustration of purpose is stated. The plaintiff argued that only part of the defendant's purpose had been frustrated since the sign remained visible by day even when not illuminated, and since it could lawfully have been illuminated by day. But the court rejected these arguments on the grounds that the sign was not in practice illuminated by day, and that its unilluminated use would not have constituted an "electrical advertising display" within the terms of the contract. It is arguable that these words may help to distinguish the case from the English *Herne Bay*[10] case, in which the contract expressly specified more than one purpose, and was not discharged when only one of these was frustrated. The court also rejected the argument that the "dim-out" regulations had merely suspended the contract until they were lifted, some 14 months after their original imposition: it applied the principle that the occurrence of a frustrating event brings about total automatic

---

[6] In this respect these cases are to be distinguished from cases of antecedent illegality such as *JM Allan (Merchandising) Ltd v Cloke* [1963] 2 Q.B. 340, where it was held that an innocent party could not enforce the contract merely because he was, as a result of a mistake of law, unaware of the illegality relating to the use of the subject-matter. In cases of supervening illegality neither party makes any mistake of law; both are the victims of an unexpected change in the law. Here again stricter standards are properly applied to antecedent obstacles as grounds of invalidity than to supervening obstacles as grounds of discharge; *cf.* above, paras 1–007, 6–004.

[7] 149 P. 2d 88 (1944).

[8] *ibid.* at 93.

[9] *ibid.* at 90.

[10] [1903] 2 K.B. 683; above, para.7–013.

discharge.[11] We shall see that in the United States this principle is subject to many qualifications,[12] so that the argument that the contract was only suspended might now have a greater chance of success. A similar point can be made about another aspect of the *20th Century Lites* case. The court there was remarkably unsympathetic to the hardship suffered by the plaintiff, who had incurred all the cost of the installation for very little reward: it was more impressed by the fact that the defendant could not make the intended use of the sign.[13] Perhaps the court's reaction is explicable on the ground that the plaintiff took the extreme position that, because it had incurred the expense of installation, "the doctrine of commercial frustration cannot be invoked"[14]; and that it was therefore entitled to the full sum payable under the contract. It may be that a claim for some less extensive form of relief would now stand a better chance of success: for example, a claim by the installer for reliance loss. This possibility is envisaged by the Restatement 2d, § 272(2) of which provides for "relief on such terms as justice requires, including protection of the parties' reliance interests".

Facts similar to those of the *20th Century Lites* case gave rise in Australia 7–016
to the case of *Scanlan's New Neon Ltd v Tooheys Ltd.*[15] A number of contracts had been made between 1937 and 1941 for the letting out of neon advertising signs for periods of five (or at the "lessee's" option a further two) years. The parties to each contract were described as "lessor" and "lessee", and "rental" began to be due as soon as the signs were installed. The rental was to be payable monthly "except as herein otherwise provided, whether or not the sign shall be used or operated by the lessee"; but it was to cease to be payable "if the sign fails to operate". The contract further provided that "it is a material consideration to the *lessor* in entering into this agreement that the *lessee* shall continue to use the sign [as contemplated]".[16] On January 19, 1942, the lighting of neon signs in one relevant state (New South Wales) was prohibited "at any time". In another such state (Victoria) a similar total prohibition was originally imposed but was later modified so as to have effect only at night, but this modification was of no significance for the purpose of the contractual dispute since discharge, if it occurred, would take effect on the happening of the frustrating event, regardless of later changes in circumstances.[17] The High Court, however, held that the contracts were not discharged, so that the "lessees" were liable for the agreed "rental". It may be possible to distinguish this case from *20th Century Lites v Goodman* by reference to the

---

[11] Below, paras 15–002, 15–010.

[12] Below paras 15–014 to 15–017, 15–023, 15–034 to 15–039.

[13] From this point of view the case may be contrasted with the equally one-sided reasoning in the English coronation case of *Blakeley v Muller* [1903] 2 K.B. 760n. (below, para.15–047), where the court stressed the hardship to the installer of the stand, without regard to that suffered by the ticket-holder.

[14] 149 P. 2d 88 at 92 (1944).

[15] (1943) 67 C.L.R. 169.

[16] Italics supplied. The words in square brackets were omitted from some of the contracts.

[17] *cf.* below, para.9–002.

special terms of the contract in the *Scanlan* case: for example, by relying on the term in that contract that payment was to be made "whether or not the sign shall be used or operated by the lessee"; though the already quoted provision, that continued use of the sign by the lessee was to be "a material consideration to the lessor", would seem to show that the use of the sign was a common purpose of the parties and would therefore seem to strengthen the case for discharge. But the interest in comparing the two cases lies, not in the possibility of drawing such fine distinctions based on a detailed analysis of the somewhat obscure contracts in them. It lies, rather, in their fundamental difference of approach, the *Scanlan* case taking a much narrower view of the scope of the doctrine of frustration of purpose than that taken in the *20th Century Lites* case. This is consistent with the somewhat critical attitude towards *Krell v Henry*[18] taken in the *Scanlan* case, where the High Court was simply reluctant to impose the risk of the change of circumstances on the lessor. Thus Latham C.J. saw no reason for saying that the lessor "whose business consisted in supplying neon signs, took the risk of losing all its business in the event of such a prohibition or limitation".[19] Indeed he regarded the court as being in a "poor position"[20] to determine which party took the risk and said that it was "much safer, when parties have contracted in absolute terms, to hold them to the terms of their contract".[21] Williams J. suggested that if this conclusion were to cause hardship to the defendant, then his "remedy, if any, [was] to apply to have the contract modified"[22] under special war-time legislation. But such modification of the contract (*e.g.* by reducing the rental payable under it) is not recognised in Australia (any more than in England) as a remedy which is available at common law to a party who is prejudiced by supervening events.[23] The court took the orthodox position that there was no half-way house between holding that the contract remained in full force and holding that it was wholly discharged. Intermediate solutions such as the reduction of one party's obligation are available only by virtue either of special legislation[24] or of express provisions in the contract to that effect.

7–017   The English black-out cases on the whole support the narrow view of the doctrine of frustration of purpose taken in the *Scanlan* case, rather than the wider view taken in the *20th Century Lites* case. The most important of the English cases is the *Leiston* case,[25] where a gas company had undertaken to provide street lamps for a local authority, to maintain them, and to light and extinguish them at set times; the contract was expressed to run for (at least) five years from August 1, 1911. In 1915 the lighting of

---

[18] [1903] 2 K.B. 740, above, paras 7–010, 7–011.
[19] (1943) 67 C.L.R. 169 at 200.
[20] *ibid.* at 199.
[21] *ibid.* at 200.
[22] *ibid.* at 231.
[23] *ibid.* at 188.
[24] *cf.* above, para.6–023, n.60.
[25] *Leiston Gas Co v Leiston-cum-Sizewell UDC* [1916] 2 K.B. 428.

street lamps was prohibited by war-time black-out regulations. It was held that the contract had not been discharged, since only a part of the promised performance (the lighting of the lamps) had been affected by the prohibition while a further part "which cannot be regarded as trivial"[26] (the maintenance of the street-lighting system) remained possible and lawful. The Court of Appeal in the *Leiston* case seems to accept an argument similar to that which was to be rejected in the *20th Century Lites* case,[27] where the contract was discharged in spite of the fact that the hirer could still derive a far from "trivial" benefit from its performance. In holding that the continued availability of such a benefit precluded discharge, the *Leiston* case applies a different, more stringent, test to partial frustration of purpose than that which is normally applied in cases of partial impossibility.[28] In *Taylor v Caldwell*[29] it was also true that it remained possible to render a part of the promised performance "which [could not] be regarded as trivial": the Gardens, and the side-shows, which the defendants had undertaken to provide, had not been affected by the fire; but discharge was not precluded by the fact that the impossibility was only partial. The application of a more stringent test in cases of partial frustration of purpose (which has already been noted in our discussion of the *Herne Bay* case,[30] and which will be further illustrated by a number of other cases to be discussed later in this chapter[31]) can be justified on the ground that discharge by frustration of purpose poses a more severe threat to the sanctity of contract than does discharge by impossibility. An alternative ground for the decision in the *Leiston* case was that, when the action was commenced, the length of the interruption in performance (nine-and-a-half months out of five years) was not yet sufficient to bring about discharge; in this respect, the case resembles cases of temporary impossibility in which the courts have applied the "proportionality test"[32] to determine the issue of frustration.[33]

The *Leiston* case was followed in *Wycombe Borough Electric Light & Power Co Ltd v Chipping Wycombe Corp*,[34] where a street lighting contract was made in 1911 and was expressed to continue until December 25, 1917. War-time black-out regulations coming into force before that date were held not to have frustrated the contract. Nor was the defendant local authority entitled to rely on a term of the contract providing for the deduction of specified sums in case any of the lamps remained unlit "for any cause whatsoever": these words were construed as extending only to causes over which the claimant company had some degree of control.

7–018

---

[26] *ibid.* at 433.
[27] 149 P. 2d 88 (1944).
[28] Above, para.5–002.
[29] (1963) 3 B. & S. 826, above, para.2–024.
[30] [1903] 2 K.B. 683, above, para.7–014.
[31] Below, paras 7–020, 7–024.
[32] Above, para.5–050.
[33] *e.g. Tamplin SS Co v Anglo-Mexican Petroleum Co* [1916] 2 A.C. 397, above, para. 5–052.
[34] (1917) 33 T.L.R. 489.

Two further cases are concerned, not with discharge under the common law doctrine, but with the interpretation of express provisions in the contracts for events which might interfere with their performance.

The first such case is *Williams v Mercer*,[35] where the contract gave the defendant a licence to erect an illuminated neon sign on the claimant's premises. The contract provided that the defendant should have the right to terminate the contract if a public authority required the sign to be "taken down, altered, removed or amended". Under black-out regulations made in 1939, it became unlawful to illuminate the sign. It was held that this event was not covered by the cancellation clause, so that the defendant remained liable for the "rent" payable under the contract. The only question discussed by the court was whether the defendant was entitled to invoke the cancellation clause. No attempt was made to argue that the defendant was discharged under the general common law doctrine of frustration, and it seems to have been assumed that he was not so discharged. The case thus lends further indirect support to the view that, in this group of cases, English courts would be likely to take the view that was taken in the Australian *Scanlan* case,[36] rather than that taken in the American *20th Century Lites* case.[37]

The second case is *Egham & Staines Electricity Co v Egham Urban District Council*,[38] the only English case in which black-out regulations were found to have had any effect on the contractual rights and duties of the parties. The case concerned a street-lighting contract (similar to that in the *Leiston* case[39]) under which the claimant company undertook to light streets and to maintain the street-lighting system. The contract provided that the company was not to be liable in damages if, "for any unavoidable cause over which the company has no control" it could not perform its obligations; and that the payments to be made under it by the defendant local authority were to abate "in the same proportion as the supply shall be curtailed" by such a cause. It was held that this provision was brought into operation by the black-out regulations of 1939, and that, as the supply had been wholly "curtailed", the local authority was wholly released from its obligation to pay. This result was, however, not reached by the application of the common law doctrine of discharge (which was not even mentioned by the House of Lords) but under an express term of the contract.

The preceding discussion shows that English courts have consistently refused or failed to apply the doctrine of frustration of purpose in the black-out cases. The only such case in which the contract was held to have been discharged on this ground is the American *20th Century Lites* case; and on the issue of partial frustration of purpose the reasoning of this case

---

[35] [1940] 3 All E.R. 293; *cf. Claude Neon Ltd v Hardie* [1970] Qd. R. 93 (where it was compulsory acquisition which interfered with performance of an advertising sign contract, but frustration was excluded by an express term in the contract).
[36] (1943) 67 C.L.R. 169.
[37] 149 P. 2d 88 (1944).
[38] [1944] 1 All E.R. 107.
[39] [1916] 2 K.B. 428.

is hard to reconcile with other American cases to be discussed later in this chapter.[40]

(3) Cases arising from other war-time legislative restrictions

Such cases are of two kinds: they arise either from restrictions on economic activity, or from restrictions on the freedom of movement of persons who had, or were suspected of having, hostile origins or associations. 7–019

(a) *Restrictions on economic activity*

The largest group of these cases concerned leases, or agreements for leases, which referred to the business to be carried on in the premises. The question was whether these contracts were discharged by frustration of purpose when war-time regulations interfered with the proposed business. One line of American cases, for example, raises the question whether leases of garages, or of show-room premises for purposes connected with the motor trade, were frustrated by war-time restrictions on the supply of cars and petroleum products. 7–020

The leading case in this group is *Lloyd v Murphy*[41] where the lease ran for five years from August 4, 1941; it provided that the premises were to be used for the "sole purpose" of selling new automobiles and of servicing them and of selling the products of a named major oil company, unless the landlord consented *in writing* to their use for another purpose. On January 1, 1942 the United States government ordered the discontinuance of sales of new automobiles, though it later relaxed these restrictions by allowing such sales to certain limited categories of persons. After the tenant had explained the effect on his business of this state of affairs to the landlord, the latter had *orally* waived the restrictions which the lease imposed on the use of the premises; but the tenant nevertheless vacated them and claimed that the lease was discharged. He later sold new cars elsewhere and it seems that his motive in claiming discharge was that he could not sell new cars (or could not do so profitably) at the premises which were the subject-matter of the lease. The court gave a number of reasons for rejecting the tenant's claim that the lease had been discharged. The first was that the interference with the use of the premises was foreseeable[42]; the Act of Congress under which the restrictions were imposed had been in force for more than a year when the contract was made, and at that time restrictions on new car production were generally anticipated. Secondly, the landlord had "waived"[43] the limitations on the use of the premises, had offered to reduce the rent, and had acted fairly: this part of the court's reasoning seems to reflect the

---

[40] *e.g.* with *Lloyd v Murphy*, 153 P. 2d 47 (1944) below, para.7–020, with *Brown v Oshiro*, 156 P. 2d 976 (1945), below, para.7–022 and with some of the "liquor prohibition" cases, below paras 7–023 to 7–024.

[41] 153 P. 2d 47 (1944).

[42] *cf.* below, para.13–009.

[43] 153 P. 2d 47, 51.

court's desire to encourage compromises of difficulties arising from war-time conditions. Thirdly, the value of the lease to the tenant had not been entirely destroyed since the intended use of the premises had not been totally prevented. This seems to have been the decisive point. The case shows yet again[44] that the courts apply a stricter standard in cases of partial frustration of purpose than in cases of partial impossibility: where the alleged ground of discharge is frustration of purpose, it is not enough for the party claiming discharge to establish that his main purpose has been frustrated. But it would be a mistake to interpret *Lloyd v Murphy* as a case which rejects the possibility of discharge by frustration of purpose. The judgment clearly accepts this possibility and explains why, on the facts, the conditions of such discharge were not satisfied. In terms of the English case law, the ground for the decision may be explained by saying that the case fell on the *Herne Bay*,[45] rather than on the *Krell v Henry*[46] side of the line. The position can be said to resemble that which would have arisen in *Krell v Henry* if only the Royal Progress, but not the coronation procession[47] had been cancelled. In that event, it is highly unlikely that the contract would have been discharged.

Similar reasoning accounts for the decision in *Mitchell v Ceazan Tires*[48] where premises were let in March 1940 for three years "for the conduct of an automobile tire business and other related businesses such as automobile supplies"; the lease also gave the tenant the right to sublet. In December 1941, government regulations severely restricted dealings in tyres. But such dealings were not wholly prohibited: for example, the regulations left open the possibility of dealing in re-treads. The main reason for holding that the contract was not discharged was that the proposed use of the premises was not wholly prohibited; a further ground of the decision was that the tenant had failed to show that the restrictions on dealing were not reasonably foreseeable.

7–021   These American cases may be contrasted with the decision of the House of Lords in *Denny Mott & Dickson Ltd v James B Fraser & Co Ltd.*[49] The parties in that case had entered into an agreement for the sale of timber; and "to enable the aforesaid trading agreement to be carried out" they then made a further agreement for the lease of a timber yard. The latter agreement gave the tenant an option to purchase the yard. War-time legislation prohibited the performance of the trading agreement, and it was held to follow that the agreement for the lease of the timber yard had been discharged, so that the tenant could no longer exercise the option to purchase. The purpose of the agreement for the lease of the yard was to enable dealings in timber to continue, and this purpose had been wholly

---

[44] Above, paras 7–014, 7–017; *cf.* below, para.7–024.

[45] [1903] 2 K.B. 683; above, para.7–013.

[46] [1903] 2 K.B. 740; above, para.7–010.

[47] See above, para.7–006.

[48] 153 P. 2d 53 (1944); *cf. Wood v Bartolino*, 146 2d 883 (1944); *Frazier v Collins*, 187 S.W. 2d 816 (1945).

[49] [1944] A.C. 265; below, para.11–024.

defeated.[50] In this respect, the case may be compared with an American case[51] in which a contract to display and distribute materials advertising the defendant's sight-seeing tours for two years from March 1941, was held to have been discharged when war-time legislation prohibited such tours with effect from September 10, 1942.

In the cases so far considered in this group, the purpose alleged to have been frustrated was either mentioned in the contract, or was obvious from the nature of the contract. Where this is not the case, the contract will not be discharged merely because war-time restrictions prevent one party from using the subject-matter for a purpose envisaged by that party alone: in such cases, there is no frustration of any *common purpose*.[52] Thus in one American case[53] a contract for the supply of coal to a manufacturer of fire-place accessories was held not to have been discharged merely because war-time regulations had restricted the supply of metals needed to make such accessories and had therefore curtailed the manufacturer's business. The decision is plainly right, for a supplier *of fuel* to a manufacturer cannot be expected to know the details of the latter's business or of his other needs. Whether the same is necessarily true of other contracts for the supply of raw materials to a manufacturer is perhaps a more open question, since the nature of some such materials may suffice to give the supplier an indication of the purpose for which they are required. But it would be difficult to convince a court that such a contract had been frustrated in circumstances of the kind here under consideration, since most raw materials can be used for more than one purpose. There seems, for example, to be no reported case in which a contract for the supply of hops to a brewer was held to have been frustrated in the United States as a result of the liquor prohibition laws (the effect of which on certain other contracts is discussed in paras 7–023 and 7–024, below). Even if hops could not be used for purposes other than brewing beer, it would presumably have been an answer to a claim of discharge that the buyer could have resold the goods, at least for export. Discharge in such cases would be brought about only by special legislative provisions to that effect.

(b) *Restriction on freedom of movement*

This group of cases concerns leases of premises which the tenant cannot put to the use intended by him because of war-time restrictions on his own freedom of movement, or on that of a group of persons to which he belongs. The typical case is that of a lease of premises for residential

7–022

---

[50] Prohibition of a main contract between A and B will not, however, necessarily discharge ancillary contracts between different parties, such as a guarantee of B's performance given by C to A or a counter indemnity given by B to C in respect of C's liability to A under the guarantee: see *Gulf Bank KSC v Mitsubishi Heavy Industrial Ltd* [1994] 1 Lloyd's Rep. 323.

[51] *Ask Mr Foster's Travel Services v Tauck Tours*, 43 N.Y.S. 2d 674 (1943).

[52] *cf.* above, para.7–013, at n.2.

[53] *Popper v Centre Brass Works*, 43 N.Y.S. 2d 107 (1943).

purposes, in which the tenant cannot lawfully reside because of his enemy alien status in wartime. The English cases on this topic are complicated by the fact that, when they were decided, English law did not recognise that leases of land could be discharged under the doctrine of frustration[54]: the tenants would therefore remain liable for rent even if it could (on the reasoning of *Krell v Henry*[55]) be said that their purpose in entering into the contracts had been frustrated. Now that English law does recognise that its doctrine of frustration can apply to leases,[56] these cases may require reconsideration; but it is unlikely that a significant number of them would now be differently decided. Leases of land are often long-term transactions, so that the parties must expect conditions to change during their currency and so to take the risk of such changes.[57] Thus an English case[58] in which it was held that a three-year lease of residential premises from late June 1914 was not discharged, when war-time legislation prevented the tenant from residing there, would probably still be followed today. A similar result was reached in the American case of *Brown v Oshiro*,[59] where a lease was granted for four years from February 1940 at a monthly rental of $175 to a Japanese tenant who operated the premises as a hotel mainly for persons of Japanese ancestry. War-time regulations, which took effect in May 1942, excluded such persons from the area in which the hotel was situated. The tenant sublet the hotel for $100 per month, and the court upheld the landlord's claim that the lease continued to bind the tenant. The decision is based partly on the view that the purpose for which the tenant intended to use the premises was merely *his* "desired object" (and not that of both parties); and partly on the ground that the tenant had attracted a substantial non-Japanese clientèle, so that even *his* purpose was only partly frustrated.[60] There seems to be little doubt that, on such facts, an English court would reach the same conclusion.

(4) The liquor prohibition cases

7–023   Most of these cases arose when, in 1920, the sale of intoxicating liquor was prohibited throughout the United States as a result of the coming into force of the 18th Amendment to the Constitution; some arose under state laws which had previously imposed similar restrictions. The cases deal with the effect of such legislation on "saloon" leases entered into before the legislation came into force; they fall into two groups.

---

[54] Below, para.11–001.

[55] [1903] 2 K.B. 740; above, para.7–010.

[56] *National Carriers Ltd v Panalpina (Northern) Ltd* [1981] A.C. 625; below, para. 11–001.

[57] *cf. Larrinaga & Co v Société Franco-Américaine des Phosphates de Medulla* (1923) 92 L.J.K.B. 455.

[58] *London & Northern Estates Ltd v Schlesinger* [1916] 1 K.B. 20.

[59] 156 P. 2d 976 (1945).

[60] For partial frustration of purpose, *cf.* above, paras 7–014, 7–017, 7–020; below para.7–024.

In the first, the leases provided that the premises were to be used only for the purpose of selling intoxicating liquor. For example, in *Industrial Development and Land Co v Goldschmidt*[61] the lease provided that the lessee would "use and occupy the said premises for the purpose of conducting thereon a general winery and/or wholesale and/or retail liquor business"; and the tenant covenanted that he "would not suffer or permit the said premises to be used for any other purposes". This was construed to mean that the premises were to be used only for the purpose of selling intoxicating liquor; and, that purpose having been frustrated when Prohibition came into force, the lease was discharged, so that the tenant ceased to be liable for rent.

In the second group of cases, the lease also permitted some other use of the premises. This was the position in *Grace v Croninger*,[62] where premises were let for "the business of a saloon and cigar store"; the lease permitted subletting "for bootblack and/or cigar store purposes". It was held that the lease was not discharged by a pre-1920 prohibition statute, because the lease allowed the tenant to use the premises for purposes other than those of a saloon and such purposes remained lawful. The court also took the (perhaps more questionable) view that even the business of a "saloon" could be carried on by selling non-intoxicating beverages. It further distinguished the *Goldschmidt* case on the ground that the tenant there had vacated the premises, and said that he could not in that case have continued in possession and "escaped payment of the rent".[63] This suggests that discharge is at the option of the tenant, a point which is hard to reconcile with the theory of automatic discharge[64]; but we shall see that American law has extensively qualified this theory.[65]

It is clear from the reasoning of *Grace v Croninger* that the distinction   7–024
between the first and the second of the above groups depends primarily on the construction of the lease; and from this point of view the meaning given in that case to the word "saloon" may be contrasted with that adopted in the earlier case of *Doherty v Monroe Eckstein Brewing Co.*[66] There the lease provided that "the only business to be carried on in the said premises is the saloon business"; and the lease was held to have been discharged when Prohibition came into force. The court rejected the suggestion that the business of a "saloon" could be carried on by selling soft drinks and other items such as tobacco, and said that "when ... the principal use for saloon purposes of the premises became unlawful, the lease became terminated by operation of law".[67] Extrinsic evidence showed that the principal business had been the sale of beer and whisky; and in the court's view it made no difference that subsidiary activities, such

---

[61] 206 P. 134 (1922).
[62] 55 P. 2d 940 (1936).
[63] *ibid.* at 941.
[64] See below, para.15–002.
[65] For references, see above, para.7–015, n.12.
[66] 191 N.Y.S. 59 (1921).
[67] *ibid.* at 61.

as the sale of soft drinks, could still be lawfully carried on. The court here applied to cases of partial frustration of purpose the same test as that which is normally applied in cases of partial impossibility.[68] We have noted that English courts have applied a stricter test in the first than in the second of these categories of cases,[69] and that this approach seems also to have been adopted in the United States: both *Lloyd v Murphy*[70] and *Grace v Croninger*[71] appear to require *total* prevention of the intended use in cases of frustration of purpose. The *Doherty* case seems to be inconsistent with this requirement, unless it can be said that the part of the contemplated purpose remaining capable of achievement was so "trivial"[72] that it could properly be disregarded.

In England a somewhat similar problem arose in *Grimsdick v Sweetman*,[73] where a lease was granted of a "beerhouse and premises with bakehouse in the rear". The tenant convenanted to "continue the said premises as a beerhouse ..." and not without the landlord's consent to use the premises "in any other manner than as a beerhouse". Under an Act of Parliament passed after the date of the lease, the tenant's licence to sell intoxicating liquor was revoked. This Act came into force when 11 of the original 21 years of the lease were unexpired, and under it compensation was paid to both parties to the lease: £100 to the tenant and £155 to the landlord. The tenant's covenant to "continue the ... premises as a beerhouse" was presumably discharged; but it was held that he remained liable for the rent. One reason for the decision was that, under the Act of Parliament, each party had received compensation for loss of the licence. This was regarded as removing any hardship which the tenant may have suffered. That hardship was that "his chief source of income from the premises had ceased"[74]; and "it must be taken that he has received compensation for that hardship".[75] Another ground for the decision was that "There is still a house in which [the tenant] can live and a bakehouse which he can use",[76] and that accordingly there had been no "total failure of consideration".[77] This reasoning illustrates yet again[78] the point that a stricter test is applied in cases of partial frustration of purpose than in cases of partial impossibility. No doubt the tenant's main purpose in taking the lease was to sell beer on the premises, but frustration of that purpose did not discharge the contract, since other, no doubt subsidiary, purposes could still be achieved.

---

[68] Above, para.5–002.
[69] Above, paras 7–014, 7–017.
[70] 153 P. 2d 47 (1944); above, para.7–020.
[71] Above, n.62.
[72] *cf.* the English *Leiston* case [1916] 2 K.B. 428 at 433, above, para.7–016.
[73] [1909] 2 K.B. 740.
[74] *ibid.* at 747.
[75] *ibid.*
[76] *ibid.*
[77] *ibid.* at 746; *cf.* above, para.2–043.
[78] Above, paras 7–014, 7–017, 7–020.

The cases in which the liquor prohibition was held to discharge the contracts have been explained on two grounds. One is that discharge occurred by frustration of purpose[79]; the other is that discharge was the result of supervening illegality.[80] The first is the broader and preferable ground, for the second could apply only if the contract imposed an affirmative obligation to sell intoxicating liquor on the premises. A merely negative obligation not to use the premises for other purposes would not make performance of either party's obligations illegal.[81]

(5) **The prohibition of export and import cases**

These cases concern contracts for the sale of goods which the buyer intends to export from, or to import into, a particular country. After the contract is made, a law is passed, either in the country of origin or in that of the intended destination, prohibiting such export or import. The courts have generally rejected the buyer's argument that such a prohibition discharged the contract on the ground of frustration of purpose.   **7–025**

(a) *Export prohibition imposed by country of origin*

This situation is illustrated by *D McMaster & Co v Cox McEuen & Co*,[82] where a contract for the sale of jute called for delivery to be made at Dundee. The buyer intended to export the jute, but was prevented from doing so by a supervening war-time prohibition of export without licence (which could not be obtained). The House of Lords held that the contract had not been discharged as the buyer could have disposed of the jute (though less advantageously) on the home market. The position is, *a fortiori*, the same if the prohibition extends only to the export of the goods to the particular country to which the buyer intended to export them. For example, in *Amtorg Trading Corp v Miehle Printing Press & Manufacturing Co*[83] American manufacturers sold printing presses to Soviet buyers for delivery at Milwaukee, knowing that the buyers intended to export the presses to the Soviet Union. After the contract had been made, United States legislation prohibited the export of the presses except under licence (which could not be obtained). It was held that the contract was not discharged, even though the buyer's "export purpose" can be said to have been frustrated. Here the prohibition left it open to the buyer not only to resell the goods in the domestic American market, but also to export them to a wide range of other destinations. Even the fact that the seller knows of the buyer's particular export purpose (as in the *Amtorg* case he no doubt did) will not suffice to discharge the contract.   **7–026**

---

[79] Corbin, 29 Jl. of Comparative Legislation and International Law, 3rd Series, p.6.

[80] *e.g.* in *Doherty v Monroe Eckstein Brewing Co*, 191 N.Y.S. 59 (1929).

[81] *cf.* above, para.7–015, n.6.

[82] 1921 S.C. (H.L.) 24.

[83] 206 F. 2d 103 (1953).

(b) *Import prohibition imposed by country of destination*

7–027   The principle of the decisions just discussed applies also to cases of import prohibitions. In the American case of *Baetjer v New England Alcohol Co*,[84] for example, molasses were bought f.o.b. Puerto Rico; the buyer intended to import them into the United States and the seller knew of this intention. It was held that the contract was not discharged when the United States authorities subsequently prohibited the import of such goods into the United States without a licence (which had not been obtained). The case shows that it makes no difference that the seller knows of the buyer's import purpose. Nor is the contract discharged merely because on its face it contains some indication of that purpose. This was the position in the American case of *Swift Canadian Co v Banet*,[85] where sheep pelts had been sold by Canadian sellers to American buyers f.o.b. Toronto; the contract contained shipping directions indicating that the goods were to be sent to Philadelphia. A subsequent United States prohibition of the import of such goods was held not to have discharged the contract. The reasons for this conclusion were that the seller had performed his part by tendering delivery at Toronto; that the shipping instructions had not altered the nature of his obligation with respect to delivery (since they could have been changed by the buyer); and that there was nothing in the American import restrictions to prevent the buyer from sending the goods to other destinations.

Similar reasoning also explains the English decision in *Congimex, etc. SARL v Tradax Export SA*,[86] perhaps the most extreme case in the present group. The question in that case was whether a contract for the sale of soyabean meal c.i.f. Lisbon had been discharged by a change in Portuguese Government policy,[87] as a result of which a licence to import the goods into Portugal had been refused. The contract was governed by English law, and required payment to be made against documents in New York, and it provided for weighing and sampling at Lisbon for the purpose of final settlement of the price. It was held that the contract had not been discharged. Performance had not become either impossible or illegal, since there was no finding that the acts of weighing and sampling of the goods (as opposed to their import into Portugal) had become illegal by Portuguese law, while there was a finding that the buyers should have considered the possibility of redirecting the goods to another country, *e.g.* to France. Nor was the case one of frustration of purpose. Under a c.i.f.

---

[84]   60 N.E. 2d 798 (1946); *cf. Maine v Lyons* (1912) 15 C.L.R. 671, where Isaacs J. referred to *Elliott v Crutchley* [1904] 1 K.B. 565; [1906] A.C. 7, one of the coronation cases, and so perhaps indicated that he had the doctrine of frustration of purpose in mind but took the view that it did not apply. Griffiths C.J. held the buyer liable on the different ground that the contract was subject to a condition subsequent which could no longer occur.

[85]   224 F. 2d 36 (1955).

[86]   [1983] 1 Lloyd's Rep. 250; *cf. Bangladesh Export Import Co Ltd v Sucden Kerry Ltd* [1995] 2 Lloyd's Rep. 1, below, n.91.

[87]   For the question when such a change may be a ground of discharge, see below, para.8–024.

contract, the seller is required to put the goods on board a ship under a contract of affreightment providing for their carriage to the destination named in the contract of sale; but he is not bound to secure their arrival or discharge there.[88] Once the goods had been duly shipped, the seller therefore had no interest in what happened to them afterwards. This was a matter of concern only to the buyer: it was only *his* purpose of importing the goods into Portugal which had been defeated. Hence the Court of Appeal rejected the argument that "the whole common object of the contracts had been destroyed".[89] In the words of Sir John Donaldson M.R.: "The short answer to this is that the frustrated expectations and intentions of one party to a contract do not necessarily or indeed usually lead to the frustration of that contract and that the ... finding that the buyers should have considered reselling the goods impliedly negatives this submission."[90] In a later case[91] it was similarly held that a contract for the sale of sugar c.i.f. Chittagong was not frustrated when the buyer's licence to import the sugar into Bangladesh was withdrawn. The contract did not oblige either the buyer to import the goods into that country or the seller to procure such import,[92] so that its performance had not become illegal by the law of the place of its performance.[93] A *fortiori*, a c.i.f. contract would not be frustrated merely because the buyer's purpose of ultimately importing the goods into a country other than that of the destination named in the contract had been defeated by a prohibition of import imposed by that other country. Thus where a Portuguese buyer had bought soyabean meal c.i.f. Rotterdam, intending ultimately to import it into Portugal, it was held that the contract was not discharged by a subsequent Portuguese import prohibition.[94]

The English and American cases discussed above may be contrasted with   **7–028** a German case[95] in which a contract had been made to supply beer to a buyer in Iran on c.i.f. terms; disputes under the contract later gave rise to a compromise agreement which provided for continued deliveries of beer over a specified period. During this period a revolution took place in Iran, one of the consequences of which was that the import of alcoholic drink into Iran was prohibited on pain of death. The court "adapted" the contract to this change of circumstances on the ground that the "commercial basis" of the contract had disappeared. The case may be

---

[88] *Benjamin's Sale of Goods* (6th ed.), paras 19–002, 19–069; for the seller's duty not to take steps to prevent delivery of the goods at the contractual destination, see *ibid.* para.19–070.

[89] [1983] 1 Lloyd's Rep. 250 at 267.

[90] *ibid.* at 253.

[91] *Bangladesh Export Import Co Ltd v Sucden Kerry SA* [1995] 2 Lloyd's Rep. 1.

[92] *ibid.* at 6.

[93] Frustration was also excluded by an express term of the contract which showed that the parties had foreseen the possibility of the lack of an effective import licence by providing that inability to *obtain* such a licence was not to be a ground of discharge: see below, para.8–019.

[94] *Congimex SARL (Lisbon) v Continental Grain Export Corp (New York)* [1979] 2 Lloyd's Rep. 346.

[95] BGH February 8, 1984, WM 1984 432.

explained on the ground either that the severity of the penalty made it an exceptional one, or that the German doctrine of the disappearance or disruption of the "commercial basis" of a contract has a wider scope, and gives rise to more flexible remedies,[96] than the common law doctrine of discharge by frustration of purpose. Even so, another German case[97] in which a similar result was reached even though there was no legal restriction on the movement of the goods at all (but only a *de facto* impossibility, brought about by the Berlin blockade, of sending them to their intended destination) has been subjected to much adverse criticism.[98]

(c) *Contractual provisions requiring export or import*

7–029   A crucial feature of all the cases in the group considered in paras 7–026 to 7–028, above was that the contracts in them did not impose any obligation on either party to export the goods from, or to import them into, the country which had imposed the prohibition. If such an obligation had been imposed, the results might have been different, *e.g.* if in the *Amtorg*[99] case the contract had provided that the goods were to be delivered at Odessa (instead of at Milwaukee), or if in the *Congimex*[1] case the seller had undertaken to deliver the soyabean meal ex ship Lisbon (instead of c.i.f. Lisbon). In such cases, the contracts would, or might, have been discharged, not by frustration of purpose, but by supervening illegality. This aspect of the prohibition of export and import cases will be further considered in Ch.8.[2]

The distinction between cases in which it is an actual term of the contract that the goods are to be exported from, or imported into, the country imposing the prohibition, and those in which this is merely the buyer's purpose, can obviously give rise to difficulty; for, even if the contract contains no express term to this effect, it may be arguable that such a term ought to be implied. In *Edward Grey & Co v Tolme & Runge*[3] a

---

[96] *e.g.* the court may modify or "adapt" the contract to the changed circumstances: see above, paras 6–011, n.66, 6–023, n.59; below, para.15–037 at n.49.

[97] BGH January 16, 1953, MDR 1953, 282.

[98] See, *e.g.* Larenz, *Geschäftsgrundlage und Vertragserfüllung*, pp.151–153; Emmerich, *Das Recht der Leistungsstörungen*, p.311. Nevertheless, the judicially developed doctrine of *Wegfall der Geschäftsgrundlage* (disappearance of the commercial basis) has been given statutory force: see the new BGB § 313 (in force from January 1, 2002) expressly authorising the adaptation (*Anpassung*) of contracts in the light of events amounting in the words of the heading of the new § 313, to *Störung der Geschäftsgrundlage* (disruption of the commercial basis).

[99] 206 F. 2d 103 (1953), above, para.7–026.

[1] [1983] 1 Lloyd's Rep. 250, above, para.7–027 at n.86.

[2] Below, paras 8–009, 8–026 to 8–031, 8–049 to 8–053.

[3] (1915) 31 T.L.R. 551; for previous proceedings, see (1915) 31 T.L.R. 137; *cf.* also *Jager v Tolme & Runge* [1916] 1 K.B. 939 (where it was held that there was no privity of contract between buyer and seller). It appears from the latter report that the defendants in both cases were a partnership of British subjects but that one of them continued after the outbreak of war to reside in Germany, so that

contract had been made for the sale of sugar f.o.b. Hamburg, on the terms that the buyer should have an option to warehouse the sugar instead of shipping it. On July 31, 1914 the German authorities prohibited the export of sugar, and war between Germany and the United Kingdom broke out on August 4. The contract was held to have been discharged since the sugar had been bought for export to this country, the export of sugar had become illegal by German law, and the warehousing of the goods for an "indefinite period" at a "prohibitive" cost "would have completely defeated the [buyers'] object and purpose".[4] One possible interpretation of this reasoning is that it was an actual term of the contract that the goods were to be exported; but in view of the buyers' option to warehouse the goods this position is hard to maintain. Nor was the argument that the buyers could have resold the sugar on the German market considered; we have seen that an argument of this kind was later to prevail in *D McMaster & Co v Cox McEuen & Co*.[5] The reason why the argument was not available in *Edward Grey & Co v Tolme & Runge* appears to be that such a resale would have been illegal as it would have involved trading with the enemy.[6] Indeed, such illegality of the contract of sale was an alternative ground for the decision and one which is, it is submitted, to be preferred to the view that discharge occurred by frustration of purpose. The sale being on f.o.b. terms, the destination of the goods would not normally be a matter of concern to the seller,[7] so that no common purpose (but only that of the buyer) appears to have been frustrated.

(6) The restriction on land use cases

Most of the cases in this group concern contracts for the sale of land; in them the purchaser argues that he should be discharged from the contract on the ground that planning or zoning restrictions have prevented him from putting the premises to their intended use. Such an argument was advanced in the *Amalgamated Investment & Property*[8] case where a contract had been made for the sale of a warehouse "for sale for occupation or redevelopment". Two days later, the warehouse was listed as being of

7–030

---

trading with him would have involved trading with the enemy: see [1916] 1 K.B. 939 at 944–945, 953.

[4] (1915) 31 T.L.R. 551 at 553.

[5] 1921 S.C. (H.L.) 24, above, para.7–026.

[6] cf. *Jager v Tolme & Runge*, above, n.3; contrast *Smith Coney & Barrett v Becker Gray & Co* [1916] 2 Ch. 87, where both parties to a similar contract were British subjects carrying on business in England and the contract provided for payment of a sum of money if physical delivery could not be effected. Hence no question of illegality arose: see *ibid.* at 92.

[7] *Benjamin's Sale of Goods* (6th ed.), para.20–021; cf. para.20–095. For an exceptional case in which the destination and even the route of shipment was a term of an f.o.b. contract, and where the contract was discharged by the supervening impossibility of using that route, see *Hackfield v Castle*, 198 P. 1041 (1921).

[8] *Amalgamated Investment & Property Co v John Walker & Sons Ltd* [1977] 1 W.L.R. 164.

architectural or historic interest, thus substantially reducing the chance of obtaining permission to redevelop it, and allegedly reducing its value from the contract price of £1.7m to £200,000. The purchaser's argument that the contract was discharged by the listing was rejected on the ground that the risk of listing was one "which inheres in all ownership of buildings".[9]

On somewhat similar facts, the same conclusion was reached in the American case of *Di Donato v Reliance Standard Life Insurance Co*,[10] where a contract for the sale of land was held not to have been discharged by "re-zoning" after the contract, so that the land could no longer be used for industrial purposes. The court relied on the doctrine of "equitable conversion"[11] (*i.e.* on the rule that the purchaser became owner of the land in equity as soon as the contract was made); and on the rule that such ownership carried with it the risk of physical harm.[12] For the present purpose, the court could see no relevant distinction between physical harm to the property and financial loss resulting from re-zoning. This reasoning could lead to different results in those American jurisdictions which do not in its full rigour apply the rule that risk passes to a purchaser of land on contract, *e.g.* in those which have adopted the Uniform Vendor and Purchaser Risk Act (which discharges the contract where "all or a material part" of the subject-matter has been destroyed); or in those States which, as a matter of common law, hold that the contract is discharged if a "large" or an "important" part of the property is destroyed.[13] Such reasoning, if it were applied to the facts of the *Amalgamated Investment & Property* case,[14] could lead to a different result from that reached in that case, where by reason of the "listing" the property was alleged to have lost over 88 per cent of its value. It should, however, be noted that, while the Uniform Vendor and Purchaser Risk Act expressly extends to the case where land is "taken by eminent domain", it does not in so many words deal with loss of value as a result of "re-zoning".

7-031   Just as, in a number of the United States, the "purchaser's risk" rule in contracts for the sale of land is modified by law, so in England it is (as we have noted in Ch.3) now common for that rule to be modified by contract.[15] The question can thus arise whether the result in a case such as the *Amalgamated Investment & Property* case (which was justified partly in terms of the "risk" of listing being on the purchaser from the time of contracting) would be affected by such provisions. The answer to this question would turn on the construction of the provisions in question. Those considered in Ch.3 seem, from their wording, to be intended to deal with the physical risks of damage to or destruction of buildings,

---

[9] *ibid.* at 173.
[10] 249 A. 2d 327 (1969). *cf. Beaton v McDivitt* (1988) 13 N.S.W.L.R. 162, where conflicting views were expressed as to the effect on an alleged contract of failure in "re-zoning" referred to in the alleged contract.
[11] 249 A. 2d 327, 329.
[12] Above, paras 3–027, 3–039.
[13] Above, paras 3–039 to 3–041.
[14] Above, n.8.
[15] Above, para.3–047.

rather than with the legal or financial risk at issue in the *Amalgamated Investment & Property* case. Construed in this way, contractual provisions which expressly left the risk on the vendor until completion would not affect the outcome on facts such as those of that case.

The *Amalgamated Investment & Property* and *Di Donato* cases may be contrasted with the further American case of *Dover Pool & Racquet Club v Brooking*[16] where a contract had been made for the sale of land which the purchaser (as the vendor knew) intended to use as a non-profit-making swimming and tennis club. In the pre-contract negotiations, zoning was discussed and the parties entered into the contract on the assumption that "everything would be alright under the existing ... by-laws". In fact, four days before the contract was made, a notice of re-zoning (precluding the intended use of the land) had been published, and this was later confirmed so as to take effect retroactively, from the date of the (pre-contract) notice. It was held that the purchaser was entitled to rescind the contract for mistake as to the "basic assumption" made by both parties that "the zoning by-laws interposed no obstacle to the [intended] use of the property".[17] But at the same time the court said that "It could not yet be said that the purchaser's principal purpose had been frustrated".[18] The distinction here drawn between mistake and frustration by antecedent events may reflect the point that American courts appear, for reasons discussed in Ch.1,[19] to be somewhat more ready to grant relief on the former than on the latter ground. In English law, by contrast, it is unlikely that a more lenient test would be applied when granting relief for mistake as to existing fact than that which would be applied to determine whether there has been discharge by supervening frustration of purpose.[20] In the *Amalgamated Investment & Property* case, the court refused to give relief on the ground of the purchaser's mistaken belief that the property was "suitable for being redeveloped". The reason why this mistake was said not to be a ground of relief was that it was not a mistake of existing fact (or even of existing law) but only one of expectation. The case differs from the *Dover Pool* case in that there the "zoning" took effect retroactively; but the effect of the "listing" or "zoning" in both cases was to impede the intended development.

In the present group of cases the purpose alleged to have been   **7-032** frustrated was that of the buyer only: this distinguishes them from the coronation cases, in which it was the common purpose of both parties which was frustrated.[21] This is also the position in a hypothetical case put in the *Cricklewood Property* case,[22] where it was said that a building lease

---

[16] 322 N.E. 2d 168 (1975).

[17] *ibid.* at 170.

[18] *ibid.* referring to what is now Restatement 2d, § 266(2), which deals with existing impracticability and frustration (above, para.1–010).

[19] Above, para.1–010.

[20] *ibid.*

[21] Above, para.7–014 at n.97.

[22] *Cricklewood Investment & Property Trust Ltd v Leighton's Investment Trust Ltd* [1945] A.C. 221.

might be discharged if the land in question were "dedicated as an open space for ever".[23] The assumption is that the "building purpose" is a term of the contract. The obligation to build might, indeed, be imposed only on the tenant, but the landlord would normally share that "building purpose" as he would have a financial interest in its achievement. In the *Amalgamated Investment & Property* case,[24] there was only an intention of one party to develop the property which had been sold. There was no undertaking by either party that development would be carried out, or that it would be possible, and no interest on the part of the vendor that the development should be carried out.

The argument that restrictions on the use of land may be a ground of frustration is not confined to contracts which create or transfer an interest in land. The point may be illustrated by further reference to the *Brisbane*[25] case, discussed in para.7–003, above, where a contractor agreed with the city to execute certain works in return for the city's help in securing permission for residential development on the contractor's land. The contractor's obligation to execute the work was discharged when compulsory acquisition of the land prevented the development from taking place. Two of the five members of the High Court[26] appear to have regarded the case as one of frustration of purpose, since they base their judgments in part on the coronation cases. This reasoning, however, gives rise to the difficulty that the proposed development can hardly be described as the common purpose of both parties: it seems to have been the purpose of one party only (*i.e.* of the contractor) and this is not normally regarded as sufficient to discharge a contract.[27] The other three members of the court based their decision on the different ground that the order giving permission for the development was of no effect as the legislation under which it was made did not bind the Crown. This reasoning seems to amount to saying that the contractors were excused by failure of a condition precedent, rather than that they were discharged by supervening events.

(7) Other miscellaneous cases

7–033   The doctrine of discharge by frustration of purpose has been applied in a number of miscellaneous American cases. One group of such cases concerns contracts to publish souvenir programmes of yacht races. These contracts were held to have been discharged when the races were cancelled because of the outbreak of the First World War.[28] In one of these cases[29] the court

---

[23] *ibid.* at 229; *cf.* at 240.
[24] [1977] 1 W.L.R. 164.
[25] *Brisbane City Council v Group Projects Pty Ltd* (1979) 145 C.L.R. 143.
[26] Stephens and Murphy JJ.; *cf.* above, para.7–003.
[27] Above, paras 7–014, 7–027 at n.90.
[28] *Alfred Marks Realty Co v "Churchills"*, 153 N.Y.S. 264 (1915); *Alfred Marks Realty Co v Hotel Hermitage Co*, 156 N.Y.S. 179 (1915).
[29] *Alfred Marks Realty Co v "Churchills"*, above.

refers with approval to *Krell v Henry*.[30] In another case,[31] a contract between a golf club and a hotel company for the use of the club's facilities by the hotel's guests was discharged when the hotel was burnt down. The case may bear some superficial resemblance to *Taylor v Caldwell*,[32] but its subject-matter was not the hotel, but the golf-club facilities, and these were not destroyed. Hence the ground of decision was frustration of purpose, rather than impossibility. It seems likely that the American decisions considered in this paragraph would be followed in England.

Other American cases, however, appear to show that the doctrine of frustration of purpose has a wider scope in American than in English law. Thus in one American case it was held that a lease of office premises, in which the tenant personally carried on his brokerage business, was discharged when the tenant was conscripted for military service[33]; it seems unlikely that this case would be followed in England[34] (even after the recognition of the possibility that leases of land can be discharged by supervening events[35]) unless the lease was a very short one. In another American case it was even held that a contract which had been made to secure a tax advantage was discharged when an adverse ruling of the tax authorities frustrated that purpose.[36] It seems unlikely that this case would be followed in England and there are indications that it may be viewed with some scepticism even in the United States.[37] However, these cases show that the view that the doctrine of discharge by frustration of purpose is more widely supported in England than in the United States[38] is the reverse of the truth. This conclusion is also supported by a comparison of the American and English "black-out" cases discussed in paras 7–015 to 7–018, above.

The American cases do, however, insist that events which merely reduce   **7–034** the profitability of a contract do not give rise to frustration of purpose. Thus it has been held that a contract which granted a licence to establish a

---

[30] [1903] 2 K.B. 740.

[31] *La Cumbre Golf Club v Santa Barbara Hotel Co*, 271 P. 2d 476 (1928).

[32] (1863) 3 B. & S. 826; above, para.2–024.

[33] *State Realty v Greenfield*, 181 N.Y.S. 511 (1920).

[34] *cf. London & Northern Estates Ltd v Schlesinger* [1916] 1 K.B. 20, above, para.7–022 at n.58.

[35] *National Carriers Ltd v Panalpina (Northern) Ltd* [1981] A.C. 675, below, para.11–001.

[36] *West Los Angeles Institute for Cancer Research v Mayer*, 366 F. 2d 220 (1966), cert. denied 385 U.S. 1010; followed in *Walker v Continental Life & Accident Co*, 445 F. 2d 1072 (1971) where tax advantages expected to accrue from an insurance scheme failed to do so as a result of a decision of the US Supreme Court, and the policy-holders were held entitled to rescind.

[37] In the Tentative Draft of Restatement 2d, § 285, Illustration 5 is evidently based on the *West Los Angeles* case, but this illustration is deleted from the corresponding place in the final version of Restatement 2d, § 265, and the case is no longer cited in this version. One may perhaps infer that the case or the illustration did not meet with the approval of the American Law Institute.

[38] *e.g.* Anderson, 3 De Paul L. Rev. 1 (1953); Birmingham, 20 Hastings L.J. 1393, 1395 (1969).

cab-rank outside a restaurant was not discharged when the restaurant failed to secure the renewal of its all-night licence[39]; that a contract to buy a restaurant was not discharged when a bar in the same building closed with the result that there was a substantial falling off in the business of the restaurant[40]; and that a lease of a grain elevator was not discharged when, in consequence of an order of the Interstate Commerce Commission, the business of the elevator fell by 50 per cent, so that it could be carried on only at a loss.[41]

The decision of the House of Lords in *National Carriers Ltd v Panalpina (Northern) Ltd*[42] falls on the same side of the line. It was there held that a 10-year lease of a warehouse was not discharged when, four-and-a-half years before the end of the lease, the only access road to the premises was closed by the local authority and remained closed for 20 months. The case was one of temporary frustration of purpose rather than one of temporary impossibility: it had not become impossible for the landlord to make the premises available for occupation or for the tenant to pay the rent, but the (no doubt mutually) intended use of the premises had been interrupted.

III. CONCLUSION

7–035   The foregoing account shows that the doctrine of discharge by frustration of purpose is recognised both in England and in the United States, but that the courts in both countries are aware of the danger that the doctrine could undermine the principle of the sanctity of contract. That danger was the basis of early criticisms of the coronation cases and also accounts for the views of those who argued that the doctrine of discharge by frustration of purpose had not been, or ought not to be, accepted in the United States. English courts have perhaps been more acutely aware of the danger than those in the United States. Although the doctrine can be said to have originated in the English coronation cases, it has scarcely ever been applied in England since those cases were decided. A retrospective glance at the illustrations of the doctrine discussed in this chapter does not show any English case in which the doctrine has been applied or in which it formed the sole basis of the decision.[43] Even the *Denny Mott*[44] case is a Scottish case, though the decision of the House of Lords is accepted as authoritative in England. The case was, however, complicated by the factor of supervening illegality, to which certain special considerations apply.[45] By contrast, the

---

[39] *The Abbaye v U S Cab Co*, 128 N.Y.S. 697 (1911).

[40] *Downing v Stiles*, 635 P. 2d 808 (1981).

[41] *Megan v Updike Grain Corp*, 94 F. 2d 551 (1938).

[42] [1981] A.C. 675.

[43] In *Edward Grey & Co v Tolme & Runge* (1915) 31 T.L.R. 551 the doctrine formed one ground for the decision, but the better ground is that the contract was discharged by supervening illegality: above, para.7–029.

[44] [1944] A.C. 265; above, para.7–021.

[45] *e.g.* discharge by certain kinds of supervening illegality cannot be excluded by express contractual provisions: *Ertel Bieber & Co v Rio Tinto Co* [1918] A.C. 260,

Amalgamated Investment & Property case[46] provides a striking illustration of the reluctance of English courts to apply the doctrine. Most of the applications of the doctrine since the coronation cases are to be found in American cases.[47] This may appear to be paradoxical, because it used to be argued that the doctrine had no place in American law,[48] and we have noted its rejection in one of the United States.[49] On the other hand, the wider scope of the doctrine in the United States (*e.g.* in the *20th Century Lites* case[50] and in some of the liquor prohibition cases[51]) is, more significantly, consistent with the greater readiness of the American (than that of the English) courts to allow a party to claim discharge on the ground of impracticability.[52] The policy arguments for, and the dangers posed by, the two doctrines of impracticability and frustration of purpose are similar: each operates in circumstances falling short of impossibility, and, because those circumstances are hard to define, each leads to uncertainty and threatens the sanctity of contract.

The stricter approach of the English courts to frustration of purpose helps also to resolve a further paradox. In this chapter we have repeatedly emphasised the close link between frustration of purpose and impracticability, indeed we have noted that the link is so close that the two doctrines are sometimes confused.[53] At first sight, it is paradoxical that English law, which first recognised the doctrine of frustration of purpose in the coronation cases, should have maintained its reluctance to recognise the doctrine of impracticability. The paradox is all the more striking in that the former doctrine, being generally available to a "buyer" of goods, services or facilities, presents a weaker case for relief than the latter doctrine: in the normal frustration of purpose case, the "buyer's" loss, if he has to perform the contract, will not exceed the contract price,[54] while the "seller's" loss in cases of impracticability is theoretically infinite. The paradox is, at least largely, resolved if one has regard to the development of the doctrine of frustration of purpose. English cases provide no illustration of discharge by "pure" frustration of purpose since the

7–036

---

below, para.8–055; while such provisions can exclude discharge by frustration of purpose: *e.g. Victoria Seats Agency v Paget* (1902) 19 T.L.R. 16, above, para.7–010.

[46] [1977] 1 W.L.R. 164, above, para.7–030.

[47] For its application by two members of the High Court of Australia in the *Brisbane* case (1979) 145 C.L.R. 143; above, paras 7–003, 7–032.

[48] Above, para.7–004.

[49] See the *Northern Indiana* case, 799 F. 2d 265 (1986), above, para.7–002.

[50] 149 P. 2d 88 (1944), above, para.7–015.

[51] *e.g. Industrial Development & Land Co v Goldschmidt*, 206 P. 134 (1922); *Doherty v Monroe Eckstein Brewing Co*, 191 N.Y.S. 59 (1929), above, paras 7–023, 7–024.

[52] Above, Ch.6.

[53] See the discussion of the *Nora Springs* case 247 N.W. 2d 744 (1976) and of the *Northern Indiana* case, 799 F. 2d 265 (1986), above, paras 7–001, 7–002 and *cf. Downing v Stiles*, 635 P. 2d 808, 811.

[54] Even the "buyer" may suffer additional reliance loss, but this is likely to be limited in extent.

coronation cases[55]; while American cases do show a number of such applications. This development is consistent with the judicial attitude in the two countries towards impracticability. It shows that certainty and the sanctity of contract are values which have been regarded as more important by the English than by the American courts.

---

[55] The *Denny Mott* case [1944] A.C. 265 was complicated by illegality, which was also an alternative (and preferable) ground in the *Edward Grey* case (1915) 31 T.L.R. 551: see above n.43 and after n.44.

CHAPTER 8

ILLEGALITY

I. INTRODUCTION: BASIS OF DISCHARGE

A contract can be discharged if, after its formation, performance of it **8–001** becomes illegal. Such supervening illegality generally arises from a change in the law which prohibits performance, or from a change in the surrounding circumstances which has the effect of prohibiting performance by virtue of the previously existing law. The distinction between these two situations may be illustrated by supposing that a contract has been made for the sale of goods on the terms that they are to be exported from England to a specified foreign country (Ruritania). If after the contract is made an Act of Parliament prohibits the export of the goods to Ruritania, the case will be one of discharge by a supervening change in the law. If after the contract is made war breaks out between the United Kingdom and Ruritania, the case will be one of discharge by a supervening change of circumstances which attracts the operation of the previously existing law against trading with the enemy.[1] In both situations the contract is discharged by supervening illegality, since in each of them a performance, which was lawful when the contract was made, later became unlawful.

A change in the law which makes performance of the contract illegal does not, however, necessarily operate even *prima facie* as a ground of discharge. We are not at this stage concerned with the question whether the principle of discharge by supervening illegality may be qualified by such factors as express contractual provisions, foreseeability or some degree of "fault" of the party claiming discharge (such as his failure to take reasonable steps to secure any permit or licence required by the supervening law).[2] Our present concern is with the more fundamental point that even the violation of an antecedent prohibition affecting the performance of a contract will not necessarily make the contract illegal. The point may be illustrated by reference to the well-known case of *St John Shipping Corp v Joseph Rank Ltd*,[3] where a shipowner committed a statutory

---

[1] Below, para.8–004.
[2] Below, paras 8–019, 8–055, 13–003.
[3] [1957] 1 Q.B. 267.

offence by overloading his ship in the course of performing a number of contracts for the carriage of goods in the ship. It was held that the contracts were not illegal (so that the shipowner was entitled to the agreed freight), since the object of the statute which prohibited the overloading was merely to prevent overloading and not to prohibit contracts; and since this object was to be achieved by imposing the fine specified in the statute, rather than by subjecting the shipowner to the much more severe financial loss which would result from invalidating the contracts of carriage with the various cargo-owners. It seems that the result would have been the same if the legislation had been passed after the conclusion of the contract. In this book, we are not concerned with the details of the rules governing antecedent illegality. The point to be made here is that a supervening prohibition will discharge a contract only where its nature is such that it would have made the contract void or unenforceable for illegality, if the prohibition had already been in force when the contract was made.

8–002   The purpose of the doctrine of discharge by supervening impossibility is to provide a legal method of allocating or distributing the loss caused by supervening events. This is true also of the extensions of that doctrine to cases of supervening impracticability and frustration of purpose. Where, however, a contract is affected by supervening illegality, the court is concerned, not merely with reaching a solution which may do justice between the contracting parties, but also with the public interest in seeing that the law is observed; and this public interest may sometimes outweigh the private interests of the parties. This point can be illustrated by reference to the history of the doctrine: we have seen that discharge by supervening illegality was recognised on grounds of public policy[4] even when it was thought that the private interests of the parties in cases of supervening impossibility were best served by adherence to the doctrine of absolute contracts.[5] Indeed, it was at one time even thought that a contract could be discharged if supervening events made its performance contrary to public policy without making it contrary to law[6]. Although there is no support in the modern cases for any such broad principle, it remains true that discharge for supervening illegality is based on public policy, or on what has been called "moral or legal impossibility"[7]: *i.e.* on the idea that performance ought not to be (though physically it could be) rendered. For this reason discharge by supervening illegality is governed by a number of special rules which do not apply in cases of supervening impossibility, impracticability or frustration of purpose.

The distinction between the two grounds of discharge was recognised in the United States by the original version of the Restatement, which dealt in separate sections with "supervening impossibility"[8] and "supervening

---

[4] Above, para.2–011.
[5] Above, para.2–002.
[6] *Atkinson v Ritchie* (1809) 10 East 530 at 534–535 (above, para.2–011); *cf. Touteng v Hubbard* (1802) 3 B. & P. 291 (above, para.5–037).
[7] *The Teutonia* (1871) L.R. 3 A. & E. 394, 416.
[8] § 457.

prohibition or prevention by law".[9] The Restatement 2d, however, treats such prohibition or prevention simply as an illustration of discharge by "impracticability",[10] thus apparently disregarding the element of public interest which enters into cases of this kind. The Uniform Commercial Code likewise subsumes cases in which performance (at least by the seller) has been prohibited under the concept of impracticability.[11] Indeed, the Code extends the excuse to cases of compliance in good faith with governmental regulation or order "whether or not it later proves to be invalid".[12] If the regulation or order did prove to be invalid, there could be no public policy grounds for excusing performance, and English law would not recognise an excuse in such circumstances.[13]

It is of course possible for a change in the law to lead to a situation in which performance becomes impossible (or impracticable), *e.g.* where the change empowers a public authority to requisition or compulsorily to acquire the subject-matter of a contract and it exercises that power before performance has been completed.[14] Similarly, a change in the law may give rise to frustration of purpose, *e.g.* where the change prohibits the use of the subject-matter for the common purpose of the parties, as in some of the liquor prohibition cases.[15] Our concern in this chapter, however, is with cases in which performance remains physically possible (or "practicable" in the sense that the penalty imposed by the new law may be small in relation to the value of the contract), and in which no question of discharge by frustration of purpose arises, but in which the contract is nevertheless discharged because its performance has become illegal.[16]

    8–003

Granted that the basis of discharge in cases of supervening illegality is public policy, it is important to bear in mind that the policy considerations raised by different types of illegality can vary considerably in weight. This point has been accepted in the law relating to antecedent illegality (which

---

[9] § 458.

[10] § 264, Comments a and c, *cf.* § 261, Illustration 1.

[11] s.2–615(a); but the Code does recognise that special provision is required for supervening prohibition in the case of obligations to pay money since performance of these cannot become impossible or impracticable: see s.2–614(2), discussed at below, paras 8–043 to 8–045. Corresponding provisions apply to chattel leases: see UCC, ss.2A–405(a), 2A–404(2).

[12] ss.2–615(a), 2A–405(a).

[13] See *Lipton Ltd v Ford* [1917] 2 K.B. 647, where much of the discussion is concerned with the validity of legislation under which goods were requisitioned.

[14] *Re Shipton Anderson & Co* [1915] 3 K.B. 676; *Bank Line Ltd v Arthur Capel & Co* [1919] A.C. 435; *West v Peoples First Nat Bank & Trust Co*, 106 A. 2d 427 (1954). *Kursell v Timber Operators & Contractors* [1927] 1 K.B. 298 appears to be a case of this kind. *cf. Islwyn BC v Newport BC* (1994) 6 Admin L.R. 386 (where the legislation on its true construction was held not to have prevented or prohibited performance). It will be recalled that the mere making of a compulsory purchase order with respect to land which is the subject-matter of a contract of sale does not discharge the contract: see above, paras 4–007 to 4–009 for the English authorities on this point.

[15] Above, para.7–023.

[16] See, *e.g.*, the discussion of the *Fibrosa* case [1943] A.C. 32, below, para.8–005.

is not of itself necessarily regarded as a ground of invalidity).[17] A similar approach is reflected in the law governing the effects of supervening illegality, so that these effects, too, may vary according to the type of illegality in question. This will become clear in the following discussion, in which a number of examples of supervening illegality will be contrasted from this point of view.

II. Trading with the Enemy

8–004   A contract made during a war to which this country is a party is illegal if it involves commercial intercourse with an enemy.[18] The public policy considerations on which the prohibition against trading with the enemy are based are of exceptional strength because observance of this prohibition can affect the very survival of the nation; and this point is reflected in a number of special rules which apply where the performance of contracts which were valid when made is later affected by this prohibition. For the purpose of the prohibition, an enemy is a person voluntarily resident or carrying on business in enemy-occupied territory.[19] Such a contract is illegal at common law on the ground of public policy that it would tend to aid the economy of the enemy country.[20] If in fact performance would not involve any further commercial intercourse with the enemy, the contract is not illegal,[21] so that it can be enforced. It is a statutory offence to trade, or to attempt to trade with an enemy.[22]

It follows from the principle of public policy on which the prohibition against trading with the enemy is based that a contract which is lawful when made will be discharged if, as a result of the outbreak of a war to which this country is a party, further performance of the contract will involve commercial intercourse with an enemy. For example, in *Esposito v Bowden*[23] a ship was chartered by a British charterer to load grain at

---

[17] *e.g.* where the illegality affects the method of performance: above, at n.3. Some dicta suggest that the court will refuse to enforce a contract on grounds of illegality only if enforcement would be an "affront to the public conscience": see *Euro-Diam Ltd v Bathurst* [1990] Q.B. 1, esp. at 35; *Howard v Shirlstar Container Transport Ltd* [1990] 1 W.L.R. 1292. But these dicta have been rejected by the House of Lords: *Tinsley v Milligan* [1994] 1 A.C. 340 at 358–361 and 358–361, *per* Lord Goff, who dissented in the result but with whose views on this point all the other members of the House of Lords directly or indirectly expressed their agreement. See also *Pitts v Hunt* [1991] 1 Q.B. 24 at 56; *Webb v Chief Constable of Merseyside Police* [2000] Q.B. 427 at 445; Treitel, *The Law of Contract* (11th ed.), pp.482–483.

[18] See *Esposito v Bowden* (1857) 7 E. & B. 763; *Duncan Fox & Co v Schrempft & Bonke* [1915] 1 K.B. 365 and 3 K.B. 355; *VO Sovfracht v Van Udens Scheepvaarten Agentur Maatschappij (NV Gebr)* [1943] A.C. 203.

[19] *Porter v Freudenberg* [1915] 1 K.B. 857.

[20] See the authorities cited above, n.18.

[21] *Tingley v Muller* [1917] 2 Ch. 144; *Cornelius v Banque Franco-Serbe* [1942] 1 K.B. 29.

[22] Trading with the Enemy Act 1939.

[23] (1857) 7 E. & B. 763.

Odessa. Subsequently the Crimean War broke out between the United Kingdom and Russia and it was held that the contract had been discharged, so that the charterer was not bound to load, since performance by him would have amounted to trading with the enemy. Performance was said to have become "unlawful and impossible".[24] It is submitted that it is the factor of supervening illegality which is in such cases the decisive one. The mere fact that war has made performance of a contract more difficult is not sufficient to discharge it where no question of illegality is involved,[25] *e.g.* because the war is neither one to which this country is a party nor one which gives rise to any illegality by the law governing the contract[26] or by the law of the place of its performance.

Conversely, the contract will be discharged by illegality if its perfor-   **8–005** mance will infringe the prohibition against trading with the enemy, even though the outbreak of war may not have made its performance impossible at all. This was the position in the *Fibrosa* case[27] where a contract had been made in July 1939, for the sale of machinery by an English seller to a Polish buyer on the terms that the goods were to be delivered c.i.f. Gdynia within three or four months. Before the goods had been shipped, war broke out between the United Kingdom and Germany, and German forces occupied Gdynia. The contract was held to have been discharged even though it might, at the time envisaged for its performance, still have been physically possible to have the goods shipped to Gdynia through a neutral country on a neutral ship; and even though the goods were ultimately destined by the buyer for Vilna which was (so far as the United Kingdom was concerned) in neutral territory at the relevant time, having been occupied by Soviet forces in 1939 and coming under German control only in 1941. The contract was discharged on the ground that it had become illegal[28] since delivery of the goods was to be made in territory held by the enemy, and so its performance would have violated the strong public interest in ensuring that no aid should be given to the economy of an enemy country in time of war. Similarly, a contract by which an English seller had undertaken to deliver goods to a German buyer was held to have been frustrated on grounds of public policy on the outbreak of the First World War, even though the goods were to have been delivered in Australia, so that delivery was plainly not impossible.[29] The

---

[24] *ibid.* at 783; *cf. Zinc Corp Ltd v Hirsch* [1916] 1 K.B. 141; *Jager v Tolme & Runge* [1916] 1 K.B. 939 at 956 (illegality) and *ibid.* at 962 (impossibility); *St Enoch Shipping Co v Phosphate Mining Co* [1916] 2 K.B. 624.

[25] *Vinava Shipping Co v Finelvet AG (The Chrysalis)* [1983] 1 W.L.R. 1469; *International Sea Tankers Inc v Hemisphere Shipping Co Ltd (The Wenjiang) (No2)* [1983] 1 Lloyd's Rep. 400.

[26] For war giving rise to such illegality, see *The Teutonia* (1871) L.R. 7 A. & E. 295.

[27] *Fibrosa Spolka Akcyjna v Fairbairn, Lawson Combe Barbour Ltd* [1943] A.C. 32.

[28] *ibid.* at 41, 68. The suggestion in *Stocznia Gdanska SA v Latvian Shipping Co* [1998] 1 W.L.R. 574 at 600 that in the *Fibrosa* case "the outbreak of war frustrated the contract" is, with respect, open to question: it was not the outbreak of war, but the enemy occupation of the contractual port of destination which was the ground of frustration.

[29] *Naylor Benzon & Co Ltd v Hirsch* (1917) 33 T.L.R. 432.

principle of public policy prohibits the import of goods from, no less than their export to, an enemy country; and a contract which envisages such import will be discharged by the outbreak of war between this country and the enemy country even though the enemy source is not specified in the contract but is only contemplated by the contracting parties.[30] If in such circumstances the contract were not discharged, parties might evade the principle of public policy in time of impending war simply by omitting from the contract any reference to the intended enemy source. The principle can apply also to a negative stipulation, such as one not to sell goods of the contract description to anyone except the person who later became an enemy subject; for "to withdraw the goods from commerce and preserve them for the enemy after the war is little removed from trading with the enemy".[31]

8–006   The rule just stated demonstrates the exceptional strength of the principle of public policy which is the basis of the prohibition against trading with the enemy: where the import of goods from an intended country of origin merely becomes impossible, or is made illegal by prohibition of export or import, it is unlikely that a contract which does not specify the source or destination of the goods would be discharged by the impossibility or prohibition.[32] A further indication of the strength of principle is provided by the rule that it cannot be excluded even by an express provision in the contract that the war is merely to suspend (and so not to discharge) it.[33] The point to be stressed here is that the rule which invalidates such express provisions in contracts which turn out to involve trading with the enemy clearly does not apply to cases of supervening impossibility or frustration of purpose: in the coronation cases, for example, clauses which made the viewing facilities available on the days of the postponed processions were held to be effective to prevent discharge.[34] From this point of view, the trading with the enemy cases again differ not only from cases of supervening impossibility or frustration of purpose, but also from cases of at least some other kinds of supervening illegality: we shall, for example, see that effect is commonly given to clauses which, in effect, suspend the obligations of sellers or buyers of goods in the event of prohibition of export or import.[35] In these two groups of cases the provisions for suspension might, indeed, cause hardship to one of the parties, but the parties are nevertheless held to their own provision for allocating the loss caused by the supervening

---

[30]   *Re Badische Co* [1921] 2 Ch. 331; *cf. Veithard & Hall Ltd v Rylands Bros Ltd* (1917) 116 L.T. 706, where the court may have regarded the contract as containing an implied reference to the enemy source by reason of previous dealings between the parties.

[31]   *Zinc Corp Ltd v Hirsch* [1916] 1 K.B. 541 at 558.

[32]   See, *e.g., Blackburn Bobbin Co Ltd v TW Allen Ltd* [1918] 2. K.B. 467, above, paras 4–053, 4–056.

[33]   Below, para.8–055.

[34]   *Victoria Seats Agency v Paget* (1902) 19 T.L.R. 16, above, para.7–010.

[35]   Below, paras 8–030, 8–056, 12–031 *et seq.*

event. In the trading with the enemy cases, public policy overrides the principle that the parties should be free in this way to allocate the loss.

A somewhat similar distinction is drawn in answering the question whether discharge may result from an event which is "foreseeable" in the sense to be discussed in Ch.13. If the event is one which merely makes performance impossible, there is at least a strong argument for the view that parties who fail in their contract to provide for the effects of a foreseeable event must be deemed to have accepted the risk that the event would occur.[36] But if the foreseeable event is a war, making the contract illegal on the ground that its performance would involve trading with the enemy, then the contract is discharged on grounds of public policy.[37]

III. OTHER SUPERVENING PROHIBITIONS

The cases provide many other illustrations of the principle that a contract may be discharged by supervening legislative prohibition. In the *Denny Mott* case,[38] *e.g.* an agreement for dealing in timber was discharged when war-time legislation prohibited such dealings. In an American case,[39] a contract to grant a free railway pass for life was discharged when an Act of Congress prohibited such arrangements. Obligations to repair or rebuild may similarly be discharged by supervening legislative prohibition on carrying out the specified work.[40] During the First World War, a commercial traveller's contract of employment was discharged when the rendering and acceptance of his services under the contract "ceased to be lawful"[41] by reason of war-time legislation, on his volunteering to join the armed forces. In principle, a contract for the sale of goods to be sent from one country to another may similarly be discharged by supervening prohibition of export or import,[42] though for reasons to be discussed later in this chapter[43] the cases provide more instances of exceptions to, than applications of, the rule. Conversely, a contract may be frustrated if after its formation it becomes illegal for one of the parties to make a payment of money due from him under it. In this sense "an obligation to pay money can be frustrated"[44]: this could, for example, be the position where payment was

8–007

---

[36] Below, paras 13–001, 13–008.

[37] Below, paras 13–003 to 13–004.

[38] *Denny Mott & Dickson v James B Fraser & Co Ltd* [1944] A.C. 265.

[39] *Louisville & Nashville RR v Crowe* (1913) 160 S.W. 759.

[40] See the cases discussed at paras 8–047 to 8–048, below.

[41] *Marshall v Glanvill* [1917] 2 K.B. 87 at 91.

[42] *Société Co-operative Suisse de Céréales v La Plata Cereal Co SA* (1947) 80 Ll.L. Rep. 530 at 542. The point is also assumed in many cases which were actually decided on other grounds, *e.g.* in *Andrew Millar & Co Ltd v Taylor & Co Ltd* [1916] 1 K.B. 402; *Congimex (etc) SARL v Tradax Export SA* [1983] 1 Lloyd's Rep. 250; *Empresa Exportadora de Azucar v Industria Azucarera Nacional SA (The Playa Larga)* [1983] 2 Lloyd's Rep. 171.

[43] Below, paras 8–035 *et seq.*

[44] See *Libyan Arab Foreign Bank v Bankers Trust Co* [1989] Q.B. 728 at 749 (where there was no illegality by the *lex loci solutionis*).

prohibited by supervening exchange control legislation,[45] or by legislation passed to give effect to economic sanctions against the country in which the payment was to be made, or for which it was destined.[46] These cases again illustrate the difference between illegality and impossibility as grounds of discharge. The payment of money cannot in law become impossible, but the contracts are discharged on grounds of public policy by the supervening prohibition. The principle of discharge can apply also to negative contracts: thus in an old case it was said that if an Act of Parliament compels a person to do what he had covenanted not to do, then "the Statute repeals the covenant".[47]

The above cases of discharge by supervening illegality must be distinguished from those (discussed in Chs 4 and 7) of alleged impossibility through failure of an intended source, or of alleged frustration of purpose. We have seen that a contract for the sale of goods is not discharged merely because supervening legislation has made it illegal for one of the parties to give effect to his intention to export the goods from[48] or to import them into[49] a particular country. It makes no difference that that party's purpose was known to the other. The contract would be discharged by such supervening illegality only if the export or import purpose formed a term of the contract, *e.g.* if the contract expressly stipulated for delivery in a country where it could no longer lawfully be made, or for the export of the goods and this was later prohibited.[50] Supervening legislation may similarly make it illegal to resort to a source or means of payment; but it will not discharge the contract where it affects a source or means intended only by the buyer, since normally this is not a matter of concern to the seller.[51] The requirement that the intended purpose or source be specified in the contract does not, however apply where the contract is made illegal by the prohibition against trading with an enemy in time of war. We have seen that, when the parties to a contract for the sale of goods to be delivered in this country contemplate that the goods will be taken from a source which, in the course of a supervening war, becomes an enemy source, then the contract will be discharged, even though it does not contain any express reference to that source.[52] This rule appears to be based on the

---

[45] See *Toprak Mahsulleri Offisi v Finagrain Cie Commerciale* [1979] 2 Lloyd's Rep. 98 (where again there was no illegality by the *lex loci solutionis*); and *Congimex SARL (Lisbon) v Continental Grain Export Corp (New York)* [1979] 2 Lloyd's Rep. 346 (where there was no supervening change in the law); see further below, para. 8–036.

[46] *Wadha Bank v Arab Bank plc, The Times*, December 23, 1992. For further proceedings in this case, see [1996] 1 Lloyd's Rep. 470.

[47] *Brewster v Kitchell* (1679) Salk. 198.

[48] *D McMaster & Co v Cox McEuen & Co*, 1921 S.C. (H.L.) 124, above, para.7–026.

[49] *Congimex (etc.) SARL v Tradax Export SA* [1983] 1 Lloyd's Rep. 250; above, para.7–027.

[50] See the examples given above, para.7–029.

[51] See the authorities cited in n.45 above; *cf. Universal Corp v Five Ways Properties Ltd* [1979] 1 All E.R. 552 (where the buyer's difficulties were due to the slow operation of machinery set up by antecedent exchange control regulations).

[52] Above, paras 4–056, 8–005.

exceptional strength of the policy of the rule against trading with the enemy. It seems to be capable of applying also where it is the contemplated source of payment which becomes an enemy source.

A supervening prohibition may affect, not the performance of the contract, but the use which one party intends to make of the subject-matter. This was, for example, the position in the black-out and liquor prohibition cases discussed in Ch.7. In some of those cases it was held in the United States that the contracts had been discharged. One view was that the basis of discharge was supervening illegality,[53] but it is submitted that the better explanation of these cases is that discharge resulted from frustration of purpose. Both parties may have contemplated the use which was to be made by one of them of the facilities or premises to be provided by the other, but the contracts imposed no positive obligation on the former party to use them in this way. There was no supervening illegality since full performance of the contracts would not have involved any violation of the law. Even where the contract did impose an obligation to use the subject-matter in a way that was subsequently prohibited, it did not necessarily follow that the whole contract was discharged. Under the rules governing partial illegality,[54] the more appropriate solution in some such cases was that the particular term imposing the obligation in question was no longer binding, but that the contract as a whole was not discharged.[55]

8–008

IV. Supervening and Antecedent Prohibitions

Our concern in this book is primarily with supervening illegality which may discharge a contract, and not with antecedent illegality which may make a contract void or unenforceable *ab initio*. Illegality is supervening when it results from a prohibition imposed *after* the contract was made; and this is true even though the prohibition was based on a state of affairs already in existence at the time of contracting.[56] The distinction between antecedent and supervening illegality may, however, become blurred where at the time of contracting the contract can be lawfully performed only if the consent of some public authority is obtained: for example, if a licence is granted for the export of goods or if planning permission is granted for building work. If such consent is sought and refused after the making of the contract, one possible view is that the case is one of supervening illegality, leading to discharge of the contract in accordance with the principles discussed in this chapter. It is, however, submitted that

8–009

---

[53] See *Doherty v Monroe Eckstein Brewing Co*, 191 N.Y.S. 59 (1929), above, para.7–024.

[54] Below, para.8–028.

[55] e.g. *Grimsdick v Sweetman* [1909] 2 K.B. 740 (above, para.7–024) where the tenant's covenant to "continue the ... premises as a beerhouse" was presumably discharged.

[56] *Gamerco SA v ICM/Fair Warning (Agency) Ltd* [1995] 1 W.L.R. 1126; below, para.8–021 at n.12; doubted on this point by Carter and Tolhurst (1996) J.C.L. 264.

those principles do not, in general,[57] apply to cases of the kind to be discussed in paras 8–010 to 8–024, below (in which the licensing requirement is already in force at the time of contracting), though it will be seen in the following discussion that failure to obtain the licence may affect the obligations of the parties in other ways. Three situations of this kind must be distinguished, of which the second is the most frequently litigated one and also the most complex; two further situations will also be discussed, in which the distinction between supervening and antecedent prohibitions gives rise to difficulty.

(1) **Intention to perform, or performance, without licence**

8–010 If it was the intention of the parties to perform the contract without the requisite consent, then the contract is illegal *ab initio*. This was, for example, the position in *Bigos v Bousted*,[58] where a contract was made to supply foreign currency in breach of exchange control regulations in force when the contract was made, and neither party intended to seek the requisite consent. The contract is similarly illegal *ab initio* if it is actually performed without the requisite licence. This possibility is illustrated by *Frank W Clifford v Garth*[59–60] where building work was done without obtaining the licence required by legislation in force at the time of contracting.

(2) **Intention to comply with licensing requirement**

8–011 More usually, contracting parties intend to comply with the licensing requirements, that is, to perform only when the required licence or consent has been obtained. In such cases, questions arise as to the incidence of the duty to obtain the licence, as to the standard of that duty, as to its content, and as to the legal effects of failure to obtain the licence.

(a) *Incidence of duty*[61]

8–012 Where a contract can be performed lawfully only if a licence (or other consent) has been granted, one of the parties will be under a duty with regard to the obtaining of that licence. The question which of the parties is under that duty may be settled by the express terms of the contract, *e.g.* by a provision requiring a seller to obtain an export licence, or the buyer to obtain an import licence.[62] In the absence of express provisions of this

---

[57] For a possible exceptions, see below, paras 8–021 at n.12, and 8–024.

[58] [1951] 1 All E.R. 92.

[59–60] [1956] 1 W.L.R. 570.

[61] For a fuller account of the law on this topic as applied to export sales, see *Benjamin's Sale of Goods* (6th ed., 1992), paras 18–274 to 18–277.

[62] See *Bangladesh Export Import Co Ltd v Sucden Kerry SA* [1995] 2 Lloyd's Rep. 1, where it is tentatively suggested at 6 that the effect of the words "licence to be obtained by the buyers" on their true construction merely relieved the sellers from the duty of obtaining the licence, without imposing it on the buyers. The point may be that any duty imposed by the above words on the buyers had been *performed* when they *obtained* a licence which was later withdrawn on grounds for which they bore no responsibility.

kind the courts will, for the purpose of determining this question, consider which of the parties was best placed, in the light of the facts known or accessible to each of them, to obtain the licence. Applying this test, the courts have, in cases involving export sales, held that the duty was on the buyers where "the facts which it was necessary to state when a licence had to be applied for were known to them but not to [the sellers]"[63]; but that where "the facts necessary to be stated [to obtain an export licence] would be known to the producer [who was the seller's supplier] and not to the buyer it would be for the seller to apply".[64] There is no general rule that export licences must be sought by sellers and import licences by buyers. The rules which *prima facie* determine the incidence of the duty may be displaced by the conduct of one of the parties, for example, a party who is under the duty may be excused from performing it by the other party's failure to co-operate with him in this respect,[65] or by the other party's wrongful repudiation of the contract and the acceptance of that repudiation by the party under the duty.[66]

In this book, our principal concern is not with the incidence of the duty, but with the effects on the contract of the failure of the party whose duty it is to apply for the licence to obtain it. These effects depend in turn on the standard of the duty.

(b) *Standard of duty*[67]

The duty with regard to the obtaining of the licence may be either one of **8–013** diligence or an absolute (or strict) one. In determining the standard of duty the court will obviously have regard in the first place to any relevant term of the contract. No doubt a guarantee by one party to obtain the licence will be held to impose an absolute duty.[68] On the other hand, the contract may expressly impose the less stringent duty to make reasonable efforts or to use best endeavours. The difficult cases are those in which the contract fails to specify the standard of duty. It may so fail either because it makes no reference to the need to obtain the licence or because, while making such reference, it does not state whether the duty to obtain the licence is to be a duty of diligence or an absolute one. In the first of these

---

[63] *HO Brandt & Co v HN Morris & Co* [1917] 2 K.B. 784 at 795.

[64] *AV Pound & Co v MW Hardy & Co Inc* [1956] A.C. 588 at 611.

[65] *Kyprianou v Cyprus Textiles Ltd* [1958] 2 Lloyd's Rep. 60; *cf. SCCMO (London) Ltd v Société Générale de Compensation* [1956] 1 Lloyd's Rep. 290. Contrast *North Sea Energy Holdings NV v Petroleum Authority of Thailand* [1999] 2 Lloyd's Rep. 483: f.o.b. buyer of oil held not to be bound to supply seller with a list of discharge ports so as to enable seller to obtain a "confirmation" that the oil could be "supplied without restriction" to buyer in country of destination.

[66] *DH Bain v Field & Co* (1920) 5 Ll.L. Rep. 16.

[67] For a fuller account of the law on this topic as applied to export sales, see *Benjamin's Sale of Goods* (6th ed.), paras 18–278 to 18–283.

[68] *Pavia & Co v Thurmann Nielsen* [1951] W.N. 533; [1951] 2 All E.R. 866 at 867; this point does not appear in the report in [1952] 2 Q.B. 84; *cf. Austin Baldwin & Co v Wilfred Turner* (1920) 36 T.L.R. 769; *BS & N Ltd (BVI) v Micado Shipping Ltd Malta (The Seaflower)* [2000] 2 Lloyd's Rep. 37 and *id. (No2)* [2001] 2 Lloyd's Rep. 341 (a charterparty case).

types of cases the question is whether any, and if so what, term can be implied, specifying the standard of duty; in the second the standard of duty turns on the construction of the term which refers to the requirement of obtaining the licence.

(i) Implied term

8–014   Where goods are sold for export and the contract contains no express reference to the need for an export licence, the general or *prima facie* rule is that the party who is obliged to take steps to obtain any necessary licence is in this respect under a duty to do no more than to exercise due diligence or to make reasonable efforts. This point was settled in *Re Anglo-Russian Merchant Traders and John Batt & Co Ltd*,[69] where aluminium was sold c.i.f. Vladivostock; the buyers and sellers were both resident in England and both knew that aluminium could not be exported without a licence. The contract made no express reference to the need to obtain the licence; and it was held that the only term which could be implied was that the sellers should use their best endeavours or reasonable diligence to obtain a licence. The reason for this general or *prima facie* rule is that the court will "only imply the least onerous obligation necessary to give the contract business efficacy".[70] The general rule may, however, be displaced by other extraneous factors. Thus in *K C Sethia (1944) Ltd v Partabmull Rameshwar*[71] c.i.f. sellers of Indian jute to Italian buyers failed to obtain an export "quota" for Italy. The sellers were held liable for failing to ship the goods and the main ground on which the *Anglo-Russian Merchant Traders* case was distinguished was that there the licensing system was at the time of contracting a matter equally within the knowledge of both parties, while in the *K C Sethia* case the workings of the quota system were within the knowledge only of the sellers, who would be likely to know the size of their own quota, how much of it had been used up, and other facts relevant to the operation of the system. The general rule may also be displaced by other terms of the contract. Thus where a contract contained elaborate provisions protecting the seller in the event of *force majeure* or prohibition of export, but no similar provisions protecting the buyer in case of prohibition of import, the court refused to imply a term that the buyer's duty to obtain an import licence was one of diligence and held that duty to be an absolute one.[72]

(ii) Construction

8–015   Where the contract does refer to the need to obtain a licence but does not specify the standard of duty, that standard depends on the construction of the relevant term or terms of the contract. Thus in the *Peter Cassidy* case[73] a contract for the sale of ant eggs to be exported from Finland provided for shipment "as soon as export licence in order", and the seller had assured

---

[69] [1917] 2 K.B. 679.
[70] *Pagnan SpA v Tradax Ocean Transportation SA* [1987] 3 All E.R. 565 at 572.
[71] [1950] 1 All E.R. 51; affirmed [1951] 2 All E.R. 352n; [1951] 2 Lloyd's Rep. 89.
[72] *Congimex Companhia Geral, etc. v Tradax Export SA* [1981] 2 Lloyd's Rep. 687 at 693, affirmed [1983] 1 Lloyd's Rep. 250 at 254.
[73] *Peter Cassidy Seed Co Ltd v Osuustukkukauppa Ltd* [1957] 1 W.L.R. 273.

the buyer that the obtaining of the licence was merely a formality". It was held that the seller had undertaken an absolute duty to obtain a licence, so that it was no excuse for him to show that licences to export ant eggs from Finland could be obtained only by members of the Finnish Ant Egg Exporters Association (of whom the seller was not one). An absolute duty may also be imposed by a contractual provision which not only refers to the need for a licence but specifies which party is to obtain it, and contains no words to qualify the duty. This was the position in *Pagnan SpA v Tradax Ocean Transportation SA*[74] where a contract for the sale of Thailand tapioca pellets contained a special typed clause which read: "Sellers to provide for export certificate enabling buyers to obtain import licence into the EEC." As the typed clause did not qualify the sellers' obligation or refer to due diligence, it was said to impose "an absolute obligation on the sellers to provide for the export certificate, save insofar as any other clause in the contract might modify the sellers' obligation or relieve [them] from the consequences of breach".[75] In fact the sellers *were* so relieved by a prohibition of export clause in the contract since the cause of their failure to obtain an export certificate was an event covered by that clause, *i.e.* a general prohibition imposed by the Thai authorities. But the sellers would have been in breach of their "absolute obligation" if the cause of that failure had been simply a refusal on the part of those authorities to issue this particular certificate, without imposing any general prohibition of export.

In the *Pagnan* case, the prohibition clause provided the seller with a specific excuse without otherwise affecting the standard of his duty. But in determining what standard is imposed by terms which specify the incidence of the duty to obtain the licence, the courts will have regard to the contract as a whole and may therefore take into account prohibition or *force majeure* clauses in the contract. In one case,[76] for example, the contract imposed a duty on the seller to obtain an export and on the buyer to obtain an import licence, and also contained a *force majeure* clause. The duty to obtain such licences seems to have been regarded as absolute[77] since the *force majeure* clause expressly provided that failure to obtain the relevant licence should not be a ground for invoking that clause. But where the *force majeure* clause contained no such provision, it was held that the duty to obtain the licence (imposed by another term of the contract) was one of reasonable diligence only.[78] The cases may be distinguished on the ground that the wording of the *force majeure* clause in the first case indicated an intention that the duties to obtain export and import licences should be absolute, while in the second, the *force majeure* clause contained no such indication. In the absence of such an indication, the courts appear to approach the question of construction (no less than that of

---

[74] [1987] 3 All E.R. 565.
[75] *ibid.* at 572.
[76] *C Czarnikow Ltd v Centrala Handlu Zagranicznego "Rolimpex"* [1979] A.C. 251.
[77] *ibid.* at 371; *cf. Atisa SA v Aztec AG* [1983] 2 Lloyd's Rep. 579 at 584.
[78] *Coloniale Import-Export v Loumidis Sons* [1978] 2 Lloyd's Rep. 560 at 562.

implication) with an inclination towards applying the "less burdensome" standard where "both are equally open for selection".[79]

There may be no indication either in the express terms of the contract,[80] or in the surrounding circumstances,[81] of the standard of duty incumbent on the party who is to obtain the licence, but the contract may contain an express stipulation that it is "subject to licence". Such words do not (like the word "subject to contract") prevent the formation of a binding contract. Their effect is "that there is introduced into the contract a condition that a licence must be obtained and that neither party is to be liable under the contract unless the licence is obtained."[82] The party who is bound to apply for the licence in such a case obviously does not warrant that one will be obtained[83]; he need do no more than use reasonable endeavours to that end.[84] It is in theory possible for the "condition" to be construed as not imposing any duty on either party to take steps to obtain the licence.[85] But in the absence of clear words to this effect, it is submitted that a contract for the sale of goods "subject to" export or import licence is unlikely to be construed in this way.[86]

(c) *Content of the duty*

8–016   Where the duty is an absolute one, no question can arise as to its content: the duty is simply one to obtain the licence.

Where the duty is one to make reasonable efforts, on the other hand, the party under the duty will be in breach of it if he fails to make any such efforts; but he can avoid liability for such a breach if he can discharge the "difficult burden"[87] of showing that any efforts which he should have made to obtain the licence would have been useless.

A high standard is required even where the duty is only one of diligence. It is no defence for the party under the duty to show merely that the steps

---

[79] *Pagnan SpA v Tradax Ocean Transportation SA* [1986] 2 Lloyd's Rep. 646 at 652, affirmed [1987] 3 All E.R. 565.

[80] See the *Pagnan* case, above, n.74.

[81] See the *Peter Cassidy* case, above, n.73.

[82] *Charles H Windschuegl Ltd v Alexander Pickering & Co Ltd* (1950) 80 Ll.L. Rep. 89 at 92.

[83] *cf. Walton (Grain & Shipping) Ltd v British Italian Trading Co* [1959] 1 Lloyd's Rep. 223.

[84] *Brauer & Co. (Great Britain) Ltd v James Clark (Brush Materials) Ltd* [1952] 2 All E.R. 497 at 501.

[85] *cf. Total Gas Marketing Ltd v Arco British* [1998] 2 Lloyd's Rep. 209, where it was conceded that a different contingent condition imposed no obligation on either party.

[86] *cf.* the regrets expressed at the result in the *Total Gas* case, above, at 233 by Lord Hope.

[87] *Charles H Windschuegl Ltd v Alexander Pickering & Co Ltd*, above, n.82, at 95; *cf. Soc. d'Avances Commerciales Ltd v A. Besse & Co Ltd* [1952] 1 Lloyd's Rep. 242 at 249; *Overseas Buyers Ltd v Grenadex SA* [1980] 2 Lloyd's Rep. 608 at 612; in the *Anglo-Russian Merchant Traders* case [1917] 2 K.B. 679 the sellers succeeded in discharging this burden.

which needed to be taken to secure the licence would have involved such expense as to turn the contract for that party into an unprofitable one. It will, for example, not be a defence for a seller merely to show that, after the contract was made, the authorities of the country from which the goods were to be exported had decided to grant him an export licence only on condition of his paying his supplier in that country more for the goods than the price payable under the seller's contract with the buyer.[88] Thus where the amount which the sellers were so required to pay to the supplier exceeded the price payable to the sellers by the buyers by some 25 per cent, it was held that this payment was one which the sellers ought to have made in the performance of their duty to make reasonable efforts to secure a licence. But it was said that if they could have obtained a licence only "on prohibitive terms or on terms entirely outside the contemplation of the parties",[89] then they would not have been obliged to do so in the performance of their duty to make reasonable efforts: they would not, for example, have been obliged for this purpose to comply with a requirement to pay the local suppliers 100 times the price which was due to them under the contract of sale.[90]

Once the licence has been obtained, the duty to obtain it is performed. The party under that duty is therefore *prima facie* not in breach if the licence is later revoked,[91] so long as the revocation is not due to that party's conduct or culpable omission. This rule appears to apply whether the duty is an absolute one or one of diligence.[92] The *prima facie* rule can be excluded by an express term of the contract[93]; and there is some support for the view that (even where the contract contains no such express term) the party under the duty must make reasonable efforts to secure the restoration of the licence.[94] No doubt a contract may expressly impose such an additional duty, but in the absence of such a term the suggested additional duty appears to be inconsistent with the view that, once the licence has been obtained, the duty of the party required to obtain it has been performed. It is submitted that a term imposing the additional duty is unlikely to be implied.

---

[88] *Brauer & Co (Great Britain) Ltd v James Clark (Brush Materials) Ltd* [1952] 2 All E.R. 497, followed in *Beves & Co Ltd v Farkas* [1953] 1 Lloyd's Rep. 103.

[89] *Brauer & Co*, case [1952] 2 All E.R. 497 at 500.

[90] *ibid.* at 501.

[91] *C Czarnikow Ltd v Centala Handlu Zagranicznego "Rolimpex"* [1979] A.C. 351; but revocation of the licence may make performance impossible and so discharge the contract, as in *Gamerco SA v ICM Fair Warning (Agency) Ltd* [1995] 1 W.L.R. 1126, above, para.8–009; below, para.8–021.

[92] The duty in the *Czarnikow* case, above, n.91, was an absolute one: see above, para.8–015.

[93] *Bangladesh Export & Import Co Ltd v Sucden Kerry SA* [1999] 2 Lloyd's Rep. 1 (where the term in question provided that "The inability to obtain import licence shall not be justification for declaration of force majeure"; and the buyer was held liable for breach of a c. & f. contract where the licence which he had obtained was later revoked: see below, para.8–019.

[94] *Provimi Hellas A.E. v Warinco A.G.* [1978] 1 Lloyd's Rep. 373.

(d) *Effects of failure to perform the duty*

8–017   In discussing these effects, it is necessary to distinguish between cases where the duty to obtain the licence is an absolute one and those in which the duty is one of diligence only.

(i) Where the duty is absolute

8–018   If the party who is under an absolute duty fails to obtain the licence, that party is liable in damages: this was, for example, the position in the *Peter Cassidy*[95] and *K C Sethia*[96] cases already discussed. So as to avoid a possible conflict with the rules relating to illegal contracts, this liability has been explained as resting on a collateral contract,[97] though the measure of damages for breach of this collateral contract appears to be the same as that for breach of the principal contract. The collateral contract reasoning makes it possible to apply the present rule to cases in which the licensing requirement arises under English (no less than where it arises under foreign[98]) law.

A further consequence of the failure to obtain the licence is that the party who was under the absolute duty cannot claim damages if (as will normally[99] be the case) the failure results in that party's inability to perform a condition precedent to, or a concurrent condition of, the other party's liability. If, for example, a seller of goods promises absolutely to obtain an export licence, and fails to secure one, he will be unable, lawfully, to deliver the goods; and, since s.28 of the Sale of Goods Act 1979 provides that delivery and payment are (unless otherwise agreed) concurrent conditions, the buyer will not become liable to pay the price. If it is the buyer who promises absolutely (and then fails) to obtain the licence, he can indeed still perform the concurrent condition of payment under s.28. But performance of his promise to obtain the licence would no doubt be held to be a condition precedent of the seller's duty to deliver if without such performance the seller could not lawfully deliver the goods in accordance with the contract.

The foregoing analysis shows that, in the cases of the kind here under discussion, failure to obtain the licence will not discharge the contract under the doctrine of frustration. The party under the duty to obtain the licence will remain liable even though the failure to obtain it was in no way due to his fault. The other party's position is not that he is discharged, but that performance from him never became due.

---

[95] [1957] 1 W.L.R. 273; above, para.8–015.

[96] [1950] 1 All E.R. 51; affirmed [1951] 2 All E.R. 352n.; [1951] 2 Lloyd's Rep. 89; above, para.8–014.

[97] *Walton (Grain & Shipping) Ltd v British Italian Trading Co* [1959] 1 Lloyd's Rep. 223 at 236; *Johnson Matthey Bankers Ltd v The State Trading Corp of India* [1984] 1 Lloyd's Rep. 427 at 434; *Pagnan SpA v Tradax Ocean Transportation SA* [1987] 3 All E.R. 565 at 577 (where, however, the "collateral contract" explanation is said at 576 to be inapplicable if at the time of shipment the parties had no reason to suppose that performance would be unlawful since in such a case there would be no intention to enter into the alleged collateral contract).

[98] As in the cases cited at nn.95 and 96, above.

[99] For exceptions see below, para.8–022.

(ii) Where the duty is one of diligence

Here a distinction must be drawn between two types of case.

In the first, the party whose duty it was to make reasonable efforts fails to make such efforts, so that no licence is obtained. That party is then liable in damages for breach of his undertaking to make those efforts, unless he can show that the efforts, if made, would have been useless.[1] Moreover he cannot claim damages from the other party, for the reasons which prevent such a claim from arising where his duty is an absolute one.[2]

In the second type of case the party whose duty it was to make reasonable efforts makes such efforts but nevertheless fails to obtain the licence. That party is plainly not liable for breach of the duty since he has done all that was required of him: the duty of diligence is not broken but is performed. The further question then arises whether either party may nevertheless be liable for breach of some other duty alleged to have arisen under the contract, such as the seller's duty to deliver or the buyer's to accept and pay.

Where the contract is expressly "subject to licence", a negative answer to this question has been given, on the ground that it was an implied condition of the contract "that a licence must be obtained and that neither party will be liable to perform the duties under the contract unless the licence is obtained".[3] This seems to mean, not that those duties were discharged, but that they were prevented from arising because the grant of the licence was a condition precedent to their accrual. Even if the case were regarded as one of discharge, this would take place under the express term that the contract was "subject to licence", and not under the common law doctrine of frustration.

Frustration may also be excluded by other terms of the contract. This is true not only when the term in question covers the event which has occurred and provides for its effect on the contract, but also when the term, though not precisely covering that event, shows that the parties contemplated it and allocated the risk of its occurrence. Such a possibility is illustrated by a case[4] in which a c. & f. contract provided that the import licence was "to be obtained by buyers" and that "inability to *obtain* [such] licence shall not be justification for declaration of force majeure". An import licence was *obtained* by the buyers but was later *revoked*; and one reason why this fact did not discharge the contract was that the term showed that the lack of an import licence "was within the contemplation of the parties and was not to constitute a frustrating event."[5]

The further, and more difficult, question is whether failure to obtain a licence, in spite of the fact that all the required reasonable efforts to obtain it were made, can discharge a contract which contains *no* express provisions for such an event. This question received some discussion in

---

[1] Above, para.8–016.
[2] Above, para.8–018 after n.99.
[3] *Charles H Windschuegl Ltd v Alexander Pickering & Co Ltd* (1950) Ll.L. Rep. 89 at 92.
[4] *Bangladesh Export Import Co Ltd v Sucden Kerry SA* [1995] 2 Lloyd's Rep. 1.
[5] *ibid.* at 6.

AV Pound & Co Ltd v M W Hardy & Co Inc,[6] where turpentine had been sold f.a.s. buyers' tanker at Lisbon; the sellers knew that the buyers intended to export the turpentine to East Germany. In the light of this knowledge, the contract was interpreted as one for the delivery in Portugal of goods which were capable of being legally exported from Portugal; indeed it is arguable that it was an express term of the contract that the goods were to be exported to East Germany since the stipulation as to payment expressly referred to the latter country.[7] However, under Portuguese law, turpentine could be exported only under licence and such licences could be applied for only by persons registered for this purpose in Portugal. The buyers and sellers were not, while the sellers' suppliers were, so registered, but their application for a licence was refused. The only point actually decided was that the buyers were not liable in damages for refusing to accept the goods since in the circumstances they were under no duty to obtain an export licence. That duty seems to have been on the sellers; but the questions whether the duty was absolute or only one of diligence, and whether the sellers were in breach of it, did not arise for decision, since the buyers' claim for damages against the sellers was not pressed in the House of Lords. It was therefore unnecessary to decide whether the contract was discharged under the doctrine of frustration.[8] Lord Kilmuir L.C. did, however say that: "it was for the sellers to do their best to obtain a licence through the suppliers and if they found that they could not, further performance of the contract was excused."[9] This seems to mean that further performance by *both* parties was excused, and one possible explanation for this result is that the contract was frustrated.[10] It is, however, submitted that the parties were excused on different grounds. Frustration refers to the discharge of an obligation after it has accrued but before it has been performed. The sellers, in the situation here under discussion, undertake unconditionally to do their best to obtain the licence, and then to deliver the goods conditionally on the grant of the licence. There can be no question of any excuse of the first obligation since, on the assumption that the sellers have done their best, that obligation is performed, even though no licence is obtained. Moreover their obligation to deliver is not discharged: it never accrues since the grant of a licence is a condition precedent to its accrual. The buyers' obligation to accept and pay can also be said not to have accrued because it, too, was conditional on the grant of a licence. Alternatively, the buyers' obligation can be said not to have accrued

---

[6] [1956] A.C. 568.

[7] See *ibid.* at 590. The stipulation as to payment was in a covering letter sent by the seller with the contract form, and it was not clear whether this letter was regarded as having been incorporated in the contract.

[8] [1956] A.C. 568 at 605.

[9] *ibid.* at 604.

[10] *cf. Walton (Grain & Shipping) Ltd v British Italian Trading Co* [1959] 1 Lloyd's Rep. 223 at 336; *Johnson Matthey Bankers Ltd v State Trading Corp of India* [1984] 1 Lloyd's Rep. 427 at 429 ("frustration in the form of ... inability to obtain a licence despite the sellers' best endeavour to do so").

because of the sellers' inability to perform a concurrent condition of the buyers' liability since (without a licence) they could not deliver goods which complied with the requirement of the contract that they should be capable of being lawfully exported to East Germany. This may be the point that Lord Simonds had in mind when he said that, without the necessary export licence, the contract "could not be performed".[11]

A contract may, however, be frustrated in the situation discussed in para.8–016 above, in which the licence requisite for its performance is first obtained and then revoked in circumstances in which the revocation does not result from or amount to any breach by the party under the duty to obtain it. This seems to have been the position in the *Gamerco* case,[12] where a contract was made to give a "rock concert" in a specified stadium in Madrid. At the time of contracting, the stadium suffered from a structural defect of which neither party was aware; and the contract was held to have been frustrated when, on discovery of the defect after that time, the use of the stadium for the intended purpose was "banned ... and the permit for [that] use was revoked".[13] Once the permit had been obtained, any conditions precedent in that respect to the reciprocal executory obligations of the parties were fulfilled; and, since the revocation of the permit neither amounted, nor gave rise, to any breach,[14] the discharge of both parties from those obligations is most plausibly explained on the ground that the contract had been frustrated by that revocation.

The question whether the contract is frustrated, or whether performance of a particular obligation is excused on some other ground, is of more than merely theoretical interest. For one thing, if there is no frustration neither party is entitled to rely on the provisions of the Law Reform (Frustrated Contracts) Act 1943.[15] For another, frustration wholly discharges the contract, whereas "excuses" falling short of frustration must be examined in relation to each particular obligation to which they are alleged to apply: they may discharge some obligations, or prevent them from arising, while leaving others unaffected. A claim for breach of such other duties may be made either *by* or *against* the party whose duty it was to make reasonable efforts to obtain the licence and who failed to obtain it in spite of making such efforts.

A claim *by* that party cannot of course succeed if his failure to obtain the licence prevents him from performing a condition precedent to, or a concurrent condition of, the other party's liability, *e.g.* if a c.i.f. seller is, by reason of his failure to obtain an export licence, prevented from lawfully shipping goods (and hence from tendering documents) the buyer will not be bound to pay. But failure to obtain the licence will not necessarily prevent the party whose duty it was to obtain it from performing such

8–021

8–022

---

[11] [1956] 2 W.L.R. 683 at 691, a passage which does not occur in the *Law Reports*. *cf.* [1956] A.C. at 607 (where the obtaining of an export licence is said to be "a condition of delivery f.a.s.").

[12] *Gamerco SA v ICM/Fair Warning (Agency) Ltd* [1995] 1 W.L.R. 1126.

[13] *ibid.* at 1233.

[14] Above, para.8–016, n.91.

[15] Below, Ch.15.

a condition precedent or concurrent condition. For example, a c.i.f. contract may impose on the buyer a duty to make reasonable efforts to obtain an import licence and those efforts may prove unavailing. The buyer can still lawfully pay and the seller may still be bound to ship goods and tender documents, since these steps may not be prevented or made unlawful by the lack of the licence. It seems therefore that the buyer could claim damages if the seller refused or failed to ship goods or to tender documents, even though the buyer's efforts to obtain the licence had remained fruitless; it might be in the buyer's interest to make such a claim if he could have profitably redirected the goods to some destination other than one in the country refusing the licence. The same principle could, it is submitted, apply where a seller on f.o.b. or f.a.s. terms failed to obtain an export licence in spite of having performed his duty to make reasonable efforts to that end. That failure would not prevent him from delivering the goods free on board or free alongside in the country of origin, for the goods might be carried coastwise to another place in the same country without contravening the export licensing requirement. Nor is the buyer normally discharged from such a contract merely because his purpose of exporting the goods, or of exporting them to a particular country, has been frustrated, whether by failure to obtain an export licence, by supervening prohibition of export, or by some other supervening event[16]; he would be discharged only if the export purpose formed a term of the contract. In *AV Pound & Co Ltd v MW Hardy & Co Inc*[17] the f.a.s. sellers' claim for damages in such circumstances was indeed dismissed, and the main reason for this result was that it was not the buyers who were under the duty to obtain the licence; this duty was apparently regarded as incumbent on the sellers.[18] The buyers therefore could not be in breach of *that* duty, but it is less clear why they were not in breach of other duties such as their duty to accept and pay for the goods against delivery f.a.s. Lisbon. The explanation for this aspect of the case appears to be that the contract was, on its true construction, a contract for the delivery of goods for export from Portugal, or that it contained an express term that the goods should be capable of being exported to East Germany.[19] Since no export licence of any kind had been obtained by the end of the shipment period, the sellers could not lawfully deliver goods in conformity with the contract, and this inability to perform a concurrent condition or a condition precedent to the buyers' liability led to the dismissal of the sellers' claim.[20]

8–023   A claim for the breach of some other duty may also be made *against* the party who was under the duty to make reasonable efforts to obtain a

---

[16] See, *e.g. Congimex Companhia Geral (etc) v Tradax Export SA* [1983] 1 Lloyd's Rep. 250; above, para.7–027.

[17] [1956] A.C. 588, above, para.8–020.

[18] See above, para.8–020, especially at n.9.

[19] See above, para.8–020, at n.9.

[20] This may be the point of Lord Simonds' statement quoted above, para.8–020 at n.11.

licence but failed to obtain one in spite of having made such efforts and of having therefore performed that duty. For example, a c.i.f. contract might impose a duty on the buyer to make reasonable efforts to obtain an import licence and the buyer might fail, in spite of making such efforts, to obtain the licence. This would not prevent the seller from lawfully shipping the goods and tendering shipping documents.[21] It would therefore not result in an inability on the seller's part to perform a condition precedent or concurrent condition to the buyer's duty to pay against documents so that the buyer would not be absolved from that duty unless some other term of the contract protected him in the events which had happened. Another possibility is that a c.i.f. contract could impose an obligation to make reasonable efforts to obtain an import licence on the *seller*. If he failed (in spite of making such efforts) to obtain the licence, he could nevertheless still lawfully ship the goods, so that *prima facie* he would not be absolved from his duties to ship goods and tender documents. Performance of these duties would not be illegal since it is no part of a c.i.f. seller's duty to ensure the actual delivery of the goods at the contractual destination.[22] It would thus be open to the buyer to claim performance and to divert the goods elsewhere. The c.i.f. seller in the situation under discussion would be discharged from his duties to ship goods and tender documents only in the unusual case in which the contract could be interpreted as giving rise to a duty to deliver the goods (at least if they were not lost in transit) at the named c.i.f. destination[23]: in that case the seller could argue that performance would involve participation in an attempt to do an unlawful act in the country of destination and that such performance ought not to be enforced.[24]

The preceding discussion shows that a failure to obtain a licence required by legislation in force at the time of contracting does not, as a general rule discharge a contract either by supervening illegality or by impossibility. But this general rule may be subject to an exception which is illustrated by the situation to be considered in para.8–024, below.

---

[21] *Congimex Companhia Geral SARL v Tradax Export SA* [1983] 1 Lloyd's Rep. 250 at 253; *cf. Bangladesh Export Import Co Ltd v Sucden Kerry SA* [1995] 2 Lloyd's Rep. 1, where the contract provided for import licence "to be obtained by buyers" and it was obtained but later revoked.

[22] *Manbré Saccharine Co Ltd v Corn Products Ltd* [1919] 1 K.B. 198 at 202 ("not by actual physical delivery of the goods ..."); *Benjamin's Sale of Goods* (6th ed.), paras 19–001, 19–002, 19–070.

[23] The existence of a duty might be inferred from stipulations (now sometimes found in c.i.f. contracts) as to the time of physical delivery: see, *e.g. Nova Petroleum International Establishment v Tricon Trading Ltd* [1989] 1 Lloyd's Rep. 312; *Benjamin, op. cit.*, para.19–071.

[24] *cf. Foster v Driscoll* [1929] 1 K.B. 470; *Ralli Bros v Compania Sota y Aznar* [1920] 2 K.B. 287, below, para.8–026; *Libyan Arab Foreign Bank v Bankers Trust Co* [1989] Q.B. 728 at 744–745 (where there was no intention to do or to procure an illegal act abroad).

(3) **Change of government policy**

8–024   The situation here to be discussed is that in which legislation imposing a licensing requirement was in force at the time of contracting; up to that time licences had been granted as a matter of course[25]; but there was then a change of government policy, so that henceforth licences were refused, or were issued only subject to new restrictions. As a result of this change of policy, the contract can no longer be lawfully performed, either because the authorities refuse to grant the licence or because they will grant it only subject to conditions which are inconsistent with the terms of the contract. If effect is given to such a change of policy by regulations having the force of law, the prohibition will be subsequent[26] and can discharge the contract by supervening illegality. There is, moreover, authority for the view that the contract can be frustrated by refusal of a licence even where no new legislation is passed to give effect to the change of policy. Such a situation arose in *Maritime National Fish Ltd v Ocean Trawlers Ltd*[27] where the charterers of a trawler which could be used only with an otter trawl claimed to be discharged on the ground that the licence needed for the use of such a trawl had not been granted. The licensing requirement was in force at the time of contracting, when licences to use otter trawls had been granted as a matter of course, but as a result of a change in the policy of the Canadian Government the issue of such licences was restricted so that the charterers obtained only three of the five licences for which they had applied. This was regarded as a potential ground of frustration though the actual decision was that the charterers were not discharged since they could have allocated one of the licences which they had obtained to the chartered trawler in question.[28] A change of government policy after the time of contracting may similarly be a ground of discharge where it introduces new and unexpected restrictions on the operation of an export or import licensing system,[29] or of an exchange control

---

[25] *cf.* the example given in *C Czarnikow Ltd v Centrala Handlu Zagranicznego "Rolimpex"* [1979] A.C. 351 at 372 (dog and television licences).

[26] As in *Nile Co for the Export of Agricultural Crops v H & J M Bennett (Commodities) Ltd* [1986] 1 Lloyd's Rep. 555.

[27] [1935] A.C. 524.

[28] See below, para.14–023.

[29] *cf. Beves & Co Ltd v Farkas* [1953] 1 Lloyd's Rep. 103, where the plea of frustration failed because it was not a term of the contract, nor a matter within the contemplation of the buyer, that the goods were to come from the country whose government had discontinued its previous practice of issuing licences; *Walton (Grain & Shipping) Ltd v British Italian Trading Co* [1959] 1 Lloyd's Rep. 223 at 236; *Congimex Companhia Geral, etc. v Tradax Export SA* [1983] 1 Lloyd's Rep. 250, where the plea of frustration failed as it was not a term of the contract that the goods were to be imported into the country whose government had changed its policy with regard to the issue of import licences; *Johnson Matthey Bankers Ltd v State Trading Corp of India* [1984] 1 Lloyd's Rep. 427 at 429.

system,[30] which was already in existence when the contract was made. The refusal of an export or import licence in such circumstances can also bring a prohibition of export clause into operation.[31]

It should be emphasised that such changes of government policy *may* discharge a contract but will not necessarily have this effect. Whether the contract is actually discharged will depend on the principles to be discussed later in this chapter, which apply in cases of truly supervening but qualified prohibitions.[32] In particular, the party whose performance is affected by the change of policy may, even after the change, be under a duty to make reasonable efforts to obtain the required licence. Moreover, the change of policy with which we are here concerned is one in the operation of a licensing or similar policy. A government may decide simply to break its contract to supply goods to a seller who has contracted to resell those goods, in the expectation of receiving them under his supply contract with the government. The contract between buyer and seller is not frustrated by such a change of policy.[33] The seller's remedy is to enforce such rights as he may have under the supply contract; if he has no such rights, he is liable to the buyer because he has failed to make an effective supply contract.

(4) Prohibition by court order

The problem of distinguishing between antecedent and supervening prohibitions is by no means confined to cases of the kind discussed in paras 8–011 to 8–024, above, concerning the refusal of licences under legislation in force when the contract was made. It can rise also where the contract requires a party to engage in a course of conduct and that party is subsequently prohibited by a court order from doing the acts in question. This was the position in the Australian *Codelfa* case[34] where a contract to build a suburban railway could be completed on time only if the contractor worked "round the clock". As a result of a misinterpretation of the relevant legislation, this method of working was believed to be lawful, but third parties later obtained an injunction against night working, on the ground that it constituted a nuisance. The majority of the High Court regarded the injunction as a supervening event which had made performance unlawful, so that the contract was discharged. Brennan J. dissented, taking the view that the contemplated method of working *constituted* a nuisance even before it had been held to be one in the

8–025

---

[30] *Congimex SARL (Lisbon) v Continental Grain Export Corp. (New York)* [1979] 2 Lloyd's Rep. 346, where no change of government policy was shown to have occurred.

[31] As in the *Walton (Grain & Shipping)* case, above n.29; *cf. Pancommerce SA v Veecheema BV* [1983] 2 Lloyd's Rep. 304, where the defence failed on grounds stated above, para.5–028.

[32] Below, paras 8–049 to 8–053.

[33] *Atisa SA v Aztec AG* [1983] 2 Lloyd's Rep. 579.

[34] *Codelfa Construction Pty Ltd v State Rail Authority of New South Wales* (1982) C.L.R. 337; above, para.4–061.

proceedings in which the injunction had been issued: hence there was no supervening event and no discharge. The majority view seems, with respect, to be the better one. For one thing, it is appropriate to regard a decision, after the time of contracting, on a disputed question of law as a supervening event: this is its practical effect, even if in theory it is merely declaratory of an antecedent state of affairs. For another, many nuisances may in practice go unchecked, so that the aggrieved party's application for an injunction which is eventually granted can of itself be regarded as a supervening event.

The application of the doctrine of discharge to a case in which an agreed or contemplated method of performance is prohibited by a court order might at first sight be open to the objection that the party claiming to be discharged should not be allowed to rely on his own wrongful conduct, on which the court order is based.[35] The point was not raised in the *Codelfa* case, presumably because it was thought to have little merit, since "round the clock" working had been contemplated by, and was in the interests of, both parties; and since the time for completion specified in the contract required this method of performance to be adopted. There is also the general point that discharge in cases of this kind is based on illegality and hence on public policy: it would be wrong for the party against whom the injunction had been issued to be held to the contract, since this might give him an incentive to disregard the injunction and so to commit contempt of court. This factor distinguishes cases of the present kind from those discussed in Ch.4 in which the subject-matter is made unavailable because it has been seized under a court order.[36] The ground of discharge in those cases is not illegality but impossibility; and in that situation it is entirely appropriate to apply the principle that a party should not be able to rely on impossibility resulting from a court order which has been induced by his own fault.

(5) Legislation passed but not yet in force

8–026 The question whether a prohibition is an antecedent or a supervening one can arise where at the time of contracting legislation has been passed which prohibits performance of the contract but which comes into force only at a later time. The answer to the question, it is submitted, depends on three factors: the machinery for bringing the legislation into force, the contractual timetable for performance, and the extent to which the parties comply with that timetable.

So far as the first of these points is concerned, the legislation which contains the prohibition may specify that it is to come into force at a fixed future date, *e.g.* six months after its enactment. If the contract is made after that legislation has been passed, and if the contract provides for performance after the expiry of the six months, then the case should, it is submitted, be regarded as one of antecedent illegality. On the other hand,

---

[35] *cf.* below, para.14–014.
[36] Above, para.4–010.

if in our example the legislation provides that it is to come into force on the making of some further order, and if such an order is made after the time of contracting so as to prohibit performance at the contractually specified time, then the case should be regarded as one of supervening illegality. The crucial distinction between the two cases is that in the first the parties could, while in the second they could not, at the time of contracting tell that performance would be affected by the prohibition. An important practical effect of the distinction is that the Law Reform (Frustrated Contracts) Act 1943 would apply to the second but not to the first of the situations described above.

A difficult intermediate situation is that in which, at the time of contracting, the legislation containing the prohibition had been passed but it was not yet certain either when the legislation would come into force or when the performance which it prohibited was to become due. This appears to have been the position in the *Ralli Bros*[37] case where a charterparty was made in July 1918, the day after a Spanish decree had been issued restricting the amount of freight which could be charged; that decree came into force, apparently as a result of some further act of the Spanish authorities, in September 1918; and the part of the freight in issue became payable on the arrival of the ship, which occurred in December 1918. The prohibition against paying more than the amount which could be charged under the decree appears to have been regarded as a supervening one, for most of the authorities discussed in the judgments concern the effect of supervening events on contracts.[38] It seems that nothing turned on the distinction between antecedent and supervening illegality, but the view that the illegality was supervening can be justified on the ground that at the time of contracting it was not clear either when the prohibition would come into force or when the payment affected by it would become due. Hence at the time of contracting the parties could not tell whether performance was or would be affected by the prohibition: this became clear only as a result of subsequent events.

V. Extent of Interference with Performance

A contract will not be discharged merely because a supervening prohibi-   8-027
tion has made full and exact performance in some respect unlawful. The prohibition may affect part only of the stipulated performance, or it may be temporary, or it may affect only one of several stipulated or contemplated methods of performance. Such supervening prohibitions give rise to problems, similar to those already discussed in relation to impossibility

---

[37] *Ralli Bros v Compania Naviera Sota y Aznar* [1920] 2 K.B. 287; and see further below, para.8-030 at n.55.

[38] *e.g. Paradine v Jane* (1647) Aleyn 26; *Ford v Cotesworth* (1868) L. R. 4 Q.B. 127; *Cunningham v Dunn* (1878) 3 C.P.D. 441; *Jacobs v Crédit Lyonnais* (1884) 12 Q.B.D. 589. *cf.* also the description of the illegality in the *Ralli Bros* case as "supervening" in *Partabmull Rameshar v KC Sethia (1944) Ltd* [1951] 2 Lloyd's Rep. 89 at 96.

which is partial or temporary[39] or which affects only the method of performance.[40] In view of the public policy element which enters into illegality cases it is, however, not safe to assume that the solutions in the cases to be discussed below will necessarily be the same as those in the corresponding impossibility cases. In particular, illegality which does not discharge the contract may nevertheless excuse performance of the obligation which can no longer be lawfully performed even where impossibility might not have this effect.

(1) Partial illegality

8–028   The question whether partial illegality frustrates the whole contract depends on whether the supervening prohibition affects the main purpose of the contract. In the *Denny Mott*[41] case, a long-term agreement for the sale of timber provided that, "to enable the aforesaid agreement to be carried out" the buyer should let a timber yard to the seller and that the seller was to have an option to purchase the yard. When the dealings in timber were prohibited by a war-time regulation, it was held that the whole contract had been frustrated since its main object (*i.e.* trading in timber) could no longer be lawfully achieved. It followed that the seller could not enforce the part of the contract which related to the letting of the yard, so that he could not exercise the option to purchase, even though that option, had it stood alone, would have been perfectly lawful. On the other hand it was said that if the illegality had affected only some minor term of the contract, and not its main purpose, then the contract would not have been discharged.[42]

8–029   A contract is not discharged by illegality merely because the common purpose of the parties is to enable or permit one or both parties to engage in a course of conduct which later becomes unlawful, without actually *requiring* either or both of them to do so. This is why the contracts in the black-out and liquor-prohibition cases[43] were not discharged by illegality (though in some of them[44] discharge occurred by frustration of purpose). To the extent that the contracts in these cases actually required acts to be done which were later prohibited, they can be explained on the ground that the doing of those acts did not constitute the main purpose of the contract. This was, for example, the position in the *Leiston*[45] case, where the contract was not discharged by illegality merely because performance of one of the claimants' obligations (that to light the street lamps at

---

[39] Above, Ch.5.

[40] *Ante,* Ch.4 (paras 4–060 to 4–085).

[41] *Denny Mott & Dickson Ltd v James Fraser & Co Ltd* [1944] A.C. 265.

[42] *ibid.* p.271.

[43] Above, paras 7–015 to 7–018, 7–023 to 7–024.

[44] See the black-out case of *20th Century Lites v Goodman,* 149 P. 2d 88 (1944), above, para.7–015; and the liquor prohibition case of *Industrial Development and Land Co v Goldshmidt* 206, P. 134 (1922), above, para.7–023.

[45] *Leiston Gas Co v Leiston-cum-Sizewell UDC* [1916] 2 K.B. 428.

specified times) had become illegal; and in *Grimsdick v Sweetman*,[46] where again the contract was not discharged by illegality merely because the tenant could not longer lawfully perform his covenant to "continue the ... premises as a beerhouse". The reasons why the contracts in those cases were not discharged by frustration of purpose have been discussed in Ch.7.[47]

The cases in which a contract is discharged because its main purpose can no longer be lawfully achieved must also be distinguished from those in which the part of the performance which has become illegal is severable, in the sense that performance of the part which remains lawful would make as much commercial sense as performance of the whole, and in which performance of the part which remains lawful is in no way dependent on the other part, the performance of which has been prohibited. The position may be illustrated by reference to the soyabean cases,[48] in many of which the American export restrictions ultimately applied to no more than 60 per cent of the quantity sold. The actual decisions in those cases turned on the operation of the express prohibition and *force majeure* clauses in the contracts. But the present point is that such a prohibition would not in any event affect the seller's liability to deliver the 40 per cent which could lawfully be delivered. In this respect, the effect of the prohibition would be the same as that of partial physical impossibility caused (for example) by partial failure of a specified crop.[49] The excuse would be subject to the same restrictions as those which apply in cases of physical impossibility. Thus it would not be available where inability to supply the full contract quantity was due to the seller's "fault": for example, to his failure to take reasonable steps to obtain a licence for the full amount,[50] or to some other culpable act or omission on his part.[51] These restrictions on the availability of the excuse are analogous to the principle which prevents a party from relying on frustration which is self-induced.[52]

The principle that performance of a severable part remains due if it is not affected by the prohibition can, it is submitted, apply also to the converse of the situation just discussed, *i.e.* where it is the obligation to pay (as opposed to that to deliver or to do some other act) which becomes illegal. The point may be illustrated by further reference to the *Ralli Bros*[53] case in which a charterparty provided for the payment of freight partly in London, and partly in Barcelona on arrival of the goods. The stipulated rate of freight exceeded that permitted by a Spanish law which came into effect after the conclusion of the charterparty, and the actual decision was that the charterer was not liable (in respect of the amount payable in   **8–030**

---

[46] [1909] 2 K.B. 740.

[47] Above, paras 7–017, 7–024.

[48] See below, paras 12–036 to 12–039.

[49] *H & R Sainsbury Ltd v Street* [1972] 1 W.L.R. 834, above, para.5–013.

[50] Above, paras 8–014, 8–015; below, para.8–051.

[51] *e.g.* if the seller's failure to obtain a licence was attributable to his criminal contravention of the prohibition on a previous occasion.

[52] Below, para.14–002.

[53] [1920] 2 K.B. 287, above, para.8–026.

Spain) for more than the amount permitted under Spanish law. References in the judgments to the modifications of "the old doctrine of *Paradine* v. *Jane*"[54] by "later authorities"[55] may have given rise to the impression that the Court of Appeal regarded the contract in the *Ralli Bros* case as having been frustrated[56]; but it is submitted that no such total discharge as would have resulted from frustration[57] occurred in that case. The charterers had in fact tendered the amount which they were permitted to pay under Spanish law; and there does not seem to be any doubt that they could have been successfully sued for this amount. The effect of the change in the law was merely to give them *pro tanto* an excuse for non-performance.

In further discussion of the soyabean cases in Ch.12, we shall see that the sellers in many of these cases were held liable for the full quantities sold.[58] Those cases were governed, not by the common law doctrine of discharge, but by the express prohibition and *force majeure* clauses in the contracts. No attempt was made in any of them to argue that the contracts were discharged by illegality under the law of the United States. One possible reason for this is that the express provisions in the contracts were regarded as displacing the common law doctrine of discharge. Another such reason is that the embargo was only partial in that it excepted certain categories of goods[59]; and sellers who failed to show that no excepted goods were available for the purpose of performance could not rely on the common law doctrine of discharge,[60] any more than on the express provisions of the contract.

8–031   Where, under the rules stated in para.8–030, above, the seller remains bound to deliver part only of the quantity sold, the buyer is not normally bound to accept such part but can reject the short delivery, even though the shortage is not due to any default on the part of the seller.[61] But if the seller is in fact able to obtain the full contract quantity under an exception to the embargo the buyer is bound to accept tender of that full amount. In one of the soyabean cases[62] the sellers had made a tender of 40 per cent of the contract quantity "in total fulfilment of 40 per cent", and the buyers had accepted this tender. This was held to amount, not to a variation of the contract, but only to a statement by the sellers of their mistaken belief

---

[54] (1647) Aleyn 26.

[55] [1920] 2 K.B. 287 at 300; and at 291. See above, para.8–026, n.38.

[56] See *Walton (Grain & Shipping) Ltd v British Italian Trading Co Ltd* [1959] 1 Lloyd's Rep. 223 at 236; *Nile Co for the Export of Agricultural Crops v H & J M Bennett (Commodities) Ltd* [1986] 1 Lloyd's Rep. 555 at 581; *Libyan Arab Foreign Bank v Bankers Trust Co* [1989] Q.B. 728 at 749.

[57] Below, para.15–010.

[58] Below, paras 12–037 to 12–038.

[59] Below, paras 8–053, 12–036 to 12–038.

[60] See above, para.6-036, n.25, for the only one of these cases in which an attempt was made (but not persisted with) to rely on the common law doctrine of discharge by supervening events.

[61] Sale of Goods Act 1979, s.30(1). This rule is subject to the exception created by s.30 (2A), discussed in above, para.5–014.

[62] *André & Cie v Cook Industries Ltd* [1987] 2 Lloyd's Rep. 463.

as to the effect of the embargo. If followed that, on the sellers' being able to ship the remaining 60 per cent, the buyers were bound to accept this further amount.

The principle of allocation of available supplies[63] seems to be capable of applying to cases of partial prohibition to the same extent to which it can apply to cases of partial physical impossibility. Indeed, many of the relevant authorities (discussed in Ch.5) are cases of supervening prohibition, though the effect of the prohibition on the contracts in the cases in question was regulated by express contractual provisions, rather than by the common law doctrine of discharge.

(2) Temporary illegality

We have seen that in cases of temporary impossibility the question of discharge often depends on the length of the delay caused by the supervening event[64]; and this test has been applied also in cases of temporary illegality. In the *Cricklewood* [65] case, for example, it was held that a building lease which was to run for 99 years from May 1936 had not been frustrated by restrictions on building which were imposed soon after the Second World War had broken out in September 1939. This conclusion was based by some members of the House of Lords on the now rejected view that leases cannot be frustrated[66]; but others based it on what (in cases of temporary impossibility) we have called the proportionality test.[67] In their view, the lease was not frustrated (so that the tenant remained liable for rent) because the duration of the building restrictions in relation to the length of the lease was not likely to be sufficiently significant to discharge it: there would probably be ample time for building during the rest of the term, after the war-time restrictions had been lifted.[68]

In discussing temporary impossibility, we distinguished[69] between cases in which a claim was made for the *balance* of the promised performance after the removal (or likely removal) of the obstacle to performance, and cases in which the claim was that, after such removal, performance should be rendered for the *whole* of the agreed period, but at a later time. In the second type of case, the question was whether performance at that later time was substantially more onerous for the party claiming to be discharged, so as to make such performance something fundamentally different from that originally undertaken. Where the obstacle to performance consists of a legal prohibition, the *Cricklewood* case resembles the first of these types of case, while an analogy to the second is provided

---

[63] Above, paras 5–022 to 5–029.

[64] Above, paras 5–036 *et seq.*

[65] *Cricklewood Property Investment Trust Ltd v Leighton's Investment Trust Ltd* [1945] A.C. 221.

[66] See below, para.11–001.

[67] Above, para.5–050.

[68] *cf. John Lewis Properties v Viscount Chelsea* [1993] 2 E.G.L.R. 77 at 80, below, para.8–046.

[69] Above, para.5–048.

by *Andrew Millar Ltd v Taylor*.[70] In that case confectionery had been sold f.o.b. Liverpool for export to Morocco and the seller claimed that the contract had been discharged when a ban on the export of such goods had been imposed on the outbreak of the First World War in 1914. It was held that the contract had not been frustrated as the embargo had been withdrawn only 15 days after it had been imposed, and before the end of the normal delivery period. This fact certainly supports the view that performance after the embargo had been lifted was not significantly (or at all) more onerous for the seller, than it would have been, had there been no embargo; and this would no doubt have been an answer to his plea of discharge, had the case been one of supervening impossibility. The question, however, is whether different considerations should apply where the plea of discharge is founded on illegality rather than on impossibility; and this is one of the aspects of the case which gives rise to some difficulty.[71] Warrington L.J. said: "If ... the performance of a contract becomes impossible by reason of its illegality, then both parties to the contract are discharged but they are only discharged because the performance of the contract has become impossible."[72] He added that there would have been "no question ... that the performance of the contract would have become impossible"[73] if the illegality had consisted in trading with the enemy; but he distinguished between illegality arising from a state of war "the duration of which it is impossible to foresee"[74] and illegality arising "from an act of the Executive Government"[75] when that act had been revoked before the end of the time fixed for performance. The reason why these remarks give rise to difficulty is that they suggest that the basis of discharge in cases of supervening illegality is impossibility. In discussing the leading *Fibrosa* case,[76] we saw that the contract there was discharged when Gdynia (the port of destination named in the contract) was occupied by the enemy. It was discharged on grounds of public policy even though its performance may not have been physically impossible at all. This element of public policy must always play some part in cases of supervening illegality, in which it may demand immediate discharge irrespective of the duration of the prohibition: this appears to be the position in the trading with the enemy cases. It must be borne in mind that the question whether a contract will involve trading with the enemy may depend, not merely on the duration of the war, but also on the movement of the armed forces of the combatants[77]; and yet it seems scarcely plausible to suggest that the outcome in the *Fibrosa* case would have been different if Polish forces had succeeded (for a short

---

[70] [1916] 1 K.B. 402.
[71] For another difficulty arising from the case, see below, para.9–006.
[72] *ibid.* at 415.
[73] *ibid.* at 416.
[74] *ibid.*; *cf. Marshall v Glanvill* [1917] 2 K.B. 87 at 91; but see above, para.5–051, nn.9,10.
[75] [1916] 1 K.B. 403 at 416.
[76] [1943] A.C. 32; above, para.8–005.
[77] *cf.* above, para.8–004, at n.19.

time) in re-occupying Gdynia in the early days of the Second World War. The distinction drawn by Warrington L.J. between illegality arising from the prohibition against trading with the enemy and illegality arising from the embargo in the *Andrew Millar* case can, however, be justified by reference to the relative weight of the public policy considerations involved. The policy considerations which underlie the prohibition against trading with the enemy are of exceptional strength,[78] so that the need to support the policy of this prohibition, by invalidating contracts whose performance would contravene it, is evidently greater than the need to support the policy of the short-lived embargo in the *Andrew Millar* case, by invalidating the contract there.

(3) **Illegal method of performance**

A contract may be discharged by supervening legislation which makes it   8–033
unlawful to comply with a stipulation in that contract as to the method of performance.

(a) *Illustrations*

The possibility of such discharge is illustrated by the *Nile Co*[79] case, in   8–034
which contracts for the sale of potatoes f.o.b. Egyptian port called for payment against documents. It was held that an agreement by which the parties had provided for the settlement of differences which had arisen under those contracts had been frustrated by Egyptian regulations which required payment to be made by confirmed documentary credits to be opened in advance. Evans J. said that "A confirmed irrevocable letter of credit in advance before shipment is a different commercial animal from the obligation to pay cash against documents after shipment and ... the difference is fundamental in this sense."[80] Another illustration of the possibility of discharge by supervening illegality in the method of performance is suggested by the cases which raise the question whether antecedent illegality of this kind is a ground of invalidity. In discussing *St John Shipping Corp v Joseph Rank Ltd*[81] we saw that a contract for the carriage of goods by sea was not invalid for antecedent illegality merely because, in performing it, the carrier had overloaded his ship; but it was said that the carrier could not have enforced the contract if, when he made it, he intended to overload his ship.[82] If his intention had been to load the ship so that a particular degree of submersion would result, and if that degree of submersion had been prohibited after the contract was made but before it was performed, then it is arguable that the contract ought to have been discharged by supervening illegality. Again, in *Ashmore*

---

[78] Above, para.8–006.
[79] *Nile Co for the Export of Agricultural Crops v H & JM Bennett (Commodities) Ltd* [1986] 1 Lloyd's Rep. 555.
[80] *ibid.* at 582.
[81] [1957] 1 Q.B. 267; above, para.8–001.
[82] At 283; *cf. Fielding & Platt v Najjar* [1969] 1 W.L.R. 357.

Benson Pease & Co v A V Dawson Ltd[83] a contract to carry 25 ton loads was performed by using lorries which could not lawfully carry loads of more than 20 tons, and it was held that the owner of the goods was not entitled to damages for breach of the contract as he knew of the antecedent illegality and "participated" in it, in the sense that he intended to benefit from it. Again it is suggested that, if the prohibition against carrying the loads in the lorries had been imposed only *after* the contracts had been made, the contracts ought to have been discharged. It is true that, in cases of antecedent illegality the result in cases of this kind to some extent depends on the relative guilt or innocence of the parties. From this point of view, the *Ashmore* case can be contrasted with *Archbolds (Freightage) Ltd v Spanglett Ltd,*[84] where goods were unlawfully carried in a van which was not licensed for the purpose, but the owner of the goods nevertheless recovered damages for breach of the contract of carriage as he did not know that the van was not properly licensed. In the two examples (given above) of suggested discharge by supervening illegality, there can be no question of relative guilt or innocence: both parties were equally "innocent" in the sense that at the time of contracting neither of them could have intended to violate the law, no illegality being then involved in the performance of the contract. Nevertheless it is submitted that considerations of public policy (which are the basis of discharge by supervening illegality) should lead to the discharge of contracts if their performance requires acts to be done which have (after the time of contracting but before that of performance) been prohibited in the interests of the safety of the public or of a section of the public.

(b) *Qualifications*

8–035   The principle of discharge by supervening illegality in the method of performance is subject to a number of limitations or qualifications.

(i) Method must be stipulated
8–036   The first such qualification is that supervening illegality must, in general, affect a *stipulated* method of performance. A contract of sale is not discharged merely because the buyer intends to use funds to be transmitted from a foreign country and a change in the exchange control regulations of that country or in the government policy which determines their operation, prevents him from transmitting those funds for payment within the time required by the contract, or at all.[85] Similarly, it does not seem that the plea of frustration would have succeeded in those of the Suez cases[86] in which the contracts contained no reference to the Canal, if the passage of the Canal had been prohibited rather than made impossible by physical obstructions.

---

[83] [1973] 1 W.L.R. 828.

[84] [1961] 1 Q.B. 374.

[85] See *Universal Corp v Five Ways Properties Ltd* [1979] 1 All E.R. 552; *Congimex SARL (Lisbon) Ltd v Continental Grain Export Corp (New York)* [1979] 2 Lloyd's Rep. 346 at 353 (where in fact no such change of policy was proved).

[86] Above, paras 4–071 *et seq.*

(ii) Requirement of fundamental change

The second qualification of the principle of discharge is that the change in   8–037
the method of performance required by the supervening legislation must
be fundamental. This requirement is recognised in the *Nile Co*[87] case and
may be illustrated by supposing that the contract there had called for
payment by letter of credit to be opened in advance at Bank X, and that
legislation had subsequently required the letter of credit to be so opened
at Bank Y. So long as this new requirement did not substantially increase
the burden of payment to the buyer, or lessen the seller's security for
obtaining payment, it is submitted that the change in the law should not
have been regarded as a ground of discharge. Similarly it is submitted that
there would have been no discharge, even in those of the Suez cases in
which it was a term of the contract that the ship should pass through the
Canal,[88] if one again assumes that passage of the Canal had been
prohibited rather than made physically impossible.

In the two situations discussed in para.8–037, above, the suggested   8–038
qualifications of the principle of discharge by supervening illegality in the
method of performance are based on the argument that performance by
the method which remains lawful is unlikely to cause serious prejudice
to the party claiming discharge. In cases of supervening illegality, that
argument may (here as elsewhere) be outweighed by considerations of
public policy. It is submitted that it would be so outweighed where the
stipulated method became illegal on the ground that performance would
involve trading with the enemy, and that this would be true even if the
method in question had been merely contemplated by both parties and
not required by the express or implied terms of the contract.[89] For
example, it is submitted that in the Suez cases contracts, with or between,
British and Egyptian residents would have been discharged (even if the
contracts had not referred to Suez) if war had broken out between the
United Kingdom and Egypt at the time of the first Suez crisis in 1956.
Considerations of public policy might similarly lead to discharge (even in
cases *prima facie* falling within the two qualifications to the principle of
discharge discussed in para.8–037, above) if the supervening prohibition
had been imposed in the interests of public safety.

(iii) Performance by substitute method

It is convenient to begin this discussion with an account of certain special   8–039
provisions of the Uniform Commercial Code concerning supervening
illegality in the method by which a buyer of goods[90] is to pay for them and

---

[87] Above para.8–034.

[88] *e.g. Palmco Shipping Inc. v Continental Ore Corp. (The Captain George K)* [1970] 2
Lloyd's Rep. 21; above, para.4–079.

[89] *cf.* the rule which applies where the prohibition against trading with the enemy
affects a source which is not specified but which is intended by both parties: *Re
Badische Co* [1921] 2 Ch. 321, above, para.4–056.

[90] Provisions similar to those to be discussed in the text below apply where the
contract under which goods are supplied is not a sale but a chattel lease: see
UCC, ss.2A–404 and 2A–405. For the sake of brevity, the discussion in the text
below is confined to the Code provisions which apply to sales; those which apply

then to consider whether they have any counterpart in English law. These provisions were presumably thought to be necessary (in spite of the fact that the Code did not, in general, distinguish between supervening impracticability and supervening illegality[91]) because it was recognised that the payment of an agreed sum of money cannot become "impracticable", any more than it can become impossible. Supervening illegality in the method of payment therefore did not fall within s.2–614(1) (which deals with certain cases of impracticability in the method of performance[92]) or within s.2–615(a) (which deals with impracticability in general). Instead, such illegality is dealt with in s.2–614(2), which applies where "the agreed means or manner of payment fails because of domestic or foreign governmental regulations". The subsection deals with two situations in which such a failure has occurred.

8–040   *(a) Method becoming illegal before delivery.*   The first is that in which the seller has not yet delivered: here s.2–614(2) provides that he can refuse to deliver "unless the buyer provides a means or manner of payment which is commercially a substantial equivalent". It follows from these words that, if the buyer does provide such an equivalent, there will be no discharge. Section 2–614(2) differs from s.2–614(1) in that s.2–614(2) does not in terms oblige the buyer to provide such an equivalent merely because it is available, while s.2–614(1) requires substitutes within its scope to be "*tendered* and accepted".

It seems unlikely that (where the seller has not yet delivered) English law would accept a rule formulated in the terms of s.2–614(2). They would almost certainly be reluctant to engage in speculation on the point whether some means of payment permitted or required by the regulation would be a commercially reasonable substitute for that specified in the contract.[93] English courts would be no more likely in the present context to accept the principle that a commercially reasonable substitute must be accepted than they are in the context of those physical obstacles to delivery which are dealt with in s.2–614(1).[94] In discussing that provision, however, we suggested that the difference between the English and American position might be one of terminology and emphasis, rather than one of substance[95]; and the question arises whether there is scope for a similar argument in the present context. One possible view is that it should be a condition of discharge in English law that the method of payment required by the supervening legislation should differ fundamentally from that specified in the contract, and that there may be little practical distinction between the case where the two methods of payment do not differ fundamentally from each other, and that in which one of

to leases raise no separate points of principle relating to the issues here to be discussed.

[91] Above, para.8–002.
[92] Above, para.4–064.
[93] For a similar difficulty in the United States, see *RC Craig Ltd v Ships of the Sea Inc* 401 F. Supp. 1051 (1975).
[94] See above, para.4–066.
[95] Above, para.4–068.

them is "commercially a substantial equivalent" of the other. In the present context, this suggestion must, however, be treated with some caution. The point may be tested by taking an example based on a case[96] in which a contract of sale called for payment by letter of credit to be opened in London and the buyer, in breach of this requirement, opened the letter of credit in Geneva. Although this breach made "no real commercial difference"[97] it was said to give the seller the right to rescind the contract.[98] The present question is what legal effects would have followed if the case had been one, not of breach, but one in which supervening legislation had required payment to be made by letter of credit to be opened in a different country from that specified in the contract. On the one hand it can be argued that a means of payment which would (but for the supervening legislation) have amounted to a repudiatory breach must differ fundamentally from (or cannot, in the words of s.2–614(a), be "commercially a substantial equivalent" for) that specified in the contract, so that the seller should not be required to accept it. On the other hand there is the argument that, where the seller can rescind even though there is "no real commercial difference" between the two methods of payment, his right to rescind in cases of breach arises in spite of the fact that the difference is *not* fundamental, under one of the many exceptions to the general rule that to justify rescission, a breach must be a serious or fundamental one.[99] It is then further arguable that a more lenient standard should be adopted where failure to comply with the contractually specified method of payment was due to circumstances over which the buyer could have no control,[1] and that therefore a non-fundamental difference imposed on him by law should not be regarded as a ground of discharge.

(b) Method of payment becoming illegal after delivery. The second situation   **8–041**
dealt with by s.2–614(2) is that in which delivery has already been taken when the governmental regulation is made which causes the agreed means or manner of payment to fail. Here the subsection first lays down the general rule that payment "by the means or in the manner provided by the regulation" discharges the buyer; and it then subjects this general rule to an exception which applies where "the regulation is discriminatory, oppressive or predatory". Neither the general rule nor the exception results in what English lawyers would call frustration of the contract. Under the general rule, the buyer remains liable to pay in accordance with the regulation (but not otherwise); under the exception he remains liable to pay in accordance with the contract, though this liability may be discharged by supervening illegality at common law.[2]

The general rule just stated differs significantly from that discussed in para.8–040 above, which applies where the regulation is made *before*

---

[96] *Enrico Furst & Co v WE Fischer Ltd* [1960] 2 Lloyd's Rep. 340.
[97] *ibid.* at 348.
[98] The actual decision was that the breach had been waived.
[99] For these exceptions, see Treitel, *The Law of Contract* (11th ed.), pp.778–826.
[1] *cf.* (in cases of supervening impossibility) above, para.4–069.
[2] Below, para.8–043.

delivery. It contains no requirement that the method of payment allowed by the regulation must be "commercially a substantial equivalent" of the stipulated method. The effect of the general rule is therefore to vary the contractual obligations of the buyer (perhaps quite substantially) in the light of the supervening illegality affecting the manner of payment. This resembles the result reached in England in the *Ralli Bros*[3] case. That case was admittedly concerned with a foreign law which restricted the *amount*, rather than the "agreed means or manner" of payment; but it seems *a fortiori* to follow from the decision that, if the Spanish decree had provided that payment could be lawfully made only in (for example) a currency other than that required by the contract, then payment in the currency specified in the decree would have discharged the charterer. The *Ralli Bros* case does not, however, conclude the question whether the same rule should necessarily apply where the contract is one for the sale of goods. If in such a case the court were to conclude that the supervening prohibition had frustrated the contract, the pre-contract position could, at least in many cases, be restored by ordering the buyer to return the goods. Such restoration could not have been achieved in the *Ralli Bros* case, where services under the charterparty had been rendered and could not, as a practical matter, be given back. However, even a contract for the sale of goods may contain a service element which cannot in practice be easily restored. Under many contracts of sale, the price may be calculated so as to cover the cost of carrying the goods to the destination named in the contract, and if, after they had been carried there, legislation interferes with the amount or manner of payment, then the seller cannot be restored to his precontract position by having the goods returned to him at that destination.

8-042 *(c) Effect of supervening illegality in method of performance on other obligations.* Under the general rule laid down by s.2-614(2) for cases in which the goods have been delivered before the governmental regulations have caused the agreed means or manner of *payment* to fail, the buyer may be discharged by a means or manner or payment even though it is not a commercial equivalent of that required by the contract. There is no corresponding provision in the Uniform Commercial Code for similarly varying or reducing the obligations of one party where the stipulated method of performing some *other* obligation than that of payment fails because of governmental regulations. Section 2-614(1), which deals with impracticability affecting the method of *delivery*, contains no reference to governmental regulations. It seems to deal only with physical obstacles to performance and requires alternative methods to be adopted only if "a commercially reasonable substitute *is* available". If no such substitute is available, delivery is simply not made and the parties are left *in statu quo*. Section 2-614(1) does not touch the problem (dealt with in s.2-614(2)) which arises where, *after* one party has performed, the agreed means or manner of performance by the other is prohibited. Section 2-615(a) does refer to cases in which performance has been made impracticable "by

---

[3] [1920] 2 K.B. 287, above, para.8-030.

compliance in good faith with foreign or domestic governmental regulation". But the only effect of such impracticability which s.2–615(a) states is that it excuses the seller; and this rule does not in terms provide for the seller's obligation to be varied[4] (in the way envisaged by s.2–614(2)) so as to discharge him if he performs, not in accordance with the contract, but in accordance with the supervening regulation. It is, however, arguable that such a solution might be available apart from the Code, as a matter of common law. In the American case of *Whitman v Anglum*[5] a buyer of milk was held to be entitled to demand delivery elsewhere than at the place specified in the contract when delivery there had become illegal in consequence of an outbreak of foot and mouth disease. The reason why he was so entitled was that the term specifying the place of delivery was regarded by the court, not as an essential term of the contract, but as one which could still be "substantially"[6] performed by delivery elsewhere. The question in that case was simply whether the buyer was entitled to demand performance by the substitute method, and not whether he would have been bound to accept it, had the seller been willing to tender it. But it seems that the same reasoning could apply to both these situations and, where it does, the seller would be entitled, no less than he was bound, to render performance by the substitute method. In English law, it is submitted that he would have this right if the substitute performance would, had it been a breach, not have been either one of condition, or one which otherwise entitled the buyer to rescind the contract.

(d) The exception.   Under the exception to the general rule laid down by s.2–614(2) for the situation in which illegality in the method of payment supervenes after delivery has been made, the buyer is not discharged *by payment* in the only manner permitted by the supervening regulation if "the regulation is discriminatory, oppressive or predatory". What this exception seems to mean is that the buyer is not discharged *by performance* in accordance with the regulation. It does not follow that he may not be discharged by supervening illegality, if payment in breach of the regulation would amount to a criminal offence. The seller's remedy in that event would not be to claim the price but to seek such relief (by way, for example, of restitution) as might be available to him in consequence of discharge by supervening events.[7] **8–043**

(e) Validity of supervening law.   In both the situations dealt with in s.2–614(2) it seems to be assumed that the governmental regulation is legally valid: this point is not affected by the disapproval of the content of the regulation which may be inferred from the words "discriminatory, oppressive or predatory".[8] In this respect s.2–614(2) differs from **8–044**

---

[4] Conceivably, s.2–615, Comment 6 (above, para.6–011) might permit such a variation.
[5] 103 A. 114 (1918), above, para.4–064. One defence pleaded was illegality.
[6] At 115.
[7] See below, paras 15–055 *et seq.*
[8] This phrase seems to refer to foreign, rather than to domestic, regulations.

s.2–615(a) which provides a seller with an excuse where his performance has become impracticable by his "compliance in good faith with any applicable foreign or domestic governmental regulation whether or not it proves to be valid". Some difficulty may, indeed be felt by reason of the fact that the principle of s.2–615(a) is capable of providing an excuse to a buyer no less than to a seller.[9] It is however submitted that s.2–615(a) should not apply where the regulation affects the contractually specified method of payment. In such a case s.2–614(2) should be the governing provision since payment of money cannot become "impracticable", though it may become illegal. There is also the practical point that a buyer should not be discharged by payment of (for example) less than the agreed price in compliance with a regulation which turned out to be invalid. Scope can be given to the words quoted above from s.2–615(a), even in providing an excuse to the buyer, for example, where he in good faith believed that a specified mode of taking delivery had been prohibited by a regulation which turned out to be invalid.

8–045   (f) *Buyer relying on illegality in method of payment.* The assumption underlying s.2–614(2) is that it is the seller who objects to the altered means or manner of payment which is required by the supervening regulation. The subsection does not deal with the situation in which the objection is raised by the buyer. This was, for example, the position in the *Nile Co* case,[10] where it was the buyer who objected to the requirement (imposed by the Egyptian regulations) of having to pay by letter of credit to be opened in advance, while the contract required payment by cash against documents. It is far from clear under which provision of the Uniform Commercial Code such a case would be dealt with in the United States.

(4) Position where contract is not discharged

8–046   The foregoing discussion has shown that there are cases of partial or temporary illegality or of illegality in the method of performance, in which the contract is not discharged, for example, because the illegality does not affect the main purpose of the contract, or because it affects only a severable part of the contractual obligation, or because the delay caused by temporary illegality is not sufficiently serious, or because the prohibited method of performance is not "fundamental". Such cases give rise to the further question whether the illegality nevertheless excuses performance of the subsidiary or severable obligation.

Where the illegality affects only a severable part[11] of the contractual obligation, this question is not thought to give rise to difficulty. If, for example, a seller is prohibited by supervening legislation from delivering more than a specified proportion of the goods sold, he is not liable for failing to deliver more than the part which can legally be delivered, and the buyer is not bound to pay for more than that part: both performance

---

[9] See s.2–615, Comment 9, above, para.4–058.
[10] [1986] 1 Lloyd's Rep. 555, above, para.8–034.
[11] In the sense discussed above, para.8–029.

and counter-performance are *pro tanto* excused.[12] Indeed, under the rules relating to delivery of the wrong quantity, the buyer is not generally bound to accept and pay for the reduced quantity which can lawfully be delivered[13]; but his release under these rules depends on his election and not on the principle of discharge by operation of law under the doctrine of frustration. Legislation restricting the amount which can lawfully be paid under a contract similarly provides a *pro tanto* excuse to the party who has undertaken to make the payment.[14]

There is similarly no difficulty where the illegality affects a method of performance which is not stipulated in the contract but is merely contemplated by one party: some other method (if available) must then be used.[15] This is also true where the method which is later prohibited is specified but is not of fundamental importance.[16] Nor would performance by the alternative method in such cases leave the party rendering it liable in damages for failing to use the contractually specified but later prohibited method. The point can be illustrated by referring again to the suggestion (made in para.8–037, above) that the contracts even in those of the Suez cases in which it was a term of the contract that the ship should pass through the Canal would not (in general) have been discharged if the passage of the Canal had been prohibited, instead of having been made physically impossible. The present point is that in such a case the carrier would not be liable in damages for failing to carry the goods via the Canal. The position is the same where temporary illegality is not sufficiently serious to frustrate the contract. In the *Cricklewood* case,[17] the only point decided by the House of Lords was that the tenant was liable for the rent as the contract had not been discharged by the temporary prohibition on building. But it is submitted that, while that prohibition lasted, it would have afforded the tenant with an excuse for failing to perform his covenant to build even if such an excuse had not been provided by an express "abeyance" clause in the lease.[18] Support for this submission is provided by a later case[19] in which a tenant had covenanted to redevelop a site by a specified date, but performance of that covenant was prevented (and made unlawful[20]) when a building on the

---

[12] This assumption underlies the soyabean cases discussed in Ch.12, below, paras, 12–036 to 12–039.

[13] Sale of Goods Act 1979 s.30(1). For the exception to this rule created by s.30(2A), see above, para.5–014.

[14] As in the *Ralli Bros* case [1920] 2 K.B. 287, above, para.8–030, and under the second of the rules contained in the UCC, s.2–614(2), above, para.8–041.

[15] Above, para.8–036.

[16] Above, para.8–037.

[17] [1945] A.C. 221, above, para.8–032.

[18] *cf. Grimsdick v Sweetman* [1909] 2 K.B. 740 so far as it concerns the tenant's covenant to "continue the ... premises as a beerhouse": above, para.7–024; *Libyan Arab Foreign Bank v Bankers Trust Co* [1989] Q.B. 728 at 772 ("suspended but not discharged"); *Arab Bank Ltd v Barclays Bank Ltd* [1954] A.C. 495.

[19] *John Lewis Properties v Viscount Chelsea* [1993] 2 E.G.L.R. 77.

[20] In the *John Lewis* case, above, it was not necessary to distinguish between supervening impossibility and illegality.

site was later listed as being of special architectural interest. The listing did not frustrate the lease,[21] but it was held to give the tenant a temporary excuse from performance of the covenant, so that his failure to carry out the redevelopment by the specified date did not amount to a breach.

8–047   The cases which give rise to the greatest difficulty are those in which the contract is not discharged because the part which has become illegal is only subsidiary and that part is not severable. A court will obviously not order specific enforcement of the part which has become illegal, but the question remains whether failure to perform that part can give rise to liability in damages. On the principle of public policy which underlies discharge by supervening illegality, it is submitted that there should be no such liability. Suppose that a charterparty required a ship to call at 10 ports, and that before the commencement of the voyage one of those ports became an enemy port. The shipowner could hardly be made liable in damages for failing to call at that port, even if it was physically possible for him to do so.[22]

Questions of this kind have also been raised in a number of cases involving leases which imposed obligations to repair or to rebuild on one of the parties. Subsequent legislation then made performance of one or more of those obligations illegal without frustrating the lease; and the question was whether the party who had undertaken the obligation to do the work which had become illegal could be made liable in damages for having failed to do it. This question gives rise to difficulty because it exposes a conflict between two policies. On the one hand, it may be unjust between the parties to allow one of them (*e.g.* the tenant) to have the benefit of the whole of the other's performance (*i.e.* possession of the premises) while being discharged by illegality from one of his own obligations. On the other hand, in cases of supervening illegality, public policy may require such discharge of the subsidiary obligation, even at the risk of not achieving ideal justice between the parties.

8–048   The first of these policies prevailed in *Eyre v Johnson*,[23] where a lease contained a covenant by the tenant to repair, but regulations made during the Second World War later made it illegal for the tenant to carry out the work which the covenant required him to do. After the War (and the lease) had come to an end, it was held that the tenant was liable in damages for having, during the War, failed to execute the repairs. No doubt this conclusion promoted justice between the parties, particularly since the tenant had been guilty of apparently deliberate delay in carrying out the repairs when he could still lawfully have done so. But unless the case can be supported on this last ground it is open to the objection that it is contrary to public policy to hold a party liable for refusing or failing to do an illegal act, for to hold him so liable would give him an incentive to

---

[21] Thus the tenant remained liable for rent: see the *John Lewis* case, above, at 82.
[22] *cf. Hindley & Co Ltd v General Fibre Co Ltd* [1940] 2 K.B. 517.
[23] [1946] K.B. 481.

violate the law. *Eyre v Johnson* has therefore been rightly doubted in later authority.[24]

An interesting contrast to *Eyre v Johnson* is provided by the Michigan case of *Cordes v Miller*[25] where a wooden building was leased for 10 years from October 1872 as a restaurant and saloon. The lease contained a covenant by the landlord to rebuild if the building should be burnt down. The building was destroyed by fire on May 26, 1874; within a week, the tenant served notice on the landlord requiring him to rebuild; but on June 15, a city ordinance prohibited the erection of wooden buildings in the area in question. The landlord accordingly rebuilt in brick; this operation was completed in November, and the tenant moved back into the premises in December. He then brought an action claiming damages for delay in rebuilding. The claim was dismissed on the ground that the landlord was under no duty to rebuild in a more expensive material than that of which the premises had been originally built. It was not even argued that he could have been held liable in damages for failing to rebuild in wood, the now prohibited material. This decision may in turn be contrasted with the similar Victorian case of *Re De Garis and Rowe's Lease*[26] where again the lessor of a wooden building covenanted to rebuild if the premises should be destroyed by fire, and they were so destroyed after a local bye-law (made under a statute in force at the time of the lease) had prohibited building in the area except in brick or stone. The lessor did not rebuild and was held liable in damages since the covenant to "rebuild" did not, on its true construction mean "reconstruct in the original materials"; and since there had been no *change* in the law (the bye-law having been made under an existing statute) so that the lessor was not discharged by supervening illegality. The latter argument is, however, hard to support, for a change in the law may result from subordinate, no less than from primary, legislation.

It is submitted that, where a subsidiary obligation has become illegal, that obligation should be discharged, on the public policy ground that a party should not be held liable in damages for having failed or refused to do an illegal act. Public policy should in this type of case prevail over considerations of justice between the parties. Any injustice which may flow from this view can at least to some extent be mitigated. Where the party to whom the performance which is now illegal is due had already paid for it (in cash or in kind) before the performance became illegal, that party can be allowed restitution in respect of a proportionate part of his payment. Such relief was given in *Louisville & Nashville R R v Crowe*,[27] where a contract by which the plaintiff had been give a railway free pass for life in exchange for a right of way granted by him to the defendant was discharged by illegality, but the defendant was held liable for the value of

---

[24] *i.e.* in the *Cricklewood* case [1945] A.C. 221 at 233, 244; *Sturcke v SW Edwards Ltd* [1971] 23 P. & C.R. 185 at 190; *cf. Brewster v Kitchell* (1691) 1 Salk. 198 ("the statute repeals the covenant").
[25] 39 Mich. 581 (1878).
[26] [1924] V.L.R. 38.
[27] 160 S.W. 759 (1913), above, para.8–007, n.39.

the right of way it had obtained, less the value of the benefit which the plaintiff had already obtained under the contract. It seems that similar relief would be available in English law.[28]

VI. QUALIFIED PROHIBITION

8–049 The situation here to be discussed is that in which, after the contract was made, legislation is passed which does not prohibit performance outright, but which does make performance illegal unless the consent of (usually) some public body is obtained. An illustration of such a qualified prohibition would be a law making the previously unrestricted export or import of goods subject to an export or import licensing requirement. The mere passing of such a law will not frustrate a contract for the sale of goods falling within its scope, for if the requisite licence is obtained the contract can be lawfully performed. In cases of this kind the court may impose on one of the parties a duty to take steps to obtain the newly required licence,[29] and this possibility gives rise to a number of problems. These resemble the problems which can arise in the situation already discussed, in which the licensing requirement is already in existence at the time of contracting.

(1) **Incidence of duty**

8–050 The first question is which of the parties is to be required to take steps to obtain the licence. There seems to be no reason why the factors which determine the incidence of the duty where the licensing requirement is already in existence at the time of contracting[30] should not also apply in the present context. In other words, the duty would (subject to any relevant terms of the contract) be on the party who was best placed (in the light of facts known or accessible to each of them) to obtain the licence.

(2) **Standard of duty**

8–051 In cases of supervening qualified prohibition, the duty of the party who is required to take steps to obtain a licence will almost invariably be one of diligence only.[31] Where the licensing requirement is already in existence at the time of contracting, it may be possible to infer, from the circumstances

---

[28] Law Reform (Frustrated Contracts) Act 1943, s.1(3), below, para.15–060.

[29] See *Dalmia Dairy Industries Ltd v National Bank of Pakistan* [1978] 2 Lloyd's Rep. 223 at 253, affirmed *ibid.* on other grounds.

[30] Above, para.8–012.

[31] The "absolute" duty imposed by cl.21 of the contract in *C Czarnikow Ltd v Centrala Handlu Zagranicznego "Rolimpex"* [1979] A.C. 351 at 371 was there expressly confined to the situation in which the licensing requirement was already in existence at the time of contracting, thus perhaps reflecting a commercial point of view that such a stringent duty was inappropriate in case of supervening illegality.

in which the contract was made, that that party intended to undertake an "absolute" duty to obtain the licence. But such an inference will not normally be drawn where the licensing requirement is imposed after the time of contracting. In *The Playa Larga*[32] one ground for holding that a contract for the sale of sugar by Cuban sellers to Chilean buyers had been discharged (with regard to the undelivered balance) was a kind of impracticability, resulting from the total breakdown of diplomatic and commercial relations between Cuba and Chile in consequence of the overthrow of the Marxist government in the latter country.[33] But another ground for the decision was that the contract had been discharged by supervening illegality arising from a Cuban law, passed after the conclusion of the contract and "freezing" all Chilean assets in Cuba. It was argued that the sellers should be held liable for breach of an "absolute" undertaking (or of a "warranty") that performance should be lawful at the place of performance.[34] However the Court of Appeal rejected the argument, saying that "clear words"[35] were required to create such an undertaking (or such a warranty) where the legislation was passed after the time of contracting. The prohibition which resulted in this case from the "freezing" of Chilean assets was supervening and *un*qualified: it was not mitigated by any licensing system. But according to a dictum in the earlier *Dalmia Industries* case,[36] the same reasoning applies to cases of supervening qualified prohibition, so that in these cases there is normally no more than a duty of diligence to obtain the licence. That general rule can, indeed, be displaced by "clear words" imposing an absolute duty. However in the absence of such words, it is plainly much harder to infer that the party under the duty to obtain the licence guaranteed that no law affecting the legality of performance should be passed in the future, than that he guaranteed compliance with existing legal requirements. To put the point in another way, that party is more likely to have accepted the risk of not being able to comply with existing legal requirements than the risk of not being able to comply with new and unforeseen obstacles arising from changes in the law made after the time of contracting. There is, indeed, support for the contrary view in the Restatement 2d where Illustration 3 to § 264 does impose the latter risk on the party required to take steps to obtain the licence even though the licensing requirement was imposed by legislation passed after the time of contracting. But this view seems to be inconsistent with the likely intention of the parties. Nor does it appear to be supported by the case on which the Illustration is based. It seems that in that case[37] the relevant legislation (requiring Department of Health approval for certain building works) was

---

[32] *Empresa Exportadora de Azucar v Industria Azucarera Nacional SA (The Playa Larga)* [1983] 2 Lloyd's Rep. 179.

[33] Above, para.6–041.

[34] The argument was based on the *Peter Cassidy* case [1957] 1 W.L.R. 273 (above, para.8–015) and on dicta in the *Walton (Grain & Shipping)* case [1959] 1 Lloyd's Rep. 223 at 236.

[35] [1983] 2 Lloyd's Rep. 171 at 191.

[36] [1978] 2 Lloyd's Rep. 223 at 253; above, n.29.

[37] *Security Sewage Equipment Co v McFerren*, 273 N.E. 2d 898 (1968).

already in force at the time of contracting, though the Department's disapproval of the works came after that time.[38]

(3) Content of the duty

8–052   The rules which determine the content of the duty in the present group of cases are generally the same as those which apply in cases of antecedent licensing requirements. The duty being normally one of diligence, the party under the duty will be under no liability if he can show that he made reasonable efforts to obtain the licence, or that such reasonable efforts as he should have made would have proved unavailing. This seems to follow from the *Anglo-Russian Merchant Traders* case[39] in which there was (1) an antecedent licensing requirement, and the seller was not liable, in spite of having failed to obtain a licence, as he had performed his duty to take reasonable steps to that end; and also (2) a supervening qualified prohibition, and the seller was not liable for having failed to obtain the licence required by this prohibition even though he had made no efforts to that end. It is not clear from the judgments exactly why the seller was not liable in respect of this second failure, but the reason seems to be that it was found as a fact that the licence would have been refused, even if the seller had applied for it. To escape liability on this ground, the party who is under the duty of diligence must show that the licence would *actually* have been refused even though reasonable efforts had been made: it is not enough for him to show that he reasonably believed that such efforts would be unavailing.[40] In this respect, these cases of supervening qualified prohibitions constitute an exception to the general principle of looking to the time of the supervening event in order to determine whether it has frustrated the contract; the extent of the exception is further discussed in Ch.9.[41] The party under the duty of diligence may, however, be able to show that the contract has been frustrated on some other ground, *e.g.* by an unqualified prohibition of the stipulated method of payment.[42] In that event the duty of diligence will be discharged along with the rest of the contract, so that the party under that duty will not be liable even if he made no efforts to secure the licence.

(4) Partial prevention

8–053   The supervening qualified prohibition may prevent only part of the contract from being lawfully performed, for example, where an export licensing system is introduced after the making of a contract of sale, and the seller obtains an export licence for only a part of the quantity sold, or where the prohibition is subject to exceptions or "loopholes" so that the seller has at his disposal some goods of the contract description but not

---

[38] *cf.* above, para.8–009.
[39] [1917] 2 K.B. 679, above, para.8–014.
[40] See the *Dalmia Dairy Industries* case, above, n.29.
[41] Below, para.9–009; for another exception see above, para.8–032.
[42] As in the *Nile Co* case [1986] 1 Lloyd's Rep. 555, above para.8–034.

enough to fulfil his obligations to the buyer. These possibilities are illustrated by the soyabean cases to be discussed in Ch.12.[43] They are governed by the general principles, discussed earlier in this chapter,[44] which apply to partial supervening illegality. That is, the seller must deliver the quantity for which he has obtained a licence and may (if other conditions are satisfied) be discharged from his duty to deliver the balance. Such "other conditions" will not be satisfied if the seller has simply made a contract for the sale of unascertained goods by description and cannot show that it was the supervening prohibition which prevented fulfilment of that contract: this was the position in many of the soyabean cases.[45] The extent of the seller's duty may also be governed by express contractual provisions (such as the "prohibition" clause in those cases) which displace the common law doctrine of discharge.

VII. FOREIGN PROHIBITION

Our primary concern in this chapter is with illegality arising under English law; but it will be obvious from the facts of the cases which have been discussed that in many of them the prohibition which prevented the contract from being lawfully performed has been one imposed by the law of a foreign country. In a substantial number of those cases, no point has been raised as to the relevant rules of the Conflict of Laws; though others do form the basis of the English Conflicts rule that a contract (though governed by English law) will not be enforced in England if or to the extent that its performance is illegal by the law governing the contract or by the law of the place of performance.[46] Conversely, illegality by the law of some other country (*e.g.* that of the country in which the party claiming to be discharged is resident or carries on business) will not prevent enforcement of the contract in England.[47] For detailed discussion of the

8–054

---

[43] Below, paras 12–036 *et seq.*

[44] Above, paras 8–029, 8–046.

[45] *i.e.* in particular, those in which the seller was not himself the prospective shipper and had failed to identify the "relevant shipper": below, para.12–037; and see next sentence of the text above.

[46] *e.g. Cunningham v Dunn* (1873) 3 C.P.D. 441; *Ralli Bros v Compania Naviera Sota y Anzar* [1920] 2 K.B. 287; *Nile Co for the Export of Agricultural Crops v H & J M Bennett (Commodities) Ltd* [1986] 1 Lloyd's Rep. 555 at 581. It follows from the formulation in the text above that a contract governed by English law will not be frustrated merely because the acts to be done under it would have become illegal by the law of a foreign country, if the contract does not require such acts to be performed there: *Bangladesh Export Import Co Ltd v Sucden Kerry SA* [1995] 2 Lloyd's Rep. 1 at 5; see above, para.7–028.

[47] *e.g. Kleinwort Sons & Co v Ungarische Baumwolle Industries A G* [1939] 2 K.B. 678; *Toprak Mahsulleri Ofisi v Finagrain Cie Commerciale etc.* [1979] 2 Lloyd's Rep. 98; *Libyan Arab Foreign Bank v Bankers Trust Co* [1989] Q.B. 728; *cf. Fox v Henderson Investment Fund Ltd* [1999] 2 Lloyd's Rep. 303 (a case of alleged antecedent illegality).

relevant Conflicts rules, reference should be made to the specialist works on that subject.[48]

Where foreign prohibitions have been held to frustrate a contract, the basis of discharge does not appear to be the same principle of public policy as that which justifies discharge on the ground of supervening illegality by English law. The point appears most clearly where illegality results from the prohibition against trading with the enemy. Where the war which brings this prohibition into operation is one to which the United Kingdom is a party, contracts, the performance of which would contravene the prohibition, are discharged because their performance might, by aiding the enemy economy, prejudice the survival of this country. But the survival of some other country cannot be a matter of such prime concern to the English courts, so that the same consideration of public policy does not apply where the war is between two or more other countries and performance of the contract would violate a prohibition against trading with the enemy imposed by the law of one of them. A similar point can be made with regard to other prohibitions: again it is obvious that English courts have a greater concern in giving effect to English than to foreign prohibitions. Nevertheless English cases recognise the existence of a somewhat analogous principle of public policy, namely that the contracting parties should be deprived of the incentive which, if the contract had remained in force, they might have had to do an illegal act in a friendly foreign country. On this ground, contracts have been held to be illegal where the prohibition existed at the time of contracting[49]; and the same reasoning should apply where the prohibition is imposed after that time. An alternative way of putting the point is that it is "an implied condition ... of the contract that at the time of performance it shall be legal for the promisor to do the act which he has promised to do"[50] or that the law of the foreign country in which that act is to be done will "not be so changed as to prevent the contract from being fulfilled".[51] It is submitted that this "implied term" is not one which is implied in fact (*i.e.* because the parties must have intended it[52]) but rather one which is implied in law[53]: in other words, that the implication arises, not because the parties must have intended to incorporate the term, but because the

---

[48] *Dicey and Morris on the Conflict of Laws* (13th ed., 1993), Ch.32; Cheshire & North, *Private International Law* (13th ed.), Ch.18.

[49] *e.g. Foster v Driscoll* [1929] 1 K.B. 470; *Regazzoni v K.C. Sethia Ltd* [1958] A.C. 301.

[50] *Walton (Grain & Shipping) Ltd v British Italian Trading Co* [1959] 1 Lloyd's Rep. 223 at 236.

[51] *Société Co-operative Suisse de Céréales, etc. v La Plata Cereal Co SA* (1947) 80 Ll.L. Rep. 530 at 542.

[52] The passage cited in the previous note does indeed apply the "officious bystander" test (which is a test of the implication of terms in fact) to the cases of the kind here under discussion. But the actual decision was based on other grounds: see *Atisa SA v Aztec AG* [1983] 2 Lloyd's Rep. 579 at 586; *cf.* also the *Kleinwort* case [1939] 2 K.B. 678 at 698, above, n.47, preferring to base the principle of discharge by supervening foreign illegality on a positive rule of law.

[53] For the distinction between terms implied in fact and terms implied in law, see Treitel, *The Law of Contract* (11th ed.), pp.207–211.

courts, as a matter of policy, have so decided. On this view, there is no substantial difference between this "implied term" explanation of the present rule and the "public policy" explanation which has been stated above.

VIII. SUPERVENING ILLEGALITY AND EXPRESS CONTRACTUAL PROVISIONS

The doctrine of discharge by supervening impossibility or frustration of purpose can clearly be excluded by express provisions in the contract which specify the effect of the supervening event on the contractual obligations of the parties. But it is settled that such an express provision cannot exclude the doctrine of discharge where supervening illegality arises on the ground that performance of the contract will involve trading with the enemy. The leading case is *Ertel Bieber Co v Rio Tinto Co Ltd*,[54] where an English company had contracted to deliver copper ore to a German company from 1911 to 1919. It was held that the contract was frustrated on the outbreak of the First World War in 1914, even though it provided that, in the event of war, certain obligations under the contract should only be suspended.[55] To give effect to this provision would or could involve continuing communication, and hence commercial relations, with the enemy and so contravene the principle of public policy against giving any aid to the enemy economy in time of war. The suspension clause itself was therefore against public policy and void, and would (it seems) have been void even if it had provided for the suspension of all (and not merely some) of the obligations of the contract. Lord Sumner stated the underlying principle when he asked rhetorically: "If upon public grounds on the outbreak of war the law interferes with private executory contracts by dissolving them, how can it be open to a subject for his private advantage to withdraw his contract from the operation of the law and claim to do what the law rejects, merely to suspend where the law dissolves?"[56]

In the United States, a similar rule appears to be laid down for cases of discharge by supervening illegality in the Civil Code prepared in 1865 by David Dudley Field and later adopted[57] by a number of States. The Field Code distinguishes between prevention (or delay) of performance by "operation of law" and "by an irresistible superhuman cause". In the

---

[54] [1918] A.C. 260; *cf. Zinc Corp Ltd v Hirsch* [1916] 1 K.B. 541; *Distington Hematite Iron Co Ltd v Possehl Co* [1916] 1 K.B. 811; *Veithardt & Hall Ltd v Rylands Bros Ltd* (1917) 116 L.T. 706; *Clapham SS Co Ltd v Naamloose, etc, Vulcan of Rotterdam* [1917] 2 K.B. 639; *Naylor Benzon & Co Ltd v Krainische Industrie Gesellschaft* [1918] 1 K.B. 331; affirmed [1918] 2 K.B. 486.

[55] For the possibility of narrowly construing such clauses so as not to refer to war between the countries of the contracting parties, see below, para.12–009.

[56] [1918] A.C. 260 at 286.

[57] The Code had been prepared for the State of New York but was not adopted there. The movement for its adoption appears to have started in California.

latter situation (*i.e.* in cases of supervening impossibility) the contract is discharged "unless the parties have expressly agreed to the contrary".[58] In the former situation, on the other hand (*i.e.* in cases of supervening illegality) the contract is discharged "even though there may have been a stipulation that this shall not be an excuse".[59] The Restatement appears, at first sight, to take an intermediate position. § 458 makes discharge by "supervening prohibition" subject to "contrary intention"[60]; but there is no such qualification in § 608 which deals with discharge by "supervening illegality". The relationship between these provisions is far from clear. The Restatement 2d seems to reject the rule which is stated for cases of supervening illegality in the legislation derived from the Field Code. It accepts the principle of discharge in cases of "prevention by governmental regulation or order"[61] but states that there is no such discharge if "the language or circumstances indicate the contrary".[62] The original Field Code rule has also been amended in California, where s.1511 of the Civil Code enables the parties expressly to provide in their contract for (*inter alia*) a procedure for claiming an extension of time in cases of prevention or delay by operation of law.

8–056   The Uniform Commercial Code in s.2–615 likewise subjects the principle of discharge by "foreign or domestic governmental regulation" to the qualification that the principle applies only "except so far as the seller may have assumed a greater obligation and subject to the preceding section on substituted performance". We have seen earlier in this chapter that part of that "preceding section" (*i.e.* s.2–614(2)) deals with failure in the agreed means or manner of payment; and that the effect of that subsection, where the seller has delivered, may be to discharge part of the buyer's duty to pay.[63] No reservation is made in s.2–614(2) for express contrary provision in the contract, but such a provision would seem to be effective by virtue of the general rule that "the effect of the provisions of the [Code] may be varied by agreement" except as otherwise provided in the Code...[64].

---

[58] § 727(2); this wording is in force in Montana: see Montana Code Annotated 2003, § 28–1–1301(2); in North Dakota: see North Dakota Century Code, § 9–11–04(2); and in South Dakota: see South Dakota Codified Laws, § 20–6–2.

[59] § 727(1); this wording is in force in Montana: see Montana Code Annotated, § 28–1–301 (1); in North Dakota: see North Dakota Century Code, § 9–11–04(1); and in South Dakota: see South Dakota Codified Laws, § 20–6–4.

[60] So that an agreement to pay compensation, if performance should be prohibited, is valid: § 456, Comment d.

[61] § 264, which regards such prevention as the failure of a basic assumption.

[62] See § 261 (stating the effect of the failure of *any* basic assumption, including one within § 264); Comment a, stating that a contrary agreement (displacing the principles of discharge) can give rise to liability in damages.

[63] Above, para.8–041.

[64] UCC, s.1–302(a), formerly s.1–102(3) (see above, para.3–017, n.57). Provisions similar to those contained in ss.2–614 and 2–615 (applicable to sale of goods) are contained in ss.2A–404 and 2A–405 (applicable to chattel leases). The latter section differs from s.2–615 in not containing words corresponding to those (quoted in the text above): "except insofar as the seller may have assumed a

The view thus seems to be gaining ground in the United States that express contractual provisions can exclude the principle of discharge even in cases of supervening illegality; and at first sight this view appears to be in direct conflict with the English rule which has been applied in the trading with the enemy cases.[65] The conflict is, however, more apparent than real. For one thing, there is some ambiguity in the references (in the Restatement 2d and Uniform Commercial Code) to "prevention by governmental regulation or order". This phrase can include cases in which the effect of the governmental order is to make performance, not illegal, but impossible[66]: for example, by the requisition or compulsory acquisition of the subject-matter, or by a court order depriving the debtor of his power of disposition over it. Thus one of the Illustrations given in the Restatement 2d[67] of such prevention is based on the English case of *Baily v De Crespigny*[68] where a lessor's covenant not to build on certain land was held to have been discharged when that land was compulsorily acquired by a railway company which built a station on the land. The ground of discharge was not illegality but impossibility through unavailability of the subject-matter; and an express term in the contract for the payment of compensation by the covenantor in the events which had happened would no doubt have been valid. Even where the ground of discharge is supervening illegality, it must again be stressed that the policy considerations underlying the prohibition which would be infringed if the contract were performed can vary considerably in strength from one type of illegality to another. It follows that these considerations will not in all cases necessarily require the invalidation of contract terms by which the parties make provision for supervening prohibitions. The trading with the enemy cases may from this point of view be contrasted with those in which performance is made illegal by supervening prohibitions of export or import. Such prohibitions may discharge the contract[69]; but in cases of this kind effect is commonly given to express contractual provisions for the event: for example, to a term requiring the party whose performance is made illegal to pay a sum of money instead of doing the prohibited act,[70] or to a "prohibition" or "*force majeure*" clause, which provides for suspension of the contract and (commonly) for its termination or cancellation if the prohibition is not lifted by the end of a specified period.[71] Such clauses are not contrary to public policy[72] since they assume that the prohibition will be observed and since the continuation of the contractual relationship in cases of this kind

---

greater obligation"; but s.1–302(a) leaves it open to a lessor of goods to assume such a "greater obligation".

[65] Above, para.8–055, at n.54.

[66] See above, paras 4–003, 8–003.

[67] § 264, Illustration 1.

[68] (1869) L.R. Q.B. 180; *cf.* above, para.4–012.

[69] Above, para.8–007.

[70] e.g. *Johnson Matthey Bankers Ltd v State Trading Corp of India* [1984] 1 Lloyd's Rep. 427 (invoicing back clause).

[71] For illustrations of such clauses, see below, paras 12–022 *et seq.*; *cf.* the *Tsakiroglou* case [1962] A.C. 93 at 95 (decided on other grounds: above, para.4–073).

[72] *Johnson Matthey* case, above, n.70, at 437.

has no tendency to subvert the purpose of the prohibition. In this respect they differ from provisions for the suspension of a contract if its performance should become illegal, in the event of war, by reason of the prohibition against trading with the enemy: such provisions are contrary to the public interest since they involve continuing relations with an enemy subject and since such relations could indirectly support the economy of the enemy country.

CHAPTER **9**

PROSPECTIVE FRUSTRATION

In one sense, the operation of the doctrine of frustration is always **9–001** prospective: it is concerned with the legal consequences of an allegedly frustrating event on the *future* obligations of the parties,[1] *i.e.* on those which, but for that event, would have accrued after its occurrence. In some cases, the effect of the event on the possibility of performing the contract can be predicted with certainty as soon as the event occurs, for example, where the event is the death of a party who has undertaken to render personal services. The same is, as a practical matter, true where the event is the destruction of the subject-matter of the contract, as in *Taylor v Caldwell*,[2] where the possibility that the Hall *might* have been rebuilt in time for the concerts[3] was so remote as to have been rightly ignored. But there are further cases, in which the effect of the event on performance of the contract is not as clear, either in the literal or in the practical senses described above, as the effect of such death or destruction; and it is with cases of this kind that the present chapter is concerned. One possibility is that the event may, when it occurs, appear to present an obstacle to performance but that this obstacle may then be unexpectedly removed. A second possibility commonly arises in cases of temporary impossibility, in many of which the question whether the contract is frustrated depends on the seriousness of the delay; and the question whether the delay will be of this kind is one that often cannot be answered with certainty as soon as the event causing the delay occurs. The first question which arises in these two groups of cases is whether the contract is discharged at all; the second (assuming an affirmative answer to the first) relates to the time of discharge.

---

[1] Below, para.15–011.
[2] (1863) 3 B. & S. 826.
[3] See above, para.6–001.

I. WHETHER CONTRACT DISCHARGED

(1) **General rule**

9–002   The general rule is that the question whether the contract is discharged is to be determined by reference to the time of the occurrence of the allegedly frustrating event. The contract will be discharged if at that time a reasonable person would have taken the view that the event would lead to a sufficiently serious interference with performance to bring about discharge. It is not necessary to wait and see whether such interference actually takes place, or would have taken place if attempts to perform had not been abandoned; indeed, the contract will be discharged even though subsequent events show that there would have been no such interference. The general rule is illustrated by *Embiricos v Sydney Reid & Co,*[4] where the Greek ship *Andriana* had been chartered to carry a cargo of grain from a port on the Sea of Azoff to the United Kingdom, a voyage which necessarily involved passage of the Dardanelles. Before the *Andriana* had been fully loaded, war broke out between Greece and Turkey, the Turkish authorities began to detain Greek ships attempting to pass through the Dardanelles, and the charterers refused to continue to load, claiming that the charterparty had been frustrated. Matters then took an unexpected turn in that the Turkish authorities announced that Greek ships would be allowed through the Dardanelles during an "escape period" of two weeks. If the charterers had loaded the cargo in accordance with the contract, the *Andriana* could have made use of this period and have accomplished the contract voyage; in fact she was trapped in the Black Sea for nearly a year, until the end of the war. It was held that the contract had been frustrated since the charterers at the time of their refusal to load were justified in believing that performance would be impossible. The ground for the decision, in the words of Scrutton J., was that: "Commercial men must not be asked to wait till the end of a long delay to find out from what in fact happens whether they are bound by the contract or not; they must be entitled to act on reasonable commercial probabilities at the time when they are called upon to make up their minds."[5]

9–003   The same principle has been stated in similar language on a number of occasions in the House of Lords. For example, in *Bank Line Ltd v Arthur Capel & Co*, Lord Sumner said that the question of frustration: "must be considered at the trial as it had to be considered by the parties when they came to know of the cause and the probabilities of the delay and had to decide what to do ... Rights ought not to be left in suspense or to hang on the chances of subsequent events."[6] Such events are relevant only "in

---

[4] [1914] 3 K.B. 45.

[5] *ibid.* at 54.

[6] [1919] A.C. 435 at 454; *cf.* also *National Carriers Ltd v Panalpina (Northern) Ltd* [1981] A.C. 675 at 706; *Wong Lai Ying v Chinachem Investment Co* (1979) 13 Build. L.R. 81.

showing what the probabilities really were".[7] These statements were in substance repeated and approved by Lord Wright in the *Denny Mott*[8] case (where frustration had resulted from a war-time Government Order prohibiting certain dealings in timber). Moreover in *Horlock v Beal*[9] Lord Atkinson had the same principle in mind in his discussion of *Jackson v Union Marine Insurance Co Ltd*,[10] where a voyage charterparty was frustrated in consequence of the ship's having gone aground and been seriously damaged on her way to the port of loading. He said that in that case the charterer "did not wait till a reasonable time had elapsed before he repudiated the contract. He did that at once when a long delay in the process of repairing [the ship] was reasonably probable"[11]. A number of decisions of the lower courts also follow the principle of the *Embiricos* case.[12]

(2) **Prospective effects distinguished from prospective events**

The *Embiricos* principle applies not only where discharge is claimed under the common law doctrine of frustration, but also where a party relies by way of excuse on an express contractual provision for the supervening event. In such cases, a distinction has been drawn between the situation in which an event falling within the provision has occurred but its effects on performance of the contract are not yet clear, and that in which the occurrence of the event itself is still a matter of speculation when the party who claims the benefit of the provision seeks to invoke it.

9–004

The first of these situations is illustrated by *Geipel v Smith*[13] where a shipowner successfully relied on an exception for restraints of princes, as justifying his refusal to load, after Hamburg (the port to which the goods were to be carried) had been blockaded by the French fleet in the course of the Franco-Prussian War. It was sufficient for this purpose that, when the blockade was imposed, it had become unlikely that it would be lifted within such time as to make performance possible.[14] Blackburn J. did, indeed say that, in refusing to take the cargo on board, the shipowner "chose to take the risk"[15] that the blockade might be lifted within such time; and this seems to mean that he would have been liable if the blockade had indeed been lifted within the time allowed for performance. But this is, it is submitted, one of the rare occasions on which Blackburn

---

[7] [1919] A.C. 435 at 454; *cf. Total Gas Marketing Ltd v Arco British Ltd* [1992] 2 Lloyd's Rep. 209 at 222; the actual decision was that the contract was discharged, under one of its express terms, by the non-occurrence of a condition.

[8] *Denny Mott & Dickson Ltd v James B Fraser & Co Ltd* [1944] A.C. 265 at 277.

[9] [1916] 1 A.C. 486.

[10] (1874) L.R. 10 C.P. 125; above, para.5–039.

[11] [1916] 1 A.C. at 502; *cf.* at 492, 508.

[12] *Anglo-Northern Trading Corp v Jones* [1917] 2 K.B. 78 at 85; *Court Line Ltd v Dant & Russell Inc* [1939] 3 All E.R. 314.

[13] (1872) L.R. 7 Q.B. 404.

[14] See *ibid.* at 410–411, 414.

[15] *ibid.* at 413.

J.'s view has not prevailed; for it seems to be inconsistent with the frequently approved principle in the *Embiricos* case.[16]

The second situation is illustrated by *Watts, Watts & Co v Mitsui & Co*[17] where a British shipowner refused on September 1, 1914 to proceed to a port of loading on the Sea of Azoff. At that time, the First World War had broken out, but Turkey was still a neutral country and the Dardanelles were not closed to shipping until September 26. It was held that the shipowner was not protected by an exception for restraints of princes since such a restraint must be "an existing fact and not a mere apprehension".[18] This does not mean that there must necessarily be actual interference with the voyage: "it may be possible to invoke the exception when a reasonable man in the face of an *existing* restraint may consider that the restraint, though it does not affect him at the moment, will do so if he continues the adventure."[19] But in applying this test the court must judge the situation as at the time of the original refusal to perform, and not "merely by the event".[20] Thus in the *Watts* case the argument that the shipowner could "take the risk of his fears being justified by the event" was rejected by Lord Sumner on the ground that this view would "give rise to a period of suspense during which neither party could be certain of his rights".[21] This part of the reasoning is similar to that of the *Embiricos* case,[22] on which Lord Sumner relies in this part of his speech,[23] though it produces the opposite effect: in other words, the shipowner's belief that an obstacle to performance *would* be imposed so as to prevent performance did not amount to a restraint of princes when no such obstacle was in fact imposed (and so did not excuse him); while in the *Embiricos* case an *existing* obstacle did give rise to frustration in spite of the fact that the charterer's belief that the obstacle would not be removed turned out to be mistaken.

(3) Borderline cases

9–005   In the *Watts* case the shipowner relied on the restraints of princes exception and made no attempt to argue that the contract had been frustrated. No doubt in principle the distinction between a belief as to the anticipated effects of a past event and the anticipated occurrence of a future event could be relevant also for the purpose of the general common law doctrine, so that for this purpose, too, a reasonable anticipation that a frustrating event was likely to occur would not, of

---

[16] Above, paras 9–002, 9–003.

[17] [1917] A.C. 227.

[18] *ibid.* at 238. This point had been settled since *Atkinson v Ritchie* (1809) East 530; see above, para.2–020, n.66.

[19] [1917] 2 A.C. 227 at 238 (italics supplied).

[20] *ibid.* at 236; *i.e.* by what happens *later*.

[21] *ibid.* at 245.

[22] [1914] 3 K.B. 45.

[23] [1917] 2 A.C. 227 at 246.

itself, suffice to discharge a contract.[24] But in borderline cases it may be hard to distinguish between the two situations here under discussion: thus threats of imminent violence by the armed forces of a belligerent power[25] or of participants in a civil war[26] may have the same effects on a contract as events in the course of the conflict which have already occurred. The possibility is illustrated by the decision of the United States Supreme Court in *The Kronprinzessin Cecilie*,[27] where a German ship left New York on July 28, 1914 with passengers and a quantity of gold which was carried under bills of lading calling for it to be delivered at Plymouth or Cherbourg. On July 31, the master learnt that Austria had declared war on Serbia and, having then just enough fuel to get back to the United States, made for a port in Maine (in accordance with advice issued by the German authorities) and there returned the gold to the consignors. If he had proceeded to Plymouth he could just have delivered the gold there before the United Kingdom declared war on Germany on August 4, and so have avoided capture. It was held that the shipowner was not in breach of the contract contained or evidenced in the bills of lading. Holmes J. said: "We are wholly unable to accept the argument that although a shipowner may give up his voyage to avoid capture after war is declared, he is never at liberty to anticipate war. In this case, the anticipation was correct and the master is not to be put in the wrong by nice calculations that if all went well he might have delivered the gold and escaped capture by a few hours."[28] It is submitted that on such facts an English court would have reached the same conclusion,[29] and would indeed have done so whether or not the anticipation was actually correct, so long as it was based on reasonable grounds.

(4) Extent of obstacle to performance unclear

The *Embiricos* case,[30] as already noted, concerned the converse situation to   9–006
that discussed in para.9–005 above, *i.e.* not that of an obstacle to performance which is expected to arise, but that of an obstacle which had already arisen; and the case shows that the unexpected removal of that obstacle does not preclude frustration. One case which is at first sight hard to reconcile with this principle is *Andrew Millar & Co Ltd v Taylor & Co Ltd*,[31] where confectionery had been sold f.o.b. Liverpool for export to Morocco; the export of confectionery was then prohibited, shortly after the outbreak of the First World War, by two Proclamations of August 5 and

---

[24] *e.g.* in the coronation cases discussed in Ch.7 a reasonable belief that the King *would* fall ill would not have been a ground of discharge.

[25] *Nobel's Explosives Co v Jenkins* [1896] 2 Q.B. 306.

[26] *Atlantic Maritime Co Inc v Gibbon* [1954] 1 Q.B. 88.

[27] *North German Lloyd v Guarantee Trust Co (The Kronprinzessin Cecilie)*, 244 U.S. 12 (1917).

[28] *ibid.* at 24.

[29] *cf. Pole v Cetcovitch* (1860) 9 C.B.N.S. 430; above, para.2–020, n.66.

[30] [1914] 3 K.B. 45.

[31] [1916] 1 K.B. 402.

10. On August 15 the sellers claimed to have been discharged by operation of law in consequence of the Proclamations; and on August 20, before the normal delivery period under the contract had expired,[32] a further Proclamation was issued, lifting the export embargo with respect to confectionery. The sellers' claim that the contract had been frustrated was rejected. Swinfen Eady L.J. said that: "if they [the sellers] had waited, the contract could have been carried out as usual without any difficulty."[33] Warrington L.J. distinguished between illegality arising from a state of war "the duration of which it is impossible to foresee" and illegality arising "from an act of the Executive Government",[34] which had not made performance impossible because the embargo had been lifted "before the time had arrived within which, even according to the ordinary practice in peace-time, the contract would have been performed".[35] In so far as these statements make the issue of frustration depend on the course of events after the sellers claimed to be discharged, they are hard to reconcile with the *Embiricos* principle, as applied in the authorities so far considered in this chapter. According to that principle, the test should have been whether, after the first two Proclamations had been issued, a reasonable person in the position of the sellers would have taken the view that performance would be prevented by them; if so, the fact that the embargo was lifted before the end of the delivery period should not have precluded frustration. The actual decision in the *Andrew Millar* case can, perhaps, be explained on the ground that the original two Proclamations were issued, and the sellers claimed to be discharged, during the first two weeks of the war; that this was a period of considerable uncertainty during which no reasonable view of the likely duration of the embargo could safely be formed; and that the sellers had therefore acted with "undue precipitation"[36] in claiming to be discharged so soon after the embargo had been imposed.

(5) **An alternative approach**

9–007   The basis of the principle of the *Embiricos* case is that it promotes commercial certainty; but (as is so often the result of the pursuit of that object) it can lead to hardship to the party who is by that principle deprived of rights under a contract which could in fact have been performed. For this reason, there is some conflict on the point in nineteenth-century American cases. In one of these,[37] an employee left his place of work, before the end of the period for which he had been employed "by reason of the alarm ... occasioned by the prevalence of cholera in the vicinity". This was held not to be a breach, even though all his fellow employees had remained at their posts and in good health, since

---

[32] No shipment period appears to have been specified in the contract.
[33] [1916] 1 K.B. 402 at 415.
[34] *ibid.* at 416
[35] *ibid.*
[36] *Atlantic Maritime Co Inc v Gibbon* [1954] 1 Q.B. 88 at 114.
[37] *Lakeman v Pollard*, 43 Me. 463, 69 Am. Dec. 77 (1857).

"the propriety of his conduct in leaving his work at that time must be determined by examining the state of facts as then existing".[38] This is in accord with the *Embiricos* principle, but a different view was taken in *Hathaway v Sabin*.[39] The defendant in that case had contracted to provide a hall for a concert to be given by a group of musicians in a town to which they were to travel on the day in question. On that day, the town seemed to have been cut off by "a snowstorm of unusual violence"[40] and the defendant accordingly gave orders for the hall not to be prepared for the concert. The musicians, however, were unexpectedly able to make the journey on an "irregular train"[41] and presented themselves at the agreed time. It was held that the contract was not discharged merely because the defendant had reasonable cause to believe that performance would be prevented. The Restatement originally took the contrary view that a reasonable apprehension of such impossibility justified suspension and eventual discharge[42]; and indeed one of the illustrations[43] supporting this view closely resembled the facts of, and the result in, the English *Embiricos* case.[44] The Restatement 2d, however, adopts a different approach: it applies to the present situation the principle of "adequate assurance of performance"[45] which was introduced into American law by s.2–609 of the Uniform Commercial Code.[46] Under this principle, as applied in the present context, the prospective prevention of the performance of one party (A) entitles the other (B) to ask A for adequate assurance of due performance. If A fails to give the assurance, B is discharged, but he has no claim for damages, since it is assumed that A's failure is excused by the supervening events.[47] Under these provisions, the decision in *Hathaway v Sabin* is accepted in principle[48]; but the defendant could have escaped liability if he had asked for an assurance that the musicians would arrive and if he had failed to receive any such assurance in time to prepare the

---

[38] *ibid.* at 78.

[39] 22 A. 663 (1891).

[40] *ibid.*

[41] *ibid.*

[42] §§ 465(1), 466.

[43] § 465, Illustration 6.

[44] [1914] 3 K.B. 45; above, para.9–002.

[45] §§ 251 and 268.

[46] See Treitel, *Remedies for Breach of Contract*, para.293. The criticism there made of the American remedy in cases of prospective *breach* (namely that mere failure to give the requested assurance gives rise to liability in damages) does not apply in the present context (where there is no such liability). UCC, s.2–609 requires the demand for assurance to be made "in writing". Under the proposed amendments for Art.2 of the Code (above, para.2–042, n.17) "in a record" is to be substituted for "in writing". The purpose of the change is to enable the demand to be made by electronic means: see the proposed s.2–103 (1)(m). See also s.2A–401, laying down for chattel leases a rule substantially similar to that laid down for sales by s.2–609.

[47] See, *e.g.* Restatement 2d, § 268, Illustration 2.

[48] *ibid.*, § 251, Illustration 1.

hall for the concert.[49] This solution is not available in English law, which does not recognise the principle of adequate assurance of performance.

The principle of the *Embiricos* case appears also not to apply in India. The reason for this departure from the principle is to be found, not in the policy grounds which underlie the American developments just described, but simply in the wording of s.56 of the Indian Contract Act 1872. This provides that a contract to do an act which after the contract is made "becomes impossible or . . . unlawful, becomes void when the act becomes impossible or unlawful". It is thought to follow from these words that the contract only "becomes void when the act is required to be done under the contract".[50]

(6) **Frustration by delay**

9–008   Even in English law, the principle of the *Embiricos* case[51] is subject to qualification in cases of what may be called "frustration by delay", that is, in certain cases of temporary impossibility.[52] We saw in Ch.5 that the question whether such impossibility constituted a ground of frustration depended (where the time of performance was not of the essence) on the length and effects of the delay[53]; and these are matters as to which it may not be possible to form a view as soon as the event giving rise to the delay occurs. In such cases, it is "often necessary to await events"; but "business men must not be required to await events too long".[54] Both of these points can be illustrated by reference to *The Nema*,[55] where a strike at the port of loading interfered with the performance of a consecutive voyage charterparty which was to run from April to December 1979. The strike began on June 6 and the contract was not immediately frustrated at that stage; but it was held that the shipowners were justified in claiming to have been discharged on August 14 since by then it was reasonable to take the view that the strike would last for so long as to frustrate the contract. In fact this view was borne out by events, the strike not being settled until October 5, so that the ratio of the performance which remained possible to that which had originally been undertaken was so low that frustration would in October have followed from the application of the "proportionality" test[56] described in Ch.5. But it is submitted that the decision should have been the same even if the strike had actually been settled on (say) August 20. The crucial point was that on August 14, it was reasonable to take the view that the delay resulting from the strike would be such as to interfere fundamentally with performance. Once this stage is reached, the

---

[49] *ibid.* Illustration 7.

[50] *Dalmia Dairy Industries Ltd v National Bank of Pakistan* [1978] 2 Lloyd's Rep. 223 at 253, affirmed *ibid.* on different grounds.

[51] [1914] 3 K.B. 45, above, para.9–002.

[52] *Pioneer Shipping v BTP Tioxide (The Nema)* [1982] A.C. 724 at 752.

[53] Above, paras 5–036 *et seq.*

[54] *The Nema*, above, n.52, at 753.

[55] Above, n.52.

[56] Above, para.5–050.

Embiricos principle applies even in these cases of "frustration by delay": that is, frustration may occur even though subsequent events show that the interference with performance was in fact less serious than the degree of interference which it had been reasonable to anticipate when the claim to be discharged was originally made. It is not, in other words, necessary to wait "to *the end* of a long delay"[57] before claiming to be discharged.

In *The Nema* the issue of frustration did not come before the courts until after the contractual time for performance had elapsed; but the same principle applies where the issue of frustration has to be decided before the end of that time. This was the position in *Metropolitan Water Board v Dick Kerr & Co*[58] where a contract for the construction of a reservoir within six years was made in 1914 and was held to have been frustrated when, after only two years (in 1916), the Government ordered the contractors to stop the work and to sell their plant. Frustration occurred at this stage since in 1916 it was reasonable to take the view that the delay would be a long one, and that, when performance again became possible, conditions in the industry would have changed to such an extent that performance then would be fundamentally different from that originally undertaken.[59]

(7) Supervening qualified prohibitions

A further qualification of the doctrine of the *Embiricos* case arises in cases of supervening qualified prohibitions.[60] These are cases in which after the contract is made its performance is prohibited, not absolutely, but unless the consent of (usually) some public authority is obtained, for example, where the previously unrestricted export of some class of goods made subject to the requirement that an export licence must be obtained. In such cases, a contract which expressly provides for the export of such goods is not frustrated (as it would be if export were absolutely prohibited) when the licensing requirement is first imposed. At this stage, one of the parties (*e.g.* the seller) will be under a duty to make reasonable efforts to obtain the licence[61]; and the seller will be able to rely on the prohibition as a ground of frustration only if he can show either that he has made such efforts or that the efforts which he should have made would have proved unavailing. It is not enough for him to show that he reasonably believed that the licence would probably have been refused even if the requisite efforts had been made.[62] To this extent, these cases of qualified prohibitions constitute an apparent departure from the general

9–009

---

[57] *Embiricos v Sydney Reid & Co* [1914] 3 K.B. 45 at 54 (italics supplied).
[58] [1918] A.C. 119.
[59] *i.e.* applying the test stated in Ch.5, para.5–042.
[60] Above, para.8–049.
[61] Above, paras 4–050, 4–051.
[62] *Dalmia Dairy Industries Ltd v National Bank of Pakistan* [1978] 2 Lloyd's Rep. 223 at 253, affirmed *ibid.* on different grounds. The actual decision at first instance was based on the position under the Indian Contract Act 1872, s.56, stated above, at n.50.

principle, of looking at the probabilities as at the time of the supervening event, in order to determine whether it frustrates the contract. The departure is probably more apparent than real, for in cases of this kind the allegedly frustrating event will be the imposition of the qualified prohibition, and at the time of this event it will generally be impossible to tell whether the seller's reasonable efforts to obtain the licence are likely to succeed. Where this is the position, the conditions for the application of the general principle of looking at the probabilities as at the time of supervening events are simply not present. If these conditions are at some later state satisfied (*e.g.* if it becomes the policy of the public authority to refuse export licences to sellers of a certain nationality to which the seller belongs, or in respect of goods destined for the country specified in the contract) it is submitted that there is then no reason why the principle of the *Embiricos* case should not be applied at this stage. This would bring cases of supervening qualified prohibition into line with those of frustration by delay. The contract in each type of case would not be discharged when the obstacle first arose, since at that stage its effect on performance would be a matter of speculation; but the contract would be frustrated once it had become possible to form a reasonable view of the effect of that obstacle on the performance of the contract

II. Time of Discharge

9–010   In cases of "frustration by delay" it may be clear (or common ground) that the contract has been frustrated, but an issue may arise as to the exact time of frustration. For example, there may be no doubt that a time charterparty has been frustrated by temporary impossibility resulting from prolonged detention of the ship; but it may be vital to establish the date of frustration in order to determine exactly when the charterer ceased to be liable for hire. The question when (no less than the question whether) frustration has occurred then depends on the tests stated in *The Nema*[63]: that is, the contract is not frustrated as soon as the detention begins, but only when it becomes reasonable to take the view that it will last for so long as to amount to a serious interference with performance in the sense in which that expression is used in the context of discharge by temporary impossibility. The point is well illustrated by a number of cases[64] in which ships which had been time-chartered were detained in the course of the Gulf War between Iran and Iraq, which is usually regarded as having begun on September 22, 1980. But for the war and the consequent detention of the ships, the charterparties would have come to an end by

---

[63] [1982] A.C. 724, above, para.9–008.

[64] *Kodros Shipping Corp v Empressa Cubana de Fletes (The Evia) (No 2)* [1983] 1 A.C. 736; *International Sea Tankers Inc v Hemisphere Shipping Co Ltd (The Wenjiang) (No 2)* [1983] 1 Lloyd's Rep. 400; *Vinava Shipping Co Ltd v Finelvet AG (The Chrysalis)* [1983] 1 W.L.R. 1469.

effluxion of time in April[65] and May[66] 1981, and, in one case arising out of a time charter trip, by redelivery of the vessel which would, in the normal course of events, have occurred in about mid-October 1980.[67] When the war began, commercial opinion was that it would soon be brought to an end and that foreign vessels would be speedily released.[68] These forecasts were falsified by later events, and there was no doubt that the very long periods of detention which in fact ensued were sufficient to frustrate the charterparties. But it was held that the contracts could be frustrated before the detention had actually gone on for such a length of time, and that they were frustrated as soon as "a sensible prognosis of the commercial probabilities"[69] could be made to the effect that the delay *would* continue for such time as to prevent the resumption of substantial services under the charterparties.[70]

The same principle determines the time of discharge where performance of a contract of employment is prevented by the supervening illness of the employee, or by his unavailability on other grounds (such as his imprisonment). Thus where an employee had suffered a heart attack, his contract of employment was not discharged at once, since "the effects of the coronary could not initially be assessed"[71]; the contract was frustrated only when it became clear that the employee would not be able to resume the performance of his duties.

---

[65] *The Wenjiang (No 2)*, above, n.64.

[66] *The Evia (No 2)*, above, n.64.

[67] *The Chrysalis*, above, n.64.

[68] *The Wenjiang (No 2)*, above, n.64, at 403; *The Chrysalis*, above, n.64, at 1472.

[69] *The Evia (No 2)* [1982] 1 Lloyd's Rep. 334 at 346, affirmed [1983] 1 A.C. 736; *cf. Adelfamar SA v Silos e Mangimi Martini (The Adelfa)* [1988] 2 Lloyd's Rep. 466 (delay in unloading due arrest of ship in legal proceedings).

[70] In the cases cited in n.64, above, commercial arbitrators had fixed the date of frustration as October 4, 1980 in *The Evia (No 2)* and as November 24 in *The Wenjiang (No 2)* and in the *Chrysalis*. The courts expressed no views of their own as to the dates of frustration, merely holding that the arbitrators had applied the correct principle of law in fixing those dates.

[71] *Notcutt v Universal Equipment Co (London) Ltd* [1986] 1 W.L.R. 641 at 644; *cf. Chakki v United Yeasts Ltd* [1982] I.C.R. 140; and see above paras 5–049, 5–056.

CHAPTER 10

ALTERNATIVES

I. GENERAL RULE

A contract is said to impose an alternative obligation if it gives one of the   **10–001**
parties the right to choose between two or more specified performances
(*e.g.* delivery of X or Y) or between two or more specified ways in which a
single performance is to be rendered (*e.g.* delivery of X today or tomorrow,
delivery of X at one of two or more specified places). The power to choose
between the alternatives may be given to either party: for example, a
contract providing for goods to be delivered during a specified month, or
at one of a range of ports, may give the power to choose the date, or place,
of delivery or shipment to either seller[1] or buyer.[2] If one or more of the
specified alternatives becomes impossible or illegal after the contract is
made, the general rule is that the contract is not discharged so long as at
least one of those alternatives remains possible and lawful.[3]

The cases provide many illustrations of this general rule. Thus where a
contract for the sale of goods provided for shipment from a Mediterranean port, it was not discharged when shipment from the port from which
the seller had intended to ship was prohibited by the authorities there, for
shipment could lawfully be made from other ports within the contractual
range.[4] Conversely, where a contract of sale provided for shipment to a
range of ports, some of which later became enemy ports, it was held that
the seller was bound to ship to a neutral port declared by the buyer, even
though the buyer had previously declared a port which, at the time of
declaration was an enemy port.[5] Similarly where an f.o.b. contract

---

[1] *e.g. Ross T Smyth (Liverpool) v W N Lindsay (Leith)* [1953] 1 W.L.R. 1280 at 1283.
[2] *e.g. David T Boyd & Co Ltd v Louis Louca* [1973] 1 Lloyd's Rep. 209; no issue of
discharge by supervening events arose in this case.
[3] *Barkworth v Young* (1856) 4 Drew. 1 at 25; *Reardon Smith Line Ltd v Ministry of
Agriculture, Fisheries & Food* [1963] A.C. 691 at 730; *Kuwait Supply Co v Oyster
Marine Management (The Safeer)* [1994] 1 Lloyd's Rep. 637 at 642; *Board of
Education v Townsend,* 59 N.E. 223 at 225 (1900); Restatement, § 469; Restatement
2d, § 261, and see the authorities cited in nn.4–19 below.
[4] *Warinco AG v Fritz Mauthner* [1978] 1 Lloyd's Rep. 151.
[5] *Hindley & Co Ltd v General Fibre Co Ltd* [1940] 2 K.B. 517; and see below, para.
10–019.

411

required the seller at the buyer's option either to ship the goods from Hamburg or to warehouse them there, the seller was not discharged by an export embargo since this prohibited only the shipment of the goods and in no way prevented him from warehousing them.[6] The same rule applies in the case of a charterparty giving the charterer the right to select one of a number of ports of discharge: if it becomes illegal for the ship to go to the selected port, but remains lawful for her to go to one or more of the others within the contractual range, fresh orders must be given.[7] Again, if a contract of carriage provides that goods are to be carried in one of two named ships, the contract will not be frustrated by loss of only one of those ships: it must be performed by use of the other.[8] The position is similar where a contract gives a party a choice as to the time of shipment, *e.g.* where a c.i.f. contract provides for shipment during "October and/or November". If shipment is prohibited on some of those days, but remains possible on others which have not yet gone by when the prohibition is imposed, then the seller must ship on one of the latter days.[9] The rule applies, again, where a contract provides for alternative methods of payment, *e.g.* "to pay in gold in New York or in sterling in London. If after the contract it becomes illegal to pay in gold in New York, [the party who was to pay] is not thereby relieved altogether from his obligation, he is merely deprived of his option".[10] Similarly, where an insurer promises to restore damaged premises or to pay the sum insured, he must make the payment if restoration becomes impossible or illegal: this is so even if he has elected to restore before the supervening impossibility or illegality, or in ignorance of it if it already existed.[11]

The position is the same where the creditor claims to be discharged on the ground of frustration of purpose: such a claim will fail if the contract provides for alternative methods of performance, one of which would, while the other would not, frustrate his purpose in entering into the contract. This was the position in one of the coronation cases, in which the contract provided that the viewing facilities were to be made available on the day originally specified for the procession in question or (in the event of its cancellation) on such other day on which that procession passed the premises from which it was to be viewed. Such express provisions were held to exclude the doctrine of discharge by frustration of purpose.[12]

---

[6] *Smith Coney & Barrett v Becker Gray & Co* [1916] 2 Ch. 87. Contrast *Edward Grey & Co v Tolme & Runge* (1915) 31 T.L.R. 551, where both alternatives had become illegal: the first by prohibition of export from the country of origin and the second by the English prohibition against trading with the enemy: see above, para.7–029.

[7] *Seabridge Shipping Ltd v Antco Shipping Ltd (The Furness Bridge)* [1977] 2 Lloyd's Rep. 377; *cf. The Safeer,* above n.3, at 642.

[8] *J Lauritzen A/S v Wijsmuller BV (The Super Servant Two)* [1990] 1 Lloyd's Rep. 1.

[9] *RT Smyth & Co Ltd (Liverpool) v W N Lindsay Ltd (Leith)* [1953] 1 W.L.R. 1280.

[10] *ibid.* at 1283; and see below, para.10–007, n.54.

[11] *Alchorne v Favill* (1825) 4 L.J.Ch. (O.S.) 47; *cf. Anderson v Commercial Union Insurance Co* (1865) 55 L.J.Q.B. 146 at 150.

[12] *Victoria Seats Agency v Paget* (1902) 19 T.L.R. 16 (first contract).

In the cases so far described, the contract expressly provided for alternative methods of performance, but the general rule equally applies where the alternative is provided by law, or inferred by law from the nature of the contract or other surrounding circumstances. Thus under a c.i.f. contract the seller can perform either by shipping goods or by appropriating to the contract goods which have already been shipped, whether by himself or by another shipper.[13] The general rule is that the seller is not discharged merely because a supervening event has made shipment impossible or illegal: if goods which had been shipped before the supervening event are available, he must (in general) buy those goods afloat and tender them to his buyer under the original contract.[14]

The general rule further applies where the party claims to be excused, not under the general doctrine of discharge, but under an express term of the contract. Thus a c.i.f. seller who is prevented by supervening events from shipping goods of the contract description will not be able to rely on an express *force majeure* clause, protecting him in the event of failure to deliver by reason of causes beyond his control, unless he can show that such causes also prevented him from buying afloat.[15] A similar rule was applied where a charterer who had undertaken to load "a cargo of wheat and/or maize and/or rye" sought to excuse his delay in loading by reference to a term providing that time during which the cargo could not be loaded by reason of certain obstructions beyond his control was not to count for the purpose of calculating demurrage. The obstruction which arose affected only wheat, which was the cargo which the charterer had decided to load (but did not affect maize or rye) and it was held that the charterer was not relieved by the clause from his obligation to load one of the other commodities[16]; and even the view that the charterer should be allowed such reasonable time as was required to enable him to decide what alternative course of action to pursue,[17] when it became clear that the supply of wheat would be delayed, has been doubted.[18] In cases of this kind, the contractual provision for alternative methods may, again, be inferred from the surrounding circumstances. Thus a contract to load a cargo at a particular port, and containing an exception for delay in loading due to ice, may not specify the method of loading. This will then be determined by reference to the method usual at that port; and if there is more than one such method the charterer will be able to rely on the exception only if *all* those methods have become physically impossible or

---

[13] *Benjamin's Sale of Goods* (6th ed.), paras 19–011, 19–136.

[14] *e.g. Ashmore & Son v C S Cox & Co* [1899] 1 Q.B. 436, as explained in *Benjamin's Sale of Goods* (6th ed.), para.19–126; for an exception to the general rule, see *Tradax Export SA v André & Cie* [1976] 1 Lloyd's Rep. 416 discussed in *Benjamin's Sale of Goods* (6th ed.), para.19–136 and above, para.4–045.

[15] *P J van der Zijden Wildhandel NV v Tucker & Cross Ltd* [1975] 2 Lloyd's Rep. 240.

[16] *Brightman & Co v Bunge y Born Limitada Sociedad* [1924] 2 K.B. 619, affirmed on another ground [1925] A.C. 799; and see below, paras 10–006 to 10–007.

[17] [1924] 2 K.B. 619 at 628, 631, 637.

[18] *Reardon Smith Line Ltd v Ministry of Agriculture, Fisheries & Food* [1963] A.C. 691 at 717, 733.

at least "commercially impracticable" as a result of the freezing of the port.[19]

II. EXCEPTIONS

10–003   It has been said that: "If one of two things which have been contracted for, subsequently becomes impossible, it becomes a question of construction whether ... the obligor is bound to perform the alternative or is discharged altogether."[20] Such a question of construction can arise in two ways. First, even where the contract imposes an alternative obligation, it may on its true construction exclude the general rule stated above. Secondly, it may be a question of construction whether the obligation imposed by a contract is indeed a true alternative one. The presence (or absence) of the disjunctive conjunction "or" is not decisive: it will be necessary, in the following discussion, to distinguish alternative obligations from a number of analogous concepts.

(1) **Contrary provision**

10–004   A contract imposing an alternative obligation may contain an express provision which, on its true construction, excludes the general rule applicable in cases of supervening impossibility affecting some (but not all) of the specified alternatives. This was, *e.g.* held to be the position where a c.i.f. contract contained a clause excusing the seller in the event of strikes preventing shipment.[21] The clause was construed so as to apply where the port of shipment which the seller intended to use became strike-bound, even though the seller had not shown that other ports from which he might have shipped were similarly affected.

(2) **Liberty to substitute**

10–005   Where a contract imposes a true alternative obligation, one cannot tell at the time of contracting which alternative the debtor is bound to perform. Such a contract must be distinguished from one which requires a party to render a specified performance but gives him a liberty to substitute a different performance. In a contract of the latter kind, the specified performance alone is originally due and remains due until the substitution

---

[19] *Owners of Steamship Matheos v Louis Dreyfus & Co* [1925] A.C. 654 at 660.

[20] *Anderson v Commercial Union Insurance Co* (1885) 55 L.J.Q.B. 146 at 150, a dictum cited with approval in *AV Pound & Co Ltd v MW Hardy & Co Inc* [1956] A.C. 588 at 612.

[21] *Sociedad Iberica de Molturacion SA v Tradax Export SA* [1978] 2 Lloyd's Rep. 545; *cf. Koninglijke Bunge v Cie Continentale d'Importation* [1973] 2 Lloyd's Rep. 44 at 50, where, however, the seller failed to prove the facts required by the exception; below, para.12–029.

is made[22]; when the substitution is made, the substituted performance becomes due (and that originally specified ceases to be due). Three things should follow. First, if the originally specified performance becomes impossible or illegal before the substitution is made, the contract should be discharged, so that the party having the liberty to substitute is not bound to render the substitute performance[23] (nor is the other party bound to accept and pay for it). Secondly, if the substitute performance becomes impossible or illegal after the substitution has been made, the contract is likewise discharged, with corresponding effects, *i.e.* the originally specified performance need no longer be rendered or accepted. Thirdly, the supervening impossibility or illegality of the substitute performance before the substitution is made has no effect on the obligations to render (and to accept and pay for) the originally specified performance: it makes no difference that the party entitled to make the substitution had intended to make it, if he had not actually made it in accordance with any relevant provisions of the contract (*e.g.* as to giving notice of the substitution). Only in this respect can the present group of cases be said to resemble those of true alternative obligations.

The situation here under discussion is illustrated by cases in which a charterparty relating to a named ship (X) gives the shipowner a "liberty to substitute"[24] or an "option to substitute"[25] another similar vessel. In one such case it was said at first instance that the object of such a provision was to ensure "that a mere accident to one particular ship is not necessarily going to bring the charterparty to an end".[26] This suggests that, in the event of such an accident, the owner is entitled (and possibly that he is bound) to make a substitution. But the only point actually decided[27] was that, after the owner had substituted vessel Y for X, and Y had had to undergo repairs during the currency of the charter, the owner was, on the true construction of the contract, entitled to make a second substitution (reverting to vessel X). There was no destruction of vessel Y, nor even any finding of frustrating delay caused by the need to repair her. The suggestion quoted above[28] was said in *The Badagry*[29] not to apply where there had been "an actual or constructive total loss of the originally

---

[22] *Coastal (Bermuda) Petroleum Ltd v VTT Vulcan Petroleum SA (The Marine Star) (No 1)* [1993] 1 Lloyd's Rep. 329; for further proceedings, see *Coastal (Bermuda) Petroleum Ltd v VTT Vulcan Petroleum SA (No 2) (The Marine Star)* [1996] 2 Lloyd's Rep. 383, below, para.12–026.

[23] See *Eridania SpA v Rudolf A Oetker* [1999] 1 Lloyd's Rep. 307 at 333–334, (carrier having liberty, but no duty, to tranship cargo; frustration was excluded as the supervening event was due to the carrier's breach); affirmed [2000] 2 Lloyd's Rep. 191 without reference to this point.

[24] *SA Maritime et Commerciale of Geneva v Anglo-Iranian Oil Co* [1953] 1 W.L.R. 1379 at 1382, affirmed without reference to this point [1954] 1 W.L.R. 497.

[25] *Terkol Rederierne v Petroleo Brasileiro SA (The Badagry)* [1985] 1 Lloyd's Rep. 395 at 396.

[26] *SA Maritime* case, above n.24, [1953] 1 W.L.R. 1379 at 1382.

[27] See [1954] 1 W.L.R. 497.

[28] At n.26.

[29] Above, n.25, at 402; *cf. ibid.* at 401.

named vessel". That case concerned a demise charter of a named ship which gave the owners an "option to substitute" a similar vessel. The named ship having become a constructive total loss, it was held that the contract was thereby discharged, so that the owners were not entitled to make the substitution. It would, of course, have been possible to exclude the doctrine of frustration by providing that the substitution could be made even in the event of the loss of the originally named ship; but that was held not to be the meaning of the substitution clause in this case.

A further distinction has been drawn between, on the one hand, a "liberty" or an "option" of the kind described above and, on the other, a contractual term which imposes an obligation on one of the parties. In the *Universal Bulk* case,[30] a voyage charter provided for a "laycan"[31] covering the first half of December "to be narrowed to 10 days spread 32 days prior of the first layday". The charterers having failed to give notice narrowing the laycan period within the required 32 days, the owners argued that this failure constituted a breach by the charterers which justified their (the owners') refusal to nominate a ship, while the charterers argued that the clause quoted above imposed no duty on them, but merely gave them an option as to the duration of the laycan spread. The Court of Appeal held (1) that the clause quoted above did "not confer an option on the charterers but impose[d] a duty"[32] so that the charterers failure to narrow the 15½ day period (comprising the first half of December) to a 10 day one was a breach; but (2) that the breach was not such as to justify the shipowners' rescission of the contract, so that they were liable in damages.[33] Our concern here is with the first part of this reasoning, which is based on the fact that the words "to be narrowed" "naturally import an obligation of some kind"[34] and were to be contrasted with another clause of the charterparty which gave the charterers an "option to 'wash out' the nominated voyage" by notice. The distinction drawn in the judgment between an "option" and an "obligation"[35] is not, however, free from difficulty; this arises in part from the fact that the word "option" has in law several meanings.[36] No doubt the grant of an "option" to purchase does not impose any obligation on the grantee either to exercise the option or to notify the grantor of his intention not to do so. But in many cases of alternative obligations, the word "option" is used to refer, not to a situation in which a party is given the choice whether to acquire a right or to incur an obligation, but to that in which his choice is between a number of specified rights or obligations, the existence of one of which is

---

[30] *Universal Bulk Carriers Ltd v Andre & Cie* [2001] EWCA Civ 588; [2001] 2 Lloyd's Rep. 65.
[31] This expression refers to "the *lay*days/*can*celling date spread": see the report at first instance [2000] 1 Lloyd's Rep. 459 at 460 (italics supplied).
[32] Above, n.30, at [17].
[33] The damages were awarded in respect of the extra cost of chartering a substitute ship on a rising market.
[34] Above, n.30, at [17].
[35] Above, n.30, after [11]; paragraph number [12] is missing from the report.
[36] See Treitel, *The Law of Contract* (11th ed.), p.153, n.74.

not in doubt but the content of which can be defined only once he has exercised his choice. This is, for example, the position where a contract for the sale of goods provides for delivery at one of a range of specified ports. Such a term no doubt gives an "option" in the sense of a choice as the place of delivery; but it may be impossible to perform the contract unless the choice is made by one party and communicated to the other.[37] Commonly, the contract will provide which party is to make the choice; and if the contract contains no such express provision, a term is likely to be implied specifying whether the choice is to be made by the buyer[38] or by the seller.[39] In such cases, the term will both confer an "option" *and* impose an "obligation"; this is *a fortiori* true where the contract expressly requires the beneficiary of the option to communicate his choice to the other party.[40] There is, in all situations of this last kind no necessary antithesis between these concepts. The position is similar where the contract is one to deliver X or Y: such a contract simply will not work unless an obligation to make the choice is imposed on the party on whom the "option" (or right of choice) is conferred. The cases of alternative obligation in which the distinction between an "option" and an "obligation" is clear-cut are those in which the contract confers a choice on one of the parties but can operate perfectly well even if that party takes no steps to exercise that choice. This is the position in the situation discussed above[41] in which a charterparty term gives the shipowner a "liberty to substitute" one vessel for another: such a term does not oblige him to exercise the liberty and, if he takes no steps to that end, his obligations under the charterparty must simply be performed by use of the originally nominated vessel. In such a case, therefore, the term can be said to confer an option but not to impose an obligation. In one respect, the *Universal Bulk* case falls into this category: failure to "narrow" the laycan would not have prevented the contract from operating, with a laycan covering the first half of December, if the shipowner had not wrongfully repudiated it; indeed, the award of damages for their repudiation must have been based on that assumption. The decision is best explained as turning simply on the wording of what Longmore J. at first instance described as "a completely one-off clause".[42]

---

[37] *e.g.* where an f.o.b. contract provides for delivery at one of a range of ports, without specifying the port at which delivery is to be made: see below, n.38.

[38] *e.g. David T. Boyd & Co Ltd v Louis Louca* [1973] 1 Lloyd's Rep. 209 (f.o.b. contract).

[39] *e.g. Bulk Trading Corp Ltd v Zenziper Grains & Foodstuffs* [2001] 1 Lloyd's Rep. 357 (f.o.t. contract).

[40] Our concern here is with contractual terms imposing an *obligation* on one party to give notice to the other of his choice between alternatives. This must be contrasted with cases in which the notice is merely a condition precedent to the exercise of an option to alter the original obligation of the beneficiary: see paras 10–009 to 10–010, especially at nn.66 and 69. In those cases, there is no obligation to give the notice: failure to give it merely has the effect that the option is not exercised.

[41] Above, after n.25.

[42] [2000] 1 Lloyd's Rep. 459 at 463.

(3) "Contract options" and "performance options"

10–006   These phrases do not introduce new concepts; they are used (at least generally) to draw the distinctions already explained between true alternative obligations and liberties to substitute. They require further explanation partly because they carry forward the discussion of how those distinctions are to be drawn, and partly because they have, unfortunately, been used in more sense than one.

     The distinction between the two kinds of "options" is derived from the speech of Lord Devlin in *Reardon Smith Line Ltd v Ministry of Agriculture, Fisheries & Food*.[43] In that case a charterparty was held on its true construction to require the charterer to load a full and complete cargo of wheat in bulk, with the "option" of loading up to one-third barley in bulk or up to one-third flour in bulk, at somewhat higher rates of freight than that specified for wheat. The charterparty contained an exception covering delays caused by strikes, and a strike at the port of loading delayed the loading of wheat, but it was assumed that the strike did not affect the loading of barley or flour. It was held that the charterer was entitled torely on the exception, so that he was not liable for delay caused by the strike in the loading of wheat. By contrast, in *Brightman & Co v Bunge y Born Limitada Sociedad*[44] a charterparty required the charterer to load "a cargo of wheat and/or maize and/or rye", with an exception covering "obstruction beyond the control of the charterers on the railways". The charterers were delayed in loading their intended cargo of wheat by industrial action which affected the railway they had intended to use, and in the end they decided instead to load maize. It was held that they were not protected by the exception (save to the minor extent of being allowed a reasonable time to consider their position and to make arrangements for loading the alternative cargo[45]). No attempt was made in either case to argue the contracts were discharged, presumably because the delays were not sufficiently serious for this purpose[46] and because in each case the cargo was actually loaded: the issue simply was as to the charterers' liability to pay demurrage. But it follows from the reasoning of the two cases that, if the delay in loading wheat had been a "frustrating" one and if no similar delay had affected the other specified commodities, then the contract would have been frustrated in the *Reardon Smith* case, but not in the *Brightman* case. It is these assumptions and the reasons for them (rather than the actual decisions) which are significant for the purpose of the present discussion.

10–007   Two tests for distinguishing between the two situations emerge from the speeches in the *Reardon Smith* case. The first concentrates on the way in which the choice open to the charterer is to be made. In the *Reardon Smith* case, the obligation was one to load wheat unless the charterer exercised

---

[43] [1963] A.C. 691.
[44] [1924] 2 K.B. 619, affirmed on another ground [1925] A.C. 799.
[45] For later doubts on this point, see above, para.10–002, n.18.
[46] *cf.* above, paras 5–036 *et seq.*

his option to substitute barley or flour, and did so in the usual way in which options are exercised, *i.e.* by notice to the other party.[47] In the *Brightman* case, by contrast, the charterer was entitled simply to load any one of the specified commodities without having to give prior notice to the carrier. It was even said that he retained his freedom of action "till the last ton was put on board."[48] Such an extreme view may be open to doubt.[49] But this does not affect the distinction between the two cases: in the *Reardon Smith* case "wheat [was] to be the basic cargo, to be displaced only if and as, the charterers decide"[50]; while in the *Brightman* case, there was no "basic cargo", so that it was not possible to tell when the contract was made which of the specified commodities the charterer was obliged to load.

The second test for distinguishing between the two situations concentrates on the purpose for which the choice is given: in Lord Devlin's words, "the question is whether or not the freedom of choice is intended solely for the benefit of the charterer"[51] or for the benefit of both parties. In the *Reardon Smith* case, Lord Devlin regarded the choice as being for the benefit of the charterer alone, as it was not the intention of the parties to oblige him to ship barley or flour, should wheat be unavailable. In the *Brightman* case the alternative was for the benefit of both parties: it was their intention to confer a right of choice on the charterer, but not to relieve him from his obligation to load merely because the commodity chosen by him was unavailable. This test may give rise to some difficulty in that what the parties intend is defined by reference to the legal consequences of that common intention; but the test of the parties' intention is not infrequently applied to contractual situations in which it gives rise to similar difficulties.[52] A factor which is relevant to the intention of the parties in the present context is whether it matters to the other party which of the alternatives is performed by the party having the right of choice.[53] If it does, the case is likely to fall on the *Reardon Smith* side of the line; if it does not, on the *Brightman* side. This is also true of the type of case, already discussed, where a c.i.f. contract provides for goods to be shipped by the seller "in October and/or November". In one such case it was said that the seller had "61 options".[54] The case would fall on the *Brightman* side of the line in that the

---

[47] See [1963] A.C. 691 at 719, 730, 731.

[48] [1924] 2 K.B. 619 at 637.

[49] Below, para.10–018.

[50] [1963] A.C. 691 at 719.

[51] *ibid.* at 730.

[52] *e.g.* in distinguishing between "mere" representations and representations which are intended to have contractual force: see Treitel, *The Law of Contract* (11th ed.), pp.353, 356.

[53] *SA Maritime et Commerciale of Geneva v Anglo-Iranian Oil Co* [1953] 1 W.L.R. 1379 at 1381, and see above, para.10–005, n.24.

[54] *R T Smyth & Co Ltd (Liverpool) v W.N. Lindsay Ltd (Leith)* [1953] 1 W.L.R. 1280 at 1283, *per* Devlin J., though in *Reardon Smith Line Ltd v Ministry of Agriculture, Fisheries and Food* [1963] 1 All E.R. 545 at 559 Lord Devlin doubted whether this description would be apt "in ordinary language".

seller would not be required to give advance notice to the buyer specifying on which of the 61 days he intended to ship the goods, and in that it would presumably not matter to a buyer who had contracted on such terms on exactly which day within the shipment period the shipment was to be made. It follows that the option as to the date of shipment is for the benefit of both parties in the sense already discussed. That is, it is for the benefit of the seller in that he can ship on any of the 61 days if no obstacle supervenes; but it is for the benefit of the buyer in that, if the seller intended to ship in October but is prevented by supervening events from doing so, and shipment in November remains possible and lawful, then the buyer is entitled to insist on shipment in November.

10–008 It thus appears from the preceding discussion that the "option" in the *Reardon Smith* case was in its legal nature similar to that in *The Badagry*.[55] The actual issues discussed in the two cases differed in the sense that in the *Reardon Smith* case the question was whether the party having the right to choose was *bound* to render the substitute performance, while in *The Badagry* the question was whether he was *entitled* to do so (and consequently whether the other party was bound to accept it). It would, however, seem that the same principle should determine the answer to both questions, for in cases of this kind the contract (unless varied at the election of the party having the "liberty" or "option") is to render the originally specified performance; and once that performance has become impossible the contract is automatically discharged,[56] so that the option or liberty is no longer capable of being exercised for the benefit of either party.[57] Thus in *The Badagry* the shipowner was no more bound than he was entitled to make the substitution, once the originally named ship had been lost.[58] Conversely in the *Reardon Smith* case the charterer would no more have been entitled than he was bound to load one of the alternative cargoes if, before exercise of his "option", an event had occurred which imposed a frustrating delay on the loading of wheat. These propositions may, indeed, require some modification where the supervening impossibility or illegality relates only to the *method* of performance. This point is further discussed below[59]; it arises not because of the nature of the option but because impossibility even in a stipulated method of performance is not necessarily a ground of discharge.[60]

Lord Devlin's speech in the *Reardon Smith* case does not actually make use of the expression "contract option" and "performance option", but it does make use of the two concepts to which these labels have been attached in

---

[55] [1985] 1 Lloyd's Rep. 395, above, para.10–005.

[56] Below, para.15–002.

[57] *cf. Blane Steamships v Minister of Transport* [1951] 2 K.B. 965 (where an option to purchase a chartered ship was held not to have survived her constructive total loss).

[58] For an apparently contrary suggestion in *SA Maritime et Commerciale of Geneva v Anglo-Iranian Oil Co* [1953] 1 W.L.R. 1379 at 1382, see above, para.10–005, nn.25 to 26.

[59] Below, paras 10–009, 10–010.

[60] See above, para.4–075.

the preceding discussion, calling the former "business options" and the latter simply (though with some unease) "options."[61] The terminological distinction between "contract" (or "contractual") and "performance" options is derived from the more recent case of the *The Didymi*[62]; but there the distinction is used in two quite different senses.

The first is that given to it by Staughton J. when he described a "contract option" as one "which alters the nature of the obligation laid down in the contract", and a "performance option" as one which arises "where only one obligation is provided by the contract and it remains unchanged; but there are different ways of performing it".[63] This distinction appears to be between what is owed and how (or by what method) it is to be performed. Thus an example of a "contract option" is said to be "a contract to load a cargo of wheat with an option to change to barley" while an example of a "performance option" would be "a contract to load a cargo in September or October, which in one sense provides a choice of 61 days".[64] If an option of the former kind is exercised, "the contract ceases to be one to load wheat and becomes one to load barley", so that if it becomes impossible to load barley the contract is discharged.[65] On the other hand, in the case of a "performance option" impossibility affecting one method of performance does not discharge the contract, which must be performed in the way (or in one of the ways) remaining possible.

The second explanation of the distinction between "contractual options" and "performance options" is that given by Sir John Donaldson M.R. in the *The Didymi*; but it will be seen that the difference between his view and that of Staughton J. is less significant than might at first sight appear. According to Sir John Donaldson, the distinction between the two types of option depends on the steps required to be taken to exercise the choice: "A 'contractual option' enables the beneficiary to define precisely what the contract requires of him. An example would be 'vessel to be redelivered at a European port to be nominated by the charterer'."[66] By contrast, a "performance option" is one which: "itself defines the alternative ways in which the contract can be performed and calls for no action upon the part of the beneficiary, save to perform the contract in a permissible way. An example would be 'vessel to be re-delivered at a European port'."[67]

Sir John Donaldson's explanation of the distinction appears to correspond (more closely than Staughton J.'s) with that drawn by Lord Devlin. It also differs from Staughton J.'s explanation in that each of the examples given by Sir John Donaldson concerns an option as to the

---

[61] [1963] A.C. 691 at 729.
[62] *Atlantic Lines & Navigation Co Ltd v Didymi Corp (The Didymi and the Leon)* [1984] 1 Lloyd's Rep. 583.
[63] *ibid.* at 585.
[64] *ibid.*
[65] *ibid.*
[66] *ibid.* at 587.
[67] *ibid.*

method of performance, rather than one as to what is owed: what the charterer has to do in each case is to redeliver the ship, and his option merely determines where he has to perform this act. Nor are the consequences of the exercise of a "contract" or "contractual" option the same under the two explanations. In Staughton J.'s example, if the charterer exercised his "contract option" to load barley, and if the loading of barley then became illegal, the contract would be discharged so that there would be no obligation to load wheat. Yet in Sir John Donaldson's example if the charterer exercised a "contractual option" by nominating a particular port, and if redelivery there subsequently became illegal, it can scarcely be supposed that there would be no obligation to redeliver the ship; the more probable solution would be that the charterer would have to make a fresh nomination of another port at which the ship could lawfully be redelivered.[68] In this respect, the effect of the exercise of a "contractual" option which related only to the method of performance may be the same as the effect of the exercise of a "performance" option.

10-010   What the judgments of Staughton J. and Sir John Donaldson M.R. have in common in their description of a "contract(ual)" option is that the exercise of such an option can alter the original obligation of the beneficiary (of the option), but that it does so only when he notifies the other party of its exercise. By contrast, no such notice need be given of the exercise of a "performance" option nor does such exercise alter the beneficiary's obligation (which remains to perform in any of the specified ways remaining possible). As Sir John Donaldson says, an option "without any requirement as to how or when the option is to be exercised has all the characteristics of a performance option".[69] Such an option may determine what is owed (no less than how it is to be performed) as in the *Brightman*[70] case (where the "option" to load wheat or maize or rye did not require the charterer to give advance notice of his choice and where, on the unavailability of wheat, he was bound to load maize or rye). Conversely, it is submitted that the selection between one of two or more methods of performance could, in principle, be a contract option if this was clearly the intention of the parties. This might be the case if a contract were made to carry goods in one of two specified ships, the choice to be made by the carrier and notified to the buyer by a specified date. If one of the ships were duly selected in accordance with these provisions, it seems that the contract would be turned into one to carry the goods in that ship, and accordingly it could be frustrated by the loss of that ship before commencement of performance.[71] But although options which relate to the method of performance can in principle be contract options, they are in practice less likely to be construed in this way than are options which

---

[68] *cf. Hindley & Co Ltd v General Fibre Co Ltd* [1940] 2 K.B. 517 (option as to port of destination to be declared by a c.i.f. buyer).

[69] [1984] 1 Lloyd's Rep. 583 at 587.

[70] [1924] 2 K.B. 619; [1925] A.C. 799, discussed above, para.10–006.

[71] The example given in the text differs from *J Lauritzen A/S v Wijsmuller BV (The Super Servant Two)* [1990] 1 Lloyd's Rep. 1 in that there no selection had been communicated before loss of one of the ships.

relate to the substance of what is to be performed. The reason for this is that the parties can generally be supposed to attach more importance to the definition of what is owed than to provisions which state how it is to be performed; and effect would be given to their intention in this respect by making discharge more likely where impossibility affects the former than where it affects the latter aspect of performance. This would be the effect of a greater readiness to classify options as to what is owed as contract options (where impossibility of performing the selected alternative is a ground of discharge) while classifying most options as to the manner of performance as performance options (where impossibility of performing the selected alternative is not a ground of discharge).

The foregoing discussion is based on the assumption that the party entitled to choose between the two alternatives is (either by the express terms of the contract, or by operation of law[72]) the debtor, *i.e.* the person who is to perform one of the alternatives. That right may also be given to the creditor, *e.g.* where A agrees to sell to B "my Rolls or my Bentley, at buyer's option". Such an option resembles a performance option in that neither alternative can be described as the primary obligation. But in two more significant ways it resembles a contract option: namely in that the option must be exercised by notice to the seller (since until this is done he cannot perform); and in that, once the option has been exercised, the contract becomes one to perform the selected alternative and that alternative only. Hence if B selects the Rolls and that car is stolen or destroyed without fault of either party before the risk has passed to the buyer, then the contract will be discharged, so that B can neither demand nor be compelled to accept the Bentley. It would clearly be unjust to require A to deliver the Bentley if he had acted in reliance on B's choice of the Rolls, *e.g.* by spending money on preparing that car for delivery or by disposing elsewhere of the Bentley; and while the argument for relieving B from any obligation to accept the Bentley is less strong, he too may have acted in reliance on his selection (*e.g.* by contracting to resell the Rolls); and his release also follows from the principle that frustration automatically discharges both parties.[73] None of these arguments applies where one of the cars is destroyed *before* the selection is made, so that in such a case B would be entitled to select the other, and A bound to deliver it. It is less clear whether or not B would be *bound* to select the surviving car: this would depend on whether the contract on its true construction merely gave B the right, or imposed on him a duty, to make the selection. The latter concept is by no means implausible: thus an f.o.b. buyer may have a duty to select a port of shipment where the contract merely specifies a range of ports.[74] In our example, it might similarly be held that B had a duty to make the selection. If so, destruction of one of the cars

10–011

---

[72] For rules of law determining which party has the option, see (for example) *Reed v Kilburn Co-operative Society* (1875) L.R. 10 Q.B. 264; *Benjamin's Sale of Goods* (6th ed.), para.20–030 (time of shipment in f.o.b. contracts).

[73] Below, para.15–002.

[74] *David T Boyd & Co Ltd v Louis Louca* [1973] 1 Lloyd's Rep. 209.

would not discharge the contract but merely narrow B's range of choice to one.

(4) Alternative methods of discharge

10–012   A contract may impose an obligation on a debtor to perform one thing (X) but give him the liberty to discharge that obligation by doing another thing (Y). Civil lawyers sometimes describe this liberty as a *facultas alternativa*[75]; it differs from an alternative obligation in that it at no stage gives rise to an obligation to do Y. Even if the debtor declares that he will do Y, he does not become bound to do it, but if he in fact does Y his obligation to perform X is discharged. It follows that if X becomes impossible or illegal, the debtor is not bound to do Y, while if Y becomes impossible the debtor must do X and loses his liberty to perform in the alternative way.

Civil lawyers illustrate this type of provision by reference to the purchase of a car for which the customer agrees to give his own car in part exchange.[76] In such a case, the customer will not normally undertake an obligation to deliver his own car: he is merely given a liberty to satisfy part of the price for the car which he is acquiring by delivery of his own car. If his own car is destroyed between the making of the contract and its performance, he must *prima facie* pay the full price in money; such a rule will not cause him any prejudice where (as will often be the case) he is put into a position to make the extra payment by his receipt of the proceeds of insurance on the destroyed car. It is of course possible for the contract expressly or by implication to provide that payment is to be made *only* on the part-exchange basis: the case would then not be one of *facultas alternativa* but one of failure in an agreed method of performance. Whether the destruction of the buyer's own car would discharge such a contract would depend on the factors discussed in Ch.5[77]; an important factor would be the proportion which the part-exchange value of the buyer's own car bore to the value of the transaction as a whole.

The converse situation to that discussed above is that in which supervening events affect the principal obligation but not the alternative method of discharge, *e.g.* if the above example of the contract for the sale of a car were varied by supposing that the money element of the price were payable on credit terms or in a foreign currency, and that legislation passed after the sale had made such payment illegal. In such a case the contract would be discharged: the buyer would not be bound to deliver his own car, even if it accounted for as much as 90 per cent of the agreed "cash" price. This follows from the concept of *facultas alternativa* as imposing *no* obligation to perform the "alternative."

---

[75] *e.g. Münchener Kommentar zum Bürgerlichen Gesetzbuch* (4th ed.), § 262, Comment III.3.

[76] *ibid.* Comment III.[8]; see the German decisions in BGHZ 46, 338, 340, BGH, January 18, 1967.

[77] Above, para.5–002.

In the examples so far discussed, the alternative method of discharge   10–013
relates to part only of the debt, but it can equally relate to the whole. This
makes no difference to the position stated above, *e.g.* where a contract
obliges a buyer to pay in cash but provides that the cash price may be
satisfied by payment wholly in kind. Supervening impossibility of making
the payment in kind does not discharge the debtor's liability to pay cash,
any more than in the case of a true alternative obligation; but the case
differs from one of alternative obligation in that, if payment in cash
became illegal, the debtor would not be bound to pay in kind. This would
be so even if he had declared his intention to pay in this way: again this
follows from the nature of the *facultas alternativa* as imposing no obligation
to perform the alternative.

So far it has been assumed that the choice between the two methods of
discharge lies entirely with the debtor. It may equally lie with the creditor,
e.g. he may be entitled to demand payment in cash or, if the creditor so
elects, by delivery of some specific thing (*e.g.* a picture). Such a case differs
from a *facultas alternativa* in that the exercise of the creditor's choice does
alter the nature of the obligation. It follows that if the creditor had elected
to seek delivery of the picture and if the picture were then destroyed the
debtor would no longer be bound to pay cash, while if, before any such
election, payment in cash became illegal the contract would be discharged
so that that creditor would lose his right to demand the picture.[78]

(5) **Alternative and contingent obligations**

An alternative obligation is often expressed by saying that "X or Y" must   10–014
be performed; but (as already noted) the use of the conjunction "or"
between two performances specified in a contract does not necessarily
mean that the obligation imposed by the contract is an alternative one. A
distinction between alternative and contingent obligations was apparently
drawn in *Deverill v Burnell*[79] where the plaintiff had shipped goods to
Rosario where they were to be delivered to one Bollaert on his accepting
certain drafts. Bills of lading covering the goods were entrusted, together
with the drafts, to the defendant for presentation to Bollaert, who
accepted the drafts but did not pay on them. The defendant promised the
plaintiff that, if the drafts were paid, he would transmit the proceeds to the
plaintiff "and if the drafts should not be paid the defendant should either
return the same to the plaintiff or pay him the amount". The defendant,
having neither returned the drafts nor paid the amount, argued that he
was liable for no more than nominal damages: his contentions were that
the obligation was alternative, that he could have performed it by
returning the drafts (which were worthless), and that damages for breach
of an alternative obligation were to be assessed by reference to the
alternative least beneficial to the claimant.[80] But the court by a majority

---

[78] The case would then be comparable to *The Badagry* [1985] 1 Lloyd's Rep. 395,
above, para.10–005.

[79] (1873) L.R. 8 C.P. 475.

[80] For this rule, see Treitel, *The Law of Contract* (11th ed.), pp.958–959.

rejected this argument and held the defendant liable for the full amount of the drafts. In the words of Grove J. (one of the majority), the defendant's undertaking "was not in the strictest sense an alternative promise, but a promise that the defendant would return the bills, and if he did not return them he would pay the amount of them".[81] Grove J. went on to give an example which he evidently regarded as *in pari materia*: "If I say to a man, I will return your horse tomorrow or pay you a day's hire of him, the only reasonable construction is that, if I do not return the horse, I will pay a day's hire."[82] The other judgments likewise treat the question whether the contract imposed an alternative obligation as one of construction. Bovill C.J. (who dissented) gave an example similar to that just quoted: a contract by which a man promised "to deliver up his horse Ajax or pay £1000"[83] would, in his view, impose an alternative obligation. He, too, treated the question whether this was the nature of the obligation as one of construction. The question, therefore, is what the parties intended to be the effect of the contract. On the majority view in *Deverill v Burnell*, the defendant had not said "I will choose between performing X or Y" but "I will perform X, but if I fail to do so I will perform Y". The duty to perform Y can be regarded as a contingent rather than as an alternative obligation. This would certainly distinguish the case from "contract options"[84] and from liberties to substitute[85] of the kind discussed above, in which X, and X alone, is due unless and until the debtor communicates his election instead to perform Y (which then alone becomes due). But the type of obligation discussed in *Deverill v Burnell* can also be said to resemble a "performance option" in one of the senses discussed above[86] in that, if the debtor does not perform X, then he must (without the need for any prior election on his part) perform Y. The two types of obligation appear, nevertheless, to be distinct. In the case of an alternative obligation of the "performance option" type, it cannot at the time of contracting be said that either X or Y is the content of the principal obligation. In the case of the type of obligation under consideration in *Deverill v Burnell*, it seems that X is the primary obligation, Y only becoming due in the event of the non-performance of X. Thus in the example given by Grove J. the primary obligation is "I will return your horse tomorrow" and the obligation to pay a day's hire is secondary and conditional on non-performance of the primary obligation. The question then arises what legal consequences would follow from the supervening impossibility or illegality of either obligation. If the supervening event affected only the secondary obligation (*e.g.* if making the payment became illegal), then the primary obligation would remain due. If on the other hand the supervening event affected the primary obligation (*e.g.* if without fault of either party the horse died or was stolen), then it is arguable that the

---

[81] (1873) L.R. 8 C.P. 475.
[82] *ibid.*
[83] *ibid.* at 480.
[84] Above, paras 10–006 to 10–010.
[85] Above, para.10–005.
[86] Above, para.10–009, at n.67.

contract would be frustrated so that the secondary obligation could not become due. This in turn is a question of construction: the contract may mean merely that if the debtor *in breach of contract* fails to do X he must do Y, or that if *for any reason* he fails to do X, then he must do Y. If it means the latter, then there is for the purpose of the doctrine of frustration no practical difference between contingent obligations of the kind discussed in *Deverill v Burnell* and alternative obligations of the "performance option" type. It is however submitted that the former is the more obvious meaning of the contract in Grove J.'s example, and that it was this meaning which he had in mind in distinguishing the case from an alternative obligation. This type of contract is also distinct from one containing a *facultas alternativa*[87] in that under a contract of the present kind Y becomes due on non-performance of X (and *only* on failure to perform X); and in that failure to perform X can give rise to an *obligation* to perform Y, while under a contract containing a *facultas alternativa* the debtor is never obliged to do Y.

A similar analysis applies where a charterparty provides that a ship is to   **10–015**
proceed to a named port (or dock) "or so near thereto as she may safely get". In such a contract the named port or dock has been described as "the primary place of discharge",[88] while the phrase "or so near thereto as she may safely get" has been referred to as an "alternative destination".[89] But a contract of this kind does not impose an alternative obligation in the true sense of that expression, since it is not open to either party to select the "alternative destination". That "alternative" in fact expresses not an alternative but a contingent obligation: the contract means that if (and only if) the ship cannot reach the "primary place of discharge", then she must (and need only) proceed to the "alternative destination". Neither party has any choice in the matter: so long as the ship can get to the primary place of discharge, the shipowner is not entitled to perform, nor is the charterer entitled to demand performance, at the "alternative destination". The "alternative" is not in fact an alternative but a substitute which becomes available only in previously defined circumstances. Indeed, it follows, from the meaning of the words "so near thereto as she may safely get", that there can be no place which answers this description if safe access to the named port (or dock) is possible. If, on the other hand, obstacles arise which prevent the ship from reaching the "primary destination" named in the contract, this will amount to the occurrence of the condition which brings the obligation to perform at the substitute destination into operation. Taken literally, the phrase "so near thereto as she can safely get" may appear to mean that the substitute destination is one of which it can never be said that it has become impossible to reach. Nevertheless it is submitted that there may be cases in which impossibility in reaching the "primary" destination could discharge the contract. This might be the position if the place of primary destination were a port which ceased wholly to exist, *e.g.* because it was totally destroyed by an earthquake.

---

[87] Above, para.10–012.
[88] *Robert H Dahl v Nelson, Donkin* (1881) 6 App. Cas. 38 at 62.
[89] *ibid.*

On the true construction of the contract, the "alternative" could be said not to apply to such a drastic change of circumstances, or perhaps to have become meaningless since one cannot get near to a place which no longer exists. This would be in accordance with the process by which express contractual provisions which might literally cover a supervening event are narrowly construed so as not to apply where that event, or its effects, are so drastic that they cannot have been in the contemplation of the parties at the time of contracting.[90] Such a process of construction would, on the other hand, be less likely to be adopted where the contract required the ship to proceed (within a named port) to a named dock or so near to that dock as she could safely get, and it was only the named dock which was destroyed. The question in each case would be whether the events which had made it impossible to reach the "primary" destination were such that it would fundamentally alter the nature of the originally agreed performance to require one party to render and the other to accept the performance at the substitute destination; and where it was only a named dock which was destroyed, a negative answer might well be given to this question.

III. EFFECT OF SELECTION

10–016   A contract which imposes an alternative obligation to do X or Y is not discharged merely because the debtor intended to do X and that performance has become impossible or illegal, while Y remains both possible and lawful. But further questions arise where the selection of X has been communicated to the other party and X (but not Y) has then become impossible or illegal. Such communication may alter the nature of the obligation from one to perform X or Y to one to perform X alone; if so, the supervening impossibility of performing X will discharge the contract. Whether the selection has this effect depends on two further points: whether the effect of making the choice is to alter, or redefine, the contractual obligation, and whether the choice has been validly made.

(1) Whether selection redefines the obligation

10–017   In some cases, the selection of one of the permitted alternatives redefines the contractual obligation so that the selected alternative alone becomes due. Whether this is the effect of the selection depends on the factors already discussed. Thus if the contract confers a liberty to substitute and the substitution is made, or if it confers a "contract option" and the option is duly exercised, the contract becomes one to perform the selected alternative. If, for example, in the *Reardon Smith*[91] case the charterer had exercised his option to load one of the commodities (other than wheat) specified in the contract, he would have become bound to load that

---

[90] See (in another context) *Metropolitan Water Board v Dick, Kerr & Co* [1918] A.C. 119, and other similar cases discussed at below, paras 12–008 to 12–009.
[91] [1963] A.C. 691.

commodity to the extent specified in the contract, and if the loading of that commodity had been delayed by strikes he would have been protected by the exception. By contrast, an indication by the debtor that he intends to exercise a "performance option"[92] or to avail himself of an alternative method of discharge does not alter the nature of the contractual obligation, so that supervening impossibility or illegality of the selected performance is not of itself a ground of discharge. Thus if in the *Brightman*[93] case the charterer had given notice to the shipowner of his intention to load wheat, this would not have altered the nature of his obligation, which would have remained one to load whichever of the specified commodities remained available. This appears from the statement of Atkin L.J. that: "In such a contract as this, there is no such thing as an appropriation of cargo binding shipowner to shipper or shipper to shipowner, nor any question of a final election of an option."[94] Scrutton L.J. seems to have had a similar point in mind when he said that he could find "nothing ... to bind the charterer to load only wheat"[95]; though this view might be based simply on the fact that the charterer's decision to load wheat had not been communicated to the shipowner.

While the mere communication of the selection does not alter the nature of the obligation imposed by a "performance option", it is arguable that subsequent events may have such an effect. In the *Brightman* case, indeed, Atkin L.J. went so far as to say that: "The shipper retains control of his powers until the final ton is put on board; and as he retains his powers, so he retains his liabilities."[96] But this statement is, with respect, open to some doubt. A shipper who has undertaken to ship "a cargo of wheat" can hardly be entitled to substitute "a cargo of maize" when almost the whole of a cargo of wheat has been shipped. In such a case the more reasonable view would appear to be that the shipper's obligation has become one to ship a cargo of wheat, not by the mere selection of that commodity, but by subsequent events. If so, he should no more be bound than he is entitled to substitute maize if supervening events made it impossible for him to complete the loading of a cargo of wheat.

(2) Whether selection was validly made

This point can arise only in the case of a "contract option", the exercise of which will redefine the contractual obligation. The point is illustrated by *Hindley & Co Ltd v General Fibre Co Ltd*[97]; where a contract for the sale of jute was made c.i.f. a range of European ports (including Bremen and Antwerp) to be declared by the buyers. Shortly after the outbreak of the Second World War, the buyers declared Bremen, but as this declaration

---

[92] Above, para.10–007.
[93] [1924] 2 K.B. 619; [1925] A.C. 799; above, para.10–006.
[94] [1924] 2 K.B. 619 at 637.
[95] *ibid.* at 630.
[96] *ibid.* at 637.
[97] [1940] 2 K.B. 517.

was illegal and hence invalid it was held that a subsequent declaration of Antwerp (then a neutral port) was valid. The declaration of Bremen being a "nullity", the buyers "were entitled to withdraw it and make the declaration which was made".[98] It follows from this reasoning that if Bremen had been *validly* selected and if it had subsequently become illegal to carry the goods to that port, then the contract would have been discharged.[99] The principle applies in cases of supervening physical impossibility just as much as in cases of illegality. Thus in the *Hindley* case it was said that the buyers' declaration of Bremen "had no more effect than if they had declared Timbuctoo"[1]; (the point being that that was a place which no ship could ever have reached). But if they had declared a port which was subsequently destroyed by an earthquake, then the contract would, it is submitted, have been discharged. This submission is supported by a case[2] in which a charterparty provided for discharge at one of a number of specified berths and contained an exception for strikes. It was held that the charterer was protected by the exception when, after he had selected one of the berths, a strike broke out there: he was not bound, after that event, to select one of the other berths. The position would be the same if a contract were made to carry goods in one of two named ships to be selected by the shipowner. If before he had made his selection one of those ships was lost, he would *prima facie* be bound to select the other[3]; and this would be so even though he had selected the first after the loss but in ignorance of that fact. But if, after a valid selection (*i.e.* one complying with any contractual terms as to the time of selection and as to its notification to the shipper) had been made, the selected ship had been lost, then it is submitted that the contract would have been discharged.

IV. EVALUATION

10–020 The general rule governing the effect of supervening events on alternative obligations[4] appears to be satisfactory; and the same may well be true of the actual results of the cases concerned with the exceptions to that rule. But objection might well be raised to the complexity of the reasoning which has been applied to some of the exceptions, particularly to that which distinguishes between "contract(ual)" and "performance" options[5] and between alternative and contingent obligations.[6] In the cases from which these distinctions are derived, the courts have done their best to make sense of obscurely drafted contracts. The tools which they have used cannot be said to have had much to do with the intention of the

---

[98] *ibid.* at 553.
[99] *cf. The Teutonia* (1872) L.R. 4 P.C. 171.
[1] [1940] 2 K.B. 517 at 553.
[2] *Bulman & Dickson v Fenwick & Co* [1894] 1 Q.B. 179.
[3] *J Lauritzen A/S v Wijsmuller BV (The Super Servant Two)* [1990] 1 Lloyd's Rep. 1.
[4] Above, para.10–001.
[5] Above, paras 10–006 to 10–011.
[6] Above, para.10–014.

parties, which should in principle be the determining factor but is in cases of alternative obligations almost impossible to discover: the very fact that an obligation is drafted in alternative terms reflects indecision rather than any firm common intention. Ideally, parties should avoid drafting contracts in alternative terms, or, where that ideal cannot be attained or where obligations are alternative by operation of law,[7] they should solve the problem of the effects on such obligations of supervening events by express contractual provisions.

---

[7] Above, para.10–002.

CHAPTER 11

LEASES OF LAND

I. INTRODUCTION

In English law, there was until 1980 considerable support for the view that   **11–001**
the doctrine of frustration could not apply to leases of land. That view was
supported by a series of decisions in the lower courts[1] and, arguably, by a
decision of the House of Lords,[2] though that case could be explained on
the narrower ground that the lease in question was not (rather than on the
ground that it could not have been) frustrated. In 1980, the House of
Lords in *National Carriers Ltd v Panalpina (Northern) Ltd* [3] rejected the view
that the doctrine could not apply to leases of land, though it held that
the doctrine did not apply in the circumstances of that case. At the same
time the speeches indicate that the doctrine will only very rarely, or hardly
ever, apply to such transactions,[4] so that there is a continuing judicial
reluctance to apply the doctrine to them. Our first task in this chapter is
to distinguish between those arguments which formerly supported the
now rejected view that leases could never be frustrated and those which
continue to restrict the operation of the doctrine of discharge in relation
to such transactions. The discussion of the two sets of arguments will be
followed by a consideration of authorities illustrating first situations in
which leases of land still would not, and secondly those in which they now
could, be frustrated.

II. ARGUMENTS FORMERLY EXCLUDING THE DOCTRINE OF DISCHARGE

Three such arguments call for discussion; none of these arguments now   **11–002**
prevails, but it is necessary to be aware of them (and of the reasons for

---

[1] For a discussion of these cases, see below, paras 11–019 to 11–021.
[2] *Matthey v Curling* [1922] 2 A.C. 180, below, para.11–020; in *Cricklewood Property and Investment Trust Ltd v Leighton's Investment Trust Ltd* [1945] A.C. 221, below, para.11–018, there had been a division of opinion on the point.
[3] [1981] A.C. 675, Lord Russell *dubitante.*
[4] *ibid.* at 689, 692, 607, 701, 715.

their rejection) so as to be able to distinguish them from those which continue in the present context to restrict the scope of the doctrine of discharge.

(1) Historical development of the doctrine

11–003   The first such argument rests on the history of the doctrine of discharge, which can be described as the gradual erosion of the doctrine of absolute contracts by the doctrine of discharge by supervening events. The classic statement of the first of these doctrines was made in 1647, in the case of *Paradine v Jane*,[5] which concerned a lease, though that was not its *ratio decidendi*.[6] In the following two centuries, the doctrine of absolute contracts was frequently applied in cases involving leases, in which supervening events were held not to have discharged covenants to pay rent or to keep the premises in repair; in particular, the tenant was commonly held liable under these covenants even though buildings on the land had been destroyed by fire.[7] Moreover, *Taylor v Caldwell*,[8] though laying the foundations of the modern doctrine of discharge, had not attempted to overrule, but on the contrary had at one point[9] explicitly recognised, the doctrine of *Paradine v Jane*. Judicial approval of that doctrine continued, even after *Taylor v Caldwell*, so that the concept of absolute contracts survived that decision to some extent. In paras 2–029 to 2–034, above, it was suggested that some such survivals of the doctrine were based simply on history, while others were based on the continuing validity of at least a variant of the reasoning of *Paradine v Jane*. The second of these possibilities will be considered, in relation to leases of land, in para.11–008, below. The present point is that the development of the doctrine of discharge in and after *Taylor v Caldwell* left unimpaired the considerable body of case law concerning leases of land, in which supervening events had not been grounds of discharge. It was therefore arguable that leases of land constituted an exception to the doctrine of discharge, but this argument was rejected in the *National Carriers* case.[10] The House of Lords there insisted that the doctrine of discharge applied to contracts generally. In earlier cases, the courts had rejected the argument that the doctrine was inapplicable to certain other transactions merely because they fell into a particular category, *e.g.* merely because they were time charters[11] or demise charters.[12] Since a demise charter amounted to a lease of a ship,[13] it was a natural continuation of that process to hold that the doctrine

---

[5] (1647) Aleyn 26; above, para.2–002.
[6] *National Carriers* case [1981] A.C. 675 at 706.
[7] For a discussion of such cases, see above, para.2–007.
[8] (1863) 3 B. & S. 826.
[9] *ibid.* at 833; above, para.2–025.
[10] [1981] 1 A.C. 675.
[11] *Bank Line Ltd v Arthur Capel & Co* [1919] A.C. 435.
[12] *Blane Steamships Ltd v Minister of Transport* [1951] 2 K.B. 965.
[13] *Scrutton on Charterparties* (20th ed.), p.59.

should not be incapable of applying to a transaction simply because it was a lease of land.

(2) Lease as a conveyance

The second argument which was formerly thought to preclude the application of the doctrine of discharge was that a lease of land was not only a contract, but also a conveyance, since it had the effect of vesting in the tenant a legal estate in the land.[14] This legal estate, it was argued, was not affected by supervening events (such as the destruction of buildings on the land or legislation regulating its use) which prevented the tenant from using the land for the intended purpose. There are, however, a number of objections to this argument and these prevailed in the *National Carriers* case.[15] First, the argument ignores what is often the commercial reality underlying the transaction. Often what the tenant bargains for is not the legal estate in the land, but its use and occupation. This is, in particular, true where the lease is for a short term and for a particular purpose which is either specified in the contract or within the contemplation of the parties.[16] Secondly, it may, in the case of such a contract, be hard to tell whether the transaction amounted to a lease or to a licence to occupy or to make some specified use of the premises. Licences are clearly subject to the doctrine of discharge, as *Taylor v Caldwell*[17] and *Krell v Henry*[18] show. The distinction between them and leases turns on the often difficult question of fact whether the parties intended the person using the premises to have "exclusive possession"[19]; and the applicability of the doctrine of discharge should not depend on the exact point where that distinction is drawn.[20] Thirdly, the lease of a chattel, such as a demise charter, can no doubt be frustrated[21]; and it would be anomalous to hold that a related lease of land could not be frustrated. For example, a demise charter of an oil tanker might be associated with the lease of a shore installation to be used together with the ship. If both were destroyed in the same explosion, it would be strange if the contract relating to the ship could, while that relating to the installation could not, be frustrated.[22] Fourthly, it has for some considerable time been recognised that an agreement for a lease of land, as opposed to an executed lease, can be frustrated.[23] This is so in spite of the fact that such an agreement, by virtue of its specific

11–004

---

[14] *e.g. Cricklewood* case [1945] A.C. 221 at 233.

[15] [1981] A.C. 675.

[16] *ibid.* at 691, 695, 702.

[17] (1863) 3 B. & S. 826, above, para.2–024.

[18] [1903] 2 K.B. 740, above, para.7–010.

[19] See, *e.g. Street v Mountford* [1985] A.C. 809; *AG Securities v Vaughan* [1990] 1 A.C. 417.

[20] *National Carriers* case [1981] A.C. 675 at 694, 701–702, 714.

[21] *Blane Steamships v Minister of Transport* [1951] 2 K.B. 965.

[22] *National Carriers* case [1981] A.C. 675 at 690, 701, 713.

[23] *Denny Mott & Dickson Ltd v James B Fraser & Co* [1944] A.C. 265, below, para. 11–024.

enforceability,[24] confers an interest in the land on the prospective tenant. That interest is, indeed, only an equitable one, but for the purpose of the doctrine of discharge the distinction between this equitable interest and the legal estate created by a lease should not be regarded as significant.

(3) **Risk**

11–005   A third argument which was formerly thought to preclude the application of the doctrine of discharge to leases of land was that risk passed to the tenant as soon as the lease was executed, on the analogy of the rule that (unless otherwise agreed) risk under a contract for the sale of land passes to the purchaser on the conclusion of the contract.[25] If risk passes to the purchaser when he becomes (by virtue of the contract) equitable owner of the land, it is said that risk should similarly pass to the tenant when, by virtue of the lease, he acquires a legal estate in the land. A contract (so the argument continues) cannot be frustrated by destruction of or damage to the subject-matter after the risk has passed; and if the risk passes as soon as the contract is made, then the contract cannot be frustrated in this way at all. But the argument is not convincing; for to say that the risk passes on contract is simply another way of saying that the contract cannot be frustrated by destruction of, or damage to, its subject-matter. It would not (in relation to leases) explain *why* they cannot be frustrated; it would simply beg that question.[26]

There are, moreover, objections as a matter of principle to applying the rule as to the passing of risk under contracts for the sale of land to leases of land. No doubt if L grants a lease to T1 who then sells that leasehold interest to T2, then the normal rules as to the passing of risk under contracts for the sale of land apply to the transaction between T1 and T2. But it by no means follows that those rules apply to the transaction between L and T1, or indeed to the relationship which may arise (as a result of the sale) between L and T2. Indeed, it seems inappropriate to apply the rules as to passing of risk to a contract under which both parties undertake continuing duties over the entire term of the contract.[27] Of course it is inherent in the notion of the passing of risk that *some* obligation or obligations remain outstanding when the passing of risk occurs.[28] If that were not the case, frustration would be excluded on the different ground that there can be no frustration of a contract after it had been fully performed. Hence under a contract of sale risk can[29] pass before delivery (in the case of goods) or conveyance (in the case of land). But there can, it is submitted, be no passing of risk where the whole essence of the transaction is the performance of mutual obligations for the

---

[24] *Walsh v Lonsdale* (1882) 21 Ch. D. 9.

[25] Above, para.3–027.

[26] *National Carriers* case [1981] A.C. 675 at 705.

[27] *ibid.*

[28] Above, para.3–007; *cf.* above, para.3–054.

[29] Except where the buyer deals as consumer: Sale of Goods Act 1979, s.20(4); above, para.3–009.

period specified under the contract. In this context it may be significant that civil law systems do not refer to the passing or transfer of risk in relation to leases, except with respect to particular objects on the land, *e.g.* where agricultural implements or animals are included in a lease of farm land.[30] It is also significant in this context that, while in English law the passing of risk is commonly discussed in connection with sales of goods, there is no counterpart to these discussions in the law relating to the hire (or hire-purchase) of goods, even though the destruction of such goods (particularly where motorvehicles are concerned) must be a matter of daily occurrence. The practical explanation why risk is not discussed in relation to such contracts is no doubt that damage to or destruction of the goods is almost invariably dealt with by the express terms which relate to the insurance of the goods[31]; and this point is also (as we shall see) relevant to leases of land.[32] But in the case of chattels it seems that such contracts could in principle be frustrated by the destruction of the subject-matter; and if this is the case the underlying assumption must be that risk has not passed. This is also true of contracts such as charterparties which may be frustrated by loss of or serious damage to the ship and this is so whether the contract is a demise charter (amounting to a contract for the hire of the ship) or a voyage or time charter (amounting to a contract for services to be rendered by the use of a particular ship).[33] In all these cases it is submitted that the nature of the contract, calling for the continuous performance of duties over a period of time, makes it inappropriate to talk of the passing of risk. The only apparent exception to this view is to be found in the law relating to building contracts, considered in Ch.3.[34] Risk is indeed discussed in relation to such contracts, but only to make the point that there is no *passing* of risk before completion of the work. That is entirely consistent with the view that it is inappropriate to talk of passing of risk where continuing duties are imposed on both parties for the duration of the contract. Moreover, the rule amounts only to saying that a building contract cannot be frustrated by the destruction of the work before

---

[30] German Civil Code (BGB) § 582a(1); except in this paragraph, the Code contains no provision as to passing of risk (under such contracts) which might be regarded as counterparts to the provision of § 446 on the transfer of risk under contracts of sale. *cf.* Esser, *Schuldrecht* (4th ed.), Vol.I, p.214 (no transfer of risk); Esser and Weyers, *Schuldrecht* (6th ed.), Vol.II, pp.142–144. Hence on destruction of the subject-matter, the general rules as to supervening impossibility (BGB, §§ 275, and the provisions referred to in § 275(4)) will apply.

[31] Guest, *The Law of Hire-Purchase*, para.495. *cf.* UCC, s.2A–219(1) laying down the general rule that, in the case of a chattel lease, "risk of loss is retained by the lessor and does not pass to the lessee". The rule is subject to the significant exception that it does not apply to a "finance lease" (as defined in s.2A–103(1)(g)), perhaps because in the case of such a transaction the lessor's function may be restricted to the single act of providing finance. The draft proposals for amendment of the Code (above, para.2–042, n.17) extend to Art.2A and, in particular, to the sections referred to in this note.

[32] Below, para.11–013.

[33] Above, para.11–003, nn.11, 12.

[34] Above, paras 3–051 *et seq.*

completion. It does not rule out the possibility of frustration on other grounds, *e.g.* by destruction of, or damage to, the object on which that work is to be done.

11–006   There is, it is submitted, a further reason why the argument that risk passes to the tenant on execution of the lease would not (even if it were accepted) be conclusive in the present context. The rules as to the passing of risk refer only to events affecting the physical integrity of the subject-matter. Issues as to frustration of leases are often raised by other supervening events such as the unavailability of the premises through requisition,[35] or legal restrictions on their use, leading to frustration of purpose.[36] Rules relating to risk of loss are not necessarily appropriate to the resolution of such issues.

Finally, the analogy of the rule that risk passes under contracts for the sale of land would suggest that, in the case of a lease, risk should pass even before execution of the lease, *i.e.* as soon as the parties enter into an agreement for a lease. But it is settled that such an agreement for a lease can be frustrated,[37] and there is no reason to suppose that this rule cannot apply where the ground of frustration is the destruction of buildings on the premises. The application of the doctrine of frustration to such a case would be quite inconsistent with the view that the risk had passed to the prospective tenant as soon as the agreement was made.

III. Factors Restricting Scope of Doctrine of Discharge

11–007   Having in the *National Carriers* case[38] established that the doctrine of frustration could apply to leases of land, the House of Lords went on to stress that the doctrine would only very rarely apply to such transactions.[39] Our present concern is with the factors which explain this restrictive approach to frustration where leases are concerned.

(1) **Partial survival of the reasoning of *Paradine v Jane***

11–008   In Ch.2 we saw that there was a group of cases in which, even today, contracts were still regarded as "absolute"[40] and that this view was justified by what may be termed a modern version of the doctrine of absolute contracts. According to the original version of that doctrine in *Paradine v Jane*, a party could not rely on a supervening event "because he *might* have provided against it by his contract"[41]; according to the narrower modern version, the party cannot so rely on such an event where it was reasonable

---

[35] *e.g. Matthey v Carling* [1922] 2 A.C. 180.
[36] *e.g.* the *Cricklewood* case [1945] A.C. 221.
[37] Above, para.11–004, n.23; below, para.11–024.
[38] [1981] A.C. 675.
[39] Above, para.11–001, at n.4.
[40] Above, paras 2–033 to 2–034.
[41] (1647) Aleyn 26, 27 (italics supplied).

to expect him to make provision in the contract for the event.[42] Such reasoning was, for example, used in the *National Carriers* case itself, where one ground for rejecting the tenant's plea of frustration was that the lease expressly provided for fire risks, that "some possible interruption from other causes cannot have been beyond the reasonable contemplation of the parties"[43] and that it was reasonable to expect them to have made provision for such other causes. Similar reasoning can be used to explain *Redmond v Dainton*,[44] where a lease of a house for 99 years from 1850 was held not to have been discharged when the house was seriously damaged in 1918 by a German bomb. The lease contained a covenant by the tenant to insure against fire, and one to repair. The court relied on *Paradine v Jane* and on the original justification for the doctrine of absolute contracts which has been quoted above[45]; but it is at least strongly arguable that, though aerial enemy attack can scarcely have been within the contemplation of the parties in 1850, they could reasonably have been expected to foresee and provide for damage from causes other than fire.

(2) **No impossibility of performance**

The most common ground of frustration is supervening impossibility of performance; and there are difficulties in applying the concept of such impossibility to leases of land. One such difficulty was that the supervening event may affect only the performance to be rendered by one party. Even the total destruction of the buildings on the land would not make it impossible for the tenant to pay rent. In *Paradine v Jane*[46] itself, there was no such impossibility.[47] This point would no longer be conclusive now that the courts have developed the concept that impossibility preventing the achievement of the "common object" of the parties can be a ground of frustration,[48] so that impossibility affecting the performance of one party can discharge both. But in *Paradine v Jane* it is doubtful whether even the landlord's obligations had become impossible to perform; for it does not seem that the supervening event put him even in *prima facie* breach of any covenant in, or obligation under, the lease.[49] A second difficulty is that even where the supervening event does affect one party's performance, its effect may be to make that performance, not impossible, but only more difficult or more expensive. This was the position in the cases discussed in Ch.2, in which tenants relied on the destruction of the premises by fire as excuses for failing to perform covenants to "repair".[50] If (as was commonly the case) such covenants *meant* that the tenant must restore the

11–009

---

[42] Above, para.2–033.
[43] [1981] A.C. 675 at 707.
[44] [1920] 2 K.B. 256; this case was not cited in the *National Carriers* case, above.
[45] At n.41, above.
[46] (1647) Aleyn 26.
[47] For discussion of this aspect of the case, see above, para.2–044.
[48] Above, para.2–039.
[49] Above, para.2–004.
[50] Above, para.2–005.

premises to the state in which they were at the beginning of the term, then clearly their destruction did not make performance impossible: on the contrary, it was precisely one of the situations in which the covenant to repair was intended to operate. "Impossibility" could, at most, affect the time of performance. A third difficulty is that the most obvious type of impossibility is that which arises (as in *Taylor v Caldwell* [51]) from the destruction of the subject-matter. Setting aside for the moment the question of just what it is that is the subject-matter of the lease, and when it can be said to have been "destroyed", we can say that "destruction" involves some considerable degree of physical impairment of the subject-matter. But in many of the cases of alleged frustration of leases there is no such impairment at all. Even in *Paradine v Jane* itself, the tenant's complaint was not that the the farm had been damaged, but that he had been prevented from occupying it. In many (though not in all) of the modern cases concerning leases (including the *National Carriers* case [52]), the allegation is similarly not one of destruction of the premises, but rather one of frustration of the tenant's purpose and, for reasons to be given in paras 11–014 and 11–015, below, a lease of land is unlikely to be discharged by such frustration.

(3) Definition of the subject-matter

11–010 Where destruction of the subject-matter is alleged to be the ground of discharge, the question arises, in the case of a lease of land, exactly how the subject-matter of the transaction is to be defined. This question can give rise to difficulty, even after the rejection of the former view that the tenant's legal estate in the land is the subject-matter of the lease. Although the subject-matter may be regarded as the thing let, it can still be open to dispute whether that subject-matter is the land itself, or the land with the buildings on it; and, even if the latter view is taken, destruction can normally affect only the buildings. The land itself is normally not "destroyed"; such destruction occurs only in the unusual cases where "some vast convulsion of nature swallowed up the property altogether ...",[53] or where it is lost in the process of coastal erosion.[54] In the more common case of destruction of the buildings alone, the impossibility will be no more than partial and (since repair or restoration will normally be possible) temporary. The question will then arise (in accordance with the principles discussed in Ch.5) whether the interference with performance is sufficiently serious to constitute a ground of discharge.[55] A negative answer to this question is likely to be given where the lease is a long one and the work of repair or restoration would occupy only a relatively minor part of the agreed term.

---

[51] (1863) 3 B. & S. 826.
[52] [1981] A.C. 675.
[53] *Cricklewood* case [1945] A.C. 221 at 229.
[54] *National Carriers* case [1981] A.C. 675 at 691; *cf.* at 700–701.
[55] Above, paras 5–002, 5–037 *et seq.*

(4) **Leases as long-term transactions**

Parties to long-term transactions must necessarily envisage the possibility   11–011
that circumstances may change, perhaps quite radically during the agreed
term of the contract. For this reason the doctrine of discharge will not
often apply to such a transaction[56]: its nature gives rise to an inference that
the parties agreed to take the risk of changes in circumstances which may
alter the relative values of performance and counter-performance, and so
make the transaction less favourable to one party (and correspondingly
more favourable to the other) than it was, or appeared to be, when it was
concluded. This argument applies with particular force to long leases of
land, for the simple reason that their specified duration is likely to exceed
that of other long-term transactions which can plausibly be imagined. The
duration even of a long-term contract for the supply of goods or services
(such as a time charterparty) does not normally approach that of a long
lease of land.[57] The length of the term not only makes it reasonable to
assume that the parties take the risk of changes of circumstances. It also
increases the possibility that such changes may be only temporary and that
the extent of interference with one party's performance, or with the
purpose for which the premises were to be used, may not be sufficiently
serious (on the "proportionality test"[58] described in Ch.5) to bring about
discharge. Such a result could follow only in extreme cases, for example,
if, after the execution of a building lease, "legislation were subsequently
passed which permanently prohibited private building in the area or
dedicated it as an open space for ever".[59] It may be objected that even
such legislation is not necessarily immutable and that expressions such as
"for ever" are not, perhaps, to be taken quite literally.[60] But in the case
put, the view that the lease is frustrated can be justified on the ground that
the question of discharge is to be judged by reference to reasonable
probabilities at the time of the allegedly frustrating event,[61] and not by
reference to what happens later. Discharge would therefore follow if,
when the legislation was passed, it was reasonable to suppose that the
prohibition would last for the whole or a major part of the remaining term
of the lease.

In para.11–004, above, we noted that one reason why the doctrine of   11–012
discharge was formerly thought to be inapplicable to leases of land was
that risk passed to the tenant on execution of the lease. One ground for
rejecting that argument was that risk did not pass at that point or indeed

---

[56] See *Larrinaga v Société Franco Américaine des Phosphates de Medalla* (1923) 92
L.J.K.B. 455; and below, para.12–003.

[57] This is true even of most contracts of indefinite duration, of the kind discussed
above, paras 6–037 to 6–040.

[58] Above, para.5–050.

[59] *Cricklewood* case [1945] A.C. 221 at 229.

[60] *cf.* the interpretation of such phrases as "at all times hereafter" and "in
perpetuity" in *Staffordshire Area Health Authority v South Staffordshire Waterworks Co*
[1978] 1 W.L.R. 1387 and *Harbinger UK Ltd v GE Information Services Ltd* [2000] 1
All E.R. (Comm) 166; above, paras 6–038, 6–040.

[61] Above, Ch.9.

at all, since it was inappropriate to talk of the passing of risk under contracts involving continuing mutual obligations.[62] At first sight, this view might seem to be inconsistent with that put forward under the present heading, *i.e.* that parties to a long-term transaction (such as a long lease) must be assumed to have taken the risk of changes in circumstances during the currency of their contract. The inconsistency is, however, more apparent than real, since in the two propositions the expression "risk" is used in a different sense. As used in paras 11–005 to 11–006, above, it refers to the consequences of an impairment of the physical integrity of the subject-matter of the contract; while in the present discussion it has a broader meaning, which includes commercial considerations affecting the relative values of the performances of the two parties. It is in this sense that parties to long-term contracts can be said to take the risk that circumstances may change during the currency of the contract. To say that the parties have taken this (commercial or financial) "risk" means no more than that, by the very fact of entering into a long-term contract, they have *allocated* in advance the risk of such changes. It does not mean that the (physical) "risk" of the destruction of the subject-matter has "passed" from one party to the other. The point may be illustrated by using the analogy of a contract for the carriage of a series of cargoes in a particular ship, under which performance is to begin some years after the conclusion of the contract. Such a contract is not frustrated by even quite radical changes in market conditions because, by entering into a contract of this kind, the parties are taken to have assumed this "risk".[63] But no one would argue that there was any "passing" of risk of loss of the ship under such a contract. Similarly, a long-term lease is a contract which, by its nature gives rise to the inference of *assumption* of risk in the first of these senses; but this does not mean that risk of loss in the second sense *passes* to the tenant on the conclusion of the contract merely because it is a lease. The first of these points merely means that long leases, like other long-term contracts, are unlikely to be frustrated; the second would mean that no lease could ever be frustrated. There is, therefore, no inconsistency between accepting the first of these points and rejecting the second.

(5) **Express provision**

11–013   Frustration may be excluded by an express provision in the contract for the supervening event. This limitation on the scope of the doctrine is more fully discussed in Ch.12; reference to one illustration of it has been made in para.11–005, above, where it was suggested that one reason why hire-purchase contracts are not in practice frustrated by the destruction of their subject-matter was that this eventuality was normally covered by provisions in the contract with regard to insurance. A similar point can be made with regard to leases of land, which commonly contain covenants to "repair" and to keep the premises insured. We saw in Ch.2 that a covenant to "repair" might, on its true construction, cover the precise

---

[62] Above, para.11–005.
[63] See the *Larrinaga* case, above, n.56.

contingency of the destruction of the premises and oblige the covenantor, in that event, to rebuild them.[64] A covenant to keep the premises insured might have a similar practical effect since by statute "any person ... interested" may require money received under the insurance policy to be laid out towards reinstating the premises[65]; and under this statutory provision a claim that the money shall be so laid out can be made by a tenant under his landlord's insurance,[66] and by a landlord under his tenant's insurance.[67] The effect of the covenant will therefore be to exclude frustration which might, if there had been no such covenant, have occurred as a result of the destruction of the premises. Covenants to repair and to keep the premises insured will of course deal only with this one possible cause of frustration. They have no direct bearing on events such as requisition or legislative prohibition of the intended use of the premises as grounds of frustration. They will be relevant to such grounds only in that they may support the argument that parties who have expressly dealt with one possible cause of frustration should have foreseen, and provided for, others as well.[68]

Reference should also be made in this context to rent review clauses. In discussing the American doctrine of discharge by "impracticability", we saw that attempts were sometimes made to invoke this doctrine where the real value of the payments to be made to a party under a long-term contract had fallen because they had been eroded by inflation.[69] Such claims have had little success even where the fall in the value of the payments was accompanied by an increase in the cost of services to be rendered by the payee (as might be the position where, under a lease, a landlord agreed to provide services such as heating); much less have they succeeded where the payee's *only* complaint was a fall in the value of money. In many leases an additional reason for rejecting claims of discharge based on such grounds would be that the fall in the value of rent is now often dealt with by rent review clauses; and that such clauses have become so common that a landlord's failure to provide for rent review would indicate an assumption by him of this commercial risk. No doubt that risk assumption would be reflected, in most cases, in the amount of the premium charged for the execution of the lease.

(6) Frustration of purpose

For the reasons given in the preceding discussion, it will only rarely be plausible to argue that a lease of land has been frustrated by impossibility resulting from the physical destruction of buildings on that land. More

11–014

---

[64] Above, para.2–005.

[65] Fires Prevention (Metropolis) Act 1774, s.83.

[66] *Portavon Cinema Co Ltd v Price and Century Insurance Co* [1939] 4 All E.R. 601; *Mark Rowlands Ltd v Berni Inns Ltd* [1986] Q.B. 211.

[67] *MacGillivray on Insurance Law* (10th ed.), paras 20–44, 20–45.

[68] For use of such an argument in the *National Carriers* case [1981] A.C. 675 at 707, see above, para.11–008, at n.43.

[69] Above, para.6–045.

commonly, the argument will rather be that discharge has resulted from frustration of purpose, *e.g.* because the tenant is prevented by physical or legal obstacles from using the premises for the intended purpose, though he can still occupy them. The chances of success with such an argument are reduced by a number of factors which restrict the scope of frustration of purpose (as opposed to impossibility or illegality) as a ground of discharge. These have been discussed in Ch.7; three of them are of special significance in the present context.

The first is that the doctrine of frustration of purpose operates only where it is the *common* purpose of both parties that is frustrated; and in the case of a long-term lease of land it is unlikely that the tenant's purpose will be one which is shared by the landlord, at least unless he stands to benefit from it. He might, indeed, so benefit in the case of a building lease, especially if the rent is to include a share of the profits of the proposed development, and in the case of such a lease the common purpose is likely to be expressed in the actual undertakings in the lease. A common purpose may also be inferred from an express term of the lease which restricts the use of the premises to that purpose: for example, from one which provides that the premises are to be used only for a specified kind of business[70] or only as a private residence. A restriction of the latter kind would not, however indicate that it was the common purpose of the parties that any particular person should reside in the premises.[71] A *fortiori* it would be hard to establish that a common purpose had been frustrated where the lease contained no reference at all (whether in the form of a positive obligation or of a negative restriction on use) to that purpose.

11–015   Secondly the alleged frustration of purpose will often, in the case of a lease of land, be only partial or temporary; and we saw in Ch.7 that the courts have applied stricter tests in cases of partial or temporary frustration of purpose than in cases of partial or temporary impossibility. In cases of partial impossibility the test of discharge is whether the main purpose of the contract has been defeated, and in many cases of temporary impossibility the question of discharge similarly depends on the length and seriousness of the interruption. But in cases of alleged frustration of purpose the courts have asked whether *any* part of the contractual purpose (so long as it was not wholly trivial) could still be achieved.[72] The application of this test to leases of land will often lead to the conclusion that the contract should not be discharged. This would, for example, be the position where the supervening event is one which interferes only with some of the purposes for which the premises were to be used: even if the purposes for which they could still be used were subsidiary to the *main* purpose, the contract would survive, so long as the surviving use was not wholly trivial. Moreover, in the case of a long lease, the temporary interference with the contractual purpose will only rarely satisfy the test stated above; for when the event occurs which interferes temporarily with the contractual purpose it will often be impossible to predict whether the

---

[70] As in the liquor prohibition cases: above, para.7–023.
[71] *London & Northern Estates Co v Schlesinger* [1916] 1 K.B. 20 at 23.
[72] Above, paras 7–014, 7–017, 7–020, 7–022, 7–024.

duration of the interference will be such as to satisfy the stringent test which applies in cases of temporary frustration of purpose. This test is likely to be satisfied only if, when the event occurs, the obstacle to the intended use can reasonably be regarded as a permanent one.[73]

Thirdly, there is the point that, although the English courts in the coronation cases[74] were the first in the common law world to recognise the concept of frustration of purpose, they have very rarely applied that concept since then. It is scarcely surprising that this reluctance should have been extended to cases of alleged frustration of purpose concerning leases of land. Indeed, the *National Carriers* case,[75] in which English law recognised the possibility that the doctrine of frustration could apply to leases of land, was one of alleged frustration of purpose, and the actual decision in that case was that the temporary interference with the contractual purpose which there took place was not sufficiently serious in its duration to discharge the lease.[76]

(7) **Effects of discharge**

The general rule of English law is that frustration discharges a contract automatically, by operation of law, and not at the option of the party who is prejudiced by the supervening event in the sense that he will not receive the performance bargained for or be able to put the subject-matter to the mutually contemplated purpose.[77] The result of this rule is that frustration is sometimes invoked by, so to speak, the "wrong" party, *i.e.* not by the party who is prejudiced (in the above sense) by the supervening event but by the other party, for whom the contract has, quite independently of that event, turned out to be a bad bargain, and who would actually make a windfall profit if the contract were held to have been frustrated. It has already been suggested[78] that to allow such a claim would be a misuse of the doctrine of discharge, the purpose of which is to provide for the satisfactory allocation of losses resulting from the supervening event, and not to enable a party to make a windfall profit. The force of that argument obviously increases with the length of the term of the contract, a long-term contract being itself an asset, the value of which is (at least *prima facie*) directly proportioned to the length of the term; and this is particularly true of long leases of land. Indeed, the value of the tenant's leasehold interest in the site could, in times of rising land values, well have increased substantially since the execution of the lease; and in such circumstances

11–016

---

[73] As in the example given in above, para.11–011, at n.59, of building being prohibited "for ever".

[74] Above, paras 7–005 to 7–014.

[75] [1981] A.C. 675.

[76] See the discussion of the *National Carriers* case (above, n.75), below para. 11–018.

[77] Below, para.15–002.

[78] See the discussion above, para.5–053, of *Tamplin SS Co v Anglo-Mexican Petroleum Co* [1916] 2 A.C. 397; and of *The Isle of Mull*, 278 F. 131 (1921) in para.15–007, below.

the result of holding that the lease had been frustrated by a supervening event, such as the destruction of buildings on the land, could paradoxically operate to the serious prejudice of the tenant. As frustration discharges a contract automatically, the effect of such a decision would be to confer a windfall profit on the landlord: he would be entitled to resume possession of the site before the end of the agreed term, even though the tenant wished to reconstruct the buildings and was content to continue to pay the agreed rent during the time taken up by this operation. To deprive the tenant of the benefit of the lease in such circumstances would be wholly inconsistent with the purpose of the doctrine of discharge.[79]

IV. THE AUTHORITIES

11–017   The narrow scope of the doctrine of frustration in relation to leases of land is illustrated by a number of English cases in which the courts have refused to apply the doctrine to such transactions. In so far as these cases are based on the view that the doctrine of frustration cannot, as a matter of law, apply to leases of land, their reasoning would no longer be followed since the rejection of that view in the *National Carriers* case.[80] But many of the earlier cases were discussed, and none was disapproved, in that case, so that it must be assumed that the actual decisions in them are still good law. Cases in which leases were held to have been frustrated are, however, to be found in other common law jurisdictions, and we shall consider the extent to which such cases might be followed in England.

(1) **Temporary interruption of use and express provisions**

11–018   It is convenient to begin with the *National Carriers* case itself, which concerned the lease of a warehouse for 10 years from January 1, 1974. The lease expressly dealt with one possible cause of frustration by providing that, if the warehouse were damaged by fire, the tenants' liability for rent was to be suspended pending reinstatement, and that, if fire caused substantial damage to, or destruction of, the premises the landlords were to have the right to determine the lease.[81] In May 1979 the only access road to the warehouse was closed by order of the local authority. At that time it seemed likely that the road would remain closed for between 12 and 20 months. For so long as the road was closed, the tenants obviously could not use the premises as a warehouse, nor did they use it for any other purpose. In an action for rent, the tenants argued that the lease had been frustrated, but the argument was rejected on two grounds. The first was that the interruption amounted at most to one-sixth of the total term of the lease, or to one-third of the remainder of the term from the

---

[79] For a similar argument in relation to the *Tsakiroglou* case [1962] A.C. 93, see above, para.4–074; *cf.* below, para.15–007.

[80] [1981] A.C. 675.

[81] cl.4(2) of the lease.

beginning of the interruption; and (applying the "proportionality test"[82] stated in Ch.5) this interruption was not sufficiently serious to constitute a ground of discharge. The second was that the parties had, in the clause relating to damage or destruction caused by fire, expressly provided against one possible cause which might interrupt the tenants' use of the premises; that no provision was made for interruption by other causes which "cannot have been beyond the reasonable contemplation of the parties"[83]; and that therefore the obligation to pay rent, being "unconditional with a sole exception for the case of fire"[84] was not affected by the events which had happened. The point to be emphasised is that the House of Lords here applied general principles governing frustration rather than special considerations affecting leases: its reasons for rejecting the plea of frustration in the *National Carriers* case would have been equally applicable in a case arising out of a contract for the hire of a chattel. Of course, in applying the "proportionality test" to cases of temporary obstacles, account must be taken of the agreed duration of the contract, and this is likely (simply because of the nature of the subject-matter) to be longer in the case of leases of land than in the case of contracts for the hire of a chattel. But the lease in the *National Carriers* case was in fact no longer than a demise charter of a ship might well be, and the grounds given by the House of Lords for rejecting the plea of frustration in that case could equally apply to the case where a demise charterer had been temporarily prevented from using the ship, assuming that the term of the contract and the length of the interruption were similar to those in the *National Carriers* case.

The "proportionality test" is obviously very hard to satisfy where the lease is for a substantially longer term than that in the *National Carriers* case. This was the position in the *Cricklewood* case,[85] where a building lease for 99 years from May 1936 was held not to have been discharged when building on the land was prohibited under emergency regulations which took effect in 1939, at the beginning of the Second World War. A claim for arrears of rent was made in April 1942 and was upheld since, "though we do not know how long the present war and the emergency regulations are going to last, the length of the interruption so caused is presumably a small fraction of the whole term".[86] The House of Lords was unanimous on this point, even though there was a difference of opinion on the general question of principle whether the doctrine of frustration applied to leases of land.

(2) Destruction by enemy action

The destruction of buildings by enemy action in the course of the two World Wars had likewise been held not to be a ground of frustration of

11–019

---

[82] Above, para.5–050.
[83] [1981] A.C. 675 at 707.
[84] *ibid.* at 698.
[85] [1945] A.C. 221.
[86] *ibid.* at 232–233.

leases, whether for residential or commerical purposes. In one of the relevant cases the judgment, apart from relying on the authority and on the reasoning of *Paradine v Jane*, may also have been based to some extent on the fact that the tenant had covenanted to insure the premises against fire and to repair them.[87] In the other two,[88] it is noteworthy that it was the landlord who claimed that the lease had been frustrated and who would, if the argument had succeeded, have made a windfall profit out of frustration. The possibility that tenants might suffer hardship (by remaining liable to pay rent for premises which they could not use) was dealt with by special war-time legislation[89] giving tenants, in cases of this kind, a statutory power to choose between disclaiming the lease and retaining it; if the tenant exercised the latter option, he was obliged to restore the destroyed buildings but was not required to pay rent until this had been done.

(3) War-time requisitioning

11-020   A further group of cases concerns the effect on leases of the war-time requisitioning of premises and again rejects the argument that this was a ground of frustration. The leases in some of these cases were relatively short: in one of them the lease was for three years[90]; in another it was "for the duration of the war"[91]; and in a third[92] it was for 21 years from March 1898, so that the lease had actually expired before the requisition was withdrawn. It is noteworthy, too, that in one of these cases[93] the landlord agreed to supply services as well as the premises, and that in another[94] the lease was of furnished accommodation. In all these cases one ground for rejecting the plea of frustration was that the tenant had received, or was entitled to receive, compensation from the requisitioning authorities. In one of them,[95] the premises had also been destroyed by fire after the requisition, but this was not regarded as a ground of frustration since the tenant had covenanted to repair, to keep the premises insured against fire, to lay out insurance moneys in reinstating the premises and, if such moneys turned out to be insufficient, to make good the deficiency; he had moreover received the insurance moneys. Having regard to these circumstances, some doubt may be expressed as to whether the case was

---

[87] *Redmond v Dainton* [1920] 2 K.B. 256.

[88] *Denman v Brise* [1949] 1 K.B. 22; *Cusak-Smith v London Corp* [1956] 1 W.L.R. 1368.

[89] See Landlord and Tenant (War Damage) Act 1939, discussed in the *Cusak-Smith* case, above.

[90] *Whitehall Court Ltd v Ettlinger* [1920] 1 K.B. 680.

[91] *Swift v Macbean* [1942] 1 K.B. 375; for the validity of such leases (in spite of the fact that their term was uncertain) see Validation of War-time Leases Act 1944; for the common law position, see *Prudential Assurance Co Ltd v London Residuary Body* [1992] 2 A.C. 386.

[92] *Matthey v Curling* [1922] 2 A.C. 180.

[93] *Whitehall Court Ltd v Ettlinger*, above, n.90.

[94] *Swift v Macbean*, above, n.91.

[95] *Matthey v Curling*, above, n.92.

indeed (as has been suggested) "a singularly harsh one from the tenants' point of view".[96]

(4) **Prevention of personal occupation**

This group of cases deals with leases of residential premises let to a tenant who is then prevented from occupying them. In one case[97] it was held that a three-year lease of a flat in a seaside resort was not frustrated when, during the First World War, the tenant, who was an enemy national, was prohibited from occupying it by an Order made under the Aliens Restriction Act 1914. One reason for the decision, which would no longer be regarded as satisfactory, was that the Order did not deprive him of his leasehold interest; but the other, which still has force, is that the tenant's "personal residence" was not "the foundation of the contract"[98] since the lease envisaged the possibility that he might (with the landlord's consent) sublet the premises. Similar reasoning was used in a California case[99] in which it was held that the lease of a hotel, which was intended to be used mainly for guests of Japanese origin, was not frustrated when, during the Second World War, government regulations excluded such persons from the area in which the hotel was situated.

11–021

In a contrasting New York case,[1] indeed, a lease of office premises, in which the tenant personally carried on his brokerage business, was held to have been discharged when the tenant was conscripted for military service; hence the landlord was not entitled to damages for the loss which he had suffered in consequence of having had to relet the premises at a rent lower than that reserved by the lease. One can understand that courts might be more inclined, in time of war, to grant such relief to tenants who had been conscripted to serve their country, than to those who had, or might be thought to have, enemy associations. But it seems unlikely that the New York case would be followed in England, where the courts would probably regard the hardship to a tenant as a matter to be dealt with by special war-time legislation.[2]

In England it has been held that even the death of a tenant of residential premises does not relieve his estate from liability for rent.[3]

(5) **Legislative restriction of use of business premises**

A group of American cases concerns the effect on leases of business premises of supervening legislative prohibitions of, or restrictions on, business activity of the kind specified in the lease. It has long been recognised in

11–022

---

[96] *National Carriers* case [1981] A.C. 675 at 715.

[97] *London & Northern Estates Co v Schlesinger* [1916] 1 K.B. 20.

[98] *ibid.* at 23.

[99] *Brown v Oshiro*, 156 P. 2d 976 (1945), above, para.7–022.

[1] *State Realty v Greenfield*, 181 N.Y.S. 511 (1920).

[2] *cf.* n.91, above.

[3] *Youngmin v Heath* [1974] 1 W.L.R. 135.

the United States that the doctrine of discharge can apply to leases of land[4]; and the question whether such supervening legislation actually was a ground of discharge has arisen there in two lines of cases which have been discussed in Ch.7: namely, the liquor prohibition cases[5] and the cases concerning the effect on leases of garage premises of the restrictions imposed during the Second World War on the trade in motorvehicles and accessories.[6] A reference back to that discussion shows that the requirements to be satisfied by the party claiming discharge were stringent ones: in particular, it had to be shown that the specified or mutually contemplated use of the premises was *wholly* prevented. Where this was established, as in some of the liquor prohibition cases,[7] the leases were held to have been discharged. In the present context, it is significant that the leases in these cases were relatively short,[8] so that there would be little force in argument that the doctrine of discharge should not apply to them because they were long-term speculations. A similar result was reached in a New York case,[9] where a lease of premises to be used "only as a tea-room" was discharged when such use of the premises was prohibited by order of the public health authority unless extensive structural repairs were undertaken.

(6) Other possible application of frustration to leases of land

11–023   There is support in a number of other jurisdictions for the view that the doctrine of frustration can apply to leases of land. In Scotland, it was held in the *Tay Salmon* case[10] that a lease of a salmon fishery for 19 seasons from 1916 was frustrated when, in 1926, the construction of a nearby bombing range prevented the tenant from using the fishery. There is also some Canadian authority for the view that leases can be frustrated[11]; and this view is further supported by a dictum in a case concerned with breach of contract that a "commercial lease" was not to be regarded "simply as a conveyance and not also a contract".[12] In some Canadian Provinces the

---

[4] See *Lloyd v Murphy*, 153 P. 2d 47 (1944); *Frazier v Collins*, 187 S.W. 2d 816 (1945). Even *Wood v Bartolino*, 146 P. 2d 883 (1944), though generally hostile to the application of the doctrine of discharge to leases of land, does not go so far as to say that it can never apply to them.

[5] Above, paras 7–023 to 7–024.

[6] Above, para.7–020.

[7] *Industrial Development and Land Co v Goldschmidt*, 206 P. 134 (1922); *Doherty v Monroe Eckstein Brewing Co*, 191 N.Y.S. 59 (1929).

[8] In the two cases cited in the previous note the leases were for respectively five and 10 years.

[9] *140 West 34th Street Corp v Davis*, 85 N.Y.S. 957 (1936).

[10] *Tay Salmon Fisheries Co v Speedie*, 1929 S.C. 593; *cf.* in South Africa, *Benjamin v Myers*, 1946 C.P.D. 655, where, however, the alleged frustration was self-induced: below, para.14–014.

[11] *Cooke v Moore* [1935] 1 W.W.R. 374, affirmed [1935] 3 W.W.R. 256 (but also explicable on the ground of the tenant's breach).

[12] *Highway Properties Ltd v Kelly, Douglas & Co Ltd* (1971) 17 D.L.R. (3d) 710 at 721, cited with approval in the *National Carriers* case [1981] A.C. 675 at 696; *cf: ibid.* at 690, 703, 716.

matter is dealt with by legislation which applies the doctrine to residential leases.[13] In Australia there is support both for and against the view that the doctrine of frustration can apply to leases of land.[14]

In England, there is no actual decision in which a lease of land was held to have been frustrated, but the speeches in the *National Carriers* case, and a number of earlier dicta there cited with approval, do give some indication of the types of cases in which such a result would be reached. The first is that of a short lease for a particular purpose, *e.g.* where a holiday cottage was rented for one month. If the cottage were, without the fault of either party, to be destroyed or so seriously damaged as to be unavailable for use for the month in question, it would be appropriate to apply the doctrine of frustration (unless, of course, that event was covered by an express term of the contract).[15] The same possibility can arise in a commercial context, as in the example already given, in which a demise charter of an oil tanker was coupled with a lease of a shore installation: it has been suggested that an explosion which destroyed both the ship and the shore installation would frustrate the lease of the installation no less than the charterparty.[16] Another analogous situation in which the doctrine of frustration might well apply in England is that which arose in the Scottish *Tay Salmon*[17] case. That case is cited with evident approval by Lord Hailsham L.C. in the *National Carriers* case,[18] though Lord Roskill there describes it as being based on principles of Scots law which have no application in England.[19]

The second type of case in which the doctrine has been said to apply is that in which the supervening event has a particularly drastic effect. This would be the position where "some vast convulsion of nature swallowed up the property altogether, or buried it in the depths of the sea",[20] or where cliff-top property was "totally lost for occupation"[21] through the less dramatic process of coastal erosion; and where, in the case of a building lease "legislation were subsequently passed which permanently prohibited building in the area or dedicated it as an open space for ever".[22] It is assumed, in this example, that when the legislation is passed

---

[13] *e.g.* in Ontario: Landlord and Tenant Act, R.S.O. 1980 c.236, s.88 (the restriction to residential tenancies results from the definition in s.81(e) of "tenancy agreement"); and in British Columbia: Landlord and Tenant Act 1974, s.9(4) (the restriction to residential tenancies results from the definition of "tenancy agreement" in s.1).

[14] See *Firth v Halloran* (1926) 38 C.L.R. 261 at 269; *Minister of State for the Army v Dalziel* (1944) 68 C.L.R. 261 at 301; *Robertson v Wilson* (1978) 75 W.N. (N.S.W.) 503; *Thearle v Keely* (1979) 76 W.N. (N.S.W.) 48.

[15] *National Carriers* case [1981] A.C. 675 at 691, 714.

[16] *ibid.* at 691, 701, 714; above, para.11–004.

[17] 1929 S.C. 593, above, n.10.

[18] [1981] A.C. 675 at 691.

[19] *ibid.* at 715–716.

[20] *Cricklewood* case [1945] A.C. 221 at 229.

[21] *National Carriers* case [1981] A.C. 675 at 701; *cf.* at 691.

[22] *Cricklewood* case [1945] A.C. 221 at 229; *cf.* at 240.

it can reasonably be regarded as likely to remain in force for the rest of the term of the lease, or at least for the major part of that time.[23]

V. AGREEMENTS FOR LEASES

11–024   Even before the *National Carriers* case recognised the applicability of the doctrine of frustration to executed leases of land, it was accepted that an agreement for such a lease could be frustrated. The leading authority was the *Denny Mott* case,[24] where a contract for the supply of timber provided that "to enable the aforesaid trading agreement to be carried out" the buyer should let a timber yard to the seller "during the period of the aforesaid trading agreement". When trading in timber was prohibited by a government Order made during the Second World War, it was held that the agreement for the lease of the yard (and hence an option to purchase contained in that agreement) had likewise been discharged. The case came before the House of Lords by way of appeal from Scotland; but no distinction was drawn in the speeches between English and Scots law, and the decision is regarded as authoritative in England no less than in Scotland.[25] It is interesting, in the present context, to note that the agreement specified no precise term for the proposed lease. This was expressed to be "for the period of the aforesaid trading agreement" and that agreement was one of indefinite duration. It specified a commencement date in 1929, but no expiry date: it merely provided for termination by notice, the periods of notice being one year if given by the seller and three years if given by the buyer. It followed that the agreement could not be regarded as the sort of long-term speculation for a fixed period to which the doctrine of frustration ought not to apply.

In the later *Rom Securities* case,[26] the claimant had entered into an agreement with the defendant for the development of a property belonging to the defendant. The agreement provided that plans for the development were to be prepared by the claimant and to be lodged with the planning authority; that completion of the development was to take place within two-and-a-half years; that the claimant was to lend £20,000 to the defendant for the period taken by the development (but for at least two years); and that the defendant was to grant a lease of the premises to the claimant for 999 years at a rent of £5,000 per annum, subject to review. Planning permission was unexpectedly refused and it was held that the claimant was entitled to the return of the money lent, while the defendant was not entitled to specific performance of the agreement to grant the lease or to arrears of rent. Goff J. is reported (rather puzzlingly) to have said that the case was "not frustration but supervening events"[27]; and he

---

[23] See above, para.11–011, at n.61 and above, para.11–015, at n.73.

[24] *Denny, Mott & Dickson v James B Fraser & Co Ltd* [1944] A.C. 265; above, para.8–028; *cf. Re Dennis Commercial Properties Ltd.* (1969) 7 D.L.R. (3d) 214.

[25] *National Carriers* case [1981] A.C. 675 at 704.

[26] *Rom Securities Ltd v Rogers (Holdings) Ltd* (1967) 205 E.G. 427.

[27] *ibid.* at 428.

based his decision on the ground that, in order to give business efficacy to the agreement, a term must be implied into it that it was to come to an end if planning permission was not obtained, at least within a reasonable time. In the *National Carriers* case, it was pointed out that this reliance on the concept of an implied term did not differ significantly from Blackburn J.'s reasoning in *Taylor v Caldwell*,[28] and that the *Rom Securities* case was therefore to be regarded as one of frustration.[29] This view in turn gives rise to the difficulty of regarding such a very long-term transaction as an agreement for a 999-year lease as discharged by frustration on the occurrence of what might seem to be no more than a temporary obstacle. One possible explanation of this aspect of the case is that the *agreement* for the lease was to be performed by the execution of the lease and was therefore not in itself a long-term transaction. The difficulty with this explanation is that even the agreement gives rise to an equitable interest the duration of which is determined by the agreed term of the prospective lease. An alternative, and preferable, explanation is that the contract provided for the development to take place within a short period of two-and-a-half years, at or near the beginning of the proposed lease, and that the loan to be made by the claimant was also evidently regarded as a short-term one, covering roughly the same period. Thus immediate, or at least early, redevelopment was an essential feature of the bargain, and frustration followed when such development was prevented.

The fact that the doctrine of frustration could apply to agreements for leases was a significant factor in the evolution of this branch of the law, for it helped to rebut two of the arguments (considered in paras 11–004 and 11–005, above) which had been advanced against the applicability of the doctrine to leases of land. The first such argument was that a lease conferred an interest in the land; but this is true also of an agreement for a lease which, being normally enforceable by an order of specific performance, confers an equitable interest in the land on the lessee.[30] For the present purpose, no significance can be attached to the difference between this equitable interest and the legal estate conferred on the tenant by an executed lease. This point is implicitly recognised in an Australian case in which the doctrine of frustration was held to be applicable to an agreement for a lease precisely because the agreement was *not* specifically enforceable (and so conferred no equitable interest) since the landlord had to render personal services under it.[31] But there is no trace of such a restriction in English law on the applicability of the doctrine of frustration to agreements for leases. The second argument was that risk passed to the tenant on execution of the lease, on the analogy of the rule that risk under a contract for the sale of land passed when the contract was made. Since that rule is in turn based on the transfer, by virtue of the contract, of an equitable interest to the purchaser, the analogy would, if applied to an agreement for a lease, suggest that risk

11–025

---

[28] [1981] A.C. 675 at 704.
[29] *ibid.* at 705 and see at 690, 694, 715.
[30] *Walsh v Lansdale* (1882) 21 Ch. D. 9; *National Carriers* case, above, n.28, at 704.
[31] *Lobb v Vasey Housing Auxiliary War Widows Guild* [1963] V.R. 239.

under it should pass as soon as the agreement was made; but the rule that such agreements can be frustrated is general in scope and therefore inconsistent with that view. It is true that the cases on frustration of agreements for leases do not directly deal with risk of *loss* (in the sense of physical impairment of the subject-matter). But there seems to be no reason to suppose that an agreement for a lease cannot be frustrated by such loss, just as it can be frustrated by legal restrictions affecting the use of the subject-matter.

VI. DISCHARGE OF PARTICULAR COVENANTS IN LEASES

11–026   For reasons stated earlier in this chapter,[32] supervening events may not frustrate the lease as a whole; but those events may nevertheless provide an excuse for not performing a particular obligation arising under the lease. One group of cases concerns supervening illegality in the performance of a particular covenant in the lease, *e.g.* in the *Cricklewood* case performance of the tenant's covenant to build would have been excused for the duration of the war-time prohibition on building,[33] even if the lease had not contained an "abeyance clause"[34] entitling him to postpone the building operations. Other cases in which the performance of particular covenants in leases had become illegal (while the leases as a whole had not) are discussed in Ch.8.[35] The same result may follow in cases of supervening impossibility. This was the position in *Baily v De Crespigny*,[36] where a landlord covenanted that neither he nor his assigns would permit building on a paddock adjoining the land let. The paddock was compulsorily acquired by a railway company, which built a station on it. It was held that the landlord was not liable in damages for breach of his covenant, first because on the true construction of the covenant "assigns" did not include assigns by compulsion of law, and secondly because it was impossible for him to secure performance of the covenant.[37]

---

[32] Above, paras 11–007 to 11–016.

[33] *cf. John Lewis Properties v Viscount Chelsea* [1993] 2 E.G.L.R. 77, above, paras 8–046, 9–009; the excuse in such a case would be no more than temporary if the prohibition were lifted well before the end of the lease and if, when it was imposed, reasonable persons would have thought that it would probably be so lifted.

[34] [1945] A.C. 221 at 233.

[35] Above, paras 8–047 to 8–048.

[36] (1869) L.R. 4 Q.B. 180.

[37] The justice of the decision is questionable: see below, paras 15–007, 15–022.

CHAPTER 12

CONTRACTUAL PROVISIONS FOR SUPERVENING EVENTS

Two main themes or policies underlie the law relating to the discharge of contracts by supervening events. The first is that the purpose of the doctrine of discharge is to find a satisfactory way of allocating the loss caused by such events. The second is that the doctrine should not be so widely applied as to undermine the sanctity of contract and that it should therefore be applied only where the change brought about by the supervening event is a fundamental one. Both these policies are, however, subject to the general principle of freedom of contract, which in the present context can operate in two ways. First, it can exclude the doctrine of discharge where the parties have contracted on terms which indicate that the contract is to remain in being in spite of the occurrence of an event which would, but for such a provision, have discharged it. Secondly, it can enable the parties to provide for discharge, or for some other form of relief, on the occurrence of an event which, but for the provision, would have had no effect on their legal rights and duties because the change of circumstances brought about by the event was not sufficiently serious or fundamental to discharge the contract under the general common law doctrine. Contractual provisions for supervening events may therefore, on the one hand, exclude frustration and, on the other, provide relief for non-frustrating events.

I. PROVISIONS EXCLUDING FRUSTRATION

(1) In general

It cannot be seriously doubted that contracting parties can by express contractual provision reverse or modify the allocation of losses which would (but for such provision) result from the doctrine of discharge. In *Taylor v Caldwell*,[1] for example, the parties could no doubt have validly provided that, in the event of the destruction of the Hall, the defendants should nevertheless compensate the hirers for their loss of profits, or indeed that

12-001

12-002

---

[1] (1863) 3 B. & S. 826; above, para.2–024.

all the obligations of both parties should have remained in force. As Lord Simon has said: "There can be no discharge by supervening impossibility if the express terms of the contract bind the parties to performance, notwithstanding that the supervening event may occur."[2] The position is the same in the United States: the doctrine of discharge is excluded, according to the Restatement, when "a contrary intention has been manifested"[3]; according to the Restatement 2d, when "the language or the circumstances indicate the contrary"[4]; and according to the Uniform Commercial Code, when "a seller may have assumed a greater obligation".[5]

These American statements of the principle refer generally to contrary indication; in this respect, they are somewhat broader than Lord Simon's statement, which refers only to *express* terms as excluding the doctrine of discharge. There is, however, no doubt that the broader formulation is accepted in England no less than in the United States, for English authorities support the view that contractual provisions which have the effect of excluding frustration need not refer in so many words to the supervening event. An intention that the risk of loss caused by at least certain kinds of supervening event are to be borne by one party rather than the other may, even after the rejection of the general doctrine of absolute contracts,[6] be inferred from the fact that an undertaking is given in unconditional and absolute terms when it could easily have been (and would normally be expected to have been) subjected to qualifications. It is, for example, no defence to a claim for demurrage under a charterparty or a bill of lading that loading was delayed by bad weather or by a strike[7] unless the contract imposing the liability is expressly subject to exceptions covering delays so caused. In one case of this kind it was said that the contract created "an absolute obligation to have the goods unloaded within the specified time, whatever the circumstances may be, unless the shipowner, or those for whom he is responsible, are in fault"; and that "the merchant takes the risk".[8] An express term can also exclude frustration, even though it does not precisely cover the supervening event,

---

[2] *Joseph Constantine SS Line Ltd v Imperial Smelting Co Ltd* [1942] A.C. 154 at 163; *cf. Kuwait Supply Co v Oyster Marine Management (The Safeer)* [1994] 1 Lloyd's Rep. 637; *Vermeer v Derby CC* [2003] EWHC 2708 at [66]; for an apparently contrary dictum in *WJ Tatem Ltd v Gamboa* [1939] 1 K.B. 132 at 138 (qualified at 139), see below, para.16–014.

[3] § 457.

[4] § 281.

[5] s.2–615. No similar words are contained in UCC, s.2A–405 (which deals with cases in which performance of a chattel lease is excused by circumstances similar to those dealt with, in cases of sale, by s.2–615). Presumably the words were regarded as unnecessary in s.2A–405 by virtue of the general rule that provisions of the Code can be varied by agreement: see s.1–302(a) and (c) in States which have adopted the (2001) revised version of Art.1 (above, para.3–017, n.57) and s.1–102(3) and (4) in States which have not adopted this version.

[6] Above, para.2–025.

[7] *Thiis v Byers* (1876) 1 Q.B.D. 244; *Budgett & Co v Binnington & Co* [1891] 1 Q.B. 35.

[8] *ibid.* at 41.

if it shows that the parties had contemplated the event and had allocated the risk of its occurrence.[9]

An inference of such risk-taking may also be drawn from the nature of the transaction as a whole. This possibility is illustrated by the *Larrinaga* case,[10] which arose out of a contract for the carriage of six cargoes of phosphates. The contract had been made in 1913, but performance was not to begin until five years later: the cargoes were to be shipped at specified dates between March 1918 and November 1920. So far as it related to shipments to be made during the First World War, the contract was abandoned by mutual consent; and the carriers argued that, so far as the contract related to the remaining cargoes, it had been discharged because of the radical change in shipping conditions which had taken place between the time when the contract was made and the time when performance was demanded. The House of Lords rejected the argument on the ground that a contract of this kind, not to be performed for many years, was an essentially speculative one, since each party to such a long-term contract had consciously taken the risk that the conditions in which performance would have to be rendered might alter. Lord Sumner described such forward contracts as a form of insurance, intended to throw the risk of changes of circumstances on whichever party might be adversely affected by them.

An agreement to exclude frustration may also be inferred from other characteristics of a transaction than its purpose of allocating commercial risks. In *The Maira (No 2)*[11] agents had undertaken to manage a ship which was later lost. At first sight, it might be thought that the ship was the subject-matter of the contract, or at least a thing, the continued existence of which was essential to the performance of the contract; and that the loss of the ship was therefore a frustrating event. Such an argument would certainly have succeeded if the contract had been one to paint or to repair the ship. But it was held that the management contract had not been frustrated since the parties could hardly have intended "that the managers should be entitled to wash their hands of all duties concerning the vessel as soon as [she] was lost"[12]: they would be expected to attend to such matters as the repatriation of the crew and the settlement of claims arising out of the loss. This reasoning may, however, not entirely exclude the doctrine of frustration in a case of this kind. If the management contract had been for a fixed term (say five years) without any provision for determination by notice, it would at least be arguable that it would have been frustrated by loss of the ship, not indeed immediately on the occurrence of that loss, but after the "clearing up" operations referred to above had been accomplished. If the parties can by implied agreement wholly exclude discharge, as in the *Larrinaga* case, there seems to be no

---

[9] *Bangladesh Export Import Co Ltd v Sucden Kerry SA* [1995] 2 Lloyd's Rep. 1.

[10] *Larrinaga & Co v Société Franco-Américaine des Phosphates de Medulla* (1923) 92 L.J.K.B. 455.

[11] *Glafki Shipping Co SA v Pinios Shipping Co No 1 (The Maira) (No 2)* [1985] 1 Lloyd's Rep. 300, affirmed on other grounds [1986] 2 Lloyd's Rep. 12.

[12] [1985] 1 Lloyd's Rep. 300 at 311.

reason of principle why they should not by such an agreement equally defer the time of discharge. An implied agreement of this kind would provide an intermediate solution between keeping the contract in being and discharging it automatically (which is the normal effect of frustration[13]): the implied agreement would have the effect of varying the rights and duties of the parties in the light of the supervening event.

This is also true of the terms implied by legislation into package travel contracts. Under the Regulations which govern such contracts,[14] there is an implied term that, if the consumer is prevented from proceeding with the package (*e.g.* by illness) he may transfer his booking to another person[15]; and a further implied term that, if the other party to the contract becomes aware that he will be unable to procure a significant proportion of the services to be provided under the contract, he must make suitable alternative arrangements at no extra cost to the consumer.[16]

12–004   Such variations of the contract are more commonly achieved by *express* provisions for the supervening event. Indeed, it is one of the principal attractions of such terms that they may provide a more sophisticated allocation of losses than that which is available under the less flexible doctrine of discharge. This was particularly true in English law before the courts were given the statutory powers of adjustment, consequent on frustration, to be discussed in Ch.15.[17] In the coronation cases,[18] for example, the only courses open to the courts were to hold the contracts either fully binding[19] or wholly discharged.[20] The parties by express contractual terms were able to provide for a variety of intermediate solutions even where (but for such express terms) the contract would have been frustrated. They could, for example, provide that the viewing facilities were to be available either on the originally specified day or (if the processions should be postponed) on such later day as they should pass the premises; or that the party who had paid for the use of the facilities should have his money back in full, or less a percentage (presumably to cover the other party's expenses) if the procession should not pass the premises. In one case,[21] such clauses were held to have excluded the doctrine of discharge and this result was preferable to the "all or nothing" solutions provided by that doctrine.[22] The same is true of

---

[13] Below, para.15–002.

[14] Package Travel, Package Holidays and Package Tours Regulations 1992 (SI 1992/3288), giving effect to EEC Council Directive 90/314.

[15] SI 1992/3288, para.10(1); above, para.4–025.

[16] SI 1992/3288, para.14(1).

[17] Below, paras 15–050 15–060, 15–071 to 15–073.

[18] Above, paras 7–006 to 7–014.

[19] *e.g. Herne Bay Steamboat Co v Hutton* [1903] 2 K.B. 683.

[20] *e.g. Krell v Henry* [1903] 2 K.B. 740.

[21] *Victoria Seats Agency v Paget* (1902) 19 T.L.R. 16.

[22] For the exclusion of frustration by an express contractual provision allowing an alternative method of performance on the occurrence of an event which could, but for such a provision, have frustrated the contract, see also *Kuwait Supply Co v Oyster Marine Management Inc (The Safeer)* [1994] 1 Lloyds Rep. 637 at 642.

another of the coronation cases[23] which was concerned with a contract for the supply of refreshments by a caterer to the defendant on board a steamer on the day of the naval review which was to form part of the celebrations.[24] The contract provided for an advance payment of £300 to be made to the caterer, but that "in the event of cancellation of the review before any expense [was] incurred by the caterer" the defendant was to be under "no liability". This was interpreted to mean that the defendant was liable for the expenses (of £20) which had been incurred by the caterer when the review was cancelled, but not for the full advance payment. But for the express provision of the contract, the court could not then have made any allowance in respect of the caterer's wasted expenses,[25] though by statute it could now do so where a payment of money had been made, or the contract contained a stipulation requiring it to be made, before the day of discharge to the party who had incurred the expenses.[26] An express contractual term has the advantage of being able to provide yet more flexible solutions, *e.g.* that if circumstances change in a way that is outside the control of a supplier of services, that supplier is to be paid a reduced remuneration (not related to expenses incurred by him) even though the services can no longer be rendered or are no longer of any use to the other party.[27]

The examples just considered illustrate the advantages and commercial convenience of contractual provisions for the effects of what would (but for such provisions) be a frustrating event; but it is also possible for such provisions to cause what may at first sight appear to be considerable hardship to one of the parties. In the Australian case of *Claude Neon Ltd v Hardie*[28] a 60-month "lease" of an illuminated sign on the "lessee's" premises provided that if the "lessee's" interest in the premises were "extinguished or transferred", the whole balance of the agreed "rental" should immediately become due. In the course of the 60 months, the premises were compulsorily acquired and demolished by a local authority. The "lessee" was held liable for the balance of the "rental" even though the supervening event had deprived him of a substantial part of the performance for which he had bargained. The express term of the contract had excluded the doctrine of discharge, and had substituted for it the parties' own risk-allocation, with which the court declined to interfere. Nor would the clause be invalid as a penalty, as it merely accelerated (and did not increase) the defendant's liability,[29] and perhaps also as the payment did not become due on breach.[30]

---

[23] *Elliott v Crutchley* [1903] 2 K.B. 477; [1906] A.C. 7.
[24] Above, para.7–006.
[25] *Civil Service Co-operation Society v General Steam Navigation Co* [1903] 2 K.B. 756.
[26] Law Reform (Frustrated Contracts) Act 1943, s.1(2), below, para.15–071.
[27] See *Tufton Associates Ltd v Dilmun Shipping* [1992] 1 Lloyd's Rep. 71.
[28] [1970] Qd. R. 93.
[29] See *Protector Loan Co v Grice* (1880) 5 Q.B.D. 529; *Wallingford v Mutual Society* (1880) 5 App. Cas. 685.
[30] See Treitel, *The Law of Contract* (11th ed.), pp.1004–1006.

(2) **Qualifications**

12–005   The possibility that express provisions for supervening events may cause hardship of the kind illustrated by the *Claude Neon* case has led the courts to restrict the operation of such provisions by a process of narrow construction. Further restrictions are based on considerations of public policy which apply in certain cases of supervening illegality. It will also be necessary to consider the effect on such provisions of legislation which restricts the validity of exemption clauses and other standard terms.

(a) *Rules of construction*

12–006   The relevant cases can be subdivided into two groups. The first is concerned with the definition of the event (specified in the clause) which would (but for that clause) have frustrated the contract. The second relates to the effect or effects which that event would, but for the clause, have had on the obligations of the parties.

(i) **Narrow construction of words defining the event**

12–007   Where a contract is capable of being frustrated by one of two or more events, a contractual provision dealing with the effects of only one of them will obviously not preclude frustration by the other or others.[31] The contract in *Krell v Henry*[32] would, for example, not have been frustrated if it had contained provisions (of the kind described above[33]) dealing with the effects on the rights and duties of the parties of the cancellation of the processions; but it could still have been frustrated if the house at 56A Pall Mall, had been destroyed by fire. Such a conclusion would merely restrict the operation of the clause in question to the literal meaning of the words of the contract.

12–008   The courts have, however, gone further in restricting the operation of such clauses by adopting a process of narrow construction of words which, if taken literally, would be wide enough to cover the event which has happened. In a number of cases, such words have been held not to cover that event, on the ground that it was not one which could at the time of contracting have been within the contemplation of the parties. That event is then capable of frustrating the contract. The leading case is *Metropolitan Water Board v Dick Kerr & Co*,[34] where a contract was made in July 1914 for the construction of a reservoir in six years. The contract provided that, in the event of delays "however occasioned", the contractors were to be given an extension of time. In February 1916, the contractors were required by a Government Order (made under war-time emergency legislation) to stop the work and to sell their construction plant. It was held that the contract was frustrated (for reasons which have been

---

[31] *Intertradex SA v Lesieur Torteaux SARL* [1978] 2 Lloyd's Rep. 509 at 515.

[32] [1903] 2 K.B. 740, above, para.7–010.

[33] Above, para.12–004, n.21.

[34] [1918] A.C. 119; *cf. C Czarnikow Ltd v Centrala Handlu Zagranicznego "Rolimpex"* [1979] A.C. 351; *BTP Tioxide Ltd v Pioneer Shipping Ltd (The Nema)* [1980] Q.B. 547 at 574, affirmed [1982] A.C. 724.

discussed in Ch.5[35]) in spite of the fact that the events which had happened were literally within the clause which provided for delays. That clause was intended to apply only to events giving rise to relatively short delays, caused by obstacles of a kind normally to be expected, such as labour shortages bad weather or failure of supplies. It, therefore, did not "cover the case in which the interruption is of such a character and duration that it vitally and fundamentally changes the conditions of the contract, and could not possibly have been in the contemplation of the parties when it was made".[36] Similarly, where a contract for the sale of flats to be built by the vendor gave him the right to rescind in case of "any unforeseen circumstances beyond the vendor's control ... whereby the vendor becomes unable to sell" it was held that the contract was nevertheless frustrated by a landslip which obliterated the work already done and made further progress with the work impossible, so that the vendor's building permit lapsed.[37] The clause was not intended to apply to such catastrophic events, even though they might literally be within its terms.

The cases illustrate many other applications of this principle. In *The Penelope*,[38] a charterparty which contained an express "strike" clause was nevertheless held to have been discharged by the *general* strike of 1926. In the *Fibrosa*[39] case, a clause which provided for an extension of time to be granted to the sellers in case of delay "by any cause ... including war" did not exclude frustration: it covered only "a minor delay as distinguished from a prolonged and indefinite interruption of contractual performance which the present war[40] manifestly and inevitably brings about".[41] On similar reasoning, it was held in *The Playa Larga*[42] that a *force majeure* clause giving a seller of sugar the right to extend the time for delivery, and the buyer the right to cancel after a specified delay, did not preclude frustration by reason of the total breakdown of diplomatic and commercial relations between the buyer's and the seller's countries. The clause was not intended to deal with events which struck "at the contract as a whole and made further performance of it unthinkable".[43] Likewise, a term which provided for the suspension of a contract of sale on the occurrence of specified obstacles to performance, but did not specify the duration of the suspension, has been construed so as not to

---

[35] Above, para.5–042.

[36] [1919] A.C. 119 at 126; *cf.* dicta in *Kuwait Supply Co v Oyster Marine Management Inc (The Safeer)* [1994] 1 Lloyd's Rep. 637 at 643–644 (where the actual decision was that the clause in question did cover the events which have happened and so excluded frustration).

[37] *Wong Lai Yin v Chinachem Investment Co* (1979) 13 Build. L.R. 81.

[38] [1928] p.180, approved, with some reservations in *BTP Tioxide Ltd v Pioneer Shipping Ltd (The Nema)* [1982] A.C. 724 at 754.

[39] *Fibrosa Spolka Akcyjna v Fairbairn, Lawson, Combe Barbour Ltd* [1943] A.C. 32.

[40] *i.e.* the Second World War.

[41] *ibid.* at 40; *cf. Veithardt & Hall Ltd v Rylands Bros Ltd* (1917) 116 L.T. 32.

[42] *Empresa Exportadora De Azucar v Industria Azucarera Nacional SA (The Playa Larga)* [1983] 2 Lloyd's Rep. 171.

[43] *ibid.* at 189.

apply (and hence not to exclude frustration) where the obstacles lasted for so long "as to make performance of the contract, if resumed a different contract from that interrupted".[44] An even clearer case is *BP Exploration (Libya) Ltd v Hunt*,[45] where a contract for the exploitation of an oilfield provided for advance payments to be made by one party to the other and for those payments to be recouped by the payor out of, *inter alia*, the oil that was to be produced. A provision in the contract that the payee was not to be personally liable to repay the advances was held not to exclude the payee's liability to make such repayments when the contract was frustrated on the expropriation of the oilfield. The provision was intended to deal with the risk that oil might not be found and not with the possibility of expropriation and consequent frustration of the contract.

12–009   The *Fibrosa* case[46] also illustrates the judicial tendency to construe "war" clauses so as not to refer to wars involving the countries to which the contracting parties belong.[47] Even where a clause did expressly refer to such a war, it was interpreted not to cover the war which actually took place. In the *Pacific Phosphate* case[48] a contract was made in 1913 to provide 12 ships for the carriage of phosphates in the years 1914 to 1918. When "the whole shipping industry had been dislocated"[49] by the First World War, it was held that the contract was frustrated in spite of the fact that it provided for suspension of performance "in the event of a war in which Great Britain is involved and which is likely to affect the steamers or their cargoes". The ground for this aspect of the decision was that the parties "never contemplated such a war as actually happened or its consequences".[50] They were presumably thinking of relatively short or localised conflicts, such as the Crimean or Boer Wars.

A similar principle of construction has been applied in employment cases. Thus it has been held that a contractual provision for the effects on the contract of illness or injury suffered by the employee did not preclude frustration where he suffered a serious heart-attack giving rise to permanent disability: "as a matter of construction" it was held that the provision did not "cover an injury which totally disabled him from performing his work".[51] Similarly a provision in an apprenticeship contract for suspension or termination on account of the misconduct of the apprentice did not preclude frustration where the apprentice was sentenced to a period of Borstal training on his conviction of a crime of violence: the contractual provision was intended to apply to misconduct related to the apprentice's

---

[44] *Acetylene Co of GB v Canada Carbide Co* (1922) 8 Ll.L. Rep. 456 at 460.

[45] [1983] 2 A.C. 352, more fully discussed below, paras 15–062 to 15–064.

[46] Above, n.39.

[47] See *Re Badische Co* [1921] 2 Ch. 221; *cf. Bolckow Vaughan & Co Ltd v Compania Minera de Sierra Minera* (1916) 33 T.L.R. 111; *Avery v Bowden* (1856) 6 E. & B. 953.

[48] *Pacific Phosphate Co Ltd v Empire Transport Co Ltd* (1920) 36 T.L.R. 750.

[49] *ibid.* at 751; *cf. Naylor Benzon & Co Ltd v Hirsch* (1917) 33 T.L.R. 432; *Scottish Navigation Co Ltd v Souter & Co* [1917] 1 K.B. 222.

[50] (1920) 36 T.L.R. 750 at 751.

[51] *Notcutt v Universal Equipment Co (London) Ltd* [1986] 1 W.L.R. 641 at 647.

work and not to the "really substantial disruption"[52] which had here taken place.

The process of narrow construction with which we are here concerned is one by which a clause which appears at first sight to provide for an event which (but for the clause) would frustrate the contract is held to apply only to events of a *less* seriously disruptive kind than that which has occurred. It follows that the clause does not preclude frustration, so that (if the other requirements of the doctrine of frustration are satisfied) both parties will be discharged. The process of narrow construction may also (as we shall see) be applied to clauses which make provision for events which would *not* (but for the clause) frustrate the contract. In cases of this kind, the process of narrow construction sometimes has the opposite effect to that just described. This will be the position where the clause is construed to apply only to events of a *more* seriously disruptive kind than those which have occurred.[53] The contract will then remain in force and neither party will be able to rely on the clause.[54]

(ii) Incomplete provision for the event

Frustration has the effect of discharging all the contractual obligations of both parties, but a contractual provision for a potentially frustrating event may deal with the effects of that event on only some of those obligations. Such a provision does not preclude the possibility that the *event* to which it refers may nevertheless discharge *obligations* to which it does not refer. Since the provision in question will usually be in the nature of an exception inserted for the benefit of one party (or, in the case of a mutual exception, for the benefit of both) there may seem to be little practical difference between saying that that party is excused by the express provision and saying that he is discharged under the doctrine of frustration. But the point may be significant in view of the fact that the Law Reform (Frustrated Contracts) Act 1943 probably applies only to cases of discharge under the doctrine of frustration.[55] Sometimes the difficulty can be avoided by applying the process of narrow construction described above, so as to restrict the express provision to events which would *not* (apart from the clause) discharge the contract. But the principle seems to go further than this and to envisage the discharge by frustration of the party who is not protected by an express provision for an event which *does* fall within the clause, precisely because that provision in terms refers only to the obligation of the other party. It seems that the latter party is then, in turn, so discharged on the theory that frustration cannot be one-sided but must automatically discharge both parties by operation of law.[56] Whether this view is correct depends on the interpretation of two difficult leading cases.

It is convenient to begin the discussion with *Bank Line Ltd v Arthur Capel*

12–010

---

[52] *FC Shepherd & Co Ltd v Jerrom* [1987] Q.B. 301 at 329; above, para.5–056.

[53] *e.g.* below, para.12–023.

[54] *e.g. Wycombe Borough Electric Light & Power Co Ltd v Chipping Wycombe Corp* (1917) 33 T.L.R. 489.

[55] Below, paras 12–019 to 12–020.

[56] Below, para.15–002.

& Co,[57] where a time charter was held to have been frustrated by the requisitioning of the ship in circumstances which have been described in Ch.5.[58] The further point to be discussed here is that the charterers argued that frustration was excluded by two clauses giving them the option to cancel the charter (i) if the ship was not delivered by April 30, 1915—as she was not; and (ii) if she was "commandeered by Government during this charter"—and she was "commandeered" (*i.e.* requisitioned), though whether this occurred "during" the charter is perhaps open to question, since it is arguable that (no date being fixed for delivery and no delivery ever having taken place) the requisition did *not* take place during the currency of the charterparty. Reliance was also placed on an exception for loss or damage due to restraint of princes. The House of Lords held that none of these provisions precluded the application of the doctrine of frustration. Lord Sumner said that a contract could not be frustrated by a contingency for which it made "full and complete"[59] provision; but he added: "A contingency may be provided for, but not in such terms as to show that the provision is meant to be all the provision for it. A contingency may be provided for but in such a way as to show that it is provided for only for the purpose of dealing with one of its effects and not with all."[60]

12–011   One possible interpretation of this passage is that the clauses referred to in para.12–010, above did not preclude frustration because the contingencies to which they referred would not necessarily be so serious as to frustrate the contract and that the clauses were to be construed as referring to such non-frustrating delays. This view is supported by Lord Sumner's statement that the second of the two cancelling clauses entitled the charterer to cancel forthwith, on the ship's being commandeered, without waiting to see whether the delay was sufficiently serious to frustrate the contract.[61] Lords Finlay and Haldane (who dissented on the issue whether the delay was sufficiently serious to frustrate the contract) seem to have taken the same view of the clause in question. On this interpretation, this aspect of the *Bank Line* case merely illustrates the process of narrow construction applied in cases such as the *Metropolitan Water Board* case.[62]

But it is submitted that this is not the most obvious meaning of the passage quoted in para.12–010, above from Lord Sumner's speech: the passage does not seem to be concerned with the *definition* of the contingency (*i.e.* with the question whether the cancelling clause covered *any* delays or only those not serious enough to qualify as frustrating delays)

---

[57] [1919] A.C. 435; and see *Hirji Mulji v Cheong Yue SS Co Ltd* [1926] A.C. 497 (where the report does not state the terms of the cancellation clause).
[58] Above, paras 5–046 to 5–047.
[59] [1919] A.C. 435 at 455.
[60] *ibid.* at 456.
[61] *ibid.*
[62] [1918] A.C. 119, above, para.12–008, at n.60; *cf. Kodros Shipping Corp of Monrovia v Empresa Cubana de Fletes of Havana (The Evia) (No 2)* [1982] 1 Lloyd's Rep. 334, affirmed [1983] 1 A.C. 736 at 767.

but with the *effects* of the contingency on the legal rights and duties of the parties. This interpretation seems also to be the most consistent with Lord Sumner's reason for concluding that the restraint of princes exception did not preclude frustration: "relief [under the exception] from liability to pay damages or hire and complete discharge from further obligation to perform the contract are different things."[63] His reasoning in relation to the first of the two cancelling clauses is similar. That clause cannot mean that the owner "should remain indefinitely at the charterers' mercy".[64] In other words, the clause deals with the effect of delay (whether frustrating or not) on the liability of the charterer but not with its effect on the liability of the owner. Lord Wrenbury makes a similar point in relation to both the cancelling clauses. There is, in his view, no inconsistency between these clauses (which entitle *the charterer* to cancel) and "an implied term which entitles *either* party to treat the contract at an end"[65] in the event of a sufficiently serious delay. The preferable reason why frustration was not excluded in the *Bank Line* case by the cancellation clauses is therefore, not that those clauses were narrowly construed, so as not to refer to the serious interruption with performance which occurred. It is rather that those clauses did not make "full and complete" provision for that interruption but provided only for some of its possible legal consequences.

That is also, it is submitted, the preferable explanation for the decision in *Jackson v Union Marine Insurance Co,*[66] where a voyage charterparty for the carriage of rails from Newport to San Francisco required the ship to proceed to Newport with all possible dispatch (dangers and accidents of navigation excepted). On her voyage to Newport the ship ran aground in circumstances falling within the exception, and she was not again ready for service for eight months. For reasons discussed in Ch.5, this temporary unavailability of the ship was held to give rise to a sufficiently serious delay to frustrate the contract.[67] The point here to be considered is that frustration was not ruled out by the fact that the delay was caused by circumstances falling within the exception for dangers and accidents of navigation. One possible reason for this conclusion is that the words of the exception were narrowly construed, so as not to cover the long delay which had actually occurred.[68] But that is not the reason given by the court. Bramwell B. said that the words of the exception "excuse the shipowner but give him no right. The charterer has no cause of action but

12–012

---

[63] [1919] A.C. 435 at 456.

[64] *ibid.* at 457.

[65] *ibid.* at 462.

[66] (1874) L.R. 10 C.P. 125.

[67] Above, para.5–039.

[68] *Sir Lindsay Parkinson & Co Ltd v Commissioners of Works* [1949] 2 K.B. 632 at 655, referring to the *Metropolitan Water Board* case [1918] A.C. 119. But it is significant that there *Jackson v Union Marine Insurance Co,* is cited, not on the point of construction stated in the text above, but only for the proposition that the length of the delay was such as to frustrate the contract.

is released from the charter. When I say he is, I think both are".[69] Other passages in the judgment are, indeed, hard to reconcile with subsequently developed views of the nature and effect of the doctrine of frustration. Thus Bramwell B. refers to the "condition precedent" that the vessel is to arrive within a reasonable time and says that: "though non-performance of a condition may be excused, it does not take away the right to *rescind* from him for whose benefit the condition was introduced."[70] This "right to rescind" is here given to one party only; but a number of other statements in the judgment make it equally available to both. One such statement is that quoted above.[71] According to a second "the exception is an excuse for him who is to do the act . . . but does not operate to take away the right the other party would have had, if the non-performance had been a breach of contract, to retire from the agreement: *and if one party may, so may the other*".[72] And, according to a third, on failure of the condition precedent "the *contract is at an end* and the charterers are discharged".[73] The italicised phrases here indicate that the case is one of discharge under the doctrine of frustration, even though the distinction between such discharge and rescission for breach was not then as clearly recognised as it generally[74] is in later authorities.[75] Thus the contract was frustrated, even though the exception did make *some* provision for the very event which had happened, because that provision was not a complete provision for the event: it prevented the delay from constituting a breach (and so protected the shipowner from liability in damages) but it did not deal with the effect of the delay as a potentially frustrating event (and so did not rule out the possibility of frustration). The fact that the shipowner was not liable for the delay did not lead necessarily to the conclusion that the contract must remain in force, so as to entitle the shipowner to enforce it in spite of the delay.[76]

12–013   Similar reasoning explains *Blane Steamships v Minister of Transport*[77] where a demise charter gave the charterers an option to purchase the ship. Clause 8 of the contract provided that, if the ship became a constructive total loss, hire was to cease from the day of the casualty resulting in such loss. After such a casualty had occurred, the charterers purported to

---

[69] (1874) L.R. 10 C.P. 125 at 144. In *Modern Transport Co Ltd v Duneric SS Co* [1917] 1 K.B. 370, it is arguable that a "restraints of princes" clause did give the shipowner rights; but the basis of that decision was that the interference with performance was not sufficiently serious to frustrate the charterparty.

[70] (1874) L.R. 10 C.P. at 145 (italics supplied).

[71] Above, at n.69.

[72] (1874) L.R. 10 C.P. 125 at 145 (italics supplied).

[73] *ibid.* (italics supplied).

[74] The distinction is still occasionally blurred: *e.g.* in the passage in *Great Peace Shipping Ltd v Tsavliris (Salvage) International Ltd (The Great Peace)* [2002] EWCA Civ 1407; [2003] Q.B. 697; discussed in para.5–060, above.

[75] Below, para.15–005 above, paras 5–049, 5–050.

[76] The actual issue was whether the shipowner was entitled to recover under an insurance of freight; it was decided in his favour on the ground that, by reason of the delay, he had lost his right to enforce the charterparty.

[77] [1951] 2 K.B. 965.

exercise the option to purchase; but it was held that they were no longer entitled to do so as the contract had been frustrated. Clause 8 did not rule out frustration by constructive total loss: it merely fixed the date on which such a loss was to be deemed to have occurred and specified *one* of its legal consequences, namely its effect on the charterers' obligation to pay hire. As in the *Bank Line* case, the clause provided for *one* effect of the loss, and not for all; as in *Jackson v Union Marine Insurance Co Ltd*, the clause excused the charterers but gave them no rights.

The principle stated by Lord Sumner in the *Bank Line* case[78] (that a contingency may be provided for, but in such a way as to show that it is provided for only for the purpose of dealing with one of its effects and not with all) is thus supported by both earlier and later authority. The only case which may appear to call that principle into question is the *Tamplin* case,[79] where (for reasons discussed in Ch.5[80]) it was held by a majority of the House of Lords that a five-year time charter had not been frustrated by the requisitioning of the ship. The point to be considered here is that the charterparty contained an exception for (*inter alia*) restraint of princes; and this exception was relied on by Lord Parker (with whom Lord Buckmaster agreed) as excluding frustration. He said: "The parties have therefore expressly contracted that for the period during which, by reason of the restraint, the owners are unable to keep the ship at the disposition of the charterers the freight is to continue payable and the owners are to be free from liability."[81] This may suggest that the exception excluded frustration because it made "full and complete" provision for the event; but there are a number of reasons for doubting this interpretation. First, Lord Haldane (who dissented on his view of the facts, but not on the principles of law to be applied) regarded the exception as providing for "merely partial or temporary suspension of certain obligations"[82] and took the view that the events which had happened were not within it.[83] Secondly, the words of the exception seem to indicate that it was intended only to protect the owner; for, after setting out a list of perils, it is stated to apply to those events "even when occasioned by the ... default ... of the master or other servants of the shipowner".[84] These words would seem to reinforce the *prima facie* rule that exceptions in a charterparty, unless expressed to be mutual, are for the benefit only of the shipowner.[85] The purpose of the exception, then, was to protect the shipowner from liability in damages for failing to provide the services of the ship while she was under requisition; but no claim for such damages was made by the charterers, who were content to pay hire (even though the ship was not available) as they were receiving larger payments by way of compensation

---

[78] [1919] A.C. 435 at 456.
[79] *Tamplin SS Co Ltd v Anglo-Mexican Petroleum Co Ltd* [1916] 2 A.C. 397.
[80] Above, para.5–052.
[81] [1916] 2 A.C. 397 at 426–427.
[82] *ibid.* at 406.
[83] *ibid.* at 411.
[84] See the report of the decision at first instance: [1915] 3 K.B. 668 at 669.
[85] *Scrutton on Charterparties* (20th ed.), pp.207–208.

from the government. Thirdly, it was said in the *Bank Line* case that the "restraint of princes" exception was not the decisive factor in the *Tamplin* case,[86] as it would have been if the exception had made "full and complete" provision for the event. If it had made such provision, the courts would not have had to consider the difficult question whether the interruption in performance was (either actually or prospectively) sufficiently serious to discharge the contract. The main reason for the decision was that the interruption had not attained this level of seriousness; it was not that frustration was precluded by an express term which made less than "full and complete" provision for the events which happened.

(b) *Supervening illegality*

12-014   A contract may be discharged by supervening illegality even though it expressly provides for the event amounting, or giving rise, to the illegality. This point has been discussed in Ch.8, where we saw that there are, in some such cases, grounds of public policy for refusing to give effect to the provision for the supervening event.[87]

(c) *Legislation*

12-015   An express term which provides that the contract is to remain in force in spite of the occurrence of an event which would, but for that term, frustrate it is not, merely for that reason, a term which excludes or restricts liability for the purposes of the Unfair Contract Terms Act 1977: on the contrary, the most obvious effect of such a term is to preserve liabilities which, but for the term, would have been discharged. In so far as the term provides for the continued operation of the contract in spite of the occurrence of the event, the term is therefore not affected by the provisions of the Act. Such a term may, however, also deal with the *effects* of an event, *e.g.* by providing that sums paid before the occurrence of the event should not be repayable to the payor, or that they should be repayable only to a limited extent. Such a provision could be said to exclude or restrict the liability of the payee to restore the payment, and the question whether the validity of a provision to this effect may be affected by the 1977 Act will be discussed in Ch.15.[88] Similar reasoning applies, *mutatis mutandis*, to those provisions of the 1977 Act which prevent a party from excluding or restricting *duties*[89] (as opposed to *liabilities*). The only section of the 1977 Act to which this reasoning does not apply is s.4, which subjects indemnity clauses to the statutory requirement of reasonableness where the liability to indemnify falls on a person who deals as consumer. If the contract in which such an indemnity clause was contained also contained an express provision excluding frustration, then the requirement of reasonableness would, under s.4, apply only to the

---

[86] *Bank Line* case [1919] A.C. 435 at 442.
[87] Above, paras 8–055 to 8–056.
[88] Below, paras 15–048, 15–084.
[89] *i.e.* ss.2, 5, 6 and 7: see the reference to these sections in s.13(1).

former term[90] (*i.e.* the indemnity clause) and it is hard to think of a realistic situation in which the presence of the latter term (*i.e.* that excluding frustration) would be relevant to the reasonableness of the indemnity clause.

The discussion in the preceding paragraph shows that the relationship between contract terms which exclude frustration and the 1977 Act is largely determined by the fact that the Act deals almost exclusively with terms which exclude or restrict liabilities or (in certain cases) duties. In this respect the Act differs from the Unfair Terms in Consumer Contracts Regulations 1999[91] which apply generally to unfair standard terms in contracts between a commercial seller or supplier and a consumer.[92] They provide that an unfair term in such a contract shall not be binding on the consumer[93] and that if the term has not been "individually negotiated" it "shall be regarded as unfair if, contrary to the requirement of good faith, it causes a significant imbalance in the parties' rights and obligations arising under the contract to the detriment of the consumer".[94] It is conceivable that a term which excluded frustration could be struck down under these Regulations: for example, they could invalidate a term such as that in the *Claude Neon* case[95] discussed in para.12-004, above if the "lessee" were a consumer and the "lessor" a commercial supplier; or if, on facts similar to those of the coronation cases,[96] the contract were to provide that the hirer's liability to pay were not to be affected by the cancellation of the procession, while making no correlative provision for the liability of the supplier. The potential unfairness of such terms, however, lies, not in the mere fact that they exclude frustration, but in the fact that they may contain one-sided provisions for the *effects* of that exclusion; and the issue is further complicated by the fact that the provisions of the Law Reform (Frustrated Contracts) Act 1943 with regard to the legal effects of frustration can, by s.2(3) of that Act, be displaced by contrary agreement. For those reasons the relationship between clauses excluding frustration and the 1999 Regulations will be further discussed in Ch.15.[97]

II. PROVISIONS FOR NON-FRUSTRATING EVENTS

(1) Purpose and nature

In the application of the doctrine of frustration, difficulty often arises in determining whether the supervening event is indeed sufficiently serious   **12–016**

---

[90] s.4(1) refers to *this* term, not to other terms of the contract.
[91] SI 1999/2083.
[92] *ibid.*, reg.4.
[93] reg.8(1).
[94] reg.5(1).
[95] [1970] Qd. R. 93.
[96] Above, paras 7–006 to 7–014.
[97] Below, paras 15–048, 15–084.

to discharge the contract; and the resulting uncertainty is no doubt inconvenient from a commercial point of view. Another source of such inconvenience appears to be the relatively strict approach of at least the English courts towards the scope of the doctrine, as exemplified by such statements as the doctrine is to be applied "within very narrow limits"[98]; by the insistence (illustrated, for example, by the Suez cases[99]) that the doctrine operates only when the supervening event brings about a "fundamental" change; and by the apparent rejection in England of "impracticability" as a ground of discharge.[1] The common law doctrine, in other words, gives rise to two distinct but related problems: that of uncertainty and that of hardship.

Both of these difficulties can be met by express provisions in the contract for some kind of relief on the occurrence of specified events: for example, of strikes, disruption of sources of supply, prohibition of export or other events beyond the control of the parties; such terms will here be referred to as *force majeure* or similar clauses. It is of course possible that some events of this kind might (but for the provision) have such a serious or fundamental effect as to discharge the contract under the general common law doctrine. But the contract terms which deal with such events are nevertheless here described as dealing with non-frustrating events, because the relief for which they provide is available whether or not the event would of itself frustrate the contract,[2] and because relief under the term may differ significantly from the automatic total discharge[3] which results from the common law doctrine. Such a clause may, for example, provide for suspension of performance, either in so many words or in effect (*e.g.* by allowing for an extension of the delivery period specified in a contract for the sale of goods); for some other variation of the contract (*e.g.* for an adjustment of the price to be paid for goods or services, as in some of the Suez cases[4]); or for cancellation at the option of one party.

12–017   It is also possible for a clause to specify an event which would not discharge the contract under the common law doctrine and then to provide for the total discharge or cancellation of the contract on the occurrence of that event.[5] Such a clause has indeed been described as a "contractual frustration clause"[6]; but the point of this description is that the *effect* of such a clause resembles that of frustration at common law to the extent that the occurrence of the event or events specified in it gives rise to automatic discharge. The question *when* the clause operates turns simply on whether the events which have occurred fall, on the true

---

[98]   *Tsakiroglou & Co Ltd v Noblee Thorl GmbH* [1962] A.C. 93 at 115.
[99]   Above, paras 4–071 to 4–082.
[1]   Above, para.6–028.
[2]   Thus in *Geipel v Smith* (1872) L.R. 7 Q.B. 404 a restraint of princes clause applied where such a restraint caused *unreasonable* delay: it was not strictly necessary to show that the delay was a *frustrating* one.
[3]   Below, para.15–002.
[4]   Above, paras 4–071, 4–082.
[5]   *e.g.* in the *Tsakiroglou* case, above, n.98.
[6]   *Bremer Handelsgesellschaft mbH v Vanden Avenne-Izegem PVBA* [1978] 2 Lloyd's Rep. 109 at 112.

construction of the clause, within its scope[7]; if so, the tests of frustration which have been developed by the general law are irrelevant, so that the contract may be discharged even though the change brought about by the event is not "fundamental" in the common law sense.

(2) Distinguished from exemption clauses

Where events occur which are covered by a clause of the kind here under consideration, the party whose performance is prevented or delayed by the supervening events is not in breach at all. In this respect, such clauses differ from exemption clauses, which assume that there has been a breach and exclude or limit liability in respect of it.[8] If, for example, a builder promised to perform "subject to strikes", and strikes prevented or delayed performance, he would not be in breach, since his undertaking would simply be one to perform (or to perform within the specified time) if strikes permitted.[9] By contrast, a clause which limited, or even one which wholly excluded, his liability for defects in the work would be an exemption clause, since it would be absurd to suppose that a building contract should impose no duty at all on the builder with respect to the standard of workmanship.[10] The distinction between clauses which define a party's duty and those which exclude or limit liability for a proved or admitted breach can obviously give rise to difficulty in borderline cases. One test which has been suggested is to ask whether the events in which the clause operates are beyond the control of the party relying on it.[11] On this test, clauses of the kind here under consideration are likely to be regarded as defining contractual duties, rather than as exemption clauses: this follows from the fact that they are normally construed so as to operate only where the event has occurred without the fault of the party relying on the clause[12] and where it is one for which he has not undertaken responsibility.[13] Two further questions arise as to the validity of such clauses.

The first is whether clauses which provide for supervening obstacles to performance must satisfy the requirement of reasonableness imposed by s.3 of the Unfair Contract Terms Act 1977. This section applies where one

12–018

---

[7] For discussion of such questions of construction, see, *e.g. Hoechong Products Ltd v Cargill Hong Kong Ltd* [1995] 1 Lloyd's Rep. 584; *Fyffes Group Ltd v Reefer Express Lines Pty Ltd (The Kriti Rex)* [1996] 2 Lloyd's Rep. 171; *Coastal (Bermuda) Petroleum Ltd v VTT Vulcan Petroleum SA (No 2) (The Marine Star)* [1996] 2 Lloyd's Rep. 383; for further discussion of such questions of construction, see below paras 12–022 *et seq.*

[8] Treitel, *The Law of Contract* (11th ed.), p.238.

[9] *cf.* in the context of deviation clauses in contracts for the carriage of goods by sea, *GH Renton & Co v Palmyra Trading Co* [1957] A.C. 149.

[10] *Trade & Transport Inc v Iino Kaiun Kaisha Ltd (The Angelia)* [1973] 1 W.L.R. 210 at 230; actual decision disapproved but on another point in *Pioneer Shipping Ltd v BTP Tioxide Ltd (The Nema)* [1982] A.C. 724.

[11] *The Angelia*, above, n.10, at 231.

[12] *Fyffes Group Ltd v Reefer Express Lines Pty Ltd (The Kriti Rex)* [1996] 2 Lloyd's Rep. 171 at 196.

[13] See below, para.12–026.

party (A) deals as consumer or on the other's (B's) written standard terms of business; and it imposes the requirement of reasonableness, not only where B is himself in breach, but also in two further situations. The first, described in s.3(2)(b)(i), is that in which B claims (by reference to the term in question) to be entitled to render a contractual performance substantially different from that reasonably expected of him. The fact that B was not in breach in failing to render that performance would not be decisive in this situation, since the rule which governs it is expressed in terms of A's reasonable expectation, rather than of B's contractual duty. But while A may reasonably expect that B will not arbitrarily vary the performance promised by him,[14] it is submitted that A cannot reasonably expect B to perform what B has promised, in spite of a supervening obstacle which is beyond B's control and on the occurrence of which the contract expressly relieves B from the duty of strict performance. The second of the situations here under discussion, in which the requirement of reasonableness applies, is described in s.3(2)(b)(ii) and is that in which B claims (by reference to the contract term) to be entitled "in respect of the whole or any part of his contractual obligation, to render no performance at all". It is submitted that this provision would not cover the case where the clause was one which defined B's contractual duty in such a way that, in consequence of the occurrence of the supervening event, no such duty arose or survived. If, for example, B promised to perform "subject to strikes" and a strike prevented performance, there would not be any "contractual obligation" on B in respect of which he would "claim to be entitled ... to render no performance at all". Accordingly, such a term would not be subject to the requirement of reasonableness under the 1977 Act.

The second question is whether a term of the kind here under discussion is open to attack on the ground of unfairness under the Unfair Terms in Consumer Contracts Regulations 1999.[15] This question arises only if the contract is one between a commercial seller or supplier and a consumer;[16] and the decided cases on *force majeure* and similar clauses provide little guidance on the present question since they are for the most part concerned with contracts between parties each of whom deals in the course of a business. The group of consumer contracts most likely to contain terms of the kind here under discussion are those for the provision to the consumer of package travel or holiday facilities. Since such contracts are governed by the Package Travel, Package Holidays and Package Tours Regulations 1992,[17] the 1999 Regulations do not apply to them.[18] By virtue of the 1992 Regulations, it is an implied term of such a

---

[14] *cf.* the situation which arose in *Anglo-Continental Holidays Ltd v Typaldos Lines (London) Ltd* [1967] 2 Lloyd's Rep. 61.

[15] SI 1999/2083, implementing Directive 99/13.

[16] 1999 Regulations, above, reg.4(1); see above, para.12–015 for other requirements of the Regulations and their effects, so far as relevant to the present discussion.

[17] SI 1992/3288.

[18] 1999 Regulations, reg.4(2)(a).

contract that the consumer is entitled to withdraw from the contract where the "organiser" is "constrained" to alter an "essential term" of it (such as the price) and as the implication is compulsory, it cannot be excluded by express agreement.[19] The sort of circumstances which are usually dealt with by *force majeure* clauses are made available by the Regulations as defences to the "other party" (than the consumer) and the defences so made available cannot be extended by the contract so as to confer wider excuses to that party.[20] The question whether, in other contracts, express provisions for supervening events which would not at common law frustrate the contract would be regarded as "unfair" within the 1999 Regulations is one to which no general answer can be given. On the one hand, it can be argued that the "indicative list" given in Regulations of terms which "may be regarded as unfair"[21] contains no explicit reference to *force majeure* or similar clauses; but this argument is clearly not conclusive since the list is expressly declared to be "non-exhaustive".[22] It can also be argued that, a *force majeure* or similar clause should not be regarded as unfair since normally it operates only in circumstances beyond the control of the party relying on it,[23] and this argument derives some slight support from one of the illustrations in the "indicative list", of terms which "may be regarded as unfair," namely a term "enabling a seller or supplier to terminate a contract of indeterminate duration without reasonable notice *except where there are serious grounds for doing so*".[24] The words here italicised seem to refer to the kind of supervening circumstances that are usually dealt with by express *force majeure* and similar clauses, and so to indicate that a term excusing the seller or supplier in the event of such changes is not, for that reason alone, "unfair" within the Regulations. On the other hand, such a term could be "unfair" if it were one-sided in its operation, *e.g.* if it excused the supplier from providing the agreed service but required the consumer nevertheless to make the agreed payment, or if it deprived him of a right to restitution in respect of payment already made.[25] It is also possible for a *force majeure* clause to protect a seller even where the event which brings it into operation does not cause any inability on his part to perform the contract.[26] If that were the effect of a term in a "pre-formulated standard contract"[27] between a commercial seller and a consumer, then the term

---

[19] 1992 Regulations, above, reg.12.

[20] *ibid.*, reg.15(2),(5).

[21] 1999 Regulations, reg.5(5), Sch.2.

[22] 1999 Regulations, reg.5(5).

[23] Above, para.12–018, at n.11; *cf.* below, para.12–026. Usually this point is made clear by the express words of such a clause.

[24] 1999 Regulations, Sch.2, para.1(g); *cf. ibid.*, para.1(j) ("without a valid reason which is specified in the contract").

[25] Example based on the *Claude Neon* case [1970] Qd. R. 93; above, para.12–004; *cf.* 1999 Regulations, Sch.2, para.1(d), 1(f) and 1(o).

[26] *cf. Ford & Sons (Oldham) Ltd v Henry Leetham & Sons Ltd* (1915) 21 Com. Cas. 55, below, paras 12–023, 12–041.

[27] The phrase is taken from 1999 Regulations, reg.5(3).

might well be regarded as unfair within the 1999 Regulations and so not binding on the consumer.

(3) Effects not governed by Law Reform (Frustrated Contracts) Act 1943

12–019   Even the effects of *force majeure* or similar clauses only resemble, and are not identical with, those of the common law doctrine; for on the occurrence of one of the specified events a party will be excused under an express term of the contract and not under the general doctrine of frustration. It follows that the effects of discharge will not be governed by s.1 of the Law Reform (Frustrated Contracts) Act 1943. That section applies where a contract has "become impossible of performance or been otherwise frustrated".[28] It is submitted that force can be given to the word "otherwise" only by interpreting the phrase in which it occurs as referring to the situation where a contract has been frustrated either because it has become impossible of performance or because it has been frustrated for some other reason (*e.g.* by supervening illegality). Neither of these conditions would be satisfied where an event had occurred which made performance impossible and the contract contained an express provision which either threw the risk of loss resulting from the event on one of the parties, or which provided for some intermediate solution for splitting the loss, such as the suspension of performance or some other variation of the contract. *A fortiori* the section will not apply where the clause provides (as such clauses commonly do) for relief even though the supervening event does *not* make performance impossible and would not "otherwise" frustrate the contract. For example, the clause may provide for automatic discharge in the event of prohibition of export or import, in circumstances in which such a prohibition would not, of itself, be a ground of frustration.[29] Even if the circumstances were such that they would, apart from the clause, frustrate the contract, discharge would take place under the clause and not under the doctrine of frustration, for that doctrine does not apply where express provision is made in the contract for the supervening event.

This last proposition has indeed been doubted, some writers[30] having taken the view that a contract can be frustrated even though it does make provision for the supervening event. But the situations on which supporters of this view rely appear to illustrate a different point: namely, one relating to the construction of the clause. We have seen earlier in this chapter[31] that a *force majeure* or similar clause may, if taken literally, appear to apply to the events which have occurred but be held, on its true construction, to cover only temporary or minor obstacles to performance; and that such a clause will not exclude frustration if the events which

---

[28] s.1(1).
[29] See above, paras 7–025 to 7–027.
[30] Williams, *The Law Reform (Frustrated Contracts) Act 1943*, 25; McKendrick, in (ed. McKendrick) *Force Majeure and Frustration of Contract*, (2nd ed), p.34.
[31] Above, paras 12–008 to 12–009.

happen go beyond those which it was intended to cover and strike at the root of the contract.[32] But where the clause does on its true construction cover the very event which has happened, it is submitted that discharge occurs under the clause and not under the common law doctrine, even if the clause provides for automatic termination on the occurrence of the event. The reason for this submission is that discharge will take place whether or not the event would, apart from the clause, have brought about a change sufficiently fundamental to frustrate the contract. The court does not have to ask this question, but simply has to ask whether the event which has happened falls, as a matter of construction, within the clause. Moreover, even clauses which provide for *total* discharge commonly make such discharge subject to procedural requirements which have no counterpart in the common law doctrine: for example, they may require the party claiming discharge to give notice of the event to the other party.[33] It has therefore been rightly held that there is no scope for the application of the common law doctrine where the contract contains elaborate provisions for the events which are alleged to have discharged it.[34]

The same view is, it is submitted, supported by s.2(3) of the Law Reform (Frustrated Contracts) Act 1943, by which the court is directed to give effect to any contractual provision: "which, upon the true construction of the contract, is intended to have effect in the event of circumstances arising which operate, or would but for the said provision operate, to frustrate the contract, or is intended to have effect whether such circumstances arise or not."[35] These words appear to cover three situations. First, the contract might simply provide that, if it should be frustrated, the normal consequences of frustration at common law (as modified by the 1943 Act) should be superseded (at least in part) by a different solution provided for in the contract. This situation would be covered by the words "in the event of circumstances arising which operate ... to frustrate the contract". It can be illustrated by supposing that the contract in *Taylor v Caldwell*[36] had provided that, if it were to become for any reason impossible to give the proposed concerts, the hirers were to be entitled to recover their wasted expenses but had left all other rights to be determined by the common law doctrine. Secondly the contract might provide that if a particular event occurred which would (but for the provision) frustrate the contract, a solution provided for in the contract should wholly displace that laid down by the general law. This situation would be covered by the words "in the event of circumstances arising which ... would but for the said provision

12–020

---

[32] The example given by Williams, above, n.30, may be intended to be of this kind.

[33] This was certainly true of the clause described as the "contractual frustration" clause in *Bremer Handelsgesellschaft mbH v Vanden Avenne-Izegem PVBA*, above, para.12–017 at n.6.

[34] See the decision at first instance in the case cited in the previous note: [1977] 1 Lloyd's Rep. 133 at 163; and *Agrokor AG v Tradigrain SA* [2000] 1 Lloyd's Rep. 497 at 504.

[35] See further below, para.15–084.

[36] (1863) 3 B. & S. 826; above, para.2–024.

operate ... to frustrate the contract". It can be illustrated by reference to those of the coronation cases in which the contract provided that, if the procession were to be postponed, the ticket-holder should have the right to use the premises on the later day on which the procession took place.[37] Thirdly the contract might make provision for discharge in circumstances which would not under the general law discharge the contract at all. This situation would be covered by the phrase "whether such circumstances arise or not". It can be illustrated by supposing that the contract in *Krell v Henry*[38] had provided that the contract should be discharged in the event of Mr Henry's illness on the days fixed for the coronation processions. Our concern in this chapter is with the second and third of the situations described above; and the Act is clearly based on the assumption that the contract in them is not frustrated.[39] Cases of the first kind (in which the parties merely envisage in general terms the possibility of frustration) appear to be rare; at any rate there seems to be no reported case of this kind.

(4) Terminology: *"force majeure"*

12–021   Clauses of the kind discussed in this part of this chapter are often described, either by the draftsman or by the courts, as *"force majeure"* clauses[40]; and reference is sometimes made in this context[41] to the rule of French law under which a debtor is not liable in damages where he has been prevented from performing by *force majeure*.[42] In *Jacobs v Crédit Lyonnais*[43] the question arose whether a seller of Esparto grass to be exported from Algeria could rely, by way of excuse for his failure to deliver, on an insurrection (which had prevented shipment by the suppliers named in the contract) as constituting *"force majeure"* under French law. The defence was rejected on the ground that the contract was governed by English law which in these circumstances provided no excuse. In a later judicial discussion of the case it was said that the obstacles on which the seller relied constituted *force majeure* only by French law and did not give rise to frustration in English law.[44] All this may seem to suggest

---

[37] *Victoria Seats Agency v Paget* (1902) 19 T.L.R. 16, above, paras 7–010, 12–004.

[38] [1903] 2 K.B. 740, above, para.7–010.

[39] Some difficulty may be felt by reason of the fact that s.1(1) provides that s.1 applies only where the contract *is* frustrated: it can be argued that it is therefore unnecessary in s.2(3) to provide for the case where the contract is *not* frustrated. But s.1(1) deals only with the scope of s.1, while s.2 deals more broadly with the scope of the whole Act; and provisions within s.2(3) can deal with many matters not dealt with in s.1 at all (such as suspension of the contract or notice requirements of the kind discussed below, at paras 12–042 to 12–046).

[40] *e.g. Peter Dixon & Sons Ltd v Henderson, Craig & Co Ltd* [1919] 2 K.B. 778.

[41] *e.g. Lebaupin v Crispin* [1920] 2 K.B. 714 at 719.

[42] French Code Civil, Art.1148; in *Lebeaupin v Crispin*, above, n.41, the reference is to Code de Commerce, Art.230.

[43] (1884) 12 Q.B.D. 589 (where the headnote is misleading: see *Ralli Bros v Compania Naviera Sota y Aznar* [1920] 2 K.B. 287 at 292, 297, 301).

[44] *ibid.* at 297.

that the French doctrine of *force majeure* is wider than the English doctrine of frustration; but this would, it is submitted, be a mistaken view. The Court in *Jacobs v Crédit Lyonnais* took an extremely narrow view of the scope of the English doctrine of discharge. It said that "The contract has absolutely provided that delivery of the esparto shall be duly made"[45]; and it further relied on *Paradine v Jane*[46] as authority for the rule that: "a person who expressly contracts absolutely to do a thing not naturally impossible, is not excused for non-performance because of being prevented by vis major."[47] This reliance on *Paradine v Jane* more than 20 years after *Taylor v Caldwell*[48] may seem to be surprising, particularly as the scope of *Taylor v Caldwell* had by then been extended beyond the simple case of destruction of the subject-matter[49]; though this aspect of the decision in *Jacobs v Crédit Lyonnais* can probably be explained on the ground that it was one of those exceptional cases[50] (discussed in Ch.2) in which it is still appropriate to apply the former doctrine of absolute contracts as stated in *Paradine v Jane*. But the subsequent development of the doctrine of frustration has been such that it is no longer true that the scope of that doctrine is narrower than that of the doctrine of *force majeure* as interpreted by the French civil courts. It has, on the contrary, been said that "the scope allowed to *force majeure* is far narrower than that of frustration in English law".[51] This view is based on the strictness with which the requirements of the doctrine are sometimes stated in French law: thus it is said that an event will be a ground of discharge only if it is unforeseeable, irresistible, and makes performance absolutely impossible.[52] It is also said to be a requirement that the obstacle must be "insurmountable"[53] and that this requirement will not be satisfied if the debtor could have performed by some substitute method, *e.g.* by air carriage where sea carriage was prevented.[54] There would seem to be no duty in English law to adopt such a fundamentally different method of performance[55]; while a "*force majeure*" clause can clearly apply even though the obstacle to performance which has arisen is not insurmountable.[56] The contrast between the two systems can be further illustrated by

---

[45] (1884) 12 Q.B.D. 589 at 604.

[46] (1647) Aleyn 26; above, para.2–002.

[47] (1884) 12 Q.B.D. 589 at 603.

[48] (1863) 3 B. & S. 826, above, para.2–024.

[49] *Jackson v Union Marine Insurance Co* (1875) L.R. 10 C.P. 125.

[50] Above, para.2–034.

[51] Nicholas, *French Law of Contract* (2nd ed.), p.202.

[52] Zweigert and Kötz (trs. Weir), *Introduction to Comparative Law* (2nd ed.), p.537; Mazeaud, Mazeaud & Chabas, *Leçons de Droit Civil* (9th ed.), Vol.II.1, No 573, 575.

[53] *ibid.* No 576.

[54] *ibid.*

[55] *e.g.* in the Suez case (above, paras 4–071 to 4–083) the results would probably have been different if the *only* means of transport remaining available had been carriage by air of commodities which, in the ordinary course of business, are invariably carried by sea.

[56] *Peter Dixon & Sons Ltd v Henderson, Craig & Co Ltd* [1919] 2 K.B. 778 at 789.

reference to the cases concerning long-term supply contracts which have been discussed in Ch.6.[57] Of course generalisations as to the relative scope of the two doctrines are not easy to substantiate; indeed, one can point to pairs of cases in which the two doctrines lead to similar results. Thus one illustration of the strict French doctrine is said to be that a seller of goods is not excused by requisition if there was the slightest chance of his having been able to deliver before the requisition took effect.[58] This may be compared with an English case[59] in which a seller was not excused by prohibition of export as the prohibition was announced 10 days before it came into force and the seller could have shipped within those 10 days, even though his intention might have been to ship later during the shipment period, which extended for a further month beyond those 10 days. It is also true that French administrative law recognises a doctrine of *imprévision*, under which contracts with public authorities may in certain circumstances be modified (rather than discharged) on account of drastic changes in economic conditions, and that this doctrine may provide relief to a contractor who would be strictly held to his contract in English law.[60] But the existence of that doctrine has no bearing on the present discussion which is concerned with the concept and terminology of "*force majeure*". The point to be emphasised is that the grounds on which relief may be available under "*force majeure*" clauses are far removed from (and wider than) those which would be a ground of discharge under the doctrine of *force majeure* as stated in the French civil code and as interpreted by the French civil courts.

(5) **Operation**

12–022 The only perfectly general statement which can safely be made about the operation of express provisions of the kind here under discussion is that their effect depends in each case on the words used and that it is, therefore, a matter of construction.

(a) *Construction in general*

12–023 Although there may be a tendency to construe a clause of the present kind narrowly against the party seeking to rely on it, there is no rule of law to this effect. The point may be illustrated by contrasting two cases. The first is *PJ van der Zijden Wildhandel NV v Tucker & Cross Ltd*,[61] where a contract for the sale of frozen Chinese rabbits on c.i.f. terms provided that "should the sellers fail to deliver ... or to effect shipment in time *by reason of* war, flood, fire or storm, heavy snow or any other causes beyond their control", they were to be entitled to cancel the contract. This clause was held not to

---

[57] Above, paras 6–037 to 6–040.

[58] Planiol & Ripert, *Traité pratique de droit civil française* (2nd ed.), Vol.VII, No 838; June 23, 1922, DP 1922.1.131.

[59] *Ross T Smyth & Co Ltd v WN Lindsay Ltd* [1953] 1 W.L.R. 1280; below, para.12–029 (n.99).

[60] See above, para.6–037, n.27.

[61] [1975] 2 Lloyd's Rep. 240.

protect the sellers when they were let down by their Chinese suppliers since this event did not prevent them from performing by other means. Under the c.i.f. contract it was their duty "to tender documents, not to ship the rabbits themselves"[62] and, although they might not have been able to ship goods of the contract description, they had failed to show that they could not have bought such goods already afloat and have tendered documents relating to those goods. The second, contrasting, case is *Ford & Sons (Oldham) Ltd v Henry Leetham & Sons Ltd*,[63] where a contract for the sale of wheat gave the seller the option of cancelling "*in case of* prohibition of export blockade or hostilities preventing delivery of wheat to this country". Shortly before and shortly after the outbreak of the First World War, prohibitions on the export of wheat were imposed by a large number of countries, including some which were substantial suppliers to this country. It was held that the seller was protected by the clause even though no such prohibition had been imposed by the United States and Canada, who were the main suppliers of wheat to the United Kingdom. The cases can be distinguished on the ground that the clause in the former case did, while that in the latter case did not,[64] require the seller to establish the relationship of cause and effect between the events specified in the clause and his inability to deliver.

A similar distinction can be drawn between clauses which protect a seller where the specified events *prevent*, and those which protect him where they merely *hinder*, performance. In the soyabean cases (to be discussed below[65]) we shall see that sellers could rely on clauses of the former kind only where they showed that at least some alternative sources of supply were not available to them. But in *Tennants (Lancashire) Ltd v CS Wilson & Co Ltd*,[66] a clause in a contract for the sale of magnesium chloride gave the sellers the right to suspend performance in the event of contingencies beyond their control "such as fire ... war strikes or the like preventing *or hindering* the manufacture or delivery of the article". It was held that the sellers could rely on this provision when, on the outbreak of the First World War, they were cut off from their principal source of supply in Germany, even though a small English source remained available from

12–024

---

[62] *ibid.* at 242; *cf.* above, para.4–044. The above reasoning would not have applied if the contract had required the sellers themselves to ship the rabbits from China: *cf. Hoechong Products Ltd v Cargill Hong Kong Ltd* [1995] 1 W.L.R. 404, where an f.o.b. seller successfully relied on a clause said at 409 to be "virtually identical" with that in the *PJ van der Zijden Wildhandel* case.

[63] (1915) 21 Com. Cas. 55.

[64] The words "by reason of" occurred in the clause in the first case, while that in the second was introduced simply by the words "In case of...".

[65] Below, paras 12–036 *et seq. cf. Re Comptoir Commercial Anversois and Power Son & Co* [1920] 1 K.B. 868 (difficulty in realising payment not a circumstance "preventing shipment"). *cf.* also *Agrokor AG v Tradigrain SA* [2000] 1 Lloyd's Rep. 497, where it was held that an announcement by the authorities of the country in question that they *intended* to impose a prohibition of export did not itself amount to a prohibition within the "prohibition of export" clause.

[66] [1917] A.C. 495.

which they could have satisfied the buyers. The events had "hindered delivery" though they might not have prevented it. In a later case the words "prevents or hinders" in a contract for the sale of Canadian wood pulp were similarly held to protect the seller when the First World War gave rise to a complete dislocation of the carrying trade[67]: performance had not been prevented (in the sense of having become impossible) but had been hindered since obstacles had arisen which would be "really difficult"[68] to overcome. The cases, however, make it clear that a mere increase in price will not of itself constitute even a hindrance.[69] Much less will it amount to a prevention: thus a steep rise in freight rates has been held not to fall within a clause which allowed a seller to suspend performance if he should be prevented from shipping "under normal conditions".[70]

(b) *Illustrations of narrow construction*

12–025   The process of narrow construction referred to above can be illustrated, in particular, by cases in which performance is prevented as a result of the fault or default of one of the parties; by cases in which the obstacle to performance is only partial, temporary or qualified[71], and by cases in which it affects only one of a number of alternative ways of performing.

(i) Fault or default of party failing to perform

12–026   In construing clauses of the kind here under discussion, the courts apply the "presumption that the expression *force majeure* is likely to be restricted to supervening events which arise without the fault of either party *and for which neither of them has undertaken responsibility*".[72] The main difficulty with the operation of this presumption arises from the words here italicised, particularly where the fault or default is that of a third party, *e.g.* where A has contracted to supply goods or services to B and A has in turn contracted with C for those goods and services to be supplied to A so that A can make use of them in performing his contract with B. The general rule in such cases is that C's fault or default in making the supply to A does not amount, for the purpose of the presumption stated above, to "fault" on the part of A and therefore does not deprive A of the benefit of a *force majeure* clause in his contract with B. This was held to be the position in the

---

[67] *Peter Dixon & Sons Ltd v Henderson, Craig & Co Ltd* [1919] 2 K.B. 778; *cf. Reardon Smith Line Ltd v Ministry of Agriculture, Fisheries & Food* [1963] A.C. 691 at 714.

[68] See the *Peter Dixon* case, above, n.67, at 780.

[69] *S Instone & Co Ltd v Speeding Marshall & Co Ltd* (1915) 32 T.L.R. 202; *Tennants (Lancashire) Ltd v CS Wilson Ltd* [1917] A.C. 495 at 509, 510, 522, 526; *Peter Dixon & Sons Ltd v Henderson, Craig & Co Ltd* [1919] 2 K.B. 778; for the possibility that a "prohibitive" price increase might bring such a clause into operation, see *Brauer & Co (Great Britain) Ltd v James Clark (Brush Materials) Ltd* [1952] 2 All E.R. 497 at 500, 501, discussed, above, para.6–035.

[70] *Blythe & Co v Richard Turpin & Co* (1916) 114 L.T. 753.

[71] For the meaning of "qualified" in this context, see above, para.8–049.

[72] *Fyffes Group Ltd v Reefer Express Lines Ltd (The Kriti Rex)* [1996] 2 Lloyd's Rep. 171 at 196; *cf. Channel Island Ferries Ltd v Sealink UK Ltd* [1988] 1 Lloyd's Rep. 323.

Marine Star (No 2)[73] where a *force majeure* clause in a contract of sale between A (the seller) and B (the buyer) referred to prevention of performance by causes "beyond the seller's control". These words were held to protect A where A's inability to deliver was brought about by the default of C, A's supplier, since "seller" in the clause could mean only "the selling party in the relevant contract containing the *force majeure* clause [*i.e.*, that between A and B] and does not refer to sellers further up the chain".[74] This approach to the construction of such clauses can of course be displaced by the express words of the clause. For example, in *Lebaupin v Crispin*[75] a contract between A and B for the sale of tinned salmon contained a *force majeure* clause referring to "any cause not under the control *of the canners [C]* or the shippers [A]" and it was held that A could not rely on C's default under the supply contract between A and C as a defence to a claim by B against A. No doubt the general rule applied in *The Marine Star (No 2)* can also be displaced by words in the *force majeure* clause which do not *specifically* refer to events beyond the control of C, or to the fault of C: for example, a clause which listed natural disasters such as floods and earthquakes or "*similar* events beyond [A's] control" would probably be construed so as not to cover C's default in making the supply to A, which A had intended to use in performing his contract with B. A case which gives rise to more difficulty, however, is *The Kriti Rex*,[76] where an f.o.b. contract limited the buyer's liability by a *force majeure* clause; and the contract went on to define *force majeure* as consisting of a series of specified events and "other events beyond the control of the parties". The vessel which the buyers had chartered and nominated to take delivery of the goods was delayed, with the result that the goods deteriorated at the port of intended shipment; and it was held that the buyers were not protected by the *force majeure* clause as the delay was due to the carrier's failure properly to maintain the ship. This conclusion was based in part on *Lebaupin v Crispin*[77]; but the clause in that case specifically referred to events not under the control *of the seller's suppliers* [C] while the clause in *The Kriti Rex* contained to no specific reference to events not under the control *of the carrier* [C] engaged by the buyer. The result in the latter case can perhaps be explained on the grounds that the specific examples which, in the contractual definition of *force majeure*, preceded the general words quoted above, showed that the *force majeure* clause was not intended to cover "aspects of the performance for which the parties [*i.e.* buyer and seller] were directly or indirectly responsible"[78]; and that under the f.o.b. contract it was the buyer's "responsibility" to provide an effective ship[79]

---

[73] *Costal (Bermuda) Petroleum Ltd v VTT Vulcan Petroleum SA (No 2) (The Marine Star)* [1996] 2 Lloyd's Rep. 383.

[74] *ibid.* at 389.

[75] [1920] 2 K.B. 174.

[76] Above, n.72.

[77] Above, n.75.

[78] [1996] 2 Lloyd's Rep. 171 at 196.

[79] See *Benjamin's Sale of Goods* (6th ed.), para.20–043.

and to tender her for loading at the appropriate time and place.[80] Yet in *The Marine Star (No 2)* the seller [A] was likewise "responsible" for delivering the goods comprised in his contract with the buyer [B] but it was nevertheless held that A *was* protected by the *force majeure* clause against liability for failure to deliver caused by the default of his supplier, C. In so far as the reasoning of *The Kriti Rex* relies on *Lebaupin v Crispin*,[81] that reasoning is, with respect, hard to reconcile with the reasoning of *The Marine Star (No 2)*[82]; though it is, no doubt, arguable that the conclusion in *The Kriti Rex* can be justified on the grounds that the events specifically enumerated in the clause showed that the clause was not intended to protect the buyer in respect of delays resulting from a plain breach of the contract of carriage between buyer and carrier.

The process of narrow construction described above is further illustrated by the meaning which has been given in other cases to words which restrict the operation of *force majeure* and similar clauses to events "beyond the control" of the party invoking the clauses. It has, for example, been held that "strikes ... beyond the control" of a party did not cover a strike which could have been settled by taking reasonable steps, such as increasing wages.[83] *A fortiori*, events are not beyond the "control" of a party who has instigated or induced the event. The point is illustrated by a case[84] in which a contract for services that related to the transport of crude oil to an inland refinery provided that neither party was to be liable for loss attributable to compliance with governmental requests "beyond the control of the party affected". These words were held not to protect a party who had taken active steps to persuade the relevant government to request him not to perform the contract.

(ii) Partial or temporary obstacle

12–027   In cases of this kind, the process of narrow construction is illustrated by the interpretation, in contracts for the sale of goods, of prohibition of export clauses which refer to prohibitions *preventing* shipment or fulfilment of the contract. The party (usually the seller) who claims to be discharged under such a clause must, in general, show that there was an "effective" prohibition, that is, one which prevents him from exporting goods in accordance with the requirements of the contract. If the prohibition does not prevent him from doing this, it is not "effective" for

---

[80] [1996] 2 Lloyd's Rep. 171 at 196.

[81] See the citation of *Lebaupin v Crispin*, above, n.75, in [1996] 2 Lloyd's Rep. 171 at 196.

[82] Above, at n.74; *Lebaupin v Crispin* was discussed in the *Marine Star (No 2)*, above, n.73, at 387 but in the event counsel did not seek to rely on the case. There is no reference in the *Kriti Rex* (decided on May 8, 1996) to the *Marine Star (No 2)* (decided on April 3, 1996). For earlier proceedings in the latter case, see [1993] 1 Lloyd's Rep. 329, above para.10–005.

[83] *Channel Island Ferries Ltd v Sealink UK Ltd* [1998] 1 Lloyd's Rep. 323.

[84] *Mamidoil-Jetoil Greek Petroleum SA v Okta Crude Oil Refinery AD (No 2)* [2003] EWCA Civ 1031; [2003] 2 All E.R. (Comm) 640.

this purpose.[85] Thus a seller cannot rely on the clause if the prohibition is imposed only for a short time and is then withdrawn when shipment in accordance with the contract is still possible[86]; or if the prohibition is only against shipment without licence and the seller has within that time obtained a licence[87]; or if his failure to obtain the licence is due to a breach of his obligation to take reasonable steps to that end[88]; or if the prohibition is subject to exceptions and the seller could have appropriated to the contract goods at his disposal which fell within,[89] or within an extension of,[90] such an exception.

The same approach is illustrated by cases concerned with the construction of *force majeure* clauses. The judicial tendency to construe such clauses strictly against the parties relying on them is illustrated by *Hong Guan & Co Ltd v R Jumabhoy*[91] where a contract for the sale of 50 tons of cloves was made "subject to *force majeure* and shipment". The sellers succeeded in procuring a shipment of 50 tons, but not in shipping enough to satisfy all their contracts for the sale of cloves. It was held that they were in breach of their contract with the buyers of the 50 tons, as the clause could not be construed to mean "subject to our shipping enough to satisfy all our contracts" or "subject to our shipping 50 tons which we allocate to you". Similarly, where a c.i.f. contract provided for an extension of the shipment period, should shipment be prevented by strikes, it was held that the seller could not rely on this provision merely because grain elevators belonging to the shipper (who was the first in a chain of buyers and sellers through whom the seller expected to acquire the goods) were affected by strikes, other elevators in the port of shipment not being so affected[92]; where a *force majeure* clause in a c.i.f. contract provided that sellers were not to be responsible for delay in shipment due to "mechanical breakdown" it was held that the sellers would be entitled to rely on the clause only if the mechanical breakdown which had

---

[85] *Samuel Sanday & Co v Cox, McEuen & Co* (1922) 10 Ll. L. Rep. 409 and 459; *Société Co-operative Suisse des Céréales v La Plata Cereal Co SA* (1947) 80 Ll. L. Rep. 530.

[86] *Samuel Sanday* case, above, n.85, at 460 (where the contract seems to have provided for loading, not within a specified period, but on a named ship which was still at the port of loading when the prohibition was lifted).

[87] These were the actual facts of the *Samuel Sanday* case, above, n.85.

[88] *Joseph Pyke & Sons (Liverpool) Ltd v Richard Cornelius & Co* [1955] 2 Lloyd's Rep. 747; *Vidler & Co (London) Ltd v R Silcock & Sons Ltd* [1960] 1 Lloyd's Rep. 509; *Agroexport v Cie Européenne de Céréales* [1947] 1 Lloyd's Rep. 409, contrast *Provimi Hellas AE v Warinco AG* [1978] 1 Lloyd's Rep. 373 (where reasonable efforts had been made to have a revoked licence restored). For the standard of the duty, see above, para.8–051.

[89] *e.g. Bremer Handelsgesellschaft mbH v C Mackprang Jr* [1979] 1 Lloyd's Rep. 114; below, para.12–036.

[90] *Raiffeisen Hauptgenossenschaft v Louis Dreyfuss & Co* [1981] 1 Lloyd's Rep. 345.

[91] [1960] A.C. 684.

[92] *Koninklijke Bunge v Cie Continentale d'Importation* [1973] 2 Lloyd's Rep. 44; contrast *BTP Tioxide Ltd v Pioneer Shipping Ltd (The Nema)* [1982] A.C. 724 (frustration of charterparty by strike affecting entire loading port).

occurred was the sole cause of the delay, *i.e.* not if some other event than one of those specified in the clause had also contributed to the delay[93]; and where a clause provided for extension of the delivery period in the event of shipment being delayed by strikes or other *force majeure* events, it was held to protect the sellers only from liability for delay in delivery, so that they were liable for damages for non-delivery.[94]

12–028   It should, however, be stressed that the cases referred to in the preceding paragraph illustrate no more than a principle of construction and do not exclude the possibility that the provision may apply even though the supervening prohibition has not wholly barred all possible methods of performance. This was the position in *Fairclough, Dodd & Jones Ltd v J H Vantol Ltd*[95] where a c.i.f. contract for the sale of cottonseed oil, to be shipped from Egypt during December 1950/January 1951, provided for an extension of the shipment period "should shipment be delayed by" prohibition of export or other causes amounting to *force majeure*. The seller's suppliers held a valid though revocable licence to export such goods, but on December 19, the Egyptian authorities prohibited the shipment of cottonseed oil and this prohibition remained in force until January 3. The seller had intended to ship the goods during the period covered by the prohibition; arrangements with a carrier to that end had been made by his suppliers; and the ship on which the shipment was to have been made had, by reason of the prohibition, to sail without the goods on board. Subsequently, on February 17, the Egyptian authorities reimposed the prohibition. It was held that the seller was entitled to rely on the clause (and hence entitled to an extension of the shipment period) and that he was subsequently discharged, either when the prohibition was reimposed or by his acceptance of the buyer's wrongful repudiation of the contract within the extended shipment period. On the true construction of the clause, shipment had been "delayed" even though the cause of the delay had not extended over the whole shipment period. A delay of such an extent would have amounted to "prevention" of shipment, while the clause on which the seller relied required him to show merely that there had been a "delay"; and by referring in another clause to war, hostilities or blockade "preventing" shipment, the contract had made it clear that the requirements of "delay" were less rigorous than those of "prevention".

(iii) Alternative ways of performing

12–029   The cases provide many illustrations of the principle that a prohibition of export or *force majeure* clause will not normally be construed to apply where the contract provides for alternative ways of performing, only some of

---

[93] *Intertradex SA v Lesieur Torteaux SARL* [1978] 2 Lloyd's Rep. 509; *cf. Huileries L'Abeille v Société des Huileries du Niger (The Kastellon)* [1978] 2 Lloyd's Rep. 203.
[94] *Re Thornett & Fehr and Yuills* [1921] 1 K.B. 219.
[95] [1957] 1 W.L.R. 136, where the House of Lords affirmed the decision of McNair J., [1955] 1 W.L.R. 642, which had been reversed by the Court of Appeal.

which are affected by the supervening prohibition or *force majeure* event.[96] This is, for example, the position where the prohibition prevents shipment only from the one particular port from which the seller intended to ship, without affecting the possibility of shipment from other ports designated as shipment ports by the contract,[97] or where the seller intended to supply goods originating in a particular country, the authorities of which prohibited the export of goods of the contract description, but that description left it open to the seller to supply goods from other sources, not affected by the prohibition.[98] Similarly, it has been held that a seller could not rely on a prohibition of export clause where the authorities of the country of origin indicated *in advance* that the export of goods of the contract description would definitely be prohibited from a future date within the shipment period: it then became his duty to ship in the part of that period remaining available before that date.[99] The position is different where those authorities have merely indicated that such a prohibition *might* be imposed: such an announcement does not require the seller to ship at once (earlier than he was originally obliged to do so), so that the subsequent imposition of the embargo will (if other necessary conditions are satisfied) bring a prohibition of export clause into operation.[1]

The general rule that a party cannot rely on a prohibition or *force majeure* clause where the supervening event does not affect all the possible methods of performance is, moreover, no more than a rule of construction; and it may therefore be displaced by the terms of the clause or by other terms of the contract. It has, for example, been said that, where a contract provided for shipment from a number of ports, the seller might be able to rely on such a clause even though he could not show that shipment from all the ports within the permitted range was impossible.[2] This might be the position, where "complete arrangements had been made for shipping during the contract period … and the performance of these is delayed by one of the specified events"[3]; or where a seller had given notice in accordance with the terms of the contract of his intention to ship from a

---

[96] *cf.* above, para.10–001; *European Grain and Shipping Ltd v J H Rayner & Co Ltd* [1970] 2 Lloyd's Rep. 239 at 243 (where the principle did not apply for reasons stated at n.3, below); *Koninklijke Bunge v Cie Continentale d'Importation* [1973] 2 Lloyd's Rep. 45.

[97] *Warinco AG v Fritz Mauthner* [1978] 1 Lloyd's Rep. 151; *cf. Seabridge Shipping Ltd v Antco Shipping Ltd (The Furness Bridge)* [1977] 2 Lloyd's Rep. 367.

[98] *Agrokor AG v Tradigrain SA* [2000] 1 Lloyd's Rep. 497, where the contract had been brought to an end by the buyer's acceptance of the seller's wrongful repudiation *before* any export prohibition had been imposed and where even after that time alternative sources of supply remained available to the seller (*cf.*, above, para.12–024, n.65).

[99] *Ross T Smyth & Co Ltd v WN Lindsay Ltd* [1953] 1 W.L.R. 1280.

[1] *Tradax Export SA v André & Cie* [1976] 1 Lloyd's Rep. 416 at 426; *Continental Grain Export Corp v STM Grain Ltd* [1979] 2 Lloyd's Rep. 460 at 474–475.

[2] *Koninklijke Bunge v Cie Continentale d'Importation* [1973] 2 Lloyd's Rep. 45 at 50.

[3] *European Grain & Shipping Ltd v JH Rayner Ltd* [1970] 2 Lloyd's Rep. 239 at 246.

particular port and shipment from that port was later prevented.[4] In one case, a seller successfully relied on a "strike" clause which was held, on its true construction, to apply on his showing that the ports through which he in fact would have shipped had been strike-bound, even though these were not the only ports through which shipment in accordance with the contract might have been made.[5]

12–030   An alternative mode of performance specified by the contract may completely alter the nature of the performance required, so that it no longer falls within the scope of the prohibition at all. This was, for example, the position where an obligation to ship or appropriate goods was converted into one to pay money by a "circle" clause which provided that if, as a result of sales and resales, a "circle" was established, then the transaction was to be settled by a monetary adjustment and failure to deliver shipping documents was no longer to be a breach. The export of goods of the contract description was prohibited only *after* such a circle had been established, and it was held that the seller could not rely on a prohibition of export clause in the contract.[6]

An option to perform in alternative ways can arise by operation of law no less than under the express terms of the contract. An obvious example of this situation arises where the contract is simply one for the sale of unascertained goods by description. The seller cannot in such a case rely on a prohibition of export clause where the prohibition merely prevents him from acquiring the goods from his intended supplier, but leaves it open to him to acquire goods of the contract description (though at a price higher than that to be paid by the buyer[7]) from other sources, *e.g.* from the foreign government which had imposed the prohibition.[8] In the case of a c.i.f. contract, the normal position is that the seller can perform either by shipping goods of the contract description or by appropriating goods which are already afloat, whether they have been shipped by himself or by a third party; and if performance by one of these methods becomes impossible, the other must be adopted.[9] It follows that normally a seller will not be able to rely on a prohibition of export clause merely because shipment of goods of the contract description has been prevented by a prohibition of export. Thus if the seller had already shipped such goods before the embargo was imposed, and had not already appropriated them to another contract, then he must appropriate those goods to the contract in question.[10] Goods of the contract description may also be available where they had been shipped by others before the embargo was imposed. Where this is the case, the general rule is that the seller must acquire such other goods and appropriate them to the contract. So long as this course

---

[4] As in the case cited in the previous note.

[5] *Sociedad Iberica de Molturacion SA v Tradax Export SA* [1978] 2 Lloyd's Rep. 545.

[6] *Tradax Export SA v Rocco Guiseppe & Figli* [1981] 1 Lloyd's Rep. 353, not following *Tradax v Carapelli* [1977] 2 Lloyd's Rep. 157 on this point.

[7] *cf.* above, paras 4–053, 8–016.

[8] *Exportelisa SA v Guiseppe Figli Soc Coll* [1978] 1 Lloyd's Rep. 433.

[9] Above, para.4–044.

[10] See the authorities cited in below, para.12–035, n.33.

of action remains possible, he will not be able to rely on a prohibition clause.[11] These are, however, only *prima facie* rules which can be excluded either by the way in which the seller's obligation is defined in the contract or by the words of the prohibition clause: for example, the contract might be one for the sale of goods to be *shipped* by the seller, and the prohibition clause might be expressed to apply in case *shipment* (as opposed to delivery, or performance) was prevented.[12] In such cases the seller could rely on a prohibition which prevented shipment by him even though goods which had been shipped by third parties, and which were in other respects in accordance with the contract, continued to be available. He could also rely on the clause if the contract provided that the goods were to come from the country which had imposed the prohibition and the only substitute goods available afloat had originated in another country. Here (as in the case where the contract called for shipment by the seller himself) the substitute goods might be of the same general commercial category as the goods which formed the subject-matter of the contract. But they would not be of the contract description; for it is settled that stipulations as to the time, place or other aspects of shipment in overseas sales form part of the description of the goods.[13]

The general rule which gives a c.i.f. seller the choice between the two   12–031
methods of performance described above, and which obliges him to adopt one if the other should be prevented, is however subject to an exception. This exception was established in the soyabean cases (to be more fully discussed later in this chapter[14]) which arose when in 1973 an embargo was imposed on the export of soyabean meal from the United States. A similar exception was held to apply when the embargo was eventually lifted.[15] The nature of the exception and its scope have been discussed in Ch.4,[16] where we saw that the reason for it was that prices would have been driven up to "unheard-of levels" if all the sellers in sometimes very lengthy strings of contracts had been required to buy the limited available quantity of goods afloat which were of the contract description. The present point is that, where the exception applied, a c.i.f. seller could in principle rely on the embargo as "preventing fulfilment" within a prohibition clause in the contract, even though there was a theoretical possibility of his acquiring afloat goods which were of the contract description.[17] This possibility did not deprive him of the protection of the clause since it did not, in the special circumstances of those cases, enable him to obtain goods of the

---

[11] *e.g. PJ van der Zijden Wildhandel NV v Tucker & Cross Ltd* [1975] 2 Lloyd's Rep. 240, above, para.12–023.

[12] *e.g. Fairclough, Dodd & Jones Ltd v JH Vantol Ltd* [1957] 1 W.L.R. 136, above para.12–028 (n.95); *cf. European Grain & Shipping Ltd v JH Rayner & Co Ltd* [1970] 2 Lloyd's Rep. 239.

[13] *Benjamin's Sale of Goods* (6th ed.), paras 18–232 to 18–237.

[14] Below, paras 12–036 to 12–039.

[15] *Cook Industries v Tradax Export SA* [1983] 1 Lloyd's Rep. 327 at 344; affirmed [1985] 2 Lloyd's Rep. 454.

[16] Above, paras 4–045 to 4–047.

[17] *e.g. Bremer Handelsgesellschaft mbH v Vanden Avenne-Izegem PVBA* [1978] 2 Lloyd's Rep. 109 at 115.

contract description "by the exercise of any means reasonably open to him".[18] It should be emphasised that the present point is that the seller was not deprived of the protection of the clause merely by the fact that he could have acquired goods afloat. In many of the soyabean cases the actual result was that the seller was deprived of that protection: the reasons for this an explained later in this chapter.[19]

(c) *Burden of proof*

12–032
The party who seeks to rely on the provision for the supervening event must prove that an event of the kind specified in the clause has happened, and that it has had the effect stated in the clause on his ability to perform the contract.[20] For example, where the clause provides a seller with an excuse in the event of "prohibition of export ... preventing fulfilment"[21] he must show not merely that a prohibition of export came into existence, but also that that prohibition prevented him from performing his part of the contract.[22] Such a causal connection must also be shown where the clause is expressed to apply in the event of the seller's failure "to deliver ... or effect the shipment *by reason of* any causes beyond their control" and such a clause may go on to provide exactly how such causal connection is to be established: it may, for example, require the seller to provide a certificate to this effect issued by a named or designated body.[23] Obviously, the questions of exactly what must be proved, and how it is to be proved, will depend on the exact words used in the clause to describe the supervening event (or the way in which it is to be proved).[24] It will be convenient to begin the discussion of the burden of proof with cases in which the clause uses the words quoted above, or expressions which have a similar meaning, and then to consider cases in which the requirements of the clause are less strict.

(i) "Prohibition of export ... preventing fulfilment"

12–033
A number of distinctions must be drawn in discussing the effect of such words. One relates to the nature of the embargo, which may be either total or partial. Another relates to the intended method of performance:

---

[18] *André & Cie v Tradax Export SA* [1983] 1 Lloyd's Rep. 254 at 258; *Continental Grain Export Corp v STM Grain Ltd* [1979] 2 Lloyd's Rep. 460 at 473.

[19] Below, paras 12–037, 12–040.

[20] *Tradax Export SA v Andre & Cie* [1976] 1 Lloyd's Rep. 416; *Thomas D Gonzalez Corp v Müller's Mühle, Müller GmbH* [1980] 1 Lloyd's Rep. 445.

[21] These were the words of Grain & Feed Trade Association Form 100, cl.21, which fell to be considered in the soyabean cases, to be discussed below, paras 12–036 to 12–039.

[22] *Tradax Export SA v André & Cie*, above, n.20 at 426; *Huileries l'Abeille v Société des Huileries du Niger (The Kastellon)* [1978] 2 Lloyd's Rep. 203; *Avimex SA v Dewulf & Cie* [1979] 2 Lloyd's Rep. 59; *Raiffeisen Hauptgenossenschaft v Louis Dreyfuss & Co Ltd* [1981] 1 Lloyd's Rep. 345; *Agrokor AG v Tradigrain SA* [2000] 1 Lloyd's Rep. 497 at 501.

[23] As in *Hoechong Products Ltd v Cargill Hong Kong Ltd* [1995] 1 W.L.R. 404.

[24] For the construction of such a requirement, see the *Hoechong* case, above.

the seller may intend either himself to ship the goods or to appropriate to the contract goods which have been or are to be shipped by another shipper.

(a) Total embargo. The seller can rely on a clause in the terms here under discussion if he can show that a total embargo had been imposed and that it lasted for the whole of the shipment period specified in the contract (or for that part of the period remaining when the embargo was imposed if at that time the seller had not yet shipped and was not in breach as a result of having failed to do so). The seller can rely on the clause even though he cannot show that he could have performed but for the embargo, *i.e.* he need not show that, when the embargo was imposed, he had goods of the contract description available and a ship to carry them.[25] This rule is analogous to that which applies in cases of alleged discharge under the common law doctrine of frustration, in which the party claiming discharge can "rely upon a frustrating event as excusing further performance of his obligations even though he would in fact have been unable to perform his obligations under the contract".[26]

The further question arises whether the position is any different if *the buyer* can show that, even if there had been no embargo, the seller could not have performed. It is submitted that the seller should certainly not be deprived of the protection of the clause merely because he was not, at the time when the embargo was imposed, in a position to ship the goods; for he would (but for the embargo) have been entitled to ship the goods later in the shipment period,[27] at least if the exact time of shipment during that period was at his rather than at the buyer's option[28]; and it would be pointless for him to continue to make efforts after the imposition of the embargo to procure goods and to make shipping arrangements in accordance with the contract. It is, perhaps, a more open question whether the seller would lose the protection of the clause if the buyer could show that the seller could not at any time within the contract period have performed, or have put himself into a position to perform, his obligations. It has been suggested that in such a situation the buyer should

---

[25] *Tradax Export SA v André & Cie* [1976] 1 Lloyd's Rep. 416 at 425, 427; so far as *contra*, a dictum in the same case at 423 was disapproved in *Bremer Handelsgesellschaft mbH v Vanden Avenne-Izegem PVBA* [1978] 2 Lloyd's Rep. 109 at 114, 121; *Bremer Handelsgesellschaft mbH v C Mackprang Jr* [1979] 1 Lloyd's Rep. 221 at 227–229. These cases all discuss the position under an absolute embargo, though they were actually concerned with an embargo which was partial in the sense explained at para.12–036, below.

[26] *Continental Grain Export Corp v STM Grain Ltd* [1979] 2 Lloyd's Rep. 460 at 471, citing *Avery v Bowden* (1855) 5 E. & B. 714.

[27] This is certainly the position where the sale is on c.i.f. terms: see *Benjamin's Sale of Goods* (6th ed.), para.19–013.

[28] Under an f.o.b. contract, the time of shipment during the shipment period is prima facie at the buyer's option, but this *prima facie* rule can be displaced by the contract: see *Benjamin's Sale of Goods* (6th ed.), paras 20–030, 20–035, 20–047 to 20–049.

be entitled to damages.[29] But there is no actual decision to this effect, and the analogy of the rule which applies where the seller relies on the common law doctrine of frustration would seem to suggest that the seller should not be liable in such a case, for the present rule appears to be one of substance rather than one which merely determines the incidence of the burden of proof.[30]

12–035   The propositions relating to burden of proof stated in para.12–034 above are based on the assumption that the *only* way in which the seller is bound to perform is by shipping goods, and that this can no longer be lawfully be done after the imposition of the embargo. It is, however, again necessary to note that, in the case of c.i.f. contracts "fulfilment" will not as a general rule be prevented merely by a prohibition of export, since normally the seller can (and must) perform either by shipping or by appropriating goods already afloat; but that this general rule is subject to an exception which was recognised in the soyabean cases as applying to certain "string contracts".[31] Under the exception, the seller is not bound to perform by *buying* afloat; and the point to be made here is that it follows that the seller need not negative the possibility that he might have bought goods afloat of the contract description, since he is under no substantive duty to do so.[32] The exception, however, does not extend to the case in which the seller *already had* such goods at his disposal when the embargo was imposed, and had not appropriated them to another contract. A seller who wishes to rely on a clause of the kind here under consideration therefore has the burden of proving that no such unappropriated goods afloat were available to him.[33]

12–036   *(b) Partial embargo.* Further complications arise when the embargo is only partial, in the sense that certain categories of goods of the contract description are excepted from it. This was the situation which arose in 1973 when, after disastrous floods in the Mississippi valley, the United States authorities first gave a warning that they might impose an embargo on the export of soyabean meal and then imposed the embargo by an official bulletin of June 27. This provided that no

---

[29]   *Bremer Handelsgesellschaft mbH v C Mackprang Jr* [1979] 1 Lloyd's Rep. 221 at 227–228.

[30]   In *Avery v Bowden* (1855) 5 E. & B. 714 (above, n.26) the charterparty was frustrated even though it was established that the charterer could not have provided a cargo.

[31]   Above, para.4–047.

[32]   Above, para.12–031, n.18.

[33]   *Continental Grain Export Corp v STM Grain Ltd* [1979] 2 Lloyd's Rep. 460 at 473; *Cook Industries Inc v Meunerie Liègeois* [1981] 1 Lloyd's Rep. 359 at 366; *Bremer Handelsgesellschaft mbH v Continental Grain Co* [1983] 1 Lloyd's Rep. 269 at 283. *cf.* also *Bremer Handeslsgesellschaft mbH v Westzucker GmbH (No 2)* [1981] 2 Lloyd's Rep. 130 (where the point was not open on appeal, not having been taken by the buyers in the court below); *Tradax Export SA v Cook Industries Inc* [1982] 1 Lloyd's Rep. 285 (where the buyer was allowed to take the point on appeal as the law relating to it had not been clarified until after the original hearing); *André & Cie SA v Tradax Export SA* [1983] 1 Lloyd's Rep. 254 (where the seller succeeded in discharging the burden of proof on this point).

soyabean meal could be exported unless it fell within one of two "loopholes": the embargo did not apply to goods on a lighter destined for an exporting vessel, or to goods for which loading aboard an exporting vessel had already commenced.[34] A further bulletin of July 2, introduced a licensing system for 40 per cent of quantities outstanding under existing contracts, but between June 27 and July 2, the embargo was subject only to the two loopholes. The resulting disruption of the soyabean trade gave rise to a great deal of litigation and it is a remarkable aspect of the history of this matter that most of this litigation took place in England[35] even though none of the events giving rise to it, and few of the parties involved, had any connection with this country. The explanation appears to be that the litigation was mainly between c.i.f. buyers and sellers whose contracts were made on terms contained in a form which had been settled by the Grain and Feeds Trade Association[36] and which provided for arbitration in London. The form contained "*force majeure*" and "prohibition" clauses, the latter of which provided for cancellation of the contracts in the event of "prohibition of export ... preventing fulfilment". The question of what sellers had to prove to bring themselves within this clause, arose in some 45 reported cases, and even these have been said to represent no more than "the tip of a massive iceberg".[37]

It is convenient to begin the discussion of these cases by considering two rules which apply where the seller intended to perform by himself shipping goods of the contract description. In this situation it was held first, that (as in the case of a total embargo) the seller need not show that he could have performed but for the embargo[38]; but secondly, that he must "close the loopholes",[39] *i.e.* that he must show that he did not have at his disposal any goods of the contract description which fell within the loopholes and which could have therefore been lawfully exported; for if such goods were at his disposal fulfilment would not be prevented by the embargo. In *Bremer Handelsgesellschaft mbH v Vanden Avenne-Izegem*

---

[34] For the later creation of a third "loophole" by the United States authorities, see the last of the cases cited in the previous note.

[35] The writer has found only two American cases which deal with the legal effects on contracts of the same natural disaster: *Bunge Corp v Recker*, 519 F. 2d 449 (1975) and *Bunge Corp v Miller*, 381 F. Supp. 176 (1974).

[36] Above, para.12–032, n.21; for a later variation of the form, see below, para.12–040.

[37] *Bremer Handelsgesellschaft mbH v Westzucker GmbH (No 3)* [1989] 1 Lloyd's Rep. 198 at 199, affirmed [1989] 1 Lloyd's Rep. 582.

[38] *Bremer Handelsgesellschaft mbH v Vanden Avenne-Izegem PVBA* [1978] 2 Lloyd's Rep. 109; *Tradax Export SA v Cook Industries Inc* [1982] 1 Lloyd's Rep. 285; for the same rule applicable in cases of total prohibitions, see above, para.12–034.

[39] *Tradax Export SA v André & Cie* [1976] 1 Lloyd's Rep. 516; *Continental Grain Export Corp v STM Grain Ltd* [1979] 2 Lloyd's Rep. 460; *Tradax Export SA v Cook Industries Inc* [1982] 1 Lloyd's Rep. 385; *Bremer Handelsgesellschaft mbH v Raiffeisen Hauptgenossenschaft* [1982] 1 Lloyd's Rep. 210; affirmed *ibid.* at 599; *Bremer Handelsgesellschaft mbH v Continental Grain Co* [1983] 1 Lloyd's Rep. 269 at 283.

PVBA,[40] the House of Lords affirmed the first of the two propositions stated above. It was, moreover, found[41] or conceded[42] that goods falling within the "loopholes" were not available to the seller; and later cases[43] make it clear that the decision of the House of Lords has not affected the rule requiring him to show that no goods within the "loopholes" were available to him.[44]

12–037   *(c) Identifying the shipper.*   Further complications can arise (and did arise in many of the soyabean cases) where the seller is not a person who intended himself to ship goods, but one who occupies (or claims that he occupies) an intermediate position between a prospective shipper and the buyer in a "string" of contracts. The burden of proof which lies on sellers who seek in such circumstances to rely on the prohibition clause is complex and was in practice rarely discharged.

In the first place, the burden is on the seller to "trace the string back to the relevant shipper".[45] This is a burden which can be an extremely difficult one to discharge where no goods were ever shipped, for in such a case the obvious method of identifying the relevant shipper by notices of appropriation passed down a string is plainly not available.[46] Although the question whether the seller had identified the relevant shipper has been

---

[40] [1978] 2 Lloyd's Rep. 109 at 114, 121. The buyer accordingly lost his claim against the seller, but was later held liable to his sub-buyer as he could not identify the "relevant shipper" (below, para.12–037, n.57): *Vanden Avenne-Izegem PVBA v Finagrain SA* [1985] 2 Lloyd's Rep. 99.

[41] [1978] 2 Lloyd's Rep. at 112, 128, 129.

[42] See *ibid.* 122; *cf. Bremer Handelsgesellschaft mbH v C Mackprang Jr* [1979] 1 Lloyd's Rep. 221 at 223, 227.

[43] See the last case cited in the previous note; *Avimex SA v Dewulf & Cie* [1979] 1 Lloyd's Rep. 57 at 58; *André & Cie v Ets. Michel Blanc & Fils* [1979] 2 Lloyd's Rep. 427; *Bunge SA v Deutsche Conti-Handelsgesellschaft mbH* [1979] 2 Lloyd's Rep. 435; *Bremer Handelsgesellschaft mbH v Westzucker GmbH (No 2)* [1981] 2 Lloyd's Rep. 130.

[44] *cf.* also *Joseph Pyke & Sons (Liverpool) Ltd v Richard Cornelius & Co* [1955] 2 Lloyd's Rep. 747; *Continental Grain Export Corp v STM Grain Ltd* [1979] 2 Lloyd's Rep. 460 at 471 (where the "prohibition of export" clause was on terms substantially similar to those of the form referred to in para.12–032, n.21, above).

[45] *Bremer Handelsgesellschaft mbH v C Mackprang Jr* [1981] 1 Lloyd's Rep. 292 at 297, where the issue arose under a *"force majeure"* clause in the same GAFTA form, but the same principle applies to the "prohibition" clause in it: see *Cook Industries Inc v Meunerie Liègeois SA* [1981] 1 Lloyd's Rep. 359; *Bremer Handelsgesellschaft mbH v Continental Grain Co* [1983] 1 Lloyd's Rep. 269 at 293. The seller succeeded on this point though he failed on others in *Bunge AG v Fuga AG* [1980] 2 Lloyd's Rep. 513 (where the point on which he failed is indicated at para.12–044, n.96 below) and in *Tradax Export SA v Cook Industries SA* [1982] 1 Lloyd's Rep. 385 (where the point on which he failed is indicated at n.39 above).

[46] *Cook Industries Inc v Meunerie Liègeois SA* [1981] 1 Lloyd's Rep. 359 at 365; *Bremer Handelsgesellschaft mbH v C Mackprang Jr* [1981] 1 Lloyd's Rep. 292 at 297.

described as one of "fact",[47] the cases yield a number of helpful guidelines on the issue. A seller who is not himself a shipper will clearly be unable to identify the relevant shipper if he simply contracts to sell goods of a particular kind and does not also contract to acquire goods of that description from a supplier[48]; for in such circumstances, it has been said that "the chain of contracts leading back to the shippers failed at its very first link".[49] Assuming that there is a series of supply (as well as of sale) contracts, one posssible way of tracing the string back to the relevant shipper is by means of notices[50] claiming excuse under the prohibition clause,[51] but this is not of itself sufficient. A person is not identified as the relevant shipper merely because the seller, *after* the embargo has been imposed, gives a notice appropriating goods shipped by that person[52]; nor does the mere fact that the seller appropriates in part fulfilment of the contract goods shipped by a particular shipper necessarily identify that shipper as the relevant one for the balance of the quantity sold,[53] nor can the seller identify himself as the relevant shipper merely by giving notice claiming excuse under the prohibition clause.[54] In holding that a seller had failed to identify himself or a third person as relevant shipper, the courts have in a number of cases stressed that the seller was not bound to appropriate goods shipped by himself or the alleged shipper but retained complete freedom to appropriate goods shipped by another.[55] It seems to follow from this reasoning that the shipper must be named or capable of being identified[56] so as to oblige the seller (either by the contract or by a notice of appropriation) to tender goods, or documents relating to goods, shipped by that shipper: it is not enough for the seller to show merely that he intended to appropriate those goods in performance of his obligations under the contract of sale.[57] If the seller cannot identify the relevant shipper, the string is incomplete: the situation is simply one where the seller (or his immediate or remote supplier) intends at some stage

---

[47] *Deutsche Conti-Handelsgesellschaft mbH v Bremer Handelsgesellschaft mbH* [1984] 1 Lloyd's Rep. 447 at 449, 450; *cf. European Grain & Shipping Ltd v Peter Cremer* [1983] 1 Lloyd's Rep. 211.

[48] *Avimex SA v Dewulf & Cie* [1979] 2 Lloyd's Rep. 57.

[49] *Bunge AG v Fuga AG* [1980] 2 Lloyd's Rep. 513 at 520.

[50] See below, paras 12–042 to 12–044.

[51] *Cook Industries Inc v Meunerie Liègeois SA* [1981] 1 Lloyd's Rep. 359 at 365.

[52] *Bremer Handelsgesellschaft mbH v Mackprang Jr* [1981] 1 Lloyd's Rep. 292.

[53] *Bremer Handelsgesellschaft mbH v Deutsche Conti-Handelsgesellschaft mbH* [1984] 1 Lloyd's Rep. 397; *Deutsche Conti-Handelsgesellschaft mbH v Bremer Handelsgesellschaft mbH* [1984] 1 Lloyd's Rep. 446.

[54] *Bremer Handelsgesellschaft mbH v Continental Grain Co* [1983] 1 Lloyd's Rep. 269 at 290.

[55] *Bremer Handelsgesellschaft mbH v Bunge Corp* [1983] 1 Lloyd's Rep. 476 at 481; *Deutsche Conti-Handelsgesellschaft mbH v Bremer Handelsgesellschaft mbH* [1984] 1 Lloyd's Rep. 447 at 449.

[56] See *Bunge AG v Fuga AG* [1980] 2 Lloyd's Rep. 513 at 520.

[57] See *Deutsche Conti-Handelsgesellschaft mbH v Bremer Handelsgesellschaft mbH* [1984] 1 Lloyd's Rep. 447 at 449; *Vanden Avenne-Izegem PVBA v Finagrain SA* [1985] 2 Lloyd's Rep. 99.

between the time of contracting and that fixed for performance to acquire goods of the contract description from an as yet undesignated shipper. In such a case the seller cannot rely on a prohibition clause merely because the embargo has been imposed.[58]

12–038   If the seller can show that there was a complete string and if he can identify the relevant shipper, he must next establish that that shipper was, by reason of the embargo, prevented from performing his obligations under the supply contract between him (the shipper) and the next person in the string. It follows that the seller must show that the relevant shipper had no goods available to him which were either within the "loopholes" or had already been shipped before the embargo was imposed but had not yet been appropriated to any other contract.[59] If there is more than one relevant shipper, the seller must show that no such goods were available to any of those shippers.[60] The burden of proof on all of these issues is on the seller: hence if he adduces no evidence as to the availability of such goods to the relevant shipper, he will be liable for breach of the contract of sale.[61] It may seem hard on a seller thus to hold him liable for failing to provide evidence that no goods within the "loopholes" were available to a third person (the relevant shipper).[62] But the result of putting the burden on the buyer to prove that goods *were* available within the "loopholes" might be to "make a breach of contract too easy".[63] The buyer would have no better access than the seller to facts relating to the availability of goods within the "loopholes" to the relevant shipper; and if the buyer failed to adduce such proof but goods within the "loopholes" were in fact available, the seller would profit from the embargo by being able to dispose of those goods at a price enhanced by it.[64]

There is, at least in theory, an alternative way in which a seller may be protected by the prohibition clause. The possibility has been judicially recognised that he could be so protected, even though he had failed to identify the relevant shipper, if he could show that no goods of the contract description could have been shipped within the "loopholes" by any possibly relevant shipper, and that no such goods were already afloat (and not appropriated to any other contract) when the embargo was

---

[58] *Bunge SA v Deutsche Conti-Handelsgesellschaft* [1979] 2 Lloyd's Rep. 435; *Bunge SA v Deutsche Conti-Handelsgesellschaft (No 2)* [1980] 1 Lloyd's Rep. 352; *Bremer Handelsgesellschaft mbH v Westzucker GmbH* [1981] 1 Lloyd's Rep. 207; *Bunge SA v Compagnie Européenne de Céréales* [1982] 1 Lloyd's Rep. 307.

[59] *Cook Industries Inc v Meunerie Liègeois* [1981] 1 Lloyd's Rep. 359; *Bremer Handelsgesellschaft mbH v Continental Grain Co* [1983] 1 Lloyd's Rep. 269 at 283; *Bremer Handelsgesellschaft mbH v Bunge Corp* [1983] 1 Lloyd's Rep. 476 at 481 (where the seller failed to identify the "relevant shipper").

[60] *Cook Industries v Tradax Export SA* [1986] 2 Lloyd's Rep. 454.

[61] *Bremer Handelsgesellschaft mbH v C Mackprang Jr.* [1979] 1 Lloyd's Rep. 221.

[62] [1979] 1 Lloyd's Rep. at 230, *per* Shaw L.J.

[63] *ibid.* at 226, *per* Stephenson L.J.

[64] *ibid.* at 224, *per* Lord Denning M.R. The argument is perhaps too strongly stated, since if the seller actually pursued this course the buyer would have little difficulty in discharging any burden of proof with regard to the "loopholes" which the law might impose on him.

imposed[65]; but there appears to be no reported case in which a seller has succeeded in discharging the difficult task of proving a multiple negative proposition of this kind.

(d) Burden of proof and substantive duties. In the case of a partial embargo, such as one which is subject to "loopholes"[66] a distinction must be drawn between two questions. The first is the question of fact whether the seller or relevant shipper had available to him goods which he could have appropriated to the contract, *e.g.* because they fell within the "loopholes", so that their shipment was not prevented by the embargo, or because they had been shipped by the seller or by the relevant shipper before the embargo took effect and had not been appropriated to another contract. It is in relation to such questions of fact that the rules as to burden of proof stated in paras 12–037 and 12–038, above apply. The second question is one of law and relates to the substantive duties of the seller, assuming that he can discharge the burden of proving that no goods of the contract description were at his or at the relevant shipper's disposal for the purpose of performing the contract. This question is whether the seller is then bound to acquire goods of the contract description from some other source, *e.g.* by buying goods which had already been shipped before the embargo took effect, or (in the case of a partial embargo) goods excepted from the embargo. We have seen that a c.i.f. seller generally is under such a duty[67]; and, where this general rule applies, the burden of proving that no such goods could have been acquired will (in accordance with the principles stated above) once again be on the seller. That burden will be extremely hard to discharge since it would require the seller to show that no unappropriated goods were available to *any* shipper or could be acquired afloat. Where, on the other hand, the case falls within an exception to the general rule requiring the seller to resort to another source, so that he is under *no* duty to make a substitute purchase, no issue as to burden of proof can arise as to the availability of another source. We have seen that one such exception was recognised in the soyabean cases, where it was held that c.i.f. sellers in "strings" of contracts were, when shipment was prevented, under no duty to buy goods then already afloat, since to require them to do this would drive prices up to "unheard-of levels".[68] In one of this group of cases, the exception was extended so as to negative the seller's duty to acquire goods which, though not already afloat and so beyond the reach of the embargo, were excepted from it because they fell within the

---

[65] This possibility is recognised in *Cook Industries Inc v Meunerie Liégeois* [1981] 1 Lloyd's Rep. 359 at 363 and in *Bremer Handelsgesellschaft mbH v Westzucker GmbH (No 3)* [1989] 1 Lloyd's Rep. 582, where the seller's attempt to prove these facts failed.

[66] As in the case of the United States embargo on the export of soyabean meal: above, para.12–036.

[67] Above, para.4–044.

[68] *Tradax Export SA v André & Cie* [1976] 1 Lloyd's Rep. 416 at 423; above, para.4–045.

"loopholes".[69] Such an extension of the exception appears in principle to be supportable on the same grounds as those which justify the original exception itself, *i.e.* that attempts by all the sellers in a string to buy the limited quantity of available "loophole" goods would create an extreme pressure on prices. But the case[70] in which the exception was extended to the present situation gives rise to difficulty in that it further holds that the seller could rely on the extended exception without having to show that the sale formed part of a "string" of contracts or that he, or a relevant shipper, had (before the embargo was imposed) made arrangements for the shipment of the goods. In so far as the case lays down a rule as to burden of proof, it is inconsistent with other decisions which require a seller claiming excuse under the clause to trace the string back to a relevant shipper.[71] In so far as it lays down a rule of substance, to the effect that a seller need not buy "loophole" goods even where his contract with the buyer is *not* one of a string of contracts, it is submitted that the case extends the instant exception too far. Normally a seller of unascertained generic goods is not relieved (even by a *force majeure* or prohibition clause) from his duty to appropriate such goods of the contract description as may be available merely because a particular source of supply intended by him (but not specified in the contract) has failed. Prohibition of export or *force majeure* will commonly make performance more expensive for the seller, and normally (where an alternative method remains open to him) he has to bear this expense.[72] It is the extremity of the increase which accounts for the exception applicable where performance of "string" contracts is affected by an embargo interfering with previously made shipping arrangements; and it is submitted that the exception should be confined to cases of this kind.[73]

(ii) Other less exacting requirements

12–040   The soyabean cases discussed above illustrate the difficulties which faced sellers who sought to rely on prohibition and similar clauses which applied only where they could show that performance had been "prevented" by the supervening event. It was, for example, often impossible for them to discharge the burden of tracing the string back to the "relevant shipper" and that of "closing the loopholes". It was probably with reference to

---

[69] *Bunge SA v Kruse* [1979] 1 Lloyd's Rep. 279; affirmed on other grounds [1980] 2 Lloyd's Rep. 142, and referred to with apparent approval on this point in *André & Cie v Tradax Export SA* [1983] 1 Lloyd's Rep. 254 at 267.

[70] *i.e. Bunge SA v Kruse*, above, n.69.

[71] Above, para.12–037; *Bremer Handelsgesellschaft mbH v C Mackprang Jr* [1979] 1 Lloyd's Rep. 221 at 228.

[72] *cf. PJ van der Zijden Wildhandel NV v Tucker & Cross Ltd* [1975] 2 Lloyd's Rep. 240.

[73] *Warinco AG v Fritz Mauthner* [1978] 1 Lloyd's Rep. 151 at 156 (*per* Bridge L.J.); *cf. ibid.* at 154 (*per* Megaw L.J.); *Bunge SA v Deutsche Conti-Handelsgesellschaft mbH* [1979] 2 Lloyd's Rep. 435 at 439. It is submitted that these views are to be preferred to the suggestion of Lord Denning M.R. in *Bremer Handelsgesellschaft mbH v Finagrain, etc SA* [1981] 2 Lloyd's Rep. 259 at 265, that *no* string need be established for the purpose of the present exception.

these difficulties that prohibitions of export were said to have been "a sellers' nightmare".[74] The source of the difficulties in the soyabean cases lay in the words "preventing . . . fulfilment" in the clause of the Grain and Feed Trade Association's standard form contract; and it was with a view to improving the seller's position that the clause was later redrafted. In its revised version it applied in case of a prohibition or of an executive act by the government of the country of origin "restricting export whether partially or otherwise"; and it provided that: "such restriction shall be deemed by both parties to apply to this contract and to the extent of such total or partial restriction, to prevent fulfilment whether by shipment or by any other means whatsoever." Taken literally, these words might be thought to apply irrespective of any causal connection between the prohibition and the seller's non-fulfilment. But in *Pancommerce SA v Veecheema BV*[75] the Court of Appeal rejected the argument that a seller could rely on this provision merely because a prohibition had been imposed, when in fact that prohibition had not prevented him from performing. The contract was one for the sale of 1,500 tons of "Spanish unmolassed sugar beet pellets" c.i.f. Ghent; before it was made the sellers had sold 1,500 tons of the same commodity to another buyer (Lucerna) to whom they had also given a "first refusal" of up to another 1,500 tons if they obtained further sugar beet pellets during the year. After the transaction with Lucerna, but before that with the present buyers, the sellers obtained an export licence for 3,000 tons, but this did not refer to any particular contracts. The Spanish Government then changed its previous policy of granting export licences as a matter of course, and refused to issue further licences. The sellers accordingly delivered only part of the 1,500 tons to the buyers and the remainder to Lucerna, to whom they regarded themselves as morally bound by their "first refusal" promise to make such delivery. When the buyers claimed damages for short delivery, the sellers relied on the prohibition clause (in the terms set out above) and argued that they were protected by that clause merely because there had been an executive act of the government restricting export. But the court rejected the argument on the ground that, though the restriction which had been imposed must be deemed to apply to the contract, that restriction did not apply to goods for which the sellers held a licence; and therefore it could not be "deemed to prevent fulfilment" within the terms of the clause.[76] In reaching this conclusion the court seems to have been influenced by the possibility that, if the sellers' argument had prevailed, they would have been entitled to cancel their contract with the buyers although they were in fact able to perform it, and so to take advantage of the rise in the market price of the goods which had resulted from the export prohibition. It should be emphasised, however, that this was not in fact what the sellers were trying to do: they had used

---

[74] *Pancommerce SA v Veecheema BV* [1983] 2 Lloyd's Rep. 304 at 306.

[75] Above.

[76] Contrast *Pagnan SpA v Tradax Ocean Transportation SA* [1947] 3 All E.R. 565, where sellers who had obtained *no* licence were protected by a clause in the same terms.

part of the goods covered by the licence to fulfil what they regarded as their moral obligation to Lucerna. No doubt, however, the buyers' legal claim must be regarded as stronger than Lucerna's purely moral one.[77]

12–041   In the *Pancommerce* case, Sir John Donaldson M.R. said that, to adopt the sellers' construction of the clause would convert prohibition of export from "a sellers' nightmare … into a sellers' dream".[78] A similar reluctance to allow a seller to rely on a prohibition clause when he can actually fulfil all his contractual obligations, in spite of the embargo, is reflected in some of the earlier authorities. In *Tennants (Lancashire) Ltd v CS Wilson & Co Ltd*,[79] for example, the main reason why a seller was entitled to rely on a clause allowing him to suspend deliveries on the occurrence of specified events "hindering … delivery" was that, as a result of the events which had happened, he was "unable to deliver *unless he breaks his other contracts*".[80] But there is no reason in principle why a clause should not (if sufficiently clear in its wording) entitle the seller to refuse to perform on the occurrence of a specified event even though the event does not in fact affect his ability to perform at all. This was, for example, the position in *Ford & Sons (Oldham) Ltd v Henry Leetham & Sons Ltd*[81] (discussed earlier in this chapter) where Bailhache J. said that the clause did not require the sellers to show any relationship of cause and effect between the prohibition and the possibility of performance of the contract. That case is not now commonly relied on, but it appears to be a correct application of the overriding principle that the operation of such clauses depends ultimately on the wording of the particular clause in each case. General policies (such as that stated in the *Pancommerce* case) may influence, but cannot in the last result determine, decisions on such questions of construction.

(d) *Requirements as to notice*

12–042   *Force majeure* and prohibition clauses commonly state that the party wishing to rely on them must give written notice to the other party of his intention to do so; and such a clause may specify in some detail the requirements with which that notice must comply. It may specify the time within which the notice must be given and the facts which it must contain[82]: for example, it may require a seller to indicate from which port or ports he had intended to ship the goods, to state that such shipment is likely to be prevented and to specify the cause of such prevention.[83] Clearly the party wishing to rely on the clause cannot do so if he simply

---

[77] For this aspect of the case, see also above, para.5–028.
[78] [1983] 2 Lloyd's Rep. 304 at 306.
[79] [1917] A.C. 495.
[80] *ibid.* at 510 (italics supplied).
[81] (1915) 21 Com.Cas. 55; above, para.12–023.
[82] This was the position under the clauses of the Grain & Feed Trade Associations Form 100 considered in the soyabean cases discussed above, paras 12–036 *et seq.*
[83] For the effects of a notice relating to part only of the quantity sold, see *Bremer Handelsgesellschaft mbH v Archer-Daniels Midland International SA* [1981] 2 Lloyd's Rep. 483.

fails to give the notice; but greater difficulty arises where he gives a notice which is defective in the sense that it fails in some way to comply with the contractual requirements. Two questions then arise: the first relates to the legal consequences of the defects in the notice, and the second to waiver of those defects.

(i) Defects in the notice

The first of the above questions has been considered in a number of cases 12–043 in which the notice was defective in being out of time. The issue in these cases was whether the contractual requirement as to the time within which the notice was to be given was a condition or an intermediate (or innominate) term. If it was a condition, the seller could not rely on the clause and so was liable for non-delivery; if it was an intermediate term he could rely on the clause (unless the delay seriously prejudiced the buyer) but he was liable to the buyer in damages, not for non-delivery, but in respect of loss suffered by the buyer in consequence of the seller's delay in giving the notice. The question whether the contractual requirement as to the time of giving notice is a condition or an intermediate term depends, as Lord Wilberforce said in *Bremer Handelsgesellschaft mbH v Vanden Avenne-Izegem PVBA*[84] on three factors: "(i) the form of the clause itself, (ii) the relation of the clause to the contract as a whole, (iii) general considerations of the law." In the present context, two such general considerations or trends are of particular significance. The first is the judicial reluctance to classify terms as conditions where the parties themselves have not clearly expressed them as such, and where they have not been previously so classified by statute or by judicial decision.[85] The second, countervailing, trend relates to stipulations as to the time of performance[86]: these have commonly (though not invariably[87]) been classified as conditions where they specify a date by, or time within, which the stipulated acts were to be done.[88] Such a classification promotes certainty: in the present context, it enables the buyer to know precisely when the seller's failure to comply with the requirement (as to giving notice) will prevent the seller from relying on the clause and so put him in breach. But such certainty is not attainable where the term in question neither specifies, nor makes it possible to determine, the *precise* time at which the notice is to be given; and a term of this kind is unlikely to be

---

[84] [1978] 2 Lloyd's Rep. 109 at 113.

[85] *e.g. Cehave NV v Bremer Handelsgesellschaft mbH (The Hansa Nord)* [1976] Q.B. 44; *Tradax Internacional SA v Goldschmidt SA* [1977] 2 Lloyd's Rep. 604 at 612; *State Trading Corp of India v M Golodetz Ltd* [1989] 2 Lloyd's Rep. 277 at 283. The trend is recognised in *Bunge Corp v Tradax Export SA* [1977] 1 W.L.R. 711 at 715, 727, though it was not applied in that case: see below, n.88.

[86] See Treitel, *The Law of Contract* (11th ed.), pp.797–800.

[87] *State Trading Corp of India v M Golodetz Ltd* [1989] 2 Lloyd's Rep. 277; *ERG Petroli SpA v Vitol SA (The Ballenita)* [1992] 2 Lloyd's Rep. 455; *Universal Bulk Carriers Ltd v Andre & Cie* [2001] EWCA Civ 588; [2001] 2 Lloyd's Rep. 65.

[88] *e.g. Bunge Corp v Tradax Export SA* [1981] 1 W.L.R. 711; *Compagnie Commerciale Sucres et Denrées v C Czarnikow Ltd (The Naxos)* [1990] 1 W.L.R. 1137; *BS & N Ltd v Micado Shipping Ltd (Malta) (No 2) (The Seaflower)* [2001] 1 All E.R. (Comm) 240.

treated as a condition.[89] The distinction between the two types of terms is illustrated by two provisions in the contract considered by the House of Lords in *Bremer Handelsgesellschaft mbH v Vanden Avenne-Izegem PVBA*. The first, contained in a prohibition of export clause, required the sellers to "advise buyers without delay" of any prohibition making shipment impossible. This was held to be an intermediate term only,[90] so that failure to give the required notice "without delay" did not prevent the sellers from relying on the clause: it would only have had this effect if the resulting delay had caused serious prejudice to the buyers. The term was not expressly made a condition and could in this respect be contrasted with other provisions in the contract which were so drafted as to take effect as conditions. Nor would certainty be significantly promoted by classifying the term as a condition, since the phrase "without delay" was inherently vague: it raised "questions of degree",[91] and therefore did not enable the buyer to tell *exactly* when the seller was in default. The second stipulation formed part of a *force majeure* clause in the same contract; it provided that notice of certain events delaying shipment was to be given within seven days of their occurrence; and that a further notice was to be given claiming an extension of the shipment period "not later than two business days after the last day of the contract period of shipment". The clause went on to give the buyer an option to cancel by notice to be received by the seller, again by a precisely specified day, and to provide exactly when the contract was to be considered void, in default of the exercise of this option. It was held that the stipulation as to the time at which notice claiming the extension must be given was a condition. Unlike the prohibition clause, it specified fixed days for the giving of various notices. It was a "complete regulatory code" and "accurate compliance with its stipulations" was "essential to avoid commercial confusion in view of the possibility of there being long strings of buyers and sellers".[92]

12–044   The cases on this topic are mostly concerned with notices which are out of time, but the notice may be defective in some other way. For example, in *Bremer Handelsgesellschaft mbH v Vanden Avenne-Izegem PVBA*[93] the notice

---

[89] See *Tradax Export SA v Italgrani di Francesco Ambrosio* [1986] 1 Lloyd's Rep. 112 at 120; *Alfred McAlpine plc v BAI (Run-off) Ltd* [2000] 1 Lloyd's Rep. 437; contrast *Société Italo-Belge pour le Commerce et l'Industrie v Palm Vegetable Oils (Malaysia) Sdn Bhd (The Post Chaser)* [1981] 2 Lloyd's Rep. 695 at 700 (criticised on this point in *Benjamin's Sale of Goods* (6th ed.), para.19–063.

[90] [1978] 2 Lloyd's Rep. 109; applied on this point in *Bunge SA v Kruse* [1979] 1 Lloyd's Rep. 279; affirmed [1981] 1 Lloyd's Rep. 207; *Bremer Handelsgesellschaft mbH v Westzucker GmbH (No 2)* [1981] 1 Lloyd's Rep. 214 at 222; affirmed [1981] 2 Lloyd's Rep. 130; *Bremer Handelsgesellschaft mbH v Finagrain, etc. SA* [1981] 2 Lloyd's Rep. 259.

[91] *The Naxos*, above, n.88, at 1347.

[92] [1978] 2 Lloyd's Rep. at 116; *Berg & Son Ltd v Vanden Avenne-Izegem PVBA* [1977] 1 Lloyd's Rep. 500 (where the seller's notice claiming extension was defective in failing to specify the port of intended shipment); contrast on this point *Alfred C Toepfer v Peter Cremer* [1975] 2 Lloyd's Rep. 118).

[93] [1978] 2 Lloyd's Rep. 109.

under the *force majeure* clause was defective not only because it was too late but also because it failed with sufficient certainty to specify the intended port or ports of shipment. This breach, too, appears to have been regarded as one of condition, probably because it formed part of the same "complete regulatory code" as the provisions as to the time of giving notice. Where the clause contains no such "code" covering more than one requirement, the question whether any particular requirement is a condition or an intermediate term will depend on the general principles on which the distinction between these two categories of terms is based.[94] In particular, it is submitted, it will depend on the words in which the requirement is expressed and (if these are equivocal) on the importance which the party to whom the notice is given may be supposed to have attached to compliance with the requirement in question.[95]

Where the notice is alleged to be in some way defective, it is usually the buyer who takes this point for the purpose of holding the seller liable. But sometimes, paradoxically, it is the seller who will seek to rely on defects in the notice; for such defects may alter the time of breach in a way that benefits him on a fluctuating market. As a general rule, the seller cannot impugn the validity of his own notice if that notice is accepted as good by the buyer.[96] It is only if the buyer treats the notice as bad that the seller, too, can rely on defects in it, to the extent that it is to his advantage to do so.[97]

(ii) Waiver of defects in the notice

Even where the notice is defective in a way that amounts to a breach   **12–045**
of condition, the seller may nevertheless be entitled to rely on the prohibition or *force majeure* clause if the buyer has waived the breach. It is well known that "waiver" is used in several senses,[98] of which two are relevant here. In the first of these, it refers to the abandonment of a right; in the second to an election between remedies, *i.e.* between enforcing a contract and rescinding it on account of the breach. The context in which waiver falls to be considered here is that of a supervening event which results in a failure on the part of the seller to deliver, and usually in an increase in the market price of the goods. In these circumstances the buyer will wish to enforce his rights under the contract, rather than to rescind or terminate it. If he has "waived" the seller's failure to comply with the requirements of the clause, then the seller will be able to rely on the clause as an excuse for not performing his obligations under the contract. It follows that "waiver" is used here to refer to the abandonment by the buyer of his right to delivery (or to damages for non-delivery), and not to the process of election between remedies which would arise if the

---

[94] See Treitel, *The Law of Contract* (11th ed.), pp.795–800.

[95] *ibid.*, p.800.

[96] *Alfred C Toepfer v Peter Cremer* [1975] 2 Lloyd's Rep. 118 at 123, 128; *Bunge AG v Fuga AG* [1980] 2 Lloyd's Rep. 513.

[97] As in *Avimex SA v Dewulf & Cie* [1979] 2 Lloyd's Rep. 57 (where the buyer relied on defects in the seller's notice invoking a *force majeure* clause on the issue of liability, though not on the issue of damages).

[98] See Treitel, *The Law of Contract* (11th ed.), pp.811–813.

buyer were seeking, not to enforce the contract, but to rescind it. The distinction is important since the conditions which must be satisfied for the operation of the two types of waiver, though similar, are not identical.[99]

To give rise to waiver in the sense of the abandonment of a right, the buyer must in the first place unequivocally represent that he is not objecting to the defects in the notice[1]; and the seller must rely on that representation so as to make it inequitable[2] for the buyer to insist on his strict legal rights to full performance of the contract by reason of the defect in the notice.[3] It has been held that the first of these requirements was not satisfied where the notice, though actually defective, was good on its face and the buyer had no means of knowing that it was defective.[4] This may seem to support a separate requirement that the buyer must have been aware of the defect in the notice at the time of the alleged waiver. But knowledge of the breach is not a separate requirement of this type of waiver[5] (though it is a requirement of waiver in the sense of election between remedies[6]). The decisions under consideration can best be explained on the ground that, if the defective notice is good on its face, the buyer's apparent acceptance of it cannot be regarded as an unequivocal representation that he will not rely on defects in it which are latent, and certainly cannot be reasonably understood in this sense by the seller who tendered the notice.

12–046   The operation of the kind of waiver here under consideration is illustrated by *Bremer Handelsgesellschaft mbH v Vanden Avenne-Izegem PVBA*[7] where the seller served a notice, which was out of time, claiming an extension of the shipment period. The buyer, while objecting to the quantity of goods specified in the notice, did not raise any point as to its being out of time. He continued to press for delivery in the extended period and during it the seller made efforts to appropriate goods to the

---

[99] *ibid.*, pp.711–721; *Motor Oil Hellas (Corinth Refineries) SA v Shipping Corp of India (The Kanchenjunga)* [1990] 1 Lloyd's Rep. 391 at 399; *Oliver Ashworth (Holdings) Ltd v Ballard (Kent) Ltd* [2000] Ch.12 at 28; *Glencore Grain Ltd v Flacker Shipping Ltd (The Happy Day)* [2002] EWCA Civ 1068; [2002] 2 Lloyd's Rep. 487, at [64–65], [67].

[1] Treitel, *op. cit.*, pp.107–109, stating this requirement for so-called "promissory estoppel", an expression now often used interchangeably with this kind of "waiver": see below, para.12–046, n.9.

[2] Treitel, *op. cit.*, pp.109–111. Merely furnishing documents in proof of *force majeure* was held not to be sufficient to satisfy this requirement in *Bremer Handelsgesellschaft mbH v Deutsche Conti-Handelsgesellschaft mbH* [1983] 1 Lloyd's Rep. 689.

[3] *Bremer Handelsgesellschaft mbH v Bunge Corp* [1983] 1 Lloyd's Rep. 476.

[4] *Avimex SA v Dewulf & Cie* [1979] 2 Lloyd's Rep. 57 at 67–68; *Cook Industries v Tradax Export SA* [1985] 2 Lloyd's Rep. 454.

[5] *The Kanchenjunga*, above, n.99, at 399.

[6] *Peyman v Lanjani* [1985] Ch. 457.

[7] [1978] 2 Lloyd's Rep. 109; *cf. Intertradex SA v Lesieur-Torteaux SARL* [1978] 2 Lloyd's Rep. 509; *Bremer Handelsgesellschaft mbH v C Mackprang Jr* [1979] 1 Lloyd's Rep. 221.

contract. It was held that the buyer had waived the seller's breach in giving notice out of time. Such a result may also be explained on the grounds of estoppel or promissory estoppel[8]; indeed, in the context of abandonment of rights, the expressions "waiver" and "promissory estoppel" are now often used interchangeably[9] and have been described as "two ways of saying exactly the same thing".[10] In whatever way the rule may be described, a buyer is not prevented by it from relying on a defect in the notice merely because he fails to object to the notice on account of the defect when he first receives the notice[11]; or merely because he calls for proof of *force majeure* after receipt of the notice[12]; or merely because, after receipt of the notice, he accepts an appropriation of part of the quantity sold (which the seller was allowed to export under an exception to the embargo).[13] In none of these cases is there any "unequivocal representation" by the buyer that he is treating the notice as valid and that he does not intend to rely on the defect in it; and even if there is such a representation the argument that the defect in the notice has been waived will still fail if the seller's alleged action in reliance consists only of some act (such as applying for an export licence) that he would have done anyway, even if the representation had not been made.[14]

---

[8] *Bremer Handelsgesellschaft mbH v Finagrain etc. SA* [1981] 2 Lloyd's Rep. 259 at 263.

[9] See Treitel, *The Law of Contract* (11th ed.), pp.117–118.

[10] *Prosper Homes v Hambro's Bank Executor and Trustee Co* (1979) 39 P. & C.R. 395 at 401.

[11] *V Berg & Son Ltd v Vanden Avenne-Izegem PVBA* [1977] 1 Lloyd's Rep. 500; *cf. Bunge SA v Companie Européenne de Céréales* [1983] 1 Lloyd's Rep. 307, where the sellers' defence failed not because of defects in the notice but because he could not identify the "relevant shipper": above, para.12–037.

[12] *Bremer Handelsgesellschaft v Deutsche Conti-Handelsgesellschaft mbH* [1983] 1 Lloyd's Rep. 689.

[13] *Bremer Handelsgesellschaft mbH v Bunge Corp* [1983] 1 Lloyd's Rep. 476.

[14] *ibid.*

CHAPTER 13

FORESEEN AND FORESEEABLE EVENTS

I. RELATION TO PURPOSES OF THE DOCTRINE

(1) Supervening impossibility

The principal purpose of the doctrine of frustration is to provide a **13–001** satisfactory means of allocating or dividing the loss caused by supervening obstacles to the performance of a contract. At the same time, the law recognises the power of the parties to make their own provision, expressly or by implication, for the effects of supervening events. If at the time of contracting the parties are aware of the risk that performance will be disrupted, then this awareness is likely to be reflected in the terms of their contract. One possible way in which it may be so reflected is by an express provision for the event in the contract: if so, the effect of the provision will be determined in accordance with the principles discussed in Ch.12. Another possibility is that the risk of disruption will be reflected in terms of the contract which do not directly refer to the event, such as the term fixing the price to be paid for the goods, facilities or services to be provided under the contract. That price may be reduced to reflect the risk that the performance promised may become valueless to the party who is to receive it, if, for example, in the coronation cases[1] there had been an interval between the announcement that the King was ill and the decision to cancel the processions, prices of tickets would no doubt have fallen during that interval. Conversely, the price may rise to reflect the risk that the cost of performance may be increased for the party who is to render it: for example where the supervening event is expected to make it impossible for that party to adopt the intended method of performance and greater costs will be incurred by his adopting a different method which remains possible.[2] If the risk of the supervening event is in this way allocated by the terms on which the parties have contracted, there seems

---

[1] Above, paras 7–006 *et seq.*
[2] As in the voyage charters affected by the closure of the Suez Canal: above, paras 4–078 *et seq.*

at least *prima facie* to be no strong reason why the law should interfere with that allocation.[3] And if the parties, knowing of the risk of disruption, nevertheless choose to contract on terms which do *not* reflect that risk, there seems likewise to be no good reason for granting relief to the party prejudiced by the event: this is one of the situations in which the old argument that that party "might have provided against it by his contract"[4] retains its force.[5]

13–002   The above reasoning may, however, be displaced: we shall see later in this chapter,[6] that frustration is not *necessarily* excluded by the fact that the supervening event was foreseeable or even foreseen. The view has even been expressed that the fact that the event "was or ought to have been foreseen ... does not prevent it from becoming a frustrating event when it occurs; the question ... is whether the new situation thus created is within or outside the scope of the contract on its true construction"[7]. But it is submitted that it would be wrong first to construe the contract and *then* to have regard to the fact that the event was foreseen, for that fact must be of crucial importance in determining "the scope of the contract", *i.e.* whether the parties contracted with reference to the event and so took the risk of its occurrence. Where they foresaw the event, the most plausible inference is that each of them did take that risk unless the contract by its express terms protected him against it. That inference is at its strongest where the risk of the occurrence is actually foreseen by the parties and they nevertheless enter into the contract without providing for it. Moreover, the law of contract often adopts objective standards, and there seems to be no good ground for wholly rejecting such standards in the present context. It follows that the doctrine of discharge may be excluded, not merely where the event giving rise to the obstacle to performance was actually foreseen, but also in at least some cases where the event was foreseeable. The exact extent of the exclusion of the doctrine of discharge from such cases gives rise to problems which will be further discussed later in this chapter.[8] The present point is that a party may be regarded as having taken the risk of the occurrence of certain events if that risk would have been appreciated by a reasonable person engaged in the type of business in question, even though the particular party claiming to be discharged was not himself subjectively aware of that risk.

In this context, it is perhaps relevant to note the analogous position in French law, where the doctrine of *force majeure* applies only where the event in question is unforeseeable,[9] that is, where there is no reason to

---

[3] See *Comptoir Commercial Anversois v Power Sons & Co* [1920] 1 K.B. 868 at 895, 901.

[4] *Paradine v Jane* (1647) Aleyn 26, 27; above, para.2–002.

[5] Above, para.2–033; *Maritime National Fish Ltd v Ocean Trawlers Ltd* [1935] A.C. 524 at 528.

[6] Below, para.13–015.

[7] *Nile Co for the Export of Agricultural Crops v H & J M Bennett (Commodities) Ltd* [1963] 1 Lloyd's Rep. 555 at 582.

[8] Below, paras 13–012 *et seq.*

[9] Mazeaud, Mazeaud & Chabas, *Leçons de Droit Civil* (8th ed.), Vol.II.1, No 576; *cf.* No 733.

think that the event will occur; and the test of foreseeability is said to be objective.[10] Too much reliance cannot, indeed, be placed on this analogy in view of the fact that the requirements of discharge under the French doctrine of *force majeure* are probably stricter than those of the English doctrine of frustration.[11] But the view that the foreseeability of the supervening event can exclude a claim for relief from contractual obligations affected by it is also found in German law,[12] where the scope of relief on account of supervening events is considerably wider than in English law. The German view is, however, subject to qualifications which (as the ensuing discussion will show) may be appropriate also in English law: for example, it has been said that relief may be given where the parties foresaw that the event might occur but regarded this possibility as so unlikely that there was no need to provide for it in their contract.[13]

(2) Certain types of supervening illegality

We saw in Ch.8 that in certain cases of supervening illegality the basis of discharge was the consideration of public policy that the parties must not be given the incentive (which they might have if the contract remained in force) to violate the rule of law giving rise to the illegality.[14] As was also pointed out in Ch.8, this consideration was particularly strong where a contract had become illegal by reason of the prohibition against trading with the enemy in time of war.[15] In such cases the principle of public policy may demand that the contract should be discharged even though this solution may not be one that achieves a satisfactory loss-allocation between the parties, and indeed even though the parties have expressly provided that the supervening illegality was not to discharge the contract but was only (for example) to suspend it.[16] If parties cannot by express contractual provisions exclude discharge arising from the war-time prohibition against trading with the enemy, it follows that discharge arising from this cause will not be excluded on the ground that the events which bring the prohibition into operation were, or could have been, foreseen when the contract was made. The argument put forward above for saying that foreseen or foreseeable events should not be grounds of discharge is that parties who contract with reference to such events must thereby be taken to have allocated the risks inherent in them. Another way

13–003

---

[10] *ibid.*, No 576.

[11] Above, para.12–021.

[12] Larenz, *Schuldrecht* (14th ed.), Vol. 1, 328; *cf.*, in Swiss law, BG, June 26, 1962, BGE 88 II 195 (seller not excused by impossibility of obtaining goods from East Berlin when both parties contracted with knowledge of the risk of such impossibility).

[13] See *Münchener Kommentar zum Bürgerlichen Gezetzbuch*, § 242, No 500, commenting on the German doctrine of *Wegfall der Geschäfsgrundlage* (disappearance of the commercial basis of the contract), now dealt with in BGB § 313 (in force January 1, 2002).

[14] Above, para.8–002.

[15] Above, para.8–006.

[16] Above, para.8–055.

of putting that point is that the parties have excluded the doctrine of discharge by implied agreement. Where, however, even an express agreement of this kind is ineffective on grounds of public policy, an implied agreement must be ineffective on the same grounds. Thus a contract may be frustrated by the prohibition against trading with the enemy even though, when it was made, the parties realised that the war which caused the prohibition to apply to the contract was imminent. For this reason, contracts made in the summer of 1939 could be frustrated as a result of the outbreak of the Second World War[17] even though this event was at that time generally regarded as likely to occur.

13–004   In Ch.8, we saw that the principle of public policy, which invalidated express provisions purporting to exclude discharge by supervening illegality which resulted from the prohibition against trading with the enemy, did not necessarily apply where the illegality resulted from some other prohibition, such as prohibition of export. Clauses which provide for suspension in such a case are not contrary to public policy because they assume that prohibitions will be obeyed and because the temporary maintenance of contractual relations in the face of such prohibitions has no tendency of itself to prejudice the public interest.[18] The present question is whether frustration in cases of this kind may be excluded on the ground that the prohibition was foreseen or foreseeable. While the *invalidity* of an express term purporting to exclude frustration leads necessarily to the view that foresight of the event should not exclude frustration, the converse is (in cases of supervening illegality) obviously not true; for to hold that the parties to a contract remain bound by it even though they foresaw or could have foreseen a supervening prohibition may be contrary to public policy, in spite of the fact that the parties could validly have provided for the event. A prohibition of export clause which suspends obligations clearly assumes that the supervening prohibition will be observed; but no such assumption could be made if the principal obligations of the contract were held to be unaffected by the prohibition on the ground that it was foreseen. The making of a contract in the face of an imminent prohibition and in the belief that performance will be affected by the prohibition comes very close to entering into the contract after the prohibition has already taken effect. On balance, the better view appears to be that such a contract should be discharged on grounds of public policy, notwithstanding foresight of the prohibition, at least if the circumstances are such that, if the illegality had been antecedent, the contract could not have been enforced by the party who claims damages for its breach. There is, of course, no question of its being specifically enforceable where such enforcement would require the defendant to do an act which had, by the time of the hearing, become illegal.

Supervening illegality is a special case which sheds no light on the general problem of discharge by foreseen or foreseeable events. In the rest

---

[17] This point is assumed in, *e.g. Monarch SS Co v A/B Karlshamns Oljefabriker* [1949] A.C. 196, where frustration was, however, excluded on the ground that it was "self-induced": below, para.14–007.

[18] Above, para.8–056.

of this chapter, the discussion will be restricted to cases in which the supervening events give rise to no illegality, but only to impossibility or to frustration of purpose.

II. APPARENTLY CONFLICTING AUTHORITIES

There is, at first sight, considerable conflict in the authorities on the question whether frustration is excluded by the fact that the event which made performance of the contract impossible (or frustrated its purpose) was foreseen or foreseeable. It will, however, be suggested that the conflict is more apparent than real; that there is a general principle excluding frustration by events which are foreseen, or foreseeable in the sense to be described below; but that the principle can be displaced by contrary indications. Decisions and dicta which appear to conflict with the general principle can be explained as falling either outside its scope or within the situations in which, though *prima facie* applicable, it is properly displaced.

13–005

(1) **Foresight or foreseeability as excluding frustration**

The cases to be discussed under this heading are of two kinds.

13–006

(a) *Event foreseen or foreseeable by one party only*

The case for excluding the doctrine of discharge is at its strongest where the allegedly frustrating event was, or could have been foreseen by the party claiming to be discharged, but not by the other party. This was the position in *Walton Harvey Ltd v Walker & Homfrays Ltd*,[19] where the defendants had granted the claimants the right to display an advertising sign on the defendants' hotel for seven years. Within this period, the hotel was compulsorily acquired, and demolished, by a local authority acting under statutory powers which had been conferred by a private Act of Parliament passed before the contract was made. The defendants "were aware of the fact that their premises might be taken under the statutory powers"; but the claimants had no such knowledge, "nor [could] such knowledge be imputed to them".[20] It was held that the contract was not frustrated, so that the defendants were liable in damages for breach of it, since they were, while the claimants were not, aware of the risk of compulsory acquisition, and since in these circumstances the defendants "could have provided against that risk but they did not".[21] Where the risk of the occurrence of the frustrating event is foreseen or foreseeable by one party but not by the other, the normal inference will, it is submitted, be that that risk is taken by the former party. In the *Walton Harvey* case, the justice of this conclusion was further reinforced by the fact that the defendants had received compensation for the compulsory acquisition of their hotel. There could be no hardship in requiring them in turn

13–007

---

[19] [1931] 1 Ch. 274.
[20] *ibid.* at 282.
[21] *ibid.*

to compensate the claimants, to whom they had in effect granted a contractual right to use a part of the premises. It would, of course, have been unjust to allow the defendants to rely on the fact that the contract was not frustrated in support of a claim by them for the payments which would have become due under it if the hotel had not been demolished; but such a claim would have failed, even though the contract was not frustrated, on the ground that the defendants had failed to perform a condition precedent to their right to the promised payments.

(b) *Event foreseen or foreseeable by both parties*

13-008   Many dicta support the view that frustration is excluded where the allegedly frustrating event was foreseen or foreseeable by both parties. This restriction on the scope of the doctrine of frustration was not indeed stated in *Taylor v Caldwell*[22] itself, but it makes its appearance only six years later in *Baily v De Crespigny*, where Hannen J. referred to a frustrating event as one which was "of such a character that it cannot reasonably be supposed to have been in the contemplation of the parties".[23] In *Krell v Henry* Vaughan Williams L.J. similarly said that "The test [of frustration] seems to be whether the event which causes the impossibility was or might have been anticipated ..."[24]; and the same view has on a number of occasions been stated in the House of Lords. Thus one element of Lord Simon's definition of a frustrating event in the *Cricklewood* case was that the event must be "entirely beyond what was contemplated by the parties when they entered into the agreement"[25]; in the *Davis Contractors* case one reason given by Lord Reid for rejecting the plea of frustration was that the delays affecting performance were no "greater in degree than was to be expected", and he added that the position might have been different if the delay had been "of a character ... different from anything contemplated"[26]; in the same case, Lord Radcliffe similarly emphasised that "The cause of the delay was not any new state of things which the parties could not reasonably have been thought to have foreseen"[27]; and

---

[22] (1863) 3 B. & S. 826.

[23] (1869) L.R. 4 Q.B. 180 at 185.

[24] [1903] 2 K.B. 740 at 752; *cf. Beaumont SS Ltd v Andrew Weir & Co* (1910) 15 Comm. Cas. 101 at 110: "No event has happened which the parties might not have reasonably contemplated"; *Re Badische Co Ltd* [1921] 2 Ch. 331 at 379 ("Impossible ... that reasonable men could have contemplated that event or those circumstances"); *cf.* in the context of setting aside consent orders in the light of supervening events, *S v S* [2002] 1 F.L.R. 992 at [48–55].

[25] *Cricklewood Investments Trust Ltd v Leighton's Investment Trust Ltd* [1945] A.C. 221 at 228; *cf. Hirji Mulji v Cheong Yue SS Co* [1926] A.C. 497 at 507: "an event ... not contemplated"; *Denmark Productions Ltd v Boscobel Productions Ltd* [1969] 1 Q.B. 699 at 725: "some supervening event not reasonably foreseeable"; *Gamerco SA v ICM/Fair Warning (Agency) Ltd* [1995] 1 W.L.R. 1126 at 1231 ("not contemplated by either party"); *Bangladesh Export Import Co Ltd v Sucden Kerry SA* [1995] 2 Lloyd's Rep. 1 at 6 (absence of import licence "was within the contemplation of the parties and was not to constitute a frustrating event").

[26] [1956] A.C. 696 at 724.

[27] *ibid.* at 731.

in *The Hannah Blumenthal*, Lord Brandon said that to bring about frustration there must be "some outside event or extraneous change of situation not foreseen or provided for by the parties at the time of contracting."[28]

In England there is no actual decision in which frustration has been excluded on the ground that the supervening event was or should have been foreseen; but this is at least one ground of decision in a number of American cases. One such case is *Baetjer v New England Alcohol Co*,[29] where molasses had been sold f.o.b. Puerto Rico and the buyer argued that the contract had been discharged because war-time conditions had made it impossible for him to ship the goods to his refinery in Massachusetts. One ground[30] for rejecting this argument (and so for holding the buyer liable for failing to take delivery) was that the contract had been made some months after the United States had become a party to the Second World War and that therefore the buyer must be taken to have assumed the risk that his arrangements for transporting the goods would be disrupted by the war. In another case,[31] a seller of Brazilian timber c.i.f. New York was similarly held liable in spite of the fact that the seller had been prevented from shipping the goods by the shortage of shipping space which had resulted from the outbreak of the Second World War in Europe: this fact was known when the contract was made, and the seller's inability to find shipping space was "a foreseeable risk which [the seller] willingly took upon himself".[32] Similarly, where coal had been sold c.i.f. Rio de Janeiro it was held that the seller was not excused by a strike in Wales which had made it allegedly "impossible" for him to find shipping space. Learned Hand J. said: "It is in the end a question of how unexpected at the time was the event which prevented performance ... This was a risk which both parties well understood and in the face of which the seller had made his engagement."[33] In fact, moreover, the seller had not established that it was impossible to find shipping space: he had shown no more than it had "become burdensome"[34] (*i.e.* unexpectedly expensive) to do so.

The effect on contracts of government regulations, imposing restric-   **13–009**
tions on business activity, or making performance less profitable, has likewise been held in a number of American cases not to be a ground of discharge since the risks in question were known,[35] not unanticipated,[36] or

---

[28] *Paal Wilson & Co A/S v Partenreederei Hannah Blumenthal (The Hannah Blumenthal)* [1983] 1 A.C. 854 at 909; *cf. FA Tamplin SS Co Ltd v Anglo-Mexican Petroleum Co Ltd* [1916] 2 A.C. 397 at 424; *Bank Line Ltd v Arthur Capel & Co* [1919] A.C. 435 at 458; *National Carriers Ltd v Panalpina (Northern) Ltd* [1981] A.C. 675 at 707.

[29] 66 N.E. 2d 748 (1946).

[30] For another, see above, para.7–027.

[31] *Madeirense do Brasil S/A v Stulman-Emrick Lumber Co*, 147 F. 2d 399 (1945).

[32] *ibid.* at 403.

[33] *Companhia de Navegaceo Lloyd Brasileiro v CG Blake Co*, 34 F. 2d 616 at 619 (1929). The strike was presumably the General Strike of 1926.

[34] *ibid.*

[35] *Essex-Lincoln Garage Inc v City of Boston*, 175 N.E. 2d 466 at 467–468 (1961).

[36] *Megan v Updike Grain Corp*, 94 F. 2d 551 at 554 (1938).

not shown to be reasonably unforeseeable.[37] In the leading case of *Lloyd v Murphy* Traynor J. said that: "The courts have required a promisor seeking to excuse himself from performance of his obligations to prove that the risk of the frustrating event was not reasonably foreseeable."[38] He explained this requirement by adding: "If it was foreseeable, there should have been provision for it in the contract, and the absence of such a provision gives rise to the inference that the risk was assumed."[39]

The same principle was applied to a "life-care" contract, *i.e.* to a contract by which the defendants undertook to look after an 84-year-old man for the rest of his life, in return for a lump sum paid in advance. The man's death was held not to frustrate the contract on the grounds that "frustration is no defense if it was reasonably foreseeable" and that "parties who have contracted with reference to known risks may not invoke the doctrine of frustration".[40]

Another line of cases concerns the American doctrine of discharge by "impracticability". We have seen that the foreseeability of the change of circumstances relied on as a ground of discharge has often been a ground on which the courts have refused to apply that doctrine.[41] In one of the American Suez cases,[42] the argument was even stronger. The case concerned a voyage charter and one reason why the shipowners could not rely on the closure of the Canal as discharging the contract was that the charterer had expressly refused to agree to the inclusion of a provision exonerating the shipowners in the events which had happened.

The views expressed in these American authorities are reflected in a number of extra-judicial statements of the doctrine of discharge. Thus the Restatement restricts the doctrine of discharge to cases where "facts that a promisor had no reason to anticipate ... render performance impossible".[43] Similarly, the Uniform Commercial Code indicates that the doctrine operates on account of "unforeseen supervening circumstances not within the contemplation of the parties at the time of contracting"[44]; and that it does "not apply when the contingency in question is sufficiently foreshadowed to be included among the business risks taken by the parties".[45]

---

[37] *Mitchell v Ceazan Tires Ltd*, 153 P. 2d 53 at 54 (1944).

[38] 153 P. 2d 47 at 50 (1944).

[39] *ibid.; cf. Western Drug Supply Co v Board of Administrators of Kansas*, 187 p.701 at 704 (1920).

[40] *Gold v Salem Lutheran Home Association*, 347 P. 2d 687 at 689 (1959).

[41] Above, paras 6–009, 6–012, 6–015; *cf. Waldinger Corp v CRS Group Engineers Inc*, 775 F. 2d 781 at 786 (1985).

[42] *Glidden v Hellenic Lines Ltd*, 275 F. 2d 253 (1960).

[43] § 457. The reason why this text refers only to foreseeability *by the promisor* lies in the American view that it is only the party whose performance becomes impossible that may be discharged *by impossibility*, the other party being discharged on other grounds discussed above, paras 2–041, 2–043.

[44] UCC, s.2–615, Comment 1.

[45] *ibid.* Comment 8.

(2) **Foresight or foreseeability not decisive**

The Restatement 2d adopts a more equivocal approach. On the one hand, it follows the authorities so far discussed in describing the doctrine of discharge as one which applies where performance becomes "vitally different from what was reasonably to be expected".[46] It further excludes from the operation of the doctrine cases where "the circumstances indicate the contrary"[47] and identifies as one such circumstance the fact that the event could have been guarded against. This is obviously the case where the event was or could have been foreseen; while "if the supervening event was not reasonably foreseeable when the contract was made, the party claiming discharge can hardly be expected to have provided against its occurrence".[48] Thus the fact that the event was foreseeable or even foreseen is relevant to the question of discharge; but the Restatement 2d repeatedly makes the point that it is not "of itself" or "necessarily" decisive.[49]

Some American decisions likewise take the view that foresight or foreseeability of the event will not, of itself, exclude discharge. One illustration of this judicial approach is to be found in one of the American Suez cases, in which it was said that "foreseeability or even recognition of a risk does not necessarily provide its allocation"[50]; though the actual decision was that discharge was excluded on other grounds,[51] and the judgment continues with the statement that the fact "that *some* abnormal risk was contemplated is probative but does not necessarily establish an allocation of the risk which actually occurs".[52] A second illustration is provided by the *Wolf Trap* case[53] where a company which had hired facilities for giving operatic performances refused to make payments under the contract, alleging that it had been discharged by a power failure which had been caused by a severe thunderstorm. At first instance the plea of discharge was dismissed on the ground that the supervening event was foreseeable; but on appeal a new trial was ordered since the proper question had not been left to the jury, who should have been asked whether the event was "of such reasonable likelihood that the obligor should not merely foresee the risk but ... have guarded against it".[54] The emphasis here is on the degree of likelihood of the occurrence of the event, a point that also appears from the court's reference to what it calls

---

[46] Introductory Note to Ch.11, p.309.

[47] §§ 261, 265.

[48] § 261, Comment c.

[49] Introductory Note to Ch.11, p.311; § 261, Comments b and c; § 265, Comment a.

[50] *Transatlantic Finance Corp v US*, 363 F. 2d 312 at 318 (1966); *cf. West Los Angeles Institute for Cancer Research v Mayer*, 366 F. 2d 220 at 225 (1966) (citing Smit, 58 Col. L. Rev. 287, 314); cert. denied 358 U.S. 1010.

[51] Above, para.4–078.

[52] 363 F. 2d 312 at 318 (1966).

[53] *Opera Company of Boston v Wolf Trap Foundation for the Performing Arts*, 817 F. 2d 1094 (1984).

[54] *ibid.* at 1103.

"the obsolete rule that foreseeability, whether reasonably likely or not, bars the application of the doctrine".[55]

(3) **Factors determining effects of foresight or foreseeability**

13–011   The judicial statements just quoted do not, any more than the Restatement 2d, deny that foresight or foreseeability may exclude the doctrine of discharge. Indeed, in saying that such a factor will not "necessarily" or "of itself" have this effect, they seem to assume that it will *prima facie* indicate that the risk of the event has been assumed, but that this *prima facie* rule may be excluded. In deciding whether it has been so excluded, three further factors, in particular, must be considered, and these factors (it is submitted) provide the most satisfactory explanation for a number of English decisions which have given rise to difficulty in the present context. The three factors are first, the degree of foreseeability, secondly the extent of foreseeability, and thirdly other indications that, even though the event was foreseen, it was not the intention of the parties or of one of them to assume the risk of its occurrence.

(a) *Degree of foreseeability*

13–012   The inference of risk assumption applies only where the event is either actually foreseen or where the degree of its foreseeability is a high one. It is not sufficient if the low degree of foreseeability, which constitutes the test of remoteness of damage in tort,[56] is satisfied. In this sense, a good deal of contemporary evidence suggests that it was "foreseeable" that King Edward VII might fall ill on the date fixed for his coronation. The King was 60 years old at the time; "a few days before the great ceremony rumours of the King's ill-health gained currency and were denied"[57]; persons who had erected stands for viewing the processions had insured against the event that happened[58]; and at least some of the contracts in the reported cases had expressly provided for it.[59] This degree of foreseeability did not exclude the operation of the doctrine of discharge where the contracts made no provision for the event. "Foreseeability" will support the inference of risk-assumption only where the supervening event is one which any person of ordinary intelligence would regard as likely to occur, or (as the point was well put in an American case) the contingency must be "one which the parties could reasonably be thought to have foreseen as a real possibility".[60] The distinction is between cases in

---

[55] *ibid.* at 1102, n.14.

[56] See *Overseas Tankships (UK) v Morts Dock & Engineering Co (The Wagon Mound)* [1961] A.C. 388.

[57] D.N.B., 2nd Supplement, 1901–1911, p.591.

[58] Above, para.7–007.

[59] *Victoria Seats Agency v Paget* (1902) 19 T.L.R. 16; *Elliott v Crutchley* [1904] 1 K.B. 565; affirmed [1906] A.C. 7.

[60] *Mishara Construction Company Inc v Transit-Mixed Concrete Corp*, 310 N.E. 2d 363 at 367 (1974).

which parties can reasonably be expected to foresee the occurrence of the event as no more than a possibility, and those in which they can be so expected to foresee it as a real likelihood. The inference of risk assumption will be drawn only in cases of the latter kind[61]; and even then it may be displaced by facts of the kind to be discussed in para.13–015, below.

(b) *Extent of foreseeability*

To support the inference of risk-assumption it is necessary to show, not only that the supervening event was foreseeable in the sense just described, but also that its consequences or effects on the contract were so foreseeable. It is, accordingly not sufficient for this purpose that *some* delay or other interference with performance could be foreseen as a likely consequence of the event, if *the* delay or interference which occurs is wholly different in extent from that which could be so foreseen. This distinction is similar to that which restricts the scope of express provisions for supervening events,[62] which may be narrowly construed so as (for example) to apply only to the relatively short delays which are expected to result from the specified event, and not to cover the very long and frustrating delays which actually occur. There is no good reason why substantially the same distinction should not apply in relation to the effects of events which were foreseeable or foreseen; and it is submitted that this point provides the most satisfactory explanation of two controversial English cases in which it was said that the contracts were, or could have been, frustrated by foreseen or foreseeable events.

 The first of these cases is *W J Tatem Ltd v Gamboa*.[63] During the Spanish Civil War, the defendant, as agent for the Republicans, chartered a ship "for the evacuation of civil population from North Spain" for 30 days from July 1. Hire was to be paid at the rate of £250 per day "until her redelivery to the owners", but was to cease if the ship was "missing". On July 14 the ship was seized by the Nationalists, who kept her until September 7, so that she was not redelivered to the owners until September 11. The charterer had paid hire in advance up to July 31, and the owner claimed further hire from August 1 to September 11. Goddard J. rejected the claim on the ground that the charterparty had been frustrated. The actual decision can be explained on the ground that it was *not* foreseeable that the ship would be detained "not only for the period of her charter but for a long period thereafter".[64] But Goddard J. added that the contract would have been frustrated even if that risk had been foreseen. "If the true foundation of the doctrine [of frustration] is that once the subject-matter of the contract is destroyed or the existence

---

[61] *Opera Company of Boston v Wolf Trap Foundation for the Performing Arts*, 187 F. 2d 1094 (1986).
[62] Above, para.12–008.
[63] [1939] 1 K.B. 132.
[64] At 135.

of a certain state of facts has come to an end, the contract is at an end,[65] that result follows whether or not the event causing it was contemplated by the parties."[66] Frustration could be prevented only by an express provision that one of the parties should bear the loss. But it is submitted that a contract is not necessarily at an end if the existence of a certain state of facts has come to an end; for the parties may have been engaged in a deliberate speculation on this point, and may thus have intended to throw on one or the other of them the risk that the relevant state of affairs would, as a result of a supervening event, be brought to an end. Where that event is actually foreseen, the natural inference is that the risk of its occurrence must be borne by the party prejudiced by it, unless that party is protected against that risk by an express term of the contract. In *W J Tatem Ltd v Gamboa* the inference that the risk of seizure and detention (to the extent to which it was foreseen or foreseeable as likely to occur) was intended to be borne by the charterer can also be supported by reference to the fact that, while the contract did *not* expressly protect him from liability if the ship should be detained, it *did* protect him from liability in respect of another foreseen risk: his liability to pay hire was to cease if the ship should be lost. Another aspect of the case which may be relevant to the issue of contractual risk-allocation is that the hire payable by the charterer was three times the normal market rate; but this fact is at best equivocal. On the one hand, it could be said that this high rate was evidence of risk-assumption by the shipowner. On the other hand, it could be said to reflect the difficulty which the charterer had experienced in procuring the desired services; this view would support the inference of risk assumption by the charterer. All this is no criticism of the actual result reached by Goddard J., so long as this is based on the fact that the *extent* of the detention of the ship was *not* foreseeable.

13–014   That result can also be supported, from a practical point of view, by making the point that the shipowner received the equivalent of three months' hire at the market rate and was deprived of the use of the ship for two-and-a-half months; and this outcome could be regarded as a satisfactory allocation of loss by the court, at least on the assumption that the loss had not been otherwise allocated by the parties. This practical justification of the result depends, however, on the fact that the charterer had paid a month's hire in advance, and that he made no claim for the return of that payment. In Goddard J.'s view any such claim would have failed even if it had been made[67]; he evidently regarded a provision in the charterparty that "Hire paid in advance and not earned to be returned to the charterers"[68] as inapplicable in the events which had happened,

---

[65] For criticism of this part of the reasoning (so far as it relates to the "true foundation" of the doctrine) see *Court Line Ltd v Dant & Russell Inc* [1939] 3 All E.R. 314 at 316. And *cf.* below, para.16–010.

[66] At 138; *cf. Palmco Shipping Inc v Continental Ore Corp (The Captain George K)* [1970] 2 Lloyd's Rep. 21 at 31.

[67] [1939] 1 K.B. at 140.

[68] cl.15 of the charterparty (as reported in (1938) 61 Ll.L. Rep. 149). For further discussion of such charterparty clauses, see below para.15–048.

presumably because these words occurred in a clause dealing with loss of the ship. The rule that money paid under a frustrated contract cannot be reclaimed by the payor no longer prevails, so that on the facts of *W J Tatem Ltd v Gamboa* the charterer could now recover back his advance payment, or at least part of it, if the contract were frustrated.[69] In this state of the law, the practical justification suggested above for the result in that case would no longer be available; and it is submitted that to allow the charterer not only to escape liability, but also to recover back his advance payment, in a case in which the risk and extent of the detention were actually foreseen, would amount to an undesirable reversal of the loss-allocation made by the parties.

The second case is *The Eugenia*,[70] where the defendants wished, in September 1956, to charter the claimants' ship to carry iron goods from Russian Black Sea ports to India. At that time "mercantile men realised that there was a risk that the Suez Canal might be closed"[71] because of the Suez crisis. The agents of the parties appreciated this risk and each made a suggestion for dealing with it.[72] But when the charterparty was concluded on September 19, nothing was expressly said about the risk of closure. The reason may be that before November 16, "mercantile men would not have formed any conclusion as to whether the obstructions in the Canal were other than temporary".[73] The actual decision was that the contract was not frustrated by the closure of the Canal on October 31, resulting in the detention of the ship: the charterers could not rely on the detention as it was due to their prior breach of contract in ordering the ship into the Canal, and thus "self-induced"[74]; nor could they rely on the extra length of the voyage which the ship would have had to make, if she had not been detained in the Canal, as the difference between a voyage via the Canal and one via the Cape was not sufficiently fundamental.[75] But Lord Denning M.R. also seemed to reject the further argument that frustration might have been excluded on the ground that at the time of contracting the closure of the Canal was foreseeable. He said: "It has often been said that the doctrine of frustration only applies where the new situation is 'unforeseen' or 'unexpected' or 'uncontemplated' as if that were an essential feature. But it is not so. The only thing that is essential is that [the

---

[69] Law Reform (Frustrated Contracts) Act 1943, s.1(2), below, para.15–050. The Act would not be excluded by s.2(5) (a), below, para.15–090, since the charter was a time charter (this fact appears more clearly from (1938) 61 Ll.L. Rep. 149 at 150 than from the *Law Reports*); nor was it a contract for the carriage of *goods* (but one for the carriage of *passengers*) by sea. The question whether the Act would be excluded by cl.15 of the charterparty (above, n.68) would depend on the construction of that clause, as to which see: above, nn.67 and 68 and below, para.15–048.

[70] *Ocean Tramp Tankers Corp v V/O Sovfracht (The Eugenia)* [1964] 2 Q.B. 226.

[71] [1963] 2 Lloyd's Rep. at 159, where the facts are more fully stated than in the *Law Reports*.

[72] [1963] 2 Lloyd's Rep. at 159.

[73] *ibid.* at 162.

[74] Below, para.14–010.

[75] Above, para.4–081.

parties] should have made no provision for it in the contract."[76] But these remarks are *obiter* and it is respectfully submitted that this aspect of the decision can be explained on other grounds. At the time of contracting, the risk of the Canal's being closed for a *very considerable time* was not foreseen; nor was it foreseeable on the high standard of foreseeability[77] required to exclude frustration. To the extent that the parties did foresee the risk, they seem to have allocated it by the terms of the charterparty. This took the form of a "time charter trip", which provided that the voyage was to be paid for by the time it took,[78] and so indicated an intention to throw the risk of delay on the charterers. There seems to be no reason why the court should, by applying the doctrine of frustration to foreseen events, reverse such an allocation of risks deliberately made by the contracting parties.

(c) *Contrary indications*

13-015   The inference that the parties have assumed or allocated the risk of foreseen (or readily foreseeable) events is only a *prima facie* one and can be excluded by evidence of contrary intention. This is most obviously the position where the parties actually include in the contract a provision that, if the foreseen event occurs, they will at that stage determine how it is to affect the contract. This was done in the American case of *Autry v Republic Productions*,[79] where a contract between a film producer and an actor was made in 1942, shortly after the United States had become a party to the Second World War. The contract provided that, if the actor were conscripted, "the parties will agree upon their mutual rights and obligations hereunder". The actor was conscripted but the parties failed to agree, and it was held that the contract had been discharged, so that the actor was not bound to resume rendering services under the contract on his demobilisation in 1945. By providing that the foreseen event was to be the subject of further negotiations, the parties had clearly indicated that they had not intended in their original contract to allocate the risk of the event's occurrence. Such a conclusion can also be based on a less formal agreement: for example, where the parties foresee the event but expressly or impliedly agree that, if it occurs, they will, "leave the lawyers to sort it out".[80] If the event does occur and the lawyers cannot "sort it out", the contract can then be frustrated, even though the event was foreseen, because in such circumstances it was again clearly not the intention of the parties to allocate the risk of its occurrence.

The inference that the parties had no such intention may also sometimes be drawn where the parties foresaw the event but made only partial provision for it. This, it is submitted, is the reason why in *Bank Line*

---

[76] [1964] 2 Q.B. at 239.

[77] Above, para.13–012.

[78] This form of charter has become common: see *Care Shipping Corp v Latin American Shipping Corp (The Cebu)* [1983] 1 Lloyd's Rep. 302 at 305. For earlier cases in which similar types of charter were involved, see below, para.15–092.

[79] 180 P. 2d. 888 (1947); above, para.5–046.

[80] *The Eugenia* [1964] 2 Q.B. at 234.

Ltd v Arthur Capel & Co,[81] a charterparty was frustrated by the requisition of the ship even though the parties had foreseen that event and had actually made *some* provision for it in the contract. One possible explanation for the decision is that it was not clear that the parties foresaw a requisition of so long a duration as would frustrate the contract. But even if they did foresee this, the very fact that they had made *some* provision for the event complicated the issue. The contract entitled the *charterer* to cancel on requisition, so that the risk of the event was clearly not meant to be on him. The effect of requisition on the *owner's* liability was not mentioned in the contract. One could infer from this silence that the parties had decided to throw the risk of requisition on him, or that they had not thought about its effect on his liability at all. If the latter inference is correct, the contract could be frustrated although requisition was foreseen, and the House of Lords so held. The normal inference that parties take the risk of foreseen events can be said to have been displaced by the special terms of the contract. General statements to the effect that. "The event need not be unforeseen and it may even be of a kind referred to in the contract"[82] should (it is submitted) be understood with reference to cases of this kind.

The inference of risk-assumption which would normally be drawn from the fact that the parties had contracted with reference to an event which was foreseen, or foreseeable as likely to occur, may also be displaced by other circumstances. The cases provided no convincing[83] illustration of this possibility; but it has been suggested[84] that the normal inference could be rebutted by the difficulty of formulating an appropriate provision for the event, or by the fact that the effect of the event on the contract, even though foreseen by the parties in extent, was regarded by them as less significant in economic terms than it actually turned out to be. But it should be emphasised that the effect of such factors is merely to displace what has here been called the normal inference, and that, in the absence of special circumstances displacing that inference, a contract will not be discharged by events which are foreseen or foreseeable as likely to occur.

III. LEGISLATIVE ANALOGIES

There is some legislative support for the relevance of foreseeability in the Regulations which govern package travel.[85] These provide that the party   13–016

---

[81] [1919] A.C. 435, above, para.12–010; *cf. Re Comptoir Commercial Anversois and Power, Son & Co* [1920] 1 K.B. 868 at 895, 901; *Hackfield v Castle*, 198 p.1041 (1921).

[82] *Adelfamar SA v Silos e Mangimi Martini (The Adelfa)* [1988] 2 Lloyd's Rep. 466 at 471.

[83] *West Los Angeles Institute for Cancer Research v Mayer*, 366 F. 2d 220 (1966), cert denied 358 U.S. 1010 may provide an illustration, but the correctness of the decision is open to doubt on other grounds: see above, para.7–033.

[84] Restatement 2d, Introductory Note to Ch.11, p.311.

[85] Package Travel, Package Holidays and Package Tours Regulations 1992 (SI 1992/3288).

contracting to supply the travel facilities is not liable in damages for failure to perform his part of the contract if this failure is due to "unusual and *unforeseeable* circumstances beyond the control of the party by whom this exception is pleaded which could not have been avoided even if all care had been exercised", or to an "event which ... even with all due care [he] could not *foresee* or forestall".[86] Under the first of these formulations, the circumstances must be unforeseeable *and* such that their consequence is unavoidable; under the second, the event must be unforeseeable *or* such that the party relying on it could not have forestalled it. The latter alternative formulation is found also in the Vienna Convention on Contracts for the International Sale of Goods. This Convention (which has not been ratified by the United Kingdom) exempts a party from liability in damages in respect of failure to perform due to an "impediment beyond his control" if "he could not reasonably be expected to have taken the impediment into account or have avoided or overcome its consequences".[87] These provisions of the Regulations and of the Convention are here relevant only by way of analogy. Their effect is not to discharge the contract but only to make available to one party a defence to a claim for damages. An English lawyer would describe them as giving rise to an excuse for non-performance rather than to frustration.[88]

---

[86] *ibid.*, reg.15(2)(c); *cf.* reg.15(2)(b).
[87] Art.79; above, para.6–048.
[88] *cf.* above, para.5–058; below, para.15–043.

CHAPTER 14

SELF-INDUCED FRUSTRATION

I. FAULT AS EXCLUDING DISCHARGE

The doctrine of frustration has been repeatedly described in this book as a legal mechanism for allocating the loss caused by a supervening event. That mechanism is, however, intended to apply only where the event is one over which the parties have no control; and it is with this limitation on the scope of the doctrine of discharge that the present chapter is concerned.

14–001

(1) **General statements of the principle**

In his original formulation of the doctrine in *Taylor v Caldwell*, Blackburn J. said that it applied where performance had become impossible "without default of the contractor"[1]; and that "The Music Hall having ceased to exist, without fault of either party, both parties are excused".[2] Obviously, the contract in that case would not have been frustrated if the defendants had deliberately set fire to the Hall,[3] since in that case there would have been no good reason for relieving the defendants from their liability to compensate the hirers for their wasted expenditure, or even for their loss of anticipated profits. Lord Sumner has expressed the same principle in the well-known statement that "Reliance cannot be placed on self-induced frustration"[4]: that is, on frustration due to the conduct of the party seeking to rely on it, or of those for whom he is responsible. The same principle is reflected in the rule of construction by which *force majeure* and similar clauses are presumed not to apply where the event which prevents

14–002

---

[1] (1863) 3 B. & S. 826 at 834.
[2] *ibid.* at 840; *cf. Appleby v Myers* (1867) L.R. 2 C.P. 651 at 659, 660.
[3] *Mertens v Home Freehold Co* [1921] 2 K.B. 526 at 537.
[4] *Bank Line Ltd v Arthur Capel & Co* [1919] A.C. 435 at 452; *Sudbrook Trading Estate Ltd v Eggleton* [1983] 1 A.C. 444, at 497; Swanton 2 J.C.L. 206.

or hinders performance is due to the fault or default of the party who should have rendered it.[5]

(a) *Negligence*

14–003   In most of the cases in which this principle has been applied, the event which prevented performance was due to the deliberate conduct of the party claiming to be discharged. It is less clear whether that party's negligence would also exclude frustration. The question has been described as an open one in the *Joseph Constantine*[6] case; according to one dictum in that case, "fault" has in previous cases been used to refer only to deliberate acts,[7] while according to another the word has, in a commercial context, been treated as equivalent to (or at least as including) negligence.[8] As a matter of general principle, the latter is, it is submitted, the preferable view. If, in *Taylor v Caldwell*, the fire had been caused by the negligence of the defendants, it is submitted that they should not have been discharged, for in that case it would have been appropriate that the loss suffered by the hirers in consequence of the fire should be borne by the defendants rather than by the hirers. Similarly, in the growing crop cases,[9] the seller could not rely as a ground of discharge on the failure of the crop if it was due, not to external causes, but to his want of proper cultivation. "Fault" thus includes negligence, and "negligence" is here used in a wider sense than that given to it in the law of tort. It is not restricted to "breach of any actionable legal duty", and includes "an event which the party relying on it had means and opportunity to prevent but nevertheless caused or permitted to come about".[10] Indeed, there are cases in which the doctrine of discharge may be excluded by reason of the defendant's breach of a duty imposing strict liability[11]; and it follows *a fortiori* that the doctrine should be excluded by his carelessness giving rise to the event which prevents performance. In the United States, the Uniform Commercial Code likewise takes the view that: " 'fault' is intended to include negligence and not merely wilful wrong."[12] This statement applies in terms only to the case where "identified" goods, or goods sold on "no arrival, no sale" terms suffer "casualty",[13] but the Restatement 2d adopts as a general principle the view that negligence amounts to "fault" for the purpose of excluding the

---

[5] *Fyffes Group Ltd v Reefer Express Lines Pty Ltd (The Kriti Rex)* [1996] 2 Lloyd's Rep. 171; above para.12–026.

[6] *Joseph Constantine SS Line Ltd v Imperial Smelting Corp Ltd* [1942] A.C. 154 at 200.

[7] *ibid.* at 195.

[8] *ibid.* at 166.

[9] Above, para.4–049.

[10] *J Lauritzen A/S v Wijsmuller BV (The Super Servant Two)* [1990] 1 Lloyd's Rep. 1 at 10.

[11] Below, para.14–007.

[12] UCC, s.2–613, Comment 1.

[13] These being the only situations dealt with in s.2–613. Under the proposed amendments to Art.2 (above para.2–042, n.17) the reference to "no arrival, no sale" terms is to be deleted from s.2–613. The corresponding s.2A–221 refers, in the case of chattel leases, only to the case where "the goods suffer casualty".

doctrine of discharge.[14] The extent to which this general principle applies where performance of a contract to render personal services is prevented by carelessly self-inflicted illness or injury will be discussed later in this chapter.[15]

(b) *Acts of third parties*

Where the conduct of a contracting party (whether deliberate or careless) would exclude the doctrine of discharge, the position would clearly be the same if the conduct in question was that of that party's servants. It has, for example, been held that a shipowner could not rely on the loss of his ship as a ground for the discharge of a contract to carry goods in her if that loss was due to the negligence of his servants.[16] It will be recalled that in *Taylor v Caldwell*[17] the fire which destroyed the Music Hall was due to the act of a careless plumber,[18] and it seems that the reason why the defendants were not responsible for his conduct was that he was not their servant but was an independent contractor. Hence the case provides an early illustration of the rule that frustration is not excluded where the cause of the obstacle to performance is the act of a third party for whose conduct the party claiming discharge is not responsible. The same principle was applied where a ship which had been chartered was arrested by the receivers of the cargo: the charterers were able to rely on the resulting long delay in unloading as a ground of discharge since they were not vicariously liable for the acts of the receivers.[19] A further application of the same principle is found in cases in which the performance of contracts with state-controlled enterprises is prevented or made illegal by a legislative or executive act of the government of the state in question. For the present purpose the enterprise and the government have been regarded as distinct bodies, so that frustration is not considered to be self-induced and the contract can be discharged by the governmental intervention.[20]

14-004

(c) *Statutory statements*

A statutory statement of the principle is contained in s.7 of the Sale of Goods Act 1979, under which an agreement for the sale of specific goods is avoided if the goods perish (before the risk has passed to the buyer) "without any fault on the part of the seller or buyer".[21] The similar rule

14-005

---

[14] § 261, Comment d.

[15] Below, para.14–019.

[16] *The Super Servant Two*, above, n.10; for another (more controversial) aspect of the case, see below, para.14–024.

[17] (1863) 3 B. & S. 826.

[18] Above, para.2–024.

[19] *Adelfamar SA v Silos e Mangimi Martini (The Adelfa)* [1988] 2 Lloyd's Rep. 466. See also above, para.4–010 and (for another aspect of the case) below, para.14–012.

[20] *C Czarnikow Ltd v Centrala Handlu Zagranicznego "Rolimpex"* [1979] A.C. 351 at 372; *Empresa Exportadora de Azucar v Industria Azucarera Nacional SA (The Playa Larga)* [1983] 2 Lloyd's Rep. 171 at 192.

[21] For the relevance of the reference to "fault" in s.20(2) of the Act in the present context, see below, para.14–015.

contained in s.2–613 of the Uniform Commercial Code likewise applies only where the "casualty" occurs "without fault of either party"; and the same phrase is found in s.2–614(1), which deals with supervening impracticability in the method of performance.[22] Curiously, s.2–615 (the principal provision on excuse by impracticability) does not in terms contain any requirement of lack of fault on the part of the seller; but the view that such a requirement is intended to restrict the operation of the section can be inferred from Comment 5. That Comment deals with failure of a particular source of supply and declares that this will not excuse the seller "unless [he] has employed all due measures to assure himself that his source will not fail". Other statutory versions of the principle are found in s.56 of the Indian Contract Act 1872, under which the doctrine of discharge is brought into operation only by an "event which the promisor could not prevent"; and by the Code of Georgia, which excludes the doctrine of discharge by supervening impossibility "where by proper prudence, such impossibility might have been avoided by the promisor".[23]

(d) *Restatement formulations*

14–006   The common law principle is further recognised in the United States by the Restatement, which provides that a promisor can rely as a ground of discharge only on facts "for the occurrence of which he was not in contributing fault".[24] The Restatement 2d similarly provides for discharge only where a party's performance becomes impracticable, or where his purpose is frustrated "without his fault".[25] This requirement is not in terms stated in the sections dealing with particular types of impracticability (such as the death or unavailability of a particular person)[26]; but these sections merely define types of events which may give rise to impracticability, and do not exhaustively state the conditions required to bring about discharge. The requirement that the event must occur without the "fault" of the party claiming discharge therefore applies to these sections of the Restatement, no less than it applies to those in which it is expressly stated.

(2) **"Fault" and "default"**

14–007   It will be recalled that in *Taylor v Caldwell* Blackburn J. stated the present requirement at one point in the form that the impossibility must occur "without default of the contractor" and at another that it must occur

---

[22] The corresponding provisions of UCC, Art.2A (applicable to chattel leases) apply only where the goods which are the subject-matter of such contracts suffer casualty, or where the method of performance becomes impracticable, "without fault" of the lessor, lessee or supplier: ss.2A–221(1), 2A–404(1).
[23] Code of Georgia (2003), s.13–4–20.
[24] § 457.
[25] §§ 261, 265.
[26] § 262; see also §§ 263, 264.

"without fault of either party".[27] In the context, it is unlikely that any distinction between these two formulations was intended; but in the light of later developments two differences between them call for discussion. In the first place, "fault" and "default" do not necessarily mean the same thing. The point is reflected in Lord Sumner's statement that "the principle of frustration of the adventure assumes that frustration arises without blame *or* fault on either side"[28]; in Lord Brandon's even clearer formulation of alternative conditions when he said that the event "must have occurred without *either* the fault *or* the default of either party"[29]; and in the definitions of "fault" in the Sale of Goods Act 1979 and in the Uniform Commercial Code (both of which contain statutory statements of the doctrine of discharge)[30]: in the Act, "fault" means "wrongful act or default"[31]; in the original version of the Code it means "wrongful act, omission or breach"[32]; and in the revised (2002) version of the Code it means "default, breach or wrongful act or omission".[33] In the present context, it seems that "fault" normally refers to conduct which amounts either to the deliberate commission of a wrong or to want of care or diligence. "Default", by contrast, normally refers simply to the breach of a legal duty, irrespective of the question whether the act or omission constituting or giving rise to the breach was deliberate or careless. Contractual duties are often strict, and a party who fails to perform such a duty will be in "default" even though he is in no way at "fault"[34]; and such "default" may exclude the doctrine of discharge. The point may be illustrated by reference to an American case[35] in which a seller of goods was unable to deliver them to the buyer because they had been taken in execution under a court order obtained against him by a third party: he was not excused because he was considered to be at "fault" in allowing the goods to become in this way unavailable for the purpose of the contract of sale. Yet the execution may be due to his inability to perform a previous contract with the third party; and that inability may be due simply to a failure of his source of unascertained generic goods, or of finance,[36] occurring without any fault on his part; and his liability to the third party

---

[27] Above, para.14–002, nn.1, 2.

[28] *Bank Line Ltd v Arthur Capel & Co* [1919] A.C. 435 at 452.

[29] *Paal Wilson & Co A/S v Partenreederei Hannah Blumenthal (The Hannah Blumenthal)* [1983] 1 A. C. 854 at 909.

[30] Above, para.14–005.

[31] Sale of Goods Act 1979, s.61(1), a definition which has been described as "not very helpful": *Joseph Constantine SS Line Ltd v Imperial Smelting Corp Ltd* [1942] A.C. 154 at 190.

[32] s.1–201(16).

[33] s.1–201(17); for the revised (2002) version, see above para.3–017, n.57.

[34] For recognition of this distinction between the meaning of "fault" and "default" in exception clauses, see *Sig Bergensen D Y A/S v Mobil Shipping & Transportation Co (The Berge Sund)* [1992] 1 Lloyd's Rep. 461 at 463, reversed on other grounds [1993] 2 Lloyd's Rep. 453.

[35] *Western Drug Supply Co v Board of Administrators of Kansas*, 187 P. 701 (1920).

[36] *cf. Klauber v San Diego Street Car Co*, 30 p.555 (1892); for strict liability in such cases, see above, para.1–003.

in respect of such failure would be strict. Similar reasoning may apply where it is argued that a voyage charter has been frustrated by detention of the ship in consequence of war. Such an argument may be rejected on the ground that the ship was unseaworthy and that the voyage would have been accomplished before the outbreak of the war, if the shipowner had not been in breach of his duty to provide a seaworthy ship.[37] Yet this duty is at common law a strict one,[38] so that again the plea of frustration may be excluded by "default" falling short of "fault" in the sense of want of care or diligence. It is to accommodate cases of this kind that the Restatement 2d defines "fault" in the present context broadly, so as to include "not only 'willful' wrongs but such other types of conduct as that amounting to breach of contract or negligence".[39] At first sight, the reference here to "breach of contract" may be thought to contain an element of circularity, *i.e.* to amount to saying that failure in performance due to impossibility is not fault (and therefore is not a breach) unless it is a breach. But the point of the inclusion of "breach of contract" in the definition of fault appears to be that impossibility is not an excuse, if it is due to antecedent breach, and such a breach can (where liability is strict) occur without "fault" in the sense of want of care or diligence. More commonly, however, "fault" in bringing about impossibility refers to deliberate or negligent conduct. Such conduct will normally prevent the party guilty of it from relying on the doctrine of discharge.

(3) **Which party's fault?**

14–008   The second way in which Blackburn J.'s two formulations in *Taylor v Caldwell*[40] of the present requirement differ from each other is that the first states that the event must occur "without default *of the contractor*" (which seems to refer to the party claiming to be excused), while the second states that it must occur "without fault *of either party*".[41] Later developments in the law have made it clear that the first of these formulations is to be preferred.[42] The second would make it possible for a party to argue that his own fault should prevent the other party from relying on the event brought about by that fault as a ground of discharge. Such an argument would, however, be wholly inconsistent with the policy of the present requirement, which is to allocate the loss caused by the supervening event to the party at fault. Lord Sumner's formulation that "reliance cannot be placed on self-induced frustration" clearly means that

---

[37] See *Monarch SS Co v A/B Karlshamns Oljefabriker* [1949] A.C. 196.

[38] *Steel v State Line SS Co* (1877) 3 App. Cas. 72 at 86; where the contract of carriage is contained in, or evidenced by, a bill of lading the duty is commonly reduced, by statute, to one of diligence: Carriage of Goods by Sea Act, 1971, s.3 and Sch., Art.III(1)(a)

[39] § 261, Comment d.

[40] Above, para.14–002, nn.1, 2.

[41] *cf. Dahl v Nelson Donkin & Co* (1881) 6 App. Cas. 38 at 53 ("neither party"), and Lord Brandon's formulation in *The Hannah Blumenthal* [1983] 1 A.C. 854 at 909, quoted above, para.14–007, at n.29.

[42] *Joseph Constantine SS Line Ltd v Imperial Smelting Corp Ltd* [1942] A.C. 154 at 191.

the plea of frustration is not available to the party who has "induced" the event. The argument that the *other* party cannot rely on such an event as a ground of discharge has therefore rightly been rejected in one of the authorities to be discussed later in this chapter.[43]

II. PRIOR BREACH OF CONTRACT

(1) **Generally sufficient to exclude discharge**

Three topics call for discussion under this heading.   14–009

(a) *Breach of one party*

In the present context, "fault" clearly includes a breach of contract which   14–010
actually is, or is the sole cause of, the frustrating event. It goes without saying that a seller of goods would not be discharged by the destruction of the goods before delivery if they had disintegrated by reason of a defect in them amounting to a breach of his undertakings as to quality, that a building contractor would not be discharged by delays occasioned by his own unjustified refusal to proceed with the work, and that a shipowner would not be discharged by delays resulting from his failure to provide a seaworthy ship.[44]

Nor would the doctrine of frustration protect a party where his own breach was only one of the factors giving rise to impossibility of a kind that would, but for that breach, be a ground of discharge. In *The Eugenia*,[45] one of the English Suez cases,[46] a ship which had been chartered for a time charter trip was ordered by the charterer to enter the Suez Canal. In giving this order, the charterer had committed a breach of a term of the charterparty that he would not order the ship into a war-zone, and this breach precluded him from relying on the subsequent prolonged detention of the ship in the Canal as a ground of frustration. Similarly, a charterer could not rely on the detention of the ship in the port into which he had ordered her, if the order to enter that port amounted to a breach of his safe-port warranty.[47] Another illustration of the point is provided by the situation already discussed, in which a ship is chartered for a voyage, the completion of which is prevented by her detention in the course of a supervening war, but would not have been so prevented, had the ship not been delayed by unseaworthiness. Here the shipowner is precluded by his own breach of contract from relying on the detention as a ground of discharge, and this is so even though the unseaworthiness would not of itself have given rise to a frustrating delay.[48] Again the

---

[43] *FC Shepherd & Co Ltd v Jerrom* [1987] Q.B. 30; below, para.14–020.

[44] *Eridania SpA v Rudolf A Oetker (The Fjord Wind)* [1999] 1 Lloyd's Rep. 307 at 335; affirmed without reference to this point [2000] 2 Lloyd's Rep. 191.

[45] *Ocean Tramp Tankers Corp v V/O Sovfracht (The Eugenia)* [1964] 2 Q.B. 226.

[46] Above, para.4–081.

[47] *Uni-Ocean Lines Pte Ltd v C Trade SA (The Lucille)* [1984] 1 Lloyd's Rep. 244.

[48] See the *Monarch SS Co* case [1949] A.C. 196, above, para.14–007, at n.37.

doctrine of discharge is excluded in such a case, even though the shipowner's breach does not amount, or of itself gives rise, to the impossibility, but is only one of the factors leading to it.

(b) *Mutual default*

14–011   The doctrine of discharge is also excluded where the circumstances relied on as grounds of discharge result partly from the breach of one party and partly from that of the other, *e.g.* where both breaches contribute to an allegedly frustrating delay. Such a situation arose, or was alleged to have arisen, in a number of cases concerning agreements to submit disputes to arbitration. Under such agreements, it was the duty of the claimants to prosecute their claims without undue delay; and if the claimants were in breach of this duty, it became in turn the duty of the respondents to take steps in the arbitration proceedings to bring that delay to an end. Where neither party took any steps in the proceedings, many years might elapse after the original formulation of the claim, making a satisfactory trial difficult or impossible. In cases of this kind, arbitrators now have a statutory power to dismiss the arbitration claim for want of prosecution[49]; but before this statutory power was created attempts were made to reach substantially the same result by a number of common law techniques.[50] The only only one of these which concerns us in this book is the argument that, where both parties had contributed to the delay, their agreement to submit the dispute to arbitration had come to an end by "frustration by mutual default".[51] This view at one time had some support in the authorities,[52] but it was rejected by *The Hannah Blumenthal*[53] where the House of Lords held that respondents to arbitration proceedings could not rely as a ground of discharge on a long delay (of some eight years) in the proceedings since they were themselves under a contractual obligation to put an end to the delay, and since the parties, in "failing to comply with ... their mutual contractual obligations to one another"[54] were clearly in default. The specific problem of delay in the conduct of arbitration proceedings is now dealt with by the statutory provision already mentioned, but it is possible to think of other situations in which each party may contribute to an allegedly frustrating event. Delays in the performance of a building contract might, for example, be the result partly of the contractor's failure to have available adequate supplies of labour, materials and machinery, and partly of the dilatoriness of the

---

[49] Arbitration Act 1996, s.41(3); the parties can exclude this statutory power by agreement: s.41(2).

[50] See Treitel, *The Law of Contract* (11th ed.), pp.10, 32 and 823.

[51] *André & Cie SA v Marine Transocean Ltd (The Splendid Sun)* [1981] Q.B. 694 at 703.

[52] *The Splendid Sun*, above, n.51; *Neptune Maritime Co Ltd v Koninklijke Bunge NV (The Argonaut)* [1982] 2 Lloyd's Rep. 214; *The Kehera* [1983] 1 Lloyd's Rep. 29.

[53] *Paal Wilson & Co A/S v Partenreederei Hannah Blumenthal (The Hannah Blumenthal)* [1983] 1 A.C. 854, where the plea of frustration failed on the further ground that the delay had not produced a radically different state of affairs; *cf.*, on this point, *Stockport MBC v O'Reilly* [1983] 2 Lloyd's Rep. 70.

[54] *The Hannah Blumenthal*, above, n.53, at 910.

client in giving instructions or supplying plans in accordance with the terms of the contract. Performance of a contract for the carriage of goods by sea might be delayed partly by the unseaworthiness of the ship and partly by the fact that the shipper had in breach of contract loaded dangerous goods. In all such cases, frustration would be excluded on the reasoning of *The Hannah Blumenthal* and it is respectfully submitted that this would be the correct result. The parties would have remedies for breach of contract and the distribution of loss should be determined under the principles relating to damages (including, in particular, those governing causation and contributory negligence) rather than under the doctrine of frustration.

(c) *Frustration wholly due to other causes*

The mere fact that a party is in breach will not preclude discharge by impossibility resulting wholly from other causes. This point is illustrated by *The Adelfa*[55] where the charterers of a ship had become liable to pay demurrage by reason of their failure to unload the cargo within the laydays. Subsequently the ship was arrested at Tripoli on the application of the receivers of the cargo, whose claims were in later English arbitration proceedings found to have been wholly unjustified and for whose conduct the charterers were not responsible. It was held that the charterers could rely on the consequences of the arrest as a ground of discharge of the charterparty (even though until such discharge their liability to pay demurrage continued); and the best explanation for this result seems to be that their own prior breach was not a contributing cause of the further frustrating delay.

14–012

(2) **Whether prior breach necessary**

The fault or default of one party may exclude frustration because it actually is the event which prevents performance: for example, where one party deliberately destroys the subject-matter of the contract. In such cases no *prior* breach is necessary to exclude frustration, though the fault will of itself amount to a breach of contract. This would have been the position if in *Taylor v Caldwell*[56] the defendants had deliberately set fire to the Music Hall. They would then have been guilty of a breach of an implied term, or of a legal duty, which has been formulated in various ways. For the present purpose it will suffice to adopt Lord Atkin's formulation of: "a positive rule of the law of contract that conduct of either promisor or promisee which can be said to amount to himself 'of his own motion'[57] bringing

14–013

---

[55] *Adelfamar SA v Silos e Mangimi Martini (The Adelfa)* [1988] 2 Lloyd's Rep. 466; *cf. Silver Coast Shipping Co v Union Nationale des Co-operatives Agricoles des Céréales (The Silver Sky)* [1981] 2 Lloyd's Rep. 95 at 97–98 (where it was said that charterers could rely on orders of a party to a civil war even though when that order was given they were in breach, through delay, of their obligation to unload).

[56] (1863) 3 B. & S. 823.

[57] This phrase is taken from *Stirling v Maitland* (1864) 5 B. & S. 840 at 852.

about the impossibility of performance is in itself a breach."[58] This principle refers to impossibility which arises where a party who has entered into a contract which can be performed only if a certain state of affairs continues to exist then puts an end to that state of affairs. It must be distinguished from the principle that a party who disables himself from performing by his "own act or default[59] thereby commits an anticipatory breach. That principle would indeed cover the case put above, of the deliberate destruction of the Music Hall, but it is wider in scope: it can cover cases in which there is no impossibility of performance at all, but only a personal inability of one party. To use the terminology discussed elsewhere in this book, a voluntary disablement of this kind would give rise at most to subjective (and not to objective) impossibility[60]; and for the purpose of the doctrine of frustration such subjective impossibility is not regarded as impossibility at all. The fault or default of one party, giving rise to impossibility of performance, may also amount to a breach even though there has been no such *deliberate* conduct preventing performance as is envisaged in Lord Atkin's statement. This would be the position in the example, given above, where before delivery goods had disintegrated because of a defect in them amounting to a breach of the seller's undertakings as to quality. Indeed, since liability for such defects is strict,[61] the seller would be in breach even though the defect was not due to his want of care or diligence.

14–014   The facts which exclude frustration on the ground that it was self-induced will thus often amount to a breach, but this is not necessarily the case. For one thing, it is far from clear whether the principle stated by Lord Atkin[62] would cover the example of the destruction of the Music Hall in *Taylor v Caldwell* through the negligence of the defendants or their servants. This would exclude frustration,[63] but the only breach in such a case might be the failure to make the Hall available, and not the antecedent negligence. For another, it is possible to point to cases in which frustration would clearly be regarded as self-induced even though the conduct of the party claiming discharge did not itself prevent performance and even though the impossibility was not the result of any prior breach of contract by that party. One such case would be that of a farmer who had contracted to sell a quantity of potatoes to be grown on his land but who failed to spray the crop so that the crop was destroyed by disease. The failure to spray would not itself be a breach,[64] but it would prevent the seller from relying on the crop failure as a ground of

---

[58] *Southern Foundries (1926) Ltd v Shirlaw* [1940] A.C. 701 at 717.
[59] *Universal Cargo Carriers Corp v Citati* [1957] 2 Q.B. 401 at 441.
[60] Above, para.3–002.
[61] *Frost v Aylesbury Diary Co* [1905] 1 K.B. 608.
[62] Above, at n.58.
[63] Above, para.14–003.
[64] Unless the contract expressly required the farmer to spray the crop, his failure to do so would not itself be a breach of duty; if he failed to spray, he would simply take the risk of being unable to deliver. It is highly unlikely that a term requiring him to spray would be implied since such an implication would satisfy neither the "officious bystander" nor the "business efficacy" tests of

frustration, since that failure would be self-induced. There is in such a case no prior breach by the party claiming discharge (as there was in *The Eugenia*[65]), nor is the impossibility brought about by conduct which is itself a breach (as it would be if the farmer had deliberately ploughed up the crop before it could be harvested).

Similar reasoning can be applied to the wholly different situation which arose where a seller of machinery, who was a party to an arbitration in Switzerland, argued that the arbitration agreement had been frustrated by delay.[66] One reason why the argument was rejected was that the delay had been caused by the seller's application to a Swiss court to remit the case to the arbitrators for further consideration and was therefore self-induced. Yet the seller could hardly be said to have committed a breach of the arbitration agreement by invoking such judicial control or supervision of the arbitration as was available to him under the law of the country in which the arbitration was being conducted. Another illustration of the point is provided by the *Denmark Productions* case,[67] in which the defendant company had entered into a contract to manage a group of musicians known as "The Kinks", and also into an agreement with the plaintiff company, by which the plaintiff and the defendant companies were to share in the task of management, the actual work of management being done by a Mr Page, one of the plaintiff's directors. The Kinks having quarrelled with Mr Page, wished to get rid of him as manager, and for this purpose terminated their management contract with the defendant company, which argued (*inter alia*) that termination of this contract had in turn frustrated the contract between it and the plaintiff company. But the argument was rejected as the action taken by The Kinks was part of a scheme agreed on between them and the defendant, the object of which was to enable them to dispense with the services of Mr Page, and not to bring to an end the management relationship between them and the defendant, which in fact continued. The termination by The Kinks of their contract with the defendant can scarcely be said to have been a breach of the contract between the plaintiff and the defendant, but it was nevertheless due to the defendant's fault, so as to exclude frustration, as the defendant had taken "a prominent part in helping The Kinks to terminate the contract",[68] had taken no steps to enforce their rights against The Kinks under that contract, and had "assisted them by acquiescing in an arrangement in which it continued to be employed as managers of the group but without liability to the plaintiffs".[69] The point

---

implication. For these tests, see Treitel, *The Law of Contract* (11th ed.), pp.201–203.

[65] Above, para.14–010.

[66] *Black Clauson International Ltd v Papierwerke Waldhof-Aschaffenburg AG* [1981] 2 Lloyd's Rep. 446.

[67] *Denmark Productions Ltd v Bosocobel Productions Ltd* [1969] 1 Q.B. 699.

[68] *ibid.* at 725, where the reference to the *Joseph Constantine* case [1942] A.C. 154 indicates that the court had in mind the principle that reliance cannot be placed on self-induced frustration.

[69] [1969] 1 Q.B. 699 at 736.

that there need be no prior breach is further illustrated by the cases of imprisoned or incapacitated employees, to be discussed later in this chapter.[70] The conduct leading to the employee's inability to render the agreed services may not in itself be a prior breach of contract, but it may nevertheless be of such a kind that the frustration is self-induced.

Further support for the view that conduct may be regarded as "inducing" frustration even though it does not of itself amount to a breach of contract is provided by the cases (already considered) in which a seller of goods was unable to deliver them because they had been taken in execution in legal proceedings brought against him by a third party.[71] The conduct giving rise to the liability to that third party may arise out of some wholly unrelated transaction. If so, it cannot be regarded as a breach of the seller's duties under the contract of sale but it nevertheless deprives him of the defence of frustration. The requirement that frustration must not be due to the conduct of the party relying on it has similarly been applied where a company was unable to transfer shares because an injunction restraining the transfer had been obtained and the company was unable to show that it could not have obtained discharge of the injunction[72]; where a tenant could not use the premises for the intended purpose because the requisite licence had been refused on the ground that he had told lies to the licensing authorities[73]; and where the tenant of a filling station was unable to obtain further supplies of petrol because he had been convicted of black-marketing.[74] Some cases of this kind may be explicable on the ground that failure to obtain the required licence was due to a prior breach in failing to take reasonable steps to that end[75]; but this explanation would not account for cases in which such efforts were bound to fail because of the previous conduct of the prospective applicant.

14–015   Under s.7 of the Sale of Goods Act 1979 an agreement for the sale of specific goods is avoided if, before the risk has passed to the buyer, the goods perish "without any fault on the part of the seller or buyer"; and under s.20(2) of the Act the passing of risk may (except where the buyer deals as consumer[76]) itself be accelerated or deferred to the extent to which delay in delivery is due to the "fault" of either party. "Fault" for this purpose need not amount to a breach of contract. The point may be illustrated by reference to sales on f.o.b. terms. Under such contracts, risk normally passes on shipment.[77] But it has been said that risk may pass

---

[70] Below, paras 14–020 to 14–021.

[71] Above, para.14–007, at n.35.

[72] *Peckham v Industrial Securities Co*, 113 A 799 (1921).

[73] *United Societies Committee v Madison Square Garden Corp*, 59 N.Y.S. 2d 475 (1946).

[74] *Benjamin v Myers*, 1946 C.P.D. 655.

[75] Above, paras 8–014, 8–051; *e.g.*, perhaps, *Amalgamated Investment & Property Co Ltd v John Walker & Co Ltd* [1977] 1 W.L.R. 164, where one ground for the decision was that the purchasers had failed to show that planning permission could not be obtained. *cf.* below, at n.83.

[76] Sale of Goods Act 1979, s.20(4), as inserted by Sale and Supply of Goods to Consumers Regulations 2002, SI 2002/3045, reg.4(2).

[77] *Benjamin's Sale of Goods* (6th ed.), para.20–086.

before this point if the buyer induces the seller to have the goods ready at the docks by telling him that the ship on which they were to be loaded would be there on a particular day during the shipment period, but she did not actually arrive there till a later day, still within the period.[78] The dictum in question deals with deterioration of the goods in the interval between those two days, but there seems to be no reason why it should not equally apply to their destruction. In such a case the "fault" of the buyer in delaying delivery would preclude him from relying on s.7 (since the risk would have passed to him) even though the delay would not of itself amount to a breach, since the buyer would have been in a position to take delivery of the goods (had they not been destroyed) within the contractual shipment period. The position is different in the United States where, under the Uniform Commercial Code, actual breach is necessary to displace the normal rules as to risk in a contract for the sale of goods.[79]

III. Omissions

Frustration may be self-induced where it is the result of an omission, no   **14–016** less than that of a positive act. Indeed, some of the situations already described are of this nature: for example, failure to obtain the discharge of an injunction affecting the subject-matter is simply an omission[80]; and breach of a carrier's obligation with regard to seaworthiness[81] is in substance an omission. The point is further illustrated by *Mertens v Home Freehold Co,*[82] where performance of a contract to build a house was prevented by war-time legislation requiring such work to be licensed. The builder deliberately worked slowly so as to ensure that the licence would be refused and it was held that he could not rely on the fact that it was refused as a ground of discharge. Again his fault was in substance a deliberate omission. In an American case, the doctrine of discharge was similarly held to be excluded on the ground that a tenant who claimed to be discharged had simply failed to object to a decision made by public officials under zoning laws when that decision had prevented his use of the premises for the intended purpose.[83] Another situation in which an omission is regarded as fault is that discussed in Ch.4, in which a seller of goods relies on failure of his intended source of supply as a ground of discharge.[84] In some cases of this kind, the fact that the seller had not

---

[78] *J & J Cunningham Ltd v Robert Munro & Co Ltd* (1922) 28 Com. Cas. 42 at 46.

[79] UCC, ss.2–509(4), 2–510. In the case of chattel leases, the rules as to risk of loss (see above, para.11–005, n.31) are displaced by "default": s.2A–220; but it seems from the wording of this section that in it "default" refers to breach.

[80] Above, para.14–014, at n.72.

[81] Above, para.14–007, at n.38.

[82] [1921] 2 K.B. 526.

[83] *McNally v Moser,* 122 A. 2d 555 (1956); *cf. the Amalgamated Investment & Property* case, above, n.75.

[84] Above, para.4–052.

ensured the availability of the goods by making an effective contract to procure such goods from his supplier has been regarded as "fault", and the doctrine of discharge has been excluded on this ground.[85] A statutory statement of the sufficiency of omissions for the present purpose is to be found in the Uniform Commercial Code, which refers to "fault" in the context of the doctrine of discharge[86] and defines that expression so as to include an omission.[87]

There must, however be limits to the principle that an omission can constitute fault or default in the present context; for in a sense it could be said that all cases of prevention of performance were due to failure to overcome obstacles. In the *Bank Line* case,[88] there seems to have been a possibility that the shipowners might have secured the early[89] release of the ship which had been requisitioned if they had offered to provide a substitute vessel,[90] but the House of Lords held that they were under no duty to take this step. Indeed, they had been asked by the requisitioning authorities which of their ships they were most ready to give up, and they had nominated the ship which was the subject-matter of the charterparty, but no attempt was made to argue that for this reason the frustration on which they successfully relied was self-induced. The question exactly when an omission will constitute fault for the present purpose is one to which the authorities provide no very clear answer. Obviously an omission will have this effect only when there is a duty to act; and it is easy to see that a carrier is under such a duty to provide a seaworthy ship, and that a builder is under a duty to carry out the agreed work without undue delay. The difficult cases are those in which it is alleged that a party is in default in failing to challenge or to seek to modify the order of a court or of a public authority which has prevented performance. In some such cases, a duty can be imposed by analogy with the rule requiring a party to make reasonable efforts to secure a licence required by supervening prohibition of export, or by similar restrictions.[91] The reason why no similar duty existed in the *Bank Line* case can perhaps be found in the degree of sacrifice which efforts to secure the early release of the ship would have required of the shipowners, or in the consideration that too severe a standard should not be imposed on a party willingly co-operating with the war effort.[92] The duty to act in such cases does not extend beyond one to take steps which are reasonable; failure to go further than this would not amount to fault in the present context. The point may be illustrated by

---

[85] *Atisa SA v Aztec A G* [1983] 2 Lloyd's Rep. 579; *cf. Canadian Industrial Alcohol Co v Dunbar Molasses Co*, 179 N.E. 383 (1932).

[86] ss.2–613, 2–614(1).

[87] s.1–201(16) in the original version; s.1–201(17) in the 2002 version (see above, para.14–003); *cf.* Vienna Convention on Contracts for the International Sale of Goods (above, para.6–048), Art.79(1): "could not reasonably be expected ... to have avoided or overcome it or its consequences."

[88] *Bank Line Ltd v Arthur Capel & Co* [1919] A.C. 435, above, para.5–046.

[89] The ship was eventually released, but too late to avoid frustration.

[90] [1919] A.C. 435 at 440, 450.

[91] Above, para.8–051.

[92] *cf. Jackson v Royal Norwegian Government*, 177 F. 2d 694 (1949).

reference to a Swiss case[93] in which it was held that the tenant of a dental surgery could not reasonably have been expected to obtain a diploma to comply with new regulations governing the use of such premises (and hence was not at fault in failing to do so) since she was 60 years old when the regulations were imposed.

IV. SELF-INFLICTED PERSONAL INCAPACITY

The circumstances in which contracts calling for personal performance may be discharged by the death, illness or incapacity of a party have been discussed in Ch.4.[94] Our present concern is with cases in which such circumstances are brought about by that party, in the sense that he has, either deliberately or negligently, inflicted the incapacity upon himself.

14–017

(1) Deliberately self-inflicted incapacity

The case for rejecting the plea of frustration is at its strongest where the party seeking to rely on it has deliberately brought about his own death or incapacity, and has done so with the motive of escaping from the contract. An incapacity "deliberately induced in order to get out of the engagement"[95] clearly cannot be a ground of discharge.

14–018

The plea of frustration was likewise rejected in the American case of *Begovitch v Murphy*,[96] where a person who had been charged with murder retained an attorney to defend him and then committed suicide. This was described as a "wilful breach"[97] on the part of the client. The view that the client was in breach may seem at first sight surprising, but it appears to be correct, once the principle is accepted that a party cannot rely on an event as a ground of frustration if he has deliberately brought it about. A party's motive for preventing performance is not usually relevant to the question of breach. This principle is not thought to give rise to any difficulty where one party physically destroys the subject-matter on which the other is to render services. If, for example, a house-owner employed a painter to paint his house, and then deliberately set fire to it, no difficulty would be felt in saying that the owner was in breach. From whatever motives the owner may have acted, the painter will suffer exactly the same prejudice as that which he would have suffered if the owner had simply repudiated the contract. As a matter of principle, it should make no difference that the services were to be rendered to the person of the party whose deliberate act made the performance of those services impossible; *Begovitch v Murphy* can be regarded as an illustration of that principle. Equally in that case the contract would not have been frustrated if it had been the attorney (rather than the client) who had committed suicide. Indeed, such a case would

---

[93] BGE 57 II 532, BG November 10, 1931.
[94] Above, paras 4–016 *et seq.*
[95] *Joseph Constantine SS Line v Imperial Smelting Corp Ltd* [1942] A.C. 154 at 166–167.
[96] 101 N.W. 2d 278 (1960).
[97] *ibid.* at 280.

have been a more obvious application (than the actual decision) of the principle that a party cannot rely on self-induced frustration. The practical importance of the distinction in these cases between frustration and breach lies in the remedies of the parties. On either analysis, the primary obligations of the parties will no doubt come to an end and restitution will be available in varying degrees[98]; but the remedy by way of damages will be available only if the case is one of breach.

(2) **Negligently self-inflicted incapacity**

14–019　　The more difficult case is that in which the self-inflicted incapacity is brought about by the negligence[99] of the party seeking to rely on it as a ground of discharge. The question whether frustration in such a case would be self-induced was raised in an example given by Lord Simon in the *Joseph Constantine* case: "Some day it may have to be finally determined whether a prima donna is excused by complete loss of voice from an executory contract to sing, if it is proved that her condition was caused by her carelessness in not changing her wet clothes after being out in the rain."[1] He seems to favour the view that the contract would be dissolved by "the fact of supervening incapacity ... without enquiring into its cause ...".[2] In the United States, the Restatement 2d seems to accept the view that negligence can, in principle, amount to fault (excluding discharge) in the present context; but it then qualifies that view by saying that "it is often so difficult to foresee the effect of conduct on health that fault in bringing about disability must be clear in order to prevent the disability from resulting in discharge".[3] In many cases this reasoning is likely to lead to the same conclusion (though from a different starting point) as that suggested by Lord Simon; but the requirement that fault must be "clear" is one which lacks precision and so makes it hard to tell when the fact that a self-inflicted disability was due to carelessness will preclude discharge. The reasoning of the Restatement 2d is also less convincing where the disability results from an injury, as opposed to an illness: for example, where the injury was caused by the careless driving of the party claiming to be discharged. It could be argued that a person who has contracted to render services owes no duty to take care of his own health or safety on occasions unconnected with the contract; but although this argument might be generally true, it would overlook the point that conduct may be negligent in the present context even though it does not of itself involve the breach of any legal duty.[4] The effect of carelessness in

---

[98] In *Begovitch v Murphy*, above, n.96, the client's estate recovered part of an advance payment of fees notwithstanding the client's breach.

[99] For the meaning of "negligence" in this context, see above, para.14–002, at n.10.

[1] Above, n.95, at 166–167.

[2] *ibid.; cf. Hare v Murphy Bros Ltd* [1974] I.C.R. 603 at 607.

[3] § 262, Comment a, *cf.* Restatement, § 459, Comment d; *Corbin on Contracts*, para.1329.

[4] Above, para.14–002, n.10.

the present context thus remains uncertain; perhaps one reason for the lack of authority on the point is that the problem is often in practice solved by other means: *e.g.* by express or implied terms which deal with the effects on the contract of illness or injury. It should be emphasised that the difficulties here discussed arise only where the supervening event affects a party's capacity to render personal services, or to receive services which can be rendered only in respect of his person. As a general principle negligence amounts to fault for the purpose of excluding frustration. Thus in the example (given above) of the contract to paint a house, it is submitted that the contract would no more be frustrated if the house were burnt down as a result of the owner's negligence than it would be if the destruction were due to his deliberate conduct.

V. Imprisoned Employees

A problem which has given rise to some difference of judicial opinion is that which arises where an employee is prevented from rendering the agreed services because of his imprisonment for a criminal offence. At first sight, it seems clear that the prevention is due to the deliberate act of the employee, so that he should not be able to rely on it as a ground of discharge. This is the position taken in the United States by the Restatement[5] and by the Restatement 2d, which gives the example of an employee who is imprisoned for burglary and concludes that he is not discharged but is liable in damages, because his inability to perform his part of the contract is due to his fault.[6]

    In England the question of the effect of imprisonment on contracts of employment has arisen (in an indirect and somewhat curious way) in cases in which employees who were told by their employers that their employment had been terminated in consequence of their imprisonment then claimed compensation for unfair dismissal.[7] Since dismissal may be unfair without being wrongful, the issue in these cases was not whether the employer was in breach but simply whether the contracts had come to an end as a result of dismissal (*i.e.* by the employer's acceptance of the employee's breach) or of frustration: on the latter analysis, no question of compensation for unfair dismissal could arise. After some conflict in the authorities, the view has prevailed that in such circumstances the contract comes to an end by frustration rather than by dismissal. The point may be illustrated by reference to *F C Shepherd & Co Ltd v Jerrom*[8] where an apprentice who had become involved in a fight between two motor-cycle

---

[5] § 458, Illustration 5.

[6] § 264, Illustration 5.

[7] Under the Employment Rights Act 1996, Pt X, consolidating earlier legislation.

[8] [1987] Q.B. 301; *cf. Harrington v Kent CC* [1980] I.R.L.R. 353; *Hare v Murphy Bros* [1974] I.C.R. 603 at 607; *Anyanwu v South Bank Student Union (No 2), The Times,* December 5, 2003; *contra, Norris v Southampton CC* [1982] I.C.R. 177. For the question whether the imprisonment is, or can reasonably be supposed to be, sufficiently long to frustrate the contract, see above, paras 5–055, 5–056.

gangs was convicted of conspiracy to commit assault and sentenced to a period of Borstal training, of which he served 39 weeks. The employers told his father that they were not prepared to take him back and subsequently resisted his claim for compensation for unfair dismissal on the ground that the contract had been frustrated. It was to rebut this defence that the apprentice argued that there had been no discharge by frustration since the alleged frustration had been self-induced. Acceptance of this argument would have entirely perverted the purpose of the rule that frustration must not be due to the fault of the party relying on it. That purpose is to prevent the party at fault from relying on an allegedly frustrating event (where it is due to his fault) and so to *impose a liability* on that party. In *F C Shepherd & Co Ltd v Jerrom* the apprentice sought to rely on his own criminal conduct in order to *establish a right* to compensation for unfair dismissal. The Court of Appeal rightly rejected his claim and held that the contract was frustrated. This is wholly consistent with Lord Sumner's formulation that "Reliance cannot be placed on self-induced frustration"[9]; for the party relying on frustration was the employer, and he had not induced the frustration.

14–021   Lord Sumner's formulation would, however, have excluded frustration if the claim had been made, not by the employee but against him, *i.e.* if the employer had been claiming damages for the employee's breach of the contract in failing to render the agreed services. In the case of an ordinary contract of employment, it may be unlikely that such a claim would be made; but the point could well arise in the context of other contracts for personal services. If, for example, a singer had contracted to sing at a "pop festival", and was then convicted and imprisoned on a drugs charge and so unable to perform, it is submitted that he should not be able to rely on his imprisonment as a ground of discharge and that the other party to the contract should be entitled to damages for its breach. In support of this submission, reliance could be placed on an analogous case in which the imprisonment of the tenant of a farmhouse was held not to excuse his failure to "reside constantly" there.[10] A contrary argument would be that frustration should not be excluded by conviction for an offence which had nothing to do with the employee's work,[11] so that a distinction would be drawn between, *e.g.* imprisonment for taking part in a weekend brawl and imprisonment for stealing from the employer. But this overlooks the point that "fault" in the present context is not restricted to a prior breach of duty (whether contractual or not) towards the other party.[12]

---

[9] *Bank Line Ltd v Arthur Capel & Co* [1919] A.C. 435 at 452.

[10] *Sumnall v Statt* (1984) 49 P. & C.R. 367.

[11] *cf. Stein v Shaw*, 79 A. 2d 310 (1951) where a disbarred attorney recovered the reasonable value of work done for a client in whose affairs he had not behaved wrongfully. The court said that the position was "not dissimilar to that when an attorney is incapacitated by reason of death, illness or incapacity", thus evidently regarding the contract as discharged in spite of the attorney's "fault". But the Restatement, § 458, Illustration 5 rejects as irrelevant the fact that the "fault" has no connection with the employment in question.

[12] Above, paras 14–002 (n.10) and 14–007.

The crucial point which emerges from *F C Shepherd & Co Ltd v Jerrom* is that the rule is not that fault of one party excludes frustration, but is that a party cannot rely on his own fault as excluding frustration. Where a party is prevented from performing his part of the contract because of his imprisonment for a criminal offence, it follows that *that* party cannot rely on the imprisonment as a ground of frustration, but the *other* party may be able to do so. Failure to appreciate this distinction led in Massachusetts to the strange nineteenth-century decision in *Hughes v Wamsutta Mills*,[13] where it was held that an employee who had been arrested for adultery was not in breach and was even entitled to wages during his imprisonment until his employment was duly terminated by notice. The correct analysis of such a case appears to be that the employee could not have relied on the imprisonment as it was due to his "fault", but that this would not preclude the employer from relying on it as a ground of discharge. Even if the contract was not discharged, the claim for wages should have been rejected as the employee had failed to perform a condition precedent to his right to be paid,[14] and no legally recognised excuse (such as illness) was available in respect of the failure. The Restatement 2d seems, rightly, to disapprove the decision.[15]

VI. Choosing Between Contracts

Frustration is sometimes said to be self-induced where it is due to the "act" or "election"[16] of the party claiming to be discharged. This way of stating the principle can give rise to difficulty where a party has entered into a number of contracts and is deprived by the supervening event of the power of performing them all, but not of the power of performing one or some of them. Where the subject-matter is physically divisible, a possible solution in such cases is to apportion it between the various claimants, in accordance with the principles discussed in Ch.5.[17] But this solution is not available where the subject-matter cannot be physically divided (at least without destroying it)[18]; and in such cases the party who is deprived by the supervening event of his capacity to perform all of his contracts may perform as many of them as his surviving capacity permits and claim that the other or others are frustrated. In favour of such a claim it can be argued that the event which prevented him from performing all the contracts occurred entirely without his "fault" and that therefore the policy of the rule which excludes frustration where it is "self-induced" does not apply. On the other hand, it can be argued that his decision to perform some of the contracts, and not the others, amounted to an "act"

---

[13] 93 Mass. (11 Allen) 201 (1869).

[14] See *Miles v Wakefield MDC* [1987] A.C. 539 at 561, 574; *Wiluszynski v Tower Hamlets LBC* [1989] I.R.L.R. 493 at 498.

[15] See Reporter's note to § 264, Illustration 5.

[16] *Maritime National Fish Ltd v Ocean Trawlers Ltd* [1935] A.C. 524 at 529.

[17] Above, paras 5–023 to 5–033.

[18] See the example given at above, para.5–029.

or "election" on his part, and that it therefore prevented him from relying on the doctrine of discharge with regard to those contracts which he had failed to perform. The second of these arguments has prevailed in the two cases which will be considered in the following discussion. But it is respectfully submitted that these cases are explicable on other grounds; and that, where the party's only effective choice is which of several contracts he will, in the altered state of things, perform, it being clear that he cannot perform them all, then the mere making of that choice should not prevent him from relying on the doctrine of discharge.

14–023   The first case is the decision of the Privy Council in *Maritime National Fish Ltd v Ocean Trawlers Ltd.*[19] The defendants operated a fleet of five trawlers for fishing with otter trawls; three of the trawlers were owned by the defendants through their subsidiaries,[20] while two were chartered from other owners; of these two, one was the *St Cuthbert.* The use of otter trawls without licence was illegal, and because of a change in government policy[21] the defendants secured only three out of the five licences for which they had applied. Having allocated two of these three licences to two of their own trawlers and one to the other chartered trawler,[22] they argued that the charter of the *St Cuthbert* had been frustrated. The argument was rejected by the Canadian courts on the ground that the defendants had taken the risk of not getting licences for all five trawlers, the licensing requirement being known to both parties at the time of contracting. The Privy Council seems to have had a similar point in mind when it said that the circumstance relied on as a ground of discharge "was known to both parties when the contract was made but the contract was absolute in its terms".[23] But it preferred to base its decision in favour of the owners of the *St Cuthbert* on the ground that frustration was self-induced: "it was the act and election of [the defendants] which prevented the *St Cuthbert* from being licensed for fishing with an otter trawl."[24] On the facts, there clearly was such an election, for the defendants could have allocated one of the three licences to the *St Cuthbert* rather than to one of their own trawlers. But suppose that the defendants had operated only the two chartered trawlers, had obtained only one licence, and that the licensing requirement had been introduced after both charterparties were concluded. The question would then have arisen whether their choice to allocate their only licence to one of the trawlers would have been an "election," so as to exclude the doctrine of frustration in relation to the charter of the other. It is submitted that the doctrine should not have been excluded in such a case. The charterer's capacity to perform both contracts is (in the case put) just as effectively removed as his capacity to perform a single contract would have been removed if he had chartered

---

[19] [1935] A.C. 524.
[20] See [1934] 1 D.L.R. 621 at 623; [1934] 4 D.L.R. 288 at 299.
[21] See above, para.8–024.
[22] See the references in n.20, above.
[23] [1935] A.C. at 528.
[24] [1935] A.C. at 529.

only one trawler and been refused a licence for that one; while the owner of the second trawler suffers no greater prejudice than he would have suffered if the charterer had contracted with him alone, and is indeed presumably unaware of the existence of the other charter. If the doctrine of frustration has merit as a means of loss-allocation, it should not be excluded merely because a supervening event which occurs without the fault of the party claiming discharge, and which prevents him from performing all his contracts, forces him to "choose" where his only choice is to perform one of those contracts rather than another.

The view that frustration is excluded in such circumstances is, nevertheless, supported by the second of the two cases here to be considered, *The Super Servant Two*.[25] In that case, a contract had been made to carry the claimant's drilling rig in, at the carrier's option, the *Super Servant One* or the *Super Servant Two*. The latter ship was lost and the carrier argued that his contract with the claimant had been frustrated by that loss because the *Super Servant One* was the subject of another fixture and hence not available for the purpose of performing the carrier's contract with the claimant. The argument was rejected on the ground that the carrier's decision to use the *Super Servant One* for the purpose of performing the other contract amounted to an "election" by him, thus precluding his reliance on the loss of the *Super Servant Two* as a ground of frustration, even if that loss was in no way due to his fault. Three lines of reasoning are given in the judgments but it is submitted with great respect that none of them is wholly convincing. First, it was said that the *Maritime National Fish* case had established that a party could not rely on frustration where his failure or inability was due to his "election"; and that the court in *The Super Servant Two* should follow that decision.[26] It is, however, submitted that the two cases are readily distinguishable: in the *Maritime National Fish* case it was possible for the charterer to perform *all* the contracts which he had made with the owners of the other trawlers, even though only three licences had been allocated to him; while in *The Super Servant Two* it was no longer possible, after the loss of the ship, for the carrier to perform all the contracts which he had made to carry drilling rigs during the period in question. Secondly, it was said that, if the carrier were given the choice which of the contracts he would perform, frustration of the other or others could come about only as a result of the exercise of that choice, and such a position would be inconsistent with the rule that frustration occurs automatically, *without* any election by either party.[27] Again, it is submitted that this line of reasoning is not conclusive since the rule that frustration operates automatically is subject to qualification precisely in cases of allegedly self-induced frustration[28]: we have seen, for example, that the

---

[25] [1990] 1 Lloyd's Rep. 1; affirming [1989] 1 Lloyd's Rep. 148; McKendrick [1990] L.M.C.L.Q. 153.
[26] [1990] 1 Lloyd's Rep. 1 at 10, 13.
[27] [1990] 1 Lloyd's Rep. 1 at 9, 14.
[28] See below, para.15–015.

imprisonment of an employee is a circumstance on which the employer, but not the employee, can rely as a ground of discharge,[29] so that discharge cannot in such cases be described as automatic. Even where the rule that frustration operates automatically does apply, we shall see that this rule forms one of the less attractive aspects of the doctrine of frustration,[30] and one which therefore should not be extended. Moreover, the element of "election" could be eliminated if the question, which of the contracts was to be discharged, were left to be determined, not by the free choice of the promisor, but by a rule of law, *e.g.* by a rule to the effect that the various contracts should for this purpose rank in the order in which they were made.[31] It may, from this point of view, be relevant that, in *The Super Servant Two*, some of the contracts which the carrier chose to perform (by the use of his other ship during the relevant period) had not been made "at any rate finally"[32] until *after* the contract with the claimant; and that, even after the loss of the *Super Servant Two*, the carrier had continued to negotiate for extra fees to be paid under one of those contracts, "before finally allocating the *Super Servant One* to the performance of these contracts".[33] The third reason given for the decision is that: "It is within the promisor's own control how many contracts he enters into and the risk should be his."[34] But this reasoning seems to undermine the whole basis of the doctrine of frustration: it has just as much force where the promisor enters into a single contract as it has where he enters into two or more, with different contracting parties. This, indeed, is the fundamental objection to the reasoning of *The Super Servant Two*, and it is submitted that the rationale of the doctrine should lead to discharge of some of the contracts where the supervening event which makes it impossible to perform them all occurs without the fault of the party claiming discharge.[35] Consistency with the reasoning of the *Maritime National Fish* case could be preserved by holding that *which* contracts were to be discharged should depend, not on the free election of the party who can no longer perform them all, but on a rule of law. On this view, the actual decision in *The Super Servant Two* could be justified by reference to the order in which the various contracts with the carrier were made.

---

[29] *FC Shepherd & Co Ltd v Jerrom* [1987] Q.B. 301 discussed above, paras 14–020, 14–021.

[30] Below, paras 15–007 to 15–009.

[31] *cf.* above, paras 5–028, 5–030.

[32] [1990] 1 Lloyd's Rep. 1 at 9.

[33] *ibid.* at 13.

[34] [1989] 1 Lloyd's Rep. 148 at 158 (at first instance); the reasoning of this judgment was approved on appeal in [1990] 1 Lloyd's Rep. 1.

[35] *cf. Bremer Handelsgesellschaft mbH v Continental Grain Co* [1983] 1 Lloyd's Rep. 269 at 292–293; the treatment of the 92 tonnes in *Bremer Handelsgesellschaft mbH v Vanden Avenne-Izegem PVBA* [1978] 2 Lloyd's Rep. 109 at 115; and see above, para.14–022.

VII. Burden of Proof

Where it is alleged that the supervening event is due to the "fault" of the party claiming to be discharged, an issue can arise as to the burden of proof. Is it up to that party to show that the event occurred without his fault, or must the other party show that the event was due to the fault of the former party? General principles relating to the incidence of the burden of proof are of limited help in answering this question. The principle that a party should not be required to prove a negative would suggest that the burden should not be on the party claiming to be discharged; while the principle that one party should not be required to prove facts peculiarly within the knowledge of the other would suggest that the burden should not be on the party denying frustration on the ground of the other's fault. It is therefore scarcely surprising that American and English law differ in their approaches to the problem.

In the United States, the burden of proof on the issue of fault is on the party who relies on the supervening event as a ground of discharge.[36] This is also the position in civil law systems,[37] where it is explained by reference to the desire to narrow the requirement of "fault" as a condition of contractual liability[38]; but this explanation will not hold in the common law, in which "fault" in the present context includes failure to perform a duty of strict liability.[39] The justification for the American rule is rather that the party claiming to be discharged is often more likely than the other party to be able to prove how the event occurred, especially if the event was the destruction of a thing which was the subject-matter of the contract, or of one which was essential for performance of the contract, and that thing was within the control of the party claiming to be discharged.[40]

English law accepts this reasoning, and reaches the same conclusion, in one special group of cases: a person to whom goods have been bailed, and who relies on their destruction as a ground of discharge, must show that the destruction was not due to any breach of his duty as a bailee.[41] But the general rule of English law is that the burden of proving fault is on the party who alleges that frustration was self-induced. The rule appears to be based on the principle that the burden of proof is, in general, on the party who alleges either that a contract has been broken,[42] or that the

---

[36] *Blount Midyette & Co v Aeroglide Corp*, 119 S.E. 2d 225 (1961).

[37] In German law, this position (formerly stated in BGB § 282, now repealed) follows from the general rule inherent in § 280(1), sentence 2 (in force January 1, 2002). See also in Switzerland Code of Obligations, Art.97; *cf.* Arts 331; in Austria ABGB, § 1298; in France, Code Civil, Art.1147 and Art.1302(3); for a possible conflict between Arts.1147 and 1137, see Treitel, *Remedies for Breach of Contract*, pp.9–10.

[38] *ibid.*

[39] Above, para.14–007.

[40] *Corbin on Contracts*, para.1330.

[41] *Aktieselskabet De Danske Sukkerfabrikker v Bajamar Compania Naviera SA (The Torrenia)* [1983] 2 Lloyd's Rep. 210 at 216.

[42] *Joseph Constantine SS Line v Imperial Smelting Corp Ltd* [1942] A.C. 154 at 174.

other party has lost the benefit of an "exception".[43] It is illustrated by the *Joseph Constantine* case,[44] where a ship was prevented by an explosion from performing the services which she was to have rendered under a charterparty. The charterers' claim for damages for breach of the charterparty was rejected: the House of Lords held that the shipowners were discharged from the contract without having to disprove fault and in spite of the fact that the cause of the explosion was never explained. This rule can be supported on the ground that generally catastrophic events which prevent performance do occur without the fault of either party. To impose the burden of disproving fault on the party relying on frustration is therefore less likely than the converse rule to lead to the right result in the majority of cases.

---

[43] *ibid.* at 192–194.

[44] Above n.42; Stone, 60 L.Q.R. 262; a contrary dictum in *FC Shepherd & Co Ltd v Jerrom* [1987] Q.B. 301 at 319 seems to have been made *per incuriam*.

CHAPTER 15

EFFECTS OF FRUSTRATION

I. INTRODUCTION

In English law, frustration discharges both parties from such of their 15–001
contractual duties as remain unperformed at the time of discharge. The
point that both parties are discharged even though the performance of
only one is affected by the supervening event has already been discussed.[1]
Three further aspects of the effects of discharge call for discussion in this
chapter. They are that discharge is automatic, that it is total, and that it
gives rise to problems of adjustment, which have been in part resolved by
legislation. It should be said at the outset that the English rules which
govern these effects of frustration have not escaped judicial criticism. Lord
Simon has suggested that: "the English doctrine of frustration could be
made more flexible" so as to avoid "the all or nothing situation, the entire
loss ... falling exclusively on one party, whereas justice might require the
burden to be shared."[2] These remarks were made with special reference
to leases of land, but were not confined to such transactions. The criticism
of the present position is perhaps too severe. We saw in Ch.2 that, in *Taylor
v Caldwell*,[3] the doctrine of discharge itself operated as a mechanism for
splitting, or "sharing" the loss[4]: it did so in the sense that, while the
claimants were not entitled to damages, the defendants were not entitled
to the promised payments. Similarly, in *Krell v Henry*[5] the outcome was that
the claimant received and retained part of the promised payment while
the defendant was released from his liability to pay the balance. But it is
arguable that these solutions either did not carry the process of "sharing"
loss far enough, or that they were due to accidents of timing.[6] Hence Lord
Simon's criticisms retain considerable force and justify further discussion

---

[1] Above, paras 2–039 to 2–043.
[2] *National Carriers Ltd v Panalpina (Northern) Ltd* [1981] A.C. 675 at 707.
[3] (1863) 3 B. & S. 826.
[4] Above, para.2–026.
[5] [1903] 2 K.B. 740; above, para.7–010.
[6] In *Krell v Henry* there would have been no loss-splitting of the kind described
above if the *whole* £75 had been payable "on" June 24: see below, para.15–069.

of the question whether the present English rules governing the effects of discharge are in a satisfactory state. For this purpose, it will be helpful to refer to alternative solutions provided in other common and civil law systems, though it would go beyond the scope of this book to attempt a detailed account of those solutions. It should also be said that criticisms of the English rules have not in recent years been frequent or widespread. The reason for this degree of acquiescence is probably to be found largely in the fact that potentially frustrating events are quite commonly the subject of express contractual provisions[7] and that such provisions often do provide for intermediate solutions by which discharge is either excluded or, if it does occur, is neither automatic nor total, and by which problems of adjustment are dealt with more flexibly than under the general law.

II. Automatic Discharge

(1) Statement of the principle

15–002   Once the requirements of frustration are satisfied, the effect of the doctrine (in English law) is to discharge the contract (in the words of Lord Sumner) "forthwith, without more and automatically".[8] This statement has been cited with approval, or paraphrased, in many later cases.[9]

(2) Parties treating contract as in force

15–003   The contract may be discharged even though both parties have, for some time after the frustrating event, continued to behave as if the contract were still in force. The law seems to be settled in this sense, even though a number of dicta on the point are not, at first sight, easy to reconcile, two apparently conflicting ones coming from the same source. In the *Hirji Mulji* case, Lord Sumner said that: "whatever the consequences of frustration may be upon the conduct of the parties, its legal effect does not depend upon their opinions, or even knowledge as to the event. ... Frustration ... operates automatically. What the parties say or do is only evidence, and not necessarily weighty evidence, of the view to be taken by informed and experienced minds."[10] But in the *Bank Line* case he said that: "Both [parties] thought its result [*i.e.* that of the requisitioning of the chartered ship] was to terminate their contractual relations ...

---

[7] Above, Ch.12.

[8] *Hirji Mulji v Cheong Yue SS Co* [1926] A.C. 497 at 505.

[9] *Maritime National Fish Ltd v Ocean Trawlers Ltd* [1935] A.C. 524 at 527; *Joseph Constantine Shipping Corp v Imperial Smelting Corp* [1942] A.C. 154 at 163, 170, 171, 187; *Denny Mott & Dickson v James B. Fraser & Co Ltd* [1944] A.C. 265 at 274; *Blane Steamships v Minister of Transport* [1951] 2 K.B. 965 at 989; *J Lauritzen A/S v Wijsmuller BV (The Super Servant Two)* [1990] 1 Lloyd's Rep. 1 at 8, 11.

[10] Above, n.8, at 509; *cf. Morgan v Manser* [1948] 1 K.B. 184 at 191.

and as they must have known more about it than I do there is no reason why I should not think so too."[11] One can resolve the apparent conflict by saying that, especially in cases of temporary impossibility, the views of the parties (whether expressed by words or by conduct) are relevant in determining whether the interruption was sufficiently serious[12] in length to frustrate the contract. Similar issues can arise in other situations in which an alleged ground of discharge raises questions of degree, *e.g.* in cases of alleged partial impossibility, or impossibility in the method of performance.[13] In determining such questions the court will take the parties' views into account but will not regard them as decisive[14]: hence it has been said that "the parties' beliefs are not determinative, but nor are they irrelevant".[15] The point that such beliefs are "not determinative" is *a fortiori*, true where the ground of discharge is the total destruction of the subject-matter: here it can make no difference to the issue of discharge that the parties, in ignorance of such destruction, continued to act as if the contract were still in existence.

The views and conduct of the parties after the frustrating event may also be relevant for purposes other than that just considered. Even if they do not prevent discharge, they may enable the court to infer that the parties have entered into a new agreement, incorporating at least some of the terms of the original contract by reference.[16] This solution was adopted in an American case[17]; but in England it would give rise to difficulty in that the courts are reluctant to find that the parties intended to enter into a new implied contract where they believed they were acting under an express contract.[18] Where a contract of employment was frustrated by an injury to the employee, it was accordingly held that no new contract was created by the employer's act of keeping the employee on the books: the parties' belief that the old contract was still in existence (when it was, in spite of that belief, frustrated) negatived any intention to enter into a new contract.[19] It is possible, however, that a party who had received requested services or other benefits after discharge would be liable on a *quantum meruit* basis even though no

---

[11] *Bank Line Ltd v Arthur Capel & Co Ltd* [1919] A.C. 435 at 460.

[12] Above, paras 5–036 *et seq.*

[13] Above, paras 5–002, 4–065, 4–078 to 4–083.

[14] *Kissavos Shipping Co SA v Empressa Cubana de Fletes (The Agathon)* [1982] 2 Lloyd's Rep. 211 at 213.

[15] *International Sea Tankers Inc v Hemisphere Shipping Co Ltd (The Wenjiang) (No 2)* [1983] 1 Lloyd's Rep. 400 at 408.

[16] *BP Exploration (Libya) Co Ltd v Hunt* [1979] 1 W.L.R. 783 at 809 (affirmed [1983] 2 A.C. 352); *cf. the Hirji Mulji* case [1926] A.C. 497 at 509.

[17] *Monite Waterproof Glue Co v Sawyer-Cleater Lumber Co*, 48 N.W. 2d 333 (1951).

[18] *cf.* in other contexts, *Beesly v Hallwood Estates Ltd* [1960] 1 W.L.R. 549 at 558; affirmed on other grounds [1961] Ch. 105; *Harvela Investments Ltd v Royal Trust of Canada (CI) Ltd* [1986] A.C. 207; *The Aramis* [1989] 1 Lloyd's Rep. 213; *Glencore Grain Ltd v Flacker Shipping Ltd (The Happy Day)* [2002] EWCA Civ 1068; [2002] 2 Lloyd's Rep. 487 at [63].

[19] *GF Sharp & Co v McMillan* [1998] I.R.L.R. 632.

implication of a new contract arose[20]; such liability could arise, irrespective of contract, on restitutionary principles. It must be distinguished from the liability, to be discussed later in this chapter, which arises by statute[21] in respect of benefits received *before* discharge.

(3) **Estoppel**

15–004   Another possible consequence of the fact that the parties have, after an allegedly frustrating event, continued to act as if the contract were still in force, or of the fact that one of them has done so, may be to give rise to an estoppel, or to amount to a waiver of frustration. According to one dictum,[22] frustration may be excluded on the ground that the party relying on it had "affirmed" the contract. In the context there seems to be no substantial distinction between affirmation and waiver. In another case,[23] buyers of a ship alleged that requisition of the ship had frustrated the contract of sale and the sellers argued that the buyers were estopped from relying on frustration by reason of their having claimed compensation from the Admiralty. This argument was rejected by the Court of Appeal,[24] apparently because the requirements of estoppel were not satisfied. The implication seems to be that, if those requirements are satisfied, estoppel can, in principle, exclude frustration. But in *BP Exploration (Libya) Co Ltd v Hunt*,[25] Robert Goff J. rejected the arguments that the claimants were estopped by their conduct from relying on frustration, or that they had waived frustration. The effect of frustration was to determine the contract at once, as a matter of law; and, while waiver or estoppel might prevent a party from relying on a legal right, they could not prevent a party from relying on frustration because "frustration is not a legal right; it is a legal doctrine".[26] Since Robert Goff J.'s decision that the contract was frustrated was upheld on appeal,[27] his view on the estoppel point must be taken to have been accepted by the Court of Appeal and by the House of Lords. Nevertheless, it is arguable that the possibility that estoppel may be relevant to the issue of frustration is not wholly to be ruled out. In particular, where impossibility is only partial or temporary, the representations (whether express or by conduct) of a party may indicate that he does not regard the impossibility as sufficiently serious to constitute a ground of discharge.[28] In an American case of this kind, waiver or estoppel was said to have precluded immediate

---

[20] *Société Tunisienne d'Armement v Sidermar SpA (The Massalia)* [1961] 2 Q.B. 278 (overruled on the issue of frustration in *Ocean Tramp Tankers Corp v V/O Sovfracht (The Eugenia)* [1964] 2 Q.B. 226); above, para.4–078.

[21] Law Reform (Frustrated Contracts) Act 1943, s.1(3), below, para.15–060.

[22] *Black Clauson International Ltd v Papierwerke Waldhof-Aschaffenburg AG* [1981] 2 Lloyd's Rep. 446 at 457.

[23] *Dale SS Co Ltd v Northern SS Co Ltd* (1918) 34 T.L.R. 271; below, para.15–030.

[24] at 272.

[25] [1979] 1 W.L.R. 783.

[26] *ibid.* at 809.

[27] [1983] 2 A.C. 352.

[28] See above, para.15–002, at nn.12, 13.

discharge[29]; and, although this case may be based on the American view that discharge is not necessarily automatic,[30] it is submitted that there is scope for the operation of estoppel even in English law in such cases of partial or temporary impossibility, for example, the conduct of the parties after the allegedly frustrating event may give rise to an estoppel by convention.[31]

(4) Frustration distinguished from rescission for breach

It further follows from the principle of automatic discharge that the doctrine can be invoked by either party to the contract, and not only by the party who is prejudiced (or adversely affected) by the supervening event (or would be so prejudiced if the contract were not discharged).[32] In this respect, frustration differs from rescission for breach, which depends on the election of the victim of the breach to treat the contract as at an end.[33] As Lord Wright has said: "where there is frustration a dissolution of the contract occurs automatically. ... It does not depend, as does rescission ... on the choice or election of either party."[34] The point is reflected in the language used by the Sale of Goods Act 1979 to describe respectively the effects of frustration and of breach of condition. In the former case, the contract "is avoided",[35] while in the latter case the breach may give the injured party "a right to treat the contract as repudiated"[36] or to "rescind"[37] it. The two processes also, of course, differ in that, though both bring the primary obligations of the parties to an end, rescission for breach leaves outstanding the guilty party's liability in damages[38] while there is no such liability after discharge by frustration. The reason for this distinction between frustration and rescission for breach is obvious enough. Breach presupposes fault or default of the party

15–005

---

[29] *West v Peoples First Nat. Bank & Trust Co*, 106 A. 2d 427 at 432 (1954).

[30] Below, para.15–014.

[31] Above, para.4–006.

[32] For the meaning, in this context, of the phrase "party prejudiced," see below, after n.39.

[33] See Treitel, *The Law of Contract* (11th ed.), p.844.

[34] *Denny Mott & Dickson v James B Fraser & Co* [1944] A.C. 265 at 274; *cf. Peter Lind & Co Ltd v Constable Hart & Co Ltd* [1979] 2 Lloyd's Rep. 248 at 253 (no "exact analogy between repudiation and frustration"); *Nitrate Corp of Chile Ltd v Pansuiza Compania de Navegacion (The Hermosa)* [1980] 1 Lloyd's Rep. 638 at 648; affirmed [1982] 1 Lloyd's Rep. 520 ("frustration and repudiation" described as "part of the same general principle" but "differentiated only by the consequences which attend discharge and the identity of the party who is entitled to assert the discharge". For further discussion of the relationship between frustration and rescission for breach, see above, para.5–060.

[35] s.7.

[36] s.11(3).

[37] s.48(4) ("rescinded") and heading before s.48 ("rescission"); ss.48A(2)(b)(ii), 48C and 48F, as inserted by Sale and Supply of Goods to Consumers Regulations 2002, SI 2002/3045, reg.5, and see reg.9, inserting similar provisions into the Supply of Goods and Services Act 1982.

[38] Treitel, *The Law of Contract* (11th ed.), p.850.

in breach but not of the victim, and this difference justifies the rule which treats the victim more favourably than the wrongdoer. In the case of frustration, no such distinction can be drawn between the parties: each is equally the victim of an event for which (by definition) neither is responsible.

There is, at first sight, some difficulty (where a contract is frustrated) in saying that one party is, to a greater extent than the other, *the* party prejudiced by the supervening event. In *Taylor v Caldwell*,[39] for example, if the contract had not been discharged, the defendants would have been prejudiced by having to pay damages in respect of their inability (by reason of an event for which they were not responsible) to provide the Music Hall, while the hirers would have been prejudiced by having to make the agreed payments without getting the use of the Hall. It is, however, submitted that there is an approach which makes it meaningful, even in cases of frustration, to talk of one party as "the party prejudiced". This is to use this expression to refer to the party who, in consequence of the supervening event, will not receive the performance for which he bargained, or will receive only such a small or subsidiary part of that performance as (in accordance with the rules relating to partial impossibility[40]) will not prevent discharge; in cases of frustration of purpose,[41] the party prejudiced will correspondingly be the party who cannot make the mutually contemplated use of the subject-matter. In other words, the hirers of the Music Hall were the party prejudiced in *Taylor v Caldwell* and the hirer of the flat was the party prejudiced in *Krell v Henry*.[42]

15–006 It will be suggested below[43] that automatic discharge sometimes produces undesirable results, and that, in cases where this is the position, an alternative solution would be to give an option to the party prejudiced to treat the contract as discharged. A possible objection to this suggestion is that this solution would, in itself, produce undesirable results, *e.g.* it could be interpreted as advocating a reversal of *Taylor v Caldwell* itself, where the hirers of the Music Hall could be said to have elected to treat the contract as still on foot by claiming damages for its breach. But even in cases of breach there is no inconsistency between rescinding the contract for breach and at the same time claiming damages for that breach[44]; and, even if this were not so, the argument would misinterpret the present suggestion, which seeks to make a narrower point. That point can be clarified by reference to a party's right to rescind a contract for non-performance, which is not so serious as to amount to frustration.[45] Such a right may arise, not only where the non-performance amounts to a breach, but also where the party failing to perform has an excuse for non-

---

[39] (1863) 3 B. & S. 826.
[40] Above, para.5–002.
[41] Above, Ch.7.
[42] [1903] 2 K.B. 740.
[43] Below, para.15–007.
[44] See Treitel, *The Law of Contract* (11th ed.) pp.850–853.
[45] Above, para.5–060.

performance, *e.g.* where temporary (but not frustrating) illness prevents performance of personal services.[46] Similarly, in *Taylor v Caldwell* a possible solution would be that the fire should provide the defendants with an excuse for their failure to supply the Hall; but it would not follow from this that the hirers should not, if they so wished, elect to affirm the contract in so far as its performance remained possible: that is, with regard to the other facilities to be provided by the defendants.[47]

This analysis could not, however, be applied where no part of the originally bargained-for performance remained possible, as in cases of time or demise charterparties, in which the ship was requisitioned for the whole of the period covered by the contract,[48] or in which the ship was destroyed.[49] We shall see that, even in such cases, the party prejudiced in the above sense (*i.e.* the charterer) has sometimes sought to affirm the contract, with a view to claiming the compensation payable by a third party to the other contracting party in consequence of the frustrating event. Again it would be possible to allow the charterer to affirm the contract for these purposes, while recognising that the supervening event protected the shipowner from liability in damages for failing to render the agreed services or to supply the ship.

(5) **Party profiting from frustration**

It follows from the automatic operation of the doctrine of frustration that   **15–007** in *Taylor v Caldwell*,[50] the hirers would not have been entitled to use the Surrey Gardens even if they had wished to do so in spite of the destruction of the Music Hall. Similarly, the defendant in *Krell v Henry*[51] would not have been entitled to use the premises even if he had wished to do so in spite of the cancellation of the coronation processions. These are, no doubt, improbable contingencies. It is scarcely plausible to suppose that the hirers would have been prepared to make the agreed payments in return for facilities which, as a result of the frustrating event, had become less valuable than those bargained for; nor would the owners have objected to providing the surviving facilities in exchange for payments which would, presumably, have exceeded the market value of the facilities after (and as reduced by) the frustrating event. But there are other cases in which it may be in the commercial interest of the party who is *prima facie* prejudiced by the frustrating event (in the sense that its occurrence will prevent him from receiving the performance that he had bargained for[52]) nevertheless to uphold the contract, and in the interest of the other party to claim that the contract has been discharged, even though he would not, if the contract were upheld after the event, be in a worse financial position

---

[46] *e.g. Poussard v Spiers and Pond* (1876) 1 Q.B.D. 410; above, para.5–060.
[47] *i.e.* the Gardens and the side-shows: above, para.2–024.
[48] *e.g. The Isle of Mull*, 278 F. 131 (1921); below, para.15–007.
[49] *e.g. Blane Steamships v Minister of Transport* [1951] 2 K.B. 965; below, para.15–007.
[50] (1863) 3 B. & S. 826.
[51] [1903] 2 K.B. 740.
[52] See above, para.15–005, after n.39.

than that in which he would have been if the event had not occurred and the contract been performed in accordance with its terms. One group of cases of this kind concerns the effects on time charters of the war-time requisitioning of the ship. If the contract were upheld, the charterer would have to pay the agreed hire without receiving the services bargained for, and it might therefore be expected that the charterer would claim to be discharged. Yet in a series of such cases it is, paradoxically, the owner who makes such a claim, even though the charterer is perfectly willing to pay the agreed hire. The owner is likely to take the course where the compensation paid by the government exceeds the agreed hire, for in such a case discharge of the contract will enable him to keep that compensation for his own benefit and so to profit from frustration. An illustration of this possibility is provided by the American case of *The Isle of Mull*.[53] A time charter for five years from May 1913, provided for payment of hire at the rate of £1,370 per month. In June 1915, the ship was requisitioned and the compensation paid by the government was nearly £1,000 per month more than the agreed hire. It was held that the shipowner was entitled to rely on the requisition as a ground of discharge, with the result that he profited from frustration to the extent of the difference between the agreed hire and the compensation for the requisition. A briefly reported English case[54] seems to reach the same result in a similar situation. Again, in *Blane Steamships v Minister of Transport*,[55] a demise charter gave the charterer an option to purchase the ship, and the charterer purported to exercise this option after the ship had become a constructive total loss. It was held that he was not entitled to do so since the loss of the ship had automatically brought the charterparty (and with it the option) to an end.[56] The shipowner's motive for claiming to be discharged was that the amount for which the ship was insured exceeded the price specified in the option; and it is arguable that the shipowner made a windfall profit out of frustration to the extent of this excess. The possibility that a party may rely on frustration to escape from a bad bargain is further illustrated by the *Orlando*[57] case (discussed in Ch.4), where a seller of goods was able to rely as a ground of discharge on the stranding of the ship named in the contract, even though the buyer was prepared to provide another ship, and even though the seller's motive in claiming discharge appears to have been that the market price of the goods had risen. Again, in *Baily v De Crespigny*[58] a lessor was able to rely, as a ground of discharge from his covenant not to build on a paddock adjacent to the land let, on the fact that the paddock had been compulsorily acquired by a railway company; and he profited from frustration in that he had received compensation for the compulsory

---

[53] 278 F. 131 (1921).
[54] *Heilgers & Co v Cambrian SN Co Ltd* (1917) 34 T.L.R. 72.
[55] [1951] 2 K.B. 965.
[56] *ibid.* at 989.
[57] *Nickoll & Knight v Ashton Edridge & Co* [1901] 2 K.B. 126; above, para.4–062.
[58] (1869) L.R. 4 Q.B. 180.

requisition[59] and was not required to pay over any part of this compensation to the tenant.

Such decisions may appear to be logical deductions from the rule that
frustration operates automatically, but they are, with respect, misapplications of the doctrine of discharge. The purpose of that doctrine is to find a satisfactory way of allocating the loss which results from the supervening event, and not to enable one of the parties to rely on that event to make a windfall profit, or to escape from a bargain merely because it has turned out, for that party, to be a disadvantageous one. In some systems of law, such a result can be avoided, at least to some extent, by applying the principle of conditional discharge or surrogate benefit, (to be discussed later in this chapter[60]) under which (for example) the shipowner in the charterparty cases discussed above could claim discharge only on terms of making over to the charterer the compensation which he had received for the requisition, or in respect of the loss, of his ship. English law does not directly recognise any such principle; but English courts have nevertheless been sensitive to the point that a party should not be allowed to rely on frustration to make a profit out of frustration; and they have in a number of cases rejected attempts to use the doctrine of discharge in this way. In the *Tamplin* case,[61] the claim that the time charter had been frustrated by the requisitioning of the ship was made by the shipowner; and the decision that the contract had not been frustrated has been explained precisely on the ground that the House of Lords saw no good reason why the shipowner should be allowed to claim discharge in order to make a profit of the kind just described.[62] In a later time charter case,[63] the rate of compensation was less than the agreed hire and the owners' claim for hire was upheld, but it is significant that they made no claim to the compensation. If owners are entitled to hire in such circumstances, it is submitted that they should not be entitled to more than the agreed hire in the converse situation, where the compensation exceeds the hire.

All this is not to say that a shipowner should never be able to claim that a time charter has been frustrated by requisition of the ship merely because the compensation paid for the requisition exceeds the agreed hire. In the *Bank Line*[64] case it was the owners who claimed frustration, and the exact reasons why that claim was upheld are not easy to discover. This difficulty has been discussed in Ch.5[65]; the point to be emphasised here is that the frustrating event in that case occurred *before* service under the charterparty had begun and the question was whether the *whole* of that service had to be rendered at some later time than that originally envisaged. Such an indefinite postponement could obviously cause prejudice to the owner if

---

[59] See *ibid.*, at 187–188.
[60] Below, paras 15–019 *et seq.*
[61] *Tamplin SS Co v Anglo-Mexican Petroleum Co* [1916] 2 A.C. 397.
[62] *Metropolitan Water Board v Dick Kerr & Co* [1918] A.C. 119 at 129; *cf.* also *Port Line Ltd v Ben Line Steamers Ltd* [1958] 2 Q.B. 146.
[63] *Modern Transport Co Ltd v Duneric SS Co* [1917] 1 K.B. 370.
[64] *Bank Line Ltd v Arthur Capel & Co* [1919] A.C. 435.
[65] Above, para.5–046.

he were required to render the services some years after the price for those services had been fixed. In the other time charter cases considered here, that was not the position. The owner was simply claiming discharge from his obligation to render services for the *balance* of the originally agreed period; and there seems to be no good reason for allowing him to escape from the term fixing the price for the services *for that period.* Where the ship is requisitioned, even the argument that the cost of performance to him has increased is one that is not open to him.

15–009   The reluctance of the courts to allow a party to profit from frustration is by no means confined to time charter cases such as the *Tamplin* case. It is further illustrated by one of the English Suez cases, discussed in Ch.4. This was the *Tsakiroglou* case,[66] in which the closure of the Suez Canal did indeed prejudice the seller by increasing his carriage costs. But that extra cost was more than outweighed by the increase in the market price of the goods, an increase which had no doubt also been brought about by the closure of the Canal. A similar argument is found in some of the American energy crisis cases.[67] In one such case,[68] for example, the court held that the crisis did not justify an oil company's refusal to continue to supply aviation fuel to an airline, and one reason for this conclusion was that the overall annual profits of the oil company had actually *increased* as a result of the crisis.

Yet another case which illustrates the reluctance of the court to allow a party to profit from frustration is the *Walton Harvey* case[69] in which a contract to display the claimants' advertising sign on the defendants' hotel was held not to have been discharged when the hotel was compulsorily acquired and demolished by a local authority acting under statutory powers. The actual ground for the decision was that the defendants knew (while the claimants did not) that the hotel might be taken under statutory powers; but it was argued in para.13–007, above, that the court was also influenced by the fact that the defendants had received compensation for the compulsory acquisition from the acquiring authority and would therefore suffer no hardship by being required, in turn, to compensate the claimants. From this point of view, the case forms a striking contrast to *Baily v De Crespigny.*[70]

This contrast well illustrates the limitation on the powers of English courts to prevent a party from using the doctrine of discharge in order, not to avoid a loss, but actually to secure a profit. An English court can prevent a party from so profiting only by holding that a contract has *not* been frustrated. Once the court has held that the requirements of frustration are satisfied, it cannot prevent either party from relying on the discharge of the contract, even though the practical result is to confer a windfall profit on the party who actually invokes the doctrine. Such a

---

[66] *Tsakiroglou & Co Ltd v Noblee Thorl GmbH* [1962] A.C. 93; above, paras 4–073 to 4–074.

[67] Above, paras 6–009 to 6–010.

[68] *Eastern Air Lines Inc v Gulf Oil,* 415 F. Supp. 429 (1975).

[69] *Walton Harvey Ltd v Walker & Homfrays Ltd* [1931] Ch. 274.

[70] (1869) L.R. 4 Q.B. 180. above, para.15–007, at n.58.

result follows logically from the principle of automatic termination, but it is submitted that it is neither a necessary nor a desirable consequence of the doctrine of discharge; and that such a consequence could and should be avoided by adopting the rule that frustration should operate only so as to give an option to terminate the contract to a party who is prejudiced by the frustrating event. Such a solution would not rule out the possibility of termination at the option of either party where both were so prejudiced; and we shall see (in discussing mitigations of the principle of automatic discharge) that the suggested solution is recognised by other systems of law[71] and so cannot be regarded as inconsistent with the concept of discharge by supervening events. That view is further supported by the fact that, in the special case of "self-induced" frustration, even English law accepts the possibility that discharge may occur at the option of one party (but not at that of the other).[72]

III. TOTAL DISCHARGE

The English common law view is that frustration operates, not only automatically (*i.e.* without the choice or election of either party) but also totally. What this means is that the obligations of both parties are wholly discharged in so far as performance of them had not fallen due when the contract was frustrated.[73] There is, consequently, thought to be no possibility of varying the contract, or of adapting it to the changed circumstances, or (in cases of temporary impossibility) of suspending its performance. The reason why such solutions have not found favour in English law,[74] seems to be that they are regarded as sources of undesirable uncertainty, or as open to the objection that they would enable the courts to make a contract for the parties.

    15–010

There is, somewhat surprisingly, little discussion of this aspect of the effects of frustration in English law. The principle of total discharge seems to be regarded simply as a logical consequence of Blackburn J.'s formulation in *Taylor v Caldwell* that "both parties are excused".[75] There is evidently thought to be no intermediate position between being fully bound and being totally discharged. This appears from metaphors in later cases referring to the life or to the death of the contract: it is said that "the life of the contract goes",[76] that frustration "kills the contract itself",[77] and that "the contract is ended and dead".[78] The principle of total discharge finds more abstract expression in such judicial statements as

---

[71] Below, para.15–014.

[72] Below, para.15–015.

[73] For the prospective operation of discharge see below, para.15–011.

[74] See below, paras 15–034, 15–040.

[75] (1863) 3 B. & S. 826 at 840.

[76] *Joseph Constantine SS Line v Imperial Smelting Corp* [1942] A.C. 154 at 187.

[77] *ibid.*, at 163; *cf. J Lauritzen A/S v Wijsmuller BV (The Super Servant Two)* [1990] 1 Lloyd's Rep. 1 at 8.

[78] *Joseph Constantine* case, above n.76, at 188.

that frustration "brings the whole contract to an end".[79] It again appears in the statutory language used in s.7 of the Sale of Goods Act 1979: the contract is "avoided". There is also some support for the principle of total discharge in the United States, *e.g.* in the rejection in one case, of the argument that the effect of the supervening event was merely to suspend the contract[80]; and in the use of the word "avoided" by the Uniform Commercial Code to refer to the effect of total destruction of the subject-matter on a contract for the sale of identified goods.[81] We shall, however, see in the ensuing discussion of mitigations of the principle of total discharge that American law has to a considerable extent rejected that principle, and that, even in English law, it is possible to point to significant departures from it.

IV. PROSPECTIVE OPERATION OF DISCHARGE

15–011   Statements of the principle of total discharge are commonly qualified so as to make the point that frustration operates only as a ground of discharge of future obligations, *i.e.* of those which would have accrued after the date of discharge. Thus it has been said that "the life of the contract goes, at least as regards future performance. The contract remains only to enforce accrued rights"[82]; that the effect of frustration is to "discharge the parties from *further* liability"[83]; and that from the moment of frustration "there is no longer any obligation as to future performance, though up to that moment obligations which have accrued remain in force".[84] The point may be illustrated by supposing that, in *Taylor v Caldwell*,[85] the Music Hall had been destroyed after the first, and before the second, of the four days specified for the grand concerts. The contract would then have been discharged with regard to the last three of those days, while each party would have remained liable for any failure to perform obligations which had fallen due on the first day. For example, the hirers would have remained liable to pay the £100 due on the evening of the first day, and the defendants would have remained liable in damages if on that day they had failed to provide the side-shows specified in the contract and had thereby reduced the box-office receipts to which the hirers were entitled under the contract.

---

[79] *National Carriers Ltd v Panalpina (Northern) Ltd* [1981] A.C. 675 at 689.

[80] *20th Century Lites v Goodman*, 149 P. 2d 88 (1944).

[81] UCC, s.2–613(a). UCC, ss.2–613(c), 2A–221(a); in the proposals for revision of the Code (above, para.2–042, n.17), "terminated" is substituted for "avoided" but only to make it clear that "pre-termination breaches are preserved": new Comment 4 to s.2–613. This aspect of the operation of the doctrine is discussed below, paras 15–011, 15–012.

[82] *Joseph Constantine* case [1942] A.C. 154 at 187.

[83] *The Super Servant Two* [1990] 1 Lloyd's Rep. 1 at 8 (italics supplied).

[84] *Denny Mott & Dickson Ltd v James B Fraser & Co Ltd* [1944] A.C. 265 at 274; *cf.* above, n.81.

[85] (1863) 3 B. & S. 826.

In the example just given, the fact that frustration has only a prospective effect gives rise to relatively little difficulty. The performances due under the contract are assumed to be regarded by the parties as equivalents for each other, and the frustrating event is assumed to have occurred after a severable part of the performance of each party, regarded as equivalent for a corresponding part of the other party's performance, ought to have been rendered. With regard to such accrued obligations, there is therefore no injustice in holding that each party remains bound. The cases which give rise to difficulty are those in which there is an interval between the times at which the parties' respective performances were to fall due, and frustration occurs in that interval. A rigid adherence to the principle that discharge is only prospective will, in such cases, lead to the result that the party who was to perform before the frustrating event remains liable while the party who was to perform after that event is discharged. This possibility gives rise to the problems of adjustment which will be discussed later in this chapter.[86] In solving these problems the courts have to some extent departed from the principle that frustration has only prospective effects,[87] and more extensive modifications of the principle have also been effected by legislation.[88] Further problems of adjustment may, as we shall see, occur even where the frustrating event takes place before any obligation of *either* party has fallen due, but after the conclusion of the contract, and after payments have been made, other benefits conferred and expenses incurred in or for the purpose of its performance.[89]

The principle that frustration has only a prospective effect may lead to the consequence that an event which prevents performance or frustrates a party's purpose does not discharge the contract at all. This possibility may be illustrated by varying the facts of *Avery v Bowden*.[90] In that case, a ship had been chartered to carry tallow from Odessa, 45 days being allowed for loading. Within that time, the charterer's agent said that he had no cargo, but the ship's captain continued, on behalf of her owner, to press for performance. Before the expiry of the 45 days, war broke out between the United Kingdom and Russia, and the charterparty was accordingly frustrated by supervening illegality. This result followed because the captain, by continuing to press for performance, had failed to accept any anticipatory breach which the charterer might have committed by saying that he had no cargo. But if that statement indeed amounted (as it seems to have done) to an anticipatory breach, then the shipowner could have accepted it and so brought the contract to an end by rescission for breach before the supervening illegality could have frustrated it. The difference between the two methods of discharge is crucial because rescission for breach would have discharged only the primary obligations of the parties

---

[86] Below, paras 15–045 *et seq.*
[87] See the *Fibrosa* case [1943] A.C. 32, below, para.15–048.
[88] Law Reform (Frustrated Contracts) Act 1942, s.1(2) (in some respects going beyond the *Fibrosa* case, above see below, para.15–050); and *ibid.*, s.1(3).
[89] Below, paras 15–069 *et seq.*
[90] (1855) 5 E. & B. 714; (1856) 6 E. & B. 953.

and have left the charterer liable in damages,[91] while no such liability can survive discharge by frustration.

15–012 The principle that acceptance of an anticipatory breach before the supervening event can prevent frustration and so leave outstanding a liability in damages can, however, give rise to somewhat surprising results. These may be illustrated by considering variations on *Krell v Henry*,[92] one of the coronation cases. Suppose that, in that case, the contract had been made on June 14, the defendant had promised to pay the whole of the agreed sum of £75 on June 22, that he had repudiated the contract (before making any payment) on June 20, and that the claimant had then accepted the repudiation on June 21 and relet the rooms on that day for only £60 payable on June 24. The subsequent cancellation of the processions on June 24 could no longer have frustrated the original contract since that contract would already have been rescinded by the claimant's acceptance of the defendant's anticipatory breach; nor would the cancellation have deprived the claimant of his right to damages for that breach since that right would have accrued three days before the cancellation. Nor, it is submitted, would the damages have been reduced by reason of the cancellation of the processions since, at the time of the acceptance of the repudiation, the cancellation was not an event which was bound to happen.[93] It follows that, although the claimant would not have been entitled to the £75 as an agreed sum (since the contract would have been rescinded before the sum became due), he would have been entitled to damages of that amount,[94] and that those damages would not have been reduced by reason either of the cancellation of the processions or of the reletting of the rooms under the second (hypothetical) contract since that contract would itself have been frustrated by the cancellation of the processions.

V. Mitigations of the Principles of Automatic and Total Discharge

15–013 Most of the mitigations of the twin principles of automatic discharge and total discharge are explicitly recognised only in systems other than English law. But they merit consideration here because of the criticisms to which the operation of those principles has been subjected. They also raise the question whether English law may not in practice sometimes recognise some such mitigations, in spite of occasional denials of this possibility.[95]

---

[91] Treitel, *The Law of Contract* (11th ed.), pp.851, 859.

[92] [1903] 2 K.B. 740; above, para.7–010.

[93] Treitel, *The Law of Contract* (11th ed.), pp.963–964, discussing *Maredelanto Compania Naviera SA v Bergbau-Handel GmbH (The Mihalis Angelos)* [1971] 1 Q.B. 164.

[94] Treitel, *The Law of Contract* (11th ed.), p.852, discussing *Daman Compania Naviera SA v Hapag-Lloyd International SA (The Blankenstein)* [1985] 1 W.L.R. 435.

[95] *The Super Servant Two* [1990] 1 Lloyd's Rep. 1 at 9.

(1) **Optional discharge**

The first possibility is to deny that discharge is automatic and to say that the supervening event merely gives an option to rescind to the party who is prejudiced by the supervening event, *i.e.* by the party who, in consequence of the event does not receive the performance for which he bargained, or who cannot use the subject-matter for the mutually contemplated purpose.[96] Cases such as *The Isle of Mull* [97] and the *Blane Steamships*[98] case may, from this point of view, be contrasted with a South African case[99] in which a contract for the sale of a business could not be performed without the consent of a public body to the transfer of the vendor's trading licence to the purchaser. No application for the transfer was made because the property was compulsorily acquired by the State. Compensation thereupon became payable and it was held that the vendor could not rely on the supervening events as a ground of discharge, the purchaser being content to perform his part of the contract and to receive the compensation payable by the State. In the United States, the Restatement 2d similarly takes the view that, where performance of services for a lump sum becomes partly impossible, their prospective recipient can enforce the contract for the balance if he is willing to pay the agreed sum in full.[1] Another way of making the same point is that the contract is "rescindable" by the party prejudiced by the supervening event.[2] It would follow from this view that, in *Taylor v Caldwell*,[3] the hirers would have been entitled to make use of the Surrey Gardens (and of the burnt-out shell of the Music Hall) on making the agreed payments of £100 per night, though the defendants would not have been liable in damages for their failure to provide the Music Hall; and that in *Krell v Henry*,[4] the defendant would have been entitled to make use of the flat on paying the agreed sum of £75, though the claimant would not have been liable in damages for the defendant's disappointed expectation of seeing the processions. It would also follow that the intentions of the parties would be relevant to the issue of discharge, so that the contract would remain in being so long as it was clear from the conduct of the parties that it was their "intention to continue to be bound"[5] by its terms; and that such conduct could give rise to a waiver of the right to treat the contract as at an end, or to an estoppel.[6]

15–014

---

[96] See above, para.15–005 for the meaning, in this context, of "party prejudiced".

[97] 278 F. 131 (1921); above, para.15–007.

[98] [1951] 2 K.B. 965; above, para.15–007.

[99] *Mnyandu v Mnynandu NO*, 1964(1) SA 418 (esp. at 425).

[1] § 270 Illustration 4, said in the Reporter's Note to be based on *Van Dusen Aircraft Supplies v Massachusetts Port Authority*, 279 N.E. 2d 717 (1972), where, however, the actual decision is based on the severable nature of the contractual obligations (below, para.15–031).

[2] *Parker v Arthur Murray Inc*, 295 N.E. 2d. 487 at 489 (1973); *cf. Grace v Croninger*, 55 P. 2d 940 at 941 (1936), above, para.7–024.

[3] (1863) 3 B. & S. 826.

[4] [1903] 2 K.B. 740.

[5] *West v Peoples First Nat Bank & Trust Co*, 106 A. 2d 427 at 432 (1954).

[6] *ibid.*; above, paras 4–006, 15–004.

15–015   The authorities considered earlier in this chapter[7] show that English law in general accepts the principle of automatic discharge and therefore rejects the idea of discharge at the option or election of one party. It does, however, exceptionally admit the possibility of discharge at the option of the party prejudiced by the supervening event in cases of alleged "self-induced"[8] frustration. Where an allegedly frustrating event is brought about by the deliberate act of one party (even by one not itself amounting to a breach[9]), that party cannot rely on it as a ground of discharge, but the other may be able to do so. This is, for example, the position where an employee is prevented from performing his part of a contract of employment in consequence of having been imprisoned for a criminal offence. The employer can plead frustration in such circumstances, but the employee cannot do so since a party cannot rely on self-induced frustration.[10] The result is that the contract is frustrated (or not) at the option of the employer.

English law has also made legislative provision for optional discharge to deal with exceptional situations: for example, with that which arose when premises which were the subject of a lease were destroyed by enemy action during the Second World War. In such cases, tenants were given a statutory power to choose between disclaiming the lease and retaining it.[11]

(2) Optional partial discharge

(a) *Partial destruction of goods*

15–016   The possibility of optional partial discharge is illustrated, in American law, by the provisions of the Uniform Commercial Code for the case where a contract is made for the sale of "identified goods" and those goods suffer casualty without the fault of either party. We have already noted that, in case of "total" loss the contract is "avoided",[12] and such avoidance appears to be both total and automatic. Our present concern is with cases in which the loss is partial or the goods have so deteriorated as no longer to conform to the contract. Section 2–613(b)[13] of the Code provides that in such cases the buyer may at his option either treat the contract as avoided or accept the goods with an allowance, *i.e.* with a price reduction in respect of the deficiency or deterioration, but without further right against the seller, so that the seller is not liable for the shortage or deterioration. This solution should be distinguished from the principle of

---

[7] Above, para.15–002.

[8] Above, Ch.14.

[9] Above, para.14–013.

[10] *FC Shepherd & Co Ltd v Jerrom* [1987] Q.B. 301; above, para.14–020.

[11] See above, para.11–016.

[12] UCC, s.2–613(a); above, para.3–016. *cf.* in the case of chattel leases, s.2A–221(a). For a proposed change in terminology, see above, para.15–010, n.81.

[13] A similar rule applies by virtue of s.2A–221(b) to chattel leases, though in the case of such contracts the second of the two options given by s.2–613(b) does not apply to a "finance lease" that is not a "consumer lease" (as defined in s.2–103(1)(g) and (e)).

optional discharge discussed above,[14] under which the party prejudiced by the supervening event can enforce the contract, but only on payment of the *full* price. Under the present solution, the option is again that of the party prejudiced by the supervening event, but he need pay only a *reduced* price.

The provisions of s.2–613(b) with regard to "partial" loss or deterioration are capable of applying in two types of cases. The first is that in which some single identified thing (such as a second-hand car) had been sold, and a part of that thing then perished or was lost, *e.g.* if after the sale the car's radio was stolen. In this situation, English law does not recognise any rule comparable to that laid down in s.2–613(b). A partial loss may, indeed, be so serious as to amount to the "perishing"[15] of the goods for the purposes of s.7 of the Sale of Goods Act 1979; but in that event avoidance of the contract is total and automatic. If (as in our example of the stolen car radio) the partial loss is less serious, it is dealt with under the rules relating to risk, and where the risk has not passed, the seller will be liable for the partial loss or deterioration in accordance with his undertakings as to quality. If under those rules he is in breach of condition, the buyer may indeed elect between avoiding the contract and affirming it, and where he affirms he can reduce the price by the amount of *damages* to which he is entitled in respect of the defect.[16] This is, however a different juristic concept from the "allowance" which is available under s.2–613(b), but "without further remedy against the seller", *i.e.* there is *no* liability in damages for breach of the contract. Under the Sale of Goods Act 1979 a buyer who deals as consumer has, in certain circumstances, the right to require the seller to reduce the price in respect of non-conformity of the goods.[17] But this right is, again, regarded as arising from a breach[18] by the seller and so again differs in its legal nature from the "allowance" available to a buyer in cases of partial loss under s.2–613(b) of the Uniform Commercial Code.

A second situation in which s.2–613(b) can apply to partial casualty to identified goods is that in which the contract was for the sale of a specified quantity of goods from a source identified in that contract,[19] and in which that source fails in part, or is partly destroyed, so that the specified quantity never becomes, or ceases to be, available to the seller.[20] In this situation, English law would reach a result similar to that for which s.2–613(b) provides, but by a different process of reasoning. If the destruction or failure, though not literally total, is so serious as to be regarded for commercial and legal purposes as total, then the contract will

15–017

---

[14] Above, para.15–014.
[15] Above, para.3–005.
[16] Sale of Goods Act 1979, s.53(1)(a).
[17] Sale of Goods Act 1979, s.48C(1) and (2), as inserted by Sale and Supply of Goods to Consumers Regulations 2002, SI 2002/3045.
[18] See the definition of non-conformity in s.48F of the 1979 Act, above, n.17.
[19] Such goods can be "identified": see UCC, s.2–501(1)(a).
[20] For the possible application of UCC, s.2–613(b) to such a case, see s.2–615, Comments 5 and 9; above, paras 3–019, 5–024.

be totally and automatically avoided in both systems.[21] If the partial destruction or failure is not of this degree of seriousness, and the quantity which remains available is less than the quantity sold, the seller will, in English law be excused to the extent of the deficiency[22] (provided that the destruction or failure was not due to his default) but he will be bound to deliver to the buyer the quantity which remains available from the specified source.[23] The buyer, on the other hand, would not normally be bound to accept that quantity, since it is less than that contracted for.[24] In this sense, therefore, the buyer has a choice between partially upholding the contract and bringing it to an end. This choice is not, however, regarded as an option to treat the contract as partly frustrated. It is regarded simply as an application of the buyer's right to choose between rescinding and affirming the contract on account of the seller's non-performance; and while on the one hand the right to rescind is not dependent on any breach by the seller,[25] it is, on the other hand, equally independent of the requirements of frustration. The buyer can rescind on account of *any* shortage (so long as it is not minimal or, if the buyer does not deal as consumer, the shortage is not so slight that it would be unreasonable for him to reject[26]); the analogy of frustration would suggest that the shortage must be at the very least such as to cause serious prejudice to the buyer and there is no such requirement in cases of the present kind.[27] If, instead of rescinding the contract, the buyer elects to accept the smaller quantity, he must (in English law) pay for it "at the contract rate".[28] Section 2–613(b) of the Uniform Commercial Code, giving him the option to take that quantity "with due allowance", lays down a more flexible rule in that the "allowance" is not necessarily assessed on a strict *pro rata* basis. But in most cases of the kind here under discussion, the English and American rules are likely to lead to similar results in financial terms.

Section 2–613 applies, not only to sales of goods which are identified at the time of contracting, but also "in a proper case" to goods sold under "no arrival, no sale" terms.[29] Under such a sale, the seller must properly ship conforming goods which will become identified only after the time of contracting[30]; if he has made such a shipment, he is not liable if, without

---

[21] UCC, s.2–613(a); *Howell v Coupland* (1876); above, para.4–049.

[22] This was the actual result in *Howell v Coupland*, above, n.21.

[23] *HR & S Sainsbury v Street* [1972] 1 W.L.R. 834; above, para.5–013.

[24] Sale of Goods Act 1979, s.30(1); for an exception, see below, at n.26.

[25] Treitel, *The Law of Contract* (11th ed.), p.759.

[26] Sale of Goods Act 1979, s.30(2A), above, para.5–014.

[27] A shortage is not necessarily sufficiently *serious* to give rise to frustration merely because it goes beyond a "slight" one for the purpose of Sale of Goods Act 1979, s.30(2A), above, at n.26.

[28] Sale of Goods Act 1979, s.30(1).

[29] Under the proposals to amend Art.2 of the Code (above, para.2–042, n.17), the reference to sales on "no arrival, no sale" terms is to be deleted from s.2–613. Under these proposals, s.2–324 (referred to below, nn.30, 31) is likewise to be deleted.

[30] See UCC, s.2–324, Comment 2.

his fault, the goods fail to arrive, or arrive late.[31] If the destruction, deterioration or delay affects part only of the goods, then the buyer has the same option as that described above in cases of partial casualty to goods identified at the time of contracting.[32] Section 7 of the Sale of Goods Act 1979 clearly would not apply to such cases since the goods would not be specific,[33] since destruction or deterioration of part is unlikely to be regarded as a constructive perishing of the whole,[34] and since delay in delivery of part clearly cannot be so regarded. In English law, the closest counterpart to the "no arrival no sale" term is to be found in cases in which goods were sold "to arrive" or "on arrival".[35] Contracts of this kind have been discussed in Ch.4.[36] They appear now to be uncommon; and there is no suggestion in the early authorities that the mere non-arrival of the goods would be a ground of frustration. Of course, contracts of this kind could be frustrated on other grounds, *e.g.* if delivery at the specified destination became illegal.[37] There is no suggestion in the English cases that failure of part of the goods to arrive would give the buyer the option to treat the contract as partially frustrated; and the question of the seller's liability in respect of the shortage would turn simply on the construction of the "arrival" condition.[38]

(b) *Other cases?*

It is questionable whether, even in the United States, the principle of   15–018
partial discharge at the option of the party prejudiced by the supervening event extends to contracts other than those for the supply[39] of goods: for example, whether on the facts of *Taylor v Caldwell*[40] it would have given the hirers the right to use the Surrey Gardens (in spite of the destruction of the Music Hall) on terms of paying a reduced nightly fee of (say) £50, instead of the £100 fee specified in the contract. It could perhaps be argued that the principle of s.2–613(b)[41] should be extended by analogy to such a situation, and such an argument could be supported by reference to other provisions of the Uniform Commercial Code which have been so extended to contracts other than those to which they directly apply.[42] English law, lacking such a statutory basis for the principle of optional partial discharge, would (as a general rule) probably, reject such

---

[31] UCC, s.2–324(a).

[32] *ibid.* ss.2–324(b), 2–613(b).

[33] Sale of Goods Act 1979, s.61(1), definition of "specific goods".

[34] Above, para.3–005.

[35] *Benjamin's Sale of Goods* (6th ed.), paras 21–022 *et seq.*

[36] Above, para.4–050.

[37] *Benjamin's Sale of Goods* (6th ed.), para.21–028.

[38] Above, para.4–050.

[39] For the application of the principle to chattel leases, see above, para.15–016, n.12.

[40] (1863) 3 B. & S. 826.

[41] Or that of its precursor, the American Uniform Sales Act, s.8(2), which gave the buyer a similar option, though in somewhat differently defined circumstances.

[42] *e.g.* UCC, s.2–609, laying down the principle of "adequate assurance of performance", which is treated by Restatement 2d, § 251 as being of general

a claim for enforcement of the part remaining possible in return for a reduced payment from the party prejudiced by the supervening event. It would be likely to allow such a claim only where the obligation to perform the part remaining possible was severable[43] from that of which performance had been prevented and where the payments to be made by the party prejudiced were apportioned or apportionable to those respective parts.

(3) **Conditional discharge**

(a) *Benefit resulting from event causing discharge*

15–019   It will be recalled that, in *Taylor v Caldwell*, the defendants appear to have had the benefit of insurance,[44] and that they may also have had a claim in tort against the plumber whose carelessness was the cause of the fire. Similarly, in some of the cases discussed earlier in this chapter we saw that a party could rely on the requisitioning,[45] or the compulsory acquisition, of the subject-matter of the contract (or of something essential for its performance[46]) or on its destruction[47] even though that party received compensation from the government or from insurance and even though the cost of his insurance had, in effect, been borne wholly or in part by the other party to the frustrated contract.[48] What all these situations have in common is that the party relying on the destruction or unavailability of the subject-matter is, on the one hand, discharged from the contract, but, on the other, is entitled to compensation from a third party in respect of the circumstances giving rise to discharge. This is by no means an uncommon situation. Where the frustrating event is brought about by some human agency, compensation in respect of it will often be legally due; and even where the event is one for which the party bringing it about is not legally liable, or one which is brought about by some natural catastrophe, the loss resulting from it will often be covered by insurance. Discharge of the contract could in all these situations be said to put the recipient of such compensation into an unduly favourable position; for he will suffer no (or only a reduced) overall financial loss, while the other party to the contract will (in consequence of the discharge) have to bear the whole of such loss as the frustrating event occasions to him. That other party is, moreover, much less likely, than the party whose performance is prevented by the frustrating event, to have acquired rights against third parties in consequence of that event. In a case such as *Taylor v Caldwell*, for example, the hirers of the Hall would be unlikely to have insured it; nor would they have a right in tort

---

application. For a possible extension of the principle of s.2–613(b) to contracts other than those for the supply of goods, see below, para.15–032, at n.25.

[43] Below, para.15–031.

[44] (1863) 3 B. & S. 826; above, para.2–028.

[45] *The Isle of Mull*, 278 F. 131 (1921).

[46] *Baily v De Crespigny* (1869) L.R. 4 Q.B. 180.

[47] *Blane Steamships v Minister of Transport* [1951] 2 K.B. 965.

[48] See below, paras 15–022, 15–081, 15–082.

against the plumber since the loss which they suffered in consequence of his carelessness was not physical harm but purely financial loss.[49]

A possible solution in cases of this kind is to apply what may be called the principle of conditional discharge: that is, to allow the party whose performance is prevented by the supervening event to rely on that event as a ground of discharge, but to require him to make over to the other party to the contract certain benefits which he has acquired in consequence of the event which has prevented performance. There are two versions of this principle. The first positively entitles the person to whom the now impossible performance was originally due (the creditor) to claim the benefits which have accrued to the party who was to have rendered that performance (the debtor). The second merely requires the debtor to make over those benefits to the creditor if he (the debtor) wishes to claim that the contract has been discharged; the debtor cannot be made to hand over those benefits, but if he fails to do so he will be liable in damages.

(b) Principle of surrogate benefit in civil law

The clearest and most comprehensive statement of the first of the above two versions of the principle of conditional discharge is contained in § 285(1) (formerly § 281(1)) of the German Civil Code. This provides that if, in consequence of the circumstances making performance of the debtor's promise impossible, the debtor obtains compensation or a claim to compensation, then the creditor is entitled to demand the transfer to himself of that compensation, or the assignment of the claim; if the creditor makes such a demand, he must, in turn, perform his part of the contract.[50] It follows that, if the creditor makes no such demand and if the impossibility is not due to circumstance for which the debtor is responsible,[51] then both parties will be discharged. This principle, commonly referred to as that of "surrogate benefit" (*stellvertretendes commodum*), is recognised also in other civil law systems.[52] A detailed account of this principle of surrogate benefit would be beyond the scope of this book; but it is generally agreed that money received from insurance

15–020

---

[49] *cf. Leight & Sillavan Ltd v Aliakmon Shipping Co Ltd (The Aliakmon)* [1986] A.C. 785; *Candlewood Navigation Corp v Mitsui OSK Lines (The Mineral Transporter)* [1986] A.C. 1; *Marc Rich AG v Bishop Rock Maritime Co Ltd (The Nicholas H)* [1994] 1 Lloyd's Rep. 492; *Hamble Fisheries Ltd v L Gardner & Sons Ltd (The Rebecca Elaine)* [1999] 2 Lloyd's Rep. 1. Nor is it likely that on facts such as those of *Taylor v Caldwell*, the claimant would now have a right against the wrongdoer under s.1 of the Contracts (Rights of Third Parties) Act 1999 to enforce a term of the contract between the defendants and the careless plumber: the claimant would probably not be a person who was expressly identified in the contract within s.1(3) or one on whom any term of the contract purported to confer a benefit within s.1(1)(b).

[50] BGB § 326(3), formerly § 323(2); Larenz, *Schuldrecht* (14th ed.), Vol.I, p.310.

[51] See BGB § 276.

[52] Bucher, *Schweizerisches Obligationenrecht, Allgemeiner Teil*, pp.419–420 (Switzerland); Koziol & Wesler, *Grundriss des Bürgerlichen Rechts* (7th ed.), Vol. I, pp.213–214 (Austria); *cf.* in France the somewhat narrower provisions of CC, Arts 1302, 1303.

of the subject-matter, from compensation for requisition,[53] or from other claims against third parties in respect of the loss or destruction of the subject-matter, can be covered by the principle.[54]

15–021   The principle of surrogate benefit is thus capable of solving some of the problems raised by the English cases considered in paras 15–007 and 15–008, above. On the other hand, the scope of the principle is limited by the requirement that there must be "identity" between the thing owed under the contract and that for which compensation is received. One German discussion of the principle begins with an example which (perhaps coincidentally) resembles *Taylor v Caldwell*[55]: if the thing owed under the contract is destroyed by fire, the debtor must (if he wishes to rely on the resulting impossibility of performance) make over to the creditor any insurance money received by him as a result of the fire, and any rights that he may have against a third party who had caused the fire.[56] The example however, differs from *Taylor v Caldwell*, in that it concerns a *sale* of the thing that was destroyed. It is unlikely that the principle of BGB § 285(1) (formerly § 281(1)) would have applied to the facts of *Taylor v Caldwell* itself; for it has been held in Germany that that principle did not apply where the contract was one by which the defendant granted the claimant the right to use certain land which was then expropriated on payment of compensation to the defendant.[57] The reason why the claimant was not entitled to this payment was that there was no "identity" between what was owed under the contract (*i.e.* the use of the land) and the thing for which the compensation was paid (*i.e.* the land itself). The principle of § 285 would apply only where the debtor had received compensation for loss of the use of the thing. That was probably not the position with regard to any insurance moneys to which the defendants in *Taylor v Caldwell* may have been entitled, though it is arguable that at least part of the damages which they might have recovered from the careless plumber could be regarded as compensation for loss of use, *i.e.* of the profits which might have been made from the use of the Hall. The concept of loss of use could also apply to cases in which charterparties were frustrated by the temporary requisition of the ship. Here the requisitioning authority compensates the shipowner for loss of the use of the ship; and in a demise charter at least that is clearly what is "owed" under the contract. The position is perhaps more doubtful in the case of a time charter,[58] where the subject-matter of the contract consists strictly speaking, of the services to be rendered by the shipowner[59]; but those

---

[53] See, *e.g.* the Swiss decision in BGE 43 II 225, May 18, 1917.

[54] Emmerich, *Das Recht der Leistungsstörungen*, 85; Von Thur/Escher, *Allgemeiner Teil des Schweitzerischen Obligationenrechts* (3rd ed.), Vol.II, p.132.

[55] (1863) 3 B. & S. 826.

[56] Larenz, *Schuldrecht* (14th ed.), Vol.I, p.309.

[57] BGHZ 25, 1, 9, 19 June, 1957, decided under BGB § 281, the precursor of the present § 285.

[58] Such as that in *The Isle of Mull*, 278 F. 131 (1921), above, para.15–007.

[59] *Ellerman Lines v Lancaster Maritime Co (The Lancaster)* [1980] 2 Lloyd's Rep. 497 at 500; *Scandinavian Trading Co AB v Flota Petrolera Ecuatoriana (The Scaptrade)*

services are to be rendered by the use of the ship. Where the compensation takes the form of insurance money payable on the destruction of the ship, it can again be argued that there is no "identity" between the subject-matter of the compensation claim (the physical thing lost) and that of the contract (the use of that thing); but the two become hard to distinguish where, as in the *Blane Steamships*[60] case, a demise charter conferred on the charterer an option to purchase the ship. Such a case might well fall within the civil law principle of "surrogate benefit", which has indeed been applied in France where a lease granted an option to purchase to the tenant and the landlord was compensated by his insurer when the premises were later destroyed by fire.[61]

(c) *Principle of conditional discharge in common law?*

(i) Generally not recognised

The principle of conditional discharge on transfer of the "surrogate benefit" obtained as a result of the supervening event has no direct counterpart in the common law. Indeed a number of decisions already considered appear either to reject it, or to be based on the assumption that the law does not recognise it. Foremost among such decisions are the charterparty cases such as *The Isle of Mull*,[62] and the *Blane Steamships*[63] case: we saw in para.15–007, above, that in these cases shipowners became, as a result of the frustrating events, entitled to payments (by way of compensation for requisition or under insurance policies) in excess of those expressed to be due to them under the contracts; and there was no suggestion that their right to treat the contracts as discharged, if established, should be subject to, or conditional on, their handing these benefits over to the charterers. In the American *Asphalt International* case[64] (discussed in Ch.6) a time charter was likewise held to have been discharged when the ship became a constructive total loss by being so severely damaged that the cost of repairing her would be twice her market value; and the court specifically rejected the argument that discharge should be excluded because it would leave the shipowners with a large windfall profit from the proceeds of their insurance on the hull of ship. The insurance moneys were, in the court's view, simply an asset of the shipowner, having no more relevance to the issue of discharge than any other asset of his; nor could the charterer complain of hardship since he could have insured his profits in the event of the constructive total loss of the ship, just as the shipowner had insured the hull. These arguments are, with respect, not entirely convincing.[65] The insurance policy was an asset

15–022

[1983] 2 A.C. 694; *Homburg Houtimport BV v Agrosin Private Ltd (The Starsin)* [2003] UKHL 12; [2004] 1 A.C. 715 at [119].

[60] [1951] 2 K.B. 965, above, para.15–007.

[61] J. Cl. Civ. Arts 1302 and 1303 No 25.

[62] 278 F. 131 (1921).

[63] [1951] 2 K.B. 965.

[64] 667 F. 2d 261 (1981); above, para.6–005.

[65] *cf.* the discussion in para.15–082 below of the policy underlying s.1(5) of the Law Reform (Frustrated Contracts) Act 1943.

of a special kind, which had acquired monetary value only as a result of the event which discharged the contract; and for this reason it is at least arguable that it should be taken into account in assessing the consequences of discharge. It is also arguable that that charter had in substance "paid" for part of the hull insurance, as the shipowner had presumably taken the cost of that insurance into account (as one of his overheads) in fixing the hire payable under the charterparty. A similar point applies (as already noted) in some of the coronation cases,[66] in which sellers of seats on stands were held to be entitled to retain money paid in advance[67] even though there is evidence that at least some such sellers were insured against the events that happened.[68] Again it seems that ticket-holders had in substance paid for such insurance in the price of their tickets. Moreover in *Baily v De Crespigny*[69] the reason why the landlord's receipt of compensation for the compulsory acquisition (which made performance of his covenant not to build impossible) did not preclude discharge was said[70] to be that the compensation bore no necessary relationship to the damages for which he would be liable if he were not discharged. This may be true, but the point of the principle requiring transfer of the surrogate benefit is not that it precludes discharge. The point is rather that discharge is conditional on the handing over of that benefit (and no more), or that the creditor is entitled, not to damages, but to that benefit.

The principle of requiring transfer of the surrogate benefit seems also by implication to be rejected by the Law Reform (Frustrated Contracts) Act 1943. In applying the restitution and apportionment provisions of that Act (to be discussed later in this chapter[71]) the court is directed by s.1(5) of the Act to disregard sums which have become payable to the claimant "under any contract of insurance" except where an obligation to insure was "imposed by an express term of the frustrated contract or by or under any enactment". It is thus, for example, possible for a claim in respect of expenses[72] or valuable benefits[73] to succeed in spite of the fact that the claimant also received insurance moneys in respect of the frustrating event. Section 1(5) is more fully discussed in paras 15–079 to 15–082 below; the present point is that the Act is plainly based on the assumption that the recipient of insurance proceeds is under no obligation to account to the other party for them, as he would be where the civil law requirement of transferring the surrogate benefit applied.

---

[66] Above, paras 7–005 to 7–014.
[67] *e.g. Blakeley v Muller & Co* [1903] 2 K.B. 760n.; see now Law Reform (Frustrated Contracts) Act 1943, s.1(2) (below, para.15–050) for a solution which has nothing to do with transfer of "surrogate benefits".
[68] Above, para.7–007.
[69] (1869) L.R. 4 Q.B. 180.
[70] *ibid.* at 187–188.
[71] Below, paras 15–050, 15–052, 15–060 to 15–066, 15–070 to 15–075.
[72] *ibid.*, s.1(2) proviso.
[73] *ibid.*, s.1(3).

(ii) Uniform Commercial Code, s.2–615, Comment 5

This Comment appears to embody the second of the two versions   15–023
(described in para.15–019, above) of the principle of conditional discharge.
The Comment deals with the situation in which a seller of goods relies on
the default of his supplier as a ground of excuse for his failure to deliver the
goods to the buyer; and it declares that "a condition to [the seller's]
making good the claim of excuse is the turning over to the buyer of his
rights against the defaulting source of supply to the extent of the buyer's
contract in relation to which excuse is being claimed." It is significant that
the reason for this requirement is to prevent the seller from making what
we have called a windfall profit, or, as Comment 5 puts it, the excuse
"should not result ... in dropping into the seller's lap an unearned bonus
of damages over": in other words, he cannot, on a rising market, rely on
failure of the source as an excuse against the buyer, while retaining his
rights against the supplier. It is scarcely fanciful to suppose that this is one
of a number of rules in the Uniform Commercial Code which are derived,
if with modifications, from German law.[74] The idea behind Comment 5 is
similar to that of § 285(1) (formerly § 281(1)) of the German Civil Code,
with the modification that the American rule gives the option of
surrendering the surrogate benefit to the debtor while the German rule
appears to give the option of claiming it to the creditor.[75]

(iii) Law of Property Act 1925, s.47(1)

An English statutory rule which at first sight bears some resemblance to the   15–024
principle of the German § 285(1) is s.47(1) of the Law of Property Act
1925. This provides that: "Where after the date of any contract for the sale
or exchange of property money becomes payable under any policy of
insurance maintained by the vendor in respect of any damage to or
destruction of property included in the contract, the money shall, on
completion of the contract, be held or receivable by the vendor on behalf
of the purchaser and paid by the vendor to the purchaser on completion of
the sale or exchange." Some of the problems arising out of this subsection
have been discussed in Ch.3.[76] The only further point to be made here is
that the practical effect of s.47(1) may be similar to that of the German §
285(1), but that the two enactments are based on wholly different theories.
The theory of § 285(1), as applied to cases of supervening destruction of
the subject-matter for which the debtor is not responsible, is that the
obligations to perform the contract are discharged and that the seller's
liability to transfer the insurance money is a legal consequence of that
discharge. The theory of s.47(1), on the other hand, is that the contract
remains in force in spite of the destruction of the subject-matter (because
the risk has passed) and that the insurance money must be paid over by the
vendor "on completion". The purchaser does not have the option (which
a creditor has under the German provision[77]) of refusing to pay the price

---

[74] See above, para.5–023, n.2.
[75] See Larenz, above, para.15–020, n.50.
[76] Above, paras 3–045 to 3–046.
[77] Larenz, *Schuldrecht* (14th ed.), Vol.1, p.309.

and leaving the insurance money with the vendor. This would obviously be a significant point if the property had been insured for less than the purchase price.

Section 47(1) is also subject to a requirement which seems to have no parallel in § 285(1): to become entitled to the insurance money, the buyer must pay "the proportionate part of the premium from the date of the contract". Moreover the subsection obviously applies only to insurance moneys: if the purchaser wishes to acquire other rights which the vendor may have against third parties, he must expressly stipulate that the vendor is to exercise those rights on his behalf, or to assign them to him.[78]

15–025   Section 47(1) is usually discussed only in relation to contracts relating to land, even though it refers more broadly to "property," an expression which includes "any interest in ... personal property".[79] It can therefore apply to a contract for the sale of goods. But the separate stages of "contract" and "completion" to which the subsection refers are scarcely apposite in relation to a contract for the sale of goods; and the total absence of any reference to s.47(1) from the leading English work on sale of goods[80] indicates that the section is not generally considered to have any significance in relation to such contracts. Even if it did apply to them, it could not apply to an agreement for the sale of specific goods which had perished before the risk had passed to the buyer; for in that case the contract would be avoided,[81] so that the stage of "completion of the contract" would never be reached. Nor, for the same reason, could the subsection apply where the goods were to be taken from an identified bulk which perished or from an identified source which wholly failed.[82] Section 47(1) could apply where specific goods were damaged, but not so seriously as to have "perished",[83] before the risk had passed, or if they were destroyed or damaged after the risk had passed. In such cases, the position would be the same as in the land cases discussed above. The contract would not be discharged so that the buyer would have to pay the price while (if the other requirements of s.47(1) were satisfied) the seller would have to pay over the insurance money to the buyer. Section 47(1) is highly unlikely to apply to a contract for the sale of unascertained goods since if goods which the seller intended to appropriate to the contract were destroyed, he would be bound to make a fresh appropriation (so that insurance on the destroyed goods would be irrelevant). This would also be generally true if goods were destroyed after appropriation, since even in such cases the seller would normally be bound to make a fresh appropriation, (so that again insurance on the destroyed goods would be irrelevant).[84] He would only be relieved from that duty where the

---

[78] cf. Leigh & Sillavan Ltd v Aliakmon Shipping Co Ltd (The Aliakmon) [1986] A.C. 785 at 819.

[79] Law of Property Act 1925, s.205(1)(xx).

[80] Benjamin's Sale of Goods (6th ed.).

[81] Sale of Goods Act 1979, s.7.

[82] Howell v Coupland (1876) 1 Q.B.D. 258.

[83] Above, para.3–016.

[84] Above, paras 3–023 to 3–024.

contract on its true construction was intended to relate only to the goods originally appropriated.[85] But in that case the contract would be discharged by the destruction of the goods, so that s.47(1) could not apply for the reason already given, *i.e.* that the stage of completion of the contract would never be reached.

(iv) Other common law rules relating to benefit of seller's insurance

The benefit of insurance effected by a seller of goods more commonly becomes available to the buyer in ways that do not involve reliance on s.47 (1). Under a c.i.f. contract, the seller is bound to procure a policy of insurance and the normal way in which the buyer will acquire rights under this policy is by its transfer to him by endorsement[86] on tender of documents.[87] In other words, the buyer will acquire rights directly against the insurer, as opposed to rights against the seller to the transfer of policy moneys received by the seller from the insurer. It is also clear that the seller cannot make a windfall profit out of the insurance: unless the contract otherwise provides, the buyer is entitled to the transfer of the policy even though its amount exceeds the value of the goods or the requirements of the contract as to the amount of insurance.[88] There is of course no question of any of these results following from frustration of the contract since a c.i.f. contract will not be frustrated by destruction of the goods save in the exceptional case where the goods are specific and perish before shipment, or where they are to be taken from a specified source which is destroyed or fails before shipment.[89] In such cases, the contract would be discharged, so that the seller would not be bound to transfer to the buyer any policy of insurance by which he might at that stage be covered.[90]

15–026

(v) Benefits other than insurance

Section 47(1) and the common law rules discussed in paras 15–025 and 15–026, above apply *only* to the benefit of insurance taken out by a seller. If a buyer (whether of land or goods) wishes to acquire rights which the seller may acquire against third parties other than insurers, various possibilities are open to him. One is to stipulate in the contract of sale that the seller must assign those rights to him.[91] In English law, this possibility gives rise to the difficulty that, as a general rule, rights of action in tort are

15–027

---

[85] *ibid.*

[86] Under Marine Insurance Act 1906, s.50(3).

[87] *Benjamin's Sale of Goods* (6th ed.), para.19–041.

[88] *ibid.*, paras 19–050, 19–058; see, *e.g. Manbré Saccharine Co Ltd v Corn Products Co Ltd* [1919] 1 K.B. 198.

[89] *Benjamin's Sale of Goods* (6th ed.,), para.19–120; *cf. ibid.* para.19–077 for the rule that destruction of the goods after shipment and appropriation does not relieve the buyer from his duty to pay the price.

[90] It is unusual, but not impossible, for a c.i.f. contract to require insurance cover to begin before shipment: see *Reinhart & Co v Joshua Hoyle & Sons Ltd* [1961] 1 Lloyd's Rep. 346.

[91] *Leigh & Sillavan Ltd v Aliakmon Shipping Co Ltd (The Aliakmon)* [1986] A.C. 785 at 819.

not assignable.[92] Where the seller's rights against third parties are of this nature, the buyer can in the contract of sale require the seller to exercise those rights on his behalf.[93] Where the rights to damages which the seller acquires against the third parties arise in contract, there is no legal difficulty in requiring the seller to assign those rights to the buyer, since such rights can be assigned to an assignee with a proprietary interest in the subject-matter[94] and also to one with a "genuine commercial interest"[95] in it; and there is no doubt that a buyer would fall into one of these categories. Even where the contract does not require the seller to transfer his rights against third parties to the buyer, the buyer may acquire the benefit of those rights in another way. A seller who has shipped goods to his buyer may remain owner of the goods after the risk has passed to the buyer and the goods may then be damaged or destroyed by the carrier's breach of contract. If the buyer has not acquired any rights against the carrier under that contract,[96] the seller can, by virtue of being owner of the goods, recover damages from the carrier in respect of the loss of, or damage to, the goods. He can do so even though he has suffered no loss by reason of having been paid (or having become entitled to be paid) for the goods by the buyer because the risk had passed to the buyer.[97] This fact does not reduce the damages recoverable by the seller to a nominal amount; it "merely affects the destination of those damages"[98]: that is, the seller must account for those damages to the buyer.[99] In this way, the buyer is once again entitled to any "surrogate benefit" which may be obtained by the seller but it must be emphasised again that he is so entitled, not on the theory that the contract of sale is discharged, but on the ground that, risk having passed, the contract remains in force notwithstanding the destruction of the goods.

---

[92] Treitel, *The Law of Contract* (11th ed.), p.696.

[93] *cf. The Aliakmon*, above, para.15–027, n.91, at 819.

[94] See, *e.g. Defries v Milne* [1913] Ch. 98; *Ellis v Torkington* [1920] 1 K.B. 399.

[95] *Trendtex Trading Ltd v Crédit Suisse* [1982] A.C. 679 at 703.

[96] If the buyer has acquired such rights, typically under s.2(1) of the Carriage of Goods by Sea Act 1992, by virtue of having become the lawful holder of the bill of lading, then the seller will in the circumstances described above, have no right to recover damages from the carrier in respect of loss of, or damage to, the goods: *Albacruz (Cargo Owner) v Albazero (Owners) (The Albazero)* [1977] A.C. 774.

[97] *Dunlop v Lambert* (1839) 2 Cl. & F. 626 at 627 (as to which see *Alfred McAlpine Construction Ltd v Panatown Ltd* [2001] 1 A.C. 518 at 523 *et seq*); *Obestain Inc v National Mineral Development Corp (The Sanix Ace)* [1987] 1 Lloyd's Rep. 465. Where the goods are carried under a contract of carriage governed by the Carriage of Goods by Sea Act 1992, s.2(4) of the Act further entitles a person who has acquired rights under the contract of carriage by virtue of s.2(1) to exercise those rights "for the benefit of" another person who has "any interest or right in or in relation to" the goods and suffers loss or damage in consequence of a breach of the contract of carriage. For a full discussion of s.2(4), see *Carver on Bills of Lading* (1st ed., 2000), paras 5–067, 5–073.

[98] *The Sanix Ace*, above, n.97, at 469.

[99] *The Albazero*, above, n.96, at 845; *Linden Gardens Trust v Lenesta Sludge Disposals Ltd* [1994] 1 A.C. 85 at 115.

The principle of the carriage cases described above[1] has been extended to cases in which defective performance by A of a building contract between A and B causes loss, not to B but to C: B can then recover damages from A (which must then be held by B for C) in respect of C's loss,[2] unless C has his own contractual right in respect of the loss against A.[3] It is theoretically possible for A's defective performance to lead to the frustration of a contract between B and C, *e.g.* where A had contracted with B to erect a building and B had in turn contracted to sell the building to C. But in such a case the defect would be likely to arise before the risk had passed to C[4] so that C would suffer no loss; and if it arose after the passing of risk there would, as in the sale of goods cases discussed in the text above, be no frustration.

(vi) Position where contract is not discharged
The foregoing discussion shows that, although English law does not
recognise the principle of conditional discharge on handing over any "surrogate benefit", it can sometimes reach similar results by denying discharge. This seems also to have been the position in the *Tamplin* case, where the time charter was not discharged by the requisition of this ship; and it was said that the shipowner would have to account to the charterer for compensation for requisition received in respect of the use of the ship,[5] and that the total compensation paid was "divisible between [owner and charterer] according to their respective rights and interests".[6] In a later time charter case, which resembled the *Tamplin* case but differed from it in that the compensation for requisition was *less* than the agreed hire, it was again held that the contract was not frustrated; and the owners conceded that any money paid by the Admiralty as compensation for use of the vessel should go to the charterers.[7]

In a further group of cases, the very fact that the party claiming discharge has, by virtue of the supervening event, acquired a right against a third party, is treated as a ground for denying discharge. One group of cases which illustrate this point concerns the alleged failure of a source of supply, in particular those cases in which A contracts to sell to B goods which are to be supplied to A by X, who then fails to make the supply in circumstances amounting to a breach of his contract with A. In an American case of this kind, A's claim to be discharged from his contract with B was denied on the ground that A had obtained an order of specific

---

[1] At n.96.

[2] See the *Linden Gardens* case, above, n.99.

[3] See the *Alfred McAlpine* case, above, n.97 and generally Treitel, *The Law of Contract* (11th ed.), pp.594–602.

[4] See above, para.3–049; the passing of risk is, in the case put, more likely to be governed by the rule stated in this paragraph than by the rule stated in above, paras 3–028 to 3–030.

[5] *Tamplin SS Co v Anglo-Mexican Petroleum Co* [1916] 2 A.C. 397 at 405; above, para.5–052.

[6] [1916] 2 A.C. 397 at 428.

[7] *Modern Transport Co Ltd v Duneric SS Co* [1917] 1 K.B. 370 at 377.

performance against X.[8] In England such a claim to be discharged has (perhaps more surprisingly) been rejected by the simple expedient of treating A "as occupying the position of"[9] X. It followed that A could not rely on a wrongful failure by X to supply the goods as a ground of discharge under the common law doctrine[10] since such reliance by X would fail on the ground that it amounted to his "default"; and X's breach was, so to speak, attributed to A and therefore amounted (by a fiction) to "default" on A's part, making A liable to B.

A somewhat similar principle is applied by the the Vienna Convention on Contracts for the International Sale of Goods to cases in which A has engaged X "to perform the whole or part of the contract"[11] with B. Article 79(1) of the Convention exempts A from liability in damages to B for failure to perform which is due to "an impediment beyond his control"[12]; but Art.79(2) then provides that A cannot rely on this exemption against B unless X would also have been entitled to the same exemption under his contract with A. This rule can, however, apply only where the contract between A and X (as well as that between A and B) is one for the sale of goods and is governed by the Convention. If, for example, X were a carrier, whose breach prevented A from fulfilling his contract with B, the case would not fall within Art.79(2). But where that provision applies, its practical effect is that A cannot keep the benefit of any rights which he might have against X while avoiding liability against B.

15–029   As a matter of common law, A would also be liable to B if A had been guilty of genuine personal default because he had failed to make an effective or adequate supply contract with X and was for this reason unable to perform his contract with B. In such a case X's failure to make the supply needed by A to perform his contract with B cannot be a ground for discharging that contract; and discharge would be excluded even though A had no rights against X.[13] Where discharge is excluded because A does have rights against X, the theory is quite different from that of the principle of conditional discharge. A's liability is not to make over his rights against X to B, nor can he escape liability to B by making over to B his rights against X; A's liability is simply to compensate B for his loss. This difference in theory should not be obscured by the fact that the value of A's right against X might be the same as the value of B's right against A, *e.g.* where both depended on the same market movements. That would be

---

[8] *El Rio Oils (Canada) Ltd v Pacific Coast Asphalt Co*, 213 P. 2d 1 (1949).

[9] *Lebaupin v Crispin* [1920] 2 K.B. 714 at 718.

[10] *i.e.* A could not rely on the application of that doctrine to cases such as *Howell v Coupland* (1876) 1 Q.B.D. 258, above, para.4–049. *Lebaupin v Crispin* decided that the seller was not protected *either* (1) by the common law doctrine *or* (2) by a *force majeure* clause in the contract. Our concern here is with the first of these points; the second is discussed above, para.12–026. But it is possible that the terms of the *force majeure* clause (the relevant part of which is quoted above para.12–026) may have had some influence on the reasoning quoted above be n.9.

[11] Art.79(2).

[12] Above, para.6–048.

[13] See *Atisa SA v Aztec AG* [1983] 2 Lloyd's Rep. 579.

a mere coincidence; there is no necessary relationship of equality between the two rights.

Cases in which compensation has been received (or been recoverable) by the party who was to supply the thing which constituted the subject-matter of the contract must be distinguished from those in which compensation may be paid or payable to the *recipient* of that subject-matter, whose only or principal duty under the contract was to pay the price or other agreed remuneration for it. The very fact that such compensation was so paid or payable has sometimes been relied on as a ground for holding that the contract was not frustrated, so that the party to whom the compensation was paid, or due, had to pay at least the contract price. We have, for example, seen that, in cases concerning leases of land one reason for denying that the requisition of the premises was a ground of discharge has been precisely that the tenant had received, or was entitled to, compensation from the requisitioning authorities.[14] Similar reasoning accounts for the rule that a contract for the sale of land is not discharged by the making of a compulsory purchase order between contract and completion[15]: the purchaser must pay the price and will be entitled to the compensation payable by the acquiring authority.

It seems equally to be true that, in cases of the present kind, the recipient of the subject-matter is not liable for more than the agreed sum out of any compensation paid to him in respect of that subject-matter. This view is supported by a case[16] which concerns the requisition, during the First World War, of a motor lorry which was the subject of a hire-purchase agrement. Compensation for the requisition had been paid to the hirer and it was held that the compensation was divisible between the parties in proportion to their respective interests, the owners being entitled to no more than the amount of the one instalment remaining unpaid. It does not seem that the contract was regarded as having been frustrated.

15–030

A similar situation arose in *Dale SS Co v Northern SS Co*[17] where a ship in the course of construction had been sold and was (while still under construction) requisitioned by the Admiralty. The Court of Appeal rejected a claim by the seller for the unpaid balance of the purchase price on the ground that the ship was not ready for delivery, so that the price had not yet become due. Swinfen Eady L.J. also said that "owing to the intervention of the Admiralty the contract could not be carried out"[18]; and that the buyer was not estopped by his conduct (in claiming compensation for the requisition) from saying that "the contract had been put to an end by the intervention of the Admiralty".[19] These remarks may suggest that the contract was discharged. But the judgment goes on to

---

[14] See above, para.11–020, after n.4; *cf. Grimsdick v Sweetman* [1909] 2 K.B. 740; above, para.7–024.

[15] Above, para.4–007.

[16] *British Berna Motor Lorries Ltd v Inter-Transport Lorries Ltd* (1915) 31 T.L.R. 200.

[17] (1918) 34 T.L.R. 271.

[18] *ibid.*

[19] *ibid.* at 272.

say that, if compensation were to be paid by the Admiralty to the buyer, then the buyer "could not then retain the whole amount without paying ... the ... unpaid purchase price"[20]; and in so far as this suggests that, in the event of the buyer's receiving such compensation, the seller could successfully have claimed the balance of the price, it is inconsistent with the notion of discharge. It is thus not wholly clear whether the contract was discharged. In any event the primary liability of the buyer (if he should receive compensation for the requisition) would have been to pay the balance of the price; and the dictum quoted above may mean merely that he could have avoided that liability on handing over the compensation. If so, the dictum gives some (if rather obscure) support to the concept of conditional discharge.

(4) Severable or divisible obligations

15–031   Obligations are for the present purpose severable or divisible if the contract which gives rise to them provides that, after a specified part of one party's performance has been rendered, a corresponding part of the other party's counter-performance is to become due. The common law rule is that if performance of a severable part of such a contract becomes impossible or illegal, only that part is discharged and the rest remains enforceable. For example, in *Stubbs v Holywell Ry Co*[21] a consulting engineer had been appointed for 15 months at a salary of £500 payable in five equal quarterly instalments. After two quarters he died and his administrators successfully claimed the £200 payable to him at the time of his death. The same principle would apply where a contract for the sale of goods provided for delivery by instalments and for payment on each delivery, and the frustrating event occurred after delivery of some of the instalments but before delivery of the others had become due.

Cases of this kind can be regarded simply as applications of the rule that discharge operates prospectively[22] and does not at common law retrospectively affect rights which had already accrued at the time of the frustrating event. But the principle of severability could apply also where performance of some (but not all) of a group of severable obligations became impossible or illegal *before* either party was due to perform, *e.g.* where a contract was made to export 10,000 tons of wheat in five equal instalments, each to be separately paid for, and then the export of more than 60 per cent of that amount was prohibited before the time fixed for delivery of, and payment for, any of the instalments. It is submitted that in such a case the principle of severability would lead to the conclusion that the contract was discharged only in respect of two of the instalments.

It seems probable, however, that the present exception to the principle of total discharge would not operate where the connection between the

---

[20] *ibid.*
[21] (1867) L.R. 2 Ex. 311; *cf. Van Dusen Aircraft Supplies v Massachusetts Port Authority*, 279 N.E. 2d 717 (1972), where part of the agreed performance became illegal; Restatement 2d, § 272, Comment b.
[22] Above, para.15–011.

severable parts was such as to make it unjust to enforce the parts which could still be performed after performance of one or more of the others had become impossible. This would be the position where a contract for the sale of machinery provided for delivery and payment in instalments and delivery of a vital part subsequently became impossible or illegal.

In the United States, obligations have been treated as "severable" for the present purpose even though they did not fall within the definition of such obligations given above. In *Mullen v Wafer*[23] a contract for the sale of an accountancy business for $30,000 provided that the seller was to help the buyer (on payment of a salary) with the conduct of the business for two years. On the death of the seller one month after the contract was made, it was held that the contract was "severable"[24] and that only the part of it relating to the physical assets of the business (worth some $4,000) was enforceable. The concept of "severability" is here used to achieve a radical alteration or adaptation of the contract in a way that cannot be justified by its terms; and it is unlikely that English courts would similarly regard a contract as severable in the absence of any indication, in its terms, of the parties' intention so to regard it. The case is more properly regarded as an extension of the principle of optional partial discharge, as expressed in s.2–613(b) of the Uniform Commercial Code, to a contract other than one for the sale of goods.[25] The option given to the buyer by that enactment in cases of partial "casualty" to goods is expressly stated to be available even though the contract is *not* a "divisible" one.[26]

15–032

The concept of severability or divisibility of a *contract* must be distinguished from that of the divisibility of the *subject-matter*. The latter concept has been discussed in Ch.5 to illustrate a limit on the principle of *pro rata* allocation in cases of partial failure of a specified source. It was there suggested that, even though the *pro rata* principle might apply where a farmer agreed to sell to each of five buyers "200 tons of wheat to be grown on my land" and only 600 tons were produced, it could not apply where he had agreed to sell to each of five buyers "one calf to be born to my herd" and only three were born.[27] The *obligations* arising under the contracts are no more severable in the first than in the second example; what distinguishes the two examples is that in the first the *subject-matter* can (while in the second it cannot) be divided without destroying it in a commercial sense. The principle of *pro rata* allocation (if it is recognised in English law)[28] must therefore be regarded as a separate exception to the concept of total discharge, and not as one that can be explained on the ground of the severability of the contractual obligations.

---

[23] 480 S.W. 2d 332 (1972).
[24] *ibid.* at 334.
[25] Above, para.15–018.
[26] See Official Comment to s.2–613 under the heading "Changes", indicating an intention to depart from the requirement of "divisibility" previously contained in the American Uniform Sales Act, s.8(2)(b).
[27] Above, para.5–029.
[28] Above, paras 5–026 to 5–030.

(5) **Ancillary obligations**

15–033   In discussing temporary impossibility, we saw that a contract to give a musical performance on a specified day could be discharged by the performer's illness on that day, but that liability was nevertheless incurred in respect of certain expenses wasted because of failure to give notice of the illness to the organiser of the concert.[29] This liability was said to be based on an implied term of the contract, and the difficulty of holding a party liable for breach of an implied term after the contract in which it was contained had been frustrated could be resolved by arguing that the implied term gave rise to a collateral contract which survived the discharge of the principal contract. A similar argument (which would be available even where the requirements for a collateral contract[30] were not satisfied) would be that the implied term gave rise to an ancillary obligation and that such an obligation can survive discharge of the principal obligations of a contract.[31]

(6) **Suspension**

15–034   There is support in the United States for the view that, in cases of temporary impossibility, the duty to perform is merely suspended; and that discharge occurs only if performance, when it again becomes possible, would be "materially more burdensome"[32] from that originally undertaken. In a sense, this resembles the practical effects of two English rules already considered: namely (1) that temporary impossibility may give a party a temporary excuse for non-performance[33]; and (2) that the contract will be discharged if performance after the end of the impossibility would (because of changes in commercial circumstances) be fundamentally different from that originally bargained for.[34] But under these rules the part of the performance which is excused never has to be rendered at all; while true "suspension" would indicate that the *whole* of the performance originally bargained for has to be rendered, though at a later time.

   In English law, the notion of "suspension" is generally viewed with hostility by the courts.[35] One reason for this hostility is that "suspension"

---

[29] *Robinson v Davison* (1871) L.R. 6 Ex. 269, above, para.5–035.

[30] For these requirements, see Treitel, *The Law of Contract* (11th ed.), pp.162–163, 180, 199–200, 356–357 and 582–584.

[31] Above, para.5–035.

[32] Restatement 2d, § 269.

[33] Above, para.5–058. This is also the effect of the excuse provided by the Vienna Convention on Contracts for the International sale of Goods, Art.79(1) (above, para.6–048); see also Art.79(3), and below, para.15–043.

[34] Above, paras 5–036 *et seq.*

[35] *cf. Daily Mirror Newspapers Ltd v Gardner* [1968] 2 Q.B. 672; *Gorse v Durham CC* [1971] 1 W.L.R. 775; *Total Gas Marketing Ltd v Arco British Ltd* [1998] 2 Lloyd's Rep. 209, where the contract was held to have been discharged by failure of condition under one of its express terms.

is "a loose expression giving rise to confusion"[36]: it is far from clear to which of the processes described in the preceding paragraph the word refers. A second reason for the judicial hostility to suspension is that it would be a source of uncertainty: in particular, it would be hard for the courts to determine for how long the "suspension" of the contract was to continue; and even if this objection could be overcome, suspension could impose, on at least one party, obligations significantly more onerous than those to which he had agreed. The force of these objections is of course reduced or eliminated where the parties have expressly provided for suspension in specified events.[37] In particular, such express provisions normally specify the nature and extent of the relief for which they provide. The terms of a contract may also in effect provide for suspension without using that expression.[38] The point may be illustrated by the *force majeure* clause in the soyabean cases,[39] which in effect suspended the seller's duty to deliver for a period not exceeding that specified in the contract, gave the buyer a right to cancel at the end of a specified time, and provided that, if that right was not exercised and shipment continued to be prevented for a further specified period, the contract was to be regarded as void. The time-table thus laid down clearly removed any objection to suspension on the score of uncertainty. Similarly some of the contracts considered in the coronation cases had the effect of suspending the contracts by providing that, if the processions should be postponed, the ticket-holder was to have the right to use the window or seat on the day on which the processions (or one of them) did eventually take place.[40] In the absence of such express provisions, the courts would have found it hard to determine whether any common law notion of "suspension" could have applied in relation to the substitute for the "Royal Progress" which took place over two months after the coronation.[41]

The concept of "suspension" must be distinguished, not only from that of a temporary excuse for non-performance, but also from that of discharge by impossibility which is temporary and the extent of which cannot be determined with certainty immediately on the occurrence of the event which interferes with performance. The latter situation arose in the Gulf War cases, discussed in Ch.9, in which the question was *when* the time charters had been frustrated by the detention of the ships in

---

[36] *Distington Haematite Iron Co Ltd v Possehl & Co* [1917] 1 K.B. 811 at 813. For special difficulties arising from the notion of "suspension" in relation to contracts of employment, see Freedland, *The Personal Employment Contract* (2003), pp.464–491, describing this notion as "often ... a highly obscure one (at 464). Only a small part of that discussion is concerned with "suspension" on account of supervening events for which neither party is responsible.

[37] *e.g. Blythe & Co v Richards Turpin & Co* (1916) 85 L.J. K.B. 1425; *Bird v British Cellulose Ltd* [1945] K.B. 336.

[38] See *Tennants (Lancashire) Ltd v CS Wilson & Co Ltd* [1917] A.C. 495 at 525.

[39] See cl.21 of the contract in *Bremer Handelsgesellschaft mbH v Vanden Avenne-Izegem PBVA* [1978] 2 Lloyd's Rep. 108; above, para.12–036.

[40] See *Victorian Seats Agency v Paget* (1902) 19 T.L.R. 16.

[41] Above, para.7–006.

consequence of the war between Iran and Iraq.[42] The result of those cases was that the charters were frustrated, not immediately on the commencement of hostilities, but from the time at which a reasonable person would take the view that the interference with performance was going to be sufficiently serious to satisfy the tests of discharge by temporary impossibility. It would, however, be wrong to regard the contracts as "suspended" in the interval between those two points: on the contrary, they remained in full force until the second point was reached, and at that stage they were totally discharged. An express provision of the contract (*e.g.* an "off-hire" clause covering the detention) could indeed provide the charterer with temporary excuse for non-performance; but this would amount to a *pro tanto* extinction, and not to a true "suspension", of his obligation to pay hire.

The concept of a temporary excuse for non-performance must further be distinguished from that of suspension in that such an excuse may affect the obligation of only one of the parties. This is, for example, the position in the case of an employee who is prevented from doing the agreed work by a temporary illness which is not sufficiently serious to frustrate the contract. The employee will not be in breach but the employer will (unless the contract otherwise provides) be liable to pay wages during sickness.[43] True "suspension" should equally affect the obligations of both parties.

(7) "Reformation"

15–035   In the United States, the term "reformation" is used to refer to a remedy analogous to that known in English law as "rectification". In some of its applications, reformation in American law can be said to be the equivalent of rectification in English law. Thus in both systems the remedy is available to correct mistakes in a document which purports to record an earlier agreement between the parties, *e.g.* where parties to a lease have agreed on a rent of £1,000, but the lease specifies a rent of only £100, per month.[44]

There is however, also some support in the United States for the "reformation" of a contract in the light of supervening events, and this use of the remedy differs quite radically from "rectification", as understood in English law. "Reformation", in this context, is available even where the terms of a document *correctly* record the agreement of the parties. It amounts to altering the terms which were actually agreed so as to adjust the operation of the contract, in the altered circumstances, as nearly as possible to that intended by the parties. For example, in one case[45] a contract for the sale of a house provided for payment of the price in specified instalments, and for conveyance of the property when the amount outstanding had been reduced to a stated sum. Because of subsequent increases in property taxes, payment of the instalments was not likely ever to achieve that reduction; and it was held that the contract

---

[42] Above, para.9–011.
[43] Above, para.5–064.
[44] Restatement 2d, § 155; Treitel, *The Law of Contract* (11th ed.), pp.321–326.
[45] *Miller v Campello Co-operative Bank*, 181 N.E. 345 (1962).

should be "reformed" so as to entitle the purchaser to conveyance on a lump-sum payment of the amount outstanding under the contract. And in the *ALCOA*[46] case (discussed in Ch.6), in which severe cost increases in the provision of services were held to give rise to "impracticability," the court did not for that reason conclude that the contract had been discharged. Instead, it substituted its own flexible pricing formula for that which had been agreed on by the parties, so as to bring the remuneration of the party rendering the services into line with the altered circumstances.

In English law, the remedy of "rectification" is governed by the principle that "Courts . . . do not rectify contracts; they may and do rectify documents".[47] The remedy is, in other words, limited to cases in which a document fails to record all the terms on which the parties had agreed, or in which it sets out different terms. Rectification cannot be used to correct other mistakes: where, for example, the actual agreement was *concluded* under a mistake but the terms so agreed were accurately *recorded* in the contractual document, then that document could not be rectified so as to embody the terms on which the parties would have agreed but for their mistake.[48] Similarly, rectification would not be available in English law to alter a contract in the light of supervening events. Rectification can be used only to bring a document into line with the actual agreement of the parties; it is irrelevant, on a claim for rectification, to consider what the parties would or might have agreed, if at the time of contracting they had taken account of the supervening event or of the probability of its occurrence.

15–036

(8) **Adaptation or alteration**

(a) *Civil law*

Civil lawyers are familiar with the concept of modifying a contract in the light of supervening events. Some examples have been given in our discussion in Ch.6 of impracticability. Thus under the German doctrine of the disappearance of the basis of the contract (*Wegfall der Geschäftsgrundlage*) it has been held that a lease could be varied by raising the rent to take account of the greatly increased cost to the landlord of his obligation to provide steam[49]; and that debts could be revalorised to take account of the severe inflation of the 1920s.[50] The German doctrine, originally developed by the courts, has now been incorporated into the Civil Code, where the relevant paragraph expressly gives the party prejudiced by the supervening event the right to demand adaptation (*Anpassung*) of the contract.[51] Similarly, under the doctrine of *imprévision* of French administrative law, severe cost increases incurred by a supplier of gas to a public authority

15–037

---

[46] *Aluminum Corp of America v Essex Group Inc*, 499 F. Supp. 53 (1980); above, para.6–018.
[47] *Mackenzie v Coulson* (1869) L.R. 8 Eq. 369 at 375.
[48] *FE Rose Ltd v WH Pim & Co Ltd* [1953] 2 Q.B. 450.
[49] Above, para.6–037, n.30.
[50] Above, para.6–044.
[51] BGB § 313 (1). See above, paras 6–011, n.66, 6–023, n.59.

have been held to be a ground for increasing the charges payable to the supplier.[52] It is striking feature of these remedies that they can actually increase the obligation of one party (at least in a literal sense): the court imposes an increase in the amount payable, without giving the party required to pay it the option of abandoning the contract and relinquishing his right to the originally agreed performance to be rendered by the other party.

(b) *American law*

15-038   The concept of adapting or altering the contract is also recognised by a number of rules of American law. One group of cases is that just considered,[53] in which American courts have "reformed" contracts in the light of supervening events. In the *ALCOA* case,[54] the result of this process was similar to that reached in the German landlord and tenant case cited above:[55] the party to whom the services were to be rendered was ordered by the court to pay for those services at a rate higher than that agreed between the parties. It is significant that this result (which does not seem to have been followed in any other case) has been subjected in the United States to much adverse criticism[56]; and that indeed similar criticism has been directed in Germany at the wide discretionary powers assumed by the courts in cases of the disappearance of the commercial basis of the contract.[57] To force a party to pay more than the sum originally agreed is clearly a much more striking judicial interference with the sanctity of contract than merely to free both parties from their obligations.

A less radical form of judicial interference with the terms agreed on by the parties is illustrated by the American view that a contract may be "suspended" in cases of temporary impossibility.[58] Here neither party is required to do *more* than he had originally undertaken; and *later* performance is not inherently more onerous than that promised (though *earlier* payment would be). Indeed, some versions of "suspension" considered earlier in this chapter restrict the performance still to be rendered to *less* than that promised, *i.e.* to that part of it remaining possible after the end of the temporary impossibility. As has been suggested above, however, this result amounts, not to true suspension, but rather to a temporary excuse for non-performance.

15-039   The adaptation or alteration of a contract in the light of supervening events may result from some of the Uniform Commercial Code provisions which have already been considered. Section 2–613(b)[59] provides that, where goods identified at the time of contracting suffer partial casualty, the buyer may take the quantity remaining available (or the deteriorated

---

[52] Above, para.6–037, n.27.
[53] Above, para.15–035.
[54] 499 F. Supp. 53 (1980), above, n.46.
[55] at n.49.
[56] Above, para.6–018.
[57] Above, para.6–011, n.66.
[58] Above, para.15–034.
[59] Above, para.15–016.

goods) "with due allowance from the contract price". Section 2–615(b) applies the principle of *pro rata* allocation[60] where a supervening event, such as partial failure of a source of supply, affects only a part of the seller's capacity to perform; in such cases the buyer is expressly given the right to "modify the contract".[61] The same rules apply to chattel leases[62]; and although they do not in terms apply to contracts generally, it is arguable that they may have a wider scope than that expressly given to them by the Code provisions: the principle of *pro rata* allocation could, for example, require a person who had agreed to render services to a number of customers, and whose capacity to perform had been reduced by supervening events, to allocate his surviving capacity among his customers on a *pro rata* basis.[63] Under the present group of rules, there is no possibility of increasing the obligations of either party. In this respect they differ significantly from the process of "reformation" discussed above, and from the Civil law process of "adaptation."

A more general principle of adaptation or modification is contained in Comment 6 to s.2–615 of the Uniform Commercial Code. This Comment has been considered in Ch.6[64]; it provides for "adjustment" where "neither sense nor justice is served by either answer when the issue is posed in flat terms of excuse or no excuse". It is hard to find illustrations of this possibility in the decided American cases[65]; but a similar theme is taken up by § 272(2) of the Restatement 2d. This provides in general terms that, where total discharge "will not avoid injustice, the court may grant such relief as justice requires ...". Cases of "suspension" for temporary impossibility are evidently regarded as illustrations of this principle[66]; and it is arguable that further illustrations of it are provided by "reformation" and by the Uniform Commercial Code provision to which reference has been made in the above discussion.

(c) *English law*

One of the authorities cited in support of the principle of Restatement 2d, § 272(2) quoted in para.15–039, above is the English case of *Minnevitch v Café de Paris (Londres) Ltd*[67]; and it might therefore be thought that the principle of judicial modification of a contract in the light of supervening events was in part derived from English law. This would not, however, be consistent with the way in which *Minnevitch's* case would be regarded in   **15–040**

---

[60] Above, para.5–023.

[61] UCC, s.2–616(1)(b).

[62] UCC, ss.2A–221(b), 2A–405(b), 2A–406(1)(b).

[63] Above, para.5–065.

[64] Above, para.6–011.

[65] Even the *ALCOA* case 499 F. Supp. 53 (1980), above, n.46, does not rely on it; *cf.* also above, para.6–018.

[66] See the citation of *Patch v Solar Corp*, 149 F. 2d 558 (1945), in Reporter's Note to Restatement 2d, § 272, Comment c; but it is submitted that the case is more properly regarded as one of temporary excuse for non-performance on account of a delay which was not sufficiently serious to attract the operation of the doctrine of discharge: see above, para.5–059.

[67] [1936] 1 All E.R. 884, cited in the Comment referred to in the previous note.

England. The case arose out of the closure of all places of public entertainment for two days following the death of King George V; and it was held that these events justified the owner of a London café in refusing to accept the services of a group of entertainers (whom he had engaged to give variety performance at the café) on those two days, but not on the following four days. In England, this result would not be analysed as a "modification" of a contract which had been frustrated. The supervening event would not be regarded as having frustrated the contract, but as having merely provided the defendant with a temporary excuse for non-performance.[68] The case does not support the view that, if the temporary impossibility had been sufficiently serious to frustrate the contract, there would in English law have been any judicial power of "adapting" or "modifying" the contract.

The many emphatic dicta cited earlier in this chapter[69] strongly indicate that English law rejects the notion that courts have any power at common law to adapt or modify contracts in the light of supervening events. If those events satisfy the requirements of discharge, the contract is wholly discharged; if they do not satisfy those requirements, the contract remains fully in force. That view is also supported by the evident reluctance of the English courts to accept the principle of *pro rata* allocation in cases of partial failure of a specified source.[70] Nor is there any hint of adaptation or modification in any of the Suez cases.[71] Indeed this is true of the American, no less than of the English, cases concerned with the closure of the Suez Canal, and this fact may be thought to raise some doubt as to the extent to which Restatement 2d, § 272(2) represents the law even in the United States. It is also worth noting that all but one of the Illustrations to § 272 are so expressed as to make the principle of modification applicable only "if the court decides that this rule [*i.e.* the rule that there must be either total discharge or no discharge at all] will not avoid injustice ...".[72] Such a vague formulation is not likely to be accepted in England; and even in the United States its application is likely to be exceptional and controversial.[73] A power to modify contracts has been overtly recognised in England only in special war-time legislation, under which (for example) the courts were given power to modify building contracts the performance

---

[68] Above, para.5–057.

[69] Above, para.15–010, at nn.76 to 79; *cf. Scanlan's New Neon Ltd v Tooheys Ltd* (1943) 67 C.L.R. 169 at 188, and see also the Report of the Committee appointed by the Board of Trade to consider the Position of British Manufacturers and Merchants in Respect of Pre-War Contracts (Cd. 8975, 1918), para.10.

[70] Above, para.5–030.

[71] Above, paras 4–071 to 4–083.

[72] These words occur in § 272, Illustrations 1–4 and 6. Illustration 5 uses the slightly different formula "*because* [not 'if'] the rules ... will not avoid injustice"; presumably this word reflects the fact that Illustration 5 is governed by the statutory rule of UCC, s.2–615(b).

[73] See the criticisms of the *ALCOA* case, 499 F. Supp. 53 (1980), above, para.15–035, n.46, cited in para.6–018 above at n.8.

of which had been disrupted during the First World War.[74] It is interesting to note that a Committee set up to consider the impact of that war on contracts was opposed to the introduction of a more general power to revise contracts, on the ground that this would impose on a party obligations to which he had never agreed.[75]

Although English law as a general rule rejects the view that frustration may be a ground for modifying or adapting contracts, it does occasionally reach conclusions which in their practical effects resemble such processes. One situation which illustrates this possibility is that in which work is done under a contract after it has been discharged, but before the parties realise that this is the position, or before discharge is established in a court of law. As noted in para.15–003, above, even though such conduct may not suffice to give rise to the inference that the parties have entered into a new (implied) contract, it may nevertheless entitle the party who has done the work to a *quantum meruit* claim on a restitutionary basis.[76] In theory this result follows even though the original contract is totally discharged. But in practical terms, the result seems to resemble what a civil lawyer might describe as an adaptation of the contract. This is particularly true where the amount recoverable by way of *quantum meruit* exceeds the agreed remuneration in order to reflect the increased costs incurred by the claimant in consequence of the circumstances leading to discharge. This was the position in one of the English Suez cases[77]; and, although the case was later overruled on the issue of frustration, it stands as an authority for the proposition that a *quantum meruit* in excess of the contract price may be recovered for work done after, and in ignorance of, frustration. The Australian *Codelfa*[78] case supports the same view.

A restitutionary award may also be made in respect of acts done in part performance of the contract *before* its discharge. We shall see that in the United States, there is power at common law to make such an award,[79] while in England such power almost certainly exists only by statute.[80] It is theoretically possible, but unlikely, for such an award to exceed the contract price.[81] If the award cannot exceed the contract price, its practical effect can at most be said to be that the contract is "modified" in the sense that a reduced payment has to be made by one party for less than full performance by the other. This falls short of the kind of modification

---

[74] *e.g.* Courts (Emergency Powers) Act 1917, s.1 *cf.* Courts (Emergency Powers) Acts 1939–1943; Liabilities (War Time Adjustments) Acts 1941–1944, restricting remedies and adopting principles of discharge apparently derived from insolvency procedures.

[75] Above, n.69.

[76] Above, para.15–003.

[77] *The Massalia* [1961] 2 Q.B. 278, as to which see above, para.15–003, n.20.

[78] *Codelfa Construction Pty Ltd v State Rail Authority of New South Wales* (1982) 149 C.L.R. 337; above, para.4–061.

[79] Below, para.15–058.

[80] Law Reform (Frustrated Contracts) Act 1943, s.1 (3); below, para.15–060.

[81] *cf.* below, para.15–059, at n.79; contrast, in cases of breach, *Boomer v Muir*, 24 P. 2d 570 (1939), doubted in Treitel, *Remedies for Breach of Contract*, p.104.

considered above[82] under which the obligation of one party may actually be increased.

15–042   In two further situations, modification of a contract can be said to be the result of supervening events which do *not* frustrate the contract. These are the cases, already considered, in which a party may have a partial or temporary excuse for non-performance,[83] and those in which the principle of *pro rata* allocation would apply if it were recognised by English law.[84] In such cases contractual obligations may indeed be varied in the light of supervening events. But such variation is, *ex hypothesi*, not a legal effect of frustration since in the cases in question the requirements of frustration are *not* satisfied. They also differ (yet again) from true modification as a remedy in cases of frustration in that they can operate only to *reduce* the obligations of at least one party. True modification must be capable also of *increasing* those obligations; indeed, that is the prime purpose of claiming such relief (in systems in which it is available) where the allegedly frustrating event has greatly increased the costs of one party's performance.[85] Even if English law were to regard such cost increases as a ground of discharge,[86] it would do no more than to relieve the party prejudiced by the increase in costs from his duty to perform. What it will not do is to modify an executory contract so as to enable that party to recover those increased costs (wholly or in part) from the other party.

The effect of supervening events on the rights and duties of the parties may be dealt with by express or implied provisions of the contract; and such provisions may have the effect of varying those rights and duties in the light of the supervening events.[87] Provisions of this kind exclude frustration, and where they come into operation they can in theory be said to give effect to the contract rather than to modify it. Their practical operation, however, can be said to resemble that of modification; and, where a term of this kind is compulsorily implied by legislation,[88] the effect of the implication comes close to a rule of law allowing some degree of modification of the contract in the light of supervening events.

(9) **Vienna Convention**

15–043   Article 79(1) of the Vienna Convention on Contracts for the International Sale of Goods exempts a party from liability "for a failure to perform any of his obligations if the failure was due to an impediment beyond his

---

[82] At n.77.

[83] Above, para.5–026.

[84] Above, paras 5–025 to 5–030.

[85] As in the German case of the landlord recovering increased rent to recover his increased costs (RGZ 100, 130 (1920)), above, para.15–037, n.49, para.6–037, n.30.

[86] *e.g.* perhaps in the variation on the Suez cases suggested in para.4–080, above.

[87] Above, para.12–003.

[88] Package Travel, Package Holidays and Package Tours Regulations 1992 (SI 1992/3288), regs 10(1) and 14, above, para.4–025.

control . . .".[89] The exemption has effect "for the period during which the impediment exists"[90]; notice of the impediment must be given to the other party within a reasonable time, and if it is not so given the party who should have given it "is liable in damages resulting from its non-receipt".[91] Article 79(5) provides that "nothing in this Article prevents a party from exercising any right other than to claim damages under this Convention."

We saw in Ch.6 that the effect of an "impediment" under the Convention was quite different from that of the total and automatic discharge which results from frustration in English law.[92] One difference between the effect of Art.79 and frustration is that the exemption may be partial: the impeded party can rely on the exemption in respect of failure to perform "*any* of his obligations".[93] Another such difference is that the exemption may be temporary (thus in effect suspending the contract): it applies "for the period for which the impediment exists".[94] The most striking difference between the exemption under Art.79 and frustration is that the exemption is expressed to apply only to the impeded party's liability in damages. The other party may therefore rely on the failure in performance as a ground for declaring the contract avoided under other provisions of the Convention[95] which govern what English lawyers would regard as the right to rescind a contract for breach or for other failure in performance not amounting to frustration. Such a failure does not (in English law) automatically bring the primary obligations of the parties to an end but does so only at the option of the party failing to receive the impeded party's performance.[96]

In all these respects, the effects of an "impediment" under Art.79 resemble those of an excuse for non-performance in English law, rather than those of frustration. The point can be illustrated by reference to cases such as *Poussard v Spiers and Pond*[97]: in that case, the singer[98] was not liable in damages because her unavailability was due to illness; the other party had (and exercised) the option to rescind; but that party could instead have affirmed the contract, and, if he had done so, the singer's failure to appear after she had recovered from her illness would have given rise to a claim for damages. A claim for damages succeeded, as we have seen, in the

---

[89] For the text of Art.79(1), see above, para.6–048. At the time of writing, the Convention has not been ratified by the United Kingdom.

[90] Art.79(3).

[91] Art.79(4).

[92] Above, para.6–048.

[93] Art.79(1); under the English doctrine of frustration, *all* obligations would be discharged.

[94] Art.79(3).

[95] Arts 49, 64, 72 and 73.

[96] Treitel, *The Law of Contract* (11th ed.), p.844.

[97] (1876) 1 Q.B.D. 410; above, para.5–058.

[98] The contract was not in fact between the singer and the defendants, but between her husband, and the defendants. This obsolete aspect of the case can now be ignored.

Minnevitch[99] case, which was again one of temporarily excused non-performance and not one of frustration. These consequences of excused non performance in English law are among those which flow from an "impediment" within Art.79.

15–044　　The wording of Art.79(5), which restricts the exemption to claims for damages, at first sight leaves it open to the other party to exercise his right, not only to declare the contract avoided, but also (instead of so doing) to "require performance"[1] from the impeded party, or, in other words, to seek specific performance. The Convention, however, restricts this remedy by providing that a court is not bound to order specific performance unless it would do so under its own law in respect of similar contracts of sale not governed by the Convention.[2] If the impediment made performance permanently impossible, specific performance would clearly not be ordered in England.[3] But the further problem arises whether specific performance would be ordered where the impossibility was only temporary but was so prolonged as to be a ground of frustration in English law. This was, for example, the position in the *Acetylene*[4] case, where a contract for the sale of carbide was held to have been frustrated by a three-year delay in shipment, resulting from the war-time requisitioning of all available ships, since by the end of the delay commercial conditions had radically changed. Under the Convention, it might seem that, as the excuse provided by Art.79 was only temporary,[5] and as it extended only to claims for damages,[6] the buyer could in such a case "require performance". But it is submitted that, where such an "impediment" existed, specific performance would not be ordered in England, even if, in cases in which there was no "impediment", the nature of the goods were such as to make the remedy an appropriate one[7]; for in English law, hardship is an independent ground on which specific performance "may ... be refused because of an unforeseen change of circumstances not

---

[99] *Minnevitch v Café de Paris (Londres) Ltd* [1936] 1 All E.R. 884, where the claim was *by* the musicians: above, para.15–040.

[1] Art.46; *cf.* Art.62.

[2] Art.28.

[3] See *Forrer v Nash* (1865) 35 Beav. 167, at 171: "the court does not compel a person to do what is impossible". *cf.* Sale of Goods Act 1979, ss.48B(3)(a) and 48E(2) as inserted by Sale and Supply of Goods to Consumers Regulations 2002, SI 2002/3045, reg.5, implementing Directive 1999/44 (no specific enforcement of consumer's right to require seller to repair or replace non-conforming goods where this would be "impossible").

[4] *Acetylene Co of CB v Canada Carbide Co* (1922) 8 Lloyd's Rep. 456, above, para.15–040.

[5] Art.79(3).

[6] Art.79(5).

[7] See Sale of Goods Act 1979, s.52 and the requirement that damages must not be an appropriate remedy (as it normally, but not invariably, would be in the case of sales of commodities readily available in the market: see Treitel, *The Law of Contract* (11th ed.), pp.1002–1005).

amounting to legal frustration"[8]. An alternative route by which refusal of specific performance could perhaps be explained is by arguing that Art.79 did not exhaustively specify the effects of "impediments" and that, while it stated their effects as excuses from liability in damages, it did not necessarily exclude the possibility of their forming grounds for total discharge under another provision of the Convention by which matters not expressly settled in it are to be settled "in conformity with the general principles on which it is based or, in the absence of such principles, in conformity with the law applicable by virtue of the rules of private international law".[9]

VI. PROBLEMS OF ONE-SIDED OR PARTIAL PERFORMANCE

Earlier in this chapter, we noted that the principle that frustration discharges only future obligations can give rise to difficulties where the contract requires one party to perform before the other and the frustrating event occurs in the interval between the times fixed for the two performances.[10] Similar difficulties can arise where one party, though not required to perform before the other, has actually done so before the time of discharge. In both these situations, a strict adherence to the principle of prospective discharge could give rise to unjust enrichment in the sense that the party who was to perform only after the time of discharge will receive the other party's performance without having to render his own performance. Even where there is no such enrichment one party may, before the time of discharge, have incurred expenses which will be wasted in consequence of discharge, and the question then arises whether the resulting loss should be borne entirely by the party who has incurred the expenses, or whether it should be split between the contracting parties.

15–045

(1) **Money paid or payable before discharge**

Two rules governing such payments were established at common law; these have been modified by statutory rules which have largely, but not entirely, superseded the common law rules.

15–046

---

[8] *Patel v Ali* [1984] Ch. 281, above, para.6–042 ; if the "change of circumstances" did amount to "legal frustration", specific performance would of course be refused on the ground that the contract had been discharged. For refusal of specific performance on grounds analogous to hardship where the contract is not discharged, see also Sale of Goods Act 1979, s.48B(3)(b) and (4), applicable to consumer sale by virtue of the Regulations cited in n.3 above.

[9] Art.7(2). Reliance could be placed on the words "nothing *in this Article*" in Art.79(5).

[10] Above, para.15–011.

(a) *Common law developments*

15–047   The original common law position was that money paid before discharge could not be recovered back by the payor and that money payable before discharge remained due. The operation of these rules is illustrated by the coronation cases.[11] A typical case was *Blakeley v Muller & Co*,[12] where tickets for seats on a stand to watch one of the processions had been bought and paid for in May 1902. The contract was frustrated on June 24 (when it was announced that the processions had been cancelled), and it was held that the ticket-holder was not entitled to the return of his money. Lord Alverstone C.J. said that it would be unfair that the loss of the expense of erecting the stand should fall wholly on the defendant.[13] Similar reasoning accounts for a number of later cases[14] in which it was held that money paid before discharge could not be recovered back by the payor and that money payable before discharge remained due. The reasoning is scarcely satisfactory, for it does not explain why the loss resulting from the cancellation of the festivities should fall wholly on the payor. The same result was justified by a more abstract line of reasoning in *Chandler v Webster*[15] where a contract for the hire of a room to watch the processions provided for payment of £141 15s. in advance. This sum had become due, and £100 of it had been paid, before the cancellation of the processions. It was held that the hirer remained liable to pay the outstanding balance of £41 15s., and that he was not entitled to recover back the £100 as money paid on a total failure of consideration. Both these conclusions were based on the principle that frustration discharges only future obligations. From this it followed that the liability to pay the £41 15s. was not discharged as it had accrued before the time of discharge; and it was also thought to follow that there was no *total* failure of consideration for the payment of the £100 since the contract was not void *ab initio*, so that the hirer had for some time had the benefit of a valid contract, giving him the right to use the room in accordance with the contract. The result was again scarcely a satisfactory way of allocating the loss,[16] which fell wholly on one party. Moreover the reasoning ignored the point that as a result of the frustrating event the performance promised to the payor in return for the payment had (in *Chandler v Webster*) become completely useless to him, and in a case of supervening impossibility could not be

---

[11] Above, paras 7–006 to 7–014.

[12] [1903] 2 K.B. 760n.

[13] *ibid.* at 761; for similar reasoning, see *Anglo-Egyptian Navigation Co v Rennie* (1875) L.R. 10 C.P. 271; and see *ibid.* at 571.

[14] *Lumsden v Barton* (1902) 19 T.L.R. 53; *Civil Service Co-operative Soc v General Steam Navigation Co* [1903] 2 K.B. 756; and see next note. *cf. Re Continental C & G Rubber Co Pty Ltd* (1919) 27 C.L.R. 184; and *Krell v Henry* [1903] 2 K.B. 740, where on appeal the defendant abandoned his counter-claim for the return of the £25 paid by him to the claimant before discharge.

[15] [1904] 1 K.B. 493.

[16] For judicial criticism, see *Lloyd Royal Belge SA v Stathatos* (1917) 33 T.L.R. 390 at 392, affirmed 34 T.L.R. 70; *Cantiare San Rocco SA v Clyde Shipbuilding and Engineering Co Ltd* [1924] A.C. 266 at 247–248, 258–259.

rendered at all, so that the payor would receive no part of what he had bargained for in exchange for the payment.

This point was stressed, and *Chandler v Webster* (so far as it held that the £100 paid before discharge could not be recovered back) was overruled in the later *Fibrosa*[17] case. An English company had agreed to sell machinery to a Polish company; delivery was to be c.i.f. Gdynia, and the price was £4,800, of which £1,600 was to be paid "with order" and the balance against shipping documents. After £1,000 of the £1,600 had been paid, and before any shipment had been made, the contract was frustrated by illegality resulting from the German occupation of Gdynia during the Second World War. The House of Lords held that the buyer could recover back the £1,000 as money paid on a consideration which had wholly failed. The failure was not prevented from being total by the fact that the buyer had at one time had the benefit of a valid contract. The point was explained by Lord Simon[18]: "In the law relating to the formation of contract, the promise to do a thing may often be the consideration, but when one is considering the law of failure of consideration and of the quasi-contractual right to recover money on that ground it is, generally speaking,[19] not the promise which is referred to but the performance of the promise." Failure of consideration thus means failure in performance; and frustration is given retrospective effect to the extent that money paid before discharge must be repaid where the payor has (in consequence of the supervening event) received no part of what he bargained for in exchange for the payment. It seems clear that the liability of the buyer to pay the unpaid balance of £600 of the stipulated advance payment was likewise discharged; for the court would not have engaged in the futile exercise of ordering him to make a payment which he would then immediately have been entitled to recover.[20]

---

[17] *Fibrosa Spolka Akcyjna v Fairbairn, Lawson, Combe, Barbour Ltd* [1943] A.C. 32. The case has been followed in a number of other common law jurisdictions: see *Robbins v Wilson & Cabeldu Ltd* [1944] 4 D.L.R. 663; *Bray v Anderson* [1956] N.Z.L.R. 347. In Australia, there is a difference of opinion on the point: see Law Reform Commission of New South Wales, Report on Frustrated Contracts, p.21 n.10; Lindgren, Carter & Harland, *Contract Law in Australia*, para.2068.

[18] At 48. The point appears to have been overlooked in *Re Goldcorp Exchange Ltd* [1995] 1 A.C. 74 at 103, where the Privy Council repeats what is in substance the reasoning of *Chandler v Webster*, without referring either to that case or to the *Fibrosa* case.

[19] A party may bargain for a promise, as opposed to its performance: *e.g.* where he insures against a possible loss. *cf.* Law Reform (Frustrated Contracts) Act 1943, s.2(5)(b), below, para.15–093.

[20] See *French Marine v Compagnie Napolitaine etc.* [1921] 2 A.C. 494 at 511 ("*frustra petis quod mox es restiturus*"), cited with approval in the *Fibrosa* case [1943] A.C. 32 at 53–54. *cf.*, in the context of breach, *McDonald v Denys Lascelles Ltd* (1933) 48 C.L.R. 457, cited with approval in (*inter alia*) *Johnson v Agnew* [1980] A.C. 367, at 396; *Hyundai Heavy Industries Ltd v Papadopoulos* [1980] 1 W.L.R. 1129 at 1141. Contrast *CT Bowring Reinsurance Ltd v MR Baxter (The M Vatan)* [1987] 2 Lloyd's Rep. 416 at 424–425, but that case concerned payments of instalments of premium under a contract of insurance, so that frustration would not have brought about a total failure of consideration (see previous note) and sums

The common law rule, as laid down in the *Fibrosa* case, applies only where the consideration for the payment has *totally* failed. The requirement that the failure must be "total" is now much attenuated[21] but it continues to be stated as the starting principle[22]: in the context of frustrated contracts it is illustrated by *Whincup v Hughes*[23] where a father apprenticed his son to a watchmaker for six years at a premium of £25. After one year the watchmaker died, and it was held that the father could not recover back any part of the premium as the failure of consideration was only partial. In the *Fibrosa* case, the buyer's claim for the return of his advance payment would similarly have failed if, before discharge of the contract, part of the machinery had been delivered, *i.e.* if part had been shipped and documents in respect of that part had been duly tendered to the buyer before the frustrating event. The claim would have failed even if that part had been a relatively minor part of the whole of the machinery which was the subject-matter of the contract.[24] The justification for this restriction on the buyer's right to restitution at common law was that the court could not easily say how much of the total price was to be attributed or apportioned to the part of the machinery which was delivered. The position would be different if the subject-matter and the terms of the contract were such that apportionment could in fact readily be made. In such cases, partial recovery of money paid could be allowed in respect of partial failure of consideration. For example, if a buyer had paid in advance for 1,000 tons of wheat which had been sold at a specified price per ton, and the contract had then been frustrated after 500 tons had been delivered, then the buyer could recover back half of the agreed payment.[25]

The requirement that the failure must be total can also be displaced by an express term of the contract. This possibility is illustrated by the situation in which a time charterparty provides that hire is to be paid in advance; that hire is to cease in the event of loss of time from specified causes for which the owner is responsible; that overpaid hire is to be repaid by the shipowner to the charterer; and that, should the vessel be

---

paid before discharge would not be recoverable by the payor on the principle of the *Fibrosa* case. Hence the question whether instalments remained due after frustration would turn on whether they had become due at the time of frustration.

[21] See Treitel, *The Law of Contract* (11th ed.), pp.1050–1052.

[22] See *Pan Ocean Shipping Ltd v Creditcorp Ltd (The Trident Beauty)* [1994] 1 W.L.R. 161 at 163, 164; *Baltic Shipping Co v Dillon* (1993) 176 C.L.R. 344 at 350–351, 367, 376, 384, 388; these were cases in which the failure resulted, not from frustration, but from breach.

[23] (1871) L.R. 6 C.P. 78.

[24] *cf. French Marine v Compagnie Napolitaine etc.* [1921] 2 A.C. 494 at 517, *per* Lord Sumner; approved in the *Fibrosa* case [1943] A.C. 32 at 54, and (*semble*) at 71 and 79 (no *total* failure of consideration where services under a time charter had been rendered for six days out of the month in respect of which the advance payment had been made).

[25] *ibid.* at 81; *cf. Ebrahim Dawood Ltd v Heath* [1961] 2 Lloyd's Rep. 512; *Clough Mill Ltd v Martin* [1985] 1 W.L.R. 111 at 117–118.

lost, "money paid and not earned shall be repaid to the charterer".[26] In the event of loss of time due to the specified causes, or of loss of the vessel, a proportionate part of the advance payment would then have to be repaid by the shipowner[27] to the charterer. The contract in such cases is not discharged under the common law doctrine of frustration, either because the event preventing the ship from rendering the services amounts to a breach,[28] or because (even where there is no breach, as in the case of loss of the vessel through accidents for which the shipowner was not responsible) the contract makes express provision for the event which, but for such provision, would have discharged it.[29] The charterer's right is therefore governed by "a contractual regime which legislates for the recovery of overpaid hire"[30] so that a "remedy in restitution" is "unnecessary and inappropriate".[31] Such a remedy would be necessary only if *either* the contract contained no provision for the repayment of hire paid in advance *or* the contract were frustrated by some event or cause other than any of those specified in the contract as giving rise to a right to repayment, *e.g.* if the ship were requisitioned [32] or detained by one of the combatants in a war or civil war.[33]

The common law rule that money can be recovered back if there has been a total failure of consideration will not apply "if ... the bargain is ... that no money will be returned".[34] Some cases of this kind will be considered later in this chapter[35]; another is that of a cricket match in which spectators are admitted to the ground on the terms that no money is to be refunded even if there is no play.[36] It seems that the terms of admission to Test Matches and to International Limited Over matches now commonly provide for refunds on a sliding scale if no play or very

---

[26] For such provisions, see cll.16 and 18 of the charterparty in *Pan Ocean Shipping Ltd v Creditcorp Ltd (The Trident Beauty)* [1994] 1 W.L.R. 161; *cf.* cll.12 and 18 of the charterparty in *French Marine v Compagnie Napolitaine etc.* [1921] 2 A.C. 494.

[27] But not by a person to whom the right to receive the advance payment had been assigned; this was the point actually decided in *The Trident Beauty*, above.

[28] *cf. The Trident Beauty*, above, where the breach took the form of a wrongful repudiation by the shipowner.

[29] Above, para.12–002.

[30] *The Trident Beauty* [1994] 1 W.L.R. 161 at 164.

[31] *ibid.*

[32] As in the *French Marine* case [1921] 2 A.C. 494, where *no* restitutionary remedy was available to the charterer by reason of the common law rule stated above, para.15–047, and now reversed by s.1(2) of the Law Reform (Frustrated Contracts) Act 1943 (below, para.15–050).

[33] As in *WJ Tatem Ltd v Gamboa* [1939] 1 K.B. 132 (above, para.13–013), where the effect of frustration was to release the charterer from liability for *future* payments but no attempt was made by him to reclaim any part of the advance payment he had made for the month during part of which he had been deprived of the use of the ship. Presumably any such claim would then have been barred by the *French Marine* case, above, n.32.

[34] *Fibrosa* case [1943] A.C. 32, at 43.

[35] Below, para.15–052.

[36] *Fibrosa* case [1943] A.C. 32 at 43.

little play takes place.[37] Contract terms which exclude the common law rule in the *Fibrosa* case would not, it is submitted, be subject to the requirement of reasonableness which s.3(2)(b)(ii) of the Unfair Contract Terms Act 1977 imposes in certain cases where a party claims "by references to any contract term ... to be entitled in respect of the whole or any part of his contractual obligation to render no performance at all"; for in cases of the kind here under discussion there is, by reason of the supervening events, *no* "contractual obligation" to perform.[38] Such terms could, however, in a consumer contract on preformulated terms, be subject to the requirement of fairness under the Unfair Terms in Consumer Contracts Regulations 1999.[39] The further question whether contract terms excluding the Law Reform Frustrated Contracts Act 1943 are subject to the 1977 Act or to the 1999 Regulations is discussed in para.15–084, below.

The right to recover money paid under a frustrated contract is recognised also in the United States[40] and in Scotland[41]; in these systems the right is not restricted by any requirement that there must be a total failure of consideration

(b) *Law Reform (Frustrated Contracts) Act 1943, s.1(2)*[42]

15–049   This subsection confirms and in some respects modifies the law as laid down in the *Fibrosa* case. That state of the law was thought to be subject to two defects.[43] It could cause injustice to the payor in denying him a right of recovery where the failure of consideration was not total; and it could cause injustice to the payee in requiring him to return the whole payment without any allowance in respect of his expenses. The first of these points will be discussed here; the second will be considered in our discussion later in this chapter of the problem of wasted expenditure.[44]

(i) Sums paid before discharge

15–050   Section 1(2) provides that sums paid in pursuance of the contract before the time of discharge shall be recoverable from the payee "as money received by him for the use of the payor". The subsection does not refer to

---

[37] See MCC Ticket Application Form (1993), Condition No 7; *The Daily Telegraph*, December 2, 1992, p.1.

[38] *cf.* above, para.12–018.

[39] SI 1999/2083. The "cricket match" example given in the text above could fall within Sch.2, para.1, of the Regulations. See also above, para.12–014.

[40] Restatement, § 468, Illustration 4; Restatement 2d, § 271(1) ("including restitution"); Palmer, *Law of Restitution*, Vol.II, p.101.

[41] *Cantiare San Rocco SA v Clyde Shipbuilding and Engineering Co* [1926] A.C. 226 at 248 (where the failure was total).

[42] For contracts to which s.1(2) does not apply (or to which it applies only with modifications) see below, paras 15–083 *et seq.* For legislation in terms virtually identical to those of the 1943 Act, see New Zealand Frustrated Contracts Act 1944; Victorian Frustrated Contracts Act 1959. The Canadian Uniform Frustrated Contracts Act closely follows the wording of the 1943 Act but departs from it to some extent.

[43] See n.45, below.

[44] Below, paras 15–070 *et seq.*

total failure of consideration and the perhaps unintended[45] consequence of its wording appears to be that the statutory right to recover back money paid before discharge extends even to cases (such as *Whincup v Hughes*)[46] in which the failure in performance is only partial. It might seem desirable that in such cases only a proportionate part of the payment ought to be recoverable, but the subsection provides that "*all* sums paid" shall be recoverable from the payee. The word "all" here suggests that the payee must repay the whole of the prepayment and seek his remedies in respect of his part performance under the provisions of the Act relating to valuable benefits and expenses; these provisions will be discussed in paras 15–060 to 15–075, below.

(ii) Sums payable before discharge

Section 1(2) also provides that sums payable in pursuance of the contract before the time of discharge shall cease to be payable. It follows that, in a case like *Chandler v Webster*,[47] the claim for the unpaid £41 15s. would now fail. This result was, for the reason given above,[48] a necessary consequence of the reasoning of the *Fibrosa* case where the failure of consideration for such a payable (but unpaid) sum, if it had been paid, would have been total. The subsection appears to extend that reasoning to cases of partial failure.

15–051

(iii) Provisions[49] to which s.1(2) does not apply

It does not follow from s.1(2) that all payments made or to be made, under a contract which is later frustrated must be repaid, or cease to be due. The subsection would not, for example, apply where the contract in terms limited the amount of the advance payment that was to be recoverable by the payor. This possibility is illustrated by the time charter provisions discussed in para.15–048, above. Another situation to which the subsection would not apply could arise where a building contract provided that liquidated damages were to be paid for delay in completing specified stages of the work. If such payments had been made by, or had become due from, the builder and the contract were later frustrated, then it is submitted that the payments would not be recoverable by the builder, or

15–052

---

[45] When introducing the Bill that was to become the 1943 Act in the House of Lords, Lord Simon L.C. referred to only "two main provisions of this Bill:" H.L.Deb., June 29, 1943, col.139; *cf.* also *ibid.* cols 140 ("the two main provisions") and 141 ("the two changes"). It is clear from his speech that these were (i) the proviso to s.1(2), relating to expenses (below, para.15–071), and (ii) s.1(3), relating to valuable benefits (below, para.15–060). However, the Law Revision Committee's 7th Interim Report, on which s.1(2), (though not s.1(3): see *BP Exploration (Libya) Ltd v Hunt* [1979] 1 W.L.R. 783 at 789, discussed in below, paras 15–062 to 15–064) is based, does not restrict its recommendation to cases of total failure of consideration.

[46] Above, para.15–048.

[47] [1904] 1 K.B. 493, above, para.15–047.

[48] Above, para.15–048, at n.20.

[49] Our concern here is with *provisions* to which s.1(2) does not apply. For *contracts* to which this subsection (among others) does not apply, see s.2(5), below, paras 15–089 *et seq.*

cease to be due from him. Section 1 of the Act is expressly subject to s.2; and s.2(3) requires the court (*inter alia*) to give effect to a provision in the contract which is intended to have effect whether or not circumstances arise which operate to frustrate the contract. The liquidated damages clause would be one which was intended to apply until the contract came to an end and would thus to this extent be excepted from the operation of s.1(2). Of course, sums paid under such a clause after discharge (in ignorance of it) would be recoverable as payments made under a mistake, and sums payable after discharge would cease to be due precisely because the contract had been discharged; but these consequences would not depend on s.1(2), which deals only with sums paid or payable before discharge.

Another possible effect of s.2(3) is that, if the parties simply exclude the operation of the Act by the terms of their contract, the common law rules stated in the *Fibrosa* case[50] may continue to apply. The right to recover back payments made before discharge would then continue to be governed by the distinction between total and partial failure of consideration. The point is probably not one of great practical importance since express terms excluding the Act are likely to make their own provisions for the fate of advance payments. A more significant point is that s.1(2) does not apply to certain contracts which are excepted from its operation by s.2(5)[51] of the Act. In such cases, the contract may well not contain any provisions for the fate of advance payments in the event of frustration; and the outcome would then depend on the unmodified common law rules laid down in the *Fibrosa* case.

15–053   Section 1(2) may also be inapplicable on the ground that an express provision in the contract excludes frustration. For example, in some of the contracts in the coronation cases frustration was excluded by the contractual provisions allowing the ticket-holder to use the viewing facilities on the days of the postponed processions.[52] In such cases s.1(2) would not now apply as the contract would not be frustrated; nor would money paid for the facilities be recoverable at common law under the rule in *Fibrosa* case.

(iv) Antecedent events

15–054   Section 1(2) would also be inapplicable in cases of *antecedent* events affecting performance of the contract.[53] In such cases relief (if any) would be available on the ground that the contract had been made under a mistake rather than on the ground that it had been discharged by frustration. In one of the coronation cases,[54] money paid under such a contract was held to be recoverable by the payor. Whether the mistake in

---

[50] [1943] A.C. 32; above, para.15–048.
[51] Below, paras 15–089 to 15–097.
[52] *Victoria Seats Agency v Paget* (1902) 19 T.L.R. 16; *cf. Clark v Lindsay* (1903) 88 L.T. 198, where the contract was made after the cancellation of the procession but in ignorance of it.
[53] *Great Peace Shipping Ltd v Tsavliris Salvage International Ltd (The Great Peace)* [2002] EWCA Civ 1470; [2003] Q.B. 697 at [161].
[54] *Griffith v Brymer* (1903) 19 T.L.R. 434.

that case would now be regarded as sufficiently fundamental to give rise to a claim for relief is (as we saw in Ch.7) an open question[55]; but where the mistake is of this nature there is no doubt that money paid under the alleged contract would be recoverable by the payor, and money expressed to be payable under it would not be due.

(2) Other benefits conferred before discharge

Our concern here is with the converse of the situation just discussed, *i.e.* with that in which a party is required to render some performance other than a payment of money and, after that performance has been rendered in part, the contract is frustrated, usually by a supervening event making it impossible or illegal for him to complete that performance. The question then arises whether the party to whom the partial performance has been rendered is required to make any payment in respect of it. In discussing this question, it will be convenient to refer to the two parties as, respectively, "the performing party" and "the recipient".   15–055

(a) *The English common law position*

This was again governed by the principle that frustration discharges the contract from the date of the frustrating event. The question, therefore, was whether by the time of discharge any payment had become due for what had been done by the performing party; and this depended on whether the obligation of the performing party was an "entire" one. Such an obligation is one which must be completely performed before the agreed counter-performance (usually a payment of money) becomes due.[56] If the obligation was an entire one, and the contract was frustrated before its complete performance, it therefore followed that the performing party was not entitled to the contract price since at the time of discharge the recipient's liability had not yet accrued. If, for example, a builder had agreed to build a house for £100,000 payable on completion and the contract was frustrated (*e.g.* by supervening illegality) before completion of the work, then the builder could not recover the £100,000. If, on the other hand, the contract provided for payment in five equal instalments as specified stages of the work were reached, and the contract was frustrated after the third, but before the fourth, stage had been completed, then the builder's obligation would not be entire, and he could recover the first three instalments, but not the other two. If the contract did not, on its true construction, require completion of the work before then, the builder would be entitled to be paid for the work which he had done.[57]   15–056

The rule that, in the example given above, the builder cannot recover the £100,000 is a perfectly reasonable one; for it would be unjust to   15–057

---

[55] Above, para.7–008.

[56] See Treitel, *The Law of Contract* (11th ed.), p.782; *cf.* (in case of breach) *Sumpter v Hedges* [1898] 1 Q.B. 673.

[57] *Menetone v Athawes* (1764) 3 Burr. 1592; *cf. Fuller v Patrick* (1849) 18 L.J. Q.B. 236; and (in case of breach) *Roberts v Havelock* (1932) 3 B. 7 Ad. 404.

require the customer to pay the full price for an unfinished house. But it was further held in England that the performing party could not recover anything at all for partial performance before frustration. He could not, where his obligation was entire, recover a *quantum meruit* as no agreement to pay a proportionate sum for doing part of the work could be implied in the teeth of an express agreement for payment only on completion. Thus in *Cutter v Powell*[58] a seaman whose wages were to become due only after completion of a voyage died during it; and his executrix recovered nothing for the services he had rendered. And in *Appleby v Myers*[59] the plaintiffs agreed "to make and erect the whole of the machinery" in the defendant's factory "and to keep the whole in order for two years from the date of completion". After part of the machinery had been erected, an accidental fire destroyed the factory with such of the machinery as was already in it, and frustrated the contract. It was held that the plaintiffs could recover nothing for the machinery which they had erected. Blackburn J. said that: "the plaintiffs, having contracted to do an entire work for a specific sum, can recover nothing unless the work be done, or unless it can be shown that it was the defendant's fault that the work was incomplete, or that there is something to justify the conclusion that the parties have entered into a fresh contract."[60]

The rule that a party who fails to complete performance of an entire obligation cannot recover anything in respect of benefits conferred by partial performance is open to the objection that it can lead to the unjust enrichment of the other party, who may be left in possession of the benefit of the partial performance without having to make any payment for it.[61] Where the failure to complete performance amounts to a breach, there is indeed the counter-argument that the rule puts pressure on the party in breach to complete performance and so protects the legitimate interests of the other party.[62] But this argument can have no force where the failure to complete performance is not a breach, but results from supervening impossibility for which neither party is responsible, or from supervening illegality, which constitutes a ground of discharge: pressure to perform will be useless where performance has become impossible and contrary to public policy where performance has become illegal. The preferable view, therefore, is that the common law rule laid down in cases such as *Appleby v Myers* is unsatisfactory, and that the performing party should have a remedy in respect of any unjust enrichment which his partial performance may have conferred on the recipient. This criticism of the rule in *Appleby v Myers* does not necessarily extend to the decision reached on the actual facts of the case, which presented the additional complication that the

---

[58] (1795) 6 T.R. 320 ; Stoljar, 34 Can. Bar Rev. 288; Dockray, 117 L.Q.R. 626.
[59] (1867) L.R. 2 C.P. 651.
[60] *ibid.* at 661.
[61] See Law Com. No 121 (dealing with cases of breach); not to be implemented: Law Commission, 19th Annual Report, para.2.11; Goff and Jones, *The Law of Restitution* (6th ed.), para.20–055; but see McFarlane and Stevens, 118 L.Q.R. 596.
[62] *e.g. Bolton v Mahadeva* [1972] 1 W.L.R. 1009.

benefit obtained before the frustrating event had been destroyed by it. It was no doubt this feature of the case which Blackburn J. had in mind when he said[63] that: "where as in the present case the premises are destroyed without fault on either side, it is a misfortune equally affecting both parties; excusing both from further performance, but giving a cause of action to neither." This aspect of the problem will be further considered later in this chapter.[64] Here it need only be pointed out that the *rule* in *Appleby v Myers* could apply to events where the benefit received by partial performance was not destroyed by the frustrating event, *e.g.* where that event was the death of the performing party.[65]

The result in *Appleby v Myers* would have been different if the contract had not been "to do an entire work for a specific sum" but had provided for payment by instalments as specified stages of the work were completed. In that case instalments due in respect of stages completed before discharge would have been recoverable,[66] but neither the instalment nor a reasonable sum would have been recoverable in respect of a stage of the work which was only partly completed at the time of discharge.[67]

(b) *The American common law position*

Criticism of the rule in *Appleby v Myers* is reinforced by contrasting it with the American rule which permits restitution in respect of benefits (of the kind here under discussion) conferred under contracts which are frustrated after part performance. Such restitution has, for example, been allowed where a builder had contracted to do work on a house which, after part of the work had been done, was destroyed[68]; where a painter had contracted to decorate a ballroom and died after doing some of the work but before completing it[69]; where a lawyer had contracted to represent a client in litigation and died after doing much of the work but before the litigation was concluded[70]; and where a railway company had acquired a right of way over land in return for a promise to grant a free pass to the landowner but the further performance of that promise became illegal.[71] Such liability is recognised as a matter of common law. It is not (as in English law and in other systems, to be discussed below) dependent on statute; though, in States which have adopted the relevant provisions of Field's Code,[72] it is recognised by the provisions of that Code.[73] One reason for the difference between the English and American common law

---

[63] (1867) L.R. 2 C.P. 651 at 659.

[64] Below, para.15–064.

[65] As, for example, in *Cutter v Powell* (1795) 6 T.R. 320; *cf.* also the American cases cited below, at nn.69–71.

[66] Above, para.15–031.

[67] This follows from *Appleby v Myers* (1867) L.R. 2 C.P. 651.

[68] *Butterfield v Byron*, 27 N.E. 667 (1891); *Dame v Wood*, 70 A. 1081 (1908); *Keeling v Shastey & Vollmer*, 25 P. 445 (1912).

[69] *Buccini v Paterno Construction Co*, 170 N.E. 911 (1930).

[70] *City of Barnsdall v Curncutt*, 174 P. 596 (1945).

[71] *Louisville & Nashville RR v Crowe*, 160 S.W. 759 (1911).

[72] See above, para.8–055.

[73] *e.g.* California Civil Code, s.1514; Montana Code Annotated 2003, s.28–1–1303.

solutions is that American law rejects the English rule which denies restitution in respect of benefits conferred in the partial performance of an entire obligation. Such restitution is available in the United States even where the failure to complete performance amounts to a breach[74]; there is obviously an even stronger case for allowing it where that failure is due to circumstances for which the claimant is not responsible. The English rule denying restitution in cases of partial performance of an entire obligation forms a crucial part of the reasoning of *Appleby v Myers*, and that reasoning clearly cannot survive in a system which rejects the rule itself.

15–059   The *measure* of restitution available under the American rule is more controversial. The authorities support at least three possible measures: the value of the benefit received by the defendant[75]; the value of the services rendered by the plaintiff[76]; and the rateable proportion of the agreed price which the work done bears to that contracted for.[77] Some cases reject the last measure on the ground that the claim is not brought "upon contract"[78]; but this is scarcely a strong argument for allowing more than a rateable proportion. The claim may not be one for breach of contract, but it is based on the contract in the more important sense that it would not be available but for the relationship created by the (now discharged) contract. The Restatement § 468 (3) combines the first and third of these measures by providing that the measure of restitution is "the benefit derived from the performance ... not exceeding, however, a ratable proportion of the contract price". It has, however, been suggested that the proportion of the contract price should not merely limit recovery where it is *less* than the reasonable value, but be recoverable as such even where it exceeds that value.[79] Since the claim is for restitution of the benefit received by the defendant, that benefit ought to be the measure of recovery under the present heading. The cost (or even the value) of a part performance which does not confer a benefit is more appropriately dealt with under the principles (to be discussed later in this chapter[80]) which govern the recovery of reliance loss or wasted expenditure. To award it in full, irrespective of the receipt of any benefit, seems unduly to favour the performing party; it shifts the *whole* of the cost (or lost value) to the other party, leaving the former to bear only the loss of profit on the part of the performance which had not yet been rendered when the contract was

---

[74] See Restatement 2d, § 374, Illustration 2.

[75] *e.g. Young v Chicopee*, 2 N.E. 63 (1904); *Dame v Wood*, 70 A. 1081 (1908); *Carroll v Bowersock*, 164 P. 143 (1917); *Kelley v Thompson Land Co*, 164 S.E. 667 (1932); *West v Peoples' First National Bank & Trust Co*, 106 A. 2d 427 (1954); *cf.* in Scotland *Richardson v Dumfriesshire Road Trs* (1890) 17 R. 805; *Cantiare San Rocco SA v Clyde Shipbuilding & Engineering Co Ltd* [1924] A.C. 226 at 237.

[76] *e.g. Angus v Scully*, 57 N.E. 674 (1900); *City of Barnsdall v Curncutt*, 174 P. 2d 596 (1945).

[77] *e.g. Butterfield v Byron*, 27 N.E. 667, 669 (1891) ("at the contract price for all he did", *i.e.* at the contract rate); *Kinzer Construction Co v State*, 125 N.Y.S. 46 (1910); California Civil Code s.1514 ("ratable proportion of the consideration").

[78] *Keeling v Schastey & Vollmer*, 124 P. 445 at 446 (1912).

[79] Palmer, *Law of Restitution*, Vol.II, p.126.

[80] Below, paras 15–068 to 15–078.

discharged. Moreover the case for upholding the performing party's claim for the benefit of part of his bargain is weakened by the fact that the contract (which must form the basis of any such claim) was discharged before any payment under it became due by the paying party, as well as by the further consideration that the latter party will, in a case of frustration, have no remedy in respect of any prejudice that he may suffer by reason of receiving only a part of the promised performance. These conflicting interests are, it is submitted, more satisfactorily resolved by allowing claims in respect of benefits conferred and expenses wasted than by allowing partial recovery in respect of the loss of one party's bargain.

(c) *Law Reform (Frustrated Contracts) Act 1943, s.1(3)*

The unsatisfactory rule in *Appleby v Myers* was modified in England by s.1(3) of the Law Reform (Frustrated Contracts) Act 1943.[81] This provides that "Where any party to the contract has, by reason of anything done by any other party thereto in, or for the purpose of, the performance of the contract, obtained a valuable benefit (other than a payment of money to which [s.1(2)] applies) before the time of discharge, there shall be recoverable from him by the said other party such sum (if any), not exceeding the value of the said benefit to the party obtaining it, as the court considers just, having regard to all the circumstances of the case" and in particular to (a) the amount of any expenses incurred by the benefited party before the time of discharge, and (b) "the effect, in relation to the said benefit, of the circumstances giving rise to the frustration of the contract".

15–060

(i) Operation of s.1(3) of the 1943 Act

The subsection would, for example, apply if A agreed to decorate B's house for £2,500 payable on completion but died after decorating half the house. It would likewise apply if, after half the work had been done, further performance of the contract were made illegal by a supervening prohibition. Similarly, it is probable that the executrix in *Cutter v Powell*[82] could now rely on the subsection, as the defendant would have had the benefit of the deceased seaman's services during part of the voyage. The point is not wholly beyond doubt since the rate of pay specified by the contract was nearly four times the normal rate. This fact, coupled with the term stating that the wages were to be paid after the completion of the voyage, led Lord Kenyon to describe the arrangements as "a kind of insurance"[83]; and the 1943 Act does not apply to "any contract of insurance".[84] It is, however, submitted that the contract in *Cutter v Powell* was not literally a "contract of insurance" within the 1943 Act. That phrase seems to refer to a contract by which money is to be paid by an insurer and the "insurance" in *Cutter v Powell* took the form of *withholding*

15–061

---

[81] For contracts to which s.1(3) does not apply (or to which it applies only with modifications) see below, paras 15–083 *et seq.*

[82] Above, para.15–057.

[83] (1795) 6 T.R. 320 at 324; but it is scarcely plausible to regard the term as an "insurance" against the death, as opposed to the desertion, of the crew.

[84] s.2(5)(b); below, para.15–093.

a payment. But it is submitted that any sum recoverable in such a case should not be based on the exceptionally high contractual rate of pay.[85]

(ii) Measure of recovery

15-062   The measure of recovery under s.1(3) was the principal issue in *BP (Exploration) Libya Ltd v Hunt.*[86] The case arose out of an elaborate agreement between BP and Mr Hunt for the exploitation of an oil concession in Libya belonging to Mr Hunt. BP were to do all the work of exploration and development and to provide the necessary finance; they were also to make certain "farm-in" payments in cash and oil. In return, they were to get a half share in the concession; and, as soon as the field began to produce oil, they were to receive "reimbursement oil" (to be taken at the rate of three-eighths of Mr Hunt's share) until they had recouped 125 per cent of their initial expenditure. A large oil field was discovered and oil began to flow from it in 1967; but in 1971 the contract between BP and Mr Hunt was frustrated when their respective interests in the concession were expropriated by Libyan decrees. At this time, BP had received only about one third of the "reimbursement oil" to which they were entitled in respect of their initial expenditure; and they brought a claim under s.1(3) of the 1943 Act. The claim was allowed by Robert Goff J., whose decision was (subject to relatively minor modifications[87]) upheld by the Court of Appeal and the House of Lords. The learned judge held that, in considering a claim under s.1(3), the court must proceed in two stages: it must first identify and value the benefit obtained, and then assess the just sum (not exceeding the value of the benefit) which it was proper to award. At the first stage, he held that "benefit," on the true construction of s.1(3), referred, not to the cost of performance incurred by the claimant, but to the end product received by the other party.[88] In the case before him, that end product was the enhancement of the value of Mr Hunt's share in the concession resulting from BP's work; but because s.1(3)(b) required the court to have regard to "the effect, in relation to the said benefit of the circumstances giving rise to ... frustration", the value of that benefit had to be reduced to take account of the expropriation. In view of this fact, the total benefit obtained by Mr Hunt was the net amount of oil he had received from the concession, plus the compensation paid to him by the Libyan Government. Of this total, half was attributed to BP's efforts and half to Mr Hunt's original ownership

---

[85] *cf.* above, para.15–059.

[86] [1979] 1 W.L.R. 783; affirmed [1981] 1 W.L.R. 236; [1983] 2 A.C. 352; Baker [1979] C.L.J. 266.

[87] Recovery of a "farm-in" payment of $2m in cash had been allowed under s.1(3) when it plainly should have been allowed under s.1(2): see [1981] 1 W.L.R. 236 at 240; [1983] 2 A.C. 352 at 370; and see below, n.90.

[88] For this reason a claim for the "time value of money"—*i.e.* for the use that Mr Hunt could have made of the proceeds of the sale of the oil—was rejected for it was not shown that he did make such use. But interest on the award from the time of frustration was allowed under Law Reform (Miscellaneous Provisions) Act 1934, s.3 (see now Supreme Court Act 1981, s.35A(1), as inserted by Administration of Justice Act 1982, s.15).

of the concession. The value of this benefit was quantified at some $85m. In assessing the "just sum" to be awarded, however, Robert Goff J. adopted a criterion which he had rejected in valuing the benefit, namely the cost to BP of the work, to the extent that it was done for Mr Hunt. To this was added the value of the "farm in" oil[89] and the resulting total was then reduced by the amount of the reimbursement oil already received by BP. On this basis, the just sum was some $34.67m.[90] and, as the valuable benefit exceeded this amount, BP recovered the just sum in full.

(iii) Definition of "valuable benefit"

It follows from the definition of valuable benefit as the "end product" that s.1(3) will not apply merely because the claimant has incurred trouble and expense in or for the purpose of the performance of the contract.[91] Thus a person who orders goods from a manufacturer does not receive a valuable benefit merely because the manufacturer has before discharge bought the raw materials and started to make the goods. The manufacturer in such a case will only be able to recover his expenses if he can bring himself within the rules to be discussed later in this chapter which govern claims for expenditure wasted in consequence of discharge.[92]

15–063

On the other hand, there can be a valuable benefit within s.1(3) even though no physical thing (such as the machinery in *Appleby v Myers*) has been transferred by the claimant to the defendant. It is clear from *BP Exploration (Libya) Ltd v Hunt*[93] that the services rendered by the claimant to the defendant there constituted at least part of the benefit obtained by the defendant. There would similarly be a valuable benefit in the case of a contract to paint a house which was frustrated by illegality after half the work had been done: indeed, this was the example given by Lord Simon L.C. to illustrate the operation of s.1(3) when he introduced the measure in the House of Lords.[94] It is submitted that services in working a ship home (as in *Cutter v Powell*) would similarly be regarded as a valuable benefit for the purposes of s.1(3), even though it might not be easy to identify any "end product" resulting from those services. There may, indeed, be disagreement on the circumstances in which services can be regarded as benefits for the purpose of giving rise to restitutionary claims in general,[95] but the legislative history of s.1(3)[96] and *BP Exploration (Libya)*

---

[89] This value seems also to be relevant to the identification of the benefit.

[90] [1981] 1 W.L.R. 236 at 241; this contrasts with the figure of some $35.40m in [1979] 1 W.L.R. 783 at 827. The difference is not explained and may be due to the adoption of different currency conversion factors at first instance and in the Court of Appeal.

[91] This was precisely the position in *Taylor v Caldwell* (1863) 3 B. & S. 826: see above, para.2–028. For the court's power to allow the recipient of the benefit to deduct expenses, see below, para.15–073.

[92] Below, paras 15–070 to 15–075.

[93] Above, n.86.

[94] H.L. Deb., June 29, 1943, col.139.

[95] See Beatson, *Use and Abuse of Unjust Enrichment*, pp.31 *et seq.*

[96] See above, n.54.

Ltd v Hunt show that they can be so regarded for the purposes of s.1(3) so long as they have resulted in some economic advantage to the party to whom they were rendered. That advantage may consist in an addition to the value of that party's property, in a reduction to that party of the cost of completing the partly finished operation (as in the case of a house painter who dies after stripping off the old paint) or in the fact that the services have helped their recipient to perform contracts with third parties (as in *Cutter v Powell* if the ship in that case was carrying goods belonging to third parties).

The approach of regarding the "end product" as the valuable benefit seems also to be adopted by the New South Wales Frustrated Contracts Act 1978.[97] The British Columbia Frustrated Contracts Act 1974, however, takes a broader view, defining "benefit" as "something done in the fulfilment of contractual obligations, whether or not the person for whose benefit it was done received the benefit".[98] The South Australian Frustrated Contracts Act 1988 seems to take the same view.[99]

The definition of "valuable benefit" in terms of an "end product" may be appropriate in a case in which the contract is one by which one party is to do work which is intended to result in the improvement of the other party's property. But there are other contexts in which it is submitted that the definition would be inappropriate, *e.g.* where the contract was one for the hire of a chattel or for services to be rendered for a fixed period under a contract such as a time charter,[1] or for the performance of a specified task under a contract of employment, as in *Cutter v Powell*. Such contracts may not be intended to leave any "end product" in the hands of the hirer, the charterer or the employer, who can nevertheless be said to have had a "valuable benefit" from the use of the chattel or the fact that the shipowner's services were rendered for part of the stipulated period or that the employee had performed part of the specified task before (in all these cases) the contract was discharged. It would be unfortunate if s.1(3) were held to be inapplicable to such contracts merely because of the definition of valuable benefit adopted, in a wholly different context, in *BP Exploration (Libya) Ltd v Hunt*.

(iv) Benefit wholly destroyed by frustrating event

15–064   The machinery of the Act worked satisfactorily in *BP Exploration (Libya) Ltd v Hunt* because the value of the benefit, even when reduced in the light of the frustrating event, exceeded the just sum. But the position would have been different if the expropriation had occurred immediately before oil had begun to flow and if no compensation for expropriation had been paid by the Libyan Government. On the reasoning of the judgment, there would then have been no valuable benefit (beyond the "farm in" oil); for that reasoning has regard to "the circumstances giving rise to the frustration" within s.1(3)(b) in *valuing the benefit* rather than in *assessing the*

---

[97] s.11(2): "has received".
[98] s.5(4).
[99] See ss.3(1)(2)(c) and 7(2).
[1] s.1(3) does not apply to voyage charters: see s.2(5)(c), below, para.15–090.

just sum. The same reasoning is adopted in an example which closely resembles *Appleby v Myers*[2]: "Suppose that a contract for work on a building is frustrated by a fire which destroys the building and which therefore destroys a substantial amount of the work already done by the plaintiff. Although it *might be thought just* to award the plaintiff a sum assessed on a *quantum meruit* basis, the effect of s.1(3)(b) will be to reduce the award to nil ...".[3] The same view is supported by a Newfoundland case[4] decided under legislation substantially similar to the English Act of 1943.[5] There may also be some support for it in the legislative history of that Act; for when introducing the Bill in the House of Lords, Lord Simon L.C. illustrated the operation of s.1(3) by reference to a case in which a contract to paint a house was frustrated after half the work had been done, but in which the cause of frustration was supervening illegality, so that a benefit was left in the hands of the house-owner.[6] If no award can be made under s.1(3) where the benefit has been destroyed by the frustrating event, then the actual decision in *Appleby v Myers* would not be affected by the Act; but in view of the evident reluctance with which Robert Goff J. (in the dictum quoted above) reached this conclusion, it is submitted that an alternative interpretation of s.1(3) is to be preferred. This would make the destruction of the benefit relevant, not to the identification of the benefit, but to the assessment of the just sum. Two points seem to support such an interpretation. First, s.1(3) is expressed to apply where a valuable benefit has been obtained "*before* the time of discharge"[7]: thus to identify the benefit in a case like *Appleby v Myers* the court must look at the facts as they were before, and not after, the fire. The partly completed installation would at least *prima facie* be a benefit, in that completion of the installation would be likely to cost less after part of the work had been done. The second point arises from the structure of the subsection. This begins by setting out the circumstances in which the court has power to make an award (*i.e.* when a valuable benefit has been obtained) and then provides guidelines for the exercise of that power. The guideline contained in s.1(3)(b) is introduced by the words "such sum as the court thinks just having regard to ... (b) ..."; and these words seem to link the guideline to the *exercise* rather than to the *existence* of the court's discretion. This interpretation cannot cause any injustice, for if the court takes the view that "in all the circumstances of the case" very little or nothing should be awarded it can exercise its discretion to that effect; and for this purpose the court can certainly take the destruction of the benefit into account so as to split the loss in such proportions as the court thinks just. But if such destruction necessarily led to the conclusion that no valuable benefit had been obtained before frustration, the court would have no discretion to

---

[2] (1867) L.R. 2 C.P. 651; above, para.15–057.
[3] [1979] 1 W.L.R. 783 at 801 (italics supplied).
[4] *Parsons Bros Ltd v Shea* (1966) 53 D.L.R. 36.
[5] Canadian Uniform Frustrated Contracts Act, s.4(1), which had been adopted in Newfoundland.
[6] H.L. Deb., June 29, 1943, col.139: "You have got your house half painted".
[7] This is also true of the Canadian Act cited in n.5 above.

award anything at all. It would be a pity if this useful discretion were restricted in a way that is neither clearly required by the words of the subsection nor necessary to promote justice. Legislation in British Columbia, New South Wales and South Australia expressly entitles the party who has conferred a benefit to make a claim in respect of it even where it has been destroyed by the supervening event; but provides that the loss resulting from such destruction is to be apportioned equally between the parties.[8] This solution looks attractive, but the arbitrariness of the rule of equal division can lead to unsatisfactory results, *e.g.* where one party (but not the other) is covered by insurance against the loss[9] or where the frustrating event, though causing him loss in relation to the particular contract in question, benefits him in other ways.[10] The New South Wales and South Australian Acts indeed recognise that the rule of equal division may not be a satisfactory one in all cases and give the court a discretion to depart from it in exceptional circumstances.[11] The British Columbia Act enables the court to reach a similar result as a matter of construction of the contract, and also provides for the total exclusion of the right to restitution by course of dealing, custom or implied term.[12]

(v) Assessing the just sum

15–065 Subject to the limitation that the sum awarded must not exceed the value of the "benefit",[13] the amount of the just sum to be awarded under s.1(3) is a matter for the discretion of the trial judge, in the sense that an appellate court will not interfere with his assessment unless it is plainly based on mistaken principles of law.[14] This follows from the reference in s.1(3) to "such sum ... as the court considers just". It seems that the position would be the same under legislation (in other common law countries) based on the English Act.[15] No such discretion is in terms

---

[8] British Columbia Frustrated Contracts Act 1974, s.5(3); New South Wales Frustrated Contracts Act 1978, s.13; see also s.11(2)(b)(ii); South Australian Frustrated Contracts Act 1988, ss.3(3), 7(2)(c).

[9] This point is not deprived of its validity by s.1(5) of the Law Reform (Frustrated Contracts) Act 1943, which directs the court to take no account of sums which have become payable (*inter alia*) to a party making a claim under s.1(3). For one thing, s.1(5) says nothing about sums becoming so payable to the other party to the frustrated contract; for another, the subsection is subject to exceptions: see below, paras 15–079 to 15–082.

[10] *e.g.* by increasing the price of his products: *cf.* above para.6–009 discussing *Eastern Airlines Inc v Gulf Oil Corp*, 415 F. Supp. 429, where this reasoning was a ground for denying discharge on the ground of alleged impracticability. Such denial might not have been possible if the ground for claiming discharge from the contract in suit had been impossibility or illegality. See also the possibility described below, para.15–072, at n.39.

[11] New South Wales Act (above), s.15; South Australian Act (above), s.7(4).

[12] ss.2 and 6(1).

[13] s.1(3) in terms imposes this limitation.

[14] This was the view of the Court of Appeal in *BP Exploration (Libya) Ltd v Hunt* [1981] 1 W.L.R. 236 at 238; in the House of Lords, the point was left open: [1983] 2 A.C. 352 at 367.

[15] See above, para.15–049, n.42.

conferred on the court by the British Columbia, New South Wales and South Australian Acts, though the lack of precise criteria for evaluating benefits will in practice involve a considerable discretionary element in the making of awards under those Acts. In New South Wales and South Australia the court is (as already noted) empowered in exceptional circumstances, to depart from the rules governing awards in respect of benefits conferred before discharge.[16]

(vi) "Payments" in kind

There is a significant difference between the structure of s.1(2) and that of s.1(3) of the 1943 Act. Under s.1(2), sums of money payable before frustration cease to be payable on frustration. The subsection applies only to "sums paid or payable", *i.e.* to payments of money. Section 1(3), by contrast, applies to other benefits, *e.g.* where A renders services or transfers property to B before frustration. But nothing in s.1(3) in terms releases A where before frustration he ought to have performed an obligation to do something other than to pay cash and has failed to do so, but would, if he had performed, have been entitled to make a claim under s.1(3). Thus if A has promised to make an advance payment in *cash* and has failed before frustration to do so, he is released by s.1(2); but if the stipulated payment had been in *kind* he would not be released by s.1(3). Nor can he, in the latter case, neutralise his liability by making a claim under s.1(3), for B has not "by reason of anything done [by A] obtained a valuable benefit ... *before* the time of discharge". On the contrary, B has failed to obtain an expected benefit by reason of something not done by A. B may *after* the time of discharge obtain a benefit by suing A, but this does not bring the case within s.1(3) as the benefit is obtained too late. Nor would it help A to argue that before the time of discharge B had a valuable benefit, namely his right to sue A, for this benefit would not have been obtained "by reason of anything done [by A] in or for the purpose of the performance of the contract". It is hard to believe that these consequences were intended. The failure of the Act to provide for the release of obligations other than those to pay cash, in circumstances in which the performance of those obligations would (if rendered before discharge) have given rise to a claim for restitution under s.1(3), seems to be a *casus omissus*.

15–066

(vii) Benefit received by another person

Section 1(6) enables the court to make an award not only against the recipient of the valuable benefit but also against a person who has assumed obligations under the contract in consideration of the conferring of a benefit on another person, whether that person is a party to the contract or not. Thus if A promises B to pay B for work which benefits C, B can, if the other requirements of s.1(3) are satisfied, make a claim under that subsection against A. If C is a party to the contract, B will also be able to make a claim against C under s.1(3); but if C is not a party to the contract B's only claim under the Act will be against A.

15–067

---

[16] New South Wales Frustrated Contracts Act 1978, s.15; South Australian Frustrated Contracts Act 1988, s.7(4).

(3) **Reliance loss**

15–068 The reliance loss with which this discussion is concerned usually takes the form of expenses incurred under a frustrated contract and wasted as a result of the events giving rise to discharge.

(a) *No remedy under English common law*

15–069 The original common law rule in England was that the party who had incurred the expenses had no remedy in respect of them. This position is illustrated by *Taylor v Caldwell*[17] itself, in which the hirers' claim was for the recovery of their wasted expenses, and that claim was rejected precisely because the contract had been discharged. The rule could be varied by the express terms of the contract, as, for example, in one of the coronation cases in which the contract provided that, if the procession were cancelled, the price of the ticket should be repaid, but with a deduction to cover the payee's expenses.[18] Even if the contract did not expressly provide for a remedy in respect of wasted expenses, it was sometimes construed so as to produce this result.[19] In the absence of such provisions, the coronation cases provided no direct remedy to the party who had incurred expenses. In a case[20] connected with the Spithead naval review, an action for the return of an advance payment was dismissed (in accordance with the law as it then stood[21]). Bigham J. suggested to the payee that he should retain no more of the payment than was necessary to cover his expenses; but the Court of Appeal held that the payee's refusal to accede to this futuristic[22] proposal was not a ground for depriving him of his costs.

The rule that the party to whom the contract price had been paid before the frustrating event was entitled to retain the payment in full was, in some of the coronation cases, justified precisely on the ground that the payee had, or was likely to have incurred expenses,[23] but the outcome in such cases was in turn open to the criticism that it went too far in protecting the payee, since his expenses were hardly likely to amount to the whole of the contract price. The only type of situation in which the rule achieved a sort of rough justice was that which arose in *Krell v Henry*,[24] in which the claimant was allowed to retain the £25 which had been paid before the time of discharge, although he had no claim to the balance of £50 which had not yet become due at that time. As the claimant had presumably incurred expenses (such as his solicitor's charges in negotiating the contract with the defendant), the result was a not wholly unsatisfactory

---

[17] (1863) 3 B. & S. 826.

[18] *Victoria Seats Agency v Paget* (1902) 19 T.L.R. 16 (second contract).

[19] *Elliott v Crutchley* [1904] 1 K.B. 565; [1906] A.C. 7, above, para.12–004.

[20] *Civil Service Co-operative Soc Ltd v General SN Co* [1903] 2 K.B. 757.

[21] Above, para.15–047.

[22] See now Law Reform (Frustrated Contracts) Act 1943, s.1(2), proviso, below, para.15–071.

[23] *e.g.* in *Blakeley v Muller & Co* [1903] 2 K.B. 760n; *Lumsden v Barton & Co* (1902) 19 T.L.R. 53.

[24] [1903] 2 K.B. 740; above, para.7–010.

form of loss-splitting. But this depended on the accident that part of the agreed price was paid before, and the balance payable after, the time of discharge, and that the part paid before that time was a relatively small part of the price. If the price had been wholly paid or payable before the time of discharge, or if it had been wholly payable after that time, the result would have been less satisfactory: in the former case, the payee would have received or been entitled to too much to cover his expenses, and in the latter he would have been entitled to nothing at all. And the result in *Krell v Henry* amounted to no more than rough justice since the amount of the prepayment (which the claimant was allowed to retain) does not seem to have borne any direct relationship to the expenses which he had incurred or was likely to incur.

Even this degree of rough justice could no longer be achieved after the House of Lords had in the *Fibrosa* case[25] held that money paid before discharge could be recovered back by the payor if there had been a total failure of consideration. It will be recalled that in that case £1,600 out of the price of £4,800 to be paid for machinery to be manufactured by the sellers was payable before discharge; and that £1,000 had been so paid. The House of Lords upheld the buyers' claim for the return of the £1,000; but at the same time it criticised[26] the resulting position under which the sellers had no remedy in respect of any expenses which had been incurred by them in performing the contract, and which would have been wholly or partly wasted if the machinery could not have been disposed of to third parties, or could only have been so disposed of at a loss. The stipulation for prepayment might have been intended precisely to protect the sellers against this risk; if so, the actual result in the *Fibrosa* case was scarcely more satisfactory than the opposite result in some of the coronation cases. On the other hand, the solution in the *Fibrosa* case was clearly preferable to that reached in those cases if the purpose of the stipulation for prepayment was merely to improve the seller's cash-flow or to reduce his credit risks.

(b) *Expenses as limiting statutory restitution claims*

The criticisms of the law in the *Fibrosa* case led, shortly afterwards, to the **15–070** passing of the Law Reform (Frustrated Contracts) Act 1943, which now governs the law relating to expenses incurred under frustrated contracts. Under the Act, such expenses are relevant almost exclusively as limits on restitution claims against the party who has incurred them; there is only one situation in which they give rise to an independent claim.[27] We shall see that independent claims in respect of expenses have a wider scope in American law.

---

[25] [1943] A.C. 32; above, para.15–048.

[26] *ibid.* at 49 and 69–72, *per* Lord Wright who had been Chairman of the Law Revision Committee which in its 7th Interim Report (Cmd. 6009) had made similar criticisms of the law.

[27] Below, at n.30 and below, para.15–076.

(i) Section 1(2) proviso: expenses and prepayments

15–071 Under the common law and statutory rules discussed earlier in this chapter, a party to whom money has been paid before the time of discharge must return it to the payor.[28] If, however, the payee has, before the time of discharge, incurred expenses in or for the purpose of the performance of the contract, the proviso to s.1(2) of the 1943 Act gives the court power, "if it considers it just to do so"[29] to allow the payee to retain "the whole or part of the sums so paid, not being an amount in excess of the expenses so incurred". The proviso also applies where money is payable[30] before the time of discharge but has not been paid: in that case, the court may allow the prospective payee to recover expenses incurred before the time of discharge, subject to the same restrictions as those which apply where a party seeks wholly or in part to retain payments already made at the time of discharge. In neither case can the amount which may be retained or recovered in respect of expenses exceed the amount which was paid or payable in pursuance of the contract before the time of discharge, nor can it exceed the amount of the expenses.[31] There is no power to make an allowance or award in respect of expenses where there was neither a prepayment nor any stipulation for prepayment. Thus the proviso would not apply on facts such as those of *Taylor v Caldwell.*[32]

15–072 Subject to the restrictions just stated,[33] the amount to be allowed or awarded is within the discretion of the court.[34] In exercising that discretion, the court will no doubt be influenced by the extent to which the expenses, or their product, have been made useless by the frustrating event. If, for example, machinery made for one customer can readily be sold to another, the court is likely to allow (or award) the payee (or prospective payee) little or nothing.[35] If, on the other hand, the expenses do not result in any product, or if the product in consequence of the frustrating event loses all or most of its value, the court is likely to award a substantial amount. Even in such a case, the court will not necessarily make the maximum award available under the Act. Suppose that in the *Fibrosa* case[36] the seller's expenses had amounted to exactly the £1,600, which was to be prepaid. To allow the seller to retain (or recover) the whole of this sum would shift the

---

[28] Above, paras 15–048, 15–050.

[29] Disregarding the proceeds of insurance payable to the claimant: s.1(5), below, para.15–079.

[30] The words "so payable" in the proviso refer back to the words "shall ... in the case of sums so payable, cease to be so payable" which occur earlier in s.1(2).

[31] These limits follow from the words of the proviso: "the whole or any part of the sums so paid or payable, not being an amount in excess of the expenses so incurred".

[32] (1863) 3 B. & S. 826.

[33] At n.31; and see n.29.

[34] This follows from the words in the proviso that the court "may, if it considers it just to do so" make an allowance or award of in respect of the expenses.

[35] *cf. Lobb v Vasey Housing Authority War Widows Guild* [1963] V.R. 239, a case decided under the Victorian Frustrated Contracts Act 1959, the language of which closely resembles that of the English 1943 Act.

[36] [1943] A.C. 32.

whole loss of the wasted expense to the buyer, and this might be as unjust as the actual result in that case, which was to leave the whole of this loss to be borne by the seller. One view is that it would be fairer to divide the loss; and a rule of equal division of loss has been laid down by statute in British Columbia, New South Wales and South Australia.[37] While the principle of dividing the loss may often be appropriate, the rule of *equal* division appears to be unnecessarily rigid (and was indeed rejected in England by the Law Revision Committee[38]). It leaves out of account the possibility that the prepayment or stipulation for prepayment reflected the intention of the parties to throw the risk that the expense might be wasted on the payor or that one of the parties was more easily than the other, able to take steps to mitigate the loss caused by the frustrating event. When, for example, a seller of goods is prohibited by supervening illegality from shipping the goods to the buyer, it is likely to be easier for the seller than for the buyer to dispose of the goods under a substitute contract and so to reduce the loss: this may well have been the position in the *Fibrosa*[39] case where, because of the war-time conditions, the buyer seems to have had no physical access to the goods and where his legal power to deal with them must have been (to say the least) reduced by those conditions. It is finally arguable that a rule of equal division fails adequately to take account of the fact that one party may have a better opportunity than the other of providing against the event by insurance or that one party may actually have the benefit of insurance, while the other has not. One possible answer to this argument[40] is that, in considering whether any sum ought to be recovered or in considering whether a party is to be allowed to recover or retain any sum in respect of (*inter alia*) expenses, s.1(5) of the Act[41] requires the court in general, to leave out of account "any sums which have, by reason of the circumstances giving rise to the frustration of the contract, become payable to that party under any contract of insurance". But in the first place this argument does not cover the case where that party has had the *opportunity* to insure and has simply failed to take it; nor, secondly, does the wording of s.1(5) apply where sums are payable under a contract of insurance, not to the party to the frustrated contract making the claim under s.1(2), but to the *other* party to that contract.[42] Both these circumstances may provide grounds for rejecting the principle of equal division, and such grounds may also exist in the exceptional cases in which under s.1(5), insurance receipts *can* be taken

---

[37] British Columbia Frustrated Contracts Act 1974, s.5(3) and (4); New South Wales Frustrated Contracts Act 1978, s.11(2)(b)(ii); *cf.* s.13; South Australian Frustrated Contracts Act 1988, s.7(2)(c); *cf.* also the German "*Bohrhämmer*" case MDR 1953, 282, BGH January 16, 1953 where the buyer was required to bear one-quarter of the seller's costs when the buyer's export purpose was frustrated. It is highly unlikely that in the circumstances of that case the contract would be discharged in English law: *cf.* above, para.7–028.

[38] 7th Interim Report (Cmd. 6009), p.7.

[39] [1943] A.C. 32. See also the possibility described in above, para.15–064, n.10.

[40] See *Gamerco SA v ICM/Fair Warning (Agency) Ltd* [1995] 1 W.L.R. 1126 at 1234.

[41] Below, para.15–079, and see paras 15–022 and 15–093, where the subsection was discussed in the previous edition of this book.

[42] See below, para.15–080 and above, para.15–064, at nn.9, 10.

into account, *i.e.* where "there was an obligation to insure imposed by the express terms of the frustrated contract or by or under any enactment". The English rule, under which all the above circumstances can be taken into account in assessing the amount to be retained or recovered is, from this point of view, preferable to a rigid rule of equal division. This point is sometimes reflected in contractual provisions relating to wasted expenses.[43] It is also recognised in the New South Wales and South Australian legislation,[44] which enables the court in exceptional circumstances to depart from the rule of equal division.

In exercising its power to make an allowance or award in respect of the payee's expenses, the court can take account of the fact that expenses have been incurred, not only by the payee, but also by the *payor*. This was the position in the *Gamerco*[45] case, where the promoter of a "pop concert" had made an advance payment to the musicians and the contract was then frustrated.[46] Exercising a "broad discretion",[47] the court allowed the promoter to recover back the advance payment in full, without any deduction in respect of the expenses incurred by the musicians for the purpose of performing the contract.[48] It did so on the ground that the promoter had also incurred expenses which exceeded the prepayment[49] and amounted to about nine times those incurred by the musicians[50]; and that as a result of the frustration of the contract, each set of expenses had been wholly wasted.

(ii) Section 1(3)(a): expenses and valuable benefits

15–073   The proviso to s.1(2) applies only where a prepayment is made, or to be made, in money. It would not, for example, apply where a "prepayment"

---

[43] In *Victoria Seats Agency v Paget* (1902) 19 T.L.R. 16 (second contract) the provision for retention of 10 per cent of the price of the ticket can scarcely have been intended to produce an equal division of the loss resulting from waste of expenditure.

[44] New South Wales Frustrated Contracts Act 1978, s.15; South Australian Frustrated Contracts Act 1988, s.7(4); *cf.* above, para.15–064, at nn.11, 12.

[45] *Gamerco SA v ICM/Fair Warning (Agency) Ltd* [1995] 1 W.L.R. 1226.

[46] Above para.8–009.

[47] [1995] 1 W.L.R. 1226 at 1236.

[48] The court was also required by s.1(5) of the Act (see above, para.15–022 and below, para.15–079), to disregard the fact that both parties to the contract had insured against cancellation and had received payments under those policies. The court seems to have regarded s.1(5) as applying in relation both to the promoter's claim to recover back the advance payment and to the musicians' claim to retain part of this prepayment in respect of their expenses: this accounts for the view expressed at 1234 that *both* parties' insurances were to be disregarded by virtue of s.1(5). It is, however, with respect, open to doubt whether the reason for disregarding the promoter's insurance lay in s.1(5); it seems that such insurance was simply irrelevant by virtue of the mandatory words of the main part of s.1(2), as opposed to the discretionary nature of the proviso to s.1(2) (to which s.1(5) no doubt applies): see below, para.15–080.

[49] The promoter's expenses exceeded $450,000; the prepayment to the musicians amounted to $412,000.

[50] The musicians' expenses appear to have been about $50,000.

was made in kind.[51] But if A made such a "payment" to B, a "valuable benefit" within s.1(3) would be received by B; and in deciding how much A can recover in respect of that benefit, the court is directed by s.1(3)(a) to have regard to "the amount of any expenses incurred before the time of discharge by the benefited party [B] in or for the purpose of the performance of the contract". So far as the allowance for expenses is concerned, the court can therefore reach the same result where a "prepayment" has been made in kind as where it has been made in cash, *i.e.* it can allow A to recover a "just sum" in respect of the "valuable benefit" obtained by B, but it can, in assessing this sum, have regard to expenses (of the kind described in s.1(3)(b)) incurred by B.

The above reasoning, however, applies only where a prepayment in kind *has* been made before the time of discharge. Where such a payment was due but had not been made before that time, A's obligation to make it is (unlike an obligation to pay cash before the time of discharge) not released.[52] Section 1(3) therefore does not give B any claim in respect of expenses as such, for under that subsection expenses are taken into account only by way of reduction of A's restitution claim in respect of a "valuable benefit" obtained by B; and in the case put A has no such claim. B's remedy appears to be to claim the "prepayment" in kind or damages for failing to make it.[53] In an action for damages, expenses saved by B could no doubt be relied on by A in reduction of B's loss. Expenses incurred by B in or for the purpose of performing the contract might at first sight seem to increase that loss, but they would not be recoverable in addition to the value of the promised "prepayment" in kind since such an award would have the effect of putting B into a position better than that in which he would have been if the contract had (up to the time of discharge) been duly performed.[54] Where B is entitled to damages in respect of A's failure to render the performance promised by A, there can be no question of B's having any further claim for expenses incurred by him in order to become entitled to that performance. In the situation here discussed a variant of the unsatisfactory rule in *Chandler v Webster*[55] appears to survive: it would, for example, seem still to apply if the "price" for the hire of the rooms had been 10 cases of champagne deliverable (but not delivered) a week before the time of discharge.

---

[51] See above, para.15–066.

[52] Above, para.15–066.

[53] In para.15–048, above, it was argued that the court should not order A to make a payment in cash to B where, on receipt of the payment, B would immediately come under an obligation to restore it. This argument would not apply directly to the case put in the text above, for if in that case A were ordered to make the prepayment in kind, B's obligation would not be one to return the "prepayment" as such: it would be no more than one to pay a "just sum" under s.1(3) to A in respect of the benefit received by B.

[54] *Cullinane v British "Rema" Manufacturing Co Ltd* [1954] 1 Q.B. 292; *C & P Haulage v Middleton* [1983] 1 W.L.R. 1461.

[55] [1904] 1 K.B. 493, above, para.15–047.

(iii) Relationship between s.1(2) and (3)

15–074 The power to make an award in respect of a valuable benefit under s.1(3) is in theory additional to the power to make an award of expenses under s.1(2). Thus if A has incurred expenses and has also conferred a valuable benefit on B and received (or stipulated for) a prepayment of money from B, then A can claim an allowance in respect of the expenses (or recover them) under s.1(2) and he can also make a claim in respect of the valuable benefit under s.1(3). But to avoid double recovery, any amount allowed or awarded in respect of expenses under s.1(2) will be taken into account in deciding how much should be awarded in respect of the valuable benefit under s.1(3); and conversely.[56]

(iv) Meaning of "expenses"

15–075 This term is broadly defined in s.1(4) so as to include overhead expenses and work or services performed personally by the party making the claim in respect of expenses.[57] The result of this definition appears to be that many forms of reliance loss are included within the concept of "expenses" for the purposes of the Act. It also suggests that the requirement that expenses must be incurred "in, or for the purpose of, the performance of the contract"[58] will be broadly interpreted, for the relationship between overhead expenses and the performance of the contract is necessarily indirect. The operation of the definition may be illustrated by reference to an American case[59] in which the plaintiff had transferred stock to the defendant who had, in return, rendered services to the plaintiff. On discharge of the contract, the plaintiff recovered part of the stock, the defendant retaining the rest in respect of the services which he had rendered. A similar result could be reached in England under s.1(3) and (4) of the 1943 Act.

It has been said that "the allowance for expenses is probably best rationalised as a statutory recognition of the defence of change of position".[60] This rationalisation may explain some of the situations discussed above, but is it respectfully submitted that it does not satisfactorily explain them all. For one thing, it would suggest that only expenses incurred *after* the time of contracting can be taken into account; but this would be inconsistent with the power of the court to include overhead expenses "in respect of any work",[61] expenses of this kind being often incurred *before* the time of contracting. For another, expenses can,

---

[56] This seems to be the result of the somewhat obscure concluding words of s.1(3)(a).

[57] s.1(4).

[58] s.1(2) proviso, s.1(3)(a).

[59] *Tulsa Opera House v Mitchell*, 24 P. 2d 997 (1933).

[60] *BP Exploration (Libya) Ltd v Hunt* [1979] 1 W.L.R. 783 at 800; affirmed without reference to this point [1983] 2 A.C. 352; for the recognition of the defence (to claims for restitution) of change of position see *Lipkin Gorman v Karpnale Ltd* [1992] 2 A.C. 548.

[61] Law Reform (Frustrated Contracts) Act 1943, s.1(4).

under the proviso to s.1(2), form the basis of an *independent claim*,[62] no less than of an allowance reducing a restitution claim; and in the former case they can hardly illustrate "the *defence* of change of position". Finally it is submitted that to exclude pre-contract expenses from the scope of the Act could lead to results which can fairly be described as capricious: for example, a c.i.f. seller to whom part of the price was paid or payable in advance[63] could retain or recover expenses relating to shipment where the goods were shipped after the time of contracting, but not if at that time they were already afloat. It seems hard, from a commercial point of view, to justify this distinction.

(c) *An independent claim for expenses?*

Under the 1943 Act, the fact that a party has incurred expenses is, in general, relevant only in that it can lead to a reduction of the restitution claims which are available against that party in respect of money paid to, or a valuable benefit obtained by, him before the time of discharge. A party who has incurred expenses has (under the Act) an independent claim in respect of them only where the contract provides for a payment of money to be made to him before discharge and that payment has not been made[64]; and even then the claim is limited by the amount of the stipulated prepayment.[65] The mere fact that a party had incurred expenses would not give rise to a claim under the 1943 Act. In *Taylor v Caldwell*[66] the hirers (and probably also the defendants) had incurred expenses, but no payment was made or had become due under the contract before the time of discharge, nor had any valuable benefit been obtained before that time by either party. The hirers' claim for damages (which was restricted to one for their wasted expenses) was rejected; and this result would not be affected by the 1943 Act.

In the United States, the courts have for some time recognised an independent claim for such expenses. A case which may be contrasted with *Taylor v Caldwell* is *Angus v Scully*,[67] where a contract had been made to move a house from one street to another. When the house had been moved about half-way to its intended new site, it was destroyed by an accidental fire for which neither party was responsible. It was held that the contractor was entitled to the reasonable cost of his work. In England, he would have no such right either at common law,[68] or under s.1(2) of the 1943 Act (since there had been no prepayment nor any stipulation for prepayment), or under (probably) s.1(3) of that Act (since his work was intended, but had failed, to leave an "end product" in the hands of the

15–076

---

[62] *i.e.* where a payment of money should under the contract have been made before the time of discharge but was not made: above para.15–071, after n.30.

[63] As in the *Fibrosa* case [1943] A.C. 32.

[64] See above, paras 15–071, after n.30 and 15–075; the words "payable" and "recover" in the proviso to s.1(2) can lead to this result.

[65] s.1(2) proviso: "the whole or any part *of the sums so . . . payable*".

[66] (1863) 3 B. & S. 826.

[67] 57 N.E. 674 (1900).

[68] *Appleby v Myers* (1867) L.R. 2 C.P. 651; above, para.15–057.

customer[69]). The English common law does not, in general, recognise any independent claim in respect of wasted expenses but may do so in exceptional circumstances, *e.g.* where the expenses were incurred after the frustrating event had occurred and this fact was known to one party but not to the other who then incurred the expenses. In one such case, the former party was held liable for the wasted expenses, and this decision can be explained on the ground that that party had impliedly undertaken, by a contract collateral to the frustrated contract and surviving its discharge, to notify the other party of the frustrating event and so to prevent him from incurring the expenses.[70]

15–077   The American tendency to compensate a party for expenses incurred before, and wasted in consequence of, discharge is also reflected in the rules governing the measure of recovery in restitution claims for benefits other than money, one possible measure being the value of services rendered by the plaintiff.[71] Application of this measure in the present context may sometimes amount to an award of reliance loss under the guise of restitution. In a case like *Angus v Scully*, it could be argued that, although nothing of value had been transferred to the house-owner, he had nevertheless received value from the contractor's part performance in the sense that, after the part performance, completion of performance would (if the house had not been destroyed by fire) have cost less than the full performance originally bargained for. But American cases have gone further than this and have allowed claims for reliance loss in cases in which nothing of value was transferred even in the sense just described. In the *Albre Marble*[72] case, work was done by a subcontractor in preparing samples and drawings and making tests. This work did not benefit the main contractor, who was nevertheless held liable to the subcontractor for the expense of the work when the contract between them was later discharged by supervening events. To the extent that the court relies on s.1(2) of the English Act,[73] its reasoning is, with respect, erroneous, for under that subsection there would be no power to allow or award expenses in the

---

[69] Thus *Angus v Scully* probably would not fall within any of the exceptions to the requirement of an "end product" for the purpose of s.1(3); for this requirement, see above, para.15–063; for suggested exceptions to it, see *ibid.* after n.99. For the defendant's possible liability in restitution on another ground, see below, para.15–077.

[70] See the discussion of *Robinson v Davison* (1876) L.R. 6 Ex. 269, above, para.5–035. Expenses incurred in the performance of ancillary obligations which survive discharge of the contract may similarly be recoverable (see above, para.15–033) Common law restitution claims may also be available in respect of services rendered after discharge: see above, para.15–041. But such claims differ in their legal nature from claims for reliance loss (in the form of wasted expenses) incurred by one party after discharge since such expenses may not result in any benefit to the other party.

[71] Above, para.15–059.

[72] *Albre Marble and Tile Co v John Bowen & Co*, 155 N.E. 2d 437 (1959); *cf.* Restatement 2d, Introductory Note to Ch.2 (Vol.II, p.311).

[73] 155 N.E. 2d 437 at 440.

absence of a prepayment or of a stipulation for prepayment. The actual decision is probably explicable on two grounds: first, that the work was specifically requested by the main contractor under a clause in the contract entitling him to make such requests; and secondly, that the main contractor was thought to have had some degree of responsibility for the supervening event, though not such a degree as to rule out the doctrine of discharge in accordance with the principles discussed in Ch.14. These factors may reconcile the case with other American decisions, especially those involving building contracts, denying recovery to contractors who could prove no more than that they had incurred reliance loss, and indicating that claims in respect of part performance before discharge could succeed only if the claimant's work and materials had been incorporated in the structure.[74] The claim would then be one for restitution rather than one for pure reliance loss.

A further possible distinction which could be used to restrict claims for reliance loss is that between *necessary* reliance (that is, costs incurred by a party in the performance of his duties under the contract) and *incidental* reliance (that is, costs incurred by a party in his own interest in reliance on the contract).[75] The successful claims in *Angus v Scully* and in the *Albre Marble* case related to costs of the first kind. But § 272(2) of the Restatement 2d makes no use of this distinction when it gives the courts a general discretion to protect "the parties' reliance interests" where simple discharge "will not avoid injustice". It is hard to predict how such a discretion might operate; but it could severely limit the operation of the doctrine of discharge. It could, for example, reverse the actual result in *Taylor v Caldwell* where the only claim made by the hirers was in respect of their reliance loss. That claim seems to have been mainly for the recovery of the hirers wasted advertising expenses, and hence one for "incidental" reliance, since the contract entitled, but did not oblige, the hirers to advertise the planned concerts, so that the advertising expenses were incurred by them simply in their own interest. But it does not seem that the claim was restricted to such expenses: it was one for the hirers' costs "in advertising the concerts, and ... in preparing for the concerts". It is at least possible that the claim included an element of "necessary" reliance in the shape of costs incurred by the hirers in performing their contractual obligation "to find and provide, at their own costs, all the necessary artistes for the said contracts"; and claims in respect of necessary reliance have been allowed in some of the American authorities discussed above. The decision in *Taylor v Caldwell*, rejecting the hirers' claim for reliance loss, has generally been regarded as the single most significant advance in the development of the common law doctrine of discharge. It would be a supreme irony if, in the United States, a court could reach the opposite conclusion on the same facts by virtue of the discretion described in

15–078

---

[74] *e.g. Young v City of Chicopee*, 72 N.E. 63 (1904); *Carroll v Bowersock*, 164 P. 143 (1917).

[75] For the use of this distinction in another context, see Fuller and Perdue, 46 Yale L.J. 52, 78; Restatement 2d, § 349, Comment a.

§ 272(2) of the Restatement 2d. There is no trace of a similar discretion in English law.

(4) **Insurance**

(a) *Section 1(5)*

15–079 This subsection of the 1943 Act provides that: "In considering whether any sum ought to be recovered or retained under the foregoing provisions of this section by any party to the contract, the court shall not take into account any sums which have, by reason of the circumstances giving rise to the frustration of the contract, become payable to that party under any contract of insurance[76] unless there was an obligation to insure imposed by an express term of the frustrated contract or by or under any enactment." It will be seen that the structure of the subsection is that of a general rule (under which insurance proceeds must be disregarded) followed by an exception (under which such proceeds can be taken into account). The assumption underlying the subsection appears to be that the insurance has been paid for by the party claiming the right to retain or recover a sum of money under s.1(1) to (4), and that the other party should not obtain a windfall benefit as a result of that payment.[77] As the following discussion will show, that assumption is by no means always well-founded.

(b) *Scope of s.1(5)*

15–080 The phrase "recovered or retained" in s.1(5) mirrors the words "to retain or ... recover" in the proviso to s.1(2), so that a claim by a person, to whom a prepayment has been or was to have been made, to retain or recover the whole or any part of that prepayment in respect of his expenses is not to be affected by the fact that sums had been paid or become payable under a contract of insurance "*to that party*" by reason of the occurrence of the frustrating event. As already noted[78] there is nothing in s.1(5) to prevent the court from taking into account for this purpose the fact that sums had been so paid or become payable to the *other* party to the frustrated contract.

Section 1(5) may operate in relation to insurance moneys which have become payable to both parties where each asks the court to exercise its

---

[76] The contract of insurance itself is not subject to the provisions to which s.1(5) refers: see s.2(5)(b), below, para.15–093.

[77] The origin of s.1(5) can be traced back to the Law Revision Committee's 7th Interim Report, Cmd. 6009 (1939), p.8, where no reasons for the recommendation that "no regard shall be had to amounts receivable under any contracts of insurance" are given. A policy reason for s.1(5) can be inferred from Lord Simon L.C.'s description of the insurance as "purely collateral" in H.L. Deb., July 8, 1943, col.368 and from its description as "quite irrelevant" by Lord Wright, *ibid.*, col.369. Such policy considerations can be compared with the rule that, in general, insurance receipts are not to be taken into account in reducing damages: *Bradburn v Great Western Railway* (1874) L.R. 10 Ex. 1.

[78] Above, para.15–072.

discretion under s.1 to allow him to recover or retain a sum of money, *e.g.* where each has conferred a valuable benefit on the other. But where only one party asks the court to exercise that discretion, s.1(5) operates only in relation to insurance moneys which have become payable to that party.

Section 1(5) is, however, not restricted to cases in which claims are made under the proviso to s.1(2) to retain or recover the whole or part of a prepayment that was, or should have been, made before the time of discharge. It can apply also where the court is called upon to decide how much, if anything, is "recoverable" under s.1(3) by a party who has, before the time of discharge, conferred a "valuable benefit" on the other party. In a case like *Appleby v Myers*,[79] for example, any insurance money received by the builder in consequence of the destruction of the factory would have to be disregarded (by virtue of s.1(5)) in assessing the "just sum" recoverable by him in respect of such a benefit under s.1(3).[80] But insurance money received by the *owner* of the factory (the benefited party) in consequence of its destruction would not fall within s.1(5)[81] since the owner would not be making any claim that "any sum ought to be recovered or retained" by him. This would be true even if the owner had incurred expenses and sought to rely on those expenses by way of reduction of the builder's restitution claim.[82] In so relying on his expenses, the owner would not be making a claim that *"any sum* ought to be recovered or retained" by him. He would not be seeking to "recover" anything (but merely to reduce the "just sum" recoverable by the other party); and the words "sum ... retained" can refer only to the case where a person has (a) received a "sum", *i.e.* a payment of money, and (b) seeks to retain part of such a "sum" in respect of his expenses; and this would not, in the case put, be the owner's position. Similarly, where a person had received (for example) a "payment" in kind, he would not have received, and cannot seek to "retain", any "sum" (of money).

Section 1(5) begins with the words "In considering whether any sum ought to be recovered or retained..." and these words give rise to two further problems. The first is whether they refer, not only to the situation in which the question which the court has to consider is whether *anything* should be recovered or retained, but also to that in which that question is *how much* (subject to the statutory limits) should be recovered or retained (*e.g.* in respect of expenses or of a valuable benefit). A narrow reading of s.1(5) might seem to indicate that the words quoted above refer only to the former question. But it is submitted that the direction to disregard insurance benefits is, from a practical point of view, at least as relevant in determining the amount to be recovered or retained as it is to the existence of a right of recovery or retention; and that the opening words of s.1(5) should be liberally interpreted to refer to the quantum of recovery

---

[79] (1867) L.R. 2 C.P. 651, above, para.15–057.

[80] For the view that such a claim would now be available to the builder on such facts, see above, para.15–064.

[81] In its original version, s.1(5) contained a proviso to this effect: H.L. Deb., July 8, 1943, col.368.

[82] By virtue of s.1(3)(a): above, para.15–073.

as well as to the existence of such a right. The second problem is whether the words quoted above apply only where the court has a *discretion* as to how much, if anything, ought to be "recovered or retained" or whether they also apply where the Act gives a party a right of recovery or retention which is not subject to any such discretion. The latter possibility is illustrated by the situation in which a party has simply made, or promised to make, a prepayment to the other and the latter has not, before the time of discharge, incurred any expenses. Section 1(2) then gives the former party an absolute right[83] to recover the payment, if he has made, and releases him from his obligation to make it if at the time of discharge it has not been made. Such a release is probably not a right to "retain" a sum of money within s.1(5) (where "retained" seems to refer to keeping a payment previously made to a party) and the subsection probably also does not apply to the payor's right under s.1(2) to recover back the payment if he has made it. Once it has been established that the payment has been made and that the contract has been frustrated, the court *must* under s.1(2) order the return of the payment: there is no scope for "considering whether any sum ought to be repaid". Hence it is submitted that s.1(5) does not apply to such a case. The fact that the payor has received insurance payments must, indeed, be disregarded in such cases, but this result follows, not from s.1(5), but from the mandatory language of s.1(2).[84] The receipt of such payments must therefore be disregarded, even in a case falling within the exception to s.1(5), discussed in para.15–081, below.

(c) *Section 1(5): the exception*

15–081   Section 1(5) does not apply where "there was an obligation to insure imposed by an express term of the frustrated contract or by or under any enactment".[85] The exception may be illustrated by reference to c.i.f. sales, which oblige the seller to insure the goods in transit and to transfer the benefit of that insurance to the buyers on tender of documents.[86] It will be recalled that the *Fibrosa* case[87] concerned such a sale and that the contract was frustrated by supervening illegality, so that the seller was discharged from his duty to transfer the benefit of his insurance to the buyer. Any sums that might have been paid or payable to the seller by insurers[88] could, under the exception to s.1(5), now be taken into account in deciding how much (if anything) the seller could retain or recover, in respect of his expenses,[89] out of any advance payment made or promised

---

[83] This follows from the words "*shall* ... be recoverable ... or cease to be so payable" in s.1(2).

[84] Above, n.83.

[85] s.1(5), concluding words.

[86] *Benjamin's Sale of Goods* (6th ed.), paras 19–001, 19–041 *et seq.*

[87] [1943] A.C. 32, above, para.15–048.

[88] There is no indication in the *Fibrosa* case itself that any payments became due under any policy of insurance (or indeed that any insurance had been effected before the contract was discharged).

[89] Under the proviso to s.1(2).

to him by the buyer. If, on the other hand, the sale had been on f.o.b. terms and the insurance cover had been effected (as would be likely in such a case) by the buyer, without his being obliged by the contract of sale to insure,[90] then any proceeds of that insurance would not have fallen within the *exception* to s.1(5). Nor, for the reasons given above,[91] would the general rule in s.1(5) apply if the buyer sought to reduce a claim by the seller in respect of a "valuable benefit"[92] conferred on the buyer by the seller (*e.g.* by part delivery before frustration) by relying on the expenses incurred by the buyer[93] in performing his duty under the contract of sale to provide the ship on which the goods were to be loaded. The *seller's* claim in respect of the "valuable benefit" would also *not* be affected by the buyer's receipt of the insurance money: such receipt affects only claims by the *recipient*[94] (or prospective recipient) of the insurance money; they do not affect claims by the *other* party.

In the first of the above examples,[95] the c.i.f. seller's contractual obligation to insure was imposed on the party making the claim that a sum of money ought to be retained or recoverable under s.1(2); but the words of the exception contained in the concluding words of s.1(5) do not specify the party on whom that *obligation* must be imposed; though it is clear from the structure of the subsection that the insurance payments must be *made or due* to the party claiming that "a sum ought to be recovered or retained." Normally the obligation to insure will rest on, and be performed by, that party; but the exception in s.1(5) can equally well apply where the contract imposes an obligation to insure for the benefit of that party on the other party to the frustrated contract, *e.g.* where a building contract requires the owner to cover the contractor against the risk of loss resulting from destruction of the works before completion.[96] The owner having paid for the insurance, it is reasonable that he should have the benefit of it in the sense of being allowed to recover any advance payment[97] that he may have made to the builder while rejecting any claim by the latter to retain any part of that payment in respect of expenses,[98] so far as these are covered by the insurance. This seems to be also the appropriate solution where the contract imposes the obligation to insure on the builder and he performs that obligation; for although in such a case he pays for the insurance in the first instance, he is likely to take the cost of that insurance into account in fixing the contract price, so that indirectly it is the owner who bears that cost and who ought therefore to

---

[90] Under a "classic" f.o.b. contract (*Benjamin*, above, n.86, para.20–002) there is no duty on either party to insure.

[91] Above, para.15–080, after n.82.

[92] Under s.1(3) of the 1943 Act.

[93] See *ibid.*, s.1(3)(a).

[94] This follows from the words "to that party" in s.1(5).

[95] Above, at n.86.

[96] Such a provision does not necessarily rule out discharge on the ground that it deals with the destruction: the contract may nevertheless be discharged *by delay: cf.* above, para.3–048.

[97] Under the main part of s.1(2), to which s.1(5) does not apply: above, at n.83.

[98] Under the proviso to s.1(2), to which s.1(5) does apply.

get the benefit of it, in the sense described above. The difficulty in accounting for the rationale of s.1(5) (including the exception) arises because the party against whom a claim is made, or a right of retention asserted, in respect of expenses, may indirectly pay for any relevant insurance even where no *obligation* is imposed on either party to insure against the circumstances giving rise to the frustration; for if the party to whom the prepayment was made or to be made has in fact insured, even without being obliged to do so by the contract which is later frustrated, or by law, then that party may still take the cost of such insurance into account in fixing his charges under the frustrated contract and in this way the other party to that contract will again indirectly have paid for the insurance but not be able to benefit from it. This process may even operate at (so to speak) one remove where the insurance is provided by a third party. The point may be illustrated by reference in *Taylor v Caldwell*[99] and by assuming that the defendants in that case had received a prepayment and had incurred expenses. It will be recalled that the defendants were not the owners, but the lessees of the Music Hall and the Hall was insured.[1] The cost of that insurance would have been incurred by the defendants directly if the policy had been taken out by them, or indirectly (by way of increased rent) if it had been taken out by their lessor (and available for their benefit).[2] In either event that cost would probably have been taken into account by the defendants in fixing the hire charge of £100 per night payable by the plaintiffs, who would in this way have indirectly paid for at least part of the insurance.

(d) *Criticism*

15–082   In many of the situations which fall within the general rule of s.1(5), the recipient (or prospective recipient) of the insurance moneys would be likely to recoup the cost of the insurance, wholly or in part, by taking it into account in fixing the contractual charge made by him to the other party to the frustrated contract. In such cases, the mandatory provision[3] of s.1(5) directing the court to disregard one party's insurance receipts when "considering whether any sum ought to be recovered or retained" by that party can lead to results of questionable justice; for it is not obvious why the other party should be deprived of the benefit of insurance for which he has, at least in part, indirectly paid. Where the frustrated contract provides for a sum of money to be paid, or where such a sum is paid, by one party, A, to the other, B, before the time of discharge, B may be able to recover or retain part of that sum in respect of his expenses[4]; and there seems to be little merit in his at the same time claiming to retain

---

[99] (1863) 3 B. & S. 826.

[1] Above, para.2–028.

[2] By virtue of Fires Prevention (Metropolis) Act 1774, s.83.

[3] For the "mandatory" nature of s.1(5), see *Gamerco SA v ICM Fair Warning (Agency) Ltd* [1995] 1 W.L.R. 1126 at 1234. In the sense that s.1(5) may be displaced by contrary agreement (see s.2(3)) it is not "mandatory".

[4] See s.1(2) proviso.

or recover insurance *premiums* by way of overhead expenses[5] while insisting that insurance *receipts* under the same insurance should be disregarded in quantifying his claim in respect to expenses. Yet the mandatory language of s.1(5) would appear to entitle B to take these apparently contradictory positions as long as the insurance was not effected under an obligation imposed by an express term of the frustrated contract or by law. To put the point in another way, the policy of the general rule stated in s.1(5) seems not to be entirely consistent with the policy underlying the exception contained in the concluding words of the subsection. Even the latter policy is not entirely clear: it seems to be based on the assumption that the insured party has himself paid for the insurance; but that (as noted in para.15–081, above) is not an express requirement of the exception, which does not specify on which party to the frustrated contract the obligation to insure must be imposed to bring the exception into play.

(5) Special cases

Our concern in this section is with cases in which the rules relating to restitution and reliance loss (discussed above) do not apply, or apply only subject to modification. The topic is most easily discussed by considering the cases to which such special treatment is given by the Law Reform (Frustrated Contracts) Act 1943. To some extent, however, the aim of the relevant provisions of the Act was to preserve existing common law rules: this is true, in particular, in relation to certain contracts for the carriage of goods by sea and to contracts of insurance. It follows that, in systems in which powers of adjustment exist at common law, these powers are likely to be similarly limited by the special rules which apply to these contracts. Express contractual provisions can likewise exclude or modify powers of adjustment which arise at common law, no less than those which arise under the Act. **15–083**

(a) *Section 2(3): contrary agreement*

The common law rule that money is recoverable on the ground of total failure of consideration can be excluded by contrary agreement: the money may be paid out-and-out, with the intention that the payee shall keep it in any event.[6] The terms of the contract can similarly exclude the provisions of the 1943 Act.[7] For example, a time charter may provide that hire is to be paid monthly in advance but that, if the ship should be lost "money paid and not earned shall be returned to the charterer at once".[8] **15–084**

---

[5] See s.1(4).

[6] *Fibrosa* case [1943] A.C. 32 at 43, 77; above, para.15–048.

[7] s.2(3). *cf.* British Columbia Frustrated Contracts Act 1974, s.2; New South Wales Frustrated Contracts Act 1978, ss.5(5), 6(1)(e); South Australian Frustrated Contracts Act 1988, s.4(1)(b). For restrictions on the effectiveness of such provisions, see above, para.12–018, below, para.15–084 at n.13–16.

[8] See cl.16 of the charterparty, in *Pan Ocean Shipping Ltd v Creditcorp Ltd (The Trident Beauty)* [1994] 1 W.L.R. 161; cl.18 gave a wider right to the charter to recover back hire paid and not earned, not restricted to cases of "*loss*" of the

If the ship is lost after having rendered services for one-quarter of the month in respect of which the advance payment is made, then three-quarters of the payment must be returned by virtue of the contractual provision to this effect; and although a similar result might follow by a more complicated process of reasoning under the Act,[9] such reasoning would not be necessary in the case put since (a) there would be no frustration by reason of the loss since the effect of this event was specifically dealt with by the contract[10] and (b) even if frustration were not excluded (*e.g.* by reason of a narrow construction of the contractual provision) that provision would, in the case put, specify the relevant *effects* of frustration and so displace the provisions of the 1943 Act by virtue of s.2(3). The Act would, however, determine the effects of frustration if the ship were prevented from rendering the agreed service by some event *other* than that specified in the contract: for example, in a variation of the case put, if the ship were prevented from rendering the services (and the contract was frustrated) by some event, such as requisition of the ship,[11] for which the contract made *no* provision.

Whether a term has excluded the Act or any part of it depends in each case on its construction. In the example last given, the answer to the question of construction is clear: "lost" does not include "requisitioned". A case of greater difficulty was *BP Exploration (Libya) Ltd v Hunt*[12] where the contract provided that the defendant was not to be personally liable to repay any advances and that the claimants' rights were to be exercisable only against the defendant's share of the oil. This provision did not exclude the Act as, on its true construction, it was not intended to deal with the risk of expropriation but with the different risk that no oil might be found.

The validity of contract terms which exclude the operation of the 1943 Act is not affected by the Unfair Contract Terms Act 1977 since such terms are "authorised" by s.2(3) of the 1943 Act.[13] In a contract between a commercial seller or supplier and a consumer, the validity of standard terms excluding s.2(3) of the 1943 Act could, however, be affected by the Unfair Terms in Consumer Contracts Regulations 1999.[14] These Regula-

---

ship. In the actual case, the cause of the failure to render the services was the shipowner's *breach*. For the effect of such provisions on the common law requirement that, to give rise to a right to restitution of money paid in advance, the failure of consideration must be "total", see above, para.15–048.

[9] The charterer's right to recover the *whole* of the advance payment under s.1(2) would be subject to reduction in respect of the shipowner's expenses and the shipowner could also make a claim under s.1(3) in respect of the "valuable benefit" which he had conferred on the charterer by rendering one-quarter of the agreed services.

[10] Above, para.12–002.

[11] *cf. French Marine v Compagnie Napolitaine, etc* [1921] 2 A.C. 494, illustrating a situation to which s.1 of the Act would now apply in the absence of a provision excluding that section by virtue of s.2(3).

[12] [1983] 2 A.C. 352; above, para.15–062.

[13] Unfair Contract Terms Act 1977, s.29(1)(a).

[14] SI 1999/2083.

tions do not, indeed, apply to "contractual terms which reflect (a) mandatory statutory provisions"[15]; but it seems that the provisions of the 1943 Act are (by reason of s.2(3)) not "mandatory" for the present purpose. The fact that s.2(3) expressly permitted the parties to exclude the 1943 Act would, however, be relevant to the question whether a term to this effect was "unfair" and so not binding on the consumer.[16]

(b) *Section 2(4): severable obligations*

We saw earlier in this chapter that, where a contract contained severable obligations, those which had accrued before the time of discharge were not affected by subsequent discharge; while those which had not then accrued did not become due.[17] Section 2(4) of the 1943 Act preserves the first limb of this proposition by providing that, if parts of a contract which have been performed[18] can properly be severed from the remainder, they are to be treated as separate contracts which have not been frustrated. The subsection then goes on to modify the previous law by providing that s.1 is to apply to the remainder of the contract.

15–085

(i) Valuable benefits and severable obligations

The operation of s.2(4) can be illustrated by referring back to *Stubbs v Holywell Ry,*[19] where a consulting engineer, who had been employed for 15 months for a payment of £500 to be made in five equal quarterly instalments, died after only two quarters. At common law, his administrator was entitled to his pay for those two quarters, and this position would not be affected by s.2(4). But at common law the administrator would not have been entitled to anything in respect of work done by the deceased before his death in (say) the first two months of the third quarter. Now such work would give rise to a claim under s.1(3) if, as a result of it, a "valuable benefit" had been obtained by the other party to the contract.

15–086

(ii) Prepayments and severable obligations

Section 2(4) also extends the rights of a person to recover back money paid under a contract imposing severable obligations. At common law, money could be recovered back if it had been paid for some severable part of the consideration which had wholly failed, even though the consideration for the whole payment had not failed[20]; as we saw earlier in this chapter,[21] a part of the consideration might be severable for this purpose either because the *obligation* to perform it was severable, or because the

15–087

---

[15] *ibid.,* reg.4(2)(a).

[16] Under *ibid.,* reg.8(1).

[17] Above, para.15–031.

[18] Thus s.2(4) would not cover the situation discussed in para.15–031, above where obligations are divisible and the frustrating event occurs before any of them have been performed.

[19] (1867) L.R. 2 Ex. 311; above, para.15–031.

[20] See *Tyrie v Fletcher* (1777) 2 Cowp. 666 at 668; Marine Insurance Act 1906, s.84(2) and (3)(b) (divisible insurance policies) and above, para.15–048, at n.25.

[21] Above, para.15–032.

subject-matter was severable in the sense of being divisible without destroying it in a commercial sense. Under the common law rule, if in *Stubbs v Holywell Ry* the whole £500 had been paid in advance, £200 could have been recovered back as no work at all had been done in the fourth and fifth quarters; but nothing could have been recovered back in respect of the third quarter if the deceased had done so much as a week's work in it. Now the third quarter would be treated as if it had been covered by a separate contract so that the £100 paid in respect of it could be recovered back under s.1(2), but the personal representative could pursue a claim under s.1(3) in respect of the week's work done by the deceased in the third quarter.

(iii) Apportionment Act 1870

15–088   Contractual obligations may be severable not only by the express terms of the contract, but also by statute. Section 2 of the Apportionment Act 1870 provides that: "All rents, annuities, dividends and other periodical payments in the nature of income ... shall ... be considered as accruing from day to day, and shall be apportionable in respect of time accordingly." By s.5, "annuities" includes "salaries[22] and pensions" and by s.7 the Act does not apply where it is "expressly stipulated that no apportionment shall take place". It is an open question whether the Act can be invoked by a party whose failure to perform his part of the contract amounts to a breach[23]; but there seems to be no reason to doubt that the Act could apply where the failure is due to an event which frustrates[24] the contract. The 1870 Act would, moreover, lead to results significantly different from those which would be reached under the 1943 Act. In the first of the above examples (of work having been done in two months of the third quarter) the administrator would under the 1870 Act be entitled to two months' salary (as opposed to a "just sum" for two months' work under s.1(3) of the 1943 Act). In the second example (of payment having been made in advance and one week's work having been done in the third quarter) the administrator would have to repay, not the whole of the third quarter's pay, but only $^{12}/_{13}$ of that sum. Where the 1870 Act applies, there is virtually no scope for the operation of s.1(3) of the 1943 Act: this provision could, in such cases, apply to no more than part of one day's work. It should be emphasised that the 1870 Act applies only to "periodical" payments; this seems to mean payments to be made at specified intervals of time, or perhaps at the end of a specified time. Payments under contracts imposing severable obligations are not necessarily of this kind. For example, payments to be made under a building contract as specified stages of the work were completed would not, it is submitted, be "periodical payments" for the purpose of the 1870 Act.

---

[22] See Matthews, 2 Legal Studies 302.
[23] *Moriarty v Regent's Garage Co* [1921] 2 K.B. 766; in the Divisional Court there had been a division of opinion on this point: see [1921] 1 K.B. 432 at 434, 448–449.
[24] *cf. Treacy v Corcorran* (1874) I.R. 8 C.L. 40.

(c) *Section 2(5): excluded contracts*

The 1943 Act does not apply to the following three types of contracts:

(i) Voyage charterparties and certain other contracts for the carriage of goods by sea

This category of excepted contracts is described in s.2(5)(a) which
provides that the Act does not apply "to any charterparty, except a time
charterparty or a charterparty by way of demise, or to any contract (other
than a charterparty) for the carriage of goods by sea".[25] It is clear from
these words that the Act does not apply to voyage charters or to contracts
contained or evidenced in bills of lading, or in sea waybills.[26] The effect of
these exclusions is to preserve two rules which are well established and
known to businessmen who are able to protect themselves (*e.g.* by express
terms of the contract, or by insurance) against any hardship which might
be thought to result from them.

The first such rule is that any freight which has become due or been
paid before frustration remains due and (if paid) cannot be recovered
back even though the cargo is lost.[27] As the Act does not apply, this
position is not affected by s.1(2). The common law rule can be excluded
by contrary agreement[28]; for example, it would not apply where on the
true construction of the contract the freight had not become due until
after the frustrating event.[29] Whether a contractual provision has this
effect can obviously give rise to difficult questions of construction,
particularly since a distinction must be drawn between the question when
freight is *earned* and when it is *payable*.[30] If frustration occurs between those
two events, the freight remains due.

The second rule preserved by s.2(5)(a) is the rule that a person who
contracts to carry goods by sea to a specified port cannot recover the
freight or any part of it if he is prevented by events outside his control
from delivering them there: he cannot, for example, recover freight *pro
rata itineris* if he is forced by such events to deliver the goods at an
intermediate port.[31] As the Act does not apply, this position is not affected
by s.1(3). Again the rule can, in effect, be excluded by the contract, *e.g.* by
a stipulation providing that freight is to be paid or earned on loading[32]

---

[25] For similar exclusions, see British Columbia Frustrated Contracts Act 1974,
s.1(2)(a); New South Wales Frustrated Contracts Act 1978, s.6(1)(b); South
Australian Frustrated Contracts Act 1988, s.4(2)(b) and (c).

[26] For a statutory definition of sea waybills, see Carriage of Goods by Sea Act 1992,
s.1(3).

[27] *Byrne v Schiller* (1871) L.R. 6 Ex. 319.

[28] *Meling v Minos Shipping Co (The Oliva)* [1972] 1 Lloyd's Rep. 458 (time charter,
but the principle could equally apply to a voyage charter).

[29] *Compania Naviera General v Kerametal Ltd (The Lorna I)* [1983] 1 Lloyd's Rep: 373.

[30] *Colonial Bank v European Grain & Shipping (The Dominique)* [1989] A.C. 1056;
Vagres Compania Maritime SA v Nissho Iwai American Corp (The Karin Vatis) [1988]
2 Lloyd's Rep. 330.

[31] *Vlierbloom v Chapman* (1844) 13 M. & W. 230; *St Enoch Shipping Co Ltd v Phosphate
Mining Co* [1916] 2 K.B. 624.

[32] Above, at n.30.

rather than on delivery. Alternatively, the carrier can protect himself by insurance of freight.[33]

15-091 It is clear from the wording of s.2(5)(a) that the Act does apply to time and demise charters. It therefore reverses the former rule that money payable under a time charter remained due in full even though it was payable in advance in respect of a period during which the contract was frustrated, so that services under the contract could be rendered only during part of that period.[34] Thus where hire was payable monthly in advance, it formerly remained due, and could not, if paid, be recovered back if the contract was frustrated after one week.[35] Section 1(2) would now apply in such a case, unless the contract itself provided for hire which had been paid but not earned to be repaid, in which case that provision would prevail by virtue of s.2(3).[36]

15-092 It is, however, an open question how, for the purposes of the Act, the hybrid now generally known as the time charter trip or trip time charter should be classified. Such a contract combines elements of a voyage charter (in that it refers to the voyage which is to be undertaken) with those of a time charter (in that it provides for payment to be calculated by reference to the time taken to accomplish the voyage, rather than by reference to the amount of cargo carried to the agreed destination). One view is that the time element should be regarded as predominant, and this view derives some support from a decision at first instance in which such a contract was said to be a time charter for the purpose of s.2(5)(a)[37] and therefore to be governed by the Act. The contrary view is that the voyage element should be regarded as predominant because the commercial object of the contract is to procure the carriage of goods between the places specified in it, the point of the stipulation as to payment by time being merely to shift the risk of delay during the voyage from the shipowner to the charterer. The classification of the contract may depend on the degree of particularity with which it describes the contemplated voyage. Thus it may be appropriate to regard the contract as a time charter if it simply describes the countries or regions between which the ship is to trade,[38] but as a voyage charter if it specifies the ports of loading and

---

[33] *Hopper v Burness* (1876) 1 C.P.D. 137 at 141.

[34] See Law Revision Committee, 7th Interim Report (Cmd. 6009), Appendix B; H.L. Deb., June 29, 1943, col.141.

[35] *French Marine v Cie Napolitaine etc.* [1921] 2 A.C. 494; *cf. Lloyd Royal Belge SA v Stathatos* (1917) 34 T.L.R. 70.

[36] See above, paras 15–048, 15–084 for the effects of such contractual provision.

[37] *Ocean Tramp Tankers Corp v V/O Sovfracht (The Eugenia)* [1963] 2 Lloyd's Rep. 155 at 171; reversed on the issue of frustration [1964] 2 Q.B. 226 (above, para.4–081), where no reference is made to s.2(5)(a) of the 1943 Act. Contracts of this kind seem also to be regarded as time charters in *Scottish Navigation Co Ltd v Souter & Co* [1917] 1 K.B. 222 and perhaps in *Lloyd Royal Belge SA v Stathatos* (1917) 34 T.L.R. 70. *cf.* also *Braemont SS Co v Andrew Weir & Co* (1910) 15 Com. Cas. 101.

[38] As in *The Eugenia* and in the *Scottish Navigation* case, above, n.37.

discharge.[39] If the contract is classified as not being a time charter, the effects of its frustration will not be governed by the Act, and the question will arise what those effects are at common law. This question is itself one to which the authorities provide no clear answer in particular, it is not clear how far the two rules of common law which s.2(5) (a) is intended to preserve in the case of voyage charters also apply to trip time charters in which the voyage element predominates. Those rules deal with the risk that the cargo may fail to reach the contractual destination and make its incidence depend on whether the freight is payable in advance or on arrival. In a trip time charter, the allocation of that risk is likely also to depend on the terms of the stipulation as to the carrier's remuneration (though the fact that it was called "freight" or "hire" would not be conclusive). That remuneration cannot under such a contract be payable wholly in advance since its amount cannot be determined till the voyage is accomplished; though it may be payable in advance at stated intervals.[40] The fact that the remuneration ultimately due depends on the number of days (or other units of time) taken by the voyage gives at least some support to the view that the obligation to get the goods to the agreed destination is not an "entire" one,[41] so that the carrier would be entitled to be paid at the contract rate for the days on which services had been rendered; and that a *pro rata* amount (but no more) of any payment which may have been made before discharge should be recoverable at common law as having been paid on a severable part of the consideration which has failed.[42] These results would be a good deal more favourable to the carrier than those which would follow from the Act, under which he would have to return the whole of any advance payment and to seek relief for part performance by arguing that he had conferred a "valuable benefit" on the cargo-owner. The outcome of such a claim is, on the authorities, uncertain[43]; but it could be argued that a "valuable benefit" had been received by the charterer in the sense that the cost of carrying the goods to the agreed destination had been reduced by their having been carried part of the way there before the contract was discharged.[44] It is, however, submitted that effect is more likely to be given to the intention of the parties by holding that their contract was not a time charter within s.2(5)(a) that therefore the Act did not apply and that the parties' rights were governed by the common law consequences (as described above) of the true construction of the payment term. This would, indeed, not enable the court to make an award or allowance in respect of expenses, but if the

---

[39] As in *Care Shipping Corp v Latin America Shipping Corp (The Cebu)* [1983] 1 Lloyd's Rep. 302 at 304 ("from Portland, Oregon to Bandar Abbas"). An intermediate possibility is illustrated by the *Lloyd Royal Belge* and *Braemont* cases, above, n.37 where the contracts specified a *port* of departure and a *region* of destination

[40] *e.g.* it was payable half monthly in advance in *The Eugenia* [1962] 2 Lloyd's Rep. 155 at 170.

[41] *cf.* above, para.15–057.

[42] *cf.* above, para.15–048. This possibility was not considered in *Lloyd Royal Belge SA v Stathatos* (1917) 34 T.L.R. 70.

[43] Above, para.15–063.

[44] Above, paras 15–063 to 15–064.

contractual rate of payment were calculated on a daily basis this restriction on the powers of the court would have little practical significance.

(ii) Contracts of insurance

15–093 Section 2(5)(b) provides that the Act shall not apply "to any contract of insurance ...".[45] The object of this exception is to preserve the rule that there can, in general, be no apportionment of premiums under an insurance policy once the risk has begun to run. The whole essence of a contract of insurance is that "the contract is for the whole entire risk, and no part of the consideration shall be returned".[46] Thus if a ship is insured but lost in some way not covered by the policy after part of the period of insurance has run, no part of the premium can be recovered back. This is obviously in accordance with the intention of the parties, for such a contract is essentially speculative. Had the ship been lost by one of the perils insured against on the first day, the insurer would have had to bear the whole loss. Conversely, he can keep the whole premium if the ship is lost by a peril that is not covered by the policy at any time during the period of insurance. At common law, there is no total (nor indeed any) failure of consideration in such a case, since in a contract of insurance the insured bargains for the insurer's promise, (rather than for its performance) and so obtains what he bargained for even if no loss at all occurs (so that no payment to him is ever made).[47] This position is preserved under s.2(5)(b) of the Act. There would be a total failure of consideration only if the insurer had never been at risk, *e.g.* if the subject-matter of the insurance had been destroyed the day before the policy had begun to run. The right of the insured to recover back his premium in such a case would arise at common law[48] and so would not be affected by the fact that the Act does not apply to contracts of insurance.

Section 2(5)(b) concludes with the words "save as is provided by subsection (5) of the foregoing section". That subsection directs the court to disregard the proceeds of insurance in exercising certain powers of restitution and adjustment conferred on it by s.1(2) and (3).[49] The concluding words of s.2(5)(b) may have been thought necessary to preserve this position, which limits the discretion of the court when dealing with the effects of frustration on a contract *other* than one of insurance. They should not be interpreted to mean that the contract of insurance (the proceeds of which the court is directed to disregard) is *itself* to be subject to the powers of the court under s.1(2) and (3).

---

[45] For similar exclusions, see British Columbia Frustrated Contracts Act 1974, s.1(2)(b), New South Wales Frustrated Contracts Act, s.6(1)(d), South Australian Frustrated Contracts Act 1988, s.4(2)(d).

[46] *Tyrie v Fletcher* (1777) 2 Cowp. 666 at 668. For a contractual provision displacing the normal rule, see *CT Bowring Reinsurance Ltd v MR Baxter (The M Vatan)* [1987] 2 Lloyd's Rep. 416.

[47] Above, para.15–048, n.19.

[48] *cf. Stevenson v Snow* (1761) 3 Burr. 1237; and see Marine Insurance Act 1906, s.84(1) and 3(a).

[49] Above, paras 15–079 *et seq.*

(iii) Certain contracts for the sale of goods

Section 2(5)(c)[50] provides that the Act shall not apply to—

(a) Any contract to which s.7 of the Sale of Goods Act 1979 applies. Under s.7 of that Act, an agreement to sell specific goods is avoided if the goods perish without any fault on the part of the seller or buyer before the risk has passed to the buyer.[51] That is, the buyer is not liable for the price and neither party is liable in damages. The same result would normally follow from the common law rules of frustration, as the destruction of the goods would frustrate the contract. The cases in which the 1943 Act would (if it were not excluded by s.2(5)(c)) make a difference are those in which there has been an advance payment or part-delivery.

If the buyer pays in advance but does not get any of the goods, he can recover back his payment on the ground of total failure of consideration.[52] The exclusion of the Act does not affect this right, but it does prevent the seller from setting off any expenses[53] which he may have incurred, *e.g.* in putting the goods into a deliverable state.

Two further problems arise from part-delivery followed by frustration.

First, a buyer of specific goods may have paid the whole price in advance and received only part-delivery. In such a case, property,[54] and hence risk,[55] is likely to have passed on payment, in which case s.7 will not apply so that the contract will not be frustrated. Section 7 would apply only if for some reason (*e.g.* because the parties had expressly or impliedly so agreed or because the sale was by a commercial seller to a buyer who dealt as consumer[56]) the risk had remained on the seller. In that case the contract could be avoided under s.7 and the question whether the buyer could recover back the advance payment or any part of it would depend (since s.1(2) of the Act would be excluded) on common law principles. These would require a distinction to be drawn according to the nature of the subject-matter. If the contract were for the sale of a specific piece of machinery to be delivered in sections, there would be no total failure of consideration after part-delivery,[57] so that *prima facie* the buyer would not be entitled to recover back any part of his payment. It has, indeed, been suggested that the buyer could recover back a proportionate part of the

---

[50] As amended by Sale of Goods Act 1979, s.63 and Sch.2, para.2.

[51] See above, paras 3–013 *et seq.*

[52] *Logan v Le Mesurier* (1846) 6 Moo. P.C. 116.

[53] Under the proviso to s.1(2) of the 1943 Act.

[54] For the tendency to link passing of property with payment, see *RV Ward Ltd v Bignall* [1967] 1 Q.B. 534 at 545; *Mitsui & Co Ltd v Flota Mercante Grancolombiana (The Ciudad de Pasto)* [1988] 1 W.L.R. 1145 at 1153.

[55] Sale of Goods Act 1979, s.20(1). If the sale is by a commercial seller to a buyer who deals as consumer, the goods remain at the seller's risk until they are delivered to the consumer: Sale of Goods Act 1979, s.20(4), as inserted by Sale and Supply of Goods to Consumers Regulations 2002, SI 2002/3045, reg.4.

[56] See n.55, above.

[57] This would have been the position in the *Fibrosa* case [1943] A.C. 32 if part delivery had been made.

price on the ground that the undelivered part was still at the seller's risk.[58] But this would give rise to the difficulty of deciding how the price was to be apportioned between the delivered and the undelivered parts, and it is precisely this difficulty which accounts for the common law requirement that failure of consideration must be total.[59] There could also be some difficulty in applying to a case of the present kind the notion of risk passing in stages. The other type of case is that in which the subject-matter is readily apportionable, *e.g.* if the contract were for the sale of 1,000 tons of wheat forming the entire contents of a particular warehouse and the contract was frustrated after delivery of 600 tons. At common law, a proportionate part of the price could be recovered back in respect of the partial failure of consideration,[60] there being no difficulty in making the proper apportionment in such a case.

Secondly, a seller of specific goods may have delivered part of the goods and been paid nothing before frustration. He cannot rely on s.1(3) of the 1943 Act (as that is excluded) to recover anything in respect of the valuable benefit obtained by the buyer. His rights apart from the Act would depend in the first place on the payment term of the contract. If this provided for payment only on complete delivery, the seller would *prima facie* have no right to be paid since the stage of complete delivery was never reached. He might be able to recover something at common law if a new contract could be implied from the buyer's keeping the goods after frustration. But it would be hard to imply such a contract if the buyer no longer had the goods, *e.g.* because he had used or resold them before frustration. The implication of a new contract might also fail for want of contractual intention where the parties believed that they were simply giving effect to the original (and now frustrated) contract.[61]

15–095   *(b) Any other contract for the sale, or the sale and delivery, of specific goods, where the contract is frustrated by reason of the fact that the goods have perished.*   These words seem to refer to a case which does not fall within s.7 of the Sale of Goods Act 1979, because, when the goods perished, the risk *had* passed to the buyer. It is difficult to see how such a contract could be frustrated by the perishing of goods; the hypothesis that risk had passed would seem to exclude frustration. Perhaps the point of excepting such a case from the 1943 Act is to make it clear that the buyer is liable for the whole price and that there is no power to order restitution or to allow (or award) anything on respect of expenses.

Section 2(5)(c) can produce some entirely capricious distinctions.

15–096   The 1943 Act is excluded only where the goods are specific. Suppose that a farmer agrees to sell 200 tons out of a crop to be grown on his land, and the crop is destroyed by events for which he is not responsible.[62] As

---

[58] Atiyah, *The Sale of Goods* (10th ed.), p.363.
[59] Above, para.15–048.
[60] *Ebrahim Dawood Ltd v Heath (Est 1927) Ltd* [1961] 2 Lloyd's Rep. 512; above, para.15–048.
[61] *cf.* above, para.15–003, at n.18.
[62] See *Howell v Coupland* (1876) 1 Q.B.D. 258; above, para.4–049.

the goods are not specific,[63] the 1943 Act is not excluded and the farmer can set off his expenses of cultivating the crop against any advance payment made by, and returnable[64] to, the buyer. But if an agreement were made to sell an identified parcel of 200 tons out of the crop after it had been lifted, or half the crop,[65] the goods would be specific so that the 1943 Act would be excluded. Hence if the agreement in such a case had provided that the farmer was to put the goods into sacks, and if the goods had been destroyed before this operation had been completed, the farmer would have to return the whole of any advance payment made by the buyer,[66] without any right to deduct any part of the expenses of packaging.

The 1943 Act is excluded only where the cause of frustration is the perishing of the goods. Thus the Act applies where the contract is frustrated by illegality or requisition.

The reason for these distinctions is far from clear; and one might ask why contracts for the sale of goods were singled out for separate treatment at all. As a matter of abstract justice, there seems to be no reason why the powers of restitution and apportionment provided by the Act should apply to a contract to build a house but not a contract to supply a specific piece of machinery. The main reason for not applying the Act to contracts for the sale of goods is that in such contracts certainty is more important than justice; and the certainty, which the rules as to the passing of risk are meant to provide, would be disrupted if their effects could be modified by the exercise of the discretionary powers conferred on the courts by the 1943 Act. But on this view contracts for the sale of goods should have been wholly excluded from the operation of the 1943 Act. Their partial exclusion does not satisfy the requirements of either certainty or justice.[67]

(d) *Commercial agents*

Many important aspects of the legal relations between "commercial agents" and their principals are dealt with by the Commercial Agents (Council Directive) Regulations 1993.[68] For the purposes of the Regulations, a "commercial agent" means: "a self-employed intermediary who has continuing authority to negotiate the sale or purchase of goods on behalf of another person (the 'principal'), or to negotiate and conclude the sale or purchase of goods on behalf of and in the name of

---

[63] Above, para.3–017.

[64] Under s.1(2) of the 1943 Act.

[65] See Sale of Goods Act 1979, s.61(1), definition of "specific goods", as amended by Sales of Goods (Amendment) Act 1995, s.2(d).

[66] Under the rule in the *Fibrosa* case [1943] A.C. 32, above, para.15–048.

[67] There is no corresponding exclusion in the British Columbia, New South Wales, and South Australian Acts cited in para.15–093 above, n.45.

[68] SI 1993/3053, as amended by Commercial Agents (Council Directive) (Amendment) Regulations 1993 and 1998 (SI 1993/3173 and SI 1998/2868). The Regulations give effect to EC Council Directive 86/653 and came into force on January 1, 1994. See generally *Bowstead and Reynolds on Agency* (17th ed.), Ch.11.

that principal.''[69] In this book, we are concerned only with those of the Regulations which may affect the legal consequences of what, at common law, would be regarded as frustration of the contract between a commercial agent and his principal.

(i) Effects of frustration in general: reg.16

15–098   This regulation provides that the Regulations: "shall not affect the application of any enactment or rule of law which provides for the immediate termination of the agency contract (a) because of the failure of one party to carry out all or a part of his obligations under the contract or (b) where exceptional circumstances arise." This provision, standing alone, would preserve the general rules of the law of contract relating to rescission for breach (or excused non-performance) and to frustration. For example, it would preserve the general rules relating to frustration where the contract was discharged by the supervening destruction of its subject-matter or of a thing essential for its performance (such as the principal's factory, if the contract related only to goods manufactured there), by supervening illegality, or by the death of the principal.

(ii) Effects of agent's death or illness: regs 17 and 18

15–099   The general principle stated in reg.16 above is, however, qualified by regs 17 and 18. Under reg.17, the commercial agent is entitled,[70] after termination of his relations with the principal, either to an "indemnity" or to "compensation for the damage he suffers as a result of" such termination.[71] Unless the contract otherwise provides, the agent is to be compensated rather than indemnified.[72] These rights are no doubt intended primarily to cover cases of termination of the agency contract by notice[73] and to provide the agent with a kind of redundancy payment in such cases.[74] But they are stated also to apply "where the agency contract[75] is terminated as a result of the death of the commercial agent."[76] This would of course be a ground of frustration at common law (unless the contract made express provision for the event) and so exclude any right to

---

[69] reg.2(1); for exclusion of certain categories of person, see regs 2(1)(i)–(iii), 2(2), 2(3) and Sch. and s.2(4).

[70] reg.17(1).

[71] reg.17(6).

[72] reg.17(2).

[73] The requisite periods of notice are set out in reg.15. This refers to termination of the "agency contract" while reg.17(6) refers to termination of the agent's "relations with his principle." Reg.17(8) (cited at n.76, below) also refers to termination of "the agency contract" and Directive 86/653, in the corresponding Arts 15 and 17 refers to termination of the "agency contract" throughout. It follows that the Regulations apply only where there is a contractual relationship between the principal and the commercial agent: *Light v Ty Europe Ltd* [2004] 1 Lloyd's Rep. 693 (CA).

[74] *Moore v Piretta PTA Ltd* [1999] 1 All E.R. 174 at 181.

[75] "Agency contract" in reg.17 has been held to mean "the agency" and so to cover the situation in which the agent has acted under a series of contracts: *Moore v Piretta PTA Ltd*, above, n.74.

[76] reg.17(8).

"compensation for ... damage", while any right analogous to that of "indemnity" would (apart from the Regulations) be limited by the Law Reform (Frustrated Contracts) Act 1943. The agent's right to "indemnity" or "compensation" is, moreover, available where termination of the agency contract by the agent is justified "on grounds of the age, infirmity or illness of the commercial agent in consequence of which he cannot reasonably be required to continue his activities".[77] These words appear to be capable of covering situations in which the contract would be frustrated at common law as a result of the serious illness of the agent.[78] It thus seems (notwithstanding reg.16) that, even where the contract is frustrated as a result of the agent's death, he will be entitled to an indemnity or to compensation under the Regulations and that these rights will be available to him also in certain cases of serious illness. The exact content of these rights is far from clear, but their scope clearly differs from that of the somewhat analogous rights which may arise under the Law Reform (Frustrated Contracts) Act 1943.

(iii) Indemnity

This expression is not here used in the normal English law sense of a right   15–100
to reimbursement in respect of expenses or liabilities incurred by the agent. An "indemnity" under the Regulations appears to be based on the benefit derived by the principal from the agent's introduction of new customers.[79] It must also be "equitable" to require the principal to pay the indemnity.[80] These rules resemble the court's power under s.1(3) of the 1943 Act to award a "just sum" in respect of a "valuable benefit"[81] but they differ from the statutory rule in that the court is to have regard under the Regulations to commission lost by the agent on business transacted with the customers in question[82] (and not merely to the benefit obtained by the principal[83]) and in that the amount of the indemnity is not to exceed one year's commission.[84]

(iv) Compensation for damage

The exact content of the agent's right to compensation for damage is far   15–101
from clear, but its scope again differs from that of the somewhat analogous rights which may arise under the Law Reform (Frustrated Contracts) Act 1943. The differences between the two sets of rules arise mainly because, in dealing with the agent's right to "compensation for ... damage", reg.17(7) provides that damage shall be "deemed to occur particularly" when termination occurs in either or both of the two following situations.

---

[77] reg.18(b)(ii); for the insertion of the words "or indemnity" into reg.18, see SI 1993/3173 above, n.68.
[78] Above, para.5–056.
[79] reg.17(3)(a).
[80] reg.17(3)(b).
[81] Above, para.15–060.
[82] reg.17(3)(b).
[83] reg.17(3)(a).
[84] reg.17(4).

The first is that in which termination takes place in circumstances which: "deprive the commercial agent of the commission which proper performance of the agency contract would have procured for him, whilst providing his principal with substantial benefits linked to the activities of the commerical agent."[85] This formulation combines a requirement of loss to the agent of commission on future transactions with one of benefit to the principal. It thus differs from the rights which would be available to the agent under s.1(3) of the 1943 Act. That subsection is satisfied if the party against whom the claim is made has obtained a "valuable benefit"; it does not in terms require the claimant to show that he has suffered loss, though no doubt in practice such loss (in the form of deprivation of rights which had not accrued at the time of discharge) will normally be suffered. A further, and probably more significant, difference between the two provisions is that s.1(3) would not be, while reg.17(7) is, satisfied by showing that benefit will accrue to the principal only *after* the time of termination.

Damage is, secondly, "deemed to occur particularly" where the termination occurs in "circumstances which ... have not enabled the commercial agent to amortise the costs and expenses that he had incurred in the performance of the agency contract[86] on the advice of his principal".[87] It follows from these words that a claim for wasted expenses can be available in cases of termination as a result of the agent's death or serious illness. Such a claim is not restricted (as it would be under s.1(2) of the 1943 Act) to cases in which there had been a prepayment of money to the agent, or a stipulation for such a prepayment.[88] The claim is, on the other hand, narrower in scope than one in respect of expenses under the 1943 Act, in that it is available only where the expenses are "incurred ... on the advice of the principal".

(v) Contrary contractual provisions

15–102   The commercial agent's rights to indemnity or compensation under the Regulations differ finally from those under the 1943 Act in that the former cannot,[89] while the latter can,[90] be excluded varied or restricted to the detriment of the commercial agent by the terms of the agency contract.

(vi) Advance commission

15–103   Commission which has been prepaid is refundable if the right to it is extinguished,[91] and the right is so extinguished if, for a reason for which the principal is not to blame, "it is established that the contract between the third party and the principal will not be executed".[92] That result clearly need not follow from the termination of the agency contract by

---

[85] reg.17(7)(a).
[86] See above, para.15–099, n.75.
[87] reg.17(7)(b).
[88] Above, para.15–071.
[89] reg.19.
[90] Law Reform (Frustrated Contracts) Act 1943, s.2(3); above, para.15–084.
[91] reg.11(2).
[92] reg.11(1)(a).

events such as the agent's death or serious illness (which would frustrate that contract at common law), so that the right to reclaim advance payments under the Regulations again differs from the corresponding right under s.1(2) of the 1943 Act, which makes the recoverability of advance payments depend, *prima facie*,[93] on whether the agency contract was discharged and on whether the payments were made before the time of discharge.[94] The non-execution of the contract between principal and third party would not be decisive for the purpose of s.1(2). Again the rules laid down by the Regulations as to the extinction of the right to commission, and hence as to the agent's duty to repay commission which has been paid in advance, cannot be excluded, varied or restricted to the agent's detriment by the terms of the contract,[95] while the rules as to the right of the principal to recover such advance payments under the 1943 Act can be so modified.[96]

---

[93] *i.e.* in the absence of contrary agreement: Law Reform (Frustrated Contracts) Act 1943, s.2(3).

[94] Above, para.15–050.

[95] reg.11(3).

[96] See n.90, above.

CHAPTER 16

NATURE OF THE DOCTRINE

Two topics form the subject-matter of this chapter. The first is the extent to which the issue of frustration is one of fact or one of law. The second concerns the theoretical or juristic basis of the doctrine of frustration. The two topics are related in that it has been suggested that the answer to the "fact or law" question may depend on which theory of the basis of the doctrine is adopted.[1]   **16–001**

I. FACT OR LAW?

The distinction between issues of "fact" and of "law" is sometimes hard to draw and has indeed been subjected to criticism where its effect is to determine substantive rights[2]; indeed, for the purpose of determining whether money paid under a mistake can be recovered back by the payor, the distinction is no longer regarded as significant.[3] Such criticism is, however, not in point in the present context, where the purpose of the distinction is to determine, not the substantive rights of the parties, but the procedural question how far the conclusions of the trier of fact on an issue of frustration are subject to the appellate or supervisory jurisdiction of the courts. The development of this branch of the law has been influenced by a change in the mode by which such issues are commonly determined. Formerly, issues of frustration were often left to juries, and the question whether frustration was a matter of fact or law was important in determining the respective functions of judge and jury. Trial by jury has become rare in civil cases, and virtually unknown in commercial disputes,   **16–002**

---

[1] Below, para.16–015.

[2] *Avon CC v Howlett* [1983] 1 W.L.R. 605 at 620, in the context of claims for the recovery of money paid under a mistake, as to which see below, n.3.

[3] *Kleinwort Benson Ltd v Lincoln CC* [1999] 2 A.C. 349; for proposals for legislative intervention, see Law Com. No. 227 (1994), now superseded by the *Kleinwort Benson* case; for the need for further reform to restrict the period of limitation for such claims, see the *Kleinwort Benson* case at 389, 401 and 418; such problems are not our concern in this book.

many of which are now submitted to arbitration. The practical significance of the question whether a finding on an issue of frustration is one of fact or one of law now lies in determining the extent to which findings made by arbitrators on questions of frustration are subject to the control of the courts, for arbitrators' findings are generally conclusive on matters of fact,[4] but are subject to the control of the courts on points of law.[5]

16–003   In *Jackson v Union Marine Insurance Co Ltd*[6] a voyage charterparty was held to have been frustrated by delay which had been caused by the stranding of the ship. The jury found that the delay was "so long as to put an end in a commercial sense to the commercial speculation"; and Bramwell B. described this finding as "all-important".[7] By contrast, in the *Tsakiroglou* case[8] (one of the Suez cases[9] discussed in Ch.4), the arbitrator found that performance of the contract of sale by shipping the goods via the Cape was "not commercially or fundamentally different from" shipping them via the Suez Canal. The House of Lords agreed with this finding but added that it did not bind the court as the question whether the difference between the two methods of performance was fundamental, was one of law,[10] or one of mixed law and fact,[11] so that it was possible for the court in the exercise of its supervisory or appellate jurisdiction to reject an arbitrator's decision on the point. This possibility is illustrated by *Re Comptoir Commercial Anversois and John Power, Son & Co*,[12] where a seller of wheat alleged that it was an implied term of the contract that he should be able to sell the buyer's draft for the price in New York, and that his inability, on account of war-time conditions, to effect such a sale was a ground of discharge. This contention was accepted by the arbitrator, but rejected by the Court of Appeal, where Bankes L.J. said that "the question whether the doctrine of 'frustrated adventure' applies must ... always be a question of law".[13] That view is reiterated in a number of later cases, even though the courts in those cases accepted the decision of the arbitrators on the questions whether, and when, the contracts had been discharged.[14]

---

[4] See, *e.g. Universal Petroleum Co Ltd v Handels und Transport Gesellschaft mbH* [1987] 1 Lloyd's Rep. 517.

[5] Below, para.16–003.

[6] (1874) L.R. 10 C.P. 125, above, para.5–039.

[7] At 141.

[8] [1962] A.C. 93.

[9] Above, para.4–062.

[10] [1962] A.C. 93 at 119, 134; *cf. Davis Contractors Ltd v Fareham UDC* [1956] 696 at 727; *Palmco Shipping Inc v Continental Ore (The Captain George K)* [1970] 2 Lloyd's Rep. 21; *Peter Lind & Co v Constable Hart & Co Ltd* [1979] 2 Lloyd's Rep. 248 at 253; *International Sea Tankers Inc v Hemisphere Shipping Co Ltd (The Wenjiang)* [1982] 2 All E.R. 437; *International Sea Tankers Inc v Hemisphere Shipping Co Ltd (The Wenjiang) (No 2)* [1983] 1 Lloyd's Rep. 400 at 402.

[11] *Tsakiroglou* case [1962] A.C. 93 at 123, 129.

[12] [1920] 1 K.B. 868, above, para.7–003.

[13] *ibid.* at 890; *cf.* at 893 ("an inference of law"), and at 898 ("a question of construction for the court").

[14] *The Wenjiang* and *The Wenjiang (No 2)*, above n.10; *Pioneer Shipping Ltd v BTP Tioxide Ltd (The Nema)* [1982] A.C. 724; *Kodros Shipping Corp v Empresa Cubana de*

One possible distinction between *Jackson*'s case and the *Tsakiroglou* case
is that the jury's finding in the former case related to the effects of a
specific factor (*i.e.* the delay) while in the latter the arbitrator's findings on
the issue of frustration were expressed in general terms.[15] But it does not
seem that a court's control over arbitrators' findings would be excluded
merely because they had made a number of findings as to the effects of
specific factors, instead of a single finding as to the effect of a group of
factors on the contract. Of course the arbitrators' findings in the Suez
cases on such questions as the greater length and cost of the voyage round
the Cape, and on the physical effects of that voyage on the goods or the
ship would clearly be findings of fact. The effects of such facts on the
contract, however, depended on the inferences to be drawn (in the light
of the legal tests governing frustration) from those facts. Since it was
formerly not uncommon to leave the drawing of such inferences to juries,
and since juries were thought of as triers of fact, these inferences, too,
were regarded as findings of fact; but they differed in nature from findings
as to the physical circumstances on which they were based. To express this
distinction, it was convenient to refer to the physical circumstances as
primary facts, and to the inferences based on them as secondary facts.[16]
When such inferences were drawn by juries, appellate courts might well
have been reluctant to interfere with them; and this reluctance appears to
account for the court's approach to the jury's finding in *Jackson*'s case. But
there has been no such reluctance on the part of the courts to exercise
their appellate or supervisory functions where such inferences were drawn,
not by juries, but by lower courts or by tribunals such as arbitrators. Thus
when issues of negligence were left to juries they might have been thought
of as issues of fact; but appeals nevertheless lie from findings of negligence
made by lower courts (which now try such issues without juries), even
where the decision of those courts are subject to appeal only on points of
law.[17] The position is the same where an arbitrator decides an issue of
frustration. An appeal lies from the decision of an arbitrator only on
points of law[18] and therefore cannot be brought against his findings of
primary fact; but the inferences that he draws from those facts as to their
effect on the contract are treated as points of law and are therefore subject
to appeal.[19] The same would, it is submitted, be true where the arbitrator
simply stated his conclusion in general terms, without clearly separating
his finding of primary fact from the inferences drawn from them. It is,

---

Fletes (The Evia) [1983] A.C. 736; Vinava Shipping Co Ltd v Finelvet AG (The
Chrysalis) [1983] 1 Lloyd's Rep. 503.
[15] See [1962] A.C. 93 at 130.
[16] See *Benmax v Austin Motor Co Ltd* [1955]A.C. 370; *National Carriers Ltd v
Panalpina (Northern) Ltd* [1981] A.C. 675 at 688; cf. *Adelfamar SA v Silos e Mangimi
Martini (The Adelfa)* [1988] 2 Lloyd's Rep. 466 at 471.
[17] Goodhart (1958) 74 L.Q.R. 402.
[18] Arbitration Act 1996, s.69; see also s.45. For the parties' power to exclude even
this degree of judicial control by agreement, see *ibid.*, ss.69(1), 45(1) and (b).
[19] See the authorities cited above, nn.12–14.

perhaps, in these circumstances that it is most appropriate to refer to the finding as one of mixed law and fact.[20]

16–005   Two further points, however, restrict the scope of appeals from arbitrators' decisions on issues of frustration. The first is that under the Arbitration Act 1996 an appeal against the decision of an arbitrator can be brought only with either the consent of the parties or the leave of the court. Such leave will not be granted merely because it is alleged that the arbitrator has gone wrong in law. It can be given only if a number of further requirements imposed by the Arbitration Act 1996 are satisfied. The point of law must be one which substantially affects the rights of one or more of the parties and which the arbitral tribunal was asked to determine; the decision of that tribunal must *either* be "obviously wrong" *or* raise questions of "general public importance" and be "at least open to serious doubt"; and it must be "just and proper . . . for the court to determine the question".[21] These requirements are based on (but go slightly beyond[22]) tests which had been developed by the courts under earlier legislation.[23] The second point is that it does not follow from the grant of leave to appeal, or from the description of the issue of frustration as one of law, that the court will substitute its own decision for that of the arbitrator merely because it disagrees with his conclusion. It has been said that, while the question of frustration is "in the ultimate analysis . . . a question of law", it is nevertheless one of such "large factual content" that the court should be careful not to substitute its own decision for that of the tribunal chosen by the parties.[24] It will reverse the arbitrator's finding only where he has either applied the wrong legal test or, while purporting to apply the correct legal test, reached a conclusion to which no reasonable person could have come on the primary facts found by him.[25]

II. THEORIES OF FRUSTRATION[26]

(1) Introduction

16–006   Much discussion is to be found in the cases of the so-called theoretical or juristic basis of the doctrine of frustration. This fact, of itself, gives rise to two preliminary puzzles. The first is why this question has attracted so much

---

[20] See the *Tsakiroglou* case [1962] A.C. 93 at 123, 129.

[21] Arbitration Act 1996, s.69(3).

[22] *CMA CGM SA v Beteiligungs–Kommanditgesellschaft mbH & Co* [2002] EWCA Civ 1878; [2003] 1 All E.R. (Comm) 204.

[23] See *Pioneer Shipping Ltd v BTP Tioxide Ltd (The Nema)* [1982] A.C. 724 at 743 and below, at nn.24, 25.

[24] *The Wenjiang (No 2)* [1983] 1 Lloyd's Rep. 400 at 402 (above, n.10).

[25] *The Nema* [1982] A.C. 724 (disapproving *Trade & Transport Inc v Iino Kaiun Kaisha Ltd* [1973] 1 W.L.R. 210 on this point); *The Wenjiang (No 2)* [1983] 1 Lloyd's Rep. 400; *The Chrysalis* [1983] 1 Lloyd's Rep. 503 (above, n.14); *Kuwait Supply Co v Oyster Marine Management Inc (The Safeer)* [1994] 1 Lloyd's Rep. 637 at 643.

[26] McNair (1940) 56 L.Q.R. 173; *The Legal Effects of War*, pp.143 *et seq.*

judicial attention. There is no very close parallel to it in other branches of the law of contract: one does not, for example, find elaborate judicial discussions of the theoretical basis of the right to rescind for misrepresentation or for breach, or even of the doctrine of consideration. Perhaps the reason why judges have engaged in such discussions in relation to the doctrine of frustration is that they have felt the need in some way to justify their departure from the doctrine of absolute contracts, or (in other words) to explain why, in cases of frustration, they do not uphold the sanctity of contract. The common law has never adopted the simple explanation that supervening impossibility, of itself, is a ground of discharge,[27] and that explanation would in any event not be adequate since the scope of the doctrine of discharge extends to cases in which performance is not impossible at all.[28]

The second puzzle is to know exactly what the discussion is about. Two questions have become, perhaps inevitably, intertwined: *why* are contracts frustrated, and *when*. Discussions of the juristic basis of the doctrine attempt sometimes to justify the doctrine, and sometimes to evolve some general formula describing the conditions in which it operates; and such formulae may well contain, or be supposed to contain, an element of justification. Thus in the *Davis Contractors* case Lord Radcliffe, after discussing and in substance rejecting the "implied term" theory (to be discussed below) went on to say: "Perhaps it would be simpler to say that frustration occurs *whenever* the law recognises that a contractual obligation has become incapable of being performed because the circumstances in which performance is called for would render it a thing radically different from that which was undertaken by the contract. *Non haec in foedera veni.* It was not this that I contracted to do."[29] This statement has been taken to support the "construction" theory,[30] which seeks to explain why frustration occurs[31]; but it is at least equally plausible from the context to suggest that Lord Radcliffe had at this stage abandoned his search for a reason *why*, and was seeking instead to formulate a test for determining *when*, the effect of the supervening event was sufficiently serious to bring about discharge.

In the following discussion we shall examine five theories which seek to answer the first of these questions (or have been thought to make this attempt) and then consider whether any practical consequences flow from the choice between them.

(2) The theories examined

The following are the theories of frustration which are found in English judicial discussions of the subject. 16–007

---

[27] Above, para.1–002.
[28] See, in particular, above, Ch.7.
[29] [1956] A.C. 696 at 729 (italics supplied).
[30] Below, para.16–011.
[31] *National Carriers Ltd v Panalpina (Northern) Ltd* [1981] A.C. 675 at 688, 717.

(a) *Implied term*

16–008   According to this theory, the contract is discharged because it impliedly provides that, in the events which have happened, it shall cease to bind. No doubt this theory owes its origin to Blackburn J.'s reference in *Taylor v Caldwell* to "an implied condition that the parties shall be excused"[32] if performance becomes impossible as a result of the perishing of the subject-matter. The theory was later elaborated by Lord Loreburn in the *Tamplin* case. While accepting that "no court has an absolving power"[33] he said that the court would not regard an obligation as absolute if the parties themselves did not intend it to be absolute. If they "must have made their bargain on the footing that a particular state of things should continue to exist, a term to that effect will be implied".[34]

This theory would clearly be untenable if it were interpreted in a purely subjective sense, *i.e.* as giving effect to the actual intentions of the parties. For one thing, they will often have no common view at all as to the effects of the frustrating event. If the party seeking to enforce the contract were in a stronger bargaining position than the other, he would probably not agree to discharge, while the other would want it. Even if the parties could reach *some* agreement on the point, they would probably not agree to total unconditional discharge. As Lord Wright has said, "they would almost certainly on the one side or the other have sought to introduce reservations or qualifications or compensations".[35] For these reasons, the implied term theory is now generally rejected.[36]

In fact, Lord Loreburn did not put forward a purely subjective version of the implied term theory. He said: "From the nature of the contract it cannot be supposed that the parties *as reasonable men* intended it to be binding under such altered conditions. Were the altered conditions such that, *as sensible men*, they would have said, 'if that happens, of course, it is all over between us?' What, in fact, was the true meaning of the contract?"[37] But in this form the implied term theory loses its chief attraction, which is that frustration merely gives effect to the intention of the parties themselves. There is an element of contradiction between

---

[32] (1863) 3 B. & S. 826 at 833–834.

[33] [1916] 2 A.C. 397 at 404.

[34] *ibid.* at 403.

[35] *Denny Mott* case [1944] A.C. 265 at 275. The court may, indeed, imply a term introducing what Lord Wright has called "qualifications", in the light of supervening events, but if it does so the legal outcome will be that the contract (so qualified) remains in force—not that it is discharged: see *Glafki Shipping Co SA v Pinios Shipping Co No 1 (The Maira) (No 2)* [1985] 1 Lloyd's Rep. 300 at 311; affirmed on other grounds [1986] 2 Lloyd's Rep. 12.

[36] *Shell UK Ltd v Lostock Garages Ltd* [1976] 1 W.L.R. 1187 at 1196; *Atisa SA v Aztec AG* [1983] 2 Lloyd's Rep. 579 at 586; *FC Shepherd & Co Ltd v Jerrom* [1987] Q.B. 301 at 322; *J Lauritzen A/S v Wijsmuller BV (The Super Servant Two)* [1989] 1 Lloyd's Rep. 145 at 154; affirmed [1990] 1 Lloyd's Rep. 1; *Great Peace Shipping Ltd v Tsavliris Salvage (International) Ltd (The Great Peace)* [2002] EWCA Civ 1407; [2003] Q.B. 697 at [73]; *cf.* in the United States, *Florida Power & Light Company v Westinghouse Electric Corp*, 826 F. 2d 239 at 263 (1987).

[37] [1916] 2 A.C. 397 at 404 (italics supplied).

saying that a court has no absolving power and saying that the court will absolve the parties if they would have agreed to this course, had they been sensible or reasonable men. The role of the parties in bringing about frustration really disappears. As Lord Radcliffe said in the *Davis Contractors* case: "By this time it might seem that the parties themselves have become so far disembodied spirits that their actual persons should be allowed to rest in peace. In their place there rises the figure of the fair and reasonable man. And the spokesman of the fair and reasonable man, who represents after all no more than the anthropomorphic conception of justice, is and must be the court itself."[38]

(b) *Just solution*

Lord Sumner once described the doctrine of frustration as "a device by which the rules as to absolute contracts are reconciled with the special exceptions which justice demands".[39] Lord Wright in the *Denny Mott* case found "the theory of the basis of the rule"[40] in this statement; he added that the doctrine of frustration did not depend on the possibility of implying a term, but was "a substantive and particular rule which the common law has evolved".[41] Moreover in the *Joseph Constantine* case he said: "The court is exercising powers, when it decides that a contract is frustrated, in order to achieve a result which is just and reasonable."[42] This "just solution theory" does not purport to explain why the courts sometimes abandon the doctrine of absolute contracts: it simply asserts that they do so. As Lord Hailsham L.C. has said: "though it admirably expresses the purpose of the doctrine, it does not provide it with any theoretical basis at all."[43] The "theory" should not, moreover, be interpreted to mean that a contract will be discharged merely because its performance in the changed circumstances will be unexpectedly burdensome or otherwise cause hardship to one of the parties. The "theory" does not, in other words, supersede the rules which determine the circumstances in which the doctrine of frustration operates.[44] Much less does it determine the type of relief which, in English law, can be given: when a contract is frustrated, both parties are at common law automatically and totally discharged[45]; and even the statutory modifica-

---

[38] [1956] A.C. 696 at 728.

[39] *Hirji Mulji v Ceong Yue SS Co Ltd* [1926] A.C. 497 at 510. In the *Bank Line* case [1919] A.C. 435 at 455 he had supported the implied term theory, which he also supports at at 504 and 506 of the *Hirji Mulji* case.

[40] [1944] A.C. 265 at 275.

[41] *ibid.* at 274.

[42] [1942] A.C. 154 at 186; *cf. National Carriers Ltd v Panalpina (Northern) Ltd* [1981] A.C. 675 at 701; *J Lauritzen A/S v Wijsmuller BV (The Super Servant Two)* [1990] 1 Lloyd's Rep. 1 at 8.

[43] *National Carriers* case, above, n.42, at 687.

[44] See *Eridania SpA v Rudolf A Oetker (The Fjord Wind)* [1999] 1 Lloyd's Rep. 307 at 328 (affirmed without reference to this point [2000] 2 Lloyd's Rep. 191); and *cf.*, for example, the discussion of "impracticability" in English law above, paras 6–026 to 6–028, and of the Suez cases above, paras 4–071 to 4–083.

[45] Above, paras 15–002, 15–010.

tions[46] of this rule can fall short of providing the comprehensive apportionment of loss which might be regarded as the "just solution".[47] The law here, as elsewhere, needs to keep in mind other goals, and in particular that of commercial certainty, which may counterbalance the search for a "just solution".

(c) Foundation of the contract

16–010   This theory, too, may be traced back to *Taylor v Caldwell,* where Blackburn J. referred to the continuing existence of the subject-matter as the "foundation of what was to be done"[48] and as the "basis"[49] on which the parties had contracted. The "foundation" theory was more fully stated by Lord Haldane in the *Tamplin* case: "When people enter into a contract which is dependent for the possibility of performance on the continued availability of a specific thing, and that availability comes to an end by reason of circumstances beyond the control of the parties, the contract is *prima facie* regarded as dissolved ... Although the words of the stipulation may be such that the mere letter would describe what has occurred, the occurrence itself may yet be of a character and extent so sweeping that the foundation of what the parties are deemed to have had in contemplation has disappeared, and the contract itself has vanished with that foundation."[50] In *WJ Tatem Ltd v Gamboa* Goddard J. regarded this as "the surest ground on which to rest the doctrine of frustration".[51]

At first sight, this theory has the merit of simplicity as it does not involve speculation as to the intention of the parties, or value judgments in seeking a "just solution". It is particularly appropriate where performance depends on the continued availability of a specific thing. But in other cases the metaphor "foundation" is scarcely helpful. How can one tell whether passage through the Suez Canal is the "foundation" of a charterparty? What is the "foundation" of a contract in which the parties take a deliberate risk as to the continued availability or existence of a specific thing or of some state of affairs? Such doubts as to what is the "foundation" of the contract can, in the last resort, be resolved only by construing the contract. If this is so, there is no practical difference between the "foundation" theory and the "implied term" theory in its objective sense. Indeed, exponents of one sometimes use the language of the other. Thus in the *Tamplin* case Lord Loreburn, after stating the "implied term" theory,[52] said that the court "can infer from the nature of

---

[46] Law Reform (Frustrated Contracts) Act 1943 especially s.1(2) and (3), above, paras 15–050, 15–060.

[47] See above, para.15–078.

[48] (1863) 3 B. & S. 826 at 833.

[49] *ibid.* at 839.

[50] [1916] 2 A.C. 397 at 406. Lord Haldane's was a dissenting speech. *Quaere* whether his formulation is in part derived from the German phrase "*Wegfall der Geschäftsgrundlage*".

[51] [1939] 1 K.B. 132 at 137.

[52] Above, para.16–008, at n.34.

the contract and the surrounding circumstances that a condition which is not expressed was a foundation of the contract".[53]

(d) Construction

All the theories so far stated depend in the last resort on the construction of the contract: to this extent, they "shade into one another".[54] After stating the "implied term" theory, Lord Loreburn proposed as the ultimate test: "what, in fact, is the true meaning of the contract?"[55] Similarly, in *Taylor v Caldwell* Blackburn J. said: "the contract is not to be *construed* as a positive contract but as subject to an *implied condition* that the parties shall be excused in case before breach performance becomes impossible."[56] Construing the contract and implying a term are here no more than alternative ways of describing the same process. Similarly, the "foundation" theory raises a question of construction whenever it is at all doubtful what the "foundation" of the contract is. And Lord Wright, in the course of stating the "just solution" theory has said: "when that happens the contract is held on its true construction not to apply at all from the time when the frustrating circumstances supervene."[57] It seems that this is the most satisfactory basis of the doctrine of frustration.[58]

(e) Failure of consideration

This theory is sometimes used to explain why *both* parties are discharged in the situation (more fully discussed in Ch.2[59]) in which the supervening event makes the performance of only *one* party's obligation impossible. Thus destruction of a specific thing may make the *supplier's* obligation impossible to perform, but it has no such effect on the *recipient's* obligation to pay; and it can be said that the recipient is discharged by failure of consideration, *i.e.* because he does not receive the performance for which he bargained.[60] In England, however, the discharge of both parties in such cases is explained on the ground that the "common object" of the parties (*i.e.* the exchange of the thing for the price) is frustrated.[61] Moreover, in so far as the present theory suggests that the failure of consideration must be total[62] it is plainly wrong since frustration can occur in cases of partial

---

[53] [1916] 2 A.C. 397 at 404.

[54] *National Carriers Ltd v Panalpina (Northern) Ltd* [1981] A.C. 675 at 693.

[55] [1916] A.C. 397 at 404.

[56] (1863) 3 B. & S. 826 at 833–834 (italics supplied).

[57] *Denny Mott* case [1944] A.C. 265 at 274; *cf. Ocean Tramp Tankers Corp v V/O Sovfracht (The Eugenia)* [1964] 2 Q.B. 226 at 239; *Occidental Worldwide Investment Corp v Skibs A/S Avanti (The Siboen and the Sibotre)* [1976] 1 Lloyd's Rep. 293 at 325.

[58] *National Carriers Ltd v Panalpina Northern Ltd* [1981] A.C. 675 at 688, *per* Lord Hailsham L.C.: "It is the formulation I personally prefer".

[59] Above, paras 2–039 *et seq.*

[60] For support for this view in the United States, see above, para.2–041.

[61] *Hirji Mulji v Yue SS Co Ltd* [1926] A.C. 497 at 507, above, para.2–039.

[62] For the meaning, and for mitigations, of the requirement that the failure of consideration must be "total" in the present context and in that of restitutionary claims for money, see above, paras 2–043, 15–048.

destruction of the subject-matter,[63] or after part performance;[64] and the theory has for this reason been rejected in the House of Lords.[65]

(3) Practical importance?

16–013   The question to be considered here is whether the discussion of the theoretical basis of the doctrine has any practical importance. It seems to have none[66] in spite of the fact that the contrary has from time to time been suggested. Three such suggestions call for discussion.

(a) *Express provision for the event*

16–014   In *WJ Tatem Ltd v Gamboa* Goddard J. said that the contract would be frustrated although the parties foresaw that the ship would be seized and detained.[67] He even said: "If the foundation of the contract goes, it goes whether or not the parties have made provision for it."[68] These statements could be made only by an adherent of the "foundation" theory. But the first has been doubted in Ch.13,[69] while the second was qualified later in the judgment: "*Unless the contrary intention is made plain*, the law imposes this doctrine of frustration."[70] The qualification contained in the words here italicised is, with respect, clearly right. A state of affairs could not be the "foundation" of the contract if the parties had (for example) expressly provided that one of them was to remain liable even though that state of affairs had ceased to exist.

(b) *Fact or law?*

16–015   In the *Davis Contractors* case, Lord Reid said that, on the "foundation" theory, no review was possible of an arbitrator's decision, as the question whether the "foundation" had disappeared was one of fact; while such review was possible on the "implied term" and "construction" theories as implication and construction were questions of law.[71] But a question of law would be involved even on the "foundation" theory if the question: what is the foundation? is itself a question of construction. Moreover the cases discussed earlier in this chapter[72] make it clear that arbitrators' decisions on issues of frustration are now regarded as raising questions of law in so

---

[63] Above, para.5–002.

[64] Above, paras 15–047 *et seq.*

[65] *National Carriers Ltd v Panalpina (Northern) Ltd* [1981] A.C. 675 at 687, 702; and see above, para.15–048.

[66] This seems to be the view of Lords Wilberforce and Roskill in *National Carriers Ltd v Panalpina (Northern) Ltd* [1981] A.C. 675 at 693, 717. Lord Hailsham L.C. (*ibid.* at 687) regards "the theoretical basis of the doctrine as clearly relevant to the point under discussion"; but he does not specify in what respect it is relevant.

[67] [1939] 1 K.B. 132 at 138.

[68] *ibid.*

[69] Above, para.13–013.

[70] [1939] 1 K.B. 132 at 139 (italics supplied).

[71] *Davis Contractors Ltd v Fareham UDC* [1956] A.C. 696 at 720.

[72] Above, paras 16–003 to 16–004.

far as they involve inferences from primary facts. With the sole exception of Lord Reid's dictum referred to above, no attempt was made in any of these cases to argue that the appellate or supervisory jurisdiction of the courts over such questions was restricted by the "foundation" (or by any other) theory of frustration.

(c) *Relevance of parties' intentions*

In the *Davis Contractors* case, Lord Reid also said that there might be a **16–016** practical difference between the "implied term" and the "construction" theories. On the former theory, it would be necessary to ask whether the parties, or reasonable persons in their position, "would certainly have agreed to an implied term bringing it [*i.e.* frustration] about".[73] But on the latter theory: "there is no need to consider what the parties thought or how they or reasonable men in their shoes would have dealt with the new situation if they had foreseen it. The question is whether the contract which they did make is, on its true construction, wide enough to apply to the new situation: if it is not, then it is at an end".[74] But in construing the contract, the court does not wholly disregard the intention of the parties. The court may not have to ask: what would the parties have said, had they thought of the frustrating event? But it does have to ask: in what circumstances did the parties intend the contract to operate? In answering this question, the court will no doubt apply an objective test[75] and may refuse to admit evidence of the parties' "subjective intent"[76]; but it is only after the question has been answered that the intention of the parties becomes irrelevant: that is, it is not necessary to go on and ask whether they would (if they had considered the event) have agreed to discharge, or to some other compromise solution. But this question does not arise under the "implied term" theory either, as frustration at common law always results in total discharge of the contract.

---

[73] [1956] A.C. 696 at 720.

[74] *ibid.* at 721.

[75] As the phrase "or reasonable men in their shoes" in the passage quoted above, at n.74, indicates.

[76] *Investors Compensation Scheme v West Bromwich BS* [1998] 1 W.L.R. 896 at 913; *cf. Mannai Investment Co Ltd v Eagle Star Life Assurance Ltd* [1997] A.C. 749 at 775.

INDEX